TUTTLE

Compact
Japanese
Dictionary

T0151736

Samuel E. Martin is the author of numerous books and papers on Japanese and Korean, including the definitive **A Reference Grammar of Japanese and A Reference Grammar of Korean**.

Sayaka Khan has a BSC (Biology, 2000) from Waseda University. She has worked as a translator and interpreter for companies in various industries, such as patent offices, science think tanks, pharmaceutical firms, film productions, game companies, etc. She has established a translation corporation with her husband, Afaque Khan.

Fred Perry has a BA (History, 1956) from Yale University as well as an MBA from St Sophia University, Tokyo (1984). He arrived in Japan in 1956, and continues to live there today. He has worked as a market researcher and consultant. Traveling throughout Japan as part of his job has provided the opportunity to learn about the local dialects spoken in different parts of the country.

TUTTLE

Compact
Japanese
Dictionary

Samuel E. Martin

Revised and Updated by Sayaka Khan and Fred Perry

TUTTLE Publishing

Tokyo │Rutland, Vermont│ Singapore

Published by Tuttle Publishing, an imprint of Periplus Editions (HK) Ltd.

www.tuttlepublishing.com

Original Edition © 2007 by Periplus Editions (HK) Ltd
This edition © 2016 by Periplus Editions (HK) Ltd

Library of Congress Control Number: 2011921097
ISBN 978-4-8053-1431-9

This title was first published by Charles E. Tuttle Publishing in 1994 as *Martin's Concise
Japanese Dictionary* (ISBN 0-8048-1912-2).

Distributed by:

Japan
Tuttle Publishing
Yaekari Bldg., 3rd Floor, 5-4-12 Osaki,
Shinagawa-ku, Tokyo 141-0032
Tel: (81) 3 5437-0171
Fax: (81) 3 5437-0755
sales@ tuttle.co.jp
www.tuttle.co.jp

North America, Latin America, and Europe
Tuttle Publishing
364 Innovation Drive, North Clarendon,
VT 05759-9436 USA.
Tel: 1 (802) 773-8930
Fax: 1 (802) 773-6993
info@tuttlepublishing.com
www.tuttlepublishing.com

Asia Pacific
Berkeley Books Pte. Ltd.
3 Kallang Sector #04-01
Singapore 349278
Tel: (65) 6741-2178
Fax: (65) 6741-2179
inquiries@periplus.com.sg
www.tuttlepublishing.com

25 24 23 22 21
7 6 5 4 3   2109VP

Printed in Malaysia

TUTTLE PUBLISHING® is a registered trademark of Tuttle Publishing, a division
of Periplus Editions (HK) Ltd.

CONTENTS

CONTENTS

INTRODUCTION

This is a dictionary based on spoken Japanese, in two parts: Japanese–English and English–Japanese. It aims to be of immediate use to the beginning student of Japanese who wants to know the meaning of an expression he has just heard or who seeks to express himself in ordinary, everyday situations. This is the place to look for the words to help you get a plumber, staples for your stapler, or sushi without the horseradish. It will also help you when you are groping for the appropriate form of a Japanese verb; here, too, you will find just which different verbs may converge in a given form, such as **itte** [行って, 要って, 言って], which can mean "going," "needing," or "saying." This dictionary cannot take the place of a textbook or a reference grammar, but it can remind you of the important points made by those books.

If you are primarily interested in reading and writing Japanese, you will need other tools, but certain features of this work will be useful to you in unexpected ways. Japanese sentences can be written using only kana—all hiragana or all katakana or a mixture of the two. However, the result is often hard to read because the Japanese do not traditionally use any device to separate words, such as the spaces we use in English. Japanese sentences written in romanized form (in any system) are easier to read because the spaces make the words stand out individually. Also, judiciously placed hyphens make the structure of compound words more accessible to the eye.

The Japanese normally write their sentences in a mixed script by using kanji (Chinese characters) for the more salient words, especially nouns, and hiragana as a kind of neutral background, appropriate for grammatical endings, particles, and the like. They also use kana as a kind of fallback, when they are uncertain or ignorant of the appropriate kanji. By using katakana for modern foreign words and other oddities, and also kanji for the words made up of elements borrowed many years ago from China, a writer can make words stand out from the background in a way that partly makes up for the absence of spaces between them.

Unfortunately, the use of kanji tempts the writer into relying entirely on the eye, forgetting that texts might be read over the telephone or listened to in the dark. For this reason, words confusing to the ear should be avoided. As a result, written Japanese today is an artificial and unstandardized medium of communication, varying in complexity with each writer and every text. If you ask ten Japanese to write out a typical long sentence read aloud from a magazine or newspaper, you will probably find you have eight to ten different versions. Many writers feel free to create new words and abbreviations based solely on the meanings associated with the kanji, and with total disregard to whether the result is meaningful to the ear.

Yet all of that is a superstructure imposed on the basic language which underlies the written text, and the basic language: Spoken Japanese. That is why it is necessary to approach the written language from a good knowledge of the sentence structure and vocabulary of the spoken language.

GUIDE TO SYMBOLS

A fall of pitch occurs after the marked syllable (denoted by the mark ´). When the accent is on the last, the syllable's fall in pitch is sometimes not apparent unless another word follows it.

| **áme** 雨 | rain |
| **ashí** 足［脚］ | foot, leg |

(vowels: **á, é, í, ó, ú**; long vowels: **ā´, ē´, ō´, ū´**)

Long vowels **ā, ē, ō,** and **ū**: Vowels with macrons (a horizontal bar above the letter) are pronounced twice as long as regular vowels.

Examples:	Meaning
byōdō (na) 平等 (な)	equal
kyūka 休暇	vacation, furlough
pēji 頁［ページ］	page
wā-puro ワープロ	word processor

Sounds: The following have suppressed vowels.

Examples:	Meaning
i, u	(These vowels are suppressed.)
hi̱to 人	person, man, fellow, people
suki̱-ma 隙間	crack; opening; opportunity

Note: A fuller explanation of the symbols shown above can be found in the Introduction.

PRONUNCIATON

In this dictionary, because we are dealing with the spoken language, the words are given in romanized form, based on the Hepburn romanization, which is traditionally favored by foreigners, with a few additional marks to help with the pronunciation. If at first the marks bother you, just disregard them; later you will probably find the notations useful as a reminder of what you have heard.

Japanese phrases are accompanied by little tunes that help the hearer know what words a phrase contains. The tunes consist of a limited number of patterns of higher and lower pitch; each phrase has an inherent pattern. For example, the following common tune is rather monotonous: the pitch is slightly lower on the first syllable, then rises and stays on a plateau for the rest of the word or phrase:

kono kodomo wa nakanai   'this child does not cry'
この 子ども は 泣かない

Yokohama e iku   'goes to Yokohama'
横浜 へ 行く

A less common tune starts high and immediately falls, staying down till the end:

áme des**u**　雨 です　'it's rain'

Méguro e mo iku　目黒 へ も 行く　'goes to Meguro too'

Other tunes rise to a plateau and then fall at some point before the end:

A**ká**saka　赤坂　'Akasaka'

I**kebú**kuro　池袋　'Ikebukuro'

ya**sumimá**shita　休みました　'rested'

When the accent, i.e., a fall of pitch, is on the last syllable, you sometimes cannot hear it unless another word, such as a particle, is attached:

ha**na (ga akai)**　鼻 (が 赤い)　'the nose (is red)'

ha**ná (ga akai)**　花 (が 赤い)　'the flower (is red)'

When the change of pitch is within a long syllable, you will probably notice a rise or fall within the syllable, as shown by these place names:

Ōsaka 大阪　= o**osaka**　　　　　Kyōto 京都　= **kyó**oto
Ryūkū 琉球　= ryu**ukyú**u　　　Taitō-ku 台東区　= ta**itó**oku

When a word has more than one accent mark that means the word has variant forms. Some people may say it with the fall at one of the syllables, others at a different syllable. When an accent mark appears in parentheses, the word is often phrased with the preceding word, which carries an accent. That accounts for the difference between **hírō shimásu** [披露します] 'performs, announces, etc.' and **riyō shimásu** [利用します] 'presumes, uses, etc.'. The accent of a particular word, especially a verb form, may change in certain contexts, as explained in the grammars; the changes often involve an accent acquired or lost on the last syllable of the form. A compound word has an inherent tune that follows rules somewhat independent of those of the component elements.

Japanese speakers often reduce the short vowels **i** and **u** in certain words by devoicing (whispering) them or even suppressing them completely. The vowel reductions are a surface phenomenon, a kind of last-minute touch when you are about to speak your sentence, and they are ignored by the traditional writing system and most transcriptions. But there are many subtleties to the rules that call for **i̠** and **u̠** instead of **i** or **u**, and they often involve word boundaries and other grammatical factors. It isn't just a matter of "whisper **i** and **u** when used between voiceless consonants (**p, t, k, f, s, h**)," though that is a good rule. You can have more than one whispered vowel in a word (**ki̠ki̠máshita** [聞きました] 'I heard it') but not in successive syllables (**ki̠kitai** [聞きたい] 'I want to hear it'). Usually it is the first of two susceptible syllables that are whispered, but not always. Syllables beginning with (**p, t, k**) are more resistant than those that begin with the affricates (**ch** and **ts**). And, syllables beginning with these affricates are more resistant than syllables that begin with fricatives (**f, h, s, sh**), in **rekishi̠-ka** [歴史家] 'historian' (from **reki̠shi** [歴史] 'history'). In the foregoing fricatives, it is the second of the susceptible syllables that is whispered.

Another general rule is that **i** and **u** are unvoiced at the end of a word that has an inherent accent when that word ends a phrase or sentence. That is why we write all the polite non-past forms as **...másu̠** [...ます].

The vowel will remain voiceless before a voiceless consonant (**dekimásu̠ ka** [できますか] 'Can you do it?') but usually will get voiced before a voiced consonant (**dekimásu ga** [できますが] 'I can, but'). For nouns, however, and for verb forms other than **...másu** [...ます], we have not marked as voiceless such cases of final **...i** and **...u**, because so often they are followed by particles or other elements that begin with a voiced consonant. For example, by itself **gásu** [ガス] 'gas' is pronounced **gásu̠** (and **dásu** [出す] 'puts it out' is pronounced **dásu̠**) but the second syllable will be voiced in the more common phrases that you hear, such as **gásu o tsu̠kéte kudasai** [ガスをつけて下さい] 'turn on the gas.'

When **shimásu̠** [します] 'does' is attached to a noun that ends in a reducible syllable, we write the voiceless vowel: **insatsu** [印刷] 'printing' that becomes **insatsu̠ shimásu̠** [印刷します] 'prints it'. (This dictionary does not always call your attention to regular situations that will bring back the voicing, as in **insatsu shi̠te** [印刷して] 'printing it'.) At

the beginning of a word (**kusá** [草] 'grass') or in the middle (**enpitsu** [え
んぴつ] 'pencil'), an unvoiced vowel remains unvoiced except when the
syllables are recited, sounded out, or sung.

The first letter represents a nasal syllable that takes its color from the
sounds around it, so that when positioned before a sound made with the
lips (**m, b, p**) it sounds like a long **m**. Before **f**, however, and in all other
situations, when the syllable contains the letter **n**, then that 'pamphlet' is
pronounced **pánfurétto** [パンフレット].

Many Japanese pronounced **fu** as **hu**. The syllable **hi** is often spoken as
a palatal fricative (like German *ich*), and you may notice that quite a few
speakers make it sound just like **shi**, especially when the **i** is devoiced; if
your ears hear **shi̥to**, be aware that it is very likely just a variant of **hi̥to**
[人] 'person.' The lips are not much rounded for the Japanese vowel **u**
and are totally disengaged in the syllables **su** and **tsu**, for which the tongue
is moved quite far forward, so that the **u** sound is somewhere between **i**
and **u**.

We have not shown the distinction between the two kinds of **g** that
are used by many speakers because the present-day situation is in flux
and the distinction, which carries little semantic weight, is missing in
many parts of the country. The prestige pronunciation, however, favors a
"softened" form of **...g...** when it is felt to be internal to a word, or begins
a particle, as in **... ga** [...が]. The softened form is pronounced through
the nose, like the **ng** at the end of English 'sing.' Some speakers use a
murmured version of **...g...**, a voiced fricative, instead of the nasal.

The long vowels **ō** and **ū** are written with a macron in virtually all
cases, though they are functionally equivalent to double vowels, **oo** and
uu and are often so transcribed. The long vowels **ā** and **ē** are similar, but
except in foreignisms, most cases of long **ē** are written as **ei**, following the
practice of the hiragana orthography, which takes into account the fact
that in some areas people pronounce **ei** as a diphthong, as once was true
everywhere.

The long vowels are written in katakana with a bar (a dash) after the
syllable; in hiragana they are written as double vowels **oo, uu, ii, ee, aa**,
but for historical reasons most often the long **ō** is written **ou**. That is why
when you use romanization to type your input for a Japanese word processor you have to write **ho u ho u** to produce the hiragana string that can

be converted into the kanji deemed appropriate for the word **hōhō** [方法] 'method.' (But you input **Ōsaka** [大阪] as **o o sa ka** because the first element of that name, the **ō** of **ōkíi** [大きい] 'big,' happens to be one of the handful of common exceptions.) We write the word for 'beer' as **bíiru** [ビール] instead of putting a long mark over a single **i** both for esthetic reasons and for linguistic considerations: most cases of long **i** consist of two grammatically different elements, as in the many adjectives that end in ...**i-i** or, less obviously, such nouns as **chíi** [地位] 'position.'

GRAMMAR

This dictionary differs from other dictionaries in a number of ways. The verb forms are cited primarily in the normal polite form (...**másu** 「...ます」), for that is what the beginning student will most often hear and practice using at the end of sentences. Other common forms are also given, such as the plain nonpast (...**u** [...う] or ...**ru** [...る]) and the gerund (...**te** [...て] or ...**de** [...で]). The nonpast forms, whether plain or polite, refer to general, repeated, or future situations ('does' or 'will do'); they are also used for situations that started in the past but continue on into the present, such as 'I have been staying here since the day before yesterday' (**ototói kara koko ni imásu** [おとといからここにいます]), or that have a result that lasts, such as 'I have gotten married' (**kekkon shite imásu** [結婚しています]), another way to say 'I am married.'

The past forms ('did') are easily made: for the polite past, change ...**másu** [...ます] to ...**máshita** [...ました], and for the plain, take the gerund and change its final **e** to **a**, with the result being ...**ta** [...た] or ...**da** [...だ]. The plain nonpast form for the [NOUN] **désu** [です] 'it is [a matter of]' is ...**dá** [...だ], but that is replaced by ... **no** [...の] or ... **na** [...な] when the expression modifies a following noun. The choice of ... **no** [...の] or ... **na** [...な] depends on a number of factors that are described in grammars and textbooks. This dictionary gives the appropriate form in parentheses in many cases. The polite past of the [NOUN] **désu** [です] is ... **déshita** [...でした], the plain past is ... **dátta** [...だった] (even when the nonpast would change to **na** [な] or **no** [の]), and the gerund is ... **dé**

[...で]). The form **... ni** [...に], in addition to its many uses as a particle ('to,' 'at,' 'for'), also functions as a form of **... désu** [...です], the infinitive in the meaning 'so as to be,' as in **jōzu ni narimáshita né** [上手になりましたね] 'has gotten good at it.'

The infinitive form of verbs (**...i** or **...e**) in spoken Japanese is mainly used to form compounds, and many nouns are derived from infinitives by a change of accent, e.g., **yasumí** [休み] 'vacation' or 'work break' from **yasúmi** [休み] 'to rest'). The common nouns and infinitives derived in this manner are included in the Japanese-English section of this dictionary. The polite negative nonpast forms of verbs are made by changing **...másu** [...ます] to **...masén** [...ません] and the past to **...masén deshita** [...ませんでした]. They are run together as if they are one word; the plain nonpast forms end in **...nai** [...ない] and the plain past forms end in **...nakatta** [...なかった]. The negative gerund is **...´náide** [...ないで], as in **Isogánaide kudasai** [急がないで] 'Don't go so fast,' but before **... mo** [...も] or **... wa** [...は], it is usually **...´ nákute** [...なくて], as in **Isogánakute wa damé desu** [急がなくてはだめです] 'You've got to go fast' and **Tabénakute mo íi desu** [食べなくてもいいです] 'We don't have to eat.' In the English-Japanese section, the citation form for verbs is the English infinitive ('to do' minus the 'to ...'), whereas most Japanese-English dictionaries use the plain nonpast as a citation form; do not confuse that with the English infinitive. This dictionary gives most English translations as third-person singular ('does'), but Japanese verbs nonspecific with reference to person.

Adjectives are cited in the plain forms **-i** [-い] (**samui** [寒い] 'it's cold') for they are often used before a noun, where the plain form is most common. The polite forms appropriate at the end of a sentence end in **...´-i desu** (**samúi desu** [寒いです] 'it's cold'). The plain past is made by replacing **-i** [-い] with **-kátta** [-かった] (**samukátta** [寒かった] 'it was cold') , and the polite past, with **-kátta desu** [-かったです] (**samukátta desu** [寒かったです] 'it was cold') . (Do not confuse **-´i desu** [-いです] and **-kátta desu** [-かったです] with the [NOUN] **désu** [(名詞)です], for which the past is [NOUN] **déshita** [(名詞)でした].) The infinitive ('so as to be') ends in **-ku** [-く], as in **sámuku narimáshita** [寒くなりました] 'it turned cold.' There are many adverbs derived from the adjective infinitive, such as **háyaku** [速く, 早く] 'quickly' or 'early.' And the

-ku ［-く］ combines with **arimasén** ［ありません］ (plain form **nái** ［ない］) to make the negative: **sámuku arimasén** ［寒くありません］ 'it isn't cold,' **sámuku nái hí ni wa** ［寒くない日には］ 'on days that are not cold.' The past of the negative is **-ku arimasén deshita** ［-くありませんでした］ (plain past **-ku nákatta** ［-くなかった］). The gerund of the adjective ('being ...' or 'is ... and') ends in **-kute** ［-くて］, and the negative gerund, as in **-ku nákute** ［-くなくて］.

But many Japanese words that translate as English adjectives belong to a different class of words and are treated more like nouns. For that reason they are sometimes called 'adjectival nouns' or 'nominal adjectives,' but you may want to think of them simply as '**na** words,' since they attach the word **na** ('that/who is ...') when they modify a following noun: **heyá ga shízuka desu** ［部屋が静かです］ 'the room is quiet,' **shízuka na heyá desu** ［静かな部屋です］ 'it is a quiet room.' As with nouns, the nonpast form of **na** words is **... désu** ［...です］ (plain form **dá** ［だ］ or nothing, but replaced by **no** ［の］ or **na** ［な］ before a noun), and the past is **... déshita** ［...でした］ (plain form **... dátta** ［...でした］). The negative is **... ja arimasén** ［...じゃありません］ (plain form **... ja nái** ［...じゃない］), the negative past is **... ja arimasén deshita** ［...じゃありませんでした］ (plain form **...ja nákatta** ［...じゃなかった］); all are usually run together with the preceding word to make one long phrase. The gerund is **... dé** ［...で］, as in **heyá ga shízuka de kírei desu** ［部屋が静かできれいです］ 'the rooms are quiet and clean,' and **kírei de shízuka na heyá** ［きれいで静かな部屋］ 'rooms that are quiet and clean.' The infinitive **... ni** ［...に］ means 'so as to be ...' as in **shízuka ni narimáshita** ［静かになりました］ 'became quiet' or '...ly' as in **shízuka ni asonde imásu** ［静かに遊んでいます］ 'is playing quietly.'

In a similar manner, Japanese nouns are often followed by some form of **... désu** ［...です］ (often called the "copula"), replacing a more specific predicate. When the predicate is a verb or an adjective, the role of the noun is marked by a particle. Because the particles go on the end of the noun, they are sometimes called "postpositions," a kind of mirror image of English prepositions: **Kyōˊto kara Nára e ikimáshita** ［京都から奈良へ行きました］ 'I went from Kyoto to Nara.' English subjects and objects are usually unmarked except by word order, but since that is not the case in Japanese, particles mark the subject and object: **Dáre ga náni o shimásu ka** ［誰が何をしますか］ 'Who does what?', **Nani o dáre ga**

shimásu ka [何を誰がしますか] 'Just who does what?'

There is often little semantic need for such marking, for you can usually tell subjects and objects from the context: it is usually people who act and things that are acted upon. So if the particles **... ga** [...が] and **... o** [...を] are omitted, as is required when you attach **... mo** [...も] 'also ..., even ...' or **... wa** [...は] 'as for ...', you usually still know who is doing what: **Watashi mo kikimáshita** [私も聞きました] 'I, too, heard it [as did others], ' **Sore mo kikimáshita** [それも聞きました] 'I heard that too [as well as other things]. '

For many nouns in spoken Japanese, it is quite common to attach a personalizing prefix **o-** [お-], which conveys a vague sense of 'that important thing.' The prefix is also used to make honorific or humble verb forms, with reference to the subject of a sentence. **O-tégami** [お手紙] often means 'your letter,' but does not tell us whether the reference is the letter you have written, or a letter that has been written *to you*; and it can mean just 'the letter' or 'letters,' said with a personalizing touch much appreciated by women and children. Another prefix **go-** [ご-] (**go-ryōshin** [ご両親] 'your parents') attaches to certain nouns (mostly of Chinese origin).

Although these personalized forms are ignored by most dictionaries, we have included many of them, because they are often irregular in accentuation or in some other way. Do not try to use the prefixes **o-** [お-] and **go-** [ご-] with new nouns unless you find the forms in this dictionary or hear them from a Japanese speaker. Honorific and humble verb forms, however, can be made up rather freely, though for certain common verbs they are replaced by euphemisms or unrelated forms; for example, **osshaimásu** [おっしゃいます] 'deigns to say' as the honorific of **iimásu** [言います] 'says.'

KANJI & KANA

Japanese kanji and kana characters have been introduced into the original dictionary and can be found immediately after the romanized forms of the entries. The most contemporary renderings of kanji have been used, including the 2,136 characters from the *jōyō* kanji [常用漢字] list. As it is unreasonable to attempt to convert all romanized words into kanji, kanji is provided only when it is commonly used by the Japanese. In some cases, the kana representation appears before the kanji, and in other cases, after. This means that in the former case kana is most commonly used but at times kanji may be preferable because it conveys the precise meaning of the original word. In the latter case this means that the word is usually written in kanji but kana may sometimes be substituted when the kanji is perceived as too difficult or too long to write.

Other dictionaries provide difficult kanji that are rarely used by native Japanese, but we have chosen to avoid this and focus on contemporary usage. It is possible to write "lemon" in kanji, for example, with the kanji 檸檬, but the katakana form レモン is much preferred.

Every effort has been made to reflect common usage of kanji and kana; thus the ordering of the kanji and kana that follows the romanization is based on frequency of usage. Centered dots mean "or," so appearance **yōsu** 様子・ようす indicates that 様子 is more frequently used but よう す is also an acceptable representation for appearance. Kanji is of course important to clarify the exact meaning of the word; as the Japanese language contains many homonyms there is a certain amount of vagueness in the usage of kana, especially out of context.

In general, romanized words are not hyphenated unless the hyphen represents a morpheme boundary within a compound word. In addition, in this dictionary we have provided kanji and kana renderings for all forms of the romanized words offered, including constituent parts of words that are abbreviated by a hyphen or substituted by a swung dash. Although this takes up extra space, it will facilitate understanding of the exact forms of the relevant word.

NUMBERS

1: **ichí** 一

2: **ní** 二

3: **san** 三

4: **yón/shí** 四

5: **gó** 五

6: **rokú** 六

7: **shichí/nána** 七

8: **hachí** 八

9: **kyū´/kú** 九

10: **jū´** 十

11: **jū-ichí** 十一

12: **jū-ní** 十二

13: **jū´-san** 十三

14: **jū´-yon/jū-shí** 十四

15: **jū´-go** 十五

16: **jū-rokú** 十六

17: **jū-shichí/jū-naná** 十七
18: **jū-hachí** 十八
19: **jū-kyū´/jū´-ku** 十九
20: **ní-jū´** 二十
30: **sán-jū** 三十
40: **yón-jū** 四十
50: **gó-jū** 五十
60: **rokú-jū** 六十
70: **naná-jū** 七十
80: **hachí-jū** 八十
90: **kyū´-jū** 九十
100: **hyakú** 百
200: **ni-hyakú** 二百
300: **sán-byaku** 三百
400: **yón-hyaku** 四百

500: **gó-hyaku** 五百
600: **rop-pyakú** 六百
700: **naná-hyaku** 七百
800: **hap-pyakú** 八百
900: **kyū´-hyaku** 九百
1,000: **sén** 千
2,000: **ni-sén** 二千
3,000: **san-zen** 三千
4,000: **yon-sén** 四千
5,000: **go-sén** 五千
6,000: **roku-sén** 六千
7,000: **nana-sén** 七千
8,000: **has-sén** 八千
9,000: **kyū´-sén** 九千
10,000: **ichi-mán** 一万

-bán 番 (numbers, orders)
1: **ichí-ban** 一番
2: **ní-ban** 二番
3: **sán-ban** 三番
4: **yón-ban/yo-ban** 四番
5: **go-ban** 五番
6: **rokú-ban** 六番
7: **naná-ban** 七番

8: **hachí-ban** 八番
9: **kyū´-ban** 九番
10: **jū´-ban** 十番
100: **hyakú-ban** 百番
1,000: **sén-ban** 千番
what number: **nán-ban** 何番

-banmé 番目 (numeral -th)
1st: **ichí-banme** 一番目
2nd: **ni-banmé** 二番目
3rd: **san-banmé** 三番目
4th: **yon-banmé/**
  yo-banmé 四番目
5th: **go-banmé** 五番目
6th: **roku-banmé** 六番目
7th: **nana-banmé** 七番目

8th: **hachi-banmé** 八番目
9th: **kyū-banmé** 九番目
10th: **jū-banmé** 十番目
100th: **hyaku-banmé** 百番目
1,000th: **sén-banmé** 千番目
what number: **nan-banmé**
  何番目

COUNTING TIME

-ji 時 (o'clock)

1: **ichí-ji** 一時
2: **ní-ji** 二時
3: **sán-ji** 三時
4: **yó-ji** 四時
5: **gó-ji** 五時
6: **rokú-ji** 六時
7: **shichí-ji/naná-ji** 七時

8: **hachí-ji** 八時;
9: **kú-ji** 九時
10: **jū´-ji** 十時
11: **jūichí-ji** 十一時
12: **jūní-ji** 十二時
what time: **nan-ji** 何時

-jikan 時間 (hours)

1: **ichí-jíkan** 一時間
2: **ní-jíkan** 二時間
3: **sán-jíkan** 三時間
4: **yo-jíkan** 四時間
5: **gó-jíkan** 五時間
6: **rokú-jíkan** 六時間
7: **shichí-jíkan/**
   naná-jíkan 七時間

8: **hachí-jíkan** 八時間
9: **kú-jíkan** 九時間
10: **jū´-jíkan** 十時間
100: **hyakú-jíkan** 百時間
1,000: **sén-jíkan** 千時間
how many: **nan-jíkan** 何時間

-fun/-pun 分 (minutes)

1: **íp-pun** 一分
2: **ni-fun** 二分
3: **sán-pun** 三分
4: **yón-pun** 四分
5: **gó-fun** 五分
6: **róp-pun** 六分

7: **naná-fun** 七分
8: **hachí-fun/háp-pun** 八分
9: **kyū´-fun** 九分
10: **júp-pun** 十分
60: **rokujúp-pun** 六十分
how many: **nán-pun** 何分

-byō 秒 (seconds)

1: **ichí-byō** 一秒
2: **ní-byō** 二秒
3: **sán-byō** 三秒
4: **yón-byō** 四秒
5: **gó-byō** 五秒
6: **rokú-byō** 六秒

7: **naná-byō** 七秒
8: **hachí-byō** 八秒
9: **kyū´-byō** 九秒
10: **jū´-byō** 十秒
60: **rokújū´-byō** 六十秒
how many: **nán-byō** 何秒

COUNTING DAYS:

-níchi 日 (days*, days of a month)

1: **tsuitachí** (ichi-nichí*) 一日
2: **f<u>u</u>tsuka** 二日
3: **mikka** 三日
4: **yokka** 四日
5: **its<u>u</u>ka** 五日
6: **muika** 六日
7: **nanoka** 七日
8: **yōka** 八日
9: **kokonoka** 九日
10: **tōka** 十日
11: **jūichí-nichi** 十一日
12: **jūní-nichi** 十二日

13: **jūsán-nichi** 十三日
14: **jū-yokka** 十四日
15: **jūgó-nichi** 十五日
16: **jūrokú-nichi** 十六日
17: **jūshichí-nichi** 十七日
18: **jūhachí-nichi** 十八日
19: **jūkú-nichi** 十九日
20: **hats<u>u</u>ka** 二十日
100: **hyakú-nichi*** 百日
365: **sán-byaku rokujū´gó-nichi**
         ***三百六十五日**
what day: **nan-nichi** 何日

Day before last (yesterday)	**ototói/issakú-jitsu** おととい・一昨日
The previous day (Yesterday)	**kinō´/sakujitsu** きのう・昨日
This day (Today)	**kyō´** きょう・今日
Next day (Tomorrow)	**ashitá/asú/myō´nichi** あした・明日
Day after next (tomorrow)	**asátte/myōgó-nichí** あさって・明後日
Everyday	**máinichí** 毎日

COUNTING WEEKS:

-shūkan 週間 (weeks)

1: **ís-shūkan** 一週間
2: **ní-shūkan** 二週間
3: **sán-shūkan** 三週間
4: **yón-shūkan** 四週間
5: **gó-shūkan** 五週間
6: **rok<u>ú</u>-shūkan** 六週間
7: **naná-shūkan** 七週間
8: **hás-shūkan** 八週間
9: **kyū´-shūkan** 九週間
10: **jús-shūkan** 十週間
how many: **nán-shūkan** 何週間

Week before last **sensén-shū**　先々週
Last week **senshū**　先週
This week **konshū**　今週
Next week **raishū**　来週
Week after next **saraishū**　再来週
Every week **maishū**　毎週

-yōbi 曜日 (days of a week)
Monday **Getsu-yōˊbi**　月曜日
Tuesday **Ka-yōˊbi**　火曜日
Wednesday **Sui-yōˊbi**　水曜日
Thursday **Moku-yōˊbi**　木曜日
Friday **Kin-yōˊbi**　金曜日
Saturday **Do-yōˊbi**　土曜日
Sunday **Nichi-yōˊbi**　日曜日

COUNTING MONTHS:
-gatsu 月 (months of the year)
January: **Ichi-gatsú**　一月
February: **Ni-gatsú**　二月
March: **San-gatsú**　三月
April: **Shi-gatsú**　四月
May: **Go-gatsú**　五月
June: **Roku-gatsú**　六月
July: **Shichi-gatsú**　七月
August: **Hachi-gatsú**　八月
September: **Ku-gatsú**　九月
Octber: **Jū-gatsú**　十月
November: **Jūichi-gatsú**　十一月月
December: **Jūní-gatsú**　十二月
what month: **nan-gatsú**　何月

-ká-getsu か月 (months)
1: **ík-ká-getsu**　一か月
2: **ni-ká-getsu**　二か月
3: **sán-ká-getsu**　三か月
4: **yon-ká-getsu**　四か月

5: **go-ká-getsu** 五か月
6: **rok-ká-getsu** 六か月
7: **nana-ká-getsu** 七か月
8: **hachi-ká-getsu/hak-ká-getsu** 八か月
9: **kyū-ká-getsu** 九か月
10: **juk-ká-getsu** 十か月
how many: **nan-ká-getsu** 何か月

Month before last **sensén-getsu** 先々月
Last month **séngetsu** 先月
This month **kongetsu** 今月
Next month **ráigetsu** 来月
Month after next **saráigetsu** 再来月
Every month **mai-tsuki** 毎月

COUNTING YEARS:
-nén 年 (years)

1: **ichí-nen** 一年	8: **hachí-nen** 八年
2: **ní-nen** 二年	9: **kyū´-nen** 九年
3: **san-nen** 三年	10: **jū´-nen** 十年
4: **yo-nen** 四年	100: **hyakú-nen** 百年
5: **go-nen** 五年	1,000: **sén-nen** 千年
6: **rokú-nen** 六年	10,000: **ichiman-nen** 一万年
7: **shichí-nen/naná-nen** 七年	how many: **nán-nen** 何年

Last year **kyónen/sakunen** 去年・昨年
Year before last **otótoshi/issakú-nen** おととし・一昨年
This year **kotoshi** ことし・今年
Next year **rainen** 来年
Year after next **sarainen** 再来年
Every year **mai-toshi/mainen** 毎年

COUNTING PEOPLE:
-mei 名 (people)
1: **ichí-mei** 一名
2: **ní-mei** 二名
3: **sán-mei** 三名
4: **yón-mei** 四名
5: **go-mei** 五名
6: **rokú-mei** 六名

7: **naná-mei** 七名
8: **hachí-mei** 八名
9: **kyū´-mei** 九名
10: **jū´-mei** 十名
100: **hyakú-mei** 百名
1,000: **sen-mei** 千名
10,000: **ichiman-mei** 一万名
how many: **nán-mei** 何名

-nin 人 (people)
1: **hitó-ri** 一人
2: **futa-rí** 二人
3: **san-nín** 三人
4: **yo-nin** 四人
5: **go-nin** 五人
6: **rokú-nin** 六人
7: **shichí-nin/naná-nin** 七人

8: **hachí-nin** 八人
9: **kyū´-nin/ku-nin** 九人
10: **jū´-nin** 十人
100: **hyakú-nin** 百人
1,000: **sén-nin** 千人
10,000: **ichiman-nin** 一万人
how many: **nán-nin** 何人

COUNTING ANIMALS:
-hiki/-biki/-piki 匹 (fish, bugs, insects or small animals)
1: **ip-pikí** 一匹
2: **ni-hiki** 二匹
3: **sán-biki** 三匹
4: **yón-hiki** 四匹
5: **gó-hiki** 五匹
6: **rop-pikí** 六匹
7: **naná-hikí** 七匹

8: **hachí-hiki/hap-pikí** 八匹
9: **kyū´-hikí** 九匹
10: **jup-pikí** 十匹
100: **hyap-pikí** 百匹
1,000: **sen-bikí** 千匹
10,000: **ichimán-bikí** 一万匹
how many: **nán-bikí** 何匹

-tō 頭 (horses, oxen or large animals)
1: **ít-tō** 一頭
2: **ní-tō** 二頭
3: **sán-tō** 三頭
4: **yón-tō** 四頭
5: **go-tō** 五頭
6: **rokú-tō** 六頭
7: **naná-tō** 七頭

8: **hachí-tō/hát-tō** 八頭
9: **kyū´-tō** 九頭
10: **jút-tō** 十頭
100: **hyakú-tō** 百頭
1,000: **sén-tō** 千頭
10,000: **ichiman-tō** 一万頭
how many: **nán-tō** 何頭

-wá/-bá/-pá 羽 (birds, rabbits)

1: **ichí-wa** 一羽	8: **hachí-wa/háp-pa** 八羽
2: **ní-wa** 二羽	9: **kyū´-wa** 九羽
3: **sán-wa/sán-ba** 三羽	10: **júp-pa/jíp-pa** 十羽
4: **yón-wa/yón-ba/shí-wa** 四羽	100: **hyáp-pa** 百羽
5: **gó-wa** 五羽	1,000: **sén-ba** 千羽
6: **rokú-wa/róp-pa** 六羽	how many: **nán-wa** 何羽
7: **shichí-wa/naná-wa** 七羽	10,000: **ichiman-ba** 一万羽

COUNTING THINGS (Objects):

-bu 部 (copies; books or documents)

1: **ichí-bu** 一部	8: **hachí-bu** 八部
2: **ní-bu** 二部	9: **kyū´-bu** 九部
3: **sán-bu** 三部	10: **jū´-bu** 十部
4: **yón-bu** 四部	100: **hyakú-bu** 百部
5: **gó-bu** 五部	1,000: **sén-bu** 千部
6: **rokú-bu** 六部	10,000: **ichiman-bu** 一万部
7: **naná-bu** 七部	how many: **nán-bu** 何部

-dai 台 (vehicles, machines)

1: **ichí-dai** 一台	8: **hachí-dai** 八台
2: **ní-dai** 二台	9: **kyū´-dai** 九台
3: **sán-dai** 三台	10: **jū´-dai** 十台
4: **yón-dai** 四台	100: **hyakú-dai** 百台
5: **gó-dai** 五台	1,000: **sen-dai** 千台
6: **rokú-dai** 六台	10,000: **ichimán-dai** 一万台
7: **naná-dai** 七台	how many: **nán-dai** 何台

-hako/-pako 箱 (boxed or boxfuls of things)

1: **hitó-hako** 一箱	8: **háp-pako** 八箱
2: **futá-hako** 二箱	9: **kyū´-hako** 九箱
3: **sán-pako/mí-hako** 三箱	10: **júp-pako** 十箱
4: **yón-hako** 四箱	100: **hyáp-pako** 百箱
5: **gó-hako** 五箱	1,000: **sén-pako** 千箱
6: **róp-pako** 六箱	10,000: **ichiman-pako** 一万箱
7: **naná-hako** 七箱	how many: **nán-pako** 何箱

-hon/-bon/-pon 本 (pencils, bottles or long objects)

1: **íp-pon** 一本	8: **hachí-hon/háp-pon** 八本
2: **ní-hon** 二本	9: **kyū´-hon** 九本
3: **sán-bon** 三本	10: **júp-pon** 十本
4: **yón-hon** 四本	100: **hyáp-pon** 百本
5: **go-hon** 五本	1,000: **sen-bon** 千本
6: **róp-pon** 六本	10,000: **ichiman-bón** 一万本
7: **naná-hon** 七本	how many: **nán-bon** 何本

-ken/-gen 軒 (houses or small buildings)

1: **ík-ken** 一軒	8: **hachí-ken/hák-ken** 八軒
2: **ní-ken** 二軒	9: **kyū´-ken** 九軒
3: **sán-gen** 三軒	10: **júk-ken** 十軒
4: **yón-ken** 四軒	100: **hyák-ken** 百軒
5: **gó-ken** 五軒	1,000: **sén-ken** 千軒
6: **rók-ken** 六軒	10,000: **ichiman-ken** 一万軒
7: **naná-ken** 七軒	how many: **nán-ken** 何軒

kire 切れ (slices, cut pieces)

1: **hitó-kire** 一切れ	7: **naná-kire** 七切れ
2: **futá-kire** 二切れ	8: **hachí-kire/hák-kire** 八切れ
3: **sán-kire/mí-kire** 三切れ	9: **kyū´-kire** 九切れ
4: **yón-kire/yó-kire** 四切れ	10: **júk-kire** 十切れ
5: **gó-kire** 五切れ	how many: **nán-kire** 何切れ
6: **rók-kire** 六切れ	

-kumí 組 (sets, pairs)

1: **hito-kumí** 一組	8: **hachí-kumi/hak-kumi** 八組
2: **futá-kumi** 二組	9: **kyū´-kumi** 九組
3: **sán-kumi/mí-kumi** 三組	10: **juk-kumi** 十組
4: **yón-kumi** 四組	100: **hyak-kumi** 百組
5: **gó-kumi** 五組	1,000: **sén-kumi** 千組
6: **rók-kumi** 六組	10,000: **ichimán-kumi** 一万組
7: **naná-kumi** 七組	how many: **nan-kumi** 何組

-ko 個, **-tsu** つ (pieces; small objects)

1: **ík-ko** 一個 (hitotsu 一つ)
2: **ní-ko** 二個 (f<u>u</u>tatsú 二つ)
3: **sán-ko** 三個 (mittsú 三つ)
4: **yón-ko** 四個 (yottsu 四つ)
5: **gó-ko** 五個 (its<u>u</u>tsu 五つ)
6: **rók-ko** 六個 (muttsu 六つ)
7: **naná-ko** 七個 (nanátsu 七つ)
8: **hachí-ko/hák-ko** 八個
          (yattsu 八つ)

9: **kyū´-ko** 九個
   (**kokonotsu** 九つ)
10: **júk-ko/jík-ko** 十個
100: **hyák-ko** 百個
1,000: **sén-ko** 千個
10,000: **ichimán-ko** 一万個
how many: **nan-ko** 何個
          (**ík<u>u</u>tsu** いくつ)

-mai 枚 (sheets; papers or flat and thin objects)

1: **ichí-mai** 一枚
2: **ní-mai** 二枚
3: **sán-mai** 三枚
4: **yón-mai/yo-mai** 四枚
5: **go-mai** 五枚
6: **rokú-mai** 六枚
7: **naná-mai** 七枚

8: **hachí-mai** 八枚
9: **kyū´-mai** 九枚
10: **jū´-mai** 十枚
100: **hyakú-mai** 百枚
1,000: **sén-mai** 千枚
10,000: **ichiman-mai** 一万枚
how many: **nán-mai** 何枚

-satsú 冊 (copies; books, magazines, or other bound things)

1: **is-satsú** 一冊
2: **ní-satsu** 二冊
3: **sán-satsu** 三冊
4: **yón-satsu** 四冊
5: **gó-satsu** 五冊
6: **rokú-satsu** 六冊
7: **naná-satsu** 七冊

8: **hás-satsu** 八冊
9: **kyū´-satsu** 九冊
10: **jús-satsu** 十冊
100: **hyakú-satsu** 百冊
1,000: **sén-satsu** 千冊
10,000: **ichiman-satsu** 一万冊
how many: **nán-satsu** 何冊

-sokú 足 (pairs of footwear)

1: **ís-soku** 一足
2: **ní-soku** 二足
3: **sán-zoku** 三足
4: **yón-soku** 四足
5: **gó-soku** 五足
6: **rokú-soku** 六足
7: **naná-soku** 七足

8: **has-soku** 八足
9: **kyū´-soku** 九足
10: **jus-soku** 十足
100: **hyakú-soku** 百足
1,000: **sén-zoku** 千足
how many: **nán-zoku** 何足

COUNTING TIMES AND OCCASIONS:

-dó 度 (times; occasions)

1: **ichí-dó** 一度
2: **ní-dó** 二度
3: **sán-dó** 三度
4: **yón-dó** 四度
5: **go-dó** 五度
6: **rokú-dó** 六度
7: **naná-do** 七度
8: **hachí-dó** 八度
9: **kyū´-dó/kú-dó** 九度
10: **jū´-dó** 十度
100: **hyakú-dó** 百度
1,000: **sén-dó** 千度
how many: **nán-dó** 何度

-hén/-bén/-pén 遍 (times; occasions)

1: **íp-pen** 一遍
2: **ni-hén** 二遍
3: **sán-bén** 三遍
4: **yón-hén/yón-pen** 四遍
5: **gò-hén** 五遍
6: **rop-pén** 六遍
7: **naná-hén** 七遍
8: **hachí-hén/hap-pén** 八遍
9: **kyū´-hén** 九遍
10: **jup-pén** 十遍
100: **hyap-pén** 百遍
1,000: **sen-pén** 千遍
10,000: **ichiman-bén** 一万遍
how many: **nán-ben** 何遍

-kái 回 (times; occasions)

1: **ik-kái** 一回
2: **ni-kái** 二回
3: **sán-kái** 三回
4: **yón-kái** 四回
5: **go-kái** 五回
6: **rok-kái** 六回
7: **naná-kái** 七回
8: **hachi-kái/hak-kái** 八回
9: **kyū´-kái** 九回
10: **juk-kái** 十回
100: **hyak-kái** 百回
1,000: **sen-kái** 千回
10,000: **ichiman-kái** 一万回
how many: **nán-kái** 何回

OTHERS:

-bái 倍 (multiples; times, -fold)

1: **ichi-bai** 一倍
2: **ni-bai** 二倍
3: **sán-bai** 三倍
4: **yón-bai** 四倍
5: **gó-bai** 五倍
6: **rokú-bai** 六倍
7: **naná-bai** 七倍
8: **hachí-bai** 八倍
9: **kyū´-bai** 九倍
10: **jū´-bai** 十倍
100: **hyakú-bai** 百倍
1,000: **sén-bai** 千倍
how many: **nán-bai** 何倍

-do 度 (degrees)

1: **ichí-do** 一度
2: **ní-do** 二度
3: **sán-do** 三度
4: **yón-do** 四度
5: **gó-do** 五度
6: **rokú-do** 六度
7: **naná-do** 七度

8: **hachí-do** 八度
9: **kyū´-do** 九度
10: **jū´-do** 十度
100: **hyakú-do** 百度
1,000: **sén-do** 千度
what's the degree: **nán-do** 何度

-en 円 (yen; money)

1: **ichí-en** 一円
2: **ní-en** 二円
3: **sán-en** 三円
4: **yón-en/yó-en** 四円
5: **gó-en** 五円
6: **rokú-en** 六円
7: **naná-en** 七円

8: **hachí-en** 八円
9: **kyū´-en** 九円
10: **jū´-en** 十円
100: **hyakú-en** 百円
1,000: **sen-en** 千円
10,000: **ichimán-en** 一万円
how much: **nán-en** 何円

-go 語 (words)

1: **ichí-go** 一語
2: **ní-go** 二語
3: **sán-go** 三語
4: **yón-go** 四語
5: **gó-go** 五語
6: **rokú-go** 六語
7: **naná-go** 七語

8: **hachí-go** 八語
9: **kyū´-go** 九語
10: **jū´-go** 十語
100: **hyakú-go** 百語
1,000: **sén-go** 千語
10,000: **ichiman-go** 一万語
how many: **nán-go** 何語

-hai/-bai/-pai 杯 (cupfuls; glassfuls; bowlfuls; spoonfuls)

1: **íp-pai** 一杯
2: **ní-hai** 二杯
3: **sán-bai** 三杯
4: **yón-hai** 四杯
5: **gó-hai** 五杯
6: **róp-pai** 六杯
7: **naná-hai** 七杯

8: **háp-pai** 八杯
9: **kyū´-hai** 九杯
10: **júp-pai** 十杯
100: **hyáp-pai** 百杯
1,000: **sén-bai** 千杯
10,000: **ichiman-bai** 一万杯
how many: **nán-bai** 何杯

-hakú 泊 (níghts of lodging)
1: **ip-paku** 一泊
2: **ní-haku** 二泊
3: **sánp-paku** 三泊
4: **yón-haku/yón-paku** 四泊
5: **gó-hakú** 五泊
6: **róp-paku** 六泊

7: **naná-hakú** 七泊
8: **háp-paku** 八泊
9: **kyū´-haku** 九泊
10: **júp-paku** 十泊
how many: **nán-paku** 何泊

-kai 階 (floors, stories)
1: **ik-kai** 一階
2: **ni-kai** 二階
3: **san-kai/san-gai** 三階
4: **yon-kai** 四階
5: **go-kai** 五階
6: **rok-kai** 六階

7: **nana-kai** 七階
8: **hachi-kai/hak-kai** 八階
9: **kyū-kai** 九階
10: **juk-kai** 十階
how many: **nan-kai** 何階

-sai 歳 (year of age)
1: **ís-sai** 一歳 (**hitotsu** 一つ)
2: **ní-sai** 二歳 (**futatsú** 二つ)
3: **sán-sai** 三歳 (**mittsú** 三つ)
4: **yón-sai** 四歳 (**yottsu** 四つ)
5: **gó-sai** 五歳 (**itsutsu** 五つ)
6: **rokú-sai** 六歳 (**muttsu** 六つ)
7: **naná-sai** 七歳 (**nanátsu** 七つ)
8: **hás-sai** 八歳 (**yattsu** 八つ)
9: **kyū´-sai** 九歳 (**kokonotsu** 九つ)
10: **jús-sai** 十歳 (**tō** 十)
100: **hyakú-sai** 百歳
how many: **nan-sai** 何歳 (**íkutsu**)

PART I
JAPANESE – ENGLISH

A

ā 1. *adv* ああ like that, that way **2.** *interj* ああ oh; yes **3.** *interj* ああ hello (*on encountering someone*)

á *interj* あっ oh! : [+ NAME and/or TITLE] **á, (o-) kā´-san da!** あっ、（お）母さんだ！ Oh, it's my mother!

abakimásu, abaku *v* 暴きます、暴く discloses

abara-ya *n* あばら屋 hovel

abaremásu, abareru *v* 暴れます、暴れる rages, storms, rampages

abare-mono *n* 暴れ者 ruffian, roughneck, wild person

abazure *n* あばずれ a real bitch

abékku *n* アベック young unmarried couple

abekobe *n* あべこべ upside down

abimásu, abiru *v* 浴びます、浴びる bathes oneself in; douses, showers

abisemásu, abiseru *v* 浴びせます、浴びせる pours on, showers

abu *n* アブ・虻 horse fly: [IDIOM] **abu hachi torazu** 虻蜂取らず falls between two stools

abuku *n* あぶく bubble
abuku-zéni *n* あぶく銭 easy money

abunaí *adj* 危ない dangerous (= **kiken (na)** 危険 (な)), Watch out!: **abunaí hashi o watarimásu** 危ない橋を渡ります walks on thin ice

abunakkashii *adj* 危なっかしい is insecure, unsteady

abunōmaru *n* アブノーマル abnormal

abura *n* 油 oil, grease

abura *n* 脂 fat (= **shibō** 脂肪): **abura o urimásu** 油を売ります shoots the breeze: **doko de abura o utte(i)tandesu(ka)?** どこで油を売って（い）たんです(か)? Where have you been goofing off?

aburá(á)ge *n* 油揚げ deep-fried bean curd

aburakkói *adj* 油っこい oily, greasy

aburakkói *adj* 脂っこい fatty

aburimásu, abúru *v* 炙ります、炙る grills

āchi(-gata) *n* アーチ(形) arch (= **yumi-gata** 弓形)

ācherii *n* アーチェリー archery

achí-kochi *adv* あちこち here and there (= **achíra-kóchira** あちらこちら)

achira *pron* あちら **1.** that one (of two) over there, the other one (over there) **2.** over there, yonder **3.** he/him, she/her, they/them

achira-gawa *n* あちら側 that (his/her/their) side, other side

ada *n* あだ meaningless: **ada to narimásu** あだとなります works negatively

ada *n* 仇 [BOOKISH] disservice, foe: **ada o uchimásu** 仇を討ちます avenges, revenges

adana *n* あだ名 nickname (= **aishō** 愛称)

adaputā *n* アダプター (electrical) adapter

adéyaka *adj* 艶やか gorgeous, fascinatingly elegant: **... no adéyaka na butai-sugata ni me o miharimashita** …の艶やかな舞台姿に目を見張り

ました …(one's) bewitching stage presence drew my attention

adobáisu *n* アドバイス advice

adobarūn *n* アドバルーン balloon from which an advertising banner is suspended

adokenai *adj* あどけない innocent, childlike
adokenai kao *n* あどけない顔 an innocent face

adoresu *n* アドレス address: **mēru-adoresu** メールアドレス e-mail address

adoribu *n* アドリブ ad lib

áeba *v* 合えば (if it fits) → **aimásu** 合います

áeba *v* 会えば (if one meets) → **aimásu** 会います

aegimásu, aégu *v* 喘ぎます、喘ぐ gasps, pants (for breath)

aéide *v* 喘いで → **aegimásu** 喘ぎます

aemásu, aéru *v* 和えます、和える dresses (vegetables, etc.)

aemásu, aéru *v* 会えます、会える can meet

aé-mono *n* 和え物 boiled or salt-rubbed fish and vegetables mixed with a dressing

áon *n* アエン・亜鉛 zinc

aénai *v* 会えない = **aemasén** 会えません (cannot meet)

aénai *v* 和えない = **aemasén** 和えません (not dress ...)

aenai *adj* 敢えない tragic, sad: **aénaku mo** 敢えなくも tragically enough

aéreba *v* 会えれば (if one can meet) → **aemásu** 会えます

aéreba *v* 和えれば (if one dresses ...) → **aemásu** 和えます

áete *v* 敢えて: **áete ... (shimásu)** 敢えて…(します) dares (*to do*)

afuremásu, afuréru *v* 溢れます、溢れる overflows

Afurika *n* アフリカ Africa
Afurika-jin *n* アフリカ人 an African

afutā-sābisu *n* アフターサービス service (*maintenance and repair*), servicing

afutā shēbu lōshon *n* アフターシェーブローション aftershave (*lotion*)

agakimásu, agaku *v* 足掻きます、足掻く struggles

agaméru *v* 崇める worships, adores, respects: **kami o agamemásu** 神を崇めます worships [adores] God.

agarí *n* 上がり **1.** a cup of green tea (*in a sushi bar*) **2.** rise **3.** product; income

agarí *n, adj* 上がり finishing, (*resulting*) finish

agarí *v* 上がり → **agarimásu** 上がります [INFINITIVE]

agarimásu, agaru *v* 上がります、上がる **1.** goes up, rises **2.** feels self-conscious, nervous; gets stage fright

agari-guchi, agari-kuchi *n* 上り口 the entrance

...-ágari (no) *adj* …上がり(の) fresh from ...,

3

right after …: **yami ágari no hitó** 病み上がりの人 a person just out of sickbed; **ame-ágari no michi** 雨上がりの道 the road right after the rain

agatte v 上がって → **agarimásu** 上がります

age-ashi n 揚げ足 fault finding

ageku n 挙句 negative outcome
  ageku no hate 挙句の果て in the end

agemásu, agerú v **1.** あげます, あげる gives
  2. …-**te agerú** …てあげる does someone's favor

agemásu, agerú v 上げます, 上げる raises up

agemásu, agerú v 揚げます, 揚げる fries; raises

age(ra)remásu, age(ra)rerú v あげ(ら)れます・あげ(ら)れる can give

age(ra)remásu, age(ra)rerú v 上げ(ら)れます・上げ(ら)れる can raise

age(ra)remásu, age(ra)rerú v 揚げ(ら)れます, 揚げ(ら)れる can fry

agereba v あげれば (if one gives) → **agemásu** あげます

agereba v 上げれば (if one raises) → **agemásu** 上げます

agereba v 揚げれば (if one fries) → **agemásu** 揚げます

age ro v 上げろ = **age yo** 上げよ [IMPERATIVE] (raise up!) → **agemásu** 上げます

agé ya/wa shinai v あげや/はしない = **agenai** あげない (not give)

agé ya/wa shinai v 上げや/はしない = **agenai** 上げない (not raise)

agé ya/wa shinai v 揚げや/はしない = **agenai** 揚げない (not fry)

ageyō v あげよう = **agemashō** あげましょう (let's give it!, I'll give it (to you).)

ago n あご・顎 jaw, chin
  ago-hige n あごひげ beard, goatee, (chin-)whiskers

agura n あぐら sitting cross-legged

áhen n アヘン・阿片 opium

ahiru n アヒル duck (*tame*)

aho, ahō n あほ(う)・阿呆 fool

ái n 愛 love (= **aijō** 愛情): **ai-shimásu** 愛します loves

ái n 藍 Japanese indigo plant
  ái zome n 藍染め Japanese indigo dye

aiaigasa n あいあい傘 sharing an umbrella

aibiki n 逢引 secret rendezvous

aibō n 相棒 partner

áibu n 愛撫 caress: ~ **shimásu** 愛撫します caresses

aichaku n 愛着 affection

aida n, *prep*, *adv* 間 interval, space, between; while

aidagara n 間柄 relationship (*between people*)

aidéa n アイデア idea

aidoku n 愛読 reading with pleasure: ~ **shimásu** 愛読します likes to read

áidoru n アイドル idol

aigo n 愛護 [BOOKISH] protection

aigoma n 合駒 piece placed to block the opponent's check

ai-hanshimásu, ai-hansuru v 相反します, 相反する conflicts

aiirenai *adj* 相容れない exclusive, incompatible, irreconcilable: **kono futatsu no kasetsu wa aiiremasen** この2つの仮説は相容れません These two suppositions are mutually exclusive

ai-jin n 愛人 mistress

aijō n 愛情 affection, love (= **ai** 愛)

aí-kagi n 合鍵 duplicate key

aikawarazu *adv* 相変わらず as usual/ever/always: **aikawarazu génki desu** 相変らず元気です stays well (as always)

aiken n 愛犬 one's (pet) dog

aikí-dō n 合気道 aikido, an art of weaponless defense

aíko n あいこ (**o-aikó** おあいこ) tie (*in sports, games*), stalemate

aikō-ka n 愛好家 lover (*devotee of …*)

aikoku-shin n 愛国心 patriotism

aikotoba n 合い言葉 password, shibboleth [INFORMAL talk]

aikyō n 愛嬌[愛敬] charm, attractiveness: **aikyō ga arimásu** 愛嬌[愛敬]があります is nice, attractive, charming

aima n 合間 spare time: **isogashii sukéjūru no aima o nutte…** 忙しいスケジュールの合間を縫って… Taking time out of one's busy schedule…

aimai (na) *adj* 曖昧(な) vague

aimasu, áu v 会います, 会う: … **ni aimasu** …に会います meets; sees (a person)

aimasu, áu v 合います, 合う: … **ni aimasu** …に合います matches with: **kuchi ni aimasu** 口に合います suits one's taste; (…**ni) ma ni aimasu** (…に) 間に合います is in time (for …)

…-**aimasu, -au/-áu** …合います, 合う [VERB INFINITIVE +] (*to*) each other

aimátte *adv* あいまって combined

ainiku *adv* あいにく unfortunately

ainiku (na) *adj* あいにく(な) regrettable

ainoko n あいの子 person of mixed race [IN NEGATIVE SENSE]

ainorí n 相乗り ride together

ainote n あいの手 short interlude

airáin n アイライン eyeliner

airashii *adj* 愛らしい lovely, sweet

airon n アイロン iron(ing)

Airurándo n アイルランド Ireland

ai-sánai v 愛さない = **ai-shimasén** 愛しません (not love)

áisatsu n 挨拶, [HONORIFIC] **go-áisatsu** ご挨拶 greeting: (…) **ni áisatsu shimásu** (…)に挨拶します greets

aisha n 愛車 one's beloved vehicle/car

aishádō n アイシャドー eye shadow

ai-shimásu, ai-súru v 愛します, 愛する (= **ai-su** 愛す) loves

ái-shite v 愛して → **ai-shimásu** 愛します

aishō n 愛称 nickname

aishō n 相性 compatibility, congeniality: **aishō ga/no íi** 相性が/のいい congenial, compatible

aisó, aisō n あいそ(う)・愛想 **1. aisó (aisō) ga/no íi** あいそ(う)[愛想]が/のいい is amiable, sociable, agreeable **2. o-aiso, o-aisō** お愛想 (*restaurant*) bill, check; incense

aisu... *prefix* アイス... iced...

aisu-hókkē *n* アイスホッケー ice hockey

aisu-kōhii *n* アイスコーヒー iced coffee

aisu-kuríimu *n* アイスクリーム ice cream

aisu-kyándii *n* アイスキャンディー popsicle

aisu-sukēto *n* アイススケート ice skating, ice skates

aisu-tii *n* アイスティー iced tea

aite *v* 開いて → **akimásu** 開きます

aite *n* 相手 (**o-aite** お相手) the other fellow; companion, partner; adversary, opponent

aite imásu (iru) *v* 開いています(いる) is open

aite imásu (iru) *v* 空いています(いる) vacant, empty

aitō *n* 哀悼 condolence: mourning: **fukai aitō** 深い哀悼 deep mourning

aitsu *pron* あいつ that guy, that creep

aitsú-ra *pron* あいつら those damn ones

aitsúide *adv* 相次いで one after another

aitii (IT) *n* IT(アイティー) information technology (*computer*)

āiu *adj* ああいう ... that kind/sort of (= **anna** あんな, **āyū** ああゆう)

aiuchí *n* 相打ち hitting/killing each other at the same time: **aiucí ni narimásu** 相打ちになります hits/kills each other at the same time

aiúeo *n* あいうえお the Japanese syllabary

áizu *n* 合図 signal, sign: **áizu shimásu/o okurimásu** 合図します/を送ります makes a sign, cues, prompts

aizúchi *n* 相槌 give responses: **aizúchi o uchimásu** 相槌を打ちます gives responses to make the conversation go smoothly

ají *n* 味 taste; flavor, seasoning: **ají ga shimásu** 味がします it tastes (has flavor) **ají ga usuidesu** 味が薄いです is bland: **ají o oboemásu** 味を覚えます acquires a taste for: **ají o shimemásu** 味をしめます gets a taste of success

áji *n* アジ・鯵 horse mackerel, saurel

Ájia *n* アジア Asia

Ajiá-jin *n* アジア人 an Asian

ajike-nái *adj* 味気ない insipid, flavorless, flat

ajísai *n* アジサイ hydrangea

ajiwaemásu, ajiwaéru *v* 味わえます, 味わえる can taste it

ajiwaimásu, ajiwáu *v* 味わいます, 味わう tastes it

áka *n* 赤 red (*color*)

aka-bō *n* 赤帽 redcap, porter

áka-chan *n* 赤ちゃん・あかちゃん baby

aká-gai *n* 赤貝 ark shell, blood(y) clam

aka-go *n* 赤子 [BOOKISH] baby : **aka-go no te o hineru yō na mono desu** 赤子の手をひねるようなものです is very easy

akai *adj* 赤い red: **akaku narimásu** 赤くなります turns red, blushes

aka-jí *n* 赤字 red letters, deficit figures: **aka-jí ni**

narimásu 赤字になります goes/gets in the red

aka-mi *n* 赤身 lean (meat/fish); unfatty (red) tuna

akan-bo, akan-bō 赤ん坊, 赤ん坊 → **áka-chan** 赤ちゃん・あかちゃん

aka-shíngo *n* 赤信号 red light (*signal*)

aká *n* あか・垢 dirt, grime

akádemii *n* アカデミー academy

akademíkku *n* アカデミック academic

aka-gane *n* あかがね・銅 copper

akanai *v* 開かない = **akimasén** 開きません (not open)

áka-no-tanin *n* 赤の他人 complete stranger, total stranger [IN NEGATIVE SENSE]: **kare wa áka-no-tanin desú** 彼は赤の他人です He's totally an outsider.

akaramemásu, akarameru *v* 赤らめます, 赤らめる blushes

akarasama (na/ni) *adj, adv* あからさま(な/に) frank(ly), plain(ly), open(ly) [IN NEGATIVE SENSE]: **kare wo akarasama na iikata ni hara ga tachimashita.** 彼のあからさまな言い方に腹が立ちました I was offended by his plain remark

akari *n* 明かり light, lamp

akarui *adj* 明るい bright, light, clear, gay, cheerful

akarumi *n* 明るみ a light place; the (open/bright) light: **akarumi ni demásu** 明るみに出ます surfaces, comes to light, is brought to light: **kaisha no (o)kane o ōryō shiteita koto ga akarumi ni demashita** 会社の(お)金を横領していたことが明るみに出ました It came to light that one had been embezzling company funds

akéba *v* 開けば (if it comes open)

ākēdo *n* アーケード arcade, roofed passageway, shopping arcade

akegata *n, adv* 明け方 daybreak, dawn

akemáshite o-medetō (gozaimásu [HONORIFIC]**)** *interj* 明けましておめでとう(ございます) Happy New Year!

akemásu, akeru *v* 開けます, 開ける opens it

akemásu, akeru *v* 空けます, 空ける leaves empty, vacates

akemásu, akeru *v* 明けます, 明ける it opens up, (the day/year) begins: **yo ga akemásu** 夜があけます (it/dawn) breaks

ake(ra)remásu, ake(ra)reru *v* 開け(ら)れます, 開け(ら)れる can open it

akeréba *v* 開ければ (if one opens it) → **akemásu** 開けます

ake ro *v* 開けろ [IMPERATIVE] (open it!) → **akemásu** 開けます

akete *v* 開けて → **akemásu** 明けます: **aketé mo kureté mo** 明けても暮れても day in and day out

aké ya/wa shinai *v* 開けや/はしない = **akenai** 開けない (not open it)

akeyō *v* 開けよう = **akemashō** 開けましょう (let's open it!)

áki *n* 秋 autumn, fall

aki-same *n* 秋雨 autumn rain

akí- *prefix* 空き empty, vacant

aki-bako *n* 空き箱 empty box

aki-beya *n* 空き部屋 empty room

aki-bin *n* 空き瓶 empty bottle

aki-chi *n* 空き地 vacant lot (*land*)

aki-kan *n* 空き缶 empty can

aki-shitsu *n* 空き室 empty room/office

aki-ya *n* 空き家 vacant/empty house

aki-su *n* あき巣狙い・空き巣 sneak thief: **akisu-nérai** あき巣狙い・空き巣狙い a sneaking thief who steals from a house in the absence of the occupants

akimásu, akíru *v* 飽きます, 飽きる wearies (*gets tired*) of; gets enough of

akimásu, aku *v* 開きます, 開く opens, comes open; it comes unbuttoned/unzipped/unlocked

akimásu, aku *v* 空きます, 空く gets empty/ vacant

akínai *v* 飽きない = **akimasén** 飽きません (not weary of)

akinaimásu, akinau *v* 商います, 商う blushes

akíndo *n* 商人 merchant

akíraka *adj* 明らか clear (*evident*): **akíraka ni shimásu** 明らかにします makes it public, reveals, explains

akirame *n* 諦め resignation, acceptance: **akirame ga warui** 諦めが悪い not knowing when to give up

akiramemásu, akiraméru *v* 諦めます, 諦める: **… o akiramemásu**…を諦めます gives up (*on*), resigns oneself to

akire *v* 呆れ → **akiremásu** 呆れます [INFINITIVE]

akiremásu, akireru *v* 呆れます, 呆れる gets amazed; gets disgusted

akirete *v* 呆れて → **akiremásu** 呆れます

akíru *v* 飽きる = **akimásu** 飽きます (wearies of)

ákite *v* 飽きて → **akimásu** 飽きます

akka *n* 悪化 worsening: **~ shimásu** 悪化します grows worse, worsens

akkan *n* 圧巻 overwhelming

akke-nái *adj* あっけない not long enough: **akke-nái ketsumatsu** あっけない結末 disappointing ending: **akkenaku makeru** あっけなく負ける is beaten too easily

akke ni toraremásu (torareru) *v* 呆気に取られます(取られる) is stunned: **yosōgai no ketsu-matsu ni akke ni toraremáshita** 予想外の結末に呆気に取られました was dumbfounded by the unexpected results

akkerakán (to) *adv* あっけらかん(と) looks unconcerned: **taisetsu na mono o nakushita noni akkerakán to shiteimásu** 大切な物をなくしたのに、あっけらかんとしています lost something important, but looks as if nothing had happened.

akogaremásu, akogaréru *v* 憧れます, 憧れる adores, admires; longs for, yearns for

akogi (ná) *adj* あこぎ(な) cruel and heartless

akú *v* 開く = **akimásu** 開きます (it opens)

áku *n* 悪 an evil

aku-bun *n* 悪文 poor writing

aku-byōdō *n* 悪平等 misapplied equality

aku-fū *n* 悪風 bad custom, bad practice, a vice

aku-heki *n* 悪癖 [BOOKISH] bad habit

aku-hō *n* 悪法 bad law

aku-hyō *n* 悪評 criticism (*unfavorable*)

áku-i *n* 悪意 ill will, malice

aku-jōken *n* 悪条件 bad/unfavorable/adverse condition

aku-júnkan *n* 悪循環 vicious circle

áku-ma *n* 悪魔 devil, evil spirit, Satan

áku-mu *n* 悪夢 nightmare, **áku-mu ni chigai arimasen** 悪夢に違いありません must be a nightmare

aku-nin *n* 悪人 an evil person

aku-ratsu (na) *adj* 悪辣(な) unscrupulous, foul, nasty, mean

aku-sei *n* 悪政 [BOOKISH] bad government

aku-sei no *adj* 悪性の malignant

aku-sen *n* 悪銭 [BOOKISH] ill-gotten gains: [IDIOM] **aku-sen mi ni tsukazu** 悪銭身につかず Ill got, ill spent./Easy come, Easy go.

aku-shitsu (ná) *adj* 悪質(な) malignant, pernicious, vicious

aku-shū *n* 悪臭 stink, smell: **aku-shū o hanachimásu** 悪臭を放ちます smells out

aku-shū *n* 悪習 abuse, bad habit: **aku-shū ni somarimásu** 悪習に染まります contracts a bad habit, gets into bad habits

aku-shumí *n* 悪趣味 bad/poor taste

aku-toku *n* 悪徳 (a) vice: **akutoku-gyōsha** 悪徳業者 dishonest business person

aku-zei *n* 悪税 [BOOKISH] unreasonable tax

akú *n* アク・灰汁 scum, lye: **akú o torimásu** 灰汁を取ります removes the scum: **akú ga tsuyoi** 灰汁が強い is self-involved

akuaríumu *n* アクアリウム aquarium

akubí *n* 欠伸 yawn(ing): **akubí (o) shimásu** 欠伸(を)します yawns

akurobátto *n* アクロバット acrobat, acrobatics

akúryoku *n* 握力 grasping power

ákuseku *adv* あくせく laboriously, (working) hard, drudging (away)

akusen-kutō *n* 悪戦苦闘 fight desperately

ákusento *n* アクセント accent

ákuseru *n* アクセル gas pedal, accelerator: **ákuseru o fumimásu** アクセルを踏みます steps on the gas

ákusesari(i) *n* アクセサリ(ー) an accessory

ákushon *n* アクション action

akushon-eiga *n* アクション映画 an action film

ákushu *n* 握手 handshake: **~ shimásu** 握手します shakes hands

ákuta *n* 芥 dirt, rubbish

amá *n* アマ・亜麻 flax plant, linen

amá iro (no) *adj* 亜麻色(の) flaxen, linen, towheaded

amá *n* 尼 nun

áma *n* 海女 woman sea diver, a pearl diver

ama-… *prefix* 雨 rain

amá-do *n* 雨戸 rain shutters

ama-gasa *n* 雨傘 umbrella (= **kasa** 傘)

amá-gutsu *n* 雨靴 rain shoes, galoshes
amá(chuá) *n* アマ(チュア) an amateur
amaemásu, amaéru *v* 甘えます, 甘える presumes on someone's goodwill, acts like a baby
amanógawa *n* あまのがわ・天の川 the Milky Way
amai *adj* 甘い sweet; lenient, permissive
amaku mimásu (míru) *v* 甘くみます(みる) kids oneself about …, underestimates
amari *n* 余り remainder, surplus, leftover
amari *adv* あまり [+ NEGATIVE verb] not very, not much, not many (= **anmari** あんまり): **amari arimasen/nai** あまりありません/ない There are not so many. I/We have not much
amari *v* 余り → **amarimásu** 余ります [INFINITIVE]
amarimásu, amáru *v* 余ります, 余る is left over, remains, is in excess, is too much/many
amarí(ni) *adv* あまり(に) too, too much, very
amatō *n* 甘党 having a sweet tooth, person who has a sweet tooth
amátte *v* 余って → **amarimásu** 余ります
amayakashimásu, amayakásu *v* 甘やかします, 甘やかす pampers, babies
amé *n* アメ・飴 candy (= **kyandi(i)** キャンディ(一))
áme *n* 雨 rain: **áme ga furimásu** 雨が降ります it rains; **áme ni narimásu** 雨になります it turns/starts to rain: **ama-yadori shimásu** 雨宿りします takes shelter from the rain
amē´ba *n* アメーバ amoeba
Amerika *n* アメリカ America, U.S.(A.): = **Amerika Gasshū´koku** アメリカ合衆国 United States of America
Ameriká-jin *n* アメリカ人 an American
amí *n* 網 net
amí-do *n* 網戸 screen door
amimásu, ámu *v* 編みます, 編む knits, braids
amí-mono *n* 編み物 knitting, knitted goods
ā´mōndo *n* アーモンド almond
án *n* 案 **1.** proposal, suggestion, idea (= **kangae** 考え, **teian** 提案) **2.** plan (= **keikaku** 計画, **kikaku** 企画)
án *n* あん・餡 bean jam/paste
án-ko *n* あんこ・餡子 bean jam/paste
aná *n* 穴 hole; slot
ana-go *n* アナゴ conger eel
ana-guma *n* アナグマ・穴熊 badger
anáta *pron* あなた you
anatá-tachi, anatá-gáta *pron* あなた達, あなた方 (all)
anatá-jíshin *pron* あなた自身 yourself
anáta(-tachi) no *pron* あなた(達)の your(s)
anáúnsā *n* アナウンサー announcer
anáúnsu *n* アナウンス announcement
andārain *n* アンダーライン underline
andāshátsu *n* アンダーシャツ undershirt
andon *n* 行灯 traditional paper-covered night-light
anadorimásu, anadoru *v* 侮ります, 侮る not think much of: **imamade … o anadotte imáshita** いままで…を侮っていました hadn't used to think much of …

ándo *n* 安堵 relief: **~ shimásu** 安堵します feels relief
áne *n* 姉 older sister (= **(o-)nē´-san** (お)姉さん)
ángai *adv* 案外 **1.** unexpectedly (much) **2.** contrary to expectations
ángai (na) *adj* 案外(な) unexpected
angō *n* 暗号 secret code
anguru *n* アングル angle (= **kakudo** 角度), viewpoint
áni *n* 兄 elder brother (= **(o-)nii´-san** (お)兄さん)
anime, animēshon *n* アニメ, アニメーション animation, animaed cartoon
anji *n* 暗示 a hint: **~shimásu** 暗示します hints, suggests
jiko-anji *n* 自己暗示 autosuggestion
ánkā *n* アンカー anchor
ankēto *n* アンケート questionnaire
ankí *n* 暗記 memorizing: **~ shimásu** 暗記します memorizes; **ankí shite** 暗記して by/from memory
ankōru *n* アンコール encore
anma *n* 按摩 masseur/masseuse (= **massá´ji** マッサージ)
an-man *n* アンマン steamed bun stuffed with bean jam
anmari *adv* あんまり too much, overly; [+ NEGATIVE] not (very) much
anmoku-no-ryōkai *n* 暗黙の了解 an unspoken agreement
anmonáito *n* アンモナイト ammonite
anna… *adj* あんな that kind of…: **anna ni** あんなに to that extent
annái *n* 案内, [HONORIFIC] **go-annai** ご案内 guidance, information: **(go-)annái shimásu** (ご)案内します guides, leads, ushers
annai-jó *n* 案内所 information booth/desk
annái-nin *n* 案内人 guide (*person*), usher (= **annai-gákari** 案内係)
annái-shó *n* 案内書 guide(book)
anó *adj* あの that (over there; *known to you and me*)
anó-hito *pron* あの人 he/him, she/her
anó-hito-tachi *pron* あの人達 they/them
anó-ko *pron* あの子 she/her, he/him
ano-yo *n* あの世 the next world, another world: **ano-yo-teki** あの世的 otherworldly
ano, anō *interj* あの, あのう (*with nervous diffidence*) well, uh …
ano né *interj* あのね (*mostly children or female*) well, listen, you know
anpáia *n* アンパイア umpire
anpán *n* アンパン sweet roll with bean jam inside
anpéa *n* アンペア ampere
anpo *n* 安保 Security: **Nichibei Anzen Hoshō Jōyaku** 日米安全保障条約 the U.S.-Japan Security Treaty
anpu *n* アンプ amplifier
anpuru *n* アンプル ampule
anraku *n* 安楽 comfort
anraku (na) *adj* 安楽(な) comfortable, easy
anraku shi *n* 安楽死 mercy killing, euthanasia

ansei *n* 安静 rest: **ansei ni shimásu** 安静にします keeps/lies quiet

anshín *n* 安心 peace of mind; relief; security; confidence, trust: **~ shimásu** 安心します not worry, relaxes (one's anxieties), is relieved (of worry)

anshitsu *n* 暗室 darkroom

anshō *n* 暗唱 recitation from memory: **~ shimásu** 暗唱します recites

ánta *pron* [INFORMAL] あんた (rude or rough (*depends on the situation*)) [FORMAL] **anáta** あなた you

antei *n* 安定 stability: **~ shimásu** 安定します stabilizes

antena *n* アンテナ antenna, aerial

ánzan *n* 安産 safe delivery, easy delivery:
~ shimásu 安産します has a safe/an easy delivery
anzan kigan *n* 安産祈願 wishing someone a safe delivery

anzán *n* 暗算 mental calculatin: **~ shimásu** 暗算します calculates mentally

anzen (na) *adj* 安全(な) safe (*harm-proof*)
anzén-pin *n* 安全ピン safety pin

anzimásu, anjiru (anzuru) *v* 案じます, 案じる (案ずる) worrys, concerns: [IDIOM] **anzuru yori umu ga yasushi** 案ずるより産むがやすし easier than one thinks

anzu *n* アンズ・杏 apricot

áo *n* 青 blue, green (color)
aói *adj* 青い blue, green, pale
ao-jáshin *n* 青写真 blueprint
ao-mi *n* 青味 blueness
ao-mushi *n* 青虫 green caterpillar
ao-nísai *n* 青二才 immature [IN NEGATIVE SENSE]:
ao-nísai no wakazō ga 青二才の若造が You're still wet behind the ears.
ao-shíngo *n* 青信号 green light (*signal*)
ao-suji *n* 青筋 blue vein: **ao-suji o tateru** 青筋を立てる bursts a blood vessel
ao-yagi *n* 青柳 (= **aoyánagi** 青柳) budding willow
ao-zóra *n* 青空 blue sky

aō´ *v* 会おう = **aimashō´** 会いましょう (let's meet!)

aogimásu, aógu *v* 扇ぎます, 扇ぐ fans; fans oneself

aogimásu, aógu *v* 仰ぎます, 仰ぐ looks up at/to; respects (= **miageru** 見上げる)

aóide *v* 扇いで → **aogimásu** 扇ぎます

aóide *v* 仰いで → **aogimásu** 仰ぎます

aomuké *n* 仰向け facing upward

aorimásu, aóru *v* 煽ります, 煽る fans; stirs up, incites

aótte *v* 煽って → **aorimásu** 煽ります

ao-zamemásu, aozameru *v* 青ざめます, 青ざめる pales, is pale

apá´to *n* アパート apartment (*house*)

appaku *n* 圧迫 pressure; oppression, suppression:
~ shimásu 圧迫します puts pressure on; oppresses, suppresses

appáre *adj, interj* あっぱれ Bravo!: **appáre na taido** あっぱれな態度 admirable attitude

áppu *n* アップ raising, up

appu-dē´to *n* アップデート update

appu-gurē´do *n* アップグレード upgrade

appu-ráito (piano) *n* アップライト(ピアノ) upright piano

appu-rō´do *n* アップロード upload: **~ shimásu** アップロードします uploads

appu-áppu *n* あっぷあっぷ grasping for breath:
~ shimásu あっぷあっぷします bobs up and down

appurú-pai *n* アップルパイ apple pie

apurō´chi *n* アプローチ approach: **~ shimásu** アプローチします

ára *interj* あら (*female*) oh!! (*shows surprise, amazement*): **árámā** あらまあ (*female*) Oh, dear!

ará *n* あら・粗 fault
ará sagashi *n* あら捜し nitpicking: **~ shimásu** あら捜しします tries to find fault with
ara-suji *n* あらすじ summary, outline, synopsis (= **gaiyō** 概要, **yōyaku** 要約)

Arabia, Árabu *n* アラビア, アラブ an Arab
Arabia-go *n* アラビア語 Arabic
Arabia-jin, Arabú-jin *n* アラビア人, アラブ人 an Arab
Arabia no *adj* アラビアの Arabian

araemásu, araeru *v* 洗えます, 洗える can wash

araí *adj* 荒い rough, coarse
ara-ara-shii *adj* 荒々しい rude, wild, rough
ara-ryōji *n* 荒療治 take drastic measures [steps]

araí *adj* 粗い rough, not smooth, coarse

araí *v* 洗い = **araimásu** 洗います [INFINITIVE]

araimásu, arau *v* 洗います, 洗う washes

arakajime *adv* あらかじめ in advance (= **maemotte** 前もって)

arakáruto *n* アラカルト a la carte (*item*)

araō *v* 洗おう = **araimashō** 洗いましょう (let's wash it!)

arare *n* 1. あられ・霰 hail: **arare ga furimásu** あられ[霰]が降ります it hails (= **hyō´** ひょう[雹]) 2. あられ rice-cracker cubes (*tidbits*)

árashi *n* 嵐 storm

arashimásu, arásu *v* 荒らします, 荒らす devastates, damages, ruins

arasoí *n* 争い controversy, contention, struggle; argument, dispute, quarrel; strife, disturbance

arasoí *n* 争い → **arasoimásu** 争います [INFINITIVE]

arasoimásu, arasóu *v* 争います, 争う struggles/contends for; argues, quarrels

arasótte *v* 争って → **arasoimásu** 争います

aratamarimásu, aratamáru *v* 改まります, 改まる to be changed, to be replaced by something new

aratamemásu, aratéru *v* 改めます, 改める changes, alters, corrects

aratámete *adv* 改めて newly, anew; again

arawaremásu, arawaréru *v* 現れます, 現れる appears, shows up, comes out

arawashimásu, arawásu *v* 現します・現す shows, reveals

arawashimásu, arawásu *v* 表します・表す expresses (= **hyōgen-shimásu** 表現します)

arawashimásu, arawásu ν 著します, 著す publishes, writes

arayúru adj あらゆる all, every (= **subete no** すべての)

aré pron あれ that one (*over there; known to you and me*)

aré-ra pron あれら those, they/them

aré ν 荒れ → **aremásu** 荒れます [INFINITIVE]

aré interj あれ! Dear! (*surprise*)

áreba ν あれば (if there be) → **arimásu** あります

areguro n アレグロ allegro

aremásu, areru ν 荒れます, 荒れる goes to ruin, falls to waste, gets dilapidated; gets rough/wild, rages

aremoyō (no) adj 荒れ模様(の) stormy, inclement

areréba ν 荒れれば (if it rages; if …) → **aremásu** 荒れます

arete ν 荒れて → **aremásu** 荒れます

aré ya/wa shinai ν 荒れや/はしない = **arénai** 荒れない (not get rough)

arí n アリ・蟻 ant

ári ν あり → **arimásu** あります

ariári (to) adv ありあり(と) vividly

ariawase n ありあわせ on hand: **ariawase no tabemono** ありあわせの食べ物 food on hand

aribai n アリバイ alibi

arifúreta adj ありふれた very common, commonplace

arigachi adj ありがち common, typical [IN NEGATIVE SENSE]

arigatai adj ありがたい appreciated, welcome; grateful: **arigata meiwaku** ありがた迷惑 unwanted favor, misplaced favor

arígatō (gozaimásu [HONORIFIC]**)** ありがとう (ございます) Thank you (very much)

árika n 在り処 whereabouts (= **yukue** 行方)

arikitari adj ありきたり commonplace, so typical [IN NEGATIVE SENSE]

arimáshita, atta ν ありました、あった there was, we had; it was (located)

arimásu, aru ν あります, ある there is, we've got; it is (located)

arí mo shinaí adj ありもしない nor is there, there even/also isn't, nonexistent

arinomama (ni/de) adv ありのまま(に/で) as is, without exaggeration: **arinomama no anata ga suki desu** ありのままのあなたが好きです I like you as you are.

ari-sama n ありさま condition, state; scene, sight

ari-sō´(na) adj ありそう(な) likely; **ari-sō´mo nái** ありそうもない unlikely

aritē´ni-iu (to) ν ありていに言う(と) frankly speaking [INFORMAL]

áritoarayúru adj ありとあらゆる every single, all kinds/sorts of

arittake n ありったけ utmost [INFORMAL]

arí wa/ya shinaí ν ありは/やしない = **arimásén** ありません = **nái** ない (is not)

arō´ ν あろう [LITERARY] = **áru darō´** あるだろう = **áru deshō** あるでしょう (probably is)

áru … adj ある certain …, some …
áru-hi ある日 n one/certain day

áru ν ある = **arimásu** あります (there is, it is located)

arubáito n アルバイト side job, sideline, part-time job (= **baito** バイト)

arufabétto n アルファベット alphabet

árugamama n あるがまま as is, for what it is: **árugamama (ni) uketorimásu** あるがまま (に)受け取ります takes things as they are

arúite ν 歩いて → **arukimásu** 歩きます

arúi-wa conj 或いは or else; maybe, possibly

arukimásu, arúku ν 歩きます, 歩く walks

arukō ν 歩こう = **arukimashó** 歩きましょう (let's walk!)

arukōru n アルコール alcohol

aruminíum n アルミニウム aluminum

áruto n アルト alto

árya ν [INFORMAL] ありゃ **1.** = **are wa** あれは (*as for that*) **2.** → **áreba** あれば

asá n 麻 flax, linen

ása n, adv morning
ása-ban (ni) n, adv 朝晩(に) morning and night/ evening
asa-yake n 朝焼け a red glow in the morning sky
asá-gao n アサガオ・朝顔 morning glory (*flower*)
asa-góhan n 朝ご飯 breakfast (= [BOOKISH] **chōshoku** 朝食, (*mostly male*) **asa-meshi** 朝飯)
ása-hi n 朝日 morning sun, rising sun
asa-meshi-máe n 朝飯前 a cinch: **sonna no (wa) asá-meshi-máe desu** そんなの(は)朝飯前で す It's a cinch.

asái adj 浅い shallow
asá-haka (na) adj 浅はか(な) shallow
asa-guroi adj 浅黒い swarthy, dark-colored, bistered
asa-se n 浅瀬 shallows

Asakusa n 浅草 Asakusa

asari n アサリ・浅蜊 short-necked clam

asátsuki n アサツキ・浅葱 scallion, green onion; chives

asátte n, adv あさって・明後日 the day after tomorrow

áse n 汗 sweat: **áse ga demásu** 汗が出ます, **áse o kakimásu** 汗をかきます sweats; **hiya-áse** 冷や汗 cold sweat

Asean n アセアン ASEAN

asemásu, aséru ν 褪せます, 褪せる fades

asénai ν 褪せない = **asemasén** 褪せません (not fade)

aseránai ν 焦らない = **aserimasén** 焦りません (not feel rushed)

aserimásu, aséru ν 焦ります, 焦る feels rushed/ pressed

aséru ν 褪せる = **asemásu** 褪せます (fades)

9

aséru *v* 焦る = **aserimásu** 焦ります (feels rushed/pressed)

ásete *v* 褪せて → **asemásu** 褪せます

asétte *v* 焦って → **aserimásu** 焦ります

áshi *n* アシ・葦 reed

ashí *n* 足 foot, 脚 leg
ashi-áto *n* 足跡 footprint
ashi-dai *n* 足台 footstool (= **ashinosé-dai** 足乗せ台)
ashi-de mátoi *n* 足手まとい a drag (*on*): **shusse no ashi-de mátoi** 出世の足手まとい a drag on one's career
ashi-kubi *n* 足首 ankle
ashi-móto *n* 足もと・足元: **ashi-móto ni ki o tsukéte** 足元に気を付けて Watch your step!: **ashi-moto o mimásu** 足元を見ます sees someone coming: … **ni ashimoto o miraremashita** …に足元を見られました … saw me coming

ashi-dome saremásu (sareru) *v* 足止めされます(される) is strained, is stuck

ashi-ga-demásu (deru) *v* 足が出ます(出る) runs over the budget: **kongetsu wa ichiman-en ashi ga demáshita** 今月は1万円足が出ました ran over the budget this month by 10,000 yen

ashí-o-araimásu (arau) *v* 足を洗います(洗う) washes one's hands of, drops one's beads, cuts one's ties with

ashí-o-nobashimásu (nobasu) *v* 足を伸ばします(伸ばす) goes a little farther

ashirai *n* あしらい treatment, hospitality, service, arrangement

ashiraimásu, ashiráu *v* あしらいます, あしらう handles, manages, deals with; receives (a guest): **hana de ashiraimásu** 鼻であしらいます turns up one's nose at (*a person*)

ashirawánai *v* あしらわない = **ashiraimásén** あしらいません (not arrange)

ashísutanto *n* アシスタント assistant (= **joshu** 助手)

ashita *n, adv* あした・明日 tomorrow: [IDIOM] **ashita wa ashita no kaze ga fuku** 明日は明日の風が吹く Tomorrow is another day.

asobi 遊び **1.** *n* fun, amusement; a game, play; a visit **2.** *v* → **asobimásu** 遊びます
asobi hanbun (de) *adv* 遊び半分(で) half-seriously

asobimásu, asobu *v* 遊びます, 遊ぶ has fun, plays; visits

asoko, asuko *pron* あそこ, あすこ (that place) over there; that place (*known to you and me*)

assári *adv* あっさり simpe/simply, plain(ly); easy/easily; frank(ly), without apparent difficulty: **assári (to) shita** + [NOUN] … あっさり(と)した… simple, plain, light, easy; fresh

assén *n* あっせん・斡旋 **1.** mediation; good offices, help (= **sewá** 世話): … **no assen de** … の斡旋で through the good offices of …, with the help of … **2.** recommendation (= **suisen** 推薦)

asshō *n* 圧勝 an overwhelming win: ~ **shimásu** 圧勝します wins an overwhelming victory

asshuku *n* 圧縮 compression: ~ **shimásu** 圧縮します compresses

asu *n, adv* あす・明日 tomorrow (= **ashita** あした・明日)

asufáruto *n* アスファルト asphalt

asupara (gásu) *n* アスパラ(ガス) asparagus

asupirin *n* アスピリン aspirin

asurechikku-kúrabu *n* アスレチッククラブ athletic club

ásu-sen *n* アース線 ground wire

asutarísuku *n* アスタリスク asterisk (such as "＊") (= **hoshi-jírushi** 星印)

asutorinzen *n* アストリンゼン astringent

ataemásu, ataeru *v* 与えます, 与える gives, provides, grants

átafuta *n* あたふた a fluster: ~ **shimásu** あたふたします gets flustered/confused (= **awatemásu, awateru** 慌てます, 慌てる)

ataisuru *v, adj* 値する deserves, deserved

átakamo *adv* あたかも as if

atákku *n* アタック attack, strenuous effort

atama *n* 頭 head
atama-dékkachi (no) *adj* 頭でっかち(の) [INFORMAL] [IN NEGATIVE SENSE] top-heavy, too many chiefs, not enough Indians, an armchair theorist, **purojekuto kankeisha wa atama-dékkachi (no) hito bakarideshita** プロジェクト関係者は頭でっかちの人ばかりでした The people involved in the project were just armchair theorists.
atama-kín *n* 頭金 down payment, up-front money; deposit
atama-wari (no/de) *adj, adv* 頭割り(の/で) per head

atama-ni-kimásu (kuru) *v* 頭にきます(くる) gets mad at, be angly with

atama-o-kakaemásu (kakaeru) *v* 頭を抱えます(抱える) tears one's hair (out), holds one's head in one's hands

atama-o-tsukaimásu (tsukau) *v* 頭を使います(使う) uses one's head/mind

atarashíi *adj* 新しい new; fresh
atarashi-gariya *n* 新しがり屋 novelty hunter

ataráshiku *adv* 新しく newly, anew, freshly

atarazu-sawarazu *adv* 当たらず障らず innocuous: **atarazu-sawarazu no henji** 当たらず障らずの返事 give a harmless answer: **atarisa-wari no nai** 当たりさわりのない innocuous

ataréba *v* 当たれば (if it hits, if it's correct) → **atarimásu** 当たります

atari 当たり **1.** *n* a hit **2.** *adj* good luck, lucky
atari-yaku *n* 当たり役 is a hit in the role
atari-kuji *n* 当たりくじ winning number
atari-doshi *n* 当たり年 lucky year
atari-hazure *adj* 当たり外れ unpredictable, risky

atari *v* 当たり → **atarimásu** 当たります [INFINITIVE]

átari *n* 辺り neighborhood: **kono átari de/wa** この辺りで/は around here

atarichirashimásu, atarichirasu *v* 当たり散らします, 当たり散らす takes out one's spite on everybody

ataridokoro-ga-warui *adj* 当たり所が悪い hitting in a vital spot

atarimae (no) *adj* 当たり前(の) natural, reasonable, proper; suitable, sensible

atarimásu, ataru *v* 当たります, 当たる hits; faces; applies; is correct

atarí ya/wa shinaí *v* 当たりや/はしない = **ataranai** 当たらない (not hit, is not correct)

atashi *pron* あたし (*mostly children or female*) I/me (= **wata(ku)shi** わた(く)し・私)

atasshu-kē su *n* アタッシュケース attache case, briefcase

atatakái *adj* 暖かい warm (*air temperature*)

atatakái *adj* 温かい warm (*liquid, heart, etc.*)

atatakáku *adv* 暖かく warmly, kindly

atatakáku *adv* 温かく warmly, kindly

atatamarimásu, atatamáru *v* 暖まります, 暖まる warms up

atatamarimásu, atatamáru *v* 温まります, 温まる warms up

atatamemásu, atataméru *v* 温めます, 温める warms it up, heats

atatte *v* 当たって → **atarimásu** 当たります

atchi *pron* [INFORMAL] あっち, [FORMAL] **achira** あちら (*the other one, over there*)

ate 当て **1.** *n* reliance, trust: **... o ate ni shite imásu** ...を当てにしています is counting on ... **2.** *n* anticipation, expectation (= **kitai** 期待) **3.** goal, object (= **mokuteki** 目的) **4.** *n* clue, trace (= **tegákari** 手掛かり)

ate 当て **1.** → **atemásu** 当てます **2. ate ro** 当てろ [IMPERATIVE] (hit!)

...-ate (nó) *suffix, adj* ...宛て(の) addressed to ... ate-na *n* 宛(て)名 address

ate-hamarimásu, ate-hamáru *v* 当てはまります, 当てはまる fits, conforms

ate-hamemásu, ate-haméru *v* 当てはめます, 当てはめる applies, conforms, adapts, fits it (*to*): **... ni ate-hámete** ...に当てはめて in conformity/accordance with ...

atekosuri *n* 当てこすり a snide remark: **kare no kotoba wa watashi e no atekosuri ni chigaiarimasen** 彼の言葉は私への当てこすりに違いありません He must have been taking a dig at me when ... said that.

atemásu, ateru *v* 当てます, 当てる guesses; hits; sets aside, appropriates, designates; touches; addresses

atenai *v* 当てない = **atemasén** 当てません (not guess)

ate(ra)remásu, ate(ra)reru *v* 当て(ら)れます, 当て(ら)れる can guess/hit/...

ateuma *n* 当て馬 dodge

ā´tisuto *n* アーティスト/アーチスト artist (= **geijutsu-ka** 芸術家)

áto (de/ni) *prep, adv* 後(で/に) after(wards), later

(= nochi ni 後に): **áto no ...** 後の...the remaining ...; **... shita áto de...** した後で... after doing

ato-máwashi *n* 後回し leaving something until later: **ato-máwashi ni shimásu** 後回しにします postpones, leaves something until later: **kono mondai wa muzukashisugiru kara ato-máwashi ni shimashō**. この問題は難しすぎるから後回しにしましょう This problem is too difficult so let's solve it later. (= ato ni mawasu 後に回す)

ató-aji *n* 後味 aftertaste: **ató-aji ga warui** 後味が悪い leaves a bad aftertaste

ato-kátazuke *n* 後片付け cleanup: **ato-kátazuke (o) shimásu** 後片付け(を)します clean up a place after using it.

áto-no-matsurí *n* 後の祭(り) The damage is done. **mō dōshiyō mo arimasen. áto-no-matsurí desu** もうどうしようもありません. 後の祭です Nothing you can do about it. The damage is done.

ato-módori *n* 後戻り retreat, back tracking: **~ shimásu** 後戻りします retreats, turns back

ato-saki *n* 後先 consequence

ato-shímatsu *n* 後始末 settling, putting in order, cleaning up after: **ato-shímatsu o shimásu** 後始末をします deal with the aftermath, pick up the pieces

áto *n* 跡 mark, track, trace; scar (= **kizu-ato** 傷跡); footprint (= **ashi-ato** 足跡)

ató-tsugi *n* あとつぎ・跡継ぎ successor

ā´to *n* アート art

atorakushon *n* アトラクション attraction, side entertainment, atelier

atorie *n* アトリエ studio, workshoip, atelier

atsuatsu (no) *adj* アツアツ(の) lovey-dovey

atsuatsu (no) *adj* 熱々(の) piping hot

atsubottai *adj* 厚ぼったい thick (= **buatsui** ぶ厚い・分厚い)

atsui *adj* 厚い thick (= **atsubottai** 厚ぼったい) atsu-zoko *n* 厚底 heavy-bottom (*things*): **atsu-zoko sandaru** 厚底サンダル platform sandals, **atsu-zoko nabe** 厚底なべ heavy-bottomed saucepan

atsúi *adj* 暑い hot (*air temperature*)

atsúi *adj* 熱い hot: **atsuku shimásu** 熱くします makes it hot

atsukamashíi *adj* 厚かましい impudent

atsukaimásu, atsukau *v* 扱います, 扱う deals with

atsumarimásu, atsumáru *v* 集まります, 集まる meets, assembles; it accumulates

atsumemásu, atsuméru *v* 集めます, 集める collects, gathers, accumulates

atsúryoku *n* 圧力 pressure

atsusa *n* 厚さ thickness

átsusa *n* 暑さ heat, warmth (*air temperature*)

átsusa *n* 熱さ heat, warmth (= **netsu** 熱)

átta *v* あった = **arimáshita** ありました (there was, we had; it was (*located*)

átta *v* 会った = **aimáshita** 会いました (met, saw (*a person*))

attakái *adj* 暖かい warm (*air temperature*) (= **atatakái** 暖かい)

attakái *adj* 温かい warm (*liquid, heart, etc.*)
(= **atatakái** 温かい)

at(a)tamemásu, at(a)taméru *v* 温めます, 温める warms it up, heats

átte *v* あって → **arimásu** あります

átte *v* 会って → **aimásu** 会います

atto-hō´mu (na) *adj* アットホーム(な) homelike atmosphere, homely

atto-mā´ku *n* アットマーク at mark (such as "@")

attō-shimásu (suru) *v* 圧倒します(する) overwhelms

attō-teki na *adj* 圧倒的な overwhelming

áu *v* 合う = **aimásu** 合います (matches with)

áu *v* 会う = **aimásu** 会います (meets; sees)

áuto *n* アウト out (*baseball*)
auto-kō´su アウトコース outer lane/track
auto-putto アウトプット output
auto-rain アウトライン outline

awa *n* 泡 bubble; foam

áwa *n* アワ・粟 millet

áwabi *n* アワビ・鮑 abalone

awánai *v* 合わない = **aimasén** 合いません (not match with)

awánai *v* 会わない = **aimasén** 会いません (not meet; not see)

áware (na) *adj* 哀れ(な) pity, pitiful

awase *n* 袷・あわせ = a lined garment

awase *v* → **awasemásu** 合わせます [INFINITIVE]

awasemásu, awaséru *v* 合わせます, 合わせる puts together, combines, joins

awásete *adv* 合わせて all together → **áwasemásu** 合わせます

awatadashii *adj* 慌ただしい hurried, flustered, confused

awatemásu, awateru *v* 慌てます, 慌てる gets flustered/confused (= **atafuta-shimásu** あたふた します)

awate-mono *n* 慌て者 a person easily flustered; a scatterbrain (= **awatenbō** あわてん坊)

áya *n* 会や → **áeba** 会えば

ayabumimásu, ayabumu *v* 危ぶみます, 危ぶむ doubts

ayafuya (na) *adj* あやふや(な) indecisive

ayamari *n* 誤り error, mistake

ayamari *n* 謝り apology

ayamari *v* 誤り → **ayamarimásu** 誤ります [INFINITIVE]

ayamari *v* 謝り → **ayamarimásu** 謝ります [INFINITIVE]

ayamarimásu, ayamáru *v* 誤ります, 誤る errs, makes a mistake

ayamarimásu, ayamáru *v* 謝ります, 謝る apologizes

ayamátte *v* 誤って → **ayamarimásu** 誤ります

ayamátte *v* 謝って → **ayamarimásu** 謝ります

ayashii *adj* 怪しい questionable, suspicious, shady; uncertain; unreliable; weird

ayashimásu, ayasu *v* あやします, あやす lulls: **akanbō o ayashite nekashitsukemáshita** 赤ん坊をあやして寝かしつけました lulled a baby to sleep

ayatóri *n* あやとり cat's cradle

ayatsurimásu, ayatsúru *v* 操ります, 操る manipulates

ayauku *adv* 危うく (*something undesirable*) about to happen or likely to happen.

āyū *adj* ああゆう ... that kind/sort of ... (= **āiu** ああ いう, **anna** あんな)

áyu *n* アユ・鮎 (= **ái** アイ・鮎) sweetfish, river trout

aza *n* 痣 bruise

azakeri *n* あざけり・嘲り mockery (= **keibetsu** 軽蔑, **azawarai** あざ[嘲]笑い, **chōshō** 嘲笑, **reishō** 冷笑)

azakerimásu, azakeru *v* あざけり・嘲ります, あざける・嘲る mocks, scorns

azárashi *n* アザラシ・海豹 seal (*animal*)

azawarai *n* あざ[嘲]笑い mockery, sneer, scornful laugh (= **azakeri** あざけり・嘲り, **keibetsu** 軽蔑, **chōshō** 嘲笑, **reishō** 冷笑)

azawaraimásu, azawarau *v* あざ[嘲]笑います, あざ[嘲]笑う mocks, sneers

azáyaka (na) *adj* 鮮やか(な) bright, vivid

azen-to-shimásu (-suru) *v* あ然とします is dumbfounded: **kodomo tachi no busahō-buri ni azen to shimáshita** 子供たちの無作法ぶりにあ然としました was speechless because the children were so rude

azukarí *v* 預り → **azukarimásu** 預かります [INFINITIVE]

azukari-jo/-sho *n* 預かり所 check room

azukarimásu, azukáru *v* 預かります, 預かる takes in trust, keeps, holds

azuke *v* 預け → **azukemásu** 預けます [INFINITIVE]

azukemásu, azukéru *v* 預けます, 預ける gives in trust, entrusts, checks, deposits

azukeraremásu, azukeraréru *v* 預けられます, 預けられる can give in trust

azukí *n* アズキ・小豆 red beans

B

...-ba *conj* ...ば [EMPHATIC] (if) indeed: **...**
nára(ba) ...なら(ば) if; **... dáttara(ba)** ...だった
ら(ば); **...-káttara(ba)** ...かったら(ば) if/when
it is (or was); **...-tára(ba)** ...たら(ば) if/when it
does (or did)

ba *n* 場 **1.** place (*for something*) (= **basho** 場所)
2. occasion, time (= **baai, bawai** 場合) **3.** scene
(= **bamen** 場面)

bā´ *n* バー bar (*for drinking*)

baai, bawai *n* 場合 situation, case, circumstance,
occasion: **... no baai/bawai** ... の場合 if

baba-núki *n* ばば抜き old maid (*card game*)

baba-shatsu *n* ばばシャツ long sleeved thermal
undershirt for female

bābékyū *n* バーベキュー barbecue

bā´bon *n* バーボン bourbon

bachí *n* 罰 retribution, punishment (= **batsu** 罰)

ba-chígai (na/no) *adj* 場違い(な/の) **1.** out of
place **2.** not from the right/best place

bā´gen *n* バーゲン bargain sale

bái *n* 倍 double; **bái ni narimásu** 倍になります
(なる) it doubles; **bái ni shimásu** 倍にします
doubles it

bai-ritsu *n* 倍率 magnification, magnifying power

...-bai *suffix* ...倍 ...times, ...-fold

bai-... *prefix* 売... selling
bái-bai *n* 売買 buying and selling
bai-meikōi *n* 売名行為 [BOOKISH] publicity
seeking, publicity stunt
bai-shun *n* 売春 prostitution: **baishún-fu** 売春婦
prostitute; whore
bai-ten *n* 売店 booth, kiosk, stand (*selling things*)

Báiburu *n* バイブル Bible (= **seisho** 聖書)

báidoku *n* 梅毒 [BOOKISH] syphilis

baikin *n* ばい菌 germ

báikingu *n* バイキング smorgasbord ("Viking")

báiku *n* バイク motorbike
báiku-bin *n* バイク便 motorcycle courier

baindā *n* バインダー binder

baiorin *n* バイオリン violin

baio-tekunórojii *n* バイオテクノロジー
biotechnology

baipasu *n* バイパス bypass

bairíngaru *n* バイリンガル bilingual

baishō´-kin *n* 賠償金 indemnity, reparation

baiyā *n* バイヤー buyer (*professional*)

bají *n* バッジ badge

báka *n* ばか・バカ・馬鹿 fool, idiot
báka na *adj* ばかな foolish, stupid
baká-ni-shimásu *v* ばかにします makes a fool of
(*a person*)
baka-bakashíi, baka-rashíi *adj* ばかばかしい
absurd, foolish (= **baka-rashíi** ばからしい)
baka-bánashi *n* ばか話 nonsense; idle talk; hot
air, bull (= **muda-bánashi** 無駄話)
báka-me *adj* ばかめ damn (fool) idiot

baka-shō´jiki (na) *adj* ばか正直(な) gullible

...bákari, ...bákkari, ... bákkashi *suffix* ...ばか
り, ...ばっかり, ...ばっかし only, just (= **dake** だ
け): **bákari de/ja naku ...mo** ...ばかりで/じゃな
く...も not only ..., but also

bakazu-o-fumimásu (fumu) *v* 場数を踏みます
(踏む) gets a lot of practical experience: **bakazu o**
fundeiru sērusuman 場数を踏んでいるセールス
マン a veteran salesman with a lot of experience

bakógaku *n* 化學・化け学 chemistry (= **kágaku**
化学)

bake-móno *n* 化け物 monster, ghost (= **obáke**
お化け・おばけ, **yōkai henge** 妖怪変化)

baken *n* 馬券 betting ticket

baketsu *n* バケツ bucket

bakkin *n* 罰金 fine, penalty

bákku *n* バック back: **~ shimásu** バックします
moves back/backward
bakku-áppu *n* バックアップ backup, support:
~ shimásu バックアップします backs up, supports
bakku mírā *n* バックミラー rearview mirror

bákku, baggu *n* バック, バッグ bag

bakuchi *n* 博打 gambling

bakudai (na) *adj* ばくだい(な) immense, vast,
huge, enormous

bakudan *n* 爆弾 bomb

bákufu *n* 幕府 (*the time of*) the shogunate

bakugeki *n* 爆撃 bombing: **~ shimásu** 爆撃します
bombs it
bakugéki-ki *n* 爆撃機 bomber

bakuhatsu *n* 爆発 explosion, bursting: **~ shimásu**
爆発します explodes, bursts

bakuteria *n* バクテリア bacteria

bakuzen (to) *adv* 漠然(と) vaguely, obscurely

bámen *n* 場面 scene (= **shiin** シーン)

ban *n* 晩 [BOOKISH] evening, night: (**hitó-ban** 一晩
one night, **futá-ban** 二晩 two nights: **íku-ban** 幾晩
some nights, how many nights? (= **nan-ban** 何晩);
kon-ban 今晩 tonight; **mai-ban** 毎晩 every night
ban-góhan, ban-meshi *n* 晩ご飯, 晩飯 evening
meal (*dinner/supper*) (= **yūshoku** 夕食)

bán *n* 番 guard, watch
ban-ken *n* 番犬 watchdog
ban-nín *n* 番人 watchman

...-ban *suffix* ...番 number: (**ichí-ban** 一番
number one, **nán-ban** 何番 what number?)
ban-chi *n* 番地 address (*house number*): **nan-**
bánchi 何番地 what house/lot number?
ban-gō´ *n* 番号 number (*assigned*)
...-banmé (no) *suffix, adj* ...番目(の) [numeral]
-th
...-ban-sen *suffix* ...番線 track number ... (*train*
station): **nan-bansen** 何番線 what (number) track?

bānā *n* バーナー burner

bánana *n* バナナ banana

ban-cha *n* 番茶 coarse green tea

bando *n* バンド **1.** strap, band (*watchband, etc.*); belt **2.** band (*music*)

bane (-jíkake) *n* ばね(仕掛け) spring (*device*)

bangaró´ *n* バンガロー bungalow

ban-gasa *n* 番傘 oilpaper umbrella

bangumi *n* 番組 program (*TV, etc.*)

Bánkoku *n* バンコク Bangkok

bánkoku *n* 万国 **1.** international **2.** all the world bánkoku-hakubútsukan, banpaku *n* 万国博物館, 万博 international exposition

bánira *n* バニラ vanilla

bannō *n* 万能 versatility, ability to do anything

bansō *n* 伴奏 musical accompaniment

bansōko, bansōkō *n* 絆創膏 adhesive plaster/tape

banzái *interj* 万歳 hurray!

bara *n* バラ・薔薇 rose (*flower*)

bára (de) *adv* ばら(で) loose, separately

barabara (ní) *adv* ばらばら(に) separate, in pieces: barabara ni narimásu ばらばらになります scatters, into pieces

baransu *n* バランス balance: baransu o torimásu バランスをとります redress the balance

barashimásu, barásu *v* ばらします, ばらす **1.** exposes (*a secret*) **2.** takes it apart, disassembles **3.** kills, shoots (*to death*)

bárē *n* バレエ ballet

barē(bō´ru) *n* バレー(ボール) volleyball

baremásu, baréru *v* [INFORMAL] ばれます, ばれる surfaces, is disclosed, is discovered: uso ga barémasu 嘘がばれます The lie comes to light.

barentáindē *n* バレンタインデー Valentine's Day

bareriina *n* バレリーナ ballerina

baré ya/wa shinai *v* [INFORMAL] ばれや/はしない = barenai ばれない (is not disclosed/discovered)

barikan *n* バリカン clippers (*barber's*)

bariki *n* 馬力 horsepower

baromē´ta *n* バロメーター barometer

barukónii *n* バルコニー balcony

basho *n* 場所 **1.** place **2.** a (*two-week*) sumo tournament: natsu-básho 夏場所 the summer sumo tournament

bassári *adv* ばっさり fast and furious, drastically, without hesitation: eda o bassári kirimásu 枝をばっさり切ります chops a branch

basshi *n* 抜歯 pulling out a tooth/teeth

basshimásu, bassuru *v* 罰します, 罰する punishes

básu *n* バス bus
basu-téi *n* バス停 bus stop
basu-gáido *n* バスガイド bus tour guide
basu-rū´mu *n* bath, bathroom (= furo 風呂)
basu-tsuki バス付き with bath

basue *n* 場末 suburb (*outskirts*)

basukétto *n* バスケット basket

basukétto bō´ru *n* バスケットボール basketball, basketball game

básuto *n* バスト bust

bátā *n* バター butter

batafurai *n* バタフライ butterfly (*swimming*)

batakusai *adj* バタ臭い has a Western air

batán (to) *adv* ばたん(と) with a bang, with a thud

batā-rō´ru *n* バターロール (butter) roll (*bread*)

bāten(dā) *n* バーテン(ダー) bartender

batomínton *n* バトミントン badminton (= badominton バドミントン)

baton *n* バトン baton: baton o watashimásu バトンを渡します passes a baton

baton tatchi バトンタッチ passing the torch, having someone take over

bátsu *n* ばつ cross (= X *"wrong"*)

bátsu *n* 罰 retribution, punishment (= bachí 罰)

batta *n* バッタ grasshopper

báttā *n* バッター batter (*baseball*): Báttā uchimashita! バッター打ちました! The batter hit the ball! (*baseball announcement*)

battári *adv* ばったり unexpectedly: senjitsu Tokyo de sensei ni battári aimashita. 先日、東京で先生にばったり会いました I ran into my teacher in Tokyo the other day.

battén *n* ばってん X (*"wrong"*), a black mark

batterii *n* バッテリー battery

battingu *n* バッティング batting (*baseball*): battingu no renshū o shimásu バッティングの練習をします practices batting

bátto *n* バット bat (*baseball*)

baundo *n* バウンド bound

bawai, baai *n* 場合 situation, case, circumstance, occasion

bázā *n* バザー bazaar: bázā o hirakimásu バザーを開きます holds a bazaar

bebiishíttā *n* ベビー・シッター baby sitter

béddo, bétto *n* ベッド、ベット bed (*Western*)

beddo-táun *n* ベット・タウン bedroom community, suburb

Bei *n* 米 America(*n*): hoku-bei 北米 North America: nan-bei 南米 South America: nich-bei 日米 Japan and America; ō-bei 欧米 Europe and America
Béi-koku *n* 米国 America (= Amerika アメリカ)
Bei-koku-jin *n* 米国人 American (= Amerika-jin アメリカ人)

beiju *n* 米寿 (*auspicious, happy event*) eighty-eighth birthday: sobo no beiju o iwaimashita. 祖母の米寿を祝いました I celebrated my grandmother's 88th birthday.

beikingu-páudā *n* ベイキング・パウダー baking powder

… béki *suffix* …べき: …-suru béki desu するべきです should do, ought to do [BOOKISH]

bekkan *n* 別館 annex (*building*)

bekkō *n* ベッコウ・鼈甲 tortoise shell

bekkyo *n* 別居 separate living: ~ shimásu 別居します lives apart (separately)

bē´kon *n* ベーコン bacon

bén *n* 弁 valve

bén *n* 便 1. convenience (= **béngi** 便宜): **bén ga íi** 便がいい convenient 2. feces

bén-jo *n* 便所 toilet

bén-ki *n* 便器 bedpan

bén-pi *n* 便秘 constipation

dai-bén *n* 大便 excrement, faces, stool

shō/shon-bén *n* 小便 urine, pee

...-bén *suffix* ...遍 = ...-**hén**, ...-**pén** 遍 (*counts times or occasions*)

bénchi *n* ベンチ bench

béngi *n* 便宜 convenience, accommodation (= **bén** 便): **béngi o hakarimásu** 便宜を図ります does someone a favor

bengóshi *n* 弁護士 lawyer

béni *n* 紅 rouge

benkai *n* 弁解 [BOOKISH] justification (= **iiwake** 言い訳): **benkai suruna!** 弁解するな! Don't give excuses!

benkyō *n* 勉強 study, (*mental*) work; cutting a price: ~ **shimásu** 勉強します studies; cuts the price

benkyō-ka *n* 勉強家 a studious person, a good student

bénri (na) *adj* 便利(な) handy, convenient

benri-ya *n* 便利屋 handyman (*or his shop*)

benron *n* 弁論 [BOOKISH] debate, speech, rhetoric: ~ **shimásu** 弁論します debates

benron-taikai *n* 弁論大会 speech contest

benshō *n* 弁償 compensation: ~ **shimásu** 弁償します recompenses

bentō *n* 弁当 (**o-bentō** お弁当) box lunch

berabō (ni) *adv* べらぼう(に) astonishingly, considerably: **berabō ni takai** べらぼうに高い extremely expensive

beranda *n* ベランダ veranda

béru *n* ベル bell, doorbell

Berurín *n* ベルリン Berlin

beruto *n* ベルト belt (= **bando** バンド): **anzen-béruto** 安全ベルト safety belt

bessō´ *n* 別荘 villa, vacation house

bēsu *n* ベース 1. base, basis 2. base (*baseball*) 3. = **bēsu gitā** ベースギター bass guitar

bēsu áppu *n* ベースアップ upping/raising the base pay; a pay raise

bēsubōru *n* ベースボール baseball (= **yakyū** 野球)

bésuto *n* ベスト best

besuto-tén *n* ベストテン best ten

besuto-serā´ *n* ベストセラー best seller

beteran *n* ベテラン veteran, expert

beteran-kyōshi *n* ベテラン教師 an experienced teacher

betsu (na/no) *adj* 別(な/の) separate, special, particular; **...wa betsu to shite** ... は別として apart/aside from ..., except for ...

betsu-betsu (na/no) *adj* 別々(な/の) separate, individual

betsu (no) *adj* 別(の) other; extra

betsu-ryō´kin *n* 別料金 extra (*charge*), separate bill

betsu (ni) *adv* 別(に) 1. [+ NEGATIVE] not

particularly 2. **... tó wa betsu ni (shite)** とは別に (して) quite apart/separately from ...

bétto *n* ベット bed (= **béddo** ベッド)

bia-hō´ru *n* ビアホール beer hall

bifuteki *n* ビフテキ = **biifu sutēki** ビーフステーキ beefsteak

bíichi *n* ビーチ beach

bíiru *n* ビール beer: **biirú-bin** ビール瓶 beer bottle: **kan-bíiru** 缶ビール canned beer: **nama-bíiru** 生ビール draft beer

bíito *n* ビート beet

bíjin *n* 美人 beautiful woman, a beauty

bíjinesu *n* ビジネス business

bíjinesu-hoteru *n* ビジネスホテル economy hotel

bíjinesu-man *n* ビジネスマン businessperson (= **kaisha-in** 会社員)

bíjon *n* ビジョン vision: **bíjon o hakkíri sasemásu** ビジョンをはっきりさせます clarifies one's vision

bíjutsu *n* 美術 art

bijútsú-kan 美術館 *n* art museum (*art gallery*)

bikkúri-shimásu (-suru) *v* びっくりします (する) gets startled, gets a surprise (= **odorokimásu** 驚きます)

bimyō (na) *adj* 微妙(な) delicate, subtle, fine, nice

bín *n* 瓶 bottle; jar

bin-bíiru *n* 瓶ビール bottled beer

ka-bin *n* 花瓶 vase

...´-bin *suffix* 便 flight (number) ...

bínbō (na) *adj* 貧乏(な) poor (*needy*)

biní(i)ru *n* ビニ(一)ル vinyl, polyvinyl; plastic

bini(i)rú-bukuro *n* ビニ(一)ル袋 plastic bag

binkan (na) *adj* 敏感(な) sensitive

binsen *n* 便箋 (letter-)writing paper, stationery

bínta *n* びんた slapping (*a person's face*): **bínta o harimásu** びんたを張ります slaps

birá *n* びら leaflet, handbill, pamphlet

bíri (no) *adj* びり(の) the last, the tail end, the rear: **bíri ni narimásu** びりになります finishes last

birōdo *n* ビロード velvet

bíru *n* ビル building

Bíruma *n* ビルマ Burma (Myanmar)

bisai (na) *adj* 微細(な) minute, detailed, fine

bishonure *n* びしょ濡れ soddenness

bisshíri *adv* びっしり cramped: **sukejūru ga bisshíri tsumatte imásu** スケジュールがびっしり詰まっています The schedule is quite packed.

bisshóri *adv* びっしょり completely soaked: **ase bisshóri** 汗びっしょり is all sweaty; **bisshóri nuremásu** びっしょり濡れます gets soaking wet through

bisukétto *n* ビスケット crackers

bitámin *n* ビタミン vitamin(s)

bitámin-zai *n* ビタミン剤 vitamin pills

bitoku *n* 美徳 virtue

bíwa *n* ビワ・枇杷 loquat (*fruit*)

bíwa *n* 琵琶 lute (*musical instrument*)

biya-hō´ru *n* ビヤホール beer hall (= **bia hō´ru** ビアホール)

biyō´in *n* 美容院 beauty parlor

bíza *n* ビザ visa (= **sashō** 査証)

bō *n* 棒 pole (*rod*); stick, club (= **bō-kire** 棒きれ, **bōkkíre** 棒つきれ)
    tetsu-bō *n* 鉄棒 (*iron*) bar

bóchi *n* 墓地 cemetery, graveyard

bōchō shimásu (suru) *v* 膨脹します(する) swells, expands

bōchū´zai *n* 防虫剤 insecticide; mothballs

bōdai (na) *adj* 膨大(な) enormous, gigantic, massive

bōdō *n* 暴動 riot

bōei *n* 防衛 defense (= **bōgyo** 防御): **~ shimásu** 防衛します defends

Bōei-shō *n* 防衛省 Ministry of Defense (DA)

bōeki *n* 貿易 commerce, trade: **~ shimásu** 貿易します conducts foreign trade
    bōeki-shōsha/gaisha *n* 貿易商社/会社 trader, trading company

bōenkyō *n* 望遠鏡 telescope

bōfū *n* 暴風 storm, gale, hurricane

bōfú-zai *n* 防腐剤 antiseptic (*substance*), preservative

bōhan-béru *n* 防犯ベル burglar alarm

bōhatéi *n* 防波堤 breakwater

bōi *n* ボーイ (bell)boy, waiter

bōi-furéndo *n* ボーイフレンド boyfriend (= **káre(-shi)** 彼(氏))

boikótto *n* ボイコット boycott

boin *n* 拇印 thumbprint

boin *n* 母音 vowel

boin *n* ボイン (*slang*) big bust

bóirā *n* ボイラー boiler

bōisukáuto *n* ボーイスカウト boy scout

bōkaru *n* ボーカル vocalist

bokashimásu, bokásu *v* ぼかします, ぼかす: **hanashí o bokashimásu** 話をぼかします beats around the bush, is noncommittal

bōken *n* 冒険 adventure
    bōken-ka *n* 冒険家 adventurer

bóki *n* 簿記 bookkeeping

bō-kire, bōkkíre *n* 棒きれ, 棒つきれ pole (*rod*); stick, club (= **bō** 棒)

bokkusu *n* ボックス
    bokkusu-seki *n* ボックス席 booth (*in a tavern etc.*)
    denwa-bókkusu *n* 電話ボックス phone booth

bókoku *n* 母国 mother country, homeland

bóku *pron* 僕 (*male*) I/me
    bóku-ra, bóku-táchi *pron* 僕ら, 僕たち we/us

bokuchiku *n* 牧畜 stockbreeding

bokujō *n* 牧場 ranch: **bokujō o itonamu** 牧場を営む keeps a ranch

bókushi *n* 牧師 (*Christian*) minister, preacher, pastor, priest; Reverend

bókushingu *n* ボクシング boxing

bokusō *n* 牧草 meadow grass

bon *n* 盆 (**o-bon** お盆) tray

Bón *n* 盆 (**O-bón** お盆) the Bon Festival (*Buddhist All Saints Day*)

...-bon *suffix* ...本 book, volume, text

...´-bon (...-hon, ...´-pon) *suffix* ...本 (*counts long objects*): → **sán-bon** 三本, (3 ~) → **sén-bon** 千本, (1,000 ~) → **mán-bon** 万本, (10,000 ~) → **nán-bon** 何本 (how many ~)

bō´nasu *n* ボーナス (*wage*) bonus

bonchi *n* 盆地 basin: **Kyōto-bonchi** 京都盆地 Kyoto basin; **bonchi wa natsu wa totemo atsuku, fuyu wa totemo samuidesu** 盆地は夏はとても暑く、冬はとても寒いです It is very hot in the summer and very cold in the winter in basins.

bóndo *n* ボンド bond: **bóndo de tomemásu** ボンドで止めます connects with bond

bōnén-kai *n* 忘年会 year-end party

bonnétto *n* ボンネット (car-) hood, bonnet

bonsai *n* 盆栽 dwarf trees (in pots)

bon'yári-shimásu (suru) *v* ぼんやりします(する) is absent-minded, daydreams

bonyū *n* 母乳 breast milk

bora *n* ボラ gray mullet

boréntia *n* ボランティア volunteer

boraremásu, boraréru *v* ぼられます, ぼられる [INFORMAL] gets overcharged (*ripped off*)

bōrei *n* 亡霊 Japanese ghost (*commonly lacks legs and feet*) (= **yūrei** 幽霊)

borimásu, bóru *v* ぼります, ぼる overcharges

bōringu *n* ボーリング bowling

bóro *n* ぼろ rag

bōru *n* ボール ball

bōru-gami *n* ボール紙 cardboard

bōru-pen *n* ボールペン ballpoint pen

boruto *n* ボルト bolt (*of nut and bolt*); volt

bō´ryoku *n* 暴力 violence (*brute force*)
    bōryoku-dan *n* 暴力団 mob, gangbanger

boryūmu *n* ボリューム volume

bō-san *n* 坊さん (**obō-sán** お坊さん) Buddhist monk (= **bō´zu** 坊主)

bósei *n* 母性 maternity

bōseki *n* 紡績 [BOOKISH] spinning
    bōseki-kō´jō *n* 紡績工場 spinning mill

bōshi *n* 帽子 hat

boshikátei *n* 母子家庭 family without a father: **boshikátei de sodachimásu** 母子家庭で育ちます grows up without a father.

boshū *n* 募集 recruitment: **~ shimásu** 募集します recruits, collects

bōsōzoku *n* 暴走族 motorcycle gang

bōsui (no) *adj* 防水(の) waterproof

bótan *n* ボタン button

bótan *n* ボタン・牡丹 tree peony

bótchan *n* 坊ちゃん (little) boy, (your) son (= **bō´ya** 坊や)

bō´to *n* ボート boat

bōtō *n* 冒頭 opening, at [in] the beginning: **bōtō o yomimasu** 冒頭を読みます reads the first parts

bōtoku *n* 冒とく sacrilege, violence: **kami e no bōtoku** 神への冒とく blasphemy

bótsubotsu *adv* ぼつぼつ **1.** *adv* (= **sórosoro** そろそろ) little by little, gradually; (leave) before

long **2.** *n* (*with*) dots, spots, bumps
bōtto-shimásu (-suru) *v* ボーっとします（する）
stupefies: **bōtto shita atama** ボーっとした頭
vacant mind
bottō-shimásu (-suru) *v* 没頭します devotes
oneself: **shigoto ni bottō-shimásu** 仕事に没頭し
ます buries oneself in one's work
bō´ya *n* 坊や (little) boy
boyakimásu, boyáku *v* ぼやきます、ぼやく
grumbles, complains
bōzen *adj* 茫然 stunned: **bōzen to shita kao** 茫然
とした顔 dazed-looking: **bōzen to shimásu** 茫然
とします is struck dumb with amazement.
bōzu *n* 坊主 Buddhist monk or priest
bōzu-atama *n* 坊主頭 shaven head
bú *n* 部 **1.** (*suffix* ...-**bu** ...部) part, division,
section
bú-bun *n* 部分 part, portion
bu-chō *n* 部長 department/division/section head,
manager, chief (*in the office*)
bu-gáisha *n* 部外者 outsider
bu-hín *n* 部品 parts
bú-ka *n* 部下 a subordinate
bu-mon *n* 部門 sector
eigyō-bu *n* 営業部 business/sales department
2. (*performance*) **hiru-no-bú** 昼の部 matinee;
yóru-no-bú 夜の部 evening performance
...-bu *suffix* **1.** ...分 (1-9) percent: **sán-wari sán-
bu** 三割三分 = **sánjū san-pāsénto** 33 パーセント
33 percent **2.** ...部 copies (*of a book*); **ichí-bu** 一
部 one copy
buai *n* 歩合 commission
buai-sei 歩合制 commission system: **buai(-sei)
de hatarakimásu** 歩合（制）で働きます works on a
commission
bu-áisō (na) *adj* 無愛想（な） unsociable, blunt,
brusque, curt
buatsuí *adj* 分厚い thick (= **atsubottai** 厚ぼっ
たい)
buchimásu, butsu *v* ぶちます、ぶつ hits
bu-chō´hō *n* 不調法 a gaffe, a blunder:
bu-chō´hō o shimásu 不調法をします makes a
blunder
bu-chō´hō-monó *n* 不調法者 abstainer
bu-chō´hō (na) *adj* 不調法（な） awkward,
clumsy, impolite
Budda *n* 仏陀 Buddha
budō *n* ブドウ・葡萄 grapes
búdō *n* 武道 martial arts (= **bújutsu** 武術)
budō-shu *n* ブドウ酒 wine
bu-énryo (na) *adj* 不遠慮（な） frank, unreserved,
forward, pushy, rude
búffe *n* ビュッフェ buffet
búgaku *n* 舞楽 traditional court dances and music
būingu *n* ブーイング booing
buji (ni) *adv* 無事（に） safely (*without incident*)
bujoku *n* 侮辱 insult(ing): ~ **shimásu** 侮辱します
insults: **bujoku sarete hara ga tachimásu** 侮辱さ
れて腹が立ちました was/got upset from an insult

bújutsu *n* 武術 martial arts (= **búdō** 武道)
búki *n* 武器 weapon, arms
bu-kimi (na) *adj* 不気味（な） ghasty, eerie:
bu-kimi na shizukesa 不気味な静けさ eerie
silence
bu-kíryō (na) *adj* 不器量（な） homely, ugly
bu-kíyō (na) *adj* 不器用（な） clumsy
bukká *n* 物価 commodity prices
bukkirábō (na) *adj* ぶっきらぼう（な） blunt,
brusque, curt
bukku *n* ブック book
bukku-fea *n* ブックフェア book fair
Búkkyō *n* 仏教 Buddhism
bū´mu *n* ブーム boom (*fad*)
bún *n* 文 sentence, text (= **búnshō** 文章)
bun-bō-gu *n* 文房具, **bunpō´-gu** 文房具
stationery supplies: **bunbōgu-ya** 文房具屋
stationery shop
bun-chin *n* 文鎮 paperweight
bún-gaku *n* 文学 literature
bún-go *n* 文語 literary language/word: **bungo-
teki (na)** 文語的（な） literary
bún-ka *n* 文化 culture, civilization; **Bunka-no-hí**
文化の日 (3 November): **bunká sai**
文化祭 cultural festival
bun-ko(-bon) *n* 文庫(本) pocketbook
bun-ken *n* 文献 literary document [FORMAL]:
bunken-mokuroku 文献目録 bibliography
bun-mei *n* 文明 civilization
bun-pō *n* 文法 grammar
bún-raku *n* 文楽 puppet play (*traditional*)
bún-shō *n* 文章 (written) sentence
bún-... *prefix* 分... part, portion, share; state,
status
bun-ben *n* 分娩 childbirth delivery: **bunben-shitsu**
分娩室 labor room
bun-dóki *n* 分度器 protractor
bun-jō *n* 分譲 sale in lots, lotting out: **bunjō-
manshon** 分譲マンション condominium
bun-kai *n* 分解 breakup (*material*): **kikai o
bunkai shimásu** 機械を分解します breaks up the
machine
bun-katsu *n* 分割 dividing, splitting: **bunkatsu-
barai de kaimásu** 分割払いで買います buys on
time
bun-pu *n* 分布 distribution
bun-retsu *n* 分裂 breakup (*countries, human
relationship*)
bun-ruí *n* 分類 classification: ~ **shimásu** 分類し
ます classifies, divides into (*types/groups*)
bun-sekí *n* 分析 analysis: ~ **shimásu** 分析します
analyzes
bún-shi *n* 分子 molecule, numerator
bun-tan *n* 分担 (taking) partial charge; allotment,
share: ~ **shimásu** 分担します takes partial charge
of, shares in; pays/does one's share
...-bun *suffix* ...分 numeral -th
yon-bun no ichí 4分の1 one-fourth
han-bun (no) *n* (*adj*) 半分（の） half

búppō *n* 仏法 the teachings of Buddhism

búrabura *adv* ぶらぶら idly dangling, idling, hang around: **~ shimásu** ぶらぶらします loafs (around); **ashi o búrabura sasemásu** 足をぶらぶらさせます swings one's leg (*back and forth*)

buraindo *n* ブラインド sunblind, window shade: **buraindo o oroshimásu** ブラインドを下ろします pulls the blind down

burá(jā) *n* ブラ（ジャー） bra(ssiere)

Burajiru *n* ブラジル Brazil

burakku *n* ブラック black coffee (= **burakku-kō´hii** ブラックコーヒー)

burakku-bókkusu *n* ブラックボックス black box

burakku-kō´hii *n* ブラックコーヒー black coffee

burakku-rísuto *n* ブラックリスト black list

burakku-yū´moa *n* ブラックユーモア black humor

búranch *n* ブランチ brunch

burandē *n* ブランデー brandy

burando *n* ブランド brand

buránketto *n* ブランケット blanket

buránko *n* ブランコ a swing (*in a park, etc.*)

burári (to) *v* ぶらり（と）drop by: **burári to tachiyorimásu** ぶらりと立ち寄ります drops by at, calls over

burasagarimásu, burasagaru *v* ぶら下がります, ぶら下がる hangs (down)

burasagemásu, burasageru *v* ぶら下げます, ぶら下げる hangs (down), suspends

búrashi *n* ブラシ brush
  ha-burashi *n* 歯ブラシ toothbrush

buratsukimásu, buratsuku *v* ぶらつきます, ぶらつく hangs around, wonders, strolls around: **machi o buratsukimásu** 町をぶらつきます wanders around/hangs around the town

buraun-kán *n* ブラウン管 TV tube

buráusu *n* ブラウス blouse

burauza *n* ブラウザ browser (*computer*)

buréi *n* 無礼 discourtesy
  burei na *adj* 無礼な impolite, rude

burēkā *n* ブレーカー circuit breaker (box): **burōkō ga ochimásu** ブレーカーが落ちます The breakers trip.

burē´ki *n* ブレーキ brake: **burē´ki o kakemásu** ブレーキをかけます puts on the brake

burézā *n* ブレザー blazer: **seifuku no burézā** 制服のブレザー blazer uniform

búri *n* ブリ・鰤 yellowtail (*fish*): *cf.* **hamachi** ハマチ, **inada** イナダ

buríifu *n* ブリーフ brief(s)

buriifu-kē´su *n* ブリーフケース briefcase

buríjji *n* ブリッジ bridge (*card game*)

buriki *n* ブリキ tin

burō´chi *n* ブローチ brooch

burōdobando *n* ブロードバンド broadband (*computer*)

burogu *n* ブログ blog, weblog (= **weburogu** ウェブログ)

burōkā *n* ブローカー agent, broker

burókkori(i) *n* ブロッコリ（ー） broccoli

buronzu *n* ブロンズ bronze

burū *adj* ブルー feeling blue: **burū na kibun** ブルーな気分 mood dip

burudóggu *n* ブルドッグ bulldog

burudō´zā *n* ブルドーザー bulldozer

burujoa *n* ブルジョア bourgeois

burūsu *n* ブルース blues (*music*)

bu-sáhō *n* 無[不]作法 a social gaffe, a faux pas
  bu-sáhō na *adj* 無[不]作法な rude, blunt

bu-sata *n* 無沙汰 neglecting to write/visit (= **go-busata** ご無沙汰): **go-busata shiteimásu** ご無沙汰しています It's been a long time./ I'm sorry I haven't written in so long [HONORIFIC]

búshi *n* 武士 Japanese warrior, samurai (= **samurai** さむらい・侍)

bushí-dō *n* 武士道 Bushido, the way of the samurai

búsho *n* 部署 department (*in the office*)

bushō (na) *adj* 無[不]精（な）lazy; slovenly
  bushō-hige *n* 無精ひげ a three-day beard, a five-o'clock shadow
  bushō-mono *n* 無精者 sluggard, sloven person

búshu *n* 部首 radical (*Chinese character*): **búshu-kensaku** 部首検索 index by radical

...-búsoku *n* ...不足 shortage (= **fusoku** 不足): **ne-busoku** 寝不足 not enough sleep

busshitsu *n* 物質 matter, substance
  busshitsu-teki (na) *adj* 物質的（な）material
  busshitsu-shúgi *n* 物質主義 materialism

busshoku *n* 物色 looking around for: **~ shimásu** 物色します looks/shops around for, seeks

bussō´(na) *adj* 物騒（な）troubled, unsafe, dangerous

búsu *n* ぶす ugly female

butá *n* ブタ・豚 pig
  buta-niku *n* 豚肉 pork

bútai *n* 舞台 stage

bútai *n* 部隊 detachment of troops, unit, outfit

butchō-zura *n* 仏頂面 a sullen face

bútikku *n* ブティック boutique

Butsu *n* 仏 Buddha (= **budda** 仏陀)
  butsu-dan *n* 仏壇 household altar (*Buddhist*)
  Butsu-zō *n* 仏像 Buddha (*statue*)

bútsu *n* ブーツ boot

bútsubutsu iimásu (iu) *v* ぶつぶつ言います（言う）complains (*muttering way, grumbling way*) [+ NEGATIVE]: **bútsubutsu monku o iimásu** ぶつぶつ文句を言います mutterings

butsubutsu-kō´kan *n* 物々交換 barter

butsukarimásu, butsukaru *v* ぶつかります, ぶつかる collides with, runs into

butsukemásu, butsukeru *v* ぶつけます, ぶつける hits

bútsuri, butsurígaku *n* 物理, 物理学 physics
  butsurigakú-sha *n* 物理学者 physicist

buttai *n* 物体 thing, matter, object, body, material body: **buttai to ryūtai no sōgo sayō** 物体と流体の相互作用 fluid-solid interaction

buttobashimásu, buttobasu *v* [INFORMAL] ぶっ飛ばします, ぶっ飛ばす beats up, burns up

buttōshi (de) *adv* [INFORMAL] ぶっ通し（で） without a break: **buttōshi de hatarakimásu** ぶっ通しで働きます works without a break (= **búttsuzuke (de)** ぶっ続け（で）)

buttsuke-honban (de) *adv* ぶっつけ本番（で） without rehearsal

buttsuzuke (de) *adv* [INFORMAL] ぶっ続け（で） without a break, continuously: **buttsuzuke de utatte nodo ga itaidesu** ぶっ続けで歌って喉が痛いです The throat is paining after singing continuously. (= **buttōshi** ぶっ通し)

búzā *n* ブザー buzzer

byákudan *n* ビャクダン・白檀 sandalwood

byō´ *n* 秒 a second (*of time*)
　byō´-yomi *n* 秒読み countdown
　byō-shin *n* 秒針 second hand, second pointer

byō´… *prefix* 病… sickness, patients

byō-in *n* 病院 hospital; clinic, doctor's office, health service: **kyūkyū-byōin** 救急病院 emergency hospital

byō-ki (no) *adj* 病気（の） sick, ill; sickness, illness: **byōki-gachi (na)** 病気がち（な） sickly, unhealthy

byō-nin *n* 病人 an invalid, a patient

byō-reki *n* 病歴 medical history

byō-shin *n* 病身 sick body: **byōshin no haha** 病身の母 my invalid/sick mother

byō-tō *n* 病棟 hospital ward

byō´ *n* 鋲 a tack; a thumbtack (= **gabyō** 画鋲)

hyōbu *n* 屏風 screen (*folding*)

byōdō (na) *adj* 平等（な） equal

byōsha *n* 描写 depiction, description: ~ **shimásu** 描写します describes: **byōsha ga umai** 描写が上手い is good at describing

C

cha *n* 茶（**o-chá** お茶） tea, green tea
　cha-bán-geki *n* 茶番劇 farce, burlesque
　cha-bín *n* 茶瓶 teapot
　cha-dái *n* 茶代（**o-chadái** お茶代） **1.** tea charges (*in café, etc.*) **2.** tip (*money*)
　cha-gará *n* 茶殻 tea leaves
　cha-gashí *n* 茶菓子（**o-chagashí** お茶菓子） tea cake
　cha-iro (no) *adj* 茶色（の） brown
　cha-me *n* 茶目（**o-cháme** お茶目） mischievous, playful [IN POSITIVE SENSE], elfish: **o-cháme na hito** お茶目な人 kidder
　cha-no-má *n* 茶の間（**o-cha-no-má** お茶の間） (*Japanese style*) living room: **o-cha-no-má de onajimi** お茶の間でお馴染み familiar to TV viewers
　cha-nomi-tómodachi *n* 茶飲み友達 coffee-drinking companion, crony
　cha-sají *n* 茶匙 teaspoon
　cha-wán *n* 茶碗（**o-cháwan** お茶碗） **1.** rice bowl **2.** tea cup (*for tea ceremony*)
　cha-wán-mushi *n* 茶碗むし steamed egg hotchpotch in a teacup (*made from broth and egg*)
　cha-zuké *n* 茶漬け（**o-chazuké** お茶漬け） a bowl of rice with hot tea and flavorings poured over it

…cha *suffix* …ちゃ = **…-téwa** …ては (doing/being, if one does/be)

cháchi (na) *adj* [INFORMAL] ちゃち（な） petty, flimsy, cheap

chā´han *n* チャーハン・炒飯 (*Chinese*) fried rice

cháimu *n* チャイム chime

chairudo-shíito *n* チャイルドシート child seat

chājí *n* チャージ charge: ~ **shimásu** チャージします charges

chákku *n* チャック zipper

chakashimásu, chakasu *v* [INFORMAL] ちゃかします、ちゃかす turns…into a joke, mimes, sends up, makes fun of, ridicules

… cháku *suffix* …着 arriving at (TIME/PLACE)

chakkarishite-(i)másu ((i)ru) *v* [INFORMAL] ちゃっかりして（い）ます（（い）る） is nimble, adroit, shrewd and calculating

chakkō *n* 着工 starting: ~ **shimásu** 着工します starts

chakuchaku (to) *adv* 着々（と） steadily

chakuchí *n* 着地 landing on: ~ **shimásu** 着地します lands on

chakufukú *n* 着服 [BOOKISH] embezzlement, misappropriation: ~ **shimásu** 着服します pockets, embezzles, have one's fingers in the till

chakugán *n* 着眼 [BOOKISH] attention: ~ **shimásu** 着眼します turns one's attention
　chakugán-ten *n* 着眼点 viewpoint

chakujítsu (na) *adj* 着実（な） steady, constant

chakunan *n* 嫡男 [BOOKISH] heir, eldest son

chakurikú *n* 着陸 (*from sky or wide water area*) landing, touching ground: ~ **shimásu** 着陸します lands on the ground

chakuséki *n* 着席 taking a seat: ~ **shimásu** 着席します takes a seat

chakushi *n* 嫡子 [BOOKISH] heir

chakushoku *n* 着色 coloring, stain, color: ~ **shimásu** 着色します stains, colors

chákushu *n* 着手 [BOOKISH] begin, start: ~ **shimásu** 着手します begins, starts

chakusō *n* 着想 [BOOKISH] conception, idea, inspiration: ~ **shimásu** 着想します conceives, comes by

chakusúi *n* 着水 landing on water, splashing down: ~ **shimásu** 着水します lands on water, splashes down

chā´mingu n チャーミング charming, attractive

…(-) chan suffix …ちゃん (*mostly attached to children's or girls' names.* [INFORMAL])

chanbará n ちゃんばら sword battle (*historical period drama*)

chánchara okashíi adj ちゃんちゃらおかしい [INFORMAL] laughable, absurd, fiddle-dee-dee

chánnerú n チャンネル channel (TV): **chánneru o kaemásu** チャンネルを替えます changes the channel

chánpion n チャンピオン champion

chánpon n ちゃんぽん alternating, skipping back and forth, mixing one's drinks/foods

chánsu n チャンス chance

chantó adv ちゃんと safe(ly) (*without incident*), firmly, securely
chantó shita adj ちゃんとした proper, secure

chárachara shita adj ちゃらちゃらした [INFORMAL] showy [IN NEGATIVE SENSE]: **chárachara shita kakkō** ちゃらちゃらした格好 showy outfits

charanporán (na) adj [INFORMAL] ちゃらんぽらん(な) [INFORMAL] irresponsible, sloppy, halfway, unreliable [IN NEGATIVE SENSE]: **charanporán na hito** ちゃらんぽらんな人 giddy fellow

charénji n チャレンジ challenge: **~ shimásu** チャレンジします challenges

charinkó n チャリンコ [INFORMAL] bicycle

cháritii n チャリティー charity

charumerá n チャルメラ noodle vendor's flute

chāshū n チャーシュー (*Chinese*) roast pork
chāshū-men n チャーシュー麺 Chinese noodles with sliced roast pork

chātā n チャーター charter: **~ shimásu** チャーターします charters
chātā-bin n チャーター便 chartered flight, charter service
chātā´-ki n チャーター機 chartered plane

chatto n チャット chatting, chat (*internet*)

chékku n チェック 1. check: **~ shimásu** チェックします checks　2. check (*bank*) (= **kogitte** 小切手)　3. check (*pattern*)

chekku-áuto n チェックアウト check-out: **~ shimásu** チェックアウトします checks out

chekkú-in n チェックイン check-in: **~ shimásu** チェックインします checks in

Chéko n チェコ Czech
Cheko-go n チェコ語 Czech (*language*)
Cheko-jín n チェコ人 a Czech

chē´n n チェーン chain, snow chain

chéro n チェロ cello

chi n 血 blood: **chi ga demásu** 血が出ます bleeds
chi-bashítta adj 血走った bloodshot
chi-dome n 血止め styptic pencil
chi-daraké adj 血だらけ bloody
chi-manakó n 血眼 bloodshot eyes: … **o chi-manakó ni nátte** … を血眼になって frantically; with bloodshot eyes
chi-namagusái adj 血生臭い bloody

chi-no-ke ga nái adj 血の気がない pale

chi-sují n 血筋 lineage, genealogy

chi n 地 ground, earth, land: **chi ni ashi o tsukemásu** 地に足をつけます grounds oneself
chi-chū´ n 地中 underground
chi-chū´-kai n 地中海 the Mediterranean
chi-hei-sén n 地平線 horizon (*on land*)
chi-hō´, chí-iki n 地方 area, region, province, district: **chi-hō´ no** 地方の local
chi-jō´ n 地上 above ground, on the ground
chí-ka n 地下 underground: **chiká-shitsu** 地下室 basement: **chiká-tetsu** 地下鉄 subway
chi-kaí n 地階 basement
chi-kakú n 地殻 (*geology*) the earth's crust
chí-ku n 地区 section, sector (*area*)
chi-méi n 地名 the name of a place/land
chi-shitsú n 地質 the geology (*of a place*): **chishitsú-gaku** 地質学 geology
chi-sō n 地層 (*geology*) stratum
chi-tai n 地帯 zone: **anzen-chitái** 安全地帯 safety zone
chí-zu n 地図 map

chián n 治安 law and order, security, public order

chiaríida n チアリーダー cheerleader

Chibetto n チベット Tibet
Chibetto-go n チベット語 Tibetan (*language*)
Chibetto-jín n チベット人 a Tibetan

chíbi n ちび [INFORMAL] midget
chibi-kko n ちびっ子 (*tiny*) tot

chibirimásu, chibiru v ちびります、ちびる [INFORMAL] wets one's pants, wets oneself

chíbu n 恥部 1. private parts, pubic area　2. source of embarrassment

chíbusa n 乳房 (woman's) breasts

chichi (oya) n 父(親) father

chichi n 乳 1. mother's milk　2. breasts and nipples
chi(chi)-bánare n 乳離れ past the breast, is weaned, become independent

chidorí-ashi n 千鳥足 swaying gait, a reeling movement: **chidorí-ashi de arukimásu** 千鳥足で歩きます walks drunkenly

chié n 知恵 wisdom
chié-okure (no) n, adj 知恵遅れ(の) mentally retarded

chién n 遅延 [BOOKISH] delay
chién-shōmeisho n 遅延証明書 train delay certificate

chífusu n チフス typhus (*fever*), typhoid (*fever*)

chigaí 違い 1. n difference, discrepancy　2. v → **chigaimásu** 違います [INFINITIVE]

chigaimásu, chigau v 違います、違う is different; is wrong; is not like that

chigatté v 違って → **chigaimásu** 違います

chigirimásu, chigiru v 千切ります、千切る tears into pieces

chigúhagú (na) adj ちぐはぐ(な), ill-assorted, mismatched, is all mixed up: **chigúhagú na kaiwa** ちぐはぐな会話 talking at cross-purposes:

chigúhagú na tebukuro ちぐはぐな手袋 odd pair of gloves

chihō (-shō´) n 痴呆(症) (*medical*) dementia

chíi n 地位 rank, position, status

chíifu n チーフ chief

chíimu n チーム team

chiimuwāku n チームワーク teamwork

chiisái, chíisa na *adj* 小さい, 小さな little, small

chíitā n チーター cheetah

chiizu n チーズ cheese

chiizu-kēki n チーズケーキ cheesecake

chíji n 知事 governor

chijimárimásu, chijimaru v 縮まります, 縮まる shrinks, shortens

chijimemásu, chijimeru v 縮めます, 縮める shortens (it)

chijimimásu, chijimu v 縮みます, 縮む (it) shrinks

chijín n 知人 [BOOKISH] acquaintance

chijiremásu, chijireru v 縮れます, 縮れる becomes curly

chijoku n 恥辱 disgrace, shame

chiká goro n, *adv* 近頃 lately, recently

chikaí n 誓い vow, pledge, oath **chikaimásu** 誓います [INFINITIVE]

chikái *adj* 近い near, close by: **chikái uchí ni** 近いうちに in the near future

chikaimásu, chikáu v 誓います, 誓う swears, vows, pledges

chikaku *adj, adv* 近く **1.** close **2.** near-by **3.** shortly

chikakú n 知覚 perception

chiká-michi n 近道 short cut

chikán n 痴漢 (*sexual*) molester, groper

chikará n 力 **1.** power, strength **2.** ability (= **nō-ryoku** 能力) **3.** effort (= **doryoku** 努力) **4.** o-chi-kara お力 influence (= **eikyōryoku** 影響力)

chika-yorimásu, chika-yoru v 近寄ります, 近寄る approaches, draws/comes near

chika-zukemásu, chika-zukéru v 近付けます, 近付ける lets one approach, brings close; associates (*keeps company*) with; can approach it

chika-zukimásu, chika-zúku v 近付きます, 近付く (= **chika-yorimásu, chika-yoru** 近寄ります, 近寄る)

chíketto n チケット ticket (= **kippu** 切符)

chikén n 知見 knowledge, learning, information

chikin n チキン chicken

chikokú n 遅刻 late: **~ shimásu** 遅刻します is late (for)

chikubi n 乳首 nipple, teat

chikuchiku-shimásu (suru) v ちくちくします (する) pricks, prickles, tickles

chikuón-ki n 畜音機 phonograph

chikúrimásu, chikuru v チクります, チクる tells, snitches on, informs on

chikusekí n 蓄積 accumulation, store

chikushō, chikishō 畜生, ちきしょう **1.** *interj* Damn! (*curse*) **2.** n beast(s)

chikuwá n チクワ broiled fish cake

chikyū´ n 地球 the Earth

chikyū´-gi n 地球儀 globe

chímachima *adv* ちまちま small and neatly arranged: **chímachima to kurashimásu** ちまちまと暮らします lives frugally: **chímachima to shita seikaku no hito** ちまちまとした性格の人 unadventurous person

chimatá n 巷 public: **chimatá no uwasa dewa…** 巷のうわさでは… People say that…

chiméikizu n 致命傷 vital wound, fatal injury

chiméiteki (na) *adj* 致命的(な) fatal, capital, mortal, deadly

chimitsú *adj* 緻密 close, minute, elaborate: **chimitsú na keikaku** 緻密な計画 careful planning

chinatsu n 鎮圧 suppression: **~ shimásu** 鎮圧します suppresses

chinbotsu n 沈没 sinking: **~ shimásu** 沈没します sinks

chínchin n ちんちん (**o-chínchin** おちんちん) penis [*baby, informal talk*]

chinden n 沈殿 deposition, settling: **~ shimásu** 沈殿します is deposited, settles out

chíngin n 賃金 wage

chinjutsú n 陳述 statement, parol: **~ shimásu** 陳述します makes a statement

chinka n 沈下 sinkage, subsidence: **~ shimásu** 沈下します subsides, settles down

chínmi n 珍味 delicacy, bonne bouche

chinmokú n 沈黙 silence: **~ shimásu** 沈黙します stops talking

chínō n 知能 intelligence

chinō-shisū n 知能指数 intelligence quotient

chinomígo n 乳飲み子 an infant, nursling: **chinomígo (o) kakaete** 乳飲み子(を)抱えて with a baby/babies

chinpánjii n チンパンジー chimpanzee

chínpira n ちんぴら・チンピラ a punk; hoodlum; juvenile delinquent

chinretsu n 陳列 exhibition, display: **~ shimásu** 陳列します exhibits, puts on display

chinseizai n 鎮静剤 sedative, tranquilizer

chinshaku n 賃借 letting and hiring, rental: **~ shimásu** 賃借します rents

chíntai n 賃貸 lease, rental, rented apartment

chíppu n チップ tip (*money*)

chírachira hikarimásu (hikaru) v チラチラ光ります(光る) glimmers

chírachira suru mono n チラチラするもの fluff stuff

chirári-to-mimásu (miru) v ちらりと見ます (見る) glances

chira(ka)shimásu, chira(ka)su v 散ら(か)します, 散ら(か)す scatters, strews

chirashí n チラシ leaflet

chirashí-zushi n ちらし寿司[鮨] sushi rice covered with fish tidbits

chiratsuki n ちらつき flicker: **gamen no chira-tsuki** 画面のちらつき screen that flickers

chiréba *v* 散れば (if they disperse/scatter/fall about) → **chirimásu** 散ります

chirí *n* 塵 dust (*on ground, floor, etc.*)
  chirí-tóri *n* ちり[塵]取り dustpan

chirí *v* 散り → **chirimásu** 散ります [INFINITIVE]

chíri *n* 地理 the geography, the lay of the land
  chirí-gaku *n* 地理学 (*the study/science of*) geography
  chiri-jō (no) *adj* 地理上(の) geographical
  chiri-teki (na) *adj* 地理的(な) geographical

chiri-gamí, chiri-kami, chiri-shi *n* ちり紙 tissues (*Kleenex*) (= **tisshu(pēpā)** ティッシュ (ペーパー))

chirimásu, chiru *v* 散ります, 散る disperses, scatters, falls about

chirí ya/wa shinai *v* 散りや/はしない = **chiranai** 散らない (not scatter)

chiryō *n* 治療 treatment (*medical*): ~ **shimásu** 治療します treats, cures

chísei *n* 知性 intellect, intelligence, mind, mentality

chiséi *n* 治世 reign

chishiteki (na) *adj* 致死的(な) death-dealing

chisetsú *n* 稚拙 childish

chíshiki *n* 知識 knowledge
  chishiki-jin *n* 知識人 intellectual(s)

Chishimá *n* 千島, **Chishíma-réttō** 千島列島 the Kurile Islands

chishíryō *n* 致死量 overdose

chísso *n* チッソ・窒素 nitrogen

chissokú *n* 窒息 suffocation: ~ **shimásu** 窒息します suffocates

chisui *n* 治水 flood control

chitchái *adj* ちっちゃい [INFORMAL] little

chíteki (na) *adj* 知的(な) intelligent, intellectual (= **chiseiteki (na)** 知性的(な))

chítsu *n* 膣 vagina

chítsujo *n* 秩序 order, discipline, system

chitté *v* 散って → **chirimásu** 散ります

chittó-mo *adv* ちっとも [+ NEGATIVE verb] [INFORMAL] not a bit, not in the least: **chittó-mo ki ni narimasén** ちっとも気になりません not care a bit

chō *n* 腸 intestines

chō´ *n* チョウ・蝶・蝶々 butterfly
  chō´chō *n* チョウチョ(ウ)・蝶々 butterfly
  chō-músubi *n* 蝶結び bow (*of a ribbon*)
  chō-nékutai *n* 蝶ネクタイ bow tie

(…-)chō´ *suffix* (…)丁 block (*or block area*) of a city: **(…-) chō-mé** (…) 丁目 (…-th) block (*of city*)

(…-) chō´ *suffix* (…)長 head, chief, leader

(…-) chō´ *suffix* (…)兆 trillion

chóbo *n* ちょぼ a dot
  chóbo-yaki *n* ちょぼ焼き (= **tako-yaki** たこ焼き) prototype of octopus balls *tako-yaki* (*Japanese food*)

chōbó *n* 帳簿 (*account*) book
  chōbo-gákari *n* 帳簿係 book-keeper

chōchín *n* 堤灯 lantern

chō´chō *n* 町長 town mayor

chōdai-shimásu (suru) *v* ちょうだい[頂戴]しま

す(する) I (humbly) *receive/accept*

…chōdái *interj* …ちょうだい [INFORMAL]
1. Please **2.** Give me…

chōdo *adj* ちょうど exactly, just: **chōdo ii toki ni kimashita** ちょうどいい時に来ました You came just at the right time.

chōgō *n* 調合 preparation: ~ **shimásu** 調合します prepares, compounds

chō´hō (na) *adj* 重宝(な) useful, convenient, valued: ~ **shimásu** 重宝します appreciates; **chō´hō garimásu** 重宝がります values, cherishes, makes full use of

chō´ji *n* 丁子 cloves

chójo *n* 長女 eldest daughter

chojō´ *n* 頂上 top, summit, peak

chō´ka *n* 超過 [BOOKISH] excess: ~ **shimásu** 超過します exceeds, goes/runs over

chōkán *n* 朝刊 morning paper

chōkán *n* 長官 chief (*head*)

chō´ki *n* 長期 long period, long range

chokín *n* 貯金 deposit, savings: ~ **shimásu** 貯金します deposits (*money*), saves
  chokin-bako *n* 貯金箱 saving box

chokkán *n* 直感 intuition

chokki *n* チョッキ vest

chóko *n* ちょこ (**o-chóko** おちょこ) saké cup

chōkoku *n* 彫刻 carving, engraving: ~ **shimásu** 彫刻します engraves

choko(rē´to) *n* チョコ(レート) chocolate

chō´ku *n* チョーク chalk

chokuryū´ *n* 直流 DC, direct current

chokusén *n* 直線 straight line

chokusetsu *n, adv* 直接 direct(ly)

chō-kyóri *n* 長距離 long distance

chō´mi *n* 調味 seasoning (*food*)
  chōmí-ryō *n* 調味料 spice

chō´nán *n* 長男 eldest son

chónbo *n* ちょんぼ・チョンボ a booboo, a goof, a blunder

chōryū *n* 潮流 current, tide, trend

chō´sa *n* 調査 examination, inquiry, investigation, research, survey: ~ **shimásu** 調査します examines, inquires, investigates, researches, surveys

chosáku-ken *n* 著作権 copyright

chōséi *n* 調整 adjustment: ~ **shimásu** 調整します adjusts

chōsén *n* 挑戦 challenge: ~ **shimásu** 挑戦します challenges
  chōsén-sha *n* 挑戦者 challenger

Chō´sén *n* 朝鮮 → **Kita Chōsén, Kankoku**

chōsetsú *n* 調節 → **chōséi**

chósha *n* 著者 writer, author

chōshí *n* 調子 tune; condition; trend; **chōshí ni norimásu** 調子に乗ります, **chōshí ga demásu** 調子が出ます gets into the swing of things: **chōshí ga ii/warui** 調子がいい/悪い is in good/bad condition

chósho *n* 著書 one's book

chō´sho *n* 長所 strong point, advantage, merit

chōshokú *n* 朝食 morning meal, breakfast (= **asa-gohan** 朝ご飯)

chōshu *n* 聴取 listening in: ~ **shimásu** 聴取します listens in
  chōshu-sha *n* 聴取者 (*radio*) listener

chōshū *n* 聴衆 audience

chōshū *n* 徴収 [BOOKISH] collection (*of taxes, etc.*), levying: ~ **shimásu** 徴収します collects, levies

chosúi-chi *n* 貯水池 reservoir

chō´ten *n* 頂点 climax, peak, high-point

chō-tsúgai *n* 蝶つがい hinge

chótto *adv* ちょっと just a little; just a minute; somewhat

chottóshitá *adj* … ちょっとした… **1.** slight, trivial **2.** quite a …, a decent/respectable …: **chottóshitá toraburu** ちょっとしたトラブル queer

chōwa *n* 調和 harmony, agreement: … **to chōwá shimásu** …と調和します is in harmony (*agrees*) with

chū *n* 注 annotation, note

chū *adj* 中 middle; medium
  chū´-bu *n* 中部 middle (*part*)
  chū-gákkō *n* 中学校 middle school (*junior high school*)
  chū-gáku-sei *n* 中学生 junior high school student
  chū-gatá (no) *n* 中型(の) medium-size (*model*)
  chū-gén *n* 中元 (**o-chūgen** お中元) midsummer gift
  chū´-i *n* 中尉 1st lieutenant; lieutenant junior grade (j.g.)
  chū-jíen *n* 中耳炎 middle ear infection
  chū´-jō *n* 中将 (*army*) lieutenant general; (*navy*) vice admiral
  chū-jún *n* 中旬 the middle of (*month*)
  chū-kán *n* 中間 middle: … (**no**) **chū-kán** … (の)中間 beween…: **chūkán-shiken** 中間試験 intermediate exam: **chūkán-kanrishoku** 中間管理職 mid-level executive, middle management
  chū-kán *n* 中巻 middle volume (*of a set of three*)
  chū-nen *n* 中年 middle age, **chū-nen (no)** 中年(の) middle-aged (*person*)
  chū-níkai *n* 中二階 mezzanine (*floor*)
  chū´-sa *n* 中佐 lieutenant colonel; (*navy*) commander
  chū´-sei *n* 中世 medieval times, the Middle Ages
  chū-shōkígyō *n* 中小企業 medium-sized and small companies
  Chū´-tō *n* 中東 the Middle East
  chū-toró *n* 中とろ・中トロ medium-fat (pink) tuna
  chū-za *n* 中座 excusing oneself, leaving in the middle: ~ **shimásu** 中座します excuses oneself

…-chū *suffix* 中 **1.** … chū (ni) …中(に) during, while, within (*time*) **2.** … chū (no) …中(の) in course …of, under (*doing*)
  kōji-chū *n* 工事中 under construction

chū´bu *n* チューブ tube

chū´cho *n* ちゅうちょ・躊躇 [BOOKISH]

hesitation: ~ **shimásu** ちゅうちょ[躊躇]します hesitates

chū´doku *n* 中毒 addiction, poisoning
  arukōru-chū´doku アルコール中毒 (= **aruchū** アル中) alcohol addiction
  shoku-chū´doku 食中毒 food poisoning

Chū´goku *n* 中国 China
  Chūgoku-jin *n* 中国人 a Chinese
  Chūgoku-go *n* 中国語 Chinese (*language*)

Chūgoku-chíhō *n* 中国地方 the Chugoku area of Japan (*Okayama, Hiroshima, Yamaguchi, Shimane, Tottori Prefectures*)

chū hai *n* 酎ハイ a *shōchū* highball

chū´i *n* 注意 attention; note, notice, reminder: ~ **shimásu** 注意します **1.** pays attention **2.** is careful of **3.** advises, warns
  chūi-bukái *adj* 注意深い careful

chūingámu *n* チューインガム chewing gum

chūjitsu (na) *adj* 忠実(な) faithful

chū´ka *n, adj* 中華 Chinese…, Chinese food
  chū´ka-gai *n* 中華街 Chinatown
  chū´ka-ryō´ri(-ten) *n* 中華料理(店) Chinese cooking (restaurant)

chūkái *n* 仲介 mediation. ~ **shimásu** 仲介します goes between
  chūkái-gyōsha *n* 仲介業者 broker, intermediary agent

chūko (no) *adj* 中古(の) secondhand
  chūkó-hin *n* 中古品 secondhand goods
  chūkó-sha *n* 中古車 used car

chūkokú *n* 忠告 advice: ~ **shimásu** 忠告します advises

chūmoku *n* 注目 attention, notice: ~ **shimásu** 注目します pays attention

chūmon *n* 注文 an order: ~ **shimásu** 注文します orders (*clothes, meal, etc.*)

chūō´ *n* 中央 the center
  chūō no *adj* 中央の central
  Chūō-sen *n* 中央線 the (JR) Chuo Line

chūritsú *n* 中立 neutral(ity)

chūséi *n* 忠誠 loyalty, fidelity, allegiance: **chūséi o chikaimásu** 忠誠を誓います pledges one's loyalty

chūséi *adj* 中性 neutral
  chūséi-aminosan *n* 中性アミノ酸 neutral amino acid

chūsén *n* 抽選 lottery, drawing

chūshá *n* 駐車 parking
  chūsha-jō *n* 駐車場 parking lot/garage
  chūsha-kinshi *n* 駐車禁止 No Parking

chūshá *n* 注射 injection: **yobō-chusha** 予防注射 preventive injection, immunization
  chūshá-ki *n* 注射器 syringe (*for injections*)

chūshí *n* 中止 suspension (*abeyance*): ~ **shimásu** 中止します suspends, stops (*in the midst*)

chūshín *n* 中心 center, heart, middle
  chūshín no *adj* 中心の central
  chūshín-chi *n* 中心地 central area

chūshō *n* 中傷 slander: ~ **shimásu** 中傷します slanders

chūshokú n 昼食 lunch (= **hiru-góhan** 昼ご飯, **ranchi** ランチ)

chūshō-teki (na) adj 抽象的(な) abstract

chūsū (shinkei) n 中枢(神経) nerve center

chūsúi-ki n 注水器 douche, syringe (*for water*)

chūto (de) adv 中途(で) on the way, halfway (= **tochū (de)** 途中(で))

  chūto-hanpa (na) adj 中途半端(な) half-done, incomplete

chūyō n 中庸 [BOOKISH] moderation: **chūyō o emásu** 中庸を得ます exercises moderation

chūzái n, 駐在 residence, presence: ~ **shimásu** 駐在します resides

  chūzái-in n 駐在員 resident officer

  chūzái-táishi n 駐在大使 ambassador

chūzetsu n 中絶 abortion: **chūzetsu-shujutsu o ukemásu** 中絶手術を受けます undergoes an abortion

D

... da suffix ...だ: → **... -ta** た

... dá v ...だ = **... désu** ...です is; it is

daben n 駄弁 idle talk: **daben o rōshimásu** 駄弁をろうします talks rubbish, talks nonsense: **daben-ka** 駄弁家 windy speaker

daberimásu, dabéru v だべります,だべる shoots the breeze/bull, chews the fat (*idly talks*)

dabétte v だべって → **daberimásu** だべります

dabingu n ダビング dubbing: ~ **shimásu** ダビングします dubs

daboku-shō n 打撲傷 [BOOKISH] bruise

dabudabu (no) adj だぶだぶ(の) baggy, loose, full, voluminous: **dabudabu no fuku** だぶだぶの服 voluminous dress

daburimásu, dabúru v ダブります, ダブる gets doubled, overlaps, repeats, is repeated (by mistake)

dáburu n ダブル **1.** = **dabururū´mu** ダブルルーム a double (*room*) **2.** double(-size) drink **3.** double-breasted suit **4. dáburusu** ダブルス (*tennis*) doubles

  daburu-béddo n ダブルベッド double bed

dabútte v ダブって → **daburimásu** ダブります

dachin n 駄賃 (**o-dachin** お駄賃) reward, tip

dada n 駄々 fretful: **dada o konemásu** 駄々をこねます is fretful, act like a baby: **dada-kko** 駄々っ子 fretful/unreasonable/spoiled child

dadappiroi adj だだっ広い rambling, too spacious

daeki n 唾液 [BOOKISH] saliva

daen n 楕円 ellipse, oval

dága conj だが [BOOKISH] but (= **shikashi** しかし)

dageki n 打撃 blow, shock: **dageki o ataemásu** 打撃を与えます hits, delivers a blow

daha n 打破 defeat: ~ **shimásu** 打破します defeats

dái- prefix 第 [+ number] number ...; (= **...-banmé** ...番目) [numeral]-th; (*separate word except when attached to a single-unit numeral*)

dái-go adj 第五 number five; (= **go-banmé** 五番目) fifth

dái-hachi adj 第八 number eight; (= **hachi-banmé** 八番目) eighth

dái-ichi adj 第一 number one; (= **ichi-banmé** 一番目) first: **dái-ichi no** 第一の (the) first; **dái-ichi ni** 第一に first (of all)

dái-jū adj 第十 number ten; (= **jūbanmé** 十番目) tenth

dai-ku adj 第九 (= **dái-kyū** 第九) number nine; (= **kyū-banmé** 九番目) ninth

dái-nana adj 第七 number seven; (= **nana-banmé** 七番目) seventh

dái-ni adj 第二 number two; (= **ni-banmé** 二番目) second: **Dái-ni-ji Sekaitaisen** 第二次世界大戦 World War II

dái-roku adj 第六 number six; (= **roku-banmé** 六番目) sixth: **dái-rokkan** 第六感 six sense

dái-san adj 第三 number three; (= **sanbanmé** 三番目) third: **dái-san-sha** 第三者 third party: **dái-san no ié** 第三の家 house number three

dái-yon adj 第四 number four; (= **yonbanmé** 四番目) fourth

dái n 題 **1.** title (= **daimei** 題名) **2.** topic, theme (= **daimokú** 題目)

dai n 代 **1.** n (**o-dai** お代) charge (*fee*), bill: **o-dai wa itadakimasen** お代はいただきません Compliments of the house.: **takushii-dai** タクシー代 taxi fare **2.** [numeral]-dai ...age, generation: **nijū´-dai** 20代 twenties; **nanajū-nen-dai** 70年代 70's (seventies); **ni-dai(me)** 2代目 The Second, junior (*family*)

... dai suffix ...だい [INFORMAL](= **... désu ka** ...ですか [FORMAL]): **dáre/nán dai** 誰/何だい who/what is it?

dai n 台 stand, (*low*) table

  fumi-dai n 踏み台 footstool

...´-dai suffix ...台 (*counts mounted machines, vehicles*)

daibā n ダイバー diver

daiben n 大便 defecation, bowel movement, feces: **daiben o shimásu** 大便をします defecates

daiben n 代弁 speaking for another: ~ **shimásu** 代弁します speaks for another

daibingu n ダイビング dive: ~ **shimásu** ダイビングします dives

daibu adv 大分 quite, very, much

dai-búbun n 大部分 most, the majority

daibutsu n 大仏 giant statue of Buddha

daidái n ダイダイ・橙 bitter orange

daidái-iro *n* 橙色 (*color*) orange

dáidai *adj, adv* 代々 generation after generation, for generations

daidokoro *n* 台所 kitchen (= **kitchin** キッチン)

  daidokoro-dō´gu *n* 台所道具 kitchen utensils

daietto *n* ダイエット diet

daifuku (mochi) *n* 大福 (もち) soft rice cake stuffed with sweet bean jam

daigaku *n* 大学 college, university

  daigakú-in *n* 大学院 graduate school: **daigakuín-sei** 大学院生 graduate student

  daigakú-kōnai *n* 大学構内 campus (= **daigaku-kyanpasu** 大学キャンパス)

  daigaku-sei *n* 大学生 college student, undergrad(uate)

daigiin *n* 代議員 deputy

daigishi *n* 代議士 Diet member

daigomi *n* 醍醐味 relish, whole point

daihitsu *n* 代筆 ghost-writing: ~ **shimásu** 代筆します writes for someone

daihon *n* 台本 script (= **kyakuhon** 脚本)

daihyō *n* 代表 representative

  daihyō-sha *n* 代表者 a representative (*person*)

  daihyō-teki (na) *adj* 代表的(な) representative, typical, model

daiji *n* 大事 a matter of importance; **daiji o torimásu** 大事をとります plays it safe: **(o-) karada o (o-)daiji ni shite kudasái** (お)体を(お)大事にして下さい take good care of yourself

  daijí (na) *adj* 大事(な) important, precious (= **taisetsu (na)** 大切(な))

dáijin *n* 大臣 minister (*cabinet*)

dai-jō´bu *adj* 大丈夫 OK, all right; safe (and sound); no need to worry, no problem: **dai-jō´bu desu** 大丈夫です It's all right.

daikei *n* 台形 trapezoid

dáikichi *n* 大吉 very good luck, excellent luck

daikin *n* 代金 the price/charge, the bill: **daikin hikikae (de)** 代金引換え(で) (= **daibiki (de)** 引引き(で)) C.O.D., collect (on delivery)

daikō *n* 代行 acting as agent

  daikō´-sha *n* 代行者 an agent (= **dairi-nin** 代理人)

daikō *n* 代講 substitute class/teacher

daikoku-bashira *n* 大黒柱 pillar, breadwinner: **ikka no daikokubashira** 一家の大黒柱 the supporter of a family

daikon *n* 大根 giant white radish

  daikon-óroshi *n* 大根おろし grated radish

dáiku *n* 大工 carpenter

daikyū *n* 代休 compensation day, substitute holiday

daiméishi *n* 代名詞 pronoun

daimoku *n* 題目 (**o-daimoku** お題目) topic (= **dái** 題)

daimyō´ *n* 大名 (**o-daimyō** お大名) feudal lord

dainamaito *n* ダイナマイト dynamite

dainamikku *n* ダイナミック dynamic

dainashi *n* 台無し ruin, spoil: **dainashi ni shimásu** 台無しにします ruins, spoils, messes

dainingu-kitchin (DK) *n* ダイニングキッチン (DK) a combined dining room-kitchen, an eat-in kitchen

dainingu-rūmu *n* ダイニングルーム dining room

daí (no) … *adj* 大(の) …, **dai-…** 大… big, great

  dai-kibo (na) *adj* 大規模(な) large scale

  dai-kirai (na) *adj* 大嫌い(な) loathing, aversion

  dái-suki (na) *adj* 大好き(な) favorite, greatly liked

  dai-tasū *n* 大多数 large number; majority

dairi *n* 代理 commission, agent, agency

  dairi-bo *n* 代理母 surrogate mother

  dairí-nin *n* 代理人 agent

  dairí-ten *n* 代理店 agency

dairiseki *n* 大理石 marble (stone)

daishi *n* 台紙 mount, board (art)

dai-shō *n* 大小 size

dai-shō *n* 代償 price, compensation

dái-sū *n* 代数 algebra, literal arithmetic

daitai *adv* 大体 in general, on the whole, approximately, almost (= **oyoso** およそ)

daitán (na) *adj* 大胆(な) bold

daite *v* 抱いて → **dakimásu** 抱きます

daitōryō *n* 大統領 president (*of a nation*)

dáiya *n* 1. ダイヤ (schedule) (*train*) 2. (= **daiyamóndo**) ダイヤ(モンド) diamond

daiyaku *n* 代役 substitute, alternate

daiyaru *n* ダイヤル dial

daiyō *n* 代用 substitution: ~ **shimásu** 代用します substitutes

daiza *n* 台座 [BOOKISH] pedestal, seat

daizai *n* 題材 material, subject matter: **kankyō-hogo o daizai ni shita eiga** 環境保護を題材にした映画 film on ecology

dáizu *n* 大豆・ダイズ soy beans

dajare *n* 駄洒落 pun, equivoque

…´-daka …高 1. quantity, volume; sum 2. higher by …: **hyakuén-daka** 百円高 100 yen up

dakanai *v* 抱かない = **dakimasén** 抱きません (not hug)

dákara (sa) *conj* だから(さ) and so; therefore; that's why

… daké *suffix* …だけ only, just: … **(-ta) daké de** …(た)だけで just from (*having done it*)

dakemásu, dakeru *v* 抱けます, 抱ける can hug, can hold in the arms

dakenai *v* 抱けない = **dakemasén** 抱けません (cannot hug)

dakete *v* 抱けて → **dakemásu** 抱けます

dakimásu, daku *v* 抱きます, 抱く holds in the arms

daki-shimemásu *v* 抱き締めます → **dakimásu** 抱きます

dakyō *n* 妥協 compromise: ~ **shimásu** 妥協します compromises

daku *v* 抱く → **dakimásu** 抱きます [INFINITIVE]

damarimásu, damáru *v* 黙ります, 黙る is/becomes silent; shuts up

damashimásu, damásu *v* 騙します, 騙す deceives, cheats

damátte *v* 黙って → **damarimásu** 黙ります

damé (na) *adj* 駄目 (な) no good, no use, won't; bad, broken, malfunctioning; don't!: **damé ni narimásu** 駄目になります gets ruined, spoiled; **damé ni shimásu** 駄目にします ruins it, spoils it

dámu *n* ダム dam

dán *n* 段 **1.** step(s); grade, order **2.** (*page*) column; scene, act **3.** (…**dán** … 段) case, event

dan-bō´ru *n* ダンボール・段ボール corrugated cardboard

dan-chō no omoi *n* 断腸の思い heartbreaking grief

dan-dán *adv* 段々 gradually

dan-kai *n* 段階 grade, rank, stage (*of a process*)

dan-raku *n* 段落 paragraph

dan-tei *n* 断定 decision, conclusion: ~ **shimásu** 断定します decides, concludes

dan-zoku-teki (na) *adj* 断続的 (な) intermittent

dan *n* 団 group, party, team

dan-chi *n* 団地 housing development

dan-chō *n* 団長 leader, head

dango *n* 団子 (**o-dango** お団子) dumpling

dan-tai *n* 団体 organization, group

dan *n* 壇 platform : **dan-jō ni agarimásu** 壇上に上がります steps onto the platform

dan *n* conversation, talk

dan-shō *n* 談笑 chatting: ~ **shimásu** 談笑します has a pleasant chat

dan-wa *n* 談話 [BOOKISH] conversation: **danwa-shitsu** 談話室 common room

dan-… *prefix* 男… male

dán-jo *n* 男女 male and female: **dánjo-kyōgaku** 男女共学 coeducation; **dánjo-byōdō** 男女平等 sexual equality

dan-kon *n* 男根 penis

dan-sei *n* 男性 male

dán-shi *n* 男子 boy: **dánshi-gakusei/seito** 男子学生/生徒 schoolboy

dan-shō *n* 男娼 male prostitute

dan-shoku *n* 男色 male homosexual love

dan-son johi *n* 男尊女卑 male chauvinism

danatsu *n* 弾圧 suppression: ~ **shimásu** 弾圧します clamps down

danbō *n* 暖房 heating (*of room, house*)

danbō-sō´chi *n* 暖房装置 heating device, radiator

danbō-sétsubi *n* 暖房設備 heating (*equipment*)

dangan *n* 弾丸 [BOOKISH] bullet

dani *n* ダニ mite, tick

danna *n* 旦那 **1.** my husband **2. danna-san/-sama** 旦那さん/様 (*your/someone else's*) husband **3.** master (*of a shop, etc.*)

danpingu *n* ダンピング dumping

danryoku *n* 弾力 elastic force

danshoku *n* 暖色 warm color(s)

dansu *n* ダンス dance: **dansu o shimásu** ダンスをします dances

dan'yaku *n* 弾薬 ammunition, powder and ball

-darake *suffix* …だらけ full of…, covered with…

daradara (to) *adj* だらだら (と) lengthy: **dara-**

dara (to) sugoshimásu だらだら (と) 過ごします slobs about

daraku *n* 堕落 corruption: ~ **shimásu** 堕落します corrupts

darari-to *adv* だらりと loosely, lollingly

darashinai *adj* だらしない slovenly, loose

dáre *pron* 誰 who: **dáre no** 誰の whose; **dáre dé mo** 誰でも anybody (at all), everybody

dáre-dare *pron* 誰々 someone or other, so-and-so, what's-his/her-name

dáre ka *pron* 誰か somebody, someone

dáre mo *adv* 誰も (not) anybody; [+ NEGATIVE verb] nobody

dáre-sore *pron* 誰それ someone or other, so-and-so, what's-his/her-name

…darō´ *suffix* …だろう probably, probably (it) is; I think; don't you think? (= **…deshō´** …でしょう)

dasai *adj* ださい tasteless, insipid, bland

dasánai *v* 出さない = **dashimasén** 出しません (not put out; not …)

dáseba *v* 出せば (if one puts out; if …) → **dashimásu** 出します

dasei *n* 惰性 inertia, (*force of*) habit

daseki *n* 打席 batter's box, trip to the plate, at-bat

dásha *v* 出しゃ → **dáseba** 出せば

dasha *n* 打者 a batter/hitter

dashí *n* だし soup stock, broth: **dashí no moto** だしの素 instant bouillon

dashi *n* 出し → **dashimásu** 出します [INFINITIVE]

dashimásu, dásu *v* 出します, 出す puts out; serves (*food/drink*); produces; pays, spends; mails; begins

dashimono *v* 出し物 play, attraction, show

dashin *n* 打診 (*medical examination by*) percussion, tapping; sounding a person out: ~ **shimásu** 打診します sounds (a person) out

dashinuke (ni) *adv* 出し抜け (に) abruptly

dashinukimásu, dashinuku *v* 出し抜きます, 出し抜く outwits, gets the better of

dáshi ya/wa shinai *v* 出しや/はしない = **dasánai** 出さない (not put out; not …)

dasoku *n* 蛇足 icing on the cake

dassen *n* 脱線 derailment: ~ **shimásu** 脱線します is derailed; gets off the track, gets sidetracked

dasshí-men *n* 脱脂綿 absorbent cotton

dasshí-nyū *n* 脱脂乳 skim milk

dasshū´-zai *n* 脱臭剤 deodorant (*personal*) (= **deodoranto** デオドラント)

dassō *n* 脱走 escape, desertion: ~ **shimásu** 脱走します escapes, deserts

dā´su *n* ダース dozen: **ichi-dā´su** 1ダース one dozen

datai *n* 堕胎 abortion: ~ **shimásu** 堕胎します has an abortion

daten *n* 打点 run batted in, RBI

datō *n* 打倒 overthrow, defeat

datō *n* 妥当 appropriate, reasonable

datsumō´-zai *n* 脱毛剤 depilatory

datsuraku *n* 脱落 omission, dropout
datsuryoku *n* 脱力 faintness, lassitude
…dátta *v* …だった was; it was (= **…déshita** …でした)
dattai *n* 脱退 withdrawal: ~ **shimásu** 脱退します withdraws
…dáttara *conj* …だったら if/when it is (or was)
…dáttari (shimásu/desu) *suffix* …だったり (します/です) being representatively/sometimes/alternately …: **dáttari…ja nákattari** …だったり…じゃなかったり (is) off and on, sometimes is and sometimes isn't
dátte *conj* だって but; however, even so, though (= **démo** でも)
…dátte *suffix* …だって even being …; … or something (= **…démo** …でも)
de *n* 出 **1.** a person's origins (*family, birthplace, school*); (… **no de** …の出) born in/of …, a graduate of … **2.** (out)flow: **mizu no de ga íi** 水の出がいい/悪い has good/bad water pressure **3.** emergence, appearance; **tsuki no de** 月の出 moonrise
…de particle …で → **…-te** …て
…dé *suffix* …で (*happening*) at, in, on; with, by (*means of*), through
…dé *conj* …で is/was and; being, its being (its being) [COPULA GERUND]
…de arimásu *v* …であります = **… désu** …です is; it is
…de gozaimashō´ *v* …でございましょう = **…deshō´** …でしょう probably is; I think it is (, sir/ma'am)
…de gozaimásu *v* …でございます [DEFERENTIAL] = **…desu** …です is; it is (sir/ma'am)
…de imásu *v* …でいます stays/keeps (*goes on*) being: **Minna génki de imásu.** みんな元気でいます We are all keeping well.
…de orimásu *v* …でおります [DEFERENTIAL/HUMBLE] (*I/we*) stay/keep (*go on*) being
deaikeisaito *n* 出会い系サイト dating service website, meet-a-mate site, online dating website (*internet*)
de-aimásu, de-áu *v* 出会います, 出会う: **… ni de-aimásu** …に出会います encounters, meets, happens to see/meet, runs/bumps into
de-átte *v* 出会って → **de-aimásu** 出会います
de-awánai *v* 出合わない = **de-aimasén** 出会いません (not encounter)
déguchi *n* 出口 exit, outlet
deiríguchi *n* 出入り口 gate(way), doorway
dekake ro *v* 出掛けろ [IMPERATIVE] (go out!) → **dekakemásu** 出掛けます
dekakemásu, dekakeru *v* 出掛けます, 出掛ける starts off/out, goes out, departs
déki *v* 出来 → **dekimásu** 出来ます [INFINITIVE]
dekiai *n* 溺愛 blind love: ~ **shimásu** 溺愛します loves blindly
dekiai (no) *adj* 出来合い(の) ready-made
dekígoto *n* 出来事 happening, accident

dekimásu, dekíru *v* 出来ます, 出来る can (*do*), is possible, produced, done, finished, through, ready
dekí-mónó, o-déki *n* できもの, おでき swelling, sore, boil, pimple
dekínai *v* 出来ない impossible = **dekimasén** 出来ません (cannot)
dekíru *v* 出来る = **dekimásu** 出来ます (can (*do*))
dekíru-dake *adv* できるだけ as much as possible
dek(k)ai *adj* で(っ)かい [INFORMAL] big (= **ōkii** 大きい)
dékki *n* デッキ deck
dekoboko (no) *adj* でこぼこ(の) **1.** bump(y), rough (*road, etc.*) **2.** uneven(ness), imbalance
déma *n* デマ false rumor
demae *n* 出前 catering, food delivered to order, restaurant delivery (*service/person*)
demaé-mochi *n* 出前持ち restaurant's delivery person
demásu, déru *v* 出ます, 出る goes/comes out, emerges, appears; is served; leaves, starts
démo *conj* でも but, however, even so, though
démo *n* デモ demonstration
… démo *suffix* …でも even/also (*being*) even if it be; …or something: **gaka démo sakka démo arimasen.** 画家でも作家でもありません is neither a painter nor a writer
de-mukaemásu, de-mukaéru *v* 出迎えます, 出迎える meets, greets, welcomes
dénai *v* 出ない = **demasén** 出ません (not go/come out; …)
denbu *n* でんぶ sweet cooked ground fish
denbu *n* 臀部 [BOOKISH] buttock, hips [*medical*]
denbun *n* 伝聞 hearsay
denbun *n* 電文 telegram, telegraphic message
dénchi *n* 電池 battery
denchō *n* 電柱 telephone/light pole
dendō *n* 伝道 conduction
    dendō-tai *n* 伝導体 conductor
    dendō-sha *n* 伝道者 a missionary
déndō *n* 電動 electric operation, electric-powered
    déndō-isu *n* 電動椅子 electric-powered wheelchair
dengáku *n* 田楽 assorted boiled foods (= **o-dén** おでん)
dengon *n* 伝言 message (= **messēji** メッセージ)
denki *n* 伝記 biography
dénki *n* 電気 electricity, power; lights
    denki-sutándo *n* 電気スタンド desk/floor lamp
    denki-sutó´bu *n* 電気ストーブ electric heater;
    denki-yō´hin *n* 電気用品 = **denki-kígu** 電気器具 electrical appliances
    denki-kámisori *n* 電気かみそり electric shaver
    denki-kónro *n* 電気コンロ hot plate
    denki-sōjíki *n* 電気掃除機 vacuum cleaner
    denki-ya (san) *n* 電気屋(さん) electrician
denkyū *n* 電球 light bulb
denmāku *n* デンマーク Denmark
dénpa *n* 電波 electric wave, radiowave

denpō *n* 電報 telegram, telegraph: **denpō o uchimásu** 電報を打ちます sends a telegram

denpun *n* でんぷん starch (*for cooking*) **denpún-shitsu (no)** *n (adj)* でんぷん質(の) starch(y)

denpyō *n* 伝票 check (*restaurant bill*)

denrai *n* 伝来 [BOOKISH] introduction, import: **senzo denrai (no)** 先祖伝来(の) descendant, patrimonial

denrei *n* 伝令 [BOOKISH] orderly, herald

dénryoku *n* 電力 electric power **denryoku-gáisha** *n* 電力会社 power company

denryū *n* 電流 electric current

densen *n* 電線 electric wire, power line

densen *n* 伝染 contagion **densen-byō** *n* 伝染病 contagious/infectious/communicable disease, epidemic

densetsu *n* 伝説 tradition (*legend*): **densetsu no otoko** 伝説の男 legendary man: **densetsu ni narimásu** 伝説になります passes into legend

dénsha *n* 電車 (*electric*) train, streetcar

dénshi (no) *adj* 電子(の) electron(ic) **denshi-manē** *n* 電子マネー electronic money, cyberbuck (*internet*) **dénshi-renji** *n* 電子レンジ microwave **denshi-shoseki** *n* 電子書籍 computer book, digital book, e-book, electronic book (*internet*)

densho-bato *n* 伝書鳩 carrier pigeon

dentatsu *n* 伝達 conveyance, transmission

dentō *n* 電灯 lamp, light, flashlight

dentō *n* 伝統 tradition **dentō-teki (na)** *adj* 伝統的(な) traditional

denwa *n* 電話 telephone (call): **denwa ni demásu** 電話に出ます answers the phone; **denwa o kakemásu/shimásu** 電話をかけます/します makes a phone call **denwa-bángō** *n* 電話番号 telephone number **denwa-bókkusu** *n* 電話ボックス phone booth **denwa-chō** *n* 電話帳 telephone book/directory **denwa-kōkánshu** *n* 電話交換手 telephone operator **denwa-sen** *n* 電話線 phone line, telephone wire(s)

deodoranto *n* デオドラント deodorant

depāto *n* デパート department store

déppa *n* 出っ歯 protruding tooth, bucktooth

déreba *v* 出れば (if one goes/comes out; if …) → **demásu** 出ます

déru *v* 出る = **demásu** 出ます (goes out, comes out, leaves, starts, attends, appears, graduates from)

deshí *n* 弟子 (**o-deshi** お弟子) apprentice, disciple

… déshita *v* …でした **1.** was; it was **2.** …**-masén deshita** …ませんでした didn't

… deshō *v* …でしょう probably, probably (it) is; I think; don't you think?

… desu, dá *v* …です、だ is, has been (and still is), will be; it is

déta *v* 出た = **demáshita** 出ました (emerged; graduated from)

dē′ta *n* データ data

detarame *n* でたらめ nonsense **detarame na** *adj* でたらめな irresponsible, unreliable

detchiagemásu, detchiagéru *v* でっちあげます、でっちあげる fake

déte *v* 出て → **demásu** 出ます [GERUND]: **déte kimásu** 出て来ます comes out; **déte ikimásu** 出て行きます goes out

dē′to *n* デート date (*time; engagement*)

dé wa *conj* では well then; in that case; and so; and now (= **ja** じゃ)

… dé wa *suffix* では (*with*) its being, it is and; if it be: **dé wa arimasén (dé wa nái)** …ではありません(ではない) = **ja arimasén (ja nái)** じゃありません(じゃない) it is not

dé ya/wa shinai *v* 出や/はしない = **dénai** 出ない (not come out)

dezáin *n* デザイン design

dezáinā *n* デザイナー designer

dezā′to *n* デザート dessert

dii-kē′ *n* ディーケー (= **DK**) → **dainingu-kítchin** ダイニングキッチン

disukáunto *n* ディスカウント discount

do *n* 度 degree; moderation; **do o sugoshimásu/ koshimásu** 度を過ごします/越します goes too far, goes to excess

do-… *prefix* ど… exactly, really **do-mannaka** *n* ど真ん中 dead center **do-konjō** *n* ど根性 a lot of guts

…-dó *suffix* …度 **1.** times (*occasions*) **2.** degrees

dō′ *adj* どう how, why; (*in*) what (*way*) **Dō′-shimáshita ka.** どうしましたか. What happened? What did you do? **Dō′-itashimashite.** どういたしまして. You're welcome.

dō′ *n* 銅 copper (= **aka-gane** あかがね・銅) **dō′-ka** *n* 銅貨 coin (*brass or copper*) **dō-sei (no)** *adj* 銅製(の) made of copper **dō-zan** *n* 銅山 copper mine **dō-zō** *n* 銅像 statue (*bronze*)

dō′ *n* 胴 torso (= **dōtai** 胴体) **dō-age** *n* 胴上げ tossing person in(*to*) the air in celebration

dō′-… *prefix* 同… the same … **dō-gaku** *n* 同額 a like amount, the same amount (of money) **dō-gi-go** *n* 同義語 = **dōi-go** 同意語 synonym **dō-gyō** *n* 同業 same trade: **dōgyō-sha** 同業者 professional brother/brethren **dō-hō** *n* 同胞 brother(s)/sister(s) with same mother, fellow countrymen/countrymen **dō-i-tai** *n* 同位体 isotope **dō-itsu (no)** *adj* 同一(の) same: **dōitsu-shi shimásu** 同一視します identifies **dō′-ji** *n* 同時 **1. dō′-ji(no)** 同時(の) simultaneous: **dōji-tsū′yaku** 同時通訳 simultaneous translation **2. ... to dō´-ji ni** ...と同時に at the same time as ...; while ..., on the other hand **3.** at a (single) time, at one time

dō-jidai (ni) *adv* 同時代 (に) (*in*) the same age/era

dō´-jidai (no) *adj* 同時代 (の) contemporaneous, same generation

dō-jō *n* 同情 sympathy, compassion: (**... ni**) **dōjō shimásu** (...に) 同情します sympathizes (with ...)

do-ka *n* 同化 elaboration, assimilation: **~ shimásu** 同化します assimilates

do-kaku *n* 同格 apposition, coordination, equal rank: **dō-kaku desu** 同格です is equal

do-kan *n* 同感 same sentiment, sympathy: **~ shimásu** 同感します sympathizes

dō´-ki *n* 同期 the same period

dō´-kí (-sei) *n* 同期 (生) classmates who joined the school in the same year (= **dōkyū´-sei** 同級生), employees who joined the company in the same year

dō-koku-jin *n* 同国人 fellow countryman/ countrymen

dō-kyū´-sei *n* 同級生 classmate

dō-ryō *n* 同僚 colleague

dō-sedai *n* 同世代 one's fellow generation

dō´-sedai (no) *adj* 同世代 (の) same generation

dō-sei (no) *adj* 同性 (の) person of the same sex: **dōseí-ai (no)** 同性愛 (の) homosexual

dō-sei (no) *adj* 同姓 (の) having the same name: **dōsei-dōmei (no)** 同姓同名 (の) person with the same family and given name

dō-shitsú *n* 同室 same room: **dōshitsú-sha** 同室者 roommate: **dōshitsú ni narimásu** 同室になります shares a room

dō-zai (no) *adj* 同罪 (の) being equally guilty: **dōzai-sha** *n* 同罪者 fellow sinners

dóa *n* ドア door
  doa-nobu *n* ドアノブ door knob

doai *n* 度合い degree, level, rate: **doai o mashimásu** 度合いを増します compounds

do-bin *n* 土瓶 teapot

dobu *n* どぶ・溝 gutter

dōbutsu *n* 動物 animal
  dōbutsu-en *n* 動物園 zoo
  dōbutsú-gaku *n* 動物学 zoology

dóchira *pron* どちら which one (*of the two*) = **dotchi** どっち; [DEFERENTIAL] where (= **dóko** どこ), who (= **dáre** 誰)

dóchira dé mo *adv* どちらでも either one of the two; [+ NEGATIVE verb] neither one of the two

dochira-gawa *n* どちら側 which one

dóchira ka *adj, adv* どちらか which one

dochira mo *adv* どちらも **1.** [+ NEGATIVE verb] neither one **2.** both

dóchira sama *n* どちら様 [DEFERENTIAL] who (are you)

dō dé mo *adv* どうでも anyhow (at all)

dōfū shimásu (suru) *v* 同封します (する) encloses (*in envelope*)

dōga *n* 動画 animation, moving image

dōgan *n* 童顔 childlike face
  dōgan no hito *n* 童顔の人 childlike faced person

dogeza *n* 土下座 kneeling on the ground: **dogeza shite ayamarimásu** 土下座して謝ります falls on one's knees to ask for pardon

dōgi *n* 道義 moral principle

dogitsui *adj* どぎつい [INFORMAL] gaudy
  dogitsui iro *n* どぎつい色 loud color
  dogitsui hyōgen *n* どぎつい表現 shocking expression

dōgú *n* 道具 tool
  dōgú-bako *n* 道具箱 tool box

dohyō *n* 土俵 sumo wrestling ring: **dohyō ni agarimásu** 土俵に上がります steps onto the sumo ring

dōi *n* 同意 agreement, approval: **~ shimásu** 同意します agrees, concurs, consents

dōin *n* 動員 mobilization, recruitment

doite *v* どいて → **dokimásu** どきます

dóitsu *pron* どいつ which damn one

Dóitsu *n* ドイツ Germany
  Doitsu-go *n* ドイツ語 German language
  Doitsú-jin *n* ドイツ人 a German
  Doitsu kei *n* ドイツ系 of German ancestry

dō´iu ... *adj* どういう... what kind/sort of ...

doji *n* どじ goof (= **hema** へま) boob

dō-jimásu, dō-jíru *v* 動じます, 動じる gets agitated, upset

dō-jinai = (**...-témo**) **dō-jimasén** (...ても) 動じません (is unfazed (by))

dojji bōru *n* ドッジボール dodge ball

dojō *n* ドジョウ loach, mudfish

dojō *n* 土壌 [BOOKISH] soil borne: **yutaka na dojō** 豊かな土壌 rich soil

dō´jō *n* 道場 martial arts hall

dō´ka *interj* どうか please: **dō´ka onegai desukara** どうかお願いですから for God's [*Christ's, Heaven's, Pete's*] sake

... dō´ka *suffix* ...どうか **... ka dō´ka** ...かどうか (whether ...) or not, **~ shiteimasu** どうかしています something wrong with, crazy, mad

dōkan *n* 導管 pipe, duct

dokanai *v* 退かない = **dokimasén** 退きません (not get out of the way)

doke *v* 退け **1.** → **dokemásu** 退けます [INFINITIVE] **2.** [IMPERATIVE] (get out of the way!) → **dokimásu** 退きます

doki *v* 退き → **dokimásu** 退きます [INFINITIVE]

dóki *n* 土器 earthenware: **Jomon-dóki** 縄文土器 Jomon ware

dōki *n* 動機 motivation, motive

dōki *n* 動悸 beat, pulse: **dōki ga shimásu** 動悸がします palpitates

dókidoki shimásu (suru) *v* どきどきします (する) one's heart throbs (beats, flutters)

dokimásu, doku *v* 退きます, 退く gets out of the way

dókku *n* ドック dock

dóko *pron* どこ where, what part/place; **Dóko e**

ikimásu ka? どこへ行きますか Where (*to what place*) are you going? **Dóko (no michi) o ikimásu ka?** どこ(の道)を行きますか What path will you take? **Dóko kara kimáshita ka?** どこから来ましたか Where did you come from?

dóko-dé-mo *adv* どこでも anywhere (at all)

dóko-doko *pron* どこどこ somewhere or other, such-and-such a place (= **dóko-soko** どこそこ)

dóko ka *n, adv* どこか somewhere

dóko made *adv* どこまで where to; how far

doko mo *adv* どこも [+ NEGATIVE verb/adj] nowhere

dóko-soko *pron* どこそこ somewhere or other (= **dóko-doko** どこどこ)

dōkoku *n* 慟哭 [BOOKISH] crying out with grief: ~ **shimásu** 慟哭します cries out with grief

...-dókoroka *adv* ...どころか = **sore-dókoroka** それどころか rather, on the contrary

dokú *n* 毒 (= **dokú-butsu** 毒物) poison

doku-késhi *n* 毒消し antidote

doku-mi *n* 毒見 tasting food/drink before offering it to the others: **dokumi-yaku** 毒見役 food taster: ~ **shimásu** 毒見します tastes food/drink before offering it to the others

dokudan *n* 独断 dogma

dokudan-teki (na/ni) *adj, adv* 独断的(な/に) dogmatic(ally)

dokudan-jō *n* 独壇場 [BOOKISH] monopoly

dokudoku nagaremásu (nagareru) *v* どくどく流れます(流れる) gurgles

dokudokushii *adj* 毒々しい gaudy, virulent

dokugaku *n* 独学 self-study: ~ **shimásu** 独学します studies by oneself

dokuhaku *n* 独白 monologue: ~ **shimásu** 独白します monologizes

dokuritsu *n* 独立 independence: ~ **shimásu** 独立します will stands on one's own two feet; **dokuritsu shite imásu** 独立しています standing on one's own two feet, being independent; **dokuritsu-shita ...** 独立した ... independent

dokuryoku (de) *adj* 独力(で) by oneself

dokusái-sha *n* 独裁者 dictator, absolute ruler

dókusha *n* 読者 reader (*person*)

dokushin *n* 独身 single, unmarried, bachelor

dokushin-sha *n* 独身者 single

dokushin-ryō *n* 独身寮 dormitory for singles

dokusho *n* 読書 reading books: **dokusho no aki** 読書の秋 autumn reading

dokusō *n* 独走 leaving all the other runners far behind, : ~ **shimásu** 独走します plays a solo

dokusō *n* 独奏 solo performance: ~ **shimásu** 独奏します plays a solo

dokusō-sei *n* 独創性 originality: **dokusō-sei ni kakeru/toboshii** 独創性に欠ける/乏しい unoriginal

dokutā kōsu *n* ドクターコース doctoral program

dokutā sutoppu *n* ドクターストップ doctor's order to stop

dokutoku (no/na) *adj* 独特(の/な) characteristic, peculiar, unique

dō´kutsu *n* 洞窟 cave

dokuzetsu *n* 毒舌 a barbed/spiteful tongue

dokuzetsu-ka *n* 毒舌家 person with a poisonous/sharp tongue

dokyumentarii dorama *n* ドキュメンタリー・ドラマ infotainment (*documentary film*)

...´-domo ...共 (*makes humble plurals*): **watakushi-dómo** わたくし[私]ども we/us

domein-mei (nēmu) *n* ドメイン名(ネーム) domain-name (*internet*)

dō´mo どうも **1.** *interj* thank you **2.** *interj* excuse me **3.** *adj* somehow, vaguely

dōmō (na) *adj* 獰猛(な) fierce, savage

domorimásu, domoru *v* どもります, どもる stammers, stutters

dón どん・ドン boom, bam (*sound*)

...-don ...丼 → **donburi** どんぶり[丼] (→ ten-don 天丼, una-don うな丼, katsu-don カツ丼)

donarimásu, donáru *v* 怒鳴ります, 怒鳴る shouts, yells

dónata *pron* どなた [DEFERENTIAL] who (= **dáre** 誰)

donburi *n* どんぶり・丼 large rice bowl

donburi-mono, don-mono *n* 丼もの a bowl of rice with some kind of topping

dóndon *adv* どんどん one right after another, in large numbers

do-nichi *n* 土日 Saturday and Sunday

dō´ni ka *adv* どうにか somehow: ~ **shimásu** どうにかします manages to do

Donmai *interj* ドンマイ Don't worry., Never mind.

dónna *adj* ... どんな... what kind of...: **dónna iró** どんな色 what color; **dónna ni** どんなに to what extent, how much

dóno ... *adj* どの... which ... (*of more than two*)

dono-gurai/kurai *adv* どの位 how many/much/far/long

dónsu *n* どんす・緞子 damask

donyori (to shita) *adj* どんより(とした) dull, gray, somber: **donyori to shita kumo** どんよりとした雲 dull sky: **donyori tto shita me** どんよりとした目 dull eyes

dorafuto *n* ドラフト draft

doraggu *n* ドラッグ drug

doraggu sutoa *n* ドラッグストア drugstore

doraibā *n* ドライバー driver

doraibu *n* ドライブ drive: ~ **shimásu** ドライブします drives

doraibu-in *n* ドライブイン roadside restaurant

doraibu-surū *n* ドライブスルー drive-through (*restaurant*)

dorai-kuríiningu *n* ドライクリーニング dry cleaning

dorái (na) *adj* ドライ(な) dry; modern, sophisticated, unsentimental

doraiyā *n* ドライヤー dryer, drier

dōrakú *n* 道楽 **1.** dissipation **2.** (**o-dōrakú** お道楽) pastime, hobby

dóre *pron* どれ which one (*of more than two*): **dóre ka** どれか some/any one of them; **dóre dé**

mo どれでも whichever/any of them; **dóre mo** ど
れも (not) any of them; **dóre-gurai/kurai** どれ
位 how many/much/far/long (= **dono-gurai/kurai**
どの位)

dorei *n* 奴隷 slave

dóresu *n* ドレス dress, frock

dórí *n* 道理 reason (*what is sensible*)

...-dórí ...通り avenue; just as (*according with*);
jikan-dórí (ni) 時間通り(に) on time ...

dóriru *n* ドリル drill (*tool; practice*)

doró *n* 泥 mud; muck (*filth, dirt*)
doro-dárake/mamire (no) *adj* 泥だらけ/まみれ
(の) muddy

dó ro *n* 道路 road
dōro-hyō´shiki 道路標識 road sign

dorobō *n* 泥棒 thief, robber, burglar

dóru *n* ドル dollar
dóru-bako *n* ドル箱 cash cow, gold mine,
moneymaker

dóryoku *n* 努力 effort: ~ **shimásu** 努力します
makes an effort, tries (*hard*), endeavors, strives

dō´sa *n* 動作 (body) movements, gestures

dosamawari *n* どさまわり road show:
dosamawari o shimásu どさ回りをします goes
on the road, goes on a tour

dō´san *n* 動産 [BOOKISH] movable property

dosanko *n* 道産子 native people/horses born in
Hokkaido

dōsei *n* 同棲 living together (*for unmarried couple*)

dosha *n* 土砂 earth and sand
dosha-buri *n* 土砂降り torrential downpour

dōshi *n* 動詞 verb

...dō´shi *suffix* ...同士 **otoko-dō´shi no yakusoku**
男同士の約束 promise between man and man:
onna-dō´shi no oshaberi 女同士のおしゃべり
girl talk, woman-to-woman chat

dō´shi *n* 同志 fellow ..., comrade

dōshin *n* 童心 juvenile mind: **dōshin ni
kaerimásu** 童心に返ります retrieves one's
childish innocence

dō´-shite *adv* どうして why; how: **dō´-shite mo**

どうしても one way or another, some how or other

dosō *n* 土葬 burial under the earth: **dosō ni
shimásu** 土葬にします buries in the ground

dōsō´-kai *n* 同窓会 alumni association; class reunion

dossari *adv* どっさり all of a heap: **dossari
ataemásu** どっさり与えます showers on: **dossari
aru shigoto** どっさりある仕事 a pile of work

dotabata *adv* どたばた noisily: ~ **shimásu** どたば
たします makes a noise, romps about: **dotabata-
kigeki** どたばた喜劇 slapstick comedy

dotanba (de) *adv* 土壇場(で) (*at*) the last moment

dótchi *pron* どっち = **dóchira** どちら which one
(*of the two*)

dote *n* 土手 dike

dōtei *n* 童貞 virgin (*male*)

dotera *n* どてら padded bathrobe (= **tanzen** 丹前)

dōtoku *n* 道徳 morals, morality
dōtoku-teki (na) *adj* 道徳的(な) moral

dótto *adv* どっと suddenly, with a rush: **dótto-
waraimásu** どっと笑います everybody laughs

dōwa *n* 童話 fairy tale

doyadoya (to) *adv* どやどや(と) ...**kara
doyadoya to detekimásu** ...からどやどやと出て
きます piles out of..., **doyadoya to hairimásu**
どやどやと入ります throngs into

doyagai *n* どや街 skid row

doyashimásu, doyasu *v* どやします, どやす
chews out

dōyō (no) *adj* 同様(の) the same

dōyō *n* 動揺 [BOOKISH] agitation, unrest:
~ **shimásu** 動揺します is agitated (*nervous*)

dōyō *n* 童謡 (*traditional*) children's song

Doyō´(bi) *n* 土曜(日) Saturday

doyomeki *n* どよめき clamor, hubbub

doyomekimásu, doyomeku *v* どよめきます, ど
よめく rings, (*a crowd of people*) makes a ruckus

dō´yū ("iu") ... *adj* どうゆう(いう)... what kind/
sort of... (= **dónna ...** どんな ...)

dó´zo *interj* どうぞ **1.** please **2.** here it is

dy... → **j...**

dz... → **z...**

E

é *n* 絵 picture, painting, drawing
e-hágaki *n* 絵葉書 picture postcard
e-hón *n* 絵本 picture book

é *v* 得 → **emásu** 得ます [INFINITIVE]

e *n* 柄 handle

e (-sá) *n* え(さ)・餌 bait : **e-zuke o shimásu**
餌付けをします feeds

e *interj* えっ eh?, what?

ē *interj* ええ yes

... e particle ...へ to (*a place*); [replaces **... ni**
...に *before* **... no** ...の...] to (*a person*)

ea-kon *n* エアコン air conditioning/conditioner

eamēru *n* エアメール airmail

earain *n* エアライン airline

earobíkusu *n* エアロビクス aerobics

eatāminaru *n* エアターミナル air terminal:
eatāminaru-basu エアターミナルバス air
terminal bus

eba-míruku *n* エバミルク evaporated milk

ebi *n* エビ・海老 shrimp: **kurumá-ebi** 車エビ
prawn; **isé-ebi** 伊勢エビ lobster; **shibá-ebi** 芝エビ
tiny shrimp

ebi-fúrai *n* エビフライ shrimp fried in bread crumbs

ebi-ten *n* エビ天 batter-fried shrimp

ē-bii-shíí *n* エービーシー・ABC alphabet (ABC)

echikétto *n* エチケット etiquette

eda *n* 枝 branch

eda-ge *n* 枝毛 outgrowth of hair, hair with split ends

eda-mame *n* 枝豆 green soy beans (*to be boiled, podded and eaten as appetizers*)

efutiipii (FTP) *n* FTP・エフティーピー File Transfer Protocol, FTP (*computer*)

egáite *v* 描いて → **egakimásu** 描きます

egakimásu, egáku *v* 描きます, 描く draws (a picture)

egao *n* 笑顔 smiling face

egetsunái *adj* えげつない [INFORMAL] gross, nasty [IN NEGATIVE SENSE]

ei-... *prefix* 英... **1.** English **2.** great

ei-bun *n* 英文 English text

ei-chi *n* 英知 wisdom

ei-dan *n* 英断 wise decision

eiei-jiten *n* 英英辞典 English-English dictionary

Ei-go *n* 英語 English (*language*)

ei-kaiwa *n* 英会話 English conversation: **eikaiwa-gakkō** 英会話学校 English conversation school

ei-ki *n* 英気 vigor, energy

Ei-koku *n* 英国 Great Britain, the United Kingdom (U.K.) = **Igirisu** イギリス England: **Eikoku-jin** 英国人 a British person = **Igirisu jin** イギリス人 an English person

ei-wa *n, adj* 英和 English-Japanese: **eiwa-jíten** 英和辞典 English-Japanese dictionary

ei-yaku *n* 英訳 English translation: **~ shimásu** 英訳します translates into English

ei-yū *n* 英雄 hero, heroine

eieiō *interj* エイエイおう Hip, hip, hurrah!

eien (no) *adj* 永遠(の) eternal, permanent

eien ni *adv* 永遠に eternally, permanently (= **eikyū (ni)** 永久(に))

eíga *n* 映画 movie, film

eigá-kan *n* 映画館 movie theater

eiga-haiyū *n* 映画俳優 movie actor/actress

eiga-sutā *n* 映画スター movie star

eiga *n* 栄華 prosperity: **eiga o kiwamemásu** 栄華を極めます is at the height of its prosperity

eigō *n* 永劫 [BOOKISH] eon: **mirai-eigō** 未来永劫 for eternity

eigyō *n* 営業 (*running a*) business

eigyō-jíkan *n* 営業時間 business hours, operating hours

eikaku *n* 鋭角 acute angle

eikan *n* 栄冠 crown, aureole

eiki *n* 鋭気 sprit

eikō *n* 栄光 glory, honor

eikyō *n* 影響 influence: **eikyō o ataemásu** 影響を与えます influences; **eikyō o ukemásu** 影響を受けます receives an influence

eikyū (ni) *adv* 永久(に) eternally, permanently, forever (= **eien (ni)** 永遠(に))

eisei *n* 衛生 hygiene, health, sanitation

eisei-teki (na) *adj* 衛生的(な) sanitary

eisei *n* 衛星 satellite: **jinkō-éisei** 人工衛星 artificial satellite

eisei chūkei *n* 衛星中継 satellite transmission

eishá-ki *n* 映写機 movie projector

éito, ē´to *n* エイト/エート eight; 8-oared racing boat

eiyō *n* 栄養 nutrition, nourishment

eizō *n* 映像 picture, image

eizoku *n* 永続 lasting for a long time, permanence: **~ shimásu** 永続します lasts for a long time

éizu *n* エイズ AIDS

éki *n* 駅 railroad station

eki-ben 駅弁 box lunches sold at railroad stations

eki-chō *n* 駅長 stationmaster: **ekichō´-shitsu** 駅長室 stationmaster's office

ekisu *n* エキス extract

ekitai *n* 液体 liquid

ekkusu-sen *n* エックス[X]線 X-ray (= **rentogen** レントゲン)

ékubo *n* えくぼ dimple

ekurea *n* エクレア éclair

emásu, éru *v* 得ます, 得る [BOOKISH] gets; can do

én *n* 円 circle (= **maru** 丸): **én gurafu** 円グラフ circle graph: **én taku** 円卓 round table

en-kei *n* 円形 circle: **enkei-datsumōshō** 円形脱毛症 *alopecia areata* (loss of har)

en-shū *n* 円周 circumference: **enshū-ritsu** 円周率 circle ratio, pi

én *n* 円, **...´-en** ...円 yen (¥): **én-daka (/-yasu)** 円高(/安) high (/low) value of the yen: **endate** 円建て yen basis

énai *v* 得ない = **emásen** 得ません (not get; cannot)

enchaku *n* 延着 delayed arrival

enbō *n* 遠望 distant view

enchō *n* 延長 extension: **~ shimásu** 延長します extends, lengthens, prolongs

enchō-kō´do 延長コード extension cord

endan *n* 縁談 marriage proposal

endan *n* 演壇 lecture platform

éndo, éndō-mame *n* エンドウ, エンドウ豆 peas

enen (to) *adv* 延々(と) endlessly: **enen to hanashimásu** 延々と話します goes on and on about

enérúgii *n* エネルギー energy

enérugísshu (na) *adj* エネルギッシュ(な) energetic

engan *n* 沿岸 the coast

engawa *n* 縁側 (*wooden*) veranda, porch (*in traditional Japanese house*)

engei *n* 園芸 gardening

engei-jō *n* 演芸場 vaudeville (*theater*)

engeki *n* 演劇 drama, play

engekí-jin *n* 演劇人 theater people

engeru-keisū *n* エンゲル係数 Engel's coefficient

engi *n* 縁起 **1.** omen, luck **2.** (*historical*) origin: **engi ga/no yoi** 縁起が/の良い is of good omen, lucky: **engi o katsugimásu** 縁起をかつぎます believes in omens, superstitious

éngi n 演技 performance; acting
  engí-sha n 演技者 = **én-ja** 演者 performer

engo n 援護 support: ~ **shimásu** 援護します
supports

engun n 援軍 rescue forces, support arms,
reinforcement

engumi n 縁組み marriage, match

énjin n エンジン engine (of automobile): **énjin ga
kakarimásu** エンジンがかかります the engine
starts; **énjin o kakemásu** エンジンをかけます
starts the engine: **énjin o fukashimásu** エンジン
を吹かします races the engine

enínia n エンジニア engineer, specialist

enjimasu, enjiru v 演じます、演じる plays, acts,
performs

énjo n 援助 support (aid), backing: ~ **shimásu**
援助します supports

enjói n エンジョイ: ~ **shimásu** エンジョイします
enjoys

enjuku n 円熟 [BOOKISH] fully maturing:
~ **shimásu** 円熟します fully matures; mellows

enka n 演歌 sad and melancholic Japanese songs
(ballad)

enkai n 宴会 party, banquet: **enkai o hirakimásu**
宴会を開きます holds a party

enkaku n 沿革 [BOOKISH] history

enkaku n 遠隔 [BOOKISH] remoteness
  enkaku-sōsa n 遠隔操作 remote handling

enkei n 遠景 [BOOKISH] distant landscape

enki n 延期 postponement: ~ **shimásu** 延期します
postpones

enkinkan n 遠近感 perspective

enkyori n 遠距離 long distance
  enkyori-ren'ai n 遠距離恋愛 long-distance love
affair

enma-daiō n エンマ(大王) the (great) King of
Hell/the Buddhist Hades, Yama

enmaku n 煙幕 smoke screen

enman (na) adj 円満(な) satisfactory

enmei n 延命 life extension
  enmei-chiryō n 延命治療 life-sustaining
treatment

enmoku n 演目 program

enmusubi n 縁結び matchmaking: **enmusubi no
kami** 縁結びの神 the god of marriage

énnichi n 縁日 a temple fair (festival)

ennō n 延納 [BOOKISH] delayed payment: **zeikin o
ennō shimásu** 税金を延納します delays payment
of taxes

enokí-dake/take n エノキダケ・榎茸 straw
mushrooms

enpitsu n 鉛筆 pencil
  enpitsu-kezuri n 鉛筆削り pencil sharpener

enro n 遠路 from a long distance: **enro harubaru**
遠路はるばる all the way

enryo n 遠慮 (**go-enryo** ご遠慮 [honorific])
reticence, social reserve, shyness: **enryo ga nái**
遠慮がない frank: ~ **shimásu** 遠慮します hesitates,

holds back, is shy; **go-enryo shimásu** ご遠慮し
ます refrains from; **Go-enryo náku.** ご遠慮なく。
Don't be shy/reticent.; **enryo shite okimásu** 遠慮
しておきます takes a rain check, declines for now

enshi n 遠視 farsighted (presbyopia): **enshi ni
narimásu** 遠視になります becomes long-sighted

enshutsu n 演出 production, staging (play,
movie): ~ **shimásu** 演出します produces, stages

énso n 塩素 chlorine

ensō n 演奏 performance (musical instrument):
~ **shimásu** 演奏します performs, plays
  ensō´-kai n 演奏会 concert

ensoku n 遠足 picnic, outing. **ensoku ni ikimásu**
遠足に行きます goes on an excursion

entai n 延滞 arrear (overdues): ~ **shimásu** 延滞し
ます being overdue
  entai-ryōkin n 延滞料金 deferred premium

entátei(n)mento n エンターテイ(ン)メント
entertainment

enten n 炎天 [BOOKISH] scorching sun/weather:
enten-ka de 炎天下で under a blazing sun

entotsu n 煙突 chimney, smokestack

enyō (no) adj 遠洋(の) pelagic, ocean, deep-sea

enzetsu n 演説 speech (public): ~ **shimásu** 演説し
ます addresses

épuron n エプロン apron

erā n エラー error
  erā-messēji n エラーメッセージ error message

erabeba v 選べば = **erabya** 選びゃ (if one
chooses/selects/elects) → **erabimásu** 選びます

erabimásu, erábu v 選びます、選ぶ chooses,
selects, elects

erabí ya/wa shinai v 選びや/はしない = **erabanai** 選ばない (not choose/elect/select)

erái adj 偉い **1.** great, grand, superior (person)
2. terrible, awful (= **hidoi** ひどい・酷い)

éreba v 得れば (if one gets) → **emásu** 得ます

erebē´tā n エレベーター elevator

ereganto (na) adj エレガント(な) elegant
(= **yūga (na)** 優雅(な))

erí n えり・襟 collar (of closing/clothes): **erí o
tadashimásu** 襟を正します straightens oneself

éro-hon n エロ本 [INFORMAL] pornography book

éru v 得る = **emásu** 得ます (gets)

ese-... adj えせ… pseudo-... (= **nise** にせ・偽[贋])

essē n エッセー essay

esu-efu n SF science fiction

esukarē´tā n エスカレーター escalator

etai-no-shirenai adj 得体の知れない strange, as
deep as a well

étchi (na) adj エッチ(な) dirty-minded: **étchi na
hanashí** エッチな話 a dirty (an off-color) story

éte v 得て → **emásu** 得ます

éte-shite adv 得てして usually: ~ ... **shimásu** 得て
して… is apt to do it

ē-to interj えーと/ええと well now, uh, let me see

ézu (ni) v 得ず(に) = **énai de** 得ないで (not
getting; unable) → **emásu** 得ます

F

fáiawōru *n* ファイアウォール firewall (*internet security*)

fáibā *n* ファイバー fiber

fáibu *n* ファイブ five

fáindā *n* ファインダー finder

fáiringu *n* ファイリング filing: **~ shimásu** ファイリングします files

fáiru *n* ファイル file

fáito *n* ファイト fight

fákkusu *n* ファックス fax, facsimile (= **fakushimiri** ファクシミリ)

fámikon *n* ファミコン Nintendo Entertainment System

fán *n* ファン fan (*enthusiast*); **yakyū-fan** 野球ファン baseball fan

   fan-kurabu *n* ファンクラブ fan club

   fan-retā *n* ファンレター fan letter

fánkushon *n* ファンクション function

fánshii *n* ファンシー fancy

fántajii *n* ファンタジー fantasy

fáshisuto *n* ファシスト fascist

fásshon *n* ファッション fashion

fásunā *n* ファスナー zipper

fāsuto-fūdo *n* ファーストフード fast food

fāsuto-nēmu *n* ファーストネーム first name

fáuru *n* ファウル foul

feisu bukku *n* フェイスブック Facebook (*internet*)

fiibā *n* フィーバー fever: **~ shimásu** フィーバーします becomes fevered

Firípin *n* フィリピン Philippines

fírumu, fuirumu *n* フィルム、フイルム film

fírutā *n* フィルター filter

fisshingu *n* フィッシング phishing (*fraud*)

fō *n* フォー、**fóa** フォア four; 4 oared racing boat

fō´ku *n* フォーク fork

fu *n* フ・麩 pieces of dried wheat gluten

fu- *prefix* 不 un-, non-

   fu-an (na) *adj* 不安(な) uneasy, anxious

   fú-ben (na) *adj* 不便(な) inconvenient, unhandy

   fu-chū´i *n* 不注意 carelessness: **fuchū´i (na)** 不注意(な) careless

   fu-dō´toku *n* 不道徳 immorality: **fudō´toku (na)** 不道徳(な) immoral

   fugō´kaku *n* 不合格 failure: **fugō´kaku (no)** 不合格(の) unqualified, failed

   fu-kánō (na) *adj* 不可能(な) impossible

   fú-kai (na) *adj* 不快(な) unpleasant, displeasing, displeased (= **fu-yúkai (na)** 不愉快(な))

   fu-kéiki *n* 不景気 depression, recession, hard times (= **fukyō** 不況)

   fu-kísóku (na) *adj* 不規則(な) irregular

   fu-kō´ *n* 不幸 misfortune: **fukō na** 不幸な unfortunate, unlucky: **fukō ni (mo)** 不幸に(も) unfortunately

   fu-kō´hei (na) *adj* 不公平(な) unfair

fu-kyō *n* 不況 business slump, depression (= **fukeiki** 不景気): **fukyō no aori o ukete** 不況のあおりを受けて due to the recession

fú-jiyū (na) *adj* 不自由(な) inconvenient, restricted; needy; weak: **okane ni fujiyū shinai** お金に不自由しない has no shortage of money

fu-jō (no/na) *n* 不浄(の/な) **1.** unclean, unhygienic **2. (go-)fujō** ご不浄・御不浄 [HONORIFIC] toilet, rest room, lavatory

fu-man(zoku) *n* 不満(足) discontent: **fuman (na)** 不満(な) discontented, dissatisfied, unhappy, unpleased (= **fuhei** 不平): **fuman na kao** 不満な顔 discontented face

fu-mei (no) *adj* 不明(の) unknown, obscure: **yukue fumei (no)** 行方不明(の) disappearance, missing

fú-ri (na) *adj* 不利(な) unfavorable, adverse: **fúri na jōkyō** 不利な状況 disadvantageous condition

fu-rin *n* 不倫 adultery

fu-ryō (no) *adj* 不良(の) bad, no good, inferior

fu-senmei (na) *adj* 不鮮明(な) obscure, unclear

fu-shin *n* 不審 doubt, suspicion: **fushin (na)** 不審(な) doubtful, suspicious

fu-shinnin shimásu *v* 不信任します nonconfidence

fu-shi (no) *adj* 不死(の) immortal(ity) (= **fujimi no** 不死身の): **fujimi no hito** 不死身の人 immortal person

fu-shízen (na) *adj* 不自然(な) unnatural

fu-shō´ji *n* 不祥事 scandal: **fushō´ji o okoshimásu** 不祥事を起こします disgraces

fu-soku *n* 不足 shortage, insufficiency, deficiency, scarcity, lack: **~ shimásu** 不足します runs short

fu-tegiwa *n* 不手際 blunder, mismanagement: **futegiwa o wabimásu** 不手際を詫びます apologies for failure/mistake: **futegiwa o owabi-shimásu** 不手際をお詫びします I apologies for the failure/mistake.

fu-tei (no) *adj* 不定(の) unfixed, uncertain, indefinite, undecided: **futei-ki (no)** 不定期(の) irregular

fu-tei (na) *adj* 不貞(な) unchaste, unfaithful (to her husband): **futei o hatarakimásu** 不貞を働きます cheats on her husband

fu-teki (na) *adj* 不敵(な) bold, lawless: **daitan-futeki (na)** 大胆不敵(な) fearless

fu-tekinin (na) *adj* 不適任(な) unfit: **futekinin-sha** 不適任者 misfit

fu-tekiō (na) *adj* 不適応(な) maladjustment (*maladaptive*)

fu-tekisetsu (na) *adj* 不適切(な) irrelevance, inappropriate: **futekisetsu na hatsugen** 不適切な発言 inappropriate remark(s)

fu-tekitō (na) *adj* 不適当(な) inadequate, unsuitable: **fu-tekitō na rei** 不適当な例 inappropriate example(s)

fu-tettei (na) *adj* 不徹底(な) not thorough, imperfect, halfway

fu-tokui (na/no) *adj* 不得意(な/の) poor/weak at

fu-tokutei (no) *adj* 不特定(の) indefinite: **futokutei-tasū (no hito)** 不特定多数(の人) general public

fu-tō (na) *adj* 不当(な) unfair, unjustified: **futō na atsuryoku** 不当な圧力 unreasonable pressure

fu-tōshiki *n* 不等式 inequality: **enerugii futōshiki** エネルギー不等式 energy inequality

fu-tōeki *n* 不凍液 antifreeze

fu-tōitsu *n* 不統一 lacking of unity, disunity

fu-tōkō *n* 不登校 nonattendance at school, truancy: **futōkō-ji** 不登校児 truant student

fu-tsuriai *n* 不釣合い imbalance

fu-un (na) *adj* 不運(な) unfortunate

fu-yō (no) *adj* 不要(の) unnecessary, unneeded

fu-yō (no) *adj* 不用(の) useless, disused

fu-yúkai (na) *adj* 不愉快(な) unpleasant, displeasing, displeased: **fuyúkai ni shimásu** 不愉快にします displeases, offends

fu-zai *n* 不在 absence: **fuzai no aida (ni)** 不在のあいだ(に) during one's absence: **fuzai-tōhyo** 不在投票 absentee vote

fú *n, suffix* 府, …´-fu … 府 an urban prefecture: **Kyōto-fu** 京都府 Kyoto Prefecture, **Ōsaka-fu** 大阪府 Osaka Prefecture

fu *n* 封 sealing: **… no fū' o shimásu** …の封をします seals a letter

… fū´ *suffix* …風, …-fū …風 air; way, fashion, manner; style

fúbo *n* 父母 father and mother, one's parents (= **ryōshin** 両親)

fúbuki *n* 吹雪 snowstorm

fuchí *n* 縁 edge, rim, frame

fuda *n* 札 label, tag, card, check: **o-fuda** お札 talisman (*of a shrine*)

fúdan *adv* 普段 usually, ordinarily, always

fúdan (no) *adj* 普段(の) usual, everyday, ordinary

fudán-gí *n* 普段着 everyday clothes

fude *n* 筆 writing/painting brush

fude-bako *n* 筆箱 pencil box/case

fudoki, fūdoki *n* 風土記 topography, records of the culture and geography of a province

fudō-myōō *n* 不動明王 [BOOKISH] Cetaka, Acala (*Buddhism*)

fudō (no) *adj* 不動(の) [BOOKISH] steadfast: **fudō no chii ni imásu** 不動の地位にいます is in an impregnable position

fudō´san *n* 不動産 real estate

fue *n* 笛 whistle; flute

fuemásu, fuéru *v* 増えます, 増える multiplies; grows in quantity/number, gets bigger, swells, increases, expands

fuéreba *v* 増えれば = [INFORMAL] **fuérya** 増えりゃ (if they grow, …) → **fuemásu** 増えます

fúe ro *v* 増えろ [IMPERATIVE] (grow!) → **fuemásu** 増えます

fuérya *v* 増えりゃ [INFORMAL] → **fuéreba** 増えれば

fúete *v* 増えて → **fuemásu** 増えます

fúe ya/wa shinai *v* 増えや/はしない, [INFORMAL]

fuérya shinai 増えりゃしない = **fuenai** 増えない (not grow/increase)

fū´fu *n* 夫婦 husband and wife, Mr. and Mrs., (*married*) couple: **fūfu-tomo(domo)** 夫婦共(々) both husband and wife

fúgú *n* フグ・河豚 blowfish, puffer

fú-gú *n* (*discriminatory term*) 不具 cripple

fui (ni) *adv* 不意(に) suddenly

fuji *n* フジ・藤 wisteria

fujin *n* 婦人 lady, woman (**go-fujin** ご婦人 [HONORIFIC])

fujin *n* 夫人 wife: **-fujin** -夫人 Mrs. …

Fuji (-san) *n* 富士(山) Mount Fuji, Fujiyama

fujo *n* 婦女 [BOOKISH] lady, woman (= **fujin** 婦人): **fujo-bōkō** 婦女暴行 sexual assault

fujo *n* 扶助 aid, support: **fujo-kin** 扶助金 benefits

fuká *n* フカ big shark (*used in western Japan*) (→ **same** サメ・鮫)

fukái *adj* 深い deep: **fukáku** 深く deeply

fukanai *v* 拭かない = **fukimasén** 拭きません (not wipe)

fukánai *v* 葺かない = **fukimasén** 葺きません (not roof)

fukánai *v* 吹かない = **fukimasén** 吹きません (not blow)

fukása *n* 深さ depth

fukashimásu, fukásu *v* 蒸かします, 蒸かす steams (*food*)

fukashimásu, fukásu *v* 吹かします, 吹かす smokes

fukashimásu, fukásu *v* 吹かします, 吹かす, **énjin o fukashimásu** エンジンを吹かします, 吹かす races the engine

fukashimásu, fukásu *v* 更かします, 更かす, **yó o fukashimásu** 夜を更かします, 更かす stays up late

fuké *v* ふけ dandruff

fuké *v* 拭け 1. → **fukemásu** 拭けます (can wipe) [INFINITIVE] 2. [IMPERATIVE] (wipe it!) → **fukimásu** 拭きます

fuké *v* 更け → **fukemásu** 更けます [INFINITIVE]

fuké *v* 老け → **fukemásu** 老けます [INFINITIVE]

fuké *v* 吹け → **fukemásu** 吹けます [INFINITIVE]

fúke *v* 吹け [IMPERATIVE] (blow!) → **fukimásu** 吹きます

fukéba *v* 拭けば (if one wipes/roofs) → **fukimásu** 拭きます

fúkeba *v* 吹けば (if it blows) → **fukimásu** 吹きます

fū´kei *n* 風景 scenery, landscape

fūkei-ga *n* 風景画 landscape painting(s)/picture(s)

fukemásu, fukeru *v* 拭けます, 拭ける can wipe

fukemásu, fukéru *v* 更けます, 更ける, **yo ga fukemásu** 夜が更けます, 更ける (*the night*) grows late

fukemásu, fukéru *v* 老けます, 老ける gets old, ages

fukemásu, fukéru *v* 吹けます, 吹ける can blow

fukenai *v* 拭けない = **fukemásen** 拭けません (cannot wipe)

fukénai *v* 更けない = **fukemasén** 更けません (not grow late)

fukénai *v* 老けない = **fukemasén** 老けません (not age)

fukénai *v* 吹けない = **fukemasén** 吹けません (cannot blow)

fukéreba *v* 更ければ (if it grows late) → **fukemásu** 更けます

fukéreba *v* 吹ければ (if one can blow) → **fukemásu** 吹けます

fukérya *v* [INFORMAL] 更けりゃ → **fukéreba** 更ければ

fukérya *v* [INFORMAL] 吹けりゃ → **fukéreba** 吹ければ

fukete *v* 拭けて → **fukemásu** 拭けます

fukéte *v* 更けて → **fukemásu** 更けます

fukéte *v* 老けて → **fukemásu** 老けます

fukéte *v* 吹けて → **fukemásu** 吹けます

fukétsu (na) *adj* 不潔(な) unclean, dirty, filthy

fuké ya/wa shinai *v* 更けや/はしない, [INFORMAL] **fukérya shinai** 更けりゃしない = **fukénai** 更けない (not grow late)

fuké ya/wa shinai *v* 老けや/はしない, [INFORMAL] **fukérya shinai** 老けりゃしない = **fukénai** 老けない (not age)

fuké ya/wa shinai *v* 吹けや/はしない, [INFORMAL] **fukérya shinai** 吹けりゃしない = **fukénai** 吹けない (cannot blow)

fuki *n* フキ・蕗 bog rhubarb

fuki *v* 拭き → **fukimásu** 拭きます [INFINITIVE]

fuki *v* 吹き → **fukimásu** 吹きます [INFINITIVE]

fukimásu, fuku *v* 拭きます, 拭く wipes

fukimásu, fuku *v* 葺きます, 葺く: **… no yáne o fukimásu** …の屋根を葺きます covers with a roof, roofs: **kawara de fukimásu** 瓦で葺きます tiles a roof: **káya/kusá/wára de fukimásu** 茅/草/藁で葺きます thatches

fukimásu, fúku *v* 吹きます, 吹く blows

fukín *n* 布きん napkin, towel, cloth, washcloth, dishcloth

fukín *n* 付近 vicinity

fukí ya/wa shinai *v* 拭きや/はしない = [INFORMAL] **fukyá shinai** 拭きゃしない = **fukanai** 拭かない (not wipe)

fúki ya/wa shinai *v* 葺きや/はしない = [INFORMAL] **fukya shinai** 葺きゃしない = **fukánai** 葺かない (not roof)

fúki ya/wa shinai *v* 吹きや/はしない = [INFORMAL] **fukya shinai** 吹きゃしない = **fukánai** 吹かない (not blow)

fukkakemásu, fukkakéru *v* ふっかけます, ふっかける overcharges: **… o fukkake-raremásu** …をふっかけられます gets overcharged for

fuku *v* 拭く → **fukimásu** 拭きます (wipes)

fukú *n* 服 clothes, suit, dress uniform

fúku *v* 吹く → **fukimásu** 吹きます (blows; plays (*instrument*))

fúku *v* 葺く → **fukimásu** 葺きます (covers with (*a roof*))

fuku *n* 福 happiness (= **kōfuku** 幸福, **shiawase** 幸せ, **saiwai** 幸い)

fuku-biki *n* 福引 lottery; raffle

fuku no kami *n* 福の神 god of wealth

fuku- *prefix* 副- vice-, assistant-

fuku-kaichō *n* 副会長 vice chairman/chairperson

fuku-shachō *n* 副社長 vice-president (*of a company*)

fuku-daitō´ryō *n* 副大統領 vice-president (*of a nation*)

fukú-sayō *n* 副作用 side-effect, after-effect

fuku- *n* 複 double

fuku-sei *n* 複製 replica, reproduction, reprint: ~ **shimásu** 複製します reproduces, reprints

fuku-sha *n* 複写 reproduction, copy: ~ **shimásu** 複写します copies (*reproduces*) it

fuku-sū *n* 複数 plural

fukugō-go *n* 複合語 compound (*word*)

fukúme *v* 含め 1. → **fukumemásu** 含めます [INFINITIVE] 2. [IMPERATIVE] (include!, hold in the mouth!) → **fukumimásu** 含みます

fukumemásu, fukuméru *v* 含めます, 含める includes, adds

fukumimásu, fukúmu *v* 含みます, 含む holds in the mouth; contains; implies; bears/keeps in mind

fukuramashimásu, fukuramásu *v* 膨らまします, 膨らます bulges, inflates

fukurami *v* 膨らみ bulge

fukuramimásu, fukuramu *v* 膨らみます, 膨らむ swells up, bulges

fukuremásu, fukureru *v* 膨れます, 膨れる swells up; pouts, sulks

fukurō *n* 袋 bag, sack

fukúrō *n* フクロウ・梟 owl

fukúshi *n* 副詞 adverb

fukúshi *n* 福祉 welfare

fukushi-séisaku *n* 福祉政策 welfare policy

fukushi-shísetsu *n* 福祉施設 welfare facility

fukushū *n* 復習 review (*study*)

fukushū *n* 復讐 revenge, vengeance

fukushū shimásu (suru) *v* 復習します(する) reviews (*study*)

fukushū shimásu (suru) *v* 復讐します(する) takes revenge, revenges

fukusō *n* 服装 dress, attirement, clothes, costume

fukuzatsu (na) *adj* 複雑(な) complicated: **fukuzatsu na shinkyō** 複雑な心境 mixed feelings: **fukuzatsu na tachiba** 複雑な立場 complicated situation

fukya *v* [INFORMAL] 拭きゃ → **fukéba** 拭けば

fukya *v* [INFORMAL] 吹きゃ → **fukéba** 吹けば

fukyū *n* 普及 diffusion, popularization: ~ **shimásu** 普及します gets diffused (*spread, popularized*): **pasokon no fukyū (ga susunde)** パソコンの普及 (が進んで) (*with*) the increase of computer users

fumanai *v* 踏まない = **fumimasén** 踏みません (not tread)

fumé *v* 踏め 1. → **fumemásu** 踏めます [INFINITIVE] 2. [IMPERATIVE] (tread it!) →

fumimásu 踏みます

fuméba v 踏めば = [INFORMAL] **fumya** 踏みや (if one treads) → **fumimásu** 踏みます

fumemásu, fumeru v 踏めます, 踏める can tread

fumi v 踏み → **fumimásu** 踏みます [INFINITIVE]

fū´mí n 風味 flavor: **fū´mí o tamochimásu** 風味を保ちます keeps/preserves a flavor: **fū´mí no aru wain** 風味のあるワイン delicate wine: **fū´mí no aru ryōri** 風味のある料理 savory dish

fumi-komimásu, fumi-kómu v 踏み込みます, 踏み込む **1.** steps into/on **2.** trespasses (*on*); raids

fumimásu, fumu v 踏みます, 踏む steps on, treads

fumí ya/wa shinai v 踏みや/はしない, [INFORMAL] **fumya shinai** 踏みゃしない = **fumanai** 踏まない (not tread)

fumotó n 麓 foot (*of a mountain*)

fumya v [INFORMAL] 踏みゃ → **fuméba** 踏めば

fún n 糞 feces, dung

…´-fun *suffix* …分 minute(s)

fúna n フナ・鮒 crucian carp

funá-… *prefix* 船… ship, vessel
 funá-bin n 船便 sea mail
 funa-ni n 船荷 ship cargo
 funá nori n 船乗り sailor, crew (*member*)
 funá-yoi n 船酔い seasick(ness): **~ shimásu** 船酔いします gets seasick

funbari n 踏ん張り effort: **mō hito funbari** もうひと踏ん張り one last effort; **funbari ga kikimasen** 踏ん張りがききません can't hold on; **funbarimásu** 踏ん張ります I (will) hold on., I (will) stand firm.

funbetsu n 分別 discretion, sense: **funbetsu ga tsukimásu** 分別がつきます cuts a tooth

funde v 踏んで → **fumimásu** 踏みます

fundoshi n ふんどし・褌 loincloth, breechcloth: **hito no fundoshi de sumō o torimásu** 人のふんどしで相撲を取ります rides on someone's back

fúne n 船[舟] boat, ship

fungai n 憤慨 [BOOKISH] indignation, resentment; **~ shimásu** 憤慨します gets indignant, resents

fun'íki n 雰囲気 atmosphere (*of a place*), mood, aura, air: **fun'íki no yoi (o)mise** 雰囲気の良い（お）店 shop with a good atmosphere: **fun'íki-zukuri** 雰囲気作り creating atmosphere

funka n 噴火 eruption: **funká-kō** 噴火口 crater; **~ shimásu** 噴火します erupts

funmatsu n 粉末 powder: **funmatsu ni shimásu** 粉末にします powder, pulverizes

funpatsu n 奮発 putting a lot of effort, spoiling oneself: **~ shimásu** 奮発します puts a lot of effort, spoils oneself

funshitsu n 紛失 loss: **~ shimásu** 紛失します loses: **funshitsu-todoke o dashimásu** 紛失届けを出します reports a missing item

funsō n 扮装 disguise: **~ shimásu** 扮装します is costumed, makes up

funsō n 紛争 conflict, dispute **funsō-chiiki** n 紛争地域 disputed area, conflict-affected region

funsui n 噴水 fountain

funtō n 奮闘 struggle: **~ shimásu** 奮闘します struggles

funuke n 腑抜け coward: **funuke-mono** 腑抜け者 coward man

furafura adv ふらふら **~ shimásu** ふらふらします swims, **furafura-kan** ふらふら感 wooziness

furai-pan n フライパン frying pan

furamenko n フラメンコ flamenco: **furamenko dansu** フラメンコダンス flamenco dance

furanai v 振らない = **furimasén** 振りません (not wave)

furánai v 降らない = **furimasén** 降りません (not precipitate)

Furansu n フランス France
 Furansu-go n フランス語 French (*language*)
 Furansú-jin n フランス人 a French

furasuko n フラスコ flask

furatsukimásu v ふらつきます staggers, sways

furé v 振れ **1.** → **furemásu** 振れます [INFINITIVE] **2.** [IMPERATIVE] (wave it!) → **furimásu** 振ります

furéba v 振れば (if one waves it) → **furimásu** 振ります

fúreba v 降れば (if it rains/snows) → **furimásu** 降ります

furemásu, fureru v 触れます, 触れる touches (= **sawaremásu** 触れます) **1.** contacts with; touches upon **2.** mentions, refers to

furemásu, fureru v 振れます, 振れる can wave it, can shake it

fureraremásu, furerareru v 触れられます, 触れられる can touch (= **sawaremásu** 触れます)

furete v 触れて → **furemásu** 触れます

furete v 振れて → **furemásu** 振れます

furi v 振り → **furimásu** 振ります [INFINITIVE]

furí n 振り manner, pretense, air

furí n 降り the rain/snow, the downpour

fúri v 降り → **furimásu** 降ります [INFINITIVE]

furi-gana n ふりがな・フリガナ readings marked (*for Chinese characters*)

furi-kae n 振(り)替(え) transfer (*of funds*)
 furikae-yókin n 振替預金 transfer deposit; furikae-kō´za n 振替口座 a transfer account furikae-kyūjitsu n 振替休日 compensating/substitute holiday

furi-kaemásu, furi-kaeru v 振(り)替えます, 振(り)替える transfers it

furi-kaerimásu, furi-kaéru v 振り返ります, 振り返る looks back (= **furi-mukimásu** 振り向きます)

furi-kake n ふりかけ flavor sprinkles (*to top rice*)

furi-káke v 振り掛け → **furi-kakemásu** 振り掛けます

furi-kakemásu, furi-kakéru v 振り掛けます, 振り掛ける sprinkles it

furimásu, furu v 振ります, 振る **1.** waves, shakes, swings **2.** wags it **3.** gives someone the ax: **kanojo ni furaremashita** 彼女に振られました My girlfriend dumped me.

furimásu̱, fúru ν 降ります, 降る falls, it precipitates (*rains, snows*)

furi-mukimásu̱, furi-múku ν 振り向きます, 振り向く looks back

fūrin *n* 風鈴 wind-chimes

furisodé *n* 振り袖 long-sleeved kimono

furí ya/wa shinai ν 振りや/はしない, [INFORMAL] **furya shinai** 振りゃしない = **furanai** 振らない (not wave)

fúri ya/wa shinai ν 降りや/はしない, [INFORMAL] **fúrya shinai** 降りゃしない = **furánai** 降らない (not rain/snow)

furo *n* 風呂 (**o-fúro** お風呂) bath: **furo ni hairimásu̱** 風呂に入ります takes a bath

furo-bá *n* 風呂場 (**o-furoba** お風呂場) bathroom

furo-shiki *n* 風呂敷 a cloth wrapper

furonto *n* フロント front desk

furonto-garasu *n* フロントガラス automobile windshield

furō´-sha *n* 浮浪者 vagabond, vagrant, tramp, homeless person

furu ν 振る = **furimásu̱** 振ります (waves)

fúru ν 降る = **furimásu̱** 降ります (rains, snows)

furue → **furuemásu̱** 震えます [INFINITIVE]

furuemásu̱, furueru ν 震えます, 震える it shakes

furui *n* ふるい sieve, sifter

furúi *adj* 古い old (*not new*), stale (*not fresh*); secondhand, used

furumai *n* 振る舞い behavior (*deportment*): **furumai másu̱** 振る舞います behaves

furui(okoshi)masu, furui(okosu), furu-u ν 奮い(起こし)ます, 奮い(起こす), 奮う summons: **yū̱ki o furuiokoshite/furutte**……勇気を奮い起こして/奮って …with gathering up of one's courage

furū´to *n* フルート flute

furū̱tsu *n* フルーツ fruit: **furū̱tsu-kakuteru** フルーツカクテル fruit cocktail: **furū̱tsu-párā** フルーツパーラー soda fountain

furya ν [INFORMAL] 振りゃ → **furéba** 振れば

fúrya ν [INFORMAL] 降りゃ → **fúreba** 降れば

fū´ryū (na) *adj* 風流(な) elegant

fu̱sá *n* 房 bunch (*cluster*)

fu̱sagarimásu̱, fu̱sagaru ν 塞がります, 塞がる gets blocked (off), clogged/stopped up, gets occupied, booked up, engaged

fu̱sagimásu̱, fu̱sagu ν 塞ぎます, 塞ぐ stops up, closes, blocks

fu̱sái *n* 夫妻 Mr. and Mrs.; husband and wife (= **fū̱fu** 夫婦)

fu̱saide ν 塞いで → **fu̱sagimásu̱** 塞ぎます

fu̱sawashíi *adj* 相応しい suitable, worthy; becoming: **fu̱sawáshiku** 相応しく suitably

fu̱segimásu̱, fu̱ségu ν 防ぎます, 防ぐ prevents; defends, protects

fu̱séide ν 防いで → **fu̱segimásu̱** 防ぎます

fu̱semásu̱, fu̱séru ν 伏せます, 伏せる covers

(up), conceals; lays it face down: **mi o fu̱séru** 身を伏せます gets down, crouches (*so as not to be seen*): **mé o fu̱sémásu̱** 目を伏せます lowers one's eyes: **fuse-ji** 伏せ字 turned letter(s), unprintable word(s)

fūsen *n* 風船 balloon: **kami-fūsen** 紙風船 paper balloon

fūsen-gámu *n* 風船ガム bubble gum

fu̱shí *n* 節 joint; gnarl, knot, knob; tune, air; point (*in a statement*)

fushi-me *n* 節目 turning point

fu̱shigi (na) *adj* 不思議(な) strange, mysterious; wonderful; suspicious, odd, funny, uncanny, weird

fu̱shin *n* 普請 building (*construction*), repairs: ~ **shimásu̱** 普請します builds, makes repairs

fu̱-shínsetsu (na) *adj* 不親切(な) unkind

fu̱shō *n* 負傷 injury: ~ **shimásu̱** 負傷します injures

fu̱sso *n* フッ素 fluorine

fu̱sumá *n* 襖 opaque sliding panel/door

futa *n* 蓋 lid, cover; flap (*of envelope, etc.*)

futa-… *adj* 二…: two: **futá-ban** 二晩 two nights: **futá-kumi** 二組 two pairs (*of*)

futago *n* 双子 twins

futamatá (no) *adj* 二又[叉](の) forked, bifurcate(d): **futamata-sokétto** 二又[叉]ソケット two-way socked, double plug

futarí *n* 二人・ふたり (**o-futari** お二人) two persons

futa-sén *n* 二千・2,000, two thousand (= **ni-sén** 二千・2,000)

futatsú *n* 二つ・2つ・ふたつ two (*pieces, small objects*) (= **ní-ko** 二個); two years old (= **ní-sai** 二歳[才])

futatsú-mi(t)tsu *n* 二つ三つ two or three

futebuteshíi *adj* ふてぶてしい impudent, audacious: **futebuteshii taido** ふてぶてしい態度 surly attitude

futekusareta *adj* ふてくされた pouty: **futeku-saremásu̱** ふてくされます has the sulks, gets sulky

futene *n* ふて寝 going to bed in a huff, staying in bed sulking: ~ **shimásu̱** ふて寝します goes to bed in a huff

futo *adv* ふと unexpectedly; by chance, suddenly: **futo ki ga tsukimásu̱** ふと気がつきます comes to a sudden realization: **futo-shitakoto kara/de** ふとしたことから/で by accident

futō *n* 埠頭 pier, wharf, quay

fūtō *n* 封筒 envelope: **henshin-yō fūtō** 返信用封筒 return-mail envelope

futodoki (na) *adj* 不届き(な) outrageous: **futodoki na okonai** 不届きな行い outrageous conduct

futō-fukutsu (na/no) *adj* 不撓不屈(な/の) indomitable, stubborn, unyielding: **futō-fukutsu no seishin** 不撓不屈の精神 indomitable sprit

futói *adj* 太い fat, plump, thick (and round)

futoji *n* 太字 boldface

futokoro *n* 懐 bosom, finance: **futokoro ga atatakai** 懐が暖かい has a heavy purse: **futokoro ga samui/sabishii** 懐が寒い/さびしい has a light purse: **futokoro ga fukai** 懐が深い is magnanimous, has deep insight, has depth

futomomo *n* 太腿 thigh

futon *n* 布団 (**o-futón** お布団) padded quilt, futon: **futon o hoshimásu** 布団を干します airs out futons: **futon o tatamimásu** 布団をたたみます folds up the bedding

futorimásu, futóru *v* 太ります, 太る gets fat: **futótte imásu** 太っています is fat

futsū *n, adv* 普通 ordinar(il)y, usual(ly), regular(ly), typical(ly), normal(ly): **futsū-dénsha** 普通電車 local (= *non-express*) train

futou *n* 不通 disconnect

futsubun *n* 仏文 French sentence, French literature

futsufutsu (to) *adv* ふつふつ(と) gradually; 勇気がふつふつと沸く gets courage gradually
futsufutsu to wakideru onsen ふつふつ湧き出る温泉 bubbling hot spring

futsuka *n* 二日・2日・ふつか **1.** 2nd day (of month) **2.** two days: **futsuka-kan** 二日間 for two days

futsū-yókin *n* 普通預金 (*ordinary*) savings account

futten *n* 沸点 boiling point

futtō *n* 沸騰 boiling. **~ shimásu** 沸騰します boils

futto bōru *n* フットボール American football

futto wāku *n* フットワーク footwork: **futto-wāku ga karui** フットワークが軽い light on one's feet

fuyáse *v* 増やせ [IMPERATIVE] (increase it!) → **fuyashimásu** 増やします

fuyáseba *v* 増やせば (if it increases) → **fuyashimásu** 増やします

fuyasha *v* [INFORMAL] 増やしゃ → **fuyaseba** 増やせば

fuyashimásu, fuyásu *v* 増やします, 増やす increases it/them

fuyō *n* 扶養 support, keeping: **~ shimásu** 扶養します supports

fuyō-kazoku *n* 扶養家族 dependent family/relatives

fuyo-teate *n* 扶養手当 family allowance

fuyú *n* 冬 winter: **fuyu-gomori** 冬ごもり winter confinement

fuyu-fuku *n* 冬服 winter clothes

fuyu-yásumi *n* 冬休み winter break/vacation

fuzakemásu, fuzakeru *v* ふざけます, ふざける fool around, kid around

fuzei *n* 風情 taste, appearance, look: **fuzei no aru keshiki/nagame** 風情のある景色/眺め tasteful view

fuzoku *n* 付属・附属 attachment, belonging, accessory

fuzokú-hin *n* 付属品 attachments, accessories

fuzoroi *n* 不揃い irregularity: **fuzoroi na katachi** 不揃いな形 irregular shape

G

ga *n* ガ・蛾 moth

ga *n* 我 oneself, ego, atman: **ga ga tsuyoi** 我が強い egotistic: **ga o tōshimásu (tōsu)** 我を通します has one's own way: **ga o orimásu** 我を折ります gives yield

...ga *...*が *particle*: marks subject (who does, what is), but marks also object of: **... ga arimásu** ...が あります (has what): **... ga irimásu** ...が要ります (needs/wants what): **... ga wakarimásu** ...が分かります (understands what): **... ga dekimásu** ...が 出来ます (can do what)

... ga *conj* ...が but (= **shikashi** しかし); and

...´-ga *suffix* ...画 painting, picture

gabugabu *adv* ガブガブ: **gabugabu nomimásu** ガブガブ飲みます gulps

gabyō *n* 画鋲 thumbtack

gachō *n* ガチョウ・鵞鳥 goose

gādeningu *n* ガーデニング gardening

gādoman *n* ガードマン guard

gādorēru *n* ガードレール guardrail

gādoru *n* ガードル girdle

gāgā *adv* ガーガー quack, croak: **gāgā iu oto** ガーガーいう音 rasping sound

gágaku *n* 雅楽 [BOOKISH] music traditional to the imperial court

gái *n* 害 damage, harm, injury

gai-... *prefix* 外... external, foreign: **gai(kokú)-jin** 外国人; **...´-gai** ...外 outside (*of*): **senmon-gai (no)** 専門外(の) unprofessional

gái-bu *n* 外部 the outside, the exterior: **gáibu (no)** 外部(の) external

gai-jin *n* 外人 = **gaikokú-jin** 外国人 foreigner

gai-kan *n* 外観 external appearance, external looks

gai-ken *n* 外見 appearance

gai-kō *n* 外交 diplomacy, diplomatic relations: **gaikō-ka** 外交家 diplomat(ic person); **gaikō´kan** 外交官 diplomat(ic officer); **gaikō-teki (na)** 外交的(な) diplomatic

gai-koku *n* 外国 foreign countries (= **ikoku** 異国): **gaikoku-go** 外国語 foreign language(s); **gaikokú-jin** 外国人 foreigner; **gaikoku-kawase** 外国為替 foreign currency operations

gai-men *n* 外面 the outside, the exterior: **gaimen (no)** 外面(の) external

gai-sen *n* 外線 outside line/extension (*phone*)

gai-shoku *n* 外食 eating out: **~ shimásu** 外食します eats out

gai-shutsu *n* 外出 going out: **~ shimásu** 外出 します goes out (= **dekakemásu** 出掛けます); **gaishutsu-chū désu** 外出中です is out

gai-tō n 外套 coat, overcoat

gai-sha n 外車 foreign car

gai-yō n 外洋 high sea

...-gai suffix ...貝 (name of) shell: **hotate-gai** ホタテガイ・帆立貝 scallop

gáido n ガイド guide

gáidoku n 害毒 [BOOKISH] evil, harm, bad influence on society

gaikan n 概観 survey, bird's-eye view

gaikotsu n 骸骨 skeleton

gaikyō n 概況 [BOOKISH] overall condition

Gaimú-shō n 外務省 Ministry of Foreign Affairs of Japan (MOFA)

gáinen n 概念 concept

gairo n 街路 broad street(s) in the town

gáisan n 概算 approximate calculation: **gaisan-chi** 概算値 estimated figure

...-gáisha n ...会社 = **kaisha** 会社 company

gaisha n 該者 = **hi-gaisha** 被害者 victim

gaitame n 外為 = **gaikoku-kawase** 外国為替 foreign currency operations

gaitō n 街頭 the street, the wayside

gaitō n 街灯 street lamp

gaiyō n 概要 outline, summary

gaka n 画家 painter, artist

...-gákari n ...係 attendant (in charge)

gake n 崖 cliff: **gake no ue** 崖の上 on a cliff

gakí n 餓鬼 [BOOKISH] hungry/begging ghost; ガキ・がき・餓鬼 brat: **gakí-daishō** がき大将 bully, little turk

gakka n 学科 subject (school): **gakka-shiken** 学科試験 examinations in academic subjects

gakkai n 学会 scholarly society, association: **gakkai-shi** 学会誌 academic journal

gakkári shimásu (suru) v がっかりします(する) is disappointed, discouraged

gakki n 学期 term (of school); semester

gakki n 楽器 musical instrument

gakkō n 学校 school → **shōgakkō** 小学校, **chūgákkō** 中学校

gakkyū n 学級 class/grade in school

gaku n 学 learning, study, science: **...´-gaku** ...学 ...-ology

gáku n 額 amount, sum

gakubu n 学部 department

gaku-buchi n 額縁 frame (of picture)

gakuchō n 学長 president of a school (college/university)

gakudan n 楽団 band (of musicians)

gakudō n 学童 school child(ren): **gakudō-hoiku** 学童保育 after-school care for children

gakuen n 学園 academy

gakufu n 楽譜 musical score

gakugei n 学芸 liberal arts: **gakugei-in** 学芸員 museum attendant

gakugyo n 学業 schoolwork, academic work

gakuha n 学派 school of thought

gakuhi n 学費 academic fees: **gakuhi o kasegimásu** 学費を稼ぎます earns academic fees

gákui n 学位 academic degree: **gakui-rónbun** 学位論文 thesis, dissertation

gakúmon n 学問 knowledge, learning, education

gakunen n 学年 school year

gakureki n 学歴 educational background

gakuryoku n 学力 academic ability

gakúsei n 学生 student: **gakuséi-fuku** 学生服 school uniform: **gakuséi-shō** 学生証 student identification card

gakusha n 学者 scholar

gákushi n 学士 bachelor's degree: **gakushi-rónbun** 学士論文 senior essay

gakushū n 学習 study, learning: **~ shimásu** 学習します studies, learns (a basic subject)

gakushū´-sha n 学習者 the student of a subject (in general): **Eigo-gakushū´-sha** 英語学習者 the student of English

gamaguchi n がま口 purse, wallet, pocketbook (= **saifu** 財布)

gáman n 我慢 patience, perseverance: **~ shimásu** 我慢します is patient, puts up with, stands, tolerates, perseveres; **gáman dekimasén (dekinai)** 我慢できません(できない) cannot stand it; **gaman-zuyói** 我慢強い is patient, persevering hard(er)

gamen n 画面 screen (of TV, computer, etc.)

gámu n ガム (chewing) gum

gán n がん・癌 cancer, carcinoma

gán n ガン・雁 wild goose

gāna n ガーナ Ghana

ganbarimásu, ganbáru n, interj 頑張ります, 頑張る stands firm, bears up, hangs in there; tries hard

gānetto n ガーネット garnet

gani-mata (no) adj がに股(の) bowlegged

ganjitsu, gantan n 元日, 元旦 New Year's day, first day of the year

gánko (na) adj 頑固(な) stubborn

gánnen n 元年 the first year of an era; Year One

gánrai adv 元来 originally, primarily

gánsho n 願書 application

gantan n 元旦 = **ganjitsu** 元日 (New Year's day, first day of the year)

gan'yaku n 丸薬 pill (= **jōzai** 錠剤)

gappei n 合併 merger, combination, union: **~ shimásu** 合併します (they) merge, unite, combine

gara n 柄 pattern

gáragara がらがら・ガラガラ 1. n rattle 2. adv rattling: **gáragara narimásu** がらがら鳴ります it rattles

garakuta n がらくた junk

garasu n ガラス glass (the substance)

garasú-bin n ガラス瓶 glass jar/bottle

gárē´ji n ガレージ garage

gári n ガリ pickled ginger slices (= **amazu-shō´ga** 甘酢生姜[ショウガ])

gāru-furéndo n ガールフレンド girlfriend (= **kánojo** 彼女)

gasorin n ガソリン gasoline: **gasorin-sutándo** ガソリンスタンド gas(oline)/service station

gassō *n* 合奏 concert: ~ **shimásu** 合奏します plays in concert

gásu *n* ガス (*natural*) gas
gasú-dai *n* ガス代 gas bill
gasú-gáisha *n* ガス会社 gas company
gasú-kónro *n* ガスこんろ (*gas*) hot plate
gasú-rénji *n* ガスレンジ gas range

…-gata …型 type, model; size

…gáta …方 [HONORIFIC PLURAL] esteemed (*persons*)

gā´tā *n* ガーター garter

gata ga kiteimásu (kiteiru) *v* がたが来ています, がたが来ている gets old and rickety

gátagata shimásu (suru) *v* がたがたします (する) clatters, rattles

gatchi *n* 合致 accordance: ~ **shimásu** 合致します corresponds

gatchiri-shita *adj* がっちりした well-built

…-gatsu …月 (*name of*) month of the year

gatten *n* 合点 consent, understanding

-gawa *n* 側 side: **hidari-gawa** 左側 the left side, **migi-gawa** 右側 the right side, **mukō-gawa** 向こう側 the other side

gāze *n* ガーゼ gauze

gazō *n* 画像 image

gé *n* 下 = **ge-kan** 下巻 last volume (*of a set of 2 or 3*)

gedoku-zai *n* 解毒剤 antidote (= **doku-késhí** 毒消し)

gehín (na) *adj* 下品(な) vulgar: **gehín na kotoba** 下品な言葉 vulgar language

géi *n* 芸 arts, accomplishments; tricks, stunts

géi *n* ゲイ gay: **gei-bā** ゲイバー gay bar

geigō *n* 迎合 assentation: ~ **shimásu** 迎合します caters to one's feelings/opinions/wishes

geijutsu *n* 芸術 art(s)
geijutsu-ka *n* 芸術家 artist
geijutsu-katsudō *n* 芸術活動 art activities

geimei *n* 芸名 screen/stage name

geinō *n* 芸能 performance arts, public entertainments
geinō´-jin *n* 芸能人 entertainer(s)

geisha *n* 芸者 geisha

geiyu *n* 鯨油 whale oil

gejun *n* 下旬 late part/end of a month

geka *n* 外科 surgery (*as a medical specialty*)
geka-i *n* 外科医 surgeon
geka-shujutsu *n* 外科手術 surgical operation

ge-kan *n* 下巻 last volume (*of a set of 2 or 3*)

géki *n* 劇 play, drama

gékido *n* 激怒 furious anger: ~ **shimásu** 激怒します gets mad

geki-ga *n* 劇画 [BOOKISH] graphic novel

gekijō *n* 劇場 theater

gekiron *n* 激論 [BOOKISH] violent controversy

gekkei *n* 月経 menstruation (= **seiri** 生理): **gekkei ga hajimarimásu** 月経が始まります one's period begins

gekkéi-ju *n* ゲッケイジュ・月桂樹 laurel

gekkyū *n* 月給 monthly salary

geko *n* 下戸 non-drinker

gekokujō *n* 下克上 forcible displacement of a superior by one's inferior: **gekokujō no jidai** 下克上の時代 period characterized by inferiors overthrowing their superiors

gē´mu *n* ゲーム game

gén *n* 弦 string
gen-gakki *n* 弦楽器 string instrument(s)

gén(-) … *prefix* 現 … present (*time*), current
gen-ba *n* 現場 site
gén-dai *n* 現代 the present: **géndai (no)** 現代(の) modern, up-to-date: **gendái-ka** 現代化 modernization
gen-eki (no-hito) *n* 現役(の人) (*person who is on*) active service
gen-jitsu *n* 現実 actuality, reality: **genjitsu (no)** 現実(の) actual, real; **genjitsu-teki (na)** 現実的(な) realistic
gen-jō *n* 現状 the present conditions/state, the status quo
gen-jú´sho *n* 現住所 current address
gen-kín *n* 現金 ready money; **genkin-kákitome** 現金書留 cash envelope (*registered mail*)
gen-kōhan (no) *adj* 現行犯(の) red-handed: **genkōhan de toulramarimásu** 現行犯で捕まります is caught red handed
gén-zai *n, adv* 現在 the present (*time*); at present, now: **génzai (no)** 現在(の) current, present

géndo *n* 限度 limit: **saidai/saikō-géndo** 最大/最高限度 the maximum/highest (degree); **saishō/saitē-gendo** 最小/最低限度 the minimum/lowest (degree)

genetsu-zai *n* 解熱剤 antipyretic agent

géngo *n* 言語 language: **gengó-gaku** 言語学 linguistics

gengō *n* 元号 era name

gen'in *n* 原因 cause, origin, root: **gen'in to kekka** 原因と結果 cause and effect

genjitsu-ka shimásu (suru) *v* 現実化します (する) realizes, materializes, brings about, carries out

genjū (na) *adj* 厳重(な) strict: **genū na keibi** 厳重な警備 very strict guard

génkan *n* 玄関 entrance (hall), porch

génki *n* 元気 (**o-géhki** お元気) energy, vigor, pep: **génki (na)** 元気(な) healthy, well, cheerful, vigorous; **génki ga ii** 元気がいい cheerful; **génki ga nai** 元気がない cheerlessly: **O-genki desu ka.** お元気ですか。 How are you?

genko *n* 拳固, **genkotsu** 拳骨 fist

genkō *n* 言行 sayings and doings: **genkō-itchi** 言行一致 behavior consonant with one's words

genkō *n* 原稿 manuscript: **genkō o shiagemásu** 原稿を仕上げます finishes one's article
genkō-yōshi *n* 原稿用紙 squared paper

genkoku *n* 原告 suitor, accuser

genkyū shimásu (suru) *v* 言及します(する) [BOOKISH] refers to …, mentions … (= **(… ni) furemásu** (… に)触れます)

génmai *n* 玄米 unpolished rice

genmai-cha *n* 玄米茶 Genmaicha, brown rice tea
genmitsu (na) *adj* 厳密(な) strict
genryō´ *n* 原料 (*raw*) materials, basic ingredient
gensaku *n* 原作 the original (*writing*)
gensan (no) *adj* 原産(の) (*plants and animals*)
　native to: **gensan-chi** 原産地 place of origin
génshi *n* 原子 atom
　genshi-bákudan *n* 原子爆弾 atomic bomb
　genshí-ryoku *n* 原子力 atomic energy
génshi (no) *adj* 原始(の) primitive
genshō *n* 現象 phenomenon
genshō *n* 減少 decrease: ~ **shimásu** 減少します
　decreases
gensoku *n* 原則 a basic principle, a rule: **gensoku**
　to shíte 原則として as a (*general*) rule
gentei *n* 限定 limitation: ~ **shimásu** 限定します
　limits, restricts
genzō shimásu (suru) *v* 現像します(する)
　develops (*film*)
geppu *n* 月賦 monthly installments/payments:
　geppu-barai 月賦払い monthly payments
géppu *n* げっぷ belch: **géppu o shimásu** げっぷ
　をします belches, burps
geragera waraimásu (warau) *v* げらげら[ゲラ
　ゲラ] 笑います(笑う) laughs with great guffaws
geretsu *adj* 下劣 rude, abusive, mean
geri *n* 下痢 diarrhea
　geri-dome *n* 下痢止め anti-diarrhetic, paregoric
geshi *n* 夏至 summer solstice
geshuku *n* 下宿 lodgings, room (and board):
　~ **shimásu** 下宿します rooms, boards, lodges
　geshuku-ya *n* 下宿屋 rooming/boarding house
gessori-shimasu (suru), gessori-yasemasu
　(yaseru) *v* げっそりします(する)、げっそりや
　せます(やせる) loses a lot of weight and becomes
　very thin
gés-súi-kin *n* 月水金 Monday-Wednesday-Friday
gesui *n* 下水 sewage; (*kitchen*) drain
　gesui-dame *n* 下水溜め cesspool
　gesui-shorijō *n* 下水処理場 sewage treatment plant
　gesui-dō *n* 下水道 sewage system
getá *n* 下駄 wooden clogs (*shoes*)
　geta-bako *n* 下駄箱 shoe box (*at entryway*)
...-getsu *suffix* ...月 month
getsumatsu *n* 月末 the end of a month
getsumen *n* 月面 surface of the moon
Getsuyō´(bi) *n* 月曜(日) Monday
gettō *n* ゲットー ghetto(s)
gezai *n* 下剤 laxative
gi-... *prefix* 偽... pseudo- ...
　gi-shō *n* 偽証 false testimony
　gi-zen *n* 偽善 hypocrisy
gi-... *prefix* 義 = **giri (no)** 義理の ...-in-law
　gí-bo *n* 義母 = **girí no haha** 義理の母 mother-in-
　law
　gí-fu *n* 義父 = **girí no chichi** 義理の父 father-in-
　law
　gi-kei *n* 義兄 = **girí no ani** 義理の兄 elder
　brother-in-law

gi-mai *n* 義妹 = **girí no imōto** 義理の妹 young
　sister-in-law
gi-tei *n* 義弟 = **girí no otōto** 義理の弟 young
　brother-in-law
gíchō *n* 議長 chairperson
gífuto *n* ギフト gift (= **okurimono** 贈り物)
gíin *n* 議員 member of parliament: **Kokkai-giin**
　国会議員 member of a national legislature
giji-dō *n* 議事堂: **kokkai giji-dō** 国会議事堂
　Diet building
gíjutsu *n* 技術 technique
　gijutu-sha *n* 技術者 technician, engineer
gíkai *n* 議会 parliament, assembly, congress;
　(*the Japanese*) Diet (= **kokkai** 国会)
gikochinái *adj* ぎこちない awkward, clumsy
gimon *n* 疑問 question, doubt
　gimón-fu *n* 疑問符 question mark
gímu *n* 義務 duty, obligation
　gimu-kyō´íku *n* 義務教育 compulsory education
gín *n* 銀 silver
　gín-gami *n* 銀紙 silver paper
　gin-iro (no) *adj* 銀色(の) silver (*color*)
　gín-ka *n* 銀貨 silver coin
　gin-sekai *n* 銀世界 snowy world
Gínga *n* 銀河 The Milky Way
ginjō *n* 吟醸 produce from the use of selected
　ingredient(s): **ginjo-shu** 吟醸酒 quality sake
　brewed from the finest rice
ginkō *n* 銀行 bank
　ginkō´-in *n* 銀行員 bank clerk
ginmi *n* 吟味 investigation: ~ **shimásu** 吟味します
　examines
ginnán *n* ギンナン・銀杏 gingko nuts
ginshō *n* 吟唱 intonation: ~ **shimásu** 吟唱します
　intones
ginyūshijin *n* 吟遊詩人 minstrel
girei *n* 儀礼 courtesy
girí *n* 義理 (**o-gíri** お義理) obligation, sense of
　obligation, honor: **girí no ...** 義理の... ...-in-law:
　girí no ane 義理の姉 elder sister-in-law
Gírish(i)a *n* ギリシャ・ギリシア Greece
　Girish(i)a-go ギリシャ・ギリシア語 Greek
　(*language*)
　Girish(i)a-jin ギリシャ・ギリシア語 Greek
　(*people*)
gíron *n* 議論 discussion: ~ **shimásu** 議論します
　discusses
giryo *n* 技量 skills, abilities
gisei *n* 犠牲 a sacrifice: **... o gisei ni shimásu** ...
　を犠牲にします makes a sacrifice/scapegoat of ...;
　gisei ni narimásu 犠牲になります falls a victim,
　is sacrificed
　giséi-sha *n* 犠牲者 victim
gíshi *n* 技師 engineer
gíshiki *n* 儀式 ceremony, ritual
gitā *n* ギター guitar
gítcho (no) *adj* (*discriminatory term*) ぎっちょ(の)
　left-handed (*person*) (= **hidari-kiki (no)** 左利き(の))
giwaku *n* 疑惑 doubt, suspicion

gí(y)a *n* ギア・ギヤ gearshift

gizō *n* 偽造 forgery

gó *n* 碁 the board game Go (= **ígo** 囲碁): **go-ban** 碁盤 a Go board

gó *n* 五・5 five

go-ban *n* 五番 number five

go-banmé (no) *adj* 五番目（の）fifth

go-dai *n* 五台 five machines/vehicles

go-dó *n* 五度 five times (= **go-kai** 五回)

gó-do *n* 五度 five degrees

gó-hiki *n* 五匹 five (*fishes/bugs, small animals*)

go-hon *n* 五本 five (*pencils/bottles, long things*)

gó-kái *n* 五回 five times

go-kai *n* 五階 five floors/stories; fifth floor

gó-ko *n* 五個 five (*pieces, small objects*)

go-mai *n* 五枚 five sheets (*flat things*)

go-nen *n* 五年 the year 5: **go nén-kan** 五年間 (*for*) five years

go-nín *n* 五人 five people

gó-satsu *n* 五冊 five copies (*books, magazines*)

go-tō *n* 五頭 five (*horses/oxen, large animals*)

gó-wa *n* 五羽 five (*birds, rabbits*)

go-... *prefix* ご・御... honorific (personalizing) *prefix (cf. o* お・御)

go-chisō *n* ごちそう・ご馳走 treat (*of food*): **~ shimásu** ごちそうします provides a treat; **gochisō-sama (deshita).** ごちそうさま（でした）. Thank you for the treat (the reply is **o-sómatsu-sama (deshita).** お粗末さま（でした）.)

go-fujo *n* ご不浄・御不浄 [HONORIFIC] toilet, rest room, lavatory (= **tóire** トイレ)

go-jibun *n* ご自分 you, yourself [HONORIFIC]

go-jísei *n* ご時世 the times [HONORIFIC] → **jísei** 時世

go-kazoku *n* ご家族 (*your/someone else's*) family [HONORIFIC] → **kázoku** 家族

go-kigen *n* ご機嫌 mood, feeling: **Go-kigen ikága desu ka** ご機嫌いかがですか How are you (feeling)?: **Go-kigen yō'** ごきげんよう. Good-bye./Hello. [HONORIFIC] → **kigen** 機嫌

go-méiwaku *n* ご迷惑 trouble, bother [HONORIFIC] → **méiwaku** 迷惑

go-mottomo *interj* ごもっとも You're absolutely right.

go-ón *n* ご恩 (*your/someone else's*) kindness, my obligation to you [HONORIFIC]: **kono go-on wa isshō wasuremasen.** このご恩は一生忘れません I will remember your kindness forever. → **ón** 恩

go-riyaku *n* ご利益 divine help/grace

go-ryō'shin *n* ご両親 (*your/someone else's*) parents [HONORIFIC] (= **oyago-san** 親御さん) → ryō'shin 両親

go-shinpai *n* ご心配 [HONORIFIC]: **go-shinpai naku** ご心配なく Don't worry about it. → **shinpai** 心配

go-shínsetsu *n* ご親切 (*your/someone else's*) kindness [HONORIFIC]: **go-shinsetsu ni dōmo arigató (gozaimásu)** ご親切にどうもありがとう（ございます）Thank you very much for your

kindness. → **shínsetsu** 親切

go-shújin *n* ご主人 (*your/someone else's*) husband [HONORIFIC] → **shújin** 主人

go-téinei (na) *adj* ご丁寧（な）polite; careful [HONORIFIC]: **go-teinei na henshin arigató gozaimásu** ご丁寧な返信ありがとうございます Thank you for your polite reply. → **téinei** 丁寧

go-tsugō *n* ご都合 convenience [HONORIFIC]: **go-tsugō ga yoroshikereba ...** ご都合がよろしければ... If you are available ...: **itsu ga go-tsugō yoroshiidesuka** いつがご都合よろしいですか When is it convenient for you? → **tsugō** 都合

go yō' *n* ご用 (*your/someone else's*) business [HONORIFIC] → **yō'** 用

gó-zen *n* ご膳 low meal table, dining tray (= **o-zen** お膳); meal (= **o-shokuji** お食事) [HONORIFIC]

go-zónji *v* ご存知: **gozónji désu ka?** ご存知ですか? Do you know? [HONORIFIC] (= **shitte(i) másuka?** 知って（い）ますか?); **zónji(age)masén** 存知（あげ）ません don't know [HONORIFIC] (= **shirimasén** 知りません)

go-... *prefix* ご・誤... wrong

go-hō *n* 誤報 false report

go-shin *n* 誤診 wrong diagnosis

go-yō *n* 誤用 inappropriate use

go-kai *n* 誤解 misunderstanding: **~ shimásu** 誤解します misunderstands

go-... *prefix* 語... language; word(s)

go-chō *n* 語調 tone of talk, intonation

gó-gaku *n* 語学 (*foreign*) language learning

go-gen *n* 語源 etymology

gó-i *n* 語彙 vocabulary (*item*): **gói o fuyashimásu** 語彙を増やします enlarges one's vocabulary

go-ro *n* 語呂 sound harmony: **goró awase** 語呂合わせ pun

-go *suffix* 後 after, later, since: **sono-go** その後 after that, since then

...-go *suffix* ...語 (*name of*) language; word(s): **Nihon-go** 日本語 the Japanese (*language*)

-gō *suffix* 号: (*magazine issues*) **...-gatsugō** ...月号; (*train numbers*) **...-gō'sha** 号車; (*room numbers*) **...-gōshitsu** ...号室

gobō *n* ゴボウ・牛蒡 burdock (*root*)

go-busata *n* ご無沙汰: **Go-busata shite orimásu** ご無沙汰しております I have been neglectful (*in keeping in touch with you*).

gochagocha (shita) *adj* ごちゃごちゃ（した）messy, jumble: **gochagocha shita heya** ごちゃごちゃした部屋 messy room

gochamaze *adj* ごちゃ混ぜ jumble (= **gotamaze** ごたまぜ)

góchō *n* 伍長 (*army*) corporal

gōdō *n* 合同 combination, union, fusion; congruence: **~ shimásu** 合同します they combine, unite, join (*forces*); **gōdō no** 合同の combined, united, joint

gofuku *n* 呉服 yard/dry goods; (*traditional Japanese clothing*) kimono: **gofuku-ya** 呉服屋 dry goods store; kimono shop

43

Gó-gatsu *n* 五月・5 月 May

gógo *n* 午後 afternoon, p.m.

góhan *n* ご飯 (*cooked*) rice; meal, dinner (= **shukuji** 食事); food

go-hyakú *n* 五百・500 five hundred

gō´i *n* 合意 agreement

gōin (na) *adj* 強引(な) forcible, highhanded: **gōin ni** 強引に forcibly, highhandedly

go-ishi *n* 碁石 a Go stone (piece)

go-jū´ *n* 五十・fifty 50

go-jū´on *n* 五十音 the Japanese *kana* syllabary

gō´ka (na) *adj* 豪華(な) luxurious, deluxe: **gō´ka na shokuji** 豪華な食事 delicious cuisine

gōkai (na) *adj* 豪快(な) dynamic: **gōkai na nomippuri** 豪快な飲みっぷり dynamic way of drinking (alcohol)

gō´ka-kenran *adj* 豪華絢爛 absolutely gorgeous: **gō´ka-kenran ni iwaimásu** 豪華絢爛に祝います celebrates with pomp and splendor

gōkaku *n* 合格 passing (*an exam*): **(shiken ni) gōkaku shimásu** (試験に)合格します passes (*an exam*)

gōkan *n* 強姦 rape: **~ shimásu** 強姦します rapes

gōkei *n* 合計 total (*sum*): **~ shimásu** 合計します totals (up)

goke (-san) *n* 後家(さん) widow

gokiburi *n* ゴキブリ cockroach

góku *adv* 極 very, exceedingly

gōkyū *n* 号泣 crying bitterly, crying out: **~ shimásu** 号泣します wails

goma *n* ゴマ・胡麻 sesame (*seeds*): **goma o surimásu** ゴマをすります grinds sesame; flatters goma-súri *n* ごますり flattery

gomakashimásu, gomakásu *v* ごまかします, ごまかす deceives, cheats, misrepresents; **tsurisen o gomakashimásu** 釣り銭をごまかします shortchanges

go-mán *n* 五万・50,000 fifty thousand

gōman (na) *adj* 傲慢(な) haughty, arrogant

gomen *interj* ごめん: **Gomen nasái.** ごめんなさい. Excuse me. (= **sumimásen** すみません); **Gomen kudasái.** ごめん下さい. **1.** Hello, anybody home? **2.** Excuse me for interrupting.

gomí *n* ゴミ trash, rubbish, garbage, house refuse, (*house*) dust
gomí-bako *n* ゴミ箱 trash box, garbage can, dustbin
gomi-búkuro *n* ゴミ袋 garbage bag
gomi-sutebá *n* ゴミ捨て場 garbage dump
gomí-ya *n* ゴミ屋 trash/garbage collector (= **gomi kaishū gyō-sha** ゴミ回収業者 ashmen)

gomoku-cháhan *n* 五目チャーハン Chinese fried rice with a variety of tidbits

gomoku-nárabe *n* 五目並べ gobang (a simplified version of the board game *Go*)

gomoku-sóba *n* 五目そば Chinese noodles with a variety of tidbits

gómu *n* ゴム rubbe: **wa-gomu** 輪ゴム rubber band
gomú-naga(gutsu) *n* ゴム長(靴) rubber boots

gondora *n* ゴンドラ gondola(s)

gonge *n* 権化 incarnation, embodiment: **... no gonge** ...の権化 ...personified

gongodōdan (na) *adj* 言語道断(な) egregious

gongu *n* ゴング gong: **gobgu o narashimasu** ゴングを鳴らします rings a gong

goraku *n* 娯楽 entertainment, recreation, amusement
goraku-shisetsu *n* 娯楽施設 amusement facility

goran *v* ご覧: **goran ni narimásu** ご覧になります [HONORIFIC] (you) see; **goran kudasai** ご覧下さい Please look/see. → **miru** を見る

gōri *n* 合理 accordance with reason: **gōri-teki (na)** 合理的(な) rational, reasonable, sensible
gōrí-ka *n* 合理化 rationalization (*making it reasonable*); streamlining: **~ shimásu** 合理化します makes it reasonable, rationalizes; streamlines (*procedures, ...*)

gorin *n* 五輪 Olympics

gorira *n* ゴリラ gorilla

... góro (ni) *suffix, adv* ...ごろ[頃](に) (*at*) about (*a time*)

goro-ne *n* ごろ寝 lying dozing, sacking out: **~ shimásu** ごろ寝します sacks out

gorotsuki *n* ごろつき cheap hoodlum(s)

gō´ru *n* ゴール goal (*sports*): **gō´ru kiipā** ゴールキーパー goalkeeper

gōruden-uíiku/wíiku *n* ゴールデンウイーク/ウィーク Golden Week holidays (29 April – 5 May)

górufā *n* ゴルファー golfer

górufu *n* ゴルフ golf
gorufu-jō *n* ゴルフ場 golf course

gōryū *n* 合流 merger, confluence: **~ shimásu** 合流します merges, join, **"Gōryū chū´i"** "合流注意" Lanes Merge (Ahead), Merge (Lanes)
gōryū-ten *n* 合流点 confluence

gó-sai *n* 五歳 five years old (= **itsutsu** 五つ)

gōsain *n* ゴーサイン go sign, green light

go-sén *n* 五千・5,000 five thousand

... -gō´sha *suffix* ...号車 train car number ...: **nan-gō´sha** 何号車 what (number) car

go-shín *n* 護身 self-defense: **goshin-jutyu** 護身術 art of self-defense

gósho *n* 御所 imperial palace (*in Kyoto*)

gotaku *n* ごたく cant: **gotaku o narabemásu** ごたくを並べます talks a load of garbage

gotamaze *n* ごたまぜ jumble (= **gochamaze** ごちゃ混ぜ)

gōtō *n* 強盗 robber; robbery: **gōtō-jiken** 強盗事件 robbery

... gótoku (ni) *suffix, adv* ...ごとく(に) [LITERARY] ... **yō´ (ni)** ...よう(に) like

... góto (ni) *suffix, adv* ...ごと(に) every ..., each ...: **koto áru góto (ni)** ことあるごと(に) every chance one gets

gō´u *n* 豪雨 heavy rain, (*torrential*) downpour: **shūchū-gō´u** 集中豪雨 local downpour, local heavy rain

gozá *n* ござ (*thin floor mat*) straw mat

gozaimásu *v* ございます [DEFERENTIAL]
= **arimásu** あります there is, we've got; it is
(located)

gózen *n* 午前 morning, a.m.: **gozen-sama** 午前様
(*person who*) comes home after midnight

gu *n* 具 ingredients, fillings

gu *n* 愚 stupidity: **gu no kotchō** 愚の骨頂 ultimate
silliness

guai *n* 具合 condition, shape, feelings (*of health*):
guai ga warúi 具合が悪い is out of order, is not
working properly, is not feeling good/right,
is upset

guchi *n* 愚痴 complaint, gripe: **guchi o
koboshimásu** 愚痴をこぼします complains, gripes

...-guchi *suffix* ...口: **mado-guchi** 窓口 window,
wicket: **deiri-guchi** 出入り口 doorway, gateway

gugen (ka) *n* 具現(化) realization

gū´gū *adv* グーグー snoring (away), Zzz

gūhatsu teki (na/ni) *adj, adv* 偶発的(な/に)
accidental(ly)

guigui (to) *adv* グイグイ(と) strongly: **guigui
to hipparimásu** グイグイと引っ張ります keeps
pulling strongly: **guigui to nomimásu/guinomi
shimásu** グイグイと飲みます/グイ飲みします
gulps down a drink

gui(t)to *adv* グイ(ッ)と with a jerk

gún *n* 軍 army, troops
gún-dan *n* 軍団 corps
gun-jin *n* 軍人 soldier, military person
gun-kan *n* 軍艦 warship
gun-puku *n* 軍服 military uniform
gún-sō *n* 軍曹 sergeant
gún-tai *n* 軍隊 troops, army; (*armed*) service (*forces*)

gún *n* 郡 county

gū-no-ne mo demasen (denai) *v* ぐうの音も出
ません(出ない) is unable to argue against

gunshū *n* 群集 crowd

gúrabu *n* グラブ → **gúrōbu** グローブ

gurafu *n* グラフ graph

... gúrai *suffix* ...位・ぐらい about (*an amount;
the same extent as*); at least

gúramu *suffix* グラム gram(s)

gúrasu *n* グラス glass (*drinking, glass, the container*)

gura(u)ndo *n* グラ(ウ)ンド playground

gurē´ (no) *adj* グレー(の) gray

gurēpufurū´tsu *n* グレープフルーツ grapefruit

guríin (no) *adj* グリーン(の) green: **guriín-sha**
グリーン車 the Green Car (*first-class seats*)

gúrōbu *n* グローブ (*baseball, boxing*) glove
(= **gúrabu** グラブ)

guruguru (to) *adv* ぐるぐる(と) round and round

gurukōsu *n* グルコース glucose

gurume *n* グルメ gourmet

gurū´pu *n* グループ group

gusaku *n* 愚策 stupid/idiotic plan

gusari-to sashimásu (sasu) *v* グサリと刺し
ます(刺す) stabs

gussúri *adv* ぐっすり (*sleeping*) soundly

gutai-rei *n* 具体例 specific example

gutai-teki (na) *adj* 具体的(な) concrete, substantial, tangible, material

gūtara (mono) *n* ぐうたら(者) lazybones, drone

gút (-to) *adv* グッ(と) with a jerk/gulp, suddenly

gūwa *n* 寓話 allegory, fable

gūzen (no) *adj* 偶然(の) accidental, fortuitous:
gūzen ni 偶然に by chance, accidentally

gūzō *n* 偶像 idol

gúzu *n* ぐず dullard

gúzuguzu iimásu (iu/yū) *v* ぐずぐず言います
(言う) complains, grumbles

gúzuguzu shimásu (suru) *v* ぐずぐずします
(する) delays, dawdles

gyaku (no/ni) *adj, adv* 逆(の/に) opposite,
contrary, backwards

gyakutai shimásu (suru) *v* 虐待します(する)
mistreats

gyáppu *n* ギャップ gap

gyo- *prefix* 御 → **go-** ご・御

gyō´ *n* **1.** 行 line (*of words*), line of the kana chart:
sá-gyō さ行 the **sa-shi-su-se-so** (さしすせそ):
gyōkan 行間 line space **2.** 行 ascetic practices,
meditation (= **shugyō** 修行)

gyō´ *n* 業 line of work (= **shokúgyō** 職業)

gyōchū *n* ギョウチュウ・ぎょう虫 pinworm

gyófu *n* 漁夫 fisherman

gyōgi *n* 行儀 behavior, manners: **gyōgi ga ii
(warui)** 行儀がいい(悪い) well (bad) mannered

gyógyō *n* 漁業 fishing (*business*)

gyōgyōshii *adj* 仰々しい pompous

gyō´ji *n* 行事 ceremony, event

gyōkai *n* 業界 industry, world: **gyōkai-shi** 業界紙
trade paper: **gyōkai-yōgo** 業界用語 industry jargon

gyōketsu *n* 凝結 [BOOKISH] condensation

gyōko *n* 凝固 [BOOKISH] coagulation

gyomin *n* 漁民 fisherperson

gyōmu *n* 業務 business, work: **gyōmu-jikan** 業務
時間 business hours

gyoro-me *n* ぎょろ目 goggling eyes: **me o gyoro-
gyoro sasemásu** 目をぎょろぎょろさせます rolls
one's eyes

gyorori to niramimasu (niramu) *v* ぎょろりと睨
みます[にらみます](睨む[にらむ]) goggles, glares

gyorui *n* 魚類 fishes

gyōsei *n* 行政 administration (*of government*):
~ kikan 行政機関 administrative agency

gyōseki *n* 業績 achievements: **gyōseki o agemásu**
業績を上げます improves performance

gyosha *n* 御者 coachman/coachmen

gyotto shimasu (suru) *v* ぎょっとします(する)
is startled

gyōza *n* ギョウザ・餃子 *chiao-tze (jiaozi)*, crescent-
shaped dumpling stuffed with ground pork, etc.

gyūgyū *adj* ぎゅうぎゅう詰め jam-packed:
gyūgyūzume no densha ぎゅうぎゅう詰めの電車
jam-packed train

gyūniku *n* 牛肉 beef

gyūnyū *n* 牛乳 (cow's) milk: **gyūnyū-ya** 牛乳屋
dairy (*shop*)

H

ha *n* 葉 leaf (= **happa** 葉っぱ): **ko-no-ha** 木の葉 leave(s) of trees: **ochi-ba** 落ち葉 fallen leave(s)
ha-maki *n* 葉巻 cigar
há *n* 歯 tooth
ha-búrashi *n* 歯ブラシ tooth brush
há-guki *n* 歯茎 gum (*teethridge*)
há-isha *n* 歯医者 dentist
ha-ita *n* 歯痛 toothache (= **shitsū** 歯痛)
ha-mígaki *n* 歯磨き brushing of teeth: **hamígaki-ko** 歯磨き粉 dentifrice, toothpaste (= **neri hamígaki** 練り歯磨き): **hamígaki (o) shimásu** 歯磨き(を)します brushes one's teeth
há *n* 刃 edge (*of knife*), blade (*of razor*)
ha *interj* は [DEFERENTIAL] yes
hā *interj* はあ **1.** aha **2.** phew
haba *n* 幅 width
habakari-nágara … *interj* はばかりながら …I beg your pardon, but …
habamemásu, habaméru *v* 阻めます, 阻める can prevent/thwart
habamimásu, habámu *v* 阻みます, 阻む prevents, thwarts
habánde *v* 阻んで → **habamimásu** 阻みます
habatsu *n* 派閥 faction, clique
hā´bu *n* ハーブ herb(s)
habúite *v* 省いて → **habukimásu** 省きます
habukimásu, habúku *v* 省きます, 省く cuts out, reduces, saves, eliminates, omits
hachi *n* ハチ・蜂 bee (= **mitsú-bachi** 蜜蜂)
hachi-mitsu *n* ハチミツ・蜂蜜 honey
hachí *n* 鉢 (**o-hachi** お鉢) bowl, basin, pot, rice bucket/tub
hachi-mono *n* 鉢物 potted plant (= **hachi-ué** 鉢植え)
hachí *n* 八・8 eight
hachí-dó *n* 八度 eight times (= **hachi-kái, hak-kái** 八回, **hap-pen** 八編)
hachi-do *n* 八度 eight degrees
hachi-hon, háp-pon *n* 八本 eight (*pencils/bottles, long objects*)
hachi-ko, hák-ko *n* 八個 eight pieces (*small objects*) (= **yáttsu** 八つ)
hachí-mai *n* 八枚 eight sheets (*flat things*)
hachí-wa, háp-pa *n* 八羽 eight (*birds, rabbits*)
Hachí-gatsu *n* 八月 August
hachi-mán *n* 八万・80,000 eighty thousand
hachūrui *n* ハ虫類・爬虫類 reptile
háda *n* 肌 skin: **hada-iro** 肌色 flesh color
hada-gí *n* 肌着 underwear
hadaka (no) *adj* 裸・はだか(の) naked: **hadaka no ō-sama** 裸の王様 **1.** naked king **2.** "The Emperor's New Clothes"
hadashi *n* 裸足 barefoot
hadé (na) *adj* 派手(な) gaudy, showy, flashy, bright, loud (*color*)
hādowéa *n* ハードウェア (*computer*) hardware:

hādowéa to sofutowea ハードウェアとソフトウェア hardware and software
hae *n* ハエ・蝿 (house)fly: **hae-tataki** ハエ叩き fly flap
háeba *v* 這えば (if one crawls) → **haimásu** 這います
haemásu, haéru *v* 生えます, 生える (*tooth, hair, mold, …*) grows
hagaki *n* はがき・葉書 (**o-hágaki** お葉書) postcard
hagane *n* ハガネ・鋼 steel
hagashimásu, hagasu *v* 剥がします, 剥がす peels off, tears off
háge *n* 禿 bald spot, baldness
hagemashimásu, hagemásu *v* 励まします 励ます encourages
hagemásu, hagéru *v* 剥げます, 剥げる it peels off
hagemásu, hagéru *v* 禿[はげ]ます, 禿げる・はげる gets/goes bald
hagemimásu, hagému *v* 励みます, 励む works hard
hagéru *v* 剥げる = **hagemásu** 剥げます (it peels off)
hagéru *v* 禿げる・はげる = **hagemásu** 禿げ[はげ]ます (it goes bald)
hageshíi *adj* 激しい violent, severe, fierce, acute
hágete *v* 禿げて・はげて → **hagemásu** 禿げ[はげ]ます: **hágete imásu** 禿げ[はげ]ています is bald
hágeta *v* 禿げた・はげた = **hagemáshita** 禿げ[はげ]ました (…bald)
hagimásu, hágu *v* 剥ぎます, 剥ぐ peels it off
hagó-íta *n* 羽子板 battledore
ha-gúruma *n* 歯車 cog (*wheel*), gear
háha, haha-oya *n* 母, 母親 mother (= **okā´-san** お母さん)
hahen *n* 破片 broken piece(s): **garasu no hahen** ガラスの破片 broken pieces of glass
hai *n* 灰 ashes
hai-zara *n* 灰皿 ash tray
hai *n* 肺 lungs
hai-byō *n* 肺病 tuberculosis, TB (= **kekkaku** 結核)
hai-en *n* 肺炎 pneumonia: **haien ni narimásu** 肺炎になります gets pneumonia
hai-gan *n* 肺がん lung cancer
hái *interj* **1.** はい yes (= **ē** ええ (*mostly female*)) **2.** here you are!
hái *v* 這い → **haimásu** 這います [INFINITIVE]
…-hai *suffix* …杯 cupful(s), bowlful(s)
haiboku *n* 敗北 defeat, loss: ~ **shimásu** 敗北します loses
haibōru *n* ハイボール highball
haibun *n* 配分 distribution: ~ **shimásu** 配分します distributes
haichi *n* 配置 layout, allocation, location, placement, setup: ~ **shimásu** 配置します puts in position

46

haifu n 配布 distribution, circulation: ~ **shimásu** 配布します distributes, circulates

haigo n 背後 rear, backside

haigō n 配合 composition: ~ **shimásu** 配合します combines; **haigō-zai** 配合剤 compounding agent

haigūsha n 配偶者 spouse

haigyō n 廃業 closure of an operation, end of a business: ~ **shimásu** 廃業します closes a business

haihiiru n ハイヒール high-heeled shoes (= **kakato no takai kutsu** かかとの高い靴)

hai-iro (no) adj 灰色(の) gray: **hai-iro no sora** 灰色の空 gray sky

haijin n 俳人 haiku poet

haijin n 廃人 cripple, wreck

háijo n 排除 removal, elimination, exclusion: ~ **shimásu** 排除します removes, eliminates, excludes

haikan n 配管 piping: ~ **shimásu** 配管します lays a pipe

haikan n 廃刊 publication discontinuation: **haikan ni narimásu** 廃刊になります discontinues the publication

haikan n 拝観 admission: ~ **shimásu** 拝観します [HUMBLE] has the honor of seeing naikan-ryo n 拝観料 admission fee

haikara (na) adj ハイカラ(な) fashionable, high-class

haikei n 背景 background, BG

háikei n 拝啓 [BOOKISH] Dear Sir/Madam (in a letter)

haiken n 拝見: ~ **shimásu** 拝見します [HUMBLE] I/We (will) look at/see (= **mimasu** 見ます)

haiki n 排気 exhaust
haiki-gásu n 排気ガス exhaust (fumes)
haikí-sen n 排気扇 exhaust fan

haiki n 廃棄 disposal, abolition, rejection: **haiki shimásu** 廃棄します scraps **haiki-butsu** 廃棄物 waste(s)

háikíngu n ハイキング hike, hiking: **háikíngu o shimásu** ハイキングをします hikes

háiku n 俳句 haiku (short (17-syllable) poem)

haikyo n 廃墟 ruin: **haikyo to narimásu** 廃墟となります ruins

haikyū n 配給 rationing: ~ **shimásu** 配給します rations

haimásu, háu v 這います, 這う crawls

háire v 入れ 1. → **hairemásu** 入れます [INFINITIVE] 2. [IMPERATIVE] (enter!) → **hairimásu** 入ります

hairemásu, hairéru v 入れます, 入れる can enter

hairimásu, háiru v 入ります, 入る enters: **furo ni hairimásu** 風呂に入ります takes a bath; **háitte imásu** 入っています is inside

hairyo n 配慮 consideration: ~ **shimásu** 配慮します considers; **go-hairyo (itadaki) arigatō-gozaimasu** ご配慮(いただき)ありがとうございます Thank you all for your help and support.

haishaku-shimásu (suru) v 拝借します(する) [HUMBLE] (I) borrow (= **karimasu** 借ります)

haishi n 廃止 abolition: ~ **shimásu** 廃止します abolishes

haishinkōi n 背信行為 [BOOKISH] treachery

haisui n 排水 drainage
haisui-ponpu n 排水ポンプ drainage pump

haita n 排他 [BOOKISH] exclusion
haita-teki (na) adj 排他的(な) exclusive
haita-shugi n 排他主義 exclusivism

haitatsu n 配達 delivery: ~ **shimásu** 配達します delivers

haite v 履いて → **hakimásu** 履きます (wears, puts on); **haite ikimásu/kimásu** 履いて行きます/来ます wears them there/here

háite v 吐いて → **hakimásu** 吐きます

haitōkin n 配当金 dividends, annuity: **haitōkin o uketorimásu** 配当金を受け取ります gets an annuity

háiya n ハイヤー limousine for hire

haiyū n 俳優 actor (= **yaku-sha** 役者), actress (= **joyū** 女優)

haji(-kko) n 端っこ edge, end (= **hashi** 端)

hají n 恥 shame: embarrassment: **hají o kakimásu** 恥をかきます disgraces/embarrasses oneself

hajikemásu, hajikéru v はじけます, はじける it pops, snaps

hajikí n はじき (o-hájiki おはじき) marbles

hajikimásu, hajíku v はじきます, はじく snaps it, repels it (water, …)

hajimari v 始まり beginning, start

hajimarimásu, hajimaru v 始まります, 始まる it begins (starts)

hajimásu, hajiru v 恥じます, 恥じる feels shame, feels embarrassed

hajime n 初め the beginning; in the beginning: **hajime no** 初めの the first …; **hajime wa** 初めは at first

hajime v 始め 1. → **hajimemásu** 始めます [INFINITIVE] 2. [IMPERATIVE] (start!) → **hajimemásu** 始めます

Hajimemáshite. interj 初めまして How do you do? (on being introduced)

hajimemásu, hajimeru v 始めます, 始める begins (starts) it

hajimeraremásu, hajimerareru v 始められます, 始められる can begin it

hajimete v 始めて → **hajimemásu** 始めます

hajímete adv はじめて・初めて for the first time

haká n 墓 (o-haka お墓) grave (tomb): **(o)haka-mairi** (お)墓参り visiting one's grave
haka-bá n 墓場 graveyard, cemetery

hakadorimásu, hakaréru v はかどります, はかどる makes good progress: **shigoto ga hakadorimásu** 仕事がはかどります gets ahead with one's work

hakai n 破壊 destruction, demolition: ~ **shimásu** 破壊します destroys, demolishes

hakaku (no) adj 破格(の) unprecedented: **hakaku no nedan** 破格の値段 rock-bottom price, bargain price

hakama *n* 袴 traditional Japanese skirtlike trousers for male

hakanai *v* 履かない = **hakimasén** 履きません (not wear)

hakanái *adj* 儚い fleeting, transitory

hakánai *v* 吐かない = **hakimasén** 吐きません (not vomit)

hakánai *v* 掃かない = **hakimasén** 掃きません (not sweep)

hakaraimás<u>u</u>, hakarau *v* 計らいます, 計らう arrange

hakáre *v* 測れ 1. → **hakaremás<u>u</u>** 測れます [INFINITIVE] 2. [IMPERATIVE] (measure it!) → **hakarimás<u>u</u>** 測ります

hakáre *v* 量れ 1. → **hakaremás<u>u</u>** 量れます [INFINITIVE] 2. [IMPERATIVE] (measure it!) → **hakarimás<u>u</u>** 量ります

hakaremás<u>u</u>, hakaréru *v* 測れます, 測れる can measure

hakaremás<u>u</u>, hakaréru *v* 量れます, 量れる can weigh

hakarí *n* 秤 (*weighting/weight*) scales

hakári *n* 測り → **hakarimás<u>u</u>** 測ります [INFINITIVE]

hakári *n* 量り → **hakarimás<u>u</u>** 量ります [INFINITIVE]

hakári *n* 図り → **hakarimás<u>u</u>** 図ります [INFINITIVE]

hakarigóto *n* 謀 plot, trick, scheme

hakarimás<u>u</u>, hakáru *v* 測ります, 測る measures

hakarimás<u>u</u>, hakáru *v* 量ります, 量る weighs

hakarimás<u>u</u>, hakáru *v* 図り[謀り]ます, 図[謀]る plans, designs; plots

hákase *n* 博士 doctor (Ph.D.) (= **hakushi** 博士): **hakase-rónbun** 博士論文 doctoral dissertation

hakátte *v* 測って → **hakarimás<u>u</u>** 測ります

hakátte *v* 量って → **hakarimás<u>u</u>** 量ります

hakátte *v* 図って → **hakarimás<u>u</u>** 図ります

haké *v* 履け 1. → **hakemás<u>u</u>** 履けます [INFINITIVE] 2. [IMPERATIVE] (wear it!) → **hakimás<u>u</u>** 履きます

haké *n* 刷毛 brush

haké 捌け 1. *n* **haké ga íi désu** 捌けがいいです it drains/sells well 2. *v* → **hakemás<u>u</u>** 捌けます [INFINITIVE]

háke *v* 掃け 1. → **hakemás<u>u</u>** 掃けます [INFINITIVE] 2. [IMPERATIVE] (sweep!) → **hakimás<u>u</u>** 掃きます

háke *v* 吐け 1. → **hakemás<u>u</u>** 吐けます [INFINITIVE] 2. [IMPERATIVE] (vomit!; spill it out!) → **hakimás<u>u</u>** 吐きます

hakéba *v* 履けば (if one wears) → **hakimás<u>u</u>** 履きます

hákeba *v* 吐けば (if one vomits) → **hakimás<u>u</u>** 吐きます

hákeba *v* 掃けば (if one sweeps) → **hakimás<u>u</u>** 掃きます

haké-k<u>u</u>chi/-guchi *n* 捌け口 outlet (*for water/emotion/goods*)

hakemás<u>u</u>, hakeru *v* 履けます, 履ける can wear (*footwear, pants, skirt, socks*)

hakemás<u>u</u>, hakéru *v* 捌けます, 捌ける it drains off; it sells (well)

hakemás<u>u</u>, hakéru *v* 吐けます, 吐ける can vomit/spill out

hakemás<u>u</u>, hakéru *v* 掃けます, 掃ける can sweep

haken *n* 派遣 dispatch: ~ **shimás<u>u</u>** 派遣します sends, dispatches; **jinzai-haken-gaisha** 人材派遣会社 temporary-employment agency

hakeréba *v* 履ければ (if one can wear) → **hakemás<u>u</u>** 履けます

hakéreba *v* 捌ければ (if it drains off) → **hakemás<u>u</u>** 捌けます

hakéreba *v* 吐ければ (if one can vomit) → **hakemás<u>u</u>** 吐けます

hakéreba *v* 掃ければ (if one can sweep) → **hakemás<u>u</u>** 掃けます

hakete *v* 履けて → **hakemás<u>u</u>** 履けます

hákete *v* 吐けて → **hakemás<u>u</u>** 吐けます

hákete *v* 掃けて → **hakemás<u>u</u>** 掃けます

haki *v* 履き → **hakimás<u>u</u>** 履きます

háki *n* 覇気 ambition (*energetic spirit*): **háki ga arimás<u>u</u>** 覇気があります is full of spirit

háki *v* 吐き → **hakimás<u>u</u>** 吐きます

háki *v* 掃き → **hakimás<u>u</u>** 掃きます

hakihaki (to) *adj* はきはき（と） lively, briskly: **hakihaki to hanashimás<u>u</u>** はきはきと話します talks clearly and briskly; **hakihaki to henji o shimás<u>u</u>** はきはきと返事をします answers clearly and crisply

haki-ké *n* 吐き気 nausea: **haki-ké ga shimás<u>u</u>** 吐き気がします, **haki-ké o moyōshimás<u>u</u>** 吐き気を催します feels nauseated/queasy

hakimás<u>u</u>, haku *v* 履きます, 履く wears (*on feet or legs*), puts/slips on (*shoes, socks, pants*)

hakimás<u>u</u>, háku *v* 吐きます, 吐く 1. vomits 2. spits out

hakimás<u>u</u>, háku *v* 掃きます, 掃く sweeps

hakimono *n* 履物 footwear

hakí ya/wa shinai *v* 履きや/はしない = **hakanai** 履かない (not wear)

háki ya/wa shinai *v* 吐きや/はしない = **hakánai** 吐かない (not vomit/spill out)

háki ya/wa shinai *v* 掃きや/はしない = **hakánai** 掃かない (not sweep)

hakka *n* ハッカ peppermint (= **pepāminto** ペパーミント)

hakkā *n* ハッカー hacker, hack (*computer*)

hak-kái, hachi-kái *n* 八回 eight times

hakken *n* 発見 discovery: ~ **shimás<u>u</u>** 発見します discovers

hakketsu-byō *n* 白血病 leukemia

hakki *n* 発揮 exertion: ~ **shimás<u>u</u>** 発揮します exerts

hakkíri *adv* はっきり plainly, clearly, distinctly, exactly: **hakkíri (to) shimás<u>u</u>** はっきり（と）します becomes clear

hák-ko, hachi-kó *n* 八個 eight pieces (*small objects*) (= **yáttsu** 八つ)

hakkō *n* 発行 publication: **hakkōsha** 発行者 publisher: **~ shimásu** 発行します publishes, issues

hakkō *n* 発光 light emission: **~ shimásu** 発光します emits light

hakkō *n* 発酵 ferment: **~ shimásu** 発酵します ferments

hakkutsu *n* 発掘 exhumation: **~ shimásu** 発掘します digs up, excavates

hakkyō *n* 発狂 derangement: **~ shimásu** 発狂します becomes insane

hako *n* 箱 box, case, chest, container

hakobi *v* 運び → **hakobimásu** 運びます [INFINITIVE]

hakobimásu, hakobu *v* 運びます, 運ぶ carries, conveys

hakonde *v* 運んで → **hakobimásu** 運びます

haku *v* 履く = **hakimásu** 履きます (wears)

haku *v* 吐く = **hakimásu** 吐きます (vomits)

haku *v* 掃く = **hakimásu** 掃きます (sweeps)

haku-... *prefix* 白... white

haku-chō *n* ハクチョウ・白鳥 swan: "**haku-chō no mizūmi**" 「白鳥の湖」 "Swan Lake"; **hakuchō-za** 白鳥座 Cygnus

hákui i *n* 白衣 white coat. hákui no tenshi 白衣の天使 nurse, angel (*not to literally mean, "angel in white"*)

haku-jin *n* 白人 Caucasian

haku-mai *n* 白米 polished rice

haku-shi *n* 白紙 blank sheet of paper: **hakushi ni modoshimásu** 白紙に戻します withdraws, takes back

haku-sho *n* 白書 white paper

...-haku *suffix* ...泊, **...-paku** ...泊 (*counts nights of lodging*)

hakuai *n* 博愛 humanitarianism: **hakuai-shugi** 博愛主義 philanthropism

hakubútsu-kan *n* 博物館 museum

hakuchūmu *n* 白昼夢 daydreaming: **hakuchūmu o mimásu** 白昼夢を見ます is spaced out

hakugai *n* 迫害 persecution: **hakugai o ukemásu** 迫害を受けます suffers from persecution

hakujaku (na) *adj* 薄弱(な) weak, tenuity: **ishi-hakujaku** 意志薄弱 weak will: **hakujaku na konkyo** 薄弱な根拠 poor reason

hákujō *n* 白状 confession: **~ shimásu** 白状します confesses

hakujō (na) *adj* 薄情(な) [BOOKISH] unfeeling, heartless, cruel: **hakujō na hito** 薄情な人 heartless person: **kono hakujō-mono!** この薄情者! You heartbreaker!

hakurai (no) *adj* 舶来(の) imported hakurai-hin *n* 舶来品 imported goods

hakurán-kai *n* 博覧会 exhibition, exposition

hakuryoku *n* 迫力 punch, power: **hakuryoku ga arimásu** 迫力があります is powerful

hakusái *n* ハクサイ・白菜 Chinese cabbage

hakushi *n* 博士 doctor (Ph.D.) (= **hakase** 博士): **hakushi-katei** 博士課程 doctoral course

hákushu *n* 拍手 clapping: **~ shimásu** 拍手します claps one's hands

hamá *n* 浜 beach: **hama-be** 浜辺 seabeach, seashore

hamachi *n* ハマチ・魚 young yellowtail (*cf.* **búri** ブリ・鰤, **inada** イナダ)

hamáguri *n* ハマグリ・蛤 clam

hame *v* はめ → **hamemásu** はめます [INFINITIVE]

hamé *n* はめ plight, fix (*one gets into*)

hamemásu, hameru *v* はめます, はめる wears (on fingers, hands (*ring, gloves, etc.*))

hame(ra)remásu, hame(ra)reru *v* はめ(ら)れます, はめ(ら)れる can wear (*on fingers, hands*)

hametsu *n* 破滅 ruin: **~ shimásu** 破滅します ruins

hamidashimásu, hamidasu *v* はみ出します, はみ出す protrudes, runs off the edge, sticks out, goes over

há-mono *n* 刃物 cutlery, knives

hámu *n* ハム ham: **hamu-éggu** ハムエッグ ham and eggs; **hamu-sándo** ハムサンド ham sandwich

hán *n* 半 half (= **hanbún** 半分): **han-...** 半 ... half a ...; **...-hán** ... 半 and a half

hán *n* 判 a "chop" = a seal (*to stamp name*) (= **hankó** 判こ)

hana *n* 鼻 (**o-hana** お鼻) nose; trunk (*of elephant*) hana-ji *n* 鼻血 nosebleed: **hana-ji ga demásu** 鼻血が出ます gets a nosebleed hana-mizú *n* 鼻水 snivel, nasal mucus: **hana-mizú ga demásu** 鼻水が出ます has a runny nose

hana *n* はな nasal mucus, snivel (= **hana-mizú** 鼻水): **hana o kamimásu** はなをかみます blows one's nose

haná *n* 花 (**o-hana** お花) flower; flower arrangement hana-mí *n* 花見 (**o-hanami** お花見) cherry blossom viewing: (**o-)hanami o shimásu** (お)花見をします goes to see the cherry blossom hana-tába *n* 花束 bouquet hana-wa *n* 花輪 wreath (*of flower*) haná-ya *n* 花屋 florist, flower shop

hána *n* はな・端 beginning, outset; edge

hána-bi *n* 花火 fireworks: **hanabí-taikai** 花火大会 big exhibition of fireworks

haná-fuda *n* 花札 (*the game of*) flower cards (= **hana-gáruta** 花がるた)

hanágata *n* 花形 a star (*in a theatrical production*): **hanágata-senshu** 花形選手 star player

hanahada *adv* はなはだ extremely

haná-michi *n* 花道 the runway to the stage (in Kabuki)

hana-múko *n* 花婿 bridegroom

hanao *n* 鼻緒 thong (on *geta*)

hanaremásu, hanaréru *v* 離れます, 離れる separates, becomes distant, leaves

hanasánai *v* 話さない = **hanashimasén** 話しません (not speak)

hanasánai *v* 放さない = **hanashimasén** 放しません (not release)

hanasánai *v* 離さない = **hanashimasén** 離しません (not separate something)

hanáseba *v* 話せば (if one speaks) → **hanase-másu** 話せます

hanáseba *v* 放せば (if one releases) → **hanase-másu** 放せます

hanáseba *v* 離せば (if one separates something) → **hanasemásu** 離せます

hanasemásu, hanaséru *v* 話せます, 話せる can speak

hanasénai *v* 話せない = **hanasemasén** 話せません (cannot speak)

hanasénai *v* 放せない = **hanasemasén** 放せません (cannot release)

hanasénai *v* 離せない = **hanasemasén** 離せません (cannot separate something)

hanashí *n* 話 talk, story, tale, speech, conversation; something to talk about: **hanashí o shimásu** 話をします talks, speaks; **Nan no hanashí desú ka.** 何の話ですか. What are you talking about?

hanashi-ái *n* 話し合い conference, discussion, negotiation

hanashi-ai *v* 話し合い → **hanashi-aimásu** 話し合います [INFINITIVE]

hanashi-aimásu, hanashi-áu *v* 話し合います, 話し合う talk together, discuss, confer, negotiate

hanashi-ka *n* 噺家 (a comic) storyteller (= **rakugo-ka** 落語家)

hanashimásu, hanásu *v* 話します, 話す speaks, talks

hanashimásu, hanásu *v* 放します, 放す release, lets loose, lets go, sets free

hanashimásu, hanásu *v* 離します, 離す separates (*something*) from, parts with; detaches, disconnects

hanáshi ya/wa shinai *v* 話しや/はしない = **hanasánai** 話さない (not speak)

hanáshi ya/wa shinai *v* 放しや/はしない = **hanasánai** 放さない (not release)

hanáshi ya/wa shinai *v* 離しや/はしない = **hanasánai** 離さない (not separate something)

hanáyaka (na) *adj* 華やか(な) colorful, showy, gorgeous, glorious, bright

haná-yome *n* 花嫁 bride

hanbā´gā *n* ハンバーガー a hamburger

hanbā´gu *n* ハンバーグ hamburger (meat)

hanbai *n* 販売 sale:~ **shimásu** 販売します deals in, sells

hanbái-ki *n* 販売機 vending machine

hanbái-daka *n* 販売高 sales volume

hanbai-moto *n* 販売元 sales agency

hanbai-in *n* 販売員 salesperson

hanbai-nin *n* 販売人 seller, dealer

hanbái-ten *n* 販売店 sales outlet

hanbai-sokushin *n* 販売促進 sales promotion (= **hansoku** 販促)

hanbai-kakaku *n* 販売価格 selling price

hanbei (no) *adj* 反米(の) anti-American

hanbún *n* 半分 half

hándán *n* 判断 judgment: ~ **shimásu** 判断します judges, gives judgment

handō *n* 反動 reaction, repercussion

handō-teki (na) *anj* 反動的(な) reactionary; handō-shugisha *n* 反動主義者 reactionary

handobággu, handobákku *n* ハンドバッグ, ハンドバック handbag, pocketbook

handoru *n* ハンドル steering wheel; handle

hane *n* 羽 feather

hane *n* 羽根 wing; shuttlecock

hané-tsuki *n* 羽根つき battledore and shuttlecock (*a kind of badminton*)

hanei *n* 反映 reflection: ~ **shimásu** 反映します is reflected

hanei *n* 繁栄 prosperity: ~ **shimásu** 繁栄します gains prosperity

hanemásu, hanéru *v* 跳ねます, 跳ねる jumps, splashes

hanga *n* 版画 woodblock print

hángā *n* ハンガー hanger

hangaku *n* 半額 half price

hangyaku *n* 反逆 rebellion: ~ **shimásu** 反逆します rebels

hangyákú-sha *n* 反逆者 rebel

hanhan *n* 半々 half-and-half

hán'i *n* 範囲 scope, range, limits: **(... no) han'í-gai/-nai** (...の)範囲外/内 beyond/within the limits (of ...)

hanigo *n* 反意語 antonym

hanikamimásu, hanikámu *v* はにかみます, はにかむ acts shy, is bashful: **hanikami-ya** はにかみ屋 shy

hánji *n* 判事 judge

hánjō *n* 繁盛 prosperity: **shōbai-hanjō** 商売繁盛 flourishing business, boom of business

hánkachi *n* ハンカチ handkerchief

hankagai *n* 繁華街 downtown area, shopping and amusement districts

hankan *n* 反感 antipathy: **hankan o kaimásu** 反感を買います provokes one's antipathy

hankei *n* 半径 radius

hanketsu *n* 判決 judgment: **hanketsu o kudashimásu** 判決を下します adjudges, gives sentence

hanki *n* 半期 half of the business year

hankó *n* はんこ・判子 a "chop" (*signature seal, name stamp*) (= **han** 判, **in** 印, **inkan** 印鑑)

hankō *n* 反抗 opposition, resistance: **... ni hankō shimásu** ...に反抗します opposes, resists (= **hanpatsu** 反発)

hankō *n* 犯行 crime, perpetration: **hankō-genba** 犯行現場 scene of a crime: **hankō-seimei** 犯行声明 criminal declaration

hankyō *n* 反響 echo: ~ **shimásu** 反響します echos: **hankyō-on** 反響音 acoustic echo

hankyōran *n* 半狂乱 frantic, partial insanity: **hankyōran ni narimásu** 半狂乱になります becomes frantic

hankyū *n* 半休 half day off: **hankyō o torimásu** 半休を取ります takes a half day off

hankyū *n* 半球 hemisphere

hánmā *n* ハンマー hammer

hanmei *n* 判明 coming-out: **~ shimásu** 判明します comes out, turns out

hanmen *n* 反面 on the other hand: **hanmen-kyōshi** 反面教師 person who serves as an example of how not to be

hanmen (no) *adj* 半面(の) half-faced

han-nichí *n* 半日 half a day, a half-day

hannichi (no) *adj* 反日(の) anti-Japanese

hánnin *n* 犯人 a criminal, culprit

hannō *n* 反応 reaction, response: **~ shimásu** 反応します reacts

hanpa *n* 半端 half: **hanpa mono** 半端物 oddments → **chūto hanpa (na)** 中途半端(な)

hanpatsu *n* 反発 **1.** repelling **2.** repulsion **3.** resistance (= **hankō** 反抗): **~ shimásu** 反発します repels; rebounds; resists

hanpén *n* ハンペン・はんぺん boiled fish cake

hanran *n* 反乱 revolt: **hanran o okosu** 反乱を起こす revolts, rebels

hanran *n* 氾濫 overflowing: **~ shimásu** 氾濫します overflows, floods

hanrei *n* 凡例 explanatory notes (*on how to use a reference work*)

hanryo *n* 伴侶 companion: **shōgai no hanryo** 生涯の伴侶 spouse (*literally, "lifetime companion"*)

hánsa (na) *adj* 煩瑣(な) troublesome, complicated

hansei *n* 反省 reflection, thinking-over: **~ shimásu** 反省します reflects (*on*), ponders

hansen (no) *adj* 反戦(の) antiwar: **hansen-katsudō** 反戦活動 antiwar activity

hansen-byō *n* ハンセン病 Hansen's disease, leprosy

hansha *n* 反射 reflection: **~ shimásu** 反射します reflects

hánshi *n* 半紙 rice paper (*stationery*)

hán-shi *v* 反し → **han-shimásu** 反します [INFINITIVE]

han-shimásu (-súru) *v* 反します is contrary (*to*), goes against, opposes: **… ni hánshite** …に反して contrary to, against, in contrast with

hanshō (no) *n* 半焼(の) partial loss by fire (= **han'yake (no)** 半焼け(の))

hanshū *n* 半周 semicircle

hansode *n* 半そで・半袖 half sleeves

hansoku *n* 反則 foul: **~ shimásu** 反則します fouls

hansoku *n* 販促 sales promotion: **hansoku-tsūru** 販促ツール sales promotion tool (= **hanbai-sokushin** 販売促進)

hantai *n* 反対 opposite, contrary, reverse (= **gyaku** 逆): **hantai-gawa** 反対側 opposite side; **hantai-go** 反対語 antonym; **hantai ni** 反対に vice versa: **~ shimásu** 反対します opposes

hantén *n* 半纏 *happi* coat (= **happi** はっぴ・法被)

hantō *n* 半島, …**-hántō** …半島 peninsula: **Izu-hántō** 伊豆半島 Izu Peninsula

han-toshí *n* 半年 half a year

han-tsukí *n* 半月 half a month

han'yake (no) *adj* 半焼け(の) **1.** medium-rare (*meat*), half-done (= **nama-yake (no)** 生焼け(の)) **2.** partial loss by fire (= **hanshō (no)** 半焼(の))

hanzai *n* 犯罪 crime: **hanzai o okashimásu** 犯罪を犯します commits a crime

hanzatsu (na) *adj* 煩雑(な) troublesome, complicated

hanzubon *n* 半ズボン short-pants

haori *n* 羽織 (**o-háori** お羽織) traditional Japanese coat

hap- *n* 八・8 eight

hap-pén *n* 八遍 eight times (= **hachí-kai** 八回, **hachí-do** 八度)

háp-pa, hachí-wa *n* 八羽 eight (*birds, rabbits*)

hap-piki *n* 八匹 eight (*fishes/bugs, small animals*)

háp-pon, hachi-hon *n* 八本 eight (*pencils/bottles, long objects*)

háp-pun *n* 八分 eight minutes

happa *n* 葉っぱ leaf (= **ha** 葉)

happi *n* 法被 *happi* (= **hantén** 半纏)

hap-pyakú *n* 八百・800 eight hundred

happyō *n* 発表 announcement, publication; (*research*) paper: **~ shimásu** 発表します announces, publishes

hā´pu *n* ハープ harp (*Western*)

hará *n* 腹 **1.** belly, stomach (= **o-naka** お腹): **hará ga herimásu** 腹が減ります gets hungry; **hará ga itamimásu** 腹が痛みます one's stomach aches **2.** mind, heart: **hará ga tachimásu** 腹が立ちます, **hará o tatemásu** 腹を立てます gets angry; **hará ga futói** 腹が太い is big-hearted; **hará ga kurói** 腹が黒い black-hearted; **hará o kimemásu** 腹を決めます makes up one's mind; **… no hará o yomimásu** …の腹を読みます reads the mind of …

hára, hárappa *n* 原, 原っぱ field

haradatashíi *adj* 腹立たしい aggravating, vexatious

haráe *v* 払え **1.** → **haraemásu** 払えます [INFINITIVE] **2.** [IMPERATIVE] (pay!) → **haraimásu** 払います

haráeba *v* 払えば (if one pays; if …) → **haraimásu** 払います

haraemásu, haraéru *v* 払えます, 払える **1.** can pay **2.** can brush aside, can shake out

harahara *adv* はらはら: **~ shimásu** はらはらします gets anxious, is scared; **harahara sasemásu** はらはらさせます scares

haraimásu, haráu *v* 払います, 払う **1.** pays **2.** brushes aside, shakes out

harái ya/wa shinai *v* 払いや/はしない = **harawanai** 払わない (not pay; not …)

harai-modoshi *n* 払い戻し a refund → **harai-modoshimásu** 払い戻します [INFINITIVE]

harai-modoshimásu, harai-modósu *v* 払い戻します, 払い戻す refunds

hará-maki *n* 腹巻き stomach band

haranai *v* 貼らない = **harimasén** 貼りません (not paste it)

haranai v 張らない = **harimasén** 張りません (not spread/stretch it)

harátte v 払って → **haraimásu** 払います

haráu v 払う = **haraimásu** 払います (pays; brushes aside, shakes out)

harawánai v 払わない = **haraimasén** 払いません (not pay; not …)

harawáta n 腸 intestines

haráya v 払や [INFOMAL] → **haráeba** 払えば

hare v 腫れ → **haremásu** 腫れます [INFINITIVE]

haré v 貼れ 1. → **haremásu** 貼れます [INFINITIVE] 2. [IMPERATIVE] (paste it!) → **harimásu** 貼ります

haré v 張れ 1. → **haremásu** 張れます [INFINITIVE] 2. [IMPERATIVE] (spread it!) → **harimásu** 張ります

haré n 晴れ fair (clear) weather

háre v 晴れ → **haremásu** 晴れます [INFINITIVE]

haréba v 貼れば (if one pastes it) → **harimásu** 貼りますす

haréba v 張れば (if one spreads/stretches it) → **harimásu** 張ります

haremásu, hareru v 腫れます, 腫れる swells up

haremásu, hareru v 貼れます, 貼れる can paste

haremásu, hareru v 張れます; 張れる can spread/stretch it

haremásu, haréru v 晴れます, 晴れる (*weather*) clears up: **hárete imásu** 晴れています is clear/fair/sunny

hare-mono n 腫れ物 swelling, boil (*on skin*)

hareréba v 腫れれば (if it swells) → **haremásu** 腫れます

haréreba v 晴れれば (if it clears up) → **haremásu** 晴れます

haretsu n 破裂 bursting: ~ **shimásu** 破裂します bursts

hari v 貼り → **harimásu** 貼ります [INFINITIVE] hari-gami n 貼り紙 poster

hari v 張り → **harimásu** 張ります [INFINITIVE]

hári n 針 needle, pin; needlework; hand (*of clock*); a staple (*of stapler*) hari-gane n 針金 wire hari-shígoto n 針仕事 needlework (*of all types*)

hári n 鍼 acupuncture

harimásu, haru v 貼ります, 貼る sticks on, pastes

harimásu, haru v 張ります, 張る spreads/stretches it

harí ya/wa shinai v 貼りや/はしない = **haranai** 貼らない (not paste it)

harí ya/wa shinai v 張りや/はしない = **haranai** 張らない (not spread/stretch it)

haru v 貼る = **harimásu** 貼ります

haru v 張る = **harimásu** 張ります

háru n 春 spring (*season*) haru-same n 春雨 bean-flour threads; spring rain haru-yásumi n 春休み spring break/vacation

harubaru adv はるばる all the way

háruka (ni) adv 遥か(に) far (off); long ago; by far háruka na adj 遥か(な) distant, far

haru-maki n 春巻 Chinese egg rolls, spring rolls

hasamarimásu, hasamáru v 挟まります, 挟まる gets caught (*in*) between, becomes sandwiched (*in*) between

hasáme v 挟め 1. → **hasamemásu** 挟めます [INFINITIVE] 2. [IMPERATIVE] (insert!) → **hasamimásu** 挟みます

hasamemásu, hasaméru v 挟めます, 挟める can insert (put between)

hasamí n はさみ・鋏 scissors, clippers

hasamí n はさみ・螯 pincer(s), claw (*of crab*)

hasámi v 挟み → **hasamimásu** 挟みます [INFINITIVE]

hasamimásu, hasámu v 挟みます, 挟む inserts, puts between: **háshi de hasamimásu** 箸で挟みます picks it up with chopsticks

hasan n 破産 bankruptcy: ~ **shimásu** 破産します goes bankrupt

hashi n 端 edge, end hashi-kko n 端っこ edge, end (= **haji(kko)** 端っこ, **hashi, haji** 端)

hashí n 橋 bridge

háshi n 箸 (**o-háshi** お箸) chopsticks: **háshi o tsukaimásu** 箸を使います uses chopsticks hashí-óki n 箸置き chopstick rest

hashigo n 梯子 ladder, stairs: **hashigó-zake** はしご酒 bar hopping; **hashigó-dan** 梯子段 wooden stairs

hashika n はしか measles

hashira n 柱 pillar, post: **ikka no hashira** 一家の柱 pillar of the family

hashíre v 走れ 1. → **hashiremásu** 走れます [INFINITIVE] 2. [IMPERATIVE] (run!) → **hashirimásu** 走ります

hashiremásu, hashiréru v 走れます, 走れる can run

hashirimásu, hashíru v 走ります, 走る runs

hashitanai adj はしたない in bad taste, shameful: **hashitanai-kuchi** はしたない口 vulgar language

hashítte v 走って → **hashirimásu** 走ります

hason n 破損 breakage failure

hassan n 発散 emanation, transpiration: ~ **shimásu** 発散します gives out, emanates, exhales, unleashes; **sutoresu hassan** ストレス発散 stress release

hás-satsu n 八冊 eight copies (*books, magazines*)

has-sén n 八千・8,000 eight thousand

hassha n 発車 departure: ~ **shimásu** 発車します departs

hasshin n 発進 (*vehicle etc.*) starts: **kuruma o hasshin sasemásu** 車を発進させます moves the car

hasshin n 発信 transmission: ~ **shimásu** 発信します sends, transmits

hasshin n 発疹 (*skin*) rash

hasu n ハス・蓮 lotus: **hasu no hana** ハスの花 lotus bloom

hasu (no) *n* 斜(の) oblique, slanting: **hasu ni** 斜に・はすに **hasu ni** obliquely (= **naname (ni)** 斜(に))

hata *n* 端 **1.** the side: (... no) **hata de** (...の)端で off to the side (*of*) **2.** the outside; **hata kara** 端から from the outside, to an outsider

hatá *n* 旗 flag

hatá *n* 機 loom

hátachi *n* 二十歳 20 years old

hatáite *v* はたいて → **hatakimásu** はたきます

hatake *n* 畑 field (*dry*): **hatake o tagayashimásu** 畑を耕します cultivates one's patch

hatáke *v* はたけ **1.** → **hatakemásu** はたけます [INFINITIVE] (= **tatakemásu** 叩けます) **2.** [IMPERATIVE] (slap/dust it!) → **hatakimásu** はたきます

hatakemásu, hata-kéru *v* はたけます, はたける can slap; can dust

hatakí *n* はたき duster

hatakí *n* はたき → **hatakimásu** はたきます [INFINITIVE]

hatakimásu, hatáku *v* はたきます, はたく slap, beat; dust (= **tatakimásu** 叩きます)

hatan *n* 破綻 bankruptcy, failure, collapse: ~ **shimásu** 破綻します falls, collapses

hatarakemásu, hatarakeru *v* 働けます, 働ける can work

hataraki *n* 働き work(ing), activity, operation, function; achievement; ability

hatarakimásu, hataraku *v* 働きます, 働く works, labors; commits (*a crime*)

hataraki-mono *n* 働き者 hard worker

hatasemásu, hataséru *v* 果たせます, 果たせる can accomplish

hatashimásu, hatásu *v* 果たします, 果たす accomplishes: **yakusoku o hatashimásu** 約束を果たします fulfills a promise

háto *n* ハト・鳩 pigeon, dove

hato-ba *n* 波止場 pier, wharf, quay (= **futō** 埠頭)

hatsu (no) *adj* 初(の) first

hatsuan *n* 発案 design idea

hatsubai *n* 発売 sale, release: ~ **shimásu** 発売します sales

hatsubai-bi *n* 発売日 sale date, release date

hatsudén-ki *n* 発電機 generator

hatsudō´-ki *n* 発動機 motor

hatsuiku *n* 発育 growth: **hatsuiku ga yoi/ii** 発育が良い/いい is well grown

hatsuka *n* 二十日 20 days; 20th of the month: **hatsuka-mé** 二十日目 the 20th day; **hatsuka-nézumi** 二十日ネズミ[鼠] mouse

hatsukoi *n* 初恋 first love

hatsumei *n* 発明 invention: ~ **shimásu** 発明します invents

... hátsu (no) *suffix* ...発(の) departing at/from (*time/place*); dispatched from/at (*place/time*)

hatsuon *n* 発音 pronunciation: ~ **shimásu** 発音します pronounces

hattatsu *n* 発達 development: **hattatsu shimásu** 発達します it develops

hatte *v* 貼って → **harimásu** 貼ります

hatte *v* 張って → **harimásu** 張ります

hátte *v* 這って → **haimásu** 這います

hátte imásu (iru) *v* 張っています(いる) is tense, taut

hátte imásu (iru) *v* 這っています(いる) is crawling

hatten *n* 発展 development, expansion, growth: ~ **shimásu** 発展します develops, expands, grows

hatten-tojō´koku *n* 発展途上国 developing nation

hát-tō *n* 八頭 eight (*horses/oxen, large animals*)

hatto (shite) *adv* はっと(して) with a sudden start (*of surprise*)

Háwai *n* ハワイ Hawaii

hawánai *v* 這わない = **haimasén** 這いません (not crawl)

hái ya/wa shinai *v* 這いや/はしない = **hawánai** 這わない (not crawl)

hayái *adj* 速い fast, quick

hayái *adj* 早い early, soon

háyaku *adv* 速く (*so as to be*) fast

háyaku *adv* 早く (*so as to be*) early, soon: **háyaku-tomo** 早くとも at the earliest

hayamé ni *adv* 早めに early (*in good time*)

hayarimásu, hayáru *v* 流行ります, 流行る gets popular, comes into fashion, spreads; (*disease*) spreads rapidly, is fast-spreading

hayari (no) *adj* 流行り(の) fashionable, popular

háyasa *n* 速さ speed

hayashi ráisu *n* ハヤシライス beef hash over rice

hayashí *n* 林 grove

hayashí *n* 囃子 (**o-hayashi** お囃し) Japanese instrument accompaniment

hayáshi *v* 生やし → **hayashimásu** 生やします

hayáshi 囃し **1.** *v* → **hayashimásu** 囃します [INFINITIVE] **2.** *n* → **o-hayashi** お囃子

hayashimásu, hayásu *v* 生やします, 生やす grows it (*hair, teeth*); lets it grow (*sprout*)

hayashimásu, hayásu *v* 囃します, 囃す (*musically*) accompanies

hayátte *v* 流行って → **hayarimásu** 流行りります

háze *n* ハゼ・沙魚 goby (*fish*)

hazenoki *n* ハゼノキ・櫨の木・黄櫨 sumac, Japanese wax tree (*plant*)

... hazu désu *v* ...はずです presumably; ought to, should

... hazu ga/wa arimasén (nái) *v* ...はずが/はありません(ない) there is no reason to expect/think that ...

hazukashíí *adj* 恥ずかしい ashamed; embarrassed, shy; shameful, disgraceful

hazumi 弾み **1.** *n* impetus, momentum; impulse; chance **2.** *v* → **hazumimásu** 弾みます [INFINITIVE]

hazumimásu, hazumu *v* 弾みます, 弾む bounces (back)

hazuremásu, hazureru *v* 外れます, 外れる gets disconnected, comes off; misses, fails

53

hazushimásu, hazusu *v* 外します, 外す disconnects, takes off, undoes, unfastens; misses: **séki o hazushimásu** 席を外します leaves one's seat

hé *n* 屁 flatulence, fart (= **onara** おなら): **hé o hirimásu/shimásu** 屁をひります／します flatulates, farts

hé *n* 経 → **hemásu** 経えます [INFINITIVE]

hē *interj* へえ oh, really, wow

hébi *n* ヘビ・蛇 snake

hechima *n* ヘチマ・糸瓜 sponge gourd, luffa (loofah)

hedatarimásu, hedatáru *v* 隔たります, 隔たる is distant, is estranged

hedatemásu, hedatéru *v* 隔てます, 隔てる estranges them, separates them, gets them apart

heddoráito *n* ヘッドライト headlight(s)

hédo *n* 反吐 vomit

hei *n* 塀 wall, fence

hei *n* 兵 soldier (= **heishi** 兵士)
hei-eki *n* 兵役 military service: **heieki ni tsukimásu** 兵役につきます serves in the army
hei-ki *n* 兵器 weapon, arms
hei-ryoku *n* 兵力 military force
héi-sha *n* 兵舎 barracks
hei-shi *n* 兵士 soldier (= **hei** 兵)
hei-tai *n* 兵隊 soldier (boy), rank: **heitai-ari** 兵隊アリ soldier ant

heibon (na) *adj* 平凡(な) commonplace, conventional, ordinary

heichi *n* 平地 flat land; (= **heiya** 平野) plain

heijitsu *n* 平日 weekday

heijō (ni) *adv* 平常(に) usually, ordinarily, generally

heijō-shin *n* 平常心 one's senses/mind: **heijō-shin o tamochimásu** 平常心を保ちます keeps one's coool/calm

heika *n* 陛下 majesty, Your Majesty.

heikai *n* 閉会 closing a meeting: **heikai-shiki** 閉会式 closing ceremony

heikin *n* 平均 average, on the average: **heikin nenrei** 平均年令 average age; **heikin jumyō** 平均寿命 average life span (*lifetime*); **heikin-ten** 平均点 average score

heiki (na) *adj* 平気(な) calm, composed, cool, unperturbed, unfazed: **heiki de** 平気で calmly

heikō *n* 平行 parallel, parallelism: **heikō-sen o tadorimásu** 平行線をたどります fails to reach an agreement, remains as far apart as ever

heikō-shimásu (suru) *v* 閉口します（する） is annoyed, is overwhelmed, gets stuck

heimen *n* 平面 flat surface: **heimen-zu** 平面図 two-dimensional diagram

heimin *n* 平民 common person: **heimin-kaikyū** 平民階級 commons

heisa *n* 閉鎖 closing: **kōjō-heisa** 工場閉鎖 factory closure

heiten *n* 閉店 closing a store: ~ **shimásu** 閉店します closes a store

heiwa *n* 平和 peace; **heiwa ni narimásu** 平和になります becomes peace; **heiwa na kuni** 平和な国 peaceful nation

haiwa na *adj* 平和な peaceful

heiya *n* 平野 plain (*flat land*)

heizen (to) *adv* 平然(と) without embarrassment: **heizen to shiteimásu** 平然としています remains unruffled

hekichi *n* 僻地 remote area (= **henpi na tochi** 辺ぴな土地)

hekieki-shimásu (suru) *v* 辟易します（する） is disgusted

hekiga *n* 壁画 wall painting

hekomimásu, hekomu *v* へこみます, へこむ gets hollow, depressed, dents: **hekonde imásu** へこんでいます is dented, depressed

héma *n* へま [INFORMAL] bungle, mess, goof: **héma (o) shimásu** へま(を)します goofs up

hemásu, héru *v* 経ます, 経る passes (by), elapses

... hen *suffix* ...辺 vicinity, nearby, neighborhood (= **chikaku** 近く)

...-hén *suffix* ...遍 (*counts times*) (= **do** 度, **kai** 回)

henai *v* 経ない = **hemasén** 経ません (not pass)

hen'átsu-ki *n* 変圧器 voltage converter, transformer

henji *n* 返事 (**o-henji** お返事) answer, reply, response: (**o-**)**henji (o) shimásu** (お)返事(を)します answers, replies, responses

hénka *n* 変化 change: **... ni hénka shimásu** ...に変化します it changes into ...

henkaku *n* 変革 innovative changes: ~ **shimásu** 変革します changes, transforms

henkan *n* 変換 conversion: **henkán-ki** 変換器 converter; **henkan-kíi** 変換キー the *kana*-to-*kanji* conversion key (*on a Japanese computer/word processor*): ~ **shimásu** 変換します converts, replaces, changes, transforms

henkan *n* 返還 return: **Hoppō ryōdo henkan** 北方領土返還 return of Russian-held northern territories: ~ **shimásu** 返還します returns

henken *n* 偏見 prejudice

henkin *n* 返金 refund (*[note]* tax refund = **kanpu** 還付): ~ **shimásu** 返金します refunds

hén (na) *adj* 変(な) strange, odd, peculiar, funny, queer

henpi (na) *adj* 辺ぴ(な) odd, off the beaten path: **hanpi na tochi** 辺ぴな土地 odd parts, places that were off the beaten track (= **hekichi** 僻地)

henryū´-ki *n* 変流器 converter (*AC-DC*)

hensei *n* 編成 organization: ~ **shimásu** 編成します organizes

henshin *n* 返信 reply, return mail: ~ **shimásu** 返信します replies

henshin *n* 変身 1. transformation: ~ **shimásu** 変身します transforms 2. the Japanese title of "The Metamorphosis"

henshū *n* 編集 editing: ~ **shimásu** 編集します edits
henshū-chō *n* 編集長 editor in chief
henshū-sha *n* 編集者 editor

hensoku-rébā *n* 変速レバー gear-shift

hentō *n* 返答 [BOOKISH] = **henjí** 返事: ~ **shimásu** 返答します

heranai v 減らない = **herimasén** 減りません (not decrease)

herashimásu, herasu v 減らします, 減らす decreases it, cuts it down, shortens, lessens, curtails

heréba v 減れば (if it decreases) → **herimásu** 減ります

heri v 減り **1.** a decrease **2.** → **herimásu** 減ります [INFINITIVE]

herí n 縁 border, edge, rim (= **fuchi** 縁)

herikoputā n ヘリコプター helicopter

herikudarimásu v へりくだります, **herikudaru** へりくだる is modest, abases oneself: **herikudatta taido** へりくだった態度 modest attitude

herikutsu n 屁理屈 sophistry, quiddity (*using clever arguments to support something that is not true*): **herikutsu o iimásu** 屁理屈を言います quibbles

herimásu, heru v 減ります, 減る decreases, dwindles, goes down

heripōto n ヘリポート heliport

herí ya/wa shinai v 減りや/はしない = **heranai** 減らない (not decrease)

heroin n ヘロイン heroin

herumetto n ヘルメット helmet

herunia n ヘルニア hernia

hérupā n ヘルパー helper

hérupesu n ヘルペス herpes

hérupu n ヘルプ help: **herupu-kinō** ヘルプ機能 (*computer*) help function

heso n へそ (**o-heso** おへそ) navel, bellybutton

hesokuri n へそくり・ヘソクリ pin money tucked away, pin money hidden away: **hesokuri ga arimásu** ヘソクリがあります has some pin money tucked away

hetá (na) adj 下手 (な); unskillful, inept, clumsy, poor, bad, inexpert: **hatá o suru to** へたをすると if you are unlucky, if you are not careful: **hatá no yokozuki** 下手の横好き dabster, likes to but is not very good at

héta v 経た = **hemáshita** 経ました (passed)

hetakuso (na) adj 下手くそ (な) → **hetá (na)** 下手 (な)

hetarikomimásu, hetarikomu v へたり込みます, へたり込む collapses, sinks down: **jimen ni hetarikomimásu** 地面にへたり込みます slumps on the ground

héte v 経て → **hemásu** 経ます: … **o héte** …を経て by way of (*through, via*) …

hetoheto adj へとへと is dead, is beaten: **hetoheto ni tsukaremásu** へとへとに疲れます is fagged out, is dead tired

hetta v 減った = **herimáshita** 減りました (decreased)

hette v 減って → **herimásu** 減ります

heyá n 部屋 (**o-heya** お部屋) room

hi n 日 day

hí-bi n 日々 every day: **híbi no seikatsu** 日々の生活 daily life

hi-goro adv 日頃 usually

hí-goto (ni) adv 日毎 (に) day by day

hi-nichi n 日にち (*fixed*) day; number of days

hi-zuke n 日付 date (*of month*): **hizuke-henkōsen** 日付変更線 change-of-day line, dateline

hi (ohi-sama) n 日 (お日様) sun (= **taiyō** 太陽): **hi no hikari** 日の光 sunshine (= **níkkō** 日光)

hi-atari n 日当たり exposure to the sun, sunniness: **hiatarí ga íi** 日当たりがいい is sunny

hi-gása n 日傘 parasol (*umbrella*)

hi-gure n 日暮れ sunset (*time*); the dark

hi-kage n 日陰 shadow (*from sunlight*)

hikage-mono 日陰者 person with a shady past

hi-nata n 日なた sunshine: **hinata-bókko** 日なたぼっこ sunbathing, basking (*in the sun*)

hi-no-de n 日の出 sunrise

hi-no-iri n 日の入り sunset

hi-ōí n 日覆い awning, sunshade, blind (= **hiyoke** 日よけ)

hi-yake n 日焼け sunburn: **hiyake o shimásu** 日焼けをします gets a sunburn

hi-yoke n 日よけ sunshade, blind, awning (= **hi-ōí** 日覆い)

hi-yori n 日和 weather (conditions): [IDIOM] **mateba kairo no hiyori ori** 待てば海路の日和あり It is a long lane that has no turning.

hi-yorimi n 日和見 waiting policy: **hiyorimi-shugi** 日和見主義 timeserving: **hiyorimi-shugi-sha** 日和見主義者 opportunist: **hiyorimi-seisaku** 日和見政策 wait-and-see policy

hí n 火 fire

hí-bachi n 火鉢 hibachi, charcoal brazier: **hí-bachi ni atarimásu** 火鉢に当たります warm oneself at a *hibachi*/charcoal brazier

hí-bana n 火花 spark: **híbana o chirashimásu** 火花を散らします gives off sparks

hí-bashi n 火箸 tongs (*for fire*)

…´-hi suffix …費 expense

hibí n ひび crack (*fine*): **hibí ga dekimásu** ひびができます crazes

hibíite v 響いて → **hibikimásu** 響きます

hibikí 響き **1.** n echo **2.** v → **hibíkimásu** 響きます [INFINITIVE]

hibikimásu, hibíku v 響きます, 響く echoes, resounds

Hibiya n 日比谷 Hibiya: **Hibiya-Kō´en** 日比谷公園 Hibiya Park

hibō n 誹謗 [BOOKISH] slander: **~ shimásu** 誹謗します defames

hibō-chūshō 誹謗中傷 mental abuse

hichíriki n ひちりき an oboe-like reed instrument (in *gagaku*)

hidari n 左 left: **hidari-dónari** 左隣り next (door) on the left; **hidari-kiki/-giki (no)** 左利き (の) left-handed (*person*); **hidari-máwari (ni)** 左回り (に) counterclockwise

hidari-gawa n 左側 left side

hidói adj ひどい severe, terrible, unreasonable, vicious, bitter, awful: **hidoi-kao** ひどい顔 face like a dropped pie

hídoku *adv* ひどく hard, cruelly, terribly: **hídoku obiemásu** ひどく脅[怯え]ます has one's heart in one's mouth

híe *v* 冷え → **hiemásu** 冷えます [INFINITIVE]

hiemásu, hiéru *v* 冷えます, 冷える gets cold

hiéreba *v* 冷えれば (if it gets cold) → **hiemásu** 冷えます

híete *v* 冷えて → **hiemásu** 冷えます

hífu *n* 皮膚 skin

higái *n* 被害 damage, injury, casualty: **higái-chi** 被害地 stricken area; **higái-sha** 被害者 victim (= **gaisha** 該者)

higashí *n* 東 east: **higashí-guchi** 東口 the east exit/entrance; **higashí-yori (no kaze)** 東寄り (の風) easterly (*wind*); **higashí-káigan** 東海岸 east coast

hige *n* ひげ・髭 beard; mustache (= **kuchí-hige** 口ひげ): **hige o hayashimásu** ひげを生やします grows a beard/mustache; **hige o sorimásu** ひげを剃ります shaves

hige *n* ひげ・ヒゲ whiskers: **neko no hige** ネコ・猫のひげ cat whiskers

hígeki *n* 悲劇 tragedy

híhan *n* 批判 judgment, criticism: **~ shimásu** 批判します judges, criticizes

hihán-sha *n* 批判者 critic, judge

híhan-teki (na) *adj* 批判的(な) critical

hihyō *n* 批評 criticism, review: **~ shimásu** 批評します reviews, critiques

hihyō-ka *n* 批評家 critic, reviewer

híiki *n* ひいき illegitimate favor, patronage: **~ shimásu** ひいきします shows preference/partiality

hiita *v* 引いた = **hikimáshita** 引きました (pulled)

híitā *n* ヒーター heater

hiite *v* 引いて → **hikimásu** 引きます

hijí *n* 肘 elbow: **hijí o harimásu** 肘を張ります bends out one's elbows: **hiji-kake isu** 肘掛け椅子 armchair

hijō *n* 非常 emergency: **hijō-burē´ki** 非常ブレーキ emergency brake; **hijō-dénwa** 非常電話 emergency phone; **hijō-guchi** 非常口 emergency exit; **hijō-kaidan** 非常階段 emergency stairs; **hijō no ba(w)ai** 非常の場合 in (the) event of emergency

hijō na *adj* 非常(な) unusual, extreme

hijō ni *adv* 非常(に) extremely

hikaemásu, hikaeru *v* 控えます, 控える refrains, withholds

hikaemé (na) *adj* 控え目(な) modest

hikaku *n* 比較 comparison: **~ shimásu** 比較します compares

hikaku-teki (ni) *adv* 比較的(に) relatively, comparatively

hikan *n* 悲観 pessimism: **~ shimásu** 悲観します awfullizes

hikan-teki (na) *adj* 悲観的(な) pessimistic

hikanai *v* 引かない = **hikimasén** 引きません (not pull)

hikaremásu, hikareru *v* 引かれます, 引かれる

gets pulled (out), gets drawn/dragged/tugged/subtracted

hikaremásu, hikareru *v* 轢かれます, 轢かれる gets run over: **torákku ni hikaremásu** トラックに轢かれます gets run over by a truck

hikaremásu, hikareru *v* 挽かれます, 挽かれる gets sawed

hikaremásu, hikareru *v* 弾かれます, 弾かれる gets played

hikaremásu, hikareru *v* ひかれます, ひかれる gets ground

hikaremásu, hikareru *v* 惹かれます, 惹かれる get attracted (*to*)

hikaremásu, hikareru *v* 光れます, 光れる can glow/shine

hikarí *n* 光 light; → **hikarimásu** 光ります

hikari-kēburu *n* 光ケーブル optical cable (*internet*)

hikarimásu, hikáru *v* 光ります, 光る it shines, glows

hike *v* 引け 1. → **hikemásu** 引けます [INFINITIVE] 2. [IMPERATIVE] (pull!) → **hikimásu** 引きます

hikéba *v* 引けば (if one pulls) → **hikimásu** 引きます

hikemásu, hikeru *v* 引けます, 引ける can pull

hikéreba *v* 引ければ (if one can pull) → **hikemásu** 引けます

hiketsu *n* 秘訣 [BOOKISH] secret, formula: **seikō é no hiketsu** 成功への秘訣 key to success

hiki- *n* 引き ("pull/take and")

…-hiki (-ppiki) …匹 (*counts small animals*, *fish*, *insects* (*bugs*))

hiki-age *n* 引き上げ refloating; rise/hike (*in price*, *wage, fee*)

hiki-age *n* 引き揚げ evacuation, repatriation; salvage

hiki-agemásu, hiki-agéru *v* 引き上げます, 引き上げる pulls up; refloats; raises (*price, wage, fee*)

hiki-agemásu, hiki-agéru *v* 引き揚げます, 引き揚げる withdraws, leaves; evacuates, gets repatriated

hikiagé-sha *n* 引(き)揚げ者 evacuee, repatriate

hikidashi *n* 引き出し drawer

hikidashimásu, hikidasu *v* 引き出します, 引き出す pulls/draws out; withdraws

hiki-fune *n* 引き(曳き)船[舟] tugboat

hikigane *n* 引き金 trigger

hiki-haraimásu, hiki-haráu *v* 引き払います, 引き払う checks out (*of hotel*)

hikiimásu, hikiíru *v* 率います, 率いる leads, commands

hikiíte *v* 率いて → **hikiimásu** 率います

hiki-kaemásu, hiki-káeru *v* 引き換えます, 引き換える exchanges, converts

hiki-kaeshimásu, hiki-káesu *v* 引き返します, 引き返す turns back, returns

hikimásu, hiku *v* 引きます, 引く pulls (out); draws; drags, tugs; catches; attracts; subtracts; deducts; looks up a word (*in dictionary*)

hi̱kimás̱u, hi̱ku *v* 轢きます, 轢く runs over
(*a person*)

hi̱kimás̱u, hi̱ku *v* 挽きます, 挽く saws

hi̱kimás̱u, hi̱ku *v* 弾きます, 弾く plays
(*a stringed instrument*)

hi̱kimás̱u, hi̱ku *v* 挽きます, 挽く grinds (*into
powder*)

hi̱kimás̱u, hi̱ku *v* 退きます, 退く retires

hi̱kinige *n* ひき[轢き]逃げ hit and run

hi̱ki-niku *n* 挽き肉 chopped/minced/ground meat

hi̱ki-torimás̱u, hiki-tóru 引き取ります, 引き取る
1. leaves, withdraws, retires **2.** takes over, looks
after, receives **3. íki o hi̱ki-torimás̱u** 息を引き取
ります takes/draws one's last breath, dies

hi̱ki-tsugimás̱u, hiki-tsúgu *v* 引き継ぎます,
引き継ぐ takes over for, succeeds (*in a projection*)

hi̱ki-ukemás̱u, hiki-ukéru *v* 引き受けます,
引き受ける undertakes, takes charge of, takes
responsibility for; guarantees: **tegata o hi̱ki-
ukemás̱u** 手形を引き受けます accepts a bill
(*of payment*)

hi̱kiwake *n* 引き分け tie, draw: **hi̱ki-wakemás̱u,
hiki-wakeru** 引き分けます, 引き分ける draws
apart; plays to a draw

hi̱ki ya/wa shinai *v* 引きや/はしない = **hikanai**
引かない (not pull)

hi̱ki-zan *n* 引き算 subtraction: **hi̱ki-zan (o)
shimás̱u** 引き算（を）します subtracts

hi̱ki-zurimás̱u, hiki-zuru *v* 引きずります, 引き
ずる drags

hi̱k-kakimás̱u, hik-káku *v* 引っ掻きます, 引っ掻
く scratches it

hi̱kken *n* 必見 must-see

hi̱kki *n* 筆記 writing down: **~ shimás̱u** 筆記します
takes notes

hikki-tai *n* 筆記体 running hand, script

hikki-yōgu *n* 筆記用具 writing instrument

hi̱kkoshi 引っ越し **1.** *n* moving (*house*) **2.** *v* →
hi̱kkoshimás̱u 引っ越します [INFINITIVE]

hi̱kkoshi-ya *n* 引っ越し屋 (house) mover

hikkoshi-torákku *n* 引っ越しトラック mover's van

hi̱kkoshimás̱u, hikkósu *v* 引っ越します, 引っ
越す moves (*house*)

hi̱kkuri-kaerimás̱u, hikkuri-káeru *v* 引っくり
返ります, 引っくり返る it tips (over); it upsets

hi̱kkuri-kaeshimás̱u, hikkuri-káesu *v* 引っく
り返します, 引っくり返す upsets (*overturns*) it

hi̱kō´ *n* 飛行 flying (*a plane*): **~ shimás̱u** 飛行します
flies (*a plane*)

hi̱kō-jō *n* 飛行場 airport (= **kū-kō** 空港)

hi̱kō´-ki *n* 飛行機 airplane: **hi̱kō´-ki ni norimás̱u**
飛行機に乗ります gets on a plane

hi̱kō-yoi *n* 飛行酔い airsick(ness)

hi̱kō *v* 引こう = **hikimashō** 引きましょう
(let's pull!)

hi̱-kō´shi̱ki (no) *adj* 非公式（の）unofficial,
informal: **hi̱-kō´shi̱ki no kaigi** 非公式の会議
informal conference

hi̱ku *v* 引く = **hikimás̱u** 引きます (pulls (out), etc.)

hi̱kúi *adj* 低い low, short

hi̱kyō´ (na) *adj* 卑怯（な）cowardly

hima *n* 暇 time; leisure, spare time; leave;
dismissal (*of servant*): **hima-tsubushi** 暇つぶし
time killing

hima na *adj* 暇（な）at leisure, unoccupied, not
busy, free (*of business*); slow (*business*)

híme *n* 姫 (**ohíme-sama** （お）姫様）princess

himei *n* 悲鳴 a scream: **himei o agemás̱u** 悲鳴を
上げます screams out

himitsu (no) *adj* 秘密（の）secret, mystery:
"Himitsu no Hanazono" 「秘密の花園」"The
Secret Garden"

himo *n* ひも string, cord, tape, strap, ribbon

himokawa(-údon) *n* ひもかわ（うどん）long thin
udon

hin *n* 品 elegance, refinement, dignity: **hin ga
arimás̱u** 品があります has class

hinagata *n* ひな形 form; pattern; shape

hina-mátsuri *n* ひな祭（り）the Dolls Festival, the
Girl's Festival (3 March)

hínan *n* 非難 blame, reproach: **~ shimás̱u** 非難し
ます blames, reproaches

hínan *n* 避難 taking refuge

hinán-sha *n* 避難者 refugee

hina-níngyō *n* ひな人形 (*festival*) dolls

hinerimás̱u, hinéru *v* 捻ります, 捻る twists;
turns

hinétte *v* 捻って → **hinerimás̱u** 捻ります

hiniku *n* 皮肉 sarcasm: **hiniku o iimás̱u** 皮肉を言
います makes ironical remarks

hiniku na *adj* 皮肉（な）sarcastic, cynical

hinin *n* 避妊 contraception: **~ shimás̱u** 避妊します
prevents pregnancy

hinín-gu *n* 避妊具 contraceptive (*device*)
(= **kondōmu** コンドーム）

hinín-yaku *n* 避妊薬 contraceptive drug/pill

hinkon *n* 貧困 poverty

hinkon na *adj* 貧困（な）needy

hinmín-kutsu/-gai *n* 貧民窟/街 slum

hinoki *n* ヒノキ・檜・桧 cypress

hinoki butai *n* 檜舞台 the stage of a major (*first-
class, leading*) show

hinshi̱ *n* 品詞 part of speech

hinshi̱ *n* 瀕死 moribundity, near death: **hinshi̱ no
kanja** 瀕死の患者 moribund patient

hinshi̱tsu *n* 品質 quality: **hinshi̱tsu o hoshō-
shimás̱u** 品質を保証します guarantees the quality

hinshuku-o-kaimás̱u (kau) *v* ひんしゅくを買い
ます（買う）invites frowns of disgust, is frowned upon

hínto *n* ヒント hint, reminder: **hínto o ataemás̱u**
ヒントを与えます gives a hint

hipparimás̱u, hippáru *v* 引っ張ります, 引っ張る
pulls, drags, tugs (*at*), takes, brings

hira-ayamari *n* 平謝り humble apology: **hira-
ayamari ni ayamarimás̱u** 平謝りに謝ります
makes a humble apology

hirágáná *n* ひらがな・平仮名 hiragana
(*the roundish Japanese letters*)

hiráite v 開いて → **hirakimásu** 開きます
hiraki 開き **1.** v → **hirakimásu** 開きます
[INFINITIVE] **2.** n open and dried fish: **sanma no hiraki** サンマの開き open and dried saury
hiraki-do n 開き戸 hinged door
hirakimásu, hiráku v 開きます, 開く opens up; has/holds (a party)
hirame n ヒラメ・平目 flounder
hiramekimásu, hirameku v ひらめきます, ひらめく comes to one in a flash
hiraoyogi n 平泳ぎ breaststroke
hira (shain) n 平(社員) rank-and-file employee
hiratai adj 平たい flat (= **tiara na** 平らな): **hiratai-hana** 平たい鼻 flat nose
hirataku adv 平たく flat: **hirataku iu to/ieba** 平たく言うと/言えば put simply
hire n ヒレ・鰭 fin
hire n ヒレ fillet (of pork, etc.): **hire-sutēki** ヒレステーキ fillet steak
hirefushimásu, hirefusu v ひれ伏します, ひれ伏す grovels, falls on one's face
hirei n 比例 proportion: **~ shimásu** 比例します is proportionate
hirimásu, híru v ひります, ひる discharges (excretes) from the body: **hé o hirimásu** 屁をひります flatulates, farts (= **dashimásu** 出します)
híró-bá n 広場 a square, a place, (public) an open space
hiroe v 拾え **1.** → **hiroemásu** 拾えます [INFINITIVE] **2.** [IMPERATIVE] (pick it up!) → **hiroimásu** 拾います
hiroemásu, hiroeru v 拾えます, 拾える can pick it up
hirogarimásu, hirogaru v 広がります, 広がる it spreads, widens
hirogemásu, hirogeru v 広げます, 広げる spreads/widens it
hiroi v 拾い → **hiroimásu** 拾います [INFINITIVE]
hirói adj 広い wide, broad; big (room, etc.)
hiroimásu, hirou v 拾います, 拾う picks it up
hiroku adv 広く wide, widely
hiromarimásu, hiromáru v 広まります, 広まる it spreads, gets diffused
hiromemásu, hiroméru v 広めます, 広める spreads/diffuses it
hírosa n 広さ width
Hiroshima n 広島 Hiroshima; **Hiroshimá-Eki** 広島駅 Hiroshima Station
hírō n 披露 presentation
   hirō´-en n 披露宴 reception, wedding banquet (engagement, wedding, etc.)
   hirō´-kai n 披露会 reception (engagement, wedding, etc.)
   hírō-shimásu (suru) v 披露します(する) announces (wedding, etc.)
hirotte v 拾って → **hiroimásu** 拾います
hirowanai v 拾わない = **hiroimasén** 拾いません (not pick up)
hirú n 昼 (**o-híru** お昼) daytime, noon: **hirú kara**

昼から after noon; **hirú no bú** 昼の部 matinee
hiru-góhan n 昼ご飯 (**o-hiru-góhan** お昼ご飯) noon meal, lunch (= **hirumeshi** 昼飯)
hiru-má n 昼間 daytime
hiru-ne n 昼寝 nap: **hiru-ne (o) shimásu** 昼寝(を)します takes a nap
hiru-súgi n 昼過ぎ afternoon
híru n ヒル・蛭 leech
hisashi-buri (ni) adv 久しぶり(に) after a long time (of absence)
hishaku n 柄杓 scoop, ladle
hishó n 秘書 secretary (private)
hi´ssha n 筆者 the writer/author (= **chosha** 著者)
hisúi n ヒスイ・翡翠 jade
hitai n 額 forehead, brow
hitashi-mono n 浸し物 (**o-hitáshi** お浸し) boiled vegetables (usually spinach or greens) served cold with seasoning
hitchaku n 必着 must-reach: **ni-gatsu muika hitchaku** 2月6日必着 due NLT (not later than) February 6
hitei n 否定 denial: **~ shimásu** 否定します denies
hito n 人, … **hitó** …人 person, man, fellow, people; someone, somebody
hitó-bito n 人々 people (in general): **hitó-bito no uwasa** 人々の噂 people's talk, rumor
hito-gara n 人柄 character, personality
hito-góroshi n 人殺し murder: **hito-góroshi o shimásu** 人殺しをします murders
hitó-tachi n 人達 people
hito-… prefix 一… one, a
hito-ánshin n ひと安心 a relief (from worry) → **anshín** 安心
hitó-ban n 一晩 one night: **hitó-ban tomari-másu** 一晩泊まります stays overnight
hito-gomi n ひとごみ・人込み crowd: **hito-gomi o sakemásu** 人込みを避けます avoids crowded places
hitó-hako n 一箱 one boxful
hitó-iki n 一息 a breath: **hitó-iki de** 一息で with a gulp: **hitó-iki iremásu/tsukimásu** 一息入れます/つきます catches one's breath
hitó-kátamari n ひと固まり・一塊 one lump/loaf: **hitó-kátamari no** 一塊の a pat of
hitó-kire n 一切れ (one) piece (a cut): **hitó-kire no pan** 一切れのパン a piece of bread
hitó-koto n 一言 a word: **hitó-koto de iuto** 一言で言うと put simply
hitó-kuchi n 一口 one mouthful; one bite; one drink, sip: **hitó-kuchi mo tabemasen** 一口も食べません does not eat a single bite; **hitó-kuchi ni iuto** 一口に言うと in a word
hitó-kumi n 一組 a set (collection): **hitó-kumi no danjo** 一組の男女 couple, pair
hitó-maki n 一巻き one (roll, bolt of cloth)
hitó-mori n 一盛り scoop (one scoopful)
hitó-nemuri n 一眠り a nap: **~ shimásu** 一眠りします takes a nap → **nemurimásu** 眠ります

hitó-oyogi *n* ひと泳ぎ a swim: ~ **shimásu** ひと泳ぎします takes a swim → **oyogimásu** 泳ぎます

hitó-ri *n* 一人 (**o-hitó-ri** お一人) one person; (**hitó-ri de** ひとりで・独りで) alone; **hitori-bótchi (no)** ひとりぼっち(の) lonely; **hitori-mónó** 独り者 single (*unmarried*) person

hitó-saji *n* 一匙 one spoonful: **hitó-saji no satō** 一匙の砂糖 one spoonful of sugar

hito-shibai *n* 一芝居 playing a trick, acting: **hito-shibai uchimásu** 一芝居打ちます plays a trick on, puts on an act → **shibai** 芝居

hito-shigoto *n* 一仕事 bout of work: ~ **shimásu** 一仕事します works → **shigoto** 仕事 (**o-shígoto** お仕事)

hito-suji *n* 一筋 shaft: **hito-suji no hikari** 一筋の光 a ray of light; **hitosuji-nawa dewa ikimasen** 一筋縄ではいきません is not an easy job

hitó-tsu *n* ひとつ・一つ one (= **ík-ko** 一個): one year old (= **ís-sai** 一歳); one and the same

hitó-yama *n* 一山 one heap/bunch: **hitóyama atemasu** 一山当てます strikes oil

hitómazu (wa) *adv* ひとまず(は) for a while; for the time being

hitori-de ni *adv* ひとりでに spontaneously, automatically, by/of itself

hitori-goto *n* 独り言 talking to oneself: **hitori-goto o iimásu** 独り言を言います says to oneself

hitosashiyubi *n* 人差し指 forefinger, index finger

hitoshíi *adj* 等しい equal, identical, similar

hitsugi *n* 棺 coffin

hitsuji *n* ヒツジ・羊 sheep: "**Hitsuji-tachi no Chinmoku**" 「羊たちの沈黙」 "The Silence of the Lambs"

Hitsuji-doshi *n* 未年 year of the Sheep

hitsujuhin *n* 必需品 necessity article: **seikatsu-hitsujuhin** 生活必需品 daily necessaries, commodities

hitsuyō *n* 必要 necessity, need: **… suru hitsuyō ga arimásu** …する必要があります needs to…: **… ga hitsuyō desu** …が必要です needs… **hitsuyō na** 必要な *adj* necessary, essential

hi´tté *v* ひって → **hirimásu** ひります

hitteki *n* 匹敵 comparison: ~ **shimásu** 匹敵します is comparable

hittó *n* ヒット a hit (*baseball*): ~ **shimásu** ヒットします hits

hittó-kyoku *n* ヒット曲 hit song

híya *n* 冷や (**o-híya** お冷や) cold water

hiya-múgi *n* 冷や麦・ひやむぎ chilled wheat-flour noodles (*cf.* **sō´men** そうめん)

hiyashimásu, hiyásu *v* 冷やします, 冷やす cools it off, refrigerates, chills: **atama o hiyashimasu** 頭を冷やします cools one's head

hiya-yákko *n* 冷ややっこ cooled bean curd

híyō *n* 費用 cost, expense: **híyó ga kakarimásu** 費用がかかります costs

hiyowa *n* ひ弱 weak: **hiyowa na kodomo** ひ弱な子供 frail child

hiza *n* 膝 knee, lap

hizamazukimásu, hizamazuku *v* ひざまずきます, ひざまずく falls on one's knees, kneels down

hizume *n* 蹄 hoof: **hizume no oto** 蹄の音 sound of hoofs

hó *n* 帆 sail

hō *interj* ほお? oh?

hō *n* 法 law (= **hōritsu** 法律); rule (= **hosoku** 法則); method (= **hōhō** 方法)

hō *n* ほお・頬 cheek (= **hoho** ほほ・頬, **hoppéta** ほっぺた)

… hō´ *n* …方 alternative, the one (*of two*) that …: **hō´ ga íi desu** …方がいいです … is better

hóbi *n* 褒美 (**go-hō´bi** ご褒美 [HONORIFIC]) prize, reward

hóbo *adj* ほぼ nearly; roughly

hóbo *n* 保母 nursery teacher

hō´bō *n, adv* 方々 everywhere, all over, every which way: **hō´bō kara** 方々から from various quarters

hōchi *n* 放置 neglect: **hōchi-jitensha** 放置自転車 illegally-parked bicycle

hóchikisu *n* ホチキス stapler: **hóchikisu no hari** ホチキスの針 strip of staples

hoehō *n* 歩調 pace: **hochō o awasemasu** 歩調を合わせます keeps pace

hōchō *n* 包丁 knife (*big*); butcher knife; cleaver (= **nikukiri-bó´chō** 肉切り包丁)

hochōki *n* 補聴器 hearing aids: **hochōki o tsukemásu** 補聴器をつけます wears a hearing aid

hōdan *n* 砲弾 bombshell

…-hōdai *suffix* 放題 can…as much as: **tabe-hōdai** 食べ放題 all-you-can-eat: **nomi-hōdai** 飲み放題 all-you-can-drink: **shitai-hōdai** したい放題 does whatever one feel like doing

hōden *n* 放電 electric(al) discharge: ~ **shimásu** 放電します discharges

(…) hodo *suffix* (…)程・ほど extent; limits; moderation; approximate time; about (*as much as*), (not) so much as; the more … the more

hodō *n* 歩道 walk(way), pavement, sidewalk: **hodō-kyō** 歩道橋 crossover bridge

hōdō *n* 報道 news report: ~ **shimásu** 報道します reports

hodóite *v* 解いて → **hodokimásu** 解きます

hodóke *v* 解け **1.** → **hodokemásu** 解けます [INFINITIVE] **2.** [IMPERATIVE] (undo/untie it!) → **hodokimásu** 解きます

hodokemásu, hodokéru *v* 解けます, 解ける **1.** can undo, can untie **2.** comes loose, comes undone

hodokimásu, hodóku *v* 解きます, 解く undoes, unties

hodokóshi *v* 施し charity: **hodokóshimásu, hodokósu** 施します, 施す gives charity: **hodokóshi o ukemásu** 施しを受けます accepts charity

hoemásu, hoéru *v* 吠えます, 吠える (*dog*) barks

hoeraremásu, hoeraréru *v* 吠えられます, 吠えられる can bark; is barked

hō´fu (na) *adj* 豊富(な) rich: **hō´fu na keiken** 豊富な経験 abundant experience

hō´gai (na) *adj* 法外(な) exorbitant, inordinate, excessive, unreasonable, steep: **hō´gai na kingaku/ nedan** 法外な金額/値段 unreasonable price

hōgaku *n* 方角 direction, one's bearings

hōgaku *n* 邦楽 Japanese music

hō´gaku (-bu) *n* 法学(部) (*science/study of*) law; School of Law

hōgan *n* 包含 inclusion, comprehension: **~ shimásu** 包含します includes, comprehends

hōgan *n* 砲丸 cannonball: **hōgan-nage senshu** 砲丸投げ選手 shot-putter

hógaraka (na) *adj* 朗らか(な) bright, sunny; cheerful

hogei *n* 捕鯨 whaling

hōgén *n* 方言 dialect

hógo *n* 保護 protection: **~ shimásu** 保護します protects, safeguards, shields

hogo-sha *n* 保護者 guardian

hoguremásu, hoguréru *v* 解れます, 解れる it loosens

hoho *n* ほほ・頬 cheek (= **hō** ほお・頬, **hoppéta** ほっぺた)

hōhō *n* 方法 method, process

hohoemashii *adj* 微笑ましい heartwarming, pleasant

hohoemí *n* 微笑み smile

hohoemimásu, hohoému *v* 微笑みます, 微笑む smiles

hoikú-en *n* 保育園 nursery school, pre-kindergarten

hoippu kuriimu *n* ホイップクリーム whipping cream

hōji *n* 法事 mass (*Buddhist*), Buddhist memorial service: **hōji o okonaimásu** 法事を行います holds a Buddhist service (*for the dead*)

hōjin *n* 法人 corporation

hōjin-zei *n* 法人税 corporation tax

hójo *n* 補助 help, assistance: **~ shimásu** 補助します helps

hojo-kin *n* 補助金 grant: **hojokin-seido** 補助金制度 bounty system

hoka *n* ほか・外・他 other, in addition to, other than (= **ta** 他): **hoka no** 他の other, another

hoken *n* 保険 insurance: **…ni hoken o kakemásu** …に保険をかけます insures

hoken-gáisha *n* 保険会社 insurance company

kenkō-hoken *n* 健康保険 health insurance

hoken-ryō *n* 保険料 insurance fee

hoken *n* 保健 healthcare, preservation of health: **sekai-hoken-kikō** 世界保健機関 World Health Organization

hōken *n* 封建 feudal(ism): **hōken-jídai** 封建時代 feudal period; **hōken-séido** 封建制度 feudal system

hoketsu *n* 補欠 substitute, alternate: **hoketsu-senshu** 補欠選手 benchwarmer: **hoketsu-shameibo** 補欠者名簿 waiting list

hō´ki *n* 放棄 abandonment: **~ shimásu** 放棄します gives up, abandons

hō´ki *n* 箒 broom: **hō´ki de hakimásu** 箒で掃きます sweeps with a broom

hōkí-boshi *n* 箒星 comet

Hokkáidō *n* 北海道 Hokkaido

hókkē *n* ホッケー hockey

hókku *n* ホック hook (*snap*): **hókku de tomemásu** ホックでとめます hooks up

hokkú *n* 発句 (a kind of) *haiku*, short poem

Hokkyoku *n* 北極 North Pole, Arctic

Hokkyoku-guma *n* ホッキョクグマ・北極グマ polar bear, white bear (= **shiro-kuma** 白熊)

Hokkyoku-gitsune *n* ホッキョクギツネ・北極ギツネ Arctic fox

Hokkyoku-kujira *n* ホッキョククジラ・北極クジラ Greenland right whale

Hokkyoku-sei *n* 北極星 North Star

Hokkyoku-ken *n* 北極圏 Arctic Circle

hōkō *n* 方向 direction

hōkoku *n* 報告 report: **~ shimásu** 報告します reports

hōkoku-sho *n* 報告書 report, statement

hokora *n* 祠 small shrine

hokorashii *adj* 誇らしい is proud

hokoremásu, hokoréru *v* 誇れます, 誇れる can brag

hokori *n* 埃 dust (*in the air*): **hokori o haraimásu** 埃を払います brushes dust off

hokorí *n* **1.** *n* pride, boast **2.** *v* → **hokorimásu** 誇ります

hokorimásu, hokóru *v* 誇ります, 誇る brags about/of

hokōsha *n* 歩行者 pedestrian: **hokōsha-tengoku** 歩行者天国 area of streets temporarily closed to vehicular traffic, pedestrian mall

hoku-… *prefix* 北… north (= **kíta no…** 北の…)

Hoku-Bei *n* 北米 = **Kíta-Ámerika** 北アメリカ North America

hóku-bu *n* 北部 the north, the northern part

hoku-hokusei *n* 北北西 north-northwest

hoku-hokutō *n* 北北東 north-northeast

hóku-i *n* 北緯 north latitude

Hoku-ō *n* 北欧 Northern Europe

hoku-sei *n* 北西 northwest

hoku-tō *n* 北東 northeast

hoku-yō *n* 北洋 northern sea: **hokuyō-gyogyō** 北洋漁業 northern sea fisheries

Hoku-riku-chíhō *n* 北陸地方 the Hokuriku area of Japan (*Toyama, Ishikawa, Fukui prefectures*)

hokuro *n* 黒子 mole (*on skin*)

hokosoemimásu, hokusoemu *v* ほくそ笑みます, ほくそ笑む chuckles, snickers to oneself

hokyō *n* 補強 reinforcement, corroboration: **~ shimásu** 補強します reinforces, corroborates

hokyū *n* 補給 supply: **~ shimásu** 補給します supplies

hōkyū *n* 俸給 [BOOKISH] pay, wages, salary (= **kyūyo** 給与, **o-kyūryō** お給料)

homé n 褒め praise: **o-homé ni azukarimasu** お褒めにあずかります is praised [HONORIFIC]

hóme v 褒め → **homemásu** 褒めます [INFINITIVE]

home-kótoba n 褒め言葉 compliment, word of praise

homemásu, homéru v 褒めます, 褒める praises, admires

hōmén n 方面, ...-hō´men ...方面 direction, quarter, district

hómo (no) adj ホモ(の) homosexual, gay

hōmon n 訪問 visit, call: ~ **shimásu** 訪問します visito, calls on

homosapiensu n ホモサピエンス Homo sapiens

hō´mu n ホーム 1. platform (at station) 2. home

hōmu-dórama n ホームドラマ soap opera

hōmuresu n ホームレス homeless: **hōmuresu ni narimásu** ホームレスになります becomes homeless

hōmushikku n ホームシック homesick: **hōmushikku ni narimásu/kakarimásu** ホームシックになります/かかります gets homesick

Hōmu-shō n 法務省 Ministry of Justice

hōmu-sutei n ホームステイ home stay: **hōmu-sutei o shimásu** ホームステイをします does home stay

hón n 本 book
  hón-bako n 本箱 bookcase
  hón-dana n 本棚 bookshelf
  hón-tate n 本立て bookends
  hón-ya n 本屋 bookshop (= **shoten** 書店)

hon-... prefix 本... main; chief; this; the; the present; real
  hon-ba n 本場 original place, area of production, real thing: **honba no nihon ryōri** 本場の日本料理 authentic Japanese food
  hon-ban n 本番 real part, real thing
  hón-bu n 本部 central office, headquarters (= **hón-sha** 本社)
  hon-dai n 本題 main issue: **hondai ni hairimásu** 本題に入ります comes to the main issue
  hon-dō n 本道 the main route
  hon-mono n 本物 the real thing: **honmono no** 本物の genuine: **honmono no aji** 本物の味 authentic flavor: **honmono no daiyamondo** 本物のダイヤモンド real diamond
  hon-ne n 本音 true (inner) feeling, real intention (= **hon-shin** 本心): **hon-ne o kikasete kudasai** 本音を聞かせて下さい Please let me know what you really think.: **hon-ne de katarimásu** 本音で語ります has heart-to-heart communication
  hon-nin n 本人 (the person) himself/herself/ myself, principal: **honnin-kakunin** 本人確認 identifying
  hón-rai n 本来 originally, from the start: **hón-rai motteiru nōryoku** 本来持っている能力 innate ability
  hon-ron n 本論 main discussion, main issue:

honron ni hairimásu 本論に入ります get down to business

hón-seki n 本籍 permanent residence: **honséki-chi** 本籍地 place of permanent residence

hon-shin n 本心 true (inner) feeling, real intention (= **honne** 本音)

hon-ten n 本店 head office, main store

...´-hon (...´-pon, ...´-bon) suffix ...本 (counts long objects)

hónbun n 本分 one's duty

honé n 骨 bone: **honé o orimásu** 骨を折ります takes (great) pains, goes to much trouble; **honé ga oremasu** 骨が折れます requires much effort, is hard/difficult
  hone-gúmi n 骨組み framework
  hone-óri n 骨折り (**o-honeori** お骨折り [HONORIFIC]) effort

hongoshi-o-iremásu (ireru) v 本腰を入れます (入れる) gets down to seriously

honki (no/de) adj, adv 本気(の/で) serious(ly), (in) earnest: **... o honki ni shimásu** ...を本気にします takes it seriously

Hónkón n ホンコン・香港 Hong Kong

honmatsu-tentō n 本末転倒 putting the cart before the horse

honmei n 本命 the favorite: **honmei no gāru-furendo/bōi-furendo** 本命のガールフレンド/ボーイフレンド main/real girlfriend/boyfriend

honmō n 本望 (one's) heart's desire, one's long-cherished desire: **honmō o togemásu** 本望を遂げます realizes one's heart's desire

honno ... adj ほんの ...just a (little), only a, a mere/slight ...: **honno sukoshi/chotto** ほんの少し/ちょっと ... just a little; just a minute

honō n 炎 flame

honomekashí n 仄めかし a hint

honomekashimásu, honomekásu v 仄めかします, 仄めかす hints

Honóruru n ホノルル Honolulu

hon-ryō n 本領 one's element/sphere: **hon-ryō o hakki shimásu** 本領を発揮します show oneself at one's best

Hónshū n 本州 Honshu

hontō (no), honto (no) adj 本当(の), ほんと(の) true, real, genuine: **hontō no koto** 本当の事 truth; **hontō ni** 本当に really, truly, indeed, absolutely

hon'yaku n 翻訳 translation: **hon'yaku shimásu** 翻訳します translates
  hon'yáku´-sha(ka) 翻訳者(家) translator

hoppéta n ほっぺた cheek (= **hō, hoho** ほお・ほほ・頬)

hoppō n 北方 the north

hóra n ホラ・法螺 1. trumpet-shell (= **horá-gai** 法螺貝) 2. exaggeration, bragging, bull (= **uso** 嘘): **hóra o fukimásu** ほらを吹きます brags, talks big

hóra interj ほら! Look!, Here!, There!, You see!

horā n ホラー horror
  horā-eiga n ホラー映画 horror movie/film

hora-ana n 洞穴 cave (= **dōkutsu** 洞窟)

horá-gai *n* 法螺貝 trumpet-shell
horánai *v* 掘らない = **horimásen** 掘りません (not dig)
hore *v* 惚れ → **horemásu** 惚れます [INFINITIVE]
hóre *v* 掘れ 1. → **horemásu** 掘れます [INFINITIVE] 2. [IMPERATIVE] (dig!) → **horimásu** 掘ります
hóreba *v* 掘れば (if one digs) → **horimásu** 掘ります
hōrei *n* 法令 law, act
horemásu, horeru *v* 惚れます, 惚れる: **... ni hore(komi)másu** …に惚れ(込み)ます falls in love (*with*)
horemásu, horéru 掘れます, 掘れる can dig
horenai *v* 惚れない = **horemásen** 惚れません (not fall in love)
horénai *v* 掘れない = **horemásen** 掘れません (cannot dig)
hōrénsō *n* ホウレンソウ・ほうれん草 spinach
horete *v* 惚れて → **horemásu** 惚れます
hórete *v* 掘れて → **horemásu** 掘れます
horí *n* 掘 ditch, moat
   hori-wari *n* 掘(り)割り canal
hóri *v* 掘り → **horimásu** 掘ります [INFINITIVE]
horidashi-mono *n* 掘り出し物 a bargain, a real find, lucky find: **horidashi-mono o sagashimásu** 掘り出し物を探します searches for bargains
horimásu, hóru *v* 掘ります, 掘る digs, carves; excavates
horimásu, hóru *v* 彫ります, 彫る carves
horí-mónó *n* 彫物 a carving, tattoo
hōritsu *n* 法律 law (*legal system*)
   hōritsu-ka *n* 法律家 jurist
hóri ya/wa shinai *v* 堀りや/はしない = **horánai** 掘らない (not dig)
hōrō *n* 放浪 wandering: **~ shimásu** 放浪します wanders, strolls
horobimásu, horobíru *v* 滅びます, 滅びる perish
horoboshimásu, horobósu *v* 滅ぼします, 滅ぼす destroy
hōrókú *n* 焙烙 [BOOKISH] earthenware pan
hóru *v* 掘る = **horimásu** 掘ります(digs)
hóru *v* 彫る = **horimásu** 彫ります(carves)
hórun *n* ホルン horn (*music*)
hōsaku *n* 方策 measures, policy
hōsaku *n* 豊作 abundant/rich harvest: **kotoshi wa hōsaku desu** 今年は豊作です We have abundant crops this year.
hosánai *v* 干さない = **hoshimásen** 干しません (not dry it)
hóseba *v* 干せば (if one dries it) → **hoshimásu** 干します
hōseki *n* 宝石 jewel, gem
   hōseki-shō *n* 宝石商 jeweler, gem dealer
   hōseki-bako *n* 宝石箱 jewel box
hosemásu, hoséru *v* 干せます, 干せる can dry it
hosénai *v* 干せない = **hosemásen** 干せません (cannot dry it)

hósete *v* 干せて → **hosemásu** 干せます
hōshanō *n* 放射能 radioactivity
hōshasen *n* 放射線 (nuclear) radiation
hoshi *n* 星 star
   hoshi-jírushi *n* 星印 star (*symbol*), asterisk (*)
   hoshi-uranai *n* 星占い astrology
   hoshi-zora *n* 星空 starry sky
hóshi *v* 干し → **hoshimásu** 干します [INFINITIVE]
hōshi *n* 奉仕 service: **~ shimásu** 奉仕します serves, gives one's service
   hōshi-katsudō *n* 奉仕活動 voluntary service, voluntary activity
hōshi *n* 胞子 spore(s)
hoshigarimásu, hoshigáru *v* 欲しがります, 欲しがる wants it
hoshíi *v* 欲しい is desired/desirable; desires, wants, would like, wishes
hoshimásu, hósu *v* 干します, 干す dries it; airs it
hōshin *n* 方針 policy, course (*of action*), aim (*direction*)
hōshin *n* 疱疹 (*medical*) herpes
hōshin *n* 放心 absent-mindedness: **hōshin jōtai** 放心状態 is lost in abstraction
hóshi (ta) *adj* 干し(た) dried
   hoshi-búdō *n* 干しブドウ[葡萄] raisin(s)
   hoshi-gaki *n* 干し柿 dried persimmons
   hoshi-kusa *n* 干(し)草 hay, dried plant
   hoshi-mono *n* 干(し)物 drying washed clothes, dried clothes
hóshite *v* 干して → **hoshimásu** 干します
hóshi ya/wa shinai *v* 干しや/はしない = **hosánai** 干さない (not dry it)
hoshō *n* 保証 guarantee, warranty: **hoshō´-sho** 保証書 letter of guarantee
hoshō *n* 補償 compensating: **~ shimásu** 補償します compensates, indemnifies
   hoshō´-kin 補償金 compensation (*money*), indemnity
hōshoku *n* 飽食 full feeding: **hōshoku no jidai** 飽食の時代 age of plenty
hōshoku *n* 宝飾 jewelry: **hōshoku-hin** 宝飾品 jewelry goods
hóshu *n* 保守 maintenance, upkeep: **~ shimásu** 保守します maintains, preserves
   hoshu-ha *n* 保守派 conservative wing
   hoshu-teki (na) *adj* 保守的(な) conservative: **hoshu-teki na kangae** 保守的な考え conservative thinking/view
hóshu *n* 捕手 catcher
hōshū *n* 報酬 reward: **hōshū o emásu** 報酬を得ます gets a reward
hōshutsu *n* 放出 emission: **~ shimásu** 放出します emits
hōsō *n* 放送 broadcasting: **hōsō´-kyoku** 放送局 broadcasting station: **~ shimásu** 放送します broadcasts
hōsō *n* 包装 packing, wrapping: **~ shimásu** 包装します packs, wraps
   hōsō´-butsu *n* 包装物 package, packet: **kogata**

(no) hōsō´-butsu 小型(の)包装物 small packet
  hōsō´-shi n 包装紙 package, wrapper
hosói adj 細い slender; narrow; thin
hōsoku n 法則 rule(s), law(s)
hosomichi n 細道 lane, path, narrow road: **"Oku
  no Hosomichi"** 「奥の細道」 "The Narrow Road
  to the Interior"
hosonagái adj 細長い long and slender/narrow
hossa n 発作 attack, seizure: **shinzō-hossa** 心臓発
  作 heart attack
hósu v 干す = **hoshimásu** 干します (dries it)
hō´su n ホース hose
hósutesu n ホステス hostess
hósuto n ホスト host
hōtai n 包帯 bandage: **hōtai o makimásu** 包帯を
  巻きます applies a bandage
hotaru n ホタル・蛍 lightning bug, firefly:
  hotaru-no-hikari 1. ホタルの光 gleam of fireflies
  2. 「ほたるの光」 "Auld Lang Syne"
hotaté-gai n ホタテガイ・帆立貝 scallop(s)
hōtei n 法廷 law court
hōteishiki n 方程式 equation
hōten n 法典 code law
hóteru n ホテル hotel: **ichiryū hoteru** 一流ホテル
  first-class hotel
hōtō n 放蕩 [BOOKISH] debauchery: **hōtō-musuko**
  放蕩息子 prodigal son
hotobashiru v ほとばしる gush: **hotobashiru-
  kanjō** ほとばしる感情 outpouring of emotion
Hotoke(-sámá) n 仏(様) Buddha (= **budda** 仏陀)
hotóndo adv ほとんど almost (all), nearly; almost
  all the time; [+ NEGATIVE verb] hardly (ever),
  seldom
hototógisu n ホトトギス・時鳥・不如帰 (little)
  cuckoo
hottan n 発端 beginning, onset: **koto no hottan
  wa...** 事の発端は… It all starts with…
hotte/hótte oku v ほって/放っておく leaves
  alone, let alone: **(watashi-no-koto wa) hótte oite
  kudasai** (私のことは)放っておいて下さい Leave
  me alone.
hotto doggu n ホットドッグ hot dog
hotto kēki n ホットケーキ pancake
hótto (na) adj ホット(な) hot: **hótto na wadai**
  ホットな話題 hot topic
hotto purēto n ホットプレート hot plate
hotto rain n ホットライン hotline
hóttó-shimásu (-suru) v ほっとします(する)
  breathes a sigh of relief
hōwa n 飽和 saturation, impregnation: ~ **shimásu**
  飽和します is saturated
  hōwa-jōtai 飽和状態 saturated state
hoyō n 保養 rest, recuperation: **me no hoyō** 目の
  保養 feast for the eyes
hu... ふ...・フ... → **fu...**
hyak-kái n 百回 a hundred times
hyakka-jíten n 百科事典 encyclopedia
hyakká-ten n 百貨店 department store (= **depáto**
  デパート)

hyákkanichi n 百か日 a memorial service 100
  days after the death
hyakú n 百・100 hundred
  hyakú-do n 百度 **1.** a hundred times (= **hyak-kái**
  百回): **(o-)hyaku-do-mairi** (お)百度参り walking
  back and forth a hundred times before a shrine
  offering a prayer each time **2.** a hundred degrees
  hyakú-doru n 百ドル a hundred dollars: **hyaku
  dorú-satsu** 百ドル札 a hundred-dollar bill
  hyaku en-dama n 百円玉 hundred yen coin
  hyaku-mán n 百万・1,000,000 one million
  hyakú-nen n 百年 100 years; a century (= **hyaku
  nén kan** 百年間)
  hyaku-nichi-seki n 百日咳 pertussis (cough)
  hyakushō n 百姓 (**o-hyakushō** お百姓) farmer
hyappatsu-hyakuchū n 百発百中 hitting the
  mark ten times out of ten: ~ **shimásu** 百発百中し
  ます hits the mark ten times out of ten
hyō n 表 table, schedule, list: **hyō ni shimásu**
  表にします lists
hyō´ n ヒョウ・豹 leopard
hyō´ n ひょう・雹 hail (= **arare** あられ・霰)
hyō´ n 票 vote: **hyō o tōjiru** 票を投じる votes,
  casts a vote
hyōban n 評判 reputation, fame: **hyōban no** 評判の
  famous, popular: **hyōban ga ii** 評判がいい money
  is on: **hyōban ga warui** 評判が悪い have a bad
  reputation
hyōdai n 表題・標題 title (of book, article, e-mail...)
hyō´ga n 氷河 glacier: **hyō´ga-ki** 氷河期 ice age:
  shūshoku hyō´ga-ki 就職氷河期 hard times for
  college-graduate job seekers
hyōgén n 表現 expression (words): ~ **shimásu**
  表現します expresses
hyōgo n 標語 slogan; motto
Hyō´go n 兵庫 Hyogo
hyōgu-ya n 表具屋 paper-hanger/-repairer,
  picture-framer
hyōhen n 豹変 [BOOKISH] sudden change: ~ **shimásu**
  豹変します changes one's spots completely
hyōhyō to adv ひょうひょうと aloof from the
  world: ~ **shiteimásu** ひょうひょうとしています
  is free as the wind
hyōjō´ n 表情 expression (on face): **hyōjō´ o
  yawaragemásu** 表情を和らげます softens one's
  expression
hyōjun n 標準 standard
  hyōjun-go n 標準語 standard Japanese (language)
hyō´ka n 評価 grade, opinion, appraisal: **hito no
  hyō´ka o kinishimasen** 人の評価を気にしません
  does not worry about what others think of
hyōkin (na) adj ひょうきん(な) funny, comical:
  hyōkin-mono ひょうきん者 a ham
hyokkori adv ひょっこり accidentally, by chance:
  hyokkori arawaremásu ひょっこり現れます
  appears unexpectedly
hyokohyoko adv ひょこひょこ lightly
hyōmén n 表面 surface: **hyōmen-chōryoku** 表面
  張力 surface tension

hyōri *n* 表裏 two faces: **hyōri-ittai** 表裏一体 two sides of the same coin: **hyōri-no-aru...** 表裏のある... two-faced

hyōron *n* 評論 criticism, comment(ary): **~ shimásu** 評論します criticizes, comments on, reviews

hyōron-ka *n* 評論家 critic, commentator, reviewer;

hyōryū *n* 漂流 drift: **~ shimásu** 漂流します drifts

hyōshi´ *n* 表紙 cover (*book, magazine, etc.*)

hyōshiki *n* 標識 sign, mark(er): **kōtsū-hyō´shiki** 交通標識 traffic sign; **dōro-hyō´shiki** 道路標識 road sign

hyōshinuke *n* 拍子抜け having the wind taken out of one's sails: **~ shimásu** 拍子抜けします suddenly feels it is pointless

hyōshō *n* 表彰 official commendation: **hyōshō-jō** 表彰状 certificate of commendation: **hyōshō-shiki** 表彰式 awarding ceremony

hyōtán *n* 瓢箪 gourd: **hyōtán kara koma** 瓢箪から駒 produces an unexpected dividend

hyōten *n* 評点 evaluation score, grade

hyōten *n* 氷点 freezing point

hyōtto-shite *adv* ひょっとして by any chance, maybe, possibly, could be. (= **hyotto-shitára** ひょっとしたら, **hyotto-suru to** ひょっとすると)

hyō´zan *n* 氷山 iceberg: **hyō´zan no ikkaku** 氷山の一角 tip of the iceberg

hyū´zu *n* ヒューズ fuse: **hyū´zu ga tobimásu** ヒューズがとびます blows out

I

i *n* 胃 = **i-búkuro** 胃袋 stomach

i-búkuro *n* 胃袋 [BOOKISH] stomach

i-chō *n* 胃腸 [BOOKISH] stomach and intestines

i-gan *n* 胃癌 (*medical*) stomach cancer

i-káiyō *n* 胃潰瘍 (*medical*) (*gastric*) ulcer

i-... *prefix* 医... medicine, medical, doctoring

í-gaku *n* 医学 medicine, medical science/studies: **igaku-sei** 医学生 medical student

í-gaku-bu *n* 医学部 medical department

i-sha *n* 医者 (**o-isha(-san/sama)** お医者(さん/様)) doctor, physician

...-i *suffix* ...医 doctor, (= **senmón-i** 専門医) medical specialist

...-i *suffix* ... 位 rank, grade

ian *n* 慰安 consolation, comfort; recreation

ibarimásu, ibáru *v* 威張ります, 威張る is/acts arrogant, haughty; swaggers

ibikí *n* いびき snore: **ibikí o kakimásu** いびきをかきます snores

ibo *n* 異母 different mother: **ibo-kyōdai** 異母兄弟 half brother(s): **ibo-shimai** 異母姉妹 half sister(s)

ibuningu-doresu *n* イブニングドレス evening dress

ibushimásu, ibusu *v* いぶします, いぶす smokes, fumigates, fumes

ibutsu *n* 異物 [BOOKISH] exogenous material, foreign body

ibutsu *n* 遺物 relics, artifact

icha *v* [INFORMAL] いちゃ = **ité wa** いては

ichí *n* 一・1 one: **ichí ka bachi ka** 一か八か all or nothing: [IDIOM] **ichí o kiite jū o shiru** 一を聞いて十を知る A word is enough to a wise man.

ichí-ban (no) *adj* 一番(の) number one; first

ichí-banme (no) *adj* 一番目(の) first

ichí-bu *n* 一部 a part, portion; a copy (*of a book*)

ichí-byō *n* 一秒 a second (*1/60 minute*)

ichí-dai *n* 一台 one (machine, vehicle)

ichi-danraku *n* 一段落 one stage: **~ shimásu** 一段落します completes one stage

ichi-dó *n* 一度 one time (= **ik-kái** 一回, **íp-pen** 一遍)

ichí-do *n* 一度 one degree

ichi-en *n* 一円 one yen

ichi-go *n* 一語 one word

ichí-ji *n* 一時 **1.** one o'clock **2.** **ichí-ji (no)** 一時(の) at one-time, once, temporary: **ichiji-shinogi** 一時しのぎ makeshift

ichi-jitsú *n* 一日 one day; someday (= **aru hi** ある日, **ichi-nichí** 一日)

ichí-mai *n* 一枚 a sheet; one sheet (*flat things*): **ichimai-uwate** 一枚上手 is a cut above

ichí-mei *n* 一名 [BOOKISH] one person (= **hitóri** 一人)

ichí-nen *n* 一年 the year 1; one year (= **ichi nén-kan** 一年間): **ichi nén-sei** 一年生 first-year student, freshman

ichi-nichí *n* 一日 one day: **ichi nichi-jū** 一日中 all day long

ichí-wa *n* 一羽 one (*bird, rabbit*)

ichí-wari *n* 一割 ten percent

íchi *n* 位置 position, location, situation

íchi(bá) *n* 市(場) market, marketplace: **boro-ichi** ぼろ[ボロ]市 rag fair

ichi-ban *n* 一番 most: **ichiban íi/warui** 一番いい/悪い best/worst

ichibu-shijū *n* 一部始終 all the details: **ichibu-shijū o katarimásu** 一部始終を語ります tells the whole story

ichidō *n* 一同 all (*who are concerned/present*)

Ichi-gatsú *n* 一月・1月 January (= **Shōgatsú** 正月)

ichigo *n* いちご・イチゴ・苺 strawberry

ichigo-ichie *n* 一期一会 [IDIOM] once in a lifetime chance

ichii *n* いちい・イチイ yew

ichi-ichi *adv* いちいち one by one, one after another, each time

ichi-ichi ga ichi, in-ichi ga ichi *interj* 1×1が1 One times one equals one.

ichí-in *n* 一員 a member

ichí-in *n* 一因 a cause

ichíjiku *n* イチジク・無花果 fig: **ichíjiku-no-ki** いちじくの木 fig tree

ichijirushíi *adj* 著しい [BOOKISH] conspicuous, prominent, remarkable, striking

ichijirúshiku *adv* 著しく [BOOKISH] conspicuously, prominently, remarkably, strikingly

ichiji-teki (na) *adj* 一時的(な) temporary

ichi-mán *n* 一万・10,000 ten thousand

ichi-mi *n* 一味 accomplice: **tōzokudan no ichi-mi** 盗賊団の一味 member(s) of a robber band

ichiō *adv* 一応・いちおう as far as it goes, to some extent, just in case, tentatively

ichi-rei *n* 一例 an example: **ichi-rei o agemásu** 一例を挙げます takes an example

ichiryū *adj* 一流(の) first-rate, topflight, elite: **ichiryū no kashu** 一流の歌手 superb singer; **ichiryū no hitobito** 一流の人々 topflight people

ichō *n* イチョウ・銀杏 gingko (*tree*)

idai (na) *adj* 偉大(な) great: **idai na hito/jinbutsu** 偉大な人(物) great person

iden *n* 遺伝 heredity
iden-shi *n* 遺伝子 gene

ideorogii *n* イデオロギー ideology

í(do) *n* 井(戸) a well: [IDIOM] **í no naka no kaeru/ kawazu** 井の中の蛙 a person who does not know much of the world

ído *n* 緯度 latitude

ie *interj* いえ (= **iie** いいえ) no

ié *v* 言え → **iemásu** 言えます **1.** [INFINITIVE] **2.** [IMPERATIVE] (say it!) → **iimásu** 言います

ié *n* 家 a house, a home

iéba *v* 言えば = **iya** 言や (if one says) → **iimásu** 言います

ie-dé *n* 家出 running away from home: ~ **shimásu** 家出します runs away
iede-nin *n* 家出人 a runaway

iemásu, ieru *v* 言えます、言える can say/tell

iemásu, iéru *v* 癒えます、癒える heals

ierō-pēji *n* イエローページ Yellow Pages

Iesu (Kirisuto) *n* イエス (キリスト) Jesus Christ

íga *n* 衣蛾 clothes moth

ígai (na) *adj* 意外(な) unexpected: **ígai na ketsumatsu** 意外な結末 unexpected ending
ígai ni *adv* 意外(に) unexpectedly

(…) ígai *suffix* (…)以外 outside (of …), except (*for*) …

igen *n* 威厳 dignity: **igen o tamochimásu** 威厳を保ちます keep one's dignity

ígi *n* 意義 [BOOKISH] significance, sense, meaning: **ígi no aru shigoto** 意義のある仕事 meaningful work

ígi *n* 異議 [BOOKISH] objection: (*in the court*) **ígi ari** 異議あり! I object! Objection!

Igirisu *n* イギリス England (= **Eikoku** 英国): **Igirisú-jin** イギリス人 an English person

ígo *n* 囲碁 the board game *Go* (= **gó** 碁)

(…) ígo *suffix* (…)以後 afterward, from … on (= (…) **ikō** (…)以降)

igokochi *n* 居心地 feeling of staying: **igokochi ga ii** 居心地がいい feels comfortable while staying: **igokochi ga warui** 居心地が悪い feels ill at ease

iguana *n* イグアナ iguana

igyō *n* 偉業 great achievement: **igyō o nashi-togemásu** 偉業を成し遂げます accomplishes a great achievement

ihan *n* 違反 violation, offense: **kōtsū-ihan** 交通違反 traffic violation: (… **ni**) **ihan shimásu** (…に)違反します violates, offends (*against*) …

ii *v* い → **imásu** います (is, stays): **1.** [INFINITIVE] **2. iró (yo)** いろ(よ) = **i yo** いよ [IMPERATIVE] (stay here!)

íi *adj* いい good; OK, right, correct (= **yoi** 良い): [NEGATIVE] **yóku arimasén** 良くありません; [PAST] **yókatta desu** 良かったです

íi-hito *n* いい人 **1.** a good person **2.** sweetheart, lover

ii-arawashimásu, ii-arawásu *v* 言い表(わ)します、言い表(わ)す expresses, puts into words

iie *interj* いいえ no

ii-kaemasu, ii-kaéru *v* 言い換えます、言い換える rephrases, puts/says it another way

ii-kagen *adj* **1.** いい加減 rather, pretty, moderate **2. ii-kagen na** いい加減(な) random, perfunctory, halfhearted, indifferent, vague, haphazard

ii-kata *n* 言い方 way of saying/telling/putting it, expression

íimasén *v* 言いません = **iwanai** 言わない not say

iimáshita *v* 言いました = **itta** 言った said

iimásu, iu/yū *v* 言います、言う(ゆう) says, tells; expresses

íin *n* 委員 committee member(s)
iin-kai *n* 委員会 committee

ii-tai *v* 言いたい wants to say: **ii-tai kotó** 言いたいこと[事] what one wants to say; **ii-tai hō´dai** 言いたい放題 says whatever one wants/feels

ii-tsukemásu, ii-tsukéru *v* 言い付けます、言い付ける commands, orders; tells on, tattles on (= **tsugeguchi-shimásu** 告げ口します)

ii-wake *n* 言い訳 explanation, excuse: **ii-wake o shinaidekudasai.** 言い訳をしないで下さい Please don't give an excuse.

íi ya/wa shinai *v* 言いや/はしない、**íya shinai** 言やしない = **iwanai** 言わない (not say)

iji *n* 意地 temper, disposition: **iji ga warúi** 意地が悪い, **iji-waru** 意地悪 ill-tempered, mean (-spirited)

iji *n* 維持 maintenance, upkeep, support: ~ **shimásu** 維持します maintains, supports

ijí-hi *n* 維持費 upkeep (*expense*)

ijime 1. *n* いじめ teasing, torment **2.** *v* → **ijimemásu** いじめます [INFINITIVE]

ijimek-ko *n* いじめっ子 bully

ijimemásu, ijimeru *v* いじめます、いじめる teases, torments

ijō 1. *n* 異状/異常 something unusual/wrong (*the*

matter), abnormality: **ijō-kishō** 異常気象 abnormal climate

ijō na *adj* 異常(な) abnormal; unusual; remarkable

(…) íjō n, *suffix* (…)以上 above, over, upwards of; the above; that's it! (*end of message/speech*) = thank you (*for your attention*): **íjō desu** 以上です That's all.

ijū n 移住 emigration, immigration: **~ shimásu** 移住します emigrates, immigrates

ijū-sha n 移住者 emigrant, immigrant (= **imin** 移民)

ika n イカ cuttlefish, squid: **ika-sumi (supagetii)** イカ墨(スパゲティ) squid ink (spaghetti)

(…) íka n, *suffix* (…)以下 below (…), less than …: **íka no tōri desu** 以下の通りです as (*described*) below, as follows

ikada n 筏 raft

ikága *adv* いかが how (about it)? [DEFERENTIAL] (= **dō´** どう): **chōshi wa ikága desuka?** 調子はいかがですか? How's it going?

ikagawashíi *adj* いかがわしい suspicious, questionable, shady: **ikagawashíi uwasa** いかがわしい噂 suspicious rumours

ika-hodo *adj* いかほど how many? (= **íkura** いく[幾]ら); how ...? (= **dono-gurai (-kurai)** どの位)

ikan n 遺憾 regret: **ikan nágara …** 遺憾ながら … I regret that …, Unfortunately …

ikanai ν 行かない = **ikimasén** 行きません (not go)

ikaremásu, ikareru ν 行かれます, 行かれる **1.** can go (= **ikemásu** 行けます) **2.** [PASSIVE] have them go (*to one's distress*); [HONORIFIC] goes (= **irasshaimásu** いらっしゃいます)

ikari n 錨 anchor

ikarí n 怒り anger: **ikarí o shizumemásu** 怒りを静めます calms the anger

ikasemásu, ikaseru ν 行かせます, 行かせる sends (*a person*); lets (*a person*) go

ikashimásu, ikásu ν 生かします, 生かす **1.** lets/makes it live, brings life to, enlivens; keeps it alive; revives **2.** makes the most of, makes good use of

iké ν 行け **1.** → **ikemásu** 行けます [INFINITIVE] **2.** [IMPERATIVE] (go!) → **ikimásu** 行きます

iké n 池 pond

íke ν 生[活]け → **ikemásu** 生[活]けます [INFINITIVE]

ikéba ν 行けば = [INFORMAL] **ikya** 行きゃ (if one goes) → **ikimásu** 行きます

ikébana n 生け花 [活花] flower arrangement

ikégaki n 生(け)垣 hedge

ikemasén, ikenai ν いけません, いけない **1.** it won't do; you mustn't; don't **2.** (*that's*) too

ikemasén, ikenai ν 行けません, 行けない (= **ikaremasén** 行かれません, **ikarenai** 行かれない) cannot go

ikemasén, ikenai ν 生[活]けません, 生[活]けない not arrange flowers

ikemásu, ikeru ν 行けます, 行ける = **ikaremásu** 行かれます, **ikareru** 行かれる can go

ikemásu, ikéru ν 生[活]けます, 生[活]ける arranges (flowers)

íken n 意見 opinion, idea: **go-íken** ご意見 (*your/ someone else's*) opinion [HONORIFIC]

íken n 違憲 constitutional violation

ikenai ν いけない = **ikemásén** いけません (it it won't do; you mustn't; don't)

ikenai ν 行けない = **ikemásén** 行けません (cannot go)

ikénai ν 生[活]けない = **ikemásén** 生[活]けません (not arrange flowers)

ike(ra)remásu, ike(ra)réru ν 生[活]け(ら)れます, **ike(ra)réru** 生[活]け(ら)れる can arrange (*flowers*)

ikéreba ν 生[活]ければ (if one arranges flowers) → **ikemásu** 生[活]けます

ikete ν 生[活]けて → **ikemásu** 生[活]けます

íkete ν 生[活]けて → **ikemásu** 生[活]けます

iki (na) *adj* 粋(な) smart, stylish

iki ν 行き → **ikimásu** 行きます [INFINITIVE]

íki n 息 breath: **íki o shimásu** 息をします breathes **iki-gire** n 息切れ shortness of breath: **hashitta ato ni iki-gire ga shimásu** 走った後に息切れがします gets out of breath after running

iki-gurushii *adj* 息苦しい stuffy

íki ν 生き → **ikimásu** 生きます [INFINITIVE]

…-iki (no) *suffix* …行き(の) bound for …

ikidōri n 憤り indignation, resentment

ikidōrimásu, ikidō´ru ν 憤ります, 憤る gets indignant, resents

ikigai n 生き甲斐 something to live for: **ikigai o kanjimásu** 生き甲斐を感じます feels one's life is worth living, feels alive

ikimásu, iku ν 行きます, 行く goes

ikimásu, ikíru ν 生きます, 生きる lives

ikímono n 生き物 living thing(s), animal(s), creature(s)

ikínai ν 生きない = **ikimásu** 生きません (not live)

ikiói n 勢い energy: **ikiói yóku** 勢いよく energetically

ikíreba 生きれば = [INFORMAL] **ikírya** 生きりゃ (if one lives) → **ikimásu** 生きます

ikíru ν 生きる = **ikimásu** 生きます (lives)

ikisatsu n いきさつ details, circumstances, complexities; complications

iki-tai ν 行きたい wants to go

iki-tai ν 生きたい wants to live

íkite ν 生きて → **ikimásu** 生きます (lives): **íkite imásu** 生きています is alive

ikí wa/ya shinai ν 行きは/やしない, [INFORMAL] **ikyashinai** 行きゃしない = **ikanai** 行かない (not go)

íki wa/ya shinai ν 生きは/やしない, [INFORMAL] **íkya shinai** 生きゃしない = **ikínai** 生きない (not live)

iki-yasúi *adj* 行きやすい accessible, easy to get to

iki-zumarimásu ν 行き詰まります, **iki-zumáru** 行き詰まる gets bogged down

ik-kai n 一階 one floor/story; first floor, ground floor

ik-kái (no) *n, adj* 一回（の）one time, once (= **ichi-dó** 一度）

ikkansei *n* 一貫性 consistency: **hanashi ni ikkansei ga arimásu** 話に一貫性があります has consistency in one's talk

ík-ken *n* 一軒 one house/building (*counter for buildings*)

ík-ken *n* 一件 one case/matter: **ik-ken-rakuchaku** 一件落着 The case is closed.

ík-ki ni *adv* 一気に with a gulp, with a dash, with a burst

ík-ko *n* 一個 one (*piece, small object*) (= **hitótsu** ひとつ・一つ)

ik-ko *n* 一戸 a house, a household: **ik-ko-date** 一戸建て detached house

ik-kō *n* 一考 consideration: **~ shimásu** 一考します considers

ik-kō (ni)... *adv* 一向（に）... [+ NEGATIVE] not at all, never: **ik-kō ni kamaimasen** 一向に構いません I don't mind at all.

ik-kyoku *n* 一曲 a piece of music, a song, a tune: **ik-kyoku utaimásu** 一曲歌います sings a song

ik-kyoku *n* 一局 a game ((i)go (*the board game Go*) and/or shōgi (*Japanese chess*)): **(i)go o ik-kyoku uchimásu** (囲)碁を一局打ちます plays a game of (i)go: **shōgi o ik-kyoku sashimásu** 将棋を一局指します plays a game of shōgi

ik-kyo-ryōtoku *n* 一挙両得 [IDIOM] Kill two birds with one stone. (= **is-seki-nichō** 一石二鳥）

ik-kyū *n* 一級 first class

ikō´ *v* 行こう = **ikimashō´** 行きましょう (let's go!)

ikō´ *v* 憩おう = **ikoimásu** 憩います (rests and relaxes)

ikō *n* 意向 one's mind, inclination, intention; one's views

(…) íkō *suffix* （…）以降 afterward, from … on (= (…) **ígo** （…）以後）

ikoi *n* 憩い rest and relaxation: **ikoi no ba(sho)** 憩いの場(所) recreation area: **ikoimásu** 憩います rests and relaxes

ikoku *n* 異国 foreign countries
ikoku-jōcho (no) *adj* 異国情緒（の）exotic

ikon *n* 遺恨 grudge

ikotsu *n* 遺骨 remains (*of person*)

iku *v* 行く = **ikimásu** 行きます (goes)

íku-... *prefix* いく・幾 … = **nán-...** 何… how many …

ikudōon (ni) *adv* 異口同音（に）unanimously

ikuji *n* 育児 child care: **ikuji-kyūka** 育児休暇 child-care leave

ikuji-nashi *n* 意気地なし coward, chicken: **ikuji (no/ga) nai** 意気地(の/が)ない is a coward, cowardly

ikura *n* イクラ salmon roe (*caviar*)

íkura *n* いくら (**o-ikura** おいくら) how much: **Oikura desu ka?** おいくらですか? How much is it?; **íkura ka** いくらか some, a little; **íkura mo** いくらも ever so much, [+ NEGATIVE] not very much; **íkura de mo** いくらでも a lot, as much as you like

ikusa *n* 戦 war (= **sensō** 戦争）

ikusei *n* 育成 fosterage, nourishment: **~ shimásu** 育成します fosters, nourishes

íkutsu *n* いくつ (**o-ikutsu** おいくつ) how many; how old: **O-ikutsu desu ka?** おいくつですか? "How old are you?" *or* "How many do you want?"; **íkutsu-ka** いくつか several, a number of; **íkutsu mo** いくつも ever so many, [+ NEGATIVE] not very many; **íkutsu de mo** いくつでも as many as you like

ikya *v* [INFORMAL] 行きゃ → **ikéba** 行けば

imá *n* 居間 living room (*Western-style*)

íma *n* 今 now, this time. **íma wa** 今は at present; **ima no tokoró wa** 今のところは for the time being, so far; **ima goro wa** 今ごろは about this time
ima-máde *adv* 今まで until now, up to the present (time)
íma-ni *adv* 今に before long, soon, by and by, presently: **íma-ni mo** 今にも at any moment
ima-sara *adv* 今さら at this point

ima-da ni *adv* 未だに still (= **mada** まだ）

imásu, iru *v* います, いる is, stays

imásu, íru *v* 射ます, 射る shoots

imḗji *n* イメージ (*psychological/social*) image (= **gazō** 画像): **imḗji torēningu** イメージトレーニング image training

iiméru *n* Eメール e-mail (= **mēru** メール）

ími *n* 意味 meaning: **... to iu ími desu** …という意味です, **... o ími shimásu** …を意味します it means …

imin *n* 移民 immigrant(s)/emigrant(s)

imó *n* イモ・芋 (**o-imo** お芋) yam; potato

imó *n* いも dork, country bumpkin (= **inaka-mono** 田舎者）

í mo shinai *v* いもしない, **í ya shinai** いやしない not stay/be; not even/also stay or be

imōtó *n* 妹 younger sister: **imōto-san** 妹さん (your) younger sister

inabíkari *n* 稲光 lightning

inada *n* イナダ baby yellowtail (*cf.* **hamachi** はまち・ハマチ, **buri** ブリ・鰤）

inai *v* いない = **imasén** いません (not stay)

(…) ínai *suffix* （…）以内 within

inaka *n* 田舎 country(side); one's home area (*hometown*): **inaka no** 田舎の rural; **inaka-mono** 田舎者 country bumpkin (= **imó** いも）

inarí-zushi *n* いなり鮨[寿司] sushi in a bag of *aburage* (fried bean-curd) (= **o-inari san** お稲荷さん）

inázuma *n* イナズマ・稲妻 lightning

inbō *n* 陰謀 [BOOKISH] dark plot(s), intrigue(s)

(…-)ínchi *suffix* （…）インチ inch(es)

ínchiki (na) *adj* いんちき（な）fake, fraud(ulent): **ínchiki na shōbai** いんちきな商売 fraud business

inchō *n* 院長 hospital head/director

Indian *n* インディアン (*American*) Indian, native American

Indo *n* インド India
Indó-jin *n* インド人 Indian (*from India*)

Indonéshia *n* インドネシア Indonesia
Indoneshia-go *n* インドネシア語 Indonesian
(*language*)
Indoneshiá-jin *n* インドネシア人 an Indonesian
íne *n* 稲 rice plant: **ine-kari** 稲刈り harvesting rice
inemúri-shimásu (suru) *v* 居眠りします(する)
dozes off
infomēshon *n* インフォメーション information
infure *n* インフレ inflation
infuruénza *n* インフルエンザ flu, influenza
íngen, ingénmame *n* インゲン・いんげん、イン
ゲンマメ・いんげん豆 kidney beans, French beans
ín(kan) *n* 印（鑑）[BOOKISH] seal, stamp (= **hán** 判,
hankó 判子)
inkei *n* 陰茎 penis [FORMAL, MEDICAL TERM]
(= **chínchin** ちんちん, **o-chínchin** おちんちん)
inki (na) *adj* 陰気(な) gloomy, glum
ínku, ínki *n* インク, インキ ink
ínku-jetto *n* インクジェット ink jet: **ínku-jetto
purintā** インクジェットプリンター inkjet printer
ínochi *n* 命 one's life (= **séimei** 生命)
inorí *n* 祈り (**o-inori** お祈り) prayer
inóri *v* 祈り → **inorimásu** 祈ります [INFINITIVE]
inorimásu, inóru *v* 祈ります, 祈る prays; wishes
for, hopes for
inpo *n* インポ sexual impotence
inreki *n* 陰暦 the lunar calendar
inryoku *n* 引力 attractive force, gravity
inryō-sui *n* 飲料水 drinking water (= **inyō-sui**
飲用水)
insatsu *n* 印刷 printing: **insatsú-butsu** 印刷物
printed matter; **insatsu shimásu** 印刷します prints
inshi *n* 印紙 revenue stamp (= **shūnyū-ínshi**
収入印紙)
inshō *n* 印象 impression
inshō-teki (na) *adj* 印象的(な) impressive
inshoku *n* 飲食 drinking and eating
inshoku-ten *n* 飲食店 restaurant(s) (= **resutoran**
レストラン)
inshuō *n* 飲酒 drinking: **inshu-unten** 飲酒運転
driving after drinking
insū-bunkai *n* 因数分解 factorization
insutanto *n* インスタント instant: **insutanto
kōhii** インスタントコーヒー instant coffee:
insutanto rāmen インスタントラーメン instant
noodles
insutorakutā *n* インストラクター instructor
insutōru *n* インストール install (*on computer*):
~ **shimásu** インストールします installs
intabyū *n* インタビュー interview: **intabyū-kiji**
インタビュー記事 interview article
intāchenji *n* インターチェンジ highway
interchange(s)
intāhai *n* インターハイ interscholastic athletic
meet
intāhon *n* インターホン intercom
intai *n* 引退 retirement: ~ **shimásu** 引退します
retires
intān *n* インターン intern

intānashonaru *n* インターナショナル
international
intānetto *n* インターネット Internet
intānetto-kafe *n* インターネットカフェ Internet
cafe (= **netto-kafe** ネットカフェ)
intānetto-tsūhan *n* インターネット通販 (= **netto
tsūhan** ネット通販) online shopping, internet
shopping
intān-shippu *n* インターンシップ internship
interi *n* インテリ intellectual; highbrow
interia *n* インテリア interior (*accessory*)
inú *n* イヌ・犬 dog: **inú-goya** 犬小屋 kennel
Inu-doshi *n* 戌年 year of the Dog
in'yō *n* 引用 quoting, quotation: ~ **shimásu** 引用し
ます quotes
in'yō *n* 陰陽 yin and yang
inyō-sui *n* 飲用水 drinking water (= **inryō-sui**
飲料水)
inzei *n* 印税 royalties (*from one's book(s)*)
iō *v* 言おう = **iimashō** 言いましょう (let's say it!)
íppai *n* いっぱい fully, full of; many, much, lots
(= **takusan** たくさん): **ippai (no)** いっぱい(の)
full, filled
-ippai *suffix* いっぱい whole, entire: **konshū-ippai**
今週いっぱい all this week, whole week
íp-pai *n* 一杯 a cupful, a glassful; a drink: **íp-pai
tsukiattekudasai** 一杯付き合って下さい Please
come have a drink with me.
ip-paku *n* 一泊 one night's lodging/stay: **ippaku-
futsuka** 一泊二日 two-day one-night (trip)
ippan (no) *adj* 一般(の) general, overall
ippan-teki (na/ni) *adj, adv* 一般的(な/に)
general, in general
ip-pén *n* 一遍 one time (= **ichi-dó** 一度, **ik-kái**
一回)
ip-piki *n* 一匹 one (*fish/bug*, *small animal*): **ippiki-
ōkami** 一匹狼 lone wolf
ippin-ryō´ri *n* 一品料理 à la carte dishes
ippō´ *n* 一方 **1.** one side **2. mō ippō´ (de wa)**
もう一方(では) the other side, on the other hand;
but, meanwhile
ippō-tsū´kō *n* 一方通行 one-way (*traffic*,
argument)
íp-pon *n* 一本 one (*pencil/bottle, long thing*),
a point
íp-pun *n* 一分 one minute
irai *n* 依頼 request; dependence, reliance; trust,
commission: ~ **shimásu** 依頼します requests, asks
for, depends/relies (*on*); entrusts, commissions
(...) írai *suffix, conj* (...)以来 (ever) since...
iranai *v* 要らない = **irimasén** 要りません (not need)
iránai *v* 炒らない = **irimasén** 炒りません (not
roast)
iraremásu, irareru *v* いられます, いられる can
stay/be
irasshái いらっしゃい → **irasshaimásu**
いらっしゃいます **1.** *v* [INFINITIVE] **2.** *interj*
= **irasshaimáse** いらっしゃいませ [IMPERATIVE]
(Welcome!)

irasshaimásu, irassháru *v* いらっしゃいます、いらっしゃる [HONORIFIC] **1.** comes (= **kimásu** 来ます) **2.** goes (= **ikimásu** 行きます) **3.** stays, is (= **imásu** います)

iráshite *v* いらして = **irasshátte** いらっしゃって → **irasshaimásu** いらっしゃいます

irásuto *n* イラスト illustration

iré *v* 入れ → **iremásu** 入れます **1.** [INFINITIVE] **2. ire ró** 入れろ、**iré yo** 入れよ [IMPERATIVE] (put it in!)

iréba *v* いれば = [INFORMAL] **irya** いりゃ (if one be/stays) → **imásu** います

iréba *v* 要れば = [INFORMAL] **irya** 要りゃ (if one needs/wants) → **irimásu** 要ります

íre-ba *v* 炒れば (if one roasts) → **irimásu** 炒ります

íre-ba *v* 射れば (if one shoots) → **imásu** 射ます

iremásu, ireru *v* 入れます、入れる puts in, lets in, admits; includes: **o-cha o iremásu** お茶を入れます makes tea; **denwa o iremásu** 電話を入れます puts in a call

  ire-ba *n* 入れ歯 false teeth: **sō-ireba** 総入れ歯 full denture

  ire-mono *n* 入れ物 container

  ire-zumi *n* 入れ墨・刺青 tattoo (= **tatū** タトゥー)

iremásu, íreru *v* 炒れます、炒れる can roast

iremásu, íreru *v* 射れます、射れる can shoot (arrow)

irenai *v* 入れない = **iremasén** 入れません (not put/let in)

irénai *v* 炒れない = **iremasén** 炒れません (cannot roast)

irénai *v* 射れない = **iremasén** 射れません (cannot shoot)

ireréba *v* 入れれば = [INFORMAL] **irerya** 入れりゃ (if one puts/lets in) → **iremásu** 入れます

iréreba *v* 炒れれば = [INFORMAL] **irérya** 炒れりゃ (if one can roast) → **iremásu** 炒れます

iréreba *v* 射れれば = [INFORMAL] **irérya** 射れりゃ (if one can shoot) → **iremásu** 射れます

íreta *v* 入れた = **iremáshita** 入れました (put/let in)

íreta *v* 炒れた = **iremáshita** 炒れました (could roast)

íreta *v* 射れた = **iremáshita** 射れました (could shoot an arrow)

irete *v* 入れて → **iremásu** 入れます

írete *v* 炒れて → **iremásu** 炒れます

írete *v* 射れて → **iremásu** 射れます

ireyō´ *v* 入れよう = **iremashó** 入れましょう (let's put it in!)

iri *v* 要り → **irimásu** 要ります [INFINITIVE]

íri *v* 炒り → **irimásu** 炒ります [INFINITIVE]

iriguchi, irikuchi *n* 入口 entrance

irimásu, iru *v* 要ります、要る is necessary; needs, wants

irimásu, íru *v* 炒ります、炒る roasts

iri-támago *n* 炒り卵 scrambled eggs

irí ya/wa shinai *v* 要りや/はしない = [INFORMAL] **irya shinai** 要りゃしない = **iranai** 要らない (not need)

íri ya/wa shinai *v* 炒りや/はしない = **iránai** 炒らない (not roast)

iri-yō (na) *adj* 入り用(な) needed (= **nyūyō (na)** 入用(な))

iró *n* 色 color; sex

  iro-ai *n* 色合い tone (*coloring*)

  iró-gami *n* 色紙 colored paper

i ró (yo) *v* いろ(よ) [IMPERATIVE] (stay!)

í ro *v* 射ろ = **í yo** 射よ [IMPERATIVE] (shoot!) → **ímásu** 射ます

iroiro (no/na) *adj* いろいろ(の/な) various

ironna ... *adj* いろんな... various

iroppói *adj* 色っぽい erotic

iru *v* いる = **imásu** います (is, stays)

iru *v* 要る = **irimásu** 要ります (needs)

íru *v* 炒る = **irimásu** 炒ります (roasts)

íru *v* 射る = **imásu** 射ます (shoots an arrow)

irya *v* [INFORMAL] いりゃ → **iréba** いれば

irya *v* [INFORMAL] 要りゃ → **iréba** 要れば

írya *v* [INFORMAL] 炒りゃ → **íreba** 炒れば

írya *v* [INFORMAL] 射りゃ → **íreba** 射れば

isé-ebi *n* 伊勢エビ[海老] lobster

isei *n* 異性 (*person of*) the opposite sex: **isei no yūjin** 異性の友人 friend(s) of the opposite sex

isei (ga/no) ii *adj* 威勢(が/の)いい spirited, buckish: **isei ga/no ii uma** 威勢が/のいい馬 dashing horse

iseki *n* 遺跡 remains

iseki *n* 移籍 [BOOKISH] transfer: **~ shimásu** 移籍します transfers

isharyō *n* 慰謝料 compensation/damages for mental suffering: **isharyō o motomemásu** 慰謝料を求めます asks for compensation

ishí *n* 石 stone, rock: **ishi-atama** 石頭 stubborn, hardhead: [IDIOM] **ishí no ue nimo sannen** 石の上にも三年 Perseverance pays in the end.

íshi *n* 意志 will, intention: **ishi-hakujaku** 意志薄弱 having no willpower: **íshi arutokoro ni michi wa aru.** 意志ある所に道はある Where there's a will, there's a way.

íshiki *n* 意識 consciousness: **íshiki o ushinai-másu** 意識を失います loses consciousness, passes out; **íshiki fumei (no)** 意識不明(の) unconscious

íshindenshin (de) *adv* 以心伝心(で) (by) telepathy

ísho *n* 遺書 will

ishō *n* 衣装 costume

íshoku *n* 移植 transplantation: **shinzō-ishoku** 心臓移植 cardiac transplantation

ishokujū *n* 衣食住 food, clothing and shelter

isogashíi *adj* 忙しい busy: **shigoto ga isogashíi** 仕事が忙しい is busy at work

isogí *n* 急ぎ haste

  isogí no *adj* 急ぎの hasty, hurried, urgent

isógi *n* 急ぎ → **isogimásu** 急ぎます [INFINITIVE]

isogimásu, isógu *v* 急ぎます、急ぐ hurries, rushes

isóida *v* 急いだ = **isogimáshita** 急ぎました (hurried, rushed)

isóide *adv* 急いで in a hurry → **isogimásu** 急ぎます

isōrō *n* 居候 freeloader: ~ **shimásu** 居候します freeloads

íssái *adj, adv* 一切 all, everything, without exception: **watashi to wa íssái kankei arimasen** 私とは一切関係ありません It's not my business at all.: **íssái kuchi ni shinaidekudasai** 一切口にしないで下さい Please don't tell anyone.

ís-sai *n* 一歳 one year old (= **hitótsu** 一つ)

issakú- 一昨-: **issakú-ban/-ya** 一昨晩/夜 night before last (= **ototói no ban/yoru** 一昨日の晩/夜); **issakú-jitsu** 一昨日 day before yesterday (= **ototói** 一昨日); **issakú-nen** 一昨年 year before last (= **ototóshi** 一昨年)

is-satsú *n* 一冊 one book (*magazine*)

ís-sei *n* 一世 1. first generation: **nikkei-issei** 日系一世 Issei, first-generation Japanese immigrants 2. … the First: **Erizabesu-issei** エリザベス一世 Elizabeth I 3. one generation: **is-sei ichidai (no)** 一世一代（の）once in a lifetime: **is-sei o fūbi shimásu** 一世を風靡します takes the world by storm, is the rage of the times

is-sei (ni) *adv* 一斉（に）all together

is-seki-nichō *n* 一石二鳥 [IDIOM] Kill two birds with one stone. (= **ikkyo-ryōtoku** 一挙両得)

is-sén *n* 一千・1,000 one thousand (= **sén** 千)

issetsú *n* 一節 passage (*of text*)

isshō *n* 一生 one's whole life: **go-on wa isshō wasuremasen** ご恩は一生忘れません I'll never forget your kindness.

ís-shō *n* 一升 1.8 liters: **isshō´-bin** 一升瓶 a 1.8-liter bottle (*of saké*)

isshō-kénmei (ni) *adv* 一生懸命（に）desperately; very hard

issho (ni) *adv* 一緒（に）together

ís-shu *n* 一種 a kind, a sort

isshun *n* 一瞬 a moment: **isshun no dekigoto** 一瞬の出来事 moment event/happening

isso *adv* いっそ rather, preferably

issō *adv* 一層 all the more…, still/much more …: **issō íi** 一層いい still better

issō *n* 一掃 sweep, cleanup: ~ **shimásu** 一掃します sweeps, cleans up

isu *n* いす・イス・椅子 chair

Isuraeru *n* イスラエル Israel
Isuraeru-jin *n* イスラエル人 Israeli

Isuramu-kyō *n* イスラム教 Islam (= **kaikyō** 回教)
Isuramu-kyōto *n* イスラム教徒 Muslim, Moslem

íta *n* 板 board, plank
ita-choko *n* 板チョコ chocolate bar

itachi *n* イタチ weasel: **itachi-gokko** イタチごっこ vicious circle

itadaite *v* いただいて・頂いて = **itadakimáshite** いただきまして・頂きまして → **itadakimásu** いただきます・頂きます

itadaki *n* 頂 peak, summit (= **chōjō´** 頂上)
itadaki *v* いただき → **itadakimásu** いただきます [INFINITIVE]

itadakimásu, itadaku *v* いただきます、いただく (*I/we humbly*) receive, eat, drink

itade *n* 痛手 damage: **itade o ukemásu** 痛手を受けます gets damage(s)

i-tai *v* いたい wants to stay

itái *adj* 痛い painful, hurting, sore

itamae *n* 板前 chef (*of Japanese food*)

itáme *v* 痛め → **itamemásu** 痛めます 1. [INFINITIVE] 2. **itamé ro** 痛めろ, **itamé yo** 痛めよ [IMPERATIVE] (hurt it!)

itáme *v* 傷め → **itamemásu** 傷めます 1. [INFINITIVE] 2. **itamé ro** 傷めろ, **itamé yo** 傷めよ [IMPERATIVE] (injure it!)

itáme *v* 炒め → **itamemásu** 炒めます 1. [INFINITIVE] 2. **itamé ro** 炒めろ, **itamé yo** 炒めよ [IMPERATIVE] (fries it!)

itamemásu, itaméru *v* 痛めます, 痛める hurts, injures: **kokóro o itamemásu** 心を痛めます worries (*oneself*), grieves

itamemásu, itaméru *v* 傷めます, 傷める damages, spoils it

itamemásu, itaméru *v* 炒めます, 炒める (pan-)fries, sautés: **itame-mono** 炒め物 stir-fry

itamí *v* 痛み → **itamimásu** 痛みます [INFINITIVE] *n* 痛み an ache, a pain

itamí *v* 傷み → **itamimásu** 傷みます [INFINITIVE] *n* 傷み damage

itamimásu, itámu *v* 痛みます, 痛む it aches
itamimásu, itámu *v* 傷みます, 傷む it spoils, rots

itamiwake *n* 痛み[傷み]分け draw caused by injury/injuries in Sumo match

itarimásu, itáru *v* 至ります, 至る arrives (*at*), reaches (*to*), goes/comes (*to*)

Itaria *n* イタリア Italy
Itaria-go *n* イタリア語 Italian (*language*)
Itariá-jin *n* イタリア人 an Italian

itashimásu, itásu *v* 致します, 致す [HUMBLE/DEFERENTIAL] do(es) (= **shimásu** します)

itatte *adv* 至って extremely

itátte *v* 至って → **itarimásu** 至ります

itazura *n* いたずら mischief, prank: **itazura-denwa** いたずら電話 prank call: **itazura (o) shimásu** いたずら（を）します gets into mischief, plays a trick: **Okashi o kurenakya itazurasuruzo!** お菓子をくれなきゃ、いたずらするぞ! Trick or treat! (*Halloween*)
itazurá-kko *n* いたずらっ子 naughty child

itazura ni *adv* いたずらに in vain, for nothing: **itazura ni toki o sugoshimásu** いたずらに時を過ごします spends one's time in idleness

itcha *adv* [INFORMAL] 行っちゃ = **ittéwa** 行っては

itchaimáshita *v* [INFORMAL] 行っちゃいました = **(itte shimaimáshita** 行ってしまいました) = **ikimáshita** 行きました (went)

itchaimáshita *v* [INFORMAL] 言っちゃいました = **itte shimaimáshita** 言ってしまいました = **iimáshita** 言いました (said)

itchaimásu, itchau *v* [INFORMAL] 行っちゃいま

す, 行っちゃう = **itte-shimaimásu, itte-shimau** 行ってしまいます, 行ってしまう will go, goes

itchaimásu, itchau *v* [INFORMAL] 言っちゃいます, 言っちゃう = **itte-shimaimásu, itte-shimau** 言ってしまいます, 言ってしまう will say, says

itchatta *v* [INFORMAL] 行っちゃった = **itte shimatta, itta** 行ってしまった, 行った went

itchatta *v* [INFORMAL] 言っちゃった = **itte shimatta, itta** 言ってしまった, 言った said

ité *v* いて → **imásu** います

ite *n* 射手 archer: **ite-za** 射手座 Sagittarius

íto *n* 糸 thread, yarn, string: **tako-ito** 凧糸 kite string

itó-maki *n* 糸巻き spool; reel

íto *n* 意図 intention, plan, purpose: **ito-shite** 意図して intentionally, on purpose (= **ito-teki ni** 意図的に)

ito-teki ni *adv* 意図的に on purpose (= **íto-shite** 意図して)

itóko *n* いとこ・従兄弟・従姉妹 cousin: **(o-)itoko-san** (お)いとこさん (*your/someone else's*) cousin

itomá *n* 暇 (**o-itoma** お暇) **1.** leave taking, farewell: **o-itoma (ita)shimásu** お暇(致)します I will take my leave **2.** free time (= **hima** 暇); leave of absence

itoshíí *adj* 愛しい dear (*beloved*)

ítsu *n, adv* いつ when

ítsu dé mo *adv* いつでも any time (*at all*): **ítsu dé mo daijōbudesu** いつでも大丈夫です Any time would be fine (*with me*).

itsu-goro *n* いつ頃 about when

itsuká *n* 五日 five days; fifth day (*of month*)

ítsu-ka *adv* いつか sometime: **mata ítsu-ka oaideikiruno o tanoshiminishiteimásu** またいつかお会いできるのを楽しみにしています I'm looking forward to seeing you again sometime in the future.

ítsu kara *adv* いつから since when, how long

itsukushimi *n* 慈しみ tender love (= **jiai** 慈愛): **itsukushimi másu** 慈しみます loves tenderly

ítsu made *adv* いつまで until when, how long

ítsu made mo *adv* いつまでも forever

ítsu made ni *adv* いつまでに by when

ítsu-mo *adv* いつも always, usually: **ítsu-mo no** いつものusual

ítsu-no-ma-ni (ka) *adv* いつの間]に(か) before one knows it

itsútsu *n* 五つ five pieces (*small objects*) (= **gó-ko** 五個); five years old (= **gó-sai** 五歳)

itsuwári *n* 偽り falsehood, lie (= **uso** 嘘)

itta *v* 行った (went) → **ikimásu** 行きます

itta *v* 言った (said) → **iimásu** 言います

ítta *v* 炒った (fried) → **irimásu** 炒ります

ítta *v* 射った (shot) → **ímásu** 射ます

ittai … *adv* 一体 … on earth, … ever … !: **ittai dōshitandesuka?** 一体どうしたんですか? What on earth happened

ittai-ka *n* 一体化 unification: ~ **shimásu** 一体化します unites

itte *v* 行って → **ikimásu** 行きます

itte *v* 言って → **iimasu** 言います

itte *v* 要って → **irimásu** 要ります

itte *v* 入って → **irimásu** 入ります

itte *v* 炒って → **irimásu** 炒ります

itte *v* 射って → **ímásu** 射ます

ittei (no) *adj* 一定(の) fixed, settled, definite

Itte(i)rasshái *interj* いって(い)らっしゃい, **Itte(i)rasshái-máse** [HONORIFIC] いって(い)らしゃいませ Good-bye! (*said to those departing home*)

Itte kimásu, Itte mairimásu *interj* 行ってきます/参ります。 Good-bye! (*said to those staying home*)

it-tō´(no) *n, adj* 一等(の) first, first class: **ittō´seki/-sha** 一等席/車 first-class seat/car

ít-tō *n* 一頭 one (*horse/ox, large animal*)

it-tsui *n* 一対 a pair

iu *v* 言う = **yū** ゆう = **iimásu** 言います (says, tells; expresses)

iwá *n* 岩 rock, crag: **iwa-ba** 岩場 rocky stretch

íwa ba *conj* いわば so to speak

iwái *n* 祝い (**o-iwai** お祝い) celebration → **iwaimásu** 祝います

iwaimásu, iwáu *v* 祝います, 祝う celebrates

iwanai *v* 言わない = **iimasén** 言いません (not say)

iwashi *n* イワシ・鰯 sardine: [IDIOM] **iwashi no atama mo shinjin kara** 鰯の頭も信心から Anything viewed through the eyes of faith seems perfect.

iwátte *v* 祝って → **iwaimásu** 祝います

iwawánai *v* 祝わない = **iwaimasén** 祝いません (not celebrate)

iwáyúru *adj* いわゆる [BOOKISH] so-called, what is known as

iya *interj* いや (*usually male*) no, nope

iya *v* [INFORMAL] 言や → **iéba** 言えば

iyá (na) *adj* 嫌(な) unpleasant; disliked; disagreeable; disgusting, nasty

iya-garimásu, iya-gáru *v* 嫌がります, 嫌がる dislikes, hates

íyaringu *n* イヤリング earring

iyashii *adj* 卑しい lowly, vulgar

í ya shinai *v* いやしない = **ínai** いない (not stay)

í ya shinai *v* 射やしない = **ínai** 射ない (not shoot)

iyō *v* いよう = **imashō´** いましょう (let's stay!)

iyó-iyo *adv* いよいよ **1.** at last, finally **2.** more and more **3.** surely

(…) ízen *suffix* (…)以前 before, up until …, ago

iza *adv* いざ when it comes to (actually do so): **iza yattemiruto (jitsu wa) kantan deshita** いざやってみると(実は)簡単でした It was (actually) easy when I did it.: **iza to iu toki** いざという時 in a pinch, in the worst case

izumi *n* 泉 fountain, spring

izure *adv* いずれ some other time; someday: **izure wakarudeshō** いずれ分かるでしょう You will see soon.; **izure mata chikaiuchini oaishimashō** いずれまた近いうちにお会いしましょう Let's meet up again sometime soon.

71

J

ja *interj, adv* [INFORMAL] じゃ、じゃあ well, well then; in that case; (well) now (= **déwa** では)

...ja *suffix* [INFORMAL] ...じゃ = **...dé wa** ...では

ja *n* 蛇 snake: **ja no michi wa hebi** 蛇の道は蛇 Set a thief to catch a thief.

jaaku (na) *adj* [BOOKISH] 邪悪(な) evil

...ja arimasen *v* [INFORMAL] じゃありません = **...ja nái** ...じゃない it is not; it is not a case of

jabu *n* ジャブ jab

...jae *interj* [INFORMAL] ...じゃえ= **...de shimae** ...でしまえ: **nónjae** 飲んじゃえ [IMPERATIVE] (drink it up!)

jagā *n* ジャガー jaguar

jagaimo *n* じゃがいも・ジャガイモ (Irish) potato

jaguchi *n* 蛇口 faucet, tap

...jai masu *v* [INFORMAL] ...じゃいます = **...de shimaimásu** ...でしまいます [INFINITIVE]: **nonjai masu** 飲んじゃいます drink it

jajauma *n* じゃじゃ馬 shrew

jāji *n* ジャージ jersey

jákétto *n* ジャケット jacket

jakén (na/ni) adj, *adv* 邪険(な/に) blunt(ly)

jakkan (no) *adj* 若干(の) some (amount of), several

jakku *n* ジャック jack

jakō *n* ジャコウ・麝香 civet, musk: **jakō-ageha** ジャコウアゲハ *byasa alcinous*: **jakō-ushi** ジャコウウシ musk-ox: **jakō-jika** ジャコウジカ musk deer: **jakō-neko** ジャコウネコ musk cat: **jakō-nezumi** ジャコウネズミ (house) musk shrew

jakuhai (mono) *n* [BOOKISH] 若輩(者) young and inexperienced person

jakunen-sha *n* [BOOKISH] 若年者 the young, a youth (= **wakamono** 若者)

jakusha *n* 弱者 the weak (person)

jakuten *n* 弱点 weak point

jama *n* 邪魔(**o-jama** お邪魔) disturbance, hindrance, obstacle: **jama (na)** 邪魔(な) intrusive, bothersome; **jama ni narimásu** 邪魔になります gets in the way, becomes a bother

Jamaika *n* ジャマイカ Jamaica

jámu *n* ジャム jam (to eat)

...ja nái *suffix, v* [INFORMAL] ...じゃない = **...ja arimasén** ...じゃありません (it) is not: **ja nái to** ...じゃないと unless it be

...ja nákereba *suffix, v* [INFORMAL] ...じゃなければ unless it be: **ja nákereba narimasén** ...じゃなければなりません it must (has to) be

...ja náku(te) *suffix, v* [INFORMAL] ...じゃなく(て) (it) is not and/but; without being

...ja nákute mo *suffix, v* [INFORMAL] ...じゃなくても even if it not be: **ja nákute mo íi desu** ...じゃなくてもいいです it need not be

...ja nákute wa *suffix, v* [INFORMAL] じゃなくては、**...ja nákya** ...じゃなきゃ not being, without

being; unless it be: **ja nákya ikemasén** ...じゃなくては(じゃなきゃ)いけません it must (has to) be

jānarisuto *n* ジャーナリスト journalist

jānarizumu *n* ジャーナリズム journalism

jānaru *n* ジャーナル journal

janbo *n* ジャンボ jumbo: **janbo jetto-ki** ジャンボジェット機 jumbo jet aircraft

jánguru *n* ジャングル jungle: **janguru-jímu** ジャングルジム jungle gym

janku-fūdo *n* ジャンクフード junk food

jánpā *n* ジャンパー windbreaker (jacket)

jánpu *n* ジャンプ jump: ~ **shimásu** ジャンプします jumps

janru *n* ジャンル genre

jarajara *adj* ジャラジャラ jangling sound

jara-shimásu, jara-su *v* じゃらします、じゃらす plays with: **(ko)neko o jarashimasu** (子)猫をじゃらします plays with a kitten/cat

jari *n* 砂利 gravel, pebbles

Járu *n* ジャル JAL (Japan Airlines)

jashin *n* [BOOKISH] 邪心 wicked heart

jashin *n* [BOOKISH] 邪神 false god(s)

Jawa *n* ジャワ Java

jazu *n* ジャズ jazz

Jei āru, Jē āru *n* ジェイアール、ジェーアール、JR (Japan Railway): **Jei āru Tōkyō eki** JR東京駅 JR Tokyo station

jettó-ki *n* ジェット機 jet (plane)

ji *n* 痔 hemorrhoids

jí *n* 字 = **moji** 文字 a letter (symbol): **kanji** 漢字 a Chinese character

jí *n* 地 land, ground; texture; fabric

ji-... *prefix* 自... self; one's own

ji-bun *n* 自分 oneself; myself; alone: **jibun-katte/gatte (na)** 自分勝手(な) selfish; **jibun de** 自分で by oneself, in person; **jibun no** 自分の (one's) own; **go-jibun** ご自分 yourself; **jibun-jishin** *n* 自分自身 time (= **jishin** 自身)

jí-ga *n* 自我 ego

jí-ko *n* 自己 (one)self

ji-sei *n* 自制 self-control

ji-shin *n* 自信 self-confidence/-assurance: **ji-shin o mótte ... (shimásu)** 自信を持って...(します) (does it) with confidence

ji-taku *n* 自宅 one's home/residence: **jitaku-taiki** 自宅待機 home standby

...-ji *suffix* ...時 o'clock: **roku-ji** 6時 six o'clock

...-ji *suffix* ...寺 temple (name): **Kinkaku-ji** 金閣寺

jiai *n* [BOOKISH] 慈愛 tender love (= **itsukushimi** 慈しみ)

jibikí *n* 字引き dictionary (= **jísho** 辞書)

jibun *n* 時分 time

jidai *n* 時代 age, period, era, time, **...-jídai** ...時代 period: **Edo-jidai** 江戸時代 the Edo period; **jidai-mono** 時代物 antique (= **kottō´-hin** 骨董品)

jídō n 児童 child (*elementary school student*)
(= **seito** 生徒)

jidō n 自動 automatic
jidō-doa n 自動ドア auto(matic) door
jidō-hanbaiki n 自動販売機 vending machine
jidō´-sha n 自動車 automobile (= **kuruma** 車)
jidō-teki (na/ni) adj 自動的(な/に) automatic;
adv automatically

jidō´-shi n 自動詞 intransitive verb

Jiei-tai n 自衛隊 the Self-Defense Forces

jigoku´ n 地獄 hell: [IDIOM] **Jigoku no sata mo
kane shidai.** 地獄の沙汰も金次第 Ready money is
a ready medicine.

jígyō n 事業 enterprise, business, undertaking

jíi n 自慰 masturbation (= **onanii** オナニー):
~ **shimásu** 自慰します masturbates

jii-pan n ジーパン blue jeans (= **jiinzu** ジーンズ)

jíjitsu n 事実 fact, truth: **jíjitsu o mitomemásu** 事
実を認めます admits the fact

jijō n 事情 circumstances; conditions: **jijō o
nomikomimásu** 事情を飲み込みます understands
the situation

jikan n 時間 (**o-jíkan** お時間) time; hour(s): **jikan
ga kakarimásu** 時間がかかります it takes time;
jikan-dō´ri (no/ni) 時間通り(の/に) on time:
jikan ni rūzu (na) 時間にルーズ(な) unpunctual

…-jikan suffix …時間 time; hour(s): **eigyō-jikan**
営業時間 business hours; **kinmu-jikan** 勤務時間
working hours

jikan-hyō n 時間表 timetable, schedule (= **jikoku-
hyō** 時刻表)

jíka ni adv 直に directly; personally (= **chokusetsu
(ni)** 直接(に))

jikan-wari (hyō) n 時間割(表) school time
schedule (*table*)

jíken n 事件 happening, incident, event, affair,
case: **jíken o kaiketsu-shimásu** 事件を解決します
solves a case/cases

jíki n 時期 time; season: **jiki-shōsō (na)** 時期尚早
(な) prematurity (premature)

jíki n 時機 opportune time, opportunity, chance:
jíki o machimásu 時機を待ちます waits for a
chance

jíki n 磁器 porcelain → **tō´ki** 陶器

jíki (no) n 磁気(の) magnetic: **jíki o obiteiru…**
磁気を帯びている… magnetize …

jiki (ni) adv 直(に) soon; immediately

jikka n 実家 one's parent's home

jikken n 実験 experiment: ~ **shimásu**
実験します experiments; **kagaku (no) jikken**
化学(の)実験 chemical experiment

jikkō n 実行 performance; practice; realization;
running: **puroguramu o jikkō shimásu** プログラ
ムを実行します runs a program

jíko n 事故 accident

jikoku n 時刻 time (*specified*)

jikoku-hyō n 時刻表 time schedule, timetable
(= **jikan-hyō** 時間表): **densha no jikoku-hyō**
電車の時刻表 railway timetable

jikú n 軸 axis, axle: **x/y/z-jikú, ekkusu/wai/zetto
-jiku** X/Y/Z軸 x/y/z axis : **chi-jiku** 地軸 earth
axis: **jiten-jiku** 自転軸 (*planet's*) rotational axis

jiman n 自慢 pride, boast: ~ **shimásu** 自慢します
boasts, brags about

jímen n 地面 ground (*surface*)

jimí (na) adj 地味(な) plain, sober

jímu n 事務 business, office work
jimu-in n 事務員 office clerk
jimu-sho n 事務所 office

jímu n ジム gym(nasium)

…-jín suffix …人 a person

jínbutsu n 人物 personage

jindō n 人道 1. humanity: **jindō-shugisha** 人道主
義者 humanitarian 2. walkway, pedestrian path

jingū´ n 神宮 (large) Shinto shrine

jinin n 人員 personnel

jínja n 神社 Shinto shrine

jínji n 人事 personnel/human affairs
jinji-ka n 人事課 personnel (section)

jínjō adj 尋常 [BOOKISH] usual, normal (= **futsū**
普通): **jinjō-de nai** 尋常でない unusual, abnormal

jinken n 人権 human rights

jinkō n 人口 population

jinkō (no) adj 人工(の) artificial

jinríkí-sha n 人力車 ricksha

jínrui n 人類 human beings, the human race:
jinrúi-gaku 人類学 anthropology

jinsei n 人生 (*one's*) life

jinshin-jiko n 人身事故 (traffic) accident of
injury and/or death: **jinshin-jiko de densha ga
okuremashita** 人身事故で電車が遅れました The
train is delayed because of an injury and/or fatal
accident.

jinshu n 人種 race (*peoples*): **jinshu sabetsu** 人種
差別 racial discrimination: **jinshu no rutsubo**
人種のるつぼ melting pot

ji-nushi n 地主 landowner

jinzō n 腎臓 kidneys

jinzō (no) adj 人造(の) artificial, imitation, false
(*man-made*): **jinzō-ningen** 人造人間 artificial human

jíppā n ジッパー zipper

jira-shimásu, jira-su v じらします, じらす
irritates someone, tantalizes, teases

jírojiro mimásu (míru) v じろじろ見ます(見る)
stares at

jísa n 時差 difference in time: **jisa-boke** 時差ぼ
け jet lag; **jisa-shukkin** 時差出勤 staggered work
hours

jisan shimásu (suru) v 持参します(する) brings
along, takes along: **(o-)bentō-jisan (de/no)** (お)弁
当持参(で/の) brown-bag

jisatsu n 自殺 suicide: ~ **shimásu** 自殺します
commits suicide: **jisatsu-ganbō** 自殺願望 desire
of suicide

jisei n 時勢 (*the trend of*) the times

jisei n 時世 (**go-jísei** ご時世) the times

jísetsu n 時節 season; (*appropriate*) time, occasion,
opportunity

jíshaku *n* 磁石 magnet

jishin *n* 地震 earthquake

jishin *n* 磁針 magnetic needle: **hōi-jishin** 方位磁針 compass

-jishin *n* 自身 oneself; myself (= **jibun-jishin** 自分自身): **kare-jishin** 彼自身 himself

jísho *n* 辞書 dictionary

jishoku *n* 辞職 resignation (*from a position*): **~ shimásu** 辞職します resigns

jisoku *n* 時速 (*per hour*) speed

jissai *n, adv* 実際 actual conditions, reality; in practice; in fact, really

ji-súberi *n* 地滑り landslide

jítai *n* 事態 situation, state of affairs

jítai *n, adv* 自体 1. the thing itself 2. originally

jítai *n* 辞退: **~ shimásu** 辞退します declines, refuses

jitchi *n* 実地 actuality, (*putting to*) practice: **jitchi (no)** 実地(の) practical, actual: **jitchi (no) keiken o tsumimásu** 実地(の)経験を積みます gets on-the-job experience(s)

jiten *n* 辞典 dictionary (= **jísho** 辞書): **kokugo-jiten** 国語辞典 Japanese dictionary: **eiwa-jiten** 英和辞典, **einichi-jiten** 英日辞典 English-Japanese dictionary

jiten *n* 事典 dictionary, subject book: **hyakka-jíten** 百科事典 encyclopedia: **jinmei-jiten** 人名事典 personal names dictionary

jitén-sha, jidén-sha *n* 自転車 bicycle: **jitensha-ya** 自転車屋 bicycle shop/dealer

jitsú *n* 実 truth: **jitsú ni** 実に truly, really, indeed; **jitsú no** 実の true, real; **jitsú wa** 実は to tell the truth, actually, in fact

jitsu-butsu *n* 実物 the real thing; the actual person: **jitsubutsu-saizu** 実物サイズ actual size, original size

jitsu-ryoku *n* 実力 (real) strength, ability, proficiency; force, power

jitsu-yō *n* 実用 practical use/application, utility: **jitsuyō-teki na** 実用的な practical

jitsugyō *n* 実業 business, enterprise: **jitsugyō-ka** 実業家 businessperson, businessman

jitto *adv* じっと intently, steadily, fixedly (*staring*); quietly, patiently: **~ shiteimásu** じっとしています holds still

jiyū´ *n* 自由 freedom, liberty: **jiyū´ (na)** 自由(な) free; fluent, at ease; **jiyū´ ni** 自由に freely; fluently; **jiyū´-gyō** 自由業 freelancing, freelance work; **jiyū´-seki** 自由席 unreserved seat

jizen *n* 慈善 charity

jō´ *n* 錠 1. (= **jō-mae** 錠前) lock: **... no jō´ o oroshimásu** …の錠を下ろします locks up 2. (= **jōzai** 錠剤) pill

jō *adj, n* 上 1. (= **jōtō (na)** 上等(な)) deluxe 2. (= **jō-kan** 上巻) first volume (*of a set of 2 or 3*)

...´-jō *suffix* …畳 (*counts room sizes by tatami mat*): **hachí-jō (ma)** 八畳(間) eight *tatami* mats (room)

...´-jō *suffix* …城 castle (*name*): 大阪城 the Osaka-jō castle

jōbu (na) *adj* 丈夫(な) sturdy, firm, healthy; safe (= **daijōbu** 大丈夫)

jochō *n* 助長 promotion, furtherance: **~ shimásu** 助長します promotes, encourages, fosters, foments

jochū *n* 女中 maid-servant

jōdán *n* 冗談 joke: **jōdán hanbun (ni)** 冗談半分(に) half in jest

jōei *n* 上映 showing (*movie*)

jōen *n* 上演 performance: **~ shimásu** 上演します performs

jo-gákusei, joshi gákusei *n* 女学生, 女子学生 female student

jōge *n* 上下 top and bottom, high and row, up and down

jōgi *n* 定規 ruler (*to measure with*)

jogingu *n* ジョギング jog(ging): **jogingu (o) shimásu** ジョギング(を)します jogs

jō´go *n* 漏斗 funnel

jōhín (na) *adj* 上品(な) elegant, refined

jōhō *n* 情報 information

jō-kan *n* 上巻 first volume (*of a set of 2 or 3*)

jōkén *n* 条件 condition, term, stipulation, provision

jō´ki *n* 蒸気 steam, vapor

jokki *n* ジョッキ jug, (*beer*) mug: **jokki ip-pai no biiru** ジョッキ一杯のビール a jug/mug of beer

jōkyaku *n* 乗客 passenger

jōkyō *n* 状況・情況 situation, circumstances, state of affairs

jo-kyō´ju *n* 助教授 assistant professor

jōkyū *n* 上級 high class, upper class: **jōkyū kōsu** 上級コース advanced course

jō-mae *n* 錠前 lock (= **kagi** 鍵)

jomei *n* [BOOKISH] 除名 excision, excommunication: **~ shimásu** 除名します expels, excommunicates

jomei *n* 助命 sparing the life/lives (= **kyūmei** 救命): **jomei-katsudō** 助命活動 rescue work: **~ shimásu** 助命します spares

jōmén *n* 上面 top (*top side*)

jōmuin *n* 乗務員 crew: **kyakushitsu jōmuin** 客室乗務員 (*airplane*) flight attendant

jōnetsu-teki (na) *adj* 情熱的(な) passionate

joō´ *n* 女王 queen

jōriku *n* 上陸 disembarking, landing: **~ shimásu** 上陸します lands, disembarks, comes ashore

jōro *n* じょうろ・ジョウロ watering can

jorō´ *n* 女郎 whore, prostitute

jōryū (no) *adj* 上流(の) classy, upper; upstream

jōryū´-sui *n* 蒸留水 distilled water

josei *n* 女性 woman, female: **josei-go** 女性語 women's language (*terms*) (= **onna kotoba** 女言葉)

joseikin *n* 助成金 grant

joseki *n* 除籍 removal from register, expulsion (*from a school/university*): **~ shimásu** 除籍します removes someone from register:; **joseki saremásu** 除籍されます gets expelled from

josetsu *n* 除雪 removing the snow: **~ shimásu** 除雪します removes the snow

jōsha *n* 乗車 getting into a car, getting on a train/bus, boarding: **~ shimásu** 乗車します boards
jōshá-ken *n* 乗車券 passenger ticket
joshi *n* 助詞 particle (*auxiliary word*)
jóshi *n* 女子 girl, woman: **joshi-dáisei** 女子大生 woman college student; **joshi-kō´sei** 女子高生 female (senior) high school student
jōshiki *n* 常識 common sense
joshō *n* 序章 introduction section (*book*)
joshu *n* 助手 helper, assistant
josō *n* 助走 running up: **~ shimásu** 助走します runs up
josō *n* 除草 weeding: **~ shimásu** 除草します eradicates weeds
josō *n* 女装 drag: **~ shimásu** 女装します is in drag
josō *n* 序奏 (*music*) introduction
jōsúi-chi *n* 浄水池 reservoir
jotai *n* 除隊 discharge: **~ shimásu** 除隊します discharges
jōtai *n* 状態 condition, situation, state, circumstances
jōtō (no) *adj* 上等(の) the best, first-rate, deluxe
joya *n* 除夜 New Year's Eve: **joya no kane** 除夜の鐘 the bells on New Year's Eve
jōyaku *n* 条約 treaty, agreement: **Washinton-jōyaku** ワシントン条約 Washington Convention
jōyō *n* 常用 common use: **jōyō-kanji** 常用漢字 Chinese characters in common use
jōyō´-sha *n* 乗用車 passenger car
jōyō´-sha *n* 常用者 addict
joyū *n* 女優 actress
jōzai *n* 錠剤 pill, tablet
jōzō-sho *n* 醸造所 brewery
jōzú (na) *adj* 上手(な) skilled, clever, good at
jū´ *n* 銃 gun: **jū-sei** 銃声 gunshot(s)
jū´ *n* 十・10 ten
　jū-bai *n* 十倍 ten times, tenfold
　jū-banmé (no) *adj* 十番目(の) tenth
　jū´-do *n* 十度 ten times (= **júk-kai** 十回); ten degrees
　jū-en-dama *n* 十円玉 ten-yen coin
　jū´-go *n* 十五・15 fifteen
　jū-hachí *n* 十八・18 eighteen
　jū-ichí *n* 十一・11 eleven
　jū´-ji *n* 十時・10時 ten o'clock
　jū´-ku, jū-kyū´ *n* 十九・19 nineteen
　jū-má *n* 十万・100,000 a hundred thousand
　jū-nána *n* 十七・17 seventeen
　jū-ní *n* 十二・12 twelve
　jū-óku *n* 十億・10億 a thousand million; (*U.S.*) a billion
　jū-rokú *n* 十六・16 sixteen
　jū´-san *n* 十三・13 thirteen
　jū-shi *n* 十四・14 fourteen (= **jū-yon** 十四)
　jū-yok-ka *n* 十四日 14 days; 14th day (*of month*)
　jū-yon *n* 十四・14 fourteen (= **jū-shi** 十四): **jū-yonen** 十四年 the year 14, for 14 years; **jū yonén-kan** 十四年間 14 years; **jū´yo-nin** 十四人 14 people
...-jū *suffix* ...じゅう・中 throughout the

(*entire*)...: **ichi-nen-jū** 一年中 throughout the year: **sekai-jū** 世界中 all over the world
jūatsu *n* 重圧 pressure
jūbako *n* 重箱 nested boxes; picnic boxes: **jūbako no sumi o tsutsukimásu** 重箱の隅をつつきます split hairs, nitpicks
jūbún (na) *adj* 十分[充分](な) enough, sufficient
jūdai (na) *adj* 重大(な) serious (*heavy, grave*); important: **jūdái-ji** 重大事 a matter of importance
jū´dō *n* 柔道 judo, jujitsu (*an art of weaponless defense*): **jūdō´gí** 柔道着 judo outfit/suit
Jū-gatsu *n* 十月・10月 October
jūgeki *n* 銃撃 gunfight
jūgun *n* 従軍 serving in an army: **~ shimásu** 従軍します serves in an army
júgyō *n* 授業 class instruction, classroom teaching: **jugyō-jíkan** 授業時間 school/teaching hours; **jugyō o okonaimásu** 授業を行います teaches (*class*): **jugyō o ukemásu** 授業を受けます attends a class
jūgyō *n* 従業 employment: **~ shimásu** 従業します is employed
jūgyō´-in *n* 従業員 employee
jūi *n* 獣医 veterinary
Jū-ichi-gatsu *n* 十一月・11月 November
jū´ji *n* 十字 a cross (*symbol*)
　jūji-ka *n* 十字架 a cross (*wooden*)
　jūjí-ro *n* 十字路 crossroad(s)
jū´ji *n* 従事 engaging in (*an activity*): **... ni jū´ji shimásu** ...に従事します engages in ...
jūkinzoku *n* 重金属 heavy metal
jūketsu *n* 充血 congestion: **me ga jūketsu shimásu** 目が充血します gets red eyes
juk-kai *n* 十階 ten floors/stories; tenth floor
júk-kai *n* 十回 ten times (= **jū´-do** 十度)
júk-ko *n* 十個 ten (*pieces, small objects*)
júku *n* 塾 a cram/tutoring school
　juku-kō(shi) *n* 塾講(師) tutor(s) in a tutoring school
jūku bokkusu *n* ジュークボックス jukebox
jukudoku *n* 熟読 reading thoroughly: **~ shimásu** 熟読します reads thoroughly
jukugo *n* 熟語 idiomatic expression
jukukō, jukkō *n* 熟考 serious thought: **~ shimásu** 熟考します considers carefully (= **jukuryo** 熟慮)
jukunen *n* 熟年 mature age: **jukunen kappuru** 熟年カップル mature couple
jukuryo *n* 熟慮 serious thought: **~ shimásu** 熟慮します considers carefully (= **jukukō, jukkō** 熟考)
jukushimásu, jukúsú *v* 熟します, 熟す ripens, gets ripe
jukusui *n* 熟睡 sound sleep: **~ shimásu** 熟睡します falls fast asleep
jukutatsu *n* 熟達 mastery: **~ shimásu** 熟達します gets in practice
Júkyō *n* 儒教 Confucianism
jukyū *n* 需給 supply and demand
jūmin *n* 住民 resident: **jūmin hyō** 住民票 residence certificate

jun *n* 順 order: **jun(ban) ni** 順(番)に in order

jún (na) *adj* 純(な) pure

junban *n* 順番 (*place in*) order, turn

júnbi *n* 準備 preparation(s), arrangements

junchō (na) *adj* 順調(な) smooth(ly going)

Jū-ni-gatsú *n* 十二月・12月 December

jun-jimásu, jun-jiru *v* [BOOKISH] 準じます, 準じる applies correspondingly (*to*); is made to accord (*with*)

júnjo *n* 順序 order, sequence

junkan *n* 循環 circulation; cycle: **~ shimásu** 循環します circulates

jun-kyō´ju *n* 準教授 associate professor

júnsa *n* 巡査 policeman, patrolman (= **omawari-san** お巡りさん)

junshō *n* 準将 brigadier general

junsui (na) *adj* 純粋(な) pure: **junsui na kokoro** 純粋な心 pure heart

jūō *n* 縦横 vertical and horizontal

     jūō-mujin (ni) *adv* 縦横無尽(に) freely

júp-pa *n* 十羽 ten (*birds*)

júp-pon *n* 十本 ten (*pencils/bottles, long things*)

júp-pun *n* 十分 10 minutes

jū´rai (wa) *adv* 従来(は) traditionally, up to now, hitherto, previously: **jū´rai (no)** 従来(の) traditional, accustomed, customary

jūryō´ *n* 重量 weight: **jūryō-age** 重量挙げ weight-lifting; **jūryōage-senshu** 重量挙げ選手 weight-lifter

juryō´-shō *n* 受領証 receipt

jū´sho *n* 住所 residence, address

jushō *n* 受賞 winning an award: **~ shimásu** 受賞します wins

     jushō´-sha *n* 受賞者 winner, awardee

jus-sai *n* 十歳 ten years old (= **tō** とお・十)

jus-satsu *n* 十冊 ten copies (*books, magazines*)

jū´su *n* ジュース juice: **orenji jūsu** オレンジジュース orange juice

jūtai *n* 渋滞 congestion: **jūtai-jō´kyō** 渋滞状況 congested (*traffic*): **jūtai shite imásu** 渋滞しています is congested (*backed up*)

jūtaku *n* 住宅 residence, house

jū´tan *n* じゅうたん・絨毯 rug, carpet (= **ka´pétto** カーペット): **kashimi(y)a jūtan** カシミア[ヤ]絨毯 cashmere carpet

jut-tō *n* 十頭 ten (*horses/oxen, large animals*)

juwá-ki *n* 受話器 (*telephone*) receiver

júyo *n* 授与 awarding, conferring: **sotsugyōshōsho o júyo shimásu** 卒業証書を授与します awards diploma

jūyō (na) *adj* 重要(な) important

juzú *n* 数珠 beads: **juzú tsunagi ni narimásu** 数珠つな[繋]ぎになります is chained together

K

ka *n* カ・蚊 mosquito: **ka-tori senkō** 蚊取り線香 mosquito coil

     ka-ya *n* 蚊帳・かや mosquito net: **ka-ya no soto** 蚊帳の外 out of scheme

ka *n* 可 pass: (*grade*) **yū, ryō, ka, fuka** 優、良、可、不可 Excellent, Good, Poor, Failing

ká *n* 課, …´**-ka** …課 section, division; lesson: **Sōmu-ka** 総務課 General Affairs Division: **Jinji-ka** 人事課 Human Resources Division: **dai ik-ka** 第1課 Lesson 1

ká *n* 科 **1.** family (*biological taxonomy*): **Saru-moku Hito-ka Hito-zoku** サル目ヒト科ヒト属 Primates Family, *Hominidae Genus, Homo Species* **2.** department: (*university*) **Eibun-ka** 英文科 Department of English Language & Literature, **Kokubun-ka** 国文科 Department of Japanese Language and Literature: (*hospital*) **Ge-ka** 外科 surgery, **Nai-ka** 内科 internal medicine

ka-… *prefix* 仮… temporary (*tentative*)

… ka *conj* …か or; (*the question*) whether

…-ka *suffix* …化 …-ization: **~ shimásu** …化します …-izes

kaba *n* カバ・河馬 hippopotamus

kabā *n* カバー cover, covering: **bukku-kabā** ブックカバー book cover: **kabā-retā** カバーレター cover letter (= **sōfu-jō** 送付状)

kabaimásu, kabau *v* 庇います, 庇う

protects, defends

kaban *n* かばん・カバン・鞄 briefcase, bag

kabayaki *n* 蒲焼き broiled eel

kabe *n* 壁 wall: **kabe-gami** 壁紙 wallpaper

kabi *n* カビ mold, mildew: **kabi– ga haete imásu** カビが生えています is moldy

kabin *n* 花瓶・かびん flower vase

kabocha *n* カボチャ pumpkin

kabu *n* 株 stock (*in a company*): **kabushiki-shijō** 株式市場 stock market

kabu *n* カブ・蕪 = **kabura** カブラ・蕪 turnip

kā´bu *n* カーブ curve (*road*)

kabuki *n* 歌舞伎 a traditional style of Japanese theater: **kabuki-za** 歌舞伎座 the Kabuki theater (*building*), Kabuki Theatrical Corporation

kabura *n* カブラ・蕪 a turnip (= **kabu** カブ・蕪)

kaburimásu, kabúru *v* 被ります, 被る wears on head; puts on

kabushiki-gáisha *n* 株式会社 joint-stock corporation

kabútte *v* 被って (*to wear a hat, etc. on one's head/shoulders*) → **kaburimásu** 被ります

káchi *n* 価値 value: **káchi ga arimásu** 価値があります is worth

kachí *n* 勝ち victory, win

kachí *v* 勝ち → **kachimásu** 勝ちます [INFINITIVE]

kachimásu, kátsu *v* 勝ちます, 勝つ wins

káchi ya/wa shinai *v* [INFORMAL] 勝ちや/はしな
い = **katánai** 勝たない (not win)

ka-chō *n* 課長 section manager

kadai *n* [BOOKISH] 課題 **1.** problem, difficult
matter (= **mondai** 問題) **2.** assignment, homework,
task **3.** subject, theme (= **daimoku** 題目)

kádan *n* 花壇 flower bed

kádan *n* 下段 [BOOKISH] lower stand

kádan *n* [BOOKISH] 果断 [BOOKISH] decisiveness:
kádan na kōi 果断な行為 decisive action

kādigan *n* カーディガン cardigan

kádo *n* 角 *(outside)* corner, street corner

kádo *n* [BOOKISH] 過度 excessiveness: **kádo no
sutoresu** 過度のストレス extreme stress: **kádo no
undō** 過度の運動 extreme exercise: **kádo ni kinchō
shimásu** 過度に緊張します is nervous excessively

kadō *n* [BOOKISH] 稼動 [BOOKISH] operating:
~ shimásu 稼動します operates

kadō *n* 華道 flower arrangement (= **furawā-
arenjimento** フラワーアレンジメント): **kadō-
kyōshitsu** 華道教室 flower arrangement class(es)

kādo *n* カード card: **messēji-kādo** メッセージカー
ド message card

kaé *v* 変え → **kaemásu** 変えます

kaé *v* 換[替]え → **kaemásu** 換え[替え]ます

kaé *v* 買え **1.** → **kaemásu** 買えます [INFINITIVE]
2. [IMPERATIVE] (buy it!) → **kaimásu** 買います

káe *v* 飼え **1.** → **kaemásu** 飼えます [INFINITIVE]
2. [IMPERATIVE] (raise it!) → **kaimásu** 飼います

kaéba *v* 買えば = [INFORMAL] **kaya** 買や (if one
buys) → **kaimásu** 買います

káeba *v* 飼えば = [INFORMAL] **káya** 飼や (if one
raises) → **kaimásu** 飼います

kaede *n* カエデ・楓 maple

kaemásu, kaeru *v* 変えます, 変える changes it

kaemásu, kaeru *v* 換え[替え]ます, 換える[替え
る] exchanges, replaces

kaemásu, kaeru *v* 買えます, 買える can buy

kaemásu *v* 飼えます, **káeru** 飼える can raise

kaenai *v* 変えない = **kaemásén** 変えません (not
change it)

kaenai *v* 換え[替え]ない = **kaemásén** 換え[替え]
ません (not exchange)

kaenai *v* 買えない = **kaemásén** 買えません
(cannot buy)

káenai *v* 飼えない = **kaemásén** 飼えません
(cannot raise)

kae(ra)remásu *v* 変え(ら)れます, **kae(ra)reru**
変え(ら)れる can change it

kae(ra)renai *v* 変え(ら)れない = **kae(ra)remásén**
変え(ら)れません (cannot change it)

káere *v* 帰れ [IMPERATIVE] (go home!) →
kaerimásu 帰ります [INFINITIVE]

kaeréba *v* 変えれば (if one changes it) →
kaemásu 変えます

kaeréba *v* 換え[替え]れば (if one exchanges) →
kaemásu 換え[替え]ます

kaeréba *v* 買えれば (if one can buy) →

kaemásu 買えます

kaéreba *v* 飼えれば (if one can raise) →
kaemásu 飼えます

káereba *v* 帰れば (if one goes home) →
kaerimásu 帰ります

kaeremásu, kaeréru *v* 帰れます, 帰れる can go
home, can return

kaerénai *v* 帰れない = **kaeremásén** 帰れません
(cannot go home)

kaerí *n* 帰り (the) return

kaeri *v* 帰り → **kaerimásu** 帰ります [INFINITIVE]

kaerimásu, káeru *v* 帰ります, 帰る goes home,
goes back, returns, leaves

kaeri ya/wa shinai *v* [INFORMAL] 帰りや/はしな
い = **kaeránai** 帰らない (not go home)

kaerō´ *v* 帰ろう = **kaerimashō´** 帰りましょう
(let's go home!)

kaeru *n* カエル・蛙 frog: **hiki-gaeru** ヒキガエ
ル toad

kaeru *v* 変える = **kaemásu** 変えます (changes it)

kaeru *v* 換える[替える] = **kaemásu** 換え[替え]ま
す (exchanges, replaces)

kaeru *v* 買える = **kaemásu** 買えます (can buy)

káeru *v* 飼える = **kaemásu** 飼えます (can raise)

káeru *v* 帰る = **kaerimásu** 帰ります (goes home)

káeseba *v* 返せば (if one returns it) →
kaeshimásu 返します

kaeshimásu, káesu *v* 返します, 返す returns it

káeshite *v* 返して → **kaeshimásu** 返します

káeshi ya/wa shinai *v* [INFORMAL] 返しや/はし
ない = **kaesánai** 返さない (not return it)

kaete *v* 変えて → **kaemásu** 変えます

kaete *v* 換え[替え]て → **kaemásu** 換え[替え]
ます

kaete *v* 買えて → **kaemásu** 買えます

káete *v* 飼えて → **kaemásu** 飼えます

kátte *adv* 却って contrary to expectations

káette *v* 帰って → **kaerimásu** 帰ります

kaeyō´ *v* 変えよう = **kaemashō** 変えましょう
(let's change it!)

kafún *n* 花粉 pollen: **kafún-shō** 花粉症 hay fever

káfusu *n* カフス cuff: **kafusu-botan** カフスボタ
ン cuff links

kagai *n* 課外 extracurricular: **kagai-katsudō**
課外活動 extracurricular activity

kágaku *n* 科学 = **sáiensu** サイエンス science:
kagaku-teki (na) 科学的(な) scientific
kagáku-sha *n* 科学者 scientist

kágaku *n* 化学 = **bake-gaku** 化け学・化学
chemistry: **kagaku-séihin** 化学製品 chemicals,
kagaku-yakuhin 化学薬品 pharmaceuticals
kagáku-sha *n* 化学者 chemist

kagamí *n* 鏡 mirror: **te-kagami** 手鏡 hand mirror

kagamimásu, kagamu *v* 屈みます, 屈む bends
over

kaganai *v* 嗅がない = **kagimásén** 嗅ぎません (not
smell it)

kagayakimásu, kagayáku *v* 輝きます, 輝く
shines, gleams, glitters

kagé v 嗅げ 1. → **kagemásu** 嗅げます [INFINITIVE] 2. [IMPERATIVE] (smell it!) → **kagimásu** 嗅ぎます

káge n 影 shadow: **hito-kage** 人影 shadow of a person, human figure: **kage-bō´shi** 影法師 shadow (of a person)

káge n 陰 shade: **ko-kage** 木陰 shade of trees

kagéba v 嗅げば (if one smells it) → **kagimásu** 嗅ぎます

kágeki n 歌劇 opera

kageki (na) adj 過激(な) excessive, extreme, radical: **kageki-ha** 過激派 the radicals, the extremists

kagemásu, kageru v 嗅げます, 嗅げる can smell it

kagen n 加減 1. (state of) one's health (= **guai** 具合): **o-kagen (wa) ikaga desuka?** お加減(は)いかがですか? (to sick person) How are you feeling?, How is your (health) condition? 2. allowance (= **tekagen** 手加減): **te-kagen shite kudasai** 手加減して下さい Please go easy on me.: **te-kagen shimasen(yo)** 手加減しません(よ) I won't go easy on you. 3. degree, extent (= **teido** 程度): **yu-kagen** 湯加減 hot water temperature: **oyu-kagen wa ikaga desuka?** お湯加減はいかがですか? How is the water temperature? (for the bath water, the water to wash customer's hair in a beauty salon, etc.) 4. adjustment, moderation (= **chōsei** 調整) (→ **ii-kagen** いい加減): **~ shimásu** 加減します adjusts, moderates, makes allowance for

kagenai v 嗅げない = **kagemasén** 嗅げません (cannot smell it)

…-ká-getsu suffix …か月・ヶ月・カ月・箇月 (counts months): **ik-ka-getsu (kan)** 1 か月(間) (for) one month

kagi v 嗅ぎ → **kagimásu** 嗅ぎます [INFINITIVE]

kagí n 鉤 hook: **kagi-tsume** 鉤つめ claw: **kagi-kakko** かぎ括弧 Japanese quotation marks (「」)

kagí n カギ・鍵 key: **(… no) kagí ga kakarimásu** (…の)鍵がかかります it locks, **(… no) kagí o kakemásu** (…の)鍵をかけます locks it

kagi-ana n 鍵穴 keyhole

kagimásu, kagu v か嗅ぎます, 嗅ぐ smells it

kágiri n 限り limit

kagirimasén, kagiranai v 限りません, 限らない not necessarily, not always

kagirimásu, kagíru v 限ります, 限る limits (delimits) it: **… ni kagirimásu** …に限ります there is nothing like (so good as, better than) …: **atsui natsu no hi (ni)wa tsumetai biiru (o ippai yaru) ni kagirimásu** 暑い夏の日(に)は冷たいビール(を一杯やる)に限ります There is nothing like a cold beer on a hot summer day.

kagitte v 限って: **… ni kagitte** …に限って it is best to …

kagí ya/wa shinai v [INFORMAL] 嗅ぎや/はしない = **kaganai** 嗅がない (not smell it)

kago n かご・籠 basket, (bird) cage: **tori-kago** 鳥かご birdcage

kagō v 嗅ごう = **kagimashō´** 嗅ぎましょう (let's smell it!)

kagu v 嗅ぐ = **kagimásu** 嗅ぎます (smells it)

kágu n 家具 furniture: **kagu-tsuki (no) apáto** 家具付き(の)アパート furnished apartment(s) **kagú-ya** n 家具屋 furniture store

kágura n 神楽 Shinto music and dances

kai v 買い → **kaimásu** 買います [INFINITIVE]

kái n カイ・貝 shellfish: **kai-gara** 貝殻 shell (of shellfish)

kái n 飼い → **kaimásu** 飼います [INFINITIVE]

… kai? interj …かい? [INFORMAL] = **desu ka?** ですか? [FORMAL](yes-or-no question)

…-kai suffix …階 (counts floors/stories)

…-kái suffix …回 (counts times/occasions)

…-kai suffix …会 society, association, club; social gathering, party, meeting: **(o-)tanjō´bi-kai** (お)誕生日会 birthday party: **nomi-kai** 飲み会 drinking party: **en-kai** 宴会 party, banquet

…-kai suffix …海 (name of) sea: **Karibu-kai** カリブ海 Caribbean Sea: **Nihon-kai** 日本海 Japan Sea

kaibatsu n 海抜 above sea level

kaibō n [BOOKISH] 解剖 autopsy: **kaibō-gaku** 解剖学 anatomy

kaibutsu n 怪物 monster (= **bake-móno** 化け物, **obáke** お化け, **mónsutā** モンスター)

kaichō n 会長 chairperson

kaichū (no) adj 懐中(の) pocket-(able): **kaichū-déntō** 懐中電灯 flashlight

kaichū (de/no) adv, adj 海中(で/の) in the sea, under the sea

kaichū n 回虫 (intestinal) worms

kaida v 嗅いだ = **kagimáshita** 嗅ぎました (smelled)

kaidan n 階段 stairs, stairway

kaidan n 会談 [BOOKISH] (official) meeting: **shunō-kaidan** 首脳会談 summit (= **samitto** サミット)

kaidan n 怪談 ghost story, scary story

kaidame n 買いだめ hoarding: **~ shimásu** 買いだめします hoards (= **kaioki** 買い置き)

kaide v 嗅いで → **kagimásu** 嗅ぎます

kaidō n 会堂 an auditorium

kaidō n 街道 main road/avenue

kaien n 開演 starting a performance: **kaien-chū** 開演中 during the performance; **kaien-jíkan** 開演時間 curtain time: **(mamonaku) kaien shimásu** (まもなく)開演します performance starts (soon)

kaifuku n 回復 recovery, recuperation: **~ shimásu** 回復します recovers, recuperates

káiga n 絵画 painting, picture

káigai n 海外 overseas, abroad: **kaigai-ryokō** 海外旅行 overseas travel

kaigan n 海岸 seashore, coast, beach: **kaigan-sen** 海岸線 shoreline, coastline

kai-gara n 貝殻 shell (of shellfish)

káigi n 会議 meeting, conference [FORMAL] (= **míitingu** ミーティング): **kaigi-chū** 会議中 in conference, in a meeting; **kaigí-shitsu** 会議室 conference room

káigun n 海軍 navy: **kaigun-kichi** 海軍基地 navy base

kaigyō n 開業 [BOOKISH] opening a business: ~ **shimásu** 開業します opens a business

kaihatsu n 開発 [BOOKISH] development: ~ **shimásu** 開発します develops

kenkyū-kaihatsu n 研究開発 research and development, R&D

kaiheitai n 海兵隊 marines, Marine Corps

kaihi n 会費 membership fee, dues: **nen-kaihi** 年会費 annual membership fee

kaihō n 解放 [BOOKISH] liberation: ~ **shimásu** 解放します liberates

kaihō n 開放 [BOOKISH] open: ~ **shimásu** 開放します opens, leaves open (*windows, doors, etc.*)

kaii adj かいい [INFORMAL] = **kayúi** かゆい・痒い (itchy)

kai-in n 会員 member: **kaiin-sei (no)** 会員制(の) membership system, members-only

kaijō n 開場 [BOOKISH] opening (*of place/event*): ~ **shimásu** 開場します opens; **kaijō-jíkan** 開場時間 opening time; **kaijō´-shiki** 開場式 opening ceremony

kaijō n 会場 hall

kaijō (de/no) adv, adj 海上(で/の) on the sea (*surface*)

kaijū n 怪獣 monster: **kaijū-eiga** 怪獣映画 monster film

kaika n 開花 flowering: ~ **shimásu** 開花します blooms

kaika n 階下 downstairs

kaikaku n 改革 [BOOKISH] reformation, reinvention

kaikan n 会館 a public hall, a building

kaikan n 開館 opening (*a hall*): ~ **shimásu** 開館します opens (*a hall*)

kaikan n 快感 [BOOKISH] pleasure, pleasant feeling: **kaikan o ajiwaimásu/oboemásu** 快感を味わいます/覚えます feels pleasure

kaikei n 会計 n **1. o-kaikei** お会計 accounts; bill, check (= **o-kanjō** お勘定): **o-kaikei/o-kanjō onegai shimásu** お会計/お勘定お願いします Check please **2.** accountant (= **kaikei-gákari** 会計係, **kaikéi-shi** 会計士)

kaiken n 会見 [BOOKISH] interview: **kisha-kaiken** 記者会見 press conference

kaiketsu n 解決 [BOOKISH] solution, settlement: ~ **shimásu** 解決します solves, settles

kaiki n 回帰 [BOOKISH] revolution, recurrence, retouring: **kita-kaiki-sen** 北回帰線 the Tropic of Cancer: **minami-kaiki-sen** 南回帰線 the tropic of Capricorn: ~ **shimásu** 回帰します returns

káiko n 解雇 [BOOKISH] dismissal (*from employment*), discharge: ~ **shimásu** 解雇します dismisses, discharges, fires, disemploys

káiko n 蚕 (**o-káiko** お蚕) silkworm

kaikyaku n 開脚 legs spread (*exercise*): ~ **shimásu** 開脚します has one's legs spread, spreads one's legs wide apart

kaikyo n 快挙 remarkable/wonderful achievement: **kaikyo o nashitogemásu** 快挙を成し遂げます has great accomplishments

kaikyō n 海峡 strait(s)

kaikyō n 回教 Islam (= **Isuramu-kyō** イスラム教)

kaikyū n 階級 class, rank: **chūryū-kaikyū** 中流階級 the middle class

kaimásu, kau v 買います, 買う buys

kaimásu, káu v 飼います, 飼う raises, keeps (*pets, farm animals, etc.*)

kaimen n 海綿 sponge

kai-mono n 買い物 shopping

kaioki n 買い置き **1.** things bought in for the future, hoarded things **2.** hoarding (= **kaidame** 買いだめ): ~ **shimásu** 買い置きします hoards

kaiō-sei n 海王星 Neptune

kairaku n 快楽 pleasure: **kairaku-shugi** 快楽主義 Epicureanism: **kairaku-shugi-sha** 快楽主義者 an Epicurean

kairi n [BOOKISH] 解離 [BOOKISH] disaggregation, dissociation: ~ **shimásu** 解離します disassociate, dissociates

kairi n 海里 nautical mile

kairyō n [BOOKISH] 改良 improvement, modification: ~ **shimásu** 改良します improves, modifies

kairyū n 海流 ocean current

kaisai n 開催 [BOOKISH] holding, opening (*an event*): ~ **shimásu** 開催します holds, opens

kaisan shimásu (suru) v 解散します(する) breaks up, disperses

kaisatsu n 改札 ticket examining/punching/collecting: **kaisatsú-guchi** 改札口 (ticket) wicket

kaisei n 改正 [BOOKISH] revision

kaisei n 快晴 clear and fine weather

kaiseki (ryōri) n 懐石(料理) an assortment of elegant ceremonial-type Japanese foods, Japanese foods in season

kaisetsu n 解説 explanation, comment: ~ **shimásu** 解説します explains, comments; **nyū´su káisetsu** ニュース解説 news commentary

kaisétsu-sha n 解説者 commentator

kaisha n 会社 company, business concern; "the office" (= **kígyō** 企業): **kaishá-in** 会社員 company employee (= **sha-in** 社員, **sararii-man** サラリーマン)

káishaku n 解釈 [BOOKISH] interpretation, explanation, exposition: ~ **shimásu** 解釈します construes, interprets, explains, expounds

kaisho n 楷書 block-style letter (*of Japanese*): **kaisho-tai** 楷書体 printed style/square of writing Chinese characters

kaisō n 海藻・海草 seaweed

kaisō n 回送 (**kaisō-chū** 回送中) **1.** forwarding (*mail matter, letter, etc.*) **2.** deadhead (*an empty car, etc.*): ~ **shimásu** 回送します forwards, deadheads; **kaisō´-sha** 回送車 a car out of service, an off-duty taxi; **kaisō´-ressha** 回送列車 deadhead train

kaisō n 回想: recollection: ~ **shimásu** 回想します recollects

kaisō shiin *n* 回想シーン retrospective scene:

kaisū *n* 回数 the number of times
kaisū´-ken *n* 回数券 ticket book (*for commuting*), coupon ticket

kaisui *n* 海水 seawater
kaisui-yoku *n* 海水浴 sea bathing: **kaisui-yoku o shimásu** 海水浴をします has a bath in the sea

kai-te *n* 買い手 buyer

kaite *v* 欠いて → **kakimásu** 欠きます

káite *v* 書いて → **kakimásu** 書きます

kaitei *n* 改訂 revision (*of documents, books, etc.*): **kaitei-ban** 改訂版 revised version: **~ shimásu** 改訂します revises

kaitei *n* 海底 bottom of the sea

kaiteki (na) *adj* 快適(な) comfortable, peasant

kaiten *n* 回転 revolution, rotation: **~ shimásu** 回転します revolves, rotates

kaiten *n* 開店 opening a shop (*for the first time or for the day*): **~ shimásu** 開店します opens shop/business

kaitō *n* 解答 answer: **~ shimásu** 解答します answers it

kaitō *n* 回答 reply: **~ shimásu** 回答します replies it

kai-torimásu, kai-tóru *v* 買い取ります, 買い取る buys up

kaiun *n* 開運 fortune, good-luck

kaiwa *n* 会話 conversation: **~ shimásu** 会話します has a conversation

kaí ya/wa shinai, kaya shinai *v* [INFORMAL] 買いや/はしない, 買やしない, **káya shinai = kawanai** 買わない (not buy)

kaí ya/wa shinai, kaya shinai *v* [INFORMAL] 飼いや/はしない, 飼やしない = **kawánai** 飼わない (not raise)

kaizen *n* 改善 [BOOKISH] improvement: **~ shimásu** 改善します improves

kaizoku *n* 海賊 pirate: **kaizoku-ban** 海賊版 pirated edition

káji *n* 火事 a fire (*accidental*): **káji ga okorimásu** 火事が起こります Fire breaks out.: **Káji da!** 火事だ! Fire!

káji *n* 舵 helm: **káji o torimásu** 舵をとります takes the helm, steers

káji *n* 家事 housework: **kaji-tetsudai** 家事手伝い housework helper

kájiki *n* カジキ swordfish

kajiránai *v* かじらない = **kajirimasén** かじりません (not gnaw)

kajirimásu, kajíru *v* かじります, かじる gnaws, nibbles

kajítte *v* かじって → **kajirimásu** かじります

kajō *n* 過剰 glut, surplus, excess: **kajō (no)** 過剰(の) superfluous, surplus: **kajō (ni)** 過剰(に) excessively: **kajō-hannō** 過剰反応 overreaction, overresponse

kakaemásu, kakaéru *v* 抱えます, 抱える **1.** holds in one's arms/under one's arm: **atama o kakaemásu** 頭を抱えます tears one's hair out **2.** keeps, retains, has; employs: **takusan no shain**

o kakaete imásu たくさんの社員を抱えています has a lot of employees **3.** has family to support/take case of (*child(ren), sick person(s), etc.*): **byōnin o kakaete imásu** 病人を抱えています has a sick person in one's family **4.** has a problem/problems: **shakkin o kakaete imásu** 借金を抱えています has debts: **(yakkaina/yamazumino) shigoto o kakaete imásu** (厄介な/山積みの)仕事を抱えています has (*difficult/piles of*) works

kakaku *n* 価格 price (= **nedan** 値段): **kakaku-kyōsō** 価格競争 price competition

kakanai *v* 欠かない = **kakimasén** 欠きません (not lack)

kakánai *v* 書かない = **kakimasén** 書きません (not write)

kakan (ni) *adv* 果敢(に) boldly, decisively: **kakan ni tatakaimásu** 果敢に戦います fights with valor

kakaránai *v* 掛からない = **kakarimasén** 掛かりません (not hang)

kakári *v* 掛かり → **kakarimásu** 掛かります [INFINITIVE]

kákari *n* 係 = **kakarí-in** 係員 attendant (*in charge*)

kakarimásu, kakáru *v* 掛かります, 掛かる **1.** it hangs **2.** it takes, requires **3.** it weighs **4.** it begins, (*engine*) starts

kakarimásu, kakáru *v* 架かります, 架かる is built

kakashi *n* カカシ・案山子 scarecrow

kakato *n* 踵 heel: **kakato no takai kutsu** 踵の高い靴 high-heeled shoes (= **haihiiru** ハイヒール)

kakátta *v* 掛かった = **kakarimáshita** 掛かりました (it hung; it took; required; it weighed; it began; (*engine*) started)

kakátte *v* 掛かって → **kakarimásu** 掛かります

kake *n* 欠け lacking, a lack, wane: **tsuki no michi-kake** 月の満ち欠け wax and wane of the moon

kake *v* 欠け → **kakemásu** 欠けます [INFINITIVE]

kaké *n* 掛け credit: **kaké de kaimásu** 掛けで買います buys on credit

káke *v* 欠け → **kakemásu** 欠けます [INFINITIVE]

káke *v* 賭け → **kakemásu** 賭けます [INFINITIVE]

káke *v* 駆け → **kakemásu** 駆けます [INFINITIVE]

káke *v* 書け → **kakemásu** 書けます [INFINITIVE]

káke *v* 書け [IMPERATIVE] (write it!) → **kakimásu** 書きます

kake-ashi *n* 駆け足 running

kakéba *v* 欠けば (if it lacks) → **kakimásu** 欠きます

kákeba *v* 書けば (if one writes) → **kakimásu** 書きます

kake-búton *n* 掛け布団 overquilt, top quilt

kakegoe *n* 掛け声 shout of encouragement: **kakegoe o kakemásu** 掛け声をかけます shouts encouragement

kaké (goto) *n* 賭け(事) gambling; a bet: **kaké (o shi)másu** 賭け(を)します bets, makes a bet

kakehiki *n* 駆け引き tactics, bargaining: **kakehiki ga umai** 駆け引きが上手い is good at bargaining

kakei *n* 家計 household budget: **kakei-bo** 家計簿

housekeeping book: **kakei o sasaemásu** 家計を支えます supports a household

kakei n 家系 one's family line: **kakei-zu** 家系図 a family tree (= **keizu** 系図)

kakéji n 掛け字 = **kaké-jiku** 掛け軸, **kaké-mono** 掛け物 scroll (*hanging*)

kakemásu, kakéru v 掛けます, 掛ける hangs it; multiplies; begins it: **… ni denwa o kakemásu** …に電話を掛けます telephones; **énjin o kakemásu** エンジンを掛けます starts (engine)

kakemásu, kakéru v 欠けます, かける・欠ける lacks it, needs

kakemásu, kakéru v 賭けます, 賭ける bets

kakemásu, kakéru v 駆けます, ・駆ける runs, gallops (*human, animal*)

kakemásu, kakéru v 書けます, 書ける can write

kaké-mono n 掛け物 scroll (*hanging*) (= **kaké-jiku** 掛け軸)

kakenai v 欠けない = **kakemasén** 欠けません (not lack it)

kakénai v 掛けない = **kakemasén** 掛けません (not hang)

kakénai v 賭けない = **kakemasén** 賭けません (not bet)

kakénai v 駆けない = **kakemasén** 駆けません (not run)

kakénai v 書けない = **kakemasén** 書けません (cannot write)

kakera n カケラ・欠片 fragment

kake(ra)remásu v 掛け(ら)れます, **kake(ra)réru** 掛け(ら)れる can hang it, can telephone

kakeréba v 欠ければ (if one lacks it) → **kakemásu** 欠けます

kakéreba v 掛ければ (if one hangs) → **kakemásu** 掛けます

kakéreba v 賭ければ (if one bets) → **kakemásu** 賭けます

kakéreba v 駆ければ (if one runs) → **kakemásu** 駆けます

kakéreba v 書ければ (if one can write) → **kakemásu** 書けます

kaketa v 欠けた = **kakemáshita** 欠けました (lacked it)

káketa v 掛けた = **kakemáshita** 掛けました (hung)

káketa v 賭けた = **kakemáshita** 賭けました (bet)

káketa v 駆けた = **kakemáshita** 駆けました (ran)

káketa v 書けた = **kakemáshita** 書けました (was able to write)

kákete v 欠けて → **kakemásu** 欠けます

kákete v 掛けて → **kakemásu** 掛けます

kákete v 賭けて → **kakemásu** 賭けます

kákete v 駆けて → **kakemásu** 駆けます

kákete v … **ni kákete** …にかけて (*extending*) through, with respect to, as regards

kake-uri n 掛け売り credit sales (= **uri-kake** 売り掛け)

kaké-ya n 賭け屋 bookie

kakeyó´ v 掛けよう = **kakemashō** 掛けましょう (let's hang it!)

kaké-zan n 掛け算 multiplication

kaki n カキ・柿 (*fruits*) persimmon

káki n カキ・牡蠣 oyster

káki n 下記 the following: **káki no tōri** 下記の通り as follows, as below

káki n 花器 flower vase

kaki n 夏期 summer (*period/term*): **kaki-kyūkā** 夏季休暇 summer holiday: **kaki-orinpikku** 夏季オリンピック Olympic Summer Games: **kaki-kōshū** 夏季講習 summer school

kaki n 火気 [BOOKISH] fire, flame: **Kaki-genkin** 火気厳禁 No Fire, Flammables

kaki v 欠き → **kakimáou** 欠きます

káki v 書き → **kakimásu** 書きます [INFINITIVE]

kakiage n かき揚げ a tangle of tidbits fried as *tempura*, fritters

kaki-atsumemásu, kaki-atsuméru v かき集めます, かき集める rakes (them up)

kaki-iremásu, kaki-iréru v 書き入れます, 書き入れる fills in (*information*)

kaki-kaemásu, kaki-kaéru v 書き換えます, 書き換える rewrites

kaki-kata n 書き方 way of writing; spelling

kakimáou, káku v 欠きます, 欠く it lacks, it is lacking/wanting

kakimásu, káku v 書きます, 書く writes

kakimásu, káku v 描きます, 描く paints, draws: **e o kakimásu** 絵を描きます draws a picture (= **egakimásu** 描きます)

kakimásu, káku v 掻きます, 掻く scratches: **senaka o kakimásu** 背中を掻きます scratches one's back

kaki-mawashimásu, kaki-mawasu v かき回します, かき回す stirs

kaki-naoshimásu, kaki-naósu v 書き直します, 書き直す rewrites

kakíne n かき根・垣根 fence

kakitome (yúbin) n 書留(郵便) registered mail

kakitori n 書き取り dictation: **kakitorimásu** 書き取ります dictates

kakí ya/wa shinai v [INFORMAL] 欠きや/はしない = **kakanai** 欠かない (not lack)

káki ya/wa shinai v [INFORMAL] 書きや/はしない = **kakánai** 書かない (not write)

kakki n 活気 liveliness, activity

kakko n 括弧 parenthesis, square bracket, brace

kakkō n 1. 格好 shape, form, appearance: **kakkō ga íi** 格好がいい = **kakko ii** かっこいい shapely, cool, stylish; **kakkō ga warúi** 格好が悪い = **kakko warui** かっこ悪い unsuitable 2. **kakkō (na/no)** 格好(な/の) suitable, moderate, reasonable (*price*)

kákkō n カッコウ cuckoo

káko n 過去 the past
kako-kei n 過去形 the past tense
kako-kanryō n 過去完了 the past perfect: **kako kanryō-kei** 過去完了形 the past perfect tense

kakō n 加工 [BOOKISH] processing (*industrially treating*): **~ shimásu** 加工します processes

kakō n 下降 [BOOKISH] descent: ~ **shimásu** 下降します descends, declines

kakō n 河口 estuary

kakō n 火口 crater (= **kurḗtā** クレーター)

kakō´ v 書こう = **kakimashō** 書きましょう (let's write it!)

kakō´-gan n 花崗岩 granite

kakoku n [BOOKISH] 過酷 [BOOKISH] too severe, harsh: **kakoku na kankyō** 過酷な環境 harsh environment: **kakoku na rōdō-jōken** 過酷な労働条件 harsh working conditions

...-kákoku suffix ...か国・ヶ国・カ国 (counts countries)

kakomi n 囲み an enclosure, a box: **kakomi-kiji** 囲み記事 column, boxed article(s) (= **koramu** コラム)

kakomimásu, kakomu v 囲みます, 囲む surrounds (= **tori-kakomimásu** 取り囲みます)

kakon n 禍根 the source of trouble, the root of evil: **kakon o tachimásu** 禍根を断ちます removes the root of an evil: **kakon o nokoshimásu** 禍根を残します creates potential problem(s) in the future

káku n 角 corner: **san-kaku(kei)/san-kakkei** 三角(形) triangle: **shikakú(kei)/shikakkei** 四角(形) square

káku (do) n 角(度) angle (= **anguru** アングル): **chok-kaku** 直角 right angle: **eikakú** 鋭角 acute angle

káku n 核 core, heart, stone: **chū-kaku** 中核 (central) core

kaku-heiki n 核兵器 nuclear weapon

káku (no) n 核(の) nucleus, nuclear: **genshi-kaku** 原子核 atomic nucleus

káku v 欠く = **kakimásu** 欠きます (it lacks)

káku v 書く = **kakimásu** 書きます (writes)

káku v 描く = **kakimásu** 描きます (draws)

káku´ v 掻く = **kakimásu** 掻きます (scratches)

káku(-) prefix 各... each, every
kakú-eki n 各駅 every station: **kakueki-téisha/ressha** 各駅停車/列車 local train (which stops at every station)
kaku-ron n 各論 each detail: **kakuron ni hairimásu** 各論に入ります gets down into specifics

...káku suffix ...覚 sense (five senses): **shi-kaku** 視覚 sense of sight: **chō-kaku** 聴覚 sense of hearing: **mi-kaku** 味覚 sense of taste: **shū-kaku** 嗅覚 sense of smell: **shok-kaku** 触覚 sense of touch

kakū (no) adj 架空(の) imaginary: **kakū no sekai** 架空の世界 imaginary world: **kakū no jinbutsu** 架空の人物 fictional character

kakudai n 拡大 enlargement: ~ **shimásu** 拡大します enlarges

kakudan (ni/no) adv, adj 格段(に/の) remarkably, remarkable: **kakudan no shinpo** 格段の進歩 remarkable progress

kakugen n 格言 maxim, wise saying

kákugo n 覚悟 resolution, resignation, premeditation: ~ **shimásu** 覚悟します, **kákugo o**

kimemásu 覚悟を決めます is resolved (to do), is prepared for, is resigned to

kakuheki n 隔壁 [BOOKISH] division wall, partition

kakuho n 確保 [BOOKISH] securement, saving: ~ **shimásu** 確保します secures, saves; **seki no kakuho** 席の確保 grabbing a seat

kakujitsu n 確実 certainly **kakujitsu (na)** 確実(な) certain, reliable, authentic (= **tashika na** 確かな)

kakumaimasu, kakumau v [BOOKISH] 匿います, 匿う harbors, shelters: **hannin o kakumaimásu** 犯人を匿います harbors a criminal

kakumaku n 角膜 cornea

kakumaku n 隔膜 diaphragm

kakumei n 革命 [BOOKISH] revolution (political, etc.)

kakunin n 確認 confirmation: ~ **shimásu** 確認します confirms

kakuran n かく乱 [BOOKISH] disturbance: ~ **shimásu** かく乱します disturbs

kakurega n 隠れ家 asylum, shelter, refuge

kakuremásu, kakuréru v 隠れます, 隠れる hides: **kakurenbo, kakurenbō** かくれんぼ, 隠れん坊 hide-and-seek

kakuri n 隔離 [BOOKISH] isolation: ~ **shimásu** 隔離します isolates
kakuri-byō´tō´ 隔離病棟 isolation ward

kakuritsu n 確立 establishment: ~ **shimásu** 確立します establishes

kakuritsu n 確率 probability: **kōsui-kakuritsu** 降水確率 probability of rain

kakusei n 覚醒 [BOOKISH] awakening, emergence, rouse: ~ **shimásu** 覚醒します awakes
kakusei-zai n 覚醒剤 stimulant drug

kakuséi-ki n 拡声器 loudspeaker

kakushimásu, kakúsú v 隠します, 隠す hides (something)

kakushin n 核心 core, heart (= **káku** 核): **kakushin ni furemásu** 核心に触れます touches the core of...

kakutei n 確定 determination, fixedness, settlement: ~ **shimásu** 確定します determines, fixes, settles
kakutei-shinkoku 確定申告 final income tax return

kákuteru n カクテル cocktail: **kakuteru-bā** カクテルバー cocktail bar: **kakuteru-pātii** カクテルパーティ cocktail party

kakutō n 格闘 fight: ~ **shimásu** 格闘します fights
kakutō-gi n 格闘技 martial art

kakutō n 確答 [BOOKISH] definite answer: ~ **shimásu** 確答します answers definitely

kakutoku n [BOOKISH] 獲得 [BOOKISH] acquisition, gain: ~ **shimásu** 獲得します acquires, gains; winning (medal/trophy)

kakuyasu n 格安 bargain, discounted: **kakuyasu-kōkūken** 格安航空券 discount airline ticket

kakuzai n 角材 block of wood

kakuzuke n [BOOKISH] 格付け rating, grading: ~ **shimásu** 格付けします rates, grades

kakyū (no) adj 下級(の) low-class: **kakyūsei** 下級生 underclassman

kamá *n* かま・窯 oven, kiln

kamá *n* かま・釜 (*Japanese style*) kettle, iron pot, cauldron, boiler: **onaji kama no meshi o taberu** 同じ釜の飯を食べる eats from the same bowl: **watashi-tachi wa onaji kama no meshi o kutta naka desu.** 私たちは同じ釜の飯を食った仲です We all ate from the same bowl. → **kamameshi** 釜飯

káma *n* 鎌 sickle: **hebi ga kama-kubi o motagemásu** 蛇が鎌首をもたげます The snake raises its head.

kamaboko *n* かまぼこ・カマボコ steamed fish cake

kamachí *n* 框 frame, rail

kamachi *n* カマチ cachema

kamado *n* かまど (*Japanese traditional*) kitchen range, stove; oven; furnace

kamaimasén, kamawánai *v* 構いません, 構わない it makes no difference; never mind; not to bother, it's o.k.

kamakiri *n* カマキリ praying mantis

kamameshi *n* 釜飯 (*cooked*) rice (*with chicken, crab, or shrimp*) served in a clay pot

kamánai *v* 噛まない = **kamimasén** 噛みません (not chew/bite)

kamasú *v* カマス barracuda, saury-pike

kamé *n* 瓶 jar (*with large mouth*)

káme *n* カメ・亀 tortoise, turtle

káme *v* 噛め 1. [INFINITIVE] 2. [IMPERATIVE] (chew!) → **kamimásu** 噛みます

kámeba *v* 噛めば (if one chews it) → **kamimásu** 噛みます

kamei *n* 仮名 an assumed name; a temporary/ tentative name

kamei *n* 加盟 affiliation: **~ shimásu** 加盟します affiliates

kamei *n* 家名 family name

kamemásu, kaméru *v* 噛めます, 噛める can chew/bite

kamen *n* 仮面 mask (= **másuku** マスク)

kaménai *v* 噛めない = **kamemasén** 噛めません (cannot chew/bite)

kámera *n* カメラ camera: **dejitaru-kamera** デジタルカメラ digital camera: **bideo-kamera** ビデオカメラ video camera

kaméreba *v* 噛めれば (if one can chew/bite) → **kamemásu** 噛めます

kamí *n* 紙 paper
  kami-básami *n* 紙ばさみ file folder; file; paperclip
  kami-búkuro *n* 紙袋 paper bag
  kami-hikōki *n* 紙飛行機 paper airplane
  kami-kúzu *n* 紙くず wastepaper
  kami-yásuri *n* 紙やすり sandpaper

kámi *n* 神 1. God, gods (= **kámi-sama** 神様) 2. divinity (= **shinsei** 神性)
  kami-dana *n* 神棚 household altar (*Shinto*)
  kámi-sama *n* 神様 God, gods, Dear Lord

kamí *v* 噛み → **kamimásu** 噛みます [INFINITIVE]

kamimásu, kamu *v* かみます, かむ: **hana o kamimásu** 鼻をかみます blows one's nose

kamimásu, kámu *v* 噛みます, 噛む chews, bites: **(fūsen) gamu o kamimásu** (風船)ガムを噛みます chews (*bubble*) gum: **shita o kamisō na kotoba** 舌をかみそうな言葉 a jawbreaker

kaminári *n* かみなり・カミナリ・雷 thunder, thunderstorm: **kaminarí ga narimásu** 雷が鳴ります it thunders

kamí (no ke) *n* 髪(の毛) hair (*on head*): **kamí (no ke) o araimásu** 髪(の毛)を洗います shampoos

kami-san *n* かみさん [INFORMAL] my wife

kamisórí *n* 剃刀 razor: **kamisórí no ha** 剃刀の刃 razor blade

kami-tsukimásu, kami-tsuku *v* 噛みつきます, 噛みつく bites

kámi ya/wa shinai *v* [INFORMAL] 噛みや/はしない = **kamánai** 噛まない (not chew/bite it)

kámo *n* カモ・鴨 wild duck

kámo *n* かも・カモ dupe, sucker

kamō´ *v* 噛もう = **kamimashō** 噛みましょう (let's chew/bite it!)

kamoku *n* 科目 subject, course (*in school*): **hisshū kamoku** 必修科目 required course/subject

Kamome *n* カモメ・鴎 seagull

… kámo (shiremasén) *suffix*, *v* …かも(しれません) = **kámo shirenai** かもしれない maybe …, perhaps …

kamu *v* かむ → **kamimásu** かみます

kámu *v* 噛む → **kamimásu** 噛みます

kán *n* 缶 can → **kan-zúme (no …)** 缶詰(の…) kan-biiru 缶ビール canned beer: kan-kírí 缶切り can opener

kán *n* 燗 (o-kan お燗) heating rice wine: **(o-)kan o tsukemásu/shimásu** (お)燗をつけます／します warms the saké

kán *n* 管 tube, pipe, duct: **suidō-kan** 水道管 water pipe: **kek-kan** 血管 blood vessel

kán *n* 巻 volume (*books, tapes*): **(dai) ik-kan** (第)一巻 vol. 1

…´- kan *suffix* …間 for the interval of; between

…´- kan *suffix* …感 feeling, sense: **go-kan** 五感 five sense: **dai-rok-kan** 第六感 sixth sense: **shok-kan** 触感 tactile (*sensation*): **shok-kan** 食感 food texture

kana *n* かな kana (*Japanese syllabic writing*) → **furi-gana** ふりがな・フリガナ

…ka na/ne *interj* …かな/かね I wonder/whether (= **deshō ka** でしょうか)

Kánada *n* カナダ Canad
  Kanadá-jin *n* カナダ人 a Canadian

kánai *n* 家内 1. my wife 2. one's family: **kanai-anzen** 家内安全 well-being/safety of one's family: **kanai-kōgyō** 家内工業 cottage industry

kanaimásu, kanáu *v* 適います, 適う accords/ agrees (*with*): **dōri ni kanaimásu** 道理にかないます it stands to reason; **mokuteki ni kanaimásu** 目的にかないます it serves the purpose

kanaimásu, kanáu *v* 敵います, 敵う is a match

(*for*), matches, is equal (*to*): **aité ni kanaimasén** 相手に敵いません is no match for the opponent

kanaimásu, kanáu v 叶います, 叶う (= **dekimásu** できます) is accomplished, attained, achieved, realized: **nozomi ga kanaimásu** 望みが叶います a desire is realized (*fulfilled*): **yume ga kanaimásu** 夢が叶います a dream comes true: **negai ga kanaimásu** 願いが叶います a wish comes true

kanamono n 金物 hardware: **kanamono-ya** 金物屋 hardware store

kanarazu adv 必ず for sure; necessity; inevitably

kánari adv かなり fairly, rather

kanaria n カナリア canary

kanashii adj 悲しい sad

kanashimi n 悲しみ sadness

kanashimimásu, kanashimu v 悲しみます, 悲しむ to be sad

kanazuchi n かなづち・カナヅチ・金槌 **1.** hammer **2.** a person who cannot swim

kanban n 看板 **1.** signboard, sign **2.** (*diner, pub*) closing time
kanban-musume n 看板娘 beautiful lady who attracts consumers/customers
kanban-yakusha n 看板役者 star actor

kanbasu n カンバス canvas (= **kyánbasu** キャンバス)

kanbatsu n かんばつ・干ばつ drought (= **hideri** ひでり・日照り)

kanben (na) n, adj 簡便(な) convenience, convenient, simple and easy

kanben shitekudasai interj 勘弁して下さい Please give me a break

kanbi n 完備 full equipment: ~ **shiteimásu** 完備しています is fully equipped

kanbi (na) adj 甘美(な) sweet, luscious, dulcet: **kanbi na kajitsu** 甘美な果実 sweet fruit: **kanbi na merodii** 甘美なメロディー dulcet melody

kanbu n 患部 [BOOKISH] diseased part, affected area

kanbu n 幹部 [BOOKISH] executive

kanbun n 漢文 Chinese classics

kanbutsu n 乾物 dry food

kanbō n 感冒 [BOOKISH] common cold: **ryūkōsei-kanbō** 流行性感冒 influenza (= **infuruénza** インフルエンザ)

kanbō n 官房 [BOOKISH] Secretariat: **naikaku kanbō-chōkan** 内閣官房長官 Chief Cabinet Secretary

kanbō n 監房 [BOOKISH] ward, jail cell

kanbojia n カンボジア Cambodia
Kanbojia-go n カンボジア語 Cambodian (*language*)
Kanbojia-jin n カンボジア人 a Cambodian

kanboku n 潅[灌]木 bush

kanbotsu n 陥没 [BOOKISH] subsidence, cave-in, sinking: ~ **shimásu** 陥没します subsides, caves

kanbyō n 看病 nursing: ~ **shimásu** 看病します nurses

kanchi n 感知 appreciation, sense: ~ **shimásu** 感知します senses

kanchi n 完治 [BOOKISH] complete cure: ~ **shimásu** 完治します cures completely

kanchō n 浣腸 enema

kánchō n 艦長 captain (*of warship*)

kánchō n 官庁 government office

kanchō n 干潮 ebb, low tide

kandai (na) adj 寛大(な) generous, lenient: **kandai na shochi** 寛大な処置 lenient judgment: **kandai na hito** 寛大な人 broad-minded person: **kandai na kokoro** 寛大な心 generous heart, big heart

kandán-kei n 寒暖計 (*room*) thermometer

kande v かんで → **(hana o) kami-másu** (鼻を)かみます v (blows nose)

kánde v 噛んで → **kamimásu** 噛みます (chews, bites)

kandō n 感動 (strong) emotion, (deep) feeling: ~ **shimásu** 感動します is impressed

kane n 金 **1.** money (= **o-kane** お金) **2.** metal (= **kinzoku** 金属)

kane n 鐘 large bell (*of church, temple, etc.*): **joya no kane** 除夜の鐘 the bells on New Year's Eve

... ka ne interj ...かね (mostly male. INFORMAL) = **... ka ne/na** ...かね/かな (I wonder/whether)

kane-bako n 金箱 **1.** cashbox, money box (= **zeni-bako** 銭箱) **2.** patron, gold mine, money-maker, cash cow (= **doru-bako** ドル箱)

kanemásu, kanéru v 兼ねます, 兼ねる combines, unites; dually/concurrently serves as

kanemóchí (no) adj 金持ち(の) rich (*wealthy*)

kan'en n 肝炎 hepatitis

kānēshon n カーネーション carnation(s): **haha-no-hi ni okuru kānēshon** 母の日に贈るカーネーション carnations gifted for Mother's Day

kanetsu n 加熱 heat, heating: ~ **shimásu** 加熱します heats
kanetsu-ki n 加熱器 heater

kangáe 考え **1.** n thought, idea, opinion **2.** v → **kangaemásu** 考えます

kangaemásu, kangáeru v 考えます, 考える thinks, considers

kangaeraremásu, kangaeraréru v 考えられます, 考えられる can think; it is thought

kangei n 歓迎 welcome (= **kantai** 歓待): ~ **shimásu** 歓迎します welcomes
kangei-kai n 歓迎会 reception (*welcome party*)

kangeki n 感激 (strong) emotion (*feeling*): ~ **shimásu** 感激します is touched; (= **kandō** 感動)

kango n 漢語 Chinese word/vocabulary (*in Japanese*)

kángo n 看護 nursing (*a patient*): ~ **shimásu** 看護します nurses
kangó-shi n 看護師 a nurse (= **kangó-fu** 看護婦)

kani n カニ・蟹 crab

kānibaru n カーニバル carnival

kanja n 患者 (*medical*) patient

kanji *n* 漢字 a Chinese character (*symbol*), kanji

kanji *n* 感じ feeling (= **kankaku** 感覚): **konna-kanji (de/no)** こんな感じ(で/の) like this; **sonna/anna-kanji (de/no)** そんな/あんな感じ(で/の) like that

kanji *v* 感じ → **kan-jimásu** 感じます

kan-jimásu, kan-jiru *v* 感じます, 感じる feels

kanjō *n* 感情 emotion

kanjō *n* 環状 [BOOKISH] loop (*shape*): **kanjō (no)** 環状(の) ring-shaped, circular; **kanjō-sen** 環状線 loop/belt line

kanjō´ *n* 勘定 (**o-kanjō** お勘定) bill, check, account: **o-kanjō/o-kaikei onegai shimásu** お勘定/お会計お願いします Check please

kanjō-gákari 勘定係 cashier

kankaku *n* 感覚 sense, sensibility, feeling, sensation

kankaku *n* 間隔 space, interval (*of time, space*)

kankei *n* 関係 connection, relationship, interest, concern, relevance: **... no kankéi-sha** ...の関係者 the people/ authorities concerned with ..., the ... people

kánki *n* 換気 ventilation: **kanki-sen** 換気扇 ventilator; **kanki sō´chi** 換気装置 ventilation system

kankō *n* 観光 sightseeing, tour: **kankō-básu** 観光バス sightseeing bus; **kankō-réssha** 観光列車 sightseeing train

kankō´-kyaku *n* 観光客 tourist, sightseer

Kánkoku *n* 韓国 South Korea

Kankoku-go *n* 韓国語 Korean (*language*)

Kankokú-jin *n* 韓国人 a Korean

kankyaku *n* 観客 audience, spectator

kankyō *n* 環境 environment: **kankyō-osen** 環境汚染 environmental pollution; **kankyō-hogo** 環境保護 environmental protection

Kankyō-shō *n* 環境省 Ministry of the Environment (MOE)

kanmatsu *n* 巻末 end of a book

kanmi *n* 甘味 sweetness: **kanmi-ryō** 甘味料 sweetening

kanna *n* かんな・カンナ plane (*tool*)

kannai (de/ni) *adv* 管内(で/に) within the jurisdiction: **ki-kannai-chūbu** 気管内チューブ endotracheal tube

kannai (de/ni) *adv* 館内(で/に) inside the building: **kannai-hōsō** 館内放送 announcements in the building: **kannai-tsuā** 館内ツアー guided tour of the building

kannen *n* 観念 **1.** idea (*Platonism*) (= **idea** イデア) **2.** concept, conception **3.** giving up **4.** meditation (*Buddhism*): ~ **shimásu** 観念します gives up, meditates

kannin *n* 堪忍 [BOOKISH] patience: ~ **shimásu** 堪忍します is patient and forgives; **kannin shitekudasai** 堪忍して下さい Please forgive me.: **kannin-bukuro no o ga kireru** 堪忍袋の緒が切れる runs out of patience

kanningu *n* カンニング (*during examination, test, etc.*) cheating: ~ **shimásu** カンニングします cheats

kanningu-pēpā *n* カンニングペーパー crib note

kannō *n* 完納 [BOOKISH] full payment: ~ **shimásu** 完納します pays up

kannō *n* 感応 [BOOKISH] response, participation: ~ **shimásu** 感応します sympathizes

kannō *n* 間脳 diencephalon

kannō teki (na) *adj* 官能的(な) sensual, erotic

kannúki *n* かんぬき bolt (*of door*)

kánnushi *n* 神主 priest (*Shinto*)

káno-jo *pron* 彼女 she/her; girlfriend, mistress

kanō (na) *adj* 可能(な) possible: **kanō-sei** 可能性 possibility

kanpa *n* カンパ fund-raising campaign (*comes from the Russian "kampaniya"*): ~ **shimásu** カンパします contributes to the fundraising campaign

kanpai *n* 乾杯 a toast, "bottoms up": ~ **shimásu** 乾杯します toasts: **Kanpai!** 乾杯 Cheers!

kanpai *n* 完敗 complete defeat: ~ **shimásu** 完敗します is completely beaten

kanpán *n* 甲板 deck (*of ship*)

kanpan *n* 乾パン hardtack

kanpeki (na) *adj* 完璧(な) perfectness, perfect

kanpi *n* 官費 government expense, government expenditure

kanpō *n* 官報 gazette

kanpō (yaku) *n* 漢方(薬) Chinese medicine

kanpu *n* 還付 refund: **kanpu-kin** 還付金 tax refund

kanpū *n* 寒風 cold wind

kanpū *n* 完封 shut-out: **kanpū-jiai** 完封試合 shutout game

kanpuku *n* 感服 admiration (= **kanshin** 感心, **kantan** 感嘆): ~ **shimásu** 感服します admires, is impressed

kanpyō´ *n* カンピョウ dried gourd strips, dried ground shavings

kanrán-seki *n* 観覧席 grandstand (*seats*)

kanren *n* 関連 relevance (= **kankei** 関係): **(... ni)** ~ **shimásu** (...に)関連します is relevant (*to*), is connected (*with*)

kánri *n* 管理 control (= **kontorōru** コントロール)

kanri-nin *n* 管理人 custodian, janitor, manager, landlord (*rental manager*)

kanri-sha *n* 管理者 administrator

kanroku *n* 貫禄 presence (= **igen** 威厳): **kanroku ga arimásu** 貫禄があります has a presence

kansai-chihō *n* 関西地方 The Kansai area of Japan (*Kyoto, Osaka, Kobe, Nara, Shiga, Hyogo, Wakayama prefecture etc.*)

kansatsu *n* 観察 [BOOKISH] observation, watching

kansatsú-sha *n* 観察者 observer

kansatsu *n* 監察 [BOOKISH] inspection

kansatsú-kan *n* 監察官 inspector

kansatsu *n* 鑑札 [BOOKISH] license (tag): **inú no kansatsu** 犬の鑑札 a dog(-license) tag

kansatsu shimásu (suru) *v* 観察します(する) observes, watches

kansatsu shimásu (suru) *v* 監察します(する) inspects

kansei *n* 完成 completion, perfection: ~ **shimásu** 完成します completes, perfects

kansetsu *n* 関節 joint (*of two bones*): **(shu)shi-kansetsu** (手)指関節 knuckle: **soku-kansetsu** 足関節 ankle (= **ashikubi** 足首): **kansetsu-en** 関節炎 arthritis

kansetsu (no) *adj* 間接(の) indirect: **kansetsu-kisu** 間接キス indirect kiss
kansetsu(-teki) ni *adj* 間接(的)に indirectly

kánsha *n* 感謝 thanks, gratitude: ~ **shimásu** 感謝します appreciates, thanks
kansha-sai *n* 感謝祭 Thanksgiving

kan-shimásu (-súru) *v* 関します relates (*to*), concerns, is connected (*with*): **... ni kánshite ...** に関して concerning, as regards, with respect to ...

kanshin *n* 関心 concern, interest (= **kyōmi** 興味): **kanshin ga arimásu** 関心があります is interested in

kanshin *n* 感心 admiration (= **kanpuku** 感服, **kantan** 感嘆): ~ **shimásu** 感心します admires, is impressed

kanshō *n* 干渉 interference, meddling: ~ **shimásu** 干渉します interferes; **kanshō shinai de kudasai** 干渉しないで下さい Please stay away from me., Please stay out of it.

kanshō *n* 鑑賞 [BOOKISH] appreciation (*art, work, music*): **(watashi no) shumi wa ongaku-kanshō/eiga-kanshō desú** (私の)趣味は音楽鑑賞/映画鑑賞です My hobby is listening to music/watching movies.

kanshō *n* 観賞 [BOOKISH] admiration, enjoyment: **kanshō-shokubutsu** 観賞植物 ornamental plant

kansoku *n* 観測 observation; opinion (= **íken** 意見): **hoshi no kansai** 星の観測 observation of the stars: **kansoku shimásu** 観測します observes

kansō *n* 感想 impression: **dokusho kansō-bun** 読書感想文 book report (*at school*)

kansō *n* 乾燥 dryness: ~ **shimásu** 乾燥します dries (*something*), It is dry weather.
kansō-ki *n* 乾燥機 dryer (*washing machine*)

kansōgei-kai *n* 歓送迎会 welcome and farewell party: **kansōgei-kai o hirakimásu** 歓送迎会を開きます holds a welcome & farewell party

kantai *n* 歓待 [BOOKISH] welcome (= **kangei** 歓迎): ~ **shimásu** 歓待します welcomes

kantan *n* 感嘆 [BOOKISH] admiration (= **kanshin** 感心, **kanpuku** 感服): ~ **shimásu** 感嘆します admires, is impressed

kantan (na) *adj* 簡単(な) easy, simple, brief

kantei *n* 鑑定 [BOOKISH] judgment: ~ **shimásu** 鑑定します judges, authenticates

kantei *n* 官邸 official residence: **shushō-kantei** 首相官邸 official residence of the prime minister

kanten *n* カンテン・寒天 gelatin from *tengusa* seaweed

kantō-chihō *n* 関東地方 the Kantō area of Japan (*Tokyō, Chiba, Saitama, Kanagawa, Ibaraki, Tochigi, Gunma, Yamanashi prefecture*) →

shutó-ken 首都圏

kantoku *n* 監督 supervision; supervisor, superintendant, overseer, manager, director: ~ **shimásu** 監督します supervises, oversees, manages (*a team*), directs (*a film*)
eiga-kantoku *n* 映画監督 film director

kantó'shi *n* 間投詞 interjection

kanzei *n* 関税 customs duty (*tariff*)

kanzen *n* 完全 perfection, completeness: **kanzen na...** 完全な... perfect...: **kanzen ni** 完全に completely

kanzō *n* 肝臓 liver

kan-zúmé (no ...) *adj* 缶詰(の...) **1.** canned (*food*), can, tin **2.** confine oneself: **hoteru ni kanzume ni natte kiji o kakimásu** ホテルに缶詰になって記事を書きます confines oneself to a hotel room to write articles

kao *n* 顔 face; looks, a look: **... (no) kao o shite imásu ...** (の)顔をしています has/wears an expression of ...
kao-iro *n* 顔色 complexion: **kao-iro no hyōjō** 顔色の表情 facial expression: **kao-iro o ukagaimásu** 顔色をうかがいます watches a person's reactions

kaō *v* 買おう = **kaimashō** 買いましょう (let's buy it!)

kaō *v* 飼おう = **kaimashō** 飼いましょう (let's raise it!)

kaomoji *n* 顔文字 Emoticon

kaori *n* 香(り) fragrance, incense (= **kō'** 香): **kōsui no kaori** 香水の香り fragrance of perfume: **kaorimásu** 香ります is fragrant

kā'pétto *n* カーペット carpet (= **jū'tan** じゅうたん・絨毯)

kappa *n* かっぱ・カッパ・河童 **1.** water imp **2.** (*sushi bar term*) cucumber (= **kyū'ri** キュウリ・胡瓜): **kappa-maki** かっぱ巻き seaweed-rolled sushi with cucumber in the center

kapparaimásu, kapparaú *v* かっぱらいます, かっぱらう [INFORMAL] swipes, steals, shoplifts

kappatsu (na) *adj* 活発(な) active, lively

kappō *n* 割烹 [BOOKISH] Japanese restaurant, Japanese cuisine: **kappō-gi** 割烹着 Japanese-style apron

káppu *n* カップ a cup (*with handle*): **kōhii-káppu** コーヒーカップ coffee cup: **magu-káppu** マグカップ mug

káppuru *n* カップル a couple (*of lovers*)

kápuseru *n* カプセル capsule: **kapuseru-hoteru** カプセルホテル capsule hotel

kara *n* 殻 shell, crust: **monuke no kara** もぬけのから[殻] completely empty (= **karappo (no)** 空っぽ(の))

kara (no) *adj* から[空](の) empty: **karappo (no)** から[空]っぽ(の) completely empty (= **monuke no kara** もぬけのから[殻])

... kará *prep, conj* ...から **1.** from..., since... (*time, space*): **... kara, ... máde** ...から...まで from ... to ... **2.** because...

kárā *n* カラー collar (= **eri** 襟)

kárā *n* カラー color (= **iro** 色)

karada *n* 体・身体 body; one's health: **karada ni ki o tsukete kudasai** (身)体に気をつけて下さい Please take care of yourself.

karái *adj* 辛い **1.** spicy, hot, peppery, pungent **2.** salty (= **shio-karai** 塩辛い; **shoppai** しょっぱい)

karakaimás<u>u</u>, karakáu *v* からかいます, からかう teases, pokes fun at

kara-kása *n* 唐傘 (*oil-paper*) umbrella

karanai *v* 刈らない = **karimasén** 刈りません (not mow)

karaoke *n* カラオケ karaoke

karashi *n* カラシ・芥子 mustard (= **masutādo** マスタード)

kárasu *n* カラス・烏 crow

karate *n* カラテ・空手 karate (*weaponless self-defense*): **karaté-gí** 空手着 karate outfit/suit

káre *pron* 彼 he/him

   kárē-ra *pron* 彼ら they/them

káre *n* 彼 boyfriend (*lover*) (= **kare-shi** 彼氏)

karē *n* カレー curry: **karē-ráisu** カレーライス rice with curry

karéba *v* 刈れば (if one mows) → **karimásu** 刈ります

kárei *n* カレイ flatfish, turbot

karemásu, kareru *v* 枯れます, 枯れる withers: **karete imásu** 枯れています is withered

karemásu, kareru *v* 刈れます, 刈れる can mow/cut

karenai *v* 枯れない = **karemasén** 枯れません (not withers)

karéndā *n* カレンダー calendar (= **koyomí** 暦)

kareréba *v* 枯れれば (if it withers) → **karemásu** 枯れます

káre-shi *n* 彼氏 boyfriend (*lover*) (= **káre** 彼)

karete *v* 枯れて → **karemásu** 枯れます

karete *v* 刈れて → **karemásu** 刈れます

kari (no) *adj* 仮(の) temporary, tentative: **kari-zumai** 仮住まい temporary residence

kári 狩り **1.** *n* hunting: **kári o shimás<u>u</u>** 狩りをします hunts **2.** *v* → **karimásu** 狩ります hunts [INFINITIVE]

kari 借り **1.** *n* borrowing: **kari ga arimás<u>u</u>** 借りがあります I owe you. **2.** *v* → **karimásu** 借ります hunts [INFINITIVE]

   karí-chin *n* 借り賃 rent (*charge*)

   kari-te *n* 借り手 the borrower/renter, the lessee, the tenant: **kari-te ga mitsukarimashita** 借り手が見つかりました I found a tenant

karimás<u>u</u>, karu *v* 刈ります, 刈る mows, cuts

karimás<u>u</u>, kariru *v* 借ります, 借りる borrows/rents it (from …)

karinai *v* 借りない = **karimasén** 借りません (not borrow)

kari(ra)remás<u>u</u>, kari(ra)reru *v* 借り(ら)れます, 借り(ら)れる can borrow

karite *v* 借りて → **karimásu** 借ります

karí ya/wa shinai *v* [INFORMAL] 刈りや/はしない

= **karanai** 刈らない (not mow)

kariyō *v* 借りよう = **karimashō'** 借りましょう (let's borrow/rent it!)

karō' *v* 刈ろう = **karimashō'** 刈りましょう (let's mow!)

karō *n* 過労 overfatigue: **karō-shi** 過労死 death from overwork

karu *v* 刈る = **karimásu** 刈ります (mows, cuts)

kāru *n* カール curl

karui *adj* 軽い light (*of weight*)

karuishi *n* 軽石 pumice

Karukatta *n* カルカッタ Calcutta (Kolkata)

kása *n* 傘・かさ umbrella: **kasa-date** 傘立て umbrella stand

kása *n* 笠 bamboo hat; (*mushroom*) cap

kasá *n* 嵩 bulk

kasabarimás<u>u</u>, kasabaru *v* かさばります, かさばる is bulky, takes up much space

kasai *n* 火災 fire (*accidental*) (= **káji** 火事): **kasai-kéihō** 火災警報 fire alarm, **kasai-hōchíki** 火災報知器 fire alarm (*device*), fire bell

kasanai *v* 貸さない = **kashimasén** 貸しません (not lend)

kasanarimás<u>u</u>, kasanaru *v* 重なります, 重なる they pile up

kasanemás<u>u</u>, kasaneru *v* 重ねます, 重ねる piles them up, puts one on top of another

kase *n* かせ shackles: **te-kase** 手かせ handcuffs; **ashi-kase** 足かせ fetters: **kase o hazushimás<u>u</u>** かせを外します unshackles

kase *v* 貸せ **1.** → **kasemásu** 貸せます [INFINITIVE] **2.** [IMPERATIVE] (lend it!) → **kashimásu** 貸します

kaséba *v* 貸せば (if one lends) → **kasemásu** 貸します

kasegimás<u>u</u>, kaségu *v* 稼ぎます, 稼ぐ earns, works for (*money*)

kasei *n* 火星 Mars

   kaséi-jin *n* 火星人 a Martian

kaséide *v* 稼いで → **kasegimásu** 稼ぎます

kaséi-fu *n* 家政婦 housekeeper, hired maid

kaseki *n* 化石 fossil(s)

kasemás<u>u</u>, kaseru *v* 貸せます, 貸せる can lend

kasen *n* 下線 underline: **kasen o hikimás<u>u</u>** 下線を引きます draws an underline

kasen *n* 化繊 [BOOKISH] synthetic fiber

kasenai *v* 貸せない = **kasemasén** 貸せません (cannot lend)

kasetto (tēpu) *n* カセット(テープ) cassette (tape)

kashí *v* 貸し → **kashimásu** 貸します [INFINITIVE]

káshi *n* 歌詞 lyrics

káshi *n* 菓子 (**o-káshi** お菓子) cakes, sweets, pastry, candy: **wa-gáshi** 和菓子 Japanese-style confection; **yō-gáshi** 洋菓子 Western-style confection

   kashí-ya *n* 菓子屋 candy store, confectionary; confectioner

kashikiri-básu *n* 貸し切りバス chartered bus
(= **chātā-basu** チャーターバス)
kashikói *adj* 賢い wise
kashikomarimáshita かしこまりました.
I understand and will comply (*with your request*).
[HONORIFIC]
kashí-ma *n* 貸間 rooms for rent; rented/rental
room(s)
kashimásu, kasu *v* 貸します, 貸す lends; rents
(it out to)
kashirá *n* 頭 (**o-kashira** お頭) head; chief, leader
… káshira *interj* …かしら (*mostly female*)
I wonder/whether
kashi-te *n* 貸し手 the lender/lessor, the landlord
kashite *v* 貸して → **kashimásu** 貸します
kashitsu *n* 過失 mistakes, errors, faults: **kashitsu-sekinin** 過失責任 negligence liability
kashi-ya *n* 貸家 house for rent; rented/rental
house
kashí ya/wa shinai *v* [INFORMAL] 貸しや/はしない = **kasanai** 貸さない (not lend)
…-kásho *suffix* …か所・箇所・個所 (*counter for places, installations, institutions*)
kashoku-shō *n* 過食症 bulimia nervosa
kashu *n* 歌手 singer: **ryūkō-kashu** 流行歌手 pop singer
kasō *n* 仮装 disguise: **kasō-pātii** 仮装パーティ
costume party: **kasō-ishō** 仮装衣装 costume
(= **kosuchūmu** コスチューム)
kasō *n* 火葬 cremation: ~ **shimásu** 火葬します
cremates
kasō *n* 仮想 [BOOKISH] virtual, imaginary: **kasō-kūkan** 仮想空間 virtual space
kasō *n* 下層 [BOOKISH] lower layer: **kasō-kaikyū** 下層階級 lower class society
kasō´ *v* 貸そう = **kashimashō** 貸しましょう (let's lend it!)
kasoku *n* 加速 acceleration: ~ **shimásu**
加速します accelerates
kasoku-pédaru 加速ペダル gas pedal (= **akuseru** アクセル)
kāsoru *n* カーソル cursor (*on the computer screen, etc.*)
kasu *v* 貸す = **kashimásu** 貸します (lends)
kásu *n* かす[滓] 1. sediment, dregs, grounds:
kōhii-kasu コーヒーかす coffee grounds 2. waste,
scum, mud, trash, rags, scrap, junk (= **kúzu** くず
[屑]): **moe-kasu** 燃えかす cinders: **ningen/seken no kásu** 人間/世間のかす the scum of the earth
3. particles: **tabe-kasu** 食べかす food particles
kásu *n* かす[糟・粕] lees: **sake-kasu** 酒粕 sake
lees
kásuka (na/ni) *adj, adv* かすか(な/に)・微か
(な/に) faint(ly), dim(ly), slight(ly)
kasumemásu, kasumeru *v* 掠めます, 掠める
skims, grazes
kasume-torimásu, kasume-toru *v* 掠め取ります, 掠め取る skims off; robs (*it of …*), cheats (*one out of …*) (= **kasumemásu** 掠めます)

kasumi *n* かすみ・霞 haze, mist
kasumimásu, kasumu *v* 霞みます, 霞む gets
dim, hazy, misty
kasurimásu, kasuru *v* かすります, かする grazes
kasutanetto *n* カスタネット castanet(s)
kasutera *n* カステラ Japanese sponge cake,
Castella
kata *n* 型 1. form, shape, size, mold, pattern: **kata ni hamemásu** 型にはめます stereotypes: **ō-gata**
大型 large-size 2. type, model: **ketsueki-gata**
血液型 blood type: **A/B/AB/O gata** A/B/AB/O
型 blood type A/B/AB/O
káta *n* 肩 shoulder(s)
kata-gaki *n* 肩書き (*business/position*) title
…-kata *suffix* …方 manner of doing, way: **yari-kata** やり方 method, process (= **hōhō** 方法):
kangae-kata 考え方 one's way of thinking, one's
point of view
… katá *n* …方 (**o-kata** お方) (*honored*) person:
ano-kata あの方 that person, **anata-gata** あなた方
you people
kata-… *prefix* 片… one (*of a pair*) (= **katáhō**
片方): **kata-ashi** 片足 one leg/foot: **kata-gawa**
片側 one side
katá-hō *n* 片方, **katáppō** 片っぽう, **katáppo** 片っ
ぽ one of a pair; the other one (*of a pair*)
kata-koto *n* 片言 imperfect language, limited
language: **katakoto de hanashimásu** 片言で話
します speaks broken language (*does not speak
fluently*)
kata-michi *n* 片道 one-way: **katamichi kíppu**
片道切符 one way ticket
katachi *n* 形 form, shape
katadoru *adj* かたど[象・模]る imitated, copied,
modeled, symbolized (= **shōchō** 象徴)
… katá-gata *suffix* …方々 (*honored*) persons
(= **… katá-tachi** …方達)
katagi (na) *adj* 堅気(な) respectable, steady,
honest
katai *n* 固い hard; tight; strong; firm; strong; strict
katai *n* 硬い hard, stiff; stilted upright
katai *n* 堅い hard; solid; sound; reliable; serious;
formal
katákana *n* カタカナ・片かな・片仮名 katakana
(*the squarish Japanese letters*)
katakúríko *n* 片栗粉 potato starch
katamari *n* 固まり・塊 a lump, a clot, a mass; a
loaf (*of bread*)
katamari *v* → **katamarimásu** 固まります
katamarimásu, katamaru *v* 固まります, 固まる
it hardens, congeals, clots, (*mud*) cakes
katamemásu, katameru *v* 固めます, 固める
hardens it, congeals it; strengthens it
katamuki *n* 傾き slant; inclination, tendency
katamukimásu, katamúku *v* 傾きます, 傾く
leans (*to one side*), slants
kataná *n* 刀 sword
katánai *adj* 勝たない = **kachimasén** 勝ちません
(not win)

katáppo *n* 片っぽ one of a pair; the other one (*of a pair*) (= **katáhō** 片方)

katarimásu *v* 語ります, **kataru** 語る relates, tells

... katá-tachi *n* ...方達 (*honored*) persons

katáwa *n* 片輪 (*discriminatory term*) cripple

kata-yorimásu *v* 片寄り[偏り]ます, **kata-yóru** 片寄る[偏る] leans (*to one side*); is partial (*to*)

kata-zukemásu, kata-zukéru *v* 片付けます, 片付ける puts in order, straightens up, tidies, cleans up

kata-zukimásu, kata-zúku *v* 片付きます, 片付く it gets tidy (put in order)

káte *v* 勝て 1. → **katemásu** 勝てます [INFINITIVE] 2. [IMPERATIVE] (win!) → **kachimásu** 勝ちます

káteba *v* 勝てば (if one wins) → **kachimásu** 勝てば

katei *n* 仮定 hypothesis, supposition: ~ **shimásu** 仮定します supposes, presumes

katei *n* 課程 process (*course, stage*)

katei *n* 家庭 home, household
katei-yō´gu/yō´hin 家庭用具/用品 home appliances

katemásu, katéru *v* 勝てます, 勝てる can win

kā´ten *n* カーテン curtain, drapes: **kāten-róddo** カーテンロッド curtain rod: **kāten-rḗru** カーテンレール curtain rail: **shawā-kāten** シャワーカーテン shower curtain

katénai *v* 勝てない = **katemasén** 勝てません (cannot win)

katō´ *v* 勝とう = **kachimashō´** 勝ちましょう (let's win!)

kātorijji *n* カートリッジ cartridge: **inku-kātorijji** インクカートリッジ ink cartridge

Katoríkku *n* カトリック Catholic

kátsu *v* 勝つ = **kachimásu** 勝ちます (wins)

kátsu *n* カツ a Japanese "cutlet" (*fried in deep fat*): **ton-katsu** 豚カツ・トンカツ pork cutlet
katsu-don *n* カツ丼 a bowl of rice with sliced pork cutlet on top

katsudō *n* 活動 action, activity, movement: ~ **shimásu** 活動します acts, moves into action

katsúgi *v* 担ぎ → **katsugimásu** 担ぎます

katsugimásu, katsúgu *v* 担ぎます, 担ぐ carries on shoulders

katsúide *v* 担いで → **katsugimásu** 担ぎます

katsuji *n* 活字 movable type: **katsuji ni shimásu** 活字にします prints, is in print

katsuo *n* カツオ・鰹 bonito: **katsuo-bushi** カツオ[鰹]節 a dried bonito fish

katsura *n* かつら・カツラ a wig

kátsute *adv* かつて at one time, formerly

katsuyaku *n* 活躍 activity: ~ **shimásu** 活躍します is active

katta *v* 買った・飼った = **kaimáshita** 買いました・飼いました (bought; raised)

katta *v* 刈った = **karimáshita** 刈りました (mowed)

kátta *v* 勝った = **kachimáshita** 勝ちました (won)

...-kátta *v* ...かった : [ADJECTIVE] **-kátta (desu)** ...かった(です) was ...

...-káttara *v* ...かったら: [ADJECTIVE] **káttara** ...かったら if/when it is

...-káttari *v* ...かったり: [ADJECTIVE] **káttari** ...かったり being representatively/sometimes/alternately: **...-ku nákattari** ...くなかったり (is...) off and on, sometimes is ... and sometimes isn't

katte *n* 勝手 kitchen
katte-dō´gu *n* 勝手道具 kitchen utensils
kátte-guchi *n* 勝手口 kitchen door, back door

katte *adj, adv* **katte (na/ni)** 勝手(な/に) selfish(ly), as one wishes

katte *v* 買って → **kaimásu** 買います

katte *v* 刈って → **karimásu** 刈ります

kátte *v* 勝って → **kachimásu** 勝ちます

kau *v* 買う = **kaimásu** 買います (buys)

káu *v* 飼う = **kaimásu** 飼います (raises pets, farm animals, etc.)

kaunserā *n* カウンセラー counselor

kauntā *n* カウンター counter

kawá *n* 川 river

kawá *n* 河 big river

kawá *n* 皮・革 skin; leather; (*tree*) bark; crust: **kawa-seihin** 革製品 leather goods

kawai-garimásu, kawai-gáru *v* かわいがり[可愛がり]ます, **kawai-gáru** かわいがる・可愛がる treats with affection, loves (*children, pets, etc.*)

kawaíi *adj* かわいい・可愛い cute, lovable, darling (= **kawairashíi** かわいらしい・可愛らしい)

kawai-sō´ (na) *adj* かわいそう(な) pitiful, poor

kawáite *v* 乾いて → **kawakimásu** 乾きます

kawakashimásu, kawakásu *v* 乾かします, 乾かす dries (out)

kawakimásu, kawáku *v* 乾きます, 乾く gets dry

kawakimásu, kawáku *v* 渇きます, 渇く: **nodo ga kawakimásu** のどが渇きます gets thirsty

kawanai *v* 買わない = **kaimasén** 買いません (not buy)

kawánai *v* 飼わない = **kaimasén** 飼いません (not raise)

kawara *n* 瓦 tile: **kawara-buki (no)** 瓦ぶき(の) tile-roofed

kawaranai *adj* 変わらない = **kawarimasén** 変わりません (not change)

kawari *n* 変わり (**o-kawari** お変わり) change (*in health*) : **o-kawari arimasénka.** お変わりありませんか。Is everything all right? (*greeting*)

kawari *n* 代わり substitute: **... no kawari ni** ...の代わりに instead of

kawari *n* かわり (**o-káwari** おかわり) a second helping (*usually of rice*): **okawari-jiyū (desu)** おかわり自由(です) has free refills

kawari *v* 変わり → **kawarimásu** 変わります [INFINITIVE]

kawarimásu, kawaru *v* 変わります, 変わる: **(... ni) kawarimásu** (...に)変わります it changes (into...)

kawarimásu, kawaru *v* 代わります, 代わる: **(... ni) kawarimásu** (...に)代わります it takes the place (*of ...*)

89

kawaru-gáwaru *adv* 代わる代わる・かわるがわる alternately

kawase *n* 為替 a money order: **kawase-rēto** 為替レート currency exchange rates

kawatta *v* 変わった = **kawarimáshita** 変わりました (changed; unusual, novel)

kawatte *v* 変わって → **kawarimásu** 変わります: **kawatte imásu** 変わっています is unusual, novel

kaya *v* 買や [INFORMAL] → **káeba** 買えば

kaya *v* 飼や [INFORMAL] → **káeba** 飼えば

kayaku *n* 火薬 gunpowder

Kayō´(bi) *n* 火曜(日) Tuesday

kayoi 通い 1. *adj* **kayoi (no)** 通い(の) commuting, live-out (help): **kayoi no o-tetsudai(-san)** 通いのお手伝い(さん) a day helper 2. *v* → **kayoimásu** 通います [INFINITIVE]

kayoimásu, kayou *v* 通います, 通う commutes, goes back and forth, goes (regularly)

kayowanai *v* 通わない = **kayoimasén** 通いません (not commute)

kayu *n* 粥・かゆ (**o-kayu** お粥) rice gruel, porridge

kayúi *adj* 痒い itchy

kázan *n* 火山 volcano: **kazán-bai** 火山灰 volcanic ash

kazari 飾り 1. *n* = **kazari-mono** 飾り物 ornament, decoration 2. *v* → **kazarimásu** 飾ります [INFINITIVE]

kazarimásu, kazaru *v* 飾ります, 飾る decorates

kazari-mono *n* 飾り物 ornament, decoration

kaze *n* 風 wind: **kaze ga tsuyói** 風が強い is windy

kaze *n* かぜ・カゼ・風邪 a cold: **kaze o hikimásu** かぜをひきます catches (a) cold

kaze-gúsuri *n* かぜ薬・風邪薬 medicine for colds

kazóe *v* 数え → **kazoemásu** 数えます [INFINITIVE]

kazoe-kirenai *adj* 数え切れない countless, innumerable

kazoemásu, kazoéru *v* 数えます, 数える counts

kazoeraremásu, kazoeraréru *v* 数えられます, 数えられる can count

kazoé ro *v* 数えろ = **kazóe yo** 数えよ [IMPERATIVE] (count!) → **kazoemásu** 数えます

kázoku *n* 家族 family: **kazoku-omoi no (hito)** 家族思いの(人) family-minded (*person*) (= **maihōmu-shugi(-sha)** マイホーム主義(者))

kázu *n* 数 number

kazu no ko *n* カズノコ・数の子 herring roe

ke *n* 毛 hair; wool; feathers

...-ke *suffix* ...家 (*name of certain*) clan, family: **Suzuki-ke** 鈴木家 Suzuki family

kē´buru *n* ケーブル cable: **kēburú-kā** ケーブルカー cable car: **kēburú-terebi** ケーブルテレビ cable TV

kecháppu *n* ケチャップ ketchup

kéchi (na) *adj* けち(な) stingy, miser

kéchinbō, kéchinbo *n* けちん坊, けちんぼ stingy person, skinflint, miser

kedamono *n* けだもの・ケダモノ・獣, **kemono**

けもの・ケモノ・獣 animal; beast

kédo *conj* けど [INFORMAL] though, but = [FORMAL] **kéredo (-mo)** けれど(も) however, though, but

kegá *n* けが・ケガ・怪我 (**o-kéga** お怪我) injury, mishap: **kegá o shimásu** 怪我をしまず gets hurt; **kegá o sasemásu** 怪我をさせます injures (someone)

ke-gawa *n* 毛皮 fur: **ke-gawa-no-kōto** 毛皮のコート fur coat

kéi *n* 刑 (*criminal*) sentence

...-kei *suffix* ...系 1. type, model: **dō-kei-shoku** 同系色 similar color 2. of ...ancestry: **kei-zu** 系図 genealogy, a family tree (= **kakei-zu** 家系図)

keiba *n* 競馬 horse racing/race

keiba-jō *n* 競馬場 racetrack

keibetsu *n* 軽蔑 contempt, despising: ~ **shimásu** 軽蔑します despises

kéibi *n* 警備 [BOOKISH] security: ~ **shimásu** 警備します guards

keibi-in *n* 警備員 security guard

keiei *n* 経営 management, operation: ~ **shimásu** 経営します runs a business

keiéi-sha *n* 経営者 manager, operator, proprietor

keigo *n* 敬語 honorific (*word*): **keigo o tsukaimásu** 敬語を使います uses honorific words

keihin *n* 景品 [BOOKISH] giveaway

keihō *n* 警報 [BOOKISH] alarm, alert, warning

keiji *n* 繋辞 [BOOKISH] copula, (*grammar term*) link

kéiji *n* 刑事 (*police*) detective

keiji *n* 掲示 bulletin: ~ **shimásu** 掲示します posts

keiji-ban *n* 掲示板 bulletin board

kéijō *n* 形状 geometry

keika *n* 経過 course (*of time*), progress, development: ~ **shimásu** 経過します (*time*) passes, elapses, expires

keikai *n* 警戒 [BOOKISH] vigilance, watch, guard; warning, caution: ~ **shimásu** 警戒します guards against (watches out (*for* ...), warns, cautions

keikaku *n* 計画 plan, scheme, program, project (= **puran** プラン): **(... no) keikaku o tatemásu** (...の)計画を立てます = **(...o) keikaku shimásu** (...を)計画します plans

keikan *n* 警官 [BOOKISH] policeman, (police) officer (= **keisatsu-kan** 警察官): **keikan-tai** 警官隊 a contingent of policemen

keiken *n* 経験 experience: ~ **shimásu** 経験します experiences, undergoes

shokumu-keiken *n* 職務経験 job experience

keiki *n* 景気 business conditions, prosperity, boom: **keiki-taisaku** 景気対策 economy-boosting measure(s): **keiki ga ii** 景気がいい Business is good.

kéiki *n* 契機 [BOOKISH] opportunity

kéiki *n* 刑期 prison term: **kéiki o oemásu** 刑期を終えます serves out one's sentence

kei(ryō)ki *n* 計(量)器 meter (*device*)

kéiko *n* 稽古 (**o-kéiko** お稽古) exercise, practice, drill (= **naraigoto** 習い事)

keikō n 傾向 [BOOKISH] tendency, trend

keikō n 経口 [BOOKISH] oral: **keikō-hinínyaku** 経口避妊薬 oral contraceptive (= **piru** ピル)

keikoku n 警告 [BOOKISH] warning: **keikoku-hyōji** 警告表示 alarm display: **keikoku shimás<u>u</u>** 警告します warns

keikō-tō n 蛍光灯 fluorescent light

keimú-sho n 刑務所 jail, prison

keireki n 経歴 career (*history*)

keirin n 競輪 [BOOKISH] bicycle race: **keirin-jō** 競輪場 bicycle racetrack

keirō n 敬老 [BOOKISH] respect for the aged Keirō-no-hí n 敬老の日 Respect-for-the-Aged Day (*Third Monday of September*)

keiryaku n 計略 [BOOKISH] plot, scheme, trick, strategy: **keiryaku o nerimás<u>u</u>** 計略を練ります engineers a plot

keiryō-kappu n 計量カップ measuring cup

keisan n 計算 calculation, computation: **~ shimás<u>u</u>** 計算します calculates, computes

keisán-ki n 計算機 calculator

keisatsu n 警察 police: **keisatsu-shó** 警察署 police station; **keisatsu-kan** 警察官 policeman, (police) officer (= **keikan** 警官)

keishiki n 形式 form, formality

keishoku n 軽食 snack, light foods

keisotsu (na) adj 軽率(な) hasty, rash

keitai n 形態 pattern, shape

keitai 1. adj 携帯 portable **2.** n 携帯 cell-phone, mobile (tele)phone (= **keitai-denwa** 携帯電話)

keitai-denwa n 携帯電話 cell-phone, mobile (tele) phone (= **keitai** 携帯): **~ shimás<u>u</u>** 携帯します carries, takes along

keiteki n 警笛 [BOOKISH] horn (*of car*) (= **kuráku-shon** クラクション)

keito n 毛糸 wool; yarn: **keito-no-tama** 毛糸の玉, **kcito-dama** 毛糸玉 ball of wool/yarn

keiyaku n 契約 contract, agreement: **~ shimás<u>u</u>** 契約します, **keiyaku o kawashimás<u>u</u>** 契約を交わします contracts, signs (up) keiyaku-sho n 契約書 contract sheet

keiyō´shi n 形容詞 adjective

… kéiyu (de/no) adv, adj …経由(で/の) by (*way of*) …, via …: **keiyu-bin** 経由便 indirect flight

kéizai n 経済 economics, finance keizái-gaku n 経済学 (*science of*) economics keizai-teki (na) adj 経済的(な) economical

Keizai-Sangyō-shō n 経済産業省 Ministry of Economy, Trade and Industry (METI)

kē´ki n ケーキ cake: **(ichigo no) shōto-kēki** (イチゴ[苺]の)ショートケーキ sponge cake (with strawberry and whipped cream) (*very popular shortcake arranged for Japanese*)

kekka n 結果 result, effect; as a result (*consequence*): **gen'in to kekka** 原因と結果 cause and effect

kekkaku n 結核 tuberculosis

kekkan n 欠陥 [BOOKISH] defect, deficiency

kekkan n 血管 blood vessel

kekkō n 欠航 [BOOKISH] cancelled flight; "flight cancelled"

kékkō (na) adj 結構(な) **1.** splendid, excellent **2.** fairly well; enough: **Kékkō desu** 結構です. No, thank you.

kekkon n 結婚 marriage (= **konin** 婚姻): **(… to) ~ shimás<u>u</u>** (…と)結婚します marries kekkón-shiki n 結婚式 wedding

kekkyokú n, adv 結局 after all, in the long run

kemono n けもの・ケモノ・獣 = **kedamono** けだもの・ケダモノ・獣 (*animal; beast*)

kemúi, kemutai adj 煙い, 煙たい smoky

kemuri n 煙 smoke

kemushi n ケムシ・毛虫 caterpillar

kén n 県 a Japanese prefecture (*like a state*), …´-ken …県: **Chiba´-ken** 千葉県 Chiba prefecture

kén n 剣 (*double-edged*) sword

…´-ken suffix …軒 (*counts houses, small buildings and shops*)

…´-ken suffix …券 ticket: **nyūjō-ken** 入場券 admission ticket

kenbái-ki n 券売機 ticket vending machine

kenbi-kyō n 顕微鏡 microscope

kenbutsu n 見物 sightseeing: **~ shimás<u>u</u>** 見物します sees the sights kenbutsu-nin n 見物人 bystander

kénchi n 見地 viewpoint

kenchiku n 建築 [BOOKISH] construction; architecture kenchiku-ka n 建築家 architect

kénchō n 県庁 the prefectural government (office)

kéndō n 剣道 the art of fencing (*with bamboo swords*)

ken'etsu n 検閲 [BOOKISH] censor(ship)

kengaku n 見学 study by observation, field study/trip/work

kénji n 検事 (*public*) prosecutor

kenjū n 拳銃 pistol

kenka n けんか・喧嘩 quarrel, argument: **~ shimás<u>u</u>** けんか[喧嘩]します quarrels, argues

kenkō n 健康 health: **kenkō-shókuhin** 健康食品 health food(s); **kenkō-hoken** 健康保険 health insurance; **kenkō-shindan** 健康診断 health check, medical examination

kenkō (na) adj 健康(な) healthy

Kenkoku-kínen-no-hi n 建国記念の日 National Foundation Day (11 February)

kenkyo (na) adj 謙虚(な) humble (*modest*)

kenkyū n 研究 research, study: **~ shimás<u>u</u>** 研究します studies, researches kenkyū-jo n 研究所 research institute, laboratory

kenmei (na) adj 賢明(な) wise

kénpō n 憲法 constitution: **Kenpō-kínénbi** 憲法記念日 Constitution (Memorial) Day (*3 May*)

kénri n 権利 right (*privilege*) kenri-kin n 権利金 "key money" (*to obtain rental lease*)

kenritsu (no) adj 県立(の) prefectural

kenryoku *n* 権力 power, authority: **kenryoku-sha** 権力者 person of power

kénsa *n* 検査 inspection, examination, check-up, test: ~ **shimásu** 検査します inspects, checks, tests

kensatsu *n* 検札 [BOOKISH] ticket examining (*on board*): **kensatsu shimásu** 検札します examines tickets

kensetsu *n* 建設 construction (*work*) (*building*)

kenshō *n* 検証 [BOOKISH] vertification

kentō *n* 拳闘 boxing (= **bókushingu** ボクシング)

kentō´ *n* 見当 aim; direction; estimate, guess: **kantō´ ga tsukimásu** 見当がつきます gets a rough idea (*of it*): **kantō´ o tsukemásu** 見当をつけます makes a guess, takes aim

kentō *n* 検討: ~ **shimásu** 検討します examines it, investigates it

…-kéntō *suffix* …見当 roughly, about, approximately

ken'yaku *n* 倹約 economy, thrift, economizing: **ken'yaku (na)** 倹約（な） thrifty, frugal: ~ **shimásu** 倹約します economizes on, saves

kénzan *n* 剣山 a frog (*pinholder*) for flowers

ke-orimono *n* 毛織物 woolen goods

keránai *v* 蹴らない = **kerimasén** 蹴りません (not kick)

kére *v* 蹴れ → **keremásu** 蹴れます [INFINITIVE]

kéreba *v* 蹴れば (if one kicks) → **kerimásu** 蹴ります

kéredo (-mo) *conj* けれど（も） however, though, but

keremásu, keréru *v* 蹴れます, **keréru** 蹴れる can kick

kerénai *v* 蹴れない = **keremasén** 蹴れません (cannot kick)

kérete *v* 蹴れて → **keremásu** 蹴れます

kéri *v* 蹴り 1. → **kerimásu** 蹴ります [INFINITIVE] 2. *n* **kéri o tsukemásu** けりをつけます winds up

kerimásu, kéru *v* 蹴ります, 蹴る kicks

kéri ya/wa shinai *v* [INFORMAL] , 蹴りや/はしない = **keránai** 蹴らない (not kick)

kerō´ *v* 蹴ろう = **kerimashō´** 蹴りましょう (let's kick!)

ké ro *v* 蹴ろ = **ké yo** 蹴よ [IMPERATIVE] (kick!) [IRREGULAR IMPERATIVE of **kerimásu** 蹴ります]

kéru *v* 蹴る = **kerimásu** 蹴ります (kicks)

késa *n, adv* 今朝 this morning

kesanai *v* 消さない = **keshimasén** 消しません (not extinguish)

kese *v* 消せ 1. → **kesemásu** 消せます [INFINITIVE] 2. [IMPERATIVE] (turn it off!, put it out!) → **keshimásu** 消します

keséba *v* 消せば (if one extinguishes) → **keshimásu** 消します

kesemásu, keseru *v* 消せます, 消せる can extinguish

kesenai *v* 消せない = **kesemasén** 消せません (cannot extinguish)

kesete *v* 消せて → **kesemásu** 消せます

keshi 消し 1. *v* → **keshimásu** 消します [INFINITIVE] 2. *adj* **tsuyakeshi (no)** つや消し matted

keshi-gomu *n* 消しゴム (*rubber*) eraser

keshi-in *n* 消印 cancellation mark/stamp

késhiki *n* 景色 scenery, view

keshimásu, kesu *v* 消します, 消す extinguishes, puts out; turns off; expunges, erases, deletes

keshite *v* 消して → **keshimásu** 消します

keshí ya/wa shinai *v* [INFORMAL] 消しや/はしない = **kesanai** 消さない (not extinguish)

keshō *n* 化粧（**o-keshō** お化粧） cosmetics, make-up

keshō-hin *n* 化粧品 cosmetics

keshō´-shitsu *n* 化粧室 restroom, bathroom, toilet, lounge

kesō *v* 消そう = **keshimashō´** 消しましょう (let's extinguish it!)

kessaku *n* 傑作 masterpiece

kessan *n* 決算 settling accounts

kesseki *n* 欠席 absence (*from school, work*): ~ **shimásu** 欠席します is absent

kessékí-sha *n* 欠席者 absentee

kesshin *n* 決心 determination, resolve: **(... shiyō to) kesshin shimásu** (…しようと) 決心します resolves (*to do*)

kesshite *adv* 決して [+ NEGATIVE] never

kesshō *n* 決勝 finals, title match: **jun-kesshō** 準決勝 semifinals

kesu *v* 消す = **keshimásu** 消します (puts out; turns off; erases)

kē´su *n* ケース case (*a particular instance*): **kēsu-bai-kē´su** ケースバイケース case by case; case (*container*)

keta *n* けた・ケタ・桁 1. (*cross*) beam, girder: **keta-shita** けた下・桁下 under the beam/girder 2. abacus rod, (*numerical*) column

ketsu *n* けつ・尻 1. = **o-ketsu, o-shiri** お尻 [POLITE FORM] buttock 2. けつ the tail end, the last (*bottom*) (= **shiri** しり・尻)

ketsuatsu *n* 血圧 blood pressure; **ketsuatsu ga takái/hikúi** 血圧が高い/低い has high/low blood pressure: **ketsuatsu o hakarimásu** 血圧を計ります takes one's blood pressure

ketsuatsu-kei *n* 血圧計 blood-pressure gauge; sphygmomanometer

ketsúeki *n* 血液 blood

ketsumatsu *n* 結末 outcome

ketsuron *n* 結論 conclusion: **ketsuron to shite** 結論として in conclusion: **ketsuron o dashimásu** 結論を出します concludes

kettei *n* 決定 determination, decision: ~ **shimásu** 決定します decides, determines (*to do*)

kettén *n* 欠点 flaw, defect, short-coming

kétta *v* 蹴った = **kerimáshita** 蹴りました (kicked)

kétte *v* 蹴って → **kerimásu** 蹴ります

kétte shimaimásu *v* 蹴ってしまいます = **kerimásu** 蹴ります (kicks)

kewashíi *adj* 険しい steep, precipitous; severe

kezuremásu, kezureru *v* 削れます, 削れる can sharpen

kezurimásu, kezuru *v* 削ります, 削る sharpens, shaves

ki *n* 気 spirit; feeling; mind, heart

ki (ga) *adv* 気(が): **kí ga mijikái** 気が短い is impatient: **kí ga omoi** 気が重い is depressed; **kí ga tachimásu** 気が立ちます gets excited; **kí ga tsukimásu** 気が付きます comes to one's senses

ki ni *adj* 気に: **kí ni irimásu** 気に入ります appeals to one, is pleasing; **(… ga) kí ni narimásu** (…が)気になります worries (*one*); **(… o) kí ni shimásu** (…を)気にします worries about …, minds; **... suru kí ni narimásu** ... する 気になります gets in the mood (*to do*)

ki o *adv* 気を: **kí o tsukemásu** 気を付けます (is) careful; **kí o ushinaimásu** 気を失います loses consciousness, faints

ki *n* 木 tree; wood

ki *v* 着 → **kimásu** 着ます [INFINITIVE]

ki *v* 来 → **kimásu** 来ます [INFINITIVE]

kibarashi *n* 気晴らし diversion, refresh (= **kibun tenkan** 気分転換)

kiben *n* 詭弁 sophistry

kibishíi *adj* 厳しい strict, severe

kibō *n* 希望 hope; **~himásu** 希望します hopes, aspires

kibō´-sha *n* 希望者 candidate, applicant

kíbun *n* 気分 feeling, mood: **kíbun-tenkan** 気分転 換 diversion, refresh (= **kibarashi** 気晴らし)

kibutori *n* 着太り looking fatter in clothes: **~ shimásu** 着太りします is looked fatter in clothes

kicháimásu *v* [INFORMAL] 来ちゃいます = **kite-shimaimásu** 来てしまいます (comes)

kichátta *v* [INFORMAL] 来ちゃった = **kite-shimatta** 来てしまった = **kitá** 来た (came)

kicháu *v* [INFORMAL] 来ちゃう = **kite-shimau** 来てしまう (comes)

kíchi *n* 基地 military base

kíchi *n* 機知 wit

ki-chigái (no) *adj* 気違い(の) mad, insane

kichín-to *adv* きちんと punctually; precisely; neat(ly)

kichō *n* 記帳 [BOOKISH] registration (*at hotel, etc.*): **~ shimásu** 記帳します checks in, registers

kichō´ *n* 機長 captain (*of an airplane*)

kichō (na) *adj* 貴重(な) valuable

　kichō-hin *n* 貴重品 valuables

kichō´men (na) *adj* 几帳面(な) meticulous, precise, particular: **jikan ni kichō´men** 時間に几 帳面 punctual

kidate-no/ga-yoi *adj* 気立ての/が良い good-natured

kído *n* 木戸 entrance gate, wicket

kídoairaku *n* [BOOKISH] 喜怒哀楽 emotions, delight, anger, sorrow and pleasure

kidorimásu, kidoru *v* 気取ります, 気取る・気 どる puts on airs: **kidotte imásu** 気取っています, **kidotta …** 気取った… affected, stuck-up

kie *v* 消え → **kiemásu** 消えます [INFINITIVE]

kiemásu, kieru *v* 消えます, 消える is extinguished, goes out; fades, vanishes

kigae *n* 着替え a change of clothing

kigaemásu, kigáéru *v* 着替えます, 着替える changes (*clothes*) [*newer form of* **ki-kaemásu** 着替えます]

kigaru (na) *adj* 気軽(な) lighthearted, casual

kígeki *n* 喜劇 comedy

kigen *n* 機嫌 (*state of*) health, mood: **kigen ga íi** 機嫌がいい cheerful; **kigen ga waruí** 機嫌が悪い unhappy, moody → **go-kigen** ご機嫌 [HONORIFIC]

kígen *n* 期限 term, period; deadline

kígen *n* 起源 origin

kigō *n* 記号 sign, mark, symbol

kígu *n* 器具 implement, fixture, apparatus

kígyō *n* 企業 company, business concern; "the office" (= **kaisha** 会社)

kíhon *n* 基本 basis, foundation: **kihon-teki (na)** 基本的(な) basic, fundamental

kíi *n* キー key: (*computer*) **kiibōdo** キーボード keyboard

kiiro (no) *adj* 黄色(の) = **kiiroi** 黄色い yellow

kiíta *v* 聞いた → **kikimashíta** 聞きました

kiite *v* 聞いて → **kikimásu** 聞きます

kí-ito *n* 生糸 raw silk

kiji *n* キジ・雉 pheasant

kíji *n* 記事 article, news item, piece, write-up: **shinbun-kiji** 新聞記事 newspaper article

kíji *n* 生地 cloth material, fabric

kíjitsu *n* [BOOKISH] 期日 appointed day; deadline

kijun *n* [BOOKISH] 基準 basis, standard

kíkai *n* 機会 chance, opportunity, occasion

kíkai *n* 機械 machine, machinery, instrument: **kikai-teki (na)** 機械的(な) mechanical

kikai *n* 器械 instrument: **kikai-taisō** 器械体操 (*apparatus*) gymnastics

kikai (na) *adj* 奇怪(な) mysterious, strange: **kikai na jiken** 奇怪な事件 mysterious case

kikaku *n* 企画 plan(ning), project: **Kikaku-bu** 企画部 planning department: **kikaku shimásu** 企画します plans

kikaku *n* 規格 norm, standard: **kikaku-ka** 規格化 standardization, **kikaku-ka shimásu** 規格化します standardizes

kíkan *n* 期間 term, period

kíkan (no) *adj* 季刊(の) quarterly: **kikán-shi** 季刊誌 a quarterly

kíkan *n* [BOOKISH] 機関 engine; instrument; agency, activity, organization: **kikan-jū** 機関銃 machine gun; **kinyū-kikan** 金融機関 financial institution

kikanai *v* 聞かない = **kikimasén** 聞きません (not listen, not ask)

kikasemásu, kikaseru *v* 聞かせます, 聞かせる lets someone hear, tells someone (*a story*); reads (*someone a book*); reasons with (*a child*)

kike *v* 聞け **1.** → **kikemásu** 聞けます [INFINITIVE] **2.** [IMPERATIVE] (listen!) → **kikimásu** 聞きます

kikéba *v* 聞けば (if one listens, …) → **kikimásu** 聞きます

kikemásu, kikeru *v* 聞けます, 聞ける can listen/hear, can ask

kiken *n* 危険 danger, peril: **kiken (na)** 危険(な) dangerous (= **abunaí** 危ない)

kiken *n* 棄権 abstention: **~ shimásu** 棄権します abstains

kikenai *v* 聞けない = **kikemasén** 聞けません (cannot listen/hear/ask)

kikete *v* 聞けて → **kikemásu** 聞けます

kiki *v* 聞き → **kikimásu** 聞きます [INFINITIVE]

kíkí *n* 危機 crisis, critical moment, emergency

kiki-ashi *n* 利き足 stronger leg

kikimásu, kiku *v* 聞きます, 聞く listens, hears; obeys; asks

kikimásu, kiku *v* 効きます, 効く takes effect, is effective, works

kiki-me *n* 効き目 effect (*effectiveness*) (= **kōyō** 効用, **kōnō** 効能): **kiki-me ga arimásu** 効き目があります is effective

kiki-te *n* 聞き手 hearer, listener

kiki-ude *n* 利き腕 stronger hand: **migi-kiki** 右利き right-hander(s): **hidari-kiki** 左利き left-hander(s)

kíkí ya/wa shinai *v* [INFORMAL] 聞きや/はしない = **kikanai** 聞かない, etc. (not listen, …)

kikkake *n* きっかけ opportunity, occasion

kikkari *adj* きっかり exactly, just (= **chōdo** ちょうど・丁度)

kikō *n* 気候 climate

kikō *n* [BOOKISH] 機構 system, organisation, structure: **kokusai-kikō** 国際機構 international organization

kikō *n* [BOOKISH] 紀行 travel: **kikō-bun** 紀行文 travel notes

kikō *n* [BOOKISH] 寄稿 contribution: **kikō-kiji** 寄稿記事 contributed article

kikō *n* [BOOKISH] 奇行 one's eccentricity: **kikō-heki** 奇行癖 eccentric habit

kikō' *v* 聞こう = **kikimashō'** 聞きましょう (let's listen/ask!)

kikoe *v* 聞こえ → **kikoemásu** 聞こえます [INFINITIVE]

kikoemásu *v* 聞こえます, **kikoeru** 聞こえる can hear; is heard

kikoenai *v* 聞こえない = **kikoemasén** 聞こえません (not hear)

kikoku *n* 帰国 returning to one's country (Japan): **~ shimásu** 帰国します returns from abroad **kikoku-shíjo** *n* 帰国子女 returnees

kikú *v* 聞く = **kikimásu** 聞きます (listens, hears; obeys; asks)

kikú *v* 聴く = **kikimásu** 聴きます (listens to music, etc.)

kikú *v* 訊く・聞く = **kikimásu** 訊[聞]きます (asks)

kikú *v* 効く = **kikimásu** 効きます (takes effect, is effective, works)

kikú *n* キク・菊 chrysanthemum

ki-kúrage *n* 木くらげ・キクラゲ・木耳 tree-ears (*an edible fungus*)

kikyū *n* 気球 balloon: **netsu-kikyū** 熱気球 hot-air balloon

kimae ga íi *adj* 気前がいい generous

kimagure *n* 気まぐれ fickle, easy to change one's mood

kimari **1.** *n* 決まり rule; settlement, arrangement; order; regulation **2.** *v* 決まり → **kimarimásu** 決まります [INFINITIVE]

kimari ga warúi *adj* きまりが悪い is/feels embarrassed

kimarimásu, kimaru *v* 決まります, 決まる is settled, is arranged

kimásu, kiru *v* 着ます, 着る wears

kimásu, kúru *v* 来ます, 来る comes

kimé *n* きめ[木目・肌理] **1.** grain, texture **2.** smooth (*human skin*) **3.** care: **kime-komakai** きめ細かい, **kime-komayaka (na)** きめ細やか(な) meticulous, attentiveness (*attentive*), tender (= **komayaka (na)** こま[細・濃]やか(な))

kimemásu, kimeru *v* 決めます, 決める settles, arranges, decides

kimi *n* 君・きみ you [*familiar*]

kimi *n* 黄身 yolk (*of egg*)

kimí *n* 気味 feeling, sensation: **kimí ga warúi** 気味が悪い nervous, apprehensive, weird (*feeling*)

kimídori (iro) *n* 黄緑(色) yellowish green (color)

Kimigayo *n* 君が代 national anthem of Japan

kimijika *n* 気短 short-tempered person (= **tanki** 短気)

kimó *n* きも[肝・胆] **1.** liver **2.** guts, courage, pluck: **kimo-dameshi** 肝試し test of courage: **kimo-ga-futoi** 肝[胆]が太い brave, gritty

kimochi *n* 気持ち feeling, sensation: **kimochi ga íi** 気持ちがいい it feels good, is comfortable; **kimochi ga warúi** 気持ちが悪い is uncomfortable, is feeling bad/unwell

ki-mono *n* 着物 clothes; a (*Japanese*) kimono

ki-músume *n* 生娘 virgin (*female*), green girl

ki-muzukashíi *n* 気難しい fussy, difficult (*person*)

kímyō (na) *adj* 奇妙(な) strange, peculiar

kín *n* 金 gold: **kin-ka** 金貨 gold coin

-kin *suffix* 金 money: **shikin** 資金 fund, capital: **shikí-kin** 敷金 security deposit (*for rental*): **shakkín** 借金 debt

kínai *n* 機内 on a plane: **kinai-shoku** 機内食 airplane meal: **kínai wa kinen desu** 機内は禁煙です Smoking on the airplane is prohibited.

kinai *v* 着ない = **kimasén** 着ません (not wear)

kínako *n* きな粉[黄な粉] soybean meal/flour: **kinako-mochi** きな粉餅 rice cake powdered with soybean

kinben (na) *adj* 勤勉(な) industrious, hardworking, diligent

kinchō *n* 緊張 strain, tension: **kinchō shite imásu** 緊張しています is tense

kinen *n* 記念 commemoration; **kinen-kítte** 記念切手 commemorative stamp

kinen-hin *n* 記念品 souvenir

kin'en *n* 禁煙 smoking prohibited, no smoking: **kin'én-sha** 禁煙車 no(n)-smoking car

kinénbi *n* 記念日 anniversary

kingaku *n* 金額 amount (*of money*)

kingan (no) *adj* 近眼(の) near-sighted, shortsighted, myopic

kíngyo *n* 金魚 goldfish: **kingyo-bachi** 金魚鉢 bowl for goldfish(es)

kiníine *n* キニーネ quinine

ki-nikúi *v* 着にくい uncomfortable (*to wear*)

kin-iro (no) *adj* 金色(の) gold (color), golden

kin-jimásu, kin-jiru *v* 禁じます, 禁じる forbids, prohibits

kínjo *n* 近所 neighborhood, vicinity

kinkán *n* キンカン・金柑 kumquat

kinki-chihō *n* 近畿地方 the Kinki area of Japan (*Osaka, Hyōgo, Kyōto, Shiga, Nara prefectures*)

kínko *n* 金庫 safe (*strongbox*), (*small*) cash box

kinkyū *n* [BOOKISH] 緊急 urgency, emergency; **kinkyū na** 緊急な urgent, critical

kinmákie *n* [BOOKISH] 金蒔絵 gold lacquer

kínmu *n* 勤務 duty, service, work: **~ shimásu** 勤務します works, is on duty

kinmú-saki *n* 勤務先 place of work/employment

kínniku *n* 筋肉 muscle: **kinniku-tsū** 筋肉痛 muscular pain, myalgia

kinō´ *n, adv* きのう・昨日 yesterday

kínō *n* 機能 function

ki-no-dóku na *adj* 気の毒な pitiful, pitiable

kíno káge *n* 木の陰 shade of trees (= **ko-kage** 木陰)

kíno kawá *n* 木の皮 bark (*of tree*)

kínoko *n* キノコ・茸 mushroom

kí-no-me *n* 木の芽 **1.** tree sprout **2.** pepper sprout

kí-no-mi *n* 木の実 nuts, tree produce (*nuts, fruits, berries*)

kinō´ **no ban** *n* きのう[昨日]の晩 last night

kinpaku shimásu (suru) *adv* 緊迫します(する) tense

kinpatsu (no) *adj* 金髪(の) blond

kinpira *n* キンピラ・きんぴら・金平 fried burdock root and carrot strips served cold

Kinrō-kánsha no hí *n* 勤労感謝の日 Labor Thanksgiving Day (23 November)

kínryoku *n* 筋力 muscle (*power*)

kinshi *n* 禁止 prohibition, ban: **~ shimásu** 禁止します prohibits, bans

kinshi *n* 近視 = **kingan** 近眼 (nearsighted)

kintamá *n* 金玉 testicle(s) [INFORMAL]

kínu *n* 絹 silk

Kin'yō´**(bi)** *n* 金曜(日) Friday

kinyū *n* 記入: **~ shimásu** 記入します fills in

kin'yū *n* 金融 finance: **kin'yū-shíjō** 金融市場 the money market

kínzoku *n* 金属 metal

kioku *n* 記憶 memory: **kiokúryoku** 記憶力 memory (*capacity*), retentiveness

kippári (to) *adv* きっぱり(と) definitely, firmly, flatly

kíppu *n* 切符 ticket: **kippu-úriba** 切符売り場 ticket office

kirai (na) *adj* 嫌い(な) disliked

kiraku (na) *adj* 気楽(な) carefree, comfortable; easygoing

kiránai *v* 切らない = **kirimasén** 切りません (not cut)

ki(ra)remásu, ki(ra)reru *v* 着(ら)れます, 着(ら)れる can wear

kirasánai *v* 切らさない = **kirashimasén** 切らしません (not exhaust)

kirashimásu, kirásu *v* 切らします, 切らす exhausts the supply of, runs out of: **... o ki(r)áshite imásu** ...を切らしています is out of ...; **shibiré o kiráshimásu** しびれを切らします loses patience

kiráshite *v* 切らして → **kirashimásu** 切らします

kiré *v* きれ・切れ a piece, a cut (*of cloth*)

kíre *v* 切れ **1.** → **kiremásu** 切れます, etc. (can cut, …) [INFINITIVE] **2.** [IMPERATIVE] (cut it!, ...) → **kírimásu** 切ります

kíreba *v* 着れば (if one wears) → **kimásu** 着ます

kíreba *v* 切れば (if one cuts) → **kirimásu** 切ります

kírei (na) *adj* きれい[綺麗](な) pretty; clean; neat, tidy; nice (looking), attractive: **Kírei ni shimásu** きれいにします cleans/tidies it

kiremasén, kirénai *v* 切れません, 切れない cannot cut; cannot run out; cannot break (off)

...-kiremasén, ...-kirénai *v* 切れません, 切れない [verb INFINITIVE +] cannot: ... **-shi-kiremasén** ...し切れません, **-shi-kirénai** し切れない cannot do it

ki(ra)remásu, ki(ra)reru *v* 着(ら)れます, 着(ら)れる can wear

kiremásu, kiréru *v* 切れます, 切れる **1.** can cut; cuts (*well*) **2.** runs out **3.** breaks (off)

kire-mé *n* 切れ目 a gap, a break, a pause

kirénai *v* 切れない **1.** dull(-edged), blunt **2.** = **kiremasén** 切れません (cannot cut; not run out; not break)

kiréreba *v* 切れれば (if one can cut; …) → **kiremásu** 切れます

kírete *v* 切れて → **kiremásu** 切れます

kiri *n* 霧 fog, mist: **kiri ga fukái (koi)** 霧が深い(濃い) is foggy

kiri *n* 桐 paulownia (*tree or wood*)

kíri *n* 錐 a hole-punch, an awl, a drill

kíri *n* 切り → **kirimásu** 切ります [INFINITIVE]

kíri *n* きり *or* 限り; limit **kirí ga nai** きりがない endless, no limit (*no boundary*)

kiri-kabu *n* 切り株 (*tree*) stump

kirimásu, kíru *v* 切ります, 切る cuts; cuts off, disconnects; hangs up (*phone*)

kirinuki *n* 切り抜き clipping (*from newspaper, etc.*)

kirisame *n* 霧雨 drizzle

Kirisuto *n* キリスト Christ **Kirisuto-kyō** *n* キリスト教 Christianity

kiritsu *n* 規律 discipline

kíri ya/wa shinai *v* [INFORMAL] 切りや/はしない = **kiránai** 切らない; etc. (not cut; …)

kíro *n* キロ **1.** kilogram **2.** kilometer **3.** kilowatt **4.** kiloliter

kirō´ *v* 切ろう = **kirimashō** 切りましょう (let's cut it!)

kiroku *n* 記録 (*historic*) record: ~ **shimásu** 記録します records (*an event*); **shin-kíroku** 新記録 a new record (*an event*)

kiru *v* 着る = **kimásu** 着ます (wears)

kíru *v* 切る = **kirimásu** 切ります (cuts)

kíryō *n* 器量 personal appearance, looks; ability

kisaku (na) *adj* 気さく(な) not put on airs

kisen *n* 汽船 steamship

kisen *n* [BOOKISH] 貴賎 rank: **shokugyō ni kisen wa arimasen** 職業に貴賎はありません Every occupation deserves respect.

kisétsu *n* 季節 season: **kisetsu-fū** 季節風 seasonal wind

kishá *n* 汽車 (*non-electric/steam*) train

kishá *n* 記者 = **shinbun-kíshá** 新聞記者 newspaper reporter, journalist

kishí *n* 岸 shore, bank

kishi-men *n* きしめん long thin udon (= **himo-kawa(-údon)** ひもかわ(うどん))

kishitsu *n* 気質 temperament

kishō *n* 気象 weather: **kishō-dai** 気象台 weather observatory

kishúkusha *n* 寄宿舎 dormitory; boarding house

kisó *n* 基礎 base, foundation (*base*)

kisoimásu, kisóu *v* 競います, 競う competes, vies: **... o kisótte** ...を競って competing (*in competition*) for ...

kisóku *n* 規則 rule, regulation

kissa-ten *n* 喫茶店 a tearoom, a coffee house, a café

kísu *n* キス kiss: ~ **shimásu** キスします kisses

kísu *n* キス・鱚 sillago (fish)

kita *v* 着た = **kimáshita** 着ました (wore)

kitá *v* 来た = **kimáshita** 来ました (came)

kita *n* 北 north: **kita-guchi** 北口 the north exit/entrance; **kita-yori (no kaze)** 北寄り(の風) northerly (wind)

Kita-Ámerika *n* 北アメリカ North America

Kita-Chōsén *n* 北朝鮮 North Korea

kita-yori *adj* 北寄り northerly: **kita-yori no kaze** 北寄りの風 northerly wind

kitáe *v* 鍛え → **kitaemásu** 鍛えます [INFINITIVE]

kitaemásu, kitaéru *v* 鍛えます, 鍛える forges, tempers; drills, disciplines

kitai *n* 期待 expectation: ~ **shimásu** 期待します expects, anticipates

kitai *n* 気体 vapor, a gas

ki-tai *v* 着たい wants to wear: **ki-taku arimasén** 着たくありません doesn't want to wear

ki-tái *v* 来たい wants to come: **ki-táku arimasén** 来たくありません doesn't want to come

kitaku *n* 帰宅 returning home: ~ **shimásu** 帰宅します returns home

kitanái *adj* 汚い dirty; untidy; messy

kite *v* 着て: **kite-ikimásu/kimásu** 着ていきます/きます wears it there/here → **kimásu** 着ます

kité *v* 来て → **kimásu** 来ます

kitei *n* [BOOKISH] 規定 regulation, rule, stipulation: **kitei no ...** 規定の... regular, stipulated, compulsory: ~ **shimásu** 規定します prescribes, stipulates, requires

kiteki *n* 汽笛 whistle (*steam*)

kiten *n* 機転 wit: **kiten no kiku** 機転の利く quick-witted

kitsuen *n* 喫煙 smoking: ~ **shimásu** 喫煙します smokes

kitsuén-sha *n* 喫煙者 smoker

kitsuén-shitsu(/-seki) *n* 喫煙室(/席) smoking room (*area/zone/seat*)

kitsúi *adj* きつい **1.** tight: **sukejūru ga kitsúi (desu)** スケジュールがきつい(です) (*one's*) schedule is tight; **uesuto ga kitsui (desu)** ウエストがきつい(です) is tight in the waist **2.** severe, hard, strict: **kitsui seikaku** きつい性格 strict character

kitsune *n* キツネ・狐 fox

kíttá *v* 切った = **kirimáshita** 切りました (cut)

kitte *n* 切手 (*postage*) stamp: **kitte-chō** 切手帳 stamp album

kítté *v* 切って → **kirimásu** 切ります

kítto *adv* きっと surely, doubtless, no doubt, undoubtedly

kiwá *n* 際 brink, edge

kiwadói *adj* 際どい delicate, dangerous, ticklish

kiwamarimásu, kiwamáru *v* 極まります, 極まる comes to an end; gets carried to extremes

kiwamemásu, kiwaméru *v* 極めます, 極める carries to extremes

kiwamemásu, kiwaméru *v* 究めます, 究める investigates thoroughly

kiwámete *adv* 極めて extremely

kiyase *adj* 着やせ looking thinner in clothes: ~ **shimásu** 着やせします is looked thinner in clothes

kí ya/wa shinai *v* [INFORMAL] 着や/はしない = **kinai** 着ない (not wear)

kí ya/wa shinai *v* [INFORMAL] 来や/はしない = **kónai** 来ない (not come)

kiyō *v* 着よう = **kimashō** 着ましょう (let's wear)

kíyō (na) *adj* 器用(な) skillful, nimble, clever

kíyū *n* 杞憂 groundless fear

kizamimásu, kizamu *v* 刻みます, 刻む chops fine; carves, engraves; notches, nicks

kizashi *n* 兆し sign(s), symptom(s), hint(s), indication(s), omen(s)

kizu *n* きず・傷・疵・瑕 wound; scratch, crack, flaw, blemish; fault, defect

kizu (ni) *v* 着ず(に) = **kináide** 着ないで (not wearing)

kizu-ato *n* 傷跡 scar

ki-zúite *v* 気付いて → **kizukimásu** 気付きます

ki-zúkai *n* 気遣い anxiety, concern, worry, care (= **hairyo** 配慮, **kokoro-kubari** 心配り)

ki-zukái *v* 気遣い → **ki-zukaimásu** 気遣います [INFINITIVE]

ki-zukaimásu, ki-zukáu v 気遣います, 気遣う is anxious/worried about, is concerned over

ki-zukátte v 気遣って → **ki-zukaimásu** 気遣います

ki-zukimásu, ki-zúku v 気付きます, 気付く notices

ki-zukimásu, ki-zúku v 築きます, 築く builds it

kizu-tsukemásu, kizu-tsukéru v 傷つけます, 傷つける wounds, injures, damages

kizu-tsukimásu, kizu-tsúku v 傷つきます, 傷つく gets wounded, injured, damaged

ko n 子 child (= (person)) kodomo 子供

ko n 仔 child (animals in particular) (→ **ko-néko** 仔猫, **ko-inu** 仔犬, **ko-buta** 仔豚)

kó, koná n 粉 flour

ko-... prefix 小… little…, small…: **ko-bako** 小箱 small box

...´-ko suffix …個 (counts small objects)

...´-ko suffix …湖 Lake…: **Biwa-ko** びわ[ビワ・琵琶]湖 Lake Biwa

kō adv こう (**kō´** こう + [PARTICLE], **kō´désu** こうです) this way, so, like this

kō´ n 香 (**o-kō** お香) incense: **o-kō o takimásu** お香を焚きます burns incense (in a temple, before the memorial tablet of the deceased, etc.)

kō-... prefix 高… high…: **kō-kétsúatsu** 高血圧 high blood pressure

...´-kō suffix …港 port (of …): **Kōbé-kō** 神戸港 the port of Kobe

...´-kō suffix …校 school, branch (school); [BOOKISH] counter for schools

kōbá, kōjō n 工場 factory, plant

kobamimásu, kobámu v 拒みます, 拒む refuses, rejects; opposes, resists

kóban n 小判 Japanese old coins made of gold (Edo period): **koban-zame** コバンザメ・小判鮫 remora (fish)

kōban n 交番 police box

kobanashi n 小話 anecdote

kobaruto n コバルト cobalt: **kobaruto-iro** コバルト色, **kobaruto-burū** コバルトブルー cobalt blue

Kōbe n 神戸 Kobe; **Kōbé-Eki** 神戸駅 Kobe Station

kobito n 小人 dwarf: **"Shirayukihime to shichinin no kobito "**「白雪姫と七人の小人」 "Snow White and the Seven Dwarfs" (The Grimm Brother's Fairy Tales)

koboremásu, koboréru v こぼれます, こぼれる it spills

koboshimásu, kobósu v こぼします, こぼす spills it: **guchi o koboshimásu** 愚痴をこぼします grumbles, complains

kobú n こぶ・瘤 bump, knob, swelling, lump, hump: **rakuda no kobú** ラクダのこぶ hump(s) on a camel

kobú-cha n 昆布茶 hot water with dried sea tangle (drink)

kó-bun n 子分 henchman, subordinate, follower

kobune n 小舟 small boat

kobura n コブラ cobra

kobushi n こぶし・拳 fist (= **nigiri-kobushi** 握り拳)

ko-buta n 子豚・仔豚 piglet(s), little pig(s): **"Sanbiki no ko-buta"**「三匹の子豚」"Three Little Pigs"

kōbutsu n 好物 favorite (food/drink)

kōcha n 紅茶 (black/red) tea

kóchi n コチ flathead (fish)

kō´chi n コーチ coach (sports)

kochira pron こちら 1. this one (of two) 2. here, this way 3. I/me, we/us; **kochira kóso** こちらこそ I am the one who should be expressing the apology/gratitude.

kochira-gawa n こちら側 this/my/our side

kōchō n [BOOKISH] 誇張 exaggeration: ~ **shimásu** 誇張します exaggerates

kōchō n 校長 principal/head of a school (elementary school, junior/senior high school)

kōchō (na) adj [BOOKISH] 好調(な) satisfactory, favorable, in a good condition: **kōchō na dedashi/suberidashi/sutāto** 好調な出だし/滑り出し/スタート flying start, good start

kódai n 古代 ancient times, **kódai no** 古代の ancient: **kodai-iseki** 古代遺跡 ancient monument(s)

ko-dakara n 子宝 child(ren): **ko-dakara ni megumaremásu** 子宝に恵まれます is blessed with child(ren), has a baby/babies

kodama n こだま echo (= **yama-biko** やまびこ)

kōdan n 公団 public corporation

kōdan n [BOOKISH] 講壇 lecture platform

kodō n 鼓動 heartbeat, pulse: **shinzō no kodō** 心臓の鼓動 beat of the heart

kō´do n コード 1. (electricity) cord 2. code

kō´do n 高度 high degree, altitude

kōdō n 公道 highway

kōdō n 行動 action, behavior

kōdō n 講堂 public (lecture) hall, auditorium

kodoku n 孤独 loneliness

kodomo n 子供 child (= **ko** 子): **kodomó-tachi** 子供たち[達] children; **Kodomo-no-hí** こどもの日 Children's Day (5 May); **kodomo no koro** 子供の頃 one's early years

koe v 超え → **koemásu** 超えます [INFINITIVE]

kóe n 声 voice; cry: **koé o dáshite** 声を出して aloud, out loud

kóe v 肥え → **koemásu** 肥えます [INFINITIVE]

koeda n 小枝 twig

koemásu, koeru v 超[越]えます, 超[越]える crosses (a height, an obstacle) → **koshimásu, kosu** 超[越]します, 超[越]す

koemásu, koéru v 肥えます, 肥える gets fat (= **futorimásu** 太ります)

kōen n 公園 public park

kōen n [BOOKISH] 講演 lecture, speech, talk

kōen n [BOOKISH] 後援 support, backing

koenai v 超[越]えない = **koemasén** 超[越]えません (not cross)

koénai v 肥えない = **koemasén** 肥えません (not get fat)

koeraremásu, koerareru v 超[越]えられます, 超[越]えられる can cross

koe ro v 超えろ = **koé yo** 超えよ [IMPERATIVE] (cross it!) → **koemásu** 超えます

koeru v 越える = **koemásu** 越えます (crosses)

koeru v 超える = **koemásu** 超えます (crosses)

koeru... adj 超える: o koeru ...(を)超える... over..., more than... (people, country, money, temperature, etc.); (sen)-nin o koeru hito (千)人を超える人 over/more than (one thousand) people

koéru v 肥える = **koemásu** 肥えます (gets fat)

koete v 超[越]えて → **koemásu** 超[越]えます

kóete v 肥えて → **koemásu** 肥えます

kōfuku n 幸福 happiness: **kōfuku (na)** 幸福(な) happy

kōfuku n 降伏 surrender: ~ **shimásu** 降伏します surrenders

kōfun n 興奮 excitement: **kōfun shite-imásu** 興奮しています is excited

kōgai n 公害 (environmental) pollution

kōgai n 郊外 suburbs, suburbia

kōgaku n 工学 engineering

kōgaku-shin n 向学心 desire to learn: **kōgaku-shin ni moeteimásu** 向学心に燃えています has a strong desire to learn

kogan n [BOOKISH] 湖岸 lakeshore

kōgan n 睾丸 testicle(s) [FORMAL]

kōgan n 紅顔 peaches and cream, rosy, fresh face (of young man): **kōgan no bishōnen** 紅顔の美少年 rosy faced handsome youth

kōgan n [BOOKISH] 厚顔 impudence: **kōgan-muchi (no)** 厚顔無恥(の) impudent and shameless

kogánai v 漕がない = **kogimasén** 漕ぎません (not row)

kōgan-zai n 抗がん剤 anticancer drug

kogashimásu, kogásu v 焦がします, 焦がす scorches it

kogata (no) adj 小型(の) small-size (model)

kóge v 焦げ → **kogemásu** 焦げます [INFINITIVE]

kóge v 漕げ → **kogemásu** 漕げます [INFINITIVE]

kóge v 漕げ [IMPERATIVE] (row!) → **kogimásu** 漕ぎます

kógeba v 漕げば (if one rows) → **kogimásu** 漕ぎます

kōgeki n 攻撃 attack: ~ **shimásu** 攻撃します attacks

kogemásu, kogéru v 焦げます, 焦げる gets scorched/burned

kogemásu, kogéru v 漕げます, 漕げる can row

kogénai v 焦げない = **kogemasén** 焦げません (not get scorched)

kogénai v 漕げない = **kogemasén** 漕げません (cannot row)

kogéreba v 焦げれば (if it gets scorched) → **kogemásu** 焦げます

kogéreba v 漕げれば (if one can row) → **kogemásu** 漕げます

kógete v 焦げて → **kogemásu** 焦げます

kógete v 漕げて → **kogemásu** 漕げます

kō gi n 講義 lecture

kō gí n 抗議 protest: ~ **shimásu** 抗議します protests

kogimásu, kógu v 漕ぎます, 漕ぐ rows (a boat)

kogítte n 小切手 (bank) check

kógi ya/wa shinai v [INFORMAL] 漕ぎや/はしない = **kogánai** 漕がない (not row)

kogō v 漕ごう = **kogimashō´** 漕ぎましょう (let's row!)

kōgo n 口語 spoken language, colloquial (word): **kōgo-teki (na)** 口語的(な) colloquial

kogoe n 小声 low voice, whisper

Kōgō´(-sama) n 皇后(様) the Empress: **Kōgō-héika** 皇后陛下 Her Majesty the Empress

kogoto n 小言 (o-kógoto お小言) scolding, complaint

kógu v 漕ぐ = **kogimásu** 漕ぎます (rows a boat)

kō´gyō n 工業 industry

kohada n コハダ shad

kōhai n 後輩 one's junior (colleague, fellow student)

kohaku n コハク・琥珀 **1.** = **kon-iro** コハク・琥珀(色) amber (color) **2.** taffeta elastic webbing **3. kohaku(san)** コハク・琥珀(酸) succinic acid

kohan n [BOOKISH] 湖畔 lakeside

kōhei (na) adj 公平(な) fair, impartial

kōhíi n コーヒー coffee: **kōhii-jáwan/-káppu** コーヒー茶碗/カップ coffee cup; **kōhii-pótto** コーヒーポット coffee pot; **kōhii-ten/-ya** コーヒー店/屋 coffee shop/house (= **kissaten** 喫茶店)

ko-hítsúji n 小羊・子羊 lamb, small sheep: **mayoeru ko-hítsúji** 迷える子羊 The Lost Sheep

kōhyō n [BOOKISH] 好評 favorable criticism

kói n 請い・乞い request (= **tanomí** 頼み)

kói n コイ・鯉 carp (fish)

kói n 恋 love (affair), romance: **kói ni ochimásu** 恋に落ちます falls in love

kói (no) adj 故意(の) deliberate; **kói ni** 故意に deliberately

kói n 濃い deep (color), strong (coffee, tea, taste), well saturated

kói n 来い [IMPERATIVE] (come!) → **kimásu** 来ます

kō´i n [BOOKISH] 好意・厚意 goodwill, favor: **kō´i o misemásu** 好意を見せます does a favor

kō´i n 行為 act, deed; behavior

koibito n 恋人 sweetheart, lover, boyfriend/girlfriend

kóida v 漕いだ = **kogimáshita** 漕ぎました (rowed)

koide v 漕いで → **kogimásu** 漕ぎます

kóin n コイン coin: **koin-rókkā** コインロッカー coin locker

kōin n 工員 factory worker

koi-nóbori n コイ[鯉]のぼり carp streamers (for Children's Day (5 May))

ko-inu n 小犬・子犬・仔犬 puppy/puppies, small dog(s)

koiru n コイル coil

koishi *n* 小石 pebble(s)

koitsu *n* こいつ this damn one: **koitsu-ra** こいつ ら these damn ones

kóji *n* 孤児 orphan: **kojí-in** 孤児院 orphanage

kō´ji *n* 工事 construction work: **kōji-chū** 工事中 under construction

kojikí *n* こじき・乞食 beggar: "**Ōji to Kojiki**" 「王子と乞食」 "The Prince and the Pauper" (*a novel by Mark Twain*)

Kojiki *n* 古事記 "Kojiki, the Records of Ancient Matters"

kójin *n* 個人 an individual

kojin-teki (na) *n* 個人的(な) individual, personal: **kojin-teki (na) iken** 個人的(な)意見 personal opinion

kojiremásu, **kojiréru** *v* こじれます、こじれる gets twisted, complicated, entangled; (*illness*) worsens

kōjitsu *n* 口実 excuse, pretext

kojō (de/no) *adv, adj* 湖上(で/の) on the lake (*surface*)

kojō *n* 古城 old castle

kōjō´ *n* 工場 factory, plant (= **kōbá** 工場)

kōjyutsu *n* 口述 dictation

kōjyutsu (no) *adj* 後述(の) after-mentioned

kokan *n* [BOOKISH] 股間 between the legs: **kokan-setsu** 股関節 hip joint

kō´ka *n* 効果 effect: **hiyō-kōka** 費用効果 cost effect

kō´ka *n* 硬貨 coin

kō´ka *n* 高価 high price: **kō´ka (na)** ... 高価(な) ... expensive ... (= **takai** 高い)

kō´kai *n* 航海 voyage: ~ **shimásu** 航海します makes a voyage, sails, navigates

kō´kai *n* 後悔 regret: ~ **shimásu** 後悔します regrets

kōkai (no) *adj* 公開(の) open to the public, open, public: ~ **shimásu** 公開します opens it to the public, discloses; **eiga no kōkai** 映画の公開 movie release

kokáin *n* コカイン cocaine

kōkan *n* 交換 exchange: ~ **shimásu** 交換します exchanges, trades; **meishi-kōkan** 名刺交換 exchanging business cards; **purezento-kōkan** プレゼント交換 exchanging gifts

kōkan-ryūgakusei *n* 交換留学生 exchange student;

kōkan-shinkei *n* 交感神経 sympathetic nerve: **fuku-kōkan-shinkei** 副交感神経 parasympathetic nerve

kōkán-shu *n* 交換手 operator (= **operēta** オペレーター): **denwa-kōkan-shu** 電話交換手 telephone operator

kōkatsu (na) *adj* 狡猾(な) sly

koké *n* 苔 moss

koké *n* こけ foolishness, a fool: **koké ni saremásu** こけにされます gets trashed

kō-kéiki *n* 好景気 prosperity, good business conditions

kō-ki *n* [BOOKISH] 好機 (*favourable*) opportunity, chance, occasion

kō-ki *n* [BOOKISH] 香気 aroma

kō-ki *n* 後期 the latter period

kō-ki *n* 後記 afterword, postscript (= **ato-gaki** 後書き): **henshū-kōki** 編集後記 editor's postscript

kō-kí (shin) *n* 好奇(心) curiosity, inquisitiveness

kō-kíatsu *n* 高気圧 high (*barometric*) pressure

kókka *n* 国家 nation

kokkai *n* 国会 assembly, parliament, congress, Diet (= **gikai** 議会)

kokkei (na) *adj* こっけい[滑稽](な) amusing, funny

kokki *n* 国旗 national flag

kokkō *n* 国交 diplomatic relations

kókku (-san) *n* コック(さん) cook, chef

kokkyō *n* 国境 border (*of country*)

koko *pron* ここ here, this place

kō-kō *n* 高校 senior high school

kókóa *n* ココア cocoa

kōkoku *n* 広告 advertisement

kókóná(t)tsu *n* ココナ(ッ)ツ coconut (= **koko-yashi no mi** ココヤシの実): **kokonáttu-miruku** ココナッツミルク coconut milk

kokonoka *n* 九日 nine days; the 9th day (*of month*)

kokónotsu *n* 九つ nine; nine years old (= **kyūsai** 九歳)

kokóro *n* 心 mind, heart, spirit, feeling: **kokoro kara (no)** 心から(の) heart-felt, sincere

kokoro-atari *n* 心当たり idea

kokoro-bosói *adj* 心細い lonely

kokoro-kubari *n* 心配り concern, care (= **hairyo** 配慮, **ki-zúkai** 気遣い)

kokoromi *n* 試み trial, attempt, test

kokoromi *v* 試み → **kokoromimásu** 試みます [INFINITIVE]

kokoromimásu, **kokoromíru** *v* 試みます、試みる tries, attempts, tests

kokoro-mochi *n* 心持ち feelings, spirit, mood

kokorozashi *n* 志 **1.** mind; intention; purpose **2.** ambition, hope **3.** goodwill, kindness; gift

kokorozashimásu, **kokorozásu** *v* 志します、志す sets one's mind

kokoro-zuke *n* 心付け tip, gratuity (= **chippu** チップ)

kokoro-zuyói *adj* 心強い encouraging, heartening: **kokoro-zuyói sonzai** 心強い存在 dependable person: **kokoro-zuyói kotoba** 心強い言葉 encouraging words

kōkō´-sei *n* 高校生 (*senior*) high-school student: **joshi/danshi kōsei** 女子/男子高生 high-school girl/boy

...´-koku *suffix* ...国 **1.** (*name of certain*) country: **Bei-koku** 米国 America (= **Amerika** アメリカ America, U.S.(A.), **Amerika-Gasshū´-koku** アメリカ合衆国 United States of America): **Ei-koku** 英国 Great Britain, the United Kingdom (U.K.) (= **Igirisu** イギリス): **Chū´-goku** 中国 China (= **Chūkajinmin-kyōwá-koku** 中華人民共和国): **Nihón-koku** 日本国 Japan (= **Nihón**, **Nippón** 日本) **2. koku-...** 国... national, state

kokuban *n* 黒板 blackboard: **kokubán-keshi** 黒板消し, **kokubán-fuki** 黒板拭き eraser

kōkū-bin *n* 航空便 = **kōkū-yū´bin** 航空郵便 airmail

kokubō *n* 国防 national defense

kokudō *n* 国道 highway

Kokudo-Kōtsū-shō *n* 国土交通省 Ministry of Land, Infrastructure, Transport and Tourism (MLIT)

kōkū-gáisha *n* 航空会社 airline company

kokujin *n* 黒人 black people, Afro-American

kokumin *n* 国民 a people, a nation; national(s), citizen(s)

kokúmotsu *n* 穀物 grain (*cereal*)

kokúnai (no) *adj* 国内(の) internal, domestic, inland

kokuritsu (-) *adj* 国立 national, government-established: **kokuritsu-toshokan** 国立図書館 national library: **kokuritsu-daigaku** 国立大学 national university

kokúrui *n* 穀類 cereal(s), grain

kokusai *n* 国際: **kokusai-dénwa** 国際電話 international phone call; **kokusai-teki (na)** 国際的 (な) international (= **intānashonaru (na)** インターナショナル(な))

Kokusai-réngō *n* 国際連合 United Nations

kokusan (no) *adj* 国産(の) domestic(ally) made, made in Japan: **kokusan-hin** 国産品 domestic product: **kokusan-sha** 国産車 domestic car: **kokusan-gyū** 国産牛 domestic beef

kokuseki *n* 国籍 nationality

kōkū-shókan *n* 航空書簡 aerogram (= **earo-guramu** エアログラム)

kōkyo *n* 皇居 palace (*in Tokyo*); the Imperial Palace

kókyō *n* 故郷 hometown, birth-place (= **furusato** ふるさと)

kōkyō (no) *adj* 公共(の) public: **kōkyō-no-ba** 公共の場 public area

kōkyō-ryō´kin *n* 公共料金 utility bills/charges

kokyū *n* 呼吸 respiration, breathing

kōkyū (na) *adj* 高級(な) high-class/grade, high-ranking; fancy: **kōkyū-hin** 高級品 fancy goods

kóma *n* こま・コマ・独楽 a toy top: **koma-máwashi** 独楽回し top-spinning

komakái *adj* 細かい **1.** fine, small **2.** detailed, exact **3.** thrifty **4.** small (*change*): **komakakú shimásu** 細かくします cashes it into smaller bills/coins

koma-mono *n* 小間物 notions, haberdashery, dime-store goods

komamónó-ya *n* 小間物屋 dime store, haberdasher

koma-nezumi *n* コマネズミ・独楽鼠 (*Japanese*) dancing mouse: **koma-nezumi no yō ni hatarakimásu** コマネズミのように働きます works like a beaver

komarasemásu, komaraséru *v* 困らせます、困らせる bothers, embarrasses

komarimásu, komáru *v* 困ります、困る gets perplexed, embarrassed, troubled; is at a loss; is in need: **komáru tokoró** 困るところ trouble (*difficulty*); **komátta-kotó** 困った事 predicament, mess, plight

komāsharu *n* コマーシャル commercial (*message*) (= **shiiému** シーエム): **terebi-komāsharu** テレビコマーシャル TV commercial

komayaka (na) *adj* こま[細・濃]やか(な) meticulous, attentive, tender: **komayaka na aijō** 細やかな愛情 tender love: **(kime-)komayaka na shidō** (きめ)細やかな指導 detailed instruction

komé *n* コメ・米 (**o-kome** お米) rice (*hulled, uncooked*)

komé-ya *n* 米屋 (**o-komeya** お米屋) rice dealer/store

kóme *v* 込め → **komemásu** 込めます [INFINITIVE]

kómeba *v* 込めば・混めば (if it gets crowded) → **komimásu** 込み[混み]ます

komemásu, koméru *v* 込めます、込める includes

koméreba *v* 込めれば (if one includes) → **komemásu** 込めます

kómete *v* 込めて → **komemásu** 込めます

komichi *n* 小道 path, lane

komi-itta *v* 込み入った complicated, intricate (*situation, subject*)

komimásu, kómu *v* 込み[混み]ます、込む・混む gets crowded

kōmin *n* 公民 citizen, civilian (= **shímin** 市民)

kōmoku *n* 項目 item: **(nyūryoku) hissu-kōmoku** (入力)必須項目 mandatory field(s)

kómon *n* [BOOKISH] 顧問 consultant, adviser: **komon-bengoshi** 顧問弁護士 a legal adviser

kōmon *n* 校門 school gate

kōmon *n* 肛門 anus

komóri *n* 子守、子守り babysitter: **komori-uta** 子守歌[唄] lullaby, cradle song

kō´mori *n* コウモリ bat (*flying mammal*) **kōmori-gása** *n* こうもり[コウモリ]傘 umbrella (*black, cloth umbrella often used by males in Japan*)

komúgi *n* 小麦 wheat: **komúgi-ko** 小麦粉 wheat flour

kōmú-in *n* 公務員 government worker/employee, official

kōmurimásu, kōmúru *v* 被ります、被る sustains, suffers, incurs (*unfair treatment, tribulation*): **dai-songai o kōmurimásu** 大損害を被ります suffers a serious loss

kón *n* 紺 = **kon-iro** 紺色 (dark blue)

koná *n* 粉 powder; flour

kona-gona *n* 粉々: ~ **shimásu** 粉々にします pulverize

kona-gúsuri *n* 粉薬 powdered medicine

kona-míruku *n* 粉ミルク powdered milk, dry milk

kónai *v* 来ない = **kimasén** 来ません (does not come)

kō´nai *n* 構内 campus: **kō´nai (no)** 構内(の) intramural

konaidá *adv* こないだ, **kono-aidá** この間 the other day, a while ago, lately

kónakatta *v* 来なかった = **kimasén deshita** 来ませんでした (didn't come)

konashimásu, konasu *v* こなします、こなす **1.** powders; digests **2.** (ful)fills, manages (*to do it*): **chūmon o konashimásu** 注文をこなします fills an order; **kázu de konashimásu** 数でこなします relies on numbers (*sales volume*)

kónban *n* 今晩 tonight: **Konban wa** こんばんは Good evening.

konbini(-ensu sutoā) *n* コンビニ（エンスストアー) convenience store

konbō *n* [BOOKISH] 棍棒 club, billy-club, bludgeon

kónbu *n* コンブ・昆布 kelp (*a kind of seaweed*)

konchū *n* 昆虫 insect

kondate *n* [BOOKISH] 献立 menu (= **ményū** メニュー)

kónde *v* 込んで・混んで → **komimásu** 込みます・混みます: **kónde-imásu** 混んでいます is crowded

kóndo *n, adv* 今度 this time; next

kondō´mu *n* コンドーム condom

kóne *n* コネ connection, "pull": (**hito ni) kóne o tsukemásu** (人に）コネを付けます establishes a connection, gets pull (*with a person*)

ko-néko *n* 小猫・子猫・仔猫 kitten(s), small cat(s)

konekutā *n* コネクター connector

kongan *n* [BOOKISH] 懇願 entreaty: **~ shimásu** 懇願します begs, implores, requests

kongari yakimásu (yaku) *v* こんがり焼きます（焼く) bakes/toasts/roasts/grills/sunburns until a beautiful brown

kongetsu *n* 今月 this month

kongō´-seki *n* [BOOKISH] 金剛石 diamond (= **daiya(mondo)** ダイヤ（モンド))

kongo (wa) *adv* 今後（は) from now on, in the future

koni (na/ni) *adj, adv* 懇意（な/に) friendly, close, intimate: **... to koni ni shiteimásu** ...と懇意にしています is very intimate with ...

konin *n* 婚姻 marriage (= **kekkon** 結婚): **konin-todoke** 婚姻届 marriage notification

kōnin (no) *adj* 公認（の) authorized, certified: **kōnin-kaikéishi** 公認会計士 certified public accountant (CPA), chartered accountant

kon (iro) *n* 紺（色) dark blue

konkai *n, adv* 今回 this time

konkan *n* 根幹 [BOOKISH] basis, foundation

konki *n* 根気 patience: **konki ga iru shigoto** 根気がいる仕事 work which requires patience

konki *n* 婚期 [BOOKISH] marriageable age: **konki o nogasu** 婚期を逃す is past marriageable age

konkurabe *n* 根比べ waiting game, endurance contest

konkuríito *n* コンクリート concrete (*cement*)

konkū´ru *n* コンクール prize contest, prize competition (= **konpe** コンペ)

kónkyo *n* 根拠 [BOOKISH] basis, grounds,

authority, evidence: **konkyo-chi** 根拠地 base, home ground: **kónkyo no nai uwasa** 根拠のない噂 groundless rumor

konkyū *n* 困窮 [BOOKISH] poverty: **~ shiteimásu** 困窮しています is in poverty, is in financial difficulties

konna ... *adj* こんな... such as, this kind of: **konna ni** こんなに to this extent, this much

kónnan *n* 困難 difficulty, trouble, hardship **kónnan (na)** *adj* 困難（な) difficult

Konnichi wa *interj* こんにちは Good afternoon; Hello!

konnyákú *n* コンニャク devil's-tongue root made into gelatin

kono... *adj* この... this ..., these... **kono-aidá** *adv* この間 the other day, a while ago, lately (= **konaidá** こないだ)
kono-goro *adv* この頃 recently (= **chiká goro** 近頃, **saikin** 最近)
kono-máe (no)... *adj* この前（の)... the last... **kono-tsúgí** *n* この次 next time (= **jikai** 次回)

kōnō *n* 効能 effect (*effectiveness*) (= **kōyō** 効用, **kiki-me** 効き目): **kōnō ga arimásu** 効能があります is effective

kónome, kí-no-me *n* 木の芽 **1.** tree sprout **2.** Japanese pepper sprout

kónomi *n* 好み (**o-konomi** お好み) liking, taste: **konomí no ...** 好みの... that one likes, that is to one's taste/liking, favorite ...: **kónomi no taipu** 好みのタイプ one's type: **o-konomi-yaki** お好み焼き seasoned pancake

konomimásu, konómu *v* 好みます、好む likes, is fond of, prefers

konónde *v* 好んで → **konomimásu** 好みます

kónpasu *n* コンパス compass (*for drafting*)

konpe *n* コンペ prize competition, prize contest (= **konkū´ru** コンクール)

konpon *n* 根本 [BOOKISH] foundation, basis: **konpon-teki (na)** 根本的（な) fundamental, basic

konpyū´ta *n* コンピュータ computer

konran *n* 混乱 [BOOKISH] mess (*disorder*), confusion, jumble: **~ shimásu** 混乱します gets confused

kónro *n* コンロ stove (*portable cooking*)

konsárutanto *n* コンサルタント consultant: **keiei-konsarutanto** 経営コンサルタント management consultant: **konsarutanto-gaisha** コンサルタント会社 consultant company

konseki *n* 痕跡 [BOOKISH] trace, mark, vestige (= **áto** 跡): **konseki o nokoshimásu** 痕跡を残します leaves a mark

kónsénto *n* コンセント **1.** (*electricity*) outlet, (*light*) plug: **kónsénto ni tsunagimásu** コンセントにつなぎます plugs in **2.** consent: **infōmudo-konsento** インフォームド・コンセント informed consent

konshín-kai *n* 懇親会 [BOOKISH] reception, get-together party

konshū *n* 今週 this week

konsome *n* コンソメ thin Western soup, consomme

kōn-sutāchi *n* コーンスターチ cornstarch

kontákuto *n* コンタクト = **kontakuto-rénzu** コンタクトレンズ contact lenses

konténa *n* コンテナ container (*for transporting goods*)

kóntesuto *n* コンテスト contest

kón'ya *n* 今夜 tonight

kon'yaku *n* 婚約 engagement (*to be married*): **konyaku-yubiwa** 婚約指輪 engagement ring (= **engēji ringu** エンゲージリング): (**... to**) **kon'yaku shite imásu** (…と)婚約しています is engaged (to …)

kon'yoku *n* 混浴 (*hot springs*) mixed bathing

kónzatsu *n* 混雑 jam, congestion: ~ **shiteimásu** 混雑しています is crowded

kópii *n* コピー copy (*photocopy*) (= **fukusha** 複写)

koppamijin-ni-narimásu (náru) *v* 木っ端微塵になります(なる) is smashed to pieces, is smashed to smithereens, is broken into pieces

koppu *n* コップ a glass, a cup

kōra *n* コウラ・甲羅 shell (*of tortoise, etc.*)

kō´ra *n* コーラ cola

koraemásu, koráeru *v* 堪えます, 堪える **1.** stands, bears **2.** controls, restrains, represses

kōran *n* コーラン the Koran, the Quran

koramu *n* コラム column, boxed article(s) (= **kakomi-kiji** 囲み記事)

kōranai *v* 凍らない = **kōrimasén** 凍りません (not freeze)

ko(ra)remásu, ko(ra)réru *v* 来(ら)れます, 来(ら)れる **1.** can come **2.** [PASSIVE] has them come (*to one's distress*); [HONORIFIC] comes (= **irasshaimásu** いらっしゃいます)

ko(ra)rénai *v* 来(ら)れない = **ko(ra)remasén** 来(ら)れません (cannot come)

ko(ra)réru *v* 来(ら)れる = **ko(ra)remásu** 来(ら)れます (can come)

kōrasemásu, kōraseru *v* 凍らせます, 凍らせる freezes it

kō´rasu *n* コーラス chorus, choir

kore *pron* これ this one: **kore kara** これから from now on; **kore kara to iu/yū ...** これという/ゆう… specific, particular

kóreba *v* 凝れば (if one gets engrossed; if it gets stiff) → **korimásu** 凝ります

koréra (no) *adj* これら(の) these (*things, matters, etc.*)

kórera *n* コレラ cholera: **korera-kin** コレラ菌 *Vibrio cholerae*

korí 凝り **1.** *n* stiffness, hardening: **káta-(no)-korí** 肩(の)こり shoulder stiffness, a stiff shoulder **2.** *v* → **korimásu** 凝ります [INFINITIVE]

kōri *n* 氷 ice : **kaki-gōri** かき氷 shaved ice (*eaten with syrup*)

kōri *v* 凍り → **kōrimásu** 凍ります [INFINITIVE]

kōri/kóri *n* 行李 wicker trunk

korimásu, kóru *v* 凝ります, 凝る **1.** gets engrossed/absorbed (*in*) **2.** (*shoulder*) gets stiff

korimásu, koriru *v* 懲ります, 懲りる learns a lesson from one's failure

kōrimásu, kōru *v* 凍ります, 凍る it freezes

kōritsu (no) *adj* 公立(の) public, municipal, prefectural

kōritsu *n* 効率 efficiency: **kōritsu-teki na** 効率的な efficient: **gyōmu no kōritsuka** 業務の効率化 streamlining

kori ya/wa shinai *v* [INFORMAL] 凝りや/はしない = **koranai** 凝らない (not get engrossed/absorbed (*in*); not get stiff)

...koro *suffix* 頃 (*at that*) time, (*at*) about (*a time*), occasion (= **... góro (ni)** …頃(に) (*at*) about (*a time*)): **aono-koro (wa)** あの頃(は) (*at*) that time, then, (*in*) those days (= **tō´ji (wa)** 当時(は), **sono-koro (wa)** その頃(は)): **kodomo no koro** 子供の頃 (*in*) one's childhood

koroai *n* 頃合い suitable time: **(sorosoro) koroai desu** (そろそろ)頃合いです It's (about) time to…

korobimásu, korobu *v* 転びます, 転ぶ falls down, tumbles

korogarimásu, korogaru *v* 転がります, 転がる it rolls, tumbles

korogashimásu, korogasu *v* 転がします, 転がす rolls it

korosaremásu, korosareru *v* 殺されます, 殺される gets killed

koroshimásu, korosu *v* 殺します, 殺す kills

kóru *v* 凝る = **kōrimásu** 凝ります (gets engrossed/absorbed (*in*); (*shoulder*) gets stiff)

kōru *v* 凍る = **kōrimásu** 凍ります (it freezes)

Korukata *n* コルカタ Kolkata (*Calcutta*)

kóruku *n* コルク = **korukú-sen** コルク栓 cork **korukú-nuki** *n* コルク抜き corkscrew

kō´ryo *n* 考慮 consideration, reflection, thought: ~ **shimásu** 考慮します considers; **kō´ryo ni iremásu** 考慮に入れます takes into consideration/ account

kō´ryō´ *n* 香料 spice (= **supaisu** スパイス)

koryōri-ya *n* 小料理屋 small traditional Japanese restaurant

kōryū *n* 交流 **1.** AC (alternating current) **2.** ~ **shimásu** 交流します exchanges, interchanges

kósa *n* 濃さ strength (*of saturation*), deepness (*of color*)

kosaemásu, kosaeru *v* こさえます, こさえる = **koshiraemásu** こしらえます makes, concocts

kōsai *n* 交際 social relations, company, association (= **kōyū** 交遊): **kōsai-hi** 交際費 an expense account: ~ **shimásu** 交際します associates, keeps company

ko-saji *n* 小さじ teaspoon (= **tii-supūn** ティースプーン)

kōsaku shimásu (suru) *v* 工作します(する) **1.** builds **2.** handcrafts

kosame *n* 小雨 light rain, drizzle

kōsan *n* 降参 surrender: ~ **shimásu** 降参します surrenders, You've got me!; gives up, goes down

(= **Máitta** 参った)

kosanai v 越さない = **koshimasén** 越しません, etc. (not go over; not …)

kosasemás<u>u</u>, kosaséru v 来させます, 来させる has/lets one come

kosasénai v 来させない = **kosasemasén** 来させません (not have/let one come)

kosásete v 来させて → **kosasemás<u>u</u>** 来させます

kōsa-ten n 交差点 an intersection (*of streets*), a crossing

kose v 越せ **1.** → **kosemás<u>u</u>** 越せます [INFINITIVE] **2.** [IMPERATIVE] (exceed it!) → **koshimás<u>u</u>** 越します

kose v **1.** 漉せ → **kosemás<u>u</u>** 漉せます [INFINITIVE] **2. kosé** 漉せ [IMPERATIVE] (strain it!) → **koshimás<u>u</u>** 漉します

koséba v 越せば (if it exceeds; if …) → **koshimás<u>u</u>** 越します

kosei n 個性 individuality, character, personality: **kosei-teki** 個性的 unique (= **yuniiku** ユニーク): **kosei o nobashimás<u>u</u>** 個性を伸ばします develops individuality: **kosei-yutaka** 個性豊か has a very distinctive personality

kōsei n 構成 constitution, construction, composition

kōsei n 更正 reclamation, reformation

kōsei n 更生 revival, reformation; regeneration, rehabilitation: **hikōshōnen no kōsei** 非行少年の更生 rehabilitation of juvenile delinquents

kōsei n 公正 impartiality
kōsei na 公正(な) *adj* impartial, fair

kōsei n 校正 proofreading: ~ **shimás<u>u</u>** 校正します proofreads
kōsei-sha, kōsei-gakari n 校正者, 校正係 proofreader

kōsei-bússhitsu n 抗生物質 antibiotic(s): **kōsei-bússhitsu o tōyoshimás<u>u</u>** 抗生物質を投与します administers

Kōsei-Rōdō-shō n 厚生労働省 Ministry of Health, Labor and Welfare

kōsei shimás<u>u</u> (suru) v 構成します(する) constitutes

kōsei shimás<u>u</u> (suru) v 更生します(する) reforms, starts a new life

kōsei shimás<u>u</u> (suru) v 校正します(する) proofreads

koseki n 戸籍 family register: **koseki-tōhon** 戸籍謄本 full copy of one's family register: **koseki-shōhon** 戸籍写本 abstract of one's family register

kosemás<u>u</u>, koseru v 越せます, 越せる can go over; can move (*house*)

kosemás<u>u</u>, koseru v 漉せます, 漉せる can filter/strain it

kōsen n 光線 ray, beam (*of light*), light

kosenai v 越せない = **kosemasén** 越せません (cannot go over; cannot move (*house*))

kosete v 越せて → **kosemás<u>u</u>** 越せます

kōsha n 後者 the latter

kōsha n 校舎 school-house

koshi n 腰 loin, hip, lower part of back
koshi-káké n 腰掛け seat, chair, bench (= **isu** いす・椅子)
koshi-maki n 腰巻き loincloth; petticoat
koshi -no-kubire n 腰のくびれ waist (= **uesuto** ウエスト)

koshi v 越し → **koshimás<u>u</u>** 越します

kō´shi n 講師 instructor(s), lecturer(s)

Kōshi n 孔子 Confucius

koshi-káke v 腰掛け → **koshikakemás<u>u</u>** 腰掛けます [INFINITIVE]

koshi-kakemás<u>u</u>, koohi kakéru v 腰掛けます, 腰掛ける sits down

koshimás<u>u</u>, kosu v 越します・越す goes/runs over, goes across, moves house (= **hikkoshimás<u>u</u>** 引っ越します)

koshimás<u>u</u>, kosu v 超します, 超す goes/runs over (= **chō´ka shimás<u>u</u>** 超過します, **ō´ba shimás<u>u</u>** オーバーします); exceeds: **do o koshimás<u>u</u>** 度を超します goes too far

koshimás<u>u</u>, kosu v 漉します, 漉す filters/strains it

kōhin n 行進 march(ing)

kōshin n 更新 renewal, update

kōshin shimás<u>u</u> (suru) v 行進します(する) marches

kōshin shimás<u>u</u> (suru) v 更新します(する) renews, updates (*a contract, website, etc.*)

koshiraemás<u>u</u>, koshiraeru v 拵えます, 拵える makes, concocts

koshite v 越して → **koshimás<u>u</u>** 越します

koshite v 漉して → **koshimás<u>u</u>** 漉します

koshí ya/wa shinai v [INFORMAL] 越しや/はしない = **kosanai** 越さない, etc. (not exceed; not …)

kosho n 古書 **1.** old book(s), antique book(s) **2.** secondhand book(s) (= **furu-hon** 古本)

koshō n 故障 **1.** breakdown, something wrong: ~ **shimás<u>u</u>** 故障します it breaks down (*gets inoperative*) **2.** hindrance

koshō´ n コショウ・胡椒 pepper

koshō n 呼称 appellation, name

koshō n 小姓 foot page

kōshō n 交渉 negotiations

kōshoku (na) *adj* 好色(な) erotic; lecherous: **kōshoku-kan** 好色漢 lecher

kōshū n 公衆 the public, the masses: **kōshū-dénwa** 公衆電話 public telephone
kōshū no *adj* 公衆の public;

kōshū(kai) n 講習(会) lecture class, course (*not regular classes in school*)

… kóso (masani) *adv* …こそ(まさに) precisely, exactly, just; certainly, really → **mása-ni** まさに・正に: **kore-koso** これこそ This is precisely/exactly/just the thing: **kare-koso** 彼こそ he is truly

kosō´ v 越そう = **koshimashō´** 越しましょう (let's go over)

kosō´ v 漉そう = **koshimashō´** 漉しましょう (let's filter!)

103

kōsō (no) *adj* 高層（の）highrise: **kōsō-bíru** 高層ビル high-rise building, skyscraper

kōsoku *n* 高速 [BOOKISH] high speed: **kōsoku-dō'ro** 高速道路 expressway, freeway; **kōsoku-gí(y)a** 高速ギア［ギヤ］high gear

kossetsu *n* 骨折 bone fracture: **~ shimásu** 骨折します fractures

kossori (to) *adv* こっそり（と）secretly, sneakily, sneakingly, on the sly

kosu *v* 越す → **koshimásu** 越します (goes/runs over, goes across, moves house)

kosu *v* 漉す → **koshimásu** 漉します (filters/strains it)

kosu *v* 超す → **koshimásu** 超します (goes/runs over)

kōsu *n* コース course; (*traffic, swim*) lane; a set series of chef's choices, a set meal: **mein-kōsu** メインコース main course: **osusume (no) kōsu** お勧めのコース recommended course

kosuchūmu *n* コスチューム costume (= **kasō** 仮装)

kōsui *n* 香水 perfume: **kōsui no kaori** 香水の香り smell of perfume

kosupure *n* コスプレ cosplay

kosúri *v* 擦り → **kosurimásu** 擦ります [INFINITIVE]

kosurimásu, kosúru *v* 擦ります, 擦る rubs, scrapes

kosu'tté *v* 擦って → **kosurimásu** 擦ります

kotáé *n* 答（え）an answer, reply, response (= **kaitō** 回答, **henjí** 返事 (**o-henji** お返事), **hentō** 返答)

kotáé *n* 応え a response, an answer (= **henjí** 返事 (**o-henji** お返事), **hentō** 返答, **ōtō** 応答) (→ **tegótae** 手応え)

kotáe *v* 答え → **kotaemásu** 答えます [INFINITIVE]

kotáe *v* 応え → **kotaemásu** 応えます [INFINITIVE]

kotaemásu, kotáéru *v* 答えます, 答える answers

kotaemásu, kotáéru *v* 応えます, 応える responds, lives up to, meets: **kitai ni kotaemásu** 期待に応えます meets one's expectations, lives up to one's expectations: **yōbō ni kotaemásu** 要望に応えます meets one's request

kotáe ro 答えろ = **kotáe yo** 答えよ [IMPERATIVE] (answer!) → **kotaemásu** 答えます

kotai *n* 固体 a solid

kōtai *n* 交替 alternation: **~ shimásu** 交替します alternates, shifts (*with*)

Kōtáishi *n* 皇太子, **Kōtáishi-sama** 皇太子さま the Crown Prince
Kōtáishi-hi *n* 皇太子妃 the Crown Princess

kōtaku *n* 光沢 luster, gloss, sheen: **kōtaku ga arimásu** 光沢があります lustrous, glossy, shiny

kotatsu *n* こたつ (**o-kóta** おこた) traditional quilt-covered heating arrangement (*foot warmer*)

kotchí *pron* こっち → **kochira** こちら

kotei *n* 固定 fixation: **~ shimásu** 固定します fixes, fastens, stabilizes

kōtei *n* 校庭 school grounds

kōtei *n* 肯定 affirmation: **~ shimásu** 肯定します affirms

kōtei *n* 皇帝 emperor: **Rōma-kōtei** ローマ皇帝 Roman emperor

kōtei *n* 工程 [BOOKISH] process, progress: **seisaku-kōtei** 製作工程 process for forming: **sagyō-kōtei** 作業工程 working process: **kōtei-kanrihyō** 工程管理表 process management timetable

kotéji *n* コテージ cottage

koteki-tai *n* 鼓笛隊 drum and fife band

koten *n* 古典 classic work (*literature, art, etc.*) (= **kurashikku** クラシック): **koten-ongaku** 古典音楽 classic music: **koten-bungaku** 古典文学 classic literature: **koten-teki na** 古典的な classical

koten *n* 個展 private exhibition: **koten o hirakimásu** 個展を開きます holds a private exhibition

kotesaki de gomakashimásu (gomakasu) *v* 小手先でごまかします（ごまかす）uses cheap tricks

kote-shirabe (ni) *adv* 小手調べ（に）(*for*) a trial, (*for*) practice

kōtetsu *n* 鋼鉄 [BOOKISH] steel (= **suchiiru** スチール)

kotó *n* こと・事 thing, matter; fact; words, sentence; case, circumstance, happening; experience: **... suru kotó ga arimásu** …することがあります does do it sometimes, has something to do; **... suru kotó ga arimasén** …することがありません has nothing to do; **... suru kotó wa arimasén** …することはありません never does it; **... shita kotó ga arimásu** …したことがあります has done it before; **... shita kotó wa arimasén** …したことはありません has never done it; **... (suru/shinai) kotó wa arimasén** …（する/しない）ことはありません it isn't that one (does/doesn't, will/won't do it); **... (suru) kotó ni shimásu** …（する）ことにします decides to (*do it*)

kóto *n* 琴 (**o-kóto** お琴) Japanese harp

koto-ji *n* 琴柱 [BOOKISH] the bridges on a Japanese harp

kóto *n* 古都 [BOOKISH] ancient capital

kō'to *n* コート 1. coat: **kō'to o haorimásu** コートを羽織ります puts on one's coat 2. (*athletic*) court: **tenisu-kō'to** テニスコート tennis court

kotō *n* 孤島 [BOOKISH] solitary island

kotobá *n* 言葉 (**o-kotoba** お言葉) 1. word, words; sentence (*spoken*); remark 2. speech 3. language (= **gengo** 言語): **o-kotoba ni amaete...** お言葉に甘えて… if you're sure it's all right, I will accept your kind offer; **o-kotoba desu ga...** お言葉ですが… not to split hairs, but…; **o-kotoba o kaesu yō desu ga...** お言葉を返すようですが… I hate to contradict you, but…, I don't mean to contradict you, but…

kōtō-gákkō *n* 高等学校 = **kōkō** 高校 high school: **kōtō-gákkō no séito** 高等学校の生徒 (= **kōkō'-sei** 高校生) high-school student

kotogara n 事柄 [BOOKISH] affair, matter (= **kotó** こと・事)

kotonarimásu, kotonáru v 異なります, 異なる is different, differs: **kotonátte imásu** 異なっています is different; **kotonátta …** 異なった… different

kóto-ni adv ことに・殊に **1.** especially (= **tóku-ni** 特に) **2.** [+ NEGATIVE] less likely **3.** moreover, what is more

kōtō (no) adj 口頭(の) oral, verbal: **kōtō-shímon** 口頭試問 oral examination

ko-tori n 小鳥 small bird

kotosara adv ことさら particularly

kotoshi n 今年 this year

kototarimásu, kototariru v 事足ります, 事足りる suffices, is enough: **… to ie ba kototarimásu** …と言えば事足ります suffice to say that …

kotowárí n 断り refusal; notice, warning; permission: **kotowárí mo náku** 断りもなく without notice/permission/leave

kotowarimásu, kotowáru v 断ります, 断る **1.** refuses, declines, begs off **2.** makes excuses **3.** gives notice **4.** dismisses, lays off, fires

kotowaza n ことわざ・諺 proverb(s)

kotozuké, kotozute n 言付け, 言づて a message (for someone) (= **méssēji** メッセージ)

kotsú n こつ[コツ] knack, trick, tip

kōtsū n 交通 traffic, transportation; communication(s): **kōtsū-hyō´shiki** 交通標識 traffic signs; **kōtsū-jū´tai** 交通渋滞 traffic jam; **kōtsū-shíngō** 交通信号 traffic signal(s)

kotsuban n 骨盤 pelvis

kotsubu n 小粒 small grain

kō-tsugō n 好都合 (convenience) expediency

kōtsūjūtai n traffic jam 交通渋滞; **kōtsūjūtai de no iraira** 交通渋滞でのイライラ road rage

kotsúzui n 骨髄 bone marrow

ko-tsúzumi n 小鼓 small hourglass-shaped drum

kótta v 凝った = **korimáshita** 凝りました (got stiff)

kōtta v 凍った = **kōrimáshita** 凍りました (it froze)

kótte v 凝って → **korimásu** 凝ります

kōtte v 凍って → **kōrimásu** 凍ります: **kōtte imásu** 凍っています is frozen

kottō´-hin n 骨董品 curious, antiques

kotton n コットン cotton (= **mén** 綿, **momen** 木綿)

kōun n 幸運 good fortune

ko-uri n 小売り retail: ~ **shimásu** 小売りします retails, sells retail
kouri-gyō n 小売業 retail business
kouri-ten n 小売店 retail store, retailer

kowagari n 怖[恐]がり a coward (= **okubyō-monó** 臆病者): **kowagarimásu** 怖[恐]がります fears, takes flight, is afraid

kowái adj こわい・怖[恐]い is afraid; frightful; terrific

kowairo n 声色 **1.** tone of voice (= **kowane** 声音)

2. impersonation: **kowairo o tsukaimásu** 声色を使います impersonates

kowane n 声音 tone of voice (= **kowairo** 声色)

kowaremásu, kowaréru v 壊れます, **kowaréru** 壊れる it breaks/smashes

kowaremono n こわれ物 fragile (article): **kowaremono-chū´i** こわれ物注意 Handle With Care

koware-yasúi adj 壊れやすい fragile, easily broken, breakable

kowashimásu, kowásu v 壊します, 壊す breaks/smashes it, destroys: **kuruma o kowashimásu** 車を壊します wrecks a car, **karada o kowashimásu** 体をこわします ruins one's health, **o-naka o kowashimásu** おなかをこわします develops stomach trouble, **(hito no) kíbun o kowashimásu** (人の)気分をこわします spoils a person's mood, makes a person feel bad

koya n 小屋 hut, shed, cabin

kōya n 荒野 [BOOKISH] wild land, wilderness

kōyaku n 公約 (public) pledge
kōyaku-sū n 公約数 common factor

koyama n 小山 hill

koyō n 雇用 [BOOKISH] employment (hiring): **koyō-keiyakusho** 雇用契約書 employment agreement

koyō´ v 来よう = **kimashō´** 来ましょう (let's come!)

kōyō n 紅葉 red leaves: **aki no kōyō** 秋の紅葉 autumnal colors of the leaves

kōyō n 効用 effect (effectiveness) (= **kiki-me** 効き目, **kōnō** 効能): **kōyō ga arimásu** 効用があります is effective

kōyō (no) adj 公用(の) official: **kōyō-go** 公用語 official language

koyomí n 暦 calendar (= **karéndā** カレンダー)

kōyu n 香油 balm

kōyu n 鉱油 mineral oil

koyū (no) adj 固有(の) characteristic

kōyū n 交友 companion, friend(s)

kōyū n 交遊 social relations, company, association (= **kōsai** 交際): ~ **shimásu** 交遊します associates, keeps company

kō yū (iu) … adj こうゆう(いう)…this kind/sort of …, such … (= **konna** こんな)

kōza n 口座 an account: **ginkō-kōza** 銀行口座 bank account: **kōza o hirakimásu** 口座を開きます opens an account

kō´zan n 鉱山 a mine

kō´zan n 高山 high mountain

ko-zara n 小皿 saucer

kōzen (no/to) adj, adv 公然(の/と) open(ly), public(ly)

ko-zeni n 小銭 small change, coins

kozō´ n 小僧 **1.** young monk **2.** = **kozō-san** 小僧さん kid

kōzō n 構造 structure, makeup, organization

kōzu n 構図 (picture) composition

kózuchi n 小槌 a small hammer: **uchide-no-**

kozuchi 打ち出の小槌 lucky mallet, magical mallet

kozue *n* 梢 treetop

kōzui *n* 洪水 flood: **kōzui ga okorimásu** 洪水が起こります floods

kózukai *n* 小使い janitor, custodian; attendant; servant

kózukai *n* 小遣い（**o-kózukai** お小遣い）pin money, pocket money

kózu (ni) *adv* 来ず（に）= **konái de** 来ないで (not coming)

kozútsumi *n* 小包 package, parcel

kú *n* 九 nine (= **kyū** 九)

kú *n* 句 phrase

kú *n* 区, ...´-**ku** ...区 **1.** a ward (*in a city*) (→ **ku-yákusho** 区役所): **Tōkyō nijūsan-ku** 東京 23 区 twenty-three wards of Tokyo, the special 23 wards which make up the core and the most populous part of Tokyo (**Adachi-ku** 足立区, **Arawkawa-ku** 荒川区, **Bunkyo-ku** 文京区, **Chiyoda-ku** 千代田区, **Chuo-ku** 中央区, **Edogawa-ku** 江戸川区, **Itabashi-ku** 板橋区, **Katsushika-ku** 葛飾区, **Kita-ku** 北区, **Koto-ku** 江東区, **Meguro-ku** 目黒区, **Minato-ku** 港区, **Nakano-ku** 中野区, **Nerima-ku** 練馬区, **Ota-ku** 大田区, **Setagaya-ku** 世田谷区, **Shibuya-ku** 渋谷区, **Shinjuku-ku** 新宿区, **Shinagawa-ku** 品川区, **Suginami-ku** 杉並区, **Sumida-ku** 墨田区, **Taito-ku** 台東区, **Toshima-ku** 豊島区) **2.** zone (= **kúiki** 区域)

ku-yákusho *n* 区役所 ward office

...-**ku** *suffix* ...く: [ADJECTIVE] ... being, so as to be, ...-ly: **taichō wa/ga amari yo-ku arimasén** 体調が/があまり良くありません one's health (*condition*) is not very good

kū´ *v* 食う (VULGAR FORM *of* eats, bites *used mainly by males*) = **kuimásu** 食います (eats, bites) (POLITE FORM **tabemásu** 食べます)

kubarimásu, kubáru *v* 配ります, 配る distributes, allots; deals (*cards*)

kúbetsu *n* 区別 difference, differentiation; discrimination: ~ **shimásu** 区別します differentiates, discriminates

kubi *n* 首 neck: **kubi ni shimásu** 首にします fires, lays off, disemploys; **kubi-kázari** 首飾り necklace

kubi-wa *n* 首輪 (*dog*) collar

kubire *n* くびれ neck (*of a bottle*), constricted place, waist

kubomi *n* くぼみ・窪み hollow, dent, depression

kuchi *n* 口 **1.** mouth: **kuchi (kará) no** 口（から）の oral **2.** words, speech: **kuchi o hasamu** 口をはさむ interrupt **3.** entrance; hole, opening, slot **4.** cork, stopper **5.** job opening

kuchi-beni *n* 口紅 lipstick

kuchi-bue *n* 口笛 whistling (*with one's lips*): **kuchi o fukimásu** 口笛を吹きます whistles

kuchi-génka *n* 口げんか[喧嘩] argument

kuchi-hige *n* 口ひげ・口髭 mustache

kuchi-komi *n* 口コミ word of mouth: **kuchi-komi de hiromarimásu** 口コミで広まります spreads by word of mouth

kuchibiru *n* 唇 lip

kuchimásu, kuchiru *v* 朽ちます, 朽ちる rots, decays

kúchite *v* 朽ちて → **kuchimásu** 朽ちます

kúda *n* 管 pipe, rube

kudáita *v* 砕いた = **kudakimáshita** 砕きました (broke it)

kudáite *v* 砕いて → **kudakimásu** 砕きます

kudáke *v* 砕け **1.** → **kudakemásu** 砕けます [INFINITIVE] **2.** [IMPERATIVE] (break it!) → **kudakimásu** 砕きます

kudakemásu, kudakéru *v* 砕けます, 砕ける **1.** it breaks, smashes, crumbles **2.** can break it

kudákete *v* 砕けて → **kudakemásu** 砕けます

kudakimásu, kudáku *v* 砕きます, 砕く breaks it, smashes it, crumbles it

kudámono *n* 果物 fruit: **kudamonó-ya** 果物屋 fruit market

kudari *n* 下り descent; outbound (*from Tokyo*), the down train

kudarimásu, kudaru *v* 下ります, 下る comes/goes down, descends; falls, drops

kudasái *v* 下さい give; (**shíte kudasái** して下さい) please (do) [IMPERATIVE of **kudasáru** 下さる = **kudasaimásu** 下さいます]

kudasaimáshite *v* 下さいまして = **kudasátte** 下さって → **kudasaimásu** 下さいます

kudasaimásu, kudasáru *v* 下さいます, 下さる gives (*he/she to you, you to me*); does as a favor (*he/she for you, you for me*), kindly (*does*)

kudasári *v* 下さり → **kudasaimásu** 下さいます [INFINITIVE]

kudasátta *v* 下さった = **kudasaimáshita** 下さいました (gave (me))

kudasátte *v* 下さって → **kudasaimásu** 下さいます

kudashi *n* 下し: **kudashi-gúsuri** 下し薬 a purgative, a laxative; **mushi-kúdashi** 虫下し a vermifuge

kudasútta *v* 下すった = **kudasátta** 下さった = **kudasaimáshita** 下さいました (gave (me))

kudasútte *v* 下すって = **kudasátte** 下さって → **kudasaimásu** 下さいます

kudatta *v* 下った = **kudarimáshita** 下りました (went down)

kudatte *v* 下って → **kudarimásu** 下ります

kudói *adj* くどい **1.** long-winded, dull **2.** thick, greasy

kúe *v* 食え **1.** → **kuemásu** 食えます [INFINITIVE] **2.** [IMPERATIVE] (eat!) → **kuimásu** 食います

kúeba *v* 食えば = [INFORMAL] **kúya** 食や (if one eats) → **kuimásu** 食います

kuemásu, kuéru *v* 食えます, 食える can eat (*polite form* **taberaremásu** 食べられます)

kuéreba *v* 食えれば (if one can eat) → **kuemásu** 食えます

kufū *n* 工夫 device, scheme, idea, invention,

artifice, ingenuity: **kufū (o kora-)shimásu** 工夫（を凝ら）します schemes, contrives

kūfuku (no) *adj* 空腹（の）hungry

Kú-gatsu *n* 九月・9月 September

kugi *n* 釘 nail, peg
  kugi-nuki *n* 釘抜き claw hammer

kugiri *n* 区切り punctuation; **kugirimásu** 区切ります divides

kūgun *n* 空軍 air force: **kūgun-kíchi** 空軍基地 air base

kugurimásu, kuguru *v* 潜ります、潜る passes under

kūhaku *n* 空白 a blank (*space*) (= **kūsho** 空所, **supēsu** スペース)

kúi *n* 杭 post, stake, pile: [IDIOM] **deru kúi wa utareru** 出る杭は打たれる A tall tree catches much wind.

kúi *v* 食い → **kuimásu** 食います [INFINITIVE]

kuichigai *n* 食い違い discrepancy

kúiki *n* 区域 zone

kuimásu, kū´ *v* 食います、食う eats (*inelegant*) (= **tabemásu** 食べます)

kúi-shínbō (na) *adj* 食いしん坊（な）glutton(ous); greedy

kuí ya/wa shinai *v* [INFORMAL] 食いや/はしない, **kúya shinai** 食やしない = **kuwánai** 食わない (not eat)

kujaku *n* クジャク・孔雀 peacock

kúji *n* くじ・クジ a lot (*in a lottery*) (= **takara-kuji** 宝くじ)

kujíite *v* 挫いて → **kujikimásu** 挫きます

kujikemásu, kujikéru *v* 挫けます、挫ける **1. ashí ga kujikemásu** 足が挫けます gets a sprained ankle **2. ki ga kujikemásu** 気が挫けます gets disheartened, discouraged **3.** (*a plan*) gets frustrated

kujikimásu, kujíku *v* 挫きます、挫く **1.** sprains: **ashí o kujikimásu** 足を挫きます sprains an ankle **2. ki o kujikimásu** 気を挫きます disheartens, discourages **3.** frustrates (*a plan*)

kujira *n* クジラ・鯨 whale

kujō *n* 苦情 complaint: **kujō o iu/yū** 苦情を言う complains

kūkan *n* 空間 space

kukí *n* 茎 stalk, stem

kū´ki *n* 空気 air

kūkō *n* 空港 airport

kúmá *n* クマ・熊 bear (*animal*)

kumade *n* 熊手 rake

kumanai *v* 汲まない = **kumimasén** 汲みません (not scoop)

kumánai *v* 組まない = **kumimasén** 組みません (not braid)

kuméba *v* 汲めば (if one scoops) → **kumimásu** 汲みます

kúmeba *v* 組めば (if one braids) → **kumimásu** 組みます

kumi *v* 汲み → **kunimásu** 汲みます [INFINITIVE]

kumí *n* 組 a set, suit, pack; a class, band, company

kúmi *v* 組み → **kumimásu** 組みます [INFINITIVE]

kumiai *n* 組合 association, guild, union: **rōdō-kumiai** 労働組合 (labor) union

kumi-awase 組み合わせ **1.** *n* assortment, mixture **2.** *v* → **kumi-awasemásu** 組み合わせます [INFINITIVE]

kumi-awasemásu, kumi-awaseru *v* 組み合わせます、組み合わせる combines, puts together, teams them up

kumimásu, kumu *v* 汲みます、汲む scoops, draws, ladles; considers, sympathizes

kumimásu, kúmu *v* 組みます、組む braids; assembles, sets up, puts together, folds (*arms*), clasps (*hands*), crosses (*legs*); teams up (*with*)

kumi-tate *n* 組み立て structure, setup, makeup, organization, framework

kumi-tatemásu, kumi-tateru *v* 組み立てます、組み立てる sets up, organizes; assembles, puts together

kumí ya/wa shinai *v* [INFORMAL] 汲みや/はしない = **kumanai** 汲まない (not scoop)

kúmi ya/wa shinai *v* [INFORMAL] 組みや/はしない = **kumánai** 組まない (not braid)

kúmo *n* 雲 cloud. **kumo-gakure** 雲隠れ disappearing, dropping out of sight

kúmo *n* クモ・蜘蛛 spider

kumō´ *v* 汲もう = **kumimashō** 汲みましょう (let's scoop!)

kumō´ *v* 組もう = **kumimashō** 組みましょう (let's braid!)

kúmo no su *n* クモ[蜘蛛]の巣 spiderweb, cobweb (= **kúmo no íto** クモ[蜘蛛]の糸 spider threads

kumori 曇り **1.** *n* cloudy weather **2.** *v* → **kumorimásu** 曇ります [INFINITIVE]

kumorimásu, kumóru *v* 曇ります、曇る gets cloudy: **kumótte imásu** 曇っています is cloudy

… kun *suffix* …君 (*mostly attached to one's juniors's or boys' names* INFORMAL)

kunda *v* 汲んだ = **kumimáshita** 汲みました (scooped)

kúnda *v* 組んだ = **kumimáshita** 組みました (braided)

kunde *v* 汲んで → **kumimásu** 汲みます

kúnde *v* 組んで → **kumimásu** 組みます

kuni *n* 国 (**o-kuni** お国) **1.** country, nation: **kuni no** 国の national, state, government **2.** native place, home area

kúnren *n* 訓練 training, drill: ~ **shimásu** 訓練します trains, drills

kuō´ *v* 食おう = **kuimashō** 食いましょう (let's eat!) (= **tabemashō** 食べましょう)

kurá *n* 鞍 saddle

kurá *n* 倉・蔵 warehouse, storeroom (*storehouse*), cellar, godown

kū´rā *n* クーラー air conditioner

kurabemásu, kuraberu *v* 比べます・較べます、比べる・較べる compares, contrasts

kúrabu *n* クラブ club (*group; card suit*); (*golf*) club: **kurabu katsudō** クラブ活動 club activities

kurage *n* クラゲ jellyfish

kurai *n* 位 grade, rank

kurai *adj* 暗い dark, gloomy; dim (*light*)

… kúrai *suffix* …くらい・位 = **… gúrai** …ぐらい・位 (about; (*an amount*); at least)

kurákkā *n* クラッカー crackers

kurákushon *n* クラクション klaxon, horn (*of car*)

kurashikku *n* クラシック classic (= **koten** 古典)

kurashimásu, kurasu *v* 暮らします, 暮らす lives, gets by; makes a living

kúrasu *n* クラス class (*group*)

kurátchi *n* クラッチ clutch (*of car*): **kuratchi-pédaru** クラッチペダル clutch pedal

kure *v* 暮れ the dark; the end of the year: **kure no** 暮れの year-end

kure *v* → **kuremásu** 暮れます [INFINITIVE]

kure *v* くれ → **kuremásu** くれます
    1. [INFINITIVE] **2.** [IMPERATIVE] (*gives; does as a favor*) (gimme!)

kúreba *v* 来れば (if one comes) → **kimásu** 来ます

kurejitto-kā´do *n* クレジットカード credit card

kuremásu, kureru *v* くれます, くれる gives (*to me/us; he to you*): **shite kuremásu** してくれます does a favor (*for me/us; he for you*)

kuremásu, kureru *v* 暮れます, 暮れる: **hi ga kuremásu** 日が暮れます it gets dark

kurē´n *n* クレーン crane (*machine*)

kurenai *v* くれない = **kuremasén** くれません (not give)

kureréba *v* くれれば (if one gives) → **kuremásu** くれます

kureréba *v* 暮れれば (if it gets dark) → **kuremásu** 暮れます

kurḗta *n* クレーター crater (= **kakō** 火口)

kurete *v* くれて → **kuremásu** くれます

kurete *v* 暮れて → **kuremásu** 暮れます

kurí *n* 栗 chestnut

kuríimu *n* クリーム cream

kuríiningu *n* クリーニング cleaning: **kuriiningu-ya** クリーニング屋 (*dry*) cleaner(s); laundry

kuri-kaeshimásu, kiri-kaesu *v* 繰り返します, 繰り返す repeats

kuríppu *n* クリップ clip

Kurísúmasu *n* クリスマス Christmas

kúro (no) *adj* 黒(の) black
    kuro-bíiru *n* 黒ビール black beer
    kuró-i *adj* 黒い black (= **kúro (no)** 黒(の))
    kuro-pan *n* 黒パン brown bread

kúrō *n* 苦労 difficulties, hardships: **Go-kúrō-sama (deshita).** ご苦労様(でした). Thank you for the hard work./Thank you for your trouble. You did good work for me.(*usually to person in a lower position than yours*) (→ **O-tsukare-sama (déshita)** お疲れ様(でした).)

kurō´ku *n* クローク cloakroom, check room

kúrō´to *n* 玄人 expert, professional

kúru *v* 来る = **kimásu** 来ます (comes)

kuruimásu, kuru'u´ *v* 狂います, 狂う gets

warped; gets out of order: **ki ga kuruimásu** 気が狂います goes mad (*insane*)

kuruma *n* 車 car; taxi; vehicle, (*hand*) cart (= **jidō´-sha** 自動車)

kurumá-ebi *n* 車エビ[海老] prawn, jumbo shrimp

kurumi *n* クルミ・胡桃 walnut; nut

kurushíi *adj* 苦しい painful; hard; heavy

kurushimemásu, kurushiméru *v* 苦しめます, 苦しめる afflicts, pains, distresses, embarrasses

kurushimí *n* 苦しみ affliction, agony, suffering, distress

kurushimí *v* 苦しみ → **kurushimimásu** 苦しみます [INFINITIVE]

kurushimimásu, kurushímu *v* 苦しみます, 苦しむ suffers; gets afflicted/distressed/embarrassed

kusá *n* 草 grass

kusái *adj* 臭い smelly, stinking; fishy, questionable

kusari *n* 鎖 chain

kusári *v* 腐り → **kusarimásu** 腐ります [INFINITIVE]

kusarimásu, kusáru *v* 腐ります, 腐る goes bad, rots, decays, spoils, sours: **kusátte imásu** 腐っています is spoiled/rotten

kusé *n* 癖・くせ a (*bad*) habit, a quirk

kūsha *n* 空車 vacant car, "(taxi) available"

kushámi *n* くしゃみ a sneeze

kushí *n* くし・櫛 a comb

kushí *n* 串 a skewer, a spit

kūsho *n* 空所 a blank (*space*) (= **kūhaku** 空白)

kusó *n* くそ・クソ・糞 dung, excrement, feces

kūsō *n* 空想 fantasy

kusugurimásu, kusuguru *v* くすぐります, くすぐる tickles

kusuguttai *adj* くすぐったい ticklish

kusuri *n* 薬 medicine, drug: **kusuri-ya (san)** 薬屋(さん) drugstore; druggist

kutabarimásu, kutabáru *v* くたばります, くたばる gets to die

kutabiremásu, kutabiréru *v* くたびれます, くたびれる gets tired

kutakuta, kuttakuta *adj* くたくた, くったくた dead tired, utterly exhausted

…-kutatte … *suffix, conj* くたって even being … (= **…-kute mo …** くても)

…-kute *suffix, conj* …くて is and (*also/so*)

kutsú *n* 靴・クツ shoes
    kutsu-béra *n* 靴べら[ベラ] shoehorn
    kutsú-himo *n* 靴ひも shoelace
    kutsu-mígaki *n* 靴磨き shoeshine
    kutsu-náoshi *n* 靴直し shoe-repair person/shop
    kutsú-shita *n* 靴下・くつ下 socks, stockings
    kutsú-ya *n* 靴屋 shoe shop/store
    kutsu-zoko *n* 靴底 shoe sole
    kutsu-zure *n* 靴ずれ a foot sore (*from shoe rubbing*)

kutsurogimásu, kutsurógu *v* くつろぎます, くつろぐ relaxes, gets comfortable

kúttá *v* 食った = **kuimáshita** 食いました (ate)

kútté v 食って → **kuimásu** 食います

...-kútte *suffix, conj* ...くって = **...-kute** ...くて

kúttsukimásu, kuttsúku v くっつきます、くっつく sticks to

kuwa n くわ・鍬 hoe

kúwa n クワ・桑 mulberry

kuwadate 企て 1. n plan, attempt, undertaking 2. v → **kuwadatemásu** [INFINITIVE]

kuwadatemásu, kuwadatéru v 企てます、企てる plans, attempts, undertakes

kuwaemásu, kuwaeru v 加えます、加える adds (*on*); imposes

kuwánai v 食わない = **kuimasén** 食いません (*not eat*) (POLITE FORM **tabenai** 食べない)

kuwasemásu, kuwaséru v 食わせます、食わせる feeds (POLITE FORM **tabe-sasemasu** 食べさせます)

kuwashíi *adj* 詳しい detailed, exact: (**... ni kuwashíi** ...に詳しい) is knowledgeable (about ...), is well versed (in ...); **kuwashíi kotó** 詳しい事 details; **kuwáshiku** 詳しく in detail

kuyamimásu, kuyamu v 悔やみます、悔やむ regrets

kuyashíi *adj* 悔しい humiliating, mortifying, vexatious

kuzu (mono) n くず [クズ] (物) waste, scum, mud, trash, rags, scrap, junk (= **kásu** かす・滓)

　kuzu-híroi n くず拾い ragpicker

　kuzú-kago n くずかご wastebasket

　kuzú-mono n くず物 waste, trash, rags, scrap, junk

kúzu n クズ・葛 arrowroot: **kuzu-yu** 葛湯 arrowroot gruel

　kuzu-ko n 葛粉 powdered arrowroot

kuzuremásu, kuzuréru v 崩れます、崩れる it crumbles, breaks (down); (*weather*) deteriorates

kuzushimásu, kuzúsu v 崩します、崩す 1. cashes, changes, breaks (*into small money*) 2. breaks it down, demolishes 3. writes (*a character*) in cursive style

kyábarē n キャバレー cabaret, night club

kyábetsu n キャベツ cabbage

kyaburétā n キャブレター carburetor

kyaku n 客 visitor, guest, company; customer (= **o-kyaku-sámá** お客様 [HONORIFIC])

　kyaku-ma n 客間 [BOOKISH] guest room

　kyaku-sha n 客車 [BOOKISH] (*railroad*) passenger car, coach

kyánbasu n キャンバス canvas (= **kanbasu** カンバス)

kyándii, kyándē n キャンディ、キャンデー candy (= **ame** アメ・飴)

kyánpasu n キャンパス campus

kyánpu n キャンプ camp(ing): **kyánpu o shimásu** キャンプをします camps

kyánseru n キャンセル cancellation: ~ **shimásu** キャンセルします cancels

kyáppu n キャップ cap (*of a pen*)

kyáputen n キャプテン captain

kyarameru n キャラメル caramel

kyátsu n きゃつ・彼奴 [INFORMAL] that damn one; **kyátsu-ra** きゃつ [彼奴] ら those damn ones (= **aitsu** あいつ; **aitsu-ra** あいつら)

kyā *interj* きゃー・キャー: **kyā(t)-to sakebimásu** きゃー（っ）[キャー（ッ）] と叫びます screams

kyō´ n 今日・きょう today

kyō´ (no miyako) n 京 (の都) Kyoto (= **Kyō´to** 京都)

...-kyō n ...教 (*name of*) religion: **Kirisuto-kyō** キリスト教 Christianity; **Isuramu-kyō** イスラム教 Islam (= **kaikyō** 回教); **Buk-kyō** 仏教 Buddhism

kyōbai n 競売 [BOOKISH] auction (= **okushon** オークション)

kyōchō n 強調 emphasis: ~ **shimásu** 強調します emphasizes

kyodai (na) *adj* 巨大 (な) huge

kyō´dai (-shimai) n 兄弟 (姉妹) brothers and/or sisters; brother; sister

kyōdan n 教壇 [BOOKISH] platform, pulpit: **kyōdan ni tachimásu** 教壇に立ちます 1. teaches at school 2. stands on a platform

kyōdan n 凶弾 [BOOKISH] bullet (*of assassin, etc.*): **kyōdan ni taoremásu** 凶弾に倒れます is shot to death (*by an assassin, etc.*)

kyōdan n 教団 [BOOKISH] religious organization

kyōdō n 共同 union, cooperation, joint (*activity*): **kyōdō-seikatsu** 共同生活 living together, living with others

kyōdō n 協同 cooperation: **kyōdō-kumiai** 協同組合 cooperative association (→ **seikatsu-kyōdō-kumiai, seikyō** 生活協同組合, 生協)

kyō´fu n 恐怖 [BOOKISH] fear, terror

kyōgeki n 京劇 classic Chinese pantomime/opera

kyōgén n 狂言 traditional Noh farce

kyō´gi n 協議 conference, discussion

kyō´gi n 競技 (*athletic*) game, match, contest, (*game*) event

　kyōgi-jō n 競技場 stadium

kyōhan(sha) n 共犯 (者) accomplice

kyóhi n 拒否 refusal, rejection, veto (= **kyozetsu** 拒絶): ~ **shimásu** 拒否します refuses, rejects, vetoes

kyōiku n 教育 education: **kyōiku o ukemásu** 教育を受けます gets an education

kyōin n 教員 [BOOKISH] teacher

kyojin n 巨人 giant (*person*): **Kyójin** 巨人 the Giants [*baseball team*]

kyōju n 教授 professor: **daigaku-kyōju** 大学教授 university professor

kyojū n 居住 [BOOKISH] residency: **kyojū-sha** 居住者 a resident; **kyojū-chi** 居住地 residence (*location*), address (= **jūsho** 住所)

kyóka n 許可 permit, permission: **kyoka-sho** 許可証 permit (*card*)

kyōkai n 教会 church

kyōkai n 協会 society, association

kyōkai n 境界 border (*of district, etc.*)

kyōká-sho n 教科書 text(book)

kyōki *n* 凶器 [BOOKISH] lethal weapon

kyōki *n* 狂気 [BOOKISH] insanity, madness, lunacy: **kyōki no sata desu** 狂気の沙汰です is sheer madness

kyōki *n* 驚喜 [BOOKISH] amazement and gladness: ~ **shimásu** 驚喜します is amazed and glad

kyokō *n* 虚構 [BOOKISH] fabrication, fiction (= **fikushon** フィクション): **kyokō no sekai** 虚構の世界 imaginary world: **genjitsu to kyokō no kondō** 現実と虚構の混同 confusion between reality and imagination

kyōkō *n* 強行 forcing: **kyōkō-toppa** 強行突破 forcing/bulldozing one's way through: **kyōkō-saiketsu** 強行採決 railroading

kyóku *n* 局, ...´-**kyoku** ...局 office, bureau, station: **terebi-kyoku** テレビ局 TV station

kyokuba *n* 曲馬 horseback stunts: **kyokubá-dan** 曲馬団 circus (= **sā´kasu** サーカス)

kyokugei *n* 曲芸 acrobat, acrobatics (= **akurobátto** アクロバット): **kyokugei-shi** 曲芸師 an acrobat, a stunt performer

kyokugen *n* 極限 [BOOKISH] limit: **kyokugen-jōtai** 極限状態 extreme situation, ultimate state

kyōkun *n* 教訓 lesson, teaching, moral: **kyōkun ni narimásu** 教訓になります learns one's lesson

kyokután (na) *adj* 極端(な) extreme: **kyokután ni** 極端に extremely

Kyokutō *n* 極東 Far East

kyōkyū *n* 供給 supply(ing), provision: ~ **shimásu** 供給します supplies; **juyō to kyōkyō** 需要と供給 supply and demand (= **jukyū** 需給)

kyō´mí *n* 興味 interest (*pleasure*): **kyōmi-bukái** 興味深い interesting

kyónen *n* 去年 last year

kyóri *n* 距離 distance

kyōryoku *n* 協力 cooperation: ~ **shimásu** 協力します cooperates

kyōryoku (na) *adj* 強力(な) strong, powerful

Kyō-ryō´ri *n* 京料理 Kyoto-style cooking/dishes

Kyōsan-shúgi *n* 共産主義 Communism: **Kyōsan shugí-sha** 共産主義者 a Communist: **Kyōsan (shugí)-koku** 共産(主義)国 communist country

kyō´shi *n* 教師 teacher, instructor, tutor: **katei-kyōshi** 家庭教師 home tutor

kyōshitsu *n* 教室 classroom

kyōshoku *n* 教職 teaching profession: **kyōshoku ni tsukimásu** 教職に就きます becomes a teacher

kyōshuku shimásu (suru) *v* 恐縮します(する) [HONORIFIC] **1.** feels grateful/obliged/ashamed: **ohome ni azukarimashite/ohome itadakimashite kyōshuku desu** お褒めにあずか[与]りまして/お褒めいただきまして恐縮です I am very grateful for your compliment., I really don't deserve your compliment., Your compliment is too much for me.; **wazawaza okoshi itadakimashite kyōshuku desu** わざわざお越しいただきまして恐縮です Thank you very much for taking the trouble to come. **2.** feels sorry/ashamed: **taihen kyōshuku desuga...** 大変恐縮ですが... I am very sorry, but...

kyoshoku-shō *n* 拒食症 anorexia

kyōsō *n* 競争 competition, rivalry, contest, race: ~ **shimásu** 競争します competes **kyōsō-áite** 競争相手 competitor

kyōson, kyōzon *n* 共存 [BOOKISH] coexistence: **minzoku kyōzon** 民族共存 ethnic coexistence

kyōten *n* 経典 **1.** sutra (*Buddhist scripture*) (= **o-kyō** お経) **2.** religious text, sacred scripture

Kyō´to *n* 京都 Kyoto (= **kyō´ (no miyako)** 京(の都)); **Kyótó-Eki** 京都駅 Kyoto Station; **Kyotó-jin** 京都人 Kyotoite

kyōtsū (no) *adj* 共通(の) common, general

kyōyo *n* 供与 grant, allowance: ~ **shimásu** 供与します grants it

kyōyō (no) *adj* 共用(の) for common use, for public use

kyōyō *n* 教養 culture, education, refinement: **kyōyō no nai** 教養のない uneducated, uncultivated

kyōyō *n* 強要 [BOOKISH] forcing: ~ **shimásu** 強要します forces, compels

kyōzai *n* 教材 teaching materials

kyozetsu *n* 拒絶 [BOOKISH] refusal, rejection, veto (= **kyóhi** 拒否): ~ **shimásu** 拒絶します refuses, rejects, vetoes

kyū *n* 灸・きゅう (**o-kyō** お灸) moxibustion (*burning moxa on the skin*)

kyū *n* 急 crisis, emergency, danger: **kyū (na)** 急(な) sudden; urgent; precipitous, steep: **kyū na (o-)shirase/renraku** 急な(お)知らせ/連絡 short notice; **kyū ni** 急に suddenly (= **totsuzen** 突然)

kyū-byō *n* 急病 sudden illness

kyū-kō *n* 急行 express (*train, etc.*): **kyūkō´-ken** 急行券 express ticket

kyū-ryū *n* 急流 (river) rapids

kyū-sei (no) *adj* 急性(の) acute (*sudden*): **kyūsei-shikkan** 急性疾患 acute disease

kyū-shi *n* 急死 sudden death

kyū-yō *n* 急用 urgent business

kyū´ *n* 級 class, grade

kyū´ *n* 九・9 nine (= **kú** 九・9)

kyū-banmé *n* 九番目 ninth

kyū´-dai *n* 九台 nine (*machines, vehicles*)

kyū´-do *n* 九度 nine degrees; nine times (= **kyū´-kái** 九回)

kyū´-hén *n* 九遍 nine times

kyū´-hon *n* 九本 nine (*pencils/bottles, long things*)

kyū-kai *n* 九階 nine floors/stories, ninth floor

kyū´-ko *n* 九個 nine pieces (*small objects*) (= **kokonotsu** 九つ)

kyū´-kái *n* 九回 nine times (= **kyū´-do** 九度)

kyū´-mai *n* 九枚 nine sheets (*flat things*)

kyū´-satsu *n* 九冊 nine copies (*books, magazines*)

kyū´-tō *n* 九頭 nine (*horses/oxen, large animals*)

kyū´-wa *n* 九羽 nine (*birds, rabbits*)

kyū(-) *prefix* 旧... ... old

kyūden *n* 宮殿 palace

kyū´dō *n* 弓道 (*the traditional art of*) archery (= **kyū´jutsu** 弓術)

kyū´-hyaku *n* 九百・900 nine hundred
kyū´ji *n* 給仕 waiter/waitress, steward, attendant, factotum
kyūjin *n* 求人 job offer(s)
kyūjitsu *n* 休日 day off, holiday
kyū´jo *n* 救助 rescue, relief: **kyūjo-tai** 救助隊 rescue party/team: ~**shimásu** 救助します rescues
kyūjō *n* 球場 ball park, (*baseball*) stadium (= **yakyū-jō** 野球場)
kyū´-jū *n* 九十・90 ninety
kyūka *n* 休暇 vacation, furlough: **kyūka o torimásu** 休暇を取ります takes day(s) off
kyūkei *n* 休憩 rest, recess, break: ~**shimásu** 休憩します takes a rest, takes a break
kyūkéi-shitsu *n* 休憩室 lounge (*room*), break room
kyūkon *n* 求婚 proposal of marriage: ~ **shimásu** 求婚します proposes (*marriage*) (= **puropōzu** プロポーズ)
kyū´kutsu (na) *adj* 窮屈(な) constrained, uncomfortable
kyūkyū (no) *adj* 救急(の) for emergencies
kyūkyū´-bako *n* 救急箱 first-aid kit
kyūkyū chiryō shitsu *n* 救急治療室 emergency room, ER
kyūkyū´-sha *n* 救急車 ambulance

kyū-mán *n* 九万・90,000 ninety thousand
kyū´ri *n* キュウリ・胡瓜 cucumber
kyū´ryō *n* 給料 (**o-kyū´ryō** お給料) salary, pay (= **sárarii** サラリー, **kyū´yo** 給与)
kyūryō´-bi 給料日 payday
kyūseishu *n* 救世主 Savior
kyū-sén *n* 九千・9,000 nine thousand
kyūshi *n* 休止 pause
kyūshi-kigō 休止記号 breath mark
kyūsh-ni-isshō-o-emasu, -eru *v* 九死に一生を得ます, 得る barely escapes death
kyūshoku (katsudō) *n* 求職(活動) job hunting, seeking employment
kyūshoku *n* 休職 leave of absence from work
kyūshoku *n* 給食 school lunch
Kyū´shū-chihō *n* 九州地方 The Kyushu area of Japan (*Fukuoka, Saga, Nagasaki, Kumamoto, Miyazaki, Kagoshima, Ōita prefectures*)
kyūsu *n* きゅうす・急須 teapot
kyūtei *n* 宮廷 (*imperial/royal*) court
Kyū-yaku seisho *n* 旧約聖書 the Old Testament
kyū´yo *n* 給与 allowance, grant, compensation, salary (= **sárarii** サラリー, **kyū´ryō** 給料): **kyūyō-meisai (sho)** 給与明細書 pay slip
kyūyō *n* 休養 rest: ~ **shimásu** 休養します rests

M

ma *n* 間 1. room; space (*available*) 2. time, interval; (= **hima** 暇) leisure: **ma o okimásu** 間を置きます gives a pause: **ma ni aimásu** 間に合います → **ma-ni-aimásu** 間に合います
ma... *prefix* 真... mid..., right..., very...
ma-fuyu *n* 真冬 midwinter
ma-hiru *n* 真昼 midday
ma-kká (na) *adj* 真っ赤(な) crimson, deep red: **ma-kká ni narimásu** 真っ赤になります crimsons, flushes deeply
ma-kkúro (na) *adj* 真っ黒(な) jet black: **ma-kkúro ni narimásu** 真っ黒になります turns to a deep black
ma-natsu *n* 真夏 midsummer
ma-yónaka *n* 真夜中 midnight
ma-n-mae (ni/de) *adv* 真ん前(に/で) right in front
ma-n-maru (no/na) *adj* 真ん丸(の/な) perfectly round
ma-n-naka *n* 真ん中 the very middle, center (= **chūshin** 中心, **sentā** センター): **ma-n-naka no** 真ん中の central, middle
ma-ssáka-sama (ni) *adj* 真っ逆さま(に) head over heels
ma-sshíro (na) *adj* 真っ白(な) snow white
ma-ssúgu (na) *adj* 真っ直ぐ(な) straight

ma´ まあ *interj* 1. oh well; I should say; perhaps, I guess 2. dear me! (*mostly female*); good heavens/grief!
ma-bátaki *n* 瞬き wink(ing), blink(ing): ~ **shimásu** 瞬きします winks, blinks
mabayui *adj* 眩い [BOOKISH] dazzling, glaring (= **mabushíí** 眩しい)
māburu *n* マーブル marble
mabushíí *adj* 眩しい dazzling, glaring (= **mabayui** 眩い)
mábuta *n* まぶた・瞼 eyelid
macchi *n* マッチ match
machí *n* 町・街 town, city: **machí no** 町の local (→ **chō´chō** 町長)
máchi *v* 待ち → **machimásu** 待ちます [INFINITIVE]
machi-ái-shitsu *n* 待合室 waiting room
machi-awasemásu, machi-awaseru *v* 待ち合わせます, 待ち合わせる makes an appointment
machibuse *n* 待ち伏せ ambush: ~ **shimásu** 待ち伏せします ambushes
machidōshíí *adj* 待ち遠しい long awaited; waiting for a long time
machigáe *n* 間違え = **machigái** 間違い (mistake, error) → **machigaemásu** 間違えます

machigaemásu, machigáéru v 間違えます, 間違える mistakes

machigaenai v 間違えない = **machigaemasén** 間違えません (not mistaken)

machigái n 間違い 1. mistake, error (= **misu** ミス, **erā** エラー) 2. → **machigaimásu** 間違います [INFINITIVE]

machigaimásu, machigáu v 間違います, 間違う is mistaken, is wrong, is in error

machigátta adj 間違った wrong (*mistaken*)

machigáu v 間違う = **machigaimásu** 間違います (is mistaken)

machigawanai v 間違わない = **machigaenai** 間違えない = **machigaemasén** 間違えません (not mistaken)

machimásu, mátsu v 待ちます, 待つ waits for, awaits, expects, anticipates

máchīnē n マチネー matinee

máda adv まだ 1. (not) yet [+ NEGATIVE verb] 2. still (*to be*)

madara n 斑 spots, speckles: **madara no** 斑の spotted: **madara-moyō** 斑模様 patchy pattern

...máde suffix, conj ...まで (*all the way*) to, till, until

... máde ni suffix, conj ...までに by, no later than, before (*it gets to be time*)

... máde ni wa suffix, conj ...までには by ... at the latest

mádo n 窓 window

mado-gárasu n 窓ガラス windowpane
madó-guchi n 窓口 window (*opening*), wicket
mado-waku n 窓枠 (*window*) sash

madoimasu, madou v 惑います, 惑う gets dazed

maekagami n 前屈み leaning forward: **maekagami ni narimásu** 前屈みになります leans forward

mae-mótte adv 前もって (*in*) advance (*beforehand*)

mae-muki (no) adj 前向き(の) 1. far-sighted (*forward-looking*) 2. positive, constructive, affirmative: **mae-muki (na) shikō** 前向き(な)思考 positive thinking (= **pojitibu shinkingu** ポジティブシンキング); **mae-muki ni** 前向きに facing front; positively

máe (ni) adv 前(に) front; in front of; before, ago: **máe no** 前の previous, former; **suru máe ni** する前に before doing; **daibu máe kara** だいぶ前から for quite a long time (now)

maeoki n 前置き introduction (= **intorodakushon** イントロダクション)

maeuri n 前売り advanced sale: **maeuri-ken** 前売り券 advanced-sale ticket

mafurā n マフラー muffler, scarf

mafia n マフィア Mafia

mafin n マフィン muffin

magao n 真顔 serious/earnest/sober/conscientious/honest look (*on one's face*) = **majime na kao** 真面目な顔, **shinken na kao** 真剣な顔

magari 曲がり 1. n a curve, a bend: **heso-magari** へそ曲がり perverse person: **magari-kado** 曲がり角 street corner 2. v → **magarimásu** 曲がります [INFINITIVE]

magari n 間借り renting a room: **~ shimásu** 間借りします rents a room

magari-nin n 間借り人 tenant (*of apartment, room*)

magarimásu, magaru v 曲がります, 曲がる 1. turns, goes around 2. it bends, curves

māgarin n マーガリン margarine

magaru v 曲がる = **magarimásu** 曲がります (turns, curves)

magemásu, mageru v 曲げます, 曲げる bends it, curves it

magiremásu, magiréru v 紛れます, 紛れる: (**... ni magiréru** ...に紛れる) gets distracted (by ...); gets confused (with ...), gets mixed up (*with*)

... mágiwa (ni/de) suffix, adv ...間際(に/で) just before ..., right on the brink of (when) ...

magó n 孫 grandchild: **o-mago-san** お孫さん (*your/someone else's*) grandchild

magó-no-te n 孫の手 back-scratcher

magó n 馬子 a packhorse driver: [IDIOM] **mago ni mo ishō** 馬子にも衣装 Clothes make the man.

magokoro n 真心 sincerity: **magokoro o komete hanashimásu** 真心を込めて話します talks sincerely

magure (atari) n まぐれ(当たり) fluke, (*dumb/good*) luck, accident, fortuity (= **gūzen** 偶然): **magure de kachimásu** まぐれで勝ちます wins by a fluke

maguro n マグロ・鮪 tuna

magusa n まぐさ[秣・馬草] hay

máhi n マヒ・麻痺 paralysis

mahō´ n 魔法 magic

mahō´-bin n 魔法瓶[びん・ビン] vacuum/thermos bottle

mai n 舞 (*Japanese*) dance: **mai o maimásu** 舞を舞います dances

mai-... prefix 毎... each, every

mai-asa n, adv 毎朝 every morning
mai-ban n, adv 毎晩 every night
mai-do n, adv 毎度 every time: **Maido arígatō gozaimásu** 毎度ありがとうございます. We appreciate your (*continuing*) patronage.
mai-getsu, mai-tsuki n, adv 毎月 every month: **mai-getsu/-tsuki no** 毎月の monthly
mai-kai n, adv 毎回 every time, each time
mai-nen, mai-toshi n, adv 毎年 every year: **mai-nen/-toshi no** 毎年の annual, yearly
mái-nichi n, adv 毎日 every day; all the time: **mái-nichi no** 毎日の daily; **mái-nichi no yō´ni** 毎日のように almost everyday
mai-shū n, adv 毎週 every week: **mái-shū no** 毎週の weekly
mai-toshi → mai-nen
mai-tsuki → mai-getsu
mai-yo n, adv 毎夜 every night (= **mai-ban** 毎晩)

...´-mai suffix ...枚 (*counts flat things*)

máigo n 迷子 a lost child: **máigo ni narimásu** 迷子になります a child becomes lost

mai-hōmu *n* マイホーム owned house, one's house and home

mai-hōmu-shugi (-sha) *n* マイホーム主義(者) family-centred person (= **kazoku-omoi no hito** 家族思いの人)

mainasu *n* マイナス less (*minus*); a minus, a disadvantage

mairimáshita *v* 参りました, [INFORMAL] **máitta** 参った You've got me!; gives up, goes down

mairimásu, máiru *v* 参ります, 参る **1.** [HUMBLE] I come/go **2.** [HUMBLE] visits, calls on **3.** is defeated, loses (= **kōsan** 降参) **4.** is floored, stumped

maisō *n* 埋葬 burial: **~ shimásu** 埋葬します buries the body

maite *v* 巻いて → **makimásu** 巻きます

máite *v* 蒔いて → **makimásu** 蒔きます

mājan *n* マージャン・麻雀 mahjong: **mājan-ya** マージャン[麻雀]屋 mahjong parlor

majime (na) *adj* 真面目(な) serious, earnest, sober, conscientious, honest

mājin *n* マージン margin

majinai *n* まじない・呪い **1.** charm (= **o-majinai** おまじない) **2.** curse (= **noroi** のろい・呪い) **3.** spell, magic, incantation (= **jujutsu** 呪術)
majinai-shi *n* まじない[呪い]師 witch doctor

majirimásu, majíru *v* 混じります, 混じる it mixes (*with*)

majiwarimásu, majiwáru *v* 交わります, 交わる associates with

majo *n* 魔女 witch

makanai *v* 巻かない = **makimasén** 巻きません (not roll it up)

makánai *v* 蒔かない = **makimasén** 蒔きません (not sow)

makasemásu, makaséru *v* 任せます, 任せる entrusts with

makashimásu, makasu *v* 負かします, 負かす defeats

make 負け **1.** *n* defeat, loss **2.** *v* → **makemásu** 負けます [INFINITIVE]: **make ro** 負けろ [IMPERATIVE] (lose!)

make *v* 巻け [IMPERATIVE] (roll it up!) → **makimásu** 巻きます

máke *v* 蒔け [IMPERATIVE] (sow!) → **makimásu** 蒔きます

makéba *v* 巻けば = [INFORMAL] **makya** 巻きゃ (if one rolls it up) → **makimásu** 巻きます

mákeba *v* 蒔けば = [INFORMAL] **makya** 蒔きゃ (if one sows) → **makimásu** 蒔きます

makemásu, makeru *v* 負けます, 負ける loses, is defeated; comes down on the price; is inferior

makemásu, makeru *v* 巻けます, 巻ける can roll it up

makemásu, makéru *v* 蒔けます, 蒔ける can sow (*seed*)

makenai *v* 負けない = **makemasén** 負けません (not lose)

makenai *v* 巻けない = **makemasén** 巻けません (cannot roll it up)

makénai *v* 蒔けない = **makemasén** 蒔けません (cannot sow)

mākétto *n* マーケット market (= **shijō** 市場)

maki *n* 薪 firewood

maki *n* **1.** 巻き a roll; a volume **2.** (...-maki ...巻き) a bolt (*of cloth*)

maki *v* 巻き → **makimásu** 巻きます [INFINITIVE]

máki *v* 蒔き → **makimásu** 蒔きます [INFINITIVE]

makimásu, maku *v* 巻きます, 巻く rolls up; winds; wraps
maki-mono *n* 巻き物 scroll
maki-tábako *n* 巻きタバコ cigarette(s)

makimásu, máku *v* 蒔きます, 蒔く sows (*seed*)
maki-e *n* 蒔(き)絵 raised lacquer

makí ya/wa shinai *v* 巻きや/はしない, [INFORMAL] **makya shinai** 巻きゃしない = **makanai** 巻かない (not roll it up)

máki ya/wa shinai *v* 蒔きや/はしない, [INFORMAL] **mákya shinai** 蒔きゃしない = **makánai** 蒔かない (not sow)

makō *v* 巻こう = **makimashō´** 巻きましょう (let's roll it up!)

makō´ *v* 蒔こう = **makimashō** 蒔きましょう (let's sow!)

makoto (no) *adj* 誠[真]まこと(の) sincere; faithful; true; genuine (= **honto (no)**, **hontō (no)** 本当(の)): **makoto ni** 誠[真]に sincerely

maku *v* 巻く = **makimásu** 巻きます (rolls up)

makú *n* 幕 (*stage*) curtain; (*play*) act: **makú ga agarimásu/akimásu** 幕が上がります/開きます the curtain goes up

máku *v* 蒔く = **makimásu** 蒔きます

maku ai *n* 幕間 intermission (*between acts*)

makunóuchi *n* 幕の内 a riceball lunch(box)

mákura *n* まくら・マクラ・枕 pillow

makya *v* [INFORMAL] 巻きゃ → **makéba** 巻けば

mákya *v* [INFORMAL] 蒔きゃ → **mákeba** 蒔けば

mama *n* ママ **1.** (*baby talk*) mommy, mom (= **kā-chan** 母ちゃん) **2.** hostess (*in a bar, etc.*)

mama-... *prefix* まま[継]... step
mama-chichi *n* まま[継]父 stepfather
mama-haha *n* まま[継]母 stepmother
mama-ko *n* まま[継]子 stepchild

mā-mā *adj, adv* まあまあ (just) so-so, not bad

... mamá (de/no) *suffix, adv, adj* ...まま(で/の) intact, untouched/undisturbed: **sono mamá de** そのままで just as it is/was, **tátta mamá de** 立ったままで without sitting down, with standing

mamé *n* マメ・豆 bean(s)

mamé *n* まめ blister

mame (na) *adj* まめ(な) diligent/dedicated (*person*)

mame (ni) *adv* まめ(に) often, frequently: **heya o mame ni sōji shimásu** 部屋をまめに掃除します cleans the room often

ma-mó-naku *adv* 間もなく soon, before long, shortly

mamorimásu, mamóru *v* 守ります, 守る defends, protects, guards

mán *n* 万 ten thousand 10,000
man-bai *n* 万倍 ten-thousandfold (*10,000 times doubled*)
man(-) ... *prefix* 満... fully ...
man-chō *n* 満潮 high tide
man-getsu *n* 満月 full moon
man'-in *n* 満員 full (*of people*)
man-jō-icchi *n* 満場一致 unanimous (*agreement*)
man-men *n* 満面 the whole face: **man-men no emi/egao o ukabemásu** 満面の笑み/笑顔を浮かべます has a big smile: **tokui man-men desu** 得意満面です is proud as a peacock, is in triumph
man-pai *adj* 満杯 is filled: **yoyaku ga man-pai desu** 予約が満杯です is fully booked: **onaka (ga) man-pai/man-puku desu** お腹（が）満杯/満腹です My stomach is full.
man-puku *n, v* 満腹 full stomach
man-rui *n* 満塁 (*baseball*) with the bases loaded: **man-rui hōmuran** 満塁ホームラン a grand slam
man-tan *n* 満タン full tank: **man-tan ni shimásu** 満タンにします fills the tank, fills it up
man-ten *n* 満点 perfect score
man-ten *n* 満天 the whole sky: **man-ten no hoshizora** 満天の星空 the whole sky full of stars
manabimásu, manabu *v* 学びます、学ぶ learns, studies
manaitá *n* まな板 chopping board (*for cooking*)
manande *v* 学んで → **manabimásu** 学びます
manazashi *n* 眼差し look in one's eyes: **yasashii manazashi** 優しい眼差し gentle look in one's eyes: **utagai no manazashi** 疑いの眼差し suspicious look in one's eyes
manbiki *n* 万引き shoplifting, shoplifter: **~ shimásu** 万引きします shoplifts
manbyō *n* 万病 all kinds of disease: [IDIOM] **kaze wa manbyō no moto** 風邪は万病のもと A cold often leads to all kinds of disease.
mane *n* 真似 imitation, mimicry; **... no mane o shimásu** ...の真似をします imitates, mimics (= **manemásu** 真似ます)
manéite *v* 招いて → **manekimásu** 招きます
máné'jā *n* マネージャー manager
manéki *v* 招き → **manekimásu** 招きます [INFINITIVE]
manekimásu, manéku *v* 招きます、招く invites
manekin *n* マネキン mannequin
manekineko *n* 招き猫 beckoning cat
manemásu, maneru *v* 真似ます、真似る imitates
manga *n* マンガ・漫画 cartoon, comics, manga: **manga-bon** マンガ[漫画]本 comic book: **manga-kissa** マンガ[漫画]喫茶 manga cafe
manhattan *n* マンハッタン Manhattan
manhōru *n* マンホール manhole
ma-ni-aimásu, ma-ni-áu *v* 間に合います、間に合う: **... ni ma-ni-aimásu** ...に間に合います is in time (*for* ...); **ma-ni-aimasén** 間に合いません arrives too late (*for* ...), misses (*the train/bus/plane*)
ma-ni-awase *v* 間に合わせ make-shift
ma-ni-awasemásu, ma-ni-awaséru *v* 間に合

わせます、間に合わせる: **... de ma-ni-awasemásu** ...で間に合わせます makes do (*with* ...)
mán'ichi *n* 万一 = **mán ga ichi** 万が一 if by any chance
Mánira *n* マニラ Manila
manjū´ *n* 饅頭 a steamed bun stuffed with ground pork (= **niku-man** 肉まん) or sweet bean paste (= **anman** あんまん)
manmosu *n* マンモス mammoth: **manmosu no kiba** マンモスの牙 mammoth tusks: **manmosu kigyō** マンモス企業 a mammoth enterprise
mannén-hitsu *n* 万年筆 fountain pen
manneri(zumu) *n* マンネリ（ズム）mannerism
manpokei *n* 万歩計 pedometer
mánshon *n* マンション a luxury apartment (*house*)
mánto *n* マント cloak
mantohihi *n* マントヒヒ hamadryas
mantora *n* マントラ mantra: **mantora o tonaemásu** マントラを唱えます chants mantra
mantsūman *n* マンツーマン one-to-one, one-on-one: **mantsūman ressun o ukemásu** マンツーマンレッスンを受けます has one-to-one lesson(s)
manugare[manukare]másu, manugareru [manukaréru] *v* まぬがれ[まぬかれ]ます・免れます、まぬがれる、まぬかれる[まぬかれる]・免れる escapes from, is exempt from, avoids: **tōsan o manugaremásu** 倒産を免れます avoids bankruptcy: **shi o manugaremásu** 死を免れます escapes death
Manyōshū *n* 万葉集 the Man'yoshu, *Collection of Ten Thousand Leaves*
manzái *n* 漫才 cross-talk comedy: **manzái konbi** 漫才コンビ a comic duo
mánzoku (na) *adj* 満足（な）satisfactory: **(... de) mánzoku shimásu** ...（で）満足します is satisfied/contented (*with* ...)
marason *n* マラソン jog(ging); (= **marason-kyō´sō** マラソン競争) marathon: **marason o shimásu** マラソンをします jogs, runs a marathon
maré (na) *adj* 稀（な）rare, infrequent: **maré ni** 稀に rarely
Marē hantō *n* マレー半島 Malay Peninsula
Marēshia *n* マレーシア Malaysia
Marēshia-jin *n* マレーシア人 a Malaysian
Marēshia-go *n* マレーシア語 Bahasa Malaysia (*language*)
mari *n* まり・マリ・鞠 ball, (*Japanese*) **temari** ball
marine *n* マリネ marinade
marifana *n* マリファナ marijuana
maru *n* 丸・まる circle, ring; zero
maru(-) ... *prefix* 丸・まる ... fully, whole...
maru-anki *n* 丸暗記 rote learning
maru-utsushi *n* 丸写し copying entirely
maru-yaki *n* 丸焼き roast whole
maru-yake *n* 丸焼け being completely burned (*by fire, etc.*)
maru de *adj* まるで **1.** completely [+ NEGATIVE]: **Nihon to maru de chigau/kotonaru bunka** 日本とまるで違う/異なる文化 quite different culture from Japanese **2.** maru de ...no yō (na) まる

で...のよう(な) as if: **maru de kodomo no yō (na)** まるで子供のよう(な) just like a child

marui *adj* 丸い round

maru ku *adv* 丸く roundly: ~ **shimásu** 丸くします makes ... round; **me o maru ku shimásu** 目を丸くします (*with*) wide eyes; **se o maru ku shimásu** 背を丸くします hunches up

maruta *n* 丸太 log

másaka まさか 1. *adv* **másaka ...dewa nai (desu) yo ne?** まさか...ではない(です)よね? Don't tell me that... 2. *interj* no kidding!; you don't say! impossible!

masanai *v* 増さない = **mashimasén** 増しません (not increase)

mása-ni *adv* まさに exactly, just; certainly, really

masarimásu, masáru *v* 勝ります, 勝る surpasses, is superior

masatsu *n* まさつ・摩擦 friction: ~ **shimásu** 摩擦します rubs (= **kosurimásu, kosuru,** 擦ります, 擦る); **karada o masatsu** 体を摩擦します rubs (oneself) down

...-máse ...ませ [IMPERATIVE of polite auxiliary] → **...-másu** ...ます [INFINITIVE]

maséba *v* 増せば = [INFORMAL] **masha** 増しゃ (if increased) → **mashimásu** 増します

...-masén *suffix*, *v* ...ません does not: **...masén deshita** ...ませんでした did not

masha *v* [INFORMAL] 増しゃ → **maséba** 増せば

mashi 増し 1. *n* an increase; a surcharge 2. *v* → **mashimásu** 増します [INFINITIVE]

mashimásu, masu *v* 増します, 増す increases, raises, swells

...-máshite *suffix* ...まして [GERUND of polite auxiliary]

mashí ya/wa shinai *v* 増しや/はしない = **masanai** 増さない (not increase)

mashumaro *n* マシュマロ marshmallow

massá´ji *n* マッサージ massage: **massá´ji´-shi** マッサージ師 masseur

massatsu *n* 抹殺 [BOOKISH] elimination, murder, killing: ~ **shimásu** 抹殺します eliminates, murders, kills

masshurūmu *n* マッシュルーム mushroom

masu *v* 増す = **mashimásu** 増します (increases)

masú *n* マス・鱒 trout

masú *n* 升 a small measuring box (*from which saké can be drunk*)

...-másu *suffix*, *v* ...ます [INFINITIVE of polite auxiliary]

masu-komi *n* マスコミ mass communication (*media*)

masukotto *n* マスコット mascot

másuku *n* マスク mask (= **kamen** 仮面)

masú-masu *adv* 益々 more and more, increasingly

masutādo *n* マスタード mustard (= **karashi** カラシ・芥子)

masuto *n* マスト mast

matá *conj, prep* また・又 again; moreover: **Mata dō´zo** またどうぞ Please (*come, etc.*) again.

matá *n* 股 crotch, groin

máta *conj* また・又 and also/another/more (= **... mo máta** ...もまた)

matagarimásu, matagáru *v* 跨がります, 跨がる: **... ni matagarimásu** ...に跨がります straddles, sits astride, mounts, rides; stretches/extends over, spans

matáge *v* 跨げ 1. → **matagemásu** 跨げます [INFINITIVE] 2. [IMPERATIVE] (stride over it!) → **matagimásu** 跨ぎます

matagemásu, matagéru *v* 跨げます, 跨げる can stride over

matági *v* 跨ぎ → **matagimásu** 跨ぎます [INFINITIVE]

matagimásu, matágu *v* 跨ぎます, 跨ぐ strides over

matáide *v* 跨いで → **matagimásu** 跨ぎます

matánai *v* 待たない = **machimasén** 待ちません (not wait for)

matátakí *n* 瞬き blink(ing) → **matátakímásu** 瞬きます blinks

mátá-wa *conj* または・又は or, or else, on the other hand; also; and/or

matcha *n* 抹茶 powdered green tea (*for tea ceremony*)

mátchi *n* マッチ 1. match(es) (*for fire*) **matchí-bako** *n* マッチ箱 matchbox

máte *v* 待て 1. → **matemásu** 待てます [INFINITIVE] 2. [IMPERATIVE] (wait!) → **machimásu** 待ちます

matemásu, matéru *v* 待てます, 待てる can wait

mato´ *n* 的 target, aim (= **tāgetto** ターゲット)

matō´ *v* 待とう = **machimashō** 待ちましょう (let's wait!)

matomarimásu, matomaru *v* まとまります, まとまる is settled, arranged, finished

matomemásu, matomeru *v* まとめます, まとめる settles, arranges, finishes

mátsu *n* マツ・松 pine tree (= **mátsu-no-kí** 松の木)

mátsu *v* 待つ = **machimásu** 待ちます (waits)

matsuba-zúe *n* 松葉杖 crutch(es)

matsuge *n* まつげ・睫(毛) eyelash(es)

matsuri *n* 祭り (**o-matsuri** お祭り) festival

matsutake *n* マツタケ・松茸 a kind of mushroom (*thumb-shaped*)

matsu-yani *n* 松脂 pine resin

mattaku *adv* 全く quite, completely, exactly (= **zenzen** 全然): **mattaku no** 全くの perfect

mátte *v* 待って → **machimásu** 待ちます: **mátte imásu** 待っています is (or *will be*) waiting/awaiting

mátto *n* マット mat

mawari *n* 周り: **(... no) mawari (ni/no)** (...の)周り(に/の) around ...

mawari... *prefix* 回り...: revolving..., rotating... **mawari-butai** *n* 回り舞台 revolving stage **mawari-dōrō** *n* 回り灯ろう・回り灯籠 revolving lantern

mawari-kaidan *n* 回り階段 spiral stairway

mawari-michi *n* 回り道 detour

mawari-kudoi *adj* 回りくどい roundabout

mawarimásu, mawaru *v* 周ります, 周る goes around

mawarimásu, mawaru *v* 回ります, 回る turns, revolves, circulates, rotates (= **kaitenshimásu, kaitensuru** 回転します, 回転する)

mawashi *n* 回し sumo wrestler's belt (*loincloth*)

mawashimásu, mawasu *v* 回します 回す turns it around, passes it around, circulates it

mawata *n* 真綿 floss silk: [IDIOM] **mawata de kubi o shimeru** 真綿で首を絞める torments one from a distance

mayaku *n* 麻薬 narcotic(s), dope (= **kusuri** クスリ・薬, **yaku** ヤク・薬, **yakubutsu** 薬物)

mayoimásu, mayóu *v* 迷います, 迷う gets lost; gets perplexed

mayonézu *n* マヨネーズ mayonnaise

mayótte *v* 迷って → **mayoimásu** 迷います

máyu *n* 眉 eyebrow(s) (= **máyuge** 眉毛)

máyu *n* マユ・繭 cocoon

mazári *v* 混ざり → **mazarimásu** 混ざります [INFINITIVE]

mazarimásu, mazáru *v* 混ざります, 混ざる it mixes

máze *v* 混ぜ 1. → **mazemásu** 混ぜます [INFINITIVE] 2. **mazé ro** 混ぜろ [IMPERATIVE] (mix it!)

mazemásu, mazéru *v* 混ぜます, 混ぜる mixes it

mazénai *v* 混ぜない = **mazemasén** 混ぜません (not mix it)

mazeyō´ *v* 混ぜよう = **mazemashō´** 混ぜましょう (let's mix it!)

mázu *adv* まず first of all, before anything else (= **saisho (ni)** 最初(に), **hajime (ni)** 初め(に))

mázu *adv* まず perhaps, nearly

mazúi *adj* 不味い untasty, bad-tasting

mazúi *adj* 1. まずい poor, awkward 2. inadvisable 3. ugly

mazushíi *adj* 貧しい poor (*needy*)

mé *n* 目 eye: **taihen na mé ni aimásu** 大変な目にあいます (*has/undergoes*) a hard experience

mé *n* 芽 bud

...-me *interj* ...め・奴 [*deprecates people*] damn (*fool*) ...: **baka-me** ばかめ・馬鹿め damn (*fool*) idiot

...-mé *suffix* ...目 [NUMERAL] -th: **itsutsu-mé** 五つ目 fifth

méate *n* 目当て a guide (*for the eye*); aim

mechamecha *adj* めちゃめちゃ・目茶目茶 in pieces, in confused, in disorder (= **mechakucha** めちゃくちゃ・目茶苦茶): **mechamecha ni shimásu** めちゃめちゃにします ruins, upsets, messes up

medachimásu, medátsu *v* 目立ちます, 目立つ stands out, becomes conspicuous

medama-yaki *n* 目玉焼き fried egg(s)

medarisuto *n* メダリスト medalist

medaru *n* メダル medal

medátta ... *v* 目立った... outstanding, conspicuous → **medachimásu** 目立ちます

medátte *adv* 目立って outstandingly, conspicuously: **medátte imásu** 目立っています is outstanding, conspicuous → **medachimásu** 目立ちます

medetái *adj* めでたい 1. happy (*events*), matter for congratulation 2. = **o-medetái** おめでたい simple-minded, optimistic; idiot

médo *n* 針孔 the eye of a needle

médo *n* 目処 aim (= **méate** 目当て)

mēdo *n* メード = **meido** メイド maid

megabaito *n* メガバイト megabyte (MB)

megakemásu, megakéru *v* 目掛けます, 目掛ける aims at: ... **o megákete** ...を目がけて (aiming) at, (going) toward

mégane *n* メガネ・眼鏡 (*eye*) glasses: **mégane o kakemásu** メガネ[眼鏡]を掛けます puts on (*wears*) glasses

megumaremásu, megumareru *v* 恵まれます, 恵まれる gets blessed: ... **ni megumárete imásu** ...に恵まれています is blessed with ...

megumi *n* 恵み blessing, mercy, charity

megumimásu, megumu *v* 恵みます, 恵む blesses with, gives mercifully (*in charity*)

megunde *v* 恵んで → **megumimásu** 恵みます

megurimásu, meguru *v* 巡ります, 巡る centers on, surrounds, concerns

me-gúsuri *n* 目薬・眼薬 eye lotion, eye drops

megutte *v* 巡って → **megurimásu** 巡ります: ... **o megutte** ...を巡って centering on, surrounding, concerning

méi *n* 姪 = **meikko** 姪っ子 niece

...´-mei *suffix* ...名 (*counts people*) [BOOKISH] (= **...-nin** ...人): **ichí-mei** 一名 one person

meibo *n* 名簿 list (*catalog*) of names, directory, register, roll

méibutsu *n* 名物 a local specialty, a special attraction, a famous product

méigo-san *n* 姪御さん (*your*) niece

meihaku (na) *adj* 明白(な) clear, obvious, explicit: **meihaku ni** 明白に clearly, obbviously, explicitly

mei-jimásu, mei-jiru *v* 命じます, 命じる commands; appoints, nominates, orders

meijín *n* 名人 expert

mei-jite *v* 命じて → **mei-jimásu** 命じます

meimon (no) *adj* 名門(の) distinguished: **meimon no de** 名門の出 person who comes from a very distinguished family: **meimon-(gak-)kō** 名門(学)校 distinguished school

meirei *n* 命令 order, command

meiro *n* 迷路 labyrinth, maze

mé-isha *n* 目・眼医者 eye doctor, oculist

meishi *n* 名刺 business card, calling card, visiting card, name card

meishí-ire *n* 名刺入れ business card case

meishi *n* 名詞 noun

meisho *n* 名所 famous place: **kankō-meisho** 観光名所 famous sightseeing spot

méiwaku *n* 迷惑 (**go-méiwaku** ご迷惑) trouble, bother, nuisance: **méiwaku na** 迷惑な troublesome; (**... ni) (go-)méiwaku o kakemásu** (...に)(ご)迷惑をかけます causes (*one*) trouble

meiwaku-mēru *n* 迷惑メール e-mail spam, junk mail (= **supamu-mēru** スパムメール)

méiyo *n* 名誉 prestige, honor, glory

mē´kā *n* メーカー maker, manufacturer

mekaké *n* 妾 (**omekake-san** お妾さん) mistress, concubine

me-kákushi *n* 目隠し a blindfold

mekata *n* 目方 weight

me-kyábetsu *n* 芽キャベツ Brussels sprouts

mēkyáppu *n* メーキャップ makeup

mémo *n* メモ note, memo(-randum) **memo-chō** *n* メモ帳 note pad, tablet

memorii *n* メモリー (*computer*) memory (= **yōryō** 容量): **memorii ga tarinai** メモリーが足りない runs out of memory

men *n* 面 1. mask 2. face, front 3. surface (= **hyōmén** 表面)

mén *n* 綿 cotton (**momen** 木綿, **kotton** コットン)
mén-bō *n* 綿棒 cotton swab

mén *n* めん・麺 (**mén-rui** めん類・麺類) noodles

ménbā *n* メンバー member

mendō *n* 面倒 trouble, bother, nuisance **mendō na** 面倒な bothersome (= **mendō-kusái** 面倒臭い)

mendori *n* メンドリ hen

menjō´ *n* 免状 license; diploma

menkai *n* 面会 interview, meeting (= **intabyū** インタビュー): **menkai-nin** 面会人 visitor: **~ shimásu** 面会します interviews, meets

ménkyo(-sho) *n* 免許(証) 1. driver's license (= **unten ménkyo(-sho)** 運転免許(証) 2. license, permit (= **menkyó-jō** 免許状)

ménseki *n* 面積 area

mentenansu *n* メンテナンス maintenance

ményū *n* メニュー menu (= **kondate** 献立)

menzei (no) *adj* 免税(の) tax-free/-exempt: **menzei-hin** 免税品 tax-free goods

mērā *n* メーラー (= **mēru sofuto** メールソフト, **mēru kuraianto** メールクライアント) mailer (*computer*)

merii gō rando *n* メリーゴーランド merry-go-round

meriyasu *n* メリヤス knitted goods

merodii *n* メロディー melody

méron *n* メロン melon

mēru *n* メール e-mail (= **ii mēru** Eメール): **mēru bokkusu** メールボックス e-mail box

mésánai *v* 召さない = **meshimasén** 召しません → **meshimásu** 召します

meshí *n* 飯 cooked rice; a meal

meshiagarimásu, meshiagaru *v* 召し上がります, 召し上がる [HONORIFIC] eats; drinks

meshí-bitsu *n* めしびつ・飯櫃 rice bucket/tub (= **o-hitsu** お櫃, **o-hachi** お鉢)

meshimásu, mésu *v* 召します, 召す [*in* FORMAL SPEECH *can replace such verbs as* **kimásu** 着ます (*wears*), **tabemásu** 食べます (*eats*), **nomimasu** 飲みます (*drinks*), **(kaze o) hikimásu** (風邪を)ひきます (*catches cold*), *etc., that involve the body*]

meshitá (no) *adj* 目下(の) inferior (*in status/rank/age*)

meshi-tsúkai *n* 召し使い servant

mésséji *n* メッセージ message (= **kotozuke** 言付け)

mesú *n* 雌・メス female animal: **... no mesú** ...の雌・メス female...

mesu *n* メス surgeon's knife

mētā *n* メーター meter (*device*)

mētoru *n* メートル meter(s) (*of length*)

mé-tsuki *n* 目付き a look (*in one's eye*): **mé-tsuki ga/no warui** 目付きが/の悪い has evil eyes

métta (na) *adj* 滅多(な) reckless, rash

métta (ni) *adv* 滅多(に) [+ NEGATIVE verb] seldom: **métta ni nakimasen** 滅多に泣きません rarely cries

mieue (no) *n* 目上(の) superior (*in status/rank/age*)

meushi *n* 雌牛 cow

me-yaní *n* 目やに matter (*gum, mucus*) from the eye

meyásu *n* 目安 1. a standard 2. guide; aim (= **méate** 目当て)

mezamashi (dokei) *n* 目覚まし(時計) alarm clock

mezamemásu, mezaméru *v* 目覚めます, 目覚める awake

mezashimásu, mezásu *v* 目指します, 目指す heads for (*a destination*): **... o mezáshite** ...を目指して heading for, aiming at

mezurashíi *adj* 珍しい rare, uncommon, novel, curious, unusual, unexpected (*but welcome*)

mezuráshiku *adv* 珍しく unusually

mi *n* 実 1. fruit (= **furūtsu** フルーツ) 2. nut (= **nattsu** ナッツ): **mi ga tawawani/takusan natteiru ki** 実がたわわに/たくさんなっている木 trees laden with fruit

mi... *prefix* 未... un...

mi-chi (no) *adj* 未知(の) unknown: **mi-chi no sekai** 未知の世界 unknown world

mi-hakken (no) *adj* 未発見(の) undiscovered

mi-hattatsu (no) *adj* 未発達(の) undeveloped

mi-kaihatsu (no) *adj* 未開発(の) undeveloped

mi-kaiketsu (no) *adj* 未解決(の) unsolved: **mikaiketsu no mondai** 未解決の問題 unsolved problem

mi-kai (no) *adj* 未開(の) uncultivated, wild: **mikai no (to)chi** 未開の(土)地 uncultivated land

mi-kakunin (no) *adj* 未確認(の) unidentified, unconfirmed: **mikakunin-hikōbuttai** 未確認飛行物体 unidentified flying object (UFO) (= **yūfō** ユーフォー): **mikakunin no hōdō** 未確認の報道 unconfirmed report

mi-kon (no) *adj* 未婚(の) unmarried: **mikon no haha** 未婚の母 unmarried mother

mi-shō (no) *adj* 未詳(の) [BOOKISH] unknown: **sakusha-mishō** 作者未詳 unknown author

mi-zō (no) *adj* 未曾有(の) [BOOKISH] unprecedented, unheard-of: **kokon-mizou (no)...** 古今未曾有(の)... ...unparalleled in history

mi *n* 身 body

mi ni amarimásu (amaru) *v* 身に余ります(余る): **mi ni amaru kōei desu** 身に余る光栄です It is an undeserved honor.

mi ni oboe ga arimasen (nai) *v* 身に覚えがありません(ない) I am innocent. / I know nothing about it. / I am not involved in the matter.

mi ni shimimásu (shimiru) *v* 身に染みます(染みる), **mi ni shimimashita (shimita)** 身に染みました(染みた) **1.** It sank deeply into my mind. / It went to my heart. **2.** pierces one's body: **samusa ga mi ni shimimásu** 寒さが身に染みます The cold pierced me.

mi ni tsukemásu (tsukeru) *v* 身につけます(つける) **1.** wears, puts on: **akusesari(i) o mi ni tsukemásu** アクセサリ(一)を身につけます wears an accessory **2.** learns, acquires: **nintairyoku o mi ni tsukemásu** 忍耐力を身につけます learns to be patient

mi ni tsumasaremásu (tsumasareru) *v* 身につまされます(つまされる) hits close to home, feels deeply, sympathizes deeply

mi no okiba ga arimasen (nai) *v* 身の置き場がありません(ない) There is no place to be/go.

mi o hikimásu (hiku) *v* 身を引きます(引く) **1.** retires **2.** recedes, stands down, backs off

mi o iremásu (ireru) *v* 身を入れます(入れる) puts oneself

mi o kiru (yō na/yō ni) *adj* 身を切る(ような/ように) cutting: **mi o kiru yō ni tsumetai kaze** 身を切るように冷たい風 biting cold wind: **mi o kirareru yō na omoi** 身を切られるような思い as if cut to the heart

mi o ko(na) ni shite hatarakimásu (hataraku) *v* 身を粉にして働きます(働く) works hard, sweats one's guts out

mi o makasemásu (makaseru) *v* 身を任せます(任せる) surrenders oneself (= **mi o yudanemásu (yudaneru)** 身をゆだねます(ゆだねる)): **unmei ni mi o makasemásu** 運命に身を任せます accepts one's fate

mi o tatemásu (tateru) *v* 身を立てます(立てる) establishes oneself (as...), makes a career

mi o yudanemásu (yudaneru) *v* 身をゆだねます(ゆだねる) surrenders oneself (= **mi o makasemásu (makaseru)** 身を任せます(任せる)): **unmei ni mi o yudanemásu** 運命に身をゆだねます accepts one's fate

mí *v* 見 **1.** → **mímásu** 見ます [INFINITIVE] **2. mí ro** 見ろ [IMPERATIVE] (look!)

miai *n* 見合い (*broker-arranged*) meeting of prospective bride and groom: **miai-kékkon** 見合い結婚 an arranged marriage

mibō´-jin *n* 未亡人 widow

mibun *n* 身分 social standing: **mibun-shōmei-sho** 身分証明書 identification card (*driver's license, insurance card, student identification card, alien registration card, etc.*)

míburi *n* 身振り gesture, movement (= **jesuchā** ジェスチャー)

mícha *v* [INFORMAL] 見ちゃ = **míte wa** 見ては: [INFORMAL] **mícha damé (desu)** 見ちゃだめ(です) = [FORMAL] **míte wa ikemasen** 見てはいけません No peeking!

mícha *v* [INFORMAL] 観ちゃ = **míte wa** 観ては: [INFORMAL] **mícha damé (desu)** 観ちゃだめ(です) = [FORMAL] **míte wa ikemasen** 観てはいけません Don't watch!

michi *n* 道 **1.** way, path: **ikiru michi** 生きる道 the way to live: **kami no michi** 神の道 path of God **2.** street, road (= **dōro** 道路): **michi ga konde-imásu** 道が混んでいます There is traffic congestion on the road.: [IDIOM] **subete no michi wa Rōma ni tsūzu** すべての道はローマに通ず All roads lead do Rome.

michi-bata *n* 道端 wayside, roadside (= **robō** 路傍)

michi-jun *n* 道順 the way, the route (*on the road*) (= **junro** 順路): **eki made no michi-jun o tazunemásu** 駅までの道順を尋ねます asks the way to the station

michi-zure *n* 道連れ travelling companion, fellow traveler

michibikimásu, michibíku *v* 導きます, 導く leads, guides

michimásu, michíru *v* 満ちます, 満ちる gets complete, full: **michite imásu** 満ちています is complete, full

midaré *n* 乱れ disorder, messiness: **kami no midaré o naoshimásu** 髪の乱れを直します fixes one's messy hair

midáre *v* 乱れ → **midaremásu** 乱れます [INFINITIVE]

midaremásu, midaréru *v* 乱れます, 乱れる gets disturbed, disordered

midashi *n* 見出し **1.** heading, caption, headline **2.** a dictionary entry; a headword (= **midashigo** 見出し語) **3.** contents (= **mokuji** 目次), index (= **sakuin** 索引), title (= **hyōdai** 標題・表題)

midáshi *v* 乱し → **midashimásu** 乱します [INFINITIVE]

midashimásu, midásu *v* 乱します, 乱す throws into disorder, upsets, disturbs

mídori (no) *adj* 緑(の) green: **midori-iro** 緑色 green color: **mídori-no-madóguchi** みどりの窓口 the Green Window (*for JR train tickets*)

Mi-doshi *n* 巳年 year of the Snake

mié *n* 見栄 show, display; (*dramatic*) pose: **mie-ppari** 見栄っぱり a show-off: **mié o harimásu** 見栄を張ります shows off, puts on air, tries to make oneself look good

míe v 見え → **miemásu** 見えます [INFINITIVE]

miemásu, miéru v 見えます, 見える **1.** is visible, can be seen **2.** appears; shows up, comes **3.** seems

miénai v 見えない = **miemásén** 見えません is invisible, cannot be seen, does not appear: **miénaku narimásu** 見えなくなります vanishes (*from sight*)

míete v 見えて → **miemásu** 見えます [INFINITIVE]

migaite v 磨いて → **migakimásu** 磨きます [INFINITIVE]

migakimásu, migaku v 磨きます, 磨く polishes, shines

migara n 身柄: **migara no kōsoku** 身柄の拘束 custody

migi n 右 right (*not left*)
migi-ashi n 右足 right leg/foot
migi-dónari n 右隣り next on the right
migi-kiki (no) adj 右利き(の) right-handed
migi-máwari (ni) adv 右回り(に) clockwise
migi-te n 右手 right hand
migi-ude n 右腕 right arm

mígoto (na) adj 見事(な) splendid, admirable, beautiful

migurushíi adj 見苦しい unseemly, unsightly

mí-hako n 三箱 three boxfuls

mihon n 見本 **1.** a sample (= **sanpuru** サンプル, **shikyōhin** 試供品) **2.** model, example (= **mohan** 模範, **tehon** 手本 (**o-tehon** お手本))

mii-hā n ミーハー lowbrow person

míira n ミイラ mummy

miíʼtingu n ミーティング meeting, conference [FORMAL] (= [BOOKISH] **káigi** 会議)

miitobōru n ミートボール meatball

mijikái adj 短い short (*not long*); brief

mijikáku adv 短く briefly, short: ~ **shimásu** 短くします shortens

mijitaku n 身支度 dressing oneself: ~ **shimásu** 身支度します dresses

Mikado n 帝 (*Japanese*) the mikado

mikagé-ishi n 見影石 granite

mikake n 見かけ appearance

mikake n 見掛け outward appearance: **mikake wa** 見掛けは outwardly, seemingly

mikaku n 味覚 sense of taste

míkan n ミカン・蜜柑 tangerine, mandarin (*orange*)

mikata n 味方 friend), accomplice, supporter, side: **...no mikata ni tsukimásu** ...の味方につきます takes sides with...

mi-kátá n 見方 a viewpoint: **...no mi-kátá o kaemásu** ...の見方を変えます changes one's viewpoint: **mi-kátá ni yotte (wa)** 見方によって(は) in a way

mikazuki n 三日月 crescent (*moon*): **mikazuki-gata** 三日月型 crescent shape

mike n 三毛 calico: **mike-neko** 三毛猫 tortoiseshell cat, calico cat

míki n 幹 trunk (*of tree*)

míki n 神酒 (**o-miki** 御神酒) saké offered to the gods

míkisā n ミキサー blender

mikka n 三日 three days; 3rd day (*of month*)

miko n 巫女 shrine maiden

mikomi n 見込み **1.** promise, hope **2.** outlook, expectation **3.** opinion, view

mikoshi n 見越し forethought

mikoshi n おみこし・御輿 (**o-míkoshi** お御輿) portable shrine (*for festival parades*)

mikuji n みくじ・神籤 (**o-mikuji** おみくじ) written fortune

mimai n 見舞い (**o-mimai** お見舞い) a visit (*of solicitude*): **mimái-kyaku** 見舞い客 visitor

... míman *suffix* ...未満 less than, below (*a quantity, an age*)

mimásu, míru v 見ます, 見る sees, looks, watches; tries doing

mimí n 耳 ear: **mimí ga tōi** 耳が遠い is hard of hearing

mimikaki n 耳かき earpick

mimi-kázari n 耳飾り earring

mimiuchi n 耳打ち whisper(ing): ~ **shimásu** 耳打ちします whispers

mimoto n 身元 one's identity: **mimoto fumei no shitai** 身元不明の死体 unidentified body

mínai v 見ない = **mimasén** 見ません (not see)

minami n 南 south: **minami-guchi** 南口 the south exit/entrance; **minami-yori (no kaze)** 南寄り(の風) southerly (wind)

Minami-Ámerika n 南アメリカ South America

mi-naraimásu, mi-narau v 見習います, 見習う follows (*learns from*) the example of

miná-san, mina-sama n 皆さん, 皆様 you all, everybody; (*you*) ladies and gentlemen

minato n 港 port: **minato-machi** 港町 port town

mine n 峰 peak, summit

mineraru-wōtā n ミネラルウォーター mineral water

mingei(-hin) n 民芸(品) folkcraft

mí ni-... *prefix*, v 見に...: **mí ni iku** 見に行く [goes] to see

minikúi adj 醜い ugly: "**Minikúi Ahiru no Ko**" 「みにくいアヒルの子」 "The Ugly Duckling"

mini-sukāto n ミニスカート miniskirt

minkan (no) adj 民間(の) civil(ian), private (*non-government*)

mi(n)ná n み(ん)な・皆 everybody, all; everything, all, completely (= **zénbu** 全部): **mi(n)ná de** み(ん)なで・皆で altogether

míno n ミノ・蓑 straw raincoat
míno-mushi n ミノムシ・蓑虫 bagworm

minori n 実り crop, harvest

minorimásu, minóru v 実ります, 実る bears fruit; ripens

minoshirokin n 身代金 ransom

mi-no-take n 身の丈 **1.** one's height (= **mitake** 身丈) **2.** one's condition: **minotake ni atta seikatsu o shimásu** 身の丈にあった生活をします lives within one's income

mi-no-ue n 身の上 one's station in life (= **misora**

身空): **minoue-banashi** 身の上話 one's life story: **minoue-sōdan** 身の上相談 consultation on one's personal affairs: **minoue-sōdan ran** 身の上相談欄 personal-advice column

minshū *n* 民衆 the masses, the people (= **shomin** 庶民, **taishū** 大衆)

minshúku *n* 民宿 bed and breakfast (B&B), family inn, hostelry

minshu-shúgi *n* 民主主義 democracy

minto *n* ミント mint

min'yō *n* 民謡 folk song, ballad (= **fōku songu** フォークソング)

mínzoku *n* 民族 race (→ **ta-minzoku (no)** 多民族(の), **tan'itsu minzoku** 単一民族)

mioboe *n* 見覚え recognition: **mioboe ga arimásu** 見覚えがあります recognizes

mi-okurimásu, mi-okuru *v* 見送ります, 見送る sees (*them*) off

miomo *n* 身重 pregnant female (= **ninpu** 妊婦)

mírai *n* 未来 future

míreba *v* 見れば = [INFORMAL] **mírya** 見りゃ (if one sees) → **mimásu** 見ます

mirin *n* ミリン・味醂 sweet rice wine (*for cooking*)

mí ro *v* 見ろ [IMPERATIVE] (look!) → **mimásu** 見ます

míru *v* 見る = **mimásu** 見ます (sees)

mirú-gai *n* ミルガイ・みる貝 surf clam, geoduck

míruku *n* ミルク milk (= **gyūnyū** 牛乳): **miruku-sēˊki** ミルクセーキ milkshake

mírya *v* [INFORMAL] 見りゃ → **míreba** 見れば

miryoku *n* 魅力 charm (*attraction*) miryoku-teki (na) *adj* 魅力的(な) charming

mísa *n* ミサ (*Catholic*) mass

misago *n* ミサゴ osprey

misairu *n* ミサイル missile

misakai-nai/naku *adj, adv* 見境ない/なく indiscriminate(ly)

misaki *n* 岬 cape, promontory, headland

misao *n* 操 chastity

mise *n* 店 (**o-mise** お店) store, shop (= **sutoa** ストア)

míse *v* 見せ **1.** → **misemásu** 見せます [INFINITIVE] **2. misé ro** 見せろ [IMPERATIVE] (show it!)

mise-kake (no) *adj* 見せかけ(の) sham, make-believe, pretend(ed)

misemásu, miséru *v* 見せます, 見せる shows

mise-mónó *n* 見せ物 show, exhibition, exhibit

misénai *v* 見せない = **misemasén** 見せません (not show)

mísete *v* 見せて → **misemásu** 見せます

míshin *n* ミシン sewing machine

mishō (no) *adj* 実生(の) seedling

míso *n* 味噌 (**o-míso** お味噌) (*fermented*) **1.** bean paste (→ **miso-shíru** 味噌汁(**omiso-shíru** お味噌汁)) **2.** child who is considered to be immature (*while playing, etc.*) (= **misokkasu** みそっかす)

misogi *n* 禊 purification

misoji *n* みそじ・三十路 thirty years old: **misoji**

o sugiruto… 三十路を過ぎると… after the age of thirty

misoka *n* 晦日 last day of month (→ **ō-mísoka** 大晦日)

misokkasu *n* みそっかす **1.** *miso* strainings **2.** good for nothing **3.** child who is considered to be immature (*while playing, etc.*) (= **miso** 味噌)

misoppa *n* 味噌っ歯 decayed tooth

misora *n* 身空 oneself, one's station in life (= **mi no ue** 身の上): **wakai misora de…** 若い身空で… …at such a young age

miso-shíru *n* 味噌汁 (**omiso-shíru** お味噌汁) soup seasoned with *miso*, *miso* soup

missetsu (na) *adj* 密接(な) thick, dense; close, intimate

misu *n* 御簾 bamboo blind

mísu *n* ミス miss, mistake

míta *v* 見た = **mimáshita** 見ました (saw)

mi-tái *v* 見たい wants to see

… mítai desu …みたいです (= **… no yóˊdesu** (/**da, na, de, ni**) …の様です(/だ, な, で ,に) seems/looks (like); [NOUN] **mítai desu** みたいです, [NOUN] **datta mítai desu** だったみたいです; verb-(**r**)**u**/-**ta mítai desu** - う(る)/たみたいです, [ADJECTIVE]-**i**/ -**katta mítai desu** い/かったみたいです

mitake *n* 身丈 **1.** total length of garment **2.** one's height (= **mi-no-take** 身の丈) **3.** one's situation

mitama *n* 御霊 [HONORIFIC] departed soul

mitame *n* 見た目 physical appearance

mitashimásu, mitásu *v* 満たします, 満たす fills up, satisfies

mitate *n* 見立て diagnosis, selection: **isha no mitate** 医者の見立て doctor's opinion: **fuku no mitate** 服の見立て choosing one's clothes (*for someone*)

míte *v* 見て → **mimásu** 見ます

mitei *n* 未定 to be determined: **shōsai wa mitei desu** 詳細は未定です The details are not yet fixed.

mitomemásu, mitomeru *v* 認めます, 認める recognizes, acknowledges, admits

mitorimásu, mitoru *v* 看取ります, 看取る **1.** cares for the sick, nurses (= **kanbyō shimásu** 看病します) **2.** attends on someone on his/her deathbed

mitorizu *n* 見取り図 blueprint, sketch

mitōshi *n* 見通し prospect, outlook

mikoshi 見越し forethought

mítsú *n* 三つ = **mittsú** 三つ (*three*) mitsu-ba *n* 三ッ葉 trefoil leaves; honewort (*stone parsley*): **mitsuba no kurōbā** 三つ葉のクローバー three-leaf clover

mítsu *n* ミツ・蜜 honey mitsú-bachi *n* ミツバチ・蜜蜂 (honey-)bee

mitsugo *n* 三つ子 **1.** triplets **2. mitsugo no tamashii hyaku made** 三つ子の魂百まで [IDIOM] The child is the father of the man.

mitsukarimásu, mitsukaru *v* 見つかります, 見つかる is found, discovered; it turns up

mitsukemásu, mitsukeru v 見つけます, 見つける finds, discovers

mi-tsumemásu, mi-tsumeru v 見つめます, 見つめる gazes at, stares at

mi-tsumori n 見積もり an estimate

mi-tsumori v 見積もり → **mi-tsumorimásu** 見積もります

mi-tsumorimásu, mi-tsumóru v 見積もります, 見積もる estimates, rates

mítsu (na) adj 密(な) dense, thick

mitsurin n 密林 jungle

mitsurō n 蜜蝋 beeswax

mitsuyu n 密輸 smuggling: ~ **shimásu** 密輸します smuggles

mittsú n 三つ three; three years old (= **san-sai** 三歳)

mittsu-mé n 三つ目 third

mittsū n 密通 adultery, intrigue: ~ **shimásu** 密通します intrigues

miuchi n 身内 family, close relatives and close friends

miugoki n, v 身動き [(usually) +NEGATIVE] **1.** moving oneself: **man'indensha de miugoki (ga) toremasen** 満員電車で身動き(が)とれません is stuck on a packed train **2.** acts freely: **shigoto ga isogashikute miugoki (ga) toremasen** 仕事が忙しくて身動き(が)とれません is tied up with busy work

mi-ukemásu, mi-ukéru v 見受けます, 見受ける observes, happens to see; appears (to be)

mi-wakemásu, mi-wakéru v 見分けます, 見分ける discriminates, distinguishes

miwaku n 魅惑 [BOOKISH] enchantment: ~ **shimásu** 魅惑します enchants, attracts **miwaku teki (na)** adj 魅惑的(な) enchanting

miya n 宮 **1.** **o-miya** お宮 Shinto shrine **2.** prince, princess

miyage n 土産 (**o-miyage** おみやげ・お土産, **o-míya** おみや) = **miyage-mono** みやげ物 souvenir: **miyage mono-ya** みやげ物屋 gift shop

miyako n 都 capital city

mí ya/wa shinai v 見や/はしない = **mínai** 見ない (not see)

mi-yasúi adj 見やすい clear (easy to see)

mí yo v 見よ = **mí ro** 見ろ [IMPERATIVE] (look!) → **mimásu** 見ます

miyō´ v 見よう = **mimashō** 見ましょう (let's look!)

miyori n 身寄り relatives: **miyori no nai kodomo** 身寄りのない子供 child who has no relatives (to rely on): **miyori no nai otoshiyori/kōrei-sha tachi** 身寄りのないお年寄り/高齢者たち old people who have no (supportive) relatives

mizo n 溝 drain, ditch, gutter

mizoochi n 鳩尾 pit of the stomach

mizore n 霙 sleet

mizu n 水 (**o-mizu** お水) (not hot) water: **tsumetai mizu** 冷たい水 cold water: **nurui mizu** ぬるい水 lukewarm water

mizu-búkure n 水膨れ blister

mizu-búsoku n 水不足 water shortage

mizu-déppō n 水鉄砲 water pistol

mizu-fūsen n 水風船 water balloon

mizu-gi n 水着 swim suit, bathing suit

mizu-iro n 水色 light blue

mizu-kíri n 水切り colander

mizu-kusa n 水草 waterweed

mizu-mushi n 水虫 athlete's foot

mizu-sáshi n 水差し water pitcher

mizu-taki n 水炊き chicken, bean curd, etc., dipped into hot broth till ready to eat

mizu-tama moyō n 水玉模様 polka dot (design)

mizu wari n 水割り (highball of) whisky and water

mizū´mi n 湖 lake (→ **kojō** 湖上, **kohan** 湖畔)

mo n 喪 mourning: **mo ni fukushimásu** 喪に服します mourns (the passing)

… mo suffix, prep …も too, also, even; (not)… either/even; indeed; number **mo** も [+ NEGATIVE] not even (so much as), [+ AFFIRMATIVE] as many/much as, all of

… mo … mo conj …も…も both …and …; [+ NEGATIVE] neither … nor …

mō´ adv もう already; now: **mō´ súgu** もうすぐ right away

mō adj もう more; (not) … any more: **mō hítori** もう一人 another (one more) person; **mō hitótsu** もう一つ another, one more, the other one; **mō ichi-dó/ík-kai** もう一度/一回 one more time, again; **mō sukóshi** もう少し (a bit) more

mócha v [INFORMAL] 持ちゃ → **móteba** 持てば

mochi n 餅 rice cake

móchi v 持ち → **mochimásu** 持ちます [INFINITIVE]

mochi-agemásu, mochi-agéru v 持ち上げます, 持ち上げる lifts

mochi-awase n 持ち合わせ what is on hand (in stock): **… no mochi-awase** …の持ち合わせ the stock of …: **ima mochi-awase ga arimasén** いま持ち合わせがありません I'm out of cash right now.

mochi-awase v 持ち合わせ → **mochi-awasemásu** 持ち合わせます

mochi-awasemásu, mochi-awaséru v 持ち合わせます, 持ち合わせる has on hand (in stock)

mochiba n 持ち場 one's post of duty

mochi-gome n もち米 glutinous rice

mochiimásu, mochiíru v 用います, 用いる uses (= **tsukaimásu** 使います)

mochimásu, mótsu v 持ちます, 持つ has, holds, carries; it lasts

mochi-mono n 持ち物 **1.** belongings **2.** what to bring: **"mochimono: hikki yōgu"**「持ち物: 筆記用具」"what to bring: writing instrument"

mochí-nushi n 持ち主 owner

mochíron adv もちろん of course, certainly

móchi ya/wa shinai v 持ちや/はしない = **motánai** 持たない (not have; not last)

mōchō n 盲腸 appendix

mōchō´(-en) n 盲腸(炎) appendicitis

mōchū *n* 喪中 mourning period

modemu *n* モデム modem

moderu *n* モデル model

mōdō-ken *n* 盲導犬 seeing-eye dog

modorimásu, modóru *v* 戻ります, 戻る goes back, returns, reverts

modoshimásu, modósu *v* 戻します, 戻す 1. vomits 2. sends back, returns

moe *v* 燃え → **moemásu** 燃えます [INFINITIVE]

moegara *n* 燃え殻 cinder(s)

moemásu, moeru *v* 燃えます, 燃える (*fire*) burns

mō´fu *n* 毛布 blanket

mōfuku *n* 喪服 mourning dress

mogi *n* 模擬 imitation

    mogi-shiken *n* 模擬試験 trial test, mock examination

mogura *n* モグラ・土竜 a mole (*rodent*)

mogurí *n* 潜り diving; a diver

mogúri *v* 潜り → **mogurimásu** 潜ります [INFINITIVE]

mogurimásu, mogúru *v* 潜ります, 潜る dives (*under*); gets into (*bed*); goes under(ground)

mohan *n* 模範 model, pattern, example (= **mihon** 見本, **tehon** 手本 (**o-tehon** お手本)): **mohan o shimeshimásu** 模範を示します gives an example

    mohan-sei *n* 模範生 model student

    mohan-kaitō *n* 模範解答 model answers

    mohan-shū *n* 模範囚 model prisoner

mohaya *adv* もはや [+ NEGATIVE verb] no longer

mójí *n* 文字 letter, character, writing: **ō-moji** 大文字 capital letter, upper-case letter: **ko-moji** 小文字 lower-case letter: (*computer*) **zenkaku-moji** 全角文字 two-byte character, full-width character: **hankaku-moji** 半角文字 one byte character, half width character

    moji-ban *n* 文字盤 dial window

    moji-dōri *adv* 文字どおり literally

mōjín *n* 盲人 blind person

mōkarimásu, mōkáru *v* 儲かります, 儲かる is profitable, it makes money

mokei *n* 模型 model, mold (= **moderu** モデル)

    mokei-hikōki *n* 模型飛行機 model airplane

    mokei-jidōsha *n* 模型自動車 model car

mōkemásu, mōkéru *v* 儲けます, 儲ける makes money, profits

mōkemásu, mōkéru *v* 設けます, 設ける prepares, sets up

Mō´ko *n* 蒙古 Mongolia (= **mongoru** モンゴル): **Mōko-jin** 蒙古人 an Mongolian: **Mōko-han** 蒙古斑 Mongolian blue spot

mokugeki *n* 目撃 witness: ~ **shimásu** 目撃します witnesses

    mokugeki-sha *n* 目撃者 a witness, an eyewitness

mokuhan (-ga) *n* 木版(画) wood-block print

mokuhyō *n* 目標 target, goal (= **tāgetto** ターゲット, **gōru** ゴール): **mokuhyō o/wa takaku mote!** 目標を/は高く持て! Shoot for the moon!

mokuji *n* 目次 (*table of*) contents (= **midashi** 見出し)

mokuroku *n* 目録 catalog, list, table, inventory (= **katarogu** カタログ)

Mokusei *n* 木星 Jupiter

mokusei (no) *adj* 木製(の) made of wood

mokusō *n* 黙想 meditation (= **meditēshon** メディテーション): ~ **shimásu** 黙想します meditates

mokután *n* 木炭 charcoal (= **sumi** 炭)

mokuteki *n* 目的 aim, objective, purpose, end, goal (= **nerai** 狙い, **mato** 的, **mokuhyō** 目標): **mokuteki no tame ni (wa) shudan o erabimasen** 目的のために(は)手段を選びません uses any trick to achieve one's ends: **mokuteki wa shudan o seitōka shimasen** 目的は手段を正当化しません The end does not justify the means

    mokuteki-chi *n* 目的地 destination, goal: **mokutekí-chi ni (tadori-)tsukimásu** 目的地に辿り着きます arrives at one's destination

    mokuteki-go *n* 目的語 (*grammar*) object

mokutō *n* 黙祷 silent prayer: **giseisha ni ippunkan/sanpun-kan no mokutō o sasagemásu** 犠牲者に1分間/3分間の黙祷を捧げます offers a one-minute/three-minutes silent prayer for the victims

Mokuyō´(bi) *n* 木曜(日) Thursday

mokuyoku *n* 沐浴 bathing, washing oneself (*to clean*): ~ **shimásu** 沐浴します washes oneself

mokuzai *n* 木材 wood

mokuzen (no) *adj* 目前(の) immediate (= **me-no-mae** 目の前): **mokuzen no rieki** 目前の利益 immediate advantage

momanai *v* 揉まない = **momimasén** 揉みません (not rub)

mome *v* 揉め 1. → **momemásu** 揉めます [INFINITIVE] 2. [IMPERATIVE] (massage it !) → **momimásu** 揉みます

moméba *v* 揉めば = [INFORMAL] **momya** 揉みや (if one massages) → **momimásu** 揉みます

mome-goto *n* 揉め事 discord, tiff, trouble: **mome-goto o okoshimásu** 揉め事を起こします causes troubles

momemásu, momeru *v* 揉めます, 揉める 1. is in discord/trouble: **ki ga momemásu** 気が揉めます feels uneasy/troubled 2. can massage (*rub with both hands*)

momen *n* 木綿 cotton (= **men** 綿, **kotton** コットン)

momete *v* 揉めて → **momemásu** 揉めます

momi *v* も揉み → **momimásu** 揉みます [INFINITIVE]

momi *n* もみ・籾 unhulled rice

mómi *n* モミ fir: **mómi no ki** モミの木 fir tree

momigara *n* もみ殻 chaff

mómiji *n* モミジ・紅葉 1. maple 2. autumn leaves

momimásu, momu *v* 揉みます, 揉む massages, rubs with both hands

momí ya/wa shinai *v* 揉みや/はしない = **momanai** 揉まない (not massage)

momo *n* モモ・桃 peach: "**Momo-tarō**" 「桃太郎」 "the Adventures of Momotaro, The Peach Boy" (*Japanese folklore*)

mómo *n* 股 thigh

momō´ *v* 揉もう = **monimáshō** 揉みましょう (let's massage it!)

momohiki *n* 股引き longjohns; drawers (= **zubón-shita** ズボン下)

momo-iro (no) *adj* 桃色(の) pink, rosy: **momo-iro no hada** 桃色の肌 pink skin

momya *v* [INFORMAL] 揉みゃ → **moméba** 揉めば

... món ... *interj* もん (*mostly female; informal, baby talk*) because (= **... monó...** もの): (*baby talk or female*) **datte sō da món (monó)** だってそうだもん(もの)

món *n* 紋 family crest (= **monshō** 紋章)

món *n* 門 gate (= **gēto** ゲート)

  món-ban *n* 門番 gatekeeper, watchman, guard, porter (= **mon'ei** 門衛)

  mon-ei *n* 門衛 gatekeeper, watchman, guard, porter (= **monban** 門番)

  mon-gen *n* 門限 curfew

Monbu-Kagaku-daijin *n* 文部科学大臣 Minister of Education, Culture, Sports, Science and Technology

Monbú-Kagaku-shō *n* 文部科学省 Ministry of Education, Culture, Sports, Science and Technology (MEXT)

mondai *n* 問題 **1.** question, topic, subject, exercise: **mondai ni naránai** 問題にならない unimportant **2.** problem, issue, trouble (= **toraburu** トラブル)

monde *v* 揉んで → **momimás<u>u</u>** 揉みます

mongái-kan *n* 門外漢 outsider, nonspecialist, layman: **keizai (ni kanshite) wa mongaikan desu** 経済(に関して)は門外漢です is a layman in economics

Mongoru *n* モンゴル Mongolia (= **mōko** 蒙古)

  Mongoru-jin *n* モンゴル人 a Mongolian

  Mongoru-go *n* モンゴル語 Mongolian (*language*)

mónku *n* 文句 **1.** phrase: **utai-monku** 謳い文句 a motto, catchphrase, slogan: **odoshi-monku** 脅し文句 threatening words **2.** complaint (= **fuhei** 不平, **fufuku** 不服, **kujō** 苦情): **mónku no tsukeyō ga arimasen** 文句のつけようがありません is perfect

monó *n* 物 thing, object, article, something, stuff

...mono *suffix* ... もの ... **shita monó/món des<u>u</u>** ...したもの/もんです used to do

monó *n* 者 person, fellow [BOOKISH] (= **hito** 人)

monogátari *n* 物語 tale, legend

monógoto *n* 物事 things, everything

monohoshisō (na/ni) *adj, adv* 物欲しそう (な/に) wistful(ly)

monohoshi-zuna (-zao) *n* 物干し綱(竿) clothesline (*laundry pole*)

monomane *n* ものまね・物真似 mimic(ry), impersonation: **monomane o shimás<u>u</u>** ものまねをします mimics, impersonates

mono-óboe *n* 物覚え memory: **mono-óboe ga ii** 物覚えがいい is quick to learn (= **nomikomi ga hayai** のみ込みが早い): **mono-óboe ga warui** 物覚えが悪い is slow to learn

mono-óki *n* 物置き shed (*store-house*)

monoraru *n* モノラル monaural sound

monorē´ru *n* モノレール monorail

monorōgu *n* モノローグ monorogue (= **dokuhaku** 独白)

monosashi *n* 物差し ruler (*foot rule*); measure; criterion

mono-sugói *adj* 物凄い terrible, awesome

mono-súgoku *adv* 物凄く terribly, extremely

monózuki (na) *adj* 物好き(な) curious, inquisitive

monshō *n* 紋章 family crest

Monsirochō *n* モンシロチョウ cabbage butterfly

moppara *adv* 専ら principally, chiefly

móppu *n* モップ mop

moraimás<u>u</u>, morau *v* もらいます, もらう receives, gets; has someone do it

mō´ra shimás<u>u</u> (suru) *v* 網羅します(する) includes, comprises, covers (*all*): **mō´ra shita ...** 網羅した... exhaustive, complete

morashimás<u>u</u>, morás<u>u</u> *v* 漏らします, 漏らす lets leak; reveals

moratta *v* もらった = **moraimásh<u>i</u>ta** もらいました (got)

moratte *v* もらって → **moraimás<u>u</u>** もらいます

morawanai *v* もらわない = **moraimasén** もらいません (not get)

more *v* 盛れ [IMPERATIVE] (heap it up!) → **morimás<u>u</u>** 盛ります

móre *v* 漏れ → **moremás<u>u</u>** 漏れます [INFINITIVE]

moremás<u>u</u>, moréru *v* 漏れます, 漏れる leaks out; is omitted; it leaks (= **morimás<u>u</u>** 漏ります)

mori *n* 森 woods, forest

mori *v* 盛り → **morimás<u>u</u>** 盛ります

mori *v* 漏り → **morimás<u>u</u>** 漏ります

morimás<u>u</u>, moru *v* 盛ります, 盛る heaps/piles it up

  mori-bana *n* 盛り花 a flower arrangement

morimás<u>u</u>, móru *v* 漏ります, 漏る it leaks

morói *adj* もろい・脆い brittle, frail

morote *n* もろて・諸手 both hands: **morote o agete sansei shimás<u>u</u>** 諸手を挙げて賛成します totally agrees

morotomo *n* もろとも together [BOOKISH]: **shinaba morotomo** 死なばもろとも go to the grave together

mō´ru *n* モール braid

moruhine *n* モルヒネ morphine

morutaru *n* モルタル (*material*) mortar

móshi (... sh<u>i</u>tára) *conj* もし (...したら) if, perchance

mō´shi-agemás<u>u</u>, mō´shi-agéru *v* 申し上げます, 申し上げる [HUMBLE] I say

mōshi-de *n* 申し出 proposal, offer; report, application, claim

mōshi-demás<u>u</u>, mōshi-déru *v* 申し出ます, 申し出る proposes, offers; reports, applies for, claims

mōshi-ire *n* 申し入れ (*public*) proposal, offering

mōshi-iremás<u>u</u>, mōshi-iréru *v* 申し入れます, 申し入れる (*publicly*) proposes, offers

moshi-ka-shitara *adv* もしかしたら, **moshi-ka-suru to** もしかすると perhaps

mōshi-komi *n* 申し込み application; reservation, subscription; proposal, offer

mōshi-komimásu, mōshi-kómu *v* 申し込みます, 申し込む applies; reserves, subscribes; proposes, offers

mōshikomí-sha *n* 申し込み者・申込者 applicant

mōshikomi-yōshi *n* 申込用紙 application form

mōshimásu, mō´su *v* 申します, 申す [HUMBLE] **1.** I say (= **mōshi-agemásu** 申し上げます) **2.** I humbly do (= **itashimásu** 致します)

móshi-moshi! *interj* もしもし! hello! hey! say there! (*on the phone*)

mō´shitate *n* 申し立て statement, testimony, allegation: **igi-mōshitate** 異議申し立て formal objection

mō´shi-wake *n* 申し訳 excuse: **mō´shi-wake arimasén/gozaimasén** 申し訳ありません/ございません I am very sorry. [FORMAL]

mō´shon *n* モーション motion; sexual overture, pass: **... ni mō´shon o kakemásu** ...にモーションをかけます makes a pass at, makes eyes at

Mosukuwa *n* モスクワ Moscow

mō´tā *n* モーター motor
　mōtā-bōto *n* モーターボート motorboat

motánai *v* 持たない = **mochimasén** 持ちません (not have; not last)

motaremásu, motaréru *v* もたれます, もたれる: (... **ni**) **motaremásu** (...に)もたれます leans (*against ...*)

motasemásu, motaséru *v* 持たせます, 持たせる lets one have, provides (*one with*), gives

mótcha *v* [INFORMAL] 持っちゃ = **mótte wa** 持っては (having; lasting)

móte *v* 持て **1.** → **motemásu** 持てます [INFINITIVE] **2.** [IMPERATIVE] (hold it!) → **mochimásu** 持ちます

móteba *v* 持てば = [INFORMAL] **mócha** 持ちゃ (if one has; if it lasts) → **mochimásu** 持ちます

motemásu, motéru *v* 持てます, 持てる **1.** is popular, well-liked **2.** can hold

motenashi *n* もてなし hospitality

mōteru *n* モーテル motel

motó *n* 元・本 origin, source; cause (*of an effect*)

motó *n* 下 (*at the*) foot (*of*), under

...-moto *suffix* ...元 the source of an activity: **shuppan-moto** 出版元 the publisher(s); **hanbai-moto** 販売元 sales agency; **seizō-moto** 製造元 the maker(s); **oroshi-moto** 卸元 the wholesaler

móto (no) *adj* 元(の) former, earlier, original: **móto kara** 元から from the beginning, always, all along

motō´ *v* 持とう = **mochimashō** 持ちましょう (let's hold it!)

motomemásu, motoméru *v* 求めます, 求める **1.** wants, looks for **2.** asks for, demands **3.** buys, gets

motomoto *n* 元々 from the start, originally; by

nature, naturally: **...-témo motomoto désu** ...ても元々です is no worse off even if ..., it will do no harm to ...

móto wa *adv* 元は originally; earlier, before (= **motomoto wa** 元々は)

mótó-yori *adv* もとより from the beginning; by nature

motozukimásu, motozúku *v* 基づきます, 基づく is based on; conforms to

mótsu *v* 持つ = **mochimásu** 持ちます (has, holds, carries)

motsuré *n* もつれ tangle, entanglement; complications

motsure *v* もつれ → **motsuremásu** もつれます [INFINITIVE]

motsuremásu, motsureru *v* もつれます, もつれる gets entangled/complicated: **shitá ga motsuremásu** 舌がもつれます lisps

mottai-nái *adj* もったいない **1.** undeserving **2.** wasteful

motte *v* 盛って → **morimásu** 盛ります

motte *v* 漏って → **morimásu** 漏ります

motte *v* 持って = **mótte** 持って (holding) [*before verbs of movement*]

mótte *v* 持って → **mochimásu** 持ちます [*but* **motte** 持って *before verbs of movement*]

motte ikimásu (iku) *v* 持って行きます(行く) takes, carries; brings (*to you, there*)

mótte imásu (iru) *v* 持っています(いる) has, holds, owns, possesses

motte itte *v* 持って行って taking it: **motte itte kudasái** 持って行って下さい please take it with you

motte kimásu (kúru) *v* 持って来ます(来る) brings (*to me, here*)

mottékite *v* 持って来て bringing it: **mottékite kudasái** 持って来て下さい please bring it here

motte kói *v* 持って来い [IMPERATIVE] (bring it here!) → **motte kimásu** 持って来ます

motte-kói (no) *adj* もってこい(の) most desirable, ideal; just the thing/ticket (= **... ni chōdo yoi** ...にちょうど良い, **uttetsuke no** うってつけ(の))

mótto *adv* もっと more, still more; longer, further: **mótto íi** もっといい better; **mótto waruí** もっと悪い worse; **mótto takusán** もっとたくさん lots more; **mótto saki (ni)** もっと先(に) further

móttomo *adv, conj* もっとも **1.** indeed, of course **2.** but, however, to be sure

móttómo *adv* 最も most; exceedingly

móya *n* もや・靄 mist, haze

moyashi *n* モヤシ bean sprouts

moyō *n* 模様 pattern, design (→ **shima-moyō** 縞模様) (= **dezain** デザイン)

moyōshimásu, moyō´su *v* 催します, 催す holds/gives (*an event*); feels

mozaiku *n* モザイク mosaic

mozō *n* 模造 imitation
　mozō-hin *n* 模造品 imitation products

mu... *prefix* 無... un-, without..., ...less
　mu-bō (na) *adj* 無謀(な) reckless

mu-chákuriku (no) *adj* 無着陸(の) non-stop (flight)

mú-cha (na) *adj* 無茶(な) unreasonable; reckless; disorderly

mú-chi *n* 無知 ignorance: **múchi (na)** *adj* 無知(な) ignorant

mu-dan (de) *adj* 無断(で) without notice, without permission

mu-ími (na) *adj* 無意味(な) meaningless

mu-íshiki (no/na) *adj* 無意識(の/な) unconscious, involuntary

mú-jaki (na) *adj* 無邪気(な) naive, innocent, unsophisticated

mú-ji (no) *adj* 無地(の) solid-color

mu-jirushi (no) *adj* 無印(の) unmarked, unbranded

mu-jō´ken (no) *adj* 無条件(の) unconditional: **mujō´ken no ai** 無条件の愛 unconditional love: **mujō´ken de** 無条件で unconditionally

mu-jō (na) *adj* 無情(な) heartless, unfeeling: **"Aa Mujō"**「ああ無情」"Les Miserables"

mu-kánkaku (na) *adj* 無感覚(な) numb

mu-kánkei (no/na) *adj* 無関係(の/な): **... to mukánkei** ...と無関係(の/な) unrelated (*unconnected, irrelevant*) to ...

mu-kánshin (no/na) *adj* 無関心(の/な): **... ni mukánshin** ...に無関心(の/な) indifferent to ..., unconcerned with ...

mu-kidō (no) *adj* 無軌道(の) reckless, trackless

mu-kigen (no/ni) *adj, adv* 無期限(の/に) indefinite(ly)

mu-kimei (no) *adj* 無記名(の) unsigned, unregistered

mu-kō (no/na) *adj* 無効(の/な) invalid (*not valid*), null

mu-sékinin (na) *adj* 無責任(な) irresponsible

mu-shoku (no) *adj* 無職(の) jobless: **mu-shoku no otoko** 無職の男 jobless man

mu-shoku (no) *adj* 無色(の) achroma, colorless(ness): **mushoku-tōmei** 無色透明 colorless and transparent

mu-teki *n* 無敵 invincibility, too strong to have as rival: **tenka-muteki** 天下無敵 having no rival in the world

mu-tón-chaku/-jaku (na) *adj* 無頓着/無自覚(な) careless

mú-yō (no) *adj* 無用(の) unnecessary; useless; having no business

mú-zai (no) *adj* 無罪(の) innocent, not guilty

mu-zō´sa (na) *adj* 無造作(な) effortless, easy: **mu-zō´sa ni** 無造作に effortlessly, easily, readily; casually, carelessly

múchi *n* 鞭 a whip: **múchi de uchimásu** 鞭で打ちます whips

muchū *n* 夢中 trance, ecstasy: **... ni muchū ni narimásu** ...に夢中になります gets entranced with (*engrossed in*) ...

muda-bánashi *n* 無駄話 idle talk, hot air, bull: **muda-bánashi o shimásu** 無駄話をします shoots the bull

muda (na) *adj* 無駄(な) futile, no good, wasteful; useless: **muda-ashi** 無駄足 fool's errand

muda (ni) *adj* 無駄(に) in vain: **muda ni shimásu** 無駄にします wastes

muda-zúkai *n* 無駄使い extravagance, waste: ~ **shimásu** 無駄使いします wastes

múgi *n* 麦 wheat, barley

mugi-wara *n* 麦わら straw

mugói *adj* むごい cruel, brutal

muika *n* 六日 six days; the 6th day (*of month*): **muika-mé** 六日目 the 6th day

muite *v* 向いて → **mukimásu** 向きます

muite *v* 剥いて → **mukimásu** 剥きます

mujun *n* 矛盾 inconsistency, contradiction: **mujun shi(te) (i)másu** 矛盾し(てい)ます is inconsistent, contradictory

mukade *n* ムカデ・百足 centipede

mukae *n* 迎え 1. *n* a welcome 2. *v* → **mukaemásu** 迎えます [INFINITIVE]

mukaemásu, mukaeru *v* 迎えます, 迎える meets; welcomes; invites

mukai *v* 向かい → **mukaimásu** 向かいます [INFINITIVE]

mukai-kaze *n* 向かい風 headwind

mukaimásu, mukau *v* 向かいます, 向かう: **... ni mukaimásu** ...に向かいます opposes; heads for

múkamuka shimásu *v* むかむか[ムカムカ]します is queasy, feels nauseated

mukanai *v* 向かない → **mukimasén** 向きません (not face)

mukashi *n* 昔 long (time) ago; ancient days mukashi no *adj* 昔の ancient, old(-en) mukashi-bánashi *n* 昔話 legend; folk tale mukashi kará no *adj* 昔からの old (*from way back*)

mukatte *v* 向かって → **mukaimásu** 向かいます

muke *v* 向け・剥け 1. → **mukemásu** 向けます・剥けます [INFINITIVE] 2. [IMPERATIVE] (turn!; pare!)

mukéba *v* 向けば = [INFORMAL] **mukya** 向きや (if one faces) → **mukimásu** 向きます

mukemásu, mukeru *v* 向けます, 向ける turns (*one's face/eyes/attention to*), directs/points it (*at*)

mukemásu, mukeru *v* 剥けます, 剥ける can skin, can pare

...-muke (no) *suffix, adj* ...向け(の)(*bound/ intended*) for ...: **kazoku-muke (no)** 家族向け(の) for family

mukete *v* 向けて・剥けて → **mukemásu** 向けます・剥けます

muki *v* 向き・剥き → **mukimásu** 向きます・剥きます [INFINITIVE]

mukimásu, muku *v* 向きます, 向く faces

mukimásu, muku *v* 剥きます,剥く (**... no kawá o mukimásu**) ... の皮を剥きます) skins, pares, peels

...-muki (no) *suffix, adj* ...向き(の) facing; (*suitable*) for ...

mukí ya/wa shinai *v* 向きや/はしない, [INFORMAL] **mukya shinai** 向きゃしない = **mukanai** 向かない (not face)

125

múko *n* 婿 son-in-law; bridegroom (= **o-muko-san** お婿さん)

mukō *prep, adv* 向こう **1.** beyond; across the way, over there: **mukō no** 向こうの opposite, facing **2.** → **mukō-gawa** 向こう側

mukō-gawa *n* 向こう側 the other side/party, the opposite side

mukō´-mizu (na) *adj* 向こう見ず(な) reckless, rash: **mukō´-mizu ni** 向こう見ずに recklessly

mukō´ *v* 向こう = **mukimashō** 向きましょう (let's face it!)

mukúi *v* 報い → **mukuimásu** 報います [INFINITIVE]

mukuimásu, mukuíru *v* 報います, 報いる [BOOKISH] repays; compensates

mukuínai *v* 報いない = **mukuimasén** 報いません (not repay/compensate)

mukúite *v* 報いて → **mukuímásu** 報います

mukya *v* [INFORMAL] 向きゃ → **mukéba** 向けば

mumei (no) *adj* 無名(の) nameless, anonymous; obscure

munashii *adj* 空しい・虚しい empty; futile, in vain

muné *n* 胸 **1.** chest, breast **2.** heart, mind

muné *n* 旨 gist, purport, intent, effect

muné *n* 棟 ridge (*of roof*)

murá *n* 村 village: **mura-bito, mura no hito** 村人, 村の人 village people: **mura hachibu** 村八分 ostracism

muragarimásu, muragáru *v* 群がります, 群がる they flock/throng together

murásaki *n* **1. murásaki (no)** 紫(の) purple **2.** 紫 soy sauce (= **shōyu** しょうゆ・醤油)

muré *n* 群れ group, throng, flock

múri 1. *n* 無理 strain, (*undue*) force: **múri (o) shimásu** 無理(を)します overdoes, overworks, forces oneself **2. múri na** 無理な unreasonable, forced; violent; overdoing; (*over-*)demanding: **múri na yōkyū** 無理な要求 unreasonable demand

muri mo arimasen (nai) *v* 無理もありません (ない) no wonder

múri ni sasemásu (saseru) *v* 無理にさせます (させる) forces one (*to do*)

múri ni shimásu *v* 無理にします strains, forces; overdoes (*it*); demands too much

múri wa nái *adj* 無理はない = **múri wa arimasén** 無理はありません: **… no mo múri …** のも無理はありません it is no wonder that…

muriyari *adv* 無理矢理 forcibly

muryō (no) *adj* 無料(の) free of charge: **muryō-chū´shajō** 無料駐車場 free parking

musánai *v* 蒸さない = **mushimasén** 蒸しません (not steam)

musen *n* 無線 radio; wireless

musen-ran *n* 無線 LAN wireless LAN, Wi-Fi (*computer*)

mushi *n* ムシ・虫 insect, bug; moth; worm: **mushi no iki** 虫の息 breathing faintly, being at death's door

mushi-kúdashi 虫下し vermifuge

mushi-megane *n* 虫眼鏡 magnifying glass

mushi-yoke *n* 虫よけ insect repellent; mothballs

mushi-yoké-ami *n* 虫よけ網 window screen (= **amido** 網戸)

mushi *n* 無視 neglect, ignorance: **~ shimásu** 無視します neglects, ignores

múshi *v* 蒸し → **mushimásu** 蒸します [INFINITIVE]

mushi-atsúi *adj* 蒸し暑い muggy, close, sultry, humid

mushi-ba *n* 虫歯 decayed tooth

mushimásu, músu *v* 蒸します, 蒸す steams it; is sultry, humid

mushí-mono *n* 蒸し物 steamed foods

múshiro *adv* むしろ rather; preferably

múshi shimásu (suru) *v* 無視します(する) ignores, neglects, disregards

múshite *v* 蒸して → **mushimásu** 蒸します

musō *n* 夢想 dream, imagination: **~ shimásu** 夢想します dreams, imagines

musō-ka *n* 夢想家 dreamer

musubi *n* むすび (**o-músubi** おむすび) riceball (= **onigiri** おにぎり)

musubi *v* 結び → **musubimásu** 結びます: **musubi-me** 結び目 knot

musubimásu, musubu *v* 結びます, 結ぶ ties, ties up: **nékutai o musubimásu** ネクタイを結びます wears a tie

musuko *n* 息子 son: **musuko-san** 息子さん (*your/someone else's*) son

musume *n* 娘 daughter; girl: **musume-san** 娘さん (*your/someone else's*) daughter, lady

musū´ (no) *adj* 無数(の) innumerable, countless

musunde *v* 結んで → **musubimásu** 結びます

mutsu *n* ムツ big eye fish

mutsukashii, muzukashii *adj* 難しい hard, difficult

muttsú *n* 六つ・6つ six (= **rok-ko** 6 個); six years old (= **roku-sai** 六歳)

múyami (ni) *adv* 無闇(に) recklessly; indiscriminately; immoderately

múzumuzu suru *adj* むずむずする itchy, crawly, creepy

myakú *n* 脈: **myakuhaku** 脈拍 pulse: **myakú o hakarimásu** 脈を計ります checks one's pulse (rate)

myō… *prefix* 明… tomorrow…

myō´-ban *n, adv* 明晩 [BOOKISH] tomorrow night (= **asu/asita no ban/yoru** 明日の晩/夜)

myō-chō *n, adv* 明朝 [BOOKISH] tomorrow morning (= **asu/ashita no asa** 明日の朝)

myō-gó-nichi *n, adv* 明後日 [BOOKISH] day after tomorrow (= **asatte** あさって・明後日)

myō´-nichi *n, adv* 明日 tomorrow (= **ashita, asu** 明日)

myōga *n* ミョウガ・茗荷 Japanese ginger (*buds*)

126

myō´ji, miyoji *n* 名字・苗字 family name [*as written*] (= **sei** 姓)

myō´(na) *adj* 妙(な) strange, queer, wondrous
myūjikaru *n* ミュージカル musical

N

n´ ("un") *n* ん(うん) uh-huh, yeah [INFORMAL] (= **hai** はい [FORMAL])
n´ ("ūn") *n* んー(うーん) hmm, well, lessee
...'n ... *suffix* ...ん... = ... **'no** ...,.,,,の,,,; ... **'n desu (da)** ...んです(だ) it's that ...
na *n* 名 name (= **namae** 名前)
na bakari (no) *adj* 名ばかり(の) nominal
na-dakái *adj* 名高い famous (= **yūmei** 有名)
na-fuda *n* 名札 name plate/tag; dog tag
na no aru *adj* 名のある famous
na no tōtta *adj* 名の通った well-known
na o nasu *v* 名を成す becomes famous, makes a name for oneself: **sakka toshite na o nashimásu** 作家として名を成さしめる makes a name for oneself as a novelist
na o nokoshimásu (nokosu) *v* 名を残します, 残す earns one's place: **kōsei ni na o nokoshimáshita** 後世に名を残しました earned one's place in history afterward
na wa tai o arawasu 名は体を表す [IDIOM] Names and natures do often agree.
ná *n* 菜 greens, vegetables; rape (= **náppa** 菜っ葉)
... na! *interj* ...な! Don't ... !
... ná/ná´ *interj* ...な/なあ (*usually male*) = ... **né/ nē´** ...ね/ねえ (*female*) isn't it, don't you think/ agree
nábe *n* 鍋 (**o-nábe** お鍋) 1. pan, pot 2. food cooked and served in a pan (= **nabé-mono** 鍋物)
nabé-mono *n* 鍋物 food cooked and served in a pan
nabigētā *n* ナビゲーター navigator
nadamemásu, nadaméru *v* 宥めます, 宥める soothes, pacifies
nadare *n* 雪崩 avalanche; snowslide (= **yuki-nádare** 雪なだれ)
náde *v* 撫で → **nademásu** 撫でます
1. [INFINITIVE] 2. **nadé ro** 撫でろ [IMPERATIVE] (stroke!, pet!)
nademásu, nadéru *v* 撫でます, 撫でる strokes, smooths, pats, pets
... nádo *suffix* ...など・等 and so forth/on, and what-not, and the like
náe *n* 苗 seedling: **nae-doko** 苗床 seedbed
náe *v* 萎え → **naemásu** 萎えます [INFINITIVE]
náe *v* なえ → **naemásu** なえます [INFINITIVE]
náeba *v* なえば (if one twists it) → **naimásu** ないます
naemásu, naéru *v* 萎えます, 萎える droops, withers
naemásu, naéru *v* なえます, なえる can twist it (*into a rope*)

naéreba *v* 萎えれば = [INFORMAL] **naérya** 萎えりゃ (if it droops) → **naemásu** 萎えます
naéreba *v* なえれば = [INFORMAL] **naérya** なえりゃ (if one can twist it) → **naemásu** なえます
naé ya/wa shinai *v* 萎えや/はしない = **naénai** 萎えない (not droop)
naé ya/wa shinai *v* なえや/はしない = **naénai** なえない (cannot twist it)
nafutarin *n* ナフタリン (*naphthalene*) mothballs
naga-... *prefix* 長...
naga-chōba *n* 長丁場 [BOOKISH] time-consuming: **naga-chōba no shigoto** 長丁場の仕事 time-consuming work
naga-gutsu *n* 長靴 boots
naga-iki *n* 長生き longevity, long life (= **chōju** 長寿)
naga-isu *n* 長椅子 couch
naga-negi *n* 長ネギ[葱] leek (*the regular* **négi** ネギ・葱, *as contrasted with* **tama-négi** タマネギ・玉葱 round onion)
naga-sode *n* 長袖 long sleeves, long-sleeved garment
naga-yu *n* 長湯 a long bath: **naga-yu o shimásu** 長湯をします takes a long bath
nagái *adj* 長い long
nagaku *adv* 長く long
nagamé *n* 眺め view, scenery
nagáme *v* 眺め → **nagamemásu** 眺めます [INFINITIVE]
nagamemásu, nagaméru *v* 眺めます, 眺める gazes/stares at, views
... (-)nágara *suffix, adv* ...ながら while (*during/ although*)
nagaré *n* 流れ a stream, a flow
nagare-sagyō *n* 流れ作業 assembly line
nagare-zu *n* 流れ図 flow chart
nagáre *v* 流れ → **nagaremásu** 流れます [INFINITIVE]
nagaré-boshi *n* 流れ星 shooting star
nagare-dama *n* 流れ弾 stray bullet
nagaremásu, nagaréru *v* 流れます, 流れる flows
nagarénai *v* 流れない = **nagaremasén** 流れません (not flow)
nagárete *v* 流れて → **nagaremásu** 流れます
nágasa *n* 長さ length
Nagásaki *n* 長崎 Nagasaki: **Nagasáki-ken** 長崎県 Nagasaki Prefecture; **Nagasáki-shi** 長崎市 Nagasaki City

nagasánai *v* 流さない = **nagashimasén** 流しません (not let flow)

nagashí *n* 流し kitchen sink

nagáshi *v* 流し → **nagashimásu** 流します [INFINITIVE]

nagashimásu, nagásu *v* 流します, 流す lets it flow, washes away

naga(t)tarashii *n* 長(っ)たらしい [IN NEGATIVE SENSE] lengthy, tedious: **naga(t)tarashii enzetsu** 長たらしい演説 lengthy speech

naga-ya *n* 長屋 tenement house

náge *v* 投げ → **nagemásu** 投げます **1.** [INFINITIVE] **2. nagé ro** 投げろ [IMPERATIVE] (throw!)

nage-ire *v* 投げ入れ a flower arrangement (*in a tall vase*)

nagéite *v* 嘆いて → **nagekimásu** 嘆きます

nagekánai *v* 嘆かない = **nagekimasén** 嘆きません (not grieve)

nagekí *n* 嘆き grief, lamentation

nagéki *v* 嘆き → **nagekimásu** 嘆きます [INFINITIVE]

nagekimásu, nagéku *v* 嘆きます, 嘆く grieves, weeps, moans, laments

nagemásu, nagéru *v* 投げます, 投げる throws

nagénai *v* 投げない = **nagemasén** 投げません (not throw)

nage-nawa *n* 投げ縄 lasso

nágete *v* 投げて → **nagemásu** 投げます

nageyō *v* 投げよう = **nagemashō´** 投げましょう (let's throw it!)

nagisa *n* なぎさ・渚 water's edge, beach, shore

nagori *n* 名残 traces, remains, remnant: **nagori-oshii** 名残惜しい hates to leave

nagurimásu, nagúru *v* 殴ります, 殴る knocks, beats, strikes

nagusame *n* 慰め comfort, consolation

nagusamemásu, nagusaméru *v* 慰めます, 慰める comforts, consoles

nagusami *n* 慰み amusement, entertainment

nagútte *v* 殴って → **nagurimásu** 殴ります

nái *v* ない = **arimasén** ありません (there is no …, lacks, has no …)

nái *v* ない → **naimásu** ないます [INFINITIVE]

nai-… *prefix* 内… within, in(-side), inner, internal

nái-bu (no) *adj* 内部(の) internal

naibu-kokuhatsu *n* 内部告発 exposuring from within, whistle-blowing: **naibu-kokuhatsusha** 内部告発者 a whistleblower

nái-chi *n* 内地 inside the country

nai-en (no) *adj* 内縁(の) common-law: **nai-en no otto/tsuma** 内縁の夫/妻 common-law husband/wife

nai-fuku *n* 内服 taking medicine orally: **~ shimásu** 内服します takes one's medicine orally: **naifuku-yaku** 内服薬 oral medicine

nai-jō *n* 内情 internal affairs (= **naibu jijō** 内部事情): **naijō ni tsújita** 内情に通じた privy

nai-ju *n* 内需 domestic demand

nai-jū gaikō *adj* 内柔外剛 (*person*) looks tough but is actually soft and sensitive at heart

nai-ka *n* 内科 internal medicine

nai-men *n* 内面 inner face, interior surface: **naimen no yasuragi** 内面の安らぎ inner peace

nai-mitsu (no) *adj* 内密(の) confidential, secret, private [FORMAL]: **naimitsu (no) jōhō** 内密(の)情報 confidential information

Nai-mō´ko, Nai-mongoru (jichi-ku) *n* 内蒙古、内モンゴル(自治区) Inner Mongolia (= **Uchi-mō´ko, Uchi-mongoru (jichi-ku)** 内蒙古、内モンゴル(自治区))

nai-ran *n* 内乱 civil strife

nai-riku *n* 内陸 inland

nai-sen *n* 内線 extension (*phone line, inside*)

nai-sen *n* 内戦 civil war, internal fighting

nai-shin *n* 内心 **1.** (*one's*) thoughts in mind: **naishin kowai** 内心怖い is scared deep down **2.** inner center (*not outer center*)

nai-shin *n* 内診 **1.** internal examination (*gynecology*) **2.** medical examination by a doctor at home (= **takushin** 宅診)

nai-shukketsu *n* 内出血 internal bleeding

nai-tei *n* 内偵 [BOOKISH] secret investigation: **~ shimásu** 内偵します investigates secretly

nai-teki (na) *adj* 内的(な) internal: **nai-teki shō´ko** 内的証拠 internal evidence

nai-ya *n* 内野 infield, baseball diamond

nai-zō *n* 内臓 internal organs

…'-nai *suffix* …内 within, in(side) (→ **kanai** 家内, **shánai (no)** 社内(の), **kokúnai (no)** 国内(の), **kō´nai** 構内)

naichingēru *n* ナイチンゲール nightingale

…-náide *suffix, adv* …ないで not [do] but instead, without [do]ing → **shináide** しないで

náifu *n* ナイフ knife

náigai *n* 内外 **1.** inside and out **2.** home and abroad (= **kokunaigai** 国内外)

…-náigai *suffix* …内外 approximately: **senen-naigai** 千円内外 approximately 1,000 yen

Naijeria *n* ナイジェリア Nigeria

Naijeria-jin *n* ナイジェリア人 a Nigerian

naiji *n* 内示 unofficial announcement (*in office*)

náikaku *n* 内閣 a government cabinet: **naikaku-sōridaijin** 内閣総理大臣 prime minister

naimásu, náu *v* ないます, なう twists (*into a rope*)

náin *n* ナイン nine; baseball team

náiron *n* ナイロン nylon

… náishi … *conj* …ないし… [BOOKISH] **1.** and/or (= **mátawa** または・又は) **2.** from … to … = **… kara…máde** …から…まで

naishin (sho) *n* 内申(書) (*one's*) school record

naishó (no) *adj* 内緒・内証(の) confidential, secret, private [INFORMAL]: **naishó no hanashí** 内緒[内証]の話, **naisho-bánashi** 内緒[内証]話 a private talk

naita *v* 泣いた = **nakimáshita** 泣きました (cried)

náitā *n* ナイター night game (*of baseball*)

naite *v* 泣いて → **nakimásu** 泣きます

naitei *n* 内定 unofficial decision, INFORMAL appointment, unofficial job offer: **naitei (no) torikeshi** 内定(の)取り消し withdrawal of a job offer

naí ya/wa shinai *v* ないや/はしない = **nawánai** なわない (not twist it)

naiyō *n* 内容 contents

náka *n, prep* 中 inside; **... no náka de/ni** …の中で/に in …
naka-darumi *n* 中だるみ slump (= **suranpu** スランプ): **~ shimásu** 中だるみします slumps
naká-mi *n* 中身・中味 contents
naka-niwa *n* 中庭 courtyard
naka-yubi *n* 中指 middle finger

náka *n* 仲 relations, terms (*between people*); **(... to) náka ga íi** (…と)仲がいい is on good terms (with …); **náka tagai** 仲違い discord
naka-dachí *n* 仲立ち go-between, intermediary: **nakadachí-nin** 仲立ち人 broker
naká-gai *n* 仲買 broker
naka-má *n* 仲間 (**o-nakama** お仲間) friend, pal, companion

nakabá *n* 半ば middle: **kokorozashi-nakaba de** 志半ばで without fulfilling one's ambition

nakanai *v* 泣かない = **nakimasén** 泣きません (not cry)

nakanaka *adv* なかなか extremely, very (*long, hard, bad, etc.*), more than one might expect

nákatta *v* なかった = **arimasén deshita** ありませんでした (was not, did not have)

...-nákatta *suffix, v* …なかった = **...-masén deshita** …ませんでした (did not)

nákattara *v* なかったら if/when there isn't/we don't; unless there is (we have)

...-nákattara *suffix, v* …なかったら if/when one doesn't; unless one does

nákattari *v* なかったり sometimes/alternately there isn't (*we don't have*)

...-nákattari (shimásu) *suffix, v* …なかったり（します） sometimes/alternately does not do

nake´ *v* 泣け **1.** → **nakemásu** 泣けます [INFINITIVE] **2.** [IMPERATIVE] (cry!) → **nakimásu** 泣きます

nakéba *v* 泣けば = [INFORMAL] **nakya** 泣きや (if one cries) → **nakimásu** 泣きます

nakemásu, nakeru *v* 泣けます, 泣ける can cry

nakeréba *v* 泣ければ = [INFORMAL] **nakerya** 泣けりゃ (if one can cry) → **nakemásu** 泣けます

nákereba *v* なければ = [INFORMAL] **nákerya** なけりゃ (unless there is, unless one has)

...-nákereba *suffix, v* …なければ = [INFORMAL] **...nákerya** …なけりゃ unless one does; **nákereba narimasén** …なければなりません has to/must do

naki *v* 泣き = **nakimásu** 泣きます [INFINITIVE]

náki ... *prefix, adj* なき… [LITERARY] = **nái ...** ない… (lacking, nonexistent)

náki ... *prefix, adj* 亡き… [LITERARY] = **nái ...** ない… (deceased): **íma wa náki ...** 今は亡き…

the late …: **náki sofu** 亡き祖父 one's dead grandfather

naki-gara *n* 亡骸 [BOOKISH] corpse

nakimásu, naku *v* 泣きます, 泣く weeps; cries
naki-dokoro *n* 泣きどころ[所] Achilles' heel (= **benkei no nakidokoro** 弁慶の泣きどころ)
naki-goe *n* 泣き声 cry, sob (*of person*): **aka-chan/akanbō no nakigoe** 赤ちゃん/赤ん坊の泣き声 baby's crying
naki-goto *n* 泣き言 complaining: **nakigoto o iimásu** 泣き言を言います complains
naki-mushi *n* 泣き虫 crybaby

nakimásu, naku *v* 鳴きます, 鳴く makes an animal sound
naki-goe *n* 鳴き声 chirp, song, chirping (*of animals, birds, insects, etc*)

nakí ya/wa shinai *v* 泣きや/はしない, **nakya shinai** 泣きゃしない = **nakimasén** 泣きません (not cry)

nakō *v* 泣こう = **nakimasho´** 泣きましょう (let's cry!)

nakō´do *n* 仲人 go-between (*matchmaker*)

náku *v* なく so that there isn't any (*we don't have any*); there not being; without
(...-)nákucha *suffix, v* (…)なくちゃ = **(...-)nákute wa** (…)なくては
...-naku (narimásu) *suffix, v* …なく（なります） (*gets*) so that one doesn't do (= **...-nai yō´ni (narimásu)** …ないように（なります）

naku-narimásu, naku-naru *v* 亡くなります, 亡くなる dies; gets lost

naku-narimásu, naku-naru *v* なくなります, なくなる vanishes (*from existence*)

nakusanai *v* なくさない = **nakushi-másén** なくしません (not lose)

nakushimásu, nakusu *v* なくします, なくす loses

nákute *adj* なくて without, lacking → **nái** ない = **arimasén** ありません

...-nákute mo *suffix, v* …なくても even not doing, even if one does not do; **shinákute mo íi** しなくてもいい need not do

...-nákute wa *suffix, v* …なくては not doing, if one does not do; **shinákute wa ikemasén** しなくてはいけません must (*ought to*) do

nakya *v* 泣きゃ → **nakéba** 泣けば

(...-) nákya *suffix, v* (…)なきゃ = [INFORMAL] **(...-) náke-rya** (…)なけりゃ = **(...-) nákereba** (…)なければ unless (*there is*)

náma *adj, n* 生 **1. náma (no/de)** 生(の/で) raw, uncooked, fresh **2.** (= **nama-bíiru** 生ビール) draft beer
nama-chūkei *n* 生中継 live coverage (= **jikkyō-chūkei** 実況中継)
nama-gomi *n* 生ごみ garbage (*kitchen waste*)
nama-gusái *adj* 生臭い fishy(-smelling)
nama-henji *n* 生返事 half-hearted reply
nama-hōsō *n* 生放送 live program, live broadcast
nama-kuríimu *n* 生クリーム (*fresh*) cream

nama-yake (no) *adj* 生焼け(の) rare (*little cooked*), underdone (= **han'yake (no)** 半焼け(の))

nama-yude (no) *adj* 生ゆで(の) half-boiled: **nama-yude tamago** 生ゆで卵 half-boiled egg (= **hanjuku-tamago** 半熟卵)

namae *n* 名前 (**o-namae** お名前) name (= **shimei** 氏名, **seimei** 姓名)

namaiki (na) *adj* 生意気(な) impertinent

namakemásu, namakéru *v* 怠けます, 怠ける idles, is lazy

namake-mono *n* 怠け者 lazy (*person*)

namari *n* ナマリ・鉛 lead (*metal*)

namarí *n* なまり・訛り dialect, accent (= **hōgen** 方言)

namarimásu, namaru *v* 鈍ります, 鈍る **1.** becomes rusty, gets dull: **hōchō ga namarimásu** 包丁が鈍ります a kitchen knife gets dull **2.** becomes weak (*one's body part*): **karada ga namarimashita** 体が鈍りました My muscle became weak.

namasu *n* ナマス・鱠 raw fish tidbits with vegetables in vinegar

namazu *n* ナマズ・鯰 catfish

náme *v* なめ → **namemásu** なめます **1.** [INFINITIVE] **2.** namé ro なめろ [IMPERATIVE] (lick it!)

namemásu, naméru *v* なめます, なめる licks, tastes

naméraka (na) *adj* なめらか(な) smooth

namí *n* 波 wave

nami-norí *n* 波乗り surfing

námida *n* 涙 tear (*in eye*): **namida-me** 涙目 teary eyes: **namida-moroi** 涙もろい easily moved to tears

namiki *n* 並木 row of trees: **namiki-michi** 並木道 tree-lined road, tree-lined street

nami (no) *adj* 並(の) ordinary, common, average, regular

nán *n* ナン nan bread

nán *n* 何 (*before* **d, t, n**) = **náni** 何 what

nán-... *prefix* 何... how many ...: **nán** [COUNTER **ka**] **(no...)** 何 [COUNTER か](の...) a number (of ...)

nán-ba 何羽 how many (*birds, rabbits*) (= **nan-wa** 何羽)

nan-bai 何倍 how many times (*doubled*)

nan-bai 何杯 how many cupfuls

nán-ban 何番 what number

nán-bén 何遍 how many times

nán-biki 何匹 how many (*fishes/bugs, small animals*)

nán-bon 何本 how many (*pencils/bottles, long objects*)

nán-byaku 何百 how many hundreds

nán-dai 何台 how many (*machines, vehicles*)

nán-do 何度 how many times

nan-gai/-kai *n* 何階/階 how many floors/stories; what (number) floor

nán-gatsu 何月 what month

nán-gen 何軒 how many (*buildings, shops,*

houses...)

nán-ji 何時 what time; **nan-jíkan** 何時間 how many hours

nán-kágetsu 何か月 how many months

nán-kai 何回 how many times

nan-kai/-gai 何階 what floor; **nankai/gai-date** 何階建て how many stories/floors

nan-kákoku 何か国 how many countries

nan-kákokugo 何か国語 how many languages

nan-kásho 何か所 how many places

nán-ko 何個 how many (*piece(s); small object(s)*)

nán-mai 何枚 how many (*flat thing(s)*)

nán-mán 何万 how many tens of thousands

nán-nen 何年 what year; how many years

nán-nichi 何日 what day (*of the month*); how many days

nán-nin 何人 how many people

nán-paku 何泊 how many nights: **~ shimásu ka** 何泊しますか How many nights will you stay?

nán-pun 何分 how many minutes

nán-sai 何歳 how (*many years*) old

nán-satsu 何冊 how many copies (*books, magazines*)

nán-seki 何隻 how many boats

nán-shoku 何食 how many meals

nán-sō 何艘 how many ships

nán-tō 何頭 how many (*large animals*)

nan-yō´bi 何曜日 what day (*of the week*)

nán-zoku/-soku 何足 how many pairs (*of footwear such as shoes, socks, etc.*)

nan-... *prefix* 南...south (= **minami no...** 南の...)

Nan-bei *n* 南米 = **Minami-Ámerika** 南アメリカ South America

nán-boku *n* 南北 north and south

nán-bu *n* 南部 the south, the southern part

nán-i *n* 南緯 the south latitude

nan-ka *n* 南下 going south: **~ shimásu** 南下します goes southward

nan-kyoku *n* 南極 South Pole

nan-sei *n* 南西 southwest

nan-tō *n* 南東 southeast

nan-pō *n* 南方 the south, south direction

nan-... *prefix* 難...difficult, tough

nan-gi *n* 難儀 difficulty, suffering, trouble [BOOKISH]

nan-ido *n* 難易度 difficulty level

nán-ji *n* 難事 difficulty

nan-kan *n* 難関 difficulty, obstacle, challenge: **nankan (kō-)kō** 難関(高)校 high school which is difficult to enter

nan-kyoku *n* 難局 difficult situation

nan-min *n* 難民 refugee

nan-sen *n* 難船 shipwreck

nan-zan *n* 難産 difficult delivery: **~ shimásu** 難産します has a difficult delivery

nan-... *prefix* 軟...soft, weak, mild

nan-jaku *adj* 軟弱 [BOOKISH] weak, soft, flaccid [IN NEGATIVE SENSE]: **nanjaku na karada** 軟弱な体 weak body nan-kin n 軟禁 [BOOKISH] house arrest: ~ shimásu 軟禁します confines (*someone*) (somewhere)

nan-kyū n 軟球 a rubber ball (*not hard ball*)

nan-sui n 軟水 soft water (*not hard water*)

nána n 七・7 seven

naná-do n 七度 1. seven degrees 2. seven times

naná-hén n 七遍 seven times

nana-kai n 七階 seven floors/stories, seventh floor

naná-kái n 七回 seven times

nana-korobi ya oki 七転び八起き [IDIOM] Have nine lives.

naná-mei n 七名 [BOOKISH] seven people (= shichí-nin, naná-nin 七人)

naná-nen n 七年 the year 7; nana nén-kan 七年間 seven years

naná-nin n 七人 → naná-mei

naná-satsu n 七冊 seven copies (*books, magazines*)

naná-hyaku n 七百・700 seven hundred

naná-jū n 七十・70 seventy

nana-mán n 七万・70,000 seventy thousand

nana-sén n 七千・7,000 seven thousand

naná-tsu n 七つ・7つ seven, seven years old (= nana-sai 七歳); nanatsu-mé 七つ目 seventh

naname (no/ni) adj, adv 斜め(の/に) aslant, oblique, diagonal

nánbā n ナンバー = nanbā puré'to ナンバープレート (*car*) license plate

nán-da-i interj 何だい what is it (= nán desu ka 何ですか)

nán-de-mo adv 何でも whatever it may be, anything (at all), everything

... nán desu (da, de) suffix, v ...なんです(だ、で) it's that it is ...

nándo n 納戸 back room, closet

náni n 何 what: náni (ga/o) ...-témo 何(が/を)...ても whatever

náni-... prefix 何...what ..., which ...
  nani-go 何語 what language
  nani-iro 何色 what color
  nani-jin 何人 what nationality

nanibun adv 何分 anyway, anyhow

nanige-nái adj 何気ない casual

náni ka n 何か something, anything

nani mo adv 何も [+ NEGATIVE] nothing, (not) anything

náninani n 何々 something or other, so-and-so, what's-it(s-name)

náni-shiro adv 何しろ after all

náni yori adv 何より than what: náni yori mo 何よりも more than anything

nánji pron 汝 [BOOKISH] thou

... nánka suffix ...なんか and so forth/on, and what-not; the likes of

Nankín-mame n 南京豆・ナンキンマメ peanut(s)

nankō n 軟膏 [BOOKISH] ointment

nankō n 難航 1. rough sailing 2. rough passage: ~ shimásu 難航します has a rough passage

nankuse n 難癖 cavil

nan-nára conj 何なら if you prefer, if you like, if you don't mind; if you don't want to

nan ni mo adv 何にも [EMPHATIC] → nani mo 何も

nán ni mo adv 何にも (= nán no ... ní mo 何の...にも [+ NEGATIVE] not to/for/at anything

nán no adj 何の what (*kind of*); of what

nanoka n 七日 seven days; the 7th day (*of month*)

... ná no ni conj ...なのに in spite of its being ..., despite that it is ...

nanpa n 難破 shipwreck: ~ shimásu 難破します shipwrecks

nanpa n ナンパ picking up (*a girl*): ~ shimásu ナンパします picks up (*a girl*)

nán-rá ka no ... adj 何らかの... some

nán-ra (no) ... adj 何ら(の)... [+ NEGATIVE] not any, not in any way

nán to ... conj 何と ... with what, what and ... ; (*saying/thinking/meaning*) what

nán to itté mo adv 何と言っても eventually, come what may

nán to ka shite adv 何とかして by some means (*or other*), somehow or other

nan to mo adv 何とも [+ NEGATIVE] nothing (at all), not ... at all

nán to shitémo adv 何としても inevitably; at any cost

náo adv 尚 still more; moreover: náo íi 尚いい still better

naóri v 直り → naorimásu 直ります [INFINITIVE]

naóri v 治り → naorimásu 治ります [INFINITIVE]

naorimásu, naóru v 直ります、直る is righted, fixed, repaired, improves

naorimásu, naóru v 治ります、治る is cured, gets well, recovers, improves

nao-sara adv 尚更 all the more, still more

naóse v 直せ [IMPERATIVE] (fix it!) → naoshimásu 直します

naoshí v 直し mending, repair(ing), correcting, correction

naóshi v 直し → naoshimásu 直します [INFINITIVE]

naóshi v 治し → naoshimásu 治します [INFINITIVE]

naoshimásu, naósu v 直します、直す 1. makes it right, corrects, repairs, mends, fixes, alters, improves it 2. [INFINITIVE +] does it over (*and better*), re-does it

naoshimásu, naósu v 治します、治す cures it

naótte v 直って → naorimásu 直ります

naótte v 治って → naorimásu 治ります

náppa n 菜っ葉 greens, vegetables; rape (*plant*)

nápukin n ナプキン 1. napkin 2. sanitary pad (= seiriyō nápukin 生理用ナプキン)

nára n ナラ・楢 Japanese oak

... nára conj ...なら, ... nára ba ...ならば if it be, provided it is [NEGATIVE ... ja nákereba/nák-erya ... じゃなければ/なけりゃ]; [VERB]-ru/-ta nára る/たなら, [ADJECTIVE]-i/katta nára い/かったなら if (it be a matter of) ...

narabe v 並べ **1.** → **narabemásu** 並べます [INFINITIVE]; **narabe ro** 並べろ [IMPERATIVE] (line them up!) **2.** [IMPERATIVE] (line up!) → **narabimásu** 並びます

narabemásu, naraberu v 並べます, 並べる arranges, lines them up

narabi v 並び **1.** row (line) **2.** → **narabimásu** 並びます [INFINITIVE]

narabimásu, narabu v 並びます, 並ぶ they line up, arrange themselves

naráe v 習え **1.** → **naraemásu** 習えます [INFINITIVE]. **2.** [IMPERATIVE] (learn it!) → **naraimásu** 習います

naraemásu, naraéru v 習えます, 習える can learn

naraigoto n 習い事 culture lesson(s)

naraimásu, naráu v 習います, 習う learns

naraku n 奈落 hell (= **jigoku** 地獄): **naraku no soko e tsukiotosaremáshita** 奈落の底へ突き落とされました was thrown into the abyss of despair

naranai v 鳴らない = **narimasén** 鳴りません (not sound)

naránai v ならない = **narimasén** なりません (not become)

narande v 並んで → **narabimásu** 並びます: **narande imásu** 並んでいます are in a row, are lined up

narase v 鳴らせ **1.** → **narasemásu** 鳴らせます [INFINITIVE] **2.** [IMPERATIVE] (sound!) → **narashi-másu** 鳴らします

narasemásu, naraseru v 鳴らせます, 鳴らせる can sound

narasenai v 鳴らせない = **narasemasén** 鳴らせません (cannot sound)

narashimásu, narasu v 鳴らします, 鳴らす sounds, rings it

narashimásu, narásu v 均します, 均す smooths, averages

narashimásu, narásu v 馴らします, 馴らす domesticates, tames

narátta v 習った = **naraimáshita** 習いました (learned)

narátte v 習って → **naraimásu** 習います

naráu v 習う → **naraimásu** 習います **naráu yori narero** 習うより慣れろ [IDIOM] Practice makes perfect.

narawánai v 習わない = **naraimasén** 習いません (not learn)

narazumono n ならず者 rogue, vagabond (= **gorotsuki** ごろつき, **buraikan** 無頼漢, **hōtō-mono** 放蕩者)

náre v 鳴れ [IMPERATIVE] (sound!) → **narimásu** 鳴ります

náre v 慣れ→ **naremásu** 慣れます [INFINITIVE]

náre v 馴れ→ **naremásu** 馴れます [INFINITIVE]

náre v **1.** なれ → **naremásu** なれます [INFINITIVE] **2.** なれ [IMPERATIVE] (become!, get to be!) → **narimásu** なります

naréba v 鳴れば = [INFORMAL] **narya** 鳴りゃ (if it sounds) → **narimásu** 鳴ります

náreba v なれば = [INFORMAL] **nárya** なりゃ (if it becomes) → **narimásu** なります

naremásu, naréru v 慣れます, 慣れる (… **ni naremásu** …に慣れます) gets used to

naremásu, naréru v 馴れます, 馴れる (= … **ni naremásu** …に馴れます) grows familiar with

naremásu, naréru v なれます, なれる can become

narénai v 慣れない = **naremasén** 慣れません (not get used to)

narenareshii adj 馴れ馴れしい too friendly, overly familiar

naréshon n ナレーション narration

naresome n 馴れ初め the thing which brought man and woman (lovers) together, trigger of love

nari v 鳴り → **narimásu** 鳴ります [INFINITIVE]

narí n なり・形 (**o-nári** おなり) form; personal appearance

nári v なり → **narimásu** なります [INFINITIVE]

narikin n 成金 nouveau riche

narimásu, náru v なります, なる becomes, gets to be, turns into; is done, completed; amounts to, is; [HONORIFIC] **o-nari ni narimásu** おなりになります, … **ni** ([ADJECTIVE]-**ku**) **narimásu** …に(…く)なります gets so it is …, gets to be …, turns into … **suru kotó ni narimásu** …する事になります it gets arranged/decided to (do) …

narimásu, naru v 鳴ります, 鳴る it sounds, rings

narimono iri (de) adv 鳴り物入り(で) with a fanfare

narí ya/wa shinai v 鳴りゃ/はしない, [INFORMAL] **narya shinai** 鳴りゃしない = **naranai** 鳴らない (not sound)

nári ya/wa shinai v なりゃ/はしない, [INFORMAL] **nárya shinai** なりゃしない = **naránai** ならない (not become)

nariyuki v 成り行き process, development, course; result: **nariyuki o mimásu** 成り行きを見ます watches how things develop (turn out)

narō´ v なろう = **narimashō** なりましょう (let's become …!)

naru-beku … adv なるべく… as … as possible

naru-hodo interj なるほど I see; quite so; you are so right; how true

narushisuto n ナルシスト narcissist

narya v [INFORMAL] 鳴りゃ → **naréba** 鳴れば

nárya v [INFORMAL] なりゃ → **náreba** なれば・成れば

nasái v なさい [IMPERATIVE] (please do it!) → **nasaimásu** なさいます

nasaimásu, nasáru v なさいます, なさる (someone honored) does

násake n 情け (**o-násake** お情け) affection, feeling, tenderness, compassion, sympathy

nasake-nái adj 情けない wretched, miserable; shameful

nasánai v 成さない = **nashimasén** 成しません (not achieve)

nasári v なさり → **nasaimásu** なさいます [INFINITIVE]

nasátta *v* なさった = **nasaimáshita** なさいました (did)

nasátte *v* なさって → **nasaimásu** なさいます

nashí *n* ナシ・梨 pear

náshi *v* 成し → **nashimásu** 成します [INFINITIVE]

náshi *v* なし [LITERARY] = **nái** ない (= **arimasén** ありません) (there is no …, lacks, has no …)

nashimásu, násu *v* 成します, 成す achieves, forms, does

… náshi ni *suffix, prep, adv* …なしに = **… ga náku(te)** …がなく(て) without, lacking, not having

násu *n* ナス [茄子・茄], **násubi** なすび eggplant

násu *v* 成す → **nashimásu** 成します (achieves, forms, does)

nasútta *v* なすった = **nasátta** なさった = **nasaimáshita** なさいました (did)

nasútte *v* なすって = **nasátte** なさって

nata *n* なた・鉈 hatches

natsú *n* 夏 summer

natsukashíi *adj* 懐かしい dear (*dearly remembered*), good old, nostalgic

natsume *n* ナツメ・棗 date (*fruit*)

natsu-míkan *n* 夏ミカン・夏蜜柑 Japanese grapefruit (*pomelo*)

natsu-yásumi *n* 夏休み summer vacation/holiday

natta *v* 鳴った = **narimáshita** 鳴りました (it sounded)

nátta *v* なった = **narimáshita** なりました (became)

nátta *v* なった = **naimáshita** ないました (twisted it)

natte *v* 鳴って → **narimásu** 鳴ります

nátte *v* なって → **narimásu** なります (becomes …)

nátte *v* なって → **naimásu** ないます (twists it)

nattō *n* ナットウ・納豆 fermented soy beans

nattoku *n* 納得 understanding, compliance, assent; **(… o) nattoku shimásu** (…を)納得します gets persuaded/convinced (*of …*), assents/ consents to, complies with; **(… o) nattoku sasemásu** (…を)納得させます persuades/convinces one (*of …*)

náttsu *n* ナッツ nuts

náu *v* なう = **naimásu** ないます (twists it)

nawá *n* 縄 rope, cord

nawabari *n* 縄張り one's territory: **nawabari-arasoi** 縄張り争い territorial fight

nawánai *v* なわない = **naimasén** ないません (not twist it)

naya *n* 納屋 barn, shed

nayamí *n* 悩み suffering, distress, torment

nayamí *v* 悩み → **nayamimásu** 悩みます [INFINITIVE]

nayamimásu, nayámu *v* 悩みます, 悩む suffers

nayánde *v* 悩んで → **nayamimásu** 悩みます

nayonayo (shita) *adj* なよなよ(した) wishy-washy, weedy [IN NEGATIVE SENSE]

náze *adv* なぜ・何故 why: **náze ka to iu to** …なぜかと言うと … the reason is that …

nazo *n* 謎 riddle, mystery

nazo-nazo *n* なぞなぞ riddle (*game*)

nazúke *v* 名付け → **nazukemásu** 名付けます **1.** [INFINITIVE] **2. nazuké ro** 名付けろ [IMPERATIVE] (name it!)

nazuke-oya *n* 名付け親 godparent

nazukemásu, nazukéru *v* 名付けます, 名付ける names, dubs

nazúkete *v* 名付けて → **nazukemásu** 名付けます

…´n desu (da) *suffix, v* …んです(だ) it's that …

ne *n* 音 (= **otó** 音) sound: **suzu no ne** 鈴の音 bell jingles; **mushi no ne** 虫の音 insects chirping **ne o agemásu** *v* 音を上げます, **ne o ageru** 音を上げる gives up

ne *n* 値 (= **nedan** 値段) price: **ne ga takái** 値が高い is expensive
ne-age *n* 値上げ price rise; raising the cost
ne-biki *n* 値引き discount (*of price*)
ne-dan *n* 値段 (**o-nédan** お値段) price

ne *n* 根 **1.** root (= **nekko** 根っこ): **ki no ne(kko)** 木の根(っこ) root of a tree; **ne mo ha mo nai uwasa** 根も葉もないうわさ groundless rumor **2.** cause (= **kongen** 根源). **3.** one's nature: **ne wa yasashii-hito desu** 根は優しい人です is basically a gentle person, is a kind person at heart, is a kind person deep down
ne-hori ha-hori *adv* 根掘り葉掘り about every detail: **ne-hori ha-hori kikaremásu/shitsumon saremásu** 根掘り葉掘り聞[訊]かれます/質問されます is questioned about every detail

ne 1. *n* 寝 (= **nemuri** 眠り) sleep(ing) **2.** *v* 寝 → **nemásu** 寝ます [INFINITIVE]; **ne ro** 寝ろ [IMPERATIVE] (sleep!)
ne-búsoku *n* 寝不足 having not enough sleep: **ne-búsoku desu** 寝不足です didn't get enough sleep
ne-isu *n* 寝椅子 couch, lounge (*chair*)
ne-maki *n* 寝巻き pajamas

… né/né´ *interj* …ね/ねえ (*mostly female*) isn't it, don't you think/agree

nébaneba shimásu (suru) *v* ねばねばします (する) is sticky

nebarí *n* 粘り stickiness: **nebari-zuyoi** 粘り強い persevering: **nebarímásu** 粘ります hangs on

necha *v* 寝ちゃ = **neté wa** 寝ては: **nechaimásu** 寝ちゃいます = **nete shimaimásu** 寝てしまいます → **nemásu** 寝ます

nechigaemásu, nechigaeru *v* 寝違えます, 寝違える gets a crick in one's neck (*while sleeping*): **nechigae mashita** 寝違えました got a crick in my neck

nechiketto *n* ネチケット netiquette (*comes from network + etiquette*)

nechizun *n* ネチズン netizen (= **netto(wāku)-shimin** ネット(ワーク)市民) (*comes from network + citizen*)

Ne-doshi *n* 子年 year of the Rat

negái *v* 願い **1.** a request **2.** → **negaimásu** 願います [INFINITIVE]

negaimásu, negáu *v* 願います, 願う asks for, requests, begs

négi *n* ネギ・葱 onion (*green*)

neiro *n* 音色 (*sound*) tone

néji *n* ねじ・ネジ screw
neji-máwashi *n* ねじ回し screw-driver

nejiránai *v* ねじらない = **nejirimasén** ねじりませ
ん (not twist)

nejirimásu, nejíru *v* ねじります, ねじる twists

nejítte *v* ねじって → **nejirimásu** ねじります

nekashimásu, nekasu *v* 寝かします, 寝かす
puts to bed/sleep; lays it on its side

nekki *n* 熱気 **1.** hot air **2.** air of excitement, fever
3. fever, pyrexia

nékkuresu *n* ネックレス necklace

nekkyō *n* 熱狂 enthusiasm: **~ shimásu** 熱狂します
gets excited

néko *n* ネコ・猫 cat
néko baba *n* 猫ばば [IDIOM] embezzlement:
~ shimásu 猫ばばします embezzles
néko-jita *n* 猫舌 [IDIOM] person who can't eat or
drink too heated/hot (*temperature*) things, the one
whose tongue is very sensitive to heat: **watashi
wa néko-jita desu** 私は猫舌です I can't handle
hot things.
néko kawaigari *n* 猫かわいがり [IDIOM] doting
on (someone): **~ shimásu** 猫かわいがりします
dotes on
néko mo shakushi mo *adv* 猫も杓子も [IDIOM]
anything or anybody (*without distinction*)
néko nade-goe (de) *n* 猫なで声 [IDIOM] in a
wheedling tone of voice
néko ni katsuobushi *n* 猫に鰹節 [IDIOM] Like
trusting a wolf to watch over sheep
néko ni koban *n* 猫に小判 [IDIOM] Casting pearls
before swine. (= **buta ni shinju** 豚に真珠)
néko no te mo karitai *v* 猫の手も借りたい
[IDIOM] busy as a bee (*not to literally mean, "I am
so busy that I would even welcome the help of a
cat."*)
néko o kaburu *v* 猫をかぶる [IDIOM] pretends to
be innocent/nice
néko-ze *n* 猫背 [IDIOM] slouch, slight stoop,
rounded back (*like that of cat*)

nékutai *n* ネクタイ necktie: **nékutai o musubimásu** ネクタイを結びます puts on (*wears*) a
necktie

nemásu, neru *v* 寝ます, 寝る goes to bed, lies
down, sleeps

ne-motó *n* 根元 (*the part*) near the root, the base
(*of a tree*)

nemui *adj* 眠い sleepy

nemuri *n* 眠り sleep(ing)

nemuri *v* 眠り → **nemurimásu** 眠ります
[INFINITIVE]

nemurimásu, nemuru *v* 眠ります, 眠る sleeps

nemutte *v* 眠って → **nemurimásu** 眠ります

nén *n* 年 year

nén-... *prefix* 年... yearly, annual

nén-do *n* 年度 year period, fiscal year: **kon-
nendo** 今年度 this fiscal year: **rai-nendo** 来年度
next fiscal year

nen-kan (no) *adj* 年間(の) for a year; annual:
nenkan-kōsuiryō 年間降水量 annual rainfall:
nenkan-uriage (-daka) 年間売上(高) annual
sales: **nenkan-shotoku** 年間所得 annual income

nen-kan *n* 年鑑 yearbook, almanac

nen-kan (no) *adj* 年刊(の) annual (*paper
publication*): **nenkan-hōkokusho** 年刊報告書
annual report

nen-matsu *n* 年末 the end of the year:
nenmatsu-nenshi kyūka 年末年始休暇 year-end
and New Year's day holidays

nen-pō *n* 年俸 annual salary

nen-ri *n* 年利 annual interest

nen-shi *n* 年始 New Year's day

nen-shō *n* 年商 annual turnover

nén *n* **1.** 念 sense, feeling; desire; caution, care,
attention; **nen no tamé (ni)** 念のため(に) to
make sure, just in case, to be on the safe side, as a
precaution, as a (*word of*) caution; (**... ni**) **nén o
iremásu** (...に)念を入れます pays attention
(to ...), is careful (*of/about ...*), **nén o oshimásu**
念を押します double-checks

nén-... *prefix* 年... **2.** age
nen-chō(-sha) *n* 年長(者) one's senior
nen-pai(-sha) *n* 年配[年輩](者) the elderly,
middle-aged person
nen-rei *n* 年齢 (*one's*) age [BOOKISH] (= **toshí**
年・歳・齢)
nen-shō (-sha) *n* 年少(者) young person, one's
junior

nen-... *prefix* 粘... sticky
nen-chaku-tē´pu *n* 粘着テープ adhesive tape
nén-do *n* 粘土 clay

nenai *v* 寝ない = **nemasén** 寝ません (not go to
bed)

nengá *n* 年賀 New Year's greetings: **nengá ni
ikimasu** 年賀に行きます makes a New Year's
call/visit
nengá-hágaki *n* 年賀葉書 a New Year greeting
postcard
nengá-jō *n* 年賀状 New Year's card

nengan *n* 念願 desire: **nengan ga kanaimásu**
念願が叶います (*one's*) dream/wish has come true

nengáppi *n* 年月日 date (*year/month/day*) (→
seinen-gáppi 生年月日)

nenki *n* 年季 one's term of service: **nenki no
haitta** 年季の入った seasoned, experienced

nenkin *n* 年金 pension: **kōsei-nenkin** 厚生年金
employee pension; **kojin-nenkin hoken** 個人年金
保険 individual annuity insurance

nenryō´ *n* 燃料 fuel: **nenryō-tanku** 燃料タンク
fuel tank

nenshō *n* 燃焼 combustion: **~ shimásu** 燃焼します
burns

nenza *n* 捻挫 sprain: **~ shimásu** 捻挫します
sprains one's ankle

134

neon n ネオン **1.** neon **2.** neon sign
Nepāru n ネパール Nepal
Nepāru-go n ネパール語 Nepalese (*language*)
Nepāru-jin n ネパール人 a Nepalese
neppū n 熱風 hot wind
nerae v 狙え **1.** → **neraemásu** 狙えます
[INFINITIVE] **2.** [IMPERATIVE] (aim!) →
neraimásu 狙います
neraemásu, neraeu v 狙えます, 狙える can aim
nerai n 狙い **1.** an aim, object; idea, intention,
what one is driving at **2.** → **neraimásu** 狙います
[INFINITIVE]
neraimásu, nerau v 狙います, 狙う aims at,
watches for, seeks
neránai v 練らない = **nerimasén** 練りません
(not knead)
neraremásu, nerareru v 寝られます, 寝られる
can go to bed, can lie down, can sleep
nerarereba v 寝られれば = [INFORMAL]
nerarerya 寝られりゃ (if one can sleep) →
neraremásu 寝られます
nerarete v 寝られて → **neraremásu** 寝られます
neratte v 狙って → **neraimásu** 狙います
nerawanai v 狙わない = **neraimasén** 狙いません
(not aim at)
nére v 練れ **1.** → **neremásu** 練れます
[INFINITIVE] **2.** [IMPERATIVE] (knead!) →
nerimásu 練ります
neréba v 寝れば = [INFORMAL] nerya 寝りゃ
(if one goes to bed) → **nemásu** 寝ます
néreba v 練れば = [INFORMAL] nérya 練りゃ
(if one kneads) → **nerimásu** 練ります
neremásu v 寝れます, nereru 寝れる =
neraremásu 寝られます (can go to bed, can sleep)
neremásu, neréru v 練れます, 練れる can knead;
can drill, train
neréreba v 練れれば (if one can knead) →
neremásu 練れます
neréreba v 練れれば = [INFORMAL] **nerérya**
練れりゃ (if one can knead) → **neremásu**
練れます
nerete v 寝れて = **nerarete** 寝られて (can go to
bed, can sleep)
néri v 練り → **nerimásu** 練ります [INFINITIVE]
neri-hamígaki v 練り歯磨き toothpaste
(= **hamigaki-ko** 歯磨き粉)
nerí-kó n 練り粉 dough
nerimásu, néru v 練ります, 練る kneads; drills,
trains
néri ya/wa shinai v [INFORMAL] 練りや/はしない
= **neránai** 練らない (not knead)
nerō v 練ろう = **nerimashō´** 練りましょう (let's
knead it!)
neru v 寝る = **nemásu** 寝ます (goes to bed, lies
down, sleeps)
néru n ネル = **furanneru** フランネル flannel
néru v 練る = **nerimásu** 練ります (kneads; drills,
trains)
nerya v [INFORMAL] 寝りゃ → **neréba** 寝れば

nérya v [INFORMAL] 練りゃ → **néreba** 練れば
nē´-san n 姉さん (**o-né´-san** お姉さん) older sister;
Miss!; Waitress!
nes-shimásu, nes-suru v 熱します, 熱する
1. gets hot, gets excited **2.** heats it, warms it
nésshin (na) adj 熱心 (な) enthusiastic
nésshin ni adv 熱心に enthusiastically
neta v 寝た = **nemáshita** 寝ました (went to bed;
slept)
netamashíi adj 妬ましい envious; enviable
netamimásu, netámu v 妬みます, 妬む envies
nete v 寝て → **nemásu** 寝ます
netsú n **1.** 熱 fever **2.** o nétsu お熱 heat
netsu-ben n 熱弁 passionate speech: **netsu-ben o
furuimásu** 熱弁を振るいます makes a passionate
speech
netsu-bō n 熱望 ambition (*hope*): ~ **shimásu**
熱望します is eager, eagerly desires
nétta v 練った = **nerimáshita** 練りました
(kneaded)
nettai (-chi´hō´) n 熱帯 (地方) tropic(s): **nettai-
urin** 熱帯雨林 tropical rainforest: **nettai-kikō** 熱帯
気候 tropical climate; **nettai-shokubutsu** 熱帯植
物 tropical plant
nétte v 練って → **nerimásu** 練ります
netto n ネット **1.** net **2.** network **3.** the Net
(= **intānetto** インターネット)
netto-bukku n ネットブック netbook (*computer*)
netto-ginkō n ネット銀行 on-line bank
netto-kafe n ネットカフェ Internet café, Net
café (= **intānetto-kafe** インターネットカフェ)
netto-ōkushon n ネット・オークション online
auction (= **onrain ōkushon** オンライン・オークシ
ョン)
netto-sāfin n ネットサーフィン net surfing
netto-tsūhan n ネット通販 online shopping,
internet shopping (= **intānetto tsūhan** インター ネ
ット通販)
nettō n 熱湯 boiling water: **nettō de yakedo o
shimásu** 熱湯で火傷をします is scalded with
boiling water
netto-wāku n ネットワーク network
netto(wāku)-shimin n ネット (ワーク) 市民
netizen (= **nechizun** ネチズン)
neuchi n 値打ち value, worth: **neuchi ga arimásu**
値打ちがあります is worth
né ya/wa shinai v 寝や/はしない = **nenai** 寝ない
(not go to bed)
neyō v 寝よう = **nemashō´** 寝ましょう (let's go
to bed!)
nezumi n ネズミ・鼠 mouse, rat
nezumi-iro (no) adj ネズミ色 (の) gray
nezumí-tori n ネズミ捕り [取り] mousetrap
ni v 似 → **nimásu** 似ます [INFINITIVE]
ní n 荷 **1.** load **2.** burden (= **nímotsu** 荷物,
o-nímotsu お荷物)
ni-zúkuri n 荷造り packing
ní n 二・2 two
ni bai n 二倍 twice (*double*)

ni-banmé (no) *adj* 二番目（の）second

ní dai *n* 二台 two (*machines, vehicles*)

ni dó *n* 二度 two times, twice; **nido-mé** 二度目 the second time

ni do *n* 二度 two degrees (*temperature*)

ni fun *n* 二分 two minutes

ní-gō (san) *n* 二号（さん）mistress, concubine

ní hai *n* 二杯 two cupfuls

ni hén *n* 二遍 two times (= **ni dó** 二度, **ni kái** 二回)

ní hon *n* 二本 two (*pencils/bottles, long objects*)

ni kai *n* 二階 second floor; upstairs

ni kái *n* 二回 two times (= **ni dó** 二度, **ni hén** 二遍); **nikai-mé** 二回目 the second time

ní ken *n* 二軒 two buildings

ní ko *n* 二個 two pieces (*small objects*)

ní mai *n* 二枚 two sheets (*flat things*)

ní-mei *n* 二名 [BOOKISH] = f̲u̲tarí 二人・ふたり two people

ní-nen *n* 二年 the year 2; = **ninén-kan** 二年間 two years; = **ninén-sei** 二年生 second-year student, sophomore

ní-sai *n* 二歳 two years old (= **futatsu** ふたつ)

ní satsu *n* 二冊 two copies (*books, magazines*)

ní-wa *n* 二羽 two (*birds, rabbits*)

... ni (´) *particle* ...に **1.** to/for (a person) **2.** at/in (*a place*), at (*a time*) **3.** (= ... é ...へ) to (*a place*) **4.** as, šo as to be, (*turns/makes*) into being, being

ni-ái *v* 似合い → **ni-aimásu** 似合います [INFINITIVE]

ni-aimásu, ni-áu *v* 似合います, 似合う: **... ni ni-aimásu**...に似合います is becoming (*to*), suits

nia misu *n* ニアミス near miss

nibúi *adj* 鈍い dull, blunt

nicha *v* 似ちゃ → **nitéwa** 似ては

Nichi-... *prefix* 日..., **...-Nichi** ...日 Japan(ese), **Nichi-Ei** 日英 Japanese-English, **Ei-Nichi** 英日 English-Japanese

...-nichi *suffix* ...日 day (*counts/names days*)

nichi-botsu *n* 日没 sunset (*time of sunset*)

Nichiyō´(-bi) *n* 日曜（日）Sunday **Nichiyō´-daiku** *n* 日曜大工 Sunday carpenter, do-it-yourself

Nichiyō-hin(-ten) *n* 日用品（店）grocery (*store*); houseware (*store*)

nie *v* 煮え → **niemásu** 煮えます [INFINITIVE]

niemásu, nieru *v* 煮えます, 煮える it boils, it cooks

niete *v* 煮えて → **niemásu** 煮えます

ní-fuda *n* 荷札 (*baggage/package*) tag

nigái *adj* 苦い bitter, wry: **nigái kōhii** 苦いコーヒー bitter coffee; **nigái keiken** 苦い経験 bitter experience; **niga-warai** 苦笑い bitter smile, wry smile; **niga-mushi o kamitsubushita yōna kao** 苦虫を噛み潰したような顔 sour face (*literally, "one's face as if chewed up a bitter bug"*)

nigaoe *n* 似顔絵 portrait

nigashimásu, nigásu *v* 逃がします, 逃がす turns loose; lets one get away, lets it slip away

nigate *adj* 苦手 (*thing, person, etc.,*) which is not one's cup of tea: **nigate na supōtsu** 苦手なスポ

ーツ sport which one is not good at: **wakaiko wa nigate desu** 若い子は苦手です I prefer not to deal with young people.

Ni-gatsú *n* 二月・2月 February

níge *v* 逃げ → **nigemásu** 逃げます
1. [INFINITIVE] **2.** nigé ro 逃げろ [IMPERATIVE] (run away!)

nigemásu, nigéru *v* 逃げます, 逃げる runs away, escapes, flees

nígeta *v* 逃げた = **nigemáshita** 逃げました (fled)

nígete *v* 逃げて → **nigemásu** 逃げます

nigirimásu, nigiru *v* 握ります, 握る grasps, grips, clutches

nigiri-meshi *n* 握り飯 riceball (= **o-nígiri** おにぎり)

nigirí-zushi *n* にぎり［握り］寿司 sushi hand-packed into small balls (*as traditional in Tokyo*)

nigitte *v* 握って → **nigirimásu** 握ります

nigíyaka (na) *adj* にぎやか・賑やか（な）merry, bustling, lively, flourishing, busy (*place, atmosphere, person, etc.*): **nigíyaka na tōri** 賑やかな通り busy street; **nigíyaka na fun'iki** 賑やかな雰囲気 lively atmosphere; **nigíyaka na hito** 賑やかな人 cheerful person

nigorimásu, nigóru *v* 濁ります, 濁る **1.** gets muddy **2.** (*a voiceless sound*) becomes voiced (k > g, f/h > b, ch/sh > j, s > z, t/ts > z)

Nihón *n* 日本 Japan (= **Nippón** 日本, **Nihón-koku** 日本国)

Nihon-fū *n* 日本風 Japanese style

Nihon-ga *n* 日本画 Japanese-style painting

Nihon-ginkō *n* 日本銀行 Bank of Japan (= **nichi-gin** 日銀)

Nihon-go *n* 日本語 Japanese (*language/word*)

Nihon-jín *n* 日本人 a Japanese

Nihon-kai *n* 日本海 the Sea of Japan

Nihon-ma *n* 日本間 Japanese-style room

Nihon-ryōri *n* 日本料理 Japanese cuisine

Nihon-sei *n* 日本製 made in Japan

Nihon-shu *n* 日本酒 saké (*rice wine*) (= **sake** 酒)

Nihon-teien *n* 日本庭園 Japanese traditional garden

ni-hyakú *n* 二百 200 two hundred

níi-san *n* 兄さん (**o-níi-san** お兄さん) older brother

niji *n* 虹 rainbow: **niji-iro** 虹色 rainbow colors

nijū-nábe *n* 二重鍋 double boiler

nijū-ago *n* 二重あご［顎］double chin

nijū-jinkaku *n* 二重人格 double personality, split personality

ní-jū *n* 二十・20 twenty: **nijū-yokka** 二十四日 24 days, 24th day (*of month*); **nijū-banmé** 二十番目 20th

nijús-sai *n* 二十歳 20 years old (= **hátachi** 二十歳・はたち)

nikawa *n* にかわ・膠 glue: **nikawa-nabe** にかわ鍋 glue pot

ni-kayoimásu, ni-kayóu *v* 似通います, 似通う **... ni/to ni-kayoimásu** ...に/と似通います closely resembles

Nikei (no) *adj* 日系(の) (*of*) Japanese ancestry; **Nikkéi-jin** 日系人 person of Japanese ancestry

níkibi *n* にきび pimple

níkki *n* にっき, **níkkei** にっけい・肉桂 cinnamon

nikki *n* 日記 (*private*) diary

níkkō *n* 日光 sunshine; **Níkkō** 日光 Nikko (*place*) (= **hi no hikari** 日の光)

nikkō-yoku *n* 日光浴 sun bathing

nikkyū *n* 日給 daily wage

nikochin *n* ニコチン nicotine

nikomi *n* 煮込み stew (*food*): **nikomi-udon** 煮込みうどん stew with Udon (*Japanese wheat noodle*)

níkoniko *adj* にこにこ smiling: **níkoniko shi(tei) másu** にこにこし(てい)ます smiles

nikú *n* 肉 (**o-níku** お肉) meat

niku-dángo *n* 肉団子 Chinese meatballs

niku-gyū *n* 肉牛 beef cattle

niku-kiri-bóʹchō *n* 肉切り包丁 butcher/carving knife, meat cleaver

niku-man *n* 肉まん steamed bun stuffed with ground pork

nikú-ya *n* 肉屋 butcher (shop)

nikú *n* **1.** 肉 (**o nílu** お肉) **2.** flesh (= **nikutai** 肉体)

niku-sei *n* 肉声 natural voice (*without a microphone, etc.*)

niku-shoku (dōbutsu) *n* 肉食(動物) carnivore

niku-shu *n* 肉腫 sarcoma

niku-tai *n* 肉体 body

niku-yoku *n* 肉欲 sexual desire

niku-zuki no ii *n* 肉付きのいい plump, fleshy

nikúi *adj* 憎い hateful

...nikúi *suffix* ...にくい・難い (...shi-nikúi ...しにくい) hard, difficult (*to do*)

nikumimásu, nikúmu *v* 憎みます, 憎む hates, detests

nikúnde *v* 憎んで → **nikumimásu** 憎みます

nikushin *n* 肉親 blood relative

níkuzure *n* 荷崩れ cargo shifting

nikuzure *n* 煮崩れ breaking up while boiling/cooking (*fishes, potatoes, etc.*)

ni-mán *n* 二万・20,000 twenty thousand

nimásu, niru *v* 似ます, 似る resembles

nimásu, niru *v* 煮ます, 煮る boils, cooks

... -ní mo *suffix* ...にも also (*even*) at/in, to, as

ni-mono *n* 煮物 boiled foods

nímotsu *n* 荷物 (**o-nímotsu** お荷物) **1.** baggage **2.** load

...(ʹ) -nin *suffix* ...人 person, people; **yo-nín** 四人 four people

nináe *v* 担え [IMPERATIVE] (carry it!) → **ninaimásu** 担います

ninái *adj* 似ない = **nimasén** 似ません (not resemble)

ninái *adj* 煮ない = **nimasén** 煮ません (not boil/cook it)

ninái *v* 担い → **ninaimásu** 担います [INFINITIVE]

ninaimásu, nináu *v* 担います, 担う carries on shoulders

ninátte *v* 担って → **ninaimásu** 担います

ninawánai *v* 担わない = **ninaimasén** 担いません (not carry)

ninchi *n* 認知 [BOOKISH] **1.** recognition, acknowledgment **2.** affiliation: **ninchi sareteinai kodomo** 認知されていない子供 child who is not affiliated by his/her parent (*usually father*)

ningen *n* 人間 human being (= **hito** 人)

ningyo *n* 人魚 mermaid: "**ningyo-hime**" 「人魚姫」 "The Little Mermaid"

ningyō *n* 人形 (**o-ningyō** お人形) doll

ningyō-shíbai *n* 人形芝居 puppet show

ningyō toukai *n* 人形使い puppeteer

nini *n* 任意 [BOOKISH] option

nínja *n* 忍者 a master of stealth, Ninja

ninjin *n* ニンジン・人参 carrot

nínjō *n* 人情 human nature, human feelings, warmheartedness: **ninjō-ka** 人情家 sympathetic person: **ninjō-mi no aru** 人情味のある human, warm-hearted: **giri to nínjō** 義理と人情 duty and sympathy

nínjutsu *n* 忍術 the art of stealth

ninka *n* 認可 [BOOKISH] permission

ninki *n* 人気 popularity. **nikki ga ai másu** 人気があります is popular

ninki *n* 任期 (*one's*) term, term of office: **ninki o tsutomemásu** 任期を務めます serves one's term

...-ninmae *suffix* ...人前 (*counts portions*)

ninmei *n* 任命 [BOOKISH] appointment: ~ **shimásu** 任命します appoints

ninmu *n* 任務 duty, assignment, task, mission: **ninmu o hatashimásu** 任務を果たします accomplishes one's errand

ninniku *n* ニンニク・大蒜 garlic

ninpu *n* 妊婦 pregnant woman

ninpu *n* 人夫 [BOOKISH] laborer

ninshiki *n* 認識 [BOOKISH] awareness, recognition: ~ **shimásu** 認識します recognizes

ninshin *n* 妊娠 pregnancy: **ninshin shite imásu** 妊娠しています is pregnant

ninshin-chūʹzetsu *n* 妊娠中絶 abortion

ninshō *n* 認証 certification

ninshō daimeishi *n* 人称代名詞 personal pronoun

ninsō *n* 人相 looks, facial features

nintai *n* 忍耐 endurance: ~ **shimásu** 忍耐します endures

nintai-ryoku 忍耐力 ability to be patient

nínzū *n* 人数 number of people; population (= **jinkō** 人口)

niō dachi *n* 仁王立ち standing firm with one's feet set apart (*like two Deva Kings stone statue*): **niō dachi ni narimásu** 仁王立ちになります stands firm with one's feet set apart

niói *adj* 臭い・匂い **1.** a smell; (...no) **niói ga shimásu** (...の)臭い[匂い]がします it smells (of ...) **2.** → **nioimásu** 臭います・匂います [INFINITIVE]

nioimásu, nióu *v* 臭います・匂います, 臭う・匂う it smells, is fragrant

niótte v 臭って・匂って → **nioimásu** 臭います・匂います

Nippón n 日本 = **Nihón(-koku)** 日本(国) Japan

nirá n ニラ a leek; a green onion

niramimásu, nirámu v 睨みます, 睨む glares, stares

nfránde v 睨んで → **niramimásu** 睨みます

níre n ニレ・楡 yew (tree)

niréba v 似れば = [INFORMAL] **nirya** 似りゃ (if it resembles) → **nimásu** 似ます

niréba v 煮れば = [INFORMAL] **nirya** 煮りゃ (if one boils/cooks it) → **nimásu** 煮ます

ni ro v 煮ろ [IMPERATIVE] (boil it!) → **nimásu** 煮ます

niru v 似る = **nimásu** 似ます (resembles)

niru v 煮る = **nimásu** 煮ます (boils, cooks)

nirya v [INFORMAL] 似りゃ・煮りゃ → **niréba** 似れば; 煮れば

ní-san (no) adj 二、三(の) two or three ...

ní-sei n 二世 second generation (Japanese emigrant); ... the Second

nisemásu, niseru v 似せます, 似せる imitates, copies; counterfeits (money), forges (a document, a signature)

ni-sén n 二千・2,000 two thousand

nise (no) adj にせ・偽(の) false, phony, fake, imitation

nise-mono n 偽物・にせもの a fake, an imitation; a forgery

nise-satsu n 偽札・贋札・にせ札 counterfeit bill (currency)

nishi n 西 west: **nishi-guchi** 西口 the west exit/entrance; **nishi-yori (no kaze)** 西寄り(の風) westerly (wind)

nishi-káigan n 西海岸 west coast

níshiki n 錦 brocade

nishime n 煮しめ(**o-níshime** お煮しめ) boiled fish and vegetables

níshin n ニシン・鰊 herring

nishoku-tsuki (no) adj 二食付き(の) with two meals incuded

nisshi n 日誌 diary, journal (of business, nursing, etc.): **gyōmu-nisshi** 業務日誌 business diary; **kango-nisshi** 看護日誌 nurse's daily record

nissū´ n 日数 the number of days

nísu n ニス = **wánisu** ワニス varnish

nita adj 似た ...similar (= **nite iru** 似ている...) → **nimásu** 似ます

nita v 煮た = **nimáshita** 煮ました (boiled)

nite v 似て → **nimásu** 似ます

nite v 煮て → **nimásu** 煮ます

... ní te particle ...にて [LITERARY] = **... de** ...で (at; ...)

nité ya shinai v 似てやしない, **nité wa inai** 似てはいない = **nicha inai** 似ちゃいない = **nitemasen, nite(i-)nai** 似てません, 似て(い)ない (not resemble)

ni-tō (no) adj 二等(の) second class; **nitō´-shō** 二等賞 the second prize

nittei n 日程 schedule, program, itinerary

niwa n 庭(**o-niwa** お庭) garden

... níwa suffix, prep, conj ...には to; at/in; as

níwaka (no/ni) adj, adv にわか(の/に) sudden(ly), unexpected(ly); **nikawa-áme** にわか雨 sudden shower

niwatori n ニワトリ・鶏 chicken

ní ya/wa shinai v 似や/はしない = **ninai** 似ない (not resemble)

ní ya/wa shinai v 煮や/はしない = **ninai** 煮ない (not boil/cook it)

niyō v 煮よう = **nimashō´** 煮ましょう (let's boil it!)

n´n interj んん 1. "un-un" (うんうん) huh-uh, uh-uh 2. "u-un" (ううん) nope

nó n 野 field (dry) (= **nó-hara** 野原)

no-... prefix 野...

nó-bana n 野花 [BOOKISH] wildflower

nó-gusa n 野草 [BOOKISH] wild grass

no-usagi n 野ウサギ・野兎 wild rabbit

...´no suffix ...の 1. the one/time/place that; (= **hitó** 人, **monó** 物, **tokí** 時, **tokoró** 所) 2. the (specific) act/fact of ... (cf. **kotó** 事) 3. which/that is ... (→ **désu** です, **dá** だ, **na** な)

nō n 脳 brain (= **nō-míso** 脳みそ・脳味噌): **dai-nō** 大脳 cerebrum: **shōnō** 小脳 cerebellum: **kan-nō** 間脳 diencephalon

nō-míso n 脳みそ・脳味噌 brain [INFORMAL] (= **nō** 脳 [FORMAL])

nō´ n 能 1. ability (= **nōryoku** 能力, **sainō** 才能): [IDIOM] **nō´ aru taka wa tsume wo kakusu** 能ある鷹は爪を隠す Who knows most speaks least. 2. **o-nō** お能 Noh (Japanese classical theater) (→ **nō-men** 能面)

nō-... prefix 農... farming, agriculture

nō´-chi n 農地 farm land

nō´-gyō n 農業 agriculture, farming

nō-jō´ n 農場 farm

nō´-ka n 農家 farm house/family; farmer

nō-min n 農民 the farmers

nobashimásu, nobásu v 伸ばします, 伸ばす extends (lengthens, stretches, deters) it

nobashimásu, nobásu v 延ばします, 延ばす prolongs

nóbe v 述べ → **nobemásu** 述べます

1. [INFINITIVE] 2. **nobé ro** 述べろ [IMPERATIVE] (tell it!)

nobemásu, nobéru v 述べます, 述べる tells, relates

nóbi v 伸び → **nobimásu** 伸びます [INFINITIVE]

nobimásu, nobíru v 伸びます, 伸びる it extends, reaches; it spreads

nobori 1. n 上り inbound (to Tokyo), the up train 2. v 登り・上り・昇り → **noborimásu** 登ります・上ります・昇ります [INFINITIVE]

noborimásu, noboru v 登ります, 登る climbs

noborimásu, noboru v 上ります, 上る goes up

noborimásu, noboru v 昇ります, 昇る rises: **hi ga noborimásu** 日が昇ります the sun rises

nóbu n ノブ knob: **doa-nobu** ドアノブ door knob

nochi *n* のち・後: **nochi-hodo** のちほど・後程 later (= **áto (de)** あと・後(で))

nódo *n* のど・喉 throat: **nódo ga kawaki-máshita** のどが渇きました is thirsty; [IDIOM] **nodo-moto sugireba atsusa wasureru** のど元過ぎれば熱さ忘れる The danger past, and God forgotten.

nō´do *n* 濃度 density, thick (*liquid*), concentration: **nisankatanso-nōdo** 二酸化炭素濃度 carbon dioxide concentration; **kō-nōdo (no) kōhii** 高濃度(の)コーヒー[珈琲] strong coffee

nódoka (na) *adj* のどか(な) tranquil, peaceful, quiet, calm

nōdō-tai *n* 能動態 the active voice (*not the passive voice*)

nó-hara *n* 野原 field

noite *v* 退いて → **nokimásu** 退きます

noirōze *n* ノイローゼ neurosis

nó-juku *n* 野宿 rough sleeping: **~ shimásu** 野宿します sleeps rough

nokanai *v* 退かない = **nokimasén** 退きません (not get out of the way)

noké *v* 退け **1.** → **nokemásu** 退けます [INFINITIVE]; **noke ro** 退けろ [IMPERATIVE] (omit it!) **2.** [IMPERATIVE] (get out of the way!) → **nokimásu** 退きます

nokemásu, nokeru *v* 退けます, 退ける removes; omits

nokenai *v* 退けない = **nokemasén** 退けません (not remove/omit)

nokete *v* 退けて → **nokemásu** 退けます

noki *n* 軒 eaves

noki *v* 退き → **nokimásu** 退きます [INFINITIVE]

nokimásu, noku *v* 退きます,退く gets out of the way

nókku shimásu (suru) *v* ノックします(する) knocks (*on door*)

nokogíri *v* のこぎり・鋸 a saw (*tool*)

nōkō (na) *adj* 濃厚(な) thick, rich, dense, passionate: **nōkō na aisukuriimu** 濃厚なアイスクリーム thick ice cream: **nōkō na miruku** 濃厚なミルク rich milk: **nōkō na kisu** 濃厚なキス passionate kiss

nokorí *n* 残り the rest, the remainder, what is left, the leftover
nokori-bi *n* 残り火 embers
nokori-ga *n* 残り香 lingering scent
nokori-monó *n* 残り物 leftovers, remains, leavings: [IDIOM] **nokori-mono niwa fuku ga aru** 残り物には福がある Last but not least.

nokorimásu, nokóru *v* 残ります, 残る remains, is left behind/over

nokoshimásu, nokósu *v* 残します, 残す leaves behind/over

nománai *v* 飲まない = **nomimasén** 飲みません (not drink)

nóme *v* 飲め **1.** → **nomemásu** 飲めます [INFINITIVE] **2.** [IMPERATIVE] (drink it!) → **nomimásu** 飲みます

nómeba *v* 飲めば = **nómya** 飲みゃ (if one drinks)

→ **nomimásu** 飲みます

nomemásu, noméru *v* 飲めます, 飲める can drink; is (very) drinkable

nō-men *n* 能面 mask (*Noh drama*)

noménai *v* 飲めない = **nomemasén** 飲めません (cannot drink)

noméreba *v* 飲めれば = [INFORMAL] **nomérya** 飲めりゃ (if one can drink) → **nomemásu** 飲めます

nomérya *v* [INFORMAL] 飲めりゃ → **noméreba** 飲めれば

nómete *v* 飲めて → **nomemásu** 飲めます

nomí *n* ノミ・蚤 flea

nómi *n* ノミ・鑿 chisel

nómi *v* 飲み → **nomimásu** 飲みます [INFINITIVE]

...nómi *suffix, adj* ...のみ (= ... **daké** ...だけ) only

nomi-komimásu, nomi-komu *v* 飲み込みます, 飲み込む swallows (*ingests*)

nomimásu, nómu *v* 飲みます, 飲む drinks; smokes; takes (*medicine*)
nomi-kai *n* 飲み会 drinking party
nomí-mizu *n* 飲み水 drinking water
nomí-mono *n* 飲み物 beverage, something to drink, refreshments
nomí-ya *n* 飲み屋 tavern, neighborhood bar

nómi ya/wa shinai *v* 飲みや/はしない, **nómya shinai** 飲みゃしない = **nománai** 飲まない (not drink)

nomō´ *v* 飲もう = **nomimashō´** 飲みましょう (let's drink!)

nómya *v* 飲みゃ → **nómeba** 飲めば

nonbē, nonbei *n* 飲兵衛・呑兵衛, のんべい a heavy drinker [INFORMAL]

nonbiri *adj* のんびり easy, leisurely: **nonbiri ya** のんびり屋 happy-go-lucky person (= **nonki** のん気[呑気]): **ie de nonbiri shimásu** 家でのんびりします relaxes at home

nónda *v* 飲んだ = **nomimáshita** 飲みました (drank)

nónde *v* 飲んで → **nomimásu** 飲みます

non-fikushon *n* ノンフィクション nonfiction

nónja *v* 飲んじゃ = **nónde wa** 飲んでは: **nónja damé (desu)** 飲んじゃだめ(です) don't drink it!

nónki (na) *adj* のん気[呑気](な) easygoing, happy-go-lucky, carefree

nonoshirimásu, nonoshíru *v* 罵ります, 罵る reviles, abuses, swears at, curses

nonoshi´tte *v* 罵って → **nonoshirimásu** 罵ります

non-sumōkā *n* ノンスモーカー non-smoker

nosutarujia *n* ノスタルジア nostalgia

nore *v* 乗れ **1.** → **noremásu** 乗れます [INFINITIVE] **2.** [IMPERATIVE] (aboard!) → **norimásu** 乗ります

noremásu, noreru *v* 乗れます, 乗れる can ride/board

noren *n* のれん・暖簾 shop curtain; credit: **noren o oroshimásu** 暖簾を下ろします closes down one's store; **noren o wakemásu** 暖簾を分けます lets the employee use the same shop name to open

his/her own shop; [IDIOM] **noren ni udeoshi** 暖簾
に腕押し unresponsive, It is like beating the air.
(= **tōfu ni kasugai** 豆腐にかすがい)
nori v 乗り → **norimásu** 乗ります [INFINITIVE]
norí n ノリ・海苔 seaweed (green)
　norí-maki n のり[海苔]巻き sushi rice in a sea-
　weed roll
norí n のり・糊 paste; starch
nori-kaemásu, nori-káeru v 乗り換えます, 乗り
換える changes (vehicles)
norimásu, noru v 乗ります, 乗る gets aboard,
rides; is carried
　nori-ba n 乗り場 boarding area/place; platform
　(at station); taxi station; bus stop
　nori-kae n 乗り換え change, transfer (of vehicle)
　nori-komi n 乗り込み drive-in
　nori-mono n 乗(り)物 vehicle
Nōrin-Suisan-shō n 農林水産省 Ministry of
Agriculture, Forestry and Fisheries of Japan (MAFF)
nōritsu n 能率 efficiency
norō´ v 乗ろう = **norimashō´** 乗りましょう (let's
get aboard!)
norói n 呪い a curse
norói n のろい slow, dull, sluggish [INFORMAL]
norói v 呪い → **noroimásu** 呪います
[INFINITIVE]
noroimásu, noróu v 呪います, 呪う curses,
utters a curse
noronoro adv のろのろ slowly, sluggishly:
　noronoro unten のろのろ運転 driving slowly:
　noronoro arukimásu のろのろ歩きます slouches
　along
norótte v 呪って → **noroimásu** 呪います
noru v 乗る = **norimásu** 乗ります (gets aboard,
rides; is carried)
noruma n ノルマ norm, quota: **noruma o**
tasseishimásu ノルマを達成します achieves one's
quota
nō´ryoku n 能力 ability (= **nō** 能, **sainō** 才能)
nosé v 乗せ → **nosemásu** 乗せます **1.**
[INFINITIVE] **2. nose ro** 乗せろ [IMPERATIVE] (load/
carry it!)
nosemásu, noseru v 乗せます, 乗せる loads,
puts aboard, ships, carries
nosemásu, noseru v 載せます, 載せる publishes
(in book, magazine, etc.), posts (an article, etc.)
nosete v 乗せて・載せて → **nosemásu** 乗せま
す・載せます
nōshuku n 濃縮 [BOOKISH] concentration (of
liquid or air)
noten (de/no) adv, adj 野天(で/の) outdoors:
　noten-búro 野天風呂 outdoor bath (= **roten-búro**
　露天風呂)
nōtenki (na) adj 能天気(な) happy-go-lucky,
easy, optimistic (person)
nō´to n ノート → **nōtobúkku** ノートブック
notebook
notta v 乗った = **norimáshita** 乗りました (got
aboard)

notte v 乗って → **norimásu** 乗ります
nottóri n 乗っ取り → **nottorimásu** 乗っ取ります
　nottóri-han n 乗っ取り犯 hijacker
　nottori-jíken n 乗っ取り事件 a hijacking; (illegal)
　takeover, seizure
nottorimásu, nottóru v 乗っ取ります, 乗っ取る
hijacks; (illegally) takes over, seizes
nottótte v 乗っ取って → **nottorimásu** 乗っ取
ります
noyama n 野山 fields and mountains
nōzei n 納税 payment of taxes: ~ **shimásu** 納税し
ます pays one's taxes
nozoite v 除いて → **nozokimásu** 除きます
nozoke´ v 覗け **1.** → **nozokemásu** 覗けます
[INFINITIVE] **2.** [IMPERATIVE] (peek!) →
nozokimásu 覗きます
nozokemásu, nozokeru v 覗けます, 覗ける can
peek/peep at
nozokemásu, nozokeru v 除けます, 除ける can
remove; can omit
nozoki v 覗き・除き → **nozokimásu** 覗きま
す・除きます [INFINITIVE]
nozokimásu, nozoku v 覗きます, 覗く peeks/
peeps at
　nozokí-ana n のぞき[覗き]穴 peephole
　nozoki-ya n のぞき[覗き]屋 peeping Tom
nozokimásu, nozoku v 除きます, 除く
eliminates, removes; omits
nozokō v 覗こう・除こう = **nozokimashō** のぞ
覗きましょう；除きましょう (let's peek!; let's
remove/omit it!)
nozomashíi adj 望ましい desirable, welcome
nozomi n 望み a desire; a hope, an expectation
nozomi v 望み・臨み → **nozomimásu** 望みま
す・臨みます [INFINITIVE]
nozomimásu, nozomu v 望みます, 望む desires,
looks to, hopes for
nozomimásu, nozomu v 臨みます, 臨む
[BOOKISH] looks out on
nozonde v 望んで・臨んで → **nozomimásu**
望みます・臨みます
nū´ v 縫う = **nuimásu** 縫います (sews)
nū´do n ヌード a nude
núe v 縫え **1.** → **nuemásu** 縫えます
[INFINITIVE]
núeba v 縫えば (if one sews) → **nuemásu**
縫えます
nuemásu, nuéru v 縫えます, 縫える can sew
nuénai v 縫えない = **nuemasén** 縫えません
(cannot sew)
nugánai v 脱がない = **nugimasén** 脱ぎません (not
take it off)
núge v 脱げ **1.** → **nugemásu** 脱げます
[INFINITIVE] **2.** [IMPERATIVE] (take it off!) →
nugimásu 脱ぎます
nugemásu, nugéru v 脱げます, 脱げる **1.**
slips/comes off **2.** can take it off
nugénai v 脱げない = **nugemasén** 脱げません
(not slip off; cannot take it off)

núgeta v 脱げた = **nugemáshita** 脱げました (it slipped; could take it off)

núgete v 脱げて → **nugemásu** 脱げます

nugimásu, núgu v 脱ぎます, 脱ぐ takes off (*clothes, shoes*)

nugō v 脱ごう = **nugimashō´** 脱ぎましょう (let's take it off!)

nuguémasu, nuguéru v 拭えます, 拭える can wipe it away

nuguénai v 拭えない = **nuguemásen** 拭えません (cannot wipe it away)

nuguimásu, nuguu´ v 拭います, 拭う wipes it away

nugútta v 拭った = **nuguimáshita** 拭いました

nugútte v 拭って → **nuguimásu** 拭います

nuguwánai v 拭わない = **nuguimasén** 拭いません (not wipe it away)

núi v 縫い → **nuimásu** 縫います

núida v 脱いだ = **nugimáshita** 脱ぎました (took it off)

núide v 脱いで → **nugimásu** 脱ぎます

nuigurumi n 縫い包み stuffed toy

nuimásu, nuu´ v 縫います, 縫う sews
　núi bari n 縫い針 sewing needle
　nui-mé n 縫い目 seam

nuita v 抜いた = **nukimáshita** 抜きました (uncorked/removed it)

nuite v 抜いて → **nukimásu** 抜きます

núi ya/wa shinai v 縫いや/はしない, **núya shinai** 縫やしない = **nuwánai** 縫わない (not sew)

nukashimásu, nukasu v 抜かします, 抜かす skips, leaves out

nuke´ v 抜け **1.** → **nukemásu** 抜けます [INFINITIVE] **2.** [IMPERATIVE] (uncork/remove it!) → **nukimásu** 抜きます

nukemásu, nukeru v 抜けます, 抜ける comes off; escapes; is omitted
　nuke-ana n 抜け穴 **1.** passage which allows one to go through **2.** passage to run away **3.** loophole

nukete v 抜けて → **nukemásu** 抜けます

...-nuki (de/no) *suffix, adj, adv* ...抜き (で/の) without (*omitting*)

nukimásu, nuku v 抜きます, 抜く uncorks; removes; omits; surpasses; selects
　nuki-ashi (sashiashi)(de) *adv* 抜き足 (差し足) (で) stealthily, on tiptoe: **nuki-ashi de arukimásu** 抜き足差し足で歩きます walks stealthily, walks on tiptoe
　nuki-uchi n 抜き打ち (*test, inspection, etc.,*) without notice: **nukiuchi-tesuto** 抜き打ちテスト popquiz: **nukiuchi-kensa** 抜き打ち検査 surprise inspection

nukō v 抜こう = **nukimashō** 抜きましょう (let's uncork/ remove it!)

numá n 沼 pond: **numa-chi** 沼地 swamp, marsh

nuno n 布 cloth: **nuno-ji** 布地 fabric

nuranai v 塗らない = **nurimasén** 塗りません (not paint it)

nurashimásu, nurasu v 濡らします, 濡らす wets, dampens

nuré v 濡れ → **nuremásu** 濡れます [INFINITIVE]

nuré v 塗れ **1.** → **nuremásu** 塗れます [INFINITIVE] **2.** [IMPERATIVE] (paint it!) → **nurimásu** 塗ります

nuréba v 塗れば = [INFORMAL] **nurya** 塗りゃ (if one paints it) → **nurimásu** 塗ります

nure-ginu n 濡れ衣 false accusation

nuremásu, nureru v 濡れます, 濡れる gets wet, damp; **nurete imásu** 濡れています is wet

nuremásu, nureru v 塗れます, 塗れる can paint it

nurenai v 濡れない = **nuremásen** 濡れません (not get wet)

nurenai v 塗れない = **nuremasén** 塗れません (cannot paint it)

nureréba v 濡れれば = [INFORMAL] **nurerya** 濡れりゃ (if it gets wet) → **nuremásu** 濡れます

nureréba v 塗れれば = [INFORMAL] **nurerya** 塗れりゃ (if one can paint it) → **nuremásu** 塗れます

nurete v 濡れて → **nuremásu** 濡れます

nurete v 塗れて → **nuremásu** 塗れます

nuri 塗り **1.** n lacquer, varnish, painting **2.** v → **nurimásu** 塗ります [INFINITIVE]

nuri-kaemásu, nuri-káéru v 塗り替えます, 塗り替える repaints

nurimásu, nuru v 塗ります, 塗る lacquers, paints, varnishes, stains; (*butter*) spreads
　nuri-gúsuri n 塗り薬 ointment [INFORMAL]
　nuri-mono n 塗り物 lacquerware

nurí ya/wa shinai v 塗りや/はしない, [INFORMAL] **nurya shinai** 塗りゃしない = **nuranai** 塗らない (not paint it)

nurō´ v 塗ろう = **nurimashō** 塗りましょう (let's paint it!)

nuru v 塗る = **nurimásu** 塗ります (paints)

nurúi *adj* ぬるい・温い lukewarm, tepid

nurya v [INFORMAL] 塗りゃ → **nuréba** 塗れば

nushi n 主 master, owner (= **aruji** 主)

nusumí n 盗み theft

nusumimásu, nusúmu v 盗みます, 盗む steals, swipes, robs, rips off

nutta v 塗った = **nurimáshita** 塗りました (painted)

nútta v 縫った = **nuimáshita** 縫いました (sewed)

nutte v 塗って → **nurimásu** 塗ります

nútte v 縫って → **nuimásu** 縫います

nuwánai v 縫わない = **nuimasén** 縫いません (not sew)

núya v 縫や → **núeba** 縫えば

... nya/nyā´ ... *suffix* にゃ/にゃあ [INFORMAL] = **... ní wa ...** には

nyō n 尿 [BOOKISH] urine, urinating (= **shíkko** しっこ, **o-shíkko** おしっこ)

nyō´bō, nyō´bo n 女房 my wife

nyū... *prefix* 入... entering
　nyū-en n 入園 entering a kindergarten/nursery: ~ **shimásu** 入園します enrolls (*in kindergarten/*

nursery); **nyūen-shiki** 入園式 (*kindergarten/ nursery*) entrance ceremony

nyū-gaku *n* 入学 admission to a school, entering a school; **nyū(gaku)-shi(ken)** 入(学)試(験) entrance exam; **nyūgaku-shiki** 入学式 school entrance ceremony: ~ **shimásu** 入学します enrolls (*in school*)

nyū-in *n* 入院 entering a hospital, hospital admission: ~ **shimásu** 入院します enters a hospital: **nyūinshite imásu** 入院しています is in a hospital

nyū-jō *n* 入場 admission (*to a place*): ~ **shimásu** 入場します is admitted, enters; **nyūjō´-ken** 入場券 admission ticket, platform (*non-passenger*) ticket; **nyūjō´-ryō** 入場料 admission fee

nyū-ka *n* 入荷 arrival (*of goods*)(*in shop, market, etc.*): ~ **shimásu** 入荷します receives (*goods*)

nyū-kai *n* 入会 admission to an association: nyūkai-kin 入会金 admission fee: ~ **shimásu** 入会します becomes a member

nyū-koku *n* 入国 entering a country; immigration: ~ **shimásu** 入国します enters a country; **nyūkoku kanri-kyoku** 入国管理局 Immigration Bureau of Japan

nyū-kyo *n* 入居 moving into an apartment: ~ **shimásu** 入居します moves into an apartment; **nyūkyó-sha** 入居者 tenant, resident (*of an apartment*)

nyū-seki *n* 入籍 registering one's marriage: ~ **shimásu** 入籍します registers one's marriage: **nyūseki shimáshita** 入籍しました We officially got married.

nyū-sen *n* 入選 winning a prize: ~ **shimásu** 入選します wins a prize

nyū-sha *n* 入社 entering (*joining*) a company: ~ **shimásu** 入社します enters a company: **nyūsha-**

shikén 入社試験 employment selection exam

nyū-shitsu *n* 入室 entering a room: ~ **shimásu** 入室します enters a room

nyū-yoku *n* 入浴 bath, taking a bath: ~ **shimásu** 入浴します takes a bath

nyūbai *n* 入梅 the rainy season (*in Japan*) (= **tsuyu** 梅雨)

nyūdō-gumo *n* 入道雲 thunderhead, cumulonimbus cloud

nyū-eki *n* 乳液 **1.** latex **2.** milky lotion, milky liquid (*cosmetic*)

nyū-gan *n* 乳がん・乳癌 breast cancer

nyū-gyū *n* 乳牛 dairy cattle

nyū-inryō *n* 乳飲料 milk beverage

nyū-ji *n* 乳児 infant

Nyūjiirándo *n* ニュージーランド New Zealand; **Nyūjiirandó-jin** ニュージーランド人 a New Zealander

nyūnen (na/ni) *adj, adv* 入念(な/に) careful(ly): **nyūnen ni shirabemásu** 入念に調べます searches carefully

nyūsan-kin *n* 乳酸菌 lactobacillus (*a type of bacteria*)

nyū-seihin *n* 乳製品 foods made from milk (*butter, cheese, etc.*)

nyūshō *n* 入賞 winning a prize: **nyūsho-sha** 入賞者 a prizewinner: ~ **shimásu** 入賞します wins a prize

nyū´su *n* ニュース news: **nyūsu-bangumi** ニュース番組 news program: **nyūsu-kyasutā** ニュースキャスター newscaster

nyū´toraru *n* ニュートラル neutral (*gear*): **(gia o) nyū´toraru ni iremásu** (ギアを)ニュートラルに入れます shifts the gear into neutral

Nyūyō´ku *n* ニューヨーク New York

nyūyō (na) *adj* 入用(な) necessary, needed

O

ó *n* 尾 = **shippó** しっぽ・尻尾 tail

ó *n* 緒 = **hanao** 鼻緒 thong, strap

o- *prefix* お・御 [HONORIFIC] (personalizing): "your" or "that important thing"

o-aiso *n* おあいそ・お愛想, **o-aisō** お愛想 **1.** compliment, flattery (= **aiso** 愛想) **2.** o-aiso おあいそ (*restaurant*) bill, check

o-bā´-san *n* おばあさん・お祖母さん grandmother (*family*) (= **bā-san** ばあさん, **obā-chan** おばあちゃん, **só-bo** 祖母)

o-bā´-san *n* おばあさん・お婆さん (*not relative*) old lady/woman (= **bā-san** ばあさん, **obā-chan** おばあちゃん)

o-bentō *n* お弁当 box lunch (= **bentō** 弁当): **(o-)bentō-bako** (お)弁当箱 lunch box

o-bon *n* お盆 tray (= **bon** 盆, **torei** トレイ)

O-bón *n* お盆 the Bon Festival (*Buddhist All Saints Day*) (= **Bon** 盆)

o-bō-san *n* お坊さん Buddhist monk (= **bō-san** 坊さん)

o-cha *n* お茶 Japanese green tea; the tea ceremony (= **cha** 茶)

o-fúro *n* お風呂 bath (= **furo** 風呂)

o-hachi *n* お鉢 rice bucket/tub (= **hachi** 鉢) (= **o-hitsu** お櫃・おひつ = **meshi-bitsu** 飯びつ)

o-hana *n* お花 **1.** flower (= **hana** 花) **2.** flower arrangement

o-hana *n* お鼻 nose (= **hana** 鼻)

o-háshi *n* お箸 chopsticks (= **hashi** 箸)

o-hima *n* お暇 (*your*) spare time, free time (= **hima** 暇): **o-hima na toki/sai ni (dōzo) oyori kudasai** お暇なとき/際に(どうぞ)お寄り下さい

Please come visit me/us when you have time.

o-kane *n* お金 money (= **kane** 金)

o-kéiko (goto) *n* お稽古（ごと）practice (*artistic*) (= **kéiko** 稽古, **naraigoto** 習い事)

o-ikura (désu ka) おいくら（ですか）What's the bill/tab/price? How much is this? (= **ikura (désu ka)** いくら（ですか）)

o-ikutsu (désu ka) おいくつ（ですか）How old (*are you*)? (= **ikutsu (désu ka)** いくつ（ですか）)

o-isha (san) *n* お医者（さん）doctor (= **isha** 医者)

o-itoko-san *n* おいとこ［従兄弟］さん (*your/ someone else's*) cousin (= **itoko** いとこ・従兄弟)

o-iwai *n* お祝い celebration (= **iwai** 祝い)

o-jama *n* お邪魔 (= **jama** 邪魔)：**O-jama deshō ga** お邪魔でしょうが Excuse me for interrupting/bothering you; **O-jama shimáshita** お邪魔しました Excuse me for having interrupted/ bothered you; **Ashita o-jama shimásu** 明日お邪魔します I will visit you tomorrow.

o-jíi-san *n* おじいさん・祖父さん grandfather (*family*) (= **jii-san** じいさん・祖父さん, **ojii-chan** おじいちゃん)

o-jíi-san *n* おじいさん・お爺さん (*not relative*) old (gentle-)man (= **jii-san** じいさん・爺さん, **ojii-chan** おじいちゃん)

o-kan *n* お燗 heating sake (= **kán** 燗)

o-kā´-san *n* お母さん・おかあさん mother [FORMAL] (= **kā´san** 母さん・かあさん, **ofukuro** お袋)

o-káshi *n* お菓子 confections, sweets, pastry, candy, cakes, cookies, biscuits (= **kashi** 菓子) (→ **wa-gáshi** 和菓子, **yō-gáshi** 洋菓子)

o-kawari *n* お変わり change (*in health*): **o-kawari arimasénka.** お変わりありませんか。Is everything all right? (*greeting*) (= **kawari** 変わり)

o-kayu *n* お粥・おかゆ gruel (*rice*) (= **kayu** 粥)

o-kome *n* お米 rice (*hulled, uncooked*) (= **kome** 米)

o-ko-san *n* お子さん (*your/someone else's*) child (= **ko** 子)

o-kyaku(-san/-sámá) *n* お客（さん/様）visitor; customer, patron (= **kyaku** 客)

o-kyō *n* お経 sutra (*Buddhist scripture*) (= **kyō** 経)

o-kyū *n* お灸 moxibustion (= **kyū** 灸)

o-matsuri *n* お祭り festival (= **matsuri** 祭り)

o-múko-san *n* お婿さん (*your/someone else's*) son-in-law; bridegroom (= **muko** 婿)

o-negai *n* お願い favor (*requested*), request (= **negai** 願い)：~ **shimásu** お願いします please

o-nē´-san *n* お姉さん older sister (= **nē´-san** 姉さん, **ane** 姉, **aneki** 姉貴)

o-níkai *n* お二階 upstairs (= **nikai** 二階)

o-níi-san *n* お兄さん older brother (= **níi-san** 兄さん, **ani** 兄, **aniki** 兄貴)

o-nō *n* お能 Noh (*Japanese classical theater*) (= **nō´** 能)

o-rei *n* お礼 an acknowledgement, a thank-you, a present (*of appreciation*) (= **rei** 礼); (*… ni*) **o-rei o iimásu** (…に) お礼を言います thanks

o-sáji *n* お匙 spoon (= **sájí** さじ・匙)

o-sake *n* お酒 saké (*Japanese rice wine*); liquor (= **sake** 酒)

o-saki ni *adv* お先に Excuse me for going first: **dó´zo o-saki ni** どうぞお先に, **o-saki ni dó´zo** お先にどうぞ Please go first; **o-saki ni shitsúrei shimásu** お先に失礼します Excuse me for being the first to leave

o-sénbei *n* お煎餅 rice crackers (= **sénbei** せんべい・煎餅)

o-séwa *n* お世話 care, assistance, help (= **sewá** 世話) (→ **o-sewa-sama** お世話様)

o-shirase *n* お知らせ report, notice, information (= **shirase** 知らせ)

o-shiri *n* お尻 buttock, hip (= **shiri** 尻)

o-shiro *n* お城 castle (= **shiro** 城)

O-shōgatsu *n* お正月 New Year; January (= **Shōgatsu** 正月)

o-soba *n* おそば・お側 near, close(-by), (be)side (= **sóba** 側)

o-soba *n* おそば・お蕎麦 buck-wheat (noodles) (= **sóba** そば・蕎麦)

o-sobaya *n* おそば［蕎麦］屋 noodle shop (= **sobá-ya** そば［蕎麦］屋)

o-sōshiki *n* お葬式 funeral (= **sōshiki** 葬式)

o-su *n* お酢 vinegar (= **sú** 酢)

o-sumō-san *n* お相撲さん sumo wrestler (= **sumō** 相撲, **rikishi** 力士)

o-súshi *n* お寿司・お鮨 = **súshi** すし・寿司・鮨 sushi (*rice seasoned with sweetend vinegar with raw fish*)

o-sushi-ya *n* お寿司［鮨］屋 = **sushí-ya** すし［寿司・鮨］屋 sushi bar

o-témae *n* お点前 tea ceremony procedures (= **temae** 点前)

o-ténki *n* お天気 **1.** weather (= **ténki** 天気) **2.** fair weather

o-tera *n* お寺 Buddhist temple (= **tera** 寺)

o-tō´-san *n* お父さん・おとうさん father (= **tō´san** 父さん・とうさん, **oyaji** 親父)

o-toshi *n* お年・お歳・(*your/someone else's*) age (= **toshi** 年・歳)

ó-tsuki-sama *n* お月さま・お月様 moon (= **tsukí** 月)

o-tsúmami *n* おつまみ appetizer (with drinks); finger food (= **tsumami** つまみ)

o-tsuri *n* おつり・お釣り change (*money returned*) (= **tsuri** つり・釣り)

o-tsutome *n* お勤め・お務め job, work(ing); duty, role (= **tsutome** 勤め・務め)

o-ukagai *n* お伺い visit; inquiry, consultation (= **ukagai** 伺い)

o-yakusho *n* お役所 government office (= **yakusho** 役所)

o-yakusoku *n* お約束 promise, agreement, appointment, engagement, date, commitment (= **yakusoku** 約束)

o-yásai *n* お野菜 vegetables (= **yasai** 野菜)

o-yasumi *n* お休み rest; holiday; recess; time off

(= **yasumí** 休み[INFORMAL], **kyūka** 休暇 [FORMAL])

o-yu *n* お湯 hot water (= **yu** 湯): **o-yu o wakashimásu** お湯を沸かします boils water

o-yome-san *n* お嫁さん (*your/someone else's*) bride (= **yome** 嫁)

o-zen *n* お膳 dining tray (= **zen** 膳)

o-zōni *n* お雑煮 rice cakes boiled with vegetables (*eaten as New Year's soup*) (= **zōni** 雑煮)

... o ...を particle: marks direct object (*gets what, loves whom*) or path traversed (*goes through/along where, using what path*)

ō´ *n* 王, **ō-sama** 王様 king

ō-chō *n* 王朝 royal dynasty

ō-dō *n* 王道 royal road: [IDIOM] **gakumon ni ōdō nashi** 学問に王道なし There is no royal road to learning.

ō-hi *n* 王妃 queen

ō-i keishō *n* 王位継承 succession to the throne

ō-ja *n* 王者 **1.** king: **riku no ōja raion** 陸の王者ライオン Lion King of the land **2.** champion: **sekai ōja** 世界王者 world champion **3.** ruler (= **hasha** 覇者)

ō-ji (-sama) *n* 王子(様) prince

ō-jo (-sama) *n* 王女(様) princess

ō-kan *n* 王冠 **1.** crown **2.** (**bin no ōkan** 瓶の王冠) bottle cap

ō-koku *n* 王国 kingdom

ō-sama *n* 王様 king

ō-shitsu *n* 王室 royal family

ō-... *prefix* 大... big, great

ō-áme *n* 大雨 heavy rain

ō-bune *n* 大船 large ship: [IDIOM] **ō-bune ni notta tsumoride itekudasai** 大船に乗ったつもりでいて下さい Please leave the matter to me and be at ease.

ō-buri *n* 大降り a downfall, heavy rain and/or snow: **ame/yuki ga ō-buri ni nattekimashita** 雨/雪が大降りになってきました It started raining/snowing heavier.

ō-buri *n* 大振り big swing

ō-buroshiki *n* 大風呂敷 very large square wrapping cloth: [IDIOM] **ō-buroshiki o hirogeru** 大風呂敷を広げる talks big, blows one's horn

ō-dáiko *n* 大太鼓 large drum

ō-dō´ri *n* 大通り main street, avenue

ō-fúbuki *n* 大吹雪 blizzard

ō-gara (na) *adj* 大柄(な) **1.** big, large (body, build) **2.** big, large patterns

ō-gata *n* 大型 large-size (*model*)

ō-gesa (na) *adj* おおげさ[大袈裟](な) exaggerated

ō´-góe (de) *adv* 大声(で) in a loud voice

ō-gosho *n* 大御所 leading figure, prominent figure: **bundan no ō-gosho** 文壇の大御所 prominent figure in the literary world: **seikai no ō-gosho** 政界の大御所 a political bigwig

ō-hiroma *n* 大広間 great hall

ō-ísogi (no/de) *adj, adv* 大急ぎ(の/で) (*in*) a great rush, a big hurry

ō-kaze *n* 大風 strong wind

ō´-mízú *n* 大水 flood (= **kōzui** 洪水)

ō-moji *n* 大文字 capital letter

ō-mono *n* 大物 a big shot

ō-mori *n* 大盛(り) large helping, large serving: **ō-mori de onegai shimásu** 大盛りでお願いします A large helping of it, please.

ō-ótoko *n* 大男 a giant of a man, big man

ō-saji *n* 大匙・大さじ tablespoon

ō-sáwagi *n* 大騒ぎ fuss, disturbance: ~ **shimásu** 大騒ぎします makes a fuss

ō-sōji *n* 大掃除 great cleaning: **nenmatsu no ō-sōji** 年末の大掃除 year-end cleaning

ō-uridashi *n* 大売出し big sale

ō-yasu-uri *n* 大安売り special bargain sale

ō-yórokobi (de) *adv* 大喜び(で) with great delight

ō-yuki *n* 大雪 heavy snow

ō-zúmō *n* 大相撲 a grand sumo tournament; an exciting match

ō-zora *n* 大空 big sky

oashisu *n* オアシス oasis

o-azuke *interj* お預け Wait! (*training one's dog*)

ō´bā *n* オーバー overcoat, (top) coat

o-báke *n* お化け・おばけ ghost, monster

ōbako *n* オオバコ (*plant*) plantain

ōbā(-kōto) *n* オーバー(コート) overcoat

ō´bā (na) *adj* オーバー(な) exaggerated, over(ly), too much

oba(-san) *n* おば[叔母](さん) aunt (*younger sister of father or mother*) (= **oba-chan** おば[叔母]ちゃん)

oba(-san) *n* おば[伯母](さん) aunt (*older sister of father or mother*) (= **oba-chan** おば[伯母]ちゃん)

oba(-san) *n* おば[小母]さん (*not relative*) lady, woman (*middle-aged*) (= **oba-chan** おばちゃん)

ō´bā shimásu (suru) *n* オーバーします(する) goes over, goes past: **jikan ga ō´bā shimásu** 時間がオーバーします runs overtime

Ōbei *n* 欧米 Europe and America: **Ōbei-shokoku** 欧米諸国 the various countries of Europe and America

obekka *n* おべっか flattery

óbi *n* 帯 girdle, sash, belt, (*Japanese*) obi

ōbii *n* オービー・OB **1.** (*abbreviation for the word "old boy"*) male graduate, alumnus **2.** (*abbreviation for the word "out of bounds"*) OB (*golf*)

obi-jō (no) *adj* 帯状(の) belt(-like), a narrow strip (*of*)

obitadashii *adj* おびただしい a great number of, immense, tremendous

ōbō (na) *adj* 横暴(な) high-handed, tyrannical

obóe *n* 覚え memory; consciousness

oboe-gaki *n* 覚(え)書(き) memo(-randum), note (= **bibóroku** 備忘録)

obóe *v* 覚え → **oboemásu** 覚えます [INFINITIVE]

oboemásu, obóeru *v* 覚えます, 覚える remembers, keeps in mind; learns

oboko (-músume) *n* おぼこ(娘) virgin (*female*)

144

oboremásu, oboreru v 溺れます, 溺れる drowns

ō'bo shimásu (suru) v 応募します(する) applies

obúi v 負ぶい → **obuimásu** 負ぶいます

obuimásu, obú v 負ぶいます, 負ぶう carries on one's back (= **seoimásu, shoimásu** 背負います)

ōbun n オーブン oven

oburāto n オブラート wafer paper

obutsu n 汚物 dirt

obútte v 負ぶって → **obuimásu** 負ぶいます

obuwánai v 負ぶわない = **obuimasén** 負ぶいません (not carry)

ōchaku (na) adj 横着(な) lazy: **ōchaku na taido** 横着な態度 lazy attitude

ochi n 落ち 1. omission, lack: **te-ochi** 手落ち oversight 2. punch line 3. the end, the result

óchi v 落ち → **ochimásu** 落ちます

ochimásu, ochíru v 落ちます, 落ちる falls, drops; is omitted; fails; is inferior **óchi-ba** n 落ち葉 fallen leaves

óchite v 落ちて → **ochimásu** 落ちます

ochi-tsuite 落ち着いて 1. adv calmly 2. v calm down!: **ochitsuite kudasai** 落ち着いて下さい Please calm down.

ochi tsukanai v 落ち着かない = **ochitsukimasén** 落ち着きません is restless

ochi-tsuki n 落ち着き: **ochitsuki ga aru (nai)** 落ち着きがある(ない) is calm; is restless

ochi-tsukimásu, ochi-tsuku v 落ち着きます, 落ち着く calms down, keeps cool, settles down, relaxes

o-chóko n おちょこ saké cup

o-chūgen n お中元 midyear present, summer gift

o-daiji ni interj お大事に: **(dōzo) o-daiji ni (shitekudasai)!** (どうぞ)お大事に(して下さい)! (Please) take care of yourself!

ōdāmeido n オーダーメイド made-to-order: **ōd'āmeido (no)** オーダーメイド(の) custom-made

ōdan n 黄疸 (medical) jaundice

ōdan n 横断 crossing, going across, intersecting: **ōdan-hodō** 横断歩道 pedestrian crossing

odate v おだて → **odatemásu** おだてます

odatemásu, odateru v おだてます, おだてる coaxes

odáyaka (na) adj 穏やか(な) quiet, calm, peaceful, gentle; moderate

odéko n おでこ forehead (= **hitai** 額)

o-dén n おでん assorted boiled foods (Japanese hot pot)

ōdio n オーディオ audio: **ōdio-mania** オーディオマニア audiophile, audio nut

ōdishon n オーディション audition

odokashimásu, odokasu v 脅かします, 脅かす threatens

odoranai v 踊らない = **odorimasén** 踊りません (not dance)

odoré v 踊れ [IMPERATIVE] (dance!) → **odorimásu** 踊ります

odoremásu, odoreru 踊れます, 踊れる can dance

odori n 踊り 1. dance, dancing 2. → **odorimásu** 踊ります [INFINITIVE]

odorimásu, odoru v 踊ります, 踊る dances

odoróite v 驚いて → **odorokimásu** 驚きます

odorokashimásu, odorokásu v 驚かします, 驚かす surprises, scares, astonishes

odorokimásu, odoróku v 驚きます, 驚く is surprised, astonished

odoshi n 脅し → **odoshimásu** 脅します [INFINITIVE]

odoshimásu, odosu v 脅します, 脅す threatens

odotte v 踊って → **odorimásu** 踊ります

oé v 終え → **oemásu** 終えます [INFINITIVE]; **oé ro** 終えろ [IMPERATIVE] (end it!) → **oemásu** 終えます

oé v 追え → **oemásu** 追えます [INFINITIVE]; [IMPERATIVE] (chase it!) → **oimásu** 追います

oé v 負え, 1. → **oemásu** 負えます [INFINITIVE] 2. **óe** [IMPERATIVE] (carry it (on your back)!) → **oimásu** 負います

ōe v 覆え → **ōemásu** 覆えます [INFINITIVE]

ō'e v 覆え [IMPERATIVE] (cover it!) → **ōimásu** 覆います

oéba v 追えば = **oya** 追や (if one chases) → **oimásu** 追います

oéba v 負えば = **oya** 負や (if one carries) → **oimásu** 負います

ō'éba v 覆えば (if one covers) → **ōimásu** 覆います

oemásu, oeru v 終えます, 終える ends it, finishes, completes

oemásu, oeru v 追えます, 追える can chase, can pursue

oemásu, oeru v 負えます, 負える can carry on one's back

ōemásu, ōéru v 覆えます, 覆える can cover

ōen n 応援 help, assistance; cheering for; support: ~ **shimásu** 応援します helps, assists; cheers for; supports

ōen-dan n 応援団 cheering party

oeréba v 終えれば・追えれば (if one ends it; if one can chase) → **oemásu** 終えます; 追えます

oeréba v 負えれば (if one can carry) → **oemásu** 負えます

ōeréba v 覆えれば (if one can cover) → **ōemásu** 覆えます

ōeru n オーエル office lady

oeta v 終えた・追えた = **oemáshita** 終えました; 追えました (ended it; could chase)

oeta v 負えた = **oemáshita** 負えました (could carry)

ō'eta v 覆えた = **ōemáshita** 覆えました (could cover)

oete v 終えて・追えて・負えて → **oemásu** 終えます; 追えます; 負えます

ō'ete v 覆えて → **ōemásu** 覆えます

oetsu n 嗚咽 sobbing: ~ **shimásu** 嗚咽します sobs

ofisu n オフィス office

ōfuku n 往復 round trip: ~ **shimásu** 往復します goes and returns ōf_u_ku-kíppu　*n* 往復切符 round-trip ticket:

ofukuro　*n* おふくろ・お袋 (*familiar, usually male*) (= **okā´-san** お母さん・おかあさん) **1.** my mother **2. ofukuro-san** お袋さん (*your/someone else's*) mother

ofureko (no)　*adj* オフレコ(の) off the record

ofu-shiizun　*n* オフシーズン off season (= **kansanki** 閑散期)

ogakuzu　*n* おが屑 sawdust

ogamimás_u_, ogámu　*v* 拝みます, 拝む worships, looks at with respect

ogánde　*v* 拝んで → **ogamimásu** 拝みます

ōganikku (no)　*adj* オーガニック(の) organic (= **yūki** 有機)

ogawa　*n* 小川 brook, stream

ógi　*n* オギ・荻 a reed

ōgí　*n* 扇 a folding fan

oginái　*n* 補い supplement

oginái　*v* 補い → **oginaimásu** 補います [INFINITIVE]

oginaimás_u_, ogináu　*v* 補います, 補う completes; complements, makes good, makes up for

ōgon　*n* 黄金 gold (= **kin** 金)

ogorimás_u_, ogoru　*v* 驕ります, 驕る is extravagant

ogorimás_u_, ogoru　*v* 奢ります, 奢る treats (*pays the bill*)

ogotte　*v* おごって → **ogorimásu** おごります

ohako　*n* おはこ・十八番 one's hobby; one's "thing", specialty, (*favorite*) trick

O-hayō (gozaimás_u_)　*interj* おはよう(ございます) Good morning!

ōhei　*n* 横柄 arrogance (= **gōman** 傲慢・ごうまん): ōhei na taido 横柄な態度 insolence

o-hína sama　*n* おひな[雛]様 (*Dolls Festival*) dolls

o-hi-sama　*n* お日様 sun (*baby talk*)

o-h_i_táshi　*n* お浸し boiled greens (*usually spinach, served cold with seasoning*)

o-h_i_tsu　*n* お櫃・おひつ rice bucket/tub (= **o-hachi** お鉢, **meshi-bitsu** 飯びつ)

o-híya　*n* お冷や cold water

Ohōtsuku-kai　*n* オホーツク海 Sea of Okhotsk

oi　*n* 甥 nephew

oi-go-san　*n* 甥御さん (*your/someone else's*) nephew

oi-kko　*n* 甥っ子 nephew (= **oi** 甥)

oi　*v* 追い → **oimásu** 追います

oi　*v* 負い → **oimásu** 負います [INFINITIVE]

oi　*v* 老い → **oimásu** 老います

ói　*interj* おい hey! (*mostly male, very* INFORMAL)

ō´i　*v* 覆い・おおい → **ōimásu** 覆います・おおいます [INFINITIVE]

ō´i　*adj* 多い many, numerous; lots
ō´ku　*adv* 多く a lot of, many

oide　*interj* おいで Come! (*training one's dog, etc.*)

oide (ni narimás_u_)　*v* おいで(になります) = **irasshaimás_u_** いらっしゃいます [HONORIFIC] **1.** comes **2.** goes **3.** is, stays

oi-káke　*v* 追い掛け → **oikakemásu** 追い掛けます [INFINITIVE]

oi-kakemás_u_, oi-kakéru　*v* 追い掛けます, 追い掛ける chases

oi-kosh_i_más_u_, oi-kósu　*v* 追い越します, 追い越す (*overtakes and*) passes

oimás_u_, ou　*v* 追います, 追う chases, pursues
oi-kaze　*n* 追い風 tail wind

oi-kosh_i_　*n* 追い越し Passing: **oi-koshi kinshi** 追い越し禁止 No Passing: **oi-koshi shasen** 追い越し車線 passing line

oimás_u_, ou　*v* 負います, 負う carries on one's back

oimás_u_, oiru　*v* 老います, 老いる grows old

ōimás_u_, oou´, ōu´　*v* 覆います, 覆う covers, shields

ōin　*n* 押韻 [BOOKISH] rhyme (= **in** 韻)

ōin　*n* 押印 [BOOKISH] putting one's seal: **~ shimás_u_** 押印します seals

ōi ni　*adv* おおいに・大いに very, greatly (= **hijō ni** 非常に, **totemo** とても)

óiru　*n* オイル oil (*for car engine*)

oishii　*adj* おいしい・美味しい tasty, nice, delicious, yummy (= **umai** うま[旨・美味]い)

oishisō　*adj* おいしそう looks tasty/nice/delicious/yummy (= **umasō** うま[旨・美味]そう)

oisoreto　*adj* おいそれと [(*usually*) + NEGATIVE verb] easily, quickly

oita　*v* 置いた = **okimásh_i_ta** 置きました (put) […-te óita …て置いた]

oitachi　*n* 生い立ち (*one's*) personal history

oitára　*v* 置いたら (if/when one puts) […-te óitara …て置いたら] → **okimásu** 置きます

oitári　*v* 置いたり (sometimes putting) […-te óitari …て置いたり] → **okimásu** 置きます

oite　*v* 置いて (puts) […-te óite …て置いて] → **okimásu** 置きます

oite　おいて: **… ni oite** … において [BOOKISH] = **… de** …で (at/in)

o-itoma　*n* お暇 leave-taking, farewell: O-itoma (ita-)shimás_u_ お暇(致)します I will take my leave.

oi-tsukimás_u_, oi-tsukú　*v* 追い付きます, 追い付く (**… ni** …に) catches up (*with*), overtakes

oí ya/wa shinai　*v* 追いや/はしない, oya shinai 追やしない = **owanai** 追わない (not chase)

ō´í ya/wa shinai　*v* 覆いや/はしない, ō ya shinai 覆やしない = **ōwanai** 覆わない (not cover)

o-jigi　*n* お辞儀 a polite bow: ojigi o shimás_u_ お辞儀をします bows

ōjii　*n* オージー (*abbreviation for the word "old girl"*) female graduate, alumna

ō-jimás_u_, ō-jiru　*v* 応じます, 応じる responds (*to*), accedes (*to*), complies (*with*)

ōji (-sama)　*n* 皇子(様) emperor's son

oji (-san)　*n* おじ[叔父](さん) uncle (*younger brother of father or mather*) (= **oji-chan** おじ[叔父]ちゃん)

oji (-san)　*n* おじ[伯父](さん) uncle (*older brother of father or mather*) (= **oji-chan** おじ[伯父]ちゃん)

oji (-san)　*n* おじ[小父]さん (*not relative*) (gentle)man, (*middle-aged*) man (= **oji-chan** おじちゃん)

146

ō-jite *v* 応じて → **ō-jimás̲u** 応じます; **… ni ō-jite** …に応じて in accordance/compliance with …

ojoku *n* 汚辱 disgrace, shame, scandal

ōjo (-sama) *n* 皇女(様) emperor's daughter

ojō-san *n* お嬢さん a young lady; (*your/someone else's*) daughter; Miss

o-jū´ *n* お重 = **jūbako** 重箱 (nested boxes; picnic boxes)

oka *n* 丘 hill

oka *n* 陸 dry land

okabu *n* お株 = **ohako** おはこ・十八番 (specialty, habit)

O-kaeri nasái! *interj* お帰りなさい! Welcome back!

okage *n* おかげ・お蔭・お陰; **… no okage de …** …のおかげ[お蔭・お陰]で thanks to …

okage-sama (de) おかげさま(で) thanks to your solicitude; thank you (*I'm very well* or *it's going very nicely*)

ōkakumaku *n* 横隔膜 diaphragm

O-kamai náku *interj* お構いなく. Don't go to any trouble.

okáme *n* おかめ moon faced/ugly woman

okámi *n* 御上・お上 the authorities, the government

okámi *n* おかみ・女将 = **okami-san** おかみ[女将]さん landlady; married woman, (*your/someone else's*) wife (= **oku-san/sama** 奥さん/様)

ō´kami *n* オオカミ・狼 wolf

okanai *v* 置かない = **okimasén** 置きません (not put)

o-kara *n* オカラ bean-curd lees

ōkare sukunakare *adv* 多かれ少なかれ more or less

okaruto *n* オカルト occult: **okaruto-eiga** オカルト映画 occult film(s)

okasánai *v* 犯さない = **okasimasén** 犯しません・(not violate)

okasánai *v* 侵さない = **okasimasén** 侵しません (not invade)

okasánai *v* 冒さない = **okasimasén** 冒しません (not braves/attacks)

okashi *v* 犯し → **okashimás̲u** 犯します [INFINITIVE]

okashi *v* 侵し → **okashimás̲u** 侵します [INFINITIVE]

okashi *v* 冒し → **okashimás̲u** 冒します [INFINITIVE]

okashíi *adj* おかしい, **okáshi na (…)** おかしな (…) **1.** amusing, funny **2.** strange, peculiar, queer

okashimás̲u, okásu *v* 犯します, 犯す commits, perpetrates; violates

okashimás̲u, okásu *v* 侵します, 侵す encroaches upon, invades

okashimás̲u, okásu *v* 冒します, 冒す braves; attacks

ōkata *adv* おおかた・大方 **1.** for the most part **2.** probably

o-káwari *n* お代わり a second helping (*usually of rice*)

o-kazari *n* お飾り (→ **kazari** 飾り) **1.** decorations and/or offerings to the gods and Buddha **2.** New Year's decorations **3.** mere figurehead: **ano ō(-sama) wa o-kazari ni sugimasen** あの王(様)はお飾りに過ぎません That king is nothing but a figurehead.

okazu *n* おかず main/side dish (*to go with the rice*)

oké *v* 置け **1.** → **okemás̲u** 置けます [INFINITIVE] **2.** [IMPERATIVE] (put it!) → **okimás̲u** 置きます

óke *n* 桶 tub, wooden bucket: **furo-oke** 風呂桶 bathtub. **kan-oke** 棺桶 coffin [INFORMAL] (= **hitsugi** 棺)

ōkē *n* オーケー okay, ok

okéba *v* 置けば (if one puts) → **okimás̲u** 置きます

okemás̲u, okeru *v* 置けます, 置ける can put

okenai *v* 置けない = **okemasén** 置けません (cannot put)

okeréba *v* 置ければ (if one can put) → **okemás̲u** 置けます

ōkesutora *n* オーケストラ orchestra

oki *n* 沖 offshore, offing

oki *v* 置き → **okimás̲u** 置きます (puts) [INFINITIVE]

oki-ba *n* 置き場 a place (*to put something*)

oki-miyage *n* 置き土産 keepsake, parting present/gift (= **senbetsu** 餞別)

oki-mono *n* 置き物 ornament; bric-a-brac

oki-tegami *n* 置き手紙 letter/note left behind: **oki-tegami o shimás̲u** 置き手紙をします leaves someone a note

óki *v* 起き → **okimás̲u** 起きます (gets up) **1.** [INFINITIVE] **2.** okí ro 起きろ, óki yo 起きよ [IMPERATIVE] (get up!)

ō-kíi *adj* 大きい big, large; loud (= **ō´ki na** 大きな) **ō´-kiku** *adv* 大きく greatly, much(ly), loudly; so as to be big/loud: **ō´k̲iku nái (arimasén)** 大きくない(ありません) small, modest

ō-ki (na) *adj* 大き(な) big, great

okimás̲u, oku *v* 置きます, 置く puts (*aside*), places, sets, lays; **shite okimás̲u** して置きます does for later, does for now (*for the time being*)

okimás̲u, okíru *v* 起きます, 起きる gets up; arises

okina *n* 翁 old man,

okínai *v* 起きない = **okimasén** 起きません (not get up; not arise)

o-ki-ni-iri *n* お気に入り favorite: **kono pēji o o-ki-ni-iri ni tsuikashimás̲u** このページをお気に入りに追加します bookmarks this page (as a favorite) (*web browser*): **o-ki-ni-iri o seirishimás̲u** お気に入りを整理します organizes bookmarks (*web browser*): **o-ki-ni-iri no terebi-bangumi wa nandesuka?** お気に入りのテレビ番組は何ですか? What is your favorite TV program?

okiraremás̲u, okiraréru *v* 起きられます, 起きられる can get up

okíreba *v* 起きれば (if one gets up; if it arises) → **okimás̲u** 起きます

147

okíru *v* 起きる = **okimásu** 起きます (gets up; arises)

ōkisa *n* 大きさ size (= **saizu** サイズ): **ōkisa o hakattekudasai** 大きさを測って下さい Please measure the size.

ókita *v* 起きた = **okimáshita** 起きました (got up)

okite *n* 掟 law, rule, regulation: **okite o mamorimásu** 掟を守ります observes a rule: **okite o yaburimásu** 掟を破ります breaks a rule

ókite *v* 起きて → **okimásu** 起きます

okiwasuréru *v* 置き忘れる forgets

óki ya/wa shinai *v* 起きや/はしない = **okínai** 起きない (not get up; not arise)

okí ya/wa shinai *v* 置きや/はしない = **okanai** 置かない (not put)

okiyō´ *v* 起きよう = **okimashō´** 起きましょう (let's get up!)

okkochimásu, okkochíru *v* 落っこちます, 落っこちる falls

okkū (na) *adj* 億劫(な) troublesome, bothersome

okō *v* 置こう = **okimashō´** 置きましょう (let's put it!)

ōkō (suru) *adj* 横行(する) rampant

okonai 行い **1.** *n* act(ion), deed, conduct: **higoro no okonai** 日ごろの行い daily behavior **2.** *v* → **okonaimásu** 行います [INFINITIVE]

okonaimásu, okonau *v* 行います, 行う acts, does, carries out, performs

okonatte *v* 行(な)って → **okonaimásu** 行(な)います

okonawanai *v* 行(な)わない = **okonaimásén** 行(な)いません (not act)

okonomi-yaki *n* お好み焼き seasoned pancake

okorí *v* 起こり origin, source, beginning: **koto no okori (wa)…** 事の起こり(は)… it happened because…, it started like this…

okorí *n* おこり ague, the shakes

okóri *v* 起こり → **okorimásu** 起こります [INFINITIVE]

okóri *v* 怒り → **okorimásu** 怒ります [INFINITIVE]

okorimásu, okóru *v* 起こります, 起こる happens, occurs, arises; springs from

okorimásu, okóru *v* 興ります, 興る starts; prospers; rises

okorimásu, okóru *v* 怒ります, 怒る gets mad/angry

okoshimásu, okósu *v* 起こします, 起こす raises; establishes; gets a person up, rouses

okoshimásu, okósu *v* 興します, 興す gives rise to, brings about

okotarimásu, okotaru *v* 怠ります, 怠る neglects, shirks; is lazy about

okótta *v* 起こった = **okorimáshita** 起こりました (happened)

okótta *v* 怒った = **okorimáshita** 怒りました (got mad)

okótte *v* 起こって → **okorimásu** 起こります

okótte *v* 怒って → **okorimásu** 怒ります

oku *v* 置く = **okimásu** 置きます (put)

óku *n* 億 a hundred million: **oku-man chōja** 億万長者 a billionaire

óku *n* 奥 the back or inside part

óku-ba *n* 奥歯 back tooth

oku-… *prefix* 屋… house, roof

oku-gai (no/de) *adj, adv* 屋外(の/で) outdoor(s), outside

oku-jō (no/de) *adj, adv* 屋上(の/で) on the roof(top), rooftop floor

oku-nai (no/de) *adj, adv* 屋内(の/で) indoor(s), inside, interior(ly)

ō´ku 多く **1.** *n* a lot, for the most part **2.** *adv* mostly

okubi *n* おくび belch

okubyō´ *n* 臆病 cowardice: **okubyō´ (na)** 臆病(な) cowardly, timid; **okubyō-mónó** 臆病者 a coward (= **kowagari** 怖[恐]がり): **okubyō´ (mono) desu** 臆病(者)です is a coward

okuranai *v* 送らない = **okurimásén** 送りません (not send)

okure *n* 後れ **1.** 後れ a lag: **okure o torimásu** 後れを取ります falls behind, gets defeated

okure *v* 遅れ → **okuremásu** 遅れます [INFINITIVE]

okure *v* 送れ [IMPERATIVE] (send it!) → **okurimásu** 送ります

o-kure *v* おくれ [HONORIFIC INFINITIVE of **kudasái** 下さい, *used as a command*] please give (*it to me*)

okuremásu, okureru *v* 遅れます, 遅れる is late, gets delayed; lags, falls behind; runs late

okuremásu, okureru *v* 送れます, 送れる can send; can spend (time)

okuremásu, okureru *v* 贈れます, 贈れる can present/award

okurenai *v* 遅れない = **okuremasén** 遅れません (is not late)

okurenai *v* 送れない = **okuremasén** 送れません (cannot send)

okurete *v* 遅れて → **okuremásu** 遅れます

okurete *v* 送れて → **okuremásu** 送れます

okuri *v* 送り → **okurimásu** 送ります [INFINITIVE]

okuri *v* 贈り → **okurimásu** 贈ります [INFINITIVE]

okurimásu, okuru *v* 送ります, 送る sends; sees a person off; spends (*time*)

okurimásu, okuru *v* 贈ります, 贈る presents, awards

okuri-mono *n* 贈り物 gift, present

okurō´ *v* 送ろう = **okurimashō** 送りましょう (let's send it!)

óku-san/-sama *n* 奥さん/様 (*your/someone else's*) wife; lady, Madam

okusoku *n* 憶測 guess

okutte *v* 送って → **okurimásu** 送ります

okutte *v* 贈って → **okurimásu** 贈ります

ō-kyū *n* 応急 emergency

ōkyū-shochi *n* 応急処置 first aid (= **ōkyū-téate** 応急手当て)

ōkyū-sochi *n* 応急措置 emergency measure

ōkyū-téate *n* 応急手当て first aid (= **ōkyū-shochi** 応急処置)

148

okuyami *n* お悔やみ condolences

O-machidō-sama déshita *interj* お待ちどうさまでした. Thank you for waiting. (*at restaurant, etc.*)

omae *pron* お前 (*mostly male. familiar or rude*) you

omake *n* おまけ extra, bonus, premium: **omake ni** おまけに to boot, in addition

o-mamori *n* お守り amulet, charm, good-luck piece

omaru *n* おまる bedpan; chamber-pot

O-matase (ita)shimáshita *interj* お待たせ(致)しました. Sorry to have made you wait.

omáwari (-san) *n* お巡り(さん)・おまわり(さん) policeman, (*police*) officer

o-me *n* お目: **o-me ni kakarimásu** お目にかかります I meet/see you; **o-me ni kakemásu** お目にかけます I show it to you

ō-medama o kuimásu (kū) *v* 大目玉を食います(食う) gets severely scolded, gets it in the neck

omedeta *n* おめでた blessed event (*pregnancy, childbirth, marriage, etc.*)

o-medetō (gozaimásu) *interj* おめでとう(ございます) congratulations: **akemáshite o-medetō (gozaimásu)** 明けましておめでとう(ございます) Happy New Year!

omei *n* 汚名 disgrace

ōme ni mimásu (miru) *v* 大目に見ます(見る) overlooks (= **minogashimásu** 見逃します): **(dōka) ōme ni mitekudasai** (どうか)大目に見て下さい Please give me a break.

o-meshi ni narimásu (náru) *v* お召しになります(なる) [HONORIFIC] **1.** wears **2.** buys **3.** invites **4. kaze o o-meshi ni narimásu** 風邪をお召しになります catches a cold

o-mi- *prefix* おみ (*for a few words*) = **o-** お・御 [HONORIFIC]

o-mi-ki *n* 御神酒 saké offered to the gods (= **miki** 神酒)

o-mí-koshi *n* お神輿 portable shrine (= **mikoshi** 神輿)

o-mi-kuji *n* おみくじ fortune (*written*)

ō-mísoka *n* 大晦日 last day of year; New Year's eve

o-miya *n* お宮 shrine (*Shinto shrine*)

o-miyage *n* おみやげ・お土産, **o-míya** おみや (*baby talk*) gift, present (*as souvenir*) (= **miyage** みやげ)

omo-... *prefix* 面... face
omo-naga (na/no) *adj* 面長(な/の) long-faced
...(na) omo-mochi *suffix*, *n* ...(な)面持ち a look on one's face: **fuan na omo-mochi** 不安な面持ち a worried look on one's face; **kinchō no omo-mochi** 緊張の面持ち a nervous look on one's face
omo-yatsure *n* 面やつれ drawn and haggard face (*due to worry and/or illness*) (= **omo-yase** 面痩せ)

omócha *n* おもちゃ・オモチャ・玩具 toy

omóe *v* 思え **1.** → **omoemásu** 思えます [INFINITIVE] **2.** [IMPERATIVE] (think!) → **omoimásu** 思います

omóeba *v* 思えば = **omóya** 思や (if one thinks) → **omoimásu** 思います

omoemásu, omoéru *v* 思えます, 思える **1.** can think **2.** = **omowaremásu** 思われます (is thought)

omoi *adj* 重い heavy; grave, serious; important

omói *n* 思い **1.** thought, idea; feeling, mind, heart; desire, will **2.** → **omoimásu** 思います [INFINITIVE]

omoi-dashimásu, omoi-dásu *v* 思い出します, 思い出す remembers, recalls
omoide *n* 思い出 memory (*a recollection*)

omoigakénai *v* 思いがけない unexpected, surprising

omoimásu, omóu *v* 思います, 思う thinks, feels

omói ya/wa shinai *v* 思いや/はしない = **omowánai** 思わない (not think)

omomuki *n* 趣 **1.** taste, flavor **2.** atmosphere, air **3.** circumstance, contents **4.** condition

omoya *n* 母屋 main building/house

omoi-yari *n* おもいやり consideration (*being kind*), solicitude

ómo (na) *adj* 主(な) principal, main: **ómo ni** 主に mainly

omo-ni *n* 重荷 burden (*on one's mind*)

omosa *n* 重さ weight

omoshi *n* 重し a weight (*object*)

omoshirói *adj* おもしろい・面白い interesting, pleasant, amusing, funny

omoté *n* 表 front (*side*), surface, outer side/surface
omote-dōri *n* 表通り main street
omote-mon *n* 表門 (*front*) gate
omote-muki (no/wa) *adj, adv* 表向き(の/は) ostensible (*ostensibly*), on the surface, official(ly)

omótta *v* 思った = **omoimáshita** 思いました (thought)

omótte *v* 思って → **omoimásu** 思います

omóu *v* 思う → **omoimásu** 思います (thinks)

omowánai *v* 思わない = **omoimasén** 思いません (not think)

omowánu ... *adj* 思わぬ...; unexpected, unanticipated

omowáre *v* 思われ → **omowaremásu** 思われます [INFINITIVE]

omowaremásu, omowaréru *v* 思われます, 思われる is thought; seems, appears

omowasemásu, omowaséru *v* 思わせます, 思わせる reminds one of, makes one think of

omóya *v* 思や → **omóeba** 思えば

ōmu *n* オウム・鸚鵡 parrot

ō-mugi *n* オオムギ・大麦 barley

omunibasu *n* オムニバス omnibus: **omunibasu-eiga** オムニバス映画 omnibus film/movie

omu-ráisu *n* オムライス omelet wrapped around rice

omuretsu *n* オムレツ omelet

omútsu *n* おむつ diapers

on *n* 音 sound; pronunciation

on-kyō n 音響 sound: **onkyō-kōka** 音響効果 sound effect

on-pa n 音波 sound wave

on-ritsu n 音律 rhythm

on-ryō n 音量 sound volume: **onryō o agete-kudasai** 音量を上げて下さい Please turn up the volume.: **onryō o sagetekudasai** 音量を下げて Please turn down the volume.

on-sa n 音叉 tuning fork

on-setsu n 音節 syllable

on-tei n 音程 musical interval

on-yomi n 音読み Chinese reading of kanji/ Chinese character in Japanese

on- prefix 御 (for a few words) = **o-** お・御 [HONORIFIC]: **on-sha** 御社 (letter) (your) good self, your esteemed institution/organization; **on-zōshi** 御曹司/御曹子 scion; ... **on-chū** ... 御中 (letter) Dear ...; **on-rei mōshiagemasu** 御礼申し上げます Thank you ... for ...

ón n 恩 (**go-ón** ご恩) obligation; kindness: **go-ón wa isshō wasuremasen** ご恩は一生忘れません I will never forget what you have done for me/your kindness.

on-gaeshi n 恩返し returning the favour, repaying the favour

on-jin n 恩人 benefactor: **inochi no onjin** 命の恩人 person to whom one owes his/her life

ón ni kimásu, ón ni kiru v 恩に着ます, 恩に着る I appreciate it. I am deeply grateful.

ón ni kisemásu, ón ni kiseru v 恩に着せます, 恩に着せる emphasizes the favor one has done: **on-kisegamashii** 恩着せがましい condescending, patronizing

on-shi n 恩師 former teacher

ōnā n オーナー owner

onaji (...) adj 同じ(...) the same (...): **onaji yō´ (na)** 同じよう(な) alike, similar

o-naka n お腹 stomach: **onaka ga sukimáshita** おなかがすきました is hungry; **onaka no guai ga warúi** おなかの具合が悪い has an upset stomach; **onaka o kowashimásu** おなかを壊します develops stomach trouble

onani n オナニー masturbation (= **jii** 自慰)

onara n おなら flatulence, fart

ónbu shimásu (suru) v おんぶします(する) carries baby on back; rides on back

onchū n 御中 [HONORIFIC] Messrs. (on envelope)

óndo n 温度 temperature; **ondo-kei** 温度計 thermometer

ondori n オンドリ・雄鶏 rooster

ōnetsu-byō n 黄熱病 (medical) yellow fever

óngaku n 音楽 music

ongak(u)-ka n 音楽家 musician

ongák(u)-kai n 音楽会 concert

oní n 鬼 **1.** demon, devil, ogre **2.** cruel, cold, and/ or heartless person **3.** fiend, person who devotes all his/her energy: **shigoto no oní** 仕事の鬼 a workaholic

oní-baba n 鬼婆 hag

oní-gokko n 鬼ごっこ tag (child game)

oní ni kanabō 鬼に金棒 [IDIOM] A good condition makes the strong much stronger.

oni no inuma ni sentaku 鬼のいぬ間に洗濯 [IDIOM] When the cat's away, the mice will play.

oni no me nimo namida 鬼の目にも涙 [IDIOM] Even the hardest heart will sometimes be moved to pity.

onkei n 恩恵 favor

onná n 女, **onna no hitó/katá** 女の人/方 woman, female; **onna no kyō´dai** 女のきょうだい sister(s) (= **shímai** 姉妹)

onna-gata n 女形, **oyáma** おやま・女形 female impersonator (in Kabuki)

onna-gokoro n 女心 woman's heart

onna-jotai n 女所帯 all female household

onna-kotoba n 女言葉 woman's language

onna-mono n 女物 women's wear

onná-no-ko n 女の子 girl (= **joshi** 女子)

onna-shújin n 女主人 hostess

onna-tárashi n 女たらし womanizer, Don Juan, Casanova, lady-killer, seducer

onna-yu n 女湯 women's (section of the) bath

óno n 斧 ax, hatchet

onóono adj 各々・おのおの each, respectively, severally; **onóono no** 各々の respective

onore n おのれ self [BOOKISH]

onozukara adv 自ずから automatically, spontaneously

onparēdo n オンパレード on parade, succession

onrain n オンライン online

onrain ōkushon n オンライン・オークション (= **netto ōkushon** ネット・オークション) online auction

onrain gēmu n オンラインゲーム online game (internet)

onrain shōsetsu n オンライン小説 online story

onrain tsūhan saito n オンライン通販サイト online shopping site

onryō n 怨霊 vengeful ghost/spirit

onsen n 温泉 hot spring; spa: **onsen-ryokō** 温泉旅行 hot spring trip: **onsen-ryōhō** 温泉療法 spa treatment: **onsen-ryokan** 温泉旅館 Japanese inn and hot-spring

onshin n 音信 contact, news: **onshin futsū desu** 音信不通です is out of contact, lost touch with

onshitsu n 温室 greenhouse

onsui n 温水 warm water

onwa n 温和 **1.** mild, moderate (climate) **2.** gentle, quiet, calm and peaceful person

on za rokku n オンザロック on the rocks (whiskey, etc.)

onzōshi n 御曹司 son of a noble/distinguished family

oō v 追おう = **oimashō´** 追いましょう (let's chase!)

oō´ v 負おう = **oimashō´** 負いましょう (let's carry it!)

oou´, ōu´ v 覆おう = **ōimashō´** 覆いましょう (let's cover it!)

opekku _n_ オペック Organization of Petroleum Exporting Countries, OPEC

ópera _n_ オペラ opera

óppai _n_ おっぱい (= (o-)chichí (お)乳 (_baby talk, slang_)) breast; milk (= chíbusa, nyūbō 乳房)

ōˊpun _n_ オープン open: ~ shimásu オープンします (_a shop, an event_) opens

ōˊpun na _adj_ オープンな open, candid

ōra _n_ オーラ aura: ōra ga arimásu オーラがあります has radiance

ōrai _n_ 往来 traffic; communication; thoroughfare

ōˊrai _n_ オーライ "all right, OK", (_all clear, go ahead_)

ōraka (na) _adj_ おおらか(な) generous, big-hearted, easygoing: ōraka na seikaku おおらかな性格 generous personality

oránai _v_ おらない = orimasén おりません (not stay)

oránai _v_ 折らない = orimasén 折りません (not break/fold/bend)

oránai _v_ 織らない = orimasén 織りません (not weave)

Oranda _n_ オランダ Holland; (= Oranda no オランダの) Dutch

Oranda-go _n_ オランダ語 Dutch (_language_)
Oranda-jin _n_ オランダ人 a Dutch

ore _pron_ おれ・俺 (_male, unrefined_) I/me

óre _v_ 1. 折れ → oremásu 折れます [INFINITIVE] 2. 折れ [IMPERATIVE] (break/fold/bend it!) → orimásu 折ります

óre _v_ 1. 織れ → oremásu 織れます [INFINITIVE] 2. 織れ [IMPERATIVE] (weave it!) → orimásu 織ります

óreba _v_ 居れば = [INFORMAL] órya 居りゃ (if one be/stays) → orimásu 居ります

óreba _v_ 折れば (if one breaks it) → orimásu 折ります

óreba _v_ 織れば (if one weaves it) → orimásu 織ります

oremásu, oréru _v_ 折れます, 折れる 1. it breaks; it folds 2. can break/fold/bend it

oremásu, oréru _v_ 織れます, 織れる can weave it

orénai _v_ 折れない = oremasén 折れません (not break/fold; cannot break it)

orénai _v_ 織れない = oremasén 織れません (cannot weave it)

orénji _n_ オレンジ orange

orenji-jūˊsú _n_ オレンジジュース orange juice/drink

oréreba _v_ 折れれば (if it breaks; if one can break it) → oremásu 折れます

oréreba _v_ 織れれば (if one can weave it) → oremásu 織れます

oresen-gurafu _n_ 折れ線グラフ line graph

órete _v_ 折れて・織れて → oremásu 折れます・織れます

óre ya/wa shinai _v_ 折れや/はしない = orénai 折れない (not break/fold; cannot break it)

óre ya/wa shinai _v_ 織れや/はしない = orénai 織れない (cannot weave it)

ori _n_ おり・澱 dregs, sediment

orí _n_ 檻 cage; jail

orí _n_ 折 time, occasion

óri _v_ 居り → orimásu 居ります [INFINITIVE]

óri _v_ 折り → orimásu 折ります [INFINITIVE]

óri _v_ 織り → orimásu 織ります [INFINITIVE]

óri _v_ 下り 1. → orimásu 下ります [INFINITIVE] 2. [IMPERATIVE] orí ro 下りろ, óri yo 下りよ (get down!) → orimásu 下ります

orientēringu _n_ オリエンテーリング orienteering

orientēshon _n_ オリエンテーション orientation

orígami _n_ おりがみ・折り紙 paper-folding (art)

oríibu _n_ オリーブ olive

oriibu-yu/-oiru オリーブ油/オイル olive oil

orimásu, óru _v_ 居ります, 居る [DEFERENTIAL/HUMBLE] is, stays (= imásu 居ます, iru 居る)

orimásu, óru _v_ 折ります, 折る breaks (_folds, bends_) it

ori-mé _n_ 折り目 fold, crease, pleat

orimásu, óru _v_ 織ります, 織る weaves it

ori-mono _n_ 織物 cloth, textile, fabric

orimásu, oríru _v_ 下ります, 下りる goes down

orimásu, oríru _v_ 降ります, 降りる gets down, gets off (_a ship/plane_), gets out (_of a car_)

ori-mono _n_ おりもの vaginal discharge

orínai _v_ 下りない = orimasén 下りません (not go down)

orínai _v_ 降りない = orimasén 降りません (not get down)

oriraremásu, oriraréru _v_ 下り[降り]られます, 下り[降り]られる can get down

orirárereba _v_ 下り[降り]られれば (if one can get down) → oriraremásu 下り[降り]られます

orirárete _v_ 下り[降り]られて → oriraremásu 下りられます・降りられます

oríreba _v_ 下りれば (if it go down) → orimásu 下ります

oríreba _v_ 降り[下り]れば (if one gets down) → orimásu 降り[下り]ます

órita _v_ 下りた = orimáshita 下りました (went down)

órita _v_ 降りた = orimáshita 降りました (got down)

ori-tatamimásu, ori-tatamu _v_ 折り畳みます, 折り畳む folds up

órite _v_ 下りて → orimásu 下ります

órite _v_ 降りて → orimásu 降ります

óri ya/wa shinai _v_ 下りや/はしない = orínai 下りない (not get down)

óri ya/wa shinai _v_ 降りや/はしない = orínai 降りない (not get down)

óri ya/wa shinai _v_ 折りや/はしない = or/らない (not break/fold/bend it)

óri ya/wa shinai _v_ 織りや/はしない = 織らない (not weave it)

oriyōˊ _v_ 降りよう = orimashōˊ 降りましょう (let's get down)

orōˊ _v_ 折ろう = orimashōˊ 折りましょう (let's break/fold/bend it!)

orō´ v 織ろう = **orimashō´** 織りましょう (let's weave it!)

óroka adj 愚か [BOOKISH] foolish (= **baka na** 馬鹿な)

ōrora n オーロラ aurora

oróse v 下ろせ [IMPERATIVE] (lower it!) → **oroshimásu** 下ろします

oroshí v おろし **1.** a grater (= **oroshí-gane** おろし金) **2.** (something) grated: **daikon-óroshi** 大根おろし] grated radish

oróshi v 下ろし → **oroshimásu** 下ろします [INFINITIVE]

oróshi v 降ろし → **oroshimásu** 降ろします [INFINITIVE]

oroshí-gane n 下ろし金 grater

oroshimásu, orósu v 下ろします, 下ろす takes down, lowers; unloads; invests; **yokin o oroshimásu** 預金を下ろします withdraws (deposited money)

oroshimásu, orósu v 降ろします, 降ろす lets one off (a ship/plane), drops off (from a car), lets out (of a car)

oroshimásu, orósu v 堕ろします, 堕ろす aborts, has an abortion

óroshi (no/de) adj, adv 卸(の/で) wholesale

óroshi-uri n 卸し売り (selling) wholesale: ~ **shimásu** 卸し売りします sells wholesale, wholesales

oróshi ya/wa shinai v 下ろしや/はしない = **orosánai** 下ろさない (not lower)

oróshi ya/wa shinai v 降ろしや/はしない = **orosánai** 降ろさない (not drop off)

orosō´ v 下ろそう = **oroshimashō´** 下ろしましょう (let's take it down/drop off!)

óru v おる = **orimásu** おります

óru v 折る = **orimásu** 折ります

óru v 織る = **orimásu** 織ります

ōrudo misu n オールドミス old maid, spinster

orugōru n オルゴール music box

ōru maitii adj オールマイティ almighty **1.** the ace of spades (card game) **2.** all-around (= **zennō** 全能)

ōru-naito adj オールナイト all-night (= **shūya** 終夜): **ōru-naito eigyō** オールナイト営業 Open all night; **ōru-naito kōgyō** オールナイト興行 all-night show

ōryō n 横領 embezzlement

osaemásu, osáeru v 押さえます, 押さえる represses; covers; holds

osaemásu, osáeru v 抑えます, 抑える controls, restrains

Ōsaka n 大阪 Osaka

　Ōsaká-Eki n 大阪駅 Osaka Station

　Ōsaká-jin n 大阪人 an Osakan

osamarimásu, osamáru v 収まります, 収まる gets reaped (collected, brought in)

osamarimásu, osamáru v 納まります, 納まる is paid

osamarimásu, osamáru v 治まります, 治まる settles (down/in)

osáme v 収め[納め] → **osamemásu** 収め[納め]ます [INFINITIVE]

osáme v 納め → **osamemásu** 納めます [INFINITIVE]

osáme v 治め → **osamemásu** 治めます [INFINITIVE]

o-samemásu, osaméru v 収め[納め]ます, 収め[納め]る reaps, harvests, collects; gets; finishes

o-samemásu, osaméru v 納めます, 納める pays (tax, premium, etc.)

o-samemásu, osaméru v 治めます, 治める governs; pacifies

o-san n お産 childbirth (= **shussan** 出産)

osanái adj 幼い infant(ile), very young; childish, green (inexperienced)

o-san shimásu (suru) v お産します(する) gives birth to (= **shussan shimásu (suru)** 出産します(する))

osarai n おさらい review [INFORMAL] (= **fukushū** 復習): ~ **shimásu** おさらいします reviews

osé v 押せ [IMPERATIVE] (push!) → **oshimásu** 押します

oséba v 押せば (if one pushes) → **oshimásu** 押します

o-séchi n おせち・お節 a season; a festival

osechi-ryō´ri n おせち料理 festival cookery (for New Year's)

o-seibo n お歳暮 year-end present, winter gift

o-seji n お世辞・おせじ compliment, flattery: **o-seji o iimásu** お世辞を言います pays compliments, flatters

o-sékkai n お節介 meddling: **o-sékkai o yakimásu** お節介を焼きます meddles; **o-sékkai (na)** お節介(な) meddlesome

osen n 汚染 [BOOKISH] contamination, pollution

ōsen n 応戦 fighting back: ~ **shimásu** 応戦します fights back

o-sewa-sama お世話様 (thank you for) your help/attention

osháberi n おしゃべり chatter-box, gossip

osháburi n おしゃぶり teething ring, pacifier

osháre n おしゃれ・お洒落 dandy: **osháre na hito** おしゃれな人 fancy dresser

oshi n おし・唖 a (deaf-)mute

oshi n 押し → **oshimásu** 押します [INFINITIVE]

oshibana n 押し花 pressed dried flower

o-shíbori n おしぼり damp hand-towel

oshie n 教え **1.** instruction, teaching(s) **2.** → **oshiemásu** 教えます [INFINITIVE]; **oshie ro** 教えろ, **oshié yo** 教えよ [IMPERATIVE] (teach!) → **oshiemásu** 教えます

oshiego n 教え子 a student (of a teacher's)

oshiemásu, oshieru v 教えます, 教える teaches, shows, tells, informs

oshieta v 教えた = **oshiemáshita** 教えました (taught, told)

oshiete v 教えて → **oshiemásu** 教えます

oshieyō v 教えよう = **oshiemashō´** 教えましょう (let's teach!)

oshíi *adj* 惜しい **1.** regrettable **2.** precious

ōshii *adj* 雄々しい manly, manful, brave, strong (*not feminine or sissy*)

oshi-ire *n* 押し入れ (*traditional Japanese*) closet, cupboard

o-shimai *n* おしまい the end (*baby talk*) (= **owari** 終わり)

oshimásu, osu *v* 押します, 押す pushes, presses (*on*)

oshíme *n* おしめ diapers

ōshin *n* 往診 house call: ~ **shimásu** 往診します makes a house call

o-shinko *n* おしんこ・お新香 radish (*etc.*) pickles

oshiroi *n* おしろい・白粉 face powder

oshíte *v* 押して → **oshimásu** 押します

oshitsukémásu, oshitsukéru *v* 押し付けます, 押し付ける pushes, presses; intrudes

oshiuri *n* 押し売り **1.** high-pressure selling: **shinsetsu no oshiuri** 親切の押し売り unwelcome kindness **2.** a high-pressure salesman: ~ **shimásu** 押し売りします pressures someone to buy

oshí ya/wa shinai *v* 押しや/はしない = **osanai** 押さない (not push)

oshí-zushi *n* 押し鮨 sushi rice and marinated fish pressed in squarish molds (*Osaka style*)

ōshoku jinshu *n* 黄色人種 Mongoloid, Asians

oshō (-san) *n* 和尚(さん) Buddhist priest

Ō´shū *n* 欧州 Europe (= **Yōróppa** ヨーロッパ)

osō *v* 押そう = **oshimashō´** 押しましょう (let's push!)

osoi *adj* 遅い late; slow

osóimásu, osou *v* 襲います, 襲う attacks, assaults; strikes, hits

osokare hayakare *adv* 遅かれ早かれ sooner or later

osoku *adv* 遅く late; slow: **osóku-tomo** 遅くとも at the latest

o-sómatsu-sama *interj* お粗末さま Please excuse the poor fare (*reply to* **gochisō-sama** ごちそうさま)

osóraku *adv* おそらく・恐らく probably, maybe, possibly

osoré *n* 恐れ fear

osóre *v* 恐れ → **osoremásu** 恐れます [INFINITIVE]

osóre-irimásu *v* 恐れ入ります **1.** excuse me **2.** thank you

osoremásu, osoréru *v* 恐れます, 恐れる fears

osoroshíi *adj* 恐ろしい fearful, dreadful, awful, terrible, horrible (= **kowái** 怖い・恐い)

osoróshiku *adv* 恐ろしく terribly

osowarimásu, osowaru *v* 教わります, 教わる is taught, studies, learns

osowatte *v* 教わって → **osowarimásu** 教わります

osshái *v* おっしゃい [IMPERATIVE] (say it!) → **osshaimásu** おっしゃいます

osshaimásu, ossháru *v* おっしゃいます, おっしゃる (*someone honored*) says; is called

osshátta *v* おっしゃった = **osshaimáshita** おっしゃいました (said)

osshátte *v* おっしゃって → **osshaimásu** おっしゃいます

osu *v* 押す = **oshimásu** 押します

osú *n* 雄・オス male animal; ... **no osú** ...の雄 a he-... (→ **o-ushi** 雄牛)

osui *n* 汚水 sewage

osui-dame *n* 汚水溜め cesspool

ōsuji *n* 大筋 outline

Ōsutorária *n* オーストラリア Australia
  Ōsutoraría-jin *n* オーストラリア人 an Australian

Ōsutoria *n* オーストリア Austria
  Ōsutoriá-jin *n* オーストリア人 an Austrian

o-suwari *interj* お座り Sit! (*training one's dog*)

otafukukaze *n* おたふく風邪 mumps

o-tagai (no) *adj* お互い(の) mutual, reciprocal: **o-tagai (ni)** お互い(に) mutually, reciprocally

otamajakushi *n* オタマジャクシ tadpole

o-taku *n* お宅 [INFORMAL] your house; you
  o-taku no *pron* お宅の your, yours

ó-te *interj* お手 Give me your paw! Shake hands! (*training one's dog*)

o-teage *n* お手上げ giving up

o-teárai *n* お手洗い washroom, toilet, restroom

o-témae *n* お手前 prowess, skill, ability

o-tenba *n* お転婆 tomboy

o-ténto-sama *n* おてんとさま・お天道さま the sun (= **táiyō** 太陽)

otétsudai (-san) *n* お手伝い(さん) (*household*) helper, maid(-servant)

otó *n* 音 sound, noise: **otó ga shimásu** 音がします it makes a noise, there is a noise

ōtō *n* 応答 reply, response, answer: ~ **shimásu** 応答します replies, responds, answers

shitsugi-ōtō *n* 質疑応答 questions and answers

ōtóbai *n* オートバイ motorcycle

otokó *n* 男 = **otoko no hitó/katá** 男の人/方 man, male, boy; **otoko no kyō´dai** 男の兄弟 brother(s)
  otoko-gokoro *n* 男心 man's heart
  otoko-jotai *n* 男所帯 all male household
  otoko-kotoba *n* 男言葉 man's language
  otoko-mono *n* 男物 menswear
  otokó-no-ko *n* 男の子 boy (= **danshi** 男子)
  otoko-tárashi *n* 男たらし seductress, man-eater, a Cleopatra
  otoko-yámome *n* 男やもめ widower
  otoko-yu *n* 男湯 men's (*section of the*) bath

ōtokuchū´ru *n* オートクチュール haute couture, high fashion

o-tokui (-san) *n* お得意(さん) good customer(s), regular customer(s)

otome *n* 乙女 **1.** (*young*) girl, lady **2.** maiden, virgin: **urawakaki otome** [BOOKISH] うら若き乙女 young maiden

o-tómo shimásu (suru) *v* お伴します(する) (*I will*) accompany (you)

otona *n* 大人・おとな adult

otonashíi *adj* おとなしい gentle, well-behaved

otonáshiku *adv* おとなしく gently

otori *n* おとり・囮 decoy; lure

otoroemásu, otoróéru *v* 衰えます, 衰える declines, fades, grows weak

otóru *adj* 劣る is inferior, worse, weak, poor (= **ototta** 劣った)

otosánai *v* 落とさない = **otoshimasén** 落としません (not drop it)

otóse *v* 落とせ [IMPERATIVE] (drop it!) → **otoshimásu** 落とします

otóseba *v* 落とせば (if one drops it) → **otoshimásu** 落とします

otoshi-dama *n* お年玉 money given as a New Year's gift

otoshimásu, otósu *v* 落とします, 落とす drops; omits

otoshimono *n* 落とし物 lost, dropped things

otoshi-támago *n* 落とし卵 poached eggs

otóshite *v* 落として → **otoshimásu** 落とします

otóshi ya/wa shinai *v* 落としや/はしない = **otosánai** 落とさない (not drop it)

otótó *n* 弟 younger brother: **otóto-san** 弟さん (*your/someone else's*) younger brother

ototói *n* おととい・一昨日 day before yesterday

otótoshi *n* おととし・一昨年 year before last

ōtotsu *n* おうとつ・凹凸 unevenness, bump (= **dekoboko** でこぼこ・凸凹)

O-tsukare-sama (déshita) *interj* お疲れ様(でした). You did good work (*today, at the end of a project, etc.*) (*One of frequently used phrases as a parting expression after work, when leaving the office or greeting to the person who is leaving*), You must be weary (*tired, exhausted*). (→ **Go-kúrō-sama (deshita).** ご苦労様(でした).)

otsu (na) *adj* おつ[乙](な) chic, stylish

otta *v* 追った = **oimáshita** 追いました (chased)

ótta *v* 負った = **oimáshita** 負いました (carried on back)

ótta *v* 織った・折った・居った = **orimáshita** 織りました; 折りました; 居りました (wove; broke; stayed)

ōtta *v* 覆った = **ōimáshita** 覆いました (covered)

otte *v* 追って → **oimásu** 追います

ótte *v* 負って → **oimásu** 負います

ótte *v* 織って・折って・居って → **orimásu** 織ります; 折ります; 居ります

ōtte *v* 覆って → **ōimásu** 覆います

otto *n* 夫 (*my*) husband

ototta *adj* 劣った is inferior, worse, weak, poor (= **otoru** 劣る)

ou *v* 追う = **oimásu** 追います (chases, pursues)

ou *v* 負う = **oimásu** 負います (carries on one's back)

ōu *v* 覆う = **ōimásu** 覆います (covers, shields)

o-ushi *n* 雄牛 bull, ox

o-úsu *n* お薄 light green tea (*tea-ceremony*) (= **usu-cha** 薄茶)

o-wakare *n* お別れ parting, farewell (= **wakaré** 別れ)

owanai *v* 追わない = **oimasén** 追いません (not chase)

owanai *v* 負わない = **oimasén** 負いません (not carry on back)

ōwanai *v* 覆わない = **ōimasén** 覆いません (not cover)

oware *v* 追われ → **owaremásu** 追われます [INFINITIVE]

oware *v* 終われ 1. → **owaremásu** 終われます [INFINITIVE] 2. [IMPERATIVE] (end it!) → **owarimásu** 終わります

owareba *v* 終われば (if (it) ends) → **owaremásu** 終われます

owaremásu, owareru *v* 終われます, 終われる can end it

owaremásu, owareru *v* 追われます, 追われる gets chased

owari *n* 終わり 1. the end: **owari no ...** 終わりの... the last, final; **owari no nai** 終わりのない endless 2. → **owarimásu** 終わります [INFINITIVE]

owarimásu, owaru *v* 終わります, 終わる it ends; ends it

owari ya/wa shinai *v* 終わりや/はしない = **owaranai** 終わらない (cannot end)

owarō´ *v* 終わろう = **owarimashō´** 終わりましょう (let's end it!)

owatta *v* 終わった = **owarimáshita** 終わりました (ended)

owatte *v* 終わって → **owarimásu** 終わります

oya *v* 追や → **oéba** 追えば

oyá *n* 親 parent

oya-baka *n* 親ばか[馬鹿] doting parent(s)

oya-fukō *n* 親不幸 unfilial behavior, unfilial child

oya-go-san *n* 親御さん (*your/someone else's*) parent (= **goryōshin** ご両親)

oya-ji *n* 親父 (*familiar, usually male*) (= (**o-)tō´-san** お父さん・おとうさん) my father: **oyaji-san** 親父さん (*your/someone else's*) father

óya-ko *n* 親子 parent and child

oya-ko-dónburi/don *n* 親子丼 rice topped with chicken and onions cooked in beaten eggs *or* rice topped with salmon and salmon roe

oya-kōkō *n* 親孝行 filial piety (*honoring one's parents*)

oya-masari *n* 親勝り talent surpassing that of one's parent(s)

oya-moto *n* 親元 (*one's*) parent's home

oya-shirazu *n* 親知らず wisdom tooth

oya-yuzuri *n* 親譲り something like constitution, character, property, etc. which is inherited from one's parents

Oya *interj* おや Gee whiz! I say! How (a)bout that!; **Oya mā!** おやまあ good heavens

óyaoya *interj* おやおや Dear dear!, Oh dear.

o ya *v* 負や → **oéba** 負えば

óyá-bun *n* 親分 boss, ringleader, chief

ōyake (no/ni) *adj, adv* 公(の/に) public(ly), open(ly), official(ly)

óyama *n* おやま・女形 female impersonator (of **Kabuki**) (= **onna-gata** 女形)

ō´ya (-san) *n* 大家(さん) landlord

O-yasumi nasái *interj* おやすみなさい. Good night.

o-yátsu *n* おやつ snacks, sweets (*for mid-afternoon*) (→ **sánji no oyatsu** 三時のおやつ)

oya-yubi *n* 親指 thumb: "**Oyayubi-hime**" 「親指姫」 "Thumbelina"

ōyō *n* 応用 application, putting to use: ~ **shimásu** 応用します applies it, puts it to use

ōyō (na) *adj* 鷹揚(な) easygoing: **ōyō na taido** 鷹揚な態度 generous attitude

oyobanai *v* およばない = **oyobimasén** およびません (not reach)

oyobi *v* および → **oyobimásu** およびます [INFINITIVE]

óyobi *prep* および and (*also*) (= **to** と)

oyobimásu, oyobu *v* およびます、および reaches, extends to, equals

oyóge *v* 泳げ 1. → **oyogemásu** 泳げます [INFINITIVE] 2. [IMPERATIVE] (swim!) → **oyogimásu** 泳ぎます

oyogemásu, oyogéru *v* 泳げます、泳げる can swim

oyógete *v* 泳げて → **oyogemásu** 泳げます

oyogí *n* 泳ぎ swimming

oyógi *v* 泳ぎ → **oyogimásu** 泳ぎます [INFINITIVE]

oyogimásu, oyógu *v* 泳ぎます、泳ぐ swims

oyogō *v* 泳ごう = **oyogimashō´** 泳ぎましょう (let's swim!)

oyóida *v* 泳いだ = **oyogimáshita** 泳ぎました (swam)

oyóide *v* 泳いで → **oyogimásu** 泳ぎます

oyonda *v* およんだ = **oyobimáshita** およびました (reached)

oyonde *v* およんで → **oyobimásu** およびます

oyoso (no) *adj* およその(の) about, roughly

ōzáppa (na) *adj* おおざっぱ(な) rough

ōzéi *n* 大勢 large crowd, throng: **ōzéi de** 大勢で in large numbers (= **takusan (no)** たくさん(の)) **ōzéi no** *adj* 大勢の many

ō´-zeki *n* 大関 champion sumo wrestler

o-zon *n* オゾン ozone: **ozon-sō** オゾン層 ozone layer

ō-zume *n* 大詰め ending: **ō-zume o mukaemásu** 大詰めを迎えます is/will be in the final stage/phase

P

pachinko *n* パチンコ pinball (*machine*): **pachinko-ya** パチンコ屋 pachinko parlor

pái *n* パイ pie (→ **appurú-pai** アップルパイ)

pái *n* パイ・ぱい・牌 a mahjong tile

paináppuru *n* パイナップル pineapple

páipu *n* パイプ pipe; cigarette holder

pairótto *n* パイロット pilot

pajama *n* パジャマ pajamas (= **nemaki** 寝巻き)

pākingu *n* パーキング parking (= **chūsha-jō** 駐車場)

pakkēji *n* パッケージ package

…-paku *suffix* …泊: **ip-paku** 一泊 one night's lodging/stay → **…-haku** …泊

pāma *n* パーマ permanent wave

pán *n* パン bread: **kashi-pan** 菓子パン sweet bun: **shoku-pan** 食パン loaf of bread, pain de mie, sandwich loaf: **pan-kēki** パンケーキ pancake **pan-kó** *n* パン粉 1. bread crumbs 2. bread flour **pan-kúzu** *n* パンくず (*bread*) crumbs **pán-ya** *n* パン屋 1. bakeshop, bakery 2. baker

pánda *n* パンダ panda

pánfu (rétto) *n* パンフ(レット) pamphlet, brochure (= **shō-sasshi** 小冊子)

pánikku *n* パニック panic **panikuru** *v* パニくる [INFORMAL] gets panicky

panku *n* パンク puncture, blowout: **taiya ga panku shimásu** タイヤがパンクします gets a flat tire

pánku *n* パンク punk: **panku rokku** パンクロック punk rock, punk music

pansuto *n* パンスト panty hose

pántaron *n* パンタロン (*women's*) slacks, pantaloons

pántii *n* パンティー underwear for ladies (*panties*)

pántsu *n* パンツ underwear (*underpants*); slacks, pants

papa *n* パパ (*baby talk*) daddy, dad (= **(o-)tō-chan** (お)父ちゃん)

parashūto *n* パラシュート parachute

Pári *n* パリ Paris

paripari (no) *adj* ぱりぱり(の) crisp; first-rate

pāsénto *n* パーセント percent

paso-kon *n* パソコン personal computer

pásu *n* パス pass(ing); **pásu shimásu** パスします passes (*an exam*) (= **gōkaku shimásu** 合格します)

pasupō´to *n* パスポート passport

patā´n *n* パターン pattern

pā´tii *n* パーティー party: **hōmu-pa-tii** ホームパーティ house party

patoka *n* パトカー patrol car, police car

pātonā *n* パートナー partner

patoron *n* パトロン patron

pāto(taimu) *n* パート(タイム) part-time work

pázuru *n* パズル puzzle: **jigusō-pazuru** ジグソーパズル jigsaw puzzle

pedaru *n* ペダル pedal: **jidensha/jitensha no pedaru** 自転車のペダル bicycle pedal

pēji *n* ページ・頁 page

Pékin *n* ペキン・北京 Beijing, Peking

pén *n* ペン pen: [IDIOM] **pén wa ken yorimo tsuyoshi** ペンは剣よりも強し The pen is mightier than the sword.

...-pén *suffix* ...遍 = **...-hén** ...遍 (*counts times*)

pénchi *n* ペンチ pliers, pincers

péndanto *n* ペンダント pendant

penki *n, prefix* ペンキ paint; (**... ni) penki o nurimásu** (...に)ペンキを塗ります paints
penki-ya *n* ペンキ屋 painter (*housepainter*)

pénshon *n* ペンション pension (*small hotel, lodge, inn, etc.*)

perapera *adj, adv* ぺらぺら・ペラペラ fluent(ly) (= **ryūchō** 流暢): **nihongo ga perapera desu** 日本語がぺらぺらです speaks Japanese fluently

péten *n* ペテン fraud (= **sagi** 詐欺, **ikasama** いかさま): **peten-shi** ペテン師 swindler (= **sagi-shi** 詐欺師, **ikasama-shi** いかさま師)

pétto *n* ペット pet: **pétto o katte imásu** ペットを飼っています has a pet/pets

piano *n* ピアノ piano: **gurando-piano** グランドピアノ grand piano

píiman *n* ピーマン green bell pepper: **aka-piiman** 赤ピーマン red bell pepper

piínát(t)su *n* ピーナ(ッ)ツ peanut(s)

pikápika (no) *adj* ピカピカ(の) flashing, glittering; **~ shimásu** ピカピカします flashes

píkuníkku *n* ピクニック picnic

pín *n* ピン pin (*for hair*)

pínchi *n* ピンチ pinch (= **kiki** 危機): **pínchi ni ochiirimásu** ピンチに陥ります gets in a pinch: **pínchi desu** ピンチです I am in a pinch.

pínku *adj* ピンク pink: **pinku-iro** ピンク色 pink color (= **momo-iro** 桃色)

pinsétto *n* ピンセット tweezers (*originally came from a French word "pincette"*)

pin (to) *adv* ぴん(と) (*stretched*) taut: **pin to kimásu** ぴんと来ます hits home with one, comes home to one, appeals to one

pinto *n* ピント focus (= **shōten** 焦点)
pin-boke *n* ピンぼけ out-of-focus

piramíddo *n* ピラミッド pyramid

písutoru *n* ピストル revolver, pistol

pittári *adv* ぴったり exactly, perfectly, closely; just right

píza *n* ピザ pizza

póchi, pótsu *n* ぽち, ぽつ a dot

pokétto *n* ポケット pocket

pomā´do *n* ポマード pomade, hair oil

ponbiki *n* ぽん引き a pimp

póndo *n* ポンド pound (*weight or money*)

pónpu *n* ポンプ pump

pónsu, ponzú *n* ポン酢 juice of bitter orange

poppukōn *n* ポップコーン popcorn

poppusu *n* ポップス pops, popular music

pori(-) *n, prefix* ポリ poly(ethylene); plastic
pori-búkuro *n* ポリ袋 (*plastic*) bag

póruno *n* ポルノ pornography; **poruno-éiga** ポルノ映画 a porno film

pósuto *n* ポスト mail box

pō´tā *n* ポーター porter

potā´ju *n* ポタージュ potage, thick Western soup

pótéto *n* ポテト potato

pótto *n* ポット pot

púragu *n* プラグ (*electric*) outlet, plug

puramómoderu *n* プラモデル plastic model

púran *n* プラン plan (= **keikaku** 計画, **kikaku** 企画): **púran o tatemásu** プランを立てます makes a plan

puranetariúmu *n* プラネタリウム planetarium

purásuchíkku *n* プラスチック plastic(s)

puratto-hōmu *n* プラットホーム (*station*) platform

purehabu-jūtaku *n* プレハブ住宅 prefabricated house

purei-gáido *n* プレイガイド a "Play Guide" theater ticket agency

purézento *n* プレゼント present, gift

púrín *n* プリン a small custard; crème brûlée

puríntā *n* プリンター printer

purinto *n* プリント printing, printout, printed matter (= **insatsú** 印刷)
purinto auto *n* プリントアウト printing, printout (= **insatsú-butsu** 印刷物)

púro *n* プロ pro(-fessional)

puroguráma *n* プログラマー programmer

purogúramu *n* プログラム program

purópan *n* プロパン propane; **puropan-gásu** プロパンガス propane gas

puro-resu *n* プロレス professional wrestling

pū´ru *n* プール **1.** swimming pool **2.** motor pool, parking lot

pusshúhon *n* プッシュホン touch-tone telephone

R

...´-ra *suffix* ...ら and others (= **nado** など・等); all of

rabel *n* ラベル label

rábo *n* ラボ lab (= laboratory)

rágubii *n* ラグビー rugby

rai-... *prefix* 来... **1.** next **2.** coming
rái-getsu *n, adv* 来月 next month
rai-nen *n, adv* 来年 next year

rai-se n 来世 afterlife, next life
rai-shū n, adv 来週 next week
rai-hō n 来訪 [BOOKISH] a visit: **raihō-sha** 来訪者 a visitor
rai-kyaku n 来客 guest, caller, visitor, company
raibaru n ライバル rival
raifurú-jū n ライフル銃 rifle
ráimu n ライム lime (*fruit*)
raion n ライオン lion
ráisensu n ライセンス license, permit
ráisu n ライス rice (*served on plate*)
raitā n ライター 1. lighter (*cigarette*) 2. writer (*professional*)
ráiu n 雷雨 [BOOKISH] thunderstorm
rajiē´tā n ラジエーター radiator (*car*)
rájio n ラジオ radio: **rájio-bangumi** ラジオ番組 radio program
rakétto n ラケット racket: **tenisu-raketto** テニスラケット tennis racket
rakkan n 楽観 optimism ~ **shimásu** 楽観します takes a favorable view (*of events, conditions, etc.*)
rakkan-teki (na) adj 楽観的(な) optimistic:
rakú adj 楽 1. comfort (= **anraku** 安楽):**Dō´zo raku ni shitekudasai** どうぞ楽にして下さい Please make yourself comfortable/at home.
rakú (na) adj 楽(な) comfortable, 2. easy (= **kantan** 簡単, **yasashii** やさしい[易しい]):
kono mondai wa rakú ni tokemásu この問題は楽に解けます can solve this problem easily
rakuda n ラクダ camel
rakudai n 落第 [BOOKISH] failure (*in a test*):
~ **shimásu** 落第します fails
rakuen n 楽園 paradise: **chijō no rakuen** 地上の楽園 earthly paradise
rakugaki n 落書き scribbling; doodling
rakugo n 落語 (*traditional Japanese*) comic story-telling: **rakugo-ka** 落語家 a comic storyteller
rā´men n ラーメン Chinese noodles (*in broth*)
ramune n ラムネ lemon soda
rán n ラン・蘭 orchid
rán n 欄 column, field: **nyūryoku-ran** 入力欄 entry field
rán n 乱 disturbance; war
ranbō n 乱暴 violence, outrage
ranbō (na) adj 乱暴(な) violent, wild, rough, disorderly
ránchi n ランチ 1. lunch 2. launch (*boat*)
ranchi-sā´bisu n ランチサービス special lunch, a luncheon special
randóseru n ランドセル knapsack for elementary school children
ranma n らんま・欄間 transom window
ranningu n ランニング running
ránpu n ランプ 1. lamp 2. ramp
rappa n ラッパ trumpet, bugle
... rashíi suffix, adj ...らしい (*seems*) like, apparent, seems to be
rashinban n 羅針盤 compass (*for directions*)
rasshu-áwā n ラッシュアワー rush hour

ratai (no) adj 裸体(の) nude (= **nūdo (no)** ヌード(の)): **ratai-ga** 裸体画 a nude (*picture*)
Raten-go n ラテン語 Latin (*language*)
réa n レア rare (*beef*)
rébā n レバー 1. liver (*to eat*) 2. lever
régyurā n レギュラー regular
rei n 礼 1. thanks, gift (= **o-rei** お礼) 2. remuneration, reward, fee (= **sharei** 謝礼)
rei-kin n 礼金 "thank-you money" (*to obtain rental*)
réi n 礼 1. greeting 2. bow (= **o-jigi** お辞儀)
rei-gí n 礼儀 courtesy, etiquette; **reigi-tadashíi** 礼儀正しい polite
rei-hai n 礼拝 worship. ~ **shimásu** 礼拝します worships
réi n 零・0 zero
réi-ji n 零時・0時 zero o'clock, twelve o'clock
réi n 例: **zenrei** 前例 precedent; **ichi-rei** 一例 example; **réi no ...** 例の... the... in question, the said ... ; the usual/customary ...
rei-gai n 例外 exception (*to the rule*)
reibō n 冷房 air conditioning
reinkō´to n レインコート raincoat
reisei (na) adj 冷静(な) calm, cool, composed
reishō n 冷笑 sneer, scoff (= **choshō** 嘲笑):~ **shimásu** 冷笑します sneers, scoffs
reitō n 冷凍 freezing: **reitō-ko** 冷凍庫 freezer: ~ **shimásu** 冷凍します freezes
reitō-shokuhin n 冷凍食品 frozen food:
reizō´ko n 冷蔵庫 refrigerator, icebox
réjā n レジャー leisure, recreation: **rejā-shisetsu** レジャー施設 leisure facilities: **rejā-yōhin** レジャー用品 leisure goods
réji n レジ cashier; checkout counter
rekishi n 歴史 history: **rekishi-teki (na)** 歴史的(な) historical
rekishi-ka n 歴史家 historian
rékkā n レッカー, **rekkā´-sha** レッカー車 wrecker (*tow truck*)
rekō´do n レコード a record (*phonograph*)
rekuriē´shon n レクリエーション recreation
rémon n レモン lemon; **remóntii** レモンティー tea with a slice of lemon
remonē´do n レモネード lemonade
ren'ai n 恋愛 love: **ren'ai-kánkei** 恋愛関係 a love affair; **ren'ai-kékkon** 恋愛結婚 a love marriage
rénchi n レンチ wrench
renchū, renjū n 連中 gang, crowd, clique
rénga n レンガ・煉瓦 brick
rengō n 連合 union, alliance, Allied; **rengō´-koku** 連合国 the Allies; **rengō´-gun** 連合軍 the Allied Forces
rénji n レンジ cooking stove, kitchen range; **denshi-rénji** 電子レンジ microwave oven
renkon n レンコン・蓮根 lotus root
renmei n 連盟 union, federation
rennyū n 練乳 condensed milk
renraku n 連絡 connection, liaison; relevance:
(... to) renraku shimásu (...と)連絡します gets in touch (*with*), contacts
renraku-saki n 連絡先 address of contact

renshū *n* 練習 training, practice, drill: **~ shimásu** 練習します trains, practices

rentákā´ *n* レンタカー rental car

rentogen *n* レントゲン, **rentogen-sen** レントゲン線 X-ray: **rentogen o torimásu** レントゲンを撮ります takes an X-ray

renzoku *n* 連続 continuity; series: **renzoku terebi dorama** 連続テレビドラマ serial TV drama: **renzoku satsujin jiken** 連続殺人事件 serial murder case

rénzu *n* レンズ lens; **kontakuto-rénzu** コンタクトレンズ contact lens

repó´to *n* レポート report (= **hōkoku(-sho)** 報告(書))

ré´sā *n* レーサー racing driver

resépushon *n* レセプション a reception

reshíito *n* レシート receipt

ressha *n* 列車 a train; **ressha-jíko** 列車事故 train accident/wreck

réssun *n* レッスン lesson: **piano (no) réssun** ピアノ(の)レッスン piano lesson: **dansu (no) réssun** ダンス(の)レッスン dance lesson

ré´su *n* レース **1.** lace: **ré´su no kâten** レースのカーテン lace curtain **2.** race: **rēsu-jō** レース場 racetracks

resukyū-tai *n* レスキュー隊 rescue team (= **kyūjo-tai** 救助隊)

résuringu *n* レスリング wrestling

résutoran *n* レストラン restaurant: **famirii-resutoran** ファミリーレストラン family restaurant

rétasu *n* レタス lettuce

rétsu *n* 列 row, line; queue

retteru *n* レッテル label

rettō *n* 列島, **...-réttō** ...列島 archipelago, chain of islands

rí *n* 利 advantage, profit, interest: [IDIOM] **gyofu no rí o shimeru** 漁夫の利を占める A third party makes off with the profits.

ríbon *n* リボン ribbon: **ribbon-musubi** リボン結び ribbon-tie

ríeki *n* 利益 benefit, advantage, profit

rihabiri *n* リハビリ rehabilitation: **rihabiri-chiryō** リハビリ治療 rehabilitation treatment

rihá´saru *n* リハーサル rehearsal: **~ shimásu** リハーサルします rehearses

rihatsu *n* 理髪 [BOOKISH] haircut(ting): **~ shimásu** 理髪します gets/gives a haircut **rihátsú-ten** *n* 理髪店 barbershop

ríidā *n* リーダー leader

ríido shimásu (suru) *v* リードします(する) leads

ríka *n* 理科 science

ríkai *n* 理解 [BOOKISH] understanding, comprehension: **~ shimásu** 理解します understands, comprehends **rikái-ryoku** *n* 理解力 comprehension (*ability*)

rikon *n* 離婚 divorce; (**... to**) **~ shimásu** (...と)離婚します gets divorced (*from ...*), divorces

rikō (na) *adj* 利口(な) clever, sharp, smart, intelligent: **rikō ni** *adv* 利口に cleverly

riku (chi) *n* 陸(地) land, dry land

rikúgun *n* 陸軍 army

rikutsu *n* 理屈 reason, argument: **he-rikutsu** へ理屈 quibble [IN NEGATIVE SENSE]

rimokon *n* リモコン remote control: **terebi no rimokon** テレビのリモコン TV remote control

rín *n* スズ・鈴 a bell, a doorbell (= **beru** ベル) suzu-mushi *n* スズムシ・鈴虫 bell cricket

ringo *n* リンゴ apple

rinji (no) *adj* 臨時(の) [BOOKISH] extraordinary, special, temporary; temporary: **rinji-nyūsu** 臨時ニュース irregular/special news: **rinji no shigoto** 臨時の仕事 temporary work: **rinji-shūnyū** 臨時収入 extra income

rínki-ōhen (ni) *adv* 臨機応変(に) depending on the time and situation, on a case-by-case basis: **rínki-ōhen ni taiōshimásu** 臨機応変に対応します responds flexibly

rinneru *n* リンネル linen

rínri *n* 倫理 ethics: **seimei-rinri** 生命倫理 bioethics: **kigyō-rinri** 企業倫理 corporate ethics

rippa (na) *adj* 立派(な) splendid, admirable, excellent, great: **rippa ni** *adv* 立派に admirably, splendidly, well

rireki *n* 履歴 a history, a record, **rireki-sho** 履歴書 one's personal history, career summary

ririku *n* 離陸 [BOOKISH] take-off (*plane*); **~ shimásu** 離陸します takes off

ríron *n* 理論 theory: **ainshutain no sōtaisei-riron** アインシュタインの相対性理論 Einstein's theory of relativity

ríshi *n* 利子 interest (*on money*) (= **risoku** 利息)

risō *n* 理想 an ideal: **risō-teki (na)** 理想的(な) ideal

risoku *n* 利息 interest (*on money*) (= **rishi** 利子)

rísu *n* リス squirrel

rísuto *n* リスト list

rítsu *n* 率 **1.** rate, proportion; average **2.** a cut, a percentage

rittai *n* 立体 solid; 3-D: **rittai-kyō** 立体鏡 stereoscope: **rittai-chūshajō** 立体駐車場 multi-story parking garage

rittoru *n* リットル liter(s)

riyō *n* 利用 use, utilization: **~ shimásu** 利用します utilizes, makes use of **riyō-sha** *n* 利用者 user

riyū *n* 理由 reason, cause, grounds; **... to iu riyū de ...** という理由で for the reason that ...

rizaya *n* 利ざや margin

rízumu *n* リズム rhythm

ro *n* 炉 furnace

... ro (yo) *interj* ...ろ(よ) [*eastern Japan*] = **... yo** ...よ (IMPERATIVE of **...i-** ...い and **... e-** ...え verb stems)

rō-... *prefix* 老... old (*not young*) **rō-gan (no)** *adj* 老眼(の) presbyopic **rō-jin** *n* 老人 old person **rō-nen** *n* 老年 old age

rō´ *n* ろう・蝋 wax; beeswax (= **mitsurō** 蜜蝋)

róba *n* ロバ donkey

róbii *n* ロビー lobby

róddo *n* ロッド rod (*curtain, etc.*)

rōdō *n* 労働 labor: **rōdō-kúmiai** 労働組合 labor union; **rōdō´-sha** 労働者 worker, laborer

rōdo-shō´ *n* ロードショー road-show attraction, first-run movie

rōgoku *n* 牢獄 jail

rōhi *n* 浪費 [BOOKISH] extravagance (= **muda-zúkai** 無駄使い): **~ shimásu** 浪費します wastes

róji *n* 路地 alley

rōka *n* 廊下 passage(way), corridor

rō´karu (na) *adj* ローカル(な) local

rokétto *n* ロケット rocket

rok-k... *prefix* 六... • 6 six
  rok-kái *n* 六回 six times
  rók-kai *n* 六階 sixth floor, six stories
  rók-ko *n* 六個 six peices (*small objects*)

rókkā *n* ロッカー locker

rókku *n* ロック rock, rock'n'roll (*music*)

roku- *n* 六 • 6 six
  roku-banme (no) *adj* 六番目(の) sixth
  roku-dai *n* 六台 six (*machines, vehicles*)
  rokú-dó *n* 六度 six times (= **rok-kái** 六回)
  rokú-do *n* 六度 six degrees
  rokú-mai *n* 六枚 six sheets (*flat things*)
  rokú-mei *n* 六名 six people (= **rokú-nin** 六人)
  rokú-sai *n* 六歳 six years old (= **muttsu** 六つ)
  rokú-satsú *n* 六冊 six copies (*books, magazines*)

rokuga *n* 録画 recording (*video*): **~ shimásu** 録画します records (*video*)

Roku-gatsú *n* 六月 • 6月 June

roku-jū *n* 六十 • 60 sixty

roku-mán *n* 六万 • 60,000 sixty thousand

rokuon *n* 録音 recording (*sound*): **~ shimásu** 録音します records (*sound*)

rokuro *n* ろくろ potter's wheel

roku-sén *n* 六千 • 6,000 six thousand

Rō´ma *n* ローマ Rome

rōmá-ji *n* ローマ字 romanization, Latin letters

rómansu *n* ロマンス romance, love affair: **romansu-shōsetsu** ロマンス小説 romance novel

romen-densha *n* 路面電車 streetcar

rón *n* 論 argument, discussion; treatise; theory
  ron-bun *n* 論文 treatise; essay; **gakui rónbun** 学位論文 dissertation, thesis

Róndon *n* ロンドン London

rōnin *n* 浪人 **1.** an unemployed samurai **2.** a student between schools: **~ shimásu** 浪人します stays out of school and studies for entrance examination for University **3.** a man without a job: **~ shimásu** 浪人します stays out of work and prepares for new job

ron-jimásu, ron-jiru *v* 論じます, 論じる discusses, argues, debates

rónri *n* 論理 logic; **ronri-teki (na)** 論理的(な) logical

ronsō *n* 論争 controversy, dispute, argument, debate, discussion

rop-p... *prefix* 六... • 6... six
  rop-pai *n* 六杯 six cupfuls
  rop-pén *n* 六遍 six times (= **rok-kái** 六回, **rokú-dó** 六度)
  róp-pon *n* 六本 six (*long objects*)
  róp-pun *n* 六分 six minutes

rop-pyakú *n* 六百 • 600 six hundred

rō´pu *n* ロープ rope

rō´rā *n* ローラー roller; **rōrā sukē´to** ローラースケート roller-skates/skating

rōru-pan *n* ロールパン roll: **batā-rō´ru** バターロール (*butter*) roll

Rosanzérusu *n* ロサンゼルス Los Angeles (= **Rosu** ロス)

rosen *n* 路線 route (*bus, train*)

Roshia *n* ロシア Russia; **Roshia-go** ロシア語 Russian (*language*); **Roshiá-jin** ロシア人 a Russian

rōsókú *n* ろうそく candle (= **kyandoru** キャンドル)

rō´suto *n* ロースト roast; **rōsuto bíifu/chíkin** ローストビーフ/チキン roast beef/chicken

rō´tarii *n* ロータリー traffic circle, rotary

rō´to *n* ろうと・漏斗 [BOOKISH] funnel (= **jō´go** じょうご)

...-rui *suffix* ...類 kinds, (*different*) species of ...
  dō-rui *n* 同類 same kind
  shin-rui *n* 親類 kindred, relative
  shu-rui *n* 種類 kind, variety: **arayuru shurui (no)** あらゆる種類(の) various kinds (*of*)
  jin-rui *n* 人類 humankind
  honyū-rui *n* 哺乳類 mammal (*class*)

rui-... *prefix* 類... similar ...
  rui-ji *n* 類似 resemblance, similarity; analogy; **...ni/to ruiji shimásu** ...に/と類似します resembles, is similar to
  rui-(gi)go *n* 類(義)語 synonym (= **dōgigo** 同義語): **rui-(gi)go-jiten** 類(義)語辞典 synonym dictionary, thesaurus

ruiseki *n* 累積 [BOOKISH] accumulation: **~ shimásu** 累積します accumulates; **ruiseki-kosuto** 累積コスト accumulated costs; **ruiseki-chi** 累積値 accumulation value; **ruiseki-ritsu** 累積率 cumulative percentage

rūmu-sā´bisu *n* ルームサービス room service (*at hotel, etc.*)

rū´ru *n* ルール rule

rúsu (no) *adj* 留守(の) absent, away from home
  rusu-ban *n* 留守番 (**o-rúsu-ban** お留守番) caretaking/caretaker; someone to take care of the house in one's absence
  rusu-ban-denwa *n* 留守番電話 answering machine

...rya *suffix* ...りゃ [INFORMAL] = **...réba** ...れば (if)

ryaku (-go) *n* 略(語) abbreviation

ryakusánai *n* 略さない = **ryakushimasen** 略しません (not abbreviate)

ryakushimásu, ryakusú *v* 略します, 略す abbreviates, shortens; omits

ryo... *prefix* 旅... travel...

ryo-kaku *n* 旅客 = **ryokyaku** 旅客 (traveler, passenger)

ryo-kan *n* 旅館 inn (*traditional*)

ryo-ken *n* 旅券 passport (= **pasupōto** パスポート)

ryo-kō *n* 旅行 travel, trip: **~ shimásu** 旅行します travels, takes a trip

ryo-kō-gaisha *n* 旅行会社 travel agency

ryo-kō´-sha *n* 旅行者 traveler; **ryokō(sha)-yō kogítte** 旅行(者)用小切手 traveler's check

ryo-kyaku *n* 旅客 traveler, passenger

ryō´ *n* 猟 hunting (*as sport*): **ryō´ o shimásu** 猟をします hunts

ryō´-shi *n* 猟師 hunter (= **hantā** ハンター)

ryō´ *n* 漁 fishing (*as sport*): **ryō´ o shimásu** 漁をします fishes

ryō´-shi *n* 漁師 fisherman

ryō´ *n* 寮 dormitory, boarding house: **gakusei-ryō** 学生寮 student dormitory: **zen-ryō-sei no gakkō** 全寮制の学校 boarding school: **dokushin-ryō** 独身寮 dormitory for singles

ryō´ *n* 陵 mound, mausoleum

ryō´ *n* 領 territory

ryō´-chi *n* 領地 territory (= **ryō´do** 領土): **sen-ryō chi** 占領地 occupied territory

ryō´-do *n* 領土 territory, domain: **ryōdo-ken** 領土権 territorial rights: **ryōdo-funsō** 領土紛争, **ryōdo-arasoi** 領土争い territorial dispute

ryō´ *n* 量 quantity, volume

ryō-... *prefix* 両 ... both

ryō-gawa *n* 両側 both sides

ryō-hō´ *n, adv* 両方 both

ryō-mén *n* 両面 both sides/directions: **ryōmen-kopii** 両面コピー two-sided copy

ryō´-shin *n* 両親 parents (*both*)

ryō-te *n* 両手 both hands

...-ryō *suffix* ...料 fee, charge: **nyūjō-ryō** 入場料 admission fee: **haikan-ryō** 拝観料 admission fee (*for temple, etc.*): **isha-ryō** 慰謝料 consolation money, palimony

ryōgae *n* 両替 money exchange/changing: **~ shimásu** 両替します changes (*money*)

ryōgaé-ki *n* 両替機 money-changing machine, money-changer

ryō´ji *n* 領事 consul

ryōjí-kan *n* 領事館 consulate

ryōkai shimásu (suru) *v* 了解します(する) consents, understands [FORMAL]

ryō´kin *n* 料金 fee, charge, fare, rate

ryō´kin-jo *n* 料金所 tollgate

ryōkō *n* 良好 good [BOOKISH]: **kenkō-ryōkō** 健康良好 good health (*mentioned on application/resume, etc.*): **yogo-ryōkō** 予後良好 good prognosis: **seiseki-ryōkō** 成績良好 good record/achievement (*at school, in office, etc.*): **gyōseki-ryōkō** 業績良好 good business performance

ryoku-cha *n* 緑茶 green tea

ryō´ri *n* 料理 cooking: **ryō´ri (o) shimásu** 料理(を)します cooks/prepares it

ryōrí-nin *n* 料理人 cook

ryōrí-ya *n* 料理屋 a restaurant (= **ryóri-ten** 料理店, **kappō** 割烹, **resutoran** レストラン)

ryōshiki *n* 良識 good sense, common sense

ryō´shin *n* 良心 conscience; **ryōshin-teki (na)** 良心的(な) conscientious: **ryō´shin no kashaku** 良心の呵責 remorse of conscience

ryōshū-sho 領収書 → **reshiíto** レシート

ryū´ *n* 竜・龍 dragon

ryūchi *n* 留置 custody: **ryūchi-jō** 留置場 detention house: **~ shimásu** 留置します keeps someone in custody, locks up

ryū´chō (na) *adj* 流暢(な) fluent [FORMAL] (= [INFORMAL] **perapera** ぺらぺら・ペラペラ)

ryūgaku *n* 留学 studying abroad: **~ shimásu** 留学します studies abroad

ryūgaku-sei *n* 留学生 foreign student(s)

ryúkku, ryukkusákku *n* リュック, リュックサック knapsack

ryūkō *n* 流行 popularity, vogue, fashion, trend: **~ shimásu** 流行します becomes popular, becomes fashionable

ryūkō (no) *adj* 流行(の) fashionable

Ryūkyū´ *n* 琉球 the Ryukyu (*Okinawa, etc.*): **Ryūkyū-rettō** 琉球列島, **Ryōkyū-shotō** 琉球諸島 Ryukyu Islands

ryūtsū *n* 流通 circulation, distribution: **ryūtsū-sentā** 流通センター distribution center: **ryūtsū-kosuto** 流通コスト distribution cost: **~ shimásu** 流通します circulates

ryū´zan *n* 流産 miscarriage: **~ shimásu** 流産します miscarries

S

sa *n* 差 difference, discrepancy (= **sai** 差異・差違, **chigai** 違い)

...-sa *suffix* ...さ ...ness (*abstract noun formed from an adjective*)

sā´ *interj* さあ well; come on; let me see

saba *n* サバ・鯖 mackerel

sābā *n* サーバー (*computer*) server

sabaku *n* 砂漠 desert

sábetsu *n* 差別 discrimination: **~ shimásu** 差別します discriminates

jinshu-sabetsu *n* 人種差別 racial discrimination

sabetsu-yōgo *n* 差別用語 discriminatory words

sabí *n* さび・サビ・錆 rust

sábi *v* 錆び → **sabimásu** 錆びます [INFINITIVE]

sabimásu, sabíru *v* 錆びます, 錆びる it rusts

sabínai *adj* 錆びない rustproof

sabishíi *adj* 寂しい・淋しい lonely: **anata ga (soba ni) inakute/anata ni aenakute (totemo) sabishíi desu** あなたが(そばに)いなくて/あなたに会えなくて(とても)さびしいです I miss you so much.

sā´bisu *n* サービス **1.** service: **sābisú-ryō** サービス料 service charge, cover charge: **sābisu-seishin** サービス精神 spirit of good service **2.** free (*as part of the service*): **sābisu-zangyō** サービス残業 unpaid overtime **3.** service (*games*) (= **sābu** サーブ)

sā´bisu-eria *n* サービスエリア **1.** service area (*tennis court, etc.*) **2.** coverage **3.** highway service area

sábite *v* 錆びて → **sabimásu** 錆びます

sabóri *v* サボり → **saborimásu** ささボります [INFINITIVE]

saborimásu, sabóru *v* サボります, サボる loafs, skives (*on the job*); cuts class, plays hookey, stays away

sabotāju *n* サボタージュ sabotage

saboten *n* サボテン cactus

sabótte *v* サボって → **saborimásu** サボります

sābu *n* サーブ serve (*games*) (= **sābisu** サービス)

sāchi raito *n* サーチライト searchlight

sadamarimásu, sadamáru *v* 定まります, 定まる is settled, fixed

sadamemásu, sadaméru *v* 定めます, 定める settles it, fixes it

sadisuto *n* サディスト sadist

sadizumu *n* サディズム sadism

sádo *n* サド **1.** sadist **2.** sadism

sádō *n* 茶道 tea ceremony

sádō *n* 作動 [BOOKISH] operation (*of machine*): ~ **shimásu** 作動します operates, works

sāfā *n* サーファー surfer, surfrider

safaia *n* サファイア sapphire

sāfin *n* サーフィン surfing, surfriding

sagaku *n* 差額 the difference (*in price*), the balance

sagan *n* 砂岩 sandstone

sagan *n* 左岸 left bank

sagári *v* 下がり → **sagarimásu** 下がります [INFINITIVE]

sagarimásu, sagáru *v* 下がります, 下がる it hangs down; goes down

sagashi *v* 探し → **sagashimásu** 探します [INFINITIVE]

sagashi *v* 捜し → **sagashimásu** 捜します [INFINITIVE]

sagashimásu, sagasu *v* 探します, 探す looks/ hunts for something/someone one wants: **shoku-sagashi** 職探し looking/hunting for a job: **takara-sagashi** 宝探し looking/hunting for treasure: **shakuya-sagashi** 借家探し looking/hunting for a house for rent

sagashimásu, sagasu *v* 捜します, 捜す searches for a missing person/thing (= **sōsaku** 捜索): **hannin-sagashi** 犯人捜し searching for the

criminal; **maigo-sagashi** 迷子捜し searching for one's lost child

sagashite *v* 探して → **sagashimásu** 探します

sagashite *v* 捜して → **sagashimásu** 捜します

sagátte *v* 下がって → **sagarimásu** 下がります

ságe *v* 下げ → **sagemásu** 下げます **1.** [INFINITIVE] **2.** sagé **ro** 下げろ [IMPERATIVE] (lower it!, bring it down!, clear from the table!)

sagemásu, sagéru *v* さげます・下げます, さげる・下げる hangs it, lowers it, brings it down, clears from the table

sagemásu, sagéru *v* 提げます, 提げる carries (*dangling from hand*)

ságete *v* 下げて → **sagemásu** 下げます

ságete *v* 提げて → **sagemásu** 提げます

sagí *n* サギ・鷺 heron

sági *n* 詐欺・サギ fraud: **sagi-shi** 詐欺師 a fraud

sagúri *v* 探り → **sagurimásu** 探ります [INFINITIVE]

sagurimásu, saguru *v* 探ります, 探る gropes

sagútte *v* 探って → **sagurimásu** 探ります

ságyō *n* 作業 **1.** work (*commonly physical labor*): **josetsu-ságyō** 除雪作業 removing the snow: **nō-ságyō** 農作業 agricultural work: **sagyō-fuku** 作業服 work clothes: **sagyō-in** 作業員 laborer **2.** operations: **sagyō-jikan** 作業時間 working hours: **sagyō-kōritsu** 作業効率 working efficiency: **sagyō-kōtei** 作業工程 working process

sáhō *n* 作法 manners, etiquette : **gyōgi-sahō** 行儀作法 manners and behaviors

sai *n* 菜 (**o-sai**お菜) side dish (*to go with the rice*) (= **okazu** おかず, **fukushoku(-butsu)** 副食(物))

sái *n* 妻 (*my*) wife: **ryōsai kenbo** 良妻賢母 a good wife and wise mother: **gusai** 愚妻 [HUMBLE] a dumb wife

sai-shi *n* 妻子 wife and child(ren)

sái *n* 差異・差違 [BOOKISH] difference (= **chigai** 違い, **sa** 差)

sái *n* 才 talent, ability: **ta-sai na** 多才な multi-talented

...´-sai *suffix*...歳・才 years of age: **nijús-sai** 二十歳[才]= **hátachi** 二十歳・はたち twenty years old, 20; **sánjús-sai** 三十歳[才]= **sánjū** 三十 thirty years old, 30

(...-)sái *n* (...)際 time, occasion: **kono-sai** この際 on this occasion: **kinkyū no sai** 緊急の際 in case of emergency

sái-shite *conj* 際して: **... ni sáishite** ...に際して on the occasion of, at the time of, when, in case of

sai- ... *prefix* 再... re- (*doing*)

sai-gen *n* 再現 reappearance: ~ **shimásu** 再現します reappears

sai-hakkō *n* 再発行 reissue: ~ **shimásu** 再発行します reissues

sai-hōsō *n* 再放送 rebroadcasting: ~ **shimásu** 再放送します rebroadcasts

sai-kai *n* 再開 resuming, restarting: ~ **shimásu** 再開します resumes, restarts

sai-kai *n* 再会 meeting again: ~ **shimásu** 再会します meets again

sai-kákunin *n* 再確認 reconfirmation: ~ **shimásu** 再確認します reconfirms

sai-kentō *n* 再検討 review: ~ **shimásu** 再検討します reviews

sai-kō *n* 再考 reconsideration: ~ **shimásu** 再考します reconsiders

sai-kon *n* 再婚 remarriage: ~ **shimásu** 再婚します marries again

sai-nyū´koku *n* 再入国 reentry (*into the country*): **sai-nyūkoku-kyokashō** 再入国許可証 reentry permission

sai-sei *n* 再生 reproduction, playback: **saisei-botan** 再生ボタン play button: **saisei-shi** 再生紙 recycled paper: ~ **shimásu** 再生します reproduces, plays

sai-shikén *n* 再試験 makeup exam (= **tsuishi (-ken)** 追試(験))

sai- ... *prefix* 最... the most

sai-ai (no) 最愛(の) one's beloved: **saiai no tsuma** 最愛の妻 one's dear wife

sai-aku (no) 最悪(の) the worst: **saiaku no jitai** 最悪の事態 worst-case scenario

sái-chū *n* 最中 midst (= **chū...** 中...): **shokuji no sáichū** 食事の最中 while eating

sai-dai (no) *adj* 最大(の) the largest, the most, the greatest: **saidai no buki** 最大の武器 the strongest weapon: **saidai-kōyakusū** 最大公約数 the greatest common divisor (GCD): **saidai-tasū no saidai-kōfuku** 最大多数の最大幸福 the greatest happiness of the greatest number

sai-dai-gén (no) *adj* 最大限(の) maximal, maximum, utmost: **saidaigén no chūi o haraimásu** 最大限の注意を払います pays the utmost attention

sái-go (no) *adj* 最後(の) last, final: **sáigo no bansan** 最後の晩餐 Last Supper: **saigo-tsūchō** 最後通牒 ultimatum (= **saigo-tsūkoku** 最後通告)

sai-jō (no) *adj* 最上(の) best, highest, topmost: **saijō-kai** 最上階 the top floor: **saijō-i** 最上位 top-level (*position, rank, etc.*)

sai-kai *n* 最下位 last place (*position, rank, etc.*)

sai-kō (no) *adj* 最高(の) the highest, the best, tops; maximal, maximum, awesome: **saikō no kibun** 最高の気分 great feeling, wonderful feeling: **shijō-saikō-kiroku** 史上最高記録 all-time high record

sai-ryō (no) *adj* 最良(の) the best: **sairyō no saku** 最良の策 the best policy

sai-shin (no) *adj* 最新(の) newest, up-to-date

sai-sho *adv* 最初 the very beginning, the outset (= **hajime** 初め): **saisho no** 最初の... the first ...

sai-shō (no) *adj* 最小(の) smallest: **saishō-gén (-do)** 最小限(度) the minimum (degree)

sai-shō (no) *adj* 最少(の) least, minimal, minimum: **saishō-nenrei** 最少年齢 minimum age

sai-shū (no) *adj* 最終(の) final, the very end (*last*): **saishū-ban** 最終版 final version: **saishū**

densha 最終電車 the last train (= **shūden** 終電)

sai-tei (no) *adj* 最低(の) lowest, worst, bottom(most); minimum: **saitei-gen(do)** 最低限(度) the minimum (degree), lowest limit: **saitei-chingin** 最低賃金 the minimum wage

sai-zen *n* 最善 the best; one's best/utmost (= **besuto** ベスト): **saizen o tsukushimásu** 最善を尽くします I'll give it my best shot.

saibai *n* 栽培 cultivation: ~ **shimásu** 栽培します cultivates

sáiban *n* 裁判 trial: ~ **shimásu** 裁判します judges

saibán-kan *n* 裁判官 judge

saiban-shó *n* 裁判所 court

sabun *n* 差分 difference: **sabun-hō** 差分法 finite difference method: **sabun-hōteishiki** 差分方程式 difference equation

sáidā *n* サイダー (*fizzy lemon*) soda (*originally came from "cider"*) (= **tansan-inryō** 炭酸飲料): **saidā-sui** サイダー水 soda water (= **tansan-sui** 炭酸水)

saidan *n* 祭壇 altar

saidan *n* 裁断 **1.** judgment: **saidan o kudashi-másu** 裁断を下します passes judgment **2.** cutting (*paper, cloth, etc.*): ~ **shimásu** 裁断します cuts out

saido-burē´ki *n* サイドブレーキ handbrake

saido-raito *n* サイドライト side light

sai-en *n* 菜園 vegetable garden

sáiensu *n* サイエンス science (= **kagaku** 科学)

saifu *n* 財布 (**o-saifu** お財布) purse, wallet

saigai *n* 災害 disaster: **shizen-saigai** 自然災害 natural disaster

sai-getsu *n* 歳月 years, time

saigi *n* 祭儀 cultus

saigishin *n* 猜疑心 suspicion: **saigishin ga tsuyoi** 猜疑心が強い is very suspicious

saihō *n* 裁縫 sewing: **saihō-dōgu** 裁縫道具 sewing set

saijitsu *n* 祭日 → **shukujitsu** 祝日

saiken *n* 債券 bond (*debenture*): **saiken-shijō** 債券市場 bond market

saikin *n* 細菌 germ: **saikin-gaku** 細菌学 bacteriology

saikin *adv* 最近 recently, lately: **saikin no** 最近の recent

saikóro *n* さいころ・サイコロ dice, a die (= **sai** さい・采・賽): **sai(kóro) o furimásu** サイ(コロ)を振ります throws a dice

saikú *n* 細工 work(manship), handiwork (= **te-záiku** 手細工), ware(s): ~ **shimásu** 細工します uses tricks

saikuringu *n* サイクリング cycling (*by bicycle*)

saikuru *n* サイクル cycle (= **shūki** 周期)

saikutsu *n* 採掘 mining, digging: ~ **shimásu** 採掘します mines

saimin *n* 催眠 hypnogenesis, hypnosis: **saimin-jutsu** 催眠術 hypnotism

saimu *n* 債務 [BOOKISH] debt: **saimu o oimásu** 債務を負います has debts

sáin *n* サイン **1.** signature (= **shomei** 署名)

2. autograph **3.** sign (= **aizu** 合図, **angō** 暗号, **kigo** 記号)

sainán n 災難 calamity, disaster: **sainan-yoke** 災難除け charm against evil; **sainán ni aimásu** 災難に遭います has a disaster

sáinō n 才能 talent, ability (= **nō** 能, **nōryoku** 能力)

sainyū n 歳入 annual revenue (*of government, local public organization, etc.*)

sáiren n サイレン siren (*sound*): **sáiren o narashimásu** サイレンを鳴らします sounds a siren **sairen-sā** n サイレンサー silencer (*gun*)

saisan n 採算 profit: **saisan ga toremásu** 採算が取れます pays, is profitable

saisan *adv* [BOOKISH] 再三 many times, repeatedly (= **nando mo** 何度も): **saisan itte imásu** 再三言っています has told over and over

saisén n さい銭・賽銭 (**o-saisen** お賽銭) money offering (*at a shrine*); **saisén-bako** さい銭箱・賽銭箱 offering box

saishin (no) *adj* 細心(の) careful: **saishin no chūi o hara(tte) kudasai** 細心の注意を払(って)下さい please pay close attention

saishoku-shugi-sha n 菜食主義者 vegetarian (= **bejitarian** ベジタリアン): **kanzen-saishoku-shugi-sha** 完全菜食主義者 vegan

saishū n 採集 collection, picking and gathering (*as specimen, data, etc.*) (= **korekushon** コレクション): **~ shimásu** 採集します collects, picks and gathers; **konchū-saishū** 昆虫採集 insect collecting

saisoku n 催促 reminding someone, urging (= **tokusoku** 督促): **~ shimásu** 催促します; **saisoku-jō** 催促状 a reminder; reminds, urges

saita v 咲いた = **sakimáshita** 咲きました (bloomed)

sáita v 裂いた = **sakimáshita** 裂きました (split it)

saite v 咲いて → **sakimásu** 咲きます

sáite v 裂いて → **sakimásu** 裂きます

saiten n 祭典 **1.** festival **2.** extravaganza

saiten n 採点 rating, grading, marking: **~ shimásu** 採点します grades, marks

saiwai n 幸い **1.** n happiness (= **kōfuku** 幸福, **shiawase** 幸せ・しあわせ): **fukō-chū no saiwai** 不幸中の幸い is lucky it wasn't worse **2.** *adv* fortunately

saiyō n 採用 employment, adoption: **~ shimásu** 採用します employs, adopts

sáizu n サイズ size (= **ōkisa** 大きさ)

sájí n さじ・サジ・匙 spoon (= **supūn** スプーン) **saji-kagen** n さじ[匙]加減 **1.** prescription **2.** allowance (= **te-kagen** 手加減) **3.** consideration (= **hairyo** 配慮) **saji o nagemásu (nageru)** v 匙を投げます(投げる) gives up (*not to literally mean, "throw a spoon"*)

saká n 坂 hill, slope: **saka-michi** 坂道 sloping road

saka-... *prefix* 酒... *drinking* **saka-bá** n 酒場 bar/pub (*for drinking*) (= **izakaya** 居酒屋, **bā** バー, **pabu** パブ) **saka-ya** n 酒屋 liquor shop

saka-mori n 酒盛(り) drinking party (= **enkai** 宴会)

sakáe v 栄え → **sakaemásu** 栄えます [INFINITIVE]

sakaemásu, sakáeru v 栄えます, 栄える thrives, flourishes, prospers

sakái n 境 boundary, border: **sakai-me** 境目 boundary line

sakan (na) *adj* 盛ん(な) flourishing, prosperous; splendid, vigorous, lively

sakana n 魚 (**o-sakana** お魚) fish **sakaná-tsuri** n 魚釣り fishing (*as sport*) **sakana-ya** n 魚屋 fish dealer/market

sakana n 肴 (**o-sakana** お肴) **1.** appetizers to go with drinks (= (**o-**)**tsumami** おつまみ) **2.** interesting story to add to the fun with drinks

sakanai v 咲かない = **sakimasén** 咲きません (not bloom)

sakánai v 裂かない = **sakimasén** 裂きません (not split)

sakanoborimásu, sakanobóru v 遡ります・溯ります, 遡る・溯る: **... ni sakanoborimásu** …に遡り[溯り]ます goes against (*the stream*), goes upstream; goes back (*in time*) to; sore o ... ni sakanoborimásu それを…に遡り[溯り]ます traces it back to …; is retroactive to

sakaraimásu, sakaráu v 逆らいます, 逆らう: **... ni sakaraimásu** …に逆らいます defies, opposes, contradicts, acts contrary to

sakari n 盛り prime: **sakari no tsuita neko** 盛りのついた猫 cat in heat **sakari-ba** n 盛り場 downtown area (= **hanka-gai** 繁華街)

sakasa(ma) (no/ni) *adj, adv* 逆さ(ま)(の/に) upside down

sá´kasu n サーカス circus

sakazukí n 杯 saké cup (= **choko** ちょこ(**o-choko** おちょこ)): **fūfu no sakazukí o kawashimásu** 夫婦の杯を交わします exchanges nuptial cups (→ **san-san-ku-do (no sakazuki)** 三三九度(の杯))

sake n 酒 (**o-sake** お酒) **1.** saké (*Japanese rice wine*) **2.** alcoholic drinks: **sake no sakana (ni)** 酒の肴(に)

sáke n サケ・鮭 salmon (= **sháke** シャケ・鮭)

sáke v 避け・裂け → **sakemásu** 避けます・裂けます

sakéba v 咲けば (if it blooms) → **sakimásu** 咲きます

sákeba v 裂けば (if one splits/tears it) → **sakimásu** 裂きます

sakebimásu, sakébu v 叫びます, 叫ぶ cries out, shouts

sakemásu, sakéru v 避けます, 避ける avoids

sakemásu, sakéru v 裂けます, 裂ける **1.** it splits, it tears **2.** can split/tear it

sakénai v 避けない = **sakemasén** 避けません (not avoid)

sakénai v 裂けない = **sakemasén** 裂けません (not split; cannot split/tear it)

163

sakénda *v* 叫んだ = **sakebimáshita** 叫びました (shouted)

sakénde *v* 叫んで → **sakebimásu** 叫びます

sakeraremásu, sakeraréru *v* 避けられます, 避けられる **1.** is avoided **2.** can avoid

sáketa *v* 避けた = **sakemáshita** 裂けました (avoided)

sáketa *v* 裂けた = **sakemáshita** 裂けました (it tore)

sákete *v* 避けて → **sakemásu** 避けます

sákete *v* 裂けて → **sakemásu** 裂けます

sakeyō´ *v* 避けよう = **sakemashō´** 避けましょう (let's avoid it!)

saki *n, adv* 先 (**o-saki** お先) **1.** front; future; ahead; first (*ahead of others*); **kono saki** この先 ahead of here; → **o-saki ni** お先に **2.** point, tip **3.** address, destination

saki-gake *n* 先駆け pioneer, forerunner, lead (→ **senku-sha** 先駆者, **paionia** パイオニア)

saki-iki, sakiyuki *n* 先行き prospect, future, outlook: **sakiyuki wa akarui desu** 先行きは明るいです has a bright future

saki-hodo 先程 [BOOKISH] a little while ago (= **sakki** さっき)

saki *v* 咲き → **sakimásu** 咲きます (blooms) [INFINITIVE]

sáki *v* 裂き → **sakimásu** 裂きます [INFINITIVE]

sakimásu, saku *v* 咲きます, 咲く blooms, blossoms

sakimásu, sáku *v* 裂きます, 裂く splits it; tears it

sakin *n* 砂金 gold dust

sakí ya/wa shinai *v* 咲きや/はしない = **sakanai** 咲かない (not bloom)

sáki ya/wa shinai *v* 裂きや/はしない = **sakánai** 裂かない (not split/tear it)

sákka *n* 作家 writer (*novelist, etc.*): **joryū-sakka** 女流作家 a woman writer

sákkā *n* サッカー soccer: **sakkā-senshu** サッカー選手 soccer player (*professional*): **sakkā-bōru** サッカーボール soccer ball

sakkaku *n* 錯覚 illusion: **me no sakkaku** 目の錯覚 optical illusion

sákki *adv* さっき a little while ago [INFORMAL] (= **saki-hodo** 先程 [FORMAL])

sakkin *n* 殺菌 sterilization (= **mekkin** 滅菌): **sakkin-kōka** 殺菌効果 antiseptic effect: **sakkin-zai** 殺菌剤 germicide

sákku *n* サック **1.** sack, case **2.** → **kondō´mu** コンドーム

sakkusu *n* サックス saxophone (= **sakusofōn** サクソフォーン)

sakkyoku *n* 作曲 music composition: ~ **shimásu** 作曲します writes music

sakkyoku-ka *n* 作曲家 a musical composer

sakō´ *v* 裂こう = **sakimashō´** 裂きましょう (let's split/tear it!)

sakoku *n* 鎖国 national isolation

sakotsu *n* 鎖骨 collarbone

saku *v* 咲く = **sakimásu** 咲きます (blooms)

sáku *v* 裂く = **sakimásu** 裂きます (splits/tears it)

saku *n* 柵 fence

saku-…, saki-… *prefix* 昨… [BOOKISH] last

sakú-ban *n, adv* 昨晩 [BOOKISH] last night (= **kinō no yoru/ban** 昨日の夜/晩)

saku-jitsu *n, adv* 昨日 [BOOKISH] yesterday (= **kinō** 昨日)

saku-nen *n, adv* 昨年 [BOOKISH] last year (= **kyonen** 去年)

saki-ototói *n, adv* さきおととい・一昨々日 [BOOKISH] three days ago (= **mikka mae** 三日前)

saki-otótoshi *n, adv* さきおととし・一昨々年 [BOOKISH] three years ago (= **sannen mae** 三年前)

sakubun *n* 作文 writing a composition (*a theme*): **sakubun o kakimásu** 作文を書きます writes a composition

sakuga *n* 作画 **1.** drawing a picture (= **byōga** 描画) **2.** taking a photograph

sakugen *n* 削減 cut, reduction: ~ **shimásu** 削減します reduces; **kosuto-sakugen** コスト削減 cost reduction; **jin'in-sakugen** 人員削減 head-count reduction

sakuhin *n* 作品 a work (*of literature or art*): **geijutsu-sakuhin** 芸術作品 a work of art: **bungaku-sakuhin** 文学作品 a literary work

sakuin *n* 索引 index (= **indekkusu** インデックス)

sakui-teki *adj* 作為的 intentional (= **ito-teki** 意図的)

sakumotsu *n* 作物 **1.** crops **2.** a piece of work (= **sakubutsu** 作物, **sakuhin** 作品)

sakura *n* 桜・サクラ cherry tree: **sakura no haná** 桜の花 cherry blossoms: **sakura-mochi** 桜餅 rice cake with bean paste wrapped in a cherry leaf (*Japanese cakes/sweets*): [IDIOM] **sakura saku** 桜咲く passes the entrance examination (*for the college/university, etc.*) (= **gōkakusuru** 合格する, **ukaru** 受かる)

sakuranbo *n* サクランボ・桜ん坊・桜桃 cherry

saku(ryaku) *n* 策(略) plot (= **kōryaku** 攻略): **sakuryaku-ka** 策略家 plotter (= **sakushi** 策士): **saku-shi** *n* 策士 plotter (= **sakuryaku-ka** 策略家)

sakusen *n* 作戦 tactics: **sakusen o tatemásu** 作戦を立てます plans one's tactics

sakusha *n* 作者 author (= **chosha** 著者)

sakushi *n* 作詞 writing the lyrics: **sakushi-ka** 作詞家 songwriter

sakushu *n* 搾取 [BOOKISH] exploitation: ~ **shimásu** 搾取します exploits; **sakushu saremásu** 搾取されます be exploited

sakusofōn *n* サクソフォーン saxophone (= **sakkusu** サックス)

sakusō(shita) *adj* 錯綜(した) complicated and intricated (= **kōsaku(shita)** 交錯(した)): ~ **shimásu** 錯綜します gets entangled; **sakusō-shita jōhō** 錯綜した情報 entangled information

sakyū *n* 砂丘 sand dune: **Tottori-sakyū** 鳥取砂丘 Tottori sand dune

… (-)sama *suffix* …様・さま [HONORIFIC] = … (-)

san …さん Mr., Ms., Mrs., Miss

samatagemásu, samatagéru *v* 妨げます, 妨げる obstructs, hinders

samayoimásu, samayóu *v* 彷徨います, 彷徨う wanders about

samáza ma (na/no) *adj* 様々 (な/の) diverse, all kinds of

same *n* サメ・鮫 shark (→ **fuká** フカ)

sáme *v* 覚め・冷め・褪め → **samemásu** 覚めます・冷めます・褪めます [INFINITIVE]

samemásu, saméru *v* 覚めます, 覚める wakes up, comes to one's senses

samemásu, saméru *v* 冷めます, 冷める gets cold, cools off

samemásu, saméru *v* 褪めます, 褪める it fades, loses color

saménai *v* 覚めない = **samemasén** 覚めません (not wake up, not come to one's senses)

saménai *v* 冷めない = **samemasén** 冷めません (not get cold, not cool off)

saménai *v* 褪めない = **samemasén** 褪めません (not fade, not lose color)

samitto *n* サミット summit (*conference*) (= **shunō-kaidan** 首脳会談)

sà-mo nàkereba *conj* さもなければ [BOOKISH] otherwise (= **sa-mo nakuba** さもなくば)

samue *n* 作務衣 traditional craftsman's outfit of long sleeve jacket tied at right side and matching loose trousers; also popular as leisure clothes

samúi *adj* 寒い cold (*air temperature*), chilly

samuke *n* 寒気 chill, rigor (= **okan** 悪寒): **samuke ga shimásu** 寒気がします feels a chill

samurai *n* サムライ・侍 samurai (*Japanese warrior*) (= **bushi** 武士)

san *n* 酸 **1.** acid **2.** sour taste: **san-mi** 酸味 sour taste, sour flavor (= **suppai aji** 酸っぱい味)

san(…) *n, prefix* 三・3 (…) three (, tri-…)

sán-ba *n* 三羽 three (*birds, rabbits*)

san-bai *adj* 三倍 triple

sán-bai *n* 三杯 three glassfuls

san-banmé *n* 三番目 third

sán-bén *n* 三遍 three times

sán-biki *n* 三匹 three (*fishes/bugs, small animals*)

sán-bon *n* 三本 three (*pencils/bottles, long objects*)

sán-dó *n* 三度 **1.** three times (= **san-kai** 三回); **sando-mé** 三度目 the third time **2.** three degrees

san-gai *n* 三階 three floors/stories; third floor

san-gánichi *n* 三が日 the first three days of the New Year

sán-gen *n* 三軒 three buildings/houses

sán-ji *n* 三時 three o'clock: **sán-ji no oyatsu** 三時のおやつ snacks, sweets for tea time at three o'clock (→ **oyatsu** おやつ)

san-jū *n* 三重 triplicity: **san-jū-sō** 三重奏 trio (= **torio** トリオ) (*musical instruments, piano, violin, cello, etc.*): **piano-sanjūsō-kyoku** ピアノ三重奏曲 piano trio

sán-kái *n* 三回 three times (= **san-do** 三度); **san**

kai-mé 三回目 the third time

san-kyaku *n* 三脚 tripod (stand): **ninin-sankyaku** 二人三脚 **1.** three-legged race (*on field day, etc.*) **2.** cooperating with singleness of purpose

sán-mai *n* 三枚 three sheets (*flat things*): **san-mai-me** 三枚目 a cutup

sán-mei *n* 三名 [BOOKISH] three people (= **sannín** 三人)

san-nen *n* 三年 the year 3; **san nén-kan** 三年間 three years; **san nén-sei** 三年生 third-year student, junior

san-nín *n* 三人 three people (= **san mei** 三名); **san-nin-shō** 三人称 third person: [IDIOM] **san-nín yoreba monju no chie** 三人寄れば文殊の知恵 "Three" heads are better than one.": [IDIOM] **san-nin san-yō** 三人三様 Each of the three is different. Everyone is different.

san-pai *n* 三拝 [HUMBLE] bowing three times, bowing several times: [IDIOM] **sanpai kyūhai suru** 三拝九拝する bows one's head several times. (*not to literally mean, "bows three times and nine times"*)

san-paku *n* 三泊 three night's lodging;

san-paku-yokka 三泊四日 four days three nights (*tour, etc.*)

sán-pun *n* 三分 three minutes

sán-sai *n* 三歳 three years old (= **mittsu** 三つ)

san-san-ku-do (no sakazuki) *n* 三三九度 (の杯) three-times-three exchange of nuptial cups: **san-san-ku-do no sakazuki o kawashimásu** 三三九度の杯を交わします exchanges nuptial cups → **sakazuki** 杯

sán-satsu *n* 三冊 three (*books, magazines, etc.*)

sán-sei *n* 三世 third generation (*of emigrant Japanese*); … the Third

san-shi-… *n* 三, 四 = **san-yo(n)-…** three or four

sán-shoku *n* 三食 three meals

san-tō *n* 三頭 three (*horses/oxen, large animals*)

san-tō *n* 三等 third class: **san-tō-shō** 三等賞 third prize

san-yo(m/n)- *n* 三, 四 = **san-shi-…** three or four: **san yon-bai** 三, 四倍 three or four times as much: **sanyo-banmé** 三, 四番目 third or fourth: **san yon-do** 三, 四度 3–4 times: **sanyo-jíkan** 三, 四時間 3–4 hours, **sán-yokka** 三, 四日 three or four days: **san yon-man** 三, 四万 thirty or forty thousand: **sanyo-nín** 三, 四人 3–4 people: **sanyo-ninmae** 三, 四人前 3–4 servings

sán-zoku/-soku *n* 三足 three pairs (*of footwear*)

sán *n* 酸 acid

san-sei *n* 酸性 acidity: **sansei-u** 酸性雨 acid rain

… (-) san …さん Mr., Ms., Mrs., Miss (= … (-) **sama** …様・さま)

…´-san, -´zan *n* …山 (*name of certain*) mountain: **Fuji-san** 富士山 Mt. Fuji: **Eberesuto (-san)** エベレスト (山) Mt. Everest: **Takao-zan** 高尾山 Mt. Takao

san-… *prefix* 山… mountain

san-myaku *n* 山脈 mountain range: **Arupusu-sanmyaku** アルプス山脈 Alps (*range*)

san-chō *n* 山頂 mountaintop

san-gaku-chitai *n* 山岳地帯 mountainous region

san-puku *n* 山腹 sidehill

san-sai *n* 山菜 edible wild plants

san-zoku *n* 山賊 bandit

sanba *n* サンバ samba

sanba *n* 産婆 (**o-sanba** お産婆) midwife (= **josanpu** 助産婦)

sanbashi *n* 桟橋 pier

sanbi *n* 賛美 admiration, worship: **sanbi-ka** 賛美歌 hymn (= **sei-ka** 聖歌, **san-ka** 賛歌)

sanbun *n* 散文 prose: **sanbun-shi** 散文詩 prose poem

sanbutsu *n* 産物 product, produce; fruit, outcome

sánbyaku *n* 三百・300 three hundred

sánchi *n* 産地 home (*of a product/crop*)

sandan-jū *n* 散弾銃 shotgun (= **shotto-gan** ショットガン)

sandaru *n* サンダル sandal

san-dii kē´ *n* 3DK three rooms and "DK" (*dinning kitchen = eat-in kitchen*)

…-sándo *suffix* …サンド sandwich (→ **sandoítchi** サンドイッチ): **tsuna-sándo** ツナサンド tuna-fish sandwich: **tamago-sando** タマゴ[卵]サンド egg sandwich: **yasai-sando** 野菜サンド vegetable sandwich: **katsu-sando** カツサンド cutlet sandwich

sandō *n* 参道 approach to a shrine; **omote-sándō** 表参道 main road to a shrine

sandō *n* 賛同 approval, support, (= **sansei** 賛成): ~ **shimásu** 賛同します agrees, approves

sandoítchi *n* サンドイッチ sandwich

sandopē´pā *n* サンド・ペーパー sandpaper

Sanfuranshísuko *n* サンフランシスコ San Francisco

Sán-gatsu *n* 三月・3月 March

sangi-in *n* 参議院 House of Councilors (= **san-in** 参院): **sangi-in-senkyo** 参議院選挙 House of Councilors' election

sango *n* サンゴ・珊瑚 coral

sango-shō *n* サンゴ[珊瑚]礁 coral reef

sangurasu *n* サングラス sunglasses

sangyō *n* 産業 industry: **sangyō-kakumei** 産業革命 industrial revolution: **sābisu-sangyō** サービス産業 service industry

sánji *n* 賛辞 [BOOKISH] praise, compliment (= **home-kotoba** 褒め[誉め]言葉): **sánji o okurimásu** 賛辞を送ります compliments

sán-jū *n* 三十・30 thirty

sanka *n* 賛歌 [BOOKISH] hymn (= **sanbi-ka** 賛美歌, **sei-ka** 聖歌)

sanka *n* 傘下 [BOOKISH] under the umbrella: **sanka-kigyō** 傘下企業 affiliated enterprise: **sanka ni hairimásu** 傘下に入ります comes under the umbrella: **sanka ni arimásu** 傘下にあります is under the umbrella

sanka *n* 参加 participation; (**…ni**) ~ **shimásu**

(**…に**)参加します participates (*in*), joins

sanká-sha *n* 参加者 participant

sánkan *n* 参観 [HUMBLE] one's visiting: **jugyō-sankan-bi** 授業参観日 open school day: **jugyō o sankan shimásu** 授業を参観します visits to observe one's child during a class

sánkaku *n* 三角 triangle: **sankaku-kei, sankak-kei** 三角形 triangular shape: **sankaku-kankei** 三角関係 a love triangle

sankē (**no shigoto**) *n* 3K (の仕事) **1.** 3Ds (*Dirty, Dangerous and Demanding*) blue collar jobs (ACRONYM of Japanese expressions, **Kitsui** きつい = Demanding, **Kiken** 危険 = Dangerous, and **Kitanai** 汚い = Dirty) **2.** (*modern*) (*IT industry, etc.*) (*can't go home, dangerous and low pay*) jobs (ACRONYM of Japanese expressions, **Kitsui** きつい demanding, **Kaerenai** 帰れない can't go home, and **Kyūryō ga yasui** 給料が安い = low pay)

sanke-zukimásu, sanke-zuku *v* 産気づきます, 産気づく goes into labor

sankō *n* 参考 reference (= **sanshō** 参照): **sankō-(to-)sho** 参考(図)書 reference book: **gakushū-sankōsho** 学習参考書 study-aid book: **sankō ni shimásu** 参考にします refers

sanma *n* サンマ・秋刀魚 mackerel pike

sanmon *n* 山門 temple gate

sanpatsu *n* 散髪・さんぱつ haircut: ~ **shimásu** 散髪します gets/gives a haircut

sanpatsu-ya *n* 散髪屋 barber(shop)

sanpo *n* 散歩 a walk, a stroll: ~ **shimásu** 散歩します takes a walk

sanpuru *n* サンプル sample (= **mihon** 見本) (→ **shikyō-hin** 試供品)

sanretsu *n* 参列 presence: ~ **shimásu** 参列します is present

sanrín-sha *n* 三輪車 tricycle

sansei *n* 賛成 approval, support (= **sandō** 賛同): ~ **shimásu** 賛成します agrees, approves

sansei *n* 参政 participation in government: **sansei-ken** 参政権 political suffrage

sanshō *n* サンショウ・山椒 Japanese pepper (*mild*)

sanshō *n* 参照 reference (= **sankō** 参考): ~ **shimásu** 参照します refers

sánso *n* 酸素 oxygen: **sanso-masuku** 酸素マスク oxygen mask: **kassei-sanso** 活性酸素 active oxygen

sansū *n* 算数 (*elementary school*) arithmetic, calculation (= **keisan** 計算), mathematics (= **sūgaku** 数学)

santora *n* サントラ sound track (= **saundo-torak-ku** サウンド・トラック)

san-zén *n* 三千 3,000 three thousand

saó *n* さお・竿・棹 pole, rod

sapō´tā *n* サポーター jockstrap, (*athletic*) supporter

sappári *adv* さっぱり [+ NEGATIVE verb] not at all:

sappári wakarimasen さっぱり分かりません I have no idea.

sappári-shita *adj* さっぱりした clean, fresh; frank: **sappári-shita aji** さっぱりした味 plain taste, lightly seasoned (*food*)

sappūkei na *adj* 殺風景な (*looks*) bare, bleak: **sappūkei na niwa** 殺風景な庭 a bleak garden

sara *n* 皿 (**o-sara** お皿) plate, dish; saucer; ashtray
 sara-arai-ki *n* 皿洗い機 dishwasher

sarabureddo *n* サラブレッド **1.** thoroughbred **2.** blue blood

sárada *n* サラダ salad

sarái-... *prefix* 再来..., ,,, after next
 sarái-getsu *adv* 再来月 [BOOKISH] month after next (= **nikagetsu-go** 二ヵ月後)
 sarai-nen *adv* 再来年 [BOOKISH] year after next (= **ni nen-go** 二年後)
 sarai-shū *adv* 再来週 [BOOKISH] week after next (= **ni shūkan-go** 二週間後)

sára-ni *adv* 更に anew; (*some*) more; further

sárarii *n* サラリー salary (= **kyū´yo** 給与)
 sararii-man *n* サラリーマン salaried man, company employee (= **kaishá-in** 会社員, **sha-in** 社員)

sarashimásu, sarasu *v* 晒します・曝します, **sarasu** 晒す・曝す **1.** exposes: **kiken ni mi o sarashimásu shimásu** 危険に身をさらし[晒し・曝し]ます exposes oneself to danger: **fūu ni sarashimásu shimásu** 風雨にさらし[晒し・曝し]ます exposes it to wind and rain **2.** bleaches: **nuno o sarashimásu shimásu** 布をさらし[晒し]ます bleaches cloth **3.** dries under the sun: **hi ni sarashimásu shimásu** 日にさらし[晒し]ます dries it in the sun **4.** reveals: **haji o sarashimásu shimásu** 恥をさらし[晒し・曝し]ます brings disgrace on oneself

sare *v* され → **saremásu** されます [INFINITIVE]

saremásu, sareru *v* されます, される **1.** has it done to one (*unwantedly*) **2.** is done; **hakai saremásu** 破壊されます is destroyed **3.** [HONORIFIC] = **nasaimásu** なさいます

sári *v* 去り → **sarimásu** 去ります [INFINITIVE]

sarimásu, sáru *v* 去ります, 去る leaves, goes away; removes it

sāroin *n* サーロイン sirloin: **sāroin-sutēki** サーロイン・ステーキ sirloin steak

sáru *v* 去る **1.** = **sarimásu** 去ります **2.** [+ DATE] last ..., most recent, (*past day*) of this month

sáru *n* サル・猿 (**o-saru** おサル・お猿) monkey

Saru-doshi *n* 申年 year of the Monkey

sarumata *n* サルマタ・猿股 loincloth

sasa *n* ササ・笹 bamboo grass: **sasa no ha** 笹の葉 bamboo leaf

sasáe *v* 支え → **sasaemásu** 支えます [INFINITIVE]

sasáe *n* 支え a support, a prop

sasaemásu, sasaeru *v* 支えます, 支える supports, props (*up*)

sásai (na) *adj* 些細(な) petty, trifling, trivial, not a big deal at all (= **torunitarinai** 取るに足りな

い): **sasai na-mondai** 些細な問題 minor problem: **sasai na-chigai** 些細な違い slight difference: **sasai na-koto de kenka/kōron shimásu** 些細なことで喧嘩/口論します quarrels about trifles

sasáyaka (na) *adj* ささやか(な) small (-*scale*), petty: **sasayaka na pātii** ささやかなパーティ little party: **sasayaka na okurimono** ささやかな贈り物 modest gift

sasayakí *n* 囁き a whisper, murmur: **sasayaki-goe** 囁き声 whispery voice

sasayakimásu *v* 囁きます → **sasayakimásu** 囁きます [INFINITIVE]

sasayakimásu, sasayáku *v* 囁きます, 囁く whispers

sase *v* させ **1.** → **sasemásu** させます [INFINITIVE] **2.** **sase ro** させろ [IMPERATIVE] (let them do it!)

sáse *v* 刺せ **1.** → **sasemásu** 刺せます (can stab) [INFINITIVE] **2.** [IMPERATIVE] (stab!) → **sashimásu** 刺します

sáseba *v* 指せば (if one points to) → **sashimásu** 指します

sáseba *v* 刺せば (if one stabs) → **sashimásu** 刺します

sasemásu, saseru *v* させます, させる makes/has/lets one do

sasemásu, saséru *v* 指せます, 指せる can point to

sasemásu, saséru *v* 刺せます, 刺せる can stab

sasenai *v* させない = **sasemasén** させません (not make/have/let one do)

sasénai *v* 指せない = **sasemasén** 指せません (cannot point to)

sasénai *v* 刺せない = **sasemasén** 刺せません (cannot stab)

saseréba *v* させれば (if one makes/has/lets them do) → **sasemásu** させます

saséreba *v* 指せれば (if one can point to) → **sasemásu** 指せます

saséreba *v* 刺せれば (if one can point stab) → **sasemásu** 刺せます

sasete *v* させて → **sasemásu** させます

sásete *v* 指せて → **sasemásu** 指せます

sásete *v* 刺せて → **sasemásu** 刺せます

saseyō *v* させよう = **sasemashō** させましょう (let's make/let them do it!)

sáshi *v* 指し → **sashimásu** 指します [INFINITIVE]

sáshi *v* 刺し → **sashimásu** 刺します [INFINITIVE]

sashi-agemásu, sashi-ageru *v* 差し上げます, 差し上げる [HUMBLE/DEFERENTIAL] presents, give (*I give you, you give them*); holds up

sashidegamashii *adj* 差し出がましい officious

sashideguchi *n* 差し出口 uncalled-for remark: **... no hanashi ni sashidéguchi o shimásu** ...の話に差し出口をします interrupts

sashi-e *n* 挿絵 illustration (*of book, newspaper, magazine, etc.*)

sashi-komi *n* 差(し)込み plug outlet (*electricity outlet*) (= **sashikomi-guchi** 差(し)込み口)

sashi-komi *v* 差(し)込み → **sashi-komimásu** 差(し)込みます

sashi-komimásu, sashi-komu *v* 差(し)込みます, 差し込む inserts

sashimásu, sásu *v* 指します, 指す points to, indicates

sashimásu, sásu *v* 差します, 差す holds (*umbrella*)

sashimásu, sásu *v* 刺します, 刺す stabs, stings

sashimí *n* 刺身・さしみ (**o-sashimi** お刺身) sliced raw fish

sashitsukae *n* 差し支え・さしつかえ **1.** hindrance, impediment **2.** previous appointment/engagement

sáshi ya/wa shinai *v* 指しや/はしない = **sasanai** 指さない (not point to)

sáshi ya/wa shinai *v* 刺しや/はしない = **sasanai** 刺さない (not stab)

sáshizu *n* 指図 directions, instructions, a command (= **shirei** 指令, **shiji** 指示): ~ **shimásu** 指図します directs, instructs, commands

sashō *n* 査証 [BOOKISH] visa (= **bíza** ビザ): **nyūkoku-sashō** 入国査証 an entry visa

sashō *n* 詐称 [BOOKISH] false statement: ~ **shimásu** 詐称します makes a false statement; **nenrei-sashō** 年齢詐称 false statement of one's age; **gakureki-sashō** 学歴詐称 false statement of one's educational background; **mibun-sashō** 身分詐称 false statement of one's status

sasō´ *v* 刺そう = **sashimashō´** 刺しましょう (let's stab!)

sasoi *n* 誘い **1.** invitation; temptation **2.** → **sasoimásu** 誘います [INFINITIVE]

sasoimásu, sasou *v* 誘います, 誘う invites; tempts

sasoō *v* 誘おう = **sasoimashō** 誘いましょう (let's invite/tempt them!)

sasotte *v* 誘って → **sasoimásu** 誘います

sasou *v* 誘う → **sasoimásu** 誘います

sasowanai *v* 誘わない = **sasoimasén** 誘いません (not invite/tempt)

sásshi, sásshu *n* サッシ, サッシュ sash (*window sash*)

sásshi *n* 冊子 brochure

shō-sasshi *n* 小冊子 pamphlet, brochure (= **pánfu(rétto)** パンフ(レット))

sas-shi *n* 察し conjecture, guess; perception, understanding; sympathy: **sasshi ga tsukimásu** 察しがつきます perceives, guesses (*correctly*); **o-sasshi no tōri** お察しの通り as you have surmised

sas-shi *v* 察し → **sas-shimásu** 察します [INFINITIVE]

sas-shinásu, sas-suru *v* 察します, 察する perceives, understands; conjectures, guesses; sympathizes

sas-shite *v* 察して → **sas-shimásu** 察します

sassokú *adv* 早速 at once, right away, promptly, immediately: **sassokú (no)** 早速(の) immediate, prompt

sásu *v* 指す → **sashimásu** 指します

sásu *v* 差す → **sashimásu** 差します

sásu *v* 刺す → **sashimásu** 刺します

sasuga *adv* さすが: **sasuga (ni)** さすが(に) as we might expect, indeed; **sasuga no kare (de)mo** さすがの彼(で)も even he

sasupendā *n* サスペンダー suspender **1.** galluses (= **zubon-tsuri** ズボンつり) **2.** garter

sasupensu *n* サスペンス suspense: **sasupensu-eiga** サスペンス映画 suspense film

sátá *n* 沙汰 (**go-sáta** ご沙汰) [BOOKISH] message; command; affair

satchū-zai *n* 殺虫剤 insecticide

sá-te *interj* さて well now/then, and now/then, as to the matter at hand

satei *n* 査定 assessment (*to decide the rank, salary, etc.*): ~ **shimásu** 査定します assesses; **satei-gaku** 査定額 assessed value

sáten *n* サテン satin

saten *n* 茶店 café (= **kissaten** 喫茶店)

sato *n* 里 **1.** village **2.** hometown (= **furusato** ふるさと・故郷, **kokyō** 故郷): **o-sato** お里 one's origin, upbringing: [IDIOM] **o-sato ga shireru** お里が知れる reveals one's upbringing **3.** countryside

sato-oya *n* 里親 foster parent

sato-gaeri *n* 里帰り goes home (*to see one's parent(s)*)

sató´ *n* 砂糖・サトウ (**o-sató** お砂糖) sugar

satori **1.** *n* 悟り enlightenment **2.** *v* → **satorimásu** 悟ります [INFINITIVE]

satorimásu, satóru *v* 悟ります, 悟る realizes (*comprehends*)

satsu *n* 札 (**o-satsu** お札) folding money, currency bill/note

satsu-iré *n* 札入れ billfold, wallet (= **saifu** 財布)

satsu-taba *n* 札束 a roll/wad of (currency) bills

...-satsú *suffix* ...冊 copy (*counts books, magazines*)

...-satsu *suffix* ...札 (currency) bill; **hyakudorú-satsu ní-mai** 百ドル札二枚 two $100 bills

satsuei *n* 撮影 shooting a film, filming, taking a photograph: **satsuei-jo** 撮影所 studio (= **sutajio** スタジオ)

satsujin *n* 殺人 murder: **satsujin-jiken** 殺人事件 murder case: **mu-sabetsu satsujin** 無差別殺人 indiscriminate murder

Satsumá-age *n* さつま[薩摩]揚げ deep-fried fish cake

Satsuma-imo *n* さつま[薩摩]芋・サツマイモ sweet potato

Saujiarabia *n* サウジアラビア Saudi Arabia

Saujiarabia-jin *n* サウジアラビア人 a Saudi Arabian

sauna *n* サウナ steam bath (*in sports center, health spa, etc.*) (originally came from Finnish term "sauna")

saundo *n* サウンド sound (= **oto** 音, **onkyō** 音響)
  saundo-efekuto *n* サウンド・エフェクト sound effect (= **onkyō-kōka** 音響効果)
  saundo-sukēpu *n* サウンドスケープ soundscape (= **oto (no) fūkei** 音（の）風景, **onkei** 音景)
  saundo-torakku *n* サウンド・トラック sound track (= **santora** サントラ)
sawagashíi *adj* 騒がしい boisterous, noisy:
  sawagashii-pātii 騒がしいパーティ noisy party:
  sawagashii-basho 騒がしい場所 noisy place
sáwagi *n* 騒ぎ **1.** noise (*boisterous*), clamor
  2. unrest, disturbance, tumult, strife; riot (= **sōdō** 騒動)
sawagimásu, sawágu *v* 騒ぎます, 騒ぐ makes lots of noise, clamors
sawáide *v* 騒いで → **sawagimásu** 騒ぎます
sawara *n* サワラ・鰆 mackerel
sawarimásu, sawaru *v* 触ります, 触る touches
sawatte *v* 触って → **sawarimásu** 触ります
sawáyaka (na) *adj* さわやか（な）・爽やか（な）
  refreshing, bracing; fluent
sáya *n* サヤ・莢 sheath, pod: **saya-endō** サヤエンドウ・さやえんどう podded pea: **saya-ingen** サヤインゲン・さやいんげん French bean
sayō *adj* さよう [DEFERENTIAL] (= **sō´** そう) like that: **Sayō de gozaimásu** さようでございます。= **Sō´desu** そうです。Yes; That's right.
sayonára, sayōnára *interj* さよなら, さようなら good-bye (= [INFORMAL] **baibai** バイバイ)
sáyori *n* サヨリ halfbeak (*fish*)
sáyū *n* 左右 right and left: **zengo-sayū** 前後左右 left to right, back and forth
sázae *n* サザエ・栄螺 wreath shell, turban shell, turbo
sé *n* 背 **1.** height, stature (= **sei** せい・背, **se-take** 背丈, **shinchō** 身長): **sé ga takái/hikúi** 背が高い/低い is tall/short **2.** back (*of body*) (= **senaka** 背中)
se-biro *n* 背広 (*man's*) business suit, lounge suit
se-bone *n* 背骨 backbone, spine
séi *n* せい・背 height, stature (= **sé** 背, **se-take** 背丈, **shinchō** 身長): **sei-kurabe** 背比べ comparing heights with someone
se-naka *n* 背中 back of body: **senaka awase ni tachimásu** 背中合わせに立ちます stands back to back
se-nobi *n* 背伸び **1.** standing on tiptoe: ~ **shimásu** 背伸びします stands on tiptoe **2.** trying to do more than one is able to do: ~ **shimásu** 背伸びします tries to do more than one is able to do
se-suji *n* 背筋 the muscles along the spine: **sesuji o (shan-to) nobashimásu** 背筋を（シャンと）伸ばします straightens up
se-take *n* 背丈 height, stature (= **sé** 背, **séi** せい・背, **shinchō** 身長): **setake o hakarimásu** 背丈を測ります measures one's height
segare *n* 倅 **1.** [HUMBLE] my son **2.** [rather IN NEGATIVE SENSE] child/young person
sehyō *n* 世評 one's reputation (= **seken no hyōka** 世間の評価)

séi (-) *n* 性 nature; sex; gender
  sei-betsu *n* 性別 gender
  sei-byō *n* 性病 venereal disease
  sei-kō *n* 性交 [BOOKISH] (*sexual*) intercourse (= **sékkusu** セックス): ~ **shimásu** 性交します has sex
  sei-teki (na) *adj* 性的（な）sexual
séi *n* 姓 family name, last name
  séi-mei *n* 姓名 (*one's*) full name (= **shi-mei** 氏名)
sei-... *prefix* 聖... sacred, holy
  sei-chi *n* 聖地 holy place
  sei-bo *n* 聖母 the Holy Mother
  sei-dō *n* 聖堂 sacred building (*temple, church, mosque, etc.*): **dai seidō** 大聖堂 cathedral
  sei-iki *n* 聖域 sanctuary
  séi-ka *n* 聖歌 hymn (= **sanbi-ka** 賛美歌, **san-ka** 賛歌)
  Séi-sho *n* 聖書 Bible (= **Baiburu** バイブル, **Shin-yaku seisho** 新約聖書, **Kyū-yaku seisho** 旧約聖書)
séi-... *prefix* 西... west, western
  séi-bu *n* 西部 the west, the western part: **seibu-geki** 西部劇 cowboy movie
  sei-hō *n* 西方 (the) west (*general direction/area*): **sei hō no** 西方の western
  sei-nan *n* 西南 southwest
  sei-reki *n* 西暦 the Western (*Christian*) calendar: **seireki ...´-nen** 西暦 ...年 the year ... A.D.
  Séi-yō *n* 西洋 the West, Europe and Americas (= **ōbei-shokoku** 欧米諸国): **séiyō-fū (no)** 西洋風（の）Western-style
sei-... *prefix* 声... voice, vocal
  sei-gaku *n* 声楽 vocal music: **sei-gaku-ka** 声楽家 vocalist
  sei-iki *n* 声域 range of voice
  sei-ryō *n* 声量 volume of one's voice
  sei-tai *n* 声帯 vocal cords
  sei-yū *n* 声優 voice actor
séi(-) *n, prefix* 生(...) life (= **seimei** 生命, **ínochi** 命)
  sei-katsu *n* 生活 life, (*daily*) living, livelihood (= **kurashi** 暮らし, **seikei** 生計); **nichijo-seikatsu** 日常生活 daily life; **seikatsú-hi** 生活費 living costs; **seikatsu-kyōdō-kumiai, seikyō** 生活協同組合, 生協 cooperative society, consumer cooperative (*coop*)
  sei-kei *n* 生計 livelihood, the way of (*earning*) one's living (= **kurashi** 暮らし): **... to shite seikei o tate(tei)másu** ...として生計を立て（てい）ます earns one's living as ...
  séi-mei *n* 生命 life (= **ínochi** 命, **sei** 生): **seimei-rinri** 生命倫理 bioethics
  séi-shi *n* 生死 life and death
... séi *suffix* ...せい [IN NEGATIVE SENSE] cause, effect, influence, fault: **... no séi de** ...のせいで because of ..., due to ...: **... séi ka** ...せいか perhaps because of ...
...´-sei *suffix* ...生 student: **shōgaku-sei** 小学生 elementary school student: **chūgaku-sei** 中学生 junior high school student: **kōkō´-sei** 高校生

169

highschool student: **daigaku-sei** 大学生 college/university student: **daigaku-in-sei** 大学院生 grad(-uate) student

…´-sei *suffix* …製 made in …, made of …: **nihon-sei** 日本製 made in Japan (= **meido in japan** メイド・イン・ジャパン): **beikoku-sei** 米国製 made in U.S.A.: **gaikoku-sei** 外国製 foreign-made: **kinzoku-sei** 金属製 made of metal: **moku-sei** 木製 made of wood

…´-sei *suffix* …星 (*name of certain, kinds of*) star: **waku-sei** 惑星 planet: **kō-sei** 恒星 fixed star

séibun *n* 成分 ingredient, component: **arukōru-seibun** アルコール成分 alcohol component

séibutsu *n* 生物 a living thing, a creature (= **ikimono** 生き物)

seibutsú-gaku *n* 生物学 biology: **seibutsugaku-teki na** 生物学的な biological

seibutsu-gáku-sha *n* 生物学者 biologist

seibutsu *n* 静物 [BOOKISH] still object: **seibutsu-ga** 静物画 still-life painting

seichō *n* 成長 growth: **~ shimásu** 成長します grows; grows up; **kodomo(-tachi) no seichō** 子供(たち)の成長 child(-ren)'s growth: **kōdo-keizai-seichō** 高度経済成長 high economic growth

séido *n* 制度 system (= **shisutemu** システム)

seidō *n* 青銅 bronze (= **buronzu** ブロンズ)

séifu *n* 政府 government

seifuku *n* 制服 uniform (*of school, office, etc.*)

seigén *n* 制限 limit, restriction ~ **shimásu** 制限します limits, restricts

seigen-jikan *n* 制限時間 time limit

seihin *n* 製品 product, manufactured goods

seii *n* 誠意 sincerity (= **magokoro** 真心): **seii o komete hanashimásu** 誠意を込めて話します talks sincerely

seiji *n* 政治 politics: **seiji-ka** 政治家 politician: **seiji-mondai** 政治問題 political issue: **kokusai-seiji** 国際政治 international politics

seijin *n* 成人 adult (= **otona** 大人・おとな): **seijin no hí** 成人の日 Coming-of-Age Day (*honoring 20-year-olds*) on 2nd Monday of January

seijitsu (na) *adj* 誠実(な) sincere

seijuku *n* 成熟 ripening, maturing: **~ shimásu** 成熟します ripens, matures

séika *n* 成果 [BOOKISH] good result, outcome (= **yoi kekka** 良い結果)

séika *n* 正価 net price

seika-ichiba *n* 青果市場 vegetable market

seikaku *n* 性格 character (*personal traits*)

seikaku (na) *adj* 正確(な) exact, accurate, correct

seikaku (na) *adj* 精確(な) minute, correct and precise

seiketsu (na) *adj* 清潔(な) **1.** clean **2.** pure

séiki *n* 世紀 century: **kon-seiki** 今世紀 this century: **rai-seiki** 来世紀 next century

seikō *n* 成功 success: **~ shimásu** 成功します succeeds

seikyū *n* 請求 claim, demand, request: **~ shimásu** 請求します claims, demands, requests

seikyū-sho *n* 請求書 bill

seimitsu (na) *adj* 精密(な) precise, detailed, minute, thorough, accurate

seimon *n* 正門 the front (*main*) gate

seinen *n* 青年 young person, youth, adolescent

seinén-ki *n* 青年期 (*one's*) youth; adolescence (= **seishún-ki** 青春期)

seinen-gáppi *n* 生年月日 date of birth

séiri *n* 生理 physiology: **séiri-teki na** 生理的な physiological; **séiri-yō nápukín** 生理用ナプキン sanitary napkin

seiri-gaku *n* 生理学 physiology

séiri *n* 整理 adjustment, arrangement: **~ shimásu** 整理します adjusts, arranges, (re-)orders, (re-)organizes

seiri-seiton *n* 整理整頓 keeping everything in order

seiritsu *n* 成立 formation, finalization, conclusion: **~ shimásu** 成立します gets formed (*organized*), comes into being, gets finalized/concluded; **kōshō-seiritsu** 交渉成立 completion of the deal

Seiron *n* セイロン Ceylon (= **Suriránka** スリランカ Sri Lanka)

seiryō *n* 清涼 [BOOKISH] refreshing: **seiryō (inryō-)sui** 清涼(飲料)水 refreshing drink

séiryoku *n* 勢力 power, energy; influence (= **iryoku** 威力)

seisaku *n* 政策 (*political*) policy

seisaku *n* 制作・製作 manufacture, production (= **purodyūsu** プロデュース): **~ shimásu** 制作[製作]します manufactures, produces

seisan *n* 生産 production, manufacture: **~ shimásu** 生産します produces

seisan *n* 清算 clearance, liquidation: **~ shimásu** 清算します clears, liquidates

seiseki *n* 成績 results, marks, grades, record: **seiseki-hyō** 成績表 report card

seishi *n* 静止 stillness: **seishi-ga(zō)** 静止画(像) still image (*photo, etc.*)

seishi *n* 精子 spermatozoon

seieki *n* 精液 semen

seishiki (no/na) *adj* 正式(の/な) formal, official

seishin *n* 精神 soul, mind, spirit, psyche: **séishin (no)** 精神(の) mental

seishitsu *n* 性質 character (*of things*), quality, disposition, nature

seishoku *n* 生殖 reproduction, procreation: **~ shimásu** 生殖します produces, procreates

seishoku-ki *n* 生殖期 reproductive period

seishún *n* 青春 adolescence: **seishun-ki** 青春期 adolescence

seisō *n* 清掃 cleaning (= **sōji** 掃除): **~ shimásu** 清掃します cleans

seisō-in *n* 清掃員 cleaning person

séito *n* 生徒 pupil, student

seitō *n* 政党 political party

seitō *n* 正当 [BOOKISH] propriety, validity, reasonableness: **seitō na riyū** 正当な理由 good/fair reason

seitō *n* 正統 legitimacy, orthodoxy (= **ōsodokkusu** オーソドックス)

seiyu *n* 製油 oil manufacturing
seiyu-gaisha *n* 製油会社 oil manufacturing company
seiyu-jo *n* 製油所 (*oil*) refinery

seiza *n* 正座 sitting straight on one's knees: ~ **shimásu** 正座します sits on the floor Japanese style (*sit with one's legs folded under one*)

seiza *n* 星座 constellation: **seiza-hayamihyō** 星座早見表 planisphere: **anata no seiza wa nandesuka** あなたの星座は何ですか? What is your sign?

seiza *n* 静座 sitting quietly, meditation. ~ **shimásu** 静座します sits quietly, meditates

séizei *adv* せいぜい at most, at best

seizō *n* 製造 production, manufacture: **seizō-moto** 製造元 maker (*manufacturer*): ~ **shimásu** 製造します manufactures, produces

seizon *n* 生存 existence, surviving: ~ **shimásu** 生存します exists, survival
seizon-ritsu *n* 生存率 survival rate

seizu *n* 星図 star chart

seizu *n* 製図 drafting a (*technical*) drawing: **kikai-seizu** 機械製図 mechanical drawing, **kenchiku-seizu** 建築製図 architectural drafting

seizui *n* 精髄 [BOOKISH] essence (= **essensu** エッセンス)

seji *n* 世辞 (**o-seji** お世辞) compliment, flattery

sékái *n* 世界 world; **sekai-jū** 世界中 throughout the world, worldwide; **sekai-teki (na)** 世界的(な) worldwide, international

séken *n* 世間 the public, people, the world, society (= **shakai** 社会, **yo-no-naka** 世の中)
seken-bánashi *n* 世間話 chat(-ting) (= **yomoyama-banashi** よもやま話)
seken-tei *n* 世間体 appearances, reputation, decency: **sekentei o kinishimásu** 世間体を気にします cares about appearances, cares what people (may) think

sekí *n* せき・咳 cough: **seki-dome shiroppu** せき止めシロップ cough syrup: **sekí o shimásu** 咳をします coughs

séki *n* 籍 1. (*one's*) family register (= **koseki** 戸籍): **séki o iremásu** 籍を入れます legally marries and has a name entered in the family register, registers one's marriage (= **nyū-seki** 入籍) → **kekkon** 結婚 2. membership: **sakkā-bu ni séki o okimásu** サッカー部に籍を置きます is a member of the football club

séki *n* 席 seat, (*assigned*) place (= **o-seki** お席)
sekí-ryō *n* 席料 cover charge

seki-... *prefix* 赤... red
seki-han *n* 赤飯 (**o-sékihan** お赤飯) rice boiled with red beans (*commonly for celebration dinner*)
Seki-jū´ji *n* 赤十字 Red Cross
seki-men *n* 赤面 a blush: ~ **shimásu** 赤面します blushes

...-seki *suffix* ...隻 (*counts ships/vessels; commonly replaced by* ...**sō** ...艘)

Seki-dō *n* 赤道 equator

sekigaisen *n* 赤外線 infrared rays

sekinin *n* 責任 responsibility, obligation; **sekinín-sha** 責任者 responsible person: **sekinin o torimásu** 責任を取ります takes responsibility

sékiri *n* 赤痢 dysentery

sekitán *n* 石炭 coal
sekitan-san *n* 石炭酸 carbolic acid

sekitatemásu, sekitateru *v* 急き立てます, 急き立てる urges

sekitórí *n* 関取 (*ranking*) sumo wrestler

sekiyu *n* 石油 petroleum, oil, kerosene: **sekiyu-sutō´bu** 石油ストーブ kerosene heater

sékkai *n* 石灰 lime (*mineral*)

sekkakú *adv* せっかく [+ NEGATIVE verb] with much effort/devotion (*but*); on purpose, taking the trouble **Sekkakúdesu ga ...** せっかくですが ... It is kind of you (*to ask*), but ...

sekkei *n* 設計 designing, planning (*of machine, etc.*): ~ **shimásu** 設計します designs, plans
shekkei-sha *n* 設計者 designer (*of machine, etc.*) (→ **dezainā** デザイナー)
shekkei-zu *n* 設計図 draft (= **zumen** 図面) blueprint (= **aojashin** 青写真)

sekken *n* 石けん・石鹸 soap (= **sōpu** ソープ)

sekkin *n* 接近 approach(ing): **sekkin-sen** 接近戦 close game, close contest (= **sessen** 接戦): **... ni sekkin o hakarimásu** ...に接近を図ります seeks access to ...; **... ni sekkin shimásu** ...に接近します approaches, draws near

sekkō *n* 石こう・石膏 plaster

sekkú *n* 節句; **Tángo no sekkú** 端午の節句 Boys Festival (5 May)

sékkusu *n* セックス sex (= **seikō** 性交): **sékkusu (o) shimásu** セックス(を)します has sex

sekkyō´ *n* 説教 (**o-sekkyō´** お説教) sermon: ~ **shimásu** 説教します preaches

sekkyoku-teki (na) *adj* 積極的(な) positive, energetic, vigorous

semái *adj* 狭い 1. narrow, tight, small (*space*): **semai-heya** 狭い部屋 small room; **semai-michi** 狭い道 narrow street, path (= **hoso-michi** 細道) 2. narrow, limited: **shiya ga semái** 視野が狭い has a narrow outlook; **katami ga semái** 肩身が狭い is ashamed 3. narrow, little, small (*mind*) (= **kyōryō** 狭量): **ryōken ga semái** 了見が狭い is narrow-minded (= **kokoro ga semái** 心が狭い)

séme *v* 攻め → **sememásu** 攻めます [INFINITIVE]

séme *v* 責め → **sememásu** 責めます [INFINITIVE]

sememásu, seméru *v* 攻めます, 攻める attacks, assaults

sememásu, seméru *v* 責めます, 責める censures, reproaches, criticizes

semento *n* セメント cement

sémete *adv* せめて at least; at most

sémete *v* 攻めて → **sememásu** 攻めます

sémete *v* 責めて → **sememásu** 責めます

semi n セミ・蝉 cicada, locust

seminā n セミナー seminar, workshop

sén n 千 1,000 (= **is-sén** 一千・1,000) thousand (= **is-sén** 一千)

　sén-ba n 千羽 1,000 (*birds, rabbits*)

　sen-bai n 千倍 a thousand-fold, 1,000 times as much

　sán-bai n 千杯 1,000 cupfuls

　sén-biki n 千匹 1,000 (*fishes/bugs, small animals*)

　sén-bon n 千本 1,000 (*pencils/bottles, long objects*)

　sen-en n 千円 a thousand yen

　sen-zoku n 千足 1,000 pairs of footwear

sén n 線 1. line (→ **shasen** 斜線): **kyoku-sen** 曲線 curved line: **choku-sen** 直線 straight line 2. outline 3. electron beam (→ **āsu-sen** アース線) 4. (*name of electric train line*): (jē āru) **Yama no te-sen** (JR) 山手線 JR Yamanote Line: (jē āru) **Chūō-kaisoku-sen** (JR) 中央快速線 (JR) Chuo Line Rapid

sén n 栓 plug, cork, stopper

　sen-nuki n 栓抜き corkscrew, bottle opener

sen-... prefix 船... ship

　sénchō n 船長 captain (*of ship*)

　sen'in n 船員 ship's crew (*member*), sailor

(...-́) sen suffix (...) 船 (*name of certain*) ship

sen-.../...-sen prefix, suffix 戦.../... 戦 war

　sen-go adv [BOOKISH] 戦後 postwar, after/since the war

　sén-ji adv [BOOKISH] 戦時 wartime; **senji-chū** 戦時中 during the war

　sen-sō n 戦争 war (= **ikusa** 戦)

　sen-tō n [BOOKISH] 戦闘 battle: **~ shimásu** 戦闘します has a battle

　sen-zen (no) adj [BOOKISH] 戦前(の) prewar, before the war

　shū-sen n [BOOKISH] 終戦 the end of a war: **shūsen ni narimásu** 終戦になります the war ends; **shūsen-go** 終戦後 after the war

(...-́) sen (...) 戦 (*name of certain*) war

sen-... prefix 先... 1. last, previous, before, former

　sen-datté adv 先立って a few days ago, recently

　sén-getsu n, adv 先月 last month

　sen-jin n 先人 1. ancestor (= **sosen** 祖先, **senzo** 先祖) 2. forerunner

　sen-jitsu n, adv 先日 the other day

　sen-ku-sha n 先駆者 pioneer, a forerunner (= **paionia** パイオニア)

　sen-nyū-kan n 先入観 preconceived idea, prejudice (= **omoikomi** 思い込み)

　sen-rei n 先例 precedent, prior example

　sen-sén-getsu n [BOOKISH] 先々月 month before last, two months ago

　sen-sén-shū n [BOOKISH] 先々週 week before last

　sen-shū n 先週 last week

　sen'-yaku n 先約 previous appointment/engagement

　sén-zo n 先祖 ancestor (= **sosen** 祖先)

sen-... prefix 先... lead, head, front, top

sen-tan n 先端 1. tip, (*pointed*) end 2. forefront:

sentan-gijutsu 先端技術 high-technology (= **hai-teku** ハイテク)

sen-tō n 先頭 lead, head, front, top (= **riido** リード): **sentō ni tachimásu** 先頭に立ちます takes the lead, takes the initiative

sénbei n せんべい・煎餅 (**o-sénbei** お煎餅) (*also* **o-sénbe** おせんべ) rice crackers

(...-) sénchi (...) センチ, **senchimē´toru** センチメートル centimeter

senchiméntaru (na) adj センチメンタル(な) sentimental (= **kanshōteki (na)** 感傷的(な))

senden n 宣伝 propaganda, publicity: **senden-kōkoku** 宣伝広告 promo

sén'i n 繊維 fiber

sén'i n 遷移 1. transition 2. succession

sénkō n 線香 (**o-sénkō** お線香) incense, joss stick: **katori-senkō** 蚊取り線香 mosquito coil; **senkō-hanabi** 線香花火 Japanese sparkler

senkō n 専攻 major (*study*): **~ shimásu** 専攻します majors (*specializes*) in

sénkyo n 選挙 election: **senkyo-ken** 選挙権 right to vote: **senkyo-undō** 選挙運動 election campaign

senkyō´ n 宣教 mission work (= **dendō** 伝道, **fukyō** 布教)

　senkyō´shi n 宣教師 missionary

senmen n 洗面 washing one's face

　senmen-jó n 洗面所 lavatory (*to wash up at/in*), bathroom

　senmen-ki n 洗面器 wash basin

senmon n 専門 specialty, major (*line/field/study*): **senmon-(yō)go** 専門(用)語 technical term, jargon; **senmon-ka** 専門家 specialist; **senmón-i** 専門医 (*medical*) specialist

senpai n 先輩 one's senior (*colleague, fellow student*)

senpō n 先方 the other side (*party*)

senpū´ n 旋風 [BOOKISH] whirlwind

senpū´-ki n 扇風機 electric fan

senritsu n 旋律 melody (= **merodii** メロディー, **fushi** 節)

senritsu n 戦慄 [BOOKISH] shudder of horror, shiver of horror: **~ shimásu** 戦慄します trembles with fear

sénro n 線路 railroad track/line

senryō n 占領 military occupation: **~ shimásu** 占領します occupies

senryū n 川柳 seventeen-syllable poem

sensai (na) adj 繊細(な) delicate, sensitive

sensaku n 詮索 prying, inquiry: **~ shimásu** 詮索します pries, inquires

　sensaku-zuki (na) adj 詮索好き(な) nosy

senséi n 先生 teacher; doctor; maestro, master (*artisan/artist*) (= **kyōshi** 教師)

sensei n 宣誓 [BOOKISH] oath (= **chikai** 誓い): **~ shimásu** 宣誓します swears an oath

sensé´shon n センセーション a sensation (*excitement*): **sensé´shon o makiokoshimásu** センセーションを巻き起こします makes a splash, creates a sensation, causes a sensation

sénshu *n* 選手 athlete; player: **orinpikku-sénshu** オリンピック選手 an Olympic athlete: **sénshu-ken** 選手権 championship, title

sensu *n* 扇子 (**o-sensu** お扇子) (*Japanese*) fan (*folding*)

sénsu *n* センス sense: **sénsu ga ii** センスがいい has good taste: **sénsu ga warui** センスが悪い has poor taste: **yūmoa no sénsu** ユーモアのセンス sense of humor

sensui *n* 潜水 submerging, diving: **~ shimás<u>u</u>** 潜水します submerges, dives
sensui-fuku *n* 潜水服 diving suit
sensui-kan *n* 潜水艦 submarine

sentaku *n* 洗濯 (**o-séntaku** お洗濯) laundry, washing (= **sentaku-mono** 洗濯物・洗たくもの)
sentáku-ki *n* 洗濯機 washer (*washing machine*)
sentaku-mono-ire *n* 洗濯物入れ clothesbag (*for laundry*)
sentaku-ya *n* 洗濯屋 a laundry

sentaku *n* 選択 selection, choice

sentaku shimás<u>u</u> (suru) *v* 洗濯します(する) launders, washes

sentaku shimás<u>u</u> (suru) *v* 選択します(する) selects

séntensu *n* センテンス sentence (*linguistic*) (= **bun** 文)

(...-) sénto *suffix* (...)セント cent(s)

séntō *n* 銭湯 public bath

seoimás<u>u</u>, seou *v* 背負います, 背負う carries on the back

seppuku *n* 切腹 *harakiri*: **~ shimás<u>u</u>** 切腹します commits 'harakiri'

seppun *n* 接吻 [BOOKISH] kiss (= **kisu** キス): **~ shimás<u>u</u>** 接吻します kisses

serí *n* 競り auction (= **ōkushon** オークション)

serí *n* せり・芹 Japanese parsley

serifu *n* せりふ・台詞 one's lines (*in a play*), dialogue

sérohan *n* セロハン cellophane: **sero(-han) tēpu** セロ(ハン)・テープ cellophane tape, scotch tape

séron *n* 世論 = **yoron** 世論 public opinion

sérori *n* セロリ celery

sē´ru *n* セール sale: **bāgen-sēru** バーゲン・セール bargain sale (= **ōyasu-uri** 大安売り)

sessen *n* 接線 tangent line

sessen *n* 接戦 close game, close contest

sésse-to *adv* せっせと diligently, hard (*laboriously*); frequently, often

ses-shimás<u>u</u> *v* 接します, **ses-suru** 接する; **(... ni) ses-shimás<u>u</u>** (...に)接します **1.** comes in contact (*with*), borders (*on*), is adjacent/contiguous (*to*) **2.** encounters, meets, receives, treats, handles

sesshoku *n* 接触 contact, touch: **...ni sesshoku shimás<u>u</u>** ...に接触します touches, comes into contact with

sesshoku *n* 節食 abstemious diet (= **daietto** ダイエット): **~ shimás<u>u</u>** 節食します goes on diet

sesshō *n* 折衝 negotiation (= **kakehiki** 駆け引き, **kōshō** 交渉): **~ shimás<u>u</u>** 折衝します negotiates

sē´tā *n* セーター sweater

setai *n* 世帯 a household (= **shotai** 所帯・世帯)

setchaku-zai *n* 接着剤 glue, adhesive

setogiwa *n* 瀬戸際 the last moment: **... no setogiwa ni arimás<u>u</u>** ...の瀬戸際にあります is on the verge of ...

setomono *n* 瀬戸物 porcelain, china(ware)

Seto-náikai *n* 瀬戸内海 the Inland Sea

sétsu *n* 節 occasion (*time or event*)

sétsu *n* 説 theory

sétsubi *n* 設備 equipment, facilities, accommodations

setsubi-gó/-ji *n* 接尾語/辞 suffix

setsudan *n* 切断 [BOOKISH] cutting, cutoff: **~ shimás<u>u</u>** 切断します cuts off

setsudo *n* 節度 moderation: **setsudo no aru** 節度のある moderate: **setsudo o mamorimás<u>u</u>** 節度を守ります is moderate

sétsuei *n* 設営 construction, setting up: **tento (no) sétsuei** テント(の)設営 setting up the tent: **~ shimás<u>u</u>** 設営します constructs, sets up

setsugen *n* 節減 reduction: **~ shimás<u>u</u>** 節減します reduces; **keihi-setsugen** 経費節減 reducing the cost; **denryoku-setsugen** 電力節減 energy conservation

setsugō *n* 接合 connection, conjugation, joining: **~ shimás<u>u</u>** 接合します connects, conjugates, joins

setsujitsu (na/ni) *adj*, *adv* 切実(な/に) urgent, serious, keenly, earnestly: **setsujitsu na mondai** 切実な問題 serious problem; **setsujitsu na yōkyū** 切実な要求 a crying need, pressing need

setsumei *n* 説明 explanation, description: **~ shimás<u>u</u>** 説明します explains, describes
setsumei-shó *n* 説明書 written explanation, instructions, manual

sétsuna *n* 刹那 [BOOKISH] moment, instant (= **shunkan** 瞬間)

setsuritsu *n* 設立 establishment, foundation: **~ shimás<u>u</u>** 設立します establishes, founds; **hōjin-setsuritsu** 法人設立 incorporation; **setsuritsu-tōki** 設立登記 organizing registration

setsuyaku *n* 節約 economizing: **~ shimás<u>u</u>** 節約します saves (*economizes on*), conserves

setsuzokú *n* 接続 connection: **~ shimás<u>u</u>** 接続します connects: **densha no setsuzokú** 電車の接続 train connections
setsuzokú-shi *n* 接続詞 a conjunction

séttai *n* 接待 business entertainment: **~ shimás<u>u</u>** 接待します entertains business guests (*clients, etc.*)

séttei *n* 設定 setup, setting (→ **shoki-settei** 初期設定): **~ shimás<u>u</u>** 設定します sets up

sétto *n* セット **1.** set (*hair, etc.*) **2.** a set meal

settō *n* 窃盗 theft: **settō-han** 窃盗犯 a thief

settō-gó/-ji *n* 接頭語/辞 prefix

settoku *v* 説得 persuasion: **~ shimás<u>u</u>** 説得します persuades, convinces

sewá *n* 世話 (**o-séwa** お世話) **1.** care, trouble, assistance, help; **(...no) sewá ni narimás<u>u</u>**

(…の)世話になります becomes obliged (*to one for help*); → **o-sewa-sama** お世話さま
2. meddling, minding other people's business

sewashíi *adj* 忙しい = **sewashi-nái** 忙しない busy, hectic

sezu *v* せず not doing (= **sezu ni** せずに, **shináide** しないで)

sha-…/…-sha *prefix, suffix* 社…/…社 company
sha-chō *n* 社長 president of a company
sha-dan *n* 社団 corporation
shá-in *n* 社員 employee (*of a company*)
shá-nai (no) *adj* 社内(の) within the office/company, internal, in-house

sha-… *prefix* 車… vehicle
sha-dō *n* 車道 road(way), drive(way), street
shá-ko *n* 車庫 garage, car barn
sha-rin *n* 車輪 wheel
sha-shō *n* 車掌 conductor

…-sha *suffix* …車 (*name of certain*) vehicle

…´-sha …者 person

shaberánai *v* 喋らない = **shaberimasén** 喋りません [INFORMAL] (not speak/talk)

shaberimásu, shabéru *v* 喋ります, 喋る [INFORMAL]speak/talk: **o-shaberi shimásu** お喋りします chatters

sháberu *n* シャベル shovel

shabétte *v* 喋って → **shaberimásu** 喋ります

shabon *n* シャボン soap (= **sekken** 石けん・石鹸)
shabon-dama *n* シャボン玉 soap bubble

shaburanai *v* しゃぶらない = **saburimasén** しゃぶりません [INFORMAL](not suck)

shaburimásu, shaburu *v* しゃぶります, しゃぶる [INFORMAL] sucks (= **suu** 吸う)

shabu-shabu *n* しゃぶしゃぶ beef slices dipped in hot broth till ready to eat

shabutte *v* しゃぶって → **shaburimásu** しゃぶります

shadan *n* 遮断 interruption: ~ **shimásu** 遮断します interrupts

shagamimásu, shagamu *v* しゃがみます, しゃがむ squats, crouches on heels

shagande *v* しゃがんで → **shagamimásu** しゃがみます

shagare-goe *n* 嗄れ声 hoarse voice

shageki *n* 射撃 shooting (*firing a rifle, shotgun, etc*)

shajitsu *n* 写実 [BOOKISH] drawing/writing realistically: **shajitsu-teki (na)** 写実的(な) realistic (= **riaru (na)** リアル(な)): **shajitsu-shugi** 写実主義 realism

Sháka *n* シャカ・釈迦 Buddha (*Sakyamuni*) (= **O-Shaka-samá** お釈迦様)

shákai *n* 社会 society (= **seken** 世間, **yo-no-naka** 世の中): **shákai no** 社会の social
shakai-kágaku *n* 社会科学 social science(s)
shakai no mado *n* 社会の窓 one's fly
shakai no shukuzu *n* 社会の縮図 society in miniature: **gakkō wa shakai no shukuzu desu** 学校は社会の縮図です School is a society in miniature.

shakai-shúgi *n* 社会主義 socialism; **shakai-shugí-sha** 社会主義者 a socialist

sháke *n* シャケ・鮭 salmon (= **sáke** サケ・鮭)

shakkín *n* 借金 debt

shákkuri *n* しゃっくり hiccup: ~ **shimásu** しゃっくりします hiccups

sháko *n* シャコ squilla, mantis shrimp

shakō *n* 社交 social intercourse, socializing

shaku *n* 酌 (**o-shaku** お酌) serving/pouring the rice wine: **o-shaku o shimásu** お酌をします serves the saké

shakuhachi *n* 尺八 vertical bamboo flute

shakunetsu *adj* 灼熱 1. burning: **shakunetsu no taiyō** 灼熱の太陽 scorching sun 2. passionate: **shakunetsu no koi** 灼熱の恋 passionate love

shaku ni sawarimásu (sawaru) *v* 癪に障ります(障る) takes offense, gets irritated/provoked; **… ga shaku ni sawarimásu** …が癪に障ります is offensive, irritating, provoking

shákushi *n* 杓子 ladle (*large wooden*): [IDIOM] **neko mo shakushi mo** 猫も杓子も all the world and his wife, everyone (= **dare mo ka(re) mo** 誰も彼も)

shákushi-jōgi *n* 杓子定規 formalism: **shákushi-jōgi ni yarimásu** 杓子定規にやります goes by the book

shamisen *n* 三味線 a three-stringed banjo

Shánhái *n* シャンハイ・上海 Shanghai

shanpán, shanpén *n* シャンパン, シャンペン champagne

shánpū *n* シャンプー shampoo

share *n* しゃれ・洒落 pun (= **dajare** 駄洒落): **share o iimásu** しゃれを言います puns

sharei (kin) *n* 謝礼(金) remuneration, reward, fee

shasei *n* 写生 sketching, sketch: ~ **shimásu** 写生します sketches

shasei *n* 射精 ejaculation, seminal emission: ~ **shimásu** 射精します ejaculates

shashin *n* 写真 photo, picture: **shashin-chō** 写真帳 photo album: **shashin-ka** 写真家 photographer: **shashin o torimásu** 写真を撮ります takes a photograph (= **shashin satsuei (o) shimásu** 写真撮影(を)します)
shashin-ki *n* 写真機 camera (= **kamera** カメラ)

shátsu *n* シャツ undershirt

sháttā *n* シャッター shutter (*camera, etc.*): **sháttā o kirimásu** シャッターを切ります releases the shutter

sháwā *n* シャワー shower: **sháwā o abimásu** シャワーを浴びます takes a shower

shi *n* 詩 poetry, poem, verse
shijin *n* 詩人 poet

shi *v* し → **shimásu** します [INFINITIVE]

… shi *suffix* …し and, and so, what with (*the fact that*) …

shí *n* 死 death
shi-gai *n* 死骸 corpse
shi-in *n* 死因 cause of death
shi-nin *n* 死人 dead person: [IDIOM] **shinin ni**

kuchi nashi 死人に口なし Dead men tell no tales.
shi-shō´-sha n 死傷者 casualties (*dead and wounded*)
shi-tai n 死体 corpse
shí n 四 four (= **yón** 四)
shi-go-… *prefix, adj* 四,五… four or five …
shi-jū n 四重 quadruplex: **shi-jū-sō** 四重奏 quartet (= **karutetto** カルテット) (*musical instruments, two violins, viola, cello, etc.*): **gengaku-shijūsō-kyoku/dan** 弦楽四重奏曲/団 string quartet
shí n 市 city (= **tóshi** 都市)
shi-chō´ n 市長 mayor
shí-gai n 市外 outside the city: **shi-gai-denwa** 市外電話 out-of-city call
shí-min n 市民 citizen, civilian (= **kōmin** 公民)
shí-nai n 市内 within the city: **shinai-denwa** 市内電話 local telephone call
shí-ritsu (no) *adj* 市立(の) municipal
shi-yákusho n 市役所 city office, city hall
shiage n 仕上げ the finish(*ing touch*)
shiáge v 仕上げ → **shiagemásu** 仕上げます [INFINITIVE]
shiagemásu v 仕上げます, **shiagéru** 仕上げる finishes up
shiagénai v 仕上げない = **shiagemasén** 仕上げません (not finish up)
shiágete v 仕上げて → **shiagemásu** 仕上げます
shiai n 試合 match, contest, meet, tournament
shiasátte n, adv しあさって・明々後日 three days from now
shiawase n 幸せ・しあわせ happiness (= **kōfuku** 幸福, **saiwai** 幸い)
shiawase (na) *adj* 幸せ(な) happy
shiba n 柴 brushwood
shiba n 芝 turf, lawn
shibá-ebi n 芝エビ[海老] tiny shrimp
shiba-fu n 芝生 lawn, grass
shiba-karí-ki n 芝刈り機 lawn mower
Shíba n 芝 Shiba; **Shiba-Kō´en** 芝公園 Shiba Park
shibai n 芝居 **1.** a play (*drama*) (= **engeki** 演劇, **engi** 演技) **2.** acting, pretending, fake: **shibai o uchimásu** 芝居を打ちます puts on an act
shibáraku *adv* しばらく (*for*) a while: **shibáraku shite** しばらくして after a while: **Shibáraku desu ne** しばらくですね It's nice to see you again.
shibaránai v 縛らない = **shibarimasén** 縛りません (not tie up)
shibarimásu, shibáru v 縛ります, 縛る tie up
shíba shíba *adv* しばしば often, repeatedly
shibátte v 縛って → **shibarimásu** 縛ります [INFINITIVE]
Shiberia n シベリア Siberia
shibin n しびん bedpan (*urinal*)
shibiré n しびれ・痺れ numbness: **shibiré o kirashimásu** しびれを切らします loses patience
shibíre v 痺れ → **shibiremásu** 痺れます
shibiremásu, shibiréru v 痺れます, 痺れる gets numb, (*a leg, etc.*) goes to sleep
shibō n 脂肪 fat (*lard, blubber*) (= **abura** 脂)

shibō n 志望 a desire, a wish: **haiyū-shibō** 俳優志望 a would-be actor: **joyū-shibō** 女優志望 a would-be actress: **daiichi-shibō no daigaku** 第一志望の大学 one's first choice college/university: **daiichi-shibō no kaisha** 第一志望の会社 one's first choice company
shiboránai v 絞らない = **shiborimasén** 絞りません not wring it
shibóri v 絞り → **shiborimásu** 絞ります [INFINITIVE]
shiborimásu, shibóru v 絞ります, 絞る wrings (*out*), squeezes, strains (*through cloth*)
shibótte v 絞って → **shiborimásu** 絞って
shibu n 支部 branch office
shibúi *adj* 渋い **1.** taste, astringent (*tea*), bitter (*wine*) rough **2.** (*face*) wry, sour: **shibúi kao o shimásu** 渋い顔をします makes a wry face **3.** appearance cool (*sedate, sober, elegant, tasteful*): **shibui engi** 渋い演技 low-keyed performance
shibui kaki n 渋い柿, **shibu-gaki** 渋柿 sour persimmon
shibui iroi n 渋い色 elegant color
Shibuya n 渋谷 Shibuya; **Shibuyá-Eki** 渋谷駅 Shibuya Station
shicha v [INFORMAL] しちゃ = **shité wa** しては
shichaimáshita v [INFORMAL] しちゃいました = **shite shimaimáshita** してしまいました = **shimáshita** しました (did)
shichaimásu v [INFORMAL] しちゃいます = **shite shimaimásu** してしまいます
shichatta v [INFORMAL] しちゃった = **shite shimatta** してしまった = **shita** した (did)
shichau v [INFORMAL] しちゃう = **shite shimau** してしまう
shichí n 七・7 seven (= **nána** 七・7)
Shichi-go-san n 七五三 the "seven-five-three" day when children of those ages visit shrines (*15 November*)
shichí n 質 a pawn (*something pawned*)
shichí-ya n 質屋 pawnbroker, pawnshop
Shichi-gatsú n 七月・7月 July
shichi-jū n 七十・70 seventy (= **naná-jū** 七十・70)
shichimen-chō n シチメンチョウ・七面鳥 turkey
shichū n シチュー stew
shída n シダ・羊歯 fern
shidai n 次第・しだい **1.** circumstances **2.** *suffix* ([NOUN, VERB] -i い) **shídai desu** 次第です it depends on …; ([VERB] -i い) - **shídai** 次第 as soon as …
shidashi-ya n 仕出し屋 caterer, catering shop
shidō n 指導 guidance, direction, leadership, counsel(*ing*), coaching: ~ **shimásu** 指導します guides, directs, leads, counsels, coaches
shidō-sha n 指導者 a guide, a director, a leader, a coach
shifuku n 私服 plain clothes; civilian clothes
shígā n シガー cigar (= **hamaki** 葉巻)

shi-gachi (na) *suffix, adj* しがち(な) apt to do, tends to

shígarétto *n* シガレット cigarette(s) (= **tabako** たばこ・タバコ・煙草): **sigaretto-kēsu** シガレットケース cigarette case

Shi-gatsú *n* 四月・4月 April

shigeki *n* 刺激 stimulation: ~ **shimásu** 刺激します stimulates: **shigeki o ukemásu** 刺激を受けます gets stimulated

shigerimásu, shigéru *v* 茂ります, 茂る it grows thick(ly)/luxuriant(ly)

shígoku *adv* 至極 extremely

shigoto *n* 仕事(**o-shígoto** お仕事) job, work, task, undertaking, business; operation: **shigoto (o) shimásu** 仕事(を)します works; **shigoto ni ikimásu** 仕事に行きます goes to work

shigure *n* 時雨 an on-and-off drizzle (*in early winter*): **semi-shigure** 蝉時雨 cicada shower, cicada chorus

shihái, shíhai *n* 支配 management, control: ~ **shimásu** 支配します rules, controls
shihái-nin *n* 支配人 manager
shihái-sha *n* 支配者 ruler

shihanki *n* 四半期 quarter (*year*): **dai ni-shi hanki** 第二四半期 the second (*business*) quarter (*of a company*)

shiharai *n* 支払い paying out, payment, disbursement

shíhei *n* 紙幣 paper money, currency (*bill*) (= (**o-)satsu** (お)札)

shihō´ (-happō) *n* 四方(八方) all sides/directions

shihon (kin) *n* 資本(金) capital, funds: **shihon-ka** 資本家 capitalist; **shihon-shúgi** 資本主義 capitalism

shiiému *n* シーエム・CM TV commercial, CM (= **komāsharu** コマーシャル)

shiin *n* 子音 consonant (= **shion** 子音)

shíin *n* シーン scene (= **bamen** 場面)

shíitake *n* シイタケ・椎茸 large brown mushrooms, shiitake mushrooms: **hoshi-shiitake** 干し椎茸 dried shiitake mushrooms

shiite *v* 敷いて → **shikimásu** 敷きます

shíite *adv* 強いて forcibly: **shíite sasemásu** 強いてさせます forces one to do

shíito *n* シート **1.** sheets; **biniiru shiito** ビニール・シート vinyl sheet **2.** seat; **shiito-béruto** シート・ベルト seatbelt

shíitsu *n* シーツ sheet (*for bed*) (= **beddo (no) shíitsu** ベッド(の)シーツ)

shíizun *n* シーズン **1.** the season (= **kisetsu** 季節) **2.** high season; **yakyū (no) shíizun** 野球(の)シーズン baseball season

shiji *n* 支持 [BOOKISH] support, maintenance (= **sapōto** サポート): ~ **shimásu** 支持します supports, endorses

shíji *n* 指示 [BOOKISH] indication, instruction, directions: ~ **shimásu** 指示します indicates, points out

shíji *n* 師事 [BOOKISH] studying under someone: …

ni shíji shimásu …に師事します studies under someone at …

shíji *n* 私事 [BOOKISH] **1.** personal matter (= **watakushi-goto** 私事) **2.** privacy

shijō *n* 市場 market (= **māketto** マーケット)

shi-jū *n* 四十・40 forty (= **yón-jū** 四十・40)

shíjū *adv* 始終 all the time

shika *n* シカ・鹿 deer

shiká *n* 歯科 dentistry
shiká-i *n* 歯科医 dentist (= **há-isha** 歯医者)

…shika *conj* …しか [+ NEGATIVE] (nothing) but, except for; (= **…daké** …だけ [+ POSITIVE]) only, just

shikake *n* 仕掛け device (*gadget*)

shikaku *n* 資格 qualification(s), competency; **zairyū shikaku** 在留資格 status of residence

shikakúi *adj* 四角い square

shiká-mo *adv* しかも moreover; and yet

shikanai *v* 敷かない = **shikimasén** 敷きません (not spread it)

shikaranai *v* 叱らない = **shikarimasén** 叱りません (not scold)

shikari *v* 叱り → **shikarimásu** 叱ります [INFINITIVE]

shikarimásu, shikaru *v* 叱ります, 叱る scolds

shikarō´ *v* 叱ろう = **shikarimashō´** 叱りましょう (let's scold!)

shikáshi *conj* しかし [BOOKISH] but, however (= **demo** でも, **keredo(mo)** けれど(も))

shi-kata *n* 仕方 way (of doing), manner, method, means: **shi-kata ga arimasén** 仕方がありません there's nothing I/we can do about it, can't be helped

shikátte *v* 叱って → **shikarimásu** 叱ります

shikéba *v* 敷けば・しけば (if one spreads it) → **shikimásu** 敷きます

shikén *n* 試験 [BOOKISH] examination, test, trial, experiment (= **tesuto** テスト)
shiken-jó *n* 試験所 (*testing*) laboratory
shiken-jō *n* 試験場 exam room/place
shikén-kan *n* 試験管 test tube

shikí *n* 式 ceremony

shiki *n* 指揮 **1.** command **2.** conducting (*orchestra*)
shikí-sha *n* 指揮者 conductor (*orchestra*)

shiki *v* 敷き → **shikimásu** 敷きます [INFINITIVE]

shikibetsu *n* 識別 discrimination: ~ **shimásu** 識別します discriminates, discerns, distinguishes

shiki-chi *n* 敷地 building lot; (*house*) site

shikii *n* 敷居 sill; threshold

shikí-kin *n* 敷金 security deposit (*for rental*)

shikimásu, shiku *v* 敷きます, 敷く spreads (*a quilt, etc.*)
shiki-búton *n* 敷布団 bottom quilt
shiki-fu *n* 敷布 (bed)sheet (= **shíitsu** シーツ, **beddo (no) shíitsu** ベッド(の)シーツ)
shiki-mono *n* 敷物 a spread; rug, mat, cushion

shikín *n* 資金 fund, capital

shi-kiremasén, shi-kirénai *v* し切れません,

し切れない = **dekimasén** できません, **dekínai**
できない (cannot do it)

shikiri n 仕切り partition (= **pātēshon** パーテーション)

shikiri ni adv しきりに incessantly; intently, hard

shikí ya/wa shinai v 敷きや/はしない
= **shikanai** 敷かない (not spread it)

shikkári adv しっかり firmly, resolutely

shikke, shikki n 湿気 dampness, humidity

shikki n 湿気 → **shikke** 湿気

shikki n 漆器 lacquer(ware)

shikko n しっこ, **o-shikko** おしっこ (slang/baby talk) urine, urinating (= **nyō** 尿)

shikkui n 漆喰 plaster, stucco, mortar

shikō n 嗜好・し好 liking, fancy, taste; **...ni shikō ga arimásu** ...に嗜好があります has a taste/liking for...

shikō-hin n 嗜好品・し好品 articles of taste, amenities of life

Shikóku n 四国 Shikoku: **Shikóku-chihō** 四国地方 the Sikoku area of Japan (*Tokushima, Kagawa, Ehime, Kōchi prefectures*)

shiku v 敷く = **shikimásu** 敷きます (spreads it)

shikyō hin n 試供品 tester, free sample (*for customers*) (→ **sanpuru** サンプル)

shikyū adv 至急 urgently: **shikyū (no)** 至急(の) urgent

shima n 島 island

shima n 縞 stripes (= **sutoraipu** ストライプ):
shima-moyō 縞模様 stripe pattern

shimai n 終い・仕舞(い) ・o-shimai おしまい・御仕舞(い) the end: **shimai (no)** しまい(の) the final/last

shimai v しまい → **shimaimásu** しまいます
[INFINITIVE]

shimaimásu, shimau v しまいます, しまう puts away, finishes; **shite shimau** してしまう finishes doing, ends up by doing (*after all*), does anyway, does it all

shimaō´ v しまおう = **shimai-mashō´** しまいましょう (let's put it away; let's finish)

shimaránai v 閉まらない = **shimarimásen** 閉まりません (not shut; not ...)

shimarimásu, shimáru v 閉まります, 閉まる it shuts, closes, locks

shimarimásu, shimáru v 締まります, 締まる gets steady, braces oneself

shimarimásu, shimáru v 締まります, 締まる gets thrifty, frugal

shimasén, shinai v しません, しない doesn't

shimasén deshita, shinákatta v しませんでした, しなかった didn't

shimáshita v しました = **shita** した (did)

shimashō´ v しましょう = **shiyō´** しよう (let's do it): **shimashō´ ka** しましょうか Shall we do it?

shimásu, suru v します, する does (it); it happens; wears
... ni ([ADJECTIVE] **-ku**) shimásu ...に...(く)します makes it so that (*it is*), makes it into; decides on

(= ... ni kimemásu ...に決めます)

... (shiyō) to shimásu ...(しよう)とします goes
(tries, is about) to do

... (suru) koto ni shimásu ...(する)事にします
decides to (do)

... to shíte(´ mo) ...として(も) (*even*) as a ...

shímatsu n 始末 managing, dealing with;
outcome, upshot, climax; **shímatsu shimásu** 始末
します deals with, manages, settles, disposes of

shimatta v しまった = **shimaimáshita** しまいました (finished)

shimátta v 閉まった・締まった = **shimarimáshita** 閉まりました・締まりました (it shut, closed, locked)

shimátta interj しまった! Damn!, Good heavens

shimau v しまう = **shimaimásu** しまいます (puts away, finishes)

shimauma n シマウマ zebra

shimawanai v しまわない = **shimaimásen** しまいません (not put away)

shime v 閉め → **shimemásu** 閉めます
[INFINITIVE]

shime v 締め → **shimemásu** 締めます
[INFINITIVE]

shime-gane n 締め金 buckle

shimei n 使命 mission (= **misshon** ミッション):
shimei-kan 使命感 sense of mission

shi-mei n 氏名 (*one's*) full name (= **sei-mei** 姓名)

shimei n 指名 designation: ~ **shimásu** 指名します nominates

shimei-tsū´wa n 指名通話 person-to-person call
shimei-tehai n 指名手配 listing a person
(*criminal*) on the wanted list: ~ **shimásu** 指名手配
します puts a person (*criminal*) on the wanted list

shimekiri n 締め切り・〆切 1. closing 2.
"Closed", deadline: **shimekiri kígen/kíjitsu** 締め
切り期限/期日 deadline, due date

shimemásu, shiméru v 閉めます, 閉める shuts
(closes, locks)

shimemásu, shiméru v 締めます, 締める 1. ties,
fastens, tightens it (*a necktie, a belt, a kimono
sash, a seatbelt, etc.*) 2. tightens up on: **neji o
shimemásu** ネジを締めます tightens up a screw
3. economizes on [IDIOM] **saifu no himo o shimeru**
財布の紐を締める tightens one's belt 4. **ki o hiki-
shimemásu** 気を引き締めます braces oneself

shiménai v 閉めない = **shimemásen** 閉めません
(not shut it)

shimeppói adj 湿っぽい damp; humid

shimerasemásu, shimerasu v 湿らせます,
湿らす moistens/dampens it, wets it

shimeri v 湿り → **shimerimásu** 湿ります
[INFINITIVE]

shimerimásu, shimeru v 湿ります, 湿る gets
damp

shiméru v 閉める = **shimemásu** 閉めます
(closes it)

shiméru v 締める = **shimemásu** 締めます
(fastens it, closes it)

shimeshimás<u>u</u>, shimésu *v* 示します, 示す shows, indicates

shímeta *v* 閉めた = **shimemásh<u>i</u>ta** 閉めました (closed it)

shímeta *v* 締めた = **shimemásh<u>i</u>ta** 締めました (fastenend it, closes it)

shímete *v* 閉めて → **shimemás<u>u</u>** 閉めます

shímete *v* 締めて → **shimemás<u>u</u>** 締めます

shimetta *v* 湿った = **shimerimásh<u>i</u>ta** 湿りました (got damp)

shimette *v* 湿って → **shimerimás<u>u</u>** 湿ります: **shimette imás<u>u</u>** 湿っています is damp

shimi *n* 染み・しみ **1.** stain, blot, blotch, spot **2.** → **shimimás<u>u</u>** 染みます [INFINITIVE]

shimi *n* 衣魚・シミ clothes moth

shimijími (to) *adv* しみじみ（と）deeply (*feels*), fully (*appreciates*)

shimimás<u>u</u>, shimiru *v* 染みます, 染みる penetrates, soaks

shimimás<u>u</u>, shimiru *v* 沁みます, 沁みる smarts, is stimulated (*body*), is deeply moved (*heart*): **... ga kokoro ni shimimás<u>u</u>** ...が心に沁みます is deeply moved by ...: **honemi ni shimimás<u>u</u>** 骨身に沁みます touches one to the quick: **hito no nasake ga mi ni shimimás<u>u</u>** 人の情けが身に沁みます deeply appreciates people's thoughtfulness

shimó *n* 霜・しも frost: **shimó ga orimás<u>u</u>** 霜が降ります frosts

shí mo *suffix* しも [+ NEGATIVE verb] **shí mo shimasén** しもしません nor do, not do either/even

shimon *n* 指紋 fingerprint

shimon *n* 諮問 [BOOKISH] inquiry: ~ **shimás<u>u</u>** 諮問します inquires, consults

shimon *n* 試問 [BOOKISH] questioning, interviewing, examination; **kōtō-shímon** 口頭試問 oral examination

shín *n* 芯 core, pith, heart: **rōsoku no shín** ロウソク［蝋燭］の芯 candlewick: **ringo no shín** リンゴ［林檎］の芯 apple core

shín-... *prefix* 心... heart, spirit

shín-chū *n* 心中 in one's heart

shin-pai *n* 心配 worry, uneasiness, concern, anxiety, fear: ~ **shimás<u>u</u>** 心配します worries about, fears; **shinpai (na)** 心配（な）uneasy; **(... ni) shinpai o kakemás<u>u</u>** (...に)心配をかけます causes (*one*) worry/concern; [HONORIFIC] **Go-shinpai náku.** ご心配なく Please do not worry about it.

shín-ri *n* 心理 psychology, mentality

shin-rí-gaku *n* 心理学 (*science/study of*) psychology; **shinri gáku-sha** 心理学者 psychologist

shín-soko *n* 心底 (*at*) the bottom of one's heart

shin-zō *n* 心臓 heart (*organ*)

shín-... *prefix* 新... ... new

shin-geki *n* 新劇 modern drama

shín-nen *n* 新年 new year: **Shín-nen akemashite omedetō (gozaimás<u>u</u>)** 新年明けましておめでとう（ございます）! Happy New Year!

shin-sen (na) *adj* 新鮮（な）fresh (= **furesshu** フレッシュ）

Shin-yaku Seisho *n* 新約聖書 the New Testament

shin-... *prefix* 神... god, deity

shin-den *n* 神殿 the sanctuary of a shrine

shín-dō *n* 神童 child prodigy

shín-pu *n* 神父 priest (*Christian*), Father, Reverend

Shín-tō, Shín-dō *n* 神道 Shinto(ism)

shin-wa *n* 神話 myth, mythology

shina *n* 品 **1.** articles, goods (= **shinamono** 品物) **2.** quality (= **hinshitsu** 品質): **ii shina** 良い品 good/high quality products

shina-mono *n* 品物 goods, articles (= **shina** 品)

shi-nagara しながら while doing

shinai *v* しない = **shimasén** しません (doesn't do it)

shináide *v* しないで not doing it, instead of doing it: **shináide imás<u>u</u>** しないでいます keeps on not doing it; **shináide kudasai** しないで下さい Please don't do it!; **shináide okimás<u>u</u>** しないでおきます neglects to do it, leaves it undone; **shináide mimás<u>u</u>** しないでみます tries not doing it; **shináide sumimás<u>u</u>** しないで済みます gets by without doing it, needs not do it, doesn't have to do it

shinai to しないと = **shinákereba** しなければ (unless one does it)

shinákatta *v* しなかった = **shimasén desh<u>i</u>ta** しませんでした (didn't do it)

shinákereba しなければ unless one does it: **shinákereba narimasén** しなければなりません must do it

shinákute mo *v* しなくても even not doing it; **shinákute mo íi des<u>u</u>** しなくてもいいです gets by without doing it, needs not do it, doesn't have to do it

shinákya *v* [INFORMAL] しなきゃ = **shinákereba** しなければ

shinanai *v* 死なない = **shinimasén** 死にません (does/will not die)

shinanákatta *v* 死ななかった = **shini-masén desh<u>i</u>ta** 死にませんでした (didn't die)

shi-naoshimás<u>u</u>, shi-naósu *v* し直します, し直す redoes it, fixes/improves it

Shínbashi *n* 新橋 Shinbashi; **Shinbashí-Eki** 新橋駅 Shinbashi Station

shínbō *n* 辛抱 [BOOKISH] endurance, patience, forbearance (= **gaman** 我慢, **nintai** 忍耐): ~ **shimás<u>u</u>** 辛抱します endures, bears, stands, puts up with

shinbun *n* 新聞 newspaper: **shinbun-k<u>í</u>shá** 新聞記者 newsperson; **shinbun-úriba** 新聞売り場 newsstand; **shinbun-úri** 新聞売り news vendor

shinbun-dai *n* 新聞代 newspaper bill

shinbún-sha *n* 新聞社 newspaper company

shinchō *n* 身長 height, stature (= **sé** 背, **séi** せい・背, **setake** 背丈): **shinchō o hakarimás<u>u</u>** 身長を測ります measures one's height

shinchū *n* 真鍮 brass

shinda v 死んだ = **shinimáshita** 死にました (died)
((*human*)) = **nakunarimashita** 亡くなりました,
o-nakunari ni narimashita [HONORIFIC] お亡くな
りになりました)

shindai n 寝台 bed, berth, bunk; **shindái-ken** 寝台
券 berth ticket; **shindái-sha** 寝台車 sleeping car

shinde v 死んで → **shinimásu** 死にます: **shinde
imásu** 死んでいます is dead

shindō n 振動 vibration (= **baiburēshon** バイブレ
ーション): **shindō shimásu** 振動します vibrates:
hageshii shindō 激しい振動 thumping vibration

Shinetsu-chihō n 信越地方 the Shinetsu area of
Japan (*Niigata, Nagano prefectures*)

shingo n 寝具 bedding

shíngo n 信号 signal: **shingō-ki** 信号機 traffic
light: **shingō-mushi** 信号無視 running a red light:
ao-shingō 青信号 green light: **aka-shingō** 赤信号
red light: [IDIOM] **aka-shingō minna de watareba
kowakunai** 赤信号皆で渡れば怖くない If
everyone crosses against the red light, then there's
nothing to be afraid of.

shíngu n 寝具 bedding

shínguru n シングル 1. = **shinguru-rū´mu** シン
グル・ルーム a single (*room*) 2. single, unmarried
(= **dokushin** 独身), bachelor

shinimásu, shinu v 死にます, 死ぬ dies (=
nakunarimásu 亡くなります, **o-nakunari ni
narimásu** [HONORIFIC] お亡くなりになります
(*for human*))

shínjá n 信者 a believer; **Kirisuto-kyō (no) shínjá**
キリスト教(の)信者 a Christian

shin-ji v 信じ → **shin-jimásu** 信じます
[INFINITIVE]

shin-jimásu, shin-jíru v 信じます, 信じる
believes in, trusts

shin-jínai v 信じない = **shin-jimasén** 信じません
(doesn't believe/trust)

shin-jínákatta v 信じなかった = **shin-jimasén
deshita** 信じませんでした (didn't believe/trust)

shínjitsu n 真実 truth (= **hontō no koto** 本当のこ
と, **makoto** 誠・真)

shinju n 真珠 pearl; **Shinjú-wan** 真珠湾 Pearl
Harbor

shinjū n 心中 double suicide, lovers' suicide

Shinjuku n 新宿 Shinjuku; **Shinjukú-Eki** 新宿駅
Shinjuku Station

shinkánsen n 新幹線 bullet train (*line*),
Shinkansen

shínkei n 神経 nerve: **shínkei ni sawarimásu** 神
経に障ります gets on one's nerves: **chūsū-shínkei**
中枢神経 central nerve

shinkéi-shitsu (na) adj 神経質(な) nervous

shinkoku (na) adj 深刻(な) serious, grave

shinobánai v 忍ばない = **shinobimasén** 忍びませ
ん (not bear, not put up with)

shinobimásu, shinóbu v 忍びます, 忍ぶ bears,
puts up with

shinónde v 忍んで → **shinobimásu** 忍びます

shínpi n 神秘 mystery; **shinpi-teki (na)** 神秘的(
な) mysterious, esoteric, miraculous

shínpo n 進歩 progress: ~ **shimásu** 進歩します
makes progress

shínpuru (na) adj シンプル(な) simple

shinrai n 信頼 trust, confidence, reliance
shinrai-sei n 信頼性 reliability: **shinrai-sei ga
takái** 信頼性が高い highly reliable

shínri n 真理 truth, veritas: **fuhen no shínri** 不変
の真理 eternal truth, everlasting truth (= **eien no
shínri** 永遠の真理)

shinrui n 親類 a relative (= **shinseki** 親戚,
shinzoku 親族)

shinryaku n 侵略 invasion, aggression: ~ **shimásu**
侵略します invades

shinsatsu n 診察 medical examination: ~ **shimásu**
診察します examines

shinsei n 申請 application (*for a permit*):
~ **shimásu** 申請します applies (*for a permit*)
shinsei-nin n 申請人 an applicant
shinsei-shó n 申請書 application form (*for a permit*)

shinseki n 親戚 a relative (= **shinrui** 親類,
shinzoku 親族)

shínsetsu n 親切 (**go-shínsetsu** ご親切) kindness,
goodwill, favor
shínsetsu na adj 親切な kind, cordial

shínshi n 紳士 gentleman

shinshitsu n 寝室 bedroom

shíntai (no) adj 身体(の) physical; **shintai-kénsa**
身体検査 physical exam; **shintai-shōgáisha** 身体
障害者 handicapped person

shinu v 死ぬ = **shinimásu** 死にます (dies)

shin'ya n, adv 深夜 late at night

shin'yō n 信用 trust, confidence; credit: ~ **shimásu**
信用します trusts

shinzoku n 親族 relatives (= **shinseki** 親戚,
shinrui 親類)

shió n 潮 tide (→ **kanchō** 干潮, **manchō** 満潮)

shió n 塩 (**o-shío** お塩) salt
shio-karái adj 塩辛い salty (= **shoppai** しょっぱ
い)
shio-yaki n 塩焼き broiled salt-coated fish

shion n 子音 consonant (= **shiin** 子音)

shiori n しおり bookmark (*a thin marker made of
paper, card, etc.*)

shippai n 失敗 failure, blunder, defeat: ~ **shimásu**
失敗します fails, misses

shippó n しっぽ・尻尾 tail (= **o** 尾)

shira-... prefix 白... white
shira-gá n 白髪 gray hair
shira-su n シラス・白子 baby sardines
shirá-taki n シラタキ・白滝 fine white threads of
Konnyaku (こんにゃく)
shira-uo n シラウオ・白魚 icefish, white fish

shírabe v 調べ → **shirabemásu** 調べます
1. [INFINITIVE] 2. **shirabe ro** 調べろ [IMPERATIVE]
(investigate!)

shirabemásu, shirabéru v 調べます, 調べる
investigates, examines, checks

shirabénai v 調べない = **shirabemasén** 調べませ
ん (not investigate)

shirábeta *v* 調べた = **shirabemáshita** 調べました (investigated)

shirábete *v* 調べて → **shirabemásu** 調べます

shirafu (no) *adj* しらふ(の) (*undrunk*) sober

shirami *n* シラミ louse, lice

shiranai *v* 知らない = **shirimasén** 知りません (not know): **shiranai hitó** 知らない人 a stranger (= **tanin** 他人)

shiraremásu, shirareru *v* 知られます, 知られる gets (*widely*) known; becomes famous

shirarenai *v* 知れない = **shiraremasén** 知れません (not get known; not be clear)

shirase *n* 知らせ **1.** (= **o-shirase** お知らせ) report, notice, information **2.** → **shirasemásu** 知らせます [INFINITIVE]; **shirase ro** 知らせろ [IMPERATIVE] (let me/someone know!)

shirasemásu, shiraseru *v* 知らせます, 知らせる announces (*informs of*), lets one know, notifies

shiréba *v* 知れば (if one learns/knows) → **shirimásu** 知ります

shiréi *n* 司令 command (*in army, etc.*) shiréi-bu *n* 司令部 headquarters

shiréi *n* 指令 command (= **meirei** 命令, **sashizu** 指図) shiréi-kan *n* 指令官 commander

shiremásu, shireru *v* 知れます, 知れる gets known; is identified; becomes clear/evident

shiri *v* 知り → **shirimásu** 知ります [INFINITIVE]

shirí *n* 尻 (**o-shiri** お尻) butt(ock), hip, bottom, seat

shiriai *n* 知り合い acquaintance

shirimasén, shiranai *v* 知りません, 知らない does not know

shirimásu, shiru *v* 知ります, 知る acquaints oneself with, finds out, learns; **shitte imásu** 知っています knows

shiri-tai *v* 知りたい curious about, want(ing) to know

shíritsu (no) *adj* 私立(の) (= **watakushí-ritsu** 私立) privately established entity/organization

shirí ya/wa shinai *v* 知りや/はしない = **shiranai** 知らない (not know)

shirizóita *v* 退いた = **shirizokimáshita** 退きました (retreated)

shirizóite *v* 退いて → **shirizokimásu** 退きます

shirizokánai *v* 退かない = **shirizokimasén** 退きません (not retreat)

shirizóki *v* 退き → **shirizokimásu** 退きます [INFINITIVE]

shirizokimásu, shirizóku *v* 退きます, 退く retreats, withdraws, retires

shiro *n* 城 (**o-shiro** お城) castle

shíro *n* 白 white: **shiro-kuma** 白熊・シロクマ white bear, polar bear (= **Hokkyoku-guma** ホッキョクグマ・北極熊)

shiró-mi *n* 白身 white (*of an egg*), albumen; white meat

shiró-i *adj* 白い white

shi ro *suffix* (*v*) しろ; [IMPERATIVE] **shi ró yo** しろよ do it! (= **sé yo** せよ) → **shimásu** します

shirō´ *v* 知ろう = **shirimashō´** 知りましょう (let's learn/know it!)

shiróppu *n* シロップ syrup

shírō´to *n* 素人 an amateur, a novice

shiru *v* 知る = **shirimásu** 知ります (learns; knows)

shíru *n* 汁 juice, gravy; broth, soup

shirukó *n* しるこ・汁粉 (**o-shiruko** おしるこ・お汁粉) a sweet redbean-paste soup

shirushi *n* 印・徴 (**o-shirushi** お印・お徴) indication, token, sign, symptom; effect(iveness)

shíryo *n* 思慮 [BOOKISH] consideration, thought (-fulness)

shíryō *n* 資料 materials; data

shíryoku *n* 視力 vision, eyesight, visual acuity

shisei *n* 姿勢 posture; attitude

shisen *n* 支線 branch (*of rail line*)

shisen *n* 視線 eye direction

shisetsu (no) *adj* 私設(の) private

shísetsu *n* 施設 facility, institution, establishment, installation

shíshi *n* シシ・獅子 lion (= **raion** ライオン)

shishū *n* 刺繍 embroidery

shishún-ki *n* 思春期 adolescence

shiso *n* シソ・紫蘇 perilla, beefsteak plant

shisō *n* 思想 thought, concept

shíson *n* 子孫 descendants; posterity

...-shi-sō (na) *suffix, adj* しそう(な) likely/about to do it: **-shi-sō mo nái** しそうもない unlikely to do it

shísso (na) *adj* 質素(な) simple, plain, frugal, rustic

shi-súgi *v* し過ぎ → **shisugimásu** し過ぎます [INFINITIVE]

shi-sugimásu, shi-sugíru *v* し過ぎます, し過ぎover(does)

shita *v* した = **shimáshita** しました (did, has done): **shita áto de** した後で after doing; **shita bákari desu** したばかりです just (now) did it; **shita hō´ga íi** した方がいい ought to do it, better do it; **shita kotóga arimasén** したことがありません has never done it; **shita monódesu** したものです used to do it

shita(-...) *n, prefix* 下(...) below, under, bottom, lower; (= **toshi-shita** 年下) younger, youngest

shita-baki *n* 下穿き underpants

shita-baki *n* 下履き (*outdoor*) shoes

shita-gi *n* 下着 underwear

shita-machi *n* 下町 downtown

shitá *n* 舌 tongue

shita-bírame *n* シタビラメ・舌平目 sole (*fish*)

shitagaimásu, shitagau *v* 従います, 従う: **... ni shitagaimásu** ...に従います conforms to ..., accords with ...

shi-tagarimásu, shi-tagáru *v* したがります, したがる wants (*is eager*) to do

shitagatte *adv, conj* 従って accordingly, therefore; **... ni shitagatte** ...に従って according to ..., in conformity with/to ...

shi-tagátte *v* したがって → **shi-tagarimásu** したがります [INFINITIVE]

shi-tai v したい wants to do it

shi-tákatta v したかった wanted to do it

shi-taku n 支度 preparation, arrangement

shi-taku v したく: **shi-taku arimasén** したくありません is unwilling to do it: **shi-taku narimásu** したくなります gets so one wants to do it

shitára v したら if/when one does it

shitári (… shimásu) v したり (…します) does/is such things as; sometimes does/is; does/is intermittently (*off and on*)

shitashíi *adj* 親しい intimate, familiar

shitate-ya n 仕立屋 tailor

shitátte v したって – **shitémo** しても even doing, even if it does

shite v して doing; does and; **shitékara** してから (next) after doing; **shitémoíi** してもいい may do it, it is OK to do it; **shité wa ikemasén/ikenai/damé** してはいけません/いけない/だめ mustn't do it, don't do it!

shitei n 指定 designation, appointment: **~ shimásu** 指定します designates, appoints

shitéi-seki n 指定席 reserved seat(s)

shitéi-shi n 指定詞 the copula (**désu, dá, ná, nó, ní, dé, …** です, だ, な, の, に, で,…)

shiteki shimásu (suru) v 指摘します(する) indicates, points out

shiten n 支店 branch shop

shitetsu n 私鉄 private railroad

shitsu n 質 quality, nature

…´-shitsu *suffix* …室 (*name of certain*) room

shitsū n 歯痛 toothache (= **ha-ita** 歯痛)

shitsubō n 失望 disappointment: **~ shimásu** 失望します disappoints

shitsúdo n 湿度 humidity

shitsugyō n 失業 unemployment; **shitsugyō´-sha** 失業者 unemployed person

shitsuke n しつけ・躾 training (*of children, …*), discipline, upbringing

shi-tsuke n 仕付け basting, tacking (*with thread*); **shitsuke-íto** 仕付け糸 basting/tacking thread

shitsukemásu, shitsukéru v しつけ[躾け]ます, しつけ[躾け]る trains (*children, …*), disciplines, brings up

shi-tsukemásu, shi-tsukéru v 仕付けます, 仕付ける bastes, tacks (*with thread*)

shitsumon n 質問 question: **~ shimásu** 質問します asks a question

shitsurakuen n 失楽園 Paradise Lost

shitsúrei n 失礼 discourtesy: **~ shimásu** 失礼します does a discourtesy, excuses oneself (*leaves*); **Shitsúrei desu ga …** 失礼ですが… Excuse me for asking, but …

shitsúrei (na) *adj* 失礼(な) impolite

shitsuren n 失恋 disappointment in love: **~ shimásu** 失恋します gets brokenhearted

shitsuteki (na) *adj* 質的(な) qualitative

shitta v 知った = **shirimáshita** 知りました (learned, found out)

shitte v 知って → **shirimasu** 知ります: **shitte**

imásu 知っています knows

shitto n 嫉妬 jealousy: **shitto bukai hito** 嫉妬深い人 jealous person

shiwa n しわ・シワ・皺 wrinkle, crease: **shiwa ga dekimásu** しわができます it wrinkles (= **shiwa ni narimásu** しわになります)

shiwaza n 仕業 act, deed: **Aitsu no shiwaza ni chigainai.** アイツの仕業に違いない I bet he is the one who is behind it.

shí ya/wa shimasén (shinai) v しや/はしません(しない) = **shimasén** しません (not do)

shi-yasúi v しやすい **1.** easy to do **2.** likely to do it, tends to do it

shi-yō n 仕様 method, means, way (= **shi-kata** 仕方); (*for products, etc.*) specifications: **shi-yō ga nái** しようがない hopeless, beyond remedy (= **shō ga nái** しょうがない)

shiyō n 使用 use, employment: **~ shimásu** 使用します uses, employs

shiyō-chū 使用中 in use, occupied (*toilet, etc.*)

shiyō-nin 使用人 servant

shiyō´-sha n 使用者 user

shiyō n 私用 private use/business (= **jibun-yō** 自分用): **shiyō no** 私用の private

shiyō v しよう = **shimashō** しましょう (let's do it): **shiyō to shimásu** しようとします tries/starts to do it

shizen n 自然 nature: **shizen (no)** 自然(の) natural; **shizen (na)** 自然(な) natural, spontaneous

shízuka (na) *adj* 静か(な) quiet, still

shizumanai v 沈まない = **shizumimasén** 沈みません (not sink)

shizumaránai v 静まらない・鎮まらない = **shizumarimasén** 静まりません・鎮まりません (not get quiet)

shizumarimásu, shizumáru v 静まります・鎮まります, 静まる・鎮まる gets quiet/calm, quiets/calms down

shizumatte v 静まって・鎮まって → **shizumarimásu** 静まります・鎮まります (gets quiet)

shizumemásu, shizuméru v 静めます・鎮めます, 静める・鎮める soothes, quiets, calms, pacifies, suppresses

shizumemásu, shizumeru v 沈めます, 沈める sinks it

shizuménai v 静めない・鎮めない = **shizumemasén** 静めません・鎮めません (not soothe it)

shizumenai v 沈めない = **shizumemasén** 沈めません (not sink it)

shizumete v 沈めて → **shizumemásu** 沈めます

shizumete v 静めて・鎮めて → **shizumemásu** 静めます・鎮めます

shizumimásu, shizumu v 沈みます, 沈む it sinks

shizunde v 沈んで → **shizumimásu** 沈みます (it sinks)

sho- *prep* 諸 [*makes definite plurals of certain nouns*]; **sho-ji** 諸事 all matters; everything; **sho-tō** 諸島 (*a group of*) islands; an archipelago

shō´ *n* 性 nature, disposition, quality

shō´ *n* 賞 prize, reward
  shō´-batsu *n* 賞罰 rewards and punishments
  shō-hin *n* 賞品 prize (*object*)
  shō-kin *n* 賞金 prize money; reward
  shō´-yo *n* 賞与 bonus; **shōyó-kin** 賞与金 bonus money

shō´ *n* 笙 a traditional Japanese reed instrument

shō-... *prefix* 商... sales, business
  shō´-bai *n* 商売 trade, business: **mizu-shobai** 水商売 chancy trade (*restaurant, bar, cabaret, etc.*)
  shó´-gyō *n* 商業 commerce, trade, business
  shō´-hin *n* 商品 goods, merchandise, (*sales*) product
  shō´-nin *n* 商人 merchant, trader
  shó´-ten *n* 商店 shop, store: **shōten-gai** 商店街 shop street(s), shopping area

...´-shō *suffix* ...商 dealer (*seller of* ...): **gyō-shō** 行商 peddling

...´-shō *suffix* ...省 **1.** (*name of certain*) Ministry **2.** (*name of certain*) province (*China*)

shōátsú-ki *n* 昇圧機 booster (*of current*)

sho´-batsu *n* 処罰 [BOOKISH] punishments: **~ shimásu** 処罰します punishes

shōbén *n* 小便 urine, urinating (*very informal. mostly male*): **~ shimásu** 小便します urinates

shōbō *n* 消防 fire fighting; **shōbō´-sha** 消防車 fire engine; **shōbō´-shi** 消防士 fire fighter; **shōbō-shó** 消防署 fire house/station, fire department

shō´bu *n* 勝負 match, contest

shō´bu *n* ショウブ・菖蒲 iris

shóbun *n* 処分 [BOOKISH] disposition, abolition: **~ shimásu** 処分します disposes of

sho´chi *n* 処置 [BOOKISH] dealing with: **~ shimásu** 処置します deals with

shōchi *n* 承知 agreement, understanding; **Shōchi shimáshita** 承知しました [HUMBLE] I understand (*and consent*). (*on business e-mail, etc.*) Yes, sir/ma'am.

shochō *n* 所長 institute director

shōchō *n* 象徴 symbol: **~ shimásu** 象徴します symbolizes

shōchū´ *n* 焼酎 distilled liquor made from yams or rice

shō´dai *n* 招待 = **shō´tai** 招待 invitation: **~ shimásu** 招待します invites

shōdaku *n* 承諾 [BOOKISH] consent, acceptance: **~ shimásu** 承諾します consents, accepts

shodō *n* 書道 calligraphy (= **shūji** 習字)

shōdokú-yaku/-zai *n* 消毒薬/剤 disinfectant

shoéba *v* [INFORMAL] しょえば = **shoya** しょや (*if one shoulders it*) → **shoimásu** しょいます

shō-fuda *n* 正札 price tag

shōga *n* ショウガ・生姜 ginger

shōgai *n* 障害 impediment, obstacle, hindrance; **shōgái-sha** 障害者 handicapped person

shō´gai *n* 生涯 life(long), for all one's life (*time*)

shōgakkō *n* 小学校 primary (*elementary*) school → **gakkō** *n* 学校

shōgáku-sei *n* 小学生 primary school student

shō ga nai *adj* [INFORMAL] しょうがない = **shi-yō ga nái** しようがない hopeless, beyond remedy; **...-kute shō ga nái** ...くてしょうがない, **... de shō ga nái** ...でしょうがない is ever so ..., is terribly ...

Shōgatsú *n* 正月 (**O-shōgatsu** お正月) January; New Year

shōgi *n* 将棋 (*Japanese*) chess: **shōgi-ban** 将棋盤 chessboard

shō´go *n* 正午 noon (*exactly*)

shōhi *n* 消費 comsumption; **shōhí-sha** 消費者 consumer

shōhi-zei *n* 消費税 consumption tax

shohō *n* 処方 prescription, prescribing: **~ shimásu** 処方します prescribes (*medicine*)

shohō-sen *n* 処方箋 prescription (slip)

shoi *v* [INFORMAL] しょい → **shoimásu** しょいます [INFINITIVE]

shō´i *n* 少尉 2nd lieutenant; ensign

shoimásu, shou *v* [INFORMAL] しょい[背負い] ます, しょう・背負う [INFORMAL] carries on the back, shoulders it

shoi ya/wa shinai *v* [INFORMAL] しょい[背負い] や/はしない = **showanai** しょわない・背わない う (*not carry on the back*)

shōji *n* 障子 translucent sliding panel/door

shōjíki (na) *adj* 正直(な) honest: **shōjíki ni** 正直に honestly

shō-jimásu, shō-jiru *v* 生じます, 生じる **1.** produces, comes about, occurs **2.** arises, happens

shōjin-ryō´ri *n* 精進料理 vegetarian cuisine

shójo *n* 処女 virgin (*female*)

shō´jo *n* 少女 young girl (= **onna no ko** 女の子)

shōjū *n* 小銃 rifle

shōka *n* 消化 digestion: **~ shimásu** 消化します digests

shōka-fúryō *n* 消化不良 indigestion

shōkai *n* 紹介 (**go-shōkai** ご紹介) introduction (*of a person*): **~ shimásu** 紹介します introduces

shōka-ki *n* 消火器 fire extinguisher

shōka-sen *n* 消火栓 fireplug, hydrant

shōken *n* 証券 security (*stock, bond*)

shóki *n* 書記 secretary

shoki *n* 初期 [BOOKISH] beginning

shoki-settei *n* 初期設定 default (*setting*)

shōki (no) *adj* 正気(の) sober, sane; in one's right mind

shōkin *n* 正金 hard cash

shōkin *n* 償金 → **baishō-kin** 賠償金 (*indemnity, reparation*)

shokken *n* 食券 meal ticket

shokki *n* 食器 tableware (*dish, plate, chopsticks, etc.*); **shokkí-dana** 食器棚 dish rack; **shokki-tódana** 食器戸棚 cupboard, **shokkí-shitsu** 食器室 pantry

shokkō *n* 職工 factory worker; workman (= **kōin** 工員)

shókku *n* ショック shock

shōko *n* 証拠 proof, evidence, witness

shō´kō *n* 将校 military officer

shoku *n* 職 office, occupation

　shokú-gyō *n* 職業 occupation, vocation, job, profession

　shoku-reki *n* 職歴 professional experience

shoku *n* (…´-shoku …食) food; (*counts meals*)

　shoku-dō *n* 食堂 dining room; restaurant

　shoku-dō´-sha *n* 食堂車 dining car, diner

　shokú-en *n* 食塩 table salt

　shoku-go (ni) *adv* 食後 (に) after a meal (= **shokuji no áto de** 食事の後で)

　shoku-hin *n* 食品 foodstuffs, groceries

　shoku-ji *n* 食事 (**o-shokuji** お食事) a meal; eating, having a meal: **~ shimásu** 食事します dines, eats (*a meal*)

　shoku (-ji) tsuki (no) *n* 食(事)付き(の) with meals (*included*); **chōshoku-tsuki (no)** 朝食付き(の) with breakfast

　shokú-motsu *n* 食物 food(s)

　shoku-pán *n* 食パン bread

　shoku-ryō-hin *n* 食料品 foodstuffs, groceries: **shokuryōhín-ten** 食料品店 grocery store

　shoku-taku *n* 食卓 dinner table; **shokutakú-en** 食卓塩 table salt

　shoku-yoku *n* 食欲 appetite

　shoku-zen *n* 食膳 (*low*) individual meal table

　shoku-zen (ni) *adv* [BOOKISH] 食前(に) before a meal (= **shokuji no máe ni** 食事の前に)

shokúbutsu *n* 植物 (*botanical*) plant; **shokubu-tsú-en** 植物園 botanical garden

shokumín-chi *n* 植民地 colony

shōkyoku-teki (na) *adj* 消極的(な) negative; conservative

shōkyū *n* 昇給 rise in pay

shōkyū *n* 昇級 promotion

shomei *n* 署名 signature: **~ shimásu** 署名します signs one's name

shōmei *n* 証明 proof, verification, attestation, certification: **~ shimásu** 証明します proves, verifies, attests, certifies

　shōmei-shó *n* 証明書 certificate; note of authentication

shōmei *n* 照明 lighting, illumination: **shōmei-kígu** 照明器具 lighting fixtures

shōmén *n* 正面 the face (*front side*)

shomotsu *n* 書物 [BOOKISH] book (= **hón** 本)

shōmyō´ *n* 声明 chanting of Buddhist scriptures

shōnen *n* 少年 boy, lad, youngster (= **otoko no ko** 男の子)

shō´ni *n* 小児 infant, child; **shōnimáhi** 小児麻痺 infantile paralysis, polio

　shōni-ka *n* 小児科 pediatrics; pediatrician (= **shōniká-i** 小児科医)

shōnin *n* 証人 a witness

shoppái *adj* [INFORMAL] しょっぱい [INFORMAL]

salty (= **shio-karai** 塩辛い)

shóppingu *n* ショッピング shopping (= **kaimono** 買い物): **shoppingu-bággu** ショッピングバッグ, **shoppingu-bákku** ショッピングバック shopping bag; **shoppingu-sénta** ショッピングセンター shopping center

shō´rai *n, adv* 将来 future (= **yukusue** 行く末, **mirai** 未来)

shōrei *n* 奨励 encouragement, promotion: **~ shimásu** 奨励します encourages, promotes

shóri *n* 処理 managing, disposing of, transacting, dealing with: **~ shimásu** 処理します manages, handles, takes care of, deals with

　shori-jō *n* 処理場 [sewage] treatment plant

shō´ri *n* 勝利 victory: **~ shimásu** 勝利します [BOOKISH] wins (= **kachimásu** 勝ちます)

　shōrí-sha *n* 勝利者 winner, victor

shorui *n* 書類 form, document, paper(s), writing

shōryaku *n* 省略 abbreviation, omission (= **ryaku** 略): **~ shimásu** 省略します abbreviates, omits

shōsa *n* 少佐 major; lieutenant commander

shosai *n* 書斎 a study, library (*room*)

shōsai *n* 詳細 [BOOKISH] details

shōseki *n* 書籍 books, publications (= **hón** 本)

shōsetsu *n* 小説 fiction, a novel

shō´shō *adv* 少々 a little [DEFERENTIAL] (= **chótto** ちょっと)

shō´shō *n* 少将 major general; rear admiral

shōshū *n* 召集・招集 conscription, (*military*) draft: **~saremásu** 召集[招集]されます gets drafted: **~ shimásu** 召集[招集]します drafts, conscripts

shōsoku *n* 消息 news, word (*from/of …*) (= **nyūsu** ニュース)

shotái *n* 所帯・世帯 a household; housekeeping (→ **onna-jotai** 女所帯, **otoko-jotai** 男所帯) (= **setai** 世帯)

shō´tai *n* 招待 invitation: **~ shimásu** 招待します invites

　shōtái-jō *n* 招待状 invitation (card)

shótchū *adv* [INFORMAL] しょっちゅう [INFORMAL] all the time

shoten *n* 書店 bookshop

shō´ten *n* 焦点 focus, focal point

shō´to *n* ショート a short (*circuit*); short story; shortstop

…-shótō *n* …諸島 (*name of certain*) islands

shotoku *n* 所得 income; **shotokú-zei** 所得税 income tax

shōtotsu *n* 衝突 collision: **~ shimásu** 衝突します collides

shotte *v* [INFORMAL] しょって → **shoimásu** しょいます・背負います

shou *v* [INFORMAL] しょう・背負う = **shoimásu** しょいます・背負います [INFORMAL] (carries on the back)

Shōwa-jidai *n* 昭和時代 Showa Period (*1926–1989*)

showanai *v* [INFORMAL] しょわない = **shoimasén** しょいません [INFORMAL] (not carry on the back)

shoyū (no) *adj* 所有(の) possessed, owned, belonging; one's own
  shoyū-butsu/-hin *n* 所有物/品 belongings, possessions
  shoyū´-sha *n* 所有者 (*legal*) owner

shōyu *n* しょうゆ・醤油 (**o-shōyu** お醤油) soy sauce

shozai *n* 所在 whereabouts

shōzō *n* 肖像 portrait
  shōzō-ga *n* 肖像画 portrait (*drawing and/or painting*)

shu *n* 朱 vermilion: **shu ni majiwareba akaku somaru/náru** 朱に交われば赤く染まる/なる [IDIOM] He who touches pitch shall be defiled.
  shu-niku *n* 朱肉 red ink pad

shū´, ...-shū *n, suffix* 州, ...州 (*name of certain*) state (*U.S., Australia*); province (*Canada*); county (*Britain*)

shū´, ...-shū *n, suffix* 週, ...週 (= **shūkan** 週間) week
  shū-matsu *n* 週末 weekend
  shū-kan *n* 週間 week: **shūkan-tenki-yohō** 週間天気予報 weather forecast for a week: **dokusho-shūkan** 読書週間 book week

shūbun *n* 秋分 autumnal equinox: **Shūbun-no-hí** 秋分の日 Autumnal Equinox Day

shuchō *n* 主張 assertion: ~ **shimásu** 主張します asserts, claims, maintains

shūchū *n* 集中 concentration: ~ **shimásu** 集中します concentrates, centers (*on*)

shúdan *n* 手段 ways, means, measures, steps (= **hōhō** 方法): **saigo no shúdan** 最後の手段 last resort

shūdan *n* 集団 group, collective body: **shūdan-seikatsu** 集団生活 group living, communal living (= **kyōdō-seikatsu** 共同生活): **busō-shūdan** 武装集団 armed group: **bo-shūdan** 母集団 a population

shūden *n* 終電 the last train (= **saishū densha** 最終電車)

shūdō´-in *n* 修道院 convent

shúfu *n* 主婦 housewife

shúfu *n* 首府 → **shutó** 首都

shūgeki *n* 襲撃 attack, charge, raid: ~ **shimásu** 襲撃します attacks, charges, raids

shúgi *n* 主義 principle, doctrine, -ism

shūgi-in *n* 衆議院 House of Representatives: **shūgi-in-senkyo** 衆議院選挙 House of Representatives election

shúgo *n* 主語 subject (*of a sentence*)

shūgō *n* 集合 assembly, gathering: ~ **shimásu** 集合します congregates, gathers, meets (*as a group*)

shugyō *n* 修行・修業 (*getting one's*) training, ascetic practices, meditation: ~ **shimásu** 修行します・修業します gets training

shūgyō *n* 就業 starting one's work(-day): ~ **shimásu** 就業します goes to (*starts*) work
  shūgyō´-jíkan *n* 就業時間 working hours

shū´ha *n* 宗派 sect

shūhen *adj* 周辺 circumference, environs, surroundings (= **shūi** 周囲): **tóshi no shūhen** 都市の周辺 outskirts (*of city*); **shūhen no ...** 周辺の... the surrounding ...

shū´i *n* 周囲 circumference; surroundings (= **shūhen** 周辺)

shuin *n* 手淫 [BOOKISH] masturbation (= **masutā-bēshon** マスターベーション, **onanii** オナニー): **shuin o shimásu** 手淫をします masturbates

shūji *n* 習字 (**o-shūji** お習字) calligraphy (*handwriting*) practice

shújin *n* 主人 **1.** husband; **go-shújin** ご主人 your husband **2.** master, owner, landlord, boss, host (**go-shújin(-sama)** ご主人(様), **danna(-san/sama)** 旦那(さん/様))

shúju (no) *adj* 種々(の) all kinds of (= **samazama (na)** 様々(な), **iroiro (na)** 色々(な), **iron na** いろんな)

shújutsu *n* 手術 surgical operation, surgery; **shújutsu (o) shimásu** 手術(を)します performs an operation, operates

shūkaku *n* 収穫 harvest, crop: ~ **shimásu** 収穫します harvests, reaps

shukan *n* 主観 subjectivity: **shukan-teki (na)** 主観的(な) subjective

shūkan *n* 習慣 custom, practice, habit (= **kuse** 癖)

shū´ki *n* 秋期 autumn (*period/term*)

shū´ki *n* 周期 cycle (*length*)

shū´ki *n* 臭気 bad smell, stink (= **akushū** 悪臭)
  shūki-dome *n* 臭気止め deodorant (*household, etc.*) (= **nioi-keshi** におい消し)

shukkin *n* 出勤 office attendance: ~ **shimásu** 出勤します goes to work

shuku-choku *n* 宿直 night duty

shukudai *n* 宿題 **1.** homework (*at school*): **natsu-yásumi no shukudai** 夏休みの宿題 summer homework **2.** unsolved problem

shukuga *n* 祝賀 congratulation: **shukuga-kai** 祝賀会 a celebration

shukujitsu *n* 祝日 national holiday

shū-kuríimu *n* シュークリーム a cream puff, an éclair: **shū-kuríimu no kawa** シュークリームの皮 puff shell

shuku-saijitsu *n* 祝祭日 → **shukujitsu** 祝日

shukuten *n* 祝典 celebration ceremony

shū´kyō *n* 宗教 religion

shūmai *n* シューマイ pork meatballs steamed in thin pastry

shúmi *n* 趣味 taste, interest, liking, hobby (= **hobii** ホビー)

shumoku *n* 種目 **1.** item: **eigyō-shumoku** 営業種目 item of business **2.** (*competition*) event: **rikujō kyōgi-shumoku** 陸上競技種目 events in athletics (*track and field*)

shunbun *n* 春分 vernal equinox: **Shunbun-no-hí** 春分の日 Vernal Equinox Day

shunga *n* 春画 pornography (*of Ukiyo-e*)

shúngiku *n* シュンギク・春菊 (*tasty leaves of*) garland chrysanthemum

shunkan *n* 瞬間 a moment, an instant (= **shunji** 瞬時, **matatakuma** 瞬く間): **tsugi no shunkan** 次の瞬間 next moment

shūnyū *n* 収入 earnings, income: **shūnyū-ínshi** 収入印紙 tax (*revenue*) stamp (= **inshi** 印紙)

shuppan *n* 出版 publishing: **~ shimásu** 出版します publishes

shuppán-butsu *n* 出版物 publication(s)

shuppán-sha *n* 出版社 publishing company

shuppán-sha *n* 出版者 publisher

shuppatsu *n* 出発 departure; **shuppátsú-ten** 出発点 point of departure: **~shimásu** 出発します departu, leaves

shuppin *n* 出品 exhibit(ing): **~ shimásu** 出品します exhibits; **shuppín-sha** 出品者 exhibitor

shū´ri *n* 修理 repair: **~ shimásu** 修理します repairs shūrí-kō 修理工 repairman, mechanic

shūrō *n* 就労 [BOOKISH] work: **~ shimásu** 就労します works (*for company, etc.*)

shúrui *n* 種類 type, sort, kind, variety

shū´shi *n* 修士 master's degree: **shūshi-rónbun** 修士論文 master's thesis: **shūshi-gō** 修士号 master's degree

ohūohi *n* 終止 [BOOKISH] ending (= **oshimai** おしまい)

shūshí-fu *n* 終止符 [BOOKISH] period, full stop (*punctuation*)

shū´shin *n* 修身 ethics, morals

shū´shin *n* 終身 all one's life (= **isshō(-gai)** 一生(涯), **shōgai** 生涯, **shūsei** 終生)

shū´shin-kei *n* 終身刑 life imprisonment

shū´shin-koyō *n* 終身雇用 lifetime employment

shushō *n* 首相 prime minister

shūshoku *n* 就職 getting a job, finding employment: **~ shimásu** 就職します gets a job, finds employment

shūshū *n* 収集 1. collecting (*trash, etc.*): **gomi-shū-shū-sha** ゴミ収集車 garbage truck 2. collection (*as one's hobby, for research, etc.*) (= **korekushon** コレクション, **saishū** 採集): **shūshū-ka** 収集家 collector (= **korekutā** コレクター): **~ shimásu** 収集します collects

shusse *n* 出世 making a success in life: **~ shimásu** 出世します makes a success in life

shussei *n* 出生 [BOOKISH] birth (= **umare** 生まれ): **shussei-chi** 出生地 (*one's*) birthplace

shusseki *n* 出席 attendance, presence (= **sanka** 参加): **~ shimásu** 出席します attends, is present shusséki-sha *n* 出席者 those present

shusshin *n* 出身 alumnus (of …); coming (*from* …): **shusshin-chi** 出身地 (*one's*) hometown

shúsu *n* 繻子 satin

shutchō *n* 出張 business trip: **~ shimásu** 出張します makes a business trip

shūten *n* 終点 terminus, end of the line, last stop, destination

shutó *n* 首都 capital city

shutó-ken *n* 首都圏 Tokyo metropolitan area (= **kantō-chihō** plus Yamanashi *prefecture* 関東地

方+山梨県) **→ kantō-chihō** 関東地方

shūtome *n* 姑 common spoken term for one's mother-in-law

shuyō (na) *adj* 主要(な) leading, chief; **shuyō-tóshi** 主要都市 major city

shūzen *n* 修繕 [BOOKISH] repair: **~ shimásu** 修繕します repairs; **shūzén-kō** 修繕工 repairman

si… → shi…

sō´ *n* 僧 Buddhist priest (= **sōryo** 僧侶, **obō-san** お坊さん)

sō´ *interj* そう [hearsay]: … (**suru, shita, dá, dátta**), **sō´** (**desu, da/na, de, ni**) …(する, した, だ, だった), そう(です, だ/な, で, に) it is reported (*said/written*) that, I hear that, they say that …; reportedly …

…-sō *suffix* …そう, **…-sō´**…そう: **shisō** (**désu, dá/na, dé, ní**) しそう(です, だ/な, で, に) looking (*as though*), about to (*happen*); will at any moment; **abuna-sō** (**désu, ni miemásu**) 危なそう(です, に見えます) looks dangerous, **jōbu-sō níwa miemasén** 丈夫そうには見えません doesn't look sturdy, **ochi-sō´desu** 落ちそうです is about to fall

…-sō *suffix* …艘 (*counts ships/boats*; commonly replaced by **…-seki** …隻)

sóba *n* そば・側 (**o-soba** お側) near/close(-by), (be-)side

sóba *n* そば・ソバ・蕎麦 (**o-soba** おそば・お蕎麦) buckwheat noodles

soba-gara *n* そば殻・ソバ殻 buck-wheat chaff (*used as pillow stuffing*)

sobá-ya (o-sobaya) *n* そば[蕎麦]屋 (おそば[蕎麦]屋) Japanese noodle shop

sōbetsu *n* 送別 farewell; send-off; **sōbétsú-kai** 送別会 farewell party (*reception*)

sobiemásu, sobiéru *v* そびえます, そびえる rises, looms

sóbo *n* 祖母 grandmother [FORMAL] (= **obā´-san** おばあさん・お祖母さん, **obā-chan** おばあちゃん)

soboku na *adj* 素朴な simple, naive

soboro *n* そぼろ・ソボロ parched minced fish; fish meal

sō´chi *n* 装置 equipment, apparatus

sochira *pron* そちら 1. there, that way 2. that one (*of two*) 3. you

sochira-gawa *n* そちら側 your side

sō´dā *n* ソーダー soda water (= **sōdá-sui** ソーダ水)

sō da *v* そうだ = **sō´ desu** そうです that's right, yes

sodachí *n* 育ち (**o-sodachi** お育ち) growing up, one's early years: **sodachi ga yoi/warui** お育ちが良い/悪い well-bred/ill-bred

sódachí *v* 育ち **→ sodachimásu** 育ちます [INFINITIVE]

sodachimásu, sodátsu *v* 育ちます, 育つ grows up, is raised (reared)

sōdai na *adj* 壮大な magnificent, grand

sōdan *n* 相談 conference (*personal*), talk, consultation, *advice*: **sōdan-aite** 相談相手 someone to turn to for *advice*; **(... to) sōdan shimásu** (...と)相談します consults (*with*), discusses, talks it over

sōdá-sui *n* ソーダ水 soda water (= **sidā** サイダー)

sodatánai *v* 育たない = **sodachimasén** 育ちません (not grow up)

sodáte *v* 育て **1.** → **sodatemásu** 育てます [INFINITIVE]; **sodaté ro** 育てろ [IMPERATIVE] (raise them!) **2.** [IMPERATIVE] (grow up!) → **sodachimásu** 育ちます

sodatemásu, sodatéru *v* 育てます、育てる raises, rears, educates

sodaténai *v* 育てない = **sodatemasén** 育てません (not raise)

sodate-no-oyá *n* 育ての親 a foster parent

sodatéru *v* 育てる = **sodatemásu** 育てます (raises, rears, educates)

sodátete *v* 育てて → **sodatemásu** 育てます

sodátsu *v* 育つ → **sodachimásu** 育ちます (grows up, is raised (reared))

sodátte *v* 育って → **sodachimásu** 育ちます

sode *n* 袖・そで (**o-sode** お袖) sleeve (→ **naga-sode** 長袖)

sō´ (desu) *v* そう(です) That's right, yes Sō´desu ka. そうですか. **1.** Oh? How interesting! **2.** Is that right/so? Sō´desu ne. そうですね. Well, now; Let me see.

sō´dō *n* 騒動 unrest, disturbance, tumult, strife; riot (= **bōdō** 暴動, **sawagi** 騒ぎ): **sō´dō ga okimásu** 騒動が起きます disturbance occurs: **oie-sōdō** お家騒動 family trouble

soéba *v* 沿えば (if it follows) → **soimásu** 沿います

soemásu, soeru *v* 添えます、添える adds, throws in extra, attaches

soenai *v* 添えない = **soemasén** 添えません (not add)

soeru *v* 添える = **soemásu** 添えます (adds, throws in extra, attaches)

soete *v* 添えて → **soemásu** 添えます

soé ya shinai *v* 添えやしない = **soé wa shinai** 添えはしない = **soenai** 添えない (not add)

soeyō *v* 添えよう = **soemashō´** 添えましょう (let's add it!)

sófu *n* 祖父 grandfather [FORMAL] (= **ojii´-san** おじいさん・お祖父さん, **ojii-chan** おじいちゃん)

sófuto-kuriimu *n* ソフトクリーム soft ice cream

sofuto(wéa) *n* ソフト(ウェア) (*computer*) software

sōgan-kyō *n* 双眼鏡 binoculars

sōgi-ya *n* 葬儀屋 undertaker (*funeral director*)

sōgō *n* 総合 synthesis sōgō-teki (na) *adj* 総合的(な) composite, comprehensive, overall, synthesized

sō´go no *adj* 相互の mutual, reciprocal sō´go ni *adv* 相互に mutually, reciprocally (= **otagai ni** お互いに)

soi *v* 沿い → **soimásu** 沿います [INFINITIVE]

sōi *n* 相違[相異] discrepancy, difference: ... ni sōi nai ...に相違[相異]ない must be ...

soimásu, sou *v* 沿います, 沿う runs along, follows

soitsu *pron* そいつ that damn one; **soitsú-ra** そいつら those damn ones

soí ya/wa shinai *v* 沿いや/はしない, **soya shinai** 沿やしない = **sowanai** 沿わない (not follow)

sō´ ja arimasén *v* [INFORMAL] そうじゃありません = **sō de wa arimasén** そうではありません not that way, not like that

sō´ ja nái to *adv* [INFORMAL] そうじゃないと = **sō de naito** そうでないと, **sō´ ja nákereba** そうじゃなければ= **sō de nakereba** そうでなければ otherwise

sōji *n* 掃除 (**o-sō´ji** お掃除) cleaning, sweeping (= **seisō** 清掃): ~ **shimásu** 掃除します cleans, sweeps: **nenmatsu no ōsōji** 年末の大掃除 year-end cleaning

sōjí-ki *n* 掃除機 a sweeper

sōjū *n* 操縦 handling, operation: ~ **shimásu** 操縦します manipulates, handles, controls, operates

sōkei *n* 総計 [BOOKISH] the grand total (= **gōkei** 合計)

sokétto *n* ソケット socket, plug

sōkin *n* 送金 remittance: ~ **shimásu** 送金します remits

sokki *n* 速記 shorthand: ~ **shimásu** 速記します takes shorthand notes

sokkō-jó *n* 測候所 weather observatory/station

sokkúri *adj* そっくり entirety, completely: **sokkúri (no)** そっくり(の) just like

sókkusu *n* ソックス anklets, socks (= **kutsushita** 靴下)

soko *pron* そこ there, that place

soko *n* 底 bottom: **umi no soko** 海の底 bottom of the ocean (= **kaitei** 海底); **kokoro no soko** 心の底 bottom of one's heart; **soko-nuke (no)** 底抜け(の) bottomless (= **soko-nashi (no)** 底無し(の)) soko-mame *n* 底まめ bunion, corn, blister

sō´ko *n* 倉庫 warehouse

sókoku *n* 祖国 homeland, mother country (= **bokoku** 母国)

sokonaimásu, sokonáu *v* 損ないます, 損なう harms, injures, hurts; [VERBS INFINITIVE +] fails in doing; **yari-sokonaimásu** やり損ないます botches, misses

...-sokú *suffix* ...足 (*counts pairs of footwear*)

sōkudo *n* 速度 speed (= **supiido** スピード); "**Sókudo otóse**" 速度落とせ Reduce Speed.

sokutatsu *n* 速達 special delivery, express

sómatsu na *adj* 粗末な crude, coarse; **o-sómatsu-sama** お粗末さま Please excuse the poor fare (*reply to gochisō-sama* ご馳走さま・ごちそうさま)

somemásu, someru *v* 染めます、染める dyes

sō´men *n* そうめん・素麺 thin white wheat-flour noodles (*cf.* **hiyamúgi** 冷や麦・ひやむぎ)

somete *v* 染めて → **somemásu** 染めます

somúite *v* 背いて → **somukimásu** 背きます

186

somukimás<u>u</u>, somúku *v* 背きます, 背く; (... **ni) somukimás<u>u</u>** (…に)背きます disobeys, goes against, violates; rebels, revolts

Sōmu-shō *n* 総務省 Ministry of Internal Affairs and Communications (MIC)

són *n* 損 damage, loss; disadvantage: **son-toku kanjō** 損得勘定 profit-and-loss arithmetic: **son'eki-keisan-sho** 損益計算書 profit and loss statement (P/L)

…´-son *suffix* …村 (*name of certain*) village

sonáé *n* 備え preparations, provisions; defenses: [IDIOM] **sonáé areba urei nashi** 備えあれば憂いなし If you are prepared, you don't have to worry.

sónae *v* 備え 1. → **sonaemás<u>u</u>** 備えます [INFINITIVE] 2. **sonáé ro** 備えろ [IMPERATIVE] (prepare it!)

sonaemás<u>u</u>, sonáéru *v* 備えます, 備える prepares, fixes, installs, furnishes; possesses

sonáénai *v* 備えない = **sonaemasén** 備えません (not prepare it)

sonáete *v* 備えて → **sonaemás<u>u</u>** 備えます

sōnan *n* 遭難 disaster, accident, shipwreck, train wreck: **~ shimás<u>u</u>** 遭難します has an accident (*a disaster*); (*a ship/train*) is wrecked

sōngai *n* 損害 damage, harm, loss

sonkei *n* 尊敬 respect, esteem: **~ shimás<u>u</u>** 尊敬します respects, esteems; **sonkei-suru-hito** 尊敬する人 someone that one respects

sonna … *adj* [INFORMAL] そんな… such (a) …, that kind of …: **sonna ni** そんなに to that extent, that much, so (very/much)

sonnára *adv* [INFORMAL] そんなら then, in that case ([FORMAL] **sore nára** それなら)

sono *adj* その … that; **sono áto** その後, **sono-go** その後 since then; **sono mamá (de/ni/no)** そのまま(で/に/の) intact

sonó-hoka *n* その他[外] and others

sonó-ta *n* その他 [BOOKISH] and others (= **sonó-hoka** その他[外])

sono-tók<u>i</u> *n, adv* その時 at that time

sono-uchi *adv* そのうち soon, before long, sometime in the future

sono-ue´ ni *adv* そのうえに moreover, also, besides

sono-yō´ na *adj* そのよう[様](な) such (*-like*); **sono-yō´ni** そのよう[様]に like that, that way

sono-koro (wa) *adv* その頃(は) (*at*) that time, then, (*in*) those days (= **tō´ji (wa)** 当時(は), **aono-koro (wa)** あの頃(は))

sore jíshin/jítai *n* それ自身/自体 itself

… sono-mónó *adv* …そのもの (*in*) itself, the very …

són-shimás<u>u</u>, són-suru *v* 損します, 損する = **són o suru** 損をする loses, suffers a loss

sonsh<u>i</u>tsu *n* 損失 a loss (= **son** 損, **rosu** ロス)

sonzai *n* 存在 existence; being/person (*in existence*), personage, figure: **~ shimás<u>u</u>** 存在します exists

sō-on *n* 騒音 noise

sóppa *n* 反っ歯 bucktooth (= **deppa** 出っ歯)

sóra *n* 空 sky

sóra de *adv* そらで by heart, from memory

soránai *v* 剃らない = **sorimasén** 剃りません (not shave)

soránai *v* 反らない = **sorimasén** 反りません (not bend/curve)

sorasánai *v* 逸らさない = **sorashimasén** 逸らしません (not dodge/warp)

soráshi *v* 逸らし → **sorashimás<u>u</u>** 逸らします

sorashimás<u>u</u>, sorásu *v* 逸らします, 逸らす 1. dodges, turns aside 2. warps it

soráohite *v* 逸らして → **sorashimasu** 逸らして

sore *pron* それ that one, it

sore dátte *adv, conj* [INFORMAL] それだって = **sore démo** それでも still, yet, even so

sore de *conj* それで and (*then/so/also*)

sore démo *conj* それでも still, yet, even so

sore hodo *conj* それほど to that extent, so

sore kara *conj* それから and (*then*); after that, since then

sore máde *conj* それまで until then: **sore máde ni** それまでに by them

sore náno ni *conj* それなのに nevertheless, nonetheless, and yet

sore nára *conj* それなら then, in that case

sore ni *conj* それに on top of that, moreover, in addition, plus

soré-ra *pron* それら those, they/them

sóre *v* 逸れ → **soremás<u>u</u>** 逸れます [INFINITIVE]

sóreba *v* 剃れば (if one shaves) → **sorimás<u>u</u>** 剃ります

sóreba *v* 反れば (if one bends) → **sorimás<u>u</u>** 反ります

sore dé wa *conj* それでは, [INFORMAL] **sore ja/jā** それじゃ/じゃあ well, well now/then; in that event: **sore dé wa sh<u>i</u>tsúrei shimás<u>u</u>** それでは失礼します excuse me but I'll be on my way; good-bye

soremás<u>u</u>, soréru *v* 逸れます, 逸れる deviates, strays, digresses

soremás<u>u</u>, soréru *v* 剃れます, 剃れる can shave

soremás<u>u</u>, soréru *v* 反れます, 反れる can bend/warp

soréru *v* 逸れる = **soremás<u>u</u>** 逸れます (deviates)

soréru *v* 剃れる = **soremás<u>u</u>** 剃れます (can shave)

soréru *v* 反れる = **soremás<u>u</u>** 反れます (can bend/warp)

sórete *v* 逸れて・剃れて・反れて → **soremás<u>u</u>** 逸れます・剃れます・反れます

sore-tómo *conj* それとも or else

sore wa sore wa *interj* それはそれは My my! My goodness!

sorézóre *adv* それぞれ respectively, severally (= **onoono** おのおの・各々)

sóri *n* そり・反り a warp, curve, bend

sóri *n* そり・剃り shaving

sóri *n* そり・ソリ sled

sóri *n* 剃り → **sorimásu** 剃ります
sóri *n* 反り → **sorimásu** 反ります
sōri-dáijin *n* 総理大臣 prime minister
sorimásu, sóru *v* 剃ります, 剃る shaves
sorimásu, sóru *v* 反ります, 反る bends (*back*), warps
sōritsu *n* 創立 establishment
sorí ya/wa shinai *v* 剃りや/はしない = **soránai** 剃らない (not shave)
sorí ya/wa shinai *v* 反りや/はしない = **soránai** 反らない (not bend)
soroban *n* そろばん・算盤 abacus, counting beads
soróé 揃え 1. *n* an array 2. *v* → **soroemásu** 揃えます [INFINITIVE]
soroemásu, soroéru *v* 揃えます, 揃える puts in order; collects; completes a set
soróí *n* 揃い 1. *n* a set (of …) 2. *v* → **soroimásu** 揃います [INFINITIVE]
sōron *n* 争論 quarrel, dispute
sōron *n* 総論 general remarks, outline, introduction
sórosoro *adv* そろそろ (*leave*) before long, it is about time to
sóru *v* 剃る = **sorimásu** 剃ります (shaves)
sóru *v* 反る = **sorimásu** 反ります (bends, warps)
sorya *conj* [INFORMAL] そりゃ = **sore wa** それは (as for that)
sō´(ryo) *n* 僧(侶) Buddhist priest
sō-ryō´ji *n* 総領事 consul general
sō´sa *n* 操作 operation, handling: ~ **shimásu** 操作します operates, handles
sōsaku *n* 創作 creation: ~ **shimásu** 創作します creates
sōsaku *n* 捜索 search, investigation: ~ **shimásu** 捜索します searches, investigates; **sōsaku-negai** 捜索願(い) an application to the police to search for (*a missing person*); **kataku-sōsaku** 家宅捜索 house search; **sōsaku-tai** 捜索隊 search party
sō´sē´ji *n* ソーセージ sausage
sósen *n* 祖先 ancestor (= **senzo** 先祖)
sóshiki *n* 組織 system, structure, setup, organization
sōshiki *n* 葬式 (**o-sōshiki** お葬式) funeral
soshite *conj* そして, **sōshite** そうして and then
soshō *n* 訴訟 lawsuit
sōshoku *n* 装飾 ornament, decoration
sosogimásu, sosogu *v* 注ぎます, 注ぐ pours (into)
sosoide *v* 注いで → **sosogimásu** 注ぎます
sō´su *n* ソース sauce, gravy
sotchí *pron* [INFORMAL] そっち = **sochira** そちら (there, that way; that one (*of two*); you)
sotchoku (na) *adj* 率直(な) frank
sóto *n* 外 outside, outdoors
sōtō (na) *adv, adj* 相当(な) 1. rather, quite, fairly 2. suitable, proper
soto-bori *n* 外堀 outer moat
soto-gawa *n* 外側 the outside: **soto-gawa (no)** 外側(の) external

soto-umi *n* 外海 high sea (= **gaikai** 外海)
sotsugyō *n* 卒業 graduation: ~ **shimásu** 卒業します graduates
   sotsugyō´-sei *n* 卒業生 a graduate
   sotsugyō´-shiki *n* 卒業式 commencement, graduation ceremony
sotta *v* 沿った = **soimáshita** 沿いました (followed)
sótta *v* 剃った = **sorimáshita** 剃りました (shaved; bent, warped)
sótta *v* 反った = **sorimáshita** 反りました (shaved; bent, warped)
sotte *v* 沿って → **soimásu** 沿います
sótte *v* 剃って, 反って → **sorimásu** 剃ります, 反ります
sou *v* 沿う = **soimásu** 沿います (it runs along, follows)
Sóuru *n* ソウル Seoul
sowanai *v* 沿わない = **soimasén** 沿いません (not follow)
sō yū (sō iu)… *adj* [INFORMAL] そうゆう(そういう) …that kind/sort of …; such … (= **sonna** そんな)
sōzō *n* 想像 imagination: ~ **shimásu** 想像します imagines
sōzōshíi *adj* 騒々しい noisy
su *n* 巣 nest
sú *n* 酢 (**o-su** お酢) vinegar
   sú-no-mono *n* 酢の物 vinegared dishes
   sú-buta *n* 酢豚 sweet and sour pork
sū´ *n* 数 number (= **kázu** 数); **sūji** 数字 numeral
   sū-gaku *n* 数学 (*junior/senior high school, college, university, graduate school*) mathematics (= **sansū** 算数); **sūgáku-sha** 数学者 mathematician
   sū-ji *n* 数字 numeral, figure (= **kazu** 数)
sū´-… *prefix* 数… several
   sū´-jitsu *n, adv* 数日 several days
   sū´-nen *n, adv* 数年 several years
   sū´-nin *n* 数人 several people
sū *v* 吸う = **suimásu** 吸います(sips, sucks, smokes, breathes in)
subarashíi *adj* すばらしい・素晴しい wonderful, splendid; **subaráshiku** すばらしく・素晴らしく splendidly
subekkói *adj* すべっこい [INFORMAL] slippery, slick, smooth (= **nameraka na** 滑らかな)
suberí-dai *n* すべり台・滑り台 a slippery-slide
suberimásu, subéru *v* 滑ります, 滑る slides, slips, skates
sube-sube (no) *adj* すべすべ(の) [INFORMAL] smooth, slippery
súbete n, *adv* すべて all
subétte *v* 滑って → **suberimásu** 滑ります
suchuwā´desu *n* スチュワーデス stewardess
suchuwā´do *n* スチュワード steward
sudare *n* すだれ・簾 curtain (*bamboo*)
sude *n* 素手 bare hands
súde ni *adv* すでに・既に already (= **mō´** もう)
sue *n* 1. 末 end, close 2. 末 future (= **shōrai** 将来):

... no yuku-sue ... の行く末 one's future: **yuku-sue wa** 行く末 is in the future

súe v 吸え 1. → **suemásu** 吸えます [INFINITIVE] 2. [IMPERATIVE] (suck!)

suéba v 吸えば (if one sips/sucks/smokes) → **suimásu** 吸います

suemásu, sueru v 据えます, 据える sets it up

suemásu, sueru v 吸えます, 吸える can sip (*suck, smoke*)

suemásu, suéru v すえます, すえる it spoils, goes bad

suete v 据えて, 吸えて → **suemásu** 据えます, 吸えます

súete v すえて → **suemásu** すえます

súgata n 姿 (**o-súgata** お姿) form, figure, shape: **hare-sugata** 晴れ姿 one in his/her Sunday best: **kimono-sugata** 着物姿 one in his/her kimono

sugi n 杉 cryptomeria, Japanese cedar

súgi v 過ぎ → **sugimásu** 過ぎます

...-sugi suffix ...過ぎ past (*the hour*)

sugimásu, sugíru v 過ぎます, 過ぎる passes, exceeds; **(shi-)sugimásu** (し)過ぎます overdoes: *adj* ... **sugimásu** ...過ぎます is overly/excessively/too

sugínai v 過ぎない = **sugimasén** 過ぎません (not pass; not exceed); **(... ni) sugínai** (...に)過ぎない is nothing more/other than, only

sugói adj すごい・凄い 1. swell, wonderful, marvelous, terrific 2. fierce, dreadful, ghastly, weird, uncanny

súgoku adv すごく・凄く awfully, terribly

sugoshimásu, sugósu v 過ごします, 過ごす passes (*time*)

súgu (ni) adv すぐ(に)at once, right away, immediately; in a minute; directly, right (*there*)

sugureteimásu, suguréru v 優れています, 優れている excels: **(... ni/yóri) sugureteimásu** (...に/より)優れています surpasses, is superior (*to*): is excellent; **sugúreta ...** 優れた... excellent ...

súgu sóba (ni) adv すぐそば(に)right near (at hand)

sui v 吸い → **suimásu** 吸います [INFINITIVE]

suichoku (no) adj 垂直(の)vertical; perpendicular

suidō n 水道 water system, water service, running water; plumbing

suidō-kan n 水道管 water pipe

suidō´-kyoku n 水道局 the Waterworks Bureau; municipal water service (*headquarters*)

suidō-ya (san) n 水道屋(さん)plumber

suiei n 水泳 swimming; **suiei-jō** 水泳場 swimming pool

suiéi-gí n 水泳着 swim suit (= **mizuki** 水着)

súifu n 水夫 seaman, sailor

suigara n 吸い殻 cigarette/cigar butt

súihei n 水兵 navy enlisted person, sailor, seaman

suihei (no) adj 水平(の)horizontal, level: **suihei-sen** 水平線 (*sea*) horizon

suii n 水位 water level

suijun n 水準 1. water level 2. standard

suika n スイカ・西瓜 watermelon

Sui, Kin, Chi, Ka, Moku, Do, Ten, Kai 水金地火木土天海 (= 水星、金星、地球、火星、木星、土星、天王星、海王星) "My Very Educated Mother Just Showed Us Nine (*planets*)" Mercury, Venus, Earth, Mars, Jupiter, Saturn, Uranus, Neptune (*eight planets in the solar system*)

sui-kuchi n 吸い口 cigarette holder

suimásu, sū v 吸います, 吸う sips, sucks, smokes, breathes in

suimasén interj すいません. [INFORMAL] 1. Excuse me. Sorry. 2. Thank you. (= **sumi-masén** すみません)

suimin n 睡眠 sleep; **suimín-zai** 睡眠剤, **suimín-yaku** 睡眠薬 sleeping pill(s)

sui-mono n 吸い物 clear soup

sui-sei adj 水性 water-based: **suisei-inku** 水性インク water based ink: **suisei-toryō** 水性塗料 water based paint

sui-sei adj 水生 aquatic: **suisei-dōbutsu** 水生動物 aquatic animal

Sui-sei n 彗星 comet: **Harē-suisei** ハレー彗星 Halley's comet

Sui-sei n 水星 Mercury

suisen n 水洗 flushing: **suisen-tóire** 水洗トイレ flush toilet

suisen n 推薦 recommendation: **~ shimásu** 推薦します recommends

suisen-jō n 推薦状 letter of recommendation

súiso n 水素 hydrogen

suisō n 水槽 water tank

suisoku n 推測 conjecture, guess, surmisal, supposition; **suisoku shimásu** 推測します guesses, surmises

Súisu n スイス Switzerland: **Súisu no** スイスの Swiss

Suisú-jin n スイス人 a Swiss

suítchi n スイッチ switch; ignition switch: **suítchi o iremásu** スイッチを入れます turns/switches it on, turns on the ignition; **suítchi o kirimásu** スイッチを切ります turns/switches it off

suitei n 推定 inference, presumption, estimation: **~ shimásu** 推定します infers, presumes, estimates

suitō-gákari n 出納係 cashier

suitorí-gami n 吸い取り紙 blotter

sui ya/wa shinai n 吸いや/はしない, **suya shinai** 吸やしない = **suwanai** 吸わない (not sip/suck/smoke)

Suiyō´(bi) n 水曜(日) Wednesday

suizókukan n 水族館 aquarium (= **akuariumu** アクアリウム)

súji n 筋 tendon, muscle, fiber, line: **ao-suji o tatete okorimásu** 青筋を立てて怒ります turns purple with rage

...súji suffix ...筋 plot (→ **ōsuji** 大筋): **arasuji** あらすじ summary, outline, synopsis

sukā´fu n スカーフ scarf; (*military*) sash

sukā´to n スカート skirt

sukébē (na) *adj* 助平(な)・すけべえ(な)・スケ
べ(な) lecherous; lewd (= **etchi (na)** エッチ(な))

sukḗ'to *n* スケート skate(s); skating: **sukēto-bōdo**
スケートボード skate board: **sukēto-gutsu** スケー
ト靴 (*a pair of*) skates: **sukéto (o) shimásu** スケー
ト(を)します skates

suki *n* すき・透き crack; opening; opportunity
(= **suki-ma** すき間・透き間・隙間)

sukí (na) *adj* 好き(な) one's favorite: **o-suki (na)**
お好き(な) (*your/someone else's*) favorite

sukí *n* 空き → **sukimásu** 空きます [INFINITIVE]

sukí *n* 鋤き → **sukimásu** 鋤きます [INFINITIVE]

sukí *n* 梳き → **sukimásu** すき[梳き]ます
[INFINITIVE]

sukídesu, sukida *v* 好きです, 好きだ likes

sukíí *n* スキー ski, skiing: **sukíi o shimásu** スキー
をします skis

suki-ma *n* すき間・透き間・隙間 crack; opening;
opportunity

sukimásu, suku *v* 空きます, 空く gets empty/clear

sukimásu, suku *v* 鋤きます, 鋤く plows

sukimásu, súku *v* すき[梳き]ます, すく・梳く
combs

sukimásu, súku *v* 好きます, 好く → **sukídesu,
sukida** 好きです, 好きだ

sukimu-míruku *n* スキムミルク skim milk

sukiyaki *n* すき焼き・すきやき thin-sliced beef
cooked in an iron pan (*with leeks, mushrooms,
bean curd, etc.*)

sukkári *adv* すっかり completely, all

sukóshi *adv* 少し a little, a bit: **sukóshi (no)** 少し
(の) some, a few; somewhat; **sukoshí mo** 少しも
[+ NEGATIVE] not in the least; **sukoshí-zútsu** 少し
ずつ bit by bit, a bit of/for each, a little at a time,
gradually

sukuimásu, sukū *v* 救います, 救う helps,
rescues, saves

sukuimásu, sukū *v* すく[掬い]います, すくう・
掬う scoops

sukunái *adj* 少ない few, meager, scarce, little;
yori sukunái より少ない fewer, less

sukúnáku *adv* 少なく (*so as to be*) few, little:
~ **shimásu** 少なくします lessens

sukúnáku-tomo *adv* 少なくとも at (*the*) least

sukuranburu-éggu *n* スクランブルエッグ
scrambled egg

sukuríín *n* スクリーン (*movie*) screen

sukutte *v* 救って → **sukuimásu** 救います

sukutte *v* すく[掬く]って → **sukuimásu** すく
[掬い]います

sukū *v* 救う → **sukuimásu** 救います

sukū *v* すくう・掬う → **sukuimásu** すく[掬い]
います

sukuwatto *n* スクワット squat (*bending and
stretching exercises, power lifting, etc.*)

sukyándaru *n* スキャンダル scandal

súmai *n* 住まい (**o-súmai** お住まい) residence

sumánai, sumimasén *v, interj* すまない, すみま
せん **1.** it never ends **2.** Thank you **3.** Excuse me

4. I apologize (for what I did).

sumasemásu, sumaséru *v* 済ませます, 済ませ
る finishes, concludes it

sumashimásu, sumásu *v* 済まします, 済ます
1. finishes, concludes it **2.** puts up with (*things as
they are*)

sumā'to (na) *adj* スマート(な) smart, stylish,
fashionable

sumātofon *n* スマートフォン smartphone
(*multifunctional mobile phone*)

súmi *n* 隅 an inside corner

sumí *n* 炭 charcoal

sumi *n* 墨 India ink, ink stick

sumí-e *n* 墨絵 Indian ink painting

sumí *n* 済み → **sumimásu** 済みます [INFINITIVE]

sumimasén *v* すみません **1.** Excuse me.
2. Sorry. **3.** Thank you. (= **sumánai** すまない)

sumimásu, súmu *v* 済みます, 済む comes to
an end

sumimásu, súmu *v* 住みます, 住む lives, takes
up residence, resides

sumire *n* スミレ・薫 violet

sumō *n* 相撲・すもう Japanese wrestling, sumo

sumō' *v* 住もう = **sumimashō'** 住みましょう
(let's reside!)

sumomo *n* スモモ・李 plum

sumō'-tóri *n* 相撲取り a sumo wrestler

súmu *v* 済む = **sumimásu** 済みます (comes to an
end)

súmu *v* 住む = **sumimásu** 住みます (lives)

...-sún *suffix* ...寸 inch (*Japanese*)

suna *n* 砂 sand

suna-búkuro *n* 砂袋 sandbag

sunákku *n* スナック **1.** a snackshop **2.** an after-
hours bar **3.** refreshment

sunakkú-gashi *n* スナック菓子 munch, snack

súnao (na) *adj* 素直(な) docile, gentle, obedient,
submissive, meek

sunáwachi *adv* すなわち・即ち namely, to wit;
that is to say; in other words

súnda *v* 済んだ = **sumimáshita** 済みました
(ended)

súnda *v* 住んだ = **sumimáshita** 住みました (lived)

súnde *v* 住んで → **sumimásu** 住みます: **súnde
imásu** 住んでいます lives, resides

suné *n* すね・臑・脛 shin, leg [IDIOM] **oya no
suné o kajiru** 親の脛をかじる sponges off one's
parents

sunpō *n* 寸法 measurements

sū'pā *n* スーパー = **sūpā-mā'ketto** スーパーマー
ケット supermarket

supái *n* スパイ spy

supai-wea *n* スパイウェア spyware (*computer*)

supaisu *n* スパイス spice (= **kōshinryō** 香辛料)

supamu-mēru *n* スパムメール (= **meiwaku-
mēru** 迷惑メール) spam e-mail, spam mail, e-mail
spam (*internet*)

supána *n* スパナ wrench

supein *n* スペイン Spain

Supein-go *n* スペイン語 Spanish (*language*)

Supeín-jín *n* スペイン人 Spaniard, a Spanish person

supéringu *n* スペリング → supéru スペル

supéru *n* スペル spell (= tsuzuri つづり・綴り)

supēsu *n* スペース 1. space (= kūkan 空間) 2. blank (= kūhaku 空白)

supíido *n* スピード speed (= sokudo 速度, hayasa 速さ): kokusai-supiido-yūbin 国際スピード郵便 EMS (*Express Mail Service*)

supíikā *n* スピーカー (loud)speaker

suponji *n* スポンジ sponge; swab: suponji-kēki スポンジケーキ sponge cake

suponsā *n* スポンサー 1. sponsor (= kōkoku-nushi 広告主, bangumi-teikyō-sha 番組提供者) 2. patron (= kōen-sha 後援者, patoron パトロン)

supōˊtsu *n* スポーツ sport(s), athletics (= undō 運動)

suppái *adj* すっぱい[酸っぱい] sour, acid: suppai-aji すっぱい[酸っぱい]味 sour flavor, sour taste (= san-mi 酸味)

suppon *n* すっぽん・スッポン snapping turtle

supponpon *n* すっぽんぽん (INFORMAL, *slang*) full monty, complete nudity (= suppadaka 素っ裸)

sūˊpu *n* スープ soup

supūˊn *n* スプーン spoon (= saji さじ・サジ・匙)

surákkusu *n* スラックス slacks

suránai *v* 擦らない = surimasén 擦りません (not rub)

suránai *v* 摺ら[摺ら]ない = surimasén 摺り[摺り]ません (not file/grind)

suránai *v* 刷らない = surimasén 刷りません (not print)

suránai *v* すらない = surimasén すりません (not pick one's pocket)

sure *v* 擦れ 1. → suremásu 擦れます [INFINITIVE] 2. [IMPERATIVE] (rub!)

sure *v* 摺れ[摺れ] 1. → suremásu 摺れ[摺れ]ます [INFINITIVE] 2. [IMPERATIVE] (file/grind!)

sure *v* 刷れ 1. → suremásu 刷れます [INFINITIVE] 2. [IMPERATIVE] (print!)

sure *v* すれ → suremásu すれます [INFINITIVE]

suréba *v* すれば = [INFORMAL] surya すりゃ (if one does) → shimásu します

súreba *v* 擦れ (if one rubs) [INFORMAL] surya 擦りゃ → surimásu 擦ります

súreba *v* 摺[摺]れば (if one files/grinds) [INFORMAL] surya 摺りゃ[摺りゃ] → surimásu 摺り[摺]ます

súreba *v* 刷れば (if one prints) [INFORMAL] surya 刷りゃ → surimásu 刷ります

súreba *v* すれば (if one picks one's pocket) [INFORMAL] surya すりゃ → surimásu すります

suremásu, suréru *v* 擦れます, 擦れる 1. it rubs/grazes 2. can rub/graze

suremásu, suréru *v* 刷れます, 刷れる can print

surénai *v* 擦れない = suremasén 擦れません (cannot rub)

surénai *v* 刷れない = suremasén 刷れません (cannot print)

suréreba *v* 擦れれば (if it rubs; if one can rub) → suremásu 擦れます

suréreba *v* 刷れれば (if it prints; if one can print) → suremásu 刷れます

surí 刷り 1. *n* print(ing) 2. *v* → surimásu 刷ります

súri *n* すり・スリ・掏り pick-pocket

súri *v* 擦り → surimásu 擦ります [INFINITIVE]

súri *v* 摺り[摺り] → surimásu 摺り[摺り]ます [INFINITIVE]

súri *v* 刷り → surimásu すります [INFINITIVE]

suríbachi *n* すり鉢 earthenware kitchen-mortar with wooden pestle

suríi *n* スリー three

surimásu, súru *v* 擦ります, 擦る rubs

surimásu, súru *v* 摺り[摺り]ます, 摺る[摺る] files; grinds

surimásu, súru *v* 刷ります, 刷る prints

surimásu, súru *v* すります, する picks one's pocket

suríppa *n* スリッパ slippers

suríppu *n* スリップ slip(ping); surippu-jíko スリップ事故 slipping accident; "Surippu-jíko ōˊshi" スリップ事故多し Slippery (*Area*)

Suriránka *n* スリランカ Sri Lanka

súriru *n* スリル thrill

súri ya/wa shinai *v* 擦りや/はしない = suránai 擦らない (not rub)

súri ya/wa shinai *v* 摺り[摺り]や/はしない = suránai 摺らない[摺らない] (not file/grind)

súri ya/wa shinai *v* 刷りや/はしない = suránai 刷らない (not print)

súri ya/wa shinai *v* すりや/はしない = suránai すらない (not pick one's pocket)

surōˊ *v* 擦ろう = surimashōˊ 擦りましょう (let's rub!)

surōˊ *v* 摺[摺]ろう = surimashōˊ 摺り[摺り]ましょう (let's file/grind it!)

surōˊ *v* 刷ろう = surimashōˊ 刷りましょう (let's print it!)

surōˊ *v* すろう = surimashōˊ すりましょう (let's steal it!)

surōˊgan *n* スローガン slogan

surōˊ (na) *adj* スロー(な) slow

surōˊpu *n* スロープ ramp

suru *v* する = shimásu します (does)

súru *v* 擦る = surimásu 擦ります (rubs)

súru *v* 摺る[摺る] = surimásu 摺り[摺り]ます (files, grinds)

súru *v* 刷る = surimásu 刷ります (prints)

súru *v* する = surimásu すります (picks one's pocket)

surudói *adj* 鋭い sharp, acute

surume *n* スルメ dried cuttlefish

surya *v* [INFORMAL] すりゃ → súreba すれば

sushi *n* すし・スシ・寿司・鮨 (o-súshi お寿司・お鮨) sushi (*rice seasoned with sweetened vinegar with raw fish*)

su̱shí-ya *n* 寿司[鮨]屋 (osu̱shi-ya お寿司[お鮨]屋) a sushi bar

suso *n* すそ・裾 hem: **suso-age (o) shimásu** 裾上げ(を)します takes a hem up

súsu *n* すす・煤 soot: **susu o haraimásu** すす[煤]を払います sweeps off soot

susume *v* 進め **1.** → **susumemásu** 進めます [INFINITIVE] **2.** [IMPERATIVE] (forward!) → **susumimásu** 進みます

susume *v* 勧め → **susumemásu** 勧めます [INFINITIVE]

susumemásu, susumeru *v* 進めます, 進める furthers, *advances*

susumemásu, susumeru *v* 勧めます, 勧める encourages, recommends, advises, counsels; persuades, urges

susumimásu, susumu *v* 進みます, 進む goes forward, progresses; goes too fast, gets ahead

susumō´ *v* 進もう = **susumimashō** 進みましょう (let's go forward!)

susunde *v* 進んで **1.** → **susumimásu** 進みます: **susunde imásu** 進んでいます is advanced, (*clock*) is fast **2.** **susunde yarimásu** 進んでやります go ahead voluntarily, willingly

sutā *n* スター star (*actor*) (= **hanagata** 花形)

sutajio *n* スタジオ studio (= **satsuei-jo** 撮影所)

sutando *n* スタンド **1.** stand (*for selling things*) **2.** (= **denki sutándo** 電気スタンド) desk/floor lamp

sute *v* 捨て **1.** → **sutemásu** 捨てます [INFINITIVE] **2. sute ro** 捨てろ [IMPERATIVE] (throw it away!, drop it!)

sute-ba *n* 捨て場 dump site (= **gomi-suteba** ごみ捨て場)

sute-mi (de) *adv* 捨て身(で) in desperation

suteki (na) *adj* すてき[素敵](な) fine, splendid, swell

sutē´ki *n* ステーキ (*beef*) steak: **sutē´ki-sando** ステーキサンド steak sandwich, **biifu sutē´ki** ビーフステーキ

sutékki *n* ステッキ walking stick, cane

sutemásu, suteru *v* 捨てます, 捨てる throws

away, abandons, dumps

sutereo *n* ステレオ stereo (*sound/player*)

sutēshon *n* ステーション railroad station (= **eki** 駅)

sutó *n* スト = **sutoráiki** ストライキ strike (*job action*)

sutō´bu *n* ストーブ stove, heater

sutōkā *n* ストーカー stalker

sutoráiku *n* ストライク strike (*baseball*)

sutóresu *n* ストレス stress, tension: **sutoresu-kaishō** ストレス解消 stress relieving, stress release (= **sutoresu hassan** ストレス発散)

sutoretchi *n* ストレッチ stretch (*exercises*)

sutoríppu *n* ストリップ striptease, strip show, burlesque

sutórō *n* ストロー straw (*to drink with*)

sū´tsu *n* スーツ suit

sūtsukē´su *n* スーツケース suitcase

sutte *v* 吸って → **suimásu** 吸います

suwanai *v* 吸わない = **suimasén** 吸いません (not sip, …)

suwaremásu, suwareru *v* 座れます, 座れる can sit; seats are available

suwarikomi(-súto) *n* 座り込み(スト) sit-in (*strike*)

suwarimásu, suwaru *v* 座ります, 座る sits (*especially Japanese style*)

suwatte *v* 座って → **suwarimásu** 座ります

suya *v* 吸や → **suéba** 吸えば

suzu *n* スズ・鈴 little bells

súzu *n* スズ・錫 tin

suzuki *n* スズキ・鱸 sea bass

suzume *n* スズメ・雀 sparrow: [IDIOM] **suzume no namida (hodo no)…** 雀の涙(ほどの)… very little bit of…

suzumé-bachi *n* スズメバチ・スズメ蜂 hornet

suzurí *n* すずり・硯 inkstone: **suzurí-bako** すずり[硯]箱 inkstone case

suzushíi *adj* 涼しい cool

sy… → **sh…**

T

tá *n* た・他 = **hoka** 他, **sono-ta**, **sono-hoka** その他 other(s)

ta-hō´ *n* 他方 a different direction, another place: **tahō´ de wa** 他方では on the other hand

tá (ni) *adv* 他(に) to/for/as others, additionally (= **hoka (ni)** 他[外](に))

ta-nin *n* 他人 outsider, stranger; others (*people*) (= **ta-sha** 他者): **aka no tanin** 赤の他人 a complete stranger

tá (no) *adj* 他(の) = **hoka (no)** 他[外](の) other

tá-sha *n* 他社 other companies

tá-sha *n* 他者 [BOOKISH] others (*people*) (= **ta-nin**

他人)

tá *n* 田 rice field (= **tanbo** 田んぼ)

ta-nbo *n* 田んぼ rice field [INFORMAL] (= **ta** 田)

ta-ué *n* 田植え rice planting

…-ta *v* …た = **…-máshita** …ました did

tába *n* 束 bundle, bunch: **satsu-taba** 札束 bundle of bills

tabako *n* タバコ・煙草 tobacco; cigarettes (= **shigaretto** シガレット)

tabakó-ire *n* タバコ[煙草]入れ cigarette case (= **sigaretto kēsu** シガレットケース)

tā´ban *n* ターバン turban

tábe v 食べ → **tabemásu** 食べます
1. [INFINITIVE] 2. **tabé ro** 食べろ, **tábe yo** 食べよ [IMPERATIVE] (eat!)

tabemásu, tabéru v 食べます, 食べる eats (= **shokuji o shimásu** 食事をします)

tabé-mónó n 食べ物 food (= **shokumotsu** 食物)

taberaremásu, taberaréru v 食べられます, 食べられる can eat

tabesasemásu, tabesaséru v 食べさせます, 食べさせる feeds

tabete v 食べて → **tabemásu** 食べます

tabeyō´ v 食べよう = **tabemashō´** 食べましょう (let's eat!)

tabi n たび・タビ・足袋 split-toe socks

tabí n 旅 journey (= **ryokō** 旅行)

tabí n 度・たび time, occasion; ... **tabí (ni)** ...度 [たび] (に) every time that ...

tabitabi adv たびたび・度々 often (= **shibashiba** しばしば, **nando-mo** 何度も)

tabō (na) adj 多忙(な) [BOOKISH] busy (= **isogashíi** 忙しい): [HONORIFIC] **go-tabō no tokoro (o) arigatō gozaimásu/gozaimáshita** ご多忙のところ(を)ありがとうございます／ございました Thank you for taking time in your busyness

tábu n タブ a tab

tabū n タブー taboo (= **kinki** 禁忌, **go-hatto** ご法度)

tábun adv たぶん・多分 probably, likely; perhaps, maybe (**tábun ... deshō´** たぶん ...でしょう, **tábun ... ká mo shiremasén** たぶん ...かも知れません)

tabun (ni) adv 多分(に) [BOOKISH] a lot, much

taburetto n タブレット 1. tablet 2. Tablet PC

taburoido n タブロイド tabloid

tácha v [INFORMAL] 立ちゃ → **táteba** 立てば

táchi n たち・質 nature, disposition

táchi v 立ち → **tachimásu** 立ちます [INFINITIVE]

táchi v 経ち → **tachimásu** 経ちます [INFINITIVE]

táchi v 断ち → **tachimásu** 断ちます [INFINITIVE]

...´-tachi suffix ...達・たち [animate plural]; and others: **watashi-tachi** わたし達[私達] we: **anata-tachi** あなた達 you (people): **kimi-tachi** 君たち[達] you guys

tachi-agarimásu, tachi-agaru v 立ち上がります, 立ち上がる rises, stands up

tachi-bá n 立場 viewpoint, standpoint, situation

tachi-domarimásu, tachi-domaru v 立ち止まります, 立ち止まる comes to a stand

"Tachiiri kinshi" n 立ち入り禁止. No Trespassing. Off Limits.

tachimachi adv たちまち immediately, instantly (= **at-toiuma ni** あっという間に, **matatakuma ni** 瞬く間に)

tachimásu, tátsu v 立ちます, 立つ stands (up)
tachi-bánashi n 立ち話 (wayside) a stand for talking, a stand for chatting: **tachi-bánashi (o) shimásu** 立ち話(を)します stands chatting, stands talking
tachi-mi n 立ち見 a stand for watching: ~ **shimásu** 立ち見します stands watching, sees

as a standee; **tachimi-kyaku** 立ち見客 standee; **tachimi-seki** 立ち見席 the gallery, standing room

tachimásu, tátsu v 発ちます, 発つ leaves (for a far place) (= **shuppatsu shimásu** 出発します)

tachimásu, tátsu v 経ちます, 経つ elapses

tachimásu, tátsu v 断ちます, 断つ [BOOKISH] cuts off

táchi ya/wa shinai v 立ちや/はしない = **tatánai** 立たない (not stand)

táda n ただ free, gratis, no fee/charge (= **muryō** 無料)

tádachi ni adv ただちに [BOOKISH] immediately

tádaima adv ただいま just now; in a minute (= **tatta-íma** たった今)
Tadaima interj ただいま I'm back!, I'm home! (said on returning to one's residence) (abbreviated phrase of "Tadaima kaerimáshita", meaning "I just came back home.")

táda (no) adj ただ(の) 1. only, just 2. ordinary

tádashi conj 但し provided

tadashíi adj 正しい right; correct; **tadáshiku** 正しく rightly, correctly

tadō´-shi n 他動詞 transitive verb

tadotadoshíi adj たどたどしい halting, not smooth (= **tsutanai** 拙い)

táe v 堪え → **taemásu** 堪えます [INFINITIVE]

táe v 絶え → **taemásu** 絶えます [INFINITIVE]

taema-náku adv 絶え間なく continuously, without interruption (= **táezu** 絶えず)

taemásu, taéru v 堪えます, 堪える bears, puts up with

taemásu, taéru v 絶えます, 絶える ceases

taénai v 堪えない = **taemasén** 堪えません (not bear)

taénai v 絶えない = **taemasén** 絶えません (not cease)

taeraremásu, taeraréru v 堪えられます, 堪えられる (can bear)

taerarénai v 堪えられない = **taeraremasén** 堪えられません (cannot bear)

taéru v 堪える = **taemásu** 堪えます (bears, puts up with)

taéru v 絶える = **taemásu** 絶えます (ceases)

táete v 堪えて → **taemásu** 堪えます

táete v 絶えて → **taemásu** 絶えます

táezu adv 絶えず continuously, without interruption (= **taema-náku** 絶え間なく)

tagá n たが a barrel hoop
taga o shimeru [IDIOM] たがを締める braces oneself
taga ga yurumu [IDIOM] たがが緩む becomes less disciplined, loses one's spirits (= **taga ga hazureru** たがが外れる)

tagai (no) adj 互い(の) (**o-tagai (no)** お互い(の)) mutual, reciprocal, for each other

tagai (ni) adv 互い(に) (**o-tagai (ni)** お互い(に)) mutually, reciprocally, with each other

tagaku n 多額 large sum

...-tagarimásu, -tagaru suffix, v ...たがります,

...たがる wants to ..., is eager to ...

tagayashimásu̲, tagayásu *v* 耕します, 耕す plows

tāgetto *n* ターゲット object, target (= **taishō** 対象)

tagu-bōto *n* タグボート tug boat

tái *n* タイ・鯛 sea bream, red snapper

Tái *n* タイ Thailand

Tai-go *n* タイ語 Thai (*language*)

Tai-jin *n* タイ人 a Thai

tái *n* 体 **1.** form: [IDIOM] **na wa tai o arawasu** 名は体を表す Names and natures do often agree. **2.** style **3.** body (= **karada** 体, **shintai** 身体)

tai-... *prep* 対..., ...´-**tai** ...対 versus, towards, against; **roku̲-tai yón** 六対四, 6対4 4 to 6 (*score*)

tai-... *prefix* 退... leaving, retire

tai-gaku *n* 退学 **1.** leaving school: ~ **shimásu** 退学します leaves school: **chūto-taigaku-sha** 中途退学者 a dropout **2.** expulsion from school (= **taigaku-shobun** 退学(処分))

tai-in *n* 退位 abdication: ~ **shimásu** 退位します abdicates

tai-in *n* 退院 leaving the hospital: ~ **shimásu** 退院します leaves the hospital

tai-goku *n* 退職 retirement: **taishoku shimásu̲** 退職します retires: **taishoku-kin** 退職金 retirement allowance: **taishoku-nenkin** 退職年金 (*retirement*) pension

tai-... *prefix* 大... great, large

tai-bō, tai-mō *n* 大望 ambition, great willingness (= **taishi** 大志)

tai-ryō *n* 大量 large quantity: **tairyō-seisan** 大量生産 mass production

tai-sa *n* 大佐 (*army*) colonel; (= **daisa** 大佐) (*navy*) captain

tái-sa *n* 大差 [BOOKISH] a great difference (= **ōkina sa** 大きな差): **tái-sa de kachimásu̲** 大差で勝ちます wins by a wide margin

tai-sen *n* 大戦 a great war, a world war (= **ōkina sensō** 大きな戦争): **dai-ichi-ji sekai-taisen** 第一次世界大戦 World War I: **dai-ni-ji sekai-taisen** 第二次世界大戦 World War II

tai-shi *n* 大志 ambition (= **taibō, taimō** 大望) [IDIOM] **shōnen yo taishi o idake** 少年よ大志を抱け Boys, be ambitious!

tái-shō *n* 大将 (*general*) admiral: **o-yama no tái-shō** お山の大将 king of the mountain: **(kinjo no) gaki-daishō** (近所の)がき[ガキ・餓鬼]大将 boss of the kids in the neighborhood

tai-shoku *n* 大食 gluttony (= **ōgui** 大食い); **taishoku-kan** 大食漢 a big eater, glutton (= **ōgurai** 大食らい)

tái-sō *adj, adv* たいそう・大層 [BOOKISH] very: **tái-sō (na)** たいそう(な) a great many/much; = **go-táisō** ごたいそう exaggerated

...-tái *suffix* ...帯 belt; zone: **anet-tai** 亜熱帯 subtropical zone: **anzen chi-tai** 安全地帯 safety zone: **kiken chi-tai** 危険地帯 danger zone

...-tai *suffix v* ...たい wants to, is eager to

tabe-tai *suffix v* 食べたい wants to eat

shi-tai *suffix v* したい, **yari-tai** やりたい wants to do: **shi-tai hōdai ni shimásu̲** したい放題にします does whatever one feels like doing [IN NEGATIVE SENSE]

taibō (no) *adj* 待望(の) long-awaited

taichō *n* 体調 (*physical condition*) tone (= **guai** 具合): **taichō ga ii/yoi** 体調がいい/良い is in good health condition; **taichō ga warui** 体調が悪い is in poor health condition

taidan *n* 対談 [BOOKISH] conversation between two people, dialogue: ~ **shimásu** 対談します has a conversation; **taidan-bangumi** 対談番組 TV talk show

táido *n* 態度 attitude, disposition, behavior: **táido ga ōkii** 態度が大きい acts big; **aimai na táido** あいまいな態度 ambiguous attitude; **kudaketa táido** くだけた態度 friendly attitude

taidō *n* 胎動 fetal movement

taifū´ *n* 台風 typhoon

taigai *adv* 大概・たいがい **1.** in general; for the most part; practically (= **taitei** たいてい・大抵) **2.** probably, like(ly), like as not

taigen *n* 体言 substantive words, indeclinable words (*grammar*)

taigū *n* 待遇 **1.** treatment, reception **2.** pay, working conditions **3.** official position, post

taihai-teki (na) *adj* 退廃的(な) decadent

Taihéiyō *n* 太平洋 Pacific Ocean (→ **taiyō** 大洋) Taiheiyō-sensō *n* 太平洋戦争 Pacific War

taihen *adv* たいへん・大変 **1.** very, exceedingly, terribly, enormously (= **hijō ni** 非常に): **Taihen osewa ni narimáshita.** 大変お世話になりました I owe you a lot., Thank you so much for everything you have done for me. **2.** laboriously, seriously, disastrously: **sorewa (hontō ni) taihen desu̲ ne** それは(本当に)大変ですね It must be (*really*) hard for you.

taihen (na) *adj* たいへん[大変](な) **1.** exceeding, enormous: **taihen na bijin desu̲** 大変な美人です is very beautiful **2.** serious, disastrous, tough, terrible, difficult: **taihen na shigoto desu̲** 大変な仕事です is tough work

taihi *n* 対比 [BOOKISH] contrast, comparison (= **hikaku** 比較): ~ **shimásu** 対比します contrasts, compares

táiho *n* 逮捕 arrest(ing): ~ **shimásu** 逮捕します arrests

taihō *n* 大砲 cannon

táii *n* 大尉 captain (*army*); lieutenant (*navy*) (= **dáii** 大尉)

taii *n* 大意 [BOOKISH] outline, summary, drift: **taii o tsukamimásu̲** 大意をつかみます catches the drift

taii *n* 体位 body position, posture (= **shisei** 姿勢)

tái(i)ku *n* 体育 physical education, athletics: **Tái(i) ku-no-hí** 体育の日 Sports Day (*2nd Monday of October*)

tai(i)kú-kan *n* 体育館 gymnasium

taiji *n* 胎児 fetus, unborn baby, embryo

taiji *n* 退治 extermination: ~ **shimásu** 退治します exterminates: **oni-taiji** 鬼退治 demon extermination

taijū *n* 体重 body weight: **shinchō to taijū** 身長と

体重 height and weight: **taijū-kei** 体重計 scales: **taijū ga fuemásu** 体重が増えます gains weight; **taijū ga herimásu** 体重が減ります loses weight

táika _n_ 大家 authority (= **kyoshō** 巨匠)

táika _n_ 対価 compensation, consideration

táika _n_ 退化 degeneration: ~ **shimásu** 退化します degenerates

taikai _n_ 大会 mass meeting; convention, conference; tournament: **zenkoku-taikai** 全国大会 national convention; **sekai-senshuken-taikai** 世界選手権大会 world championships

taikai _n_ 大海 ocean, high sea (= **taiyō** 大洋)

taikaku _n_ 体格 body build, physique

taikei _n_ 体系 a system

taiken _n_ 体験 personal experience: ~ **shimásu** 体験します experiences

taiko _n_ 太鼓 (_Japanese_) drum

taikō _n_ 対抗 confrontation, opposition; … **ni** ~ **shimásu** …に対抗します opposes, stands against, confronts; … **ni taikō shite** …に対抗して in opposition to, against, in rivalry with

taikutsu (na) _adj_ 退屈(な) boring, dull

taiman (na) _adj_ 怠慢(な) negligent, careless, neglectful

táimatsu _n_ たいまつ・松明 torch

taimen _n_ 対面 interview

taimen _n_ 体面 one's dignity, sense of honor, "face": **taimen o tamochimásu** 体面を保ちます keeps up appearances

taimingu _n_ タイミング timing (= **ma-ai** 間合い)

taiō _n_ 対応 1. correspondence, handling; (… **ni**) **taiō shimásu** (…に)対応します corresponds (_to_) 2. equivalent (= **sōō** 相応): (… **ni**) **taiō shimásu** (…に)対応します is equivalent (_to_)

taion _n_ 体温 body temperature; **taion-kei** 体温計 (_clinical_) thermometer

taipo _n_ タイポ typo, typing error

táipu _n_ タイプ 1. type, style (= **kata** 型): **atarashii táipu** 新しいタイプ new type (= **shin-gata** 新型) 2. one's type: **kare wa watashi no táipu dewa arimasen** 彼は私のタイプではありません He's not my type. 3. typewriting, typewriter

taipuráitā _n_ タイプライター typewriter (= **taipu** タイプ)

tairagemásu, tairageru _v_ 平らげます, 平らげる [INFORMAL] eats up

taira-gi _n_ タイラギ pin/razor/fan shell (_a kind of scallop_)

taira (na) _adj_ 平ら(な) even, smooth, flat; **taira ni shimásu** 平らにします flattens

tairiku _n_ 大陸 continent: **tairiku (no)** 大陸(の) continental

tairitsu _n_ 対立 confronting, opposing: ~ **shimásu** 対立します confronts, opposes

táiru _n_ タイル tile (_floor, wall_)(_made of plastic, etc._)

tairyoku _n_ 体力 stamina (= **sutamina** スタミナ): **tairyoku ga arimásu** 体力があります has stamina

taisei _n_ 体制 system: **seiji-taisei** 政治体制 political

system: **kyōiku-taisei** 教育体制 education system

taisei _n_ 体勢 posture (= **shisei** 姿勢): **taisei o kuzushimásu** 体勢を崩します loses one's balance: **taisei o tatenaoshimásu** 体勢を立て直します regains one's balance

taisei _n_ 耐性 tolerance: **arukōru-taisei** アルコール耐性 tolerance to alcohol: **yakubutsu-taisei** 薬物耐性 drug resistance

taisei _n_ 大勢 general situation (= **nariyuki** なりゆき)

taisei _n_ 態勢 preparedness: **taisei ga totonoimásu** 態勢が整います is ready

Taiséiyō _n_ 大西洋 Atlantic Ocean (→ **taiyō** 大洋)

taisen _n_ 対戦 match, competition: **taisen-aite** 対戦相手 one's opponent: **taisen-gata kakutō-gēmu** 対戦型格闘ゲーム V.S. fighting game

taisetsu (na) _adj_ 大切(な) 1. important (= **daiji (na)** 大事(な), **jūyō (na)** 重要(な)): **taisetsu na shorui** 大切な書類 important documents 2. valuable, precious (= **daiji (na)** 大事(な), **kichō (na)** 貴重(な)): **taisetsu na omoide** 大切な思い出 precious memories

taisetsu-ni-shimásu (suru) _v_ 大切にします(する) cherishes, treats carefully, gives importance (= **daiji-ni-shimásu** 大事にします): **kazoku o taisetsu ni shimásu** 家族を大切にします gives importance to family: (**dōzo**) **o-karada o taisetsu ni shitekudasai** (どうぞ)お体を大切にして下さい Please take care of yourself.

táishaku _n_ 貸借 debit and credit, lending and borrowing

táishaku-taishō hyō _n_ 貸借対照表 balance sheet (B/S)

táishi _n_ 大使 ambassador

taishí-kan _n_ 大使館 embassy

tái-shi _v_ 対し → **tai-shimásu** 対します [INFINITIVE]

tai-shimásu, tai-súru _v_ 対します, 対する: (… **ni**) **tai-shimásu** (…に)対します, 対する: opposes; … **ni tái-shite** …に対して 1. against; toward; as against, as compared with, in contrast to 2. with respect to, in regard to

tái-shita … _adj_ たいした・大した… important; serious; immense

taishitsu _n_ 体質 (_physical_) constitution

taisho _n_ 対処 handling of matters: ~ **shimásu** 対処します handles, copes with

taishō _n_ 対象 object, target (= **tāgetto** ターゲット)

taishō _n_ 対照 contrast: ~ **shimásu** 対照します contrasts; **hikaku-taishō** 比較対照 comparison and contrast (→ **táishaku-taishō-hyō** 貸借対照表)

taishō _n_ 対称 symmetry: **sayū-taishō** 左右対称 bilateral symmetry: … **to taishō o nashimásu** …と対称をなします is symmetrical to …

Táishō-jidai _n_ 大正時代 Taisho Period (_1912–1926_)

taishū _n_ 体臭 body odor (BO)

taishū _n_ 大衆 the general public, the masses: **taishū (no)** 大衆(の) popular, mass: **taishū-ka** 大衆化 popularization

taisō *n* 体操 calisthenics, physical exercises:
~ **shimásu** 体操します does calisthenics, does
physical exercise

taita *v* 炊いた = **takimáshita** 炊きました (cooked)

taite *v* 炊いて → **takimásu** 炊きます

taite *v* 焚いて → **takimásu** 焚きます

taitei *adv* たいてい・大抵 usually: **taitei no ...**
たいていの ...the usual ..., most ...

taitō (no) *adj* 対等（の）equal, equivalent (= **dōtō
(no)** 同等（の）)

táitoru *n* タイトル **1.** title (= **hyōdai** 表題) **2.** title,
championship: **taitoru-matchi** タイトルマッチ
title match **3.** caption, subtitle (= **jimaku** 字幕)

taiwa *n* 対話 conversation, dialogue

Taiwán *n* 台湾 Taiwan; **Taiwan-jín** 台湾人
a Taiwanese

taiya *n* タイヤ a tire: **kuruma no taiya** 車のタイヤ
car tires: **jitensha/jidensha no taiya** 自転車のタイ
ヤ bicycle tires

taiyō *n* 大洋 ocean (= **taikai** 大海): **go-taiyō**
五大洋 five oceans (*Pacific Ocean, Indian Ocean,
Atlantic Ocean, Arctic Ocean, Antarctic Ocean*)
(→ **Taiheiyō** 太平洋, **Taiseiyō** 大西洋)

taiyō *n* 大要 summary (= **gaiyō** 概要, **yōyaku**
要約, **samarii** サマリー)

táiyō *n* 太陽 **1.** sun (= **ohisama** お日様) **2.** joy to
someone

taiyō-enerugii *n* 太陽エネルギー solar energy

taiyō-kei *n* 太陽系 solar system

táiyō-kōsen 太陽光線 [FORMAL] sunshine (= **nikkō**
日光, **taiyō no hikari** 太陽の光)

táiyō no hikari 太陽の光 sunshine (= **nikkō** 日光,
taiyō-kōsen 太陽光線)

taiyō-nensū *n* 耐用年数 lifespan of thing,
expected lifetime

taiyō-sei *n* 耐用性 durability

taizai *n* 滞在 a stay (*away from home*), a sojourn:
~ **shimásu** 滞在します stays (*away from home*),
sojourns; **taizai-saki** 滞在先 place of sojourn

taka *n* タカ・鷹 hawk (→ **nō aru taka wa tsume
wo kakusu** 能ある鷹は爪を隠す)

taka no tsume *n* タカノツメ・鷹の爪 red pepper
(= **tōgarashi** トウガラシ・唐辛子)

táká *n* 高 quantity: **táká ga shireteimásu** 高が知れ
ています is limited, not amount to a hill of beans

takaga *adj* たかが no(thing) more than

takái *adj* 高い high, tall; costly, expensive; loud

takanai *v* 炊かない = **takimasén** 炊きません (not
cook)

takará *n* 宝 (**o-takara** お宝) a treasure (= **takara-
mono** 宝物)

takará-kuji *n* 宝くじ lottery

takara-mono *n* 宝物 a treasure

tákasa *n* 高さ height (= **kōdo** 高度)

take *n* 竹 bamboo

take-fū′rin *n* 竹風鈴 bamboo wind-chimes

take-no-ko *n* タケノコ・竹の子・筍 bamboo
shoot

take-záiku *n* 竹細工 bambooware

take *n* タケ・茸 (*compounds/dialect*) mushroom
(= **kínoko** キノコ)

take *v* 炊け → **takemásu** 炊けます [INFINITIVE]

take *v* 焚け → **takemásu** 焚けます [INFINITIVE]

take *v* 炊け [IMPERATIVE] (cook it!) → **takimásu**
炊きます

takéba *v* 焚けば (if one makes a fire) →
takimásu 焚きます

takéba *v* 炊けば (if one cooks/burns it) →
takimásu 炊きます

takemásu, takeru *v* 焚きます, 焚ける can make
a fire

takemásu, takeru *v* 炊きます, 炊ける can cook;
can burn it

taki *n* 滝 waterfall

taki *v* 炊き → **takimásu** 炊きます [INFINITIVE]

taki *v* 焚き → **takimásu** 焚きます [INFINITIVE]

takigi *n* たきぎ・薪 firewood, fuel

takimásu, taku *v* 焚きます, 焚く makes a fire
taki-bi *n* 焚き火 bonfire
taki-tsuke *n* 焚き付け kindling

takimásu, taku *v* 炊きます, 炊く cooks; burns it
takikomi-góhan *n* 炊き込みご飯 a rice dish that
includes adding seasonal ingredients to the rice

takishiido *n* タキシード tuxedo

takí ya/wa shinai *v* 焚きや/はしない = **takanai**
焚かない (not make a fire)

takí ya/wa shinai *v* 炊きや/はしない = **takanai**
炊かない (not cook/burn it)

takkuru *n* タックル tackle

táko *n* タコ octopus
tako-yaki *n* たこ焼き griddled dumplings with
octopus bits inside

táko *n* 凧・たこ kite: **táko o agemásu** 凧を揚げま
す flies a kite
takó-áge *n* 凧揚げ kite-flying

táko *n* たこ callus, corn

takō′ *v* 焚こう = **takimashō′** 焚きましょう (let's
make a fire!)

takō′ *v* 炊こう = **takimashō′** 炊きましょう (let's
cook!; let's burn it!)

takokuseki (no) *adj* 多国籍（の）multinational:
takokuseki-kigyō 多国籍企業 multinational
company

taku *n* 宅 **1.** my house **2.** (*your/someone else's*)
house (= **o-taku** お宅) **3.** [HUMBLE] my husband
tak-kyū-bin *n* 宅急便 express delivery service
taku-hai-bin *n* 宅配便 delivery service

taku *v* 焚く = **takimásu** 焚きます (cooks; burns)

taku *v* 炊く = **takimásu** 炊きます (makes a fire)

taku *n* 卓 table, desk
tak-kyū *n* 卓球 table tennis
taku-jō *n, adv* 卓上 on one's table/desk

takúan, takúwan *n* たくあん, たくわん yellow
pickles made from sliced daikon

takumashii *adj* たくましい・逞しい **1.** strong,
robust (*body*) **2.** strong (*will*)

takumi *n* 巧み skill
takumi na *adj* 巧み（な）skillful

takumi ni *adv* 巧みに skillfully

takurami *n* 企み plan, scheme, plot

takurámi *v* 企み → **takuramimásu** 企みます [INFINITIVE]

takuramimásu, takurámu *v* 企みます, 企む plans, schemes, plots

takuránde *v* 企んで → **takuramimásu** 企みます **1.** intentionally, on purpose, with forethought **2. (… to takuránde)** …と企んで in collusion/cahoots with …

taku̱sán (no) *adj* たくさん[沢山] (の) lots (*of*), much/many, a lot (*of*)

táku̱shii *n* タクシー taxi: **takushii (no) untenshu** タクシー(の)運転手 taxi driver: **takushii noriba** タクシー乗り場 taxi stand: **takushii-dai** タクシー代 taxi fare (= **takusii-unchin** タクシー運賃, **takusii-ryōkin** タクシー料金)

takuwae *n* 蓄え savings, a reserve, a stock (= **chochiku** 貯蓄)

takuwáe *v* 蓄え → **takuwaemásu** 蓄えます [INFINITIVE]

takuwaemásu, takuwaéru *v* 蓄えます, 蓄える saves up, hoards

takúwan *n* たくわん, takuan たくあん yellow pickles made from sliced daikon

tamá *n* **1.** 玉 **1.** ball: **keito no tamá** 毛糸の玉 ball of wool: **pachinko no tamá** パチンコの玉 pachinko ball **2.** round thing: **tamá no ase** 玉の汗 beads of sweat **3.** testicle(s) (= **kōgan** 睾丸, **kintama** 金玉) **4.** precious and/or lovely thing: **tamá no yō na akanbō/aka-chan** 玉のような赤ん坊/赤ちゃん sweetest baby

tamá *n* 玉・珠 jewel; bead; drop: **ryū no tamá** 竜[龍]の玉 dragon ball (= **ryū-gyoku** 龍玉) tamá no koshi ni noru [IDIOM] 玉の輿に乗る marries a rich man, becomes a Cinderella

tamá *n* 球 **1.** globe (= **chikyū** 地球) **2.** (*light*) bulb (= **denkyū** 電球)

tamá *n* 弾 bullet (= **dangan** 弾丸): **pisutoru no tamá** ピストルの弾 pistol bullet

tamágo *n* 卵・玉子・タマゴ egg: **tamágo no kara** 卵の殻 eggshell: **tamago-yaki** 卵[玉子]焼き rolled egg

tama-négi *n* タマネギ・玉葱 onion (*round bulb*)

tama (no/ni) *adj, adv* たま (の/に) occasional(ly), infrequent(ly), now and then, at times, once in a while

tamaranai *v* 溜らない = **tamarimásén** 溜りません (does/will not accumulate)

amaranai *v* 貯まらない = **tamarimásén** 貯まりません (does/will not save)

amaranai *v* 堪らない = **tamarimásén** 堪りません (is intolerable, insufferable, unbearable)

tamari *n* 溜まり・たまり = **tamari-ba** たまり場 (a gathering place (*hangout, haunt*))

tamari *v* 貯まり → **tamarimásu** 溜まります [INFINITIVE]

tamari *v* 貯まり → **tamarimásu** 貯まります [INFINITIVE]

tamari-ba *n* たまり場 a gathering place (*hangout, haunt*)

tamarimásén, tamaranai *v* 溜りません, 溜らない does/will not accumulate

tamarimásén, tamaranai *v* 貯まりません, 貯まらない does/will not save (*money*)

tamarimásén, tamaranai *v* たまりません, たまらない is intolerable, insufferable, unbearable; **(…-te tamanai** …てたまらない does/is) unbearably, insufferably

tamarimásu, tamaru *v* 溜まります, 溜まる it accumulates

tamarimásu, tamaru *v* 貯まります, 貯まる it saves (*money*)

támashii *n* 魂 soul

tamatama たまたま occasionally

tamá-tsuki *n* 玉突き billiards (= **biriyādo** ビリヤード) tamá-tsukí jiko *n* 玉突き事故 pileup

tamatte *v* 溜まって → **tamarimásu** 溜まります

tamatte *v* 貯まって → **tamarimásu** 貯まります

… tanbí (ni) *suffix, adv* [INFORMAL] …たんび(に), **tabí (ni)** 度・たび(に) every time that …

tame *v* 溜め → **tamemásu** 溜めます **1.** [INFINITIVE] **2. tame ro** 溜めろ, **tamé yo** 溜めよ [IMPERATIVE] (amass it!; accumulate it!)

tame *v* 貯め → **tamemásu** 貯めます **1.** [INFINITIVE] **2. tame ro** 貯めろ, **tamé yo** 貯めよ [IMPERATIVE] (save it!)

… tamé *suffix* …為・ため **1.** for the sake (good, benefit) of **2.** for the purpose of **3.** because (*of*), due to

tameiki *n* ため息 sigh

tamemásu, tameru *v* 溜めます, 溜める amasses/accumulates

tamemásu, tameru *v* 貯めます, 貯める saves (*money*)

tameraimásu, tameráu *v* ためらいます, ためらう hesitates

tameshí *n* 試し trial, test, experiment: **tameshí ni** 試しに as a trial/test

tameshí *v* 試し → **tameshimásu** 試します [INFINITIVE]

tameshimásu, tamésu *v* 試します, 試す tries, attempts, experiments with

tamete *v* 溜めて → **tamemásu** 溜めます

tamete *v* 貯めて → **tamemásu** 貯めます

tāminaru *n* ターミナル terminal: **narita-kūkō dai-ichi-tāminaru kita/minami wingu** 成田空港第1ターミナル北/南ウィング Narita Airport Terminal 1 North/South Wing: **narita-kūkō dai-ni-tāminaru kita/minami wingu** 成田空港第2ターミナル北/南ウィング Narita Airport Terminal 2 North/South Wing

ta-minzoku (no) *adj* 多民族(の) multiracial: **ta-minzoku-kokka** 多民族国家 multiracial country

tamóchi *v* 保ち → **tamochimásu** 保ちます [INFINITIVE]

tamochimásu, tamótsu *v* 保ちます, 保つ keeps, preserves, maintains

tamotánai *v* 保たない = **tamochimasén** 保ちません (not keep)

tamotó *n* たもと・袂 sleeve; edge, end

tamótte *v* 保って → **tamochimásu** 保ちます

tamushi *n* 田虫 ringworm; athlete's foot

…´-tan *suffix* …反 bolt (*of cloth*)

tana *n* 棚 shelf, rack (→ **shokkí-dana** 食器棚)

tana-age *n* 棚上げ shelving: **mondai o tana-age shimásu** 問題を棚上げします shelves the issue

tana kara botamochi *n* 棚からぼた餅 windfall (= **tana-bota** 棚ぼた)

tana-oroshi *n* 棚卸し stocktaking

Tanabata *n* 七夕・たなばた the Festival of the Weaver Star (*7 July*)

tandoku *n* 単独 alone (= **tanshin** 単身): **tandoku-kōdō** 単独行動 independent action

táne *n* 種 **1.** seed **2.** source, cause **3.** material **4.** secret, trick to it **5. hanashi no táne** 話の種 subject, topic

tango *n* 単語 word(s), vocabulary

tango *n* タンゴ tango (*music*)

Tángo no sekku *n* 端午の節句 Boys' Festival (*5 May*)

tani, tani-ma *n* 谷, 谷間 valley

tán'i *n* 単位 unit

tanitsu-minzoku *n* 単一民族 single race

tanjō´bi *n* 誕生日 (**o-tanjō´bi** お誕生日) birthday: **(o-)tanjōbi-pātii** (お)誕生日パーティ birthday party

tanjun (na) *adj* 単純(な) simple; simplehearted, simpleminded (*not complicated*): **tanjun-ka** 単純化 simplification: **tanjun-meikai** 単純明快 simple and clear

tánka *n* 短歌 31-syllable poem (*traditional Japanese poem*)

tánka *n* 担架 stretcher, litter: **tánka de hakobaremásu** 担架で運ばれます is carried on a stretcher

tánka *n* 単価 unit cost, unit price

tánka *n* 啖呵 [BOOKISH] caustic words (*during a quarrel*): **tánka o kirimásu** 啖呵を切ります blusters out

tanki *n* 短期 short period

tanki-dáigaku *n* 短期大学 junior college, two-year college

tankō *n* 炭鉱 coal mine

tanmatsu *n* 端末 computer terminal

tanmono *n* 反物 draperies, dry goods

tán naru … *adj* 単なる… only, mere [BOOKISH] = **táda no** ただの: **tán naru uwasa ni sugimasén** 単なる噂にすぎません That's just a rumor.

tán ni *adv* 単に: **tán ni … dake/nomi** 単に…だけ/のみ only, merely (= **táda** ただ)

tannin *n* 担任 (*teacher*) in charge; **… o tannin shimásu** …を担任します takes charge (*is in charge*) of …

tanomí *n* 頼み a request (= **tanomi-goto** 頼みごと, **onegai** お願い): **tanomí no tsuna** 頼みの綱 one's one and only hope, lifesaver: **o-tanomi-shitai**

koto ga arunodesuga… お頼みしたいことがあるのですが… Would you mind doing me a favor?

tanómi *v* 頼み → **tanomimásu** 頼みます [INFINITIVE]

tanomimásu, tanómu *v* 頼みます, **tanómu** 頼む **1.** requests, begs **2.** relies upon, entrusts with **3.** hires, engages (*a professional*)

tanónde *v* 頼んで → **tanomimásu** 頼みます

tanoshíi *adj* 楽しい pleasant, enjoyable

tanoshími *n* 楽しみ (**o-tanoshimi** お楽しみ) a pleasure, an enjoyment; **… (surú no) o tanoshími ni shimásu** …(するの)を楽しみにします **1.** takes pleasure in (doing) **2.** looks forward to …ing

tanoshimimásu, tanoshímu *v* 楽しみます, **tanoshímu** 楽しむ enjoys, takes pleasure in

tanoshínde *v* 楽しんで → **tanoshimimásu** 楽しみます

tanpakú-shitsu *n* 蛋白質・たんぱく質 protein

tanpen-shōsetsu *n* 短編小説 short story (*novel*)

tánpo *n* 担保 mortgage, pledge (= **teitō** 抵当): **butteki-tanpo** 物的担保 collateral on property: **jinteki-tanpo** 人的担保 guarantee: **tanpo-bukken** 担保物件 collateral: **mu-tanpo rōn** 無担保ローン unsecured loan (= **mu-tanpo** 無担保融資)

tánpon *n* タンポン tampon

tánpopo *n* タンポポ・たんぽぽ dandelion

tansan *n* 炭酸 carbonic acid

tansán-sui *n* 炭酸水 soda water

tanseki *n* 胆石 gall stone

tanshi *n* 端子 a terminal (*electronics*)

tanshin *n* 単身 [BOOKISH] alone (= **tandoku** 単独)

tanshin-funin *n* 単身赴任 job transfer away from one's home

tánsho *n* 短所 shortcoming, fault, weak point: **tánsho to chōsho** 短所と長所 weak and strong points

tansu *n* たんす・タンス・箪笥 chest of drawers

tantei *n* 探偵 detective: **tantei-shōsetsu** 探偵小説 detective fiction: **shiritsu-tantei** 私立探偵 private eye

tantō *n* 担当 responsibility, charge: **~ shimásu** 担当します takes charge of

tantō´-sha *n* 担当者 person in charge, responsible person (→ **tannin** 担任)

tantō-chokunyū (na) *adj* 単刀直入(な) point-blank: **tantō-chokunyū na iken** 単刀直入な意見 straightforward opinion: **tantō-chokunyū ni iu to** *adv* 単刀直入に言うと put bluntly

tánuki *n* タヌキ・狸 **1.** raccoondog (*not badger* **anaguma** 穴熊) **2.** sly person

tanuki neiri *n* 狸寝入り [IDIOM] play possum

toranu tanuki no kawa-zanyō *n* 取らぬ狸の皮算用 [IDIOM] Count one's chickens before they are hatched

tánzen *n* 丹前 padded bathrobe (= **dotera** どてら)

taóre *v* 倒れ → **taoremásu** 倒れます [INFINITIVE]

taoremásu, taoréru *v* 倒れます, 倒れる falls down, tumbles, collapses

táoru *n* タオル towel: **basu-taoru** バスタオル bath towel

taóse *v* 倒せ [IMPERATIVE] (knock it down!) → **taoshimásu** 倒します

taóshi *v* 倒し → **taoshimásu** 倒します [INFINITIVE]

taoshimásu, taósu *v* 倒します, 倒す knocks down, overthrows

tapesutorii *n* タペストリー tapestry

tappú-dansu *n* タップダンス tap dance

tappúri *adv* たっぷり fully, more than enough

tára *n* タラ・鱈 cod (*fish*)

…-tára *suffix, conj* …たら if, when

tarafuku *adv* たらふく [INFORMAL] (*eat, drink*) one's fill

tarai *n* たらい tub, basin
tarai-mawashi ni saremásu *n* たらい回しにされ ます is shifted from one section to another

tarako *n* タラコ・鱈子 cod roe

taráppu *n* タラップ gangway

tarashimásu, tarásu *v* 垂らします, 垂らす dangles, drops, spills

tarashimásu, tarásu *v* たらします, たらす = tarashi-komimásu たらし込みます, tarashi-komu たらし込む seduces; wheedles

taré *n* たれ・タレ gravy, (*cooking*) sauce

taremásu, taréru *v* 垂れます, 垂れる hangs down, dangles; drips

tarento *n* タレント a TV personality, (*person of*) talent

tari *v* 足り → **tarimásu** 足ります [INFINITIVE]

…tári (shimásu/desu) …たり (します/です) doing representatively/sometimes/alternately: **tári …-nákáttari** …たり…なかったり doing off and on, sometimes does and sometimes doesn't

tarimásu, tariru *v* 足ります, 足りる is enough/ sufficient, suffices

tarinai *v* 足りない = tarimasén 足りません (is not enough, is insufficient)

tariru *v* 足りる = tarimásu 足ります (is enough/ sufficient, suffices)

tarite *v* 足りて → **tarimásu** 足ります

taru *n* たる・樽 barrel, keg, cask

taru *v* 足る [*dialect, literary*] → **tarimásu** 足りま す (is enough/sufficient, suffices)

tāru *n* タール tar: **kōru-tāru** コール・タール coal tar: **sekiyu-tāru** 石油タール petroleum tar

tarumi *n* 弛み → **tarumimásu** 弛みます [INFINITIVE]

tarumimásu, tarumu *v* 弛みます, 弛む gets slack (*loose*), relaxed

tarunde *v* 弛んで → **tarumimásu** 弛みます

taruto *n* タルト tarte

taryō *n* 多量 large quantity

tasanai *v* 足さない = tashimasén 足しません (not add)

tase *v* 足せ [IMPERATIVE] (add!) → **tashimásu** 足します

taséba *v* 足せば (if one adds) → **tashimásu** 足します

tashi *v* 足し → **tashimásu** 足します [INFINITIVE]

táshika *adv* 確か if I remember rightly, probably

táshika ni *adj* 確かに for sure, surely, undoubtedly; indeed

táshika na *adv* 確かな safe, sure, certain

tashikamemásu, tashikaméru *v* 確かめます, 確かめる makes sure, ascertains

tashimásu, tasu *v* 足します, 足す **1.** adds; **ní ni san o tashimásu** 二に三を足します adds three to two, adds three and two **2. yō o tashimásu** 用を足 します does one's business, relieves oneself, goes to the bathroom

tashite *v* 足して → **tashimásu** 足します

tashi ya/wa shinai *v* 足しや/はしない = tasanai 足さない (not add)

tashō *adj* 多少 **1.** (*large and/or small*) number, quantity, amount **2. tashō (no)** 多少(の) more or less; somewhat; some

tasogare *n* たそがれ・黄昏 **1.** twilight (= **yūgure** 夕暮れ)

tassha (na) *adj* 達者(な) healthy; skillful, expert, good at

tas-shimásu, tas-suru *v* 達します, 達する accomplishes; reaches

tas-shinai *v* 達しない = tas-shimasén 達しません (not accomplish/reach)

tasū´ *n* 多数 large number; majority

tasukarimásu, tasukáru *v* 助かります, 助かる is saved; is relieved

tasuké *v* 助け → **tasukemásu** 助けます **1.** [INFINITIVE] **2. tasuké ro** 助けろ, **tasuké yo** 助けよ [IMPERATIVE] (help!)

tasukemásu, tasukéru *v* 助けます, 助ける **1.** helps **2.** saves

tasukénai *v* 助けない → tasukemasén 助け ません

tasukéte *v* 助けて → **tasukemásu** 助けます

tasuki *n* タスキ・襷 a sleeve cord

tatáite *v* 叩いて → **tatakimásu** 叩きます

tatakaemásu, tatakaéru *v* 戦えます, 戦える can fight

tatakaenai *v* 戦えない = tatakaemasén 戦えませ ん (cannot fight)

tatakaete *v* 戦えて → **tatakaemásu** 戦えます

tatakaimásu, tatakau *v* 戦います, 戦う fights; makes war/game: **teki to tatakaimásu** 敵と戦いま す battles an enemy

tatakaimásu, tatakau *v* 闘います, 闘う struggle, fights (*with, against*): **byōki to tatakaimásu** 病気 と闘います fights the disease

tatakánai *v* 叩かない = tatakimasén 叩きません (not strike)

tatákátte *v* 戦って → **tatakaimásu** 戦います

tatákátte *v* 闘って → **tatakaimásu** 闘います

tatakau *v* 戦う = tatakaimásu 戦います (fights; makes war/game)

tatakau *v* 闘う = tatakaimásu 闘います (fights, struggle)

tatakawanai *v* 戦わない = tatakaimasén 戦いま せん (not fight/make war/game)

tatakemásu, tatakéru *v* 叩けます, 叩ける

199

tatakénai ν 叩けない = **takemasén** 叩けません (cannot strike)

tatákete ν 叩けて → **takemásu** 叩けます

tataki *n* **1.** 叩き pounding; bashing; mincing; **Nihon-tátaki** 日本叩き Japan-bashing **2.** たたき concrete/cement floor

takimásu, tatáku ν 叩きます, 叩く strikes, hits, knocks; pounds (*fish/meat to tenderize or mince it*), minces; **té o takimásu** 手を叩きます claps

tatami 1. *n* 畳 floor mat(ting), matted floor **2.** ν 畳み → **tatamimásu** 畳みます [INFINITIVEd]

tatamimásu, tatamu ν 畳みます, 畳む folds up

tatánai ν 立たない = **tachimasén** 立ちません (not stand)

tatanda ν 畳んだ = **tatamimáshita** 畳みました (folded up)

tatande ν 畳んで → **tatamimásu** 畳みます

tátchi *n* タッチ touch; **tátchi no sa de** タッチの差で by the turn of a hair

tate *n* 盾・楯 shield

tate ni toru *n* 盾[楯]に取る [IDIOM] use something as an excuse

tate no hanmen *n* 盾[楯]の半面 [IDIOM] one side of the issue (*not to literally mean, "one side of the shield"*)

tate no ryōmen o miyo *n* 盾[楯]の両面を見よ [IDIOM] Look on both sides of the issue. (*not to literally mean, "Look on both sides of the shield."*)

tate *n* 縦 length, height, longitudinal

tate-gaki *n* 縦書き vertical writing

tate-ito *n* 縦糸 warp (*vertical threads*)

táte no 縦の *adj* vertical

táte ni 縦に *adv* vertically, lengthwise

táte ν 建て → **takemásu** 建てます **1.** [INFINITIVE] **2. taté ro** 建てろ, **táte yo** 建てよ [IMPERATIVE] (build it!)

táte ν 立て **1.** → **takemásu** 立てます [INFINITIVE] **2.** [IMPERATIVE] 立て (stand up!) → **tachimásu** 立ちます

...-tate (no) *adj* ...たて(の) fresh from ...

táteba ν 立てば = [INFORMAL] **tácha** 立ちゃ (if one stands) → **tachimásu** 立ちます

taté-fuda *n* 立(て)札 signboard

tatekae *n* 立(て)替え paying for someone: **takaemásu** 立(て)替えます pays for someone tatekae-kin *n* 立(て)替え金 advance money

tatekae *n* 建(て)替え reconstruction, rebuilding: **tatekae imásu** 建(て)替えます rebuilds

tatémae *n* 建て前 principle, policy: **... o tatémae to shimásu** ...を建て前とします makes ... one's policy

tate-mashi *n* 建て増し house addition/extension, annex

tatemásu, tatéru ν 建てます, 建てる erects, builds, raises; sets up, establishes

tatemásu, tatéru ν 立てます, 立てる can stand

taté-móno *n* 建物 building

taténai ν 建てない = **tatemasén** 建てません (not build)

tateraremásu, tateraréru ν 建てられます, 建てられる can build it

tateraréreba ν 建てられれば (if one can build) → **tateraremásu** 建てられます

tatéreba ν 建てれば (if one builds) → **tatemásu** 建てます

tatéreba ν 立てれば = [INFORMAL] **tatérya** 立てりゃ (if one can stand) → **tatemásu** 立てます

taté-tsubo *n* 建て坪 floor space

táte ya/wa shimasén (shinai) ν 建てや/はしません(しない), [INFORMAL] **tatérya shimasén** 建てりゃしません = **tatemasén** 建てません won't build

táte ya/wa shimasén (shinai) ν 立てや/はしません(しない), [INFORMAL] **tatérya shimasén** 立てりゃしません = **tatemasén** 立てません cannot stand

taté yo ν 建てよ = **taté ro** 建てろ [IMPERATIVE] (build it!)

tateyō´ ν 建てよう = **tatemashō´** 建てましょう (let's build it!)

tatō´ ν 立とう = **tachimashō´** 立ちましょう (let's stand!)

tatoé *conj* たとえ even if

tatóe 例え・たとえ **1.** *n* an example, an instance; a simile, an analogy **2.** → **tatoemásu** 例えます・喩えます [INFINITIVE]

tatóeba *adv* 例えば・たとえば for example, for instance

tatoemásu, tatoéru ν 例えます・喩えます, 例える・喩える gives an example, compares (*draws a simile to*)

tátsu ν 立つ → **tachimásu** 立ちます

tátsu ν 発つ → **tachimásu** 発ちます

tátsu ν 経つ → **tachimásu** 経ちます

tátsu ν 断つ → **tachimásu** 断ちます

tatsu *n* 竜・龍 dragon (= **doragon** ドラゴン)

Tatsu-doshi *n* 辰年 year of the Dragon

tatsu no otoshigo *n* タツノオトシゴ・竜の落とし子 sea horse (= **umi-uma, kaiba** 海馬)

tatta *adj* たった just, merely, only

tátta ν 立った = **tachimáshita** 立ちました; etc. (stood up; ...)

tatta-íma *n, adv* たった今 just now; in (*just*) a minute

tátte ν 立って → **tachimásu** 立ちます: **tátte imásu** 立っています is standing

tawā *n* タワー tower, pagoda (= **tō** 塔); **Tōkyō-tawā** 東京タワー Tokyo Tower

tawará *n* たわら・俵 straw bag; bale

tawashi *n* たわし scrub(bing) brush; swab

tayasúku *adv* たやすく easily

tayoránai ν 頼らない = **tayorimasén** 頼りません (not rely on)

táyori 頼り **1.** *n* reliance: **táyori ni shite(i)másu** 頼りにして(い)ます I'm counting on you.: **tayori nai** 頼りない undependable, unreliable **2.** ν →

tayorimás<u>u</u> 頼ります [INFINITIVE]

táyori *n* 便り communication, correspondence, a letter, word (*from someone*), news (= **shōsoku** 消息); **kaze no táyori** 風の便り a little bird, rumor: **kaze no táyori ni kikimashita** 風の便りに聞きました I heard through the grapevine.

tayorimás<u>u</u>, tayóru *v* 頼ります, 頼る relies on, depends on

tayō-sei *n* 多様性 diversity: **seibutsu-tayōsei no hozen** 生物多様性の保全 biodiversity conservatory

tayótte *v* 頼って → **tayorimás<u>u</u>** 頼ります

tazuna *n* 手綱 reins: **tazuna o shimemás<u>u</u>** 手綱を締めます tightens the reins

tazúne *v* 尋ね → **tazunemás<u>u</u>** 尋ねます
1. [INFINITIVE] **2.** [IMPERATIVE] **tazuné ro** 尋ねろ, **tazúne yo** 尋ねよ ask!

tazúne *v* 訪ね → **tazunemás<u>u</u>** 訪ねます
1. [INFINITIVE] **2.** [IMPERATIVE] **tazuné ro** 訪ねろ, **tazúne yo** 訪ねよ visit!

tazunemás<u>u</u>, tazunéru *v* **1.** 尋ねます, 尋ねる asks (*a question*) **2.** 尋ねます, 尋ねる looks for

tazunemás<u>u</u>, tazunéru *v* 訪ねます, 訪ねる visits

té *n* 手 **1.** hand, arm **2.** trick, move **3.** kind **4.** person **5.** help: **té ni** 手に; **sore ga té ni hairimás<u>u</u>** それが手に入ります = **sore o té ni iremás<u>u</u>** それを手に入れます obtains, gets it

te-árai *n* 手洗い **1.** hand wash **2.** o-teárai お手洗い washroom, rest room, toilet (= **keshō-shitsu** 化粧室, **toire** トイレ)

te-áte *n* 手当て treatment; reparation, provisione

te-áte *n* 手当 (**o-téate** お手当) allowance

te-búkuro *n* 手袋 gloves

te-dori *n* 手取り take-home pay

te-f<u>u</u>kí *n* 手拭き (**o-téfuki** お手拭き) hand towel (= **te-nugui** 手拭い)

te-gákari *n* 手掛かり a hold, a place to hold on; a clue (= **itoguchi** 糸口)

te-gami *n* 手紙 (**o-tégami** お手紙) letter (= **shokan** 書簡 [BOOKISH])

te-gata *n* 手形 a note, a bill: **yakusoku-tegata** 約束手形 promissory note: **kawase-tegata** 為替手形 draft bill of exchange

te-gatái *adj* 手堅い safe; reliable; steady

te-gókoro *n* 手心 discretion

te-gótae *n* 手応え response, effect: **tegótae ga aru** 手応えがある response on my fishing rod

té-guchi *n* 手口 way (*of doing bad things*), trick

te-gúruma *n* 手車 hand cart

te-hái *n* 手配 (*setting up*) a search for a criminal, a dragnet: ~ **shimás<u>u</u>** 手配します sets up a dragnet; **tehai-sháshin** 手配写真 photograph of a wanted criminal

té-hazu *n* 手はず・手筈 arrangements

te-hón *n* 手本 (**o-tehon** お手本) model, pattern (= **mihon** 見本)

té-kubi *n* 手首 wrist

té-mane *n* 手まね・手真似 gesture with hand(s) (= **(te no) jesuchā** (手の)ジェスチャー)

te-máneki *n* 手招き beckoning

té-mari *n* 手まり・手毬 (*decorated small*) handball

te-nímotsu *n* 手荷物 hand luggage

té-nó-hira *n* 手のひら・掌 palm (*of hand*)

te-nugui *n* 手拭い hand towel (= **te-fuki** 手拭き (**o-tefuki** お手拭き))

te-ono *n* 手斧 hatchet, hand axe

te-ori (no) *adj* 手織り(の) handweaving

te-sage *n* 手提げ・手さげ handbag

te-sei (no) *adj* 手製(の) homemade, handcrafted (= **te-zukuri (no)** 手作り(の), **hōmu meido (no)** ホームメイド(の), **hando meido (no)** ハンドメイド(の))

te-záiku *n* 手細工 handiwork

te-zawari *n* 手ざわり texture, touch, hand feeling

te-zúkuri (no) *adj* 手作り(の) homemade, made by hand (= **hōmu meido (no)** ホームメイド(の), **hando meido (no)** ハンドメイド(の), **te-sei (no)** 手製(の))

...-te *suffix* ...て (*does/did*) and, and then, and so; doing; [+ AUXILIARY] (→ **sh<u>i</u>te** して)

tēburu *n* テーブル table; **tēburú-kake** テーブル掛け tablecloth (= **tēburu kurosu** テーブルクロス); **dainingu tēburu** ダイニングテーブル dining table (= **shoku-taku** 食卓)

tei-... *prefix* 定... fixed, appointed, set

tei-ka *n* 定価 the set price, fixed price

téiki (no) *adj* 定期(の) **1.** fixed, regular, periodic, scheduled **2.** → **tei-kí-ken** 定期券

tei-kí-ken *n* 定期券 pass (*commuter ticket*), season ticket: **teiki-yokin** 定期預金 time deposit

tei-shoku *n* 定食 a set meal, table d'hôte; a complete meal

tei-... *prefix* 低... low

tei-ka *n* 低下 fall, drop, decline, descent: ~ **shimás<u>u</u>** 低下します falls, drops, declines, descends

tei-kétsúatsu *n* 低血圧 low blood pressure

tei-kíatsu *n* 低気圧 low (*barometric*) pressure

tei-soku *n* 低速 low speed: **teisoku-gia** 低速ギア, **teisoku-giya** 低速ギヤ low gear

tei-... *prefix* 停... stop

tei-den *n* 停電 power failure/outage

tei-ryū *n* 停留 stop, stopping: **tei-ryū-jo** 停留所 stop (*of bus, streetcar, etc.*)

tei-sha *n* 停車 stopping (*of a vehicle*): ~ **shimás<u>u</u>** 停車します stops (*a vehicle*)

tei-shi *n* 停止 suspension, interruption: ~ **shimás<u>u</u>** 停止します suspends; **ichiji-teishi** 一時停止 pause, suspension

...-tei *suffix* ...てい → **...-te imás<u>u</u>** ...ています [INFINITIVE]

teian *n* 提案 proposal, suggestion: ~ **shimás<u>u</u>** 提案します proposes

teibō *n* 堤防 dike, embankment (= **tsutsumi** 堤)

téido *n* 程度 degree, extent, level

teikei *n* 提携 [BOOKISH] cooperation, affiliation: ~ **shimás<u>u</u>** 提携します cooperates, affiliates

teikō *n* 抵抗 resistance: ~ **shimás<u>u</u>** 抵抗します resists

téikoku *n* 帝国 empire
téikoku (no) *adj* 帝国(の) imperial
teikoku-shúgi *n* 帝国主義 imperialism
téinei (na) *adj* ていねい[丁寧](な) (**go-téinei (na)** ごていねい[丁寧](な)) polite; careful
te-iré *n* 手入れ repair; upkeep, care
teisai *n* 体裁 appearance, get-up, form, format, layout
teisetsu (na) *adj* 貞節(な) chaste, principled: **teisetsu na tsuma** 貞節な妻 faithful wife
téishu *n* 亭主 **1.** host (*at Japanese tea ceremony*) **2.** landlord **3.** (*my*) husband
teitō *n* 抵当 mortgage, pledge (= **tanpo** 担保)
téjina *n* 手品 jugglery, magic (*tricks*)
tejiná-shi *n* 手品師 juggler, magician
tejun *n* 手順 order, procedure, program (= **dandori** 段取り)
...-té kara *suffix* ...てから after (do)ing, after one does/did, does/did and then (*next*)
teki *n* 敵 **1.** enemy, foe **2.** opponent; **kō-teki-shu** 好敵手 rival (= **raibaru** ライバル)
teki ni shio o okuru *n* 敵に塩を送る [IDIOM] help one's enemy when they are in trouble
...-teki *suffix* ...滴 a drop
...-teki *suffix, adj* 的(な) ...ic, ...ical, ...al, ...ly: **chi-teki (na)** 知的(な) intellectual: **shi-teki (na)** 私的(な) private, personal (= **kojin-teki (na)** 個人的(な)): **shi-teki (na)** 詩的(な) poetic: **-teki ni** ...的に ...ically, ...ally: **kanjō-teki ni narimásu** 感情的になります gets emotional: **kiseki-teki ni tasukarimashita** 奇跡的に助かりました miraculously survived
tékido *n* 適度 [BOOKISH] moderation: **tékido na/no** 適度な/の reasonable, moderate: **tékido na undō** 適度な運動 moderate exercise
tékigi *adv* 適宜 [BOOKISH] suitably, fitly, properly (= **tekitō (ni)** 適当(に)): **tékigi (no)** 適宜の suitable, fit, proper
tekikaku (na) *adj* 適格(な) qualified, eligible: **tekikaku-sha** 適格者 qualified person (= **teki-nin** 適任)
tekikaku (na/ni) *adj, adv* 的確・適確(な/に) precise(ly), accurate(ly), exact(ly): **tekikaku na handan** 的確[適確]な判断 accurate judgement
teki-nin *n* 適任 qualified person (= **tekikaku-sha** 適格者)
teki-sánai *v* 適さない = **tekishimasén** 適しません (is not suitable)
tekisetsu (na) *adj* 適切(な) appropriate, to the point
teki-shimásu, teki-su *v* 適します, 適す is suitable, qualified
teki-shite *v* 適して → **teki-shimásu** 適します
tékisuto *n* テキスト **1.** textbook (= **kyōka-sho** 教科書) **2.** original text
tekitō (na) *adj* 適当(な) **1.** suitable, proper **2.** irresponsible, haphazard, random, half-hearted: **tekitō na henji** 適当な返事 vague answer
tekitō (ni) *adv* 適当(に) **1.** suitably, properly (= **tekigi** 適宜) **2.** irresponsibly, haphazardly,

randomly, half-heartedly (= **iikagen (ni)** いい加減(に)): **tekitō ni erabimásu** 適当に選びます chooses randomly: **tekitō ni kikinagashimásu** 適当に聞き流します pretends to listen: **tekitō ni wakete-kudasai** 適当に分けて下さい Please distribute as you see fit.
tekk(-...) *n, prefix* 鉄(...) iron, steel
tek-ka(-maki) *n* 鉄火(巻き) seaweed-rolled sushi with tuna inside
tek-ki *n* 鉄器, **tekkí-rui** 鉄器類 hardware (items)
tek-kyō *n* 鉄橋 iron bridge
teko *n* てこ・挺・挺子 lever
teko demo ugokanai てこでも動かない [IDIOM] will not move at all
...-te kudasái *interj* ...て下さい please (*do*)
temá *n* 手間(**o-téma** お手間) time and effort (*taken up*); one's trouble (= **tesū** 手数(**o-tesū** お手数))
tē´ma *n* テーマ theme, topic (= **shudai** 主題): **tēma-songu** テーマソング theme song (= **shudai-ka** 主題歌)
temae *n* **1.** 手前・てまえ this side (of ...); I/me **2.** 手前(**o-témae** お手前) prowess, skill, ability
temae *n* 点前(**o-témae** お点前) tea ceremony procedures
...-temásu *suffix, v* ...てます = **...-te imásu** ...ています
temáwari *n* 手回り personal effects; luggage (= **temawarí-hin** 手回り品)
...-témo *suffix* ...ても even doing/being, even if (*one does/is*); **shitémo íi** してもいい it is OK to do, one may do
ten *n* 点 point, dot, spot; score (*points*)
ten-sū´ *n* 点数 score, points
tén *n* 天 **1.** sky **2.** heaven (= **ten-goku** 天国)
tén-goku *n* 天国 paradise, heaven (= **ten** 天)
ten-jō *n* 天井 ceiling
tén-ki *n* 天気(**o-ténki** お天気) **1.** weather; **ten-ki-yóhō** 天気予報 weather forcecast **2.** fair weather
ten-kō *n* 天候 weather
ten-mon (no) *n* 天文(の) astronomical: **ten-mon-dai** 天文台 (*astronomical*) observatory: **ten-mon-gaku** 天文学 astronomy
tén-shi *n* 天使 angel
tén *n* テン ten; **besutó-tén** ベストテン the best ten
ten-.../...-ten *prefix, suffix* 天.../...天 → **ten-pura** 天ぷら・天麩羅
ten-don *n* 天丼 a bowl of rice with tenpura shrimp on top
ten-pura *n* テンプラ・天ぷら・天麩羅 tenpura, food fried in batter, especially shrimp
ten-.../...-ten *prefix, suffix* 店.../...店 shop
ten'in *n* 店員 shop clerk, salesclerk, salesperson
ten-po *n* 店舗 [BOOKISH] store, shop (= **mise** 店(**o-mise** お店))
ten-shu *n* 店主 shopkeeper
ten-tō *n* 店頭 store front
tenbō *n* 展望 **1.** looking over, a view **2.** prospecting, prospects
tenbō-dai *n* 展望台 (*sightseeing*) observatory

tengu *n* テング・天狗 **1.** a long-nosed goblin **2.** conceited person

ténisu *n* テニス tennis: **tenisu-kōto** テニスコート tennis court: **tenisu-shūzu** テニスシューズ tennis shoes

tenjí *n* 展示 exhibit: ~ **shimásu** 展示します exhibits

tenjí-kai *n* 展示会 exhibition

ten-jimásu, ten-jiru *v* 転じます、転じる [BOOKISH] changes, shifts; gets transferred

ten-kin *n* 転勤 job transfer (= **tennin** 転任): ~ **shimásu** 転勤します gets transferred (*to another location*)

ten-kō *n* 転校 school transfer: ~ **shimásu** 転校します transfers to another school

ten-nin *n* 転任 job transfer (= **tenkin** 転勤): ~ **shimásu** 転任します gets transferred

tennen *n* 天然 nature (= **shizen** 自然)

tennen-boke *n* 天然ボケ goofy, dopey by nature [IN POSITIVE SENSE]

tennen-gasu *n* 天然ガス natural gas

tennen (no) *adj* 天然(の) natural

tennen-tō *n* 天然痘 smallpox

Tennō´ *n* 天皇 the Emperor: **Tennō héika** 天皇陛下 His Majesty the Emperor

Tennō-tanjō´bi *n* 天皇誕生日 the Emperor's Birthday (*national holiday in Japan*)

tenōru *n* テノール tenor

tenōru-kashu *n* テノール歌手 a tenor (*singer*)

ténpi *n* 天火 oven (= **ōbun** オーブン)

tenpo *n* テンポ tempo

tenrán-kai *n* 展覧会 exhibition (= **tenji-kai** 展示会)

tensai *n* 天才 genius

ténsei *n* 天性 disposition, temperament

ténto *n* テント tent

tepp-... *prefix* 鉄... iron, steel

tep-pan *n* 鉄板 iron plate: **teppan-yaki** 鉄板焼き sliced meat, etc. grilled at table

tep-pō *n* 鉄砲 gun, rifle: **mizu-deppō** 水鉄砲 squirt gun, water pistol

teppén *n* てっぺん top, highest part [INFORMAL] (= **chōjō** 頂上)

tē´pu *n* テープ tape; **sero(han)-tēpu** セロ(ハン)テープ scotch tape; **tēpu-rekō´dā** テープレコーダー tape recorder

terá *n* 寺 (**o-tera** お寺) Buddhist temple (= **jiin** 寺院)

teránai *v* 照らない = **terimasén** 照りません (not shine)

terashi-awasémásu, terashi-awaséru *v* 照らし合わせます、照らし合わせる collates

terashimásu, terásu *v* 照らします、照らす illuminates, lights it up, shines on; compares, collates, checks; **... ni teráshite** …に照らして in the light of…, in view of…

térasu *n* テラス terrace, balcony

tére *v* 照れ → **teremásu** 照れます [INFINITIVE]

...-teréba …てれば = **...-te iréba** …ていれば: **sō**

shite(i)réba yokatta そうして(い)ればよかった if one does so

téreba *v* 照れば (if it shines) → **terimásu** 照ります

térebi *n* テレビ television

terebi-bangumi *n* テレビ番組 TV show

terebi-denwa *n* テレビ電話 videophone

terebi-gēmu *n* テレビゲーム video game

terebi-kaigi *n* テレビ会議 teleconference

terehonkādo *n* テレホンカード telephone card

teremásu, teréru *v* 照れます、照れる feels embarrassed, awkward, flustered

terénai *v* 照れない = **teremasén** 照れません (not feel embarrassed)

terepashii *n* テレパシー telepathy

teréreba *v* 照れれば (if one feels embarrassed) → **teremásu** 照れます

térete *v* 照れて → **teremásu** 照れます

téri *v* 照り → **terimásu** 照ります [INFINITIVE]

terimásu, téru *v* 照ります、照る it shines

teriyaki *n* 照り焼き (*fish, chicken, etc.*) broiled with soy sauce and sweeteners

téri ya/wa shinai *v* 照りや/はしない = **teránai** 照らない (not shine)

téro (rīsuto) *n* テロ(リスト) terrorism, terrorist

...-teru *suffix, v* …てる [INFORMAL] = **...-te iru** …ている = **...-te imásu** …ています

...-terya *suffix, v* [INFORMAL] …てりゃ [INFORMAL] = **...-te irya** …ていりゃ = **...-te iréba** …ていれば

tesū´ *n* 手数 (**o-tesū** お手数) [BOOKISH] trouble (taken up), time and effort (= **tema** 手間 (**o-tema** お手間)): **o-tesū okakeshite mōshiwake gozaimasen** お手数おかけして申し訳ございません [HUMBLE] I apologize for bothering you.: **o-tesū okakeshite sumimasen** お手数おかけしてすみません I'm sorry for bothering you.

tesú´-ryō *n* 手数料 handling/service charge

tésuto *n* テスト test [INFORMAL] (= **shiken** 試験)

...-téta *suffix, v* …てた = **...-te ita** …ていた = **-te imáshita** …ていました (was doing)

...-téte *suffix, v* …てて = **...-te ite** …ていて (was doing)

tetsu *n* 鉄 iron, steel

tetsu-bō *n* 鉄棒 **1.** horizontal bar **2.** iron bar

tetsu-dō *n* 鉄道 railroad, railway

tetsudáe *v* 手伝え [IMPERATIVE] (you should help!) → **tetsudaimásu** 手伝います

tetsudái *n* 手伝い **1. o-tétsudai** お手伝い assistance, help **2.** → **tetsudaimásu** 手伝います [INFINITIVE]

tetsudaimásu, tetsudáu *v* 手伝います、 tetsudáu 手伝う helps

tetsudaō´ *v* 手伝おう = **tetsudaimashō´** 手伝いましょう (let's help!)

tetsudátte *v* 手伝って → **tetsudaimásu** 手伝います

tetsúgaku *n* 哲学 philosophy; **tetsugákú-sha** 哲学者 philosopher

tetsuya *n* 徹夜 staying up all night: ~ **shimásu** 徹夜します stays up all night

te-tsúzuki *n* 手続き formalities, procedure (= **tejun** 手順)

tétte *v* 照って → **terimásu** 照ります

tettei-teki (na/ni) *adj, adv* 徹底的(な/に) thorough(ly)

…-té wa *suffix, v* …ては doing/being, if one does/ be [+ NEGATIVE verb] : **-té wa ikemasén** …ては いけません mustn't

ti… → **chi…**

tii-kappu *n* ティーカップ Western-style tea cup

tii-supūn *n* ティースプーン Western-style teaspoon (= **ko-saji** 小匙・小さじ)

tisshu(-pē´pā) *n* ティッシュ(ペーパー) tissue(s) (= **chiri-kami**, **chiri-gami**, **chiri-shi** ちり紙)

to *n* 戸 door

to-dana *n* 戸棚 cupboard, enclosed shelves

to *n* 都 **1.** capital (= **shu-to** 首都) **2.** Tokyo (= **Tōkyō-to** 東京都)

to-chi-ji *n* 都知事 Governor of Tokyo

to-chō *n* 都庁 the Tokyo Metropolitan Government

to-den *n* 都電 Toei (*Tokyo metropolitan*) streetcar

to-ei *n* 都営 Toei, metropolitan (*run by Tokyo*), metro; **Toei-sen** 都営線 (subway) Toei Line; **Toei-basu** 都営バス Toei Bus

to-kai *n* 都会 city, town; **tokái-jin** 都会人 city dweller, urbanite

to-min *n* 都民 Tokyoite (= **Tōkyō-tomin** 東京都 民)

tó-nai *n, adv* 都内 within the metropolis (of Tokyo)

tó-shi *n* 都市 city; **toshi (no)** 都市(の) urban; **toshi-gasu** 都市ガス city gas; **toshi-ginkō** 都市銀 行 city bank

… to *prep* …と with [CONCATENATES A NOUN]: **… to issho ni** …と一緒に … with (someone)

… to … *conj* …と and [CONCATENATES A NOUN]: **anata to watashi** あなたと私 you and I

… to *suffix* …と (*said/thought/seemed*) that …; "…" (*quote-*) unquote: **kare wa … to itta** 彼は… と言った he said that …

… to iu *suffix* …という which says; which is (*called*), called; which is (*in effect*)

to iú no wa … *suffix* というのは… What that means (What that amounts to) is that …

… to *suffix* …と **1. (su)-ru to** (す)ると when(ever), if; …and thereupon, …whereupon: **moshikasuru to** もしかすると perhaps, possibly **2. (shi)-nai to** (し)ないと unless: **nantoka shi-nai to** なんとかしないと have to do something

tō´ *n* 十 ten (= **jū** 十)

tō´ *n* 藤 rattan, cane

tō´ *n* 塔 tower, pagoda (= **tawā** タワー); **Efferu-tō** エッフェル塔 Eiffel Tower

tō´-… *prefix* 東… east, eastern

tō´-bu *n* 東部 the east, the eastern part

tō-hō *n* 東方 the east

tō-nan *n* 東南 southeast: **tōnan-ajia** 東南アジア Southeast Asia

Tō´-yō *n* 東洋 the East, the Orient

tō-zai *n* 東西 east and west, the East and the West

…´-tō *suffix* …頭 (*counts large animals*) head [**go-tō** 五頭 *unaccented* (five heads)]

…-tō *suffix* …等 class

Tō´a *n* 東亜 → **Higashi-Ájia** 東アジア

tobaku *n* 賭博 [BOOKISH] gambling (= **ganburu** ギャンブル, **bakuchi** 博打)

tō´ban *n* 当番 (**o-tō´ban** お当番) person on duty

tobanai *v* 跳ばない = **tobimasén** 跳びません (not jump)

tobanai *v* 飛ばない = **tobimasén** 飛びません (not fly)

tobashimásu, tobasu *v* 飛ばします, 飛ばす lets fly; skips, omits; hurries

tobe *v* 跳べ **1.** → **tobemásu** 跳べま す [INFINITIVE] **2.** [IMPERATIVE] (jump!) → **tobimásu** 跳びます

tobe *v* 飛べ **1.** → **tobemásu** 飛べます [INFINITIVE] **2.** [IMPERATIVE] (fly!) → **tobimásu** 飛びます

tobéba *v* 跳べば = [INFORMAL] **tobya** 跳びゃ (if one jumps) → **tobimásu** 跳びます

tobéba *v* 飛べば = [INFORMAL] **tobya** 飛びゃ (if one flies) → **tobimásu** 飛びます

tobemásu, toberu *v* 跳べます, 跳べる can jump

tobemásu, toberu *v* 飛べます, 飛べる can fly

tobete *v* 跳べて → **tobemásu** 跳べます

tobete *v* 飛べて → **tobemásu** 飛べます

tobi *v* 跳び → **tobimásu** 跳びます [INFINITIVE]

tobi *v* 飛び → **tobimásu** 飛びます [INFINITIVE]

tobi-dashimásu, tobi-dásu *v* 跳び出します・跳 び出す jumps out

tobi-dashimásu, tobi-dásu *v* 飛び出します, 飛び出す runs/bursts out; it sticks out, protrudes; **uchi o tobi-dashimásu** 家を飛び出します runs away (*from home*) (= **iede shimásu** 家出します)

tobimásu, tobu *v* 跳びます, 跳ぶ jumps

tobimásu, tobu *v* 飛びます, 飛ぶ flies

tobira *n* 扉 **1.** a door wing, a door of a gate **2.** title page

tobí ya/wa shinai *v* 跳びや/はしない = **tobanai** 跳ばない (not jump)

tobí ya/wa shinai *v* 飛びや/はしない = **tobanai** 飛ばない (not fly)

toboshíi *adj* 乏しい scarce, meager, scanty

tobu *v* 跳ぶ = **tobimásu** 跳びます (jumps)

tobu *v* 飛ぶ = **tobimásu** 飛びます (flies)

tōbun *n* 糖分 [BOOKISH] sugar content

tōbun *n* 等分 dividing equally: **~ shimásu** 等分し ます divides equally

tōbun *n* 当分 for the time being

tōchaku *n* 到着 arrival: **~ shimásu** 到着します arrives

tochi *n* 土地 ground, earth, soil; a piece of land

tochū (de/no) *adv, adj* 途中(で/の) on the way; **tochū-gesha** 途中下車 stopover (*train*)

tōdai *n* 燈台 lighthouse

Tō-dai *n* 東大 Tokyo University (= **Tōkyō-Dáigaku** 東京大学)

todóite *v* 届いて → **todokimásu** 届きます

todoké *n* 届け (**o-todoke** お届け) notification, notice, report

todóke *v* 届け → **todokemásu** 届けます
1. [INFINITIVE] **2. todóke ro** 届けろ, **todóke yo** 届けよ [IMPERATIVE] (deliver! notify!)

todokemásu, todokéru *v* 届けます, 届ける
1. delivers **2.** reports it (*to*), notifies

todokeraremásu, todokeraréru *v* 届けられます, 届けられる can deliver

todoke-saki *n* 届け先 address (for delivery)

todókete *v* 届けて → **todokemásu** 届けます

todóki *v* 届き → **todokimásu** 届きます [INFINITIVE]

todokimásu, todóku *v* 届きます, 届く reaches; arrives; gets delivered

todomári *v* とどまり → **todomarimásu** とどまります [INFINITIVE]

todomarimásu, todomáru *v* とどまります, とどまる it stops; it remains

todomátte *v* とどまって → **todomarimásu** とどまります

todóme *v* とどめ → **todomemásu** とどめます
1. [INFINITIVE] **2. todomé ro** とどめろ, **todomé yo** とどめよ [IMPERATIVE] (stop it!)

todomemásu, todómeru *v* とどめます, とどめる stops it

todómete *v* とどめて → **todomemásu** とどめます

todoróite *v* 轟いて → **todorokimásu** 轟きます

todoróki *v* 轟き → **todorokimásu** 轟きます [INFINITIVE]

todorokimásu, todoróku *v* 轟きます, 轟く [BOOKISH] roars, rumbles

tóeba *v* 問えば (if one inquires) → **toimásu** 問います

tōfú *n* 豆腐 (**o-tōfu** お豆腐) bean curd

togamé *n* とがめ (**o-togame** おとがめ) [BOOKISH] rebuke, censure, blame

togáme *v* とがめ・ → **togame-másu** とがめます [INFINITIVE]

togamemásu, togaméru *v* とがめます, とがめる [BOOKISH] blames, rebukes, reproves, finds fault with: **ki ga togamemásu** 気がとがめます suffers from a guilty conscience

togarasemásu, togaráseru *v* とがらせ[尖らせ] ます, とがらせる・尖らせる sharpens, points

togarimásu, togáru *v* とがります[尖ります]・尖ります, とがる・尖る gets sharp (*pointed*)

togé *n* とげ・刺・棘 thorn

tóge *v* 遂げ・研げ → **togemásu** 遂げます・研げます [INFINITIVE]

tóge *v* 研げ [IMPERATIVE] (sharpen it!) → **togimásu** 研ぎます

tōgé *n* 峠 mountain pass; **...-tō´ge** ...峠 ...Pass

tōgei *n* 陶芸 ceramic art, ceramics

togemásu, togéru *v* 遂げます, 遂げる achieves, accomplishes

togemásu, togéru *v* 研げます, 研げる can sharpen (*grind, polish*)

tógete *v* 遂げて → **togemásu** 遂げます

tógete *v* 研げて → **togemásu** 研げます

tógi *v* 研ぎ → **togimásu** 研ぎます [INFINITIVE]

togimásu, tógu *v* 研ぎます, 研ぐ sharpens, grinds, polishes

tōhenboku *n* 唐変木 damned fool

tōhoku-chihō 東北地方 The Tōhoku area of Japan (*Aomori, Iwate, Miyagi, Akita, Yamagata, Fukushima prefectures*)

tōhon *n* 謄本 full copy: **koseki-tōhon** 戸籍謄本 full copy of one's family register

tōhyō *n* 投票 ballot, vote

toi *v* 問い → **toimásu** 問います [INFINITIVE]

tói *n* とい・樋 drain pipe, gutter

tōi *adj* 遠い **1.** far-off, distant **2. mimí ga tōi** 耳が遠い is hard of hearing

toiawase *n* 問い合わせ (**o-toiawase** お問い合わせ) inquiry

tóida *v* 研いだ = **togimáshita** 研ぎました (sharpened it)

tóide *v* 研いで → **togimásu** 研ぎます

toimásu, tóu *v* 問います, 問う inquires

tóire *n* トイレ toilet, bathroom

tóiretto-pé´pā *n* トイレットペーパー toilet paper

tóita *v* 解いた = **tokimáshita** 解きました (undid;...) → **tokimásu** 解きます

...-tóita ...といた = **...-te óita** ...ておいた = **...-te okimáshita** ...ておきました: **yametóita [yamete óita] hō ga ii** 止めといた[止めておいた] 方がいい You'd be better off just giving up.

...-tóita ra ...といたら = **...-te óita ra** ...ておいた ら: **yametóita ra [yamete óitara] yokatta** 止めといたら[止めておいたら]良かった It just had to give it up.

...-tóita ri ...といたり = **...-te óita ri** ...ておいた り: **koko ni oltólta ri shinaide kudasái** ここに置 いといたりしないで下さい don't put it here please

...-tóite ...といて = **...-te óite** ...ておいて: **himitsu ni shitóite kudasái** 秘密にしといて下さ い Keep it on the downlow.

tóite *v* 解いて → **tokimásu** 解きます

tōitsu *n* 統一 unification, standardization: **~ shimásu** 統一します unifies, standardizes

toí ya/wa shinai *v* 問いや/はしない = **towanai** 問わない (not inquire)

tóji *v* 閉じ → **tojimásu** 閉じます [INFINITIVE]

tōji *n* 冬至 winter solstice

tōji *n* 湯治 hot-spring cure: **tōji-ba** 湯治場 spa; **~ shimásu** 湯治します takes (*goes for*) the baths (= **tōji ni ikimásu** 湯治に行きます)

tō´ji (wa) *adv* 当時(は) (*at*) that time, then, (*in*) those days (= **anokoro (wa)** あの頃(は), **sono-koro (wa)** その頃(は))

tojimásu, tojíru *v* 閉じます, 閉じる closes (*a book, door wings, ...*)

tojínai *v* 閉じない = **tojimasén** 閉じません (not close)

tójite *v* 閉じて → **tojimásu** 閉じます

205

tōjitsu *n* 当日 the day in question, that very day, on the day

tōjō *n* 搭乗 boarding a plane: **tōjō-chū** 搭乗中 (*in the midst of*) boarding: **~ shimásu** 搭乗します boards

tōjṓ´-ken *n* 搭乗券 boarding pass

tōjō *n* 登場 entry onto the stage: **~ shimásu** 登場 します appears on stage

… tóka …とか or something (*like it*)

tōka *n* 十日 **1.** 10th day (*of a month*) **2.** (*for*) ten days (= **tōka-kan** 十日間)

tokage *n* トカゲ・蜥蜴 lizard

tokai *n* 都会 city: **dai-tókai** 大都会 metropolis (= **tóshi** 都市)

tōkai-chíhō *n* 東海地方 The Tōkai area of Japan (*Mie, Aichi, Gifu, Shizuoka prefectures*)

tokaku (… shimásu) *adv* とかく (…します) apt/liable (*to do*): **tokaku no uwasa** とかくの噂 unsavory rumors

tokánai *v* 解かない = **tokimasén** 解きません (not undo it; not…)

tokasánai *v* 溶かさない = **tokashimasén** 溶かし ません (not melt/dissolve)

tokasánai *v* とかさ[梳かさ]ない = **tokashimasén** とかし[梳かし]ません (not comb)

tokáse *v* 溶かせ **1.** → **tokasemásu** 溶かせ ます [INFINITIVE] **2.** [IMPERATIVE] (melt it!) → **tokashimásu** 溶かします

tokáse *v* とかせ・梳かせ **1.** → **tokasemásu** とかせ[梳かせ]ます [INFINITIVE] **2.** [IMPERATIVE] (comb it!) → **tokashimásu** とかし[梳かし]ます

tokasemásu, tokaséru *v* 溶かせます, 溶かせる can melt/dissolve it

tokasemásu, tokaséru *v* とかせ[梳かせ]ます, とかせる・梳かせる can comb it

tokasénai *v* 溶かせない = **tokasemasén** 溶かせま せん (cannot melt/dissolve)

tokasénai *v* とかせ[梳かせ]ない = **tokasemasén** とかせ[梳かせ]ません (cannot comb)

tokáshi *v* 溶かし → **tokashimásu** 溶かします [INFINITIVE]

tokáshi *v* とかし・梳かし → **tokashimásu** とか し[梳かし]ます [INFINITIVE]

tokashimásu, tokásu *v* 溶かします, 溶かす melts/thaws/dissolves it

tokashimásu, tokásu *v* とかし[梳かし]ます, とかす・梳かす combs

tóke *v* 溶け → **tokemásu** 溶けます [INFINITIVE]

tóke *v* 解け → **tokemásu** 解けます [INFINITIVE]

tóke *v* 解け [IMPERATIVE] (undo!; …!) → **tokimásu** 解きます

tókeba *v* 解けば, etc. (if one undoes it; if …) → **tokimásu** 解きます, etc.

tokei *n* 時計 time piece; clock; watch

tōkei *n* 統計 statistics

tokemásu, tokéru *v* 溶けます, 溶ける it melts/ thaws/dissolves

tokemásu, tokéru *v* 解けます, 解ける comes undone; gets solved

tókete *v* 溶けて → **tokemásu** 溶けます

tókete *v* 解けて → **tokemásu** 解けます

tokí *n* 時 time

tóki *n* トキ・朱鷺・鴇 crested ibis (*bird*)

tóki *v* 解き → **tokimásu** 解きます [INFINITIVE]

tóki *v* 説き → **tokimásu** 説きます [INFINITIVE]

tóki *v* とき・梳き → **tokimásu** とき[梳き]ます [INFINITIVE]

tō´ki *n* 陶器 pottery, ceramics, china → **jíki** 磁器

tō´ki *n* 登記 registration: **~ shimásu** 登記します enregisters

tō´ki *n* 冬期 winter (*period/term*): **tōki-orinpikku** 冬季オリンピック Winter Olympics

tō´ki *n* 投機 speculation: **~ shimásu** 投機します speculates

tō´ki *n* 投棄 dumping: **~ shimásu** 投棄します dumps, throws away

tokidoki 時々・ときどき sometimes

tokimásu, tóku *v* 解きます, 解く undoes, unties; solves

tokimásu, tóku *v* 説きます, 説く explains, persuades, preaches

tokimásu, tóku *v* とき[梳き]ます, とく・梳く comb

…-tókimásu *v* …ときます = **…-te okimásu** … ておきます: **yametókimásu** やめときます will pass

tóki ni *adv* …時に at the time that …, when …

tokí ni *adv* ときに・時に by the way, incidentally; sometimes

tóki ya/wa shinai *v* 解きゃ/はしない = **tokánai** 解かない (not undo it)

tokkakari *n* 取っ掛かり a hold, a place to hold on; a clue (= **tegakari** 手掛かり)

tokkan kōji *n* 突貫工事 eleventh-hour job

tokki *n* 突起 projection, protuberance

tokki *n* 特記 special mention: **tokki-jikō** 特記事項 special comments, special instruction: **tokki-nai kagiri** 特記ない限り unless specified otherwise

tokku (ni) *adv* とっく(に) long before (= **tokku no mukashi (ni)** とっくの昔(に))

tokkumiaimásu, tokkumiau *v* 取っ組み合いま す, 取っ組み合う grapple

tokkuri *n* とっくり・徳利 saké bottle/pitcher, ceramic decanter for serving saké

tokkyo *n* 特許 patent

tokkyū *n* 特急 special express (*train*); **tokkyū´-ken** 特急券 special-express ticket

tokkyū *n* 特級 special class; (*best*) quality

toko *n* 床 (**o-toko** お床) bed: **toko ni tsukimásu** 床に就きます takes to one's bed, goes to bed

… tokó *suffix* …とこ [INFORMAL] place (= **… tokoró** …所)

tokonoma *n* 床の間 alcove in Japanese room

tokoro, … tokoró *suffix* 所, …所 **1.** place **2.** address

tokoro, … tokoró ところ, …ところ circumstance, time: **shíta tokoró desu** したところ です has just done it; **shíte iru tokoró desu** して

いるところです is (*in the midst of*) doing it; **suru tokoró desu** するところです is about to do it

tokoró-de *conj* ところで by the way; well now

tokoro-dókoro *n, adv* ところどころ various places, here and there

tokoró-ga *conj* ところが but, however

... tokoró ga *suffix, conj* ...ところが however

tokoro-gaki *n* 所書き [BOOKISH] address (*written*) (= **atesaki** 宛先, **jū´sho** 住所)

tokoroten *n* ところてん seaweed gelatin strips served cold in a tangy soy sauce

toko-ya *n* 床屋 barber(shop)

toku-... *prefix* 特 special (= **tokubetsu** 特別)

toku-betsu (no) *adj* 特別(の) special, particular, extra: **tokubetsu ni** 特別に especially

toku-chō *n* 特徴 special feature/quality, (*a distinguishing*) characteristic

toku *n* 徳 virtue

toku *n* 得 (**o-toku** お得) profit, advantage, gain: **toku (na)** 得(な) profitable, advantageous

tóku *v* 説く = **tokimásu** 解きます (undoes)

tóku *v* 説く = **tokimásu** 説きます (explains)

tóku *v* とく・梳く = **tokimásu** とき[梳き]ます (combs)

...-toku *suffix, v* ...とく [INFORMAL] = ...-**te oku** ...ておく: **ato de yattoku** あとでやっとく I will do it later.

tōkú *adv* 遠く **1.** the distance, far off **2.** so as to be far/distant → **tōi** 遠い

tokuhon *n* 読本 reader, reading book

tokúi *n* 得意 **1.** pride; forte, strong point: **tokúi (na)** 得意(な) favorite, proud, exultant **2. o-tokui** お得意 (regular) customer, patron **3.** prosperity

tokúi (na/no) *adj, adv* 特異(な/の) unique, peculiar

tóku (ni) *adv* 特(に) in particular, especially

toku-nítō *n* 特二等 special second class

tokushoku *n* 特色 special feature, characteristic

tokushu (na) *adj* 特殊(な) special, particular

tokuten *n* 得点 points obtained, score (= **sukoa** スコア)

tokuyū (no) *adj* 特有(の) special, particular

tókya *v* [INFORMAL] 解きゃ → **tókeba** 解けば, etc.

Tōkyō *n* 東京 Tokyo
  Tōkyō´-Dáigaku *n* 東京大学 Tokyo University (= **Tō-dai** 東大)
  Tōkyō´-Eki *n* 東京駅 Tokyo Station
  Tōkyō´-jin *n* 東京人 a Tokyoite
  Tōkyō´-to *n* 東京都 the metropolis of Tokyo

tō´kyoku *n* 当局 the authorities

tománai *v* 富まない = **tomimasén** 富みません (not abound)

tomare *v* 止まれ **1.** → **tomaremásu** 止まれます [INFINITIVE] **2.** [IMPERATIVE] (stop) → **tomari-másu** 止まります

tomare *v* 泊まれ **1.** → **tomaremásu** 泊まれます [INFINITIVE] **2.** [IMPERATIVE] (stay over for the night!) → **tomarimásu** 泊まります

tomaremásu, tomareru *v* 泊まれます, 泊まれる can stay overnight

tomaremásu, tomareru *v* 止まれます, 止まれる can stop

tomarete *v* 泊まれて → **tomaremásu** 泊まれます

tomarete *v* 止まれて → **tomaremásu** 止まれます

tomari *n* 泊まり staying overnight; night duty

tomari *v* 止まり → **tomarimásu** 止まります [INFINITIVE]

tomari *v* 泊まり → **tomarimásu** 泊まります [INFINITIVE]

tomarimásu, tomaru *v* 止まります・止まる it stops

tomarimásu, tomaru *v* 泊まります, 泊まる stays overnight

tomarō´ *v* 泊まろう = **tomarimashō´** 泊まりましょう (let's stay overnight!)

tomaru *v* 泊まる = **tomarimásu** 泊まります (stays overnight): **tomaru tokoró** 泊まる所 accommodation(s), place to stay

tomatte *v* 止まって → **tomarimásu** 止まります

tomatte *v* 泊まって → **tomarimásu** 泊まります

tōmáwari *n* 遠回り detour

tōmáwashi *n* 遠回し oblique statement

tome *v* 止め → **tomemásu** 止めます [INFINITIVE]

tome *v* 泊め → **tomemásu** 泊めます [INFINITIVE]

tome *v* 留め → **tomemásu** 留めます [INFINITIVE]

tómeba *v* 富めば (if it abounds) → **tomimásu** 富みます

tōmei (na) *adj* 透明(な) transparent, clear

tomemásu, tomeru *v* 止めます, 止める stops it

tomemásu, tomeru *v* 泊めます, 泊める puts one up overnight

tomemásu, tomeru *v* 留めます, 留める fastens (*firmly attaches*)

tome-bári *n* 留め針 pin

tōmen *adv* 当面 for now (= **sashiatari** 差し当たり)

tōmen (no) *adj* 当面(の) immediate, present; **tōmen no mondai** 当面の問題 immediate problem

tomenai *v* 止めない = **tomemasén** 止めません, etc. (not stop it; ...)

tomerare *v* 止められ → **tomeraremásu** 止められます [INFINITIVE]

tomerare *v* 泊められ → **tomeraremásu** 泊められます [INFINITIVE]

tomeraremásu, tome(ra)reru *v* 止められます, 止められる can stop it

tomeraremásu, tome(ra)reru *v* 泊められます, 泊められる can put one up overnight

tomerarenai *v* 止められない = **tomeraremasén** 止められません, etc. (cannot stop it; ...)

tomeyō *v* 止めよう = **tomemashō´** 止めましょう (let's stop it!; ...)

tómi *n* 富 wealth, fortune, riches, abundance

tómi *v* 富み → **tomimásu** 富みます [INFINITIVE]

tomimásu, tómu *v* 富みます, 富む is rich; abounds

tōmin *n* 冬眠 hibernation

tómi ya/wa shinai *v* 富みや/はしない = **tománai** 富まない (not abound)

tómo *n* 友 [BOOKISH] friend (= **yūjin** 友人)
  tomodachi *n* 友達 (**o-tomodachi** お友達) friend

tómo *n* 伴 (**o-tómo** お伴) one's companion, company (= **dōhan-sha** 同伴者)

... tó-mo! *interj* ...とも！: **ii tó mo** いいとも
  Of course!

tó-mo-kaku *adv* ともかく anyway, anyhow, at any rate

tomonaimásu, tomonáu *v* 伴います、伴う; **... ni tomonaimásu** ...に伴います accompanies

tomo ni *adv* 共に together (= **issho ni** 一緒に)

tō-mórokoshi *n* トウモロコシ corn (*on the cob*) (= **kōn** コーン); **tōmorokoshí-ko** とうもろこし粉 cornstarch

tomoshimásu, tomósu *v* 灯します、灯す burns (*a light*)

tómu *v* 富む = **tomimásu** 富みます (is rich; abounds)

tonáe *v* 唱え → **tonaemásu** 唱えます
  1. [INFINITIVE] **2. tonáé ro** 唱えろ、**tonáe yo** 唱えよ [IMPERATIVE] (advocate!; shout!; recite!; call!; claim!)

tonaemásu, tonáéru *v* 唱えます、唱える advocates; shouts; recites; calls; claims

tonáete *v* 唱えて → **tonaemásu** 唱えます

tōnan *n* 盗難 [BOOKISH] (*suffering*) theft

tonari *n* 隣 next-door, neighbor(ing)

tonbo *n* トンボ・蜻蛉 dragonfly

tonda *adj* とんだ outrageous, terrible, shocking

tonda *v* 跳んだ = **tobimáshita** 跳びました (jumped)

tonda *v* 飛んだ = **tobimáshita** 飛びました (flew)

tónda *v* 富んだ = **tomimáshita** 富みました (was rich; abounded)

tonde *v* 跳んで → **tobimásu** 跳びます

tonde *v* 飛んで → **tobimásu** 飛びます

tónde *v* 富んで: **tónde imásu** 富んでいます is rich, abundant → **tomimásu** 富みます

tonde-mo arimasén *adj* とんでもありません Oh, no. No way.

tonde-mo nái *adj* とんでもない = **tonde-mo arimasén** とんでもありません outrageous, terrible, shocking

tó-ni-kaku とにかく anyway, anyhow

ton-katsu *n* 豚カツ・トンカツ pork cutlet

tónma *n* とんま・トンマ・頓馬 idiot, fool

tonma *n* とんま dullness, fool, idiot, boob (= **manuke** まぬけ, **noroma** のろま)

tonneru *n* トンネル tunnel

ton-ya *n* 問屋 wholesale store (= **oroshi-uri** 卸売り): [IDIOM] **sō wa ton-ya ga orosanai** そうは問屋が卸さない It won't work the way you expect.

tōnyō-byō *n* 糖尿病 diabetes

tōnyū *n* 豆乳 soybean milk

tōnyū *n* 投入 [BOOKISH] **1.** a throw (*into*) **2.** investment, investing: **~ shimásu** 投入します throws into, invests

toppatsu *n* 突発 [BOOKISH] outbreak: **toppatsu-jiko** 突発事故 sudden accident; **toppatsu-jiken** 突発事件 unforeseen accident; bombshell

toppu *n* トップ top

tora *n* トラ・虎 tiger

toraberāzu chekku *n* トラベラーズチェック traveler's check

toraburu *n* トラブル trouble: **toraburu-mēkā** トラブルメーカー troublemaker

Tora-doshi *n* 寅年 year of the Tiger

torάe *v* 捕らえ → **toraemásu** 捕らえます [INFINITIVE]

toraemásu, toráéru *v* 捕らえます、捕らえる catches, seizes, captures, arrests

toraiaru *n* トライアル trial: **toraiaru-koyō** トライアル雇用 trial employment

torákku *n* トラック **1.** truck **2.** track (*for running*)

torakutā *n* トラクター tractor

toránai *v* 取らない = **torimasén** 取りません, etc. (not take; not ...)

toránku *n* トランク (*clothes/car*) trunk

toránkusu *n* トランクス trunks

toranpétto *n* トランペット trumpet

toranporin *n* トランポリン trampoline

toránpu *n* トランプ playing cards

toranshiibā *n* トランシーバー transceiver, walkie-talkie

tóre *v* 取れ **1.** → **toremásu** 取れます [INFINITIVE] **2.** [IMPERATIVE] (take it!; ... !) → **torimásu** 取ります

tóreba *v* 取れば = [INFORMAL] **tórya** 取りゃ (if one takes) → **torimásu** 取ります

torei *n* トレイ tray

toremásu, toréru *v* 取れます、取れる **1.** (*button, etc.*) comes off **2.** can take

torēnā *n* トレーナー sweatshirt

torénai *v* 取れない = **toremasén** 取れません (not come off; cannot take)

torendo *n* トレンド trend (*fashion, etc.*) (= **keikō** 傾向)

torēningu *n* トレーニング training (*exercise, etc.*) workout: **torēningu-uea** トレーニングウエア training wear: **torēningu-shūzu** トレーニングシューズ training shoes: **torēningu-jimu** トレーニングジム training gym

toréreba *v* 取れれば = [INFORMAL] **torérya** 取れりゃ (if it comes off; if one can take) → **toremásu** 取れます

torēshingu-pēˊpa *n* トレーシングペーパー = **torepe** トレペ tracing paper

tórete *v* 取れて → **toremásu** 取れます

tori *n* トリ・鳥 bird (→ **ko-tori** 小鳥)
  tori-kago *n* トリカゴ・鳥籠 bird cage
  torí-gai *n* トリガイ・鳥貝 Japanese cockle
  tori-i *n* 鳥居 the gate to a Shinto shrine
  tori *n* トリ・鶏 chicken (= **niwa-tori** 鶏・ニワトリ)
  tori-niku *n* トリニク・鶏肉 chicken meat

tóri *v* 取り → **torimásu** 取ります [INFINITIVE]

tóri *v* 撮り → **torimásu** 撮ります [INFINITIVE]

tori-... *prefix* 取り ... [verb PREFIX]: takes and ...

tōri *n* 通り street, avenue; passage (= **michi** 道)

tōˊri *n* とおり・通り way (of doing), manner: ...

208

no tố'ri ni …のとおりに like … (= **(no) yō ni** (の)よう[様]に)

tố'ri *n* 通り → **tōrimásu** 通ります [INFINITIVE]

tori-agemásu, tori-ageru *v* 取り上げます、取り上げる takes up; takes away

tori-atsúkai *n* 取り扱い handling, treatment, management, transaction

tori-atsúkai *v* 取り扱い → **toriatsukaimásu** 取り扱います [INFINITIVE]

tori-atsukaimásu, tori-atsukau *v* 取り扱います、取り扱う handles, deals with, manages

tori-awase *n* 取り合わせ assortment

tori-bun *n* 取(り)分 share (~ **torimae** 取り前)

Tori-doshi *n* 酉年 year of the Rooster

tórí-hiki *n* 取り引き・取引 transaction, deal, business, trade

tori-kae *n* 取り替え change, replacement

tori-kae *v* 取り替え → **tori-kaemásu** 取り替えます **1.** [INFINITIVE] **2. tori-kae ro** 取り替えろ, **tori-kaé yo** 取り替えよ [IMPERATIVE] (replace it!)

tori-kaemásu, tori-kaeru *v* 取り替えます、取り替える replaces it

tori-kaenai *v* 取り替えない = **tori-kaemásén** 取り替えません (not replace it)

tori-kaerare *v* 取り替えられ → **tori-kaeraremásu** 取り替えられます

tori-kaeraremásu, tori-kaerareru *v* 取り替えられます、取り替えられる can replace it

tori-kaerarenai *v* 取り替えられない = **tori-kaeraremasén** 取り替えられません (cannot replace it)

tori-kesanai *v* 取り消さない = **tori-keshimásén** 取り消しません (not cancel)

tori-keshi *n* 取り消し cancellation, revocation; deletion, erasure

tori-keshi *v* 取り消し → **tori-keshimásu** 取り消します [INFINITIVE]

tori-keshimásu, tori-kesu *v* 取り消します、取り消す cancels, revokes; deletes, erases

tori-keshite *v* 取り消して → **tori-keshimásu** 取り消します

tori-kesō' *v* 取り消そう → **tori-keshimashō'** 取り消しましょう (let's cancel it!, I will cancel it)

toriko *n* とりこ・虜 **1.** captive, prisoner (= **horyo** 捕虜) **2.** person who is crazy about something/someone; **koi no toriko** 恋の虜 captive of love

tori-kumi *n* 取り組み・取組み wrestling match/bout/program

torimásu, tóru *v* 取ります、取る **1.** takes; takes away, removes **2.** passes (*the salt, sugar, etc.*) **3.** takes (*a course*)

torimásu, tóru *v* 撮ります、撮る takes (*a picture*)

tōrimásu, tō´ru *v* 通ります、通る passes by, passes through

tōrimásu, tō´ru *v* 透ります、透る penetrates

tōri-michi *n* 通り道 passage(way) (= **tsūro** 通路)

torishimari *n* **1.** 取り締まり・取締り control, management, supervision **2.** 取締 (= **torishimari-yaku** 取締役) managing director

tori-shimari *v* 取り締まり → **tori-shimarimásu** 取り締まります [INFINITIVE]

tori-shimarimásu, tori-shimaru *v* 取り締まります、取り締まる controls, manages, supervises, directs

toritsugi 1. 取り次ぎ・取次ぎ answering the door **2.** 取次 an usher; an agency

toriwake *adv* とりわけ especially, in particular

tóri ya/wa shinai *v* 取りや/はしない、[INFORMAL] **tórya shinai** 取りゃしない = **toránai** 取らない (not take)

tóro *n* とろ・トロ fatty tuna (*cf.* **chū-toro** 中とろ・中トロ, **aka-mi** 赤身)

torō´ *v* 取ろう = **torimashō´** 取りましょう (let's take it!)

torō *n* 徒労 vain effort

tōrō *n* 灯籠 a stone lantern: **tōrō nagashi** 灯籠流し floating lanterns on a river

tōroku *n* 登録 registration: ~ **shimásu** 登録します registers, enrolls

tō´ron *n* 討論 [BOOKISH] debate, discussion, dispute

tororo *n* トロロ・とろろ grated yam; **tororo-kónbu** とろろ昆布 kelp flakes

tóru *v* 取る = **torimásu** 取ります (takes; takes away)

tō´ru *v* 通る = **tōrimásu** 通ります (passes by, passes through)

tō´ru *v* 透る = **tōrimásu** 透ります (penetrates)

Tóruko *n* トルコ Turkey

tórya *v* [INFORMAL] 取りゃ → **tóreba** 取れば

toryō *n* 塗料 coating compositions (*paint, Japanese lacquer, varnish, etc.*)

tōsaku *n* 倒錯 [BOOKISH] perversion: **seiteki-tōsaku** 性的倒錯 paraphilia

tōsaku *n* 盗作 plagiarism

tōsan *n* 倒産 bankruptcy (= **hasan** 破産): ~ **shimásu** 倒産します goes bankrupt

tōsan *n* 父さん (*mostly male*) dad (= **oyaji** 親父, **tō-chan** 父ちゃん)

tōsánai *v* 通さない = **tōshimásen** 通しません (not let through/in)

tō´se *v* 通せ **1.** → **tōsemásu** 通せます [INFINITIVE] **2.** [IMPERATIVE] (let them through/in!) → **tōshimásu** 通します

tōsei *n* 統制 control (*of prices, etc.*)

tōsemásu, tōséru *v* 通せます、通せる can let through/in

tōsemásu, tōséru *v* 透せます、透せる can pierce/penetrate

tōsénai *v* 通せない = **tōsemasén** 通せません (cannot let through/in)

tōsenbo, tōsenbō *n* 通せんぼ・通せん坊 blocking a person's way

toshi *n* 年 **1.** year **2.** 年・歳 (お年・お歳) age: **toshí o torimásu** 年を取ります gets old

toshi-ake *n* 年明け new year

toshi-koshi soba *n* 年越しそば[蕎麦] buckwheat noodles eaten traditionally on New Year's Eve

toshi-otoko *n* 年男 a man born in a year with the same Chinese zodiac sign as the current year

toshi-onna *n* 年女 a woman born in a year with the same Chinese zodiac sign as the current year

toshi-go *n* 年子 child born within a year of another

toshi-kakkō *n* 年格好 one's age (= **toshi-goro** 年頃): **toshi-kakkō ga rokujū kurai no dansei** 年格好が60くらいの男性 a man of about 60: **toshi-kakkō ga musume to niteiru otoko-no-ko** 年格好が娘と似ている男の子 a boy of about my daughter's age

toshi-ma *n* 年増 middle-aged woman

toshi-shita (no) *adj* 年下（の） younger, junior

toshi-ue (no) *n* 年上（の） older, senior

toshi-yóri *n* 年寄り (**o-toshiyori** お年寄り) an old person (= **kōrei-sha** 高齢者)

tóshi *n* 都市 city: **dai-tóshi** 大都市 big city, metropolis (= **tokai** 都会)

tōshí (no) *adj* 通し（の） direct, through (*to destination*): **tōshi de ikimásu** 通しで行きます goes direct (*through to destination*); **tōshi-gíppu** 通し切符 a through ticket; **tōshi-bangō** 通し番号 serial number

tōshi *n* 投資 investment, investing: **~ shimásu** 投資します invests

tōshi *n* 凍死 freezing to death, frost-killing: **~ shimásu** 凍死します is frozen dead

tō'shi *n* 闘志 [BOOKISH] fighting spirit

tōshi *v* 通し → **tōshimásu** 通します [INFINITIVE]

tōshi *v* 透し → **tōshimásu** 透します [INFINITIVE]

tōshimásu, tō'su 通します, 通す lets through/in, admits; shows in; pierces

tōshimásu, tō'su 透します, 透す penetrates

tōshin-dai *n* 等身大 life size

tōshin (jisatsu) *n* 投身（自殺） committing suicide by throwing oneself (*into water, off the platform, etc.*) (= **minage** 身投げ)

tō'shite *v* 通して → **tōshimásu** 通します

tósho *n* 図書 library (*book collection*): **tósho-gákari** 図書係 the librarian (*in charge*), (*book*) custodian

toshó-kan *n* 図書館 library (*building*); **toshokán-in** 図書館員 a librarian

toshó-shitsu *n* 図書室 library (*book room*)

tō'sho *n* 投書 letter to the editor

tō'sho (wa) *adv* 当初（は） [BOOKISH] at first, initially, originally (= **saisho (wa)** 最初（は）, **hajime** (wa) 初め（は））

tōshu *n* 党首 party leader

tōshu *n* 投手 a pitcher (*baseball, etc.*) (= **pitchā** ピッチャー)

tōshū *n* 踏襲 following predecessor's way: **~ shimásu** 踏襲します follows, adheres

tóso *n* とそ・屠蘇 (**o-tóso** お屠蘇) spiced saké drunk at New Year's

tōsō *n* 闘争 fight, labor struggle: **~ shimásu** 闘争します fights, struggles

tōsō *n* 逃走 [BOOKISH] escape: **~ shimásu** 逃走します escapes, runs away

tossa no *adj* とっさの prompt

tossa ni *adv* とっさに in an instant, promptly, immediately

tō'su *v* 通す = **tōshimásu** 通します (lets through/in, admits; shows in)

tō'su *v* 透す = **tōshimásu** 透します (lets pierce, penetrates)

tō'sutā *n* トースター toaster

tō'suto *n* トースト toast

tō'ta *v* 問うた = **toimáshita** 問いました (inquired)

… totan ni …途端に (*at*) the instant/moment that …

tō'te *v* 問うて → **toimásu** 問います

tōtei *adv* 到底 [+ NEGATIVE VERB] absolutely (not)

tō'te mo *adv* 問うても even inquiring

totemo *adj* とても very [INFORMAL] (= **tottemo** とっても, **taihen** 大変)

tō'tō *adv* とうとう at last, finally (= **tsuini** ついに)

totonóe *v* 整え → **totonoemásu** 整えます [INFINITIVE]

totonoemásu, totonóeru *v* 整えます, 整える regulates, adjusts; prepares

totonóenai *v* 整えない = **totonoemásén** 整えません (not regulate/adjust/prepare)

totonói *v* 整い → **totonoimásu** 整います [INFINITIVE]

totonoimásu, totonóu *v* 整います, 整う is in order; is ready

totonowánai *v* 整わない = **totonoimasén** 整いません (is not ready)

totsuzen *adv* 突然 suddenly, abruptly (= **kyū ni** 急に): **totsuzen no** 突然の sudden, abrupt

tótta *v* 取った = **torimáshita** 取りました (took)

totte *v* 取って = **tótte** 取って (taking) [*before verbs of movement*]

totté *n* 取っ手・把手 a handle, knob

tótte *v* 取って → **torimásu** 取ります [*but* **totte** 取って *before verbs of movement*]

tótte *v* とって: **…ni tótte** (…に)とって (*with reference*) to, for

totte ikimásu (iku) *v* 取っていきます（いく） takes, brings it there

totte kimásu (kúru) *v* 取ってきます（くる） brings it (here)

tottemo *adj* とっても terribly, extremely, completely (= **totemo** とても)

tótte okimásu (oku) *v* 取っておきます（おく） puts aside, reserves, holds

tóu *v* 問う = **toimásu** 問います (inquires)

tōwaku *n* 当惑 embarrassment, puzzlement (= **konwaku** 困惑): **~ shimásu** 当惑します gets embarrassed, gets puzzled

towanai *v* 問わない = **toimasén** 問いません (not inquire)

tó ya *v* 問や → **tóéba** 問えば

tōza *n* 当座, **tōza-yókin** 当座預金 current deposit, checking account

tōza no *adj* 当座（の） [BOOKISH] temporary

tózan *n* 登山 mountain-climbing (= **yama-nobori**

山登り): ~ **shimásu** 登山します climbs a mountain
tozán-sha n 登山者 mountain-climber

tōzen adv 当然 naturally, surely; **tōzen no** 当然の
proper, deserved

tōzoku n 盗賊 burglar

tsū n 通 1. an authority, an expert 2. (counts
letter): **ít-tsū** 一通 one letter

tsúa n ツアー tour 1. group tour (= **dantai-ryokō**
団体旅行) 2. short trip (= **shō-ryokō** 小旅行)

tsúbá n つば・唾 spit, saliva

tsúba n つば・鍔 sword-guard

tsubaki n つばき・唾 = **tsúbá** つば・唾 (spit)

tsúbaki n ツバキ・椿 camellia

tsubame n ツバメ・燕 swallow (bird)

tsubasa n つばさ・翼 wing

tsubo n つぼ・壺 jar, crock

tsubo n 坪 tsubo (6 sq. ft.)

tsubomarimásu, tsubomaru v つぼまります、つ
ぼまる it puckers up; gets puckered up, is shut; it narrows

tsubome v つぼめ → **tsubomeru** つぼめる
1. [INFINITIVE] 2. **tsubome ro** つぼめろ, **tsubomé
yo** つぼめよ [IMPERATIVE] (pucker it!)

tsubomemásu, tsubomeru v つぼめます、つぼ
める puckers it; shuts it; narrows it

tsubomi n つぼみ・蕾 flower bud

tsúbu n 粒 grain

tsuburemásu, tsubureru v 潰れます、潰れる
it collapses/smashes

tsuburemásu, tsubureru v つぶれます、つぶれ
る can shut/close one's eyes: **mé ga tsuburemásu**
目がつぶれます lose one's eyesight

tsuburimásu, tsuburu v つぶります、つぶる:
mé o tsuburimásu 目をつぶります shuts/closes
one's eyes

tsubushimásu, tsubusu v 潰します、潰す
smashes (crushes, squeezes) it

tsubuyakimásu, tsuyaku v つぶやきます、つぶ
やく murmur; **(tsuittā de) tsubuyaku** (ツイッタ
ーで)つぶやく tweet (internet)

tsuchí n 土 earth, ground

tsuchí n 槌 hammer (= **hánmā** ハンマー, **hánma**
ハンマ)

tsūchi n 通知 report, notice, notification

tsūchō n 通帳 passbook, bankbook: **yokin-tsūchō**
預金通帳 deposit book: **chokin-tsūchō** 貯金通帳
savings book

tsúe n 杖 cane, walking stick

tsuganai v 注がない = **tsugimasén** 注ぎません;
etc. (not pour it; not …)

tsūgaku n 通学 commuting to school: ~ **shimásu**
通学します commutes to school
tsūgaku-ro n 通学路 school route

tsuge n つげ・ツゲ・柘植 boxwood

tsuge 告げ → **tsugemásu** 告げます
1. v [INFINITIVE] 2. v **tsuge ro** 告げろ, **tsugé yo**
告げよ [IMPERATIVE] (tell it!) 3. n = **o-tsuge**
御告げ revelation, divine message

tsuge v 注げ [IMPERATIVE] (pour it!) →
tsugimásu 注ぎます

tsuge-guchi (ya) n 告げ口(屋) (tattle)tale,
(= **chikuri-ya** チクリ屋 [INFORMAL]): ~ **shimásu**
告げ口します tattles (= **chikurimásu** チクリます
[INFORMAL])

tsugemásu, tsugeru v 告げます、告げる tells,
informs

tsugemásu, tsugeru v 注げます、注げる can pour

tsugemásu, tsugeru v 継げます、継げる
can inherit

tsugemásu, tsugeru v 接げます、接げる can
join it

tsugenai v 告げない = **tsugemasén** 告げません
(will not tell)

tsugenai v 注げない = **tsugemasén** 注げません
(cannot pour)

tsugenai v 継げない = **tsugemasén** 継げません
(cannot inherit)

tsugenai v 接げない = **tsugemasén** 接げません
(cannot join it)

tsugi n 継ぎ patch; (… ni) tsugi o atemásu
(…に)継ぎを当てます patches it

tsugí n 次 (o-tsúgi お次) next, the following; **tsugí
no** 次の the next one

tsugí v 注ぎ → **tougimóou** 注ぎます [INFINITIVE]

tsugí v 継ぎ → **tsugimásu** 継ぎます [INFINITIVE]

tsugí v 接ぎ → **tsugimásu** 接ぎます [INFINITIVE]

tsugimásu, tsugu v 注ぎます、注ぐ pours it

tsugimásu, tsugu v 継ぎます、継ぐ inherits,
succeeds to

tsugimásu, tsugu v 接ぎます、接ぐ joins it,
grafts, glues

tsugi-me n 継ぎ目 joint, seam

tsugi-me n 接ぎ目 joint, seam

tsugitashi-kō´do n 継ぎ足しコード extension
cord (= **enchō-kō´do** 延長コード)

tsugí-tsugi (ni) adv 次々(に) one after another

tsugō n 都合 (**go-tsugō** ご都合) circumstances,
convenience, opportunity; **tsugō ga íí/warúi** 都合
がいい/悪い (it is) convenient/inconvenient; **tsugō
no yoi** 都合のよい expedient: **go-tsugō shugi** ご都
合主義 expediency, opportunism

tsui n 対 a pair (= **pea** ペア): **tsui ni narimásu**
対になります becomes/makes/forms a pair

tsúi adv つい 1. unintentionally, inadvertently
2. just (now): **tsúi imashígata** つい今しがた just
now; **tsúi saki-hodo** つい先程 [BOOKISH] just a
little while ago (= **tsúi sakki** ついさっき)

tsuide v 注いで → **tsugimásu** 注ぎます

tsuide v 継いで → **tsugimásu** 継ぎます

tsuide v 接いで → **tsugimásu** 接ぎます

tsúide adv 次いで next, in succession,
subsequently; **… ni tsúide** …に次いで following
…, next after/to … (in importance)

tsuide n ついで opportunity, occasion,
convenience: **tsuide no setsu/sai/toki ni** ついでの
節/際/時に at your/one's convenience; **tsuide ga
arimásu** ついでがあります has occasion to…

… tsuide (ni) suffix …ついで(に) on the occasion
of/that …, incidentally to …; while …; along the way

tsuihō *n* 追放 purge: **~ shimásu** 追放します purges

tsúin *n* ツイン, **tsuin-rū´mu** ツインルーム twin(-bed)room

tsuin-béddo *n* ツインベッド twin beds

tsúi ni *adv* ついに at last, finally (= **tōtō** とうとう)

tsuiraku *n* 墜落 (*plane*) crash: **~ shimásu** 墜落します (*a plane*) crashes

tsui-shi(kén) *n* 追試(験) makeup exam (= **sai-shi(ken)** 再試(験))

tsuitachí *n* 一日 first day of a month

tsuitate *n* 衝立 partition

tsuite *v* 突いて → **tsukimásu** 突きます

tsúite *suffix* ついて **... ni tsúite (no)** …について (の) about, concerning; **... ni tsúite (wa)** …について(は) as far as … is concerned

tsúite *v* 付いて → **tsukimásu** 付きます

tsúite imasén (inai) *v* ついていません(いない) is unlucky, fails to strike it lucky (= **tsúite masén** ついてません)

tsúite imasén (inai) *v* 付いていません(いない) is not attached; un-.... (= **tsúite masén** 付いてません)

tsúite imasén (inai) *v* 点いていません(いない) is not turn on (lights) (= **tsúite masén** 点いてません)

tsúite nai *v* ついてない = **tsúite masén** ついてません (is unlucky, fails to strike it lucky)

tsuittā *n* ツイッター Twitter (*internet*)

tsuji *n* 辻 crossroads; road(side), street: **yotsu-tsuji** 四つ辻 crossroad (= **jūji-ro** 十字路)

tsū-ji *n* 通じ 1. (**o-tsū´-ji** お通じ) bowel movement 2. effect

tsū-ji *v* 通じ → **tsū-jimásu** 通じます [INFINITIVE]

tsū-jimásu, tsū-jiru *v* 通じます, 通じる gets through, communicates; transmits; connects, runs; is understood; one's bowels move; **(... o) tsū-ji te** (…を)通じて through (*the medium of*)

tsūjín *n* 通人 an expert, an authority; a man of the world

tsūjō *adv* 通常 usually, ordinarily (= **futsū** 普通, taitei たいてい・大抵)

tsūjō (no) *adj* 通常(の) usual, ordinary

tsuká *n* 塚 mound

tsuka *n* つか・柄 hilt

tsūka *n* 通貨 currency (*money*) (= **kahei** 貨幣)

tsūkā no naka *n* つーかー[ツーカー]の仲 those who are very close and know what each other is thinking

tsukae *v* 使え 1. → **tsukaemásu** 使えます [INFINITIVE] 2. [IMPERATIVE] (use it!) → **tsukaimásu** 使います

tsukáé *n* つかえ obstruction

tsukaeba *v* 使えば (if one uses it) → **tsukaimásu** 使います

tsukaemásu, tsukaeru *v* 使えます, 使える can use it; be useful

tsukaemásu, tsukáéru *v* つかえます, つかえる 1. gets clogged up, obstructed, busy: **nodo ga tsukaemásu** 喉がつかえます has difficulty in swallowing: **mune ga tsukaemásu** 胸がつかえます 2. feels stuffed up (*physically*) 3. feels a pressure on one's chest (*mentally*)

tsukaenai *v* 使えない = **tsukaemasén** 使えません (cannot use it)

tsukáénai *v* つかえない = **tsukaemasén** つかえません (not get obstructed)

tsukaeréba *v* 使えれば = [INFORMAL] **tsukaerya** 使えりゃ (if one can use it) → **tsukaemásu** 使えます

tsukaéreba *v* つかえれば (if it is obstructed) → **tsukaemásu** つかえます

tsukaete *v* 使えて → **tsukaemásu** 使えます

tsukáete *v* つかえて → **tsukaemásu** つかえます

tsukae ya/wa shinai *v* 使えや/はしない, [INFORMAL] **tsukaerya shinai** 使えりゃしない = **tsukaenai** 使えない (cannot use it)

tsukáe ya/wa shinai *v* つかえや/はしない, [INFORMAL] **tsukáerya shinai** つかえりゃしない = **tsukáénai** つかえない (not get obstructed)

tsukai *n* 使い 1. message, errand 2. messenger 3. *v* → **tsukaimásu** 使います [INFINITIVE]

tsukai-hashiri, tsukai-bashiri *n* 使い走り, **tukai-ppashiri** 使いっ走り errand runner

tsukaimásu, tsukau *v* 使います, 使う uses; spends; employs; handles

tsukamae *v* 捕まえ → **tsukamaemásu** 捕まえます 1. [INFINITIVE] 2. **tsukamae ro** 捕まえろ, **tsukamaé yo** 捕まえよ [IMPERATIVE] (catch!)

tsukamaemásu, tsukamaeru *v* 捕まえます, 捕まえる catches, seizes, arrests

tsukamaenai *v* 捕まえない = **tsukamaemasén** 捕まえません (not catch)

tsukamánai *v* つかまない = **tsukamimasén** つかみません (not seize)

tsukamemásu, tsukaméru *v* つかめます, つかめる can seize

tsukaménai *v* つかめない = **tsukamemasén** つかめません (cannot seize)

tsukámete *v* つかめて → **tsukamemásu** つかめます

tsukamimásu, tsukámu *v* つかみます, つかむ seizes, grasps, clutches

tsukamō´ *v* つかもう = **tsukamimashō** つかみましょう (let's seize it!)

tsukanai *v* 突かない = **tsukimasén** 突きません (not stab, …)

tsukánai *v* 付かない = **tsukimasén** 付きません (not come in contact, …)

tsukánde *v* つかんで → **tsukamimásu** つかみます

tsukaō *v* 使おう = **tsukaimashō´** 使いましょう (let's use it!)

tsukaremásu, tsukaréru *v* 疲れます, 疲れる gets tired

tsukatte *v* 使って → **tsukaimásu** 使います

tsukau v 使う = **tsukaimásu** 使います (uses)

tsukawanai v 使わない = **tsukaimasén** 使いません (not use)

tsuke v 漬け → **tsukemásu** 漬けます **1.** [INFINITIVE] **2. tsuke ro** 漬けろ, **tsuké yo** 漬けよ [IMPERATIVE] (soak it!)

tsuke v 突け [IMPERATIVE] (stab it!) → **tsukemásu** 突けます, **tsukimásu** 突きます

tsuké n 付け bill, account **1. tsuké de kaimásu** 付けで買います buys it on credit **2.** → **tsukemásu** 付けます [INFINITIVE] **3. tsuké ro/yo** 付けろ/よ [IMPERATIVE] (attach it!)

tsuké v 着け → **tsukomáou** 着けます **1.** [INFINITIVE] **2.** [IMPERATIVE] (arrive!) → **tsukimásu** 着きます

tsukeawase n 付け合わせ garnish, relish

tsukéba v 突けば = [INFORMAL] **tsukya** 突きゃ (if one stabs) → **tsukimásu** 突きます

tsukéba v 付けば = [INFORMAL] **tsukya** 付きゃ (if it comes in contact) → **tsukimásu** 付きます

tsukemásu, tsukeru v 漬けます, 漬ける pickles; soaks

tsukemásu, tsukeru v 突けます, 突ける can stab, can thrust, can poke, can push

tsukemásu, tsukéru v 付けます, 付ける attaches, sticks on, adds, applies

tsukemásu, tsukéru v 点けます, 点ける turns on (lights)

tsukemásu, tsukéru v 着けます, 着ける = **mi ni tsukemásu** 身に着けます puts on, wears

tsuke-mono n 漬物 Japanese pickles

tsukenai v 漬けない = **tsukemásen** 漬けません (not pickle/soak)

tsukenai v 突けない = **tsukemásen** 突けません (cannot stab/thrust/poke/push)

tsukénai v 付けない = **tsukemásen** 付けません (not attach/stick on/add/apply)

tsukénai v 点けない = **tsukemásen** 点けません (not turn on (lights))

tsukénai v 着けない = **tsukemásen** 着けません (not puts on/wears)

tsukete v 漬けて → **tsukemásu** 漬けます

tsukete v 突けて → **tsukemásu** 突けます

tsukéte v 点けて → **tsukemásu** 点けます

tsukéte v 着けて → **tsukemásu** 着けます

tsukeyō v 漬けよう = **tsukemashō´** 漬けましょう (let's pickle/soak it!)

tsukeyō´ v 付けよう = **tsukemashō´** 付けましょう (let's attach/… it!)

tsukeyō´ v 点けよう = **tsukemashō´** 点けましょう (let's turn on (lights)!)

tsukeyō´ v 着けよう = **mi ni tsukemashō´** 身に着けましょう (let's put on/wear!)

tsuki v 突き → **tsukimásu** 突きます [INFINITIVE]

tsuki v 着き → **tsukimásu** 着きます [INFINITIVE]

tsukí n 月 moon; month

tsukí-hi n 月日 time (days and years)

tsuki-mí n 月見 (**o-tsuki-mi** お月見) moon viewing

tsukí-yo n 月夜 moonlight (night)

tsukí v 付き → **tsukimásu** 付きます [INFINITIVE]

…-tsuki (no) …付き(の) with (… attached)

tsuki-ai 付き合い **1.** n **o-tsukíai** お付き合い association, social company, friendship (= **kōsai** 交際) **2.** v → **tsuki-aimásu** 付き合います [INFINITIVE]

tsuki-aimásu, tsuki-áu v 付き合います, 付き合う: **… to tsuki-aimásu** …と付き合います associates (with), enjoys the company of, goes out (with one's lover)

tsuki-atari 突き当たり **1.** n the end of a street/corridor **2.** v → **tsuki-atarimásu** 突き当たります [INFINITIVE]

tsuki-atarimásu, tsuki-atáru v 突き当たります, 突き当たる runs into; comes to the end of (a street)

tsuki-dashimásu, tsuki-dásu v 突き出します, 突き出す makes it protrude, sticks it out

tsuki-demásu, tsuki-déru v 突き出ます, 突き出る protrudes, sticks out

tsukimásu, tsuku v 突きます, 突く stabs, thrusts, pokes, pushes

tsukimásu, tsúku v 付きます, 付く **1.** comes in contact **2.** sticks to; joins; follows; touches

tsukimásu, tsúku v 着きます, 着く arrives (= **tōchaku shimásu, tōchaku suru** 到着します, 到着する)

tsukimásu, tsúku v 点きます, 点く burns, is turned (on), is lit

tsukimásu, tsukíru v 尽きます, 尽きる comes to an end, runs out

tsūkin n 通勤 commuting to work: **~ shimásu** 通勤します commutes to work; **tsūkin-jíkan** 通勤時間 commuting time

tsukínai v 尽きない = **tsukimásén** 尽きません (not come to an end)

tsukíru v 尽きる = **tsukimásu** 尽きます (comes to an end)

tsuki-sáshi v 突き刺し → **tsuki-sashimásu** 突き刺します [INFINITIVE]

tsuki-sashimásu, tsuki-sásu v 突き刺します, 突き刺す stabs

tsukíte v 尽きて → **tsukimásu** 尽きます

tsukí ya/wa shinai v 突きや/はしない, [INFORMAL] **tsukya shinai** 突きゃしない = **tsukanai** 突かない (not stab)

tsukí ya/wa shinai v 付きや/はしない, [INFORMAL] **tsukya shinai** 付きゃしない = **tsukánai** 付かない (not come in contact)

tsukiyō´ v 尽きよう → **tsukimásu** 尽きます; **tsukiyō´ to shiteimásu** 尽きようとしています is about to come to an end

tsukō´ v 付こう → **tsukimásu** 付きます: **tsukō´ to shimásu** 付こうとします is about to come in contract, …

213

tsukō´ ν 突こう = **tsukimáshō´** 突きましょう (let's stab/poke/thrust!)

tsūkō n 通行 passing, passage, transit: ~ **shimásu** 通行します = **tōrimásu** 通ります passes (by/through); **tsūkō-dome** 通行止め closed to traffic, No Passage; **tsūkō-nin** 通行人 passer-by

Tsukúba n つくば・筑波 Tsukuba; **Tsukuba-Dáigaku** n 筑波大学 Tsukuba University

tsukuda-ni n ツクダニ・佃煮 conserves boiled down from fish or seaweed

tsukue n 机 desk (= **desuku** デスク)

tsukuránai ν 作らない = **tsukurimásén** 作りません (not make it)

tsukúre ν 作れ **1.** → **tsukuremásu** 作れます [INFINITIVE] **2.** [IMPERATIVE] (make it!) → **tsukurimásu** 作ります

tsukúreba ν 作れば = [INFORMAL] **tsukúrya** 作りゃ (if one makes it) → **tsukurimásu** 作ります

tsukuremásu, tsukuréru ν 作れます, 作れる can make it

tsukurénai ν 作れない = **tsukuremásén** 作れません (cannot make it)

tsukuréreba ν 作れれば = [INFORMAL] **tsukurérya** 作れりゃ (if one can make it) → **tsukuremásu** 作れます

tsukúrete ν 作れて → **tsukuremásu** 作れます

tsukure ya/wa shinai ν 作れや/はしない, [INFORMAL] **tsukurérya shinai** 作れりゃしない = **tsukurénai** 作れない (cannot make it)

tsukurí 作り **1.** n makeup, toilette **2.** n artistically arranged slices of raw fish

tsukurí 作りν → **tsukurimásu** 作ります [INFINITIVE]

tsukurí 造り **1.** n a structure, build **2.** ν → **tsukurimásu** 造ります [INFINITIVE]

tsukúri-banashi n 作り話 (stories) fiction

tsukurimásu, tsukúru ν 作ります, **tsukúru** 作る makes, forms, creates, produces, grows, manufactures, prepares (fixes) (small or intangible things); **jikan o tsukurimásu** 時間を作ります makes (sets aside) time, sets up a time

tsukurimásu, tsukúru ν 造ります, 造る makes, forms, creates, grows, manufactures, builds (big things)

tsukuri ya/wa shinai 作りや/はしない, [INFORMAL] **tsukúrya shinai** 作りゃしない = **tsukuránai** 作らない (not make it)

tsukuróe ν 繕え **1.** → **tsukuroemásu** 繕えます [INFINITIVE] **2.** [IMPERATIVE] (mend it!) → **tsukuroimásu** 繕います

tsukuróeba ν 繕えば (if one mends it) → **tsukuroimásu** 繕います

tsukuroemásu, tsukuroeru ν 繕えます, 繕える can mend it

tsukuroénai ν 繕えない = **tsukuroemásén** 繕えません (cannot mend it)

tsukuroéreba ν 繕えれば (if one can mend it) → **tsukuroemásu** 繕えます

tsukurói 繕い **1.** n mending, repair **2.** ν → **tsukuroimásu** 繕います [INFINITIVE]

tsukuroimásu, tsukuróu ν 繕います, 繕う mends, repairs

tsukuroō´ ν 繕おう = **tsukuroimashō´** 繕いましょう (let's mend it!)

tsukurowánai ν 繕わない = **tsukuroimásén** 繕いません (not mend)

tsukúrya ν [INFORMAL] 作りゃ → **tsukúreba** 作れば

tsukusánai ν 尽くさない = **tsukushimásén** 尽くしません (not exhaust)

tsukúse ν 尽くせ [IMPERATIVE] (exert yourself!) → **tsukushimásu** 尽くします

tsukúseba ν 尽くせば (if one exhausts) → **tsukushimásu** 尽くします

tsukusemásu, tsukuséru ν 尽くせます, 尽くせる can exhaust

tsukusénai ν 尽くせない = **tsukusemásén** 尽くせません (cannot exhaust)

tsukuséreba ν 尽くせれば (if one can exhaust) → **tsukusemásu** 尽くせます

tsukúsete ν 尽くせて → **tsukusemásu** 尽くせます

tsukúsha ν [INFORMAL] 尽しゃ → **tsukúseba** 尽くせば

tsukúshi ν 尽くし → **tsukushimásu** 尽くします [INFINITIVE]

tsukushimásu, tsukúsu ν 尽くします, 尽くす exhausts, runs out of; exerts oneself, strives

tsukúshite ν 尽くして → **tsukushimásu** 尽くします

tsukúshi ya/wa shinai ν 尽くしや/はしない, [INFORMAL] **tsukúsha shinai** 尽くしゃしない = **tsukusánai** 尽くさない (not exhaust)

tsukusō´ ν 尽くそう = **tsukushimashō´** 尽くしましょう (let's exert ourselves!)

tsukútta ν 作った = **tsukurimáshita** 作りました (made it)

tsukútte ν 作って → **tsukurimásu** 作ります

tsukya ν [INFORMAL] 突きゃ → **tsukéba** 突けば

tsukya ν [INFORMAL] 付きゃ → **tsukéba** 付けば

tsúma n 妻 wife **1.** my wife (= **kanai** 家内) **2.** (your/someone else's) wife = **oku-san** 奥さん

tsumá n つま・褄 skirt (of Kimono)

tsumá n ツマ sashimi garnishings

tsumamanai ν 摘まない = **tsumamimásén** 摘みません (not pinch)

tsumami 摘み・つまみ **1.** n a knob; a pinch **2.** n = **tsumamimono** つまみ物, **o-tsúmami** おつまみ things to nibble on while drinking (= **sakana** さかな・肴) **3.** ν → **tsumamimásu** 摘みます [INFINITIVE]

tsumamimásu, tsumamu ν 摘みます, 摘む pinches, picks; summarizes

tsumanai ν 積まない = **tsumimásén** 積みません (not pile it up)

tsumanai ν 摘まない = **tsumimásén** 摘みません (not gather/pluck)

tsumánnai *adj* つまんない [INFORMAL] → **tsumaránai** つまらない

tsumaránai *adj* つまらない worthless, no good, boring, trivial

tsumaránai *v* 詰まらない = **tsumarimasén** 詰まりません (is not clogged)

tsumári *v* 詰まり → **tsumarimásu** 詰まります [INFINITIVE]

tsúmari *adv* つまり after all; in short (= **kekkyoku (no tokoro)** 結局(のところ), **yōsuruni** 要するに)

tsumarimásu, tsumáru *v* 詰まります, 詰まる is clogged up, choked; is stuck; is shortened; is crammed

tsumáru tokoro つまるところ = **tsúmari** つまり (after all)

tsumasaki *n* つま先・爪先 toe, toe tip(s)

tsumashíi *adj* つましい・倹しい is thrifty, frugal

tsumátte *v* 詰まって → **tsumarimásu** 詰まります

tsuma-yōji *n* つまようじ・爪楊枝 toothpick

tsuma-zuite *v* つまずいて → **tsuma-zukimásu** つまずきます

tsuma-zukánai *v* つまずかない = **tsuma-zukimasén** つまずきません (not stumble)

tsuma-zukimásu, tsuma-zuku *v* つまずきます, つまずく stumbles

tsume *n* 爪 **1.** claw (= **kagizume** 鉤爪) (→ **taka-no-tsume** 鷹の爪): **tora no tsume** トラ[虎]の爪 tiger's claw **3.** hoof
tsume-kíri *n* 爪切り nail clippers
tsume-yásuri *n* 爪やすり nail file, emery board

tsume *v* 積め [IMPERATIVE] (pile it up!) → **tsumimásu** 積みます

tsume *v* 摘め [IMPERATIVE] (pluck it!) → **tsumimásu** 摘みます

tsúme *v* 積め → **tsumemásu** 積めます [INFINITIVE]

tsúme *v* 詰め → **tsumemásu** 詰めます **1.** [INFINITIVE] **2. tsumé ro** 詰めろ, **tsumé yo** 詰めよ [IMPERATIVE] (stuff it!)

tsumemásu, tsumeru *v* 積めます, 積める can pile it up; accumulates

tsumemásu, tsumeru *v* 摘めます, 摘める can gather/pluck it

tsumemásu, tsuméru *v* 詰めます, 詰める **1.** stuffs, crams **2.** cans

tsumenai *v* 積めない = **tsumemasén** 積めません (cannot pile it up)

tsumenai *v* 摘めない = **tsumemasén** 摘めません (cannot gather/pluck it)

tsumenai *v* 詰めない = **tsumemasén** 詰めません (not stuff/cram, not can it)

tsuménai *v* 積めない = **tsumemasén** 積めません (not accumulate)

tsumeraremásu, tsumerareru *v* 詰められます, 詰められる can stuff/can it

tsumeraremásu, tsumeraréru *v* 詰められます, 積められる can accumulate

tsumerarénai *v* 詰められない = **tsumerare-masén** 詰められません (cannot stuff)

tsumerárete *v* 詰められて → **tsumeraremásu** 詰められます

tsumeru *v* 積める = **tsumemásu** 積めます (can pile up; can gather/pluck it)

tsumeru *v* 摘める = **tsumemásu** 摘めます (can pile up; can gather/pluck it)

tsuméru *v* 詰める = **tsumemásu** 詰めます, etc. (stuffs, …)

tsumeta *v* 積めた = **tsumemáshita** 積めました; etc. (*could pile it up; …*)

tsúmeta *v* 詰めた = **tsumemáshita** 詰めました, etc. (stuffed, …)

tsumetai *adj* 冷たい cold (*to the touch*)

tsumete *v* 積めて → **tsumemásu** 積めます; etc.

tsúmete *v* 詰めて → **tsumemásu** 詰めます; etc.

tsumeyō´ *v* 詰めよう = **tsumemashō´** 詰めましょう (let's stuff it!)

tsumi *v* 積み → **tsumimásu** 積みます [INFINITIVE]

tsúmi *n* 罪 crime, sin, guilt, fault: "**Tsumi to Batsu**" 「罪と罰」 "Crime and Punishment"; **tsumi-bukai** 罪深い sinful

tsumi-(i)re *n* つみれ (つみいれ) fishballs (*for soup*)

tsumimásu, tsumu *v* 積みます, 積む piles it up, accumulates it; deposits; loads

tsumimásu, tsumu *v* 摘みます, 摘む gathers, plucks, clips, picks

tsumitate-kin *n* 積立金 reserve fund: = **tsumi-tate-chókin** 積立貯金 installment savings

tsumō´ *v* 積もう = **tsumi-mashō´** 積みましょう (let's pile it up!)

tsumō´ *v* 摘もう = **tsumi-mashō´** 摘みましょう (let's pluck it!)

…-tsumori …つもり intention, plan, (*what one has in*) mind, purpose, expectation: (**watashi wa) mada wakai-tsumori desu.** (私は)まだ若いつもりです I think I am still young.: **chikajika, nomikai o suru tsumoridesu.** 近々、飲み会をするつもりです We're/I'm having a drinking party soon.

…-tsumori (de)wa/ja... …つもり(で)は/じゃ [+ NEGATIVE verb] didn't/don't mean to, had/have no intention of: **kau-tsumori wa arimasendeshita** 買うつもりはありませんでした I didn't mean to buy: **kau-tsumori wa arimasen** 買うつもりはありません I have no intention of buying: **sumimasen, ki o warukusaseru-tsumori wa nakattandesu** すみません、気を悪くさせるつもりはなかったんです Sorry, I didn't mean to offend you.: **kare o kizutukeru-tsumori wa arimasendeshita** 彼を傷つけるつもりはありませんでした I didn't mean to hurt him.

tsumu *v* 積む = **tsumimásu** 積みます

tsumu *v* 摘む = **tsumimásu** 摘みます

tsumují-kaze *n* つむじ風・旋風 whirlwind

tsuná *n* 綱 rope, cord, cable (= **rōpu** ロープ) (→ **tanomi no tsuna** 頼みの綱, **tazuna** 手綱)

tsuna watari *n* 綱渡り walking a tightrope, balancing act
tsúna *n* ツナ tuna(fish) (*canned*)
tsuna-sándo *n* ツナサンド tuna-fish sandwich
tsunagari つながり・繋がり **1.** *n* connection, relation **2.** *v* → **tsunagarimásu** つながります [INFINITIVE]
tsunagarimásu, tsunagaru *v* つながります, つながる is connected, linked
tsunagatte *v* つながって → **tsunagaru** つながる; in a string (*line, chain*), in succession, in a row
tsunage *v* つなげ **1.** → **tsunagemásu** つなげます [INFINITIVE] **2.** [IMPERATIVE] link them! → **tsunagimásu** つなぎます
tsunagemásu, tsunageru *v* つなげます, つなげる can connect, link, tie
tsunagete *v* つなげて → **tsunagemásu** つなげます
tsunagi つなぎ **1.** *n* a link, a connection **2.** *v* → **tsunagimásu** つなぎます [INFINITIVE]
tsunagimásu, tsunagu *v* つなぎます, つなぐ connects, links, ties: **naisen ichi-ni-san ban ni o-tsunagi-shimásu** 内線 123 番におつなぎします I'll put you through to extension 123.
tsunaide *v* つないで → **tsunagimásu** つなぎます
tsunami *n* 津波 tsunami
tsunda *v* 積んだ = **tsumimáshita** 積みました (piled it up; …)
tsunde *v* 積んで → **tsumimásu** 積みます
tsunde *v* 摘んで → **tsumimásu** 摘みます
tsúne (no) *adj* 常(の) usual, ordinary
tsunerimásu, tsunéru *v* つねります, つねる pinches
tsunézune *n* つねづね・常々 all the time, usually (= **fudan** 普段, **itsumo** いつも)
tsunó *n* 角 horn (*of an animal*): **sai no tsunó** サイの角 rhinoceros horn
tsū-píisu *n* ツーピース a two-piece woman's suit
tsurá *n* 面・つら (*slipshod Japanese*) **1.** face (= **kao** 顔): [IDIOM] **tsurá no kawa ga atsui** 面の皮が厚い is thick-skinned, is brazenfaced **2.** surface, appearance (= **uwa(t)-tsura** 上(っ)面, **uwa-be** うわべ・上辺): **uwat-tsura dake de handan shimásu** 上っ面だけで判断します judges only by appearances
tsurai *adj* つらい・辛い painful, cruel, hard
tsuranai *v* 吊らない → **tsurimasén** 吊りません (not hang it)
tsuranai *v* 釣らない → **tsurimasén** 釣りません (not fish)
tsuranukimásu, tsuranuku *v* 貫きます, 貫く **1.** goes through, penetrates (= **kantsū shimásu**, 貫通します, **kantsū suru**, 貫通する): **dangan ga karada o tsuranukimashita** 弾丸が体を貫きました the bullet went through the body **2.** accomplishes: **shinnen o tsuranukimásu** 信念を貫きます has the courage of one's convictions
tsurara *n* ツララ・氷柱 icicle
tsure 連れ **1.** *n* **o-tsúre** お連れ company, companion **2.** *v* → **tsuremásu** 連れます [INFINITIVE]
tsure 吊れ **1.** *v* → **tsuremásu** 吊れます [INFINITIVE] **2.** [IMPERATIVE] (hang it!) → **tsurimásu** 吊ります
tsure *v* 釣れ **1.** → **tsuremásu** 釣れます [INFINITIVE] **2.** [IMPERATIVE] (fish!) → **tsurimásu** 釣ります
tsuréba *v* 吊れば = [INFORMAL] **tsurya** 吊りゃ (if one hangs) → **tsurimásu** 吊ります
tsuréba *v* 釣れば = [INFORMAL] **tsurya** 釣りゃ (if one fishes) → **tsurimásu** 釣ります
tsurimásu, tsureru *v* 連れます, 連れる brings along, is accompanied by (= brings/takes one along)
tsurimásu, tsureru *v* 吊れます, 吊れる can hang it
tsurimásu, tsureru *v* 釣れます, 釣れる can fish
tsurenai *v* 連れない = **tsuremasén** 連れません (not bring along)
tsurenai *v* 吊れない = **tsuremasén** 吊れません (cannot hang)
tsurenai *v* 釣れない = **tsuremasén** 釣れません (cannot fish)
tsurenái *adj* つれない coldhearted, cruel
tsureraremásu, tsurerareru *v* 連れられます, 連れられる **(… ni) tsureraremásu** (…に)連れられます gets brought along (by …)
tsureréba *v* 連れれば = [INFORMAL] **turerya** 連れりゃ (if one brings along) → **tsuremásu** 連れます
tsureréba *v* 吊れれば= [INFORMAL] **turerya** 吊れりゃ (if one can hang) → **tsuremásu** 吊れます
tsureréba *v* 釣れれば = [INFORMAL] **turerya** 釣れりゃ (if one can fish) → **tsuremásu** 釣れます
tsurete *v* 連れて → **tsuremásu** 連れます
tsurete *v* 吊れて → **tsuremásu** 吊れます
tsurete *v* 釣れて → **tsuremásu** 釣れます
tsureyō *v* 連れよう **1.** = **tsuremashō´** 連れましょう (let's bring him along!) **2.** = **o-tsureshimashō´** お連れしましょう (I'll take you along.)
tsuri *n* つり・釣り (**o-tsuri** おつり, **tsuri-sen** つり銭) (*small*) change
tsuri 釣り **1.** *n* fishing: **sakana-tsuri** 魚釣り fishing: **ippon-zuri** 一本釣り single hook fishing **2.** *v* → **tsurimásu** 釣ります [INFINITIVE]
tsuri-bari *n* 釣り針 fishhook
tsuri-dōgu *n* 釣り道具 fishing gear
tsuri-ito *n* 釣り糸 fishing line
tsuri-zao *n* 釣り竿 fishing rod
tsuri *n* つり・吊り hanging (things), hanging tool: **kubi-tsuri jisatsu** 首吊り自殺 suicide by hanging: **zubon-tsuri** ズボンつり［吊り］ suspender, galluses
tsuri-bashi *n* つり［吊り］橋 suspension bridge
tsuri-gane *n* つり［吊り］鐘 big bell (*temple, etc.*)
tsuri-kawa *n* つり［吊り］革 strap to hang on to (*electric train, bus, etc.*)
tsuriai *n* 釣(り)合い・つりあい balance, equilibrium, symmetry (= **baransu** バランス, **chōwa** 調和)

tsurimásu, tsuru v 吊ります, 吊る hangs it (*by a line*), suspends, strings up

tsurimásu, tsuru v 釣ります, 釣る fishes

tsurí ya/wa shinai v 吊りや/はしない = **tsuranai** 吊らない (not suspend it)

tsurí ya/wa shinai v 釣りや/はしない, [INFORMAL] **tsurya shinai** 釣りゃしない = **tsuranai** 釣らない (not fish)

tsū´ro n 通路 1. passage(way) (= **tōri-michi** 通り道) 2. aisle (= **rōka** 廊下) 3. thoroughfare

tsuru v 吊る = **tsurimásu** 吊ります (hangs it)

tsuru v 釣る = **tsurimásu** 釣ります (fishes)

tsurú n ツル・蔓 vine; carpices of a glass frame

tsurú n つる・弦 string (*of bow or violin*)

tsurú n つる・鉉 handle

tsúru n ツル・鶴 crane (*bird*)

tsurugí n 剣・つるぎ sword

tsurya v [INFORMAL] 吊りゃ → **tsuréba** 吊れば

tsurya v [INFORMAL] 釣りゃ → **tsuréba** 釣れば

tsūshin n 通信 1. correspondence: **tsūshin-kōza** 通信講座 correspondence course: **tsūshin-hanbai** 通信販売 mail order 2. report, news: **gakkyūtsūshin** 学級通信 class report/news 3. communications. **tsūshin-shudan** 通信手段 means of communication

tsutá n ツタ・蔦 ivy

tsutaé n 伝え (**o-tsutae** お伝え) → **dengon** 伝言, **messēji** メッセージ

tsutáe v 伝え → **tsutaemásu** 伝えます 1. [INFINITIVE] 2. **tsutae ro** 伝えろ, **tsutáe yo** 伝えよ [IMPERATIVE] (trasmit!)

tsutaemásu, tsutaeru v 伝えます, 伝える passes it on to someone else; reports, communicates; transmits; hands down

tsutaenai v 伝えない = **tsutaemasén** 伝えません (not transmit)

tsutaeraremásu, tsutaerareru v 伝えられます, 伝えられる can transmit it

tsutaerarenai v 伝えられない = **tsutaerare-masén** 伝えられません (cannot transmit it)

tsutaerarete v 伝えられて → **tsutaeraremásu** 伝えられます

tsutaeréba v 伝えれば = [INFORMAL] **tsutaerya** 伝えりゃ (if one transmits it) → **tsutaemásu** 伝えます

tsutaete v 伝えて → **tsutaemásu** 伝えます

tsutanai adj つたない・拙い halting, unskillful, poor (= **heta** 下手): **tsutanai Nihongo de sumimasén** つたない日本語ですみません [HUMBLE] Sorry for my poor Japanese.

tsutawaranai v 伝わらない = **tsutawarimasén** 伝わりません (not get transmitted)

tsutawáreba v 伝われば = [INFORMAL] **tsutawárya** 伝わりゃ (if it be transmitted) → **tsutawarimásu** 伝わります

tsutawari v 伝わり → **tsutawarimásu** 伝わります [INFINITIVE]

tsutawarimásu, tsutawaru v 伝わります, 伝わる is passed on; is reported, communicated; is transmitted; is handed down

tsutawatte v 伝わって → **tsutawarimásu** 伝わって

tsuto n つと・苞 straw wrapping, straw-wrapped package

tsuto adv つと [BOOKISH] quickly

tsutóme v 勤め → **tsutomemásu** 勤めます 1. [INFINITIVE] 2. **tsutomé ro** 勤めろ [IMPERATIVE] (work!)

tsutóme v 努め 1. → **tsutomemásu** 努めます [INFINITIVE] 2. **tsutomé ro** 努めろ [IMPERATIVE] (endeavor!)

tsutomé n 勤め (**o-tsutome** お勤め) [BOOKISH] work(ing), job (*post*)

tsutome-nin n 勤め人 office worker

tsutome-saki n 勤め先 place of employment, one's office

tsutomé n 務め (**o-tsutome** お務め) duty, role

tsutomemásu, tsutoméru v 勤めます, 勤める [BOOKISH] is employed, works; works as; **ginkō´-in o tsutomemásu** 銀行員を勤め[務め]ます works as a bank clerk

tsutomemásu, tsutoméru v 努めます, 努める [BOOKISH] exerts oneself, strives, endeavors

tsutómete v 勤めて → **tsutomemásu** 勤めます

tsutómete v 努めて → **tsutomemásu** 努めます

tsutomeyō´ v 努めよう = **tsutome-mashō´** 努めましょう (let's exert ourselves!)

tsutsu n 筒 cylinder, pipe (= **kuda** 管, **kan** 管)

…´tsútsu suffix …つつ [LITERARY] 1. = …-nágara …ながら (while doing) 2. … (shi)tsutsu arimásu …(し)つつあります is about to … (= …-te imásu …ています)

tsutsúji n ツツジ azalea

tsutsukimásu v つつきます → **tsu(t)tsukimásu** つ(っ)つきます

tsutsumánai v 包まない = **tsutsumi-masén** 包みません (not wrap it up)

tsutsúme v 包め 1. → **tsutsumemásu** 包めます [INFINITIVE] 2. [IMPERATIVE] (wrap it up!) → **tsutsumimásu** 包みます

tsutsúmeba v 包めば (if one wraps it up) → **tsutsumimásu** 包みます

tsutsumemásu, tsutsuméru v 包めます, 包める can wrap it up

tsutsuménai v 包めない = **tsutsumemasén** 包めません (cannot wrap it up)

tsutsuméreba v 包めれば (if one can wrap it up) → **tsutsumemásu** 包めます

tsutsúmete v 包めて → **tsutsumemásu** 包めます

tsutsumí n 包み package, bundle: **tsutsumi-gami** 包み紙 package paper (= **hōsō-shi** 包装紙)

tsutsumí n 堤 1. dike, bank, embankment (= **dote** 土手, **teibō** 堤防) 2. reservoir (= **chosui-chi** 貯水池)

tsutsumí n 包み → **tsutsumimásu** 包みます [INFINITIVE]

tsutsumimásu, tsutsúmu v 包みます, 包む wraps it up

tsutsúmi ya/wa shinai ν 包みや/はしない
= **tsutsumánai** 包まない (not wrap it up)

tsutsumō´ ν 包もう = **tsutsumimashō´** 包みましょう (let's wrap it up!)

tsutsúnde ν 包んで → **tsutsumimásu** 包みます

tsutsushími n 慎み prudence, discretion

tsutsushími ν 慎み → **tsutsushimimásu** 慎みます [INFINITIVE]

tsutsushími ν 謹み → **tsutsushimimásu** 謹みます [INFINITIVE]

tsutsushimimásu, tsutsushimu ν 慎みます, 慎む is discreet, is careful; refrains from: **kotoba o tsutsushimimásu** 言葉を慎みます is careful about how one speaks and behaves

tsutsushimimásu, tsutsushimu ν 謹みます, 謹む is humble, is reverent: **tsutsushinde go-meifuku o oinoriitashimásu** 謹んでご冥福をお祈りいたします I offer my deepest condolences

tsutsushínde ν 慎んで → **tsutsushimimásu** 慎みます

tsutsushínde ν 謹んで → **tsutsushimimásu** 謹みます

tsutte ν 吊って → **tsurimásu** 吊ります

tsutte ν 釣って → **tsurimásu** 釣ります

tsu(t)tsúite ν つ(っ)ついて = **tsu(t)tsukimásu** つ(っ)つきます [INFORMAL]

tsu(t)tsukimásu, tsu(t)tsúku ν つ(っ)つきます, つ(っ)つく pecks at [INFORMAL]

tsuya n ツヤ・艶 gloss, shine, luster (= **gurosu** グロス, **kōtaku** 光沢)

tsuya-keshi n ツヤ[艶]消し matte

tsuya n 通夜 (**o-tsuya** お通夜) lyke-wake

tsū´yaku n 通訳 interpreter; interpreting: **tsūyaku-sha** 通訳者 an interpreter: **~ shimásu** 通訳します interprets

tsuyo-bi n 強火 high flame

tsūyō shimásu (suru) ν 通用します(する) 1. is used commonly 2. is accepted among people, is valid: **sekai dewa tsūyō shimásén** 世界では通用しません is not accepted in the world

tsuyói adj 強い strong; **tsúyosa** 強さ strength

tsuyu n つゆ・梅雨 rainy season (in Japan)

tsúyu n 露 dew

tsúyu n つゆ・汁 (**o-tsúyu** おつゆ) light (clear) soup

tsuzuite ν 続いて → **tsuzukimásu** 続きます

tsuzukanai ν 続かない = **tsuzukimasén** 続きませ

ん (it does/will not continue)

tsuzuke ν 続け → **tsuzukemásu** 続けます [INFINITIVE]

tsuzukemásu, tsuzukeru ν 続けます, 続ける continues it, goes on (with it)

tsuzukenai ν 続けない = **tsuzukemasén** 続けません (does not continue it)

tsuzukerarenai ν 続けられない = **tsuzukeraremasén** 続けられません (cannot continue it)

tsuzukerarete ν 続けられて → **tsuzukeraremásu** 続けられます

tsuzukete 続けて 1. adv continuously, in succession, going on (to the next) 2. → **tsuzukemásu** 続けます

tsuzukeyō ν 続けよう = **tsuzukemashō´** 続けましょう (let's continue!)

tsuzuki n 続き continuation, sequel, series

tsuzukimásu, tsuzuku ν 続きます, 続く it continues (will continue); adjoins

tsuzuku n 続く To Be Continued

tsuzumarimásu, tsuzumáru ν つづまります, つづまる [BOOKISH] it shrinks, gets shortened (= **chijimarimásu**, 縮まります, **chijimaru** 縮まる)

tsuzumí n 鼓・つづみ drum (hourglass-shaped)

tsuzuranai ν 綴らない = **tsuzurimasén** 綴りません (not spell/… it)

tsuzure n 綴れ 1. rags 2. hand-woven brocade

tsuzúre ν 綴れ 1. → **tsuzuremásu** 綴れます [INFINITIVE] 2. [IMPERATIVE] (spell/… it!) → **tsuzurimásu** 綴ります

tsuzuremásu, tsuzureru ν 綴れます, 綴れる can spell; can compose; can patch, bind, sew (together)

tsuzurenai ν 綴れない = **tsuzuremasén** 綴れません (cannot spell/… it)

tsuzuri n 綴り・つづり 1. spelling (= **superu** スペル) 2. binding, bound (sewn) pages

tsuzuri ν 綴り → **tsuzurimásu** 綴ります

tsuzurimásu, tsuzuru ν 綴ります, 綴る 1. spells 2. composes, writes 3. patches; binds; sews (together/up)

tsuzurō´ ν 綴ろう = **tsuzurimashō´** 綴りましょう (let's spell/compose/bind it!)

tsuzutte ν 綴って → **tsuzurimásu** 綴ります

tu… → **tsu…**

ty… → **ch…**

U

u *n* ウ・鵜 cormorant (*fishing bird*)
u-kai *n* 鵜飼い cormorant fishing
u no me taka no me *v* 鵜の目鷹の目 [IDIOM] keeps one's eyes peeled
u-nomi ni suru *v* 鵜呑みにする [IDIOM] swallows (*someone's words, talk, etc.*), believes every word someone says

uba *n* 乳母 nanny (*who cares for baby/babies in a household*)
uba-guruma *n* 乳母車 baby carriage (= bebii-kā ベビーカー)

ubaimásu, ubáu *v* 奪います, 奪う seizes, robs, plunders
ubátte *v* 奪って → **ubaimásu** 奪います
ubawánai *v* 奪わない = ubaimasén 奪いません (not seize)
úcha *v* [INFORMAL] 打ちゃ → **úteba** 打てば
úchi *v* 打ち → **uchimásu** 打ちます [INFINITIVE]
uchi *n* うち・家 1. o-uchi おうち[お家] house, home; family: uchi no náka de/ni うち[家]の中 で/に indoors 2. ... uchí, ... uchi (no) うち (の) [INFORMAL] we/us; I/me; our, my: uchi no kazoku うちの家族 my family
uchi *n* 内: ... no uchí (de) ... の内(で) inside; among
uchi *n* うち: ...-(shi)nai uchí ni ... (し)ないうち に before it happens (*while it has not yet happened*)
uchi-... *prefix* 内... inside, inner
uchi-benkei *n* 内弁慶 [IDIOM] a lion at home and a mouse abroad
uchi-bori *n* 内堀 inner moat
uchi-gawa *n* 内側 the inside
uchi-ki (na) *adj* 内気(な) shy (= shai (na) シャイ (な)) [IN POSITIVE SENSE]: uchiki na seikaku 内気 な性格 shy disposition
Uchi-mṓko, Uchi-mongoru (jichi-ku) *n* 内蒙 古, 内モンゴル（自治区) Inner Mongolia (= Nai mṓko, Nai-mongoru (jichi-ku) 内蒙古, 内モンゴ ル（自治区))
uchi-wa *n* 内輪 1. the family circle; the inside: uchiwa (no) 内輪(の) private: uchiwa no hanashi 内輪の話 private matter, family affair 2. uchiwa (na) 内輪(な) moderate, modest, conservative
uchi-wake *n* 内訳 breakdown, particulars, details (= meisai 明細): shishutsu no uchiwake 支出の内 訳 breakdown of expenditures
uchi-age *n* 打ち上げ 1. launch (*rocket*) 2. close (*performance, project, etc.*)
uchi-akemásu, uchi-akeru *v* 打ち明けます, 打 ち明ける confesses, frankly reveals, confides
uchi-awase *n* 打ち合わせ・打合せ consultation, meeting (*in the office, etc. by appointment*) (= kaigi 会議, miitingu ミーティング)
uchi-awasemásu, uchi-awaséru *v* 打ち合わせ ます, 打ち合わせる hold a meeting/consultation
uchi-keshi *n* 打ち消し denial; negation, negative

uchi-keshimásu, uchi-kesu *v* 打ち消します, 打 ち消す denies (*a rumor, etc.*), takes back a remark
uchi-koroshimásu, uchi-korósu *v* 撃ち殺しま す, 撃ち殺す shoots to death
uchimásu, útsu *v* 打ちます, 打つ hits, strikes, hammers; sends a telegram
uchí-mí *n* 打ち身 bruise
uchimásu, útsu *v* 撃ちます, 撃つ fires, shoots (*a gun*)
uchiwa *n* うちわ・団扇 (*Japanese*) a flat fan
úchi ya/wa shinai *v* 打ちや/はしない, [INFORMAL] úcha shinai 打ちゃしない = utánai 打たない (not hit)
uchōten *n* 有頂天 rapturous delight, going into raptures, being beside oneself with joy, being in seventh heaven, being carried away, being overjoyed: uchōten ni narimásu 有頂天になります goes into raptures
úchū *n* 宇宙 universe, (*outer*) space
uchū-fuku *n* 宇宙服 spacesuit
uchū hikō-shi *n* 宇宙飛行士 astronaut
uchū-sen *n* 宇宙船 spaceship
udé *n* 腕 1. arm 2. special skill
ude-dókei *n* 腕時計 wristwatch
ude-gumi *n* 腕組み folding one's arms; ~ shimásu 腕組みします folds one's arms
ude-jiman (no) *adj* 腕自慢(の) proud of one's skill
ude-kiki (no) *adj* 腕利き(の) skilled, competent, able
ude-maé *n* 腕前 prowess, skill, ability
ude-wa *n* 腕輪 bracelet (= buresuretto ブレスレ ット)
ude-zuku (de) *adv* 腕ずく(で) forcibly
údo *n* ウド・独活 Japanese celery
udon *n* うどん (o-údon おうどん) Japanese wheat-flour noodles: udon-ya うどん屋 Japanese noodle shop
U-doshi *n* 卯年 year of the Rabbit
ue *n* 上 1. ...ué ...上 above, upper part, surface, top: ... no ue (de/ni/no) ...の上(で/に/の) on, on top of 2. ué 上 (= toshi-ue 年上) older, oldest
ue *v* 植え → **uemásu** 植えます [INFINITIVE]
ue *v* 飢え 1. hanger, starvation 2. → **uemásu** 飢えます [INFINITIVE]
uédingu-... *prefix* ウエディング... wedding
uédingu-doresu *n* ウエディングドレス wedding dress (= hanayome-ishō 花嫁衣裳)
uédingu-kēki *n* ウエディングケーキ wedding cake
uédingu-pātii *n* ウエディングパーティ wedding party (= kekkon-shukuga-kai 結婚祝賀会, kekkon-hirōen 結婚披露宴)
uédingu-ringu *n* ウエディングリング wedding ring (= kekkon-yubiwa 結婚指輪)
uehāsu *n* ウエハース wafer
ueki *n* 植木 garden/potted plant

uekí-bachi *n* 植木鉢 flowerpot

ueki-ya *n* 植木屋 gardener

uemásu, ueru *v* 植えます, 植える plants, grows plant

uemásu, uéru *v* 飢えます, 飢える starves (*hungers*)

uenai *v* 植えない = **uemasén** 植えません (not plant)

uénai *v* 飢えない = **uemasén** 飢えません (not starve)

Ueno *n* 上野 Ueno; **Uenó-Eki** 上野駅 Ueno Station; **Ueno-Kṓen** 上野公園 Ueno Park

uerare *v* 植えられ → **ueraremásu** 植えられます [INFINITIVE]

ueraremásu, uerareru *v* 植えられます, 植えられる can plant

ueréba *v* 植えれば (if one plants) → **uemásu** 植えます

uéreba *v* 飢えれば (if one starves) → **uemásu** 飢えます

uérudan *n* ウエルダン well-done (beef)

uésuto *n* ウエスト waist (= **koshi** 腰); **uesuto-pōchi** ウエストポーチ belt bag

ueta *v* 植えた = **uemáshita** 植えました (planted)

úeta *v* 飢えた = **uemáshita** 飢えました (starved)

uḗtā *n* ウエーター waiter

uete *v* 植えて → **uemásu** 植えます

úete *v* 飢えて → **uemásu** 飢えます

uḗtoresu *n* ウエートレス waitress

ueyō *v* 植えよう = **uemashō´** 植えましょう (let's plant it!)

ugai *n* うがい a gargle

ugai (o) shimásu (suru) *v* うがい(を)します(する) gargles

ugóita *v* 動いた = **ugokimáshita** 動きました (one/it moved)

ugóite *v* 動いて → **ugokimásu** 動きます

ugokánai *v* 動かない = **ugokimasén** 動きません (not move)

ugokasánai *v* 動かさない = **ugokashimasén** 動かしません (not move it)

ugokáse *v* 動かせ **1.** → **ugokasemásu** 動かせます [INFINITIVE] **2.** [IMPERATIVE] (move it!) → **ugokashimásu** 動かします

ugokasemásu, ugokaséru *v* 動かせます, 動かせる can move it

ugokasénai *v* 動かせない = **ugokasemasén** 動かせません (cannot move it)

ugokásete *v* 動かせて → **ugokase-másu** 動かせます

ugokashimásu, ugokásu *v* 動かします, 動かす moves it

ugokáshite *v* 動かして → **ugokashimásu** 動かします

ugóke *v* 動け **1.** → **ugokemásu** 動けます [INFINITIVE] **2.** [IMPERATIVE] (move!) → **ugokimásu** 動きます

ugokemásu, ugokéru *v* 動けます, 動ける one/it can move

ugokénai *v* 動けない = **ugokemasén** 動けません (cannot move)

ugókete *v* 動けて → **ugokemásu** 動けます

ugoki *n* 動き movement, motion; trend

ugóki *v* 動き → **ugokimásu** 動きます [INFINITIVE]

ugokimásu, ugóku *v* 動きます, 動く one/it moves

ugúisu *n* ウグイス・鶯 bush warbler

uindo-burē´kā *n* ウインドブレーカー windbreaker

uindō shoppingu *n* ウィンドウショッピング window shopping

uinkā *n* ウインカー car turn signal

uínku *n* ウインク wink(ing) (= **wínku** ウインク, **mekubase** 目配せ): ~ **shimásu** ウインクします winks

uirusu *n* ウイルス virus; **uirusu-taisaku-sofuto** ウイルス対策ソフト antivirus software (= **anchi uirusu sofuto (-uwea)** アンチウイルスソフト (ウェア))

uísúkíi *n* ウイスキー, **wísukii** ウイスキー whisky

uita *v* 浮いた = **ukimáshita** 浮きました (floated)

uite *v* 浮いて → **ukimásu** 浮きます

úji *n* 氏 clan, family; family name (= **sei** 姓)

uji-gami *n* 氏神 tutelary deity (*guardian spirit*)

uji (mushi) *n* ウジ(ムシ)・蛆(虫) maggot

ukabanai *v* 浮かばない = **ukabimasén** 浮かびません (not float)

ukabasemásu, ukabaseru *v* 浮かばせます, 浮かばせる lets float it

ukabe *v* 浮かべ **1.** → **ukabemásu** 浮かべます [INFINITIVE] **2. ukabe ro** 浮かべろ, **ukabé yo** 浮かべよ [IMPERATIVE] (float it!) **3.** [IMPERATIVE] (float!) → **ukabimásu** 浮かびます

ukabéba *v* 浮かべば (if it floats) → **ukabimásu** 浮かびます

ukabemásu, ukaberu *v* 浮かべます, 浮かべる lets/makes it float, floats it; shows (*a look*); brings to mind

ukabenai *v* 浮かべない = **ukabemasén** 浮かべません (not float it)

ukaberéba *v* 浮かべれば (if one floats it) → **ukabemásu** 浮かべます

ukabete *v* 浮かべて → **ukabemásu** 浮かべます

ukabimásu, ukabu *v* 浮かびます, 浮かぶ floats

ukagae *v* 伺え → **ukagaemásu** 伺えます [INFINITIVE] → **ukagaimásu** 伺います

ukagae *v* 窺え → **ukagaemásu** 窺えます [INFINITIVE] → **ukagaimásu** 窺います

ukagaemásu, ukagaeru *v* 伺えます, 伺える can visit; can inquire

ukagaemásu, ukagaeru *v* 窺えます, 窺える can watch for

ukagaenai *v* 伺えない = **ukagaemasén** 伺えません (cannot visit/inquire)

ukagaenai *v* 窺えない = **ukagaemasén** 窺えません (cannot watch for)

ukagaete *v* 伺えて → **ukagaemásu** 伺えます

ukagaete *v* 窺えて → **ukagaemásu** 窺えます

ukagai *n* 伺い (**o-ukagai** お伺い) visit; inquiry, consultation

ukagai *n* 伺い → **ukagaimásu** 伺います [INFINITIVE]

ukagai *n* 窺い → **ukagaimásu** 窺います [INFINITIVE]

ukagaimásu, ukagau *v* 伺います, 伺う [HUMBLE] I visit (*you*); I inquire; I hear

ukagaimásu, ukagau *v* 窺います, 窺う keeps a watchful eye on (*the situation*); (**ki̱kái/chansu o ukagaimásu** 機会/チャンスを窺います) watches for (*an opportunity*)

ukagatte *v* 伺って → **ukagaimásu** 伺います

ukagatte *v* 窺って → **ukagaimásu** 窺います

ukagawanai *v* 伺わない = **ukagaimasén** 伺いません (not visit/inquire)

ukagawanai *v* 窺わない = **ukagaimasén** 窺いません (not watch for)

ukai *n* 迂回・う回 detour: **~ shimásu** 迂回します detours

ukanai *v* 浮かない = **ukimasén** 浮きません (not float)

ukande *v* 浮かんで → **ukabimásu** 浮かびます

ukárimásu, ukáru *v* 受かります, 受かる passes, succeeds

ukatsu *n* うかつ・迂闊 carelessness, inattentiveness, thoughtlessness: **ukatsu ni mo** うかつ[迂闊]にも carelessly, inattentively, thoughtlessly

uke *v* 浮け **1.** → **ukemásu** 浮けます [INFINITIVE] **2.** [IMPERATIVE] (float!) → **ukimásu** 浮きます

úke *v* 受け **1.** → **ukemásu** 受けます [INFINITIVE] **2. uké ro** 受けろ, **uké yo** 受けよ [IMPERATIVE] (*accept it!*)

ukéba *v* 浮けば (if one floats) → **ukimásu** 浮きます

uke-iremásu, uké-ireru *v* 受け入れます, 受け入れる accepts

ukemásu, ukeru *v* 浮けます, 浮ける can float

ukemásu, ukéru *v* 受けます, 受ける accepts; receives; takes; gets; suffers, incurs

ukemi *n* 受身 **1.** passive voice (= **judō-tai** 受動態) **2.** passive (*attitude*)

uke-mochimásu, uke-mótsu *v* 受け持ちます, 受け持つ takes/accepts/has charge of

ukenai *v* 浮けない = **ukemasén** 浮けません (cannot float)

ukénai *v* 受けない = **ukemasén** 受けません (not accept)

uke-óe *v* 請け負え **1.** → **uke-oemásu** 請け負えます [INFINITIVE] **2.** [IMPERATIVE] (contract to do it!) → **uke-oimásu** 請け負います

uke-óeba *v* 請け負えば (if one contracts to do it) → **uke-oimásu** 請け負います

uke-oemásu, uke-oéru *v* 請け負えます, 請け負える can contract to do it

uke-oénai *v* 請け負えない = **uke-oemasen** 請け負えません (cannot contract to do it)

uke-óereba *v* 請け負えれば (if one can contract to do it) → **uke-oemásu** 請け負えます

uke-óete *v* 請け負えて → **uke-oemásu** 請け負えます

uke-oi *n* 請負・請け負い a contract (*to undertake work*)

ukeoi-gyōsha *n* 請(け)負(い)業者 a contractor

ukeoi-shigoto *n* 請(け)負(い)仕事 contract work

uke-ói *v* 請け負い → **uke-oimásu** 請け負います [INFINITIVE]

uke-oimásu, uke-óu *v* 請け負います, 請け負う contracts (*to undertake work*)

ukeoi-nin *n* 請負人 contractor

uke-oō´ *v* 請け負おう = **uke-oimashō´** 請け負いましょう (let's contract to do it!)

uke-ótte *v* 請け負って → **uke-oimásu** 請け負います

uke-owánai *v* 請け負わない = **uke-oimasén** 請け負いません (not contract to do it)

ukeraremásu, ukeraréru *v* 受けられます, 受けられる can accept; can receive; …

ukerárénai *v* 受けられない = **ukerare-masén** 受けられません (cannot accept)

ukerárete *v* 受けられて → **ukeraremásu** 受けられます

ukeréba *v* 浮ければ = [INFORMAL] **ukerya** 浮けりゃ (if one can float) → **ukemásu** 浮けます

ukéreba *v* 受ければ = [INFORMAL] **ukerya** 受けりゃ (if one accepts) → **ukemásu** 受けます

ukeru *v* 浮ける = **ukemásu** 浮けます (can float)

ukéru *v* 受ける = **ukemásu** 受けます (accepts)

uketamawarimásu, uketamawáru *v* 承ります, 承る I (*humbly*) hear/listen/consent

ukete *v* 浮けて → **ukemásu** 浮けます

úkete *v* 受けて → **ukemásu** 受けます

uke-toranai *v* 受け取らない = **uke-torimásen** 受け取りません (not accept)

uke-tóre *v* 受け取れ **1.** → **uketore-másu** 受け取れます [INFINITIVE] **2.** [IMPERATIVE] (receives it!) → **uke-torimásu** 受け取ります

uke-toréba *v* 受け取れば (if one accepts) → **uke-torimásu** 受け取ります

uke-toremásu, uke-toréru *v* 受け取れます, 受け取れる can accept/take

uke-torénai *v* 受け取れない = **uke-toremasén** 受け取れません (cannot accept)

uke-toréréba *v* 受け取れれば (if one can accept) → **uke-toremásu** 受け取れます

uke-tori *n* 受け取り・受取 receipt

uke-tori *v* 受け取り → **uke-torimásu** 受け取ります [INFINITIVE]

uke-torimásu, uke-toru *v* 受け取ります, 受け取る accepts, receives, takes; takes it (= understand it)

uke-torō´ *v* 受け取ろう = **uke-torimashō´** 受け取りましょう (let's accept it!)

uke-tótte *v* 受け取って → **uke-torimásu** 受け取ります

uketsugimásu, uketsugu *v* 受け継ぎます, 受け継ぐ succeeds to

uke-tsu̱ke *n* 受付 acceptance; information desk; receptionist

uke-tsu̱kemásu, uke-tsu̱kéru *v* 受け付けます, 受け付ける accepts, receives

uke-uri n 受け売り borrowing someone else's ideas
uké ya/wa shinai v 浮けや/はしない = **ukenai** 浮けない (cannot float)
úke ya/wa shinai v 受けや/はしない = **ukénai** 受けない (not accept)
ukeyō´ v 受けよう = **ukemashō´** 受けましょう (let's accept it!)
uké-zara n 受け皿 saucer (for cup)
uki n 雨季・雨期 rainy season
ukiashi dachimásu (dátsu) v 浮き足立ちます (立つ) is wavering, is ready to run away (= **nige-goshi ni narimásu (náru)** 逃げ腰になります (なる))
uki-bori n 浮き彫り relief (*sculpture consisting of shapes carved on a surface*) (= **reriifu** レリーフ): **shinjutsu o ukibori ni shimásu** 真実を浮き彫りにします call attention to the fact that ...
ukimásu, uku v 浮きます, 浮く floats
ukiwa n 浮き輪 inner tube (*swimming*)
ukí ya/wa shinai v 浮きや/はしない = **ukanai** 浮かない (not float)
ukiyo n 浮世 [BOOKISH] this fleeting world, transient world
　ukiyo-banare n 浮世離れ unworldliness
　ukiyo-e n 浮世絵 Japanese woodblock prints
ukkári adv うっかり absentmindedly (= **tsui** つい)
ukō´ v 浮こう = **ukimashō** 浮きましょう (let's float!)
ukya v [INFORMAL] 浮きゃ → **ukéba** 浮けば
umá n ウマ・馬 horse
　umá no mimi ni nenbutsu n ウマ[馬]の耳に念仏 [IDIOM] in one ear and out the other
Uma-doshi n 午年 year of the Horse
uma ga aimásu (au) v ウマ[馬]が合います(合う) gets on well, gets along well
umái adj うまい・旨い・美味い (*commonly male*) tasty, delicious (= **oishii** 美味しい)
umái adj うまい・上手い 1. skillful, good (= **jōzu** 上手) 2. successful, profitable
úmaku adv うまく・旨く・美味く so as to be tasty
úmaku adv うまく・上手く 1. skillfully 2. successfully
umanai v 産まない = **umimasén** 産みません (not bear)
umánai v 膿まない = **umimasén** 膿みません (not fester)
ūman ribu n ウーマンリブ women's liberation
umare n 生まれ・産まれ 1. n birth 2. v → **umaremásu** 生まれます・産まれます [INFINITIVE]
umaremásu, umareru v 生まれ[産まれ]ます, 生まれ[産まれ]る is born
umarimásu, umaru v 埋まります, 埋まる gets buried (= **uzumarimásu** うずまり[埋まり]ます)
ume n ウメ・梅 Japanese apricot ("plum")
　ume-boshi n 梅干し pickled plum/apricot
　ume-shu n 梅酒 apricot wine
ume n 埋め → **umemásu** 埋めます [INFINITIVE]
ume n 産め → **umemásu** 産めます [INFINITIVE]

ume n 産め [IMPERATIVE] (bear!) → **umimásu** 産みます
uméba v 産めば = [INFORMAL] **umya** 産みゃ (if one bears) → **umimásu** 産みます
úmeba v 膿めば (if it festers) → umimásu 膿みます
umeite v うめいて・呻いて → **umekimásu** うめきます・呻きます
umekí n うめき・呻き a groan
umekimásu, uméku v うめきます・呻きます, うめく・呻く groans
umemásu, umeru v 埋めます, 埋める buries (= **uzumemásu** うずめます・埋めます)
umemásu, umeru v 生め[産め]ます, 生め[産め]る can give birth to, can bear (*a baby*)
umenai v 埋めない = **umemasén** 埋めません (not bury)
umenai v 生め[産め]ない = **umemasén** 生め[産め]ません (cannot bear)
umereba v 埋めれば = [INFORMAL] **umerya** 埋めりゃ (if one buries) → **umemásu** 埋めます
umereba v 生め[産め]れば = [INFORMAL] **umerya** 生め[産め]りゃ (if one can bear) → **umemásu** 生め[産め]ます
umete v 埋めて → **umemásu** 埋めます
umete v 生め[産め]て → **umemásu** 生め[産め]ます
umeyō v 埋めよう = **umemashō** 埋めましょう (let's bury it!)
umi n 生み・産み 1. birth: umi (no) 生み・産み (の) (*by giving*) birth, natal 2. → **umimásu** 生みます・産みます [INFINITIVE]
umí n うみ・膿 pus
úmi n 海 sea
　umibe n 海辺 (sea-) shore, seaside
　umi ni sen-nen yama ni sen-nen 海に千年山に千年 1. knowing every trick in the book 2. a sly old fox (= **umi-sen yama-sen** 海千山千)
　umi no hi n 海の日 Marine day, Ocean Day (*3rd Monday of July*)
úmi v 膿み → **umimásu** 膿みます [INFINITIVE]
umimásu, umu v 生みます・産みます, 生む・産む gives birth to, bears
umimásu, úmu v 膿みます, 膿む festers
umí ya/wa shimasén v 生み[産み]や/はしません = **umimasén** 生みません・産みません (not bear)
úmi ya/wa shimasén v 膿みや/はしません = **umimasén** 膿みません (not fester)
umō n 羽毛 feather
umō´ v 生もう・産もう = **umimashō´** 生み[産み]ましょう (let's give birth!)
umu v 生む・産む = **umimásu** 生みます・産みます (gives birth)
úmu n 有無 existence (*or non-existence*): **úmu o iwasazu** 有無を言わさず forcibly (= **muriyari** 無理やり)
úmu v 膿む = **umimásu** 膿みます (festers)
umya v [INFORMAL] 生みゃ・産みゃ → **uméba** 生めば・産めば

úmya *v* [INFORMAL] うみゃ・膿みゃ → **úmeba** うめば・膿めば

ún *n* 運 fate, luck (→ **fu-un (na)** 不運(な), **kōun** 幸運)

ún ga íi *adj* 運がいい lucky

ún ga warui *adj* 運が悪い unlucky (= **fu-un** 不運, **tsuiteinai** ついて(い)ない・ツイて(い)ない)

ún-mei *n* 運命 destiny, fate (= **shukumei** 宿命): **únmei no itazura** 運命のいたずら[悪戯] quirk of fate: **únmei no akai-ito** 運命の赤い糸 red string of fate, red thread of destiny

ún-waruku *adv* 運悪く unluckily

ún-yoku *adv* 運良く luckily (= **saiwai** 幸い)

ún *interj* うん = **n ん** [INFORMAL] yeah, yes

unagashimásu, unagásu *v* 促します, 促す stimulates, urges (*on*)

unagi *n* ウナギ・鰻 eel

una-don *n* うな丼 a bowl of rice topped with broiled eel

uná-jū *n* うな重 broiled eel on rice in a lacquered box

unagi nobori *n* うなぎ登り[上り]・鰻登り[上り] rising rapidly and steadily (*prices, etc.*)

unarí *n* 唸り・うなり a roar; a growl; (= **umekí** うめき・呻き) a groan

unarimásu, unáru *v* 唸ります, 唸る roars; growls; (= **umekimásu** うめきます・呻きます) groans

unazukimásu *v* うなずきます・頷きます, **unazuku** うなずく・頷く nods

únchin *n* 運賃 fare (*transportation*)

unda *v* 生んだ・産んだ = **umimáshita** 生み[産み]ました (gave birth)

únda *v* 膿んだ = **umimáshita** 膿みました (festered)

unde *v* 生んで・産んで → **umimásu** 生みます・産みます

únde *v* 膿んで → **umimásu** 膿みます

undei no sa *n* 雲泥の差 [IDIOM] great difference (= **taisa** 大差)

undō *n* 運動 **1.** movement: **shakai-undō** 社会運動 social movement: **senkyo-undō** 選挙運動 election campaign **2.** exercise; sports; athletics: **undō-jō** 運動場 athletic field, playground; **undō-senshu** 運動選手 athlete

únga *n* 運河 canal

úni *n* ウニ・雲丹 sea urchin (*roe*)

unpan *n* 運搬 transport(-ation) (*of goods and/or people*): ~ **shimásu** 運搬します transports

unsō *n* 運送 transport(-ation) (*of goods*) (= **unpan** 運搬): ~ **shimásu** 運送します transports

unsō-gyō-sha 運送業者 *n* transportation company

unsō-ya *n* 運送屋 express/forwarding agent; (*house*) mover (= **hikkoshi-ya** 引っ越し屋)

unten *n* 運転 operation, operating, running, working, driving: ~ **shimásu** 運転します operates (*a vehicle*), drives

untén-menkyo (-shō) *n* 運転免許(証) driver's license

untén-shu *n* 運転手 driver (= **doraibā** ドライバー)

unto *adv* うんと much, a good deal, greatly

unubore ga tsuyói *adj* うぬぼれが強い vain, conceited

"un-un" *interj* うんうん = **n´n** んん

unyu *n* 運輸 transport(ation) (*of goods*) (= **unsō** 運送): ~ **shimásu** 運輸します transports

unzári shimásu (suru) *v* うんざりします(する) gets bored, gets sick and tired

uo *n* ウオ・魚 fish (= **sakana** サカナ・魚)

uo no me *n* うおのめ・魚の目 foot corn

uppun *n* うっぷん・鬱憤 frustration, pent-up anger, pent up discontent. **uppun o harashimásu** うっぷんを晴らします vents one's anger

urá *n* 裏 reverse (*side*), back; lining; what's behind it; the alley

urá *n* 裏 sole (*of foot*): **ashi no urá** 足の裏 sole of foot

ura-dō´ri *n* 裏通り back street, alley

ura-gáeshi (no) *adj* 裏返し(の) inside-out

ura-gáeshimásu, ura-gáesu *v* 裏返します, 裏返す turns over; turns inside out

ura-guchi *n* 裏口 back door: **ura-guchi-nyūgaku** 裏口入学 buying one's way into a school

ura-ji *n* 裏地 lining (*material*)

ura-kata *n* 裏方 sceneshifter

ura-me ni demásu *v* 裏目に出ます, **ura-me ni deru** 裏目に出る backfires, turns out badly

ura-mon *n* 裏門 back gate

ura-omote no aru hito *n* 裏表のある人 two-faced person

urá *n* 浦 bay (= **irie** 入り江)

urabon *n* うら[盂蘭]盆 the Bon Festival (= **o-bón** お盆)

ura-girí *n* 裏切り a double-cross, betrayal, treachery

ura-girimásu, ura-gíru *v* 裏切ります, 裏切る betrays, double crosses

uramí *n* 恨み grudge, resentment, ill will, enmity **urami o kaimásu (kau)** *v* 恨みを買います (買う) incurs someone's enmity

uramimásu, urámu *v* 恨みます, 恨む begrudges, resents

uranai *v* 売らない = **urimasén** 売りません (not sell)

uranái *n* 占い fortune-telling; **uranái-shi** 占い師 fortune-teller

urayamashíi *adj* 羨ましい・うらやましい enviable; envious

urayamimásu, urayámu *v* 羨みます・うらやみます, 羨む・うらやむ envies

ure *v* 売れ **1.** → **uremásu** 売れます [INFINITIVE] **2.** [IMPERATIVE] (sell it!) → **urimásu** 売ります

uréba *v* 売れば = [INFORMAL] **urya** 売りゃ (if one sells) → **urimásu** 売ります

ure-kuchi *n* 売れ口 sales outlet

uremásu, ureru *v* 売れます, 売れる **1.** it sells, is in demand; thrives; is popular **2.** Can sell

urenai *v* 売れない = **uremasén** 売れません (not sell; cannot sell)

ureréba v 売れれば, [INFORMAL] **urerya** 売れりゃ (if it sells; if one can sell) → **uremásu** 売れます

ureshíi adj うれしい・嬉しい glad, delightful, pleasant, wonderful, happy

urete v 売れて → **uremásu** 売れます

uré ya/wa shinai v 売れや/しない = **urenai** 売れない (it doesn't sell; one cannot sell)

úri n ウリ・瓜 fruit of the gourd family, *Cucurbitaceae*, melon (*cucumbers* (= **kyūri** キュウリ[胡瓜]), watermelons (= **suika** スイカ[西瓜]), pumpkin (= **kabocha** カボチャ[南瓜]), loofah (= **hechima** ヘチマ[糸瓜]), wax gourd (= **tōgan** トウガン[冬瓜]), *etc.*)

úri futatsu n ウリ[瓜]二つ like two peas in a pod (*not to literally mean, "two melons"*) (= **sokkuri** そっくり)

uri-uri ga uri uri ni kite urinokori, uri uri-kaeru uri-uri no koe n 瓜売りが瓜売りに来て売り残り、売り売り帰る瓜売りの声 (*play on words*) A melon salesman came to sell his melons, but couldn't sell out. We hear his voice selling on his way back home.

uri v 売り → **urimásu** 売ります [INFINITIVE]
uri-ba n 売り場 (*shop*) counter, stand; shop, store
uri-dashi n 売り出し (*special*) sale; **uri-dashimásu** 売り出します puts on sale/market; launches
uri-kake n 売り掛け credit sales
uri-kire n, adj 売り切れ sellout; sold out
uri-ko n 売り子 salesclerk (*salesgirl/saleswoman/salesman*); shopgirl; (**shinbun úriko** 新聞売り子) news vendor (*newsboy/newsgirl*)
uri-mono n 売り物 sales goods/item, (*something*) for sale
uri-nushi n 売り主 seller (= **uri-te** 売り手)
uri-te n 売り手 seller (= **uri-nushi** 売り主)

uri-kíre v 売り切れ → **urikiremásu** 売り切れます [INFINITIVE]

uri-kiremásu, uri-kiréru v 売り切れます, 売り切れる sells out, runs out of

urimásu, uru v 売ります, 売る sells

urí ya/wa shinai v 売りや/はしない, [INFORMAL] **urya shinai** 売りゃしない = **uranai** 売らない (not sell)

urō´ v 売ろう = **urimashō** 売りましょう (let's sell!)

uroko n ウロコ・鱗 scales (*on a fish*)

urotsukimásu, urotsuku v うろつきます, うろつく hangs around

ū´ru n ウール wool

urū´-doshi n うるう[閏]年 leap year

urume (-íwashi) n ウルメ(イワシ)・潤目(鰯) large (*and usually dried*) sardine

urusái adj うるさい annoying, noisy (= **sawagashii** 騒がしい)

urushi n ウルシ・漆 lacquer; **urushi-nuri no utsuwa** 漆塗りの器 lacquerware (= **shikki** 漆器)

uruwashii adj うるわしい・麗しい [BOOKISH] 1. beautiful 2. heartwarming

urya v [INFORMAL] 売りゃ → **uréba** 売れば

usa-barashi n 憂さ晴らし distraction (*from emotional pain, suffering, etc.*), diversion, break, something to cheer one up: **usa-barashi o shimásu** 憂さ晴らしをします diverts oneself

usagi n ウサギ・兎 rabbit, hare

usan kusai adj うさんくさい・胡散臭い fishy, suspicious-looking

usetsu shimásu (suru) v 右折します(する) turns right

ushi n ウシ・牛 ox, oxen; cow, cattle

Ushi-doshi n 丑年 year of the Ox

ushinai v 失い → **ushinaimásu** 失います [INFINITIVE]

ushinaimásu, ushinau v 失います, 失う loses

ushinatte v 失って → **ushinaimásu** 失います

ushiro n 後ろ behind; (*in*) back

úso n うそ・嘘 lie, fib, false(hood)
úso mo hōben うそ[嘘]も方便 [IDIOM] a lie is sometimes expedient
usó-tsuki n うそつき・嘘つき liar

úsu n うす・臼 (*utensil*) mortar

usu-cha n 薄茶 weak powdered tea (= **o-úsu** お薄)

usui adj 薄い thin

utá n 歌 1. song 2. (*Japanese*) 31-syllable poem

utá n 詩 modern poem

utaemásu, utaeru v 歌えます, 歌える can sing

utaenai v 歌えない = **utaemásén** 歌えません (cannot sing)

utagaemásu, utagaeru v 疑えます, 疑える can doubt

utagaenai v 疑えない = **utagaemásén** 疑えません (cannot doubt)

utagai adj 疑い 1. a doubt: **utagai náku** 疑いなく undoubtedly, doubtless 2. v → **utagaimásu** 疑います [INFINITIVE]

utagaimásu, utagau v 疑います, 疑う doubts

utagawanai v 疑わない = **utagaimásén** 疑いません (not doubt)

utagawashíi v 疑わしい doubtful

utai n 謡 [BOOKISH] chanting a Noh libretto

utai v 歌い → **utaimásu** 歌います [INFINITIVE]

utaimásu, utau v 歌います, 歌う sings; recites, chants

utaimásu, utau v うたい[謳い]ます, うたう・謳う expressly states; extols

utánai v 打たない = **uchimásén** 打ちません (not hit)

utaō v 歌おう = **utaimashō´** 歌いましょう (let's sing!)

utawanai v 歌わない = **utaimasen** 歌いません (not sing)

útcha v [INFORMAL] 打っちゃ = **útte wa** 打っては (hitting)

úte v 打て 1. → **utemásu** 打てます [INFINITIVE] 2. [IMPERATIVE] (hit it!) → **uchimásu** 打ちます

úte v 撃て 1. → **utemásu** 撃てます [INFINITIVE] 2. [IMPERATIVE] (shoot it!) → **uchimásu** 撃ちます

úteba v 打てば = [INFORMAL] **úcha** 打ちゃ (if one hits) → **uchimásu** 打ちます

utemásu, utéru v 打てます, 打てる can hit; can send (*a telegram*)

utemásu, utéru v 撃てます, 撃てる can shoot (*a gun*)

uten n 雨天 [BOOKISH] rainy weather: **uten-kekkō** 雨天決行 rain or shine: **uten-jun'en** 雨天順延 Postponed in case of rain.: **uten-chūshi** 雨天中止 Canceled in case of rain.

uténai v 打てない = **utemasén** 打てません (cannot hit)

uténai v 撃てない = **utemasén** 撃てません (cannot shoot)

utéreba v 打てれば = [INFORMAL] **utérya** 打てりゃ (if one can hit) → **utemásu** 打てます

utéreba v 撃てれば = [INFORMAL] **utérya** 撃てりゃ (if one can shoot) → **utemásu** 撃てます

utō´ v 打とう = **uchimashō** 打ちましょう (let's hit!)

utō´ v 撃とう = **uchimashō** 撃ちましょう (let's shoot!)

utói adj うとい・疎い; **... ni utói** ...に疎い[うとい] out of touch with ..., not abreast of ...; estranged from...

útouto adv うとうと drowsing (off) (= **utsura utsura** うつらうつら); **~ shimásu** うとうとします drowses, dozes

útsu v 打つ = **uchimásu** 打ちます (hits)

utsubuse n うつぶせ・俯せ lying on one's stomach

utsukushíi adj 美しい beautiful

utsumukemásu, utsumukeru v うつむけます, うつむける; **kao o utsumukemásu** 顔をうつむけます turns one's face down

utsumukimásu, utsumúku v うつむきます, うつむく lowers one's eyes, looks down, hangs one's head

utsurí n 映り reflection, picture quality; (*a becoming*) match

utsúri v 移り → **utsurimásu** 移ります [INFINITIVE]

utsúri v 映り → **utsurimásu** 映ります [INFINITIVE]

utsurimásu, utsúru v 移ります, 移る 1. one/it moves, shifts (= **idō shimásu (suru)** 移動します(する)) 2. changes 3. moves house/residence (= **hikkoshimásu** 引越します, **hikkosu** 引越す)

utsurimásu, utsúru v 映ります, 映る is reflected; can be seen (*through*); is becoming

utsurimásu, utsúru v 写ります, 写る comes out (*photograph*)

utsuro (na) adj うつろ・虚ろ(な) hollow, empty, vacant: **utsuro na hyōjō´ o mísete** うつろ[虚ろ]な表情を見せて with a blank look

utsúse v 移せ [IMPERATIVE] (move it!) → **utsushimásu** 移します

utsúshí v 移し → **utsushimásu** 移します [INFINITIVE]

utsúshí 写し 1. n copy (= **kopii** コピー, **fukusha** 複写) 2. v → **utsushimásu** 写します [INFINITIVE]

utsúshí v 映し → **utsushimásu** 映します [INFINITIVE]

utsushimásu, utsúsú v 移します, 移す moves/transfers it

utsushimásu, utsúsú v うつします, うつす infects, gives another person a disease (*illness*)

utsushimásu, utsúsú v 写します, 写す copies; takes a picture of; projects a picture

utsushimásu, utsúsú v 映します, 映す reflects, mirrors

utsúshite v 移して → **utsushimásu** 移します

utsúshite v 写して → **utsushimásu** 写します

utsúshite v 映して → **utsushimásu** 映します

utsutsu o nukashimásu (nukasu) v うつつを抜かします(抜かす) is engrossed, is addicted

utsútte v 移って → **utsurimásu** 移ります

utsútte v 映って → **utsurimásu** 映ります

utsuwa n 器 1. receptacle, utensil, container (= **yōki** 容器) 2. tool (= **kigu** 器具, **dōgu** 道具) 3. ability, personality: **utsuwa ga/no ōkii hito** 器が/の大きい人 person of high caliber

utta v 売った = **urimáshita** 売りました (sold)

útta v 打った = **uchimáshita** 打ちました (hit)

uttae n 訴え complaint, lawsuit

uttaemásu, uttaéru v 訴えます, 訴える accuses, sues: **kujō o uttaemásu** 苦情を訴えます complains

utte v 売って → **urimásu** 売ります

útte v 打って → **uchimásu** 打ちます

uttetsuke (no) adj うってつけ(の) the most suitable; just right, just the ..., just the one/ticket

uttóri (to) adv うっとり(と) absorbed, fascinated: **~ shimásu** うっとりします is fascinated, spellbound, is enchanted

uttōshíi adj うっとうしい gloomy, dismal, dreary: **uttōshíi tenki** うっとうしい天気 gloomy weather

uwabaki n 上履き・上ばき indoor footwear (*slippers, etc.*): **kōnai dewa uwabaki ni hakikaete kudasai** 校内では上履きに履き替えて下さい Please change into your indoor shoes in the school building.: **uwabaki jisan** 上履き持参 Bring your indoor shoes.

uwabe n 上辺・うわべ 1. surface (= **hyōmen** 表面) 2. outer appearances (= **gaikan** 外観): **uwabe o tsukuroi másu** うわべをつくろい[繕い]ます puts up a front

uwagaki n 上書き 1. address (*written on envelope, etc.*) 2. overwriting: **uwagaki-hozon** 上書き保存 overwrite save: **uwagaki-mōdo** 上書きモード overwrite mode

uwagi n 上着 coat, jacket, blouse

uwagoto n うわごと・うわ言 raving, delirium

uwaki adj 浮気 1. uwaki (na) 浮気(な) fickle 2. uwaki (o) shimásu 浮気(を)します is unfaithful, has an (*extramarital*) affair

uwa-mawarimásu, uwa-mawaru v 上回ります, 上回る exceeds

uwasa n うわさ・噂 rumor, gossip (= **goshippu** ゴシップ)

uyamai *n* 敬い reverence, respect
uyamái *v* 敬い → **uyamaimásu** 敬います [INFINITIVE]
uyamaimásu, uyamáu *v* 敬います, 敬う reveres, respects
uyamátte *v* 敬って → **uyamaimásu** 敬います
uyamuya *n* うやむや obscurity, vagueness (= **aimai** あいまい・曖昧)
uyamuya ni shimásu (suru) *v* うやむやにします (する) is wishy-washy, obscures the issue
uyoku *n* 右翼 (*political party*) the right wing, rightists

úzu *n* 渦, **uzú-maki** 渦巻き whirlpool
(uzu-maki) rōru-kēki *n* (渦巻き)ロールケーキ swiss roll
uzu-shio *n* 渦潮 whirling current: **Naruto no uzushio** 鳴門の渦潮 Naruto whirlpool
uzumarimásu, uzumaru *v* うずまります・埋まります, うずまる・埋まる gets buried
uzumemásu, uzumeru *v* うずめます・埋めます, うずめる・埋める buries
uzura *n* ウズラ・鶉 quail: **uzura no tamago** ウズラ[鶉]の卵 quail egg

W

wá *n* 輪 circle; wheel; link; ring; loop (= **wak-ka** 輪っか)
wa-gomu *n* 輪ゴム rubber band
wak-ka *n* 輪っか・わっか [INFORMAL] circle; wheel; link; ring; loop (= **wa** 輪)
wa 2. *n* 和 **1.** peace (= **hei-wa** 平和, **wa-hei** 和平) **2.** harmony (= **chō-wa** 調和, **kyō-wa** 協和)
wa-hei kōshō *n* 和平交渉 [BOOKISH] peace negotiations
wa-hei jōyaku *n* 和平条約 [BOOKISH] peace treaty
wa-... *prefix* 和 ... Japanese ...
wa-ei *n* 和英 Japanese-English (= **nichi-ei** 日英); **waei-jíten** 和英辞典 Japanese-English dictionary
wa-fū *n* 和風 [BOOKISH] Japanese style
wa-fuku *n* 和服 Japanese traditional clothes; kimono
wa-gáshi *n* 和菓子 Japanese cakes/sweets
wá-ka *n* 和歌 (*Japanese*) 31-syllable poem
wa-sei-eigo *n* 和製英語 "Made in Japan" English, Japanese English (= **japaniizu ingurisshu** ジャパニーズイングリッシュ)
wá-shi *n* 和紙 Japanese paper
wa-shitsu *n* 和室 Japanese-style room
wa-shoku *n* 和食 Japanese food
wa-yaku *n* 和訳 translation into Japanese; **ei-bun wa-yaku** 英文和訳 translation from English into Japanese
...-wa *suffix* ...羽 (*counts birds, rabbits*)
... wa *particle* ...は as for ..., speaking of ..., let's talk about (*change the subject to*) ...; ..., guess what —; if it be (= **...déwa** ... では = **... nára** ... なら)
... wa *interj* ...わ (*mostly female*) indeed, you see
wā *interj* わあ (*female or children*) Wow!; Gee!; Gosh!
wabí *n* わび・侘び a liking for simple things; simple tastes
wabi *n* 詫び **1.** o-wabi お詫び apology **2.** *v* → **wabimásu** 詫びます [INFINITIVE]
wabimásu, wabiru *v* 詫びます, 詫びる [BOOKISH]

apologize (= **o-wabishimasu** お詫びします)
wabínai *v* 詫びない = **wabimasén** 詫びません (not apologize)
wabishíi *v* わびしい・侘しい miserable; lonely
wábite *v* 詫びて → **wabimásu** 詫びます
wa-chū *n* [BOOKISH] busy (*on the phone*) (= **hanashi-chū** 話し中): **wachū-on** 話中音 busy tone
wa-dachi *n* わだち・ワダチ・轍 (*wheel*) ruts
wadai *n* 話題 topic of conversation, subject (*of talk*)
wá-ga ... *adj* 我が・わが... [BOOKISH] my, our: **wá-ga kuni** 我が国・わが国 our (*this*) country (*commonly Japan*)
wá-ga-hai *pron* 我(が)輩・吾(が)輩 [BOOKISH] (*archaic or obsolete. male*) I/me: "**wa-ga-hai wa neko de aru**"「吾輩は猫である」 "I am a cat"
waga-mámá (na) *adj* わがまま・我が侭(な) selfish (= **mi-gatte (na)** 身勝手(な), **jibun-katte (na)** 自分勝手(な))
wágon (sha) *n* ワゴン(車) station wagon
wai-fai *n* ワイ・ファイ (= **musen-ran** 無線LAN) Wi-Fi, wireless LAN (*computer*)
wáin *n* ワイン wine: **aka-wain** 赤ワイン red wine: **shiro-wain** 白ワイン white wine: **wain-gurasu** ワイングラス wine glass
wáipā *n* ワイパー windshield wiper
wáiro *n* わいろ・賄賂 bribe(ry); graft
waisetsu *n* わいせつ obscenity (= **midara** 淫ら, **iyarashii** いやらしい): **waisetsu (na)** わいせつ (な) obscene
wai-shatsu *n* Yシャツ shirt
waita *v* 沸いた = **wakimáshita** 沸きました (boiled)
waita *v* 湧いた = **wakimáshita** 湧きました (gushed)
waite *v* 沸いて → **wakimásu** 沸きます
waite *v* 湧いて → **wakimásu** 湧きます
wakai *n* 和解 reconciliation: ~ **shimásu** 和解します is reconciled
wakái *adj* 若い young

waka-ba *n* 若葉 young leaves: **Wakaba-māku** 若葉マーク Wakaba mark (*a mark displayed on the windshield to indicate brand new driver*)

waka-dori *n* 若鶏 broiler chicken

waka-mono *n* 若者 young person, youth

waka-te *n* 若手 young person; **wakate-sákka** 若手作家 young writer

wakame *n* ワカメ・若布 a kind of seaweed

wakanai *v* 沸かない = **wakimasén** 沸きません (not boil)

wakanai *v* 湧かない = **wakimasén** 湧きません (not gush)

wakaránai *v* 分からない・解らない = **wakarimasén** 分かりません・解りません (not understand)

wakaré *n* 別れ (**o-wakare** お別れ) parting, farewell

wakaré *n* 分かれ branch(ing), fork(ing), division

wakáre *n* 別れ breakup; farewell; leave

wakáre *v* 別れ **1.** → **wakaremásu** 別れます [INFINITIVE] **2. wakaré ro** 別れろ [IMPERATIVE] (part!)

wakáre *v* 分かれ [IMPERATIVE] (understand!) → **wakarimásu** 分かります

wakaremásu, wakaréru *v* 別れます, 別れる they part, separate

wakaremásu, wakaréru *v* 分かれます, 分かれる it branches off, splits

wakareme *n* 分かれ目 turning point

wakarénai *v* 別れない = **wakaremasén** 別れません (not part)

wakarí *n* 分かり comprehension (= **nomikomi** 呑み込み): **wakarí ga hayái** 分かりが早い quick-witted, **wakarí ga íi** 分かりがいい intelligent; **(mono)wakarí ga warúi** (もの)分かりが悪い dull(-witted), stupid

wakári *v* 分かり → **wakarimásu** 分かります [INFINITIVE]

Wakarimáshita *v* 分かりました. **1.** Yes, I see. **2.** Yes, I will (*comply with your request*).

wakarimásu, wakáru *v* 分かります, 分かる it is clear (*understood*); understands; finds out; has good sense

wakari-yasúi *v* 分かりやすい clear, easy to understand

wakashimásu, wakasu *v* 沸かします, 沸かす boils it

wakátta *v* 分かった = **wakarimáshita** 分かりました (understood)

wakátte *v* 分かって → **wakarimásu** 分かります: **wakátte imásu** 分かっています it is understood, it is (*now*) clear

wáke *n* わけ・訳 **1.** reason (= **riyū** 理由) **2.** meaning (= **imi** 意味), content (= **naiyō** 内容) **3.** case, circumstance (= **jijō** 事情)

wáke *v* 分け **1.** → **wakemásu** 分けます [INFINITIVE] **2. waké ro** 分けろ [IMPERATIVE] (divide it!)

wáke *n* 訳: (… **suru/shinai**) **wáke ni wa ikanai** …(する/しない) 訳にはいかない cannot help (doing)

wakéba *v* 沸けば (if it boils) → **wakimásu** 沸きます

wakéba *v* 湧けば (if it gushes) → **wakimásu** 湧きます

wakemae *n* 分け前 share, portion

wakemásu, wakéru *v* 分けます, 分ける divides (*splits, distributes*) it; separates them

wake-mé *n* 分け目 dividing line, part(ing) (*in hair*)

wáke arimasén (nái) *v* 訳ありません(ない) is no problem, is a cinch; easy

wakénai *v* 分けない = **wakemasén** 分けません (not divide it; not separate them)

wáke-nai *v* 訳ない・わけない easy, simple, ready; **wake-naku** 訳なく・わけなく easily, simply, readily, with no problem

wakeraremásu, wakeraréru *v* 分けられます, 分けられる **1.** it gets divided; they get separated **2.** can divide it

wakerarénai *v* 分けられない = **wakeraremasén** 分けられません (cannot divide it)

wakeraréreba *v* 分けられれば [INFORMAL] **wakerarerya** 分けられりゃ (if it gets divided; if we can divide it) → **wakeraremásu** 分けられます

wakerárete *v* 分けられて → **wakeraremásu** 分けられます

wakereba *v* 分ければ = [INFORMAL] **wakerya** 分けりゃ (if we divide it) → **wakemásu** 分けます

wákete *v* 分けて → **wakemásu** 分けます

wakeyō´ *v* 分けよう = **wakemashō´** 分けましょう (let's divide it!)

wakí *n* わき・脇 side (= **yoko** 横)

waki-bara *n* わき腹・脇腹 flank (= **yoko-bara** 横腹)

waki-mi *n* わき見・脇見 looking off (= **yoso-mi** よそ見); **wakimi-unten** 脇見運転 inattentive driving

waki-michi *n* わき道・脇道 sideroad; **hanashi ga wakimichi ni soremásu** 話が脇道にそれます strays from the subject

wakí *n* わき・腋 side of the body

waki-ga *n* わきが・腋臭 armpit smell, body odor

waki-nó-shita *n* わき[脇・腋]の下 **1.** armpit **2.** under one's arms

wakí *v* 沸き → **wakimásu** 沸きます [INFINITIVE]

wakí *v* 湧き → **wakimásu** 湧きます [INFINITIVE]

waki-mizu *n* 湧き水 spring water

waki aiai *n* 和気あいあい in happy harmony

wakimásu, waku *v* 沸きます, 沸く it boils: **o-yu ga wakimásu** お湯が沸きます the water boils (→ **o-yu o wakashimásu** お湯を沸かします, **o-yu ga wakimáshita** お湯が沸きました)

wakimásu, waku *v* 湧きます, 湧く it gushes, springs forth: **yūki ga wakimáshita** 勇気が湧きました I was given courage., I got courage.: **kibō ga wakimáshita** 希望が湧きました I was given hope., I got hope.

wakí ya/wa shinai *v* 沸きや/はしない, [INFORMAL] **wakya shinai** 沸きゃしない = **wakanai** 沸かない (not boil)

wakí ya/wa shinai ν 湧きや/はしない, [INFORMAL] **wakya shinai** 湧きゃしない = **wakanai** 湧かない (not gush)

waku ν 沸く = **wakimásu** 沸きます

waku ν 湧く = **wakimásu** 湧きます

wakú n 枠 **1.** frame, framework (= **waku-gumi** 枠組) **2.** reel, limit, a confine

waku-gumi n 枠組 **1.** frame, framework (= **waku** 枠) **2.** outline (= **autorain** アウトライン, **ōsuji** 大筋)

wákuchin n ワクチン vaccine

wakusei n 惑星 planet

waku-waku shimásu (suru) ν わくわくします（する）is thrilled, is excited

waméite ν わめいて・喚いて → **wamekimásu** わめきます・喚きます

wamekimásu, waméku ν わめきます・喚きます, わめく・喚く yells

wan n 碗 (**o-wan** お碗) bowl: **cha-wan** 茶碗 rice-bowl: **cha-wan-mushi** 茶碗蒸し pot-steamed hotchpotch

wán n 湾 bay, gulf: **Tōkyō-wan** 東京湾 Tokyo Bay

wan-gan n 湾岸 gulf coast: **wangan-sensō** 湾岸戦争 Gulf War

wán n ワン one

wán-man n ワンマン **1.** one-man, operator-only (*bus*); **wanman-shō´** ワンマンショー one-man show, solo performance **2.** dictator: **wanman-keiei** ワンマン経営 Caesar management

wan-píisu n ワンピース (*one-piece*) dress

wan-rū´mu n ワンルーム one-room (*studio*) apartment

wána n わな・ワナ・罠 trap; lasso: **wána ni kakarimásu** わな[罠]にかかります gets trapped/snared

wáni n ワニ crocodile, alligator

waní-ashi (no) adj わに足(の) bowlegged

wánisu n ワニス varnish

wanpaku n わんぱく・腕白 rudeness: **wanpaku-kozō** わんぱく[腕白]小僧 brat, mischievous boy

wanpaku (na) adj 腕白・わんぱく(な) naughty, mischievous (*commonly used for children*) (= **yancha (na)** やんちゃ(な))

wánryoku n 腕力 [BOOKISH] arm strength, physical force, physical strength

wán-wan interj ワンワン bow-wow! (*bark*)

wappu n 割賦 allotment, installment (= **kappu** 割賦)

wā-puro n ワープロ word processor

wára n ワラ・藁 rice straw

wára ni mo sugaru omoi de adv ワラ[藁]にもすがる思いで [IDIOM] grasping at straws

warabanshi n わら半紙 coarse paper, rough paper

warabe n わらべ・童 [BOOKISH] child(ren) (= **jidō** 児童): **warabe-uta** わらべ歌・童歌 Japanese traditional children's song

warabi n ワラビ bracken

warae ν 笑え **1.** → **waraemásu** 笑えます [INFINITIVE] **2.** [IMPERATIVE] (laugh!) → **waraimásu** 笑います

waraéba ν 笑えば (if one laughs) → **waraimásu** 笑います

waraémásu, waraeru ν 笑えます, 笑える can laugh

waraenai ν 笑えない = **waraemasén** 笑えません (cannot laugh)

waraéreba ν 笑えれば (if one can laugh) → **waraemásu** 笑えます

warai 笑い **1.** n a laugh, laughter; smile **2.** ν → **waraimásu** 笑います [INFINITIVE] warai-banashi n 笑い話 funny story

warai わらい・嘲い **1.** n a ridicule, sneer, mockery **2.** ν → **waraimásu** わらい[嘲い]ます [INFINITIVE]

waraimásu, warau ν 笑います, 笑う laughs; laughs at; smiles

waraimásu, warau ν わらい[嘲い]ます, わらう・嘲う ridicules, sneers, mocks (= **chōshō shimásu (suru)** 嘲笑します(する), **aza-warai másu** 嘲笑います, **aza-warau** 嘲笑う)

waraí ya/wa shinai ν 笑いや/はしない = **wara-wanai** 笑わない (not laugh)

waraí ya/wa shinai ν わらい[嘲い]や/はしない = **warawanai** わら[嘲]わない (not ridicule)

waranai ν 割らない = **warimasén** 割りません (not break/divide/dilute it)

waraō ν 笑おう = **waraimashō´** 笑いましょう (let's laugh!)

warawanai ν 笑わない = **waraimasén** 笑いません (not laugh)

warawanai ν わらわ[嘲わ]ない = **waraimasén** わらい[嘲い]ません (not ridicule)

waraware ν 笑われ → **warawaremásu** 笑われます [INFINITIVE]

waraware ν わらわ[嘲わ]れ → **warawaremásu** わらわ[嘲わ]れます [INFINITIVE]

warawaremásu, warawareru ν 笑われます, 笑われる gets laughed at

warawaremásu, warawareru ν わらわ[嘲わ]れます, わらわ[嘲わ]れる is ridiculed at

warawarenai ν 笑われない = **warawaremasén** 笑われません (not get laughed at)

warawarenai ν わらわ[嘲わ]れない = **warawaremasén** わらわ[嘲わ]れません (is not ridiculed at)

warawareréba ν 笑われれば (if one gets laughed at) → **warawaremásu** 笑われます

warawareréba ν わらわ[嘲わ]れれば (if one is ridiculed at) → **warawaremásu** わらわ[嘲わ]れます

warawarete ν 笑われて → **warawaremásu** 笑われます

warawarete ν わらわ[嘲わ]れて → **warawaremásu** わらわ[嘲わ]れます

wáre pron 我 [BOOKISH] **1.** oneself **2.** I/me (= **wata(ku)shi** わた(く)し・私) ware ni kaerimásu (kaeru) ν 我に返ります (返る) comes to oneself ware omou, yue ni ware ari 我思う、ゆえに

我あり (*famous saying*) I think, therefore I am. (*Cogito, ergo sum.*)
ware o wasuremásu (wasureru) *v* 我を忘れます (忘れる) **1.** is hooked on, is carried away (= **muchū ni narimásu (náru)** 夢中になります (なる)) **2.** is stunned (= **bōzen-jishitsu to narimásu (náru)** 茫然自失となります (なる))
ware-ware *pron* 我々・われわれ [BOOKISH] we; us
ware *v* 割れ **1.** → **waremásu** 割れます [INFINITIVE] **2.** [IMPERATIVE] (divide it!) → **warimásu** 割ります
waremásu, wareru *v* 割れます, 割れる **1.** it cracks, it splits **2.** can divide/break/dilute it
ware-me *n* 割れ目 crack, crevice, gap
ware-mono *n* 割れ物 fragile
warenai *v* 割れない = **waremasén** 割れません (not crack; cannot divide/break/dilute)
warete *v* 割れて→ **waremásu** 割れます
wari *n* 割 **1.** (**...-wari** ...割) tens of percent; percentage: **sán-wari** 三割 = **sanjup-pāsénto** 30パーセント・30% thirty percent **2.** profit(ability): **wari ni aimasén** 割に合いません it doesn´t pay (off); **wari ga íi** 割がいい profitable: **wari ga warúi** 割が悪い unprofitable
wari-ai *n* 割合 rate, percentage: **wari-ai (ni)** 割合 (に) comparatively, relatively
wariate *n* 割り当て quota, allotment
waribashi *n* 割り箸 throwaway chopsticks
wari-biki *n* 割引 discount
wari-kan *n* 割り勘 splitting the bill; (*going*) Dutch treat: **warikan ni shimáshō** 割り勘にしましょう Let's split the bill.
warikómimásu, warikómu *v* 割り込みます, 割り込む 割り込む cuts in (*into*), breaks in; breezes in
wari-mae *n* 割り前 share, portion
warimásu, waru *v* 割ります, 割る divides/splits it, breaks it, dilutes it
wari (ni) *adv* わり (に)・割 (に) relatively, comparatively (= **wariai (ni)** 割合 (に))
warízan *n* 割り算 division
warō´ *v* 割ろう = **warimashō**´ 割りましょう (let's divide/break/ dilute it!)
warú *n* 悪 bad, evil (= **aku** 悪)
warú-i *adj* 悪い **1.** bad, poor; wrong; vicious **2.** at fault
Warú-i! *interj* 悪い! Sorry.
warú-fuzake *n* 悪ふざけ practical joke
warú-gashikoi *adj* 悪賢い sly, cunning, crafty, wily (*person*) (= **zuru-gashikoi** ずる賢い, **kōkatsu (na)** 狡猾 (な))
warú-gi *n* 悪気 evil intent, malice (= **akui** 悪意)
warú-jie *n* 悪知恵 cunning, craft
warú-kuchi/-guchi *n* 悪口 (*verbal*) abuse, slander: **warúguchi o iimásu** 悪口を言います speaks ill (*of*)
waru-mono *n* 悪者 bad guy/fellow, villain, scoundrel: **warumono atsukai** 悪者扱い demonize
warú-yoi *n* 悪酔い getting sick from drink: **~ shimásu** 悪酔いします gets sick from drink

warutsu *n* ワルツ waltz
wásabi *n* ワサビ・山葵 horseradish
washi *n* ワシ・鷲 eagle
washi *pron* わし (*archaic old male*) I/me (= **wata(ku)shi** わた (く) し・私)
Washínton *n* ワシントン Washington
wasure *v* 忘れ **1.** → **wasuremásu** 忘れます [INFINITIVE] **2. wasure ro** 忘れろ [IMPERATIVE] (forget it!)
wasuremásu, wasureru *v* 忘れます, 忘れる forgets
wasure-mono *n* 忘れ物 **1.** leaving something behind **2.** a thing left behind (*forgetfully*)
wasurenái de *v* 忘れないで: **wasurenái de (... shite) kudasái** 忘れないで(...して)下さい don't forget (*to do* ...)
wasurep-pói *adj* 忘れっぽい forgetful
wasureraremásu, wasurerareru *v* 忘れられます, 忘れられる can forget
wasurerarenai *v* 忘れられない = **wasureraremasén** 忘れられません (cannot forget)
wasurerareréba *v* 忘れられれば (if one can forget) → **wasureraremásu** 忘れられます
wasureta *v* 忘れた = **wasuremashíta** 忘れました (I forgot).
wasurete *v* 忘れて → **wasuremásu** 忘れます
wasureyō´ *v* 忘れよう = **wasuremashō**´ 忘れましょう (let's forget it!)
watá *n* 綿 cotton (= **kotton** コットン)
watá-ame *n* 綿アメ cotton candy (= **wata-gashi** 綿菓子)
wata-bokori *n* 綿ぼこり dustball
watá-gashi *n* 綿菓子 cotton candy (= **wata-ame** 綿アメ)
wata-ge *n* 綿毛 fluff, cotton fiber: **tanpopo no watage** タンポポの綿毛 pappus of a dandelion
wata-íre *n* 綿入れ (*cotton*) padded garment
watá *n* 腸 guts, intestines (= **harawátá** はらわた・腸)
watakushi *pron* わたくし・私 [BOOKISH], **watashi** わたし・私 [HUMBLE] I/me; **watakushi-tachi** わたくし [私] 達, **watáshí-táchi** わたし [私] 達 we/us
watakushí-ritsu (no) *adj* 私立 (の) private(-ly established); **watakushí-ritsu (no) gakkō** 私立 (の) 学校 private school
watakushi-shōsetsu *n* 私小説 I-Novel (*a novel writing about oneself*) (= **shi-shōsetsu** 私小説)
wataranai *v* 渡らない = **watarimasén** 渡りません (not cross over)
watare *v* 渡れ **1.** → **wataremásu** 渡れます [INFINITIVE] **2.** [IMPERATIVE] (cross over!) → **watarimásu** 渡ります
wataremásu, watareru *v* 渡れます, 渡れる 渡れる can cross over
watarenai *v* 渡れない = **wataremasén** 渡れません (cannot cross over)
waterete *v* 渡れて → **wataremásu** 渡れます
watari *v* 渡り **1.** crossing, ferry (*place*): **watari o tsukemásu** 渡りをつけます forms an understanding with, gets in touch with; **watari**

ni fúne 渡りに舟 a timely rescue, a convenient escape/excuse 2. → **watarimásu** 渡ります [INFINITIVE]

watarimásu, wataru v 渡ります, 渡る crosses over

watarō´ v 渡ろう = **watarimashō´** 渡りましょう (let's cross over!)

watasanai v 渡さない = **watashimasén** 渡しません (not hand it over; not ferry)

watase v 渡せ 1. → **watasemásu** 渡せます [IMPERATIVE] 2. → **watashimásu** 渡します [IMPERATIVE] (hand it over!)

wataséba v 渡せば (if one hands it over; if one ferries) → **watashimásu** 渡します

watasemásu, wataseru v 渡せます, 渡せる can hand it over; can ferry

watasenai v 渡せない = **watasemasén** 渡せません (cannot hand it over; cannot ferry)

wataseréba v 渡せれば (if one can hand it over; if one can ferry) → **watasemásu** 渡せます

watásete v 渡せて → **watasemásu** 渡せます

watashi pron 私・わたし = [BOOKISH] **watakushi** 私・わたくし I/me

watashi v 渡し → **watashimásu** 渡します [INFINITIVE]

watashi-búne n 渡し舟 ferryboat

watashimásu, watasu v 渡します, 渡す hands it over; ferries

watáshí-táchi pron わたし[私]達 we, us (= **watakushí-tachi** わたくし[私]達)

watashite v 渡して → **watashimásu** 渡します

watasō v 渡そう = **watashimashō´** 渡しましょう (let's hand it over!; let's ferry them over!)

watasu v 渡す → **watashimásu** 渡します

watatte v 渡って → **watarimásu** 渡ります

watta v 割った = **warimáshita** 割りました (divided/ … it)

watte v 割って → **warimásu** 割ります

watto n ワット watt

waza n 業 trick, feat

waza n 技 skill, technique, art (= **gijutsu** 技術)

wáza-to adv わざと deliberately, on purpose, intentionally (= **ito-teki ni** 意図的に, **koi ni** 故意に, **aete** あえて)

wazawai n 災い misfortune, mishap, disaster, calamity (= **sainan** 災難)

wázawaza adv わざわざ expressly, especially; purposely (= **wáza-to** わざと, **ito-teki ni** 意図的に, **koi ni** 故意に, **aete** あえて)

wazuka adj わずか a few, a little (= **sukoshi** 少し)

wazurai n 煩い・わずらい [BOOKISH] trouble, worry

wazurai n 患い [BOOKISH] illness (= **byōki** 病気)

wazurai v 煩い → **wazuraimásu** 煩います [INFINITIVE]

wazurai v 患い → **wazuraimásu** 患います [INFINITIVE]

wazuraimásu, wazurau v 煩います, 煩う worries about, is troubled by

wazuraimásu, wazurau v 患います, 患う has trouble with (one's eyes), suffers from (an ailment): **mé o wazuraimásu** 目を患います has trouble with one's eyes

wazuratte v 煩って → **wazuraimásu** 煩います

wazuratte v 患って → **wazuraimásu** 患います

wazurawanai adj 煩わない = **wazuraimasén** 煩いません (not worry …)

wazurawashíi adj 煩わしい troublesome; complicated

web n ウェブ World Wide Web, internet

websaito n ウェブサイト website

weburogu n ウェブブログ (= **burogu** ブログ) weblog, blog (internet)

wísukii n ウィスキー whisky

witto n ウィット wit (= **kichi** 機知, **tonchi** とんち・頓知・頓智)

Y

yá n 矢 arrow

ya-jirushi n 矢印 arrow sign (such as "→", "←", "↑", "↓")

ya-…, …-ya prefix, suffix 夜…, …夜 night (= **ban** 晩): **shū-ya** 終夜 all night (= **ōru-naito** オールナイト)

yá-gu n 夜具 [BOOKISH] bedclothes; top quilt

yá-kan n 夜間 [BOOKISH] (at) night

ya-kei n 夜景 night view

ya-kin n 夜勤 nightwork

ya-kō-ressha n 夜行列車 night train

ya-… prefix 野… wild, field

ya-chō n 野鳥 wild bird

ya-ei n 野営 camp, bivouac

yá-gai n 野外 outdoors, in the field (= **auto-doa** アウトドア): **yagai-katsudō** 野外活動 outdoor activity

ya-jū n 野獣 [BOOKISH] wild beast: **"Bijo to Yajū"** 「美女と野獣」 "Beauty and the Beast"

ya-ken n 野犬 wild dog

ya-sei (no) adj 野性(の) wild, not cultivated

ya-sen n 野戦 open battle: **yasen-byōin** 野戦病院 field hospital

… ya … conj …や … and … and … (choosing typical items)

… ya interj …や [INFORMAL] 1. = **…i ya** …いや = **… i wa** …いは 2. = **…e ba** …えば (if)

… -ya suffix …屋 (name of certain) shop, shopkeeper, dealer; house (→ **(o-)sobá-ya** (お)蕎

麦屋: **rāmen-ya** ラーメン屋 Ramen shop: **karē-ya** カレー屋 curry shop

yā´ *interj* やあ hi! hello! (*mostly male. Very informal. Cannot be used to address a superior*)

yabái *adj* やばい **1.** (*mostly male.* VERY INFORMAL) dangerous (*will get you into trouble*) **2.** (*mostly young people.* SLANG) awesome

yaban (na) *adj* 野蛮(な) barbarous, barbarian, savage: **yaban-jín** 野蛮人 a barbarian, a savage

yabō *n* 野望 ambition [IN NEGATIVE SENSE] (= **yashin** 野心) (= **taishi** 大志, **taibō** 大望 [IN NEGATIVE SENSE])

yábo (na) *adj* 野暮(な) [INFORMAL] rustic, inelegant; **yabo-yō** 野暮用 small errand to run

yabu *n* ヤブ・薮 bush, thicket

yabu-hebi *n* やぶ蛇 boomerang (*something injures the originator*), waking a sleeping giant

yabu-isha *n* ヤブ[薮]医者 quack doctor

yabu-ka *n* ヤブカ・薮蚊 striped mosquito

yabúite *v* 破いて → **yabukimásu** 破きます

yabukánai *v* 破かない = **yabukimasén** 破きません (not tear it)

yabúke *v* 破け **1.** → **yabukemásu** 破けます [INFINITIVE] **2.** [IMPERATIVE] (tear it!) → **yabukimásu** 破きます

yabukemásu, yabukéru *v* 破けます、破ける **1.** it tears, bursts; is frustrated **2.** can tear/burst it (= **yaburemásu** 破れます)

yabukénai *v* 破けない = **yabukemasén** 破けません (it does not tear)

yabúkete *v* 破けて → **yabukemásu** 破けます

yabúki *v* 破き → **yabuki másu** 破きます [INFINITIVE]

yabukimásu, yabúku *v* 破きます、破く tears (*bursts*) it; frustrates; violates; defeats → **yabuki másu** 破きます

yaburánai *v* 破らない = **yaburimasén** 破りません (not tear it)

yabure *v* 破れ **1.** → **yaburemásu** 破れます [INFINITIVE] **2.** [IMPERAITIVE] tear it! (= **yaburimásu** 破ります)

yabure-kabure *n* やぶれ[破れ]かぶれ desperation (= **jibōjiki** 自暴自棄)

yaburemásu, yabúreru *v* 破れます、破れる **1.** it tears, bursts; is frustrated **2.** can tear/burst it

yaburemásu, yabúreru *v* 敗れます、敗れる loses

yaburénai *v* 破れない = **yaburemasén** 破れません (it does not tear)

yaburénai *v* 敗れない = **yaburemasén** 敗れません (it does not lose)

yabúrete *v* 破れて → **yaburemásu** 破れます

yabúrete *v* 敗れて → **yaburemásu** 敗れます

yaburimásu, yabúru *v* 破ります、破る tears (*bursts*) it; frustrates; violates; defeats

yabusaka de (wa) arimasen (nai) *v* やぶさかで(は)ありません (ない) is willing to do

yabútte *v* 破って → **yaburimásu** 破ります

yá-chin *n* 家賃 house rent

yádo, yado-ya *n* 宿, 宿屋 inn

yagate *adv* やがて before long; in time (= **mamonaku** まもなく)

yági *n* ヤギ・山羊 goat

yahári *adv* やはり also; either; after all; just we/I thought! (= **yappari** やっぱり)

yaiba *n* やいば・刃 blade; sword

yaite *v* 焼いて → **yakimásu** 焼きます

yaite *v* 妬いて → **yakimásu** 妬きます

yáji *n* やじ・野次 heckling

yajiuma *n* やじうま・野次馬 rubbernecker: **yajiuma-konjō** やじうま根性 extreme curiosity

yakamashíi *adj* やかましい [INFORMAL] noisy, boisterous, clamorous, annoying, overly strict, demanding [IN NEGATIVE SENSE]

yakan *n* やかん teakettle

yakanai *v* 焼かない = **yakimasén** 焼きません (not burn it)

yakanai *v* 妬かない = **yakimasén** 妬きません (is not jealous, not envy)

yake *v* 焼け **1.** → **yakemásu** 焼けます [INFINITIVE] **2.** [IMPERATIVE] (burn/broil it!) → **yakimásu** 焼きます

yáke *n* やけ・自棄 desperation (= **jibō-jiki** 自暴自棄) **yáke ni** やけに excessively, unbearably, terribly; **yáke(-kuso) ni nátte** やけ(くそ)になって desperately, from (*out of*) despair

yakéba *v* 焼けば (if one burns/broils it) → **yakimásu** 焼きます

yakéba *v* 妬けば (if one is jealous, if one envies) → **yakimásu** 妬きます

yakedo *n* やけど・火傷 burn, scald (*on the skin*) (= **nesshō** 熱傷)

yakemásu, yakeru *v* 焼けます、焼ける **1.** it burns; it is baked **2.** can burn it

yakemásu, yakeru *v* 妬けます、妬ける is jealous, envies

yakenai *v* 焼けない = **yakemasén** 焼けません (it does not burn; cannot burn it)

yakenai *v* 妬けない = **yakemasén** 妬けません (is not jealous, not envy)

yakete *v* 焼けて → **yakemásu** 焼けます

yakete *v* 妬けて → **yakemásu** 妬けます

yaki 焼き **1.** *n* baking, burning, broiling; tempering; exposure **2.** *v* → **yakimásu** 焼きます [INFINITIVE]

yaki *v* 妬き → **yakimásu** 妬きます [INFINITIVE]

yaki-... *prefix* 焼き... roast: (**ishi-)yaki imo** (石)焼き芋 (stone-)baked yam

yaki-dō´fu *n* 焼き豆腐 broiled bean curd

yakí-guri *n* 焼き栗 roasted chestnuts

yaki-gushi *n* 焼き串 skewer, spit

yaki-meshi *n* 焼き飯 fried rice

yaki-móchi *n* やきもち・焼き餅 jealousy (= **shitto** 嫉妬)

yakí-mochi *n* やきもち・焼き餅 toasted rice-cake

yaki-mono *n* 焼き物 **1.** pottery **2.** broiled food/dishes

yaki-niku *n* 焼き肉・焼肉 grilled slices of meat

yaki-soba *n* 焼きそば・やきそば chow mein; fried Chinese noodle

yaki-tori *n* 焼き鳥・やきとり chicken shishkebab (*skewers*): **yaki tori-ya** 焼き鳥屋 a *yakitori* shop/stand

...-yaki *suffix* ...焼 (*ceramic*) ware from ...; **Imari-yaki** 伊万里焼 Imari (*ware*), **Kutani-yaki** 九谷焼 Kutani (*ware*)

yakimásu, yaku *v* 焼きます, 焼く burns/broils it, bakes (*roasts, toasts*) it

yakimásu, yaku *v* 妬きます, 妬く is jealous, envies

yakí ya/wa shinai *v* 焼きや/はしない, [INFORMAL] **yakya shinai** 焼きゃしない = **yakanai** 焼かない (not burn)

yakí ya/wa shinai *v* 妬きや/はしない, [INFORMAL] **yakya shinai** 妬きゃしない = **yakanai** 妬かない (is not jealous, not envy)

yákkai *n* 厄介・やっかい (**go-yákkai** ご厄介) trouble, bother (= **meiwaku** 迷惑, **go-meiwaku** ご迷惑): **yákkai (na)** 厄介・やっかい(な) troublesome, annoying

yakko *n* やっこ・奴 **1.** servant, slave **2.** [IN NEGATIVE SENSE] (*undesirable*) person/one: **yakko-san** やっこ[奴]さん that guy, he/him (= **yatsu** やつ・奴, **aitsu** あいつ) **3.** = **yakko-dō'fu** やっこ[奴]豆腐 (*parboiled*) tofu (*bean-curd cubes*); **hiya-yakko** 冷や奴 cold tofu

yakkyoku *n* 薬局 pharmacy, drugstore

yaku *v* 焼く = **yakimásu** 焼きます (burns it, bakes it)

yaku *v* 妬く = **yakimásu** 妬きます (is jealous, envies)

yaku *n* ヤク yak (*animal*)

yakú *n* 訳 translation, translated word (→ **honyaku** 翻訳, **tsūyaku** 通訳)

yáku(...) *adj* 約(...) approximately, about ... (= **oyoso** およそ, **daitai** 大体)

yaku *n* 役 **1.** (*cast of*) players **2.** part, role, duty **yaku-mé** *n* 役目 (**o-yakume** お役目) duty, function (= **yakuwari** 役割)

yaku-sha *n* 役者 actor (= **haiyū** 俳優), actress (= **joyū** 女優)

yaku-wari *n* 役割 role, part (= **yakume** 役目)

yaku-... 役...(**o-yaku...** お役...) service (*government, official*), use

o-yaku ni tatereba saiwai desu お役に立てれば幸いです [HUMBLE] I hope I/it can be of some help to you.

o-yaku ni tatezu (ni) sumimasen お役に立てず(に)すみません [HUMBLE] I am sorry for not being able to help you.

yaku-nin *n* 役人 (**o-yaku-nin** お役人) public servant, government official (= **kōmuin** 公務員)

yaku-sho *n* 役所 (**o-yaku-sho** お役所) government office (→ **shi-yakusho** 市役所, **ku-yakusho** 区役所)

yaku *n* 薬 drug(= **mayaku** 麻薬) (→ **kusuri** 薬)

...-yaku, yaku-... *suffix, prefix* ...-薬, 薬... medicines, drugs

yaku-hin 薬品 drugs; chemicals

yaku-mi *n* 薬味 **1.** spice (→ **supaisu** スパイス, **kōshin-ryō** 香辛料), condiment **2.** drug ingredient

yaku-sō 薬草 medicinal herb

yaku-zai *n* 薬剤 [BOOKISH] pharmaceuticals, medicines (= **kusuri** 薬): **yakuzai-shi** 薬剤師 pharmacist

yaku-dachimásu, yaku-dátsu *v* 役立ちます, 役立つ serves a purpose, is useful

yaku-datánai *v* 役立たない = **yaku-dachimasén** 役立ちません (not useful)

yakú-datemásu, yakú-dáteru *v* 役立てます, 役立てる puts it to use

yakú ni tachimásu (tátsu) *v* 役に立ちます(立つ) → **yaku-dachimásu** 役立ちます

yakú ni tatemásu (tatéru) *v* 役に立てます(立てる) puts it to use (= **yakú-datemásu** 役立てます)

yakusánai *v* 訳さない = **yakushimasén** 訳しません (not translate)

yakúse *v* 訳せ **1.** → **yakusemásu** 訳せます [INFINITIVE] **2.** [IMPERATIVE] (translate!) → **yakushimásu** 訳します

yakusemásu, yakuséru *v* 訳せます, 訳せる can translate

yakusénai *v* 訳せない = **yakusemasén** 訳せません (cannot translate)

yakúsete *v* 訳せて → **yakusemásu** 訳せます

yakúshi *v* 訳し → **yakushimásu** 訳します

yakushimásu, yakúsú *v* 訳します, 訳す translates

yakúshite *v* 訳して → **yakushimásu** 訳します

yakusō' *v* 訳そう = **yakushimashō'** 訳しましょう (let's translate!)

yakusoku *n* 約束 (**o-yakusoku** お約束) promise, agreement, appointment, engagement, date, commitment: **~ shimásu** 約束します promises, agrees

yakusoku-goto *n* 約束事 a promise

yákuza *n* やくざ gangster, hoodlum

yákuza (na) *adj* やくざ(な) no-good, worthless; **yákuza na kagyō** やくざな稼業 improper work; coarse

yakya *v* [INFORMAL] 焼きゃ → **yakéba** 焼けば

yakya *v* [INFORMAL] 妬きゃ → **yakéba** 妬けば

yakyū *n* 野球 baseball (= **bēsu bōru** ベースボール)

yakyū-jō *n* 野球場 ball park, (*baseball*) stadium

yamá *n* 山 **1.** mountain **2.** heap, pile, bunch: **shorui no yamá** 書類の山 pile of documents **3.** speculation, venture **4.** → **yamá(-ba)** 山(場)

yama-arashi *n* ヤマアラシ・山荒 porcupine

yama-arashi *n* 山嵐 mountain storm

yama-aruki *n* 山歩き trekking (= **haikingu** ハイキング)

yamá(-ba) *n* 山(場) climax

yama-biko *n* やまびこ・山彦 echo (= **kodama** こだま・木霊)

yama-buki *n* ヤマブキ・山吹 Japanese rose: **yamabuki-iro** 山吹色 bright yellow

yama-goya *n* 山小屋 cabin, mountain lodge

yama-imo *n* ヤマイモ・山芋 yam

yama-neko *n* ヤマネコ・山猫 wild cat

yama-nóbori *n* 山登り mountain-climbing (= **tozan** 登山)

yama no fumoto *n* 山のふもと[麓] the base of a mountain (= **yamasuso** 山裾)

yama-otoko *n* 山男 1. mountaineer 2. woodsman 3. monster living in the heart of a mountain

yama-suso *n* 山裾 the base of a mountain (= **yama no fumoto** 山のふもと[麓])

yamanai *v* やまない = **yamimasén** やみません (not stop)

yama-shi *n* 山師 speculator

yamashii *adj* やましい ashamed of oneself; has guilty feeling

yama-te *n* 山手, **yama-no-te** 山手・山の手 uptown; the bluff: **Yama-no-te-sen** 山の手線 Yamanote Line

Yámato *n* 大和 Japan (*an ancient name*)

yamato-kotoba *n* 大和言葉 words of Japanese origin, native Japanese words (= **wago** 和語)

yamato-nadeshiko *n* ヤマトナデシコ・大和撫子 1. dianthus (*flower*) 2. beautiful and modest Japanese woman

yame *v* 止め → **yamemásu** 止めます 1. [INFINITIVE] 2. **yame ro** 止めろ, **yamé yo** 止めよ [IMPERATIVE] (stop it!)

yaméba *v* 止めば = [INFORMAL] **yamya** 止めや (if it stops) → **yamimásu** 止めます

yamemásu, yameru *v* 止めます, 止める stops it; abolishes, abstains from, gives up

yamemásu, yameru *v* 辞めます, 辞める resigns, quits

yamenai *v* 止めない = **yamemasén** 止めません (not stop it)

yameraremásu, yamerareru *v* 止められます, 止められる can stop it

yamerarenai *v* 止められない = **yameraremasén** 止められません (cannot stop it)

yameréba *v* 止めれば = [INFORMAL] **yamérya** 止めりゃ (if one stops it) → **yamemásu** 止めます

yamete *v* 止めて → **yamemásu** 止めます

yame ya/wa shinai *v* 止めや/はしない, [INFORMAL] **yamérya shinai** 止めりゃしない = **yamemasén** 止めません (not stop it)

yameyō *v* 止めよう = **yamemashō´** 止めましょう (let's stop it!)

yami *v* 止み → **yamimásu** 止みます [INFINITIVE]

yamí *n* 闇 1. darkness (= **kurayamí** 暗闇) 2. disorder 3. black market (= **yamí-ichí** 闇市) 4. anything illicit, the dark (= **fuhō na** 不法な)

yamí-ichí(ba) *n* 闇市(場) black market

yamí-kumo (ni) *adv* 闇雲(に) at random, in a blind way

yamí-sōba *n* 闇相場 black-market price

yamimásu, yamu *v* 止みます, 止む it stops

yamí ya/wa shinai *v* 止みや/はしない, [INFORMAL] **yamya shinai** 止みやしない = **yamanai** 止まない (not stop)

yamō´ *v* 止もう → **yamimásu** 止みます (about to stop)

yamome *n* やもめ widow

yámori *n* ヤモリ・守宮 gecko

yamu *v* 止む = **yamimásu** 止みます (it stops)

yamu-o-énai *v* やむを得ない = **yamu-o-émasén** やむを得ません unavoidable (= **sakerarénai** 避けられない)

yanagi *n* ヤナギ・柳 willow

yancha (na) *adj* やんちゃ(な) naughty, mischievous (*commonly used for boys*) (= **wanpaku (na)** 腕白・わんぱく(な))

yanda *v* 止んだ → **yamimáshita** 止みました (it stopped)

yande *v* 止んで → **yamimásu** 止みます

yáne *n* 屋根 roof

yaní *n* やに・脂 resin, gum → **meyaní** 目やに・目脂

yánushi *n* 家主 landlord, landlady (= **ōya(-san)** 大家(さん))

yaochō *n* 八百長 fixed game

yaoya *n* 八百屋 greengrocer, vegetable market

yappári *adv* やっぱり [INFORMAL] also; either; as I thought (= **yahári** やはり)

yarakashimásu, yarakasu *v* やらかします, やらかす [INFORMAL][IN NEGATIVE SENSE] does it [*demeans the object*] (= **shimásu** します); **héma o yarakashimásu** へまをやらかします makes a damn mess of it

yaranai *v* やらない = **yarimasén** やりません (not give/send/do/...)

yararemásu, yarareru *v* やられます, やられる gets had/hit (= *beaten*), outwitted, robbed, ripped off, beset (*by illness*), wounded, killed, ...

yare *v* やれ 1. → **yaremásu** やれます [INFINITIVE] 2. [IMPERATIVE] (give/send/do/... !) → **yarimásu** やります

yaréba *v* やれば, [INFORMAL] **yarya** やりゃ (if one does) → **yarimásu** やります

yaremásu, yareru *v* やれます, やれる 1. can give 2. can do

yaremásu, yareru *v* 遣れます, 遣れる can send

yarenai *v* やれない = **yaremasén** やれません (cannot give/do)

yarete *v* やれて → **yaremásu** やれます

yari *n* やり・槍 spear

yari *v* やり → **yarimásu** やります [INFINITIVE]

yari-kata *n* やり方 way, method, process, manner

yarimásu, yaru *v* やります, やる does

yarimásu, yaru *v* やり[遣り]ます, やる・遣る 1. gives 2. sends: **tegami o yarimásu** 手紙をやります send a letter 3. **íp-pai yarimásu** 一杯やります has a drink 4. has sex

yari-naoshimásu *v* やり直します, **yari-naósu** やり直す redoes it, does it over (*again*)

yari-sokonaimásu *v* やり損ないます, **yari-sokonáu** やり損なう botches, misses

yarí ya/wa shinai *v* やりや/はしない, [INFORMAL]

yarya shinai やりゃしない = **yaranai** やらない (not do)

yarō´ v やろう = **yarimashō´** やりましょう (let's do …!)

yarō´ n 野郎 (very INFORMAL) scoundred, so-and-so

yaru v やる = **yarimásu** やります [INFORMAL] (does; gives; sends, etc.)

yarya v [INFORMAL] やりゃ → **yaréba** やれば

yasai n 野菜 (**o-yásai** お野菜) vegetables

yasashii adj 優しい・やさしい gentle; kind, ˋgenerous (= **shinsetsu** 親切)

yasashii adj 易しい・やさしい easy, simple

yasashiku adj 優しく・やさしく gently; politely

yase v 痩せ → **yasemásu** 痩せます [INFINITIVE]

yase-gaman n やせ[痩せ]我慢 playing the martyr: ~ **shimásu** やせ我慢します plays the martyr

yasemásu, yaseru v 痩せます, 痩せる gets thin; **yasete imásu** 痩せています is thin

yáshi n ヤシ・椰子 (coconut) palm

yáshin n 野心 ambition [IN NEGATIVE SENSE] (= **yabō** 野望; **taishi** 大志, **taibō** 大望)

yashinai 養い 1. n foster(ing) 2. v → **yashinaimásu** 養います [INFINITIVE]

yashinaimásu, yashinau v 養います, 養う brings up, rears; fosters; nourishes

yashinatte v 養って → **yashinaimásu** 養います

yashinawanai v 養わない = **yashinaimasén** 養いません (not rear)

…´-yasu, yasu-… suffix, prefix …安, 安… cheap(er/lower) by … ; **hyakuén-yasu** 百円安 down/off by ¥100

yasúi adj 安い cheap, low(-priced)

yasu-mono n 安物 cheap stuff [IDIOM] **yasu-mono-gai no zeni-ushinai** 安物買いの銭失い Penny wise and pound foolish

yasu-ne n 安値 low price

yasu-ukeai n 安請け合い easy promise

yasu-uri n 安売り bargain (= **bāgen** バーゲン)

yasude n ヤスデ millipede (animal)

yasúi adj やすい・易い (= **shi-yasúi** しやすい) easy (to do)

yasúi adj やすい (= **shi-yasúi** しやすい) likely/apt to (do), tends to

yasúme v 休め 1. → **yasumemásu** 休めます [INFINITIVE] 2. [IMPERATIVE] (rest!) → **yasumimásu** 休みます

yasúmeba v 休めば (if one rests) → **yasumimásu** 休みます

yasumemásu, yasuméru v 休めます, 休める 1. rest/relax it, let it rest; ease it 2. can rest

yasuméreba v 休めれば (if we let it rest) → **yasumemásu** 休めます

yasumeyō´ v 休めよう = **yasumemashō** 休めましょう (let's let it rest!)

yasumí n 休み (**o-yasumi** お休み) 1. rest (= [BOOKISH] **kyūkei** 休憩) 2. break, pause (= **teishi** 停止, **chūdan** 中断) 3. recess (= **kyūkei**

jikan 休憩時間) 4. time off, vacation, holiday (= **kyūka** 休暇) 5. → **O-yasuminasái** おやすみなさい

yasúmi v 休み → **yasumimásu** 休みます [INFINITIVE]

yasumimásu, yasúmu v 休みます, 休む rests, relaxes, takes time off; stays away (from school); goes to bed, sleeps

yasumō´ v 休もう = **yasumimashō´** 休みましょう (let's rest!)

yasúnde v 休んで → **yasumimásu** 休みます

yasuraka (na/ni) adj, adv 安らか(な/に) peaceful(ly)

yasuri n やすり file, rasp

yasurí-gami n やすり紙 sandpaper (= **kami-yásuri** 紙やすり)

yatai n 屋台 street stall; stand

yatara adv やたら: **yatara na** やたらな indiscriminate, reckless, random: **yatara ni** やたらに indiscriminately, randomly, recklessly, blindly, unduly

yatō n 野党 opposition party

yatóe v 雇え 1. → **yatoemásu** 雇えます [INFINITIVE] 2. [IMPERATIVE] (hire them!) → **yatoimásu** 雇えます

yatóeba v 雇えば (if one hires) → **yatoimásu** 雇います

yatoéreba v 雇えれば (if one can hire) → **yatoemásu** 雇えます

yatoéru v 雇える = **yatoemásu** 雇えます (can employ/hire)

yatói 雇い 1. n employment 2. v → **yatoimásu** 雇います [INFINITIVE]

yatoimásu, yatóu v 雇います, 雇う employs, hires

yatótte v 雇って → **yatoimásu** 雇います

yatóu v 雇う = **yatoimásu** 雇います (employs)

yatowánai v 雇わない = **yatoimasén** 雇いません (not hire)

yatsú n 八つ eight (= **yattsú** 八つ)

    yatsuatari n 八つ当たり・やつあたり taking out on: ~ **shimásu** 八つ当たりします takes out on

yátsu n やつ・奴 [INFORMAL] 1. guy, fellow, wretch, [IN NEGATIVE SENSE] (undesirable) person/one (= **aitsu** あいつ) 2. (undesirable) thing/one 3. he/him

yatsude n ヤツデ fatsia

yattekimásu, yattekúru v やってきます, やってくる comes, comes along

yatto adv やっと at last; barely, with difficulty

yattoko n やっとこ pincers, pliers

yattsú n 八つ eight; eight years old

yawarakái adj 軟らかい・柔らかい soft, mild

yáya adj やや a little, slightly: **yáya átte** ややあって after a little while

yaya(k)koshíi adj やや(っ)こしい complicated; puzzling; tangled; troublesome

ye… → **e…**

yó n 世 the world at large, the public

yo-nó-naka *n* 世の中 the world at large, society

yó-ron *n* 世論 public opinion

yó *n* 代 the age, the times; one's lifetime

yó *n* 夜 night (= **yóru** 夜)

yo-aké *n* 夜明け dawn

yo-fúkashi *n* 夜更かし staying up late:
yo-fúkashi o shimásu 夜更かしをします stays up late

yo-máwari *n* 夜回り night watchman

yo-naká *n* 夜中 middle of the night

yóru *n* 夜 night

yo-… *prefix* 四 four

yó-ji *n* 四時 four o'clock

yó-jo -han *n* 四畳半 four-and-a-half mat area, a small Japanese room

yo-ban, yón-ban *n* 四番 number four

yo-nen *n* 四年 **1.** fourth year **2.** four years (= **yonén-kan** 四年間)

yon-én-sei 四年生 **1.** fourth-year student (*at elementary school*) **2.** senior (*at university/college*)

yo-nín *n* 四人 four people

… yo *interj* …よ **1.** indeed, mind you, I tell/warn/alert you **2.** (*reinforces* IMPERATIVE)

yō´ *n* 要 gist (= **yō´shi** 要旨, **yōryō´** 要領)

yō *n* 用 (**go-yō** ご用) **1.** business; errand (= **yōji** 用事) **2.** use, service **3.** going to the bathroom

yō-ji *n* 用事 business, errand

yō-ken *n* 用件 business (*something to tell, something to do*): "**Yoroshikereba go-yōken o uketamawarimasu ga**" 「よろしければ、ご用件を承りますが」 (*on the phone, in the reception, etc.*) "What can we/I do for you?", "May I help you?"

yō-mú-in *n* 用務員 custodian, janitor, servant (*in the school, office, etc.*)

yō-táshi *n* 用足し business, errand

yō-… *prefix* 洋… Western

yō-fuku *n* 洋服 (**o-yófuku** お洋服) (Western-style) clothes, a suit, a dress (= **fuku** 服): (**yō**) **fuku-ya** (洋)服屋 tailor, clothing shop; **yófuku-burashi** 洋服ブラシ cloth-brush; **yófuku-dansu** 洋服ダンス wardrobe

yō-ga *n* 洋画 **1.** foreign movie **2.** Western-style painting

yō-gaku *n* 洋楽 Western-style music

yō-gása *n* 洋傘 (*Western-style*) umbrella (= **kasa** 傘)

yō-gáshi *n* 洋菓子 Western cakes/sweets

yō-hin *n* 洋品 haberdashery

yō-kan *n* 洋館 Western-style building

yō-ma *n* 洋間 Western-style room

yō-sai *n* 洋裁 dressmaking; **yōsáishi** 洋裁師 dressmaker

yō-shi *n* 洋紙 Western paper

yō-shoku *n* 洋食 foreign (*Western*) food

yō-shu *n* 洋酒 liquor (*Western*)

yō-… *prefix* 養… foster, protection

yō-fubo *n* 養父母 adoptive parents

yó´-jo *n* 養女 adopted daughter; (**… o**) **yō´jo ni shimásu** (…を)養女にします adopts (*a girl*)

yō-shi *n* 養子 adopted child; (**… o**) **yōshi ni shimásu** (…を)養子にします adopts a child

yō-iku *n* 養育 [BOOKISH] **1.** bringing up children, education: ~ **shimásu** 養育します brings up; **yōiku-hi** 養育費 expense of bringing up children **2.** protection (*of old people, orphan children, sick people, etc.*); **yōiku-in** 養育院 asylum

yō-rōin *n* 養老院 old people's home (= **rōjin hōmu** 老人ホーム)

yobanai *v* 呼ばない = **yobimasén** 呼びません (not call/invite)

yobe *v* 呼べ **1.** → **yobemásu** 呼べます [INFINITIVE] **2.** [IMPERATIVE] (call!) → **yobimásu** 呼びます

yobéba *v* 呼べば (if one calls/invites) → **yobimásu** 呼びます

yobemásu, yoberu *v* 呼べます, 呼べる **1.** can call **2.** can invite

yobenai *v* 呼べない = **yobemásen** 呼べません (cannot call/invite)

yobete *v* 呼べて → **yobemásu** 呼べます

yobi *v* 呼び → **yobimásu** 呼びます [INFINITIVE]

yóbi *n* 予備 preparation: **yóbi (no)** 予備(の) reserve, spare

yobi-kō *n* 予備校 prep school, cram school

yobi-sénkyo *n* 予備選挙 a primary election

yobimásu, yobu *v* 呼びます, 呼ぶ **1.** calls; names; summons **2.** invites

yobi ya/wa shinai *v* 呼びや/はしない = **yobanai** 呼ばない (not call/invite)

yobō *v* 呼ぼう = **yobimashō´** 呼びましょう (let's call/invite!)

yobō *n* 予防 precaution, prevention: ~ **shimásu** 予防します prevents, wards off

yobō-sesshu *n* 予防接種 = **yobō-chū´sha** 予防注射 inoculation, vaccination (*injection*)

yōbō *n* 要望 strong desire

yōbō *n* 容貌 facial appearance

yobun (no/ni) *adj, adv* 余分(の/に) extra, excess

yōbun *n* 養分 nutrient substance (= **eiyōbun** 栄養分)

yobya *v* [INFORMAL] 呼びゃ → **yobéba** 呼べば

yóchi *n* 余地 [BOOKISH] room, space, margin, leeway (= **yutori** ゆとり, **yoyū** 余裕): **giron no yóchi ga arimasen** 議論の余地がありません There is no room for debate.: (**mattaku**) **utagai no yóchi ga arimasen** (まったく)疑いの余地がありません There is no doubt about it (at all).

yóchi *n* 予知 prediction: ~ **shimásu** 予知します predicts, forecasts, foresees, foretells

yochi-nōryoku *n* 予知能力 ability to foresee the future

yōchi (na) *adj* 幼稚(な) childish: **yōchi na kangae** 幼稚な考え childish idea

yōchi-en *n* 幼稚園 kindergarten

yodare *n* よだれ drool: **yodare ga déru** よだれが出る drool comes out

yōdai *n* 容態・容体・様態 health condition (*commonly of patient*) (= **yōtai** 容態, **hyōjō** 病状)

yōʹdo *n* ヨード iodine

yóeba *v* 酔えば = **yóya** 酔や (if one gets drunk) → **yoimásu** 酔います

yōeki *n* 溶液 liquid solution

yōen *adj* 妖艶 seductive beauty, frascinatingly elegant, bewitching (= **adeyaka** あでやか・艶やか)

yoga *n* ヨガ yoga

yōʹgan *n* 溶岩 lava

yogen *n* 予言 prediction: ~ **shimásu** 予言します predicts; **nosutoradamusu no dai-yogen** ノストラダムスの大予言 the great prophecies of Nostradamus

yōgí-sha *n* 容疑者 a suspect

yogo *n* 予後 prognosis: **yogo-furyō** 予後不良 poor prognosis: **yogo-ryōkō** 予後良好 good prognosis: **yogo-inshi** 予後因子 prognostic factor

yōgo *n* 擁護 [BOOKISH] protection, support: ~ **shimásu** 擁護します protects, supports; **jinken-yōgo** 人権擁護 protection of human rights; **dōbutsu-yōgo-dantai** 動物擁護団体 animal protection association

… yōgo *suffix* …用語 (*special*) term (*technical word, etc.*): **kōyōgo** 公用語 national language: **senmon-yōgo** 専門用語 technical term: **sabetsu-yōgo** 差別用語 discriminatory words

yogore *n* 汚れ **1.** dirt, smudge, blot, blotch **2.** → **yogoremásu** 汚れます [INFINITIVE]

yogoremásu, yogoreru *v* 汚れます, 汚れる gets soiled, smudged; **yogorete imásu** 汚れています is dirty

yogorenai *v* 汚れない = **yogoremásen** 汚れません (not get soiled)

yogosanai *v* 汚さない = **yogoshimásen** 汚しません (not soil)

yogoshi *v* 汚し → **yogoshimásu** 汚します [INFINITIVE]

yogoshimásu, yogosu *v* 汚します, 汚す soils, dirties, stains

yōʹgu *n* 用具 tools, implements, instruments, kit; **yōgu-búkuro** 用具袋 kit bag; **yōgú-bako** 用具箱 tool box

yōguruto *n* ヨーグルト yogurt

yoha *n* 余波 after-effect (*of typhoon, etc.*), aftermath

yohaku *n* 余白 margin, blank (*space*) (= **supésu** スペース)

yōhin *n* 用品 = **…-yōʹhin** …用品 utensils, appliances, supplies, necessities; **nichi-yohin** 日用品 daily necessities; **jimu-yōhin** 事務用品 office supplies

yohō *n* 予報 forecast, prediction; **tenki-yóhō** 天気予報 weather forecast

yohodo *adv* よほど・余程 considerably, a good deal (= **yoppodo** よっぽど); **yohodo no koto ga nai kagiri** よほどのことがない限り unless something really important comes up

yoi *n* 宵 [BOOKISH] early part of the night, just after nightfall; **yoi no myōjō** 宵の明星 Venus in the evening sky

yói *adj* 良い・よい (= **íi** いい) good [NEGATIVE] **yóku arimasén** 良くありません; (*past*) **yókatta desu** 良かったです was good

yoi *n* 酔い **1.** intoxication, drunkenness **2.** motion sickness (*seasick, carsick, airsick, etc.*); **kuruma-yoi** 車酔い car sickness; **norimono-yói** 乗り物酔い travel sickness

yói *adj* 酔い → **yoimásu** 酔います [INFINITIVE]

yōʹi *n* 用意 preparation; caution (= **junbi** 準備); **… no yōʹi o shimásu** …の用意をします prepares for …

yoimásu, yóu *v* 酔います, 酔う gets drunk; gets seasick, carsick, airsick

yoisho *interj* よいしょ upsy-daisy!, alley-oop!, heave-ho!

yói ya/wa shinai *v* 酔いや/はしない, **yóya shinai** 酔やしない = **yowánai** 酔わない (not get drunk)

yōji *n* 楊枝・ようじ toothpick (= **tsuma-yōʹji** つまようじ・爪楊枝)

yōʹji *n* 幼児 [BOOKISH] infant

yōʹji *n* 幼時 [BOOKISH] childhood: **yōji-taiken** 幼時体験 childhood experiences

yōʹjin *n* 用心 precaution, caution, care; **"hi no yōʹjin"** 「火の用心」 "Be careful of fire!"

yōjin-bō *n* 用心棒 bodyguard (= **bodii gādo** ボディガード)

yōjin-bukái *adj* 用心深い cautious, careful (= **shinchō** 慎重)

yoka *n* 余暇 [BOOKISH] spare time (= **hima (na jikan)** 暇(な時間))

yōka *n* 八日 **1.** 8th day (*of a month*) **2.** (*for*) eight days (= **yōka-kan** 八日間)

yokan *n* 予感 premonition, foreboding: **yokan ga shimásu** 予感がします forebodes

yōʹkan *n* ヨウカン・羊羹 sweet bars of bean paste and agar-agar flavored with chestnut, plum, etc.

yóke *v* 避け → **yokemásu** 避けます [INFINITIVE]

yokei (na) *adj* 余計(な) superfluous, unnecessary, uncalled-for: **yokei ni** 余計に unnecessarily

yokemásu, yokéru *v* 避けます, 避ける avoids, keeps away from

yoken *n* 予見 prediction (= **yochi** 予知): ~ **shimásu** 予見します predicts, forecasts

yokénai *v* 避けない = **yokemásen** 避けません (not avoid)

yokeyōʹ *v* 避けよう = **yoke-mashōʹ** 避けましょう (let's avoid)

yoki *n* 予期 expectation, anticipation: ~ **shimásu** 予期します expects, anticipates

yōki *n* 容器 container, receptacle (= **iremono** 入れ物, **utsuwa** うつわ・器)

yōki *n* 陽気 **1.** weather **2.** cheerfulness, brightness, liveliness

yōki (na) *adj* 陽気な cheerful, bright, lively

yokin *n* 預金 deposit (*of money*): ~ **shimásu** 預金します deposits (*money*)

yokin-kōʹza *n* 預金口座 bank account

yokin-tsūʹchō *n* 預金通帳 bankbook

yokka *n* 四日 **1.** 4th day (*of a month*) **2.** (*for*) four days (= **yokka-kan** 四日間)

yokkyū n 欲求 greed; desire, want (= **yoku** 欲, **yokubō** 欲望, **negai** 願い): **sandai-yokkyū** 三大欲求 three basic desires (*food appetite, sexual desire, and desire to sleep*) (*also known as part of the four Primitive Fountains: Food, Sleep, and Sex*)

yokkyū-fuman n 欲求不満 frustration (= **furasutorēshon** フラストレーション)

yoko n 横 1. side (= **soba** 側, **waki** 脇) 2. the width (= **haba** 幅) 3. sideways 4. sidewise

yoko-chō n 横町 sidestreets, alley

yoko-ito n 横糸 woof (*horizontal threads*)

yoko girimáou, yoko gíru v 横切ります, 横切る crosses, cuts across, intersects, passes

Yokohama n 横浜 Yokohama

Yokohamá-Eki n 横浜駅 Yokohama Station

Yokohamá-kō n 横浜港 the port of Yokohama

yokoku n 予告 advance notice; **eiga no yokoku-hen** 映画の予告編 movie trailer (= **torērā** トレーラー)

yoko ni narimásu (náru) v 横になります(なる) lies down (= **yoko-tawárimásu** 横たわります)

yoko ni shimásu (suru) v 横にします(する) lays down (= **yokotaemásu** 横たえます)

yokoshimásu, yokósu v 寄越します, 寄越る sends (*here*), hands over to me

Yṓkoso. interj ようこそ Welcome!; **Nihon e Yōkoso** 日本へようこそ Welcome to Japan! (= **Yōkoso Nihon e** ようこそ日本へ)

yokozuna n 横綱 grand champion sumo wrestler

yokú n 欲 greed; desire, want (= **yokubō** 欲望)

yokubō n 欲望 greed; desire, want (= **yoku** 欲)

yoku o ieba 欲を言えば [IDIOM] if I am allowed to wish more

yoku o kaku 欲をかく [IDIOM] gets greedy (= **yoku baru** 欲張る)

... yoku suffix ...欲 desire: **shoku-yoku** 食欲 food appetite, desire for food or drink: **sei-yoku** 性欲 sexual desire: **suimin-yoku** 睡眠欲 desire to sleep (→ **sandai-yokkyū** 三大欲求)

yóku adv 良く・よく well, better; **kare no koto wa yóku shitte imasu** 彼のことはよく知っています I know him very well.; **hayaku yóku narimasuyōni** 早く良くなりますように Hope you feel better soon. (*to a sick person*)

yóku adv よく lots, much, thoroughly, carefully; **yóku yonde kudasai** よく読んで下さい Please read it carefully.

yóku adv よく lots, often, frequently; **Eiga-kan ni wa yóku ikimasu** 映画館にはよく行きます I often go to the (*movie*) theater.

yóku (-) ... prefix 翌... the next (*day, night, month, year;* date)

yoku-ban n 翌晩 [BOOKISH] the following night, the next night

yoku-getsu n 翌月 [BOOKISH] the following month, the next month

yoku-jitsu n 翌日 [BOOKISH] the following day, the next day

yoku-shū n 翌週 [BOOKISH] the following week, the next week

yoku-toshi n 翌年 [BOOKISH] the following year, the next year

yokubári n 欲張り a greedy person

yokubárí (na) adj 欲張り(な) greedy

yokubári v 欲張り → **yokubarimásu** 欲張ります [INFINITIVE]

yokubarimásu, yokubáru v 欲張ります, 欲張る is greedy

yoku (-) ... prefix 湯... bath (→ **yukata** 浴衣)

yoku-jō n 浴場 [BOOKISH] bathhouse; **kōshū-yokujō** 公衆浴場 public bath (= **(o-)furo-ya** (お)風呂屋)

yoku-shitsu n 浴室 bathroom (= **(o-) furo-ba** (お)風呂場)

yoku-sō n 浴槽 bathtub

yōkyū n 要求 requirement, demand, claim, request (= **yōsei** 要請)

yome n 嫁 1. daughter-in-law 2. bride (= **o-yome-san** お嫁さん) 3. **yome-san** 嫁さん [INFORMAL] (*my*) wife (= **oku-san** 奥さん)

yómeba v 読めば (if one reads) → **yomimásu** 読みます

yomi n 読み 1. reading 2. expectation, forecast 3. pronunciation; **on-yomi** 音読み Chinese pronunciation of Kanji/Chinese characters; **kun-yomi** 訓読み Japanese pronunciation of Kanji/Chinese characters

yomi-kata n 読み方 1. how to read 2. how to pronounce the Kanji/Chinese characters

yomimásu, yómu v 読みます, 読む 1. reads 2. reads out, pronounces 3. foresees, guesses

yomi ya/wa shinai v 読みや/はしない, [INFORMAL] **yómya shinai** 読みやしない = **yománai** 読まない (not read)

yōmō n 羊毛 wool

yómya v [INFORMAL] 読みゃ → **yómeba** 読めば

yón n 四・4 four

yon-bai n 四倍 four-fold, four times as much

yon-banmé (no), yo-banmé (no) adj 四番目(の) fourth

yón-ban, yo-ban n 四番 number four

yón-dai n 四台 four (*machines, vehicles*)

yón-do n 四度 four degrees; four times (= **yón-kái** 四回, **yón-hén** 四遍)

yón-do-mé n 四度目 the fourth time

yón-fun, yón-pun n 四分 four minutes

yón-hai n 四杯 four cupfuls

yón-hén n 四遍 four times

yón-hiki n 四匹 four (*fishes/bugs, small animals*)

yón-hon n 四本 four (*pencils/bottles, long objects*)

yon-kágetsu n 四か月 four months

yon-kai n 四階 four floors/stories; fourth floor

yón-kái n 四回 four times; **yon kai-mé** 四回目 the fourth time

yón-mai n 四枚 four sheets (*flat things, papers, dishes, etc.*)

yon-méi n 四名 four people (*also* **yo-mei** 四名, **yo-nín** 四人)

yón-pun n 四分 four minutes (*also* **yón-fun** 四分)

yón-satsu n 四冊 four copies (*books, magazines*)

yón-tō n 四頭 four (*horses/oxen, large animals*)

yón-wa n 四羽 four (*birds, rabbits*) (*also* **yón-ba** 四羽)

... yō´ (na) *suffix, adj* ...よう[様](な) seem(ing) to be: **yō ni** ...よう[様]に (*so as to be*) like ...; **suru yō ni iimásu** するよう[様]に言います tells one to do it

yondokoro-nai *adj* よんどころない inevitable

yón-hyaku n 四百・400 four hundred

yōniku n 羊肉 [BOOKISH] lamb (*meat, includes mutton*)

yón-jū n 四十・40 forty

yon-mán n 四万 40,000 forty thousand

...-yō (no) *adj* ...用(の) for the use of ...

yon-sén n 四千・4,000 four thousand

yopparai n 酔っ払い drunk (*person*)

yopparaimásu, yopparau *v* 酔っ払います, 酔っ払う gets drunk

yoppodo *adv* よっぽど considerably, a good deal (= **yohodo** よほど・余程)

yoranai *v* 寄らない → **yorimasén** 寄りません (not drop in)

yoranai *v* 拠らない = **yorimasén** 拠りません (not rely)

yoránai *v* 撚らない = **yorimasén** 撚りません (not twist)

yore *v* 寄れ 1. → **yoremásu** 寄れます [INFINITIVE] 2. [IMPERATIVE] (drop in!) → **yorimásu** 寄ります

yóre *v* 撚れ 1. → **yoremásu** 撚れます (can twist) [INFINITIVE] 2. [IMPERATIVE] (twist it!) → **yorimásu** *v* 撚ります

yoréba *v* 拠れば= [INFORMAL] **yorya** 拠りゃ (if one relies) → **yorimásu** 拠ります

yoréba *v* 寄れば= [INFORMAL] **yorya** 寄りゃ (if one drops in) → **yorimásu** 寄ります

yóreba *v* 撚れば (if one twists) → **yorimásu** 撚れば

yoremásu, yoreru *v* 寄れます, 寄れる can drop in; can approach

yoremásu, yoréru *v* 撚れます, 撚れる can twist/twine

yorenai *v* 寄れない = **yoremasén** 寄れません (cannot drop in)

yorénai *v* 撚れない = **yoremasén** 撚れません (cannot twist)

yoreréba *v* 寄れれば (if one can drop in) → **yoremásu** 寄れます

yoréreba *v* 撚れれば (if one can twist) → **yoremásu** 撚れます

yorete *v* 寄れて → **yoremásu** 寄れます

yórete *v* 撚れて → **yoremásu** 撚れます

yori *v* 寄り → **yorimásu** 寄ります (drops in) [INFINITIVE]

yori *v* 拠り → **yorimásu** 拠ります (relies) [INFINITIVE]

yóri *v* 撚り → **yorimásu** 撚ります (twists) [INFINITIVE]

yori-... *adj* より... [+ADJECTIVE] more ..., ...-er [BOOKISH]

... yóri *conj* ...より 1. (*more/rather/other*) than ... 2. from, out of; since

yoridori-midori n よりどりみどり・選り取り見取り choosing whichever one likes

yorigónomi n より好み・選り好み choosiness: **yorigónomi o shimásu** より好みをします is choosy

yorimásu, yoru *v* 寄ります, 寄る drops in; approaches, comes near; meets

yorimásu, yoru *v* 拠ります, 拠る relies on; ... ni yotte ...によって, ... ni yoru to ...によると, ... ni yoréba ...によれば according to ...: **tenki-yohō ni yoreba asu wa ame dasō desu** 天気予報によれば明日は雨だそうです According to the weather forecast, it will rain tomorrow.

yorimásu, yóru *v* 撚ります, 撚る twists, twines (= **nejirimasu** 捻ります, **nejiru** 捻る)

yorí ya/wa shinai *v* 拠りや/はしない = **yoranai** 拠らない (not rely)

yorí ya/wa shinai *v* 寄りや/はしない, [INFORMAL] **yorya shinai** 寄りゃしない = **yoranai** 寄らない (not drop in)

yóri ya/wa shinai *v* 撚りや/はしない = **yoránai** 撚らない (not twist)

yorō´ *v* 寄ろう = **yorimashō´** 寄りましょう (let's drop in!; let's approach!)

yorō´ *v* 撚ろう = **yorimashō´** 撚りましょう (let's twist it!)

yoroi n 鎧 armor

yoroi-do n よろい戸・鎧戸 shutter (*house*) (= **shattā** シャッター)

yorokobi 喜び 1. n joy. 2. v → **yorokobimásu** 喜びます [INFINITIVE]

yorokobimásu, yorokóbu *v* 喜びます, 喜ぶ is glad, happy, delighted; rejoices

yorokónde *v* 喜んで → **yorokobimásu** 喜びます; gladly

yoro-mekí n よろめき an (*extramarital*) affair

yoro-mekimásu, yoro-méku *v* よろめきます, よろめく totters, falters, staggers; has an (*extramarital*) affair

Yōróppa n ヨーロッパ Europe (= **Ōshū** 欧州)

yoroshii *adj* よろしい・宜しい very well; satisfactory

yoroshikáttara *adv* よろしかったら if you don't mind; if you like

yoroshiku *v* よろしく・宜しく 1. (... ni) **yoroshiku (itte kudasái/o-tsutae kudasái)** (...に)よろしく(言って下さい/お伝え下さい) Give my regards to ... 2. → **yoroshii** よろしい・宜しい 3. **Dō´zo yoroshiku.** どうぞよろしく. How do you do?; Please favor (*my request, me, mine*).

yóroyoro (to) *adj, adv* よろよろ(と) tottering, faltering, staggering; having an affair: **~ shimásu** よろよろします → **yoromekimásu** よろめきます

yoru *v* 寄る = **yorimásu** 寄ります (drops in)

yoru *v* 拠る・因る = **yorimásu** 拠る[因り]ます (relies); **... ni yoru to ...** によると according to ...

yóru *v* 撚る = **yorimásu** 撚ります (twists)

yorya *v* [INFORMAL] 拠りゃ[因りゃ] → **yoréba** 拠れ[因れ]ば

yorya *v* [INFORMAL] 寄りゃ → **yoréba** 寄れば

yórya *v* [INFORMAL] 撚りゃ → **yóreba** 撚れば

yōryō *n* 要領 **1.** gist: **yōryō o enai kaitō** 要領を得ない回答 pointless answer, unclear answer **2.** knack: **yōryō ga ii** 要領がいい is efficient (person)

yōsai *n* 要塞 fortress (*military facility*)

yosan *n* 予算 budget

yōsan *n* 養蚕 raising silkworms, silk farming, sericulture

yosánai *v* よさない = **yoshimasén** よしません (not stop doing it) (= **yamemasén** やめません)

yose *n* 寄席 vaudeville (*theater*)

yose *v* 寄せ → **yosemásu** 寄せます **1.** [INFINITIVE] **2. yose ro** 寄せろ, **yosé yo** 寄せよ [IMPERATIVE] (let them approach!)

yóse *v* 止せ [IMPERATIVE] (stop doing it!) → **yoshimásu** 止します

yóseba *v* 止せば = [INFORMAL] **yósha** 止しゃ (if they stop doing it) → **yoshimásu** 止します

yōseki *n* 容積 volume of a container

yosemásu, yoseru *v* 寄せます、寄せる **1.** lets approach, brings near **2.** collects, gathers **3.** adds **4.** sends

yosen *n* 予選 preliminary; primary

yose-nabe *n* 寄せ鍋 chowder

yosenai *v* 寄せない = **yosemasén** 寄せません (not let approach; ...)

yose-nami 寄せ波 surf

yoseréba *v* 寄せれば = [INFORMAL] **yoserya** 寄せりゃ (if we let them approach; ...) → **yosemásu** 寄せます

yosete *v* 寄せて → **yosemásu** 寄せます (lets approach; ...)

yósha *v* [INFORMAL] 止しゃ → **yoséba** 止せば

yóshi *n* 由 reason; meaning; circumstance; means

yóshi *v* 止し → **yoshimásu** 止します [INFINITIVE]

Yóshi! *interj* よし! OK; very well

yō´shi *n* 用紙 forms, blanks, papers: **genkō-yōshi** 原稿用紙 manuscript paper used for writing Japanese vertically (*commonly one page of 400-characters or 200-characters*): **ankēto-yōshi** アンケート用紙 questionnaire (*originally came from French word "enquete"*)

yō´-shi *n* 要旨 summary, abstract (*gist*) (= **shu-shi** 主旨)

yoshimásu, yósu *v* 止します、止す stops doing it (= **yamemásu** 止めます)

yō-shimásu, yō-súru *v* 要します、要する needs, requires, takes, costs; summarizes, sums it up

yóshite *v* よして → **yoshimásu** よします (can stop doing it)

yōshoku *n* 養殖 raising, farming, culture: **yōshoku-shínju** 養殖真珠 cultured pearls

yoshū *n* 予習 preparatory study: **~ shimásu** 予習します prepares, studies (*ahead*)

yosó *n* よそ・余所 somewhere else; alien, strange: **yosó no hitó** よその人 outsider, stranger (= **yoso-mono** よそ者・余所者)

yoso-mono *n* よそ者・余所者 outsider, stranger

yosō *n* 予想 expectation, presumption: **~ shimásu** 予想します expects, presumes, presumes; **yosō íjō** 予想以上 above/beyond expectations

yosō´ *v* よそう = **yoshimashō´** よしましょう (let's stop doing it)

yō´so *n* 要素 element

yosoku *n* 予測 forecast, prediction, estimate: **~ shimásu** 予測します forecasts, predicts, estimates

yósu *v* 止す [INFORMAL] = **yoshimásu** 止します (stops doing it)

yōsu *n* 様子・ようす circumstances; aspect; appearance, look

yōsui *n* 用水 diversion of water, service water, irrigation water

yōsui-ro *n* 用水路 irrigation canal

yō-súru *v* 要する = **yō-shimásu** 要します (needs, requires, takes, costs; summarizes, sums it up)

yō-súru ni *v* 要するに in summary, to sum it up, in short; in effect, what it amounts to (*boils down to*) is ...; after all

yotamono *n* よた者・与太者 hoodlum

yotei *n* 予定 expectation, plan: **~ shimásu** 予定します schedules, plans

yōtén *n* 要点 gist, point

yotō *n* 与党 ruling party

yotsu-kado *n* 四つ角 intersection (*of two streets*), crossroads

yotta *v* 寄った = **yorimáshita** 寄りました (dropped in)

yotta *v* 拠った = **yorimáshita** 拠りました (relied)

yótta *v* 撚った = **yorimáshita** 撚りました (twisted)

yótta *v* 酔った = **yoimáshita** 酔いました (got drunk)

yotte *v* 寄って → **yorimásu** 寄ります (drops in)

yotte *v* 拠って → **yorimásu** 拠ります (relies)

yótte *v* 撚って → **yorimásu** 撚ります (twists)

yótte *v* 酔って → **yoimásu** 酔います (gets drunk)

yotto *n* ヨット yacht

yottsú *n* 四つ four

yóu *v* 酔う = **yoimásu** 酔います (gets drunk; gets seasick, etc.)

yowái *adj* 弱い weak; frail; poor at (*math, etc.*); **sake ni yowái** 酒に弱い easily intoxicated

yowa-mi *n* 弱み weakness, weak point

yowa-mushi *n* 弱虫 a cream puff, wimp

yowánai *v* 酔わない = **yoimasén** 酔いません (not get drunk)

yowasemásu, yowaséru *v* 酔わせます, 酔わせる gets one drunk, lets one get drunk

yoyaku *n* 予約 reservation, subscription, booking, appointment: **~ shimásu** 予約します makes a reservation

yōyaku *adv* ようやく finally, at last; barely

yōyaku *n* 要約 a summary: **~ shimásu** 要約します summarizes

yoyū *n* 余裕 room, leeway, margin, excess, surplus

yú *n* 湯 (**o-yu** お湯) **1.** hot water, warm water: **o-yu o wakashimásu** お湯を沸かします boils water

yu-dō´fu *n* 湯豆腐 tofu (*bean-curd*) cubes boiled in an earthen-ware pot

yu-ge *n* 湯気 steam

yu-nomi *n* 湯飲み, **yunomi-jáwan** 湯飲み茶碗 Japanese teacup

yu-tánpo *n* 湯たんぽ hot-water bottle

yu-wákashi *n* 湯沸かし teakettle, boiler (*for heating water*)

yu-zámashi *n* 湯冷まし cooled boiled water

yú *n* 湯 (**o-yu** お湯) **2.** bath: **o-yu ga wakimáshita** お湯が沸きました The bath is ready.: **otoko-yu** 男湯 men's section of a bathhouse: **on'na-yu** 女湯 women's section of a bathhouse

yú-bune *n* 湯船 bathtub

yu-zame *n* 湯冷め feeling chilly after taking a bath

yū *n* ゆう・言う [INFORMAL] = **iu** 言う, **iimásu** 言います (says)

yū *n* 結う = **yuu** 結う, **yuimásu** 結います does up one's hair

yū *n* 優 excellent: (*grade*) **yū, ryō, ka, fuka** 優、良、可、不可 Excellent, Good, Poor, Failing

yū´-retsu *n* 優劣 relative merits (*superiority or inferiority*)

yū-ryō (na) *adj* 優良な superior

yū-shō *n* 優勝 (*winning*) the victory/championship; **~ shimásu** 優勝します wins (*the victory*); **yūshō-sha** 優勝者 the winner, victor

yū-shū (na) *adj* 優秀な excellent, superior

yū-tō-sei *n* 優等生 model student

yū *n* 夕 evening (= **yū-gata** 夕方)

yū-bé *n* 夕べ evening

yū-dachi *n* 夕立 a sudden shower during afternoon or evening

yū-gao *n* 夕顔 moonflower

yū-gata *n* 夕方 evening

yū-giri *n* 夕霧 evening mist

yū-gure *n* 夕暮れ twilight (= **tasogare** たそがれ・黄昏); **yū-gure-doki** 夕暮れ時 evening during the twilight hours

yū-han *n* 夕飯 [INFORMAL] = **yū-meshi** 夕飯 supper, dinner (= **yū-shoku** 夕食)

yū-hi *n* 夕日・夕陽 **setting sun**

yū-kan *n* 夕刊 **evening paper**

yū-kaze *n* 夕風 **evening breeze**

yū-meshi *n* 夕飯 (*commonly male. Very informal*) → yū-han 夕飯

yū-moya *n* 夕もや・夕靄 evening fog

yū-shoku *n* 夕食 evening meal (*supper, dinner*) (= **yū-han, yū-meshi** 夕飯)

yū-yake *n* 夕焼け (*red sky at*) sunset

yū-… *prefix* 友… friend

yū-jin *n* 友人 [BOOKISH] friend (= **tomo** 友, **tomodachi** 友だち・友達)

yū-jō *n* 友情 friendship

yū-kō *n* 友好 [BOOKISH] (*official*) friendship, friendly relationship (*among countries, etc.*)

yū-be *n* ゆうべ・昨夜 last night (= **kinō no ban/yoru** 昨日の晩/夜, **saku-ban/ya** 昨夜/晩)

yūben *n* 雄弁 eloquence: **yūben (na)** 雄弁(な) eloquent

yūben-ka *n* 雄弁家 eloquent speaker

yubí *n* 指 **1.** finger (= **te no yubí** 手の指) **2.** toe (= **ashi no yubí** 足の指)

yubi-ningyō *n* 指人形 finger puppet

yubi-núki *n* 指貫き thimble

yubi-saki *n* 指先 fingertip

yubi-sashimásu, yubi-sasu *v* 指差します, 指差す points (*commonly indicates something with an extended index finger*)

yubi-wa *n* 指輪 ring: **konyaku-yubiwa** 婚約指輪 engagement ring

yūbin *n* 郵便 mail: **yūbin-chókin** 郵便貯金 postal savings; **yūbin-fúrikae** 郵便振替 postal transfer; **yūbin-ká wase** 郵便為替 (*postal*) money order; **yūbin-uke** 郵便受け mailbox

yūbin-bako *n* 郵便箱 mailbox

yūbin-bángō *n* 郵便番号 zip code; ZIP Code

yūbín-butsu *n* 郵便物 mail

yūbín-kyoku *n* 郵便局 post office

yūbín-posuto *n* 郵便ポスト Red post box (= **posuto** ポスト)

yūbín-ya (san) *n* 郵便屋(さん) mail carrier, mailman, postman

yū´bi (na) *adj* 優美(な) elegant, graceful

yūboku *n* 遊牧 nomadism: **yūboku-min** 遊牧民 nomad

yūbō (na) *adj* 有望(な) promising (= **zento yūbō (na)** 前途有望(な)): **yūbō-kabu** 有望株 growth stock: **yūbō (na) senshu** 有望(な)選手 promising player

yudan *n* 油断 negligence, carelessness, sloppines

yudáne *v* 委ね → **yudanemásu** 委ねます **1.** [INFINITIVE] **2. yudané ro** 委ねろ, **yudáne yo** 委ねよ [IMPERATIVE] (entrust it!)

yudanemásu, yudanéru *v* 委ねます, 委ねる entrusts, commits

Yudayá-jin *n* ユダヤ人 Jew; **Yudaya-kyō** ユダヤ教 Judaism

yudemásu, yudéru *v* 茹でます, 茹でる boils (*food*)

yude-támago *n* ゆで卵・茹で卵 boiled egg

yúdete *v* 茹でて → **yudemásu** 茹でます

yue *v* 結え **1.** → **yuemásu** 結えます [INFINITIVE] **2.** [IMPERATIVE] (do up your hair!) → **yuimásu** 結います

yué *n* 故・ゆえ [BOOKISH] reason, grounds; **… yué ni** …故に・ゆえに for the reason that …, because …

yuéba v 結えば = **yuya** 結や (if one does up one's hair) → **yuimásu** 結います

yuemásu, yueru v 結えます, 結える can do up one's hair

yuenai v 結えない = **yuemásén** 結えません (cannot do up one's hair)

yūenchi n 遊園地 amusement park

yueréba v 結えれば (if one can do up one's hair) → **yuemásu** 結えます

yū´fuku (na) adj 裕福(な) rich, wealthy

yūfō n ユーフォー・UFO unidentified flying object (= **mi-kakunin hikō-buttai** 未確認飛行物体)

yū´ga (na) adj 優雅(な) elegant, refined

yugamanai v 歪まない = **yugamimásén** 歪みません (not get distorted/warped)

yugamemásu, yugameru v 歪めます, 歪める distorts, warps

yugamenai v 歪めない = **yugamemásén** 歪めません (not distort/warp)

yugámete v 歪めて → **yugamemásu** 歪めます

yugami n 歪み distortion, warp

yugami v 歪み → **yugamimásu** 歪みます [INFINITIVE]

yugamimásu, yugamu v 歪みます, 歪む gets distorted/warped

yugande v 歪んで → **yugamimásu** 歪みます

yūga-tō n 誘蛾灯 light trap

yūgi n 遊戯 (**o-yūgi** お遊戯) playgame: **yūgi-shitsu** 遊戯室 playroom

yūhei n 幽閉 confinement: ~ **shimásu** 幽閉します confines

yūhodō n 遊歩道 promenade (= **puromunādo** プロムナード)

yui v 結い → **yuimásu** 結います [INFINITIVE]

yuigon n 遺言 1. leaving a will 2. a will, testament (= **yuigon-jō** 遺言状, **yuigon-sho** 遺言書)

yúiitsu (no) adj 唯一(の) [BOOKISH] the only (= **tada hitotsu no** ただひとつの・唯一つの)

yuimásu, yū (yuu) v 結います, 結う does up one's hair

yuí ya/wa shinai v 結いや/はしない, **yuya shinai** 結やしない = **yuwanai** 結わない (not do up one's hair)

yūjū-fudan n 優柔不断 indecisiveness

yuka n 床 floor (= **furoa** フロア): **yuka-ita** 床板 floor board

yúkai (na) adj 愉快(な) merry, happy, gay; funny, droll

yūkai n 誘拐 kidnap(ping): ~ **shimásu** 誘拐します kidnaps

yūkai-han n 誘拐犯 kidnapper

yūkaku n 遊郭 red-light district

yūkan (na) adj 勇敢(な) brave

yūkari n ユーカリ eucalyptus

yukata n 浴衣・ゆかた (light) bathrobe

yuketsu n 輸血 blood transfusion

yuki v 行き・ゆき [LITERARY] = **iki** 行き (goes) [INFINITIVE]

yukí n 雪 snow: **yukí ga furimásu** 雪が降ります it snows

yuki-dama n 雪玉 snowball

yuki-daruma n 雪だるま snowman

yuki-doke n 雪解け 1. melting snow 2. thaw (reduction or easing in tension or hostility)

yuki-gassen n 雪合戦 snowball fight

yuki-nádare n 雪なだれ snowslide, avalanche (= **nadare** 雪崩・なだれ)

yuki-onna n 雪女 snow woman (spirit of snow)

yuki-otoko n 雪男 yeti

yū´ki n 勇気 courage

yukimásu v 行きます ゆきます [LITERARY] = **ikimásu** 行きます (goes)

yū´ki (no) adj 有機(の) organic: **yūki-yasai** 有機野菜 organic vegetables: **yūki-kagaku** 有機化学 organic chemistry

yukkúri adv ゆっくり 1. slowly 2. at ease; **Go-yukkúri.** ごゆっくり. Take it easy. Don't feel you have to rush.

yūkō (na) adj 有効(な) effective, valid

yūkō-kigen n 有効期限 expiration date (except food. → **shōmi-kigen** 賞味期限)

yuku v 行く・ゆく [INFORMAL] [LITERARY] = **iku** 行く (goes)

yukue-fumei n 行方不明 missing (person, pet, etc.): yukue-fumei-sha 行方不明者 a missing person

yumé n 夢 dream 1. succession of images during sleep; **kinō no yoru … no yumé o mimáshita** 昨日の夜 … の夢を見ました Last night I had a dream of … 2. aspiration, wish; **yumé ga kanaimashita** 夢が叶いました (My) dream came true!

yūmei (na) adj 有名(な) famous, well-known

yumí n 弓 bow (for archery or violin)

yumi-gata n 弓形 curve, arch, bow

yū´moa n ユーモア humor, wit

yunifōmu n ユニフォーム uniform (of athlete, etc.)

yuniiku n ユニーク unique (= **kosei-teki** 個性的, **dokutoku** 独特)

yunikōdo n ユニコード unicode

yunikōn n ユニコーン unicorn (= **ikkaku-jū** 一角獣)

yunitto basu n ユニットバス prefabricated bath

yūnō (na) adj 有能(な) capable, efficient: **yūnō na hisho** 有能な秘書 efficient secretary

yunyū n 輸入 import(ing): ~ **shimásu** 輸入します imports

yunyū-hin n 輸入品 imported goods

yunyū´-zei n 輸入税 (import) duty

yūran n 遊覧 excursion

yūrashia n ユーラシア Eurasia

yure 揺れ 1. n tremor, shock 2. v → **yuremásu** 揺れます

yū´rei n 幽霊 Japanese ghost (commonly lacks legs and feet) (= **bō-rei** 亡霊)

yuremásu, yureru v 揺れます, 揺れる it shakes, sways, swings, rocks, rolls

yurenai v 揺れない = **yuremasén** 揺れません (not shake it)

yureréba v 揺れれば (if it shakes) → **yuremásu** 揺れます

yurerya v [INFORMAL] 揺れりゃ → **yureréba** 揺れれば

yurete v 揺れて → **yuremásu** 揺れます

yuri n ユリ・百合 lily

yuri-kago n 揺りかご・揺り籠 cradle
   yuri-kago kara hakaba made 揺りかご[揺り籠]から墓場まで (slogan) From the cradle to the grave

yū´ri (na) adj 有利(な) profitable, advantageous

yurúi adj 緩い・ゆるい loose, slack; lenient; slow

yurushí n 許し (**o-yurushí** お許し) permission

yurushimásu, yurúsu v 許します, 許す allows, permits, lets; pardons, forgives

yūryō n 有料 pay (not free), charge, fee: **yūryō-chū´shajō** 有料駐車場 paid parking

yūryoku (na) adj 有力(な) strong, powerful, influential

yusaburimásu, yusaburu v 揺さぶります, 揺さぶる shakes (sways, swings, rocks, shocks) it

yūsen n 優先 priority: **yūsen-jun'i** 優先順位 order of priority

yūsha n 勇者 brave man (→ **yūkan** 勇敢)

yūshi n 融資 financing (of bank, etc.): ~ **shimásu** 融資します finances

yūshi n 有志 volunteer, supporter, interested person

yūshí-téssen n 有刺鉄線 barbed wire

yushutsu n 輸出 export(ing): ~ **shimásu** 輸出します exports
   yushutsu-hin n 輸出品 export goods
   yushutsu-zei n 輸出税 (export) duty

yūshoku-jinshu n 有色人種 colored races

yusō n 輸送 transport(ation): ~ **shimásu** 輸送します transports

yūsō n 郵送 mailing: ~ **shimásu** 郵送します mails
   yūsō´-ryō n 郵送料 postage

yusuburimásu, yusuburu v 揺すぶります, 揺すぶる shakes (sways, swings, rocks) it

yusugimásu, yusugu v ゆすぎます, ゆすぐ rinses (= **susugu** すすぐ)

yūsu-hósuteru n ユースホステル youth hostel

yusuranai v 揺すらない = **yusurimasén** 揺すりません (not shake it)

yusuréba v 揺すれば (if one shakes it) → **yusurimásu** 揺すります

yusuré ya/wa shinai v 揺すれや/はしない = **yusuranai** 揺すらない (not shake it)

yusuri n ゆすり・強請り blackmail, extortion

yusuri v 揺すり → **yusurimásu** 揺すります
   [INFINITIVE]: **binbō-yusuri** 貧乏揺すり nervous shaking of one's leg(s)

yusurimásu, yusuru v 揺すります, 揺する shakes (sways, swings, rocks) it

yusurimásu, yusuru v 強請ります, 強請る blackmails, extorts

yusurō´ v 揺すろう = **yusurimashō´** 揺すりましょう (let's shake it!)

yusurya v [INFORMAL] 揺すりゃ → **yusuréba** 揺すれば

yútaka (na) adj 豊か(な) abundant, plentiful; wealthy (= **hōfu (na)** 豊富(な))

yū-tā´n n ユー[U]ターン U-turn

Yuta-shū n ユタ州 Utah

yutori adj ゆとり leeway, breadth of mind, space; **yutori-kyōiku** ゆとり教育 less strenuous education (primary education with reduced hours and/or content of the curriculum)

yútte v 結って → **yuimásu** 結います (does up one's hair)

yutte v ゆって・言って = **itte** 言って (saying, says and)

yūutsu (na) adj 憂うつ・憂鬱(な) melancholy, gloom

yūwaku n 誘惑 temptation; seduction: ~ **shimásu** 誘惑します seduces

yuwanai v 結わない = **yuimasén** 結いません (not do up one's hair)

yuwanai v ゆわない・言わない = **iwanai** 言わない (not say)

yūzai (no) adj 有罪(の) guilty

yúzu n ユズ・柚子 citron

yūzū n 融通 **1.** financing: ~ **shimásu** 融通します finances, lends/advances money **2.** adaptability, versatility
   yūzū no/ga kiku adv 融通の/がきく adaptable, versatile

yuzuranai v 譲らない = **yuzurimasén** 譲りません (not cede)

yuzure v 譲れ **1.** → **yuzuremásu** 譲れます [INFINITIVE] **2.** [IMPERATIVE] (cede!) → **yuzurimásu** 譲ります

yuzuréba v 譲れば (if one cedes) → **yuzurimásu** 譲ります

yuzuremásu, yuzureru v 譲れます, 譲れる can give up/in; can cede

yuzurenai v 譲れない = **yuzuremasén** 譲れません (cannot cede)

yuzuréreba v 譲れれば (if we can cede) → **yuzuremásu** 譲れます

yuzurete v 譲れて → **yuzuremásu** 譲れます (can cede)

yuzuri v 譲り **1.** → **yuzurimásu** 譲ります [INFINITIVE] **2.** inheritance; ... **yuzuri no** ...譲りの inherited from ...

yuzurimásu, yuzuru v 譲ります, 譲る gives up; gives in; yields; cedes; is inferior

yuzutte v 譲って → **yuzurimásu** 譲ります

Z

zá *n* 座 **1.** theater (→ **kabuki-za** 歌舞伎座) **2.** seat

za-búton *n* 座布団 Japanese flat square cushion to sit on

za-dan *n* 座談 [BOOKISH] chat; **zadán-kai** 座談会 round-table discussion

za-isu *n* 座椅子 backrest (= *legless chair*)

za-kō *n* 座高 sitting height

za-kyō *n* 座興 entertainment (*at drinking party, etc.*)

za-seki *n* 座席 seat: **zaseki-bángō** 座席番号 seat number; **kōbu-zaseki-béruto** 後部座席ベルト rear seat belts (= **kōbu-zaseki (no) sutoberuto** 後部座席 (の)シートベルト)

za-shiki *n* 座敷 (**o-zashiki** お座敷) **1.** tatami room, drawing room **2.** tatami-floored seating area in Japanese-style restaurant

za-zen *n* 座禅 meditation (*Zen*)

za-... *prefix* 雑... miscellaneous

zak-ka *n* 雑貨 miscellaneous goods, sundries: **zakka-ten** 雑貨店 variety shop

za-tsuon *n* 雑音 noise(s), static, miscellaneous sounds

zap-pi *n* 雑費 miscellaneous expenses

zas-shi *n* 雑誌 magazine, periodical, miscellaneous articles

zas-sō *n* 雑草 (*miscellaneous*) weeds

zatsudan *n* 雑談 (*miscellaneous*) chat: ~ **shimásu** 雑談します has a chat

zat-ta (na) *adj* 雑多 (な) sundry, miscellaneous

zái *n* 材 (= **zaimoku** 材木) lumber; (= **zairyō** 材料) material

zai-moku *n* 材木 lumber, wood

zai-ryō´ *n* 材料 raw material(s), ingredient(s): **kenchiku-zairyō** 建築材料 building materials: **sūpu no zairyō** スープの材料 ingredients for the soup

zái *n* 財 (= **záisan** 財産) wealth

zai-batsu *n* 財閥 a big financial group

zai-dan *n* 財団 a foundation

zai-gen *n* 財源 financial resources

zai-hō *n* 財宝 treasures, riches (*money, jewels, etc.*)

zai-kai *n* 財界 financial circles

zai-ryoku *n* 財力 financial power, economic power

zái-san *n* 財産 one's property, wealth, fortune

zai-sei *n* 財政 finance

zai-... *prefix* 在... (*resident*) in

zai-gaku(-chū) *adv* 在学(中) in school; in college; at university: **zaigaku-shōmeisho** 在学証明書 certificate of enrollment

zai-ryū *n* 在留 [BOOKISH] residing, residence: **zairyū-shíkaku** 在留資格 status of residence

zai-seki(-chū) *adv* 在籍(中) **1.** in school; in college; at university (= **zai-gaku(-chū)** 在学(中)): **zaiseki-sha** 在籍者 registered student **2.** in association: **zaiseki-sha** 在籍者 registered person

zai-taku *n* 在宅 [BOOKISH] being at home: ~ **shimásu** 在宅します stays at home; **zaitaku-kinmu** 在宅勤務 working at home

zai-... *prefix* 罪... sin, crime

zái-aku *n* 罪悪 sin: **záiaku-kan** 罪悪感 feeling/sense of guilt

zai-nin *n* 罪人 criminal

zaiko *n* 在庫 inventory

zaiko-hyō *n* 在庫表 inventory list

zaiko-shobun se¯ru *n* 在庫処分セール clearance sale (= **zaiko-issō sēru** 在庫一掃セール)

Zaimu-shō *n* 財務省 Ministry of Finance

záiru *n* ザイル a mountain-climbing rope

zamā´-miro *interj* ざまあ見ろ (*mostly male. very informal*) It serves you/them right!

zandaka *n* 残高 (*remaining money*) balance: (**ginkō**) **yokin-zandaka** (銀行)預金残高 bank balance

zangai *n* 残骸 **1.** wreck(age) which does not preserve its original shape **2.** thrown corpse which does not preserve its original shape: **teki-hei no zangai** 敵兵 の残骸 enemy's corpse

zángé *n* 懺悔 confession (*of sins*): ~ **shimásu** 懺悔します confesses

zangyaku (na) *adj* 残虐 (な) merciless and cruel/brutal (*to animals, people*), atrocious; **zangyaku-kō´i** 残虐行為 an atrocity

zangyō *n* 残業 overtime (*work*): ~ **shimásu** 残業します works late

zankoku (na) *adj* 残酷 (な) cruel to, brutal to, harsh towards (*animals, people*): **zankoku na shiuchi** 残酷 な仕打ち cruel treatment

zannén (na) *adj* 残念 (な) regrettable, disappointed; too bad, a pity; **zannen-nagara** 残念ながら regrettably (= **ikan-nagara** 遺憾ながら [BOOKISH])

zannin (na) *adj* 残忍 (な) brutal, cruel (= **zankoku (na)** 残酷 (な)): **zannin na hito** 残忍な人 cruel person

zara ni *adv* ざらに found everywhere, very common

zárazara (shita) *adj* ざらざら (した) rough (-textured)

zarigani *n* ザリガニ crawfish

zarú *n* ざる・ザル a bamboo sieve/colander

zāsai *n* ザーサイ Chinese pickles

zasetsu *n* 挫折 falling by the wayside, frustration, setback, fail; **zasetsú-kan** 挫折感 feeling of frustration, sense of failure; **zasetsu shimásu** 挫折 します gets frustrated, falls by the wayside, fails; **zasetsu sasemásu** 挫折させます frustrates, defeats

zatsu (na) *adj* 雑 (な) coarse, crude

zatto *adv* ざっと roughly; briefly

... ze *interj* ...ぜ (*mostly male. Very informal*) indeed, I tell you

zé-hi *adv* ぜひ・是非 **1.** without fail, for sure: (**watashi-tachi no ie ni**) **zehi itsudemo asobini kite kudasai** (私たちの家に)は是非いつでも遊び に来て下さい Please come visit us (*our home*) anytime. **2.** [BOOKISH] right and wrong, pros and cons; **shikei (seido) no zehi** 死刑(制度)の是非 pros and cons of the death penalty

zéi _n_ 税 tax (= **zei-kin** 税金); **shōhi-zei** 消費税 consumption tax; **shotoku-zei** 所得税 income tax; **gensen-chōshū-zei** 源泉徴収税 withholding income tax; **jūmin-zei** 住民税 resident tax
zei-kan _n_ 税関 customs, custom house
zei-kin _n_ 税金 tax (= **zei** 税)
zei-mu sho _n_ 税務署 tax office

zeitákú _n_ ぜいたく・贅沢 luxury, extravagance: **zeitákú (na)** ぜいたく・贅沢(な) luxurious
zeitaku-hin _n_ ぜいたく[贅沢]品 luxury (goods), luxuries

zékken _n_ ゼッケン an athlete's number: **zékken o tsukemásu** ゼッケンを付けます attaches/assigns a number (_to an athlete_)

zekkō (no) _adj_ 絶好(の) best; **zekkō-chō** 絶好調 best condition

zémi _n_ ゼミ, **zeminā´ru** ゼミナール seminar

zén _n_ 善 goodness; **zén-aku** 善悪 good and evil, right and wrong
zén-i _n_ 善意 goodwill
zén-sho _n_ 善処 [BOOKISH]: **Zénsho shimásu** 善処します "I will do my best" (_about the matter_) = Don't expect me to do anything.

Zén _n_ 禅 Zen (Buddhism)

zen _n_ 膳 (**o-zen** お膳, **gó-zen** 御膳) (_traditional individual low_) meal table, dining tray

zén-... _prefix_ 全... all, total, whole, complete, the whole
zén-bu _adv_ 全部 everything, completely: **zén-bu de** 全部で altogether
zen'-in _n_ 全員 everyone
zén-koku (no) _adj_ 全国(の) nation-wide
zen-men _n_ 全面 the entire surface
zen-metsu _n_ 全滅 annihilation
zen-shin _n_ 全身 the whole body, body as a whole
zen-tai _n_ 全体 the whole, entirety: **zentai no** 全体の entire, whole; **zentai ni** 全体に wholly, generally
zén-tai _adv_ 全体 originally, primarily (= **gánrai** 元来)
zen-yaku _n_ 全訳 complete translation
zen-zen _adv_ 全然・ぜんぜん 1. [+ NEGATIVE verb] (not) at all, (not) ever 2. [INFORMAL] completely, utterly, entirely, altogether

zén-... _prefix_ 前...[BOOKISH] former, earlier (= **máe no** ...前の...)
zen-chō _n_ 前兆 omen, sign
zén-go _n_ 前後 1. before and after; ahead and behind; back and forth 2. sequence, order
...-zén-go _suffix_ ...前後 approximately, around, about (= **teido** 程度)
zen-han _n_ 前半 the first half
zen-men _n_ 前面 the front side
zen-pō _n_ 前方 the front direction
zen-rei _n_ 前例 precedent, prior example
zén-sha _n_ 前者 the former
zen-shin _n_ 前進 advance: **~ shimásu** 前進します advances
zen-tei _n_ 前提 premise
zén-to _n_ 前途 the future, prospects: **zento yūbō (na)** 前途有望(な) promising (= **yūbō (na)** 有望 (な))

zén'-ya _n_ 前夜 the night before

zenmai _n_ ぜんまい・ゼンマイ 1. a spring, hair-spring, clock-spring 2. royal fern, osmund

zensoku _n_ ぜんそく・喘息 asthma

zeppeki _n_ 絶壁 precipice

zérii _n_ ゼリー jelly

zéro _n_ ゼロ zero

zetsubō _n_ 絶望 despair: **~ shimásu** 絶望します despairs

zetsuen shimásu _v_ 絶縁します insulates

zettai (no) _n_ 絶対(の) absolute: **zettai ni** 絶対に totally, absolutely

zi... → j...

... zo _interj_ ...ぞ (_mostly male_. VERY INFORMAL) indeed, I tell you

zō _n_ 像 1. statue (= **chō-zō** 彫像) 2. image: **terebi ei-zō** テレビ映像 images on TV screen: **ga-zō** 画像 picture, image 3. portrait (= **shō-zō** 肖像)

zō _n_ ゾウ・象 elephant

zō-... _prefix_ 増... increase
zō-dai _n_ 増大 enlargement, increase: **~ shimásu** 増大します enlarges, increases
zō´-ho _n_ 増補 supplement: **~ shimásu** 増補します supplements
zō-ka _n_ 増加 increase, growth: **(...ga) ~ shimásu** (...が)増加します increases
zō-ryō _n_ 増量 increase (_quantity_): **(...o) ~ shimásu** (...を)増量します increases it
zō-satsu _n_ 増刷 reprint (_publishing_): **(...o) ~ shimásu** (...を)増刷します reprints
zō-shin _n_ 増進 promotion, betterment, increase: **~ shimásu** 増進します promotes

zōgan _n_ 象眼 inlaid work; damascene

zōgo _n_ 造語 coined word

zōka _n_ 造花 artificial flower

zōkei _n_ 造詣 profound knowledge (_of academics, arts, technologies, etc._): **zōkei ga fukai** 造詣が深い is well versed

zōkin _n_ ぞうきん・雑巾 rag, dustcloth

zoku _n_ 賊 robber, bandit, thief (→ **kai-zoku** 海賊, **tō-zoku** 盗賊, **san-zoku** 山賊)

...´-zoku _suffix_ ...族 (_name of certain_) tribe/gang/group of ...; the ...s

zokugo _n_ 俗語 slang (= **surangu** スラング)

zoku (na) _adj_ 俗(な) common, vulgar; popular

zokusánai _v_ 属さない = **zokushimasén** 属しません (not belong)

zoku-shimásu, zoku-súru _v_ 属します, 属する belongs (= **zokúsú** 属す)

zokú(-)shite _v_ 属して → **zoku(-) shimásu** 属します

zokú zoku _adv_ ぞくぞく・続々 one right after another, in rapid succession

zóku zoku shimásu (suru) _v_ ぞくぞくします (する) 1. is thrilled with excitement 2. shivers with chill

zonbún (ni) _adv_ 存分(に) as much as one likes

zóngai _adv_ 存外 beyond expectations

zōni _n_ 雑煮・ぞうに (**o-zōni** お雑煮) rice cakes

boiled with vegetables (*eaten as New Year's soup*)

zon-ji *v* 存じ → **zon-jimásu** 存じます
[INFINITIVE]; → **go-zon-ji** ご存じ

zon-jiagemásu, zon-jiageru *v* 存じあげます, 存
じあげる [HUMBLE] thinks, feels; knows

zon-jimásu, zon-jíru *v* 存じます, 存じる [HUMBLE/
DEFERENTIAL] thinks, feels; knows

zon-jínai *v* 存じない = **zon-jimasén** 存じません
(not think/feel/know)

zón-jite *v* 存じて → **zon-jimásu** 存じます

zonzái (na) *adj* ぞんざい(な) slovenly, rough,
carelessly, sloppy

zóri *n* 草履 straw sandals

zórozoro *adv* ぞろぞろ in streams/crowds, in large
numbers

zōsen *n* 造船 shipbuilding: ~ **shimásu** 造船します
builds a ship

zōsen-jó *n* 造船所 shipyard

zōsho *n* 蔵書 book collection, library

zōsui *n* 雑炊 rice boiled in a soup

zo⁻-tei *n* 贈呈 [HUMBLE] presentation: ~ **shimásu**
贈呈します presents

zotto *adv* ぞっと with a shudder/shiver: ~ **shimásu**
ぞっとします shudders, shivers, thrills (*is thrilled*)

zu *n* 図 picture, drawing, chart, map, diagram, figure:
zu ni norimásu 図に乗ります pushes a good thing
too far, takes advantage of a person

zu-an *n* 図案 sketch, design

zu-hyō *n* 図表 chart, diagram (= **chāto** チャート)

zu-kai *n* 図解 illustration, diagram

...-zu *suffix* ...ず, **...-zu ni** ...ずに = **...-nái de** ...な
いで (not doing, instead of doing)

zubari *adv* ずばり [INFORMAL] frankly: **zubari
iimásu** ずばり言います comes directly to the point

zubón *n* ズボン trousers, pants, slacks

zubon-shita *n* ズボン下 underpants, shorts

zubon-tsuri *n* ズボン吊り suspenders

zubutoi *adv* 図太い thick-skinned, impudent: ~
shinkei 図太い神経 nerves of steel

zúibun *adv* ずいぶん・随分 **1.** fairly, rather
2. very, quite, extremely (= **kanari** かなり)

zuihitsu *n* 随筆 essays (= **essei** エッセイ)

zúii (no) *adj* 随意(の) voluntary, optional (= **nin'i
(no)** 任意(の))

zúiji *adv* 随時 as needed, at anytime as one likes

-zuke *suffix* 付け dated

...-zuki *suffix* ...好き a lover of ..., a great ... fan

zúkku *n* ズック canvas; duck (*fabric*)

...-zúkuri *suffix* ...造り made of ...

zūmu *n* ズーム zoom (*camera*)

zúnō *n* 頭脳 [BOOKISH] brains, head, intellect
(= **atama** 頭)

zurashimásu, zurasu *v* ずらします, ずらす shifts

zuró *n* ずれ discrepancy, lag, gap

zúre *v* ずれ → **zuremásu** ずれます [INFINITIVE]

zuremásu, zuréru *v* ずれます, ずれる slips out of
place, gets loose

zurénai *v* ずれない = **zuremasén** ずれません (not
get loose)

zúrereba *v* ずれれば (if it gets loose) →
zuremásu ずれます

zúrete *v* ずれて → **zuremásu** ずれます

zuró⁻su *n* ズロース panties; drawers

zúru *n* ずる cheating

zuru gashikoi *adj* ずる賢い cunning, wily

zurúi *adj* ずるい sly, cunning, tricky

zuru-yásumi *n* ずる休み skipping (*school*):
~ **shimásu** ずる休みします skips (*school*)

zusan (na) *adj* ずさん(な) sloppy, slipshod,
careless, slovenly

...´zutsu *suffix* ...ずつ (*off/for*) each, apiece, at a time

zutsū *n* 頭痛 headache: **zutsū no táne** 頭痛の種
one's biggest headache; **zutsū ga shimásu** 頭痛が
します has a headache

zutto *adv* ずっと **1.** directly **2.** by far, much (*more*):
zutto máe ずっと前 way back (*before*), a long time
ago **3.** all the way through, all the time

zūzūshíi *adj* ずうずうしい・図々しい brazen,
shameless, bold, impudent (= **atsukamashii**
厚かましい)

zy... → **j...**

245

PART II
ENGLISH–JAPANESE

A

a, an → **one** (*but usually omitted in Japanese*)
aardvark *n* tsuchíbutá ツチブタ
abacus *n* soroban そろばん
  abacus rod *n* keta けた・桁
abalone *n* áwabi アワビ
abandon *v* sutemásu (suteru, sutete) 捨てます
  (捨てる, 捨てて)
  abandoned cat *n* suteneko 捨て猫
abase *v* otoshimásu (otósu, otoshite) 落とします
  (落とす, 落として), (*be humble*) hige shimásu
  (suru, shite) 卑下します(する, して)
abate *v* **1.** (*lose steam*) osamarimásu 治まります,
  yawaragimásu 和らぎます **2.** herashimásu 減らし
  ます **3.** (*exclude*) haijo shimásu (suru, shite) 排
  除します(する, して); (*resolve*) mukō ni shimásu
  (suru, shite) 無効にします(する, して) **4. ~ *a tax***
  genzei shimásu (suru, shite) 減税します(する,
  して)
abbreviate *v* ryakushimásu (ryakúsu, ryakushite)
  略します(略す, 略して)
abbreviation *n* ryakugo 略語, shōryaku 省略
abdicate *v* **1.** shirizokimásu (shirizoku, shirizoite)
  退きます(退く, 退いて), jinin shimásu (suru,
  shite) 辞任します(する, して) **2. ~ *the throne***
  taii shimásu (suru, shite) 退位します(する, して)
abdomen *n* onaka おなか・お腹, fukubu 腹部,
  hara 腹
abduct *v* yūkai shimásu (suru, shite) 誘拐します
  (する, して)
aberration *n* dassen 脱線, itsudatsu 逸脱, seishin
  ijō 精神異常
abet *v* keshikakemásu (keshikakeru, keshikakete)
  けしかけます(けしかける, けしかけて)
abeyance *n* ichiji teishi 一時停止, horyū 保留
abhor *v* **1.** (*dislike intensely*) nikumimásu
  (nikumu, nikunde) 憎みます(憎む, 憎んで), (*not
  favored*) kiraimásu (kirau, kiratte) 嫌います(嫌う,
  嫌って) **2.** ... o sakemásu (sakeru, sakete) ...を避
  けます(避ける, 避けて)
abide *v* **1.** (*stay*) nokórimásu (nokoru, nokotte)
  残ります(残る, 残って), todomarimásu (todomaru,
  todomatte) 留まります(留まる, 留まって) **2.** (*dwell*)
  sumimásu (sumu, sunde) 住みます(住む, 住んで)
  3. (*suffer*) gaman shimásu (suru, shite) 我慢しま
  す(する, して), ...ni taemásu (taeru, taete) ... に耐
  えます(耐える, 耐えて) **4.** (*accept*) ukeiremasu
  (ukeireru, ukeirete) 受け入れます(受け入れる,
  受け入れて)
ability *n* **1.** (*skill*) nōryoku 能力, udemae 腕前,
  temae 手前 (o-témae お手前); (*stuff*) kíryō 器量,
  utsuwa 器・うつわ **2.** (*function*) hataraki 働き;
  (*proficiency*) jitsuryoku 実力 **3.** (*talent*) sái(nō)
  才(能)
abject *adj* **1.** mijime (na) 惨め(な), hisán (na)
  悲惨(な), zetsubō-teki (na) 絶望的(な) **2.** iyashii
  卑しい **3.** hikutsu na 卑屈な

ablaze *adj* **1.** (*shiny*) kagayaiteiru 輝いている
  2. (*burning*) moeteiru 燃えている **3.** (*excited*)
  kōfun 興奮している
able → **can**
abnormal *adj* (*abnormality*) ijō (na) 異常(な)
aboard *v gets* ~ norimásu (noru, notte) 乗ります
  (乗る, 乗って); *puts* ~ nosemásu (noseru, nosete)
  乗せます(乗せる, 乗せて)
abode *n* ie 家, jūkyo 住居, jūtaku 住宅
abolish *v* **1.** (*demolish*) haishi shimásu (suru,
  shite) 廃止します(する, して), yamemásu
  (yameru, yamete) 止めます(止める, 止めて)
  2. (*destroy*) ... o horoboshimásu (suru, shite) ...を
  滅ぼします(滅ぼす, 滅ぼして)
aborigine *n* aborijini アボリジニ, aborijinii アボ
  リジニー, genjūmin 原住民, senjūmin 先住民
abort *v* chūshi shimásu (suru, shite) 中止します
  (する, して)
abortion *n* datai 堕胎, ninshin chū´zetsu 妊娠中絶;
  has an ~ oroshimásu (orósu, oróshite) 下ろします
  (下ろす, 下ろして)
abound *v* tomimásu (tómu, tónde) 富みます(富む,
  富んで)
about *prep* **1.** (*an amount*) yáku ... 約..., ... gúrai
  ...位, ... hodo ...程, ...-zéngo... 前後, ...-kéntō ...見
  当 → **almost, around 2.** (*a time*) góro (ni) ...
  頃(に) **3.** (*concerning*) ... ni tsúite (no)... につい
  て(の); *talk* ~ ... ni tsúite hanashimásu (hanasu,
  hanashite) ...について話します(話す, 話して)
  is about to happen (su-)ru tokoró desu (す)ると
  ころです, (shi-)yō to shimásu (し)ようとします,
  (shi-)sō désu (し)そうです
  about when itsu goro いつ頃
above *prep* ... (no) ué (ni) ...(の)上(に)
aboveground *n* chijō 地上
abrade *v* **1.** (*to wear down*) surihera shimásu
  (suriherasu, suriherashite) すり減らします(すり
  減らす, すり減らして), (*to be worn away*) mamō
  sasemásu (saseru, sasete) 磨耗させます(させる,
  させて) **2.** (*chafe*) iraira sasemasu (saseru, sasete)
  イライラさせます(させる, させて)
abreast *adv* yokó ni narande 横に並んで; *not ~ of*
  ...ni utói ...に疎い・うとい
abridge *v* (*shorten*) tanshuku shimásu (suru,
  shite) 短縮します(する, して), yōyaku shimásu
  (suru, shite) 要約します(する, して); (*abate*) hera
  shimásu (herasu, herashite) 減らします(減らす,
  減らして)
abroad *adv* gaikoku (de) 外国(で), káigai (de)
  海外(で)
  study abroad *n* ryūgaku 留学
abrupt *adj* totsuzen (no) 突然(の)
abruptly *adv* totsuzen 突然
abscess *n* nōyō 膿瘍
abscond *v* nigemásu (nigeru, nigete) 逃げます
  (逃げる, 逃げて)

absence *n* kesseki (no) 欠席(の), (*from home*) rúsu (no) 留守(の)

absent *v* kesseki shimásu (suru, shite) 欠席します (する, して)

absentee *n* absséki-sha 欠席者

absent-minded *adj* bon'yári shimásu (suru, shite) ぼんやりします

absent-mindedly *adv* ukkári shite うっかりして

absolute *adj* zettai (no) 絶対(の)

absolutely *adv* zettai ni 絶対に, honto (hontō) ni 本当・ほんと(ほんとう)に; **~ cannot** tōtei 到底 + [NEGATIVE]

absorbed *adj* (*fascinated*) uttóri (to) うっとり (と); **gets ~ in** ... ni korimásu (kóru, kótte) ...に凝 ります(凝る, 凝って)

absorbent cotton *n* dasshí-men 脱脂綿

absorption *n* kyūshū 吸収

abstain *v* **1.** (*stop*) yamemásu (yameru, yamete) やめます・止めます(止める, 止めて), (*refrain from*) tsutsushimimasu (tsutsushimu, tsutsushinde) 慎みます(慎む, 慎んで); **~ from** ... o yamemásu (yameru, yamete) ... をやめます(やめる, やめて), tachimásu (tátsu, tátte) 断ちます(断つ, 断って) **2.** (*do not vote*) kíken shimásu (suru, shite) 棄権し ます(する, して)

abstainer *n* kinshu-ka 禁酒家

abstention *n* kiken 棄権

abstinence *n* jisei 自制, sessei 節制, kinshu 禁酒

abstract 1. *adj* chūshō-teki (na) 抽象的(な) **2.** *n* (*summary*) yōˊshi 要旨

absurd *adj* baka-rashíi ばからしい

abundance *n* tómi 富

abundant *adj* yútaka (na) 豊か(な) → **abound**

abuse 1. *n* warú-kuchi/-guchi 悪口 **2.** → **scold, mistreat**

abusive *adj* ranbō (*na*) 乱暴(な), kuchigitanai 口汚い, warui 悪い

abut *v* sesshimásu (sessu(ru), sesshite) 接します (接す(る), 接して)

abysmal *adj* hidói ひどい・酷い, sokonuke (no) 底抜けの, hakarishirenai 計り知れない; *abysmal darkness* (mak-)kurayami (no) (真っ)暗闇(の)

abyss *n* chi no soko 地の底, shin'en 深遠, naraku 奈落, donzoko どん底

AC, alternating current *n* kōryū 交流

academic *adj* akádemikku アカデミック, gakumon 学問

academy *n* gakkōˊ 学校

accede *v* tsugimásu (tsugu, tsuide) 継ぎます (継ぐ, 継いで), dōi shimásu (suru, shite) 同意し ます(する, して)

accede to *v* ... ni ō-jimásu (ō-jiru, ō-jite) ...に応 じます(応じる, 応じて)

accelerate *v* kasóku shimásu (suru, shite) 加速し ます(する, して)

accelerator *n* ákuseru アクセル

accent *n* ákusento アクセント → **pronunciation, dialect**

accept *v* **1.** ukemásu (ukéru, úkete) 受けます (受ける, 受けて), uke-torimásu (uke-toru, uke-totte) 受け取ります(受け取る, 受け取って), uke-tsukemásu (uke-tsukeru, uke-tsukete) 受け付 けます(受け付ける, 受け付けて) **2.** (*consents*) shōdaku shimásu (suru, shite) 承諾します(する, して); **~ a bill** (*of payment*) tegata o hiki-ukemásu (hiki-ukeru, hiki-úkete) 手形を引き受けます(引き 受ける, 引き受けて)

acceptance *n* **1.** shōdaku 承諾 **2.** (*resignation*) akirame 諦め

access; seeks ~ to ... ni sekkin o hakarimásu (hakáru, hakátte) ...に接近を図ります(図る, 図って)

accessible *adj* (*easy to get to*) iki-yasúi 行きや すい

accessory *n* (*clothing accessory*; *belt, handbag, etc.*) akusesarii アクセサリー, (*car accessory, etc.*) kā akusesarii カーアクセサリー

accident *n* **1.** jíko 事故, dekígoto 出来事 **2.** (*disaster*) sōnan 遭難; *has an* ~ sōnan shimásu (suru, shite) 遭難します(する, して)

accidental *adj* gūzen (no) 偶然(の)

accidentally *adv* gūzen ni 偶然に, hyótto ひょ っと

acclaim 1. *n* shōsan 称賛 **2.** *v* shōsan shimásu (suru, shite) 称賛します(する, して)

accommodate *v* shukuhaku sasemásu (saseru, sasete) 宿泊させます(させる, させて), tekiō shimásu (suru, shite) 適応します(する, して)

accommodation *n* (*place to stay*) shukuhaku shisetsu 宿泊施設; (*facilities*) sétsubi 設備

accompany *v* **1.** **~ ... to** issho ni ikimásu (iku, itte) (...と)一緒に行きます(行く, 行って), o-tómo shimásu (suru, shite) お供します(する, して); ...ni tomonaimásu (tomonáu, tomonátte) ...に伴います(伴う, 伴って) **2.** *is accompanied by* (= *brings along*) ... o tsuremásu (tsureru, tsurete) ... を連れます(連れる, 連れて)

accomplice *n* kyōhansha 共犯者, ichimi 一味

accomplish *v* **1.** (shite) shimaimásu (shimau, shimatte) (して)しまいます(しまう, しまって); hatashimásu (hatásu, hatáshite) 果たします (果たす, 果たして), togemásu (togéru, tógete) 遂げます(遂げる, 遂げて) **2.** (*attains*) ...ni tas-shimásu (tas-suru, tas-shite) ...に達します(達する, 達して); ... ga kanaimásu (kanáu, kanátte) ... がか ないます(かなう, かなって)

accord *v* **~ with** (...ni) kanaimásu (kanáu, kanátte) (...に)かないます(かなう, かなって); (... to) itchi shimásu (suru, shite) (...と)一致します (する, して)

accordance *n* itchi 一致; *in ~ with* ... ni ō-jite ...に応じて; ... ni shitagátte ...にしたがって・従 って

according (to) *adj* **1.** (*relying on*) ... ni yoru to ...によると, ... no hanashíde (wa) ...の話で(は) **2.** (*in conformity with*) ... ni shitagatte ...に従って

accordingly *adv* shitagátte したがって・従って

accordion n acōdion アコーディオン

accost v kóe o kakemásu (koe o kakeru, koe o kakete) 声をかけます(声をかける, 声をかけて), hanashikakemásu (hanashikakeru, hanashikakete) 話しかけます(話しかける, 話しかけて)

account n **1.** (bill) kanjō´ 勘定 (o-kanjō お勘定) **2.** (credit) tsuké つけ **3.** (bank account) kōza 口座, yokin 預金
on account of ... no séi de ... のせいで → **because** → **sake (for the)**
takes into account kō´ryo ni iremásu (ireru, irete) 考慮に入れます(入れる, 入れて)

accountable adj sekinin ga aru 責任がある, setsumei dekíru 説明できる

accountant n kaikei (-gákari) 会計(係), kaikéi-shi 会計士

accounts n (o-)kaikei (お)会計

accumulate v **1.** (it accumulates) tsumorimásu (tsumóru, tsumótte) 積もります(積もる, 積もって), tamarimásu (tamaru, tamette) たまります(たまる, たまって); tsumemásu (tsumeru, tsumete) つめます(つめる, つめて); atsumarimásu (atsumáru, atsumátte) 集まります(集まる, 集まって) **2.** (accumulates it) tsumimásu (tsumu, tsunde) 積みます(積む, 積んで), tamemásu (tameru, tamete) ためます(ためる, ためて), atsumemásu (atsúmeru, atsúmete) 集めます(集める, 集めて)

accurate adj seikaku (na) 正確(な)

accuse v uttaemásu (uttaeru, uttaete) 訴えます(訴える, 訴えて); (criticizes) hínan shimásu (suru, shite) 非難します(する, して)

accustom v **~ oneself to** ... ni naremásu (naréru, nárete) ... に慣れます(慣れる, 慣れて)

accustomed adj jū´rai no 従来の

ache **1.** v (it aches) itamimásu (itámu, itánde) 痛みます(痛む, 痛んで) **2.** n (an ache) itamí 痛み

achieve → **accomplish**

achievement n (work) hataraki 働き

acid **1.** n sán 酸 **2.** adj suppái 酸っぱい

acknowledge v mitomemásu (mitomeru, mitomete) 認めます(認める, 認めて)

acorn n dónguri どんぐり・ドングリ

acoustic n **1.** akō´sutíkku (gakki) アコースティック(楽器); acoustic guitar akōsutikku gitā アコースティック・ギター **2.** onkyō 音響

acquaint v **~ oneself with** (... o) shirimásu (shiru, shitte) (...を)知ります(知る, 知って); is acquainted with ... o shitte imásu (iru, ite) ... を知っています(いる, いて)

acquaintance n shiriai 知り合い, chijin 知人

acquiesce v fukujū shimásu (suru, shite) 服従します(する, して)

acquire → **get**

acquit v shakuhō´ shimásu (suru, shite) 釈放します(する, して), kaihō shimásu (suru, shite) 解放します(する, して), muzai ni shimásu (suru, shite) 無罪にします(する, して)

acre n ēkā エーカー

acrobat n akurobátto アクロバット, kyokugei 曲芸

acronym n kashira moji 頭文字

across prep, adv ... (no) mukō(ni) ...(の)向こう (に), múkō 向こう goes across → **cross**
across the way mukō 向こう, mukō-gawa 向こう側; cuts ~ yoko-girimásu (yoko-gíru, yoko-gítte) 横切ります(横切る, 横切って); goes ~ ōdan shimásu (suru, shite) 横断します(する, して)

act n **1.** → **do 2.** (deed) shiwaza しわざ・仕業, okonai 行い, kō´i 行為; ~ like a child amaemásu (amáeru, amáete) 甘えます(甘える, 甘えて); ~ of God fuka kō´ryoku 不可抗力 **3.** (of play) makú 幕; dán 段 **4.** hōritsu 法律; ~ of Congress kokkai seiteihō 国会制定法

acting **1.** n (play acting) éngi 演技 **2.** → **temporary 3.** → **agent**; acting as agent daikō 代行

action n **1.** katsudō 活動 **2.** (conduct) okonai 行い; (behavior) kō´dō 行動 → **activity**

activate v ugokashimásu (ugokasu, ugokashite) 動かします(動かす, 動かして), sádō sasemásu (saseru, sasete) 作動させます(させる, させて)

active adj kappatsu (na) 活発(な); is ~ katsuyaku shimásu (suru, shite) 活躍します(する, して)

activity n **1.** katsudō 活動, katsuyaku 活躍 **2.** (work) hataraki 働き **3.** (agency) kikán 機関 → **exercise** → **movement**

actor n yakusha 役者, haiyū 俳優

actress n joyū 女優

actual adj jissai (no) 実際(の); actual conditions genjitsu 現実

actuality n jitchi 実地

actually adv jitsú wa 実は, jitsu ní 実に

acupuncture n hári はり・鍼

acute adj **1.** (sharp) surudói 鋭い **2.** (severe) hageshíi 激しい **3.** (sudden) kyūsei (no) 急性 (の)

ad → **advertisement**

adage n kotowaza ことわざ・諺, kakugen 格言

adamant adj katái かたい・硬い・固い, gánko (na) 頑固(な), dánko (to shita) 断固(とした)

adapt v tekigō´ sasemásu (saseru, sasete) 適合させます(させる, させて)

adaptability n yūzū 融通; is adaptable yūzū ga kikimásu (kiku, kiite) 融通がききます(きく, きいて)

adapter n adáputā´ アダプター

add v kuwaemásu (kuwaeru, kuwaete) 加えます (加える, 加えて); (supplements it with) soemásu (soeru, soete) 添えます(添える, 添えて), yosemásu (yoseru, yosete) 寄せます(寄せる, 寄せて); (attaches) tsukemásu (tsukéru, tsukéte) 付けます(付ける, 付けて)

addict n jōyō´-sha 常用者, chūdoku (-sha) 中毒 (者), izón-sha 依存者; drug addict mayaku jō´yō´/ chūdoku (-sha) 麻薬常用者/中毒(者)

addition n tsuiká 追加, tenká 添加; house addi-

tion tate-mashi 建て増し; *in ~ to* ...no hoka (ni) ...の他(に), [BOOKISH]... no tá (ni) ...の他(に); *food additive* shokuhin tenkábutsu 食品添加物

additionally *adv* hoka ni 他に, [BOOKISH] táni 他に

address *n* **1.** jūsho 住所, (...) saki (...)先, (*house number*) banchi 番地, (*written*) tokoro-gaki 所書き, adoresu アドレス; (*on envelope*) uwagaki 上書き
contact address *n* renraku-saki 連絡先
e-mail address *n* mēru ádoresu (meru-ado) メールアドレス(メルアド)
address book *n* adoresu chō´ アドレス帳
addressed to ...-ate (no) ...あて・宛て(の)
2. enzetsu 演説 **3.** *v* torikumimásu (torikumu, torikunde) 取り組みます(取り組む, 取り組んで)

addressee *n* uketori-nin 受取人, jushin-sha 受信者

adequate *adj* ...-no tame (ni) ...のため(に)

adhere *v* kuttsukimásu (kuttuku, kuttuite) くっつきます(くっつく, くっついて); fucháku shimásu (suru, shite) 付着します(する, して)

adhesive tape *n* nenchaku tē´pu 粘着テープ; bansōkō ばんそうこう・絆創膏

ad hoc *adj* tokubetsu (no) 特別(の), sonoba shinogi (no) その場しのぎ(の)

adios *adj* sayōnará さようなら

adjacent *adj* **1.** → next **2.** *is ~ to* ...ni ses-shimásu (ses-suru, ses-shite) ...に接します(接する, 接して)

adjective *n* keiyō´shi 形容詞

adjoining → next

adjust *v* totonoemásu (totonóeru, totonóete) 整えます(整える, 整えて), chōsei/séiri/kagen shimásu (suru, shite) 調整/整理/加減します(する, して)

adjustment *n* chōsei 調整, séiri 整理, kagen 加減, chōsetsu 調節

administer *v* (*of government*) osámemásu (osámeru, osámete) 治めます(治める, 治めて); kánri shimásu (suru, shite) 管理します(する, して)

administration *n* **1.** (*of government*) gyōsei 行政 **2.** (*of business*) keiei 経営, kánri 管理

admirable *adj* mígoto (na) 見事(な), rippa (na) 立派(な)

admirably *adv* mígoto ni 見事に, rippa ni 立派に

admiral *n* táishō 大将; *vice admiral* chū´jō 中将; *rear admiral* shō´shō 少将

admire *v* kanshin shimásu (suru, shite) 感心します(する, して), homemásu (homéru, hómete) 褒めます(褒める, 褒めて), akogaremásu あこがれ[憧れ]ます(あこがれる, あこがれて)

admission *n* (*to hospital*) nyūin 入院; (*to school*) nyūgaku 入学; (*to a place*) nyūjō 入場
admission fee *n* nyūjō´-ryō 入場料
admission ticket *n* nyūjō´-ken 入場券

admit *v* **1.** (*lets in*) iremásu (ireru, irete) 入れます(入れる, 入れて), tōshimásu (tō´su, tō´shite) 通します(通す, 通して) **2.** (*acknowledges*)

mitomemásu (mitomeru, mitomete) 認めます(認める, 認めて); (*confesses*) uchi-akemásu (uchi-akeru, uchi-akete) 打ち明けます(打ち明ける, 打ち明けて)

admittance *n* nyūjō (kyoka) 入場(許可), nyūkai 入会

admonish *v* chūkoku shimásu (suru, shite) 忠告します(する, して), chūi shimásu (suru, shite) 注意します(する, して), kankoku shimásu (suru, shite) 勧告します(する, して)

adolescence *n* seinén-ki 青年期, seishún-ki 青春期, shishún-ki 思春期

adolescent *n* seinen 青年

adopt *v* (*a boy*) yōshi ni shimásu (suru, shite) 養子にします(する, して); (*a girl*) yō´jo ni shimásu (suru, shite) 養女にします(する, して)

adopted *adj* (*son*) yōshi (ni natta) 養子(になった); (*daughter*) yō´jo (ni natta) 養女(になった)

adorable *adj* kawaíi かわいい・可愛い, kawairashíi かわいらしい・可愛らしい, airashíi 愛らしい

adore *v* akogaremásu (akogaeru, akogarete) あこがれ[憧れ]ます(あこがれる, あこがれて)

adrenalin *n* adorenarín アドレナリン

adult *n* otona おとな・大人, seijin 成人

adultery *n* kantsū 姦通, furin 不倫

advance 1. *n* zenshin 前進 **2.** *n in ~* sono máe ni その前に; (*beforehand*) mae motte 前もって, jizen ni 事前に **3.** *v* (*goes ahead*) susumimásu (susumu, susunde) 進みます(進む, 進んで); (*advances it*) susumemásu (susumeru, susumete) 進めます(進める, 進めて), (*lends money*) yūzū shimásu (suru, shite) 融通します(する, して)
advance notice *n* yokoku 予告

advanced sale *n* maeuri 前売り
advanced-sale ticket maeuri-ken 前売り券

advantage *n* **1.** toku 得 (o-toku お得), (*benefit*) ríeki 利益; *takes ~ of* ... o riyō shimásu (suru, shite) ...を利用します(する, して) **2.** (*merit*) chō´sho 長所

advantageous *adj* yū´ri (na) 有利(な), toku (na) 得(な)

advent *n* shutsugen 出現, tōrai 到来, kirisuto no kōrin キリストの降臨

adventure *n* bōken 冒険

adverb *n* fukushi 副詞

advergame *n* ado(ba) gēmu アド(ば)ゲーム

adversary *n* aité 相手 (o-aite お相手)

adverse *adj* fúri (na) 不利(な), gyakkyō (no) 逆境(の)

advertisement *n* kōkoku 広告

advice *n* **1.** adobáisu アドバイス, chūkoku 忠告 **2.** (*consultation*) sōdan 相談

adviser *n* (*consultant*) komon 顧問, sōdan aite 相談相手

advocate *v* tonaemásu (tonáeru, tonáete) 唱えます(唱える, 唱えて)

aerial → antenna

aerobics *n* earobíkusu エアロビクス

aerology *n* kishōgaku 気象学

Aesop *n* isóppu イソップ

aesthetic *adj* bi-teki (na) 美的な

afar *adv* tōku (ni) 遠く(に), enpō 遠方; *from ~* tōku kara 遠くから

affable *adj* áiso/áisō ga íi あいそ/あいそう[愛想]がいい, hitoatari no ii 人当たりのいい, hitozuki no suru 人好きのする, shitashimiyasui 親しみやすい

affair *n* 1. kotó 事, kotogara 事柄, jíken 事件, shigoto 仕事 2. *(love affair) (extramarital)* uwaki 浮気; *has an ~ with …* … to uwaki o shimásu (suru, shíte) …と浮気をします(する, して)

affect → influence

affectation *n* kidorí 気取り, furí ふり, kíza きざ・気障

affected *adj* kidotta ... 気取った...; *is ~* kidotte imásu (iru, ite) 気取っています(いる, いて)

affection *n* nasake 情け (o-násake お情け), aijō 愛情; *treats with ~ (… o) kawai-garimásu (kawaigáru, kawai-gátte) (...を)かわいがります(かわいがる, かわいがって)

affiliate 1. *v* kamei shimásu (suru, shíte) 加盟します(する, して) 2. *n* ko-gáisha 子会社, shiten 支店

affirmation *n* kōtei 肯定

affix *v* setsuji 接辞, tenkábutsu 添加物

afflict *v* kurushimemásu (kurushiméru, kurushímete) 苦しめます(苦しめる, 苦しめて)

affliction *n* kurushimi 苦しみ

afford *v* (jūbun na) (o-)kane ga arimásu (áru, átte) (十分な)(お)金があります(ある, あって); yoyū ga arimásu (áru, átte) 余裕があります(ある, あって)

affront 1. *v* bujoku shimásu (suru, shite) 侮辱します(する, して) 2. *n* bujoku 侮辱

Afghan 1. *(person)* Afuganísután-jin アフガニスタン人 2. *(language)* Afuganisután-go アフガニスタン語

Afghanistan *n* Afuganísutan アフガニスタン

afire *adv* moete 燃えて, kōfunshite 興奮して

afloat *adj, adv* ukan da/de 浮かんだ/で
afloat cargo *n* okini 沖荷

**afraid; *is ~ of* ... (...ga) kowái desu (...が)怖いです, (...o) kowagari-másu (kowagáru, kowagátte) (...を)怖がります(怖がる, 怖がって)

Africa *n* Afurika アフリカ

Afro-American *n* kokujin 黒人

after 1. *prep* ... kará ...から, ... (no) áto de ... (の)後で; *~ doing* shítékara してから, shita áto de した後で; -go 後; *~ that* sono-go その後 2. *adv* ... shita ato ni/de ...した後に/で

after a long time *adv (of absence)* hisashi-buri ni 久しぶりに

after a meal *n, adv* shokuji no áto 食事の後, [BOOKISH] shokugo 食後

after a while *adv* shibáraku shite しばらくして

after all *adv* kekkyokú 結局; yappári やっぱり, [INFORMAL] yappáshi やっぱし; tsúmari つまり, [BOOKISH] tsumáru tokoro つまるところ,

[BOOKISH] yō-súru ni 要するに; [BOOKISH] shosen しょせん

aftercare *n* afutā kea アフターケア

after the war *n, adv* sensō no áto 戦争の後, [BOOKISH] sengo 戦後

After you! *interj* Dōzo o-saki ni どうぞお先に

after-hours bar *n* sunákku スナック

afterlife *n* 1. anoyo あの世, ráise 来世, shígo no sekai 死後の世界 2. bannen 晩年

afternoon *n, adv* hirú kara 昼から, gógo 午後

afters *n* dezáto デザート

after-school *adj* hōkago (no) 放課後(の)

aftershave (lotion) *n* afutā-shēbu (rōshon) アフターシェーブ(ローション)

aftertaste *n* ató-aji 後味; *leaves a bad ~* atóaji ga waruí 後味が悪い

after(ward) *adv* ato 後

afterwards *adv* áto de 後で

afterworld *n* anoyo あの世, ráise 来世, shígo no sekai 死後の世界

again *adv* mō ichi-dó もう一度, mō ik-kái もう一回; matá また・又; arátamete 改めて, kurikaeshimásu (ga) 繰り返します(が)

against *prep* 1. *(in contrast to)* ...ni táisuru ...に対する; ...ni táishite ...に対して; *(contrary to)* ...ni hán-shite ...に反して; *(opposing)* ... ni hantai/taikō shite ...に反対/対抗して 2. *(running into)* ... ni butsukatte ...にぶつかって 3. *(leaning on)* ...ni motárete (no) ...にもたれて(の)

age 1. *n* toshí とし・年・歳, nenrei 年齢; *your age* (o-)toshi (お)年, [BOOKISH] nenrei 年齢 2. *n (era)* jidai 時代 3. *v (gets old)* toshí o torimásu (tóru, tótte) 年を取ります(取る, 取って), fukemásu (fukéru, fukéte) 老けます(老ける, 老けて)

agency *n* 1. dairi 代理, dairí-ten 代理店 2. *(organization)* kikán 機関

agent *n* dairi 代理, dairi-nin 代理人; *(proxy)* daikō´-sha 代行者; *(broker)* burō´kā ブローカー

aggravating *adj* haradatashíi 腹立たしい

aggression *n* shinryaku 侵略

aggressor *n (person)* shinryáku-sha 侵略者

agile *adj* kibin (na) 機敏(な), binshō (na) 敏捷(な), subayái すばやい・素早い

agitated; *v gets ~* dōyō shimásu (suru, shíte) 動揺します(する, して) → flustered

agitation *n* 1. dōyō 動揺 2. kōfun 興奮

agitator *n (person)* sendō-sha 扇動者

agnate *n, adj* chichigata (no shinzoku) 父方 (の親族)

ago *adv* ...máe ni ...前に; *a little while ~* (tsui) sákki (つい)さっき, [BOOKISH] (tsui) saki-hodo (つい)先程

agony *n* kurushimi 苦しみ, kutsū 苦痛

agrarian *adj* nōgyō (no) 農業(の), nōchi (no) 農地(の), nōson (no) 農村(の), nōmin (no) 農民(の)

agree *v* 1. *(approves)* sansei shimásu (suru, shíte) 賛成します(する, して); *(concurs)* dōi shimásu (suru, shíte) 同意します(する, して)

2. (*promises*) yak<u>u</u>soku shimás<u>u</u> (suru, sh<u>i</u>te) 約束します(する、して) **3.** (*accords with*) ... ni kanaimás<u>u</u> (kanáu, kanátte) ...にかないます(かなう、かなって), ... to itchi shimás<u>u</u> (suru, sh<u>i</u>te) ...と一致します(する、して); ~ *with* (*in harmony*) ... to chōwa shimás<u>u</u> (suru, sh<u>i</u>te) ...と調和します(する、して)

agreeable *adj* aisó/aisō´ ga íi あいそ/あいそう [愛想]がいい

agreement *n* **1.** (*promise*) yak<u>u</u>soku 約束; (*contract*) keiyaku 契約; (*treaty*) jōyaku 条約 **2.** (*understanding*) shōchi 承知; (*consensus*) itchi 一致, dōi 同意, gō´i 合意 **3.** (*harmony*) chōwa 調和

agriculture *n* nō´gyō 農業

ague *n* okóri おこり, mararia netsu マラリア熱, okán 悪寒

ahead *adv* saki (ni) 先(に) (o-saki (ni) お先(に)); *gets ~* s<u>u</u>sumimás<u>u</u> (s<u>u</u>sumu, s<u>u</u>sunde) 進みます(進む、進んで)

ahead and behind zén go (ni) 前後(に)

aid → **help**

AIDS *n* éizu エイズ, AIDS

aikido *n* aikídō 合気道

ail → **sick**

ailing *adj* byōki de 病気で, byōki ryōyōchū (no) 病気療養中(の)

aim *n* **1.** nerai 狙い, méate 目当て; médo 目度・目途, meyasu 目安, kentō´ 見当; (*target*) mato 的; *takes ~* kentō´ o ts<u>u</u>kemás<u>u</u> (ts<u>u</u>kéru, ts<u>u</u>kéte) 見当をつけます(つける、つけて) **2.** (*goal*) mok<u>u</u>teki 目的; (*direction*) hōshin 方針

aim at ... *v* **1.** o neraimás<u>u</u> (nerau, neratte) ...を狙います(狙う、狙って) **2.** ...o megakemás<u>u</u> (megakéru, megákete) ...を目掛けます(目掛ける、目掛けて)

aimless *adj* mok<u>u</u>teki ga/no nái 目的が/のない

air 1. *n* kū´ki 空気 **2.** *n* (*manner*) furí ふり; (*appearance*) fū´ 風 **3.** *n* (*tune*) f<u>u</u>shí 節 **4.** *v ~ it* (*dry*) hoshimás<u>u</u> (hósu, hósh<u>i</u>te) 干します(干す、干して)

air base *n* kūgun k<u>í</u>chi 空軍基地

air conditioner, air conditioning *n* kū´rā クーラー, eakon エアコン, reibō (sō´chi) 冷房(装置)

aircraft *n* hikōki 飛行機
aircraft carrier *n* kōkū bokan 航空母艦

air force *n* kūgun 空軍

airline *n* (*company*) kōkū-gáisha 航空会社

airmail *n* kōkū-bin 航空便, kōkū yū´bin 航空郵便, eamēru エアメール

airplane *n* h<u>i</u>kō´-ki 飛行機

airport *n* kūkō 空港, hikōjō 飛行場

airsick *adv gets ~* h<u>i</u>kōki ni yoimás<u>u</u> (yóu, yótte) 飛行機に酔います(酔う、酔って)

airsick(ness) *n* h<u>i</u>kō-yoi 飛行酔い

airspace *n* ryōkū 領空

air terminal *n* tāminaru ターミナル

airy *adj* **1.** kaze tōshi no yoi 風通しのよい **2.** keikai (na) 軽快(な) **3.** keihaku (na) 軽薄(な)

aisle *n* tsū´ro 通路

ajar *adj* **1.** sukoshi hiráite 少し開いて, hanbiraki (de) 半開き(で) **2.** chōwa shinái (de) 調和しない(で)

akin *adj* **1.** ketsuen (no) 血縁(の), ketsuzoku (no) 血族(の) **2.** dōshu (no) 同種(の), ruiji (no) 類似(の)

à la carte *adj, adv* ippin ryō´ri 一品料理, arakaruto (no) アラカルト(の)

alarm *n* keihō (sō´chi) 警報(装置)

alarm clock *n* arāmu アラーム, mezámashi 目覚し, mezamashi-dókei 目覚し時計

alas *prep* áa ああ, āá あーあ

album *n* (*photograph*) arubamu アルバム; (*stamp*) k<u>i</u>tte-chō 切手帳

alchemy *n* renkinjutsu(shi) 錬金術(師), arukemísuto アルケミスト

alcohol *n* arukōru アルコール

alcoholic *adj* arukōru chūdoku-sha アルコール中毒者

alcove *n* (*in Japanese room*) toko no ma 床の間

alert *n* (*alarm*) keihō 警報, arāto アラート

algebra *n* dáisū (gaku) 代数(学)

alias *n* gimei 偽名, betsumei 別名, tsūshō 通称

alibi *n* aribái アリバイ

alien *n* **1.** yosó (no) よそ(の) **2.** (*an alien*) → **foreigner 3.** uchūjin 宇宙人, éirian エイリアン

alienate *v* sogai shimás<u>u</u> (suru, shite) 疎外します(する、して), tōzakemás<u>u</u> (tōzakeru, tōzakete) 遠ざけます(遠ざける、遠ざけて), sodéni shimás<u>u</u> (suru, shite) そでにします(する、して)

align *v* seiretsu shimás<u>u</u> (suru, shite) 整列します(する、して), narabimás<u>u</u> (narabu, narande) 並びます(並ぶ、並んで)

alike *adj* onaji (yō´na) 同じ(ような), nitéiru 似ている

alimentary *adj* eiyō (no) 栄養(の), tabemono (no) 食べ物(の)

alimony *n* bekkyo téate 別居手当, rikon téate 離婚手当, fujoryō 扶助料

alive *adj* **1.** *is* ~ íkite imás<u>u</u> (iru, ite) 生きています(いる、いて) **2.** *keeps* ~ ikashimás<u>u</u> (ikásu, ikásh<u>i</u>te) 生かします(生かす、生かして)

all *pron* **1.** minna みんな・皆, zen'in 全員; *all* (*concerned/present*) ichidō 一同 **2.** zénbu 全部, súbete 全て・すべて; (*everything*) íssái 一切, arayúru あらゆる; *not at all* どういたしまして **3.** (*completely*) s<u>u</u>kkári すっかり

all along *adv* (*from the beginning*) móto kara 元から

all day (*long*) *adv* ichinichi-jū 一日中

all directions, all sides *adv* sh<u>i</u>hō 四方

all kinds of *adj* samazama (na) さまざま(な)・様々(な), iroiro (na/no) いろいろ・色々(な/の), shúshu (no) 種々(の)

all-out *adj* zenmen-teki (na) 全面的な, zenryoku o ageta 全力をあげた

all over *adv* **1.** (*everywhere*) hōbō ほうぼう・方々(に); ...-jū ...中 **2.** (*finished*) → **end**

all of a sudden *adv* totsuzen (ni) 突然(に), fuini 不意に, ikinari いきなり

all the more *adv* issō いっそう・一層, nao-sara なおさら・尚更

all the time *adv* zutto ずっと, shótchū しょっちゅう, shíjū/始終; (*usually*) tsunezune 常々・つねづね

all the way to *adv* ... máde ...まで

all the way through *adv* zutto ずっと

all together *adv* awásete 合わせて

allay *v* shizumemásu (shizumeru, shizumete) 静めます(静める, 静めて), yawáragemásu (yawárageru, yawáragete) 和らげます(和らげる, 和らげて)

allegation *n* **1.** shuchō 主張 **2.** mōshitate 申し立て

allege *v* **1.** shuchō shimásu (suru, shite) 主張します(する, して) **2.** mōshitatemásu (suru, shite) 申し立てます(申し立てる, 申し立てて)

allegory *n* gūwa 寓話

allergy *n* arérúgii アレルギー

alleviate *v* **1.** yawáragemásu (yawárageru, yawáragete) 和らげます(和らげる, 和らげて) **2.** shizumemásu (shizumeru, shizmete) 静めます(静める, 静めて) **3.** kanwa shimásu (suru, shite) 緩和します(する, して)

alley *n* róji 路地; (*back street*) urá 裏, ura-dō´ri 裏通り; (*side street*) yokochō 横町[横丁]

alliance *n* rengō 連合

allied *adj* rengōkoku no 連合国の, dōmeikoku no 同盟国の

Allies *n* Rengōkoku 連合国

alligator *n* wáni ワニ

allocate *v* wariatemásu (suru, shite) 割り当てます (する, して), haibun shimásu (suru, shite) 配分します(する, して)

allot *v* kubarimásu (kubáru, kubátte) 配ります (配る, 配って)

allotment *n* wariate 割り当て; (*share*) buntan 分担

allow *v.* **1.** (*permits*) yurushimásu (yurúsu, yurúshite) 許します(許す, 許して) **2.** → **give**

allowance *n* (*bonus*) téate 手当(o-téate お手当); (*grant*) kyō´yo 供与; *makes ~ for* ...o kagen shimásu (suru, shite) ...を加減します(する, して)

alloy *n* gōkin 合金

all right *adj* (*OK*) daijōbu (na) 大丈夫(な); (*permissible*) íi いい・良い, yoroshii よろしい

allude *v* honomeka shimásu (su, shite) ほのめかします(す, して), anji shimásu (suru, shite) 暗示します(する, して)

allure 1. *n* miryoku 魅力, miwaku 魅惑 **2.** *adj* alluring miryoku-teki (na) 魅力的な, miwaku-teki (na) 魅惑的な

ally *n* dāmeikoku 同盟国

almanac *n* koyomi 暦, nenkan 年鑑

almond *n* āmondo アーモンド

almost *adv* hotóndo ほとんど・殆ど; daitai 大体

almost all, almost all the time *n* hotóndo ほとんど・殆ど

almost every day *n* máinichi no yō ni 毎日のように

alms *n* hodokoshi (mono) 施し(もの)

aloft *adv, adj* kūchū ni/de 空中に/で, takaitokoro ni/de 高いところに/で

alone *adv* hitóri (de) 一人[独り]で・ひとり(で); (*leave alone*) *let ~* hotte/hōtte okimásu (oku, oite) 放っておきます(おく, おいて)

along 1. *prep, adv* ...ni sotte ...に沿って; (*somewhere*) ...no doko ka (de) ...のどこか(で) **2.** *adv* *brings/takes* jisan shimásu (suru, shite) 持参します(する, して); ... o tsurete ikimásu (iku, itte) ...を連れて行きます(行く, 行って)

alongside *prep* ... no sóba ni ...のそばに

aloof *adj* takabisha (na) 高飛車(な), otákaku tomatta お高くとまった

aloud *adv* kóe o/ni dáshite 声を/に出して

alphabet (ABC) *n* arufabetto アルファベット, ē bii shíi エービーシー

alphabetical *adj* ē-bii-shii jun (no) ABC 順(の), arufabetto jun (no) アルファベット順(の)

already *adv* mō´ もう, súde-ni すでに・既に

Alps *n* arupusu アルプス

also *conj* **1.** ...mo ...も,, mátá また **2.** [INFORMAL] yappári やっぱり, [BOOKISH] yahári やはり,

altar *n* saidan 祭壇
household altar *n* (*Buddhist*) butsudan 仏壇; (*Shinto*) kami-dana 神棚

alter *v* **1.** (*clothing*) naoshimásu (naósu, naóshite) 直します(直す, 直して) **2.** aratamemásu (aratáméru, aratámete) 改めます(改める, 改めて), kaemásu (kaeru, kaete) 変えます(変える, 変えて)

alternate; *v ~ (with)* kōtai shimásu (suru, shite) 交代[交替]します(する, して)

alternately *adv* kawaru-gáwaru 代わる代わる

alternating current *n* kōryū 交流

alternation *n* kōtai 交代・交替

alternative *adj, n* ... (no) hō´ (ga) ...(の)方(が)

although *conj* ... no ni ...のに, ... daga ... だが, ... towaie ... とはいえ

altitude *n* kō´do 高度

altogether *adv* **1.** zénbu de 全部で; minná de みんなで・皆で **2.** (*completely*) mattakú まったく・全く

altruism *n* ritá shugi 利他主義, ritá-teki (na) kōi 利他的(な)行為

aluminum *n* arumi(niumu) アルミ(ニウム)

alumna *n* joshi sotsugyōsei 女子卒業生, josei no sotsugyōsei 女性の卒業生

alumni *n* sotsugyōsei 卒業生
alumni association *n* dōsō-kai 同窓会

alumnus (*of* ...) *n* (...no) sotsugyō(-sei) ...(の)卒業(生), shusshin 出身

always *adv* **1.** ítsu-mo いつも, (*usually*) fúdan ふだん・普段 **2.** (*from the beginning*) móto kara 元から
as always *n* aikawarazu 相変わらず

am → **is**

a.m. *adv* (*morning*) gozen 午前, ē emu AM

amalgamate *v* **1.** gappei shimásu (suru, shite) 合併します(する, して), heigō shimásu (suru, shite) 併合します(する, して) **2.** yūgō shimásu (suru, shite) 融合します(する, して), mazemásu (mazeru, mazete) 混ぜます(混ぜる, 混ぜて)

amass *v* tamemásu (taméru, támete) ため[貯め・溜め]ます(ためる, ためて)

amateur *n* amachua アマチュア; (*novice*) shíró'to しろうと・素人

amaze *v gets amased* akiremásu (akireru, akirete) 呆れます(呆れる, 呆れて), bikkuri shimásu (suru, shite) びっくりします(する, して)

amazement *n* odoroki おどろき・驚き, kyōtan 驚嘆

ambassador *n* táishi 大使

amber *n* kohaku (iro) こはく(色)・琥珀(色)

ambition *n* (*hope*) netsubō 熱望, yashin 野心; (*energetic spirit*) háki 覇気

ambitious *adj* yashin-teki (na) 野心的(な)

ambivalent *adj* kokoro ga fuántei (na) 心が不安定(な), ánbibarensu (no) アンビバレンス(の), kattō-teki (na) 葛藤的な

ambulance *n* kyūkyū-sha 救急車

ambush **1.** *n* machibuse 待ち伏せ, harikomi 張り込み, fuiuchi 不意打ち, kishū kōgeki 奇襲攻撃 **2.** *v* machibuse shimásu (suru, shite) 待ち伏せします(する, して), kishū kōgeki o kakemásu (kakeru, kakete) 奇襲攻撃をかけます(かける, かけて)

amenable *adj* jūjun (na) 従順(な), sunao (na) 素直(な)

amend *v* shūsei shimásu (suru, shite) 修正します(する, して), kaisei shimásu (suru, shite) 改正します(する, して)

amendment *n* shūsei 修正, kaisei 改正

amenity *n* **1.** kokochiyosa 心地よさ, kaiteki-sa/sei 快適さ/性 **2.** reigi 礼儀 **3.** benri na shisetsu 便利な施設

America *n* Amerika アメリカ, Beikoku 米国

American *n* Ameriká-jin アメリカ人

amiable *adj* shakō-teki (na) 社交的(な), hitozukai no yoi 人付き合いのよい, hitoatari no yoi 人当たりのよい, kanji no yoi 感じのよい, aiso/aisō ga íi あいそ/あいそう[愛想]がいい

amiss *adv* machigatte 間違って, futekitō ni 不適当に, futsugō ni 不都合に, hazurete はずれて・外れて

amity *n* yūkō 友好, shinboku 親睦, shinzen 親善

ammonia *n* ánmonia アンモニア

ammunition *n* **1.** dan'yaku 弾薬, buki 武器 **2.** kōgeki shudan 攻撃手段, bōei shudan 防衛手段

amnesia *n* kioku sōshitsu 記憶喪失, kenbō-shō 健忘症

amnesiac *adj* kiokusōshitsu (no) 衛記憶喪失(の)

amnesty **1.** *n* onsha 恩赦 **2.** *v* onsha o ataemásu (ataeru, ataete) 恩赦を与えます(与える, 与えて)

among *prep* ... no náka/uchí (ni) ... の中/内(に)

amoral *adj* dōtoku kannen no nai 道徳観念のない

amorous *adj* **1.** iroppoi 色っぽい, namámekashii なまめかしい **2.** kōshoku (na) 好色(な) **3.** koi (no) 恋(の), ren'ai (no) 恋愛(の)

amortize *v* shōkyaku shimásu (suru, shite) 償却します(する, して), kenbō-shō 健忘症

amount **1.** *n* (*sum*) gáku 額, kingaku 金額 **2.** *n* (*large and/or small*) *amount* tashō 多少 **3.** *v ~ to* (*how much*) (íkura/o-ikura) ni narimásu (náru, nátte) いくら(おいくら)になります(なる, なって) **4.** *v what it amounts to is* ...yōsúru ni 要するに

amour **1.** *n* ren'ai 恋愛, jōji 情事 **2.** aijin 愛人

ample *adj* **1.** *n* hiroi 広い, kōdai na 広大な **2.** futotta 太った **3.** jūbun (na) じゅうぶん(な)・十分(な) → **enough**

amplifier *n* anpu アンプ

amplify *v* kakudai shimásu (suru, shite) 拡大します(する, して)

amulet *n* o-mamori お守り

amuse *v* warawasemásu (warawaseru, warawasete) 笑わせます(笑わせる, 笑わせて), tanoshimasemásu (tanoshimaseru, tanoshimasete) 楽しませます(楽しませる, 楽しませて)

amusement *n* **1.** asobi 遊び **2.** nagusami 慰み, goraku 娯楽

amusement park *n* 遊園地

amusing *adj* omoshirói おもしろい・面白い; (*funny*) okashíi おかしい, kokkei (na) こっけい・滑稽な

an → **a**

anal *adj* kōmon no 肛門の

analog *n, adj* anarogu (shiki) (no) アナログ(式)(の)

analogy *n* **1.** tatoe 例え・たとえ・喩え **2.** ruiji 類似

analysis *n* bunseki 分析

ancestor *n* sósen 祖先, sénzo 先祖

ancestry; *of ... ~ ...*-kei (no) ... 系(の)
    an American of Japanese ancestry n Nikkei (no) Ameriká-jin 日系(の)アメリカ人, (Amerika no) Nikkéi-jin (アメリカの)日系人
    an American of German ancestry n Doitsu-kei (no) Ameriká-jin ドイツ系(の)アメリカ人

anchor *n* ikari いかり・錨・碇

anchor man *n* nyūsu kyásutā ニュースキャスター

ancient *adj* mukashi no 昔の, kodai no 古代の
    ancient days ōmukashi 大昔
    ancient times kodai 古代

and *conj* ... (*including each item*) ... to ...と; (*choosing typical items*) ...ya ...や; (*does/did*) *and* [VERB]-te て; [VERB]-rú/-tá shi る/たし; (*is/was*) *and* [NOUN] de で, [ADJECTIVE]-kute くて; [NOUN] dá/dátta shi だ/だったし, [ADJECTIVE]-í/-kátta shi い/かったし
    and also ... oyobi ...および・及び
    and now/then sá-te さて/それから
    and/or mátá-wa または・又は, ...ya ...や

and others ... -ra...ら;... nádo ...など・等; sonó-hoka その他・そのほか, [BOOKISH] sonó-ta その他

and so forth/on, and the like, and what-not ... nádo ...など・等, ... nánka ...なんか

and yet sore démo それでも, shiká-mo しかも, sore náno ni それなのに

anemia *n* hinketsu(-shō) 貧血(症)

anesthetic *n* másui(-yaku/zai) 麻酔(薬/剤)

anew *adv* ataráshiku 新しく, aratámete 改めて, sára-ni さらに・更に

angel *n* ténshi 天使, enjeru エンジェル

angel fish *n* énzeru fisshu エンゼルフィッシュ

anger *n* ikari 怒り

angina *n* angina アンギナ, kyōshin-shō 狭心症

angle *n* 1. kákudo 角度, kakú 角 2. (*viewpoint*) kénchi 見地

angry; gets ~ okorimásu (okóru, okótte) 怒ります(怒る, 怒って), hará o tatemásu (tatéru, tátete) 腹を立てます(立てる, 立てて), atáma ni kimásu (atáma ni kuru, atáma ni kite) 頭にきます(頭にくる, 頭にきて), kiremásu (kiréru, kirete) キレます(キレる, キレて)

animal *n* dōbutsu 動物, ikimono 生き物; [IN NEGATIVE SENSE] ke(da)mono けだもの・獣 (1: ip-piki 一匹, 2: ní-hiki 二匹, 3: sán-biki 三匹, *how many* nán-biki 何匹)

animation *n* 1. animé アニメ, animēshon アニメーション, dōga 動画 2. kakki 活気

ankle *n* ashí-kúbi 足首

anklets *n* sókkusu ソックス (*how many* nán-soku/-zoku 何足)

annex *n* 1. (*building*) bekkan 別館 2. (*new*) shinkan 新館 3. (*addition*) tate-mashi 建て増し

annihilation *n* zenmetsu 全滅

anniversary *n* (*day*) kinén-bi 記念日

annotation *n* chū 注

announce *v* 1. (*inform*) shirasemásu (shiraseru, shirasete) 知らせます(知らせる, 知らせて) 2. (*publish*) happyō shimásu (suru, shite) 発表します(する, して) 3. (*wedding, etc.*) hírō shimásu (suru, shite) 披露します(する, して)

announcement *n* happyō 発表, anáunsu アナウンス

announcer *n* anaúnsā アナウンサー

annoyance *n* (*trouble*) méiwaku 迷惑

annoying *adj* urusái うるさい, yakamashíi やかましい, méiwaku (na) 迷惑(な), wazurawashíi わずらわしい

annual 1. *adj* ichinen (no) 一年(の) 2. *n* nenkan 年刊, nenpō 年報

annuity *n* nenkin 年金

annul *v* haishi shimásu (suru, shite) 廃止します(する, して), mukō ni shimásu (suru, shite) 無効にします(する, して)

anomalous *adj* hensóku (no) 変則(の), tókui (na) 特異(な)

anonymous *adj* mumei (no) 無名(の)

anorak *n* 1. anorákku アノラック 2. otáku オタク

another *pron* mō hitótsu もう一つ, mō ichi-... もう一...

another person mō hitóri もう一人

another place yoso よそ

another time (*some other time*) ítsu-ka いつか, izure いずれ

answer 1. *n* (*an answer*) kotáé 答え, kaitō 解答, (*a reply*) henji 返事(o-henji お返事), [BOOKISH] hentō 返答 2. *v* (*answers it*) kotaemásu (kotáéru, kotáete) 答えます(答える, 答えて), kaitō shimásu (suru, shite) 解答します(する, して), ~ *the phone* denwa ni demásu (déru, déte) 電話に出ます(出る, 出て)

ant *n* ari アリ・蟻 (1: ip-piki 一匹, 2: ní-hiki 二匹, 3: sán-biki 三匹; *how many* nán-biki 何匹)

antagonism *n* tekii 敵意, tairitsu 対立, hánkan 反感, kikkō 拮抗

Antarctica *n* nánkyoku (tairiku) 南極(大陸)

antenna *n* antena アンテナ

anthropology *n* jinrúi-gaku 人類学

anti- *n* han- 反

anti-American *n, adj* hanbei (no) 反米(の)

antibiotic(s) *n* kōsei bússhitsu 抗性物質

antic(s) *n* kokkei na shigusa こっけいな・滑稽な しぐさ・仕草, odoketa shigusa おどけたしぐさ・仕草, fuzaketa taido ふざけた態度

anticipate *v* machimásu (mátsu, mátte) 待ちます(待つ, 待って), kitai shimásu (suru, shite) 期待します(する, して); (*presume*) yosō shimásu (suru, shite); 予想します(する, して)

anticipation *n* → **expectation** → **hope**

anti-diarrhetic *n* geri-dome 下痢止め

antidote *n* 1. gedókuzai 解毒剤, dok(u)-késhí 毒消し 2. bōei shudan 防衛手段

antifreeze *n* futōeki 不凍液

antihistamine *n* kōhisutamín-zai 抗ヒスタミン剤

anti-Japanese *adj* hannichi (no) 反日(の)

antipathy *n* hankan 反感, ken'o 嫌悪, fuítchi 不一致, tairitsu 対立

antiquated *adj* kyūshiki (no) 旧式(の), táiko (no) 太古(の), kódai (no) 古代(の); [IN NEGATIVE SENSE] jidai okure (no) 時代遅れ (の); [IN POSITIVE SENSE] kófū (na) 古風(な)

antique *n* jidai-mono 時代物; (*curio*) kottō-hin 骨董品

antiquity *n* ōmukashi 大昔

antiseptic *n* bōfu-zai 防腐剤

antithesis *n* seihántai 正反対, taishō 対照, anchi-tēze アンチテーゼ

antiwar *n, adj* hansen (no) 反戦(の)

antler *n* edazunó 枝角, tsunó 角

antonym *n* hantai-go 反対語

anus *n* kōmon 肛門

anxiety *n* ki-zúkái 気遣い, shinpai 心配 → **worry**

anxious *adj* gets ~ harahara shimásu (suru, shite) はらはらします(する, して) → **worried, worry** → **eager**

any *adj* ... ka ...か, ... mo ...も (*but often omitted*) → **anything**

anybody *pron* hito 人, dáre ka 誰か; (*not anyody*)
dare mo 誰も
anybody (at all) dare de mo 誰でも

anyhow *adv* **1.** (*nevertheless*) tónikaku とにかく;
(*anyway*) tómokaku ともかく, nanibun なにぶん,
nánishiro なにしろ **2.** (*at all*) dō de mo どうでも

anyone → **anybody**

anyplace → **anywhere**

anything *pron* **1.** (*something*) náni ka 何か
(*but often omitted*); (*not anything*) nani mo 何も
2. (*at all*) nan de mo 何でも

any time *adv* itsu de mo いつでも

anyway *adv* → **anyhow**

anywhere *adv* (*somewhere*) dóko ka (…) どこか
(...); *anywhere (at all)* doko de mo どこでも;
not anywhere → **nowhere**

apart; *adv* *lives* ~ bekkyo shimásu (suru, shite)
別居します(する, して); ~ *from ...* ...wa betsu
to shite ...は別として; *quite ~ from ...* ... tó wa
betsu ni (shite) ... とは別に(して); *takes it ~*
barashimásu (barásu, baráshite) ばらします
(ばらす, ばらして)

apartment (house) *n* apáto アパート, (*luxury*)
mánshon マンション
apartment complex *n* danchi 団地

apathetic *adj* mukándō (no) 無感動(の), mukánjō
(no) 無感情(の), mukánshin (no) 無関心(の)

apathy *n* mukándō 無感動, mukánjō 無感情,
mukánshin 無関心

ape 1. *n* sáru サル・猿 **2.** *n* noróma na hito のろま
な人 **3.** *v* ... o mane(su)ru ... をまね(す)る・真似
(す)る, ... no mane o suru ... のまね[真似]をする

aperitif *n* aperitifu/aperichifu アペリティフ/アペ
リチフ, shokuzen-shu 食前酒

aphorism *n* kakugen 格言, kingen 金言, keiku 警句

aphrodisiac *n* biyaku 媚薬, horegusuri ほれ薬,
[FORMAL] seishin kyōsōzai 精神強壮剤

apiece *adv* (onóono/sorezore) ...zútsu (おのおの/
それぞれ) ...ずつ

apologize *v* owabishimásu (suru, shite) おわび
[お詫び]します(する, して), ayamarimásu
(ayamáru, ayamátte) 謝ります(謝る, 謝って);
I apologize (*for what I did*). Mōshiwaké arimasen/
gozaimasen 申し訳ありません/ございません,
sumimasen すみません, gomennasái ごめんな
さい

apology *n* wabi わび・詫び (o-wabi おわび・
お詫び), ayamári 謝り

apoplexy *n* (nō) sotchū (脳)卒中, (nō) ikketsu
(脳)溢血

appall *v* zotto shimásu (suru, shite) ぞっとします
(する, して), gakuzen to shimásu (suru, shite) が
くぜん・愕然とします(する, して)

apparatus *n* sō'chi 装置; kígu 器具

apparel *n* (i)fuku (衣)服
apparel industry *n* apareru gyōkai アパレル業界

apparent(ly) *adv* ... rashíi ...らしい

apparition *n* **1.** yúrei 幽霊, bōrei 亡霊
2. shutsu-gen 出現

appeal *v* (*appeal to one*) pin to kimásu (kúru,
kíte) ぴんときます(くる, きて), ki ni irimásu
(ki ni iru, ki ni itte) 気に入ります(気に入る,
気に入って)

appear *v* **1.** (*looks, seems*) miemásu (miéru,
míete) 見えます(見える, 見えて) **2.** (*shows
up*) demásu (déru, déte) 出ます(出る, 出て),
arawaremásu (arawaréru, arawárete) 現れます
(現れる, 現われて); (*occurs*) hassei shimásu
(suru, shite) 発生します(する, して); ~ *on stage*
bútai ni demásu (déru, déte) 舞台に出ます(出る,
出て), tōjō shimásu (suru, shite) 登場します
(する, して)

appearance *n* **1.** yōsu 様子・ようす, ...sama
...様 **2.** gaiken 外見; (*outer appearances*) uwabe
うわべ・上辺, omoté 表 **3.** (*get-up, form*) teisai
体裁; (*shape*) kakkō かっこう・格好・恰好
personal appearance 4. (*air, manner*) ...fū´...風

appease *v* nadámemásu (nadameru, nadamete)
なだめます(なだめる, なだめて), yawaragemásu
(yawarageru, yawarageru) 和らげます(和らげる,
和らげて), iyashimásu (iyasu, iyashite) いやし
・癒します(癒す, 癒して)

append *v* fuka shimásu (suru, shite) 付加します
(する, して), tsuketashimásu (tsuketasu, tsuke-
tashite) 付け足します(付け足す, 付け足して),
soemásu (soeru, soete) 添えます(添える, 添えて)

appendage *n* fuzoku-butsu 付属物

appendectomy *n* mōchō setsujo-jutsu 盲腸切
除術, mōchō-en (no) shujutsu 盲腸炎(の)手術,
chūsui setsujo-jutsu 虫垂切除術, chūsui-en (no)
shujutsu 虫垂炎(の)手術

appendicitis *n* mōchō-en 盲腸炎, chūsui-en
虫垂炎

appetite *n* shokuyoku 食欲

appetizers *n* zensai 前菜; (*to go with drinks*)
sakana さかな・肴, tsumami(mono) つまみ
(もの), o-tsúmami おつまみ

appetizing *adj* oishisō (na) おいしそう(な)

applaud *v* hákushu shimásu (suru, shite) 拍手し
ます(する, して), hákushu o okurimásu (okuru,
okutte) 拍手を送ります(送る, 送って)

applause *n* hákushu 拍手

apple *n* ringo りんご・リンゴ (*how many* nán-ko
何個)
apple pie *n* appuru pai アップルパイ

appliances *n* (katei) yō'gu (家庭)用具, katei
yō'hin 家庭用品, (*electric*) denki-yō'hin 電気用品,
katei-yō denki kigu 家庭用電気器具

applicant *n* mōshikomí-sha 申し込み者, kibō-sha
希望者

application *n* **1.** (*for a job, etc.*) mōshi-komi 申し
込み, gánsho 願書; (*claim*) mōshi-de 申し出; (*for
a permit*) shinsei-sho 申請書 **2.** (*putting to use*)
ōyō 応用, jitsuyō 実用; (*for computer*) sofutowea
ソフトウェア

apply *v* **1.** (*it applies*) atarimásu (ataru, attate)
当たります(当たる, 当たって); (*accordingly*)
jun-jimásu (jun-jiru, jun-jite) 準じます(準じる,

準じて) **2.** (*applies it*) atemásu (ateru, atete) 当てます(当てる, 当てて), tsukemásu (tsukéru, tsukéte) 付けます(付ける, 付けて); ōyō shimásu (suru, shite) 応用します(する, して) **3.** (*applies for*) mōshi-komimásu (mōshi-komu, mōshi-konde) 申し込みます(申し込む, 申し込んで), ōbo shimásu (suru, shite) 応募します(する, して); (*claims*) mōshi-demásu (mōshi-deru, mōshi-dete) 申し出ます(申し出る, 申し出て)

appoint *v* (*nominates*) mei-jimásu (mei-jiru, mei-jite) 命じます(命じる, 命じて); (*designates*) shitei shimásu (suru, shite) 指定します(する, して)

appointed day *n* kíjitsu 期日

appointment *n* (*engagement, date, visit to a customer*) yakusoku 約束; (*to see doctor, ...*) yoyaku 予約

apportion *v* ... o wariatemásu (wariateru, wariatete) ... を割り当てます(割り当てる, 割り当てて), ... o bunpai shimásu (suru, shite) ... を分配します(する, して)

appraisal *n* hyōka 評価

appraise *v* hyōka shimásu (suru, shite) 評価します(する, して), kantei shimásu (suru, shite) 鑑定します(する, して)

appreciable *adj* kánari (no) かなり(の), sōtō (no) 相当(の)

appreciate *v* arigátaku omoimásu (omóu, omótte) ありがたく[有り難く]思います(思う, 思って), kansha shimásu (suru, shite) 感謝します(する, して)

appreciation *n* kánsha 感謝, hyōka 評価

apprehend *v* **1.** ríkai shimásu (suru, shite) 理解します(する, して), sasshimásu (su(ru), shite) 察します(す(る), して) **2.** tsukamaemásu (tsukamaeru, tsukamaete) 捕まえます(捕まえる, 捕まえて), taiho shimásu (suru, shite) 逮捕します(する, して) **3.** shinpai shimásu (suru, shite) 心配します(する, して)

apprehensive *adj* kimí ga warúi 気味が悪い

apprentice *n* deshí 弟子

approach *v* (...ni) chika-zukimásu (chika-zúku, chika-zúite) (...に)近付きます(近付く, 近付いて), yorimásu (yóru, yótte) 寄ります(寄る, 寄って); sekkin shimásu (suru, shite) 接近します(する, して); *lets one ~* (... o) chika-zukemásu (chika-zukéru, chika-zúkete) (...を)近付けます(近付ける, 近付けて)

approach to a shrine sandō 参道

appropriate 1. *adj* (*suitable*) tekísetsu (na) 適切 (な), tekitō (na) 適当(な) **2.** *v* (*sets aside* (*for*)) atemásu (ateru, atete) 当てます(当てる, 当てて) **3.** *v* → **seize**

approval *n* dōi 同意

approve *v* sansei shimásu (suru, shite) 賛成します (する, して)

approximate 1. *adj* daitai (no) 大体(の), gaisan (no) 概算(の), chikái 近い **2.** *v* chikazukimásu (chikazuku, chikazuite) 近づきます(近づく, 近づいて), chikazukemásu (chikazukeru, chikazukete) 近づけます(近づける, 近づけて)

approximately *adv* daitai 大体; yáku ... 約...; ... gúrai ...位; ...-zéngo ...前後; ... -kéntō ...見当; ...-náigai (de) ...内外(で)

apricot *n* anzu あんず・杏

April *n* Shi-gatsú 四月・4 月

apron *n* épuron エプロン

apropos *adv* tekisetsu na/ni 適切な/に

apt; adj *~ to (do)* (shi-)yasúi (し)やすい・易い; [BOOKISH] tokaku (...shimásu) とかく(...します); [BOOKISH] ete-shite (...shimásu) 得てして(します)

aptitude *n* keikō 傾向, sáinō 才能, rikairyoku 理解力

aquarium *n* suizóku kan 水族館

Aquarius *n* (*star sign*) Mizugame-za 水瓶座

Arab, Arabian *n, adj* Árabu (no) アラブ(の), (*person*) Arabú-jin (no) アラブ人(の)

Arabic *n* (*language*) Arabia-go アラビア語

arbiter *n* cyūsái-sha 仲裁者

arbitrary *adj* nin-i (no) 任意の, dokudan-teki (na) 独断的(な), kímama (na) 気まま(な)

arbor *n* kokáge 木陰

arc *n* (en)ko (円)弧

arcade *n* ākēdo アーケード

archaeologist *n* kōko gákusha 考古学者

archaic *adj* sutáreta 廃れた

arch *n* yumi-gata 弓形, āchi(-gata) アーチ(形)

archer *n* ite/shashu 射手, yumí o iruhito 弓を射る 人; yumí no meijin 弓の名人

archery *n* (*the traditional art*) kyūdō 弓道, kyūjutsu 弓術

archetype *n* genkei 原型, tenkei 典型

archipelago *n* rettō 列島, ...-réttō ...列島

architect *n* kenchiku-ka 建築家

architecture *n* kenchiku 建築

archive *n* kiroku (sho) 記録(書)

Arctic *n* Hokkyoku 北極

ardent *adj* nesshin (na) 熱心(な), netsuretsu(teki) (na) 熱烈(的)(な)

ardor *n* netsui 熱意, jōnetsu 情熱, nesshin 熱心, ikigomi 意気込み

arduous *adj* kónnan (na) 困難(な)

arid *adj* kánsō shita/shiteiru 乾燥した/している, fumō no/na 不毛の/に

are → is

area *n* **1.** ménseki 面積 **2.** (*district*) chíhō 地方, chiiki 地域, eria エリア, chitai 地帯 → **place** → **vicinity**

argue *v* kenka shimásu (suru, shite) けんか[喧嘩] します(する, して); (*discusses, debates*) ron-jimásu (ron-zuru, ron-jite) 論じます(論ずる, 論じて)

argument *n* **1.** kenka けんか・喧嘩, kuchi-génka 口げんか・口喧嘩 **2.** (*discussion*) rón 論, ronsō 論争 **3.** (*logic*) rikutsu 理屈

Aries *n* (*star sign*) O-hitsuji-za 牡羊座

arise *v* okimásu (okíru, ókite) 起きます(起きる, 起きて); (*happens*) shō-jimásu (shō-jiru, shō-jite) 生じます(生じる, 生じて)

ark shell *n* (*blood clam*) aká-gai 赤貝

arm *n* udé 腕

armor *n* yoroi よろい・鎧

armory *n* buki ko 武器庫, heiki ko 兵器庫

armpit *n* waki nó shita 腋の下・わきの下

  armpit smell *n* (*body odor*) waki-ga わきが・腋臭

arms *n* heiki 兵器, buki 武器

army *n* gúntai 軍隊; (*vs. navy*) rikú-gun 陸軍

aroma *n* ároma アロマ, (yoi) kaori (よい)香り, hōkō 芳香

around 1. *adv* (... no) mawari ni (...の)周りに; *goes ~* (... o) mawarimásu (mawaru, mawatte) (...を)回ります(回る, 回って) 2. → **about**, **approximately**

arouse *v* shigeki shimásu (suru, shite) 刺激します (する, して), kōfun shimásu (suru, shite) 興奮します(する, して), kōfun sasemásu (saseru, sasete) 興奮させます(させる, させて)

arrange *v* 1. (*lines them up*) narabemásu (naraberu, narabete) 並べます(並べる, 並べて); *~ themselves* narabimásu (narabu, narande) 並び ます(並ぶ, 並んで) 2. (*decides, sets*) kimemásu (kimeru, kimete) 決めます(決める, 決めて), (*a meeting/consultation*) uchi-awasemásu (uchi-awaséru, uchi-awásete) 打ち合わせます(打ち合わ せる, 打ち合わせて) 3. (*puts together*) matomemásu (matomeru, matomete) まとめます(まとめる, まとめて) 4. (*flowers*) (haná o) ikemásu (ikéru, íkete) (花を)生けます(生ける, 生けて)

arranged *v* 1. *gets ~* (*is put together*) matomarimásu (matomaru, matomatte) まとま ります(まとまる, まとまって), (*as a set/array*) soroimásu (soróu, sorótte) 揃います(揃う, 揃 って); (*gets decided/set*) kimarimásu (kimaru, kimatte) 決まります(決まる, 決まって) 2. *it has been ~ that ...* kotó ni natte (i)másu ...ことになっ て(い)ます

arranged marriage *n* (o-)miai kékkon (お)見合い結婚

arrangement *n* 1. (*settlement*) kimari 決まり; (*adjustment*) séiri 整理 2. *arrangements* (*preparations*) júnbi 準備, shitaku 支度・仕度; (*plans*) téhazu 手はず・手筈

  flower arrangement *n* ikébana 生け花・生花

  prior arrangement *n* uchi-awase 打ち合わせ

array *n* soroé 揃え

arrears *n* tainō(kin) 滞納(金)

arrest *v* toraémásu (toráéru, toráete) 捕えます (捕える, 捕えて), tsukamaemásu (tsukamaeru, tsukamaete) 捕まえます(捕まえる, 捕まえて), táiho shimásu (suru, shite) 逮捕します(する, して)

arrival *n* tōchaku 到着; ... cháku ...着

arrive (at) *v* 1. (... ni) tsukimásu (tsukú, tsúite) (...に)着きます(着く, 着いて), tōchaku shimásu (suru, shite) 到着します(する, して), itarimásu (itaru, itatte) 至ります(至る, 至って) 2. (*is delivered*) todokimásu (todóku, todóite) 届きます(届く, 届いて)

arriving at (TIME/PLACE) ... cháku (no) ...着(の)

arrogant *adj* gōman (na) 傲慢(な); *is/acts ~* ibarimásu (ibáru, ibátte) 威張ります(威張る, 威張って)

arrow *n* yá 矢; (*sign*) ya-jírushi 矢印

arrowroot *n* kuzu くず・葛

  powdered arrowroot *n* kuzuko くず粉・葛粉

art *n* bíjutsu 美術, geijutsu 芸術

artery *n* 1. dōmyaku 動脈 2. kansen dōro 幹線道路

artful *adj* kōmyō (na) 巧妙(な), takumi (na) 巧み (な), kōkatsu (na) 狡猾(な), jinkō (no) 人工(の)

arthritis *n* kansetsu-en 関節炎

article *n* (*thing*) monó 物, (*goods*) shina(-mono) 品(物); (*writeup*) kíji 記事; (*scholarly*) ronbun 論文

articulate 1. *adj* hakkírishita はっきりした, meikai (na) 明快(な) 2. *v* hakkíri iimásu (iu, itte) はっきり言います(言う, 言って)

artifice *n* sakuryaku 策略, kōmyō sa 巧妙さ

artificial *adj* jinkō (no) 人工(の), jinkō-teki (na) 人工的(な)

artillery *n* taihō 大砲, buki 武器

artisan *n* shokunin 職人

artist *n* geijutsu-ka 芸術家; (*painter*) gaka 画家

arts *n* géi 芸, waza 技, āto アート

as 1. *conj* (*like*) ... (no) yō´ (ni) ... (の)よう(に) 2. (*so as to be*) ...ni..に 3. (*in the role of*) ... to shite ... として

  as far as ... is concerned ... ni kákete wa ... に かけては; ...ni kan-shite wa... に関しては

  as for ... wa ...は

  as much as ... gúrai ...位; ...hodo ...程・ほど; *~ one likes* zonbun (ni) 存分(に)

  as much as possible dekiru-dake 出来るだけ・できるだけ

  as regards ... ni kákete wa ...にかけては; ... ni kán-shite ...に関して; ni tsúite …については

  as to/for the matter at hand sá-te さて

  as soon as ... (suru) to (súgu) ...(する)と(すぐ) (shíté) kara súgu (して)からすぐ, ([VERB]-i い) -shídai (ni) 次第(に)

  as usual/ever/always aikawarazu 相変わらず

Asakusa *n* Asakusa 浅草

ascent *n* jōshō 上昇, agáru koto 上がること

ascertain *v* tashikamemásu (tashikaméru, tashikámete) 確かめます(確かめる, 確かめて)

ascetic practices *n* shugyō 修行, gyō´ 行

ashamed *adj* hazukashíi 恥ずかしい; (*guilty feeling*) yamashíi やましい; *is ~* of hajimásu (hajíru, hajíte) 恥ます(恥じる, 恥じて)

ash(es) *n* hai 灰; *volcanic ash* kazán-bai 火山灰

ashen *adj* hai iro (no) 灰色(の), aojiroi 青白い, masáao (na) 真っ青(な)

ashore *adv* kishi (ni) (mukatte) 岸(に)(向か って), riku (ni) (mukatte) 陸(に)(向かって)

ashtray *n* hai-zara 灰皿

Asian 1. *adj* Ajia (no) アジア(の) 2. *n* (*person*) Ajiá-jin アジア人

aside (from) *adv* ... wa betsu to shite ...は別として

ask v 1. (*a favor of a person*) (... ni ...o) tanomimásu (tanómu, tanónde) (...に ...を)頼みます(頼む、頼んで)、negaimásu (negau, negatte) 願います(願う、願って); (*requires*) motomemásu (motoméru, motómete) 求めます(求める、求めて) 2. (*a person a question*) (... ni) kikimásu (kiku, kiite) (...に)聞きます(聞く、聞いて)、tazunemásu (tazunéru, tazúnete) 尋ねます(尋ねる、尋ねて)、ukagaimásu (ukagau, ukagatte) 伺います(伺う、伺って)

askance 1. adv utagatte 疑って 2. adj naname (no) 斜め(の)

aslant adv, adj nanáme (no/ni) 斜め(の/に)

asleep adv, adj nemutte (iru) 眠って(いる)

asparagus n asupara (gásu) アスパラ(ガス)

aspect n 1. yōsu 様子 2. (*grammatical*) ásupékuto アスペクト, (soku/kyoku) men (側/局)面

aspersions n chūshō 中傷, hinan 非難

asphalt n asufáruto アスファルト

asphyxiate v chissoku shimásu (suru, shite) 窒息します(する、して)、chissoku sasemásu (saseru, sasete) 窒息させます(させる、させて)

aspiration n ganbō 願望, yashin 野心, akogare 憧れ

aspire → hope

aspirin n asupirin アスピリン

ass 1. n róba ろば・ロバ 2. n gankomono 頑固者; báka ばか 3. n (o-)shíri (お)しり・(お)尻 4. v (*act dumb*) báka na mane o shimásu (suru, shite) ばかな真似をします(する、して)

assail v kōgeki shimásu (suru, shite) 攻撃します(する、して)、hínan shimásu (suru, shite) 非難します(する、して)

assault v osóimásu (osou, osotte) 襲います(襲う、襲って) **→ attack**

assemble v 1. (*they collect*) atsumarimásu (atsumáru, atsumátte) 集まります(集まる、集まって)、shūgō shimásu (suru, shite) 集合します(する、して); (*collects them*) atsumemásu (atsuméru, atsúmete) 集めます(集める、集めて) 2. (*fits parts together to make a whole*) kumi-awasemásu (kumi-awaseru, kumi-awasete) 組(み)合せます(組(み)合わせる、組(み)合わせて)、kumi-tatemásu (kumi-tateru, kumi-tatete) 組(み)立てます(組(み)立てる、組(み)立てて)

assembly n 1. (*gathering*) shūgō 集合 2. (*parliament*) kokkai 国会

assent v nattoku shimásu (suru, shite) 納得します(する、して) **→ consent**

assert v shuchō shimásu (suru, shite) 主張します(する、して)

assertion n shuchō 主張

assimilate v dōka shimásu (suru, shite) 同化します(する、して); kyūshū shimásu (suru, shite) 吸収します(する、して)

assist v ōen shimásu (suru, shite) 応援します(する、して); tasukemásu (tasukéru, tasukete) 助けます(助ける、助けて) **→ help**

assistance n sewá 世話 （o-séwa お世話）; tetsudái 手伝い(o-tétsudai お手伝い); hójo 補助, ōen 応援

assistant n joshu 助手, ashísutanto アシスタント

assistant professor n jo-kyō´ju 助教授

associate professor n jun-kyō´ju 准教授

associate with ...to tsuki-aimásu (tsuki-áu, tsuki-átte) ...と付き合います(付き合う、付き合って); ...to majiwarimásu (majiwáru, majiwátte) ...と交わります(交わる、交わって); ... o chika-zukemásu (chika-zukéru, chika-zúkete) ...を近付けます(近付ける、近付けて)

association n 1. kyōkai 協会; (*academic*) gakkai 学会; (*guild, union*) kumiai 組合 2. (*social company*) tsuki-ai 付き合い(o-tsukíai お付き合い) 3. (*of thought*) rensō 連想

assortment n kumi-awase 組み合わせ, tori-awase 取り合わせ

assumed name n gimei 偽名

asterisk n hoshi-jírushi 星印; asutarisuku アスタリスク

asthma n zensoku 喘息

astonished; adj gets ~ odorokimásu (odoróku, odoróite) 驚きます(驚く、驚いて)

astringent adj shibúi 渋い

astringent n (*facial*) asutorínzen アストリンゼン

astronomy n tenmón-gaku 天文学

asylum n hinán-jo 避難所, seishin byōin 精神病院

at prep ... de...で; (*being located at*) ... ni ...に
at any rate tómokaku ともかく
at best séizei せいぜい
at ease yukkúri ゆっくり
at last iyoiyo いよいよ, yōyaku ようやく, tsúi-ni ついに; (*after difficulty*) yatto やっと
at least sukúnáku-tomo 少なくとも, sémete せめて
at most 1. ōku-temo 多くても, séizei せいぜい 2. sémete せめて
at once sassokú 早速・さっそく
at one time kátsute かつて

atelier n atorie アトリエ, gashítsu 画室

athlete n (undō) sénshu (運動)選手

athlete's foot n mizumushi 水虫, tamushi 田虫

athletic field n undō-jō 運動場, kyōgi-jō 競技場

athletics n undō 運動, supó´tsu スポーツ; (*physical education*) tai(i)ku 体育・たいく, asurechíkku アスレチック

athletic supporter n sapōtā サポーター

Atlantic Ocean n Taiséiyō 大西洋

atmosphere n fun'íki 雰囲気

atom n génshi 原子

atomic adj genshí (-ryoku) 原子力(の)
atomic bomb n genshi bákudan 原子爆弾
atomic energy n genshí-ryoku 原子力

atomizer n supurē スプレー

atrocious adj (*brutal*) zangyaku (na) 残虐(な)

atrocity n zangyaku kō´i 残虐行為

attach 1. v (*sticks on*) tsukemásu (tsukéru, tsukéte) 付けます(付ける、付けて) 2. (*adds*) soemásu (soeru, soete) 添えます(添える、添えて)

attached file *n* tenpu fáiru 添付ファイル

attachment *n* fuzoku 付属・附属, fuzoku-hin 付属品・附属品

attack 1. *n* (*an attack*) kōgeki 攻撃, shūgeki 襲撃 **2.** *v* (*makes an attack*) osóimásu (osou, osotte) 襲います(襲う, 襲って); sememásu (seméru, sémete) 攻めます(攻める, 攻めて); kōgeki/shūgeki shimásu (suru, shite) 攻撃/襲撃します(する, して)

attain → reach → accomplish

attempt 1. *n* tameshí 試し, kokoromi 試み; (*plot, scheme*) kuwadate 企て **2.** *v* (*attempts it*) tameshimásu (tamésu, taméshite) 試します(試す, 試して), kokoromimásu (kokoromíru, kokorómite) 試みます(試みる, 試みて); kuwadatemásu (kuwadatéru, kuwadátete) 企てます(企てる, 企てて)

attend *v* demásu (deru, dete) 出ます(出る, 出て); shusseki shimásu (suru, shite) 出席します(する, して)

attendance *n* shusseki 出席
office attendance *n* shukkin 出勤

attendant 1. *n* (*in charge*) kákari 係, kakarí-in 係員, ...-gákari ...係 **→ clerk**
flight attendant *n* furaito aténdanto フライトアテンダント, suchuwādesu スチュワーデス, kyabin aténdanto キャビンアテンダント, kyakushitsu jōmu-in 客室乗務員

attention *n* **1.** chū´i 注意, chūmoku 注目 **2.** omoiyari 思いやり

attest *v* shōmei shimásu (suru, shite) 証明します(する, して)

attestation *n* shōmei 証明

attitude *n* táido 態度, shisei 姿勢

attorney *n* bengóshi 弁護士

attract *v* hikimásu (hiku, hiite) 引きます(引く, 引いて); (*charming*) miryoku ga arimásu (áru, átte) 魅力があります(ある, あって)

attraction *n* atorakushon アトラクション

attractive *adj* (*nice-looking*) kírei (na) きれい・綺麗(な); (*charming*) miryoku-teki (na) 魅力的(な)

attractiveness *n* (*charm*) aikyō あいきょう・愛嬌

auction *n* serí 競り・セリ, kyōbai 競売, ōkushon オークション

audience *n* chōshū 聴衆, kankyaku 観客

audio *n*, *adj* onsei (no) 音声(の), ōdio オーディオ

audition *n* ōdishon オーディション, shínsa 審査

auditorium *n* kaidō 会堂, kōdō 講堂

aunt *n* (*father's or mather's elder sister*) obá(-san) 伯母(さん); (*father's or mather's younger sister*) obá(-san) 叔母(さん); (*in general*) obá(-san) おば(さん)

auspicious *adj* medetái めでたい・目出度い (o-medetái おめでたい・お目出度い)

Australia *n* ōsutorária オーストラリア

Australian 1. *n* (*person*) ōsutorariá-jin オーストラリア人 **2.** *adj* ōsutorariá no オーストラリアの

authentic *adj* kakujitsu (na) 確実(な), honmono (nó) 本物(の), shōshinshōmei (no) 正真正銘(の)

authentication *n* (*certificate*) shōmei-sho 証明書

author *n* chó-sha 著者, sáku-sha 作者 **→ writer**

authority *n* **1.** (*expert*) táika 大家, tsū´ 通 **2.** (*power*) ken'i 権威 **3.** (*basis*) kónkyo 根拠
the authorities tōkyoku 当局, okámi お上;
the authorities/people concerned with ... ... no kankéi-sha ...の関係者

authorized *adj* kōnin (no) 公認(の)

automatic *adj* jidō-teki (na) 自動的(な)

automatically *adv* jidō-teki ni 自動的に; (*spontaneously*) hítori-de ni ひとりでに・独りでに, onozukara おのずから・自ずから

automation *n* ōtomēshon オートメーション, jidō (ka) 自動(化)

automobile *n* jidō-sha 自動車, kuruma 車 (*how many* nán-dai 何台)

autosuggestion *n* jiko anji 自己暗示

autumn *n* áki 秋
autumn leaves mómiji もみじ・紅葉
autumn period/term shū´ki 秋期

autumnal equinox *n* shūbun 春分
Autumnal Equinox Day Shūbun-no-hí 秋分の日

available *adj* (*things*) riyō dekiru 利用できる, (*person*) áiteiru 空いている; *seats are ~* suwaremásu (suwareru, suwarete) 座れます(座れる, 座れて)
available room(s) aki-beya/-ma/-shitsu 空き部屋/間/室
available space aki-ma 空き間
available taxi kūsha 空車

avalanche *n* nadare なだれ・雪崩; (*snowslide*) yuki-nádare 雪なだれ

avenue *n* tōrí 通り, ōdō´ri 大通り, kaidō 街道; michi 道

average 1. *n* (*on the average*) heikin 平均
average age heikin nenrei 平均年令; (*life span, lifetime*) heikin jumyō 平均寿命
average score heikin ten 平均点
2. *adj* (*ordinary*) nami (no) 並(の), heibon (na) 平凡(な) **3.** *v averages it* narashimásu (narásu, naráshite) ならし[均し]ます(ならす, ならして)

avert *v* **1.** sakemásu (sakéru, sákete) 避けます(避ける, 避けて) **2.** me o sorashimásu (sorasu, sorashite) 目をそらします(そらす, そらして)

aviary *n* torígoya 鳥小屋

aviation *n* kōkū (ki) 航空(機)

avoid *v* sakemásu (sakéru, sákete) さけます・避けます(さける, さけて), yokemásu (yokéru, yókete) よけます・避けます(よける, よけて)

await → wait for

awake *v*, (*comes awake*) mezamemásu, (mezaméru, mézámete) 目覚めます(目覚める, 目覚めて); *is awake* (*not asleep*) nemurimasén (nemuranai, nemuranaide) 眠りません(眠らない, 眠らないで)

award 1. *n* shō 賞
Academy Award academí shō アカデミー賞
2. *v* (*gives*) (shō o) júyo shimásu (suru, shite)

(賞を)授与します(する,して); okurimásu (okuru, okutte) 贈ります(贈る,贈って)

awardee *n* jushō´-sha 受賞者

away *adj* tōku (ni) 遠く(に)

away from home rúsu (no) 留守(の)

right away súgu すぐ

go away ikimásu (iku, itte) 行きます(行く, 行って)

run away (*flees*) nigemásu (nigéru, nígete) 逃げます(逃げる,逃げて)

take away torimásu (tóru, tótte) 取ります(取る, 取って); tōku (ni) 遠く(に)

awesome *adj* (mono)sugói (もの)すごい・

(物)凄い, subárashíi すばらしい・素晴らしい, saikō 最高

awful *adj* osoroshíi 恐ろしい, hidói ひどい

awfully *adv* → **very**

awkward *adj* mazúi まずい, gikochinai ぎこちない, buzama (na) ぶざま(な)

awl *n* kiri きり・キリ・錐

awning *n* hi-ōí 日覆い, hiyoke 日よけ, tenmaku 天幕

ax *n* ono おの・オノ・斧

axis, axle *n* jikú 軸; *x/y/z axis/axle* ekkusu/wai/zetto jiku X/Y/Z 軸

azalea *n* tsutsúji つつじ

B

babble *n* o-shaberi おしゃべり

baby 1. *n* áka-chan 赤ちゃん, akanbo 赤ん坊・赤んぼ 2. (*lover*) koibito 恋人 3. *v* (*pampers one*) ama-yakashimásu (ama-yakasu, ama-yakashite) 甘やかします(甘やかす,甘やかして)

babysitter *n* bebii shittā ベビーシッター, (*professional*) komóri 子守

baby stroller *n* bebii kā ベビーカー

bachelor *n* 1. dokushin dansei 独身男性, hitori mónó ひとり者・独り者 2. gákushi 学士

bachelor's degree *n* gákushi (gō) 学士(号)

back 1. *adv* (*behind*) ... no ushiro (de/ni) ... の後ろ(で/に) 2. *n* (*of body*) senaka 背中, (*lower part*) koshi 腰; (*of room etc.*) óku 奥; (*reverse side*) urá 裏 → **support**

back; go ~ modorimásu (modóru, modótte) 戻ります(戻る, 戻って); (*to one's usual place*) kaerimásu (káeru, káette) 帰ります(帰る, 帰って); ~ *up* bákku shimásu (suru, shite) バックします(する, して); bákku-appu shimásu (suru, shite) バックアップします(する, して)

I'll be right back. *interj* Chótto itte kimásu. ちょっと行って来ます。

I'm back. *interj* Tadáima (kaerimáshita). ただいま(帰りました).

back and forth *adv* zéngo (ni) 前後(に); *goes* ~ kayoimásu (kayou, kayotte) 通います(通う, 通って)

backbencher *n* hira-giin 平議員

backbone *n* sebone 背骨

backdate *v* hizuke o sakanoborasemásu (sakanoboraseru, sakanoborasete) 日付をさかのぼらせます(せる, せて)

back door *n* ura-guchi 裏口

back down *v* 1. (*retreat*) kōtai shimásu (suru, shite) 後退します(する, して) 2. (*withdraw*) hiki sagarimásu (sagaru, sagatte) 引き下がります(下がる, 下がって)

backdrop *n* haikei (maku) 背景(幕)

backed up *v* (*traffic*) jūtai shite imásu (iru, ite) 渋滞しています(いる, いて)

backfire *n* ura-me ni demásu (deru, dete) 裏目に出ます(出る, 出て)

back gate *n* ura-mon 裏門

background *n* 1. haikei 背景, bákku バック 2. (*one's origin, education, experience, etc.*) keireki 経歴 3. (*circumstances of the event, information*) yobi chishiki 予備知識, bákku gura(u)ndo バックグラ(ウ)ンド

backhand *n* (*sports*) bakku hando バックハンド

backhanded *adj* 1. (*sports*) bakku hando (no) バックハンド(の) 2. (*ambiguous meaning*) aimai (na) あいまい(な)・曖昧(な) 3. (*roundabout, indirect*) mawarikudoi 回りくどい 4. *n* (*backhanded slap*) bakku hando バックハンド

backhander *n* (*bribe*) wáiro わいろ・賄賂

backing 1. *n* (*support*) kōen 後援; enjo 援助 2. → **lining**

back issue *n* (*out-of-date or previous issue of a periodical*) bakku nanbā バックナンバー

backlash *n* handō 反動, hanpatsu 反発

backlog *n* 1. (*reserve*) bichiku 備蓄 2. (*stock*) zaiko 在庫 3. (*work*) yarinokoshi no shigoto やり残しの仕事

back number *n* (*out-of-date or previous issue of a periodical*) bakku nanbā バックナンバー

back-order *n* toriyose chūmon 取り寄せ注文

backpack *n* ryukku-sakku リュックサック

back pay *n* mibarai kyūyo 未払給与, mibarai chingin 未払賃金

backrest *n* (*legless chair*) za-isu 座椅子

back room *n* nándo 納戸

back seat *n* kōbu zaseki 後部座席

backside *n* 1. ushiro 後ろ, [BOOKISH] kōhō 後方 2. (*buttock*) shiri 尻 (o-shiri お尻)

backstage *adj, adv* butai ura (no/de) 舞台裏(の/で), gakuya (no/de) 楽屋(の/で)

backstop *n* (*baseball*) bakku netto バックネット

back street *n* ura-dō´ri 裏通り

backstroke *n* seoyogi 背泳ぎ

backup *n* **1.** (*computer*) bákku appu バックアップ **2.** yobi 予備, hikae 控え

backwards *adv* (*contrariwise*) gyaku (ni) 逆(に); *move* ~ bákku shimásu (suru, shite) バックします(する, して), ushiro e/ni sagarimásu (sagáru, sagátte) 後ろに下がります(下がる, 下がって)

backwater *n* **1.** (*stagnant place*) teitai chi 停滞地 **2.** (*stagnant state*) teitai 停滞 **3.** (*held water*) yodonda mizu よどんだ水

backyard *n* ura-niwa 裏庭

bacon *n* bē´kon ベーコン
bacon and egg bēkon eggu ベーコンエッグ

bacteria *n* bakuteria バクテリア, saikin 細菌

bad *adj* **1.** warúi 悪い, damé (na) だめ・駄目(な); furyō (na) 不良(な); (*inept*) hetá (na) へた・下手(な) **2.** fu- 不 一
bad custom, bad practice *n* akushū 悪習
bad guy furyō 不良, warumono 悪者
bad-tasting *adj* mazúi まずい
bad temper *n* tanki 短気

bad; *goes* ~ (*rots*, *sours*) kusarimásu (kusáru, kusátte) 腐ります(腐る, 腐って); *too* ~ (*regrettable*) zannen (na) 残念(な), ikemasén (ikenai) いけません(いけない)

badge *n* bajji バッジ

badger *n* anaguma アナグマ・穴熊 (*not raccoon-dog* tánuki タヌキ・狸)

badly *adv* **1.** waruku 悪く **2.** (*very*) *totemo* とても

badminton *n* badominton バドミントン; (*traditional Japanese version*) hané-tsukí 羽根突き

bag *n* **1.** fukuró 袋; (*paper*) kamibúkuro 紙袋, (*plastic*) poribúkuro ポリ袋 **2.** → **suitcase** **3.** → **handbag; purse**

baggage *n* nímotsu 荷物 (o-nímotsu お荷物)

baggy *adj* dabudabu (no) だぶだぶ(の)

Bahama Islands *n* bahama shotō バハマ諸島

bailiff *n* teiri 廷吏・ていり

bait *n* esa えさ・餌

bake *v* **1.** yakimásu (yaku, yaite) 焼きます(焼く, 焼いて) **2.** *gets baked* yakemásu (yakeru, yakete) 焼けます(焼ける, 焼けて)

baker, bakery, bakeshop *n* pán-ya パン屋, bēkarii ベーカリー

baking *n* yaki 焼き
baking powder *n* bēkingu paudā ベーキングパウダー

balance *n* **1.** (*equilibrium*) tsuriai 釣り合い, baransu バランス **2.** (*remaining money*) zandaka 残高
balance sheet *n* (*B/S*) taishaku-taishō hyō 貸借対照表, bii-esu B/S

balcony *n* barukonii バルコニー

bald **1.** *adj* hágeta ... はげた[禿げた]... **2.** *v* (*gets bald*) hagemásu (hagéru, hágete) はげます・禿げます(はげる, はげて); (*is bald*) hágete imásu (iru, ite) はげて[禿げて]います(いる, いて)

baldness *n* háge はげ・禿げ (*bald spot*)

bale *n* tawará 俵

baleful *adj* yūgai (na) 有害(な)

ball *n* **1.** tamá 玉; *dragon ball* ryū no tama 竜・龍の玉; (*traditional Japanese handball*) mari まり・鞠, temari てまり・手鞠 **2.** (*sports*) bō´ru ボール; *tennis ball* tenisu bōru テニスボール; *basket ball* basuketto bōru バスケットボール; *rugby ball* ragubii (no) bōru ラグビー(の)ボール **3.** kyū 球; *ball sport* kyūgi 球技
ball park *n* yakyū-jō 野球場, kyūjō 球場

ballad *n* (*Japanese traditional music*) min'yō 民謡; (*Western-style*) barādo バラード

ballerina *n* (*female ballet dancer*) bareriina バレリーナ

ballet *n* bárē バレエ
ballet company *n* barē dan バレエ団
ballet composition *n* barē kyoku バレエ曲
ballet dancer *n* barē dansā バレエダンサー, (*female dancer*) bareriina バレリーナ

balloon *n* **1.** fūsen 風船 (*hot-air balloon*) (netsu)kikyū (熱)気球 **3.** (*toy balloon*) fūsen-dama 風船玉 **4.** (*water balloon*) mizu-fūsen 水風船

ballot *n* tōhyō 投票
ballot paper *n* tōhyō yōshi 投票用紙
ballot results *n* tōhyō kekka 投票結果

ballpoint pen *n* bōru-pen ボールペン

balm *n* kōyu 香油

bamboo *n* take 竹 (**1:** íp-pon 一本, **2:** ní-hon 二本, **3:** sánbon 三本, *how many* nán-bon 何本)
bamboo blind *n* (*Japanese traditional*) misu みす・御簾, sudare すだれ・簾 → **blind**
bamboo hat *n* kása 笠
bamboo shoot *n* take-no-ko タケノコ・竹の子・筍
bamboo tea whisk *n* chasen 茶せん・茶筅
bamboo wind-chimes *n* take-fūrin 竹風鈴

bambooware *n* take-záiku 竹細工

ban **1.** *n* kinshi 禁止. **2.** *bans it* v kinshi shimásu (suru, shite) 禁止します(する, して)

banal *adj* heibon (na) 平凡(な), arifureta ありふれた

banana *n* banana バナナ; *banana shake* banana sheiku バナナシェイク

band *n* **1.** (*group*) kumí 組 **2.** (*of musicians*) (*Western style*) gakudan 楽団, bando バンド **3.** (*Japanese style*) hayashí はやし・囃し (o-hayashi おはやし・お囃し) **4.** (*watchband, etc.*) (tokei) bando (時計)バンド **5.** beruto ベルト
band leader bando masutā バンドマスター

Band-Aid *n* bando-eido バンドエイド

bandage *n* hōtai 包帯

bandit *n* zoku 賊

bandwagon *n* gakutai-sha 楽隊車

bandy-legged *adj* ō-kyaku (no) O脚(の), ganimata (no) がに股(の)

bang *n* (*sound*) ban バン, batan バタン

bangle *n* **1.** (*wristlet*) ude wa 腕輪 **2.** kazari 飾り

banish *v* tsuihō shimásu (suru, shite) 追放します(する, して)

banister *n* tesuri 手すり

banjo *n* banjo バンジョー; ***three stringed banjo*** shamisen しゃみせん・三味線

bank *n* **1.** ginkō 銀行 **2.** *(special storage place)* banku バンク **3.** *(bank of a river or lake)* kishí 岸

bank account *n* ginkō-kóza 銀行口座, yokin-kóza 預金口座

bankbook *n* tsū´chō 通帳, yokin-tsū´chō 預金通帳

bank clerk *n* ginkō´-in 銀行員

bank rate *n* ginkō waribiki-buai 銀行割引歩合

blood bank *n* ketsueki banku 血液バンク

sperm bank *n* seishi banku 精子バンク

bankruptcy *n* hasan 破産; ***goes bankrupt*** hasan shimásu (suru, shite) 破産します(する、して)

banner *n* **1.** *(flag)* hata 旗 **2.** *(motto, slogan, etc.)* hyōshiki 標識 **3.** *(hanging cloth or curtain over a street, entrance, etc.)* taremaku 垂れ幕 **4.** *(advertising)* banā (kōkoku) バナー (広告)

banquet *n* enkai 宴会

baptism *n* semei 洗礼

bar *n* **1.** *(for drinking)* saka-ba 酒場, *(Western style)* bā バー, *(neighborhood pub)* nomí-ya 飲み屋, *(after-hours)* sunákku スナック **2.** bō 棒

bartender *n* bāten(-dā) バーテン(ダー)

iron bar *n* tetsu-bō 鉄棒

wood bar *n* ki no bō 木の棒

a bar of soap *n* sekken ík-ko せっけん[石鹸]一個

barbarian *n* yaban-jín 野蛮人

barbarous *adj* yaban (na) 野蛮(な)

barbecue *n* bābekyū バーベキュー

barbed wire *n* yūshi-téssen 有刺鉄線

barber(shop) *n* tokoya 床屋, rihátsú-ten 理髪店, sanpatsu-ya 散髪屋

bar-code *n* bā-kōdo バーコード

bare 1. *adj (scarce)* toboshii 乏しい **2.** *(mere)* honno wazuka (no) ほんのわずか(の)
3. → naked **4.** → reveal

barefoot *adj* hadashi (no) はだし・裸足 (の/で); *adv* hadashi (de) はだし・裸足(で)

barely *adv* karōjite かろうじて・辛うじて, nantoka なんとか, girigiri ぎりぎり

bargain *n (a real find)* horidashi mono 堀出し物, bāgen バーゲン; *(cut the price)* bāgen sēru バーゲンセール

barge *n* hashike はしけ

bar hopping *n* hashigó-zake はしご酒, hashigo はしご・梯子

baritone *n (male singing voice or a singer with the voice)* bariton バリトン

barium *n* bariumu バリウム

barium study bariumu kensa バリウム検査

bark 1. *n (of tree)* kí no kawá 木の皮, [BOOKISH] juhi 樹皮 **2.** *v (a dog barks)* hoemásu (hóeru, hóete) 吠えます(吠える、吠えて)

barley *n* ō-mugi 大麦

barley tea *n* mugi-cha 麦茶

barn *n* naya 納屋

barometer *n* **1.** *(indicator)* baromētā バロメーター **2.** *(atmospheric pressure measurement instrument)* kiatsu-kei 気圧計

baron *n (man with a barony)* danshaku 男爵

baroness *n* **1.** *(wife of a baron)* danshaku fujin 男爵夫人 **2.** *(woman with a barony)* onna danshaku 女男爵

baroque 1. *n (music, architecture)* barokku バロック **2.** *adj* barokku (yōshiki) no バロック (様式)の

baroque architecture *n* barokku kenchiku バロック建築

baroque music *n* barokku ongaku バロック音楽

barracks *n* **1.** héisha 兵舎 **2.** barakku バラック

barracuda *n* kamasu カマス

barrage *n* shūchū hōka 集中砲火

barrel *n* taru 樽; ***barrel hoop*** tagá たが

barren *adj* **1.** *(land)* yaseta やせた, fumō (na/no) 不毛(な/の) **2.** *(sterile)* funin (no) 不妊(の) **3.** *(dull)* ajike nai 味気ない, mumikansō (na) 無味乾燥(な)

barricade *n* barikēdo バリケード

barrier *n* **1.** *(fence)* saku 柵 **2.** *(obstacle)* shōgai-butsu 障害(物) **3.** *(limit)* genkai 限界 **4.** *(limit or boundary)* genkai 限界, kyōkai 境界

barrow *n (wheelbarrow)* teoshi-guruma 手押し車

barter *n* butsubutsu kōkan 物々交換

base *n* **1.** *(military, etc.)* kíchi 基地
military base *n* gunji-kichi 軍事基地 **2.** *(of a tree)* ne-motó 根元 **3.** *(foundation)* kiso 基礎
based on *is ~* ... ni motozukimásu (motozúku, motozúite) ...に基づきます(基づく、基づいて) **4.** *(baseball)* rui 塁, bē´su ベース

baseball *n* yakyū 野球, bēsubō´ru ベースボール

baseball stadium *n* yakyū-jō 野球場, kyūjō 球場

baseball team *n* náin ナイン, chiimu チーム

basement *n (floor)* chikai 地階; *(room)* chiká (-shitsu) 地下(室)

bash *v* tatakimásu (tatáku, tatáite) 叩きます(叩く、叩いて)

bashful → shy

bashing *n* tatakí 叩き, basshingu バッシング

basic *adj* kíhon-teki (na) 基本的(な), konpon-teki (na) 根本的(な)

basically *adv* kihon-teki (ni) 基本的(に)

basin *n* **1.** *(for washing face)* senmén-ki 洗面器 **2.** tarai たらい **3.** hachí 鉢 **4.** *(flat land surrounded by higher land)* bonchi 盆地
Kyoto basin *n* Kyōto bonchi 京都盆地

basis *n* **1.** kíhon 基本, konpon 根本, kijun 基準, kiso 基礎 **2.** *(grounds)* kónkyo 根拠

basket *n* kago かご・籠, basuketto バスケット

basketball *n* basuketto bōru バスケット・ボール, basuke バスケ

basking *(in the sun)* *n* hinatabókko ひなたぼっこ

bass *n* **1.** *(sea bass)* suzuki スズキ **2.** *(music)* basu バス, bēsu ベース

bastard *n* **1.** *(illegitimate child)* [BOOKISH] hi-chakushutsu-shi 非嫡出子, *(discriminatory word)* shisei-shi/shisei-ji 私生子/私生児 **2.** *(baseball)* bátto バット

baste   1. *v* (*sewing*) ~ *with thread* shi-tsu̱kemás̱u (shi-tsu̱kéru, shi-tsu̱kéte) 仕付けます(仕付ける, 付けて); *basting thread* shitsu̱ke-íto 仕付け糸
2. *v* (*cooking*) tare o kakemás̱u (kakéru, kakete) タレをかけます(かける, かけて)

bat   *n* 1. kō´mori コウモリ 2. (*baseball*) bátto バット

bath   *n* fúró 風呂(o-fúro お風呂), yokujō 浴場
bathing *n* nyūyoku 入浴; *bathing suit* mizu-gi 水着
bathrobe *n* basurōbu バスローブ
bathroom *n* 1. (*for bathing*) furoba 風呂場 (o-furoba お風呂場), yoku-jō/s̱hitsu 浴場/室
2. (*toilet*) tóire トイレ, keshō´-s̱hitsu 化粧室, (o-) teárai (お)手洗い, (o-)benjó (お)便所; *goes to the* ~ yō´ o tashimás̱u (tasu, tasẖite) 用を足します(足, 足して)
bathtub *n* yúbune 湯舟, yokus̱ō 浴槽
public bath *n* séntō 銭湯, kōshū yokujō 公衆浴場
steam bath *n* sauna(-buro) サウナ(風呂)
taking a bath *n* nyūyoku 入浴; *takes a* ~ fúró ni hairimás̱u (háiru, háitte) 風呂に入ります(入る, 入って), nyūyoku shimás̱u (suru, sẖite) 入浴します (する, して)

baton   1. (*sports, such as race and rhythmic gymnastics*) baton バトン 2. (*music*) shiki-bō 指揮棒

battalion   *n* (*military*) daitai 大隊

batter   *n* (*baseball*) battā バッター, dásha 打者
battery   *n* denchi 電池, bátteri バッテリー
batting   *n* (*baseball*) battingu バッティング
batting practice *n* furii batting フリーバッティング

battle   1. *n* takatai 戦い, arasoi 争い, [BOOKISH] sentō 戦闘 2. *v* takakaimás̱u (tatakau, tatakatte) 戦います(戦う, 戦って)

battledore   *n* hagó-íta 羽子板 (*wooden paddle used to play traditional Japanese badminton* hané-tsu̱kí 羽根突き)

bay   *n* wán 湾, urá 浦

bay area   *n* wángan chiiki 湾岸地域; beieria ベイエリア

be → **is** → **go** → **come**

beach   *n* hama 浜, bíichi ビーチ; (*seashore*) kaigan 海岸

bead   *n* 1. tamá 玉, biizu ビーズ; (*prayer*) *beads* juzú じゅず・数珠 2. *counting beads* → **abacus**

beagle   *n* (*dog*) biiguru-ken ビーグル犬

beak   *n* kuchibashi くちばし

beam   *n* 1. (*crossbeam*) keta けた・桁; *under the beam* keta-shita 桁下・けた下 2. (*beam of light*) kōsen 光線

bean   *n* mamé マメ・豆; (*soy beans*) daizu ダイズ・大豆

bean curd   *n* tōfu 豆腐(o-tōfu お豆腐); (*pot-boiled squares*) yu-dō´fu 湯豆腐; (*cooled cubes*) hiya-yakko ひややっこ(冷や奴); (*broiled*) yaki-dō´fu 焼き豆腐; (*deep-fried*) aburá-age 油揚げ
bean-curd lees   *n* o-kara おから
bean-flour threads   *n* harusame 春雨

bean jam/paste   *n* (*sweet*) án(ko) アン(コ)・餡 (こ); (*fermented*) míso みそ・味噌 (o-míso おみそ・お味噌)

bear   1. *n* (*animal*) kúmá 熊 2. *v* (*puts up with*) shinobimás̱u (shinobu, shinonde) 忍びます(忍ぶ, 忍んで), taemás̱u (táeru, táete) 耐えます(耐える, 耐えて), shínbō shimás̱u (suru, sẖite) 辛抱します (する, して) 3. → **carry** 4. → **give birth** 5. *bears fruit* minorimás̱u (minoru, minotte) 実ります(実る, 実って)
bear up (*stands firm*) ganbarimás̱u (ganbáru, ganbátte) がんばり[頑張り]ます(がんばる, がんばって)

beard   *n* hige ひげ・鬚; (*chin-whiskers*) ago-hige あごひげ・顎鬚

bearings; *one's bearings* hōgaku 方角

beat   *v* 1. (*hits*) nagurimás̱u (nagúru, nagútte) なぐり[殴り]ます(なぐる, なぐって); (*slaps*) hatakimás̱u (hatáku, hatáite) はたきます・叩きます(はたく, はたいて) 2. (*defeats*) makashimás̱u (makasu, makasẖite) 負かします(負かす, 負かして) 3. (*heart throbs*) dókidoki shimás̱u (suru, sẖite) どきどきします(する, して); ~ *around the bush* (*is non-committal*) hanasẖí o bokashimás̱u (bokás̱u, bokásẖite) 話をぼかします(ぼかす, ぼかして)

beaten; *v gets* ~ yararemás̱u (yarareru, yararete) やられます(やられる, やられて)

beautiful   *adj* uts̱uku̱shíi 美しい, kírei (na) きれい・綺麗(な) 見事(な)

beauty   *n* 1. [BOOKISH] bi 美, uts̱uku̱shí-sa 美しさ 2. (*beautiful woman*) bi-jin 美人, bi-jo 美女

beauty parlor   *n* biyō´in 美容院

beaver   *n* biibā ビーバー
eager beaver *n* ganbari-ya 頑張り屋

because   *conj* ... kara ...から, ... tame ...ため・為, ... mono ... もの, ... no de ... ので, [BOOKISH] ... yúé ni ... ゆえに・故に; *perhaps* ~ *of* ... (no) séi ka ... (の)せいか

beckoning   *n* temáneki 手招き

become   *v* (... ni, ... -ku) narimás̱u (náru, nátte) (... に, ... く)なります(なる, なって); [HONORIFIC] o-nari ni narimás̱u (náru, nátte) おなりになります(なる, なって); *is becoming to* ... (*suits*) ... ni ni-aimás̱u (ni-áu, ni-átte) ... に似合います(似合う, 似合って)

bed   *n* toko 床; (*Western*) béddo (bétto) ベッド (ベット), shindai 寝台; *goes to* ~ nemás̱u (neru, nete) 寝ます(寝る, 寝て), yasumimás̱u, (yasúmu, yasúnde) 休みます(休む, 休んで); *takes to one's* ~ toko ni tsu̱kimás̱u (tsu̱kú, tsúite) 床に就きます (就く, 就いて)
bed-and-breakfast *n* minshu̱ku 民宿
bedclothes, bedding *n* shíngu 寝具, yágu 夜具; (*Japanese quilt*) fu̱ton 布団 (o-fu̱ton お布団)
bed making *n* beddo mēkingu ベッドメーキング
bedroom *n* shinshitsu 寝室
bedroom community *n* beddotáun ベッドタウン

bedsheet n shíitsu シーツ, shikifu 敷布
bedside n makura-moto 枕元
bedspread n beddo kabā ベッドカバー
bedtime n shūshin jikoku 就寝時刻
bedlam n **1.** sawagi 騒ぎ; sōran 騒乱 **2.** (confusion) konran 混乱
bedpan n benki 便器; (urinal) shibin しびん; (fecal) omaru おまる
bedraggled adj **1.** (limp and wet) hikizutte nurashita 引きずって濡らした **2.** (limp and soiled) hikizutte yogoshita 引きずって汚した
bee n hachi 蜂・ハチ
  beehive n mitsubachi no subako ミツバチ「蜜蜂」の巣箱
  beeswax n mitsurō みつろう・蜜蝋
  honey bee mitsú-bachi 蜜蜂・ミツバチ
beef n gyūniku 牛肉, biifu ビーフ
  beef hash (over rice) hayashi-ráisu ハヤシライス
  beef slices dipped in hot broth shabu-shabu しゃぶしゃぶ・シャブシャブ
  roast beef rōsuto biifu ローストビーフ
  beefsteak n sutēki ステーキ
  beefsteak plant n (perilla) shiso シソ・紫蘇
been → **is** → **go** → **come** *Where have you been?* Dóko e/ni itte kimáshita ka. どこへ／に行ってきましたか.
beep n **1.** (sound) bii-tto iu oto ビーッという音 **2.** (answering machine) pii-tto iu oto ピーッという音 **3.** yobidashi-on 呼び出し音
beer n bíiru ビール
  beer bottle/can n biirú-bin/kan ビール瓶/缶
  beer hall n bia/ya hō´ru ビア/ビヤホール
  draft beer n nama-bíiru 生ビール, náma 生
beet n bíito ビート
beetle n (insect) kabutomushi カブトムシ
  black beetle n gokiburi ゴキブリ
before adv (... no) máe (ni) (...の)前(に); ~ *it happens* (shi-) nai uchí (ni) (し)ないうちに); *Eat ~ you go.* Tábete kara itte kudasái. 食べてから行って下さい.
  before a meal n, adv taberu mae (ni) 食べる前(に), [BOOKISH] shokuzen (ni) 食前(に)
  before and after adv zéngo (ni) 前後(に); máe mo áto mo 前も後も
  before anything else adv mázu まず・先ず
  before long adv ma-mó-naku まもなく・間もなく, sórosoro そろそろ; (eventually) yagate やがて
  before the war adv sensō no mae (no) 戦争の前(の), [BOOKISH] senzen (no) 戦前(の)
beforehand adv mae-motte 前もって, jizen (ni) 事前(に)
beg v tanomimásu (tanómu, tanónde) 頼みます (頼む, 頼んで), negaimásu (negáu, negátte) 願います(願う, 願って)
  I beg your pardon, but ... interj shitsúrei desu ga ... 失礼ですが..., [BOOKISH] habakari-nagara ... はばかりながら...
beggar n kojikí こじき・乞食

begin v (it begins) hajimarimásu (hajimaru, hajimatte) 始まります(始まる, 始まって); (begins it) hajimemásu (hajimeru, hajímete) 始めます(始める, 始めて)
beginner n shoshin-sha 初心者, biginā ビギナー
beginning n hajime 初め, (outset) saisho 最初, [INFORMAL] shoppána しょっぱな・初っぱな, hajimari 始まり; *from the ~* hajime (k)kara 初め(っ)から, móto kara もとから・元から, [BOOKISH] mótó-yori もとより・元より
begrudge v uramimásu (urámu, uránde) 恨みます(恨む, 恨んで); (be jealous of another's good fortune, etc.) hito no kōun o netamimásu (netamu, netande) 人の幸運をねたみます(ねたむ, ねたんで)
behalf n **1.** (support) shiji 支持 **2.** (benefit) rieki 利益; *in/on ~ of ...* (... no) tamé (... の)ため・為 **3.** (representative) *in/on ~ of ...* [INFORMAL] (... no) kawari (ni) ...の代わり(に), (... no) dairi (de) ...の代理(で), [FORMAL] (... o) daihyō shite ...を代表して
behavior n **1.** (actions) kōdō 行動 **2.** (act) kōi 行為 **3.** (deportment) furumai ふるまい・振る舞い **4.** (manners) (o-)gyōgi (お)行儀 **5.** (attitude) táido 態度
behind 1. prep (... no) ushiro (de/ni) (... の)後ろ(で/に); (the other side) urá 裏 **2.** falls/gets ~ okuremásu (okureru, okurete) 遅れます(遅れる, 遅れて); gets left ~, stay ~ nokorimásu (nokóru, nokótte) 残ります(残る, 残って); leaves ~ nokoshimásu (nokósu, nokóshite) 残します(残す, 残して), (forgets) wasuremono o shimásu (suru, shite) 忘れ物をします(する, して)
beige n bēju ベージュ
Beijing n pekin 北京
being 1. n (in existence; person) sonzai 存在; *human being* ningen 人間 **2.** (creature) ikimono 生き物 **3.** → **is** v *comes into ~* seiritsu shimásu (suru, shite) 成立します(する, して) **5.** *... ~ what it is* (who one is) sasuga no ... さすがの...
belch 1. n geppu げっぷ **2.** v geppu o shimásu (suru, shite) げっぷ(をします;する, して)
belfry n shōrō 鐘楼
Belgium n berugii ベルギー
believe v **1.** ~ (in) (... o) shinjimásu (shinjiru, shinjite) (... を)信じます(信じる, 信じて) **2.** → **think**
bell n **1.** (large) kane 鐘 **2.** (small) rín/suzu 鈴 **3.** (doorbell) béru ベル, yobi-rin 呼び鈴 **4.** (temple bell) tsurigane 釣り鐘
  the bells on New Year's Eve joya no kane 除夜の鐘
bellboy n bōi ボーイ
bell pepper n píiman ピーマン
belly n hará 腹; fuku-bu 腹部; onaka お腹
bellybutton n heso へそ (o-heso おへそ)
belong (to) v (... ni) zokushimásu (zokusú(ru), zokúshite) (... に)属します(属す(る), 属して)

belonging *adj* (*possessed*) shoyū (no) 所有 (の); *belongings* n mochímono 持ち物

beloved n 1. (*person* or *pet*) itoshii いとしい・愛しい, saiai (no) 最愛 (の) 2. (*thing*) aiyō (no) 愛用 (の) 3. (*thing* or *place*) okiniiri (no) お気に入りの, daisuki (na) 大好き (な)

beloved daughter mana-musume 愛娘
beloved dog ai-ken 愛犬
beloved vehicle ai-sha 愛車
beloved wife ai-sai 愛妻

below *prep, adv* (... no) shíta (ni) (... の) 下 (に); (*less than*) ... íka (... no) ... 以下 (... の), ... míman (... no) ... 未満 (... の)

belt n 1. beruto ベルト, óbi 帯 2. (*sumo wrestler's*) mawashi まわし・回し 3. (*zone*) (chi)tai 地帯

belt conveyor n = **conveyor belt** beruto konbeya ベルト・コンベヤ, beruto konbeyā ベルト・コンベヤー, beruto konbea ベルト・コンベア, beruto konbeā ベルト・コンベアー

belt line n kanjō-sen 環状線

beltway n kanjō dōro 環状道路

bemused *adj* 1. (*confused*) konwakushita 困惑した, tōwakushita 当惑した 2. (*lost in thought*) mono-omoi ni fuketta 物思いにふけった

bench n benchi ベンチ

bend v 1. (*it bends*) oremásu (oréru, órete) 折れます (折れる, 折れて), (*curves*) magarimásu (magaru, magatte) 曲がります (曲がる, 曲がって), (*warps*) sorimásu (sóru, sótte) 反ります (反る, 反って) 2. (*bends it*) orimásu (óru, ótte) 折ります (折る, 折って), magemásu (mageru, magete) 曲げます (曲げる, 曲げて), sorashimásu (sorásu, soráshite) 反らします (反らす, 反らして), (*branch, etc.*) tawamemásu (tawameru, tawamete) たわめます (たわめる, たわめて)

bend backward v karada o sorashimásu (sorasu, sorashite) 体を反らします (反らす, 反らして)
bend down v kagamimásu (kagamu, kagande) 屈みます (屈む, 屈んで)
bend forward v mae-kagami ni narimásu (naru, natte) 前屈みになります (なる, なって)
bend over v kagamimásu (kagamu, kagande) 屈みます (屈む, 屈んで)

beneath → **below**

benefactor n onjin 恩人

benefit n ríeki 利益; (... no) tamé (... の) 為

benign 1. n (*pathology*) ryōsei 良性 2. *adj* (*gracious*) shinsetsu (na) 親切 (な)

bent *adj* (*curved*) magatta 曲がった

beret n berē-bō ベレー帽

Berlin n Berurín ベルリン

berm n (*road shoulder*) rokata 路肩

berry n kí-no-mi 木の実, berii ベリー (*includes nuts, fruits*) → **strawberry** → **mulberry**

berth n shindai 寝台
berth ticket n shindái-ken 寝台券

beset (*stricken*); *gets ~* (*by illness*) yararemásu (yarareru, yararete) やられます (やられる, やられて)

beside *prep, adv* (*next to*) ... no sóba (de/ni) ... のそば (で/に) , ... no tonari (de/ni) ...の隣り (で/に), ... no waki (de/ni) ... のわき (で/に)

besides *prep, adv* (*in addition to*) sono ué (ni) その上 (に), (sono) hoka (ni) (その) 他 (に)

best *adj* 1. ichiban íi 一番いい [良い, 善い]; sairyō (no) 最良 (の) 2. (*highest*) saikō (no) 最高 (の) 3. (*top-class*) jōtō (no) 上等 (の) 4. (*special-quality*) tokkyū (no) 特級 (の), zekkō (no) 絶好 (の) 5. bésuto ベスト

at best *adv* séizei せいぜい
the best, one's best n saizen 最善
best-seller n besuto-serā ベストセラー
Please give my best wishes to ... ... ni yoroshíku (itte kudasái, o-tsutae kudasái) ... によろしく (言って下さい, お伝え下さい)
ten best n besutó-tén ベストテン

bet 1. n (*act of betting*) kake 賭け 2. n (*money*) kake-kin 賭け金 3. v kakemásu (kakéru, kákete) 賭けます (賭ける, 賭けて), kaké o shimásu (suru, shite) 賭けをします (する, して)

betray v ura-girimásu (ura-gíru, ura-gítte) 裏切ります (切る, 切って)
betrayal n ura-giri 裏切り
betrayer n ura-giri-mono 裏切り者

betrothal n konyaku 婚約
betrothed n konyaku-sha 婚約者

better *adj* 1. mótto íi/yoi もっといい/良い, (...) yóri íi/yoi (...) よりいい/良い 2. (*preferable*) ... (no hō') ga íi/yoi ... (の方) がいい/良い 3. *had ~ do it* shita hō ga íi/yoi した方がいい/良い, *had ~ not do it* shinai hō' ga íi/yoi しない方がいい/良い 4. (*sick person, etc.*) *feel ~* kibun ga (mae yori) ii/yoi 気分が (前より) いい/良い

betterment n zōshin 増進

between *prep, adv* (... no) aida (ni) (... の) 間 (に); ...-kan (...) ...間
between acts maku no aida 幕の間, makuai ni 幕あいに・幕間 [合] に

beverage n nomí-mono 飲み物

beware v chūi shimásu (suru, shite) 注意します (する, して)
(Please) beware ki o tsukete (kudasai) 気をつけて (ください)

beyond *prep, adv* (... no) mukō (ni) (... の) 向こう (に); *beyond expectations* zongai 存外
beyond remedy shō (shi-yō) ga nái しょう (しよう・仕様) がない

BGM n (*background music*) bii jii emu ビージーエム

bias n 1. (*prejudice*) henken 偏見, sennyū-kan 先入観 2. (*statistics*) baiasu バイアス

Bible n Séisho 聖書, Báiburu バイブル

bibliography n tosho mokuroku 図書目録, bunken mokuroku 文献目録

bicycle n jitén-sha, jidén-sha 自転車
bicycle races n keirin 競輪
bicycle shop n jitensha-ya, jidensha-ya 自転車屋

bid 1. v (*to offer*) nyūsatsu shimásu (suru, shite)

入札します(する, して) **2.** v (to command) meirei shimásu (suru, shite) 命令します(する, して)
3. v (to express) ii másu (iu, itte) 言います(言う, 言って) **4.** n nyūsatsu 入札

bidder n nyūsatsu-sha 入札者

bidding n nyūsatsu 入札, seri 競り

big adj **1.** ōkíi 大きい, [INFORMAL] dekai (dekkai) でかい(でっかい) **2.** (spacious) hirói 広い

big brother áni 兄, (o-)nii-san (お)兄さん

big dipper n jettokōsutā ジェットコースター

big-head n unubore うぬぼれ

big news n sukūpu スクープ

big ohot n ō-mono 大物

big sister ane 姉, (o-)nē´-san (お)姉さん

bigot n henkutsu-mono 偏屈者, ganko-mono 頑固者

bike n **1.** (bicycle) jitén-sha, jidén-sha 自転車 **2.** (motorbike) baiku バイク, ōtobai オートバイ (abbreviation for the word "autobike")

bilingual n, adj bairingaru (no) バイリンガル(の)

bill n **1.** (to pay) kanjō 勘定 (o-kanjō お勘定); denpyō 伝票, o-aiso お愛想・おあいそ; daikin 代金, ...-dai ...代; (account) tsuké つけ
ooparate bill/charge (restaurant) betsu-ryōkin 別料金; (Dutch treat) warikan 割り勘
2. (bank bill, promissory note) tegata 手形 **3.** (currency note) (o-)satsu (お)札 **4.** (handbill) bira びら・ビラ

billfold → **wallet**

billiards n biriyādo ビリヤード

billion n jū´-oku 十億 (U.S.); chō´ 兆, ít-chō 一兆 (Britain)

billy-club n konbō 棍棒・こん棒

bin n trash bin gomi-bako ゴミ箱

bind v **1.** (pages, sheets) tsuzurimásu (tsuzuru, tsuzutte) 綴ります(綴る, 綴って) **2.** → **tie**

binding (a book) n **1.** seihon 製本 **2.** (bound pages) tsuzuri 綴り

bine n tsuru ツル・蔓

binge n donchan-sawagi どんちゃん騒ぎ

bingo n (game) bingo ビンゴ

binoculars n sōgan-kyō 双眼鏡

biography n denki 伝記

biological adj seibutsugaku-teki (na) 生物学的(な)

biologist n seibutsu gáku-sha 生物学者

biology n seibutsú-gaku 生物学

biotechnology n baio(-tekunorojii) バイオ(テクノロジー), seibutsu kōgaku 生物工学

bird n tori 鳥, (... -wa ...羽, **1:** ichí-wa 一羽, **2:** ní-wa 二羽, **3:** sánba 三羽, **6;** róp-pa 六羽, **10;** júp-pa 十羽; **how many** nán-ba 何羽)
bird-watching n bādo uotchingu バードウオッチング; yachō-kansatsu 野鳥観察
small bird n ko-tori 小鳥

birth n **1.** (being born) umare 生まれ, [BOOKISH] shussei 出生 **2.** (origin) tanjō 誕生; **give ~ to ...** o umimásu (umu, unde) ... を生みます(生む, 生んで), o-san shimásu (umu, shite) お産します

(する, して) **3.** (roots) hassei/hasshō 発生

birthstone n tanjō´seki 誕生石

birthday n tanjō´bi 誕生日 (o-tanjō´bi お誕生日); bāsudē バースデー

birthday cake n (o-)tanjō´bi kēki (お)誕生日ケーキ; bāsudē kēki バースデーケーキ

birthday card n (o-)tanjō´bi kādo (お)誕生日カード; bāsudē kādo バースデーカード

birthday present n (o-)tanjō´bi purezento (お)誕生日プレゼント, bāsudē purezento バースデープレゼント

birthplace n kókyō 故郷, furusato 故郷・ふるさと

biscuit n (cookie) bisuketto ビスケット

bisexual n (ambisexual) bai-sekushuaru バイセクシュアル, bai-sekusharu バイセクシャル, ryōseiai-sha 両性愛者

bit n **1.** (a little) sukóshi 少し, [INFORMAL] chótto ちょっと

bitch n **1.** (female dog) mesu-inu 雌犬 **2.** (malicious and lewd woman) abazure あばずれ

bite 1. v kamimásu (kámu, kánde) かみます・噛みます(かむ, かんで), kami-tsukimásu (kami-tsúku, kami-tsuite) かみつきます・噛みつきます(かみつく, かみついて) **2.** n one bite hitó-kuchi ひとくち・一口 **3.** n (hurt) sashikizu 刺傷

bitter adj **1.** (taste, hard to bear, painful) nigái 苦い **2.** (awful) hidói ひどい・酷い
bitter experience nigai keiken 苦い経験
bitter orange n daidai ダイダイ・橙; **bitter orange juice** pónsu/ponzú ポン酢
bitter taste nigai aji 苦い味

bivouac n yaei 野営, bibāku ビバーク

black adj kurói 黒い; kúro (no) 黒(の); **jet black** makkúro (na) 真っ黒(な)

black box n burakku bokkusu ブラックボックス

black coffee n burakku kōhii ブラックコーヒー

blacklist n burakku risuto ブラックリスト

black mark n batten ばってん

black market n yami-ichi 闇市, yamí-íchiba 闇市場

black person (people) n kokujin 黒人

black tea n kōcha 紅茶

blackboard n kokuban (usually in school) 黒板

black-hearted adj hara gurói 腹黒い

blackmail n yusuri ゆすり, kyōkatsu 恐喝

bladder n bōkō 膀胱

blade n **1.** (razor) (kamisóri no) há (かみそりの)刃 **2.** (sword) yaiba やいば・刃 **3.** (leaf) ha 葉 **4.** (metal part of an ice skate) burēdo ブレード **5.** (swordsman) ken-shi 剣士

blah adj tsumaranai つまらない, taikutsu (na) 退屈(な)

blah blah blah adj nantoka (kantoka) 何とか(かんとか), kakukakushikajika かくかくしかじか

blame 1. n (censure) togamé とがめ (o-togame おとがめ), hínan 非難 **2.** v (rebukes one) togamemásu (togaméru, togámete) とがめます(とがめる, とがめて), hínan shimásu (suru, shite) 非難します(する, して); **I'm** (the one who is) **to**

blame Watashi ga warúi no desu わたし[私]が悪いのです **3. → responsibility**

blanch *v* (*bleach*) hyōhaku shimásu (suru, shite) 漂白します(する, して)

bland *adj* **1.** (*tasteless*) aji ga usui 味が薄い **2.** (*gentle*) odayaka (na) 穏やか(な) **3.** (*insipid*) tsumaranai つまらない, omoshirokunai おもしろくない・面白くない

blank **1.** *n* (*space*) kūsho 空所, yohaku 余白 **2.** *n* (*form*) yōshi 用紙 **3.** *adj* hakushi (no) 白紙(の) **4.** *adj* (*expression*) utsuro (na) うつろ(な)・空ろ(な)・虚ろ(な); *with a ~ look* utsuro na hyōjō o mísete うつろな[虚ろな]表情を見せて

blanket *n* mō'fu 毛布, buranketto ブランケット

blast-off *n* hassha 発射

bleach *n* hyōhaku-zai 漂白剤

bleak *adj* **1.** (*hopeless*) kibō no nai 希望のない; *bleak future* kurai shōrai 暗い将来 **2.** (*desolate*) wabishii わびしい, sappūkei (na) 殺風景(な) **3.** (*cold*) samui 寒い

bleed *v* chi ga demásu (déru, déte) 血が出ます(出る, 出て), shukketsu shimásu (suru, shite) 出血します(する, して)

blemish *n* **1.** (*scarring*) kizu 傷 **2.** (*defect*) ketten 欠点 **3.** (*stain*) oten 汚点

blend *n* burendo ブレンド, kongō 混合

blender *n* míkisā ミキサー

bless *v* **1.** *~ with* ... o megumimásu (megumu, megunde) ...を恵みます(恵む, 恵んで) **2.** *gets blessed with* ...ni megumaremásu (megumareru, megumarete) ...に恵まれます(恵まれる, 恵まれて) Bless you. *interj* (*to sneezer*) Odaiji ni お大事に

blessed *adj* **1.** megumareta 恵まれた, shukufuku sareta 祝福された **2.** (*holy*) shinsei (na) 神聖(な), seinaru 聖なる; *Blessed Virgin Mary* seibo maria 聖母マリア

blessed event (*pregnancy, childbirth, marriage, etc.*) omedeta おめでた, keiji 慶事

blessedly *adv* saiwai 幸い

blessing *n* megumi 恵み, shukufuku 祝福

blind *n* **1.** (*person*) mōjin 盲人 **2.** (*sun-shade*) hi-ō'í 日覆い, hi-yoke 日よけ, buraindo ブラインド **→ bamboo blind**

blindfold *n* me-kákushi 目隠し

blindly *adv* yatara (ni) やたら(に)

blink *v* ma-tátaki/ma-bátaki shimásu (suru, shite) またたき/まばたき/瞬きします(する, して)

blister *n* mizu-búkure 水膨れ; (*corn*) mamé まめ, soko mame 底まめ

blizzard *n* (mō-/ō-) fúbuki (猛/大)吹雪

bloc *n* ken 圏, burokku ブロック

block **1.** *n* (*city block*) *The closest equivalent is* chōme 丁目, *a square of several blocks. For distances, use* ... -chō ... 町; *It is three [stretches of] blocks from here.* ... Michi o mittsu watari-másu ... 道を三つ渡ります. *... You cross three streets.* **2.** *n* *block of wood* kakuzai 角材 **3.** *n* (*toy*) tsumiki 積み木, burokku ブロック **4.** *v* (*clogs, impedes*) fusagimásu (fusagu, fusaide)

ふさぎます(ふさぐ, ふさいで), burokku shi-másu (suru, shite) ブロックします(する, して)

blocked (off) *v* *gets ~* fusagarimásu (fusagaru, fusagatte) ふさがります(ふさがる, ふさがって); *the road is ~* dō'ro ga fusagátte imásu 道路がふさがっています

blockade **1.** *n* fūsa 封鎖 **2.** *v* fūsa shimásu (suru, shite) 封鎖します(する, して)

blond *adj* kinpatsu (no) 金髪(の), burondo (no) ブロンド(の)

blood *n* chi 血, [BOOKISH] ketsueki 血液 blood type *n* ketsueki-gata 血液型

bloodless *adj* mu-ketsu (no) 無(血)の

blood pressure *n* ketsuatsu 血圧; *blood pressure gauge* ketsuatsu-kei 血圧計, *takes one's ~* ketsuatsu o hakarimásu (hakáru, hakátte) 血圧を計ります(計る, 計って)

bloodshot; *adj* *with ~ eyes* chimánako ni nátte 血眼になって

bloody *adj* chinamagusái 血生臭い

bloom *v* sakimásu (saku, saite) 咲きます(咲く, 咲いて)

blossom → bloom → flower

blot, blotch *n* shimi しみ・染み, yogore 汚れ

blotter *n* suitorí-gami 吸い取り紙

blouse *n* (*woman's, child's*) buráusu ブラウス

blow *v* fukimásu (fukú, fúite) 吹きます(吹く, 吹いて); *blows one's nose* hana o kamimásu (kamu, kande) 鼻をかみます(かむ, かんで)

blowfish *n* fúgu フグ・河豚

blowout *n* panku パンク

blowup *n* bakuhatsu 爆発, bakuha 爆破

bludgeon *n* konbō 棍棒・こん棒

blue *adj* **1.** áoi 青い; áo (no) 青(の) **2.** (*feel blue*) burū ブルー, yūutsu 憂うつ dark (navy) blue kon-iro (no) 紺色(の) light (sky) blue sora-iro (no) 空色(の) blue-collar worker *n* burū karā ブルーカラー; nikutai rōdō-sha 肉体労働者 bluejeans *n* jii-pan ジーパン blueprint *n* ao-jáshin 青写真

blunder *n* shippai 失敗; chónbo ちょんぼ; (*faux pas*) bu-sáhō 不作法・無作法

blunt *adj* (*dull-edged*) kirénai 切れない; (*dull-pointed*) nibúi 鈍い; (*rude*) bu-sáhō (na) 不作法・無作法(な); (*curt*) bu-áiso (na) 無愛想 (な), bukkírábō (na) ぶっきらぼう(な)

blush *v* kao ga akaku narimásu (náru, nátte) 顔が赤くなります(なる, なって), [BOOKISH] sekimen shimásu (suru, shite) 赤面します(する, して)

board 1. *n* (*plank*) íta 板 **2.** *n* (*meals*) (o-)shokuji (お)食事 **3.** *v* (*gets on a train/bus*) jōsha shimásu (suru, shite) 乗車します(する, して), (*a plane*) tōjō shimásu (suru, shite) 搭乗します(する, して)

boarder *n* geshuku-nin 下宿人

boarding area/place *n* nori-ba 乗り場

boarding house *n* **1.** geshuku (-ya) 下宿(屋) **2.** (*dormitory*) kishúkusha 寄宿舎, ryō' 寮

boarding pass *n* tōjō´-ken 搭乗券, bōdingu-kādo ボーディングカード, bōdingu-pasu ボーディングパス

boarding school *n* zenryōsei (no) gakkō 全寮制(の)学校

boast *v* jiman shimásu (suru, shite) 自慢します(する, して)

boat *n* fúne 舟・船; (*small*) kobune 小舟・小船, bō´to ボート; (*how many*) nán-sō/seki 何艘/隻)
boat people *n* bōto-piipuru ボートピープル
boat race *n* bōto-rēsu ボートレース

bock beer *n* kuro-bíiru 黒ビール

body *n* **1.** karada 体・身体; *whole body* zenshin 全身; *body build* taikaku 体格; *body odor* waki-ga わきが・腋臭; taishū 体臭; *body temperature* taion 体温; *body weight* taijū 体重 **2.** (*collective body, group*) shūdan 集団
bodybuilding *n* bodii-biru ボディビル
bodyguard *n* bodii-ga´do ボディガード, goei 護衛
body lotion *n* bodii-rōshon ボディー・ローション

bog down, gets bogged down *v* iki-zumari-másu (iki-zumáru, iki-zumátte) 行き詰まります(行き詰まる, 行き詰まって)

bog rhubarb *n* fuki フキ・蕗

bohemian *n* bohemian ボヘミアン

boil *v* **1.** *boils water* o-yu o wakashimásu (wakasu, wakashite) お湯を沸かします(沸かす, 沸かして); *water boils* o-yu ga wakimásu (waku, waite) お湯が沸きます(沸く, 沸いて) **2.** *boils* (*food*) nimásu (niru, nite) 煮ます(煮る, 煮て), yudemásu (yudéru, yúdete) ゆでます・茹でます(ゆでる, ゆでて); (*soup, rice*) takimásu (taku, taite) 炊きます(炊く, 炊いて) **3.** *it boils* niemásu (nieru, niete) 煮えます(煮える, 煮えて); *what it boils down to* (*is ...*) yō-súru ni 要するに

boil *n* (*on skin*) hare-mono はれもの, dekí-móno できもの(o-déki おでき)
boiled eggs *n* yude-támago ゆで卵
boiled fish *n* nizakana 煮魚
boiled foods *n* ni-mono 煮物; (*assorted*) o-dén おでん, dengaku 田楽
boiled greens *n* (*usually spinach, served cold with seasoning*) o-hitáshi おひたし
boiled vegetables *n* nishime 煮しめ, o-níshime お煮しめ
boiled water *n* o-yu お湯, (*cooled for drinking*) yu-zámashi 湯冷まし

boiler *n* bóirā ボイラー; (*gas-fired instant hot-water maker*) shunkan yu-wa´kashiki 瞬間湯沸かし器; (*hot-water maker*) yu-wakashiki 湯沸かし器; (*pot*) kama かま・釜, nábe 鍋

boisterous *adj* yakamashíi やかましい, sawagashíi 騒がしい

bok choi *n* (*Chinese cabbage*) hakusai 白菜

bold *adj* daitán (na) 大胆(な), (*na*) yūkan (na) 勇敢(な)

bolt *n* (*of door*) kannuki かんぬき・閂; (*of nut and bolt*) boruto ボルト; (*of cloth*) ... -maki ... 巻き, -tan 反

bomb 1. *n* (*a bomb*) bakudan 爆弾 **2.** *n* (*bombing*) bakugeki 爆撃 **3.** *v* (*bombs it*) bakugeki shimásu (suru, shite) 爆撃します(する, して)

bomber *n* bakugéki-ki 爆撃機

bombing *n* bakugeki 爆撃

bombshell *n* bakudan 爆弾; *bombshell statement* bakudan hatsugen 爆弾発言

Bon; the Bon Festival (o-)bón (お)盆, urabon うら盆

bond *n* (*debenture*) saiken 債券

bone *n* honé 骨

bonehead *n* baka ばか・馬鹿

bonfire *n* taki-bi たき火

bong *n* gōn ゴーン

bonito *n* katsuo カツオ・鰹; (*dried*) katsuo-bushi かつお節・鰹節

bonnet → hat → (*car*) **hood**

bonus *n* **1.** (*wage*) bō´nasu ボーナス, shō´yo 賞与 **2.** (*extra*) omake おまけ

booboo *n* chónbo ちょんぼ

boo-hoo *interj* (*sound of crying*) **1.** ēn ēn エーンエーン (*mostly children's crying*), wān wān ワーンワーン (*louder*) **2.** ōi ōi オーイオーイ

book 1. *n* hon 本 (*how many* nán-satsu 何冊), [BOOKISH] shómotsu 書物; (*publications*) shoseki 書籍 **2.** *n ~ of* (*commuting*) *tickets* kaisū-ken 回数券 **3.** *n* (*book of account*) chōbo 帳簿 **4.** *books* (*reserves*) yoyaku shimásu (suru, shite) 予約します(する, して)

bookcase *n* hónbako 本箱
book collection *n* zōsho 蔵書, tósho 図書
book cover *n* hon no hyōshi 本の表紙
book up *v* *gets ~* fusagárimásu (fusagaru, fusagatte) ふさがります(ふさがる, ふさがって)
bookends *n* hón-tate 本立て
bookfair *n* bukku-fea ブックフェア
bookie *n* kaké-ya 賭け屋, nomiya ノミ屋
booking *n* **1.** yoyaku 予約 **2.** bóki 簿記
bookshelf *n* hón-dana 本棚
bookshop, bookstore *n* hón-ya 本屋, shoten 書店
book title *n* sho-mei 書名

bookkeeper *n* chōbo-gákari 帳簿係

bookkeeping *n* bóki 簿記

bookmark *n* shiori しおり

bookworm *n* hon no mushi 本の虫

boom *n* **1.** (*prosperity*) (niwaka) keiki (にわか)景気; keiki (ga ii) 景気(がいい) **2.** (*fad*) bū´mu ブーム (= ryūkō 流行) **3.** (*sound*) dón ドン

boomerang *n* būmeran ブーメラン

booster *n* (*of current*) shōátsú-ki 昇圧器

booth *n* **1.** (*selling things*) baiten 売店 **2.** (*in a tavern, etc.*) bókkusu-seki ボックス席 **3.** (*telephone*) denwa bókkusu 電話ボックス **4.** (*office*) būsu ブース

boot(s) *n* naga-gutsu 長靴, būtsu ブーツ, (*rubber*) gomu-naga ゴム長; *to boots* (*extra*) omake (ni) おまけに

border 1. *n* (*boundary*) sakái 境; (*of a district, etc.*) kyōkai 境界; (*of a country*) kokkyō 国境;

(*edging*) herí へり・縁 **2. ~ on** *v* ... ni ses-shimásu (ses-suru, ses-shíte) ... に接します(接する, 接して), rinsetsu shimásu (suru, shite) 隣接します (する, して)

borderline 1. *n* kyōkai-sen 境界線, bōdārain ボーダーライン **2.** *adj* kyōkai-senjō no 境界線上の, girigiri no ぎりぎりの

bore *v gets bored* unzári sasemásu (saseru, sasete) うんざりさせます(させる, させて)

boring *adj* (*dull*) taikutsu (na) 退屈(な), tsumaránai つまらない

born 1. *gets ~ v* umaremásu (umareru, umarete) 生まれます(生まれる, 生まれて) **2. ~ in/of** *adj* ... no de/umare ... の出/生まれ, ... -úmare (no) ... 生まれ(の)

borrow (*from* ...) *v* (... ni) karimásu (kariru, karite) (... に)借ります(借りる, 借りて); [HUMBLE] haishaku shimásu (suru, shite) 拝借します(する, して)

bosom *n* futokoro 懐・ふところ

boss *n* **1.** shújin 主人 **2.** (*head of company*) shachō 社長 **3.** (*a leader*) jōshi 上司 **4.** (*ring-leader*) óyá-bun 親分, bosu ボス

Boston *n* bosuton ボストン

Boston bag *n* bosuton-baggu ボストンバッグ

botanical garden *n* shokubutsú-en 植物園, botanikaru gāden ボタニカルガーデン

botch *v* yari-sokonaimásu (yari-sokonáu, yari-sokonátte) やり損ないます(損なう, 損なって)

both 1. *pron* ryōhō 両方 **2.** *adj* ryōhō no 両方の **3.** *adv* dochira mo どちらも; **~ ... and ...** ... mo ... mo ... も...も

both directions/sides n ryōmen 両面, ryō-gawa 両側

bother *n* mendō´ 面倒, méiwaku 迷惑; (*intrusion*) jama じゃま・邪魔, (*care*) sewá 世話(o-séwa お世話), o-sewa-sama お世話様, yákkai やっかい・厄介 (go-yákkai ごやっかい・ご厄介) → **worry**; **~ a person** hito no jama e[邪魔]をします(する, して)

bothersome *adj* mendō-kusái 面倒くさい[臭い], yákkai (na) やっかい・厄介(な); jama (na) じゃま・邪魔(な)

bottle *n* **1.** bín 瓶 **2.** (*a bottle of liquor*) *a bottle of whiskey* wisukii-botoru (ippon) ウィスキーボトル (一本); *a bottle of beer* bíiru íp-pon ビール一本, *1.8-liter bottle* (*of saké*) isshō´-bin 一升瓶; *keeping one's own bottle of liquor at a bar for the next time to come* botoru-kiipu ボトルキープ

bottle cap *n* (bín no) kyáppu (瓶の)キャップ, (bín no) ōkan (瓶の)王冠

bottle opener *n* sen-nuki 栓抜き

bottom *n* soko 底, (*underneath*) shita 下, ... shitá ...下; (*buttock*) shirí 尻(o-shiri お尻); (*bottommost, minimum, minimal*) *adj* saitei (no) 最低(の)

bottoms up (*toast*) kanpai 乾杯

bottom-up management *n* botomu-appu ボトムアップ

bounce *v* hazumimásu (hazumu, hazunde) 弾みます(弾む, 弾んで)

bound 1. *v* → **bind**; *bound pages* tsuzuri 綴り **2.** → **jump**

bound for ... -iki (no) ... 行き(の); *is ~ ...* ...e ikimásu (iku, itte) ... へ行きます(行く, 行って)

bound to (*do*) *v* kitto ...(suru) deshō きっと... (する)でしょう

boundary *n* sakái 境

bouquet *n* haná-tába 花束

bourbon *n* bā´bon バーボン

boutique *n* butikku ブティック

bow *n* (*archery or violin*) yumí 弓; (*shape*) yumi-gata 弓形; (*of ribbon*) chō-músubi ちょう結び・蝶結び

bow 1. *n* (*of head, etc.*) o-jigi おじぎ・お辞儀 **2.** *v* o-jigi o shimásu (suru, shite) おじき・お辞儀をします(する, して)

bowel *n* chō 腸; *bowels* naizō 内臓, *bowel movement* tsū-ji 通じ(o-tsū´-ji お通じ), *has a ~ movement* tsū-ji ga arimásu (arú, atte) 通じがあります(ある, あって)

bowl *n* wan 碗(o-wan お碗); (*ricebowl*) chawan 茶碗 (o-cháwan お茶碗); (*basin, pot*) hachí 鉢

bowl of rice with topping *n* donburi どんぶり・丼, ...-don ...どん・丼

bowlegged *adj* gani-mata (no) がにまた(の), waní-ashi (no) わに足(の)

bowl(ful) *n* ...-hai ... 杯 (**1:** íp-pai 一杯, **2:** ní-hai 二杯, **3:** sánbai 三杯)

bowling *n* bōringu ボウリング; *bowling competition* bōringu-taikai ボウリング大会, *bowling alley* bōringu-jō ボウリング場, *bowling ball* bōringu (no) bōru ボウリング(の)ボール

bow-wow! *n* wán-wan ワンワン

box *n* hako 箱, *box lunch* bentō 弁当 (o-bentō お弁当), (*sold at station*) eki-ben 駅弁; *small measuring box* masú 升

boxer *n* bokusā ボクサー

boxing *n* kentō 拳闘, bókushingu ボクシング; *boxing glove* gurōbu グローブ

box office 1. (*ticket office*) chiketto-uriba チケット売り場 **2.** (*receipts from a play, film, etc.*) kōgyō-shūnyū 興行収入, bokkusu-ofisu ボックスオフィス

boxtree, boxwood *n* tsuge つげ

boy *n* **1.** otokó-no-ko 男の子, shōnen 少年, bō´ya 坊や, bótchan 坊ちゃん; *big boy* (*male*) otokó 男 **2.** (*waiter*) bōi ボーイ

boyfriend *n* bōi-furéndo ボーイフレンド; káreshi 彼氏

Boy Scouts *n* bōi sukauto ボーイスカウト

Boys' Festival (*5 May*) *n* Tángo no sekku 端午の節句

boycott *n* boikotto ボイコット

boyish *adj* bōisshu ボーイッシュ, otoko-no-ko rashii 男の子らしい

bra *n* bura ブラ = burajā ブラジャー

bracelet *n* ude-wa 腕輪, buresuretto ブレスレット

brace oneself *v* shimarimásu (shimaru, shimatte) 締まります(締まる, 締まって)

bracing *adj* (*refreshing*) sawáyaka (na) さわやか・爽やか(な)

bracket *n* kakko 括弧; *square bracket (such as "[]")* kaku-kakko 角括弧

brag *v* hóra o fukimásu (fukú, fúite) ほらを吹きます(吹く, 吹いて)

brag about *v* jiman (o) shimásu (suru, shite) 自慢(を)します(する, して), hokorimásu (hokóru, hokótte) 誇ります(誇る, 誇って)

braid *v* amimásu (ámu, ánde) 編みます(編む, 編んで)

brain(s) *n* nō(-míso) 脳(みそ), zunō 頭脳, atamá 頭 (= *head*)

brainstorming *n* burein sutōmingu ブレインストーミング

brake *n* burēˊki ブレーキ

branch *n* **1.** (*of tree*) eda 枝 **2.** (*of store*) shiten 支店 **3.** (*of rail line*) shisen 支線 **4.** (*of school*) bún-kō 分校 **5.** (*of office*) bu 部
branch off *v it branches off* wakaremásu (wakaréru, wakárete) 分かれます(分かれる, 分かれて)

brand *n* burando ブランド, meigara 銘柄, shōhyō 商標; *famous brand goods* yūmei burando-hin 有名ブランド品

brandy *n* burandē ブランデー

brand-new *adj* shinpin no 新品の

brass *n* shinchū 真ちゅう・真鍮

brassiére *n* burájā ブラジャー

brat *n* wanpaku-kozō わんぱく[腕白]小僧, gakí がき・餓鬼

brave *adj* yūkan (na) 勇敢(な), tsuyói 強い

bravo *interj* burabō ブラボー

brazen *adj* zūzūshíí ずうずうしい

brazier *n* híbachi 火鉢

Brazil *n* Burajiru ブラジル

bread *n* pán パン, shoku-pan 食パン
bread crumbs *n* pan-kó パン粉, pan-kúzu パンくず[屑]
bread flour *n* kyōriki-kó 強力粉, pan senyō-ko パン専用粉

breadth *n* haba 幅

break *n* **1.** (*rift or pause*) kire-mé 切れ目 **2.** (*rest*) yasumí 休み(o-yasumi お休み), kyūkei 休憩

break *v* **1.** *it breaks v* kowaremásu (kowaréru, kowárete) 壊れます(壊れる, 壊れて), (*in two*) oremásu (oréru, órete) 折れます(折れる, 折れて), (*it splits*) waremásu (wareru, warete) 割れます(割れる, 割れて), (*it smashes*) kudakemásu (kudakéru, kudákete) 砕けます(砕ける, 砕けて), (*it opens up, it dawns*) akemásu (akeru, akete) 開け[明け]ます(開け[明け]る, 開け[明け]て) **2.** *breaks it v* kowashimásu (kowású, kowáshite) 壊します(壊す, 壊して), (*in two*) orimásu (óru, ótte) 折ります(折る, 折って), (*splits*) warimásu (waru, watte) 割ります(割る, 割って), (*smashes it*) kudakimásu (kudáku, kudáite) 砕きます(砕く,

砕いて); ~ *in* wari-kómimásu (wari-kómu, wari-kónde) 割り込みます(割り込む, 割り込んで)

break down 1. *it breaks down* (*crumbles*) kuzuremásu (kuzuréru, kuzúrete) 崩れます(崩れる, 崩れて), (*stops working*) koshō shimásu (suru, shite) 故障します(する, して) **2.** *breaks* (*demolishes*) *it* kuzushimásu (kuzúsu, kuzúshite) 崩します(崩す, 崩して)

break off (*ends it*) kirimásu (kíru, kítte) 切ります(切る, 切って); (*it ends*) kiremásu (kiréru, kírete) 切れます(切れる, 切れて)

break out (*appears*) hassei shimásu (suru, shite) 発生します(する, して)・ **occur**

breakable *adj* koware-yasúi 壊れやすい

breakdown *n* **1.** (*crash*) koshō 故障 **2.** (*item by item*) meisai 明細, uchiwake 内訳

breakfast *n* chōshoku 朝食, asa-góhan 朝ご飯; (*mostly male,* [INFORMAL]) asa-meshi 朝飯

bream *n sea bream* tái タイ・鯛

breast *n* (*chest*) muné 胸; (*woman's*) chichí 乳, chibusa 乳房, (*baby talk, slang*) óppai おっぱい; *breast cancer* nyū-gan 乳がん・乳癌

breath *n* íki 息; *a breath* hitó-iki 一息; *draws/takes one's last* íki o hiki-torimásu (hiki-tóru, hiki-tótte) 息を引き取ります(引き取る, 引き取って)

breathe *v* íki o shimásu (suru, shite) 息をします(する, して); kokyū shimásu (suru, shite) 呼吸します(する, して); *breathe a sigh of relief* shimásu (suru, shite) ほっとします(する, して)

breathe (it) in *v* (... o) suimásu (sū, sutte) (...を)吸います(吸う, 吸って)

breechcloth *n* fundoshi ふんどし・褌

breed *n* **1.** (*species of plant, etc.*) hinshu 品種 **2.** (*kind*) shurui 種類 **3.** (*lineage*) kettō 血統

breeze *n* (soyó-)kaze (そよ)風; *shoots the ~* daberimásu (dabéru, dabétte) だべります(だべる, だべって); ~ *in* wari-komimásu (wari-kómu, wari-kónde) 割り込みます(割り込む, 割り込んで)

brevity *n* kanketsu (sa) 簡潔(さ), mijikasa 短さ

brew *n* jōzō 醸造

brewery *n* jōzō-sho 醸造所

bribe(ry) *n* wáiro わいろ・賄賂

bric-a-brac *n* oki-mono 置物

brick *n* rénga レンガ・煉瓦

bride *n* haná-yome(-san) 花嫁(さん), (o-)yome (-san) お嫁(さん)

bridegroom *n* hana-múko(-san) 花婿(さん), (o-)múko(-san) (お)婿(さん)

bridge *n* **1.** hashí 橋, (*steel*) tekkyō 鉄橋; *the bridges on a Japanese harp* koto-ji 琴柱; *"The Bridges of Madison County"* "Madison-gun no hashi" 『マディソン郡の橋』; *Rainbow Bridge* (*Tokyo*) Reinbō-burijji レインボーブリッジ **2.** (*card*) burijji ブリッジ

bridle *n* baroku 馬勒

brief *adj* (*short*) mijikái 短い; (*simple*) kantan (na) 簡単(な)

briefcase n kaban かばん・鞄, buriifu kēsu ブリーフケース

briefing n jōkyō setsumei 状況説明

briefly adj (in brief) zatto ざっと

brier n ibara イバラ

brigadier general n júnshō 准将

bright adj 1. akarui 明るい 2. (sunny) hogáraka (na) 朗らか(な) 3. (colorful) hanáyaka (na) 華やか(な) 4. (gaudy) hadé (na) はで・派手(な) 5. (of spirit) yōki (na) 陽気(な)

brilliant adj subarashii すばらしい・素晴らしい, sugoi すごい・凄い

brim n fuchi ふち・縁, heri へり・縁

brine n shiomizu 塩水

bring v (a thing) motte/tótte kimásu (kúru, kité) 持って/取って来ます(来る, 来 て); ~ along (a person) tsurete kimásu (kúru, kité) 連れて来ます (来る, 来て). – But "bring to you/them" motte/tótte/tsurete ikimásu (iku, itte) 持って/取って/連れて行きます(行く, 行って)

bring about v okoshimásu (okósu, okóshite) 起こします(起こす, 起こして)

bring close/near v chika-zukemásu (chika-zukéru, chika-zúkete) 近付けます(近付ける, 近付けて), yosemásu (yoseru, yosete) 寄せます(寄せる, 寄せて)

bring up v (rears) sodatemásu (sodatéru, sodátete) 育てます(育てる, 育てて); yashinai-másu (yashinau, yashinatte) 養います(養う, 養って); yōiku shimásu (suru, shite) 養育します(する, して); (trains) shitsukemásu (shitsukéru, shitsúkete) しつけます(しつける, しつけて)

brink n kiwá 際

Britain → England

British → English

brittle adj morói もろい・脆い

broad adj hirói 広い

broadband n, adj burōdo-bando ブロードバンド, [BOOKISH] kōtai-iki 広帯域

broadcast 1. n hōsō 放送 2. v hōsō shimásu (suru, shite) 放送します(する, して)

broadcasting station n hōsō´-kyoku 放送局

broadly adj hiróku 広く

broad-minded n kanyō (na) 寛容(な)

brocade n níshiki 錦

broccoli n burokkorii ブロッコリー

brochure n panfuretto パンフレット, katarogu カタログ

broil v yakimásu (yaku, yaite) 焼きます(焼く, 焼いて)

broiled foods n yaki-mono 焼物; broiled salt-coated fish shioyaki 塩焼き

broke adj (without money) kinketsu 金欠

broken adj (not working) damé desu (da/na, de, ni) だめ[駄目]です(だ/な, で, に); koshō shita 故障した

brokenhearted; gets ~ shitsuren shimásu (suru, shite) 失恋します(する, して)

broker n burōkā ブローカー, nakagai 仲買い, nakadachí 仲立ち

brokerage n (commission) tesūryō 手数料, komisshon コミッション

bronze n seidō 青銅, buronzu ブロンズ

brooch n burōchi ブローチ

brook n ogawa 小川

broom n hōki ほうき・箒

broth n sūpu スープ

brother n (otoko) kyō´dai (男)兄弟; (older) (o-)níí-san (お)兄さん, áni 兄; (younger) otótó 弟, (your younger brother) otōto-san 弟さん

brother-in-law n gíri no áni/otōtó (kyō´dai) 義理の兄/弟

brothers and sisters n kyō´dai 兄弟, (female sisters) shimai 姉妹

brought up; gets ~ (is reared) sodachimásu (sodátsu, sodátte) 育ちます(育つ, 育って)

brow n 1. (eyebrow) máyu 眉 2. (forehead) hitai 額

brown adj cha-iro (no/i) 茶色(の/い)

brown bread n kuro-pan 黒パン

bruise n uchímí 打ち身, daboku-shō 打撲傷

brush 1. n búrashi ブラシ, haké はけ・刷毛; (for writing or painting) fude 筆 2. v ~ aside haraimásu (haráu, harátte) 払います(払う, 払って)

brushing n burasshingu ブラッシング

brush up n burasshu appu ブラッシュアップ

brushwood n shiba 柴

brusque adj bu-áisō (na) 無愛想(な), bukkírabō ぶっきらぼう(な)

Brussels sprouts n me-kyábetsu 芽キャベツ

brutal adj mugói むごい, zankoku (na) 残酷(な), zangyaku (na) 残虐(な), zannin (na) 残忍(な)

brutality n mugósa むごさ, zankoku 残酷, zangyaku 残虐, zannin 残忍, mujihi 無慈悲

bubble n awá 泡, abukú あぶく; (soap) shabon-dama シャボン玉; bubble economy baburu (keizai) バブル(経済)

bubble bath n baburu-basu バブルバス; awa-buro 泡風呂

bubble gum n fūsen-gámu 風船ガム

bucket n 1. baketsu バケツ 2. (rice) (o)-hachi お鉢, (o)-hitsu おひつ・お櫃, meshi-bitsu 飯びつ・飯櫃

buckle n shime-gane 締め金, bákkuru バックル

buck private n heisotsu 兵卒

buck tooth n déppa 出っ歯, sóppa 反っ歯

buckwheat n soba そば・蕎麦

buckwheat chaff n soba-gara そばがら

buckwheat noodles n (o-)sóba (お)そば[蕎麦]

bud n 1. (of leaf) mé 芽 2. (of flower) tsubomi つぼみ・蕾

Buddha n Hotoke(-sámá) 仏(様), (Sakyamuni) Shaka 釈迦 = O-shakasama お釈迦様; (statue of Buddha) Butsu-zō 仏像

Buddhism n Bukkyō 仏教

Buddhist n Bukkyō-to 仏教徒
Buddhist priest n (o-)bō-san (お)坊さん, sō´ryo 僧侶, [INFORMAL] bō´zu 坊主
Buddhist temple n (o-)terá (お)寺

budding willow n ao yagi 青やぎ・青柳, ao-yánagi 青柳

buddy → **friend**

budge → **move**

budget n yosan 予算

buffet n byuffe ビュッフェ

bug n mushi 虫・ムシ (**1:** ip-pikí 一匹, **2:** ní-hiki 二匹, **3:** sánbiki 三匹; **how many** nán-biki 何匹)

bugle n rappa ラッパ

build v (*erects*) tatemásu (tatéru, tátete) 建てます (建てる, 建てて), ki-zukimásu (ki-zúku, ki-zúite) 築きます (築く, 築いて); (*creates*) tsukurimásu (tsukúru, tsukutte) 造ります (造る, 造って); *body build* taikaku 体格

builder n (*person*) kenchiku-sha 建築者; kenchiku-gyōsha 建築業者

building n taté-mono 建物, bíru ビル

building lot n shiki-chi 敷地

bulb n tamá 玉; *light bulb* denkyū 電球

bulge n fukurami ふくらみ・膨らみ

bulk n ōkisa 大きさ, kasá かさ; *in ~* bára de ばらで・バラで

bull n **1.** (*bullshit*) baka/muda-hánashi げか/無駄話, (*bragging*) hóra ほら・ホラ; *shoots the ~* daberimásu (daberu, dabétte) だべります (だべる, だべって), muda-bánashi o shimásu (suru, shite) 無駄話をします (する, して) **2.** o-ushi 雄牛

bulldozer n burudózā ブルドーザー

bullet n tamá 弾, [BOOKISH] dangan 弾丸

bulletin n keiji 掲示

bulletin board n keiji-ban 掲示板

bulletproof adj bōdan (no) 防弾 (の)

bullet train n shinkánsen 新幹線

bullfight(ing) n tōgyū 闘牛

bully n (*children*) ijimekko いじめっ子

bump n **1.** (*swelling*) kobú こぶ・瘤; *(with) bumps* bótsubotsu (ga dekite) ぽつぽつ (ができて) **2.** (*in road*) dekoboko でこぼこ・凸凹

bump into v ... ni butsukarimásu (butsukaru, butsukatte) ... にぶつかります (ぶつかる, ぶつかって); (*happens to meet*) de-aimásu (de-au, de-atte) 出会います (出会う, 出会って)

bun n (*steamed*) manjū まんじゅう; (*pork-stuffed*) niku-man 肉まん; (*beanjam-stuffed*) an-man あんまん

bunch n **1.** (*cluster*) fusá 房 **2.** (*pile*) yamá 山 **3.** (*bundle*) tába 束 **4.** (*group*) muré 群れ
bunch of n (*lots of*) takusan (no) たくさんの

bundle n tsutsumí 包み; (*bunch*) tába 束

bungalow n (*cottage*) bangarō バンガロー

bungle 1. n héma へま **2.** v héma o shimásu (suru, shite) へまをします (する, して)

bunion n mamé まめ, soko-mame 底まめ

bunk n (*bed*) shindai 寝台

bunny n **1.** (*rabbit*) usagi (chan) ウサギ (ちゃん) **2.** (*alluring young woman*) sekushii na onna (no ko) セクシーな女 (の子); *bunny girl* banii gāru バニーガール

burden n ní 荷, (*on one's mind*) omo-ni 重荷

burdock (*root*) n gobō ゴボウ; *fried burdock and carrot strips* kinpira キンピラ・金平

bureau n **1.** (*department*) kyóku 局, ...-kyoku ...局 **2.** (*chest*) tansu たんす・箪笥

bureaucracy n kanryō-seido 官僚制度

bureaucrat n kanryō 官僚

burglar n dorobō 泥棒・どろぼう

burglar alarm n bōhan béru 防犯ベル, (*tōnan*) keihō-ki (盗難) 警報器

burial n maisō 埋葬

buried → **bury**

burlesque n **1.** outoríppu ストリップ **2.** (*parody*) parodii パロディ

Burma n Bíruma ビルマ

burn 1. v (*it burns*) yakemásu (yakeru, yakete) 焼けます (焼ける, 焼けて); (*fire burns*) moemásu (moeru, moete) 燃えます (燃える, 燃えて) **2.** v (*burns it*) yakimásu (yaku, yaite) 焼きます (焼く, 焼いて); (*burns a fire; wood, coal*) takimásu (taku, taite) 焚きます (焚く, 焚いて), (*burns a light*) tomoshimásu (tomósu, tomóshite) ともし [点し] ます (ともす, ともして) **3.** n (*on the skin*) yakedo やけど・火傷

burp n geppu (o shimásu; suru, shite) げっぷ (をします; する, して)

burst v (*it bursts*) yaburemásu (yaburéru, yaburete) 破れます (破れる, 破れて), (*explodes*) bakuhatsu shimásu (suru, shite) 爆発します (する, して); (*bursts it*) yaburimásu (yabúru, yabútte) 破ります (破る, 破って); *burst out* tobi-dashimásu (tobi-dásu, tobi-dáshite) 飛び出します (飛び出す, 飛び出して)

bury v uzumemásu (uzumeru, uzumete) うずめます・埋めます (うずめる, うずめて), umemásu (umeru, umete) 埋めます (埋める, 埋めて); *gets buried* uzumarimásu (uzumaru, uzumatte) うずまります・埋まります (うずまる, うずまって), umarimásu (umaru, umatte) 埋まります (埋まる, 埋まって)

bus n básu バス

bus driver n básu no untenshu バスの運転手

bus information booth n básu no annai-jo バスの案内所

bus stop n teiryū-jo 停留所; básu nori-ba バス乗り場

bus terminal n basu tāminaru バスターミナル

bus tour guide n basu gaido(-san) バスガイド (さん)

bush n [BOOKISH] kanboku 灌木・灌木, shigemi 茂み

Bushido n bushi-dō 武士道

bush warbler n ugúisu ウグイス

business n **1.** (*job*) shigoto 仕事 (o-shígoto お仕事), bijinesu ビジネス **2.** (*line of business*) shṓbai 商売 **3.** (*office work*) jímu 事務 **4.** (*transaction*) tórí-hiki 取り引き・取引 **5.** (*errand*) yōji 用事, (go-)yṓ (ご) 用, yō-táshí 用足し **6.** (*enterprise*) jígyō 事業, jitsugyo 実業

7. (*commerce*) shōˊgyō 商業 **8.** *having no* ~ muyō (no) 無用(の) **9.** *It's not your business.*, *Mind your own business.* Yokei na o-sewa désu 余計な お世話です。

business concern *n* shōsha 商社
business conditions *n* keiki 景気
business hours *n* eigyō-jíkan 営業時間
businesslike *adj* bijinesu raiku ビジネスライク, jimu-teki(na) 事務的(な)
businessman *n* jitsugyō-ka 実業家, bijinesu-man ビジネスマン
business suit *n* sebiro 背広
business trip *n* shutchō 出張
bust → **burst**
bustle *n* (*energetic activity*) kakki 活気
bustling *adj* nigíyaka (na) にぎやか・賑やか(な)
busy *adj* isogashíi いそがしい・忙しい, sewashíi せわしい・忙しい, sewashí nai せわしない; [BOOKISH] tabō (na) 多忙(な); (*in the midst of work*) shigoto-chū 仕事中, (*in conference*) kaigi-chū 会議中; *The line is busy* (O-)hanashi-chū désu (お)話中です
busybody *n* osekkai-yaki (na hito) おせっかい焼き(な人), sewa-zuki 世話好き
but *conj* **1.** [BOOKISH] shikáshi しかし, tokoró-ga ところが **2.** démo でも **3.** ([INFORMAL] or *child talk*) dátte だって; ... ga ... が, (...) kéredo (-mo) (...) けれど(も), ... tokoróga ... ところが; ippōˊ (de) 一方(で)
butcher (*shop*) *n* nikú-ya 肉屋
butcher knife *n* nikukiri-bōˊchō 肉切り包丁
butt **1.** *n* (*cigarette*, *cigar*) suigara 吸いがら **2.** → **buttock**
butter *n* bátā バター, báta バタ; *butter roll* batā-rōˊru バターロール
butterfly *n* chōˊ ちょう・蝶, chōchō ちょうちょう・蝶々, chōcho ちょうちょ
buttock *n* shirí 尻 (o-shiri お尻), (*mostly male* [VERY INFORMAL]) ketsu けつ・尻・穴
button **1.** *n* botan ボタン **2.** *v* (*buttons it*) ... no

botan o kakemásu (kakéru, kákete) ... のボタンをかけます(かける, かけて)
buxom *n* (*full-bosomed*) hōman na mune (no) 豊満な胸の, fukuyoka (na) ふくよか(な)
buy *v* kaimásu (kau, katte) 買います(買う, 買って); motomemásu (motoméru, motómete) 求めます(求める, 求めて); ~ *up* kai-torimásu (kai-tóru, kai-tótte) 買い取ります(買い取る, 買い取って)
buyer *n* **1.** kai-te 買い手 **2.** (*professional*) báiyā バイヤー
buzz *n* **1.** (*phone call*) denwa no yobidashi-on 電話の呼び出し音 **2.** (*rumor*) uwasa 噂・うわさ **3.** (*humming sound of insect*) (mushi no) haoto (虫の)羽音
buzzer *n* búzā ブザー
by 1. *prep* (*no later than*) ... máde ni ... までに; (*means of*) ... de ... で; **by and by** → **soon**
by ... at the latest *adv* ... máde ni wa ... までには
by chance *adv* hyótto suruto ひょっと(すると), gūzen (ni) 偶然(に), fúto ふと
by far *adv* zutto ずっと; háruka (ni) はるか(に)
gets by *v* (*lives*) kurashimásu (kurasu, kurashite) 暮らします(暮らす, 暮らして)
by heart/memory *adv* sóra de そらで・空で
by itself/nature *adv* hítori-de ni ひとりでに・独りでに, motomoto もともと・元々, mótó-yori もと[元]より
by oneself *adv* jibun de 自分で
by the way → way
bye (-bye) → **good-bye**
bygone *n* kako no koto 過去のこと, sugita koto 過ぎたこと
bylaw *n* kisoku 規則
bypass *n* (*highway*, *surgery*) baipasu バイパス
by-product *n* fukusanbutsu 副産物
bystander *n* kenbutsu-nin 見物人
byte *n* (*computer*) baito バイト

C

cab → **taxi**
cabaret *n* kyábarē キャバレー
cabbage *n* kyábetsu キャベツ; (*Chinese*) hakusai 白菜・ハクサイ
cabin *n* koya 小屋; (*mountain lodge*) yama-goya 山小屋
cabin cruiser *n* ōgata mōtā bōto 大型モーターボート
cabinet *n* (*government*) náikaku 内閣
cable *n* **1.** tsunái 綱, kēˊburu ケーブル **2.** (*telegram*) kaigai-dénpō 海外電報
cable car *n* kēburú-kāˊ ケーブルカー

cable television *n* kēburú-terebi ケーブルテレビ, yūsen-terebi 有線テレビ
cache *n* (*computer*) kyasshu キャッシュ
cactus *n* saboten サボテン
cadaver *n* shitai 死体
caddie *n* kyadii キャディー
cadence *n* rizumu リズム, hyōshi 拍子
cadet *n* shikan kōho sei 士官候補生
cadge *v* nedarimásu (nedaru, nedatte) ねだります(ねだる, ねだって); takarimásu (takaru, takatte) たかります(たかる, たかって)
cafe *n* (*coffee shop*) kissa-ten 喫茶店, kafe カフェ

cafeteria *n* kafeteria カフェテリア, shokudō 食堂; *school cafeteria* gaku-shoku 学食, gakusei shokudō 学生食堂; *company cafeteria* shain-shokudō 社員食堂

caffeine *n* kafein カフェイン

cage *n* **1.** (*for bird*) kago かご・籠, tori-kago 鳥かご・鳥籠 **2.** (*for animal*) orí おり・檻

cagey *adj* nukemenonai 抜け目のない, yōjin-bukai 用心深い

cagoule *n* (*raincoart*) kagūru カグール

cahoots; *in ~ with* ... to takuránde ... と企[たくら]んで

Cairo *n* kairo カイロ

cajole *v* odatemásu (odateru, odatete) おだてます（おだてる, おだてて）; kangen de damashimásu (damasu, damashite) 甘言でだまします・騙します（騙す, 騙して）

cajolery *n* obekka おべっか, kuchi-guruma 口車, [BOOKISH] kangen 甘言,

cake 1. *n* kē'ki ケーキ; (*spongecake*) kasutera カステラ **2.** *n* (o-)káshi （お）菓子・(*Japanese*) wa-gáshi 和菓子 **3.** *n* (*rice cake*) mochi もち・餅 **4.** *v it cakes* (*mud*) (doró ga) katamarimásu (katamaru, katamatte) (泥が) 固まります（固まる, 固まって） **5.** *n* → **bar** (*of soap*)

calamity *n* sainán 災難, wazawai 災い

calcium *n* karushium カルシウム

calculate *v* keisan shimásu (suru, shíte) 計算します（する, して）

calculation *n* **1.** keisan 計算 **2.** (*estimate*) mitsumori 見積もり

calculator *n* keisán-ki 計算機; *desk calculator* dentaku 電卓

calculus *n* **1.** (*mathematics*) bisekibun-gaku 微積分学 **2.** (*pathology*) kesseki 結石

calendar *n* koyomí 暦; karéndā カレンダー

calf *n* **1.** (*young cow*) ko ushi 子牛 **2.** (*leg below the knee*) fukurahagi ふくらはぎ

calfskin *n* ko-ushi no kawa 子牛の皮

caliber *n* **1.** (*bore caliber*) kōkei 口径 **2.** (*ability*) sainō 才能

calisthenics *n* biyō taisō 美容体操, jūnan taisō 柔軟体操

call 1. *n* (*phone call*) denwa 電話 **2.** *n* (*visit*) hōmon 訪問; (*of solicitude*) (o-)mimai （お）見舞 **3.** *v* yobimásu (yobu, yonde) 呼びます（呼ぶ, 呼んで）; (*phone*) denwa o shimásu (suru, shíte) 電話をします（する, して） **4.** *v* (*call on*) → **visit; call to mind** → **recall**

call box *n* hijōyō denwa 非常用電話

call center *n* kōru sentā コールセンター

call girl *n* kōru gāru コールガール

called; *is called* ... to iimásu (iu, itte/yutte) ... と言います（言う, 言って/ゆって）

caller *n* (*visitor*) raikyaku 来客

calligraphy *n* shodō 書道; (*hand-writing practice*) (o-)shūji （お）習字

calling *n* **1.** (*vocation*) shokugyō 職業 **2.** (*summons*) shōshū 召集

calling card *n* meishi 名刺 (= *business card*, *name card*)

calling-card case *n* meishí-ire 名刺入れ

callous *adj* **1.** (*having calluses*) táko no dekita たこのできた **2.** (*insensitive, unfeeling*) mu-shinkei (na) 無神経（な）, mu-kankaku (na) 無感覚（な） **3.** (*unsympathetic*) omoiyari ga nai 思いやりがない, mu-jō (na) 無情（な）

callus *n* táko たこ

calm *adj* (*quiet*) shízuka (na) 静か・しずか（な）, odáyaka (na) 穏やか・おやだや（な）, reisei (na) 冷静（な）; nódoka (na) のどか（な）; *gets calm* shizumarimásu (shizumáru, shizumatte) 静まります（静まる, 静まって）; *calms, makes ~* shizumemásu (shizuméru, shizúmete) 静めます（静める, 静めて）; *calms down* (*regains composure*) ochitsukimásu (ochi-tsuku, ochitsuite) 落ち着きます（落ち着く, 落ち着いて）

calmly *adv* ochi-tsuite 落ち着いて; (*unperturbed*) heiki de 平気で

calorie *n* karorii カロリー

calorie calculation *n* karorii keisan カロリー計算

Cambodia *n* kanbojia カンボジア

camcorder *n* bideo kámera ビデオカメラ

came → come

camel *n* rakuda ラクダ

camellia *n* tsúbaki ツバキ・椿

cameo *n* kameo カメオ

camera *n* kámera カメラ, shashín-ki 写真機

cameraman *n* kamera-man カメラマン

camouflage *n* kamufurāju カムフラージュ

camp 1. *n* kyánpu キャンプ; (*bivouac*) yaei 野営 **2.** *v* kyánpu (o) shimásu (suru, shíte) キャンプ（を）します（する, して）

campaign *n* kyanpēn キャンペーン, undō 運動

camper *n* **1.** (*a person who camps*) kyanpu (o) suru hito キャンプ（を）する人 **2.** (*vehicle*) kyanpingukā キャンピングカー, kyanpā キャンパー

campfire *n* kyánpu-faia キャンプファイア, kyánpu-faiya キャンプファイヤ, kyánpu-faiyā キャンプファイヤー

camping *n* kyánpu キャンプ, kyanpu-seikatsu キャンプ生活

campsite *n* kyanpu-jō キャンプ場; yaei-chi 野営地

campus *n* kyánpasu キャンパス, (*within the university*) daigakú-kōnai 大学構内; kōtei 校庭

can 1. *n* (*tin can*) kán 缶・かん (**1:** íp-pon 一本, **2:** ní-hon 二本, **3:** sánbon 三本, *how many* nán-bon 何本) **2.** *cans it* *v* (kán ni) tsumemásu (tsuméru, tsúmete) (缶に) 詰めます（詰める, 詰めて）

canned beer *n* kan bíiru 缶ビール

can opener *n* kan-kírí 缶切り

can *modal v* (*can do it*) (... ga) dekimásu (dekíru, dékite) (... が) 出来ます・できます（出来る, 出来て）, (suru) kotó ga dekimásu （する）事[こと]が

出来ます・できます; (... ga) kanaimás<u>u</u> (kanáu, kanátte) (... が)叶います(叶う, 叶って) [NOTE] *A potential ("can") version of almost every verb can be made by replacing ... -ru ...る with ... -(ra)reru ... (ら)れる, or ...-u ...う with ...-eru ...える. Most of the potentials will be found in the Japanese-English section. Some Japanese frown upon the ...-reru ...れる forms, and use only the longer ...-rareru ...られる; some use ...-areru ...あれる (for ...-eru ...える) as well as ...-rareru (=...-reru) ...られる (=...れる)*

can see (... ga) miemás<u>u</u> (miéru, míete) (... が)見えます(見える, 見えて)

can hear (... ga) k<u>i</u>koemás<u>u</u> (k<u>i</u>koeru, k<u>i</u>koete) (... が)聞こえます(聞こえる, 聞こえて)

Canada *n* Kánada カナダ

Canadian *n* Kanadá-jin カナダ人

canal *n* únga 運河

canary *n* kanari(y)a カナリア[ヤ]

cancel *v* tori-keshimás<u>u</u> (tori-kesu, tori-kesh<u>i</u>te) 取り消します(取り消す, 取り消して); keshimás<u>u</u> (kesu, kesh<u>i</u>te) 消します(消す, 消して)

cancellation *n* tori-keshi 取り消し; kyánseru キャンセル;
  cancellation mark/stamp *n* keshi-in 消印

cancelled flight *n* kekkō 欠航 = *flight cancellation*

cancer *n* gán がん・癌; (*lung*) haigan 肺がん・肺癌; (*stomach*) i-gan 胃がん・胃癌; (*breast*) nyū´gan 乳がん・乳癌

Cancer *n* (*star sign*) Kani-za カニ座

candid *adj* sotchoku (na) 率直(な)

candidate *n* kōhō-sha 候補者

candid(ly) *adv* sotchoku (ni) 率直に, ō´pun (ni) オープン(に) → **frank**

candle *n* rōsók<u>u</u> ろうそく, kyándoru キャンドル
  candleholder *n* rōsók<u>u</u> date ろうそく立て, shoku-dai 燭台
  candlelight *n* rōsók<u>u</u> no hikari ろうそくの光
  candlestick *n* rōsók<u>u</u>-date ろうそく立て, shokudai 燭台

candor *n* socchoku (sa) 率直(さ)

candy *n* kyándii キャンディー, (*wheat-gluten*) ame アメ・飴
  candy floss *n* (*sweet*) watagashi 綿菓子
  candy store *n* (o-)kashí-ya (お)菓子屋

cane 1. *n* (*walking stick*) s<u>u</u>tékki ステッキ; (*staff*) tsúe 杖 **2.** *n* (*rattan*) tō´ 藤・トウ

canine *n* **1.** (*dog*) inu 犬; *canidae* inu-ka 犬科 **2.** (*canine teeth*) kenshi 犬歯

canister *n* yōki 容器, kan 缶

canna *n* kanna カンナ

cannabis *n* taima 大麻, marifana マリファナ

canned (*food*) *adj* kanzúmé (no) 缶詰(の);
  canned pineapple pain-kan パイン缶

cannibal *n* kanibaru カニバル, hitokui 人食い

cannon *n* taihō 大砲

cannot *modal v* [NEGATIVE] dekimasén (dekínai) でき[出来]ません(でき[出来]ない); (shi-)

kiremasén (sh<u>i</u>-kirénai) (し)切れません(し切れない); ~ **stand it** gáman dekimasén (dekínai) がまん[我慢]でき[出来]ません(でき[出来]ない), tamarimasén (tamaranai) たまりません(たまらない)

canoe *n* kanū カヌー

canon *n* (*music*) kanon カノン

canopy *n* tengai 天蓋・てんがい

cantaloupe *n* kantarōpu meron カンタロープ・メロン

cantankerous *adj* kimuzukashii 気難しい, tsumujimagari (no) つむじ曲がり(の)

canteen *n* shokudō 食堂

canvas *n* kyanbasu キャンバス
  canvas shoes *n* (*sneakers*) suniikā スニーカー

canyon *n* kyōkoku 峡谷・きょうこく; *Grand Canyon* Gurando kyanion グランドキャニオン

cap *n* **1.** → **hat 2.** (*of a pen*) kyáppu キャップ **3.** (*of a bottle*) kyáppu キャップ, ōkan 王冠 **4.** (*of a mushroom*) kása かさ・笠

capability *n* **1.** (*ability*) nōryoku 能力 **2.** (*possibility*) kanō-sei 可能性 **3.** (*potential*) shōrai-sei 将来性

capable *adj* nōryoku ga aru 能力がある; yūnō (na) 有能(な)

capacity *n* kyapa(sitii) キャパ(シティー) **1.** (*ability*) nōryoku 能力 **2.** (*measure of contents*) yōseki 容積

cape *n* **1.** (*promontory*) misaki 岬 **2.** (*sleeveless garment*) kēpu ケープ

caper *n* kēpā ケーパー

capital *n* **1.** (*city*) shútó 首都 **2.** (*money*) shihon 資本

capitalism *n* shihon-shúgi 資本主義

capitalist *n* shihon-ka 資本家

capitalize *v* **1.** (*write or print in capital letters*) ōmoji de kakimás<u>u</u> (kaku, ka<u>i</u>te) 大文字で書きます(書く, 書いて) **2.** (*supply with capital*) shusshi shimás<u>u</u> (suru, sh<u>i</u>te) 出資します(する, して)

capital letter *n* ōmoji 大文字

capital punishment *n* shi-kei 死刑

capitulate *v* kōfuku shimás<u>u</u> (suru, sh<u>i</u>te) 降伏します(する, して), kōsan shimás<u>u</u> (suru, sh<u>i</u>te) 降参します(する, して)

caprice *n* kimagure 気まぐれ

capricious *adj* kimagure (na) 気まぐれ(な)

Capricorn *n* (*star sign*) Yagi-za 山羊座

capsize *v* tenpuku shimás<u>u</u> (suru, shite) 転覆します(する, して), tenpuku sasemás<u>u</u> (saseru, sasete) 転覆させます(させる, させて)

capsule *n* káp<u>u</u>seru カプセル

captain *n* (*army*) táii 大尉; (*navy*) taisa 大佐; (*airplane*) k<u>i</u>chō 機長; (*ship*) sénchō 船長, (*warship*) kanchō 艦長; (*team*) kyáputen キャプテン

caption *n* kyapushon キャプション **1.** (*situation*) midashi 見出し **2.** (*text of a speech of movie, etc*) jimaku 字幕 **3.** (*explanation*) setsumei bun 説明文

captivate *v* miwaku shimás<u>u</u> (suru, shite) 魅惑します(する, して)

captive n horyo 捕虜
captivity n kankin 監禁
capture v toraemásu (toráeru, toráete) 捕らえます（捕らえる、捕らえて）
car n kuruma 車, jidō-sha 自動車 (*how many* nándai 何台); *Car Number (Six)* (roku)-gō´sha (六)号車; *what (number) car* nan-gō´sha 何号車
　car barn n sháko 車庫
　car ferry n kā ferii カーフェリー
　car park n chūsha-jō 駐車場
carafe n mizu-sashi 水差し
caramel n kyarameru キャラメル
carat n karatto カラット
caravan n 1. taishō 隊商, kyaraban キャラバン 2. (*large vehicle*) kyaraban-kā キャラバンカー, kanpingu-kā キャンピングカー
carbohydrate n tansuikabutsu 炭水化物
carbolic acid n sekitan-san 石炭酸
carbon n tanso 炭素
　carbon copy n kābon-kopii カーボンコピー; (*e-mail*) shiishii CC
　carbon dioxide n ni-sanka-tanso 二酸化炭素
　carbon monoxide n issanka-tanso 一酸化炭素
　carbon paper n kābon-shi カーボン紙
　carbonated drink n tansan inryō 炭素飲料
　carbonated water n tansan sui 炭素水
　carbonic acid n tansan 炭酸
carburetor n kyaburétā キャブレター
carcass n shitai 死体, shigai 死骸
card n 1. fuda 札, kā´do カード; (*playing card*) toránpu (ichí-mai) トランプ（一枚）2. (*calling card, name card*) meishi 名刺 3. (*postcard*) hagaki はがき・葉書 (o-hágaki おはがき・お葉書); *New Year's card* nengajō 年賀状
　card game n toranpu トランプ
　card index n kādo-shiki sakuin カード式索引
cardboard n bōru-gami ボール紙; (*corrugated*) danbō´ru 段ボール
cardiac 1. n (*medicine*) kyōshin-zai 強心剤 2. adj shizō (no) 心臓（の）
cardigan n kādigan カーディガン
cardinal adj shuyō (na) 主要（な）, kihonteki (na) 基本的（な）
care n (*caution*) yōjin 用心, nén 念; (*upkeep*) te-iré 手入れ; *take ~ of* (*a person*) ... no sewá o shimásu (suru, shite) ... の世話(o-séwa お世話)をします（する、して）, ... no mendō o mimásu (míru, míte) ... の面倒を見ます（見る、見て）; (*a matter*) ... o shóri shimásu (suru, shite) ... を処理します（する、して）
　care for v → **like, love, want** → **look after**
career n (*occupation*) shokúgyō 職業; kyaria キャリア; (*history*) rireki 履歴; (*summary, resume*) keireki 経歴; shoku-reki 職歴
carefree adj kiraku (na) 気楽（な）, nónki (na) のんき・呑気（な）
careful adj chūibukai 注意深い; *is ~* ki o tsukemásu (tsukéru, tsukéte) 気を付けます（付ける、付けて）; nén o iremásu (ireru, irete) 念を入れます（入れる、入れて）; chūi-bukái 注意深い
carefully adv chūibukaku 注意深く
careless adj mutón-chaku/-jaku (na) 無頓着（な）, zusan (na) ずさん（な）, zonzái (na) ぞんざい（な）, taiman (na) 怠慢（な）, fuchū´i (na) 不注意（な）
carelessly adv (*casually*) muzō´sa ni 無造作に
carelessness n fuchū´i 不注意, yudan 油断
carer n kaigo-nin 介護人
caress 1. n aibu 愛撫, hōyō 抱擁 2. v aibu/hōyō shimásu (suru, shite) 愛撫/抱擁します（するして）
caretaker 1. n (*custodian*) kanri-nin 管理人 2. (*person who takes care of another*) kaigo-nin 介護人, sewa-nin 世話人
carnival n kānibaru カーニバル, shaniku-sai 謝肉祭
carouse v (*drink deeply*) dáiku 大工
carp n (*fish*) kói コイ・鯉
　carp streamers n (*for the Boys' Festival*) koi-nóbori こいのぼり・鯉のぼり・
carpenter n dáiku 大工
carpentry n daiku shigoto 大工仕事
carpet n jū´tan じゅうたん・絨毯, kā´pétto カーペット
carpet bombing n jū´tan bakugeki じゅうたん［絨毯］爆撃
carpet sweeper n jū´tan sōji-ki じゅうたん［絨毯］掃除機
carriage n 1. (*four-wheeled horse-drawn passenger*) basha 馬車 2. (*transporting*) unpan 運搬 3. (*carrying expense*) unsōryō 運送料 4. (*movable part of a machine*) (kikai no) kadōbu (機械の) 可動部 5. (*bearing*) mi no konashi 身のこなし
carrier n 1. (*transportation*) yusō 輸送, unsō 運送 2. (*of disease*) hokin-sha 保菌者, hoin-sha 保因者 3. (*mail carrier*) yūbin haitatsu-nin 郵便配達人 4. (*newspaper carrier*) shinbun haitatsu-nin 新聞配達人 5. (*aircraft carrier*) kōkū bokan 航空母艦, kūbo 空母
carrot n ninjin ニンジン・人参
carry v 1. motte/tótte ikimásu (iku, itte) 持って/取っていきます（いく、いって）; (*loads aboard*) nosemásu (noseru, nosete) 載せます（載せる、載せて）; (*conveys*) hakobimásu (hakobu, hakonde) 運びます（運ぶ、運んで）2. (*dangling from the hand*) sagemásu (sagéru, ságete) 提げます（提げる、提げて）; *~ on one's back/shoulders* shoimásu (shou, shotte) しょいます（しょう、しょって）, ninaimásu (nináu, ninátte) 担います（担う、担って）, katsugimásu (katsúgu, katsúide) 担ぎ［かつぎ］ます（担ぐ、担いで）; (*piggyback*) oimásu (ou, otte) 負います（負う、負って）, obuimásu (obū´, obútte) おぶ［負ぶ］います（おぶう、おぶって）, ónbu shimásu (suru, shite) おんぶします（する、して）
　carry out v (*performs*) okonaimásu (okonau, okonatte) 行います（行う、行って）; (*brings about*) genjitsu-ka shimásu (suru, shite) 現実化します（する、して）

carry-cot *n* keitai bebii beddo 携帯ベビーベッド

carry-on 1. *n* (*luggage*) te-nimotsu 手荷物
2. *adj* kinai-mochikomi (yō no) 機内持ち込み
(用の)

carsick; gets ~ (kuruma ni) yoimás<u>u</u> (yóu, yótte)
(車に)酔います(酔う, 酔って)

cart *n* teoshi-gúruma 手押し車, daisha 台車

cartel *n* karuteru カルテル

cartilage *n* nankotsu 軟骨

carton → box

cartoon *n* manga 漫画・マンガ・まんが

cartridge *n* **1.** (*ink cartridge*) kātorijji カートリッ
ジ **2.** (*cartridge in gun*) danyaku-tō 弾薬筒

carve *v* (*inscribe*) kizamimás<u>u</u> (kizamu, kizande)
刻みます(刻む, 刻んで), horimás<u>u</u> (hóru, hótte)
彫ります(彫る, 彫って)

carving *n* horí-mónó 彫り物, (*sculpture*) chōkoku
彫刻

carving knife *n* nikukiri-bō´chō 肉切り包丁;
chōkokutō 彫刻刀

cascade *n* (*small waterfall*) chiisana taki
小さな滝

case *n* **1.** (*situation*) ba(w)ai 場合, ... wáke... 訳・
わけ, (*event*) ... dán ... 段; (*matter*) kotó 事・こと,
jiken 事件, (*particular instance*) kē´su ケース
2. (*box*) hako 箱

case by case kēsu-bai-kē´su ケース・バイ・ケ
ース

in this case kono ba(w)ai この場合

in that case sorenára それなら; (sore) déwa
(それ)では, ja じゃ, jā じゃあ

in case of ... ni sái-sh<u>i</u>te... に際して; ... no bāi/
tokí ni... の場合/時に

just in case nen no tame 念のため, ichiō 一応

cash 1. *n* (*money*) genkín 現金; *petty cash* koguchi
genkin 小口現金 **2.** *n* shōkin 賞金
cashbook *n* genkin-suitō-chō 現金出納帳
cashbox *n* (chiisai) kinko (小さい)金庫
cash card *n* kyasshu-kādo キャッシュカード
cash dispenser *n* genkin jidō shiharai-ki 現金自
動支払機
cash envelope *n* (*registered mail*) genkin-
kák<u>i</u>tome 現金書留
cash flow *n* kyasshu furō キャッシュフロー
cash register *n* reji レジ
3. *v* (*a check*) genkín ni kaemás<u>u</u> (kaéru, káete)
現金にかえます・換えます(換える, 換えて),
genkín ni shimás<u>u</u> (suru, sh<u>i</u>te) 現金にします(する,
して) **4.** *v* (*into smaller bills/coins*) komakáku
shimás<u>u</u> (suru, sh<u>i</u>te) 細かくします
(する, して), kuzushimás<u>u</u> (kuzúsu, kuzúsh<u>i</u>te)
くずします・崩します(くずす, くずして)

cashew nut *n* kashū nattsu カシューナッツ

cashier *n* suitō-gákari 出納係, réji-gákari レジ係

cashmere *n* kashimia(/ya) カシミア(/ヤ)

casino *n* kajino カジノ

cask *n* taru たる・樽

casket *n* **1.** (*coffin*) hitsugi 棺・ひつぎ **2.** (*jewel
box*) hōseki-bako 宝石箱

casserole *n* mushiyaki nabe 蒸し焼きなべ

cassette *n* kasetto (tēpu) カセット(テープ)

cast 1. *n* (*throwing*) hito nage 一投げ **2.** *n*
(*selecting actors, selected actors*) kyasuto
キャスト, haiyaku 配役 **3.** *v* (*throw*) nagemás<u>u</u>
(nagéru, nágete) 投げます(投げる, 投げて)
4. *v* (*select actors*) kyasutingu shimás<u>u</u> (suru,
sh<u>i</u>te) キャスティングします(する, して),
haiyaku o kimemás<u>u</u> (kimeru, kimete) 配役を決め
ます(決める, 決めて)

castaway *n* **1.** (*shipwrecked person*) hyōryū-sha
漂流者 **2.** (*outcast*) misuterareta hito 見捨てら
れた人

caste *n* kāsuto カースト

cast iron *n* chū-tetsu 鋳鉄・ちゅうてつ

castle *n* (o-)shiro (お)城; (*name of certain*) ...-jō
... 城

castor oil *n* himashi-abura ヒマシ油

castrate *n* kyosei-sha 去勢者

casual *adj* nanige-nái 何気ない; kigaru (na) 気軽
(な); kajuaru (na) カジュアル(な)
casual clothes *n* kajuaru na hukusō カジュアル
な服装, kajuaru na kakkō カジュアルな格好
casual sex *n* yukizuri no sekkusu 行きずりのセ
ックス
casuals *n* fudan-gi 普段着

casually *adv* (*effortlessly*; *carelessly*) muzō´sa ni
無造作に

casualty *n* (*injury, damage*) higai 被害; (*victim*)
higái-sha 被害者; (*dead and injured*) shishō´-sha
死傷者

cat *n* néko 猫・ネコ (**1:** ip-pík<u>í</u> 一匹, **2:** ní-h<u>i</u>ki
二匹, **3:** sánbiki 三匹, *how many* nán-biki 何匹)
cat's cradle *n* ayatori あやとり
cat's-eye *n* nekome-ishi 猫目石

catalog *n* katarogu カタログ; mokuroku 目録;
(*directory*) meibo 名簿

catalyst *n* shokubai 触媒

catapult *n* (*airplane*) funsha-ki 噴射機, kataparuto
カタパルト

cataract *n* **1.** (*large waterfall*) ookina taki 大きな
滝 **2.** (*downpour*) gōu 豪雨 **3.** (*ophthalmology*)
hakunai-shō 白内障

catarrh *n* kataru カタル

catastrophe *n* dai-sanji 大惨事, dai-saigai
大災害, katasutorofi カタストロフィ

catastrophic *adj* hakyoku-teki (na) 破局的(な)

catch 1. *v* (*seizes*) tsukamaemás<u>u</u> (tsukamaeru,
tsukamaete) 捕まえます(捕まえる, 捕まえて);
torimás<u>u</u> (tóru, tótte) 取ります(取る, 取って);
(*attracts*) h<u>i</u>kimás<u>u</u> (h<u>i</u>ku, hiite) 引きます(引く,
引いて) **2.** *v* (*a disease*) (byōki ni) kakarimás<u>u</u>
(kakáru, kakátte) (病気に)かかります(かかる, か
かって) **3.** *n a good catch* 獲物・えもの
4. *n* (*trap*) wana わな・ワナ **5.** *n* (*clasp*)
tomegane 留め金

catch a cold kaze o h<u>i</u>kimás<u>u</u> (h<u>i</u>ku, hiite) かぜ
[風邪] をひきます(ひく, ひいて), [HONORIFIC]
kaze o o-meshi ni narimás<u>u</u> (náru, nátte) かぜ

［風邪］をお召しになります(なる、なって)
catch-phrase n kyacchi furēzu キャッチフレーズ
catch up (with) (... ni) oi-tsukimásu (oi-tsukú, oi-tsúite) (... に)追いつきます(追いつく、追いついて)
category n kategorii カテゴリー
caterer, catering shop n shidashi-ya 仕出し屋
catering n (food delivered to order) demae 出前, kētaringu ケータリング
caterpillar n kemushi 毛虫・ケムシ
catfish n namazu ナマズ
cathedral n dai-seidō 大聖堂
Catholic n Katoríkku (kyō) カトリック(教)、(person) Katoríkku kyōto カトリック教徒
cattle n (bulls and cows) ushi 牛・ウシ (how many nán-tō 何頭)
catty adj ijiwaru (na) 意地悪(な)、zurui ずるい
caucho n gomu ゴム
caucus n tōin shūkai 党員集会
cauldron n kama かま・釜
cauliflower n karifurawā カリフラワー
cause n (of an effect) gen'in 原因、moto 元; (negative effect) ... séi ... せい; (source) táne 種; (reason) wáke 訳、riyū 理由; (purpose benefit) tame ため・為
cause (one) concern/worry (... ni) shinpai o kakemásu (kakéru, kákete) (... に)心配をかけます(かける、かけて)
cause (one) trouble (... ni) méiwaku o kakemásu (kakéru, kákete) (... に)迷惑をかけます(かける、かけて)
cause (someone to do) ... ni sasemásu (saseru, sasete) ... にさせます(させる、させて)
caustic 1. n fushoku-zai 腐食剤 2. adj fushoku-sei (no) 腐食性(の)
caution 1. n yōjin 用心; (precaution) yō'i 用意、nén 念; as (a word of) caution nen no tamé (ni) 念のため[に](に) 2. v (warns) keikai shimásu (suru, shite) 警戒します(する、して)
cautious adj yōjin-bukái 用心深い
cautiously adv shinchō (ni) 慎重に、yōjin-bukaku 用心深く、chūi-bukaku 注意深く
cavalier adj gōman (na) 傲慢(な)、ōhei (na) 横柄(な)
cavalry n 1. (horsemen) kihei-tai 騎兵隊 2. (military) kikō-butai 機甲部隊
cave n hora-ana 洞穴・ほら穴、hórá 洞・ほら; ... -dō ... 洞
caveman n 1. (human living in caves) kekkyo-jin 穴居人)、genshi-jin 原始人 2. (crude man) soya na otoko 粗野な男、(brutal man) yaban na otoko 野蛮な男
cavern n dai-dōkutsu 大洞窟
caviar n (roe) kábia キャビア; (salmon/trout roe) ikura イクラ、sujiko 筋子、suzuko すずこ; (cod roe) tarako たらこ
cavity n 1. (hole) ana 穴 2. (hollow area) kūdō 空洞 3. (tooth cavity) mushiba 虫歯
CD player n shii-dii pureiyā CDプレイヤー

cease v yamimásu (yamu, yande) やみます・止みます(止む、止んで)、taemásu (taéru, táete) 絶えます(絶える、絶えて)
cease-fire n teisen 停戦
ceaseless adj taemanai 絶え間ない
cedar; cryptomeria, Japanese cedar n sugi 杉・スギ
cede v yuzurimásu (yuzuru, yuzutte) 譲ります(譲る、譲って)
ceiling n tenjō 天井
celeb, celebrity n serebu セレブ、yūmei-jin 有名人
celebrate v iwaimásu (iwáu, iwátte) 祝います(祝う、祝って)
celebration n (party) iwái 祝い (o-iwai お祝い)
celery n sérori セロリ; Japanese celery údo ウド・独活
celestial adj ten (no) 天(の)、tentai (no) 天体(の)
celibacy 1. n (single person/people) dokushin-sha 独身者 2. adj dokushin (no) 独身(の)
cell n 1. (biology) saibō 細胞 2. (prison) dokubō 独房、rōya 牢屋
cellar n (storehouse) kurá 倉・蔵; (basement) chiká shitsu 地下室
cello n chéro チェロ
cellophane n sérohan セロハン
cellophane tape n serohan-tēpu セロハンテープ
Celt n 1. (a Celt) keruto-jin ケルト人 2. (ethnic) keruto-zoku ケルト族
cement n semento セメント
cement floor n tatakí たたき
cemetery n haka-bá 墓場、bóchi 墓地
cenotaph n (senbotsu-sha) kinen-hi (戦没者)記念碑
censor 1. n ken'etsu-kan 検閲官 2. v ken'etsu shimásu (suru, shite) 検閲します(する、して)
censorship n ken'etsu 検閲
censure 1. n (blame) hínan 非難 2. v (blames one) hínan shimásu (suru, shite) 非難します(する、して)、sememásu (seméru, sémete) 責めます(責める、責めて)
census n kokusei-chōsa 国勢調査
cent n sénto セント; percent pāsénto パーセント
centennial n hyakushūnen 百周年
center n mannaka 真ん中・まんなか、chūō 中央、chūshin 中心; (institution) séntā センター
centigrade n sésshi 摂氏、seshi セ氏; ... -do ... 度
centimeter n sénchi センチ、senchi-mē'toru センチメートル
centipede n mukade ムカデ・百足
central adj mannaka no 真ん中の・まんなかの、chūshin no 中心の、chūō no 中央の
Central America n chūbei 中米、chūō-amerika 中央アメリカ
central area n chūshín-chi 中心地
central heating n sentoraru hiitingu セントラルヒーティング
central office n hónbu 本部

central park n chūō kōen 中央公園; *(Manhattan) Central Park* sentoraru pāku セントラルパーク

central reservation n chūō-bunri-tai 中央分離帯

century n séiki 世紀

ceramics n seramikku セラミック; *(ceramic art)* tōgei 陶芸; *(ceramic ware)* tōʹki 陶器; *(pottery)* yaki-mono 焼き物

cereal n 1. kokúmotsu 穀物, kokúrui 穀類 2. *(breakfast food prepared from grain)* siriaru シリアル

cerebral adj nō (no) 脳(の)

ceremony n shiki 式, gíshiki 儀式; *wedding ceremony* kekkon-shiki 結婚式

certain adj táshika (na) 確か・たしか(な); kakujitsu (na) 確実(な); *(specific, particular)* áru ... áru ...

certainly adv mochíron もちろん・勿論; táshika ni 確かに; mása-ni まさに

certainty n kakujitsu 確実, kakujitsu-sei 確実性

certificate n shōmei-sho 証明書

certification n shōmei 証明

certified adj kōnin (no) 公認(の)
  certified public accountant (CPA) n kōnin-kaikéishi 公認会計士
  certified mail n kakitome yūbin 書留郵便

certify v shōmei shimásu (suru, shite) 証明します(する, して)

cervical adj shikyū-keibu (no) 子宮頸部(の)・子宮けい部(の)

cesarean n teiō-sekkai 帝王切開

cesspool n osui-dame 汚水溜め・汚水だめ, gesui-dame 下水溜め・下水だめ

Ceylon n Seiron セイロン = *Sri Lanka* Surivánka スリランカ

chafe v surimukimásu (surimuku, surimuite) すりむきます(すりむく, すりむいて)

chaff n momigara もみ殻・もみがら

chagrin n kuyashísa 悔しさ・くやしさ

chain n kusari 鎖・くさり, chēn チェーン; *(linked) in a ~* tsunagatte つながって
  chain smoker n chēn sumōkā チェーンスモーカー
  chain store n chēn-ten チェーン店, chēn sutoa チェーンストア
  chain mail n chēn mēru チェーンメール
  chain of islands rettō 列島

chair n isu 椅子・イス, koshi-káke 腰掛け

chair-lift n *(ski lift)* sukii rifuto スキーリフト

chairperson n kaichō 会長, gichō 議長

chalet n sharē シャレー, sansō 山荘

chalk n chōʹku チョーク *(piece of chalk; 1: íp-pon 一本, 2: ní-hon 二本, 3: sánbon 三本, how many nán-bon 何本)*

challenge 1. n chárenji チャレンジ, chōsen 挑戦 2. v *(tries)* idomimásu (idómu, idonde) 挑みます(挑む, 挑んで), chárenji shimásu (suru, shite) チャレンジします(する, して); *(tests)* tameshimásu (tamésu, tamédu) 試します(試す, 試して)

challenger n charenjā チャレンジャー, chōsen-sha 挑戦者

chamber 1. n *(room)* heya 部屋 2. n *(meeting hall)* kaigi-shitsu 会議室 3. n *(compartment in a firearm)* yakushitsu 薬室 4. n *(palace room)* ō-shitsu 王室 5. n *(legislative hall)* giin 議院 6. n *(legislative officer)* giin 議員 7. v *(enclose bullets)* tama o komemásu (komeru, komete) 弾をこめます(こめる, こめて)

chamber of commerce n shōkō kaigisho 商工会議所

chamber-pot n omaru おまる

chameleon n kamereon カメレオン

champagne n shanpán シャンパン, shanpén シャンペン

champion n yūshō-sha 優勝者, chanpion チャンピオン; *(sumo wrestler)* ōʹ-zeki 大関; *grand champion sumo wrestler* yokozuna 横綱

championship n senshu-ken 選手権, chanpion shippu チャンピオンシップ

chance n 1. *(opportunity)* kikái 機会, chánsu チャンス 2. *(impulse)* hazumi 弾み → **by chance**

chancellor n *(minister)* daijin 大臣

chandelier n shanderia シャンデリア

change 1. n *(small money)* kozeni 小銭, komakái (o)kane 細かい(お)金 2. n *(money returned)* o-tsuri お釣り・おつり, tsuri-sen 釣り銭 3. n hénka 変化; *(in health)* o-kawari お変わり; *(abnormality)* ijō 異常; *(of trains)* norikae 乗り換え; *(of clothing)* kigae 着替え 4. v *it changes* kawarimásu (kawaru, kawatte) 変わります(変わる, 変わって); hénka shimásu (suru, shite) 変化します(する, して); utsurimásu (utsúru, utsútte) 移ります(移る, 移って) 5. v *changes it* kaemásu (kaeru, kaete) 変えます(変える, 変えて); aratamemásu (aratáméru, aratámete) 改めます(改める, 改めて) 6. v *(clothes)* kigaemásu (kigáeru, kigáete) 着替えます(着替える, 着替えて) 7. v *(train, bus, plane)* nori-kaemásu (nori-káeru, nori-káete) 乗り換えます(乗り換える, 乗り換えて)

for a change adj kibun-tenkan (ni) 気分転換(に), ikinuki (ni) 息抜き(に)

changeable n kōi-shitsu 更衣室

channel n 1. *(for radio or television)* channeru チャンネル 2. kaikyō 海峡; suiro 水路

chant v utaimásu (utau, utatte) 歌い[謡い]ます(歌[謡]う, 歌[謡]って); *chanting Buddhist scriptures* shōmyō 声明; *chanting a Noh libretto* utai 謡

chaos n kaosu カオス, muchitsujo 無秩序, konton 混沌

chaotic adj muchitsujo (no) 無秩序(の), konton to shita 混沌とした

chap n 1. *(crack)* hibi ひび 2. *(capped skin)* akagire あかぎれ 3. *(fellow)* yatsu やつ

chapel n chaperu チャペル, reihai-dō 礼拝堂

chapter n *(book)* shō 章, chaputā チャプター

char v 1. *become charred* kogemásu (kogeru, kogete) 焦げます(焦げる, 焦げて) 2. *chars it*

kogashimásu (kogasu, kogashite) 焦がします
（焦がす，焦がして）

character *n* 1. (*quality*) seishítsu 性質
2. (*personal traits*) seikaku 性格, kosei 個性
3. (*written*) jí 字, móji 文字; *Chinese character*
kanji 漢字 **4.** (*part or role in a play or film*)
kyarakuta キャラクタ, kyarakutā キャラクター

characteristic *n* (*an earmark*) tokushoku
特色, (*a distinguishing characteristic*) tokuchō
特徴 **2.** *adj* (*typical*) daihyō-teki (na) 代表的
（な）; (*specific*) koyū (no) 固有（の）, tokuchō-teki
(na) 特徴的（な）

characterize *v* tokuchō zukemásu (zukeru,
zukete) 特徴づけます（づける，づけて）

charade *n* misekake 見せかけ

charcoal *n* sumí 炭・スミ, mokután 木炭
charcoal brazier *n* híbachi 火鉢

charge 1. *n* (*fee*) ryōkin 料金, daikin 代金, ... -ryō
... 料, ... -dai ... 代; (*with fee*) yūryō (no) 有料（の;
no charge muryō (no) 無料（の）, [INFORMAL] tada
(no) ただ（の）; *Is there a charge?* Yūryō désu ka.
有料ですか. **2.** *n in* ~ (*teacher*) tannin 担任; tantō
担当; *takes/accepts* (*is in*) ~ *of* ... o tannin/tantō
shimásu (suru, shite) ... を担任/担当します
（する・して）, uke-mochimásu (uke-mótsu, uke-
mótte) 受け持ちます（受け持つ，受け持って）;
takes (*is in*) *partial* ~ *of* ... o buntan shimásu (suru,
shite) ... を分担します（する・して） **3.** *n* (*an
attack*) shūgeki 襲撃 **4.** *v* seikyū shimásu (suru,
shite) 請求します（する・して） **5.** *v* (*attacks*)
shūgeki shimásu (suru, shite) 襲撃します（する，
して） **6.** *v* (*fill or furnish*) (*rechargeable public
transport card*) chāji shimásu (suru, shite) チャー
ジします（する・して）, (*cellphone*) jūden shimásu
(suru, shite) 充電します（する・して）

charisma *n* karisuma カリスマ

charitable *adj* jizen (no) 慈善（の）

charity *n* hodokoshi 施し, jizen 慈善, charitii
チャリティー; (*mercy*) megumi 恵み
charity concert *n* charitii konsáto チャリティー
コンサート

charm 1. *v* (.. o) uttori-sasemásu (uttori-saseru,
uttori-sasete) うっとりさせます（うっとりさ
せる，うっとりさせて） **2.** *n* (*good-luck piece*)
o-mamori お守り; (*attraction*) miryoku 魅力,
(*attractiveness*) aikyō´ あいきょう・愛敬・愛嬌

charming *adj* chāmingu チャーミング, miryoku-
teki na 魅力的な; *is* ~ miryoku/aikyō´ ga arimásu
(áru, átte) 魅力/あいきょう［愛嬌・愛敬］があり
ます（ある・あって）

chart *n* zuhyō 図表, zu 図, chāto チャート

charter *n* tokkyo jō 特許状, chātā チャーター

chartered *adj*
  chartered accountant *n* kōninkaikéishi 公認会
計士
  chartered plane *n* chātā´-ki チャーター機
  chartered bus *n* kashikiri-básu 貸し切りバス

chase *v* oi-kakemásu (oi-kakéru, oi-kákete)
追いかけます（追いかける・追いかけて）, oimásu

(ou, otte) 追います（追う・追って）, [FORMAL]
tsuisekishimásu (suru, shite) 追跡します（する・
して）

chasm *n* wareme 割れ目

chaste *adj* teisetsu (na) 貞節（な）, junsui (na)
純粋（な）

chastise *v* korashimemásu (korashimeru,
korashimete) 懲らしめます（懲らしめる・懲ら
しめて）

chastity *n* teisetsu 貞節, junketsu 純潔

chat 1. *n* oshaberi おしゃべり・お喋り, sekenbá-
nashi 世間話, muda-banashi 無駄話, zatsudan 雑
談 **2.** *v* oshaberi o shimásu (suru, shite) おしゃべ
り・お喋り（世間話/無駄話/雑談）をします（す
る，して）

chatter *v* shaberimásu (shabéru, shabétte) しゃべ
ります・喋ります（しゃべる，しゃべって）

chatterbox *n* o-shaberi おしゃべり・お喋り

chauffeur *n* okakae unténshu お抱え運転手

chauvinism *n* 1. (*aggressive patriotism*) kyōshin-
teki aikokushin 狂信的愛国心 **2.** (*sexism*) sei-
sabetsu shugi 性差別主義

cheap *adj* yasúi 安い; *cheaper by ¥100* hyakuén-
yasu 百円安

cheat *v* (*deceives*) damashimásu (damásu,
damashíte) だまします・騙します（だます, だま
して）, gomakashimásu (gomakásu, gomakáshite)
ごまかします（ごまかす, ごまかして）; (*dissembles,
shirks, tricks*) zúru o shimásu ずる［ズル］をし
ます; (*on one's spouse*) fūtei o hatarakimásu
(hataraku, hataraite)
不貞をはたらきます（はたらく, はたらいて）

cheating *n* kan'nin'gu カンニング

check 1. *n* (*bank*) kogítte 小切手, chékku チェッ
ク **2.** *n* (*chit*) fuda 札 **3.** *n* (*pays money at the
restaurant*) kanjó´ 勘定 (o-kanjō お勘定), denpyō
伝票, (o-)aisó, (o-)aisó （お）あいそ（う）・（お）愛想;
Check please! O-ikura désu ka. おいくらですか.
4. *v* ~ *it* (*baggage*) azukemásu (azukéru, azúkete)
預けます（預ける, 預けて） **5.** (*investigates*)
shirabemásu (shirabéru, shirábete) 調べます
（調べる, 調べて）, chékku shimásu (suru, shite)
チェックします（する, して）, (*inspects*) kénsa
shimásu (suru, shite) 検査します（する, して）,
(*compares*) terashimásu (terásu, teráshite) 照らし
ます（照らする, 照らして）

check in (*registers*) chekkúin shimásu (suru,
shite) チェックインします（する, して）

check out (*of hotel*) chekkuáuto shimásu (suru,
shite) チェックアウトします（する, して）

checkbook *n* (*bank*) kogítte chō 小切手帳

checking account *n* tōza-yókin 当座預金

checkpoint *n* kenmon-jo 検問所

check room *n* (*cloakroom*) kurō´ku クローク;
azukari-jo 預かり所

check-up *n* 1. kénsa 検査 **2.** (*medical checkup*)
kenkō shindan 健康診断

cheek *n* hō´ 頬・ほお, hoho 頬・ほほ, [INFORMAL]
hoppéta ほっぺた

cheekbone n hoho-bone, hō-bone 頬骨[ほほ骨，ほお骨]

cheeky adj namaiki (na) 生意気(な)

cheer n ōen 応援; **~ for** ōenshimásu (suru, shite) 応援します(する，して)

cheerful adj (in a good mood) kigen ga íi 機嫌がいい, (full of energy) genki ga ii 元気がいい, (merry, blitheful) hogáraka (na) 朗らか・ほがらか (な), yōki (na) 陽気(な)

cheerleader n (female) chia gāru チアガール

cheerless adj genki ga nai 元気がない

Cheers interj **1.** (See you later) mata (ne) また (ね) **2.** (toast) kanpai! 乾杯!

cheese n chíizu チーズ

cheesecloth n kanreisha 寒冷紗

chef n shefu シェフ, ryōri chō 料理長, (chef of Japanese food) itamae(-san) 板前(さん)

chemicals n kagaku-séihin 化学製品; (pharmaceuticals) yakuhin 薬品, kagaku-yakuhin 化学薬品

chemist n **1.** kágaku-sha 化学者 **2.** (pharmacist) yakuzai-shi 薬剤師

chemistry n kágaku 化学, bakegaku 化学

chemotherapy n kagaku ryōhō 化学療法

cherish v daiji ni shimásu (suru, shite) 大事にします(する，して), [FORMAL] chō´hō shimásu (suru, shite) 重宝します(する，して), chōhō-garimásu (chōhō-gáru, chōhō-gátte) 重宝がります(重宝がる，重宝がって)

cherry n (tree) sakura no ki 桜の木; (fruit) sakuranbo サクランボ・桜んぼ

cherry blossoms n sakura (no haná) 桜(の花)

cherry tree n sakura no ki 桜の木

chess n **1.** chesu チェス **2.** (Japanese chess) shōgi 将棋

chessboard n (Japanese chess) shōgi-ban 将棋盤

chest n **1.** (of body) muné 胸 **2.** (box) hako 箱; (drawers) tansu たんす・タンス

chestnut 1. n kurí 栗・クリ; **roasted chestnut** yaki-guri 焼き栗 **2.** adj (color) kuri iro (no) 栗色(の)

chew v kamimásu (kámu, kánde) 噛みます・かみます(噛む，噛んで); **~ the fat** (idly talk) daberimásu (dabéru, dabétte) だべります・駄弁ります(だべる，だべって)

chewing gum n gamu ガム, chūingamu チューインガム

chiao-tze n (jiaozi) gyōza 餃子・ギョーザ

chic adj shikku (na) シック(な), iki (na) 粋(な), jōhin (na) 上品(な)

chicken n tori 鶏・トリ, niwatori 鶏・ニワトリ; **chicken** (etc.) **dipped into hot broth** mizutaki 水炊き; **skewered grilled chicken** yaki-tori 焼き鳥・やきとり, (shop) yakitori-ya 焼き鳥屋

chide v tashinamemásu (tashinameru, tashinamete) たしなめます(たしなめる，たしなめて), shikarimásu (shikaru, shikatte) 叱ります(叱る，叱って)

chief 1. n (head) chō 長, chōkan 長官, chiifu チーフ, (ringleader) óyá-bun 親分 **2.** adj (main) shuyō (na) 主要(な), ómo na 主な, hon-... 本...

chiefly adv moppara 専ら・もっぱら, ómo ni 主に

chieftain n **1.** (of a group) shuchō 首長 **2.** (of a clan or a tribe) zokuchō 族長

child n kodomo 子供・こども・子ども, ko 子, (elementary school student) jídō 児童; **your child** o-ko-san/sama お子さん/さま・様

childhood n kodomo no tokí 子供の時, kodomo no koro 子供の頃, kodomo jidai 子供時代

childish adj osanái 幼い; yōchi (na) 幼稚(な); kodomoppoi 子供っぽい

childlike adj kodomo rashii 子供らしい; junshin (na) 純真(な)

children n kodomó-tachi 子供たち; **Children's Day** (5 May) Kodomo no hí こどもの日・子供の日

chili n chiri チリ

chili pepper n chiri peppā チリペッパー, tōgarashi トウガラシ・唐辛子

chili powder n chiri paudā チリパウダー

chill v **~ it** hiyashimásu (hiyásu, hiyáshite) 冷やします(冷やす，冷やして)

chilled wheat-flour noodles n hiyamúgi ヒヤムギ・冷麦

chilly adj samúi 寒い, hieru 冷える

chime n chaimu チャイム

chimney n entotsu 煙突・えんとつ

chimpanzee n chinpanjii チンパンジー

chin n agó あご・顎

China n Chū´goku 中国

China dress n Chaina doresu チャイナドレス

Chinatown n Chaina taun チャイナタウン

china (ware) n (porcelain) setomono 瀬戸物

Chinese n (language) Chugoku-go 中国語; (person) Chugokú-jin 中国人

Chinese;

Chinese cabbage n (bok choi) hakusai 白菜・ハクサイ

Chinese character n kanji 漢字, jí 字

Chinese cooking n chūka-ryō´ri 中華料理

Chinese egg rolls n haru-maki 春巻・ハルマキ

Chinese fried noodles n yakisoba 焼きそば

Chinese fried rice n chā´han チャーハン

Chinese meatballs n niku-dángo 肉団子

Chinese noodles n (with soup) rā´men ラーメン, chūkamen 中華麺; (with tidbits) gomoku-sóba 五目そば

Chinese pickles n zāsai ザーサイ

Chinese restaurant n chūka-ryórí-ten 中華料理店, Chūka resutoran 中華レストラン

Chinese word/vocabulary (in Japanese) n kango 漢語

chip n (of wood) kóppá 木っ端; (crack) kizu 傷; (electronic engineering) chippu チップ

chips n (potato chip) poteto chíppusu ポテトチップス

chirp n saezuri さえずり

chisel n nómi ノミ

chives n asátsūki アサツキ・浅葱

chlorine n énso 塩素

chocolate n choko(rē´to) チョコ（レート）
   chocolate bar n ita-choko板チョコ
   chocolate milk n míruku-kokoa ミルクココア

choice 1. n (*selection*) sentaku 選択 2. adj (*best-quality*) jōtō (na) 上等（な）

choir n 1. (*chorus group*) gasshō-dan 合唱団
   2. (*chorus group in church*) seika-tai 聖歌隊

choke v 1. (*he chokes*) íki ga tsumarimásu (tsumaru, tsumátte) 息がつまります・詰まります（詰まる、詰まって）2. (*chokes him*) ... no íki o tomemásu (tomeru, tomete) ... の息を止めます（止める、止めて）

cholera n kórera コレラ

cholesterol n koresuterōru コレステロール

choose v 1. [INFORMAL] erabimásu (erábu, eránde) えらびます・選びます（選ぶ、選んで）; [FORMAL] sentaku shimásu (suru, shite) 選択します（する、して）2. (*decides on*) ... ni shimásu (suru, shite) ... にします（する、して）

choosy adj yorigónomi ga hageshíi より好みがはげしい・激しい, yorigónomi o shimásu (suru, shite) より好みをします（する、して）

chop 1. v (*chops it*) kizamimásu (kizamu, kizande) 刻みます（刻む、刻んで）; (*fire wood*) (takigi o) warimásu (waru, watte) 薪を割ります（割る、割って）2. n (*signature seal*) hankó はんこ、hánhan・判

chopped meat n hiki-niku 挽き肉・ひき肉

chopping board n manaita まないた

choppy adj (*having many waves*) nami no arai 波の荒い

chopstick rest n hashí-óki 箸置き・はし置き

chopsticks n (o-)háshi（お）はし・箸; (*throw-away*) wari-bashi 割り箸・わりばし（1 pair ichízen 一膳）

chorale n 1. (*choir*) gasshō tai 合唱隊 2. (*chorus*) gasshō-kyoku 合唱曲

chord n 1. (*music*) waon 和音; (*guitar chord*) kōdo コード 2. (*emotion*) kokoro no kinsen 心の琴線

chore n zatsuyō 雑用

choreography n furitsuke 振り付け

chorus n kō´rasu コーラス, (*music sang by a group*) gasshō-kyoku 合唱曲, (*group of singers*) gasshō-dan 合唱団

chow → **food**

chowder n chaudā チャウダー, (*Japanese style*) yose-nabe 寄せなべ・寄せ鍋

chow mein n yaki-soba 焼きそば

Christ n Kirisuto キリスト

Christian 1. adj Kirisuto-kyō no ... キリスト教の... 2. n (Kirisuto-kyō no) shínjá （キリスト教の）信者

Christianity n Kirisuto-kyō キリスト教

Christian name n senrei mei 洗礼名, kurisuchan nēmu クリスチャンネーム

Christmas n Kurísúmasu クリスマス
   Christmas card n kurisumasu kādo クリスマスカード
   Christmas Eve n kurisumasu ibu クリスマスイブ
   Christmas present n kurisumasu purezcnto クリスマスプレゼント
   Christmas tree n kurisumasu tsurii クリスマスツリー

chromosome n senshokutai 染色体

chronic adj mansei (no) 慢性（の）

chronicle n nendai-ki 年代記

chronological adj nendai-jun (no) 年代順（の）

chrysalis n sanagi さなぎ・蛹

chrysanthemum n kikú 菊・キク; (*tasty leaves*) *garland chrysanthemum* shungiku 春菊・シュンギク

chubby adj fukkurashita ふっくらした, futome (no) 太めの

chuck v 1. (*throws*) nagemásu (nageru, nagete) 投げます（投げる、投げて）2. (*tosses*) hōrimásu (hōru, hōtte) 放ります（放る、放って）

church n kyōkai 教会

cider n (*fizzy lemon soda*) sáidā サイダー, ringo shu リンゴ酒

cigar n shígā シガー, ha-maki 葉巻
   cigar shop/store n tabako-ya たばこ屋

cigarette n tabako たばこ・タバコ・煙草, maki-tábako 巻きたばこ, shígarétto シガレット（1: íppon 一本, 2: ní-hon 二本, 3: sánbon 三本, *how many* nán-bon 何本; (*packs*) 1: hitó-hako 一箱, 2: futá-hako 二箱, 3: mí-hako, san-pako 三箱, *how many packs* nán-pako 何箱）
   cigarette/cigar butt n suigara 吸い殻
   cigarette case n tabakó-ire たばこ入れ
   cigarette holder n páipu パイプ, sui-kuchi 吸い口
   cigarette lighter n raitā ライター

cinch n (*an easy thing to do*) wáke mo nái (kotó) わけもない（こと）

cinder(s) n moegara 燃えがら

cinema → **movies**

cinnamon n shinamon シナモン

cipher n 1. (*zero*) zero ゼロ・零 2. (*secret code*) angō 暗号

circle 1. n maru 丸, én 円, (*ring*) wá 輪, (*orbit*) kidō 軌道; *traffic circle* rō´tarii ロータリー 2. v maru/en de kakomimásu (kakomu, kakonde) 丸/円で囲みます（囲む、囲んで）

circular adj kanjō (no) 環状（の）

circulate v (*it circulates*) mawarimásu (mawaru, mawatte) 回ります（回る、回って）; (*circulates it*) mawashimásu (mawasu, mawashite) 回します（回す、回して）

circulation n (*cycle*) junkan 循環; (*of money*) ryūtsū 流通

circumference n shū´í 周囲, shūhen 周辺, enshū 円周

circumstance *n* **1.** ba(w)ai 場合; kotó 事・こと, ... wáke ... 訳・わけ, ... tokoró ... 所・ところ **2.** jijō 事情, jōtai 状態, jōkyō 状況; yóshi 由・よし, ... shidai ... 次第・しだい **3.** yōsu 様子・ようす **4.** (*convenience*) tsugō 都合 (go-tsugō ご都合)

circumstances *n* (*details*) ikisatsu いきさつ・経緯

circus *n* sá′kasu サーカス

cistern *n* suisō 水槽, chosui tanku 貯水タンク

citation *n* inyō bun 引用文

cite *v* **1.** (*quotes*) inyō shimásu (suru, shite) 引用します (します, して) **2.** (*refers*) genkyū shimásu (suru, shite) 言及します (します, して)

citizen *n* shímin 市民; (*national*) kokumin 国民

citizenship *n* shimin-ken 市民権

citron *n* yúzu ユズ・柚; ***citron bath*** ユズ湯

citrus *n* kankitsu-rui かんきつ類・柑橘類・カンキツ類

city **1.** *n* shí 市, (*town*) machí 町, (*metropolis*) tóshi 都市, tokai 都会 (*dweller*) tokái-jin 都会人
   city office *n* shi-yákusho 市役所
   city council *n* shi-gikai 市議会
2. *adj.* (*within the city*) shí-nai (no) 市内(の)

civilian *n* minkan no hito 民間の人, minkan-jin 民間人

civilian clothes *n* shifuku 私服, heijō-fuku 平常服

civility *n* reigi tadashisa 礼儀正しさ

civilization *n* bummei 文明, (*culture*) búnka 文化

civilize *v* **1.** bunmei-ka shimásu (suru, shite) 文明化します (する, して) **2.** senren shimásu (suru, shite) 洗練します (する, して)

claim **1.** *n* (*demands*) yōkyū/seikyū 要求/請求, suru, shite) 要求/請求 (します; する, して) **2.** *v* (*maintains*) shuchō shimásu (suru, shite) 主張します (する, して), tonaemásu (tonáéru, tonáete) 唱えます (唱える, 唱えて)

clairvoyant **1.** *n* senrigan 千里眼 **2.** *adj* senrigan (no) 千里眼(の)

clam *n* hamáguri ハマグリ・蛤; ***short-necked clam*** asari アサリ・浅蜊; ***blood(y) clam*** aká-gai 赤貝・アカガイ

clamber *v* yojinoborimásu (yojinoboru, yojinobotte) よじ登ります (よじ登る, よじ登って)

clamor **1.** *n* (*a clamor*) sáwagi 騒ぎ, kensō 喧騒; **2.** *v* (*makes a clamor*) sawagimásu (sawágu, sawáide) 騒ぎます・さわぎます (騒ぐ, 騒いで)

clamorous *adj* sōzōshii 騒々しい

clamp **1.** *n* (*a piece of metal for fastening*) tomegane 留め金 **2.** *v* (*fastens or fixes*) koteishimásu (suru, shite) 固定します (する, して)

clan *n* ichizoku 一族, ikka 一家 (*historically, a social grouping affiliated through blood and allegiance relationships*)

clandestine *adj* himitsu (no) 秘密(の)

clang **1.** *n* gachan ガチャン **2.** *v* (*rings loudly*) (gachan to) narashimásu (narasu, narashite) (ガチャンと) 鳴らします (鳴らす, 鳴らして)

3. *v* (*sounds*) narimásu (naru, natte) 鳴ります (鳴る, 鳴って)

clannish *adj* haitateki (na) 排他的(な)

clap (*one's hands*) *v* té o tatakimásu (tatáku, tatáite) 手を叩きます (叩く, 叩いて), hákushu shimásu (suru, shite) 拍手します (する, して)

clarification *n* setsumei 説明

clarify *v* **1.** (*makes clear*) akiraka ni shimásu (suru, shite) あきらか[明らか]にします (する, して) **2.** (*becomes clear*) akiraka ni narimásu (naru, natte) あきらか[明らか]になります (なる, なって), hakkiri shimásu (suru, shite) はっきりします (する, して)

clarinet *n* kurarinetto クラリネット

clarity *n* **1.** (*transparency*) tōmei do 透明度 **2.** seichō sa 清澄さ **3.** meiryō sa 明瞭さ

clasp (*one's hands*) *v* (té o) kumimásu (kúmu, kúnde) (手を) 組みます (組む, 組んで)

class **1.** kúrasu クラス, kyū′ 級, (*in school*) gakkyū 学級
   class instruction *n* júgyō 授業, kōshū 講習 **2.** kaikyū 階級; **the middle ~** chūryū kaikyū 中流階級
   classmate *n* dōkyū′-sei 同級生, (*former classmate*) dōki-sei 同期生
   class reunion *n* dōsō′-kai 同窓会
   classroom *n* kyōshitsu 教室; **classroom teaching** júgyō 授業

classic *n* kurashikku クラシック, koten 古典

classical *adj* koten (no) 古典(の)
   classical music *n* kurashikku ongaku クラシック音楽, koten ongaku 古典音楽
   classical literature *n* koten bungaku 古典文学, (*Japanese*) kobun 古文

clatter *v* gátagata shimásu (suru, shite) がたがたします (する, して)

claw *n* tsume 爪・ツメ; (*of crab*) hasamí ハサミ; (*animal*) kagitsume 鉤爪(かぎづめ)

claw hammer *n* kugi-nuki 釘抜き

clay *n* néndo 粘土

clean **1.** *adj* kírei (na) きれい[綺麗](な), seiketsu (na) 清潔(な); (*fresh*) sappári shita さっぱりした **2.** *v* (*cleans it up*) kírei ni shimásu (suru, shite) きれい[綺麗]にします (する, して), (*tidies*) katazukemásu (katazukéru, katazúkete) 片付けます・かたづけます (片付ける, 片付けて), (*sweeps*) sōji shimásu (suru, shite) 掃除します (する, して)

cleaner *n* seiso-in 清掃員; cleaners *n* kuriininigu-ya クリーニング屋

cleaning *n* (*dry*) (dorai-) kuríningu (ドライ) クリーニング; (*sweeping up*) sōji 掃除・そうじ (o-sō′ji お掃除)

clear **1.** *adj* (*bright*) akarui 明るい; (*sunny*) hárete imásu 晴れています, harete ... 晴れた ...; (*transparent*) tōmei (na) 透明(な) **2.** *adj* (*evident*) akíraka (na) 明らか(な), (*obvious, explicit*) meihaku (na) 明白(な); (*understood*) wakátte imásu 分かっています, wakátta 分かった... **3.** *adj* (*easy to see*) miyasúi 見やすい; (*easy to*

understand) wakari-yasúi 分かりやすい
4. *adj* (*unimpeded*) jama ga nái じゃま[邪魔]が
ない **5.** *v* (*takes away from the table*) sagemásu
(sagéru, ságete) 下げます(下げる, 下げて)
6. gets ~ (*empty*) sukimásu (suku, suite) すきます・
空きます(すく, すいて) **7. becomes ~** (*evident*)
shiremásu (shireru, shirete) 知れます(知れる,
知れて)

clearly *adv* (*distinctly*) hakkíri はっきり;
(*obviously, explicitly*) meihaku ni 明白に

clear soup *n* sui-mono 吸い物, (o-)tsúyu (お)つ
ゆ・汁

clear weather *n* haré 晴れ

cleaver *n* hochō 包丁; *meat cleaver* nikukiri-
bō´chō 肉切り包丁

clerk *n* (*in shop*) ten'in 店員; (*in office*) jimú-in
事務員; (*in bank*) ginkō´-in 銀行員

clever *adj* rikō (na) 利口・りこう(な); (*nimble
with fingers*) kíyō (na) 器用(な); (*skilled*) jōzú
(na) じょうず・上手(な)

cliff *n* gake がけ・崖

climate *n* kikō 気候

climax *n* yamá 山, chō´ten 頂点; (*upshot*)
ketsumatsu 結末; shímatsu 始末

climb *v* noborimásu (noboru, nobotte) 登ります
(登る, 登って)

clinic *n* byōin 病院

clinch *n* (*boxing*) kurinchi クリンチ

cling *v* kuttsukimásu (kuttsuku, kuttsuite) くっつ
きます(くっつく, くっついて), shigamitsukimásu
(shigamitsuku, shigamitsuite) しがみつきます(し
がみつく, しがみついて)

clip 1. *clips it* *v* tsumimásu (tsumu, tsunde) 摘み
ます(摘む, 摘んで), kirimásu (kíru, kitté) 切り
ます(切る, 切って) **2.** *n* kuríppu クリップ →
paperclip

clippers *n* hasami はさみ・鋏; (*nail*) tsumekíri
爪切り; (*barber's*) barikan バリカン

clipping *n* (*from newspaper, etc.*) kirinuki 切り
抜き

clique *n* renchū 連中, habatsu 派閥

cloak *n* mánto マント
  cloakroom *n* kurō´ku クローク, (*tenimotsu*) azu-
karijo (手荷物)預かり所

clock *n* tokei 時計; *alarm clock* mezamashi dokei
目覚まし時計; *around the clock* nijūyojikan 24時
間, ichinichi-jū 一日中

clockspring *n* zemmai ぜんまい

clockwise *adv* migi-máwari (ni) 右回り(に)

clogged; *gets ~ (up)* fusagarimásu (fusagáru, fusagátte) ふさがります(ふさがる, ふさがって)

clogs 1. *n* (*wooden shoes*) getá げた・下駄
  2. *v* (*it clogs up, gets clogged*) tsumarimásu
(tsumáru, tsumátte) 詰まります(詰まる, 詰まっ
て), tsukaemásu (tsukáéru, tsukáete) つかえます
(つかえる, つかえて)

cloisonné *n* shippō-yaki 七宝焼

close 1. *v closes it* (*shuts*) shimemásu (shiméru,
shímete) 閉めます(閉める, 閉めて), (*a book, etc.*)

tojimásu (tojiru, tójite) 閉じます(閉じる, 閉じて);
~ one's eyes mé o tsuburimásu (tsuburu, tsubutte)
目をつぶります(つぶる, つぶって);
(*obstructs*) fusagimásu (fusagu, fusaide) ふさぎま
す(ふさぐ, ふさいで); (*ends*) owarimásu (owaru,
owatte) 終わります(終わる, 終わって) **2. *it closes***
shimarimásu (shimáru, shimátte) 閉まります(閉ま
る, 閉まって) → **end 3.** *adj* (*near*) chikái 近い; **~
by** sóba (no) そば(の) (o-soba (no) おそば(の));
(*intimate*) missetsu (na) 密接(な) **4.** *adj* (*humid*)
mushi-atsúi 蒸し暑い **5.** *n* (*the end*) owari 終わり,
sue 末, matsu 末

closely *adv* pittári (to) ぴったり・ピッタリ(と)

closet *n* (*Japanese*) oshi-ire 押し入れ, nándo
納戸; (*Western*) kurōzetto クローゼット

clot 1. *n* (*a clot*) katamari 固まり・塊・かたまり;
(*it clots*) **2.** *v* katamarimásu (katamaru, katamatte)
固まります(固まる, 固まって)

cloth *n* ori-mono 織物, kíji 生地, nuno 布; (*a piece
of*) kiré 切れ, nuno-gire 布切れ; (*dustcloth*) zōkin
ぞうきん・雑巾; (*dishcloth*) fukín ふきん・布巾;
(*traditional wrapper*) furoshiki ふろしき・風呂敷

clothes *n* fukú 服, fukusō 服装; (*Western*) yō-fuku
洋服・(*Japanese traditional style*) kimono 着物,
wafuku 和服
  clothes moth *n* íga いが, shimi 衣魚・しみ

clothesbag *n* (*for laundry*) sentakumono-ire
洗濯物入れ

clothesbrush *n* yō-fuku-búrashi 洋服ブラシ

clothesline *n* monohoshi-zuna 物干し綱

clothing shop *n* yōfuku-ya 洋服屋

cloud *n* kúmo 雲

cloudburst *n* gōu 豪雨

cloudiness *n* kumori 曇り・くもり

cloudy; *gets ~* kumorimásu (kumóru, kumótte)
曇ります・くもります(曇る, 曇って); *cloudy
weather* kumorí 曇り・くもり

clover *n* kurōba¯ クローバー; *four-leaf clover*
yotsuba no kurōbā 四つ葉のクローバー

cloves *n* chō´ji 丁字・チョウジ, kurōbu クローブ

clown *n* dōke-shi 道化師

club *n* **1.** (*group; card suit*) kúrabu クラブ
  2. (*stick*) konbō 棍棒・こん棒; (*golf*) (gorufu)
kurabu (ゴルフ)クラブ

clue *n* tegákari 手掛かり, itóguchi 糸口

clump *n* katamari 塊・かたまり

clumsy *adj* hetá (na) へた[下手]な, bu-kíyō (na)
不器用(な); gikochi-nái ぎこちない

cluster → bunch

clutch 1. *v* (*grasps*) nigirimásu (nigiru, nigitte)
握ります(握る, 握って), tsukamimásu (tsukámu,
tsukánde) つかみます(つかむ, つかんで)
  2. *n* (*of car*) kurátchi クラッチ, (*pedal*) kuratchí-
pédaru クラッチペダル

CM → commercial (*message*)

coach 1. *v* (*coaches them*) shidō shimásu (suru,
shite) 指導します(する, して) **2.** *n* (*director*)
shidō´-sha 指導者; (*sports*) kō´chi コーチ
3. *n* (*railroad*) kyakusha 客車

coach station *n* (*depot*) basu no hatchaku-jō バスの発着場

coal *n* sekitán 石炭
  coal mine *n* tankō 炭鉱

coarse *adj* arai 粗い[荒い]; sómatsu (na) 粗末(な); zatsu-... 雑...

coast *n* engan 沿岸, kaigan 海岸

coat *n* uwagi 上着, kō´to コート; (*overcoat*) gaitō 外套, ō´bā オーバー; (*traditional Japanese*) haori 羽織

coax *v* odatemásu (odateru, odatete) おだてます (おだてる, おだてて)

cobweb *n* kúmo no su クモの巣; kúmo no íto クモの糸

cocaine *n* kokáin コカイン

cock *n* ondori オンドリ・雄鶏

cockle *n* torí-gai トリガイ[貝]

cockpit *n* kokkupitto コックピット, sōjū-seki 操縦席, sōjū-shitsu 操縦室

cockroach *n* gokiburi ゴキブリ

cocktail (party) *n* kákuteru (pātii) カクテル(パーティー)

cocky *adj* unuboreta うぬぼれた, namaiki (na) 生意気(な)

cocoa *n* kókóa ココア

coconut *n* kókonáttsu ココナッツ
  coconut palm *n* yáshi ヤシ・椰子

cocoon *n* máyu マユ・繭

C.O.D. (*collect on delivery*) *n* daikin hiki-kae (de) 代金引き換え(で)

cod *n* (*fish*) tára タラ・鱈
  cod roe *n* tarako タラコ

code *n* kō´do コード; (*secret*) angō 暗号

co-ed *n* jo (-shi) gákusei 女(子)学生

coeducation *n* dánjo kyōgaku 男女共学

co-existence *n* kyōson 共存, kyōzon 共存

coffee *n* kōhíi コーヒー
  coffee cup *n* kōhii-káppu/jáwan コーヒーカップ/茶碗
  coffee pot *n* kōhii-pótto コーヒーポット

coffee machine *n* **1.** kōhii-mēkā コーヒーメーカー **2.** *n* (*vending machine*) kōhii-jidōhanbaiki/jihanki コーヒー自動販売機/自販機

coffee shop/house *n* kōhii-ten コーヒー店, kissa-ten 喫茶店

coffin *n* hitsugi 棺・ひつぎ

cog *n* (*wheel*) ha-gúruma 歯車

coherence *n* (shubi) ikkan-sei 首尾一貫性

coherent *adj* (shubi) ikkan shita 首尾一貫した

cohesion *n* danketsu 団結, ketsugō 結合

coil *n* koiru コイル

coin *n* kō´ka 硬貨, kóin コイン; (*brass or copper*) dō´ka 銅貨; (*¥10*) jū-en-dama 十円玉; (*¥100*) hyaku-en-dama 百円玉; *tosses a coin* kōka/koin o nagete ura-omote de kimemásu (kimeru, kimete) 硬貨/コインを投げて裏表で決めます(決める, 決めて)
  coin locker *n* koin-rókkā コインロッカー

coincidence *n* gūzen 偶然

coincidental *adj* gūzen itchi shita 偶然一致した

coincidentally *adv* gūzen 偶然, gūzen itchi shite 偶然一致して

coitus *n* seikō 性交

cola *n* kō´ra コーラ

colander *n* mizu-kírí 水切り; (*bamboo*) zarú ざる

cold 1. *adj* samúi 寒い; (*to touch*) tsumetái 冷たい; *gets ~* sámuku/tsumetáku narimásu (náru, nátte) 寒く/冷たくなります(なる, なって); samemásu (saméru, sámete) 冷めます(冷める, 冷めて); hiemásu (hiéru, híete) 冷えます(冷える, 冷えて) **2.** *n* kaze かぜ[風邪]; *catches a ~* kaze o hikimásu (hiku, hiite) かぜ[風邪]をひきます(ひく, ひいて), [HONORIFIC] kaze o omeshi ni narimásu (náru, nátte) かぜ[風邪]をお召しになります(なる, なって)
  cold medicine *n* kaze-gúsuri かぜ[風邪]薬

cold-blooded *adj* reiketsu (no) 冷血(の), reikoku (na) 冷酷(な), chi mo namida mo nai 血も涙もない

coldhearted *adj* turenái つれない

coldness *n* tsumetasa 冷たさ, samusa 寒さ

cold water *n* mizu 水, (o-)híya (お)冷や

coleslaw *n* kōru-surō コールスロー, kyabetsu-sárada キャベツサラダ

colic *n* sentsū 疝痛

collaborate *v* **1.** (*cooperates*) kyōryokushimásu (suru, shite) 協力します(する, して) **2.** (*works collaboratively*) kyōdōsagyōshimásu (suru, shite) 共同作業します(する, して)

collaboration *n* kyōryoku 協力

collapse *v* taoremásu (taoréru, taórete) 倒れます(倒れる, 倒れて); (*gets smashed*) tsuburemásu (tsubureru, tsuburete) つぶれます・潰れます(つぶれる, つぶれて)

collar *n* **1.** (*of coat*) kárā カラー, erí えり・襟 **2.** (*of dog*) kubi-wa 首輪

collarbone *n* sakotsu 鎖骨

collate *v* (*compares*) terashimásu (terásu, terá-shite) 照らします(照らす, 照らして), terashi-awasémásu (terashi-awaséru, terashi-awaséte) 照らし合わせます(照らし合わせる, 照らし合わせて)

collateral *n* tanpo 担保

colleague *n* **1.** (*professional colleague*) (shokuba no) dōryō (職場の)同僚 **2.** (*academic colleague*) gakuyū 学友

collect *v* **1.** *collects them* atsumemásu (atsuméru, atsúmete) 集めます(集める, 集めて), yosemásu (yoseru, yosete) 寄せます・よせます(寄せる, 寄せて), (*completes a set*) soroemásu (soroéru, soróete) そろえます・そろえます(揃える, 揃えて); (*gathers up*) shūshū shimásu (suru, shite) 収集します(する, して); (*recruits*) boshū shimásu (suru, shite) 募集します(する, して); (*reaps, brings in*) osamemásu (osaméru, osámete) 納めます(納める, 納めて), (*levies taxes etc.*) chōshū shimásu (suru, shite) 徴収します(する, して); *~ tickets* shūsatsu shimásu (suru, shite) 集札します(する, して) **2.** *they collect* (*come together*) atsumarimásu (atsumáru, atsumátte) 集まります(集まる, 集まって)

collect call *n* korekuto kōru コレクトコール

collect (*on delivery*), **C.O.D.** *adv* daikin hiki-kae (de) 代金引き換え(で) , dai-biki (de) 代引き(で), chakubarai (de) 着払い(で)

collection *n* 1. (*of books*) zōsho 蔵書, korekushon コレクション 2. (*of taxes etc.*) chōshū 徴収

collector *n* shūshū-ka 収集家, korekutā コレクター

college *n* daigaku 大学; karejji カレッジ; *in ~* zaigaku(-chū) 在学(中)

college student *n* daigáku-sei 大学生

collide *v* shototsu shimásu (suru, shite) 衝突します(する, して)

collision *n* shōtotsu 衝突

colloquial 1. *n* (*language, word*) kōgo 口語 2. *adj* kōgo-teki (na) 口語的(な)

collusion; *in ~ with* ... to takuránde ... と企んで

colonel *n* taisa 大佐

colony *n* shokumín-chi 植民地

color *n* iró 色, kárā カラー; *what ~* nani-iro (no) 何色(の), dónna iró (no) どんな色(の)

color-blind *adj* 1. (*ophthalmology*) shikikaku ijō (no) 色覚異常(の) 2. (*nonracialism*) jinshusabetsu o shinai 人種差別をしない

colored paper *n* irógami 色紙

colorful *adj* (*bright*) hanáyaka (na) 華やか(な), karafuru (na) カラフル(な)

colorless *adj* 1. (*without color*) mushoku (no) 無色(の) 2. (*lacking animation*) seiki no nai 生気のない 3. (*insipid*) tsumaranai つまらない

colossal *adj* kyodai (na) 巨大(な)

colt *n* (*young male horse*) osu no ko-uma 雄の子馬

column 1. *n* rán 欄, koramu コラム; (*page column*) dán 段; (*numerical column*) keta けた・桁 2. → **pillar**

columnist *n* koramunisuto コラムニスト

coma *n* konsui 昏睡

comb 1. *n* kushí くし・櫛 2. *v* (*the hair*) kamí o sukimásu (suku, suite) 髪をすきます(すく, すいて), tokimásu (tóku, tóite) ときます・梳きます(とく, といて), tokashimásu (tokásu, tokáshite) とかします・梳かします(とかす, とかして)

combat *n* sentō 戦闘

combatant *n* sentō-in 戦闘員

combination *n* 1. kumi-awase 組み合わせ, konbinēshon コンビネーション 2. (*union*) gappei 合併, gōdō 合同

combine 1. *v* (*combines them*) kumi-awasemásu (kumi-awaseru, kumi-awasete) 組み合わせます(組み合わせる, 組み合わせて), awasemásu (awaséru, awásete) 合わせます(合わせる, 合わせて); (*dually serves as*) kanemásu (kanéru, kánete) 兼ねます(兼ねる, 兼ねて) 2. *v* (*they unite*) gappei/gōdō shimásu (suru, shite) 合併/合同します(する, して)

combined *adj* gōdō no ... 合同の...

combustion *n* 1. (*burning*) nenshō 燃焼

2. (*oxidation*) sanka 酸化 3. (*tumult*) sawagi 騒ぎ・さわぎ 4. (*agitation*) dōyō 動揺

come *v* kimásu (kúru, kité) 来ます(来る, 来て); (*I/we come to you*) ikimásu (iku, itte) 行きます(行く, 行って)

come about shō-jimásu (shō-jiru, shō-jite) 生じます(生じる, 生じて); genjitsu-ka shimásu (suru, shite) 現実化します(する, して)

come along yatte-kimásu (yatte-kúru, yatte-kíte) やってきます(くる, きて)

come back itte kimásu (kúru, kíte) 行ってきます(くる, きて); kaerimásu (káeru, káette) 帰ります(帰る, 帰って)

come down kudarimásu (kudaru, kudatte) 下ります・おります(下る, 下って); (*on the price*) makemásu (makeru, makete) 負けます(負ける, 負けて)

come in hairimásu (háiru, háitte) 入ります(入る, 入って), háitte kimásu (kúru, kíté) 入ってきます(くる, きて)

come near yorimásu (yoru, yotte) 寄ります・よります(寄る, 寄って), chika-zukimásu (chika-zúku, chika-zúite) 近づきます(近づく, 近づいて)

come off (*button, etc.*) toremásu (toréru, tótte) 取れます・とれます(取れる, 取れて); nukemásu (nukeru, nukete) 抜けます(抜ける, 抜けて); hazuremásu (hazureru, hazurete) 外れます・はずれます(外れる, 外れて)

come on, ...! (*urging an invitation*) sā´ さあ, hora ほら

come out demásu (déru, déte) 出ます(出る, 出て), déte kimásu (kúru, kíté) 出てきます(くる, きて); (*appears*) arawaremásu (arawaréru, arawárete) 現れます(現れる, 現れて); (*photographs*) utsurimásu (utsúru, utsútte) 写ります(写る, 写って)

come to (*reaches*) ni itarimásu (itaru, itatte) ...に至ります・いたります(至る, 至って)

come to an end sumimásu (súmu, súnde) 済みます・すみます(済む, 済んで), owarimásu (owaru, owatte) 終わります(終わる, 終わって), tsukimásu (tsukiru, tsukíte) 尽きます・つきます(尽きる, 尽きて)

come to the end of (*a street*) tsuki-atarimásu (tsuki-ataru, tsuki-atatte) 突き当たります・つきあたります(突き当たる, 突き当たって)

come what may nán to itté mo なんと言っても

comedy *n* kígeki 喜劇, komedii コメディ

comely *n* 1. (*pleasing in appearance*) yōshi no ii 容姿のいい, kiryō no yoi 器量の良い 2. (*attractive*) miryoku-teki (na) 魅力的(な)

comet *n* hōkí-boshi ほうき星, suisei 彗星・すい星

comfort 1. *n* anraku 安楽, kiraku 気楽 2. *n* (*consolation*) nagusame 慰め, ian 慰安 3. *v* (*consoles*) nagusamemásu (nagusameru, nagusamete) 慰めます(慰める, 慰めて)

comfortable 1. *adj* rakú (na) 楽(な), anraku (na) 安楽(な), kiraku (na) 気楽(な); kaiteki (na) 快適

(な), kimochi ga íi 気持ちがいい **2.** → **relax**
3. *adj* (*easy to wear*) ki-yasúi 着やすい, (*easy to sit on*) suwariyasúi 座りやすい・すわりやすい
comforter *n* **1.** (*down quilt*) hane-buton 羽布団
2. (*person that comforts*) nagusameru hito 慰める人 **3.** (*thing that comforts*) nagusameru mono 慰めるもの **4.** *Comforter* seirei 聖霊
comic;
  comic book *n* manga (-bon) 漫画(本); komikku コミック
  comics *n* manga 漫画・まんが
  comic storytelling *n* rakugo 落語
  comic storyteller *n* rakugo-ka 落語家
  comic strip *n* koma wari manga こま割り漫画・まんが
comical *adj* hyōkín (na) ひょうきん(な) → **funny**
Coming-of-Age Day (*2nd Monday of January*) *n* Seijin no hí 成人の日
comma *n* konma コンマ
command 1. *n* (*order, instructions*) meirei 命令; (*historic term*) sátá さた・沙汰 **2.** *v* (*orders a person*) ... ni ii-tsukemásu (ii-tsukéru, ii-tsukéte) ...に言い付けます(言い付ける、言い付けて), mei-jimásu (mei-jiru, mei-jite) 命じます(命じる、命じて) **3.** *v* (*leads*) hikiimásu (hikiíru, hikíite) 率います(率いる、率いて)
commander *n* shiréi-kan 司令官; (*navy*) chūsa 中佐
commemorate *v* kinen shimásu (suru, shite) 記念します(する、して)
commemoration *n* kinen 記念
commemorative stamp *n* kinen-kítte 記念切手
commencement *n* (*ceremony*) sotsugyō´-shiki 卒業式
commend *v* (*praises*) homemásu (homeru, homete) ほめます・褒めます(褒める、褒めて)
comment 1. *n* (*explanation*) kaisetsu 解説
2. *n* (*critique, opinion*) hyōron 評論 **3.** *n* komento コメント → **remark 4.** *~ on v* (*explains*) kaisetsu shimásu (suru, shite) 解説します(する、して); (*criticizes*) hyōron shimásu (suru, shite) 評論します(する、して)
commentary *n* **1.** (*interpretation*) kaisétsu 解説 **2.** (*explanatory note*) chūshaku 注釈 **3.** (*records*) kiroku 記録 **4.** (*on-the-spot broadcasting*) jikkyō hōsō 実況放送
commentator *n* komentētā コメンテーター
1. (*explicator*) kaisétsu-sha 解説者 **2.** (*critic*) hyōron-ka 評論家, hyōron-sha 評論者
commerce *n* shō´gyō 商業; (*trade*) bōeki 貿易
commercial *n* komāsharu コマーシャル, shiiému (*CM*) シーエム
commercialize *v* **1.** (*makes commercial*) shōgyō-ka shimásu (suru, shite) 商業化します(する、して) **2.** (*makes profitable*) eiri-ka shimásu (suru, shite) 営利化します(する、して) **3.** (*makes profitable at the expense of quality*) hinshitsu o gisei ni shite eiri-ka shimásu (suru, shite) 品質を犠牲にして営

利化します(する、して)
commission 1. *n* (*handling charge*) tesū-ryō 手数料; (*brokerage fee*) sáya さや **2.** *v* (*commissions ... to do it*) (sore o ... ni) irai shimásu (suru, shite)(それを... に) 依頼します(する、して)
commissioner *n* riji 理事, chōkan 長官
commit *v* **1.** (*entrusts*) yudanemásu (yudanéru, yudáhete) ゆだねます・委ねます(ゆだねる、ゆだねて) **2.** (*perpetrates*) okashimásu (okasu, okashite) 犯します(犯す、犯して); hatarakimásu (hataraku, hataraite) 働きます(働く、働いて) → **do 3. commit oneself → promise → say**
commitment *n* **1.** (*promise*) yakusoku 約束 **2.** (*duty*) gimu 義務 **3.** (*responsibility*) sekinin 責任
committee *n* iín-kai 委員会
  committee member(s) *n* íin 委員
commodity *n* shōhin 商品
commodity prices *n* bukka 物価
common *adj* futsū (no) 普通(の); kyōtsū (no) 共通(の); (*average*) nami (no) 並(の); (*vulgar, popular*) zoku (na) 俗(な); *very common* (*is prevalent*) hayari (no) はやり・流行(の); [IN NEGATIVE SENSE](*is found everywhere*) arifureta ありふれた(no) ありきたり(の)
commoner *n* shomin 庶民, ippan-jin 一般人
commonplace *adj* heibon (na) 平凡(な); arifureta ありふれた
common sense *n* (*ippan*) jōshiki 一般常識
commonwealth *n* renpō 連邦
commotion *n* **1.** (*tumult*) sawagi 騒ぎ **2.** (*agitation*) dōyō 動揺 **3.** (*confused movement*) konran 混乱
commune 1. *v* danwa shimásu (suru, shite) 談話します(する、して) **2.** *n* chihō jichitai 地方自治体
communicate *v* tsutaemásu (tsutaeru, tsutaete) 伝えます(伝える、伝えて); tsūjimásu (tsū-jiru, tsū-jite) 通じます(通じる、通じて)
communicated; gets ~ tsutawari-másu (tsutawaru, tsutawatte) 伝わります(伝わる、伝わって)
communication *n* (*traffic*) kōtsū 交通, ōrai 往来; (*message, news*) táyori 便り, tsūshin 通信
communique *n* kōshiki seimei 公式声明
Communism *n* kyōsan -shúgi 共産主義
  Communist *n* kyōsan shugí-sha 共産主義者
community *n* komyuniti コミュニティ, komyunitii コミュニティー, (*society*) shákai 社会 → **town, village**
community college *n* (*junior college*) tanki-dáigaku 短期大学
commute *v* kayoimásu (kayou, kayotte) 通います(通う、通って); *~ to work* tsūkin shimásu 通勤します(する、して)
commuter *n* **1.** (*to work*) tsūkin-sha 通勤者 **2.** (*goes to school*) tsūgaku-sha 通学者
commuting;
  commuting to work *n* tsūkin 通勤

commuting hours n tsūkin-jíkan 通勤時間; *peak commuting hours* tsūkin-jíkan-tai 通勤時間帯

companion n nakamá 仲間; tsure 連れ(o-tsure お連れ), tómo 供 (o-tómo お供), tomodachi 友達; aité 相手 (o-aite お相手)

company n (*firm*) kaisha 会社, ... -sha ... 社; (*within the office/company*) shánai (no) 社内(の); (*group*) kumí 組; (*social*) tsuki-ai 付き合い・つきあい, kōsai 交際; (*guests*) raikyaku 来客, (o-) kyaku (お)客, o-kyaku-san/sámá お客さん/さま・様

company secretary n sōmu buchō 総務部長

keep one company ... to tsuki-aimásu (tsuki-áu, tsuki-átte) ... と付き合います・つきあいます(付き合う, 付き合って)

keep company with ... o chika-zukemásu (chika-zukéru, chika-zúkete) ... を近付けます (近付ける, 近付けて)

comparatively adv hikaku-teki (ni) 比較的(に), wari ni 割に, wariai (ni) 割合(に)

compare v kurabemásu (kuraberu, kurabete) 比べます(比べる, 比べて), hikaku shimásu (suru, shite) 比較します(する, して); taishō/taihi shimásu (suru, shite) 対照/対比します(する, て); (*collates*) terashimásu (terásu, teráshite) 照らします(照らす, 照らして); *as compared with* ... ni tái-shite ... に対して

comparison n hikaku 比較; taishō 対照, taihi 対比

compass n (*for directions*) rashinban 羅針盤; (*for drafting*) konpasu コンパス

compassion n nasake 情け (o-násake お情け)

compatibility n aishō´ 相性

compatible adj aishō´ ga(/no) íi 相性が(/の)いい

compensate v mukuimásu (mukuíru, mukuite) 報います(報いる, 報いて); (*indemnifies*) hoshō shimásu (suru, shite) 補償します(する, して); (*certify*) hoshō shimásu (suru, shite) 保証します(する, して)

compensation n (*indemnity money*) hoshō-kin 補償金, benshō 弁償, baishō 賠償; (*allowance*) kyō´yo 供与

compete v kisoimásu (kisóu, kisótte) 競います(競う, 競って), kyōsō shimásu (suru, suite) 競争します(する, して)

competency n (*qualification*) shikaku 資格

competition n kyōsō 競争

competitive adj 1. (*fiercely-competitive*) kyōsō no hageshii 競争の激しい 2. (*strong desire to compete*) kyōsō-shin no tsuyoi 競争心の強い

competitor n kyōsō-áite 競争相手

complain v (*gives utterance*) fuhei/mónku o iimásu (iu, itte/yutte) 不平/文句を言います(言う, 言って/ゆって); (*guchi o*) kobashimásu (kobósu, kobóshite)(ぐち・愚痴を)こぼします(こぼす, こぼして); (*mutters to oneself*) butsu-butsu iimásu (iu, itte) ぶつぶつ言います(言う, 言って); kujō o iimásu (iu, itte) 苦情を言います(言う, 言って); (*makes a formal accusation*)

uttaemásu (uttaeru, uttaete) 訴えます(訴える, 訴えて)

complaint n fuhei 不平, mónku 文句, kujō 苦情, kogoto 小言 (o-kógoto お小言), guchi ぐち・愚痴; (*lawsuit*) uttae 訴え

complement n hosoku 補足, hojū 補充

complete 1. *becomes ~* v (*full*) michimásu (michíru, míchite) 満ちます(満ちる, 満ちて) **2.** *completes it* v kansei shimásu (suru, shite) 完成します(する, して); (*a set*) soroemásu (soroéru, soróete) 揃えます(揃える, 揃えて) **3.** oginaimásu (ogináu, oginatte) 補います(補う, 補って)

complete adj (*exhaustive*) mō´ra chita ... 網羅した...

completely adv mattakú 全く・まったく, to(t) temo と(っ)ても, sukkári すっかり, sokkúri そっくり; (+ [NAGATIVE]) zenzen 全然; (*all*) zénbu 全部・ぜんぶ, minná みんな・皆; (*the whole...*) zén(-) ... 全...

completion n kansei 完成

complex n konpurekkusu コンプレックス, rettō-kan 劣等感

complexation n sakuka 錯化

complexion n kao iro 顔色

complexities n (*details*) ikisatsu いきさつ・経緯

compliance; *in ~ with* ... ni ō-jite ... に応じて, ... ni junkyo shite ... に準拠して

complicated adj fukuzatsu (na) 複雑(な), komi-itta 込み入った・こみいった, yaya(k)koshíi やや(っ)こしい, wazurawashii 煩わしい; hánsa (na) はんさ[煩瑣](な), hanzatsu (na) 煩雑・はんざつ (な); *gets* ~ kojiremásu (kojiréru, kojírete) こじれます(こじれる, こじれて), motsuremásu (motsureru, motsurete) もつれます(もつれる, もつれて)

complications n (*details*) ikisatsu いきさつ・経緯; (*entanglements*) motsure もつれ

compliment n seji 世辞, o-seji お世辞, home kotoba ほめ言葉

comply; *~ with* v ... ni ō-jimásu (ō-ji ru, ō-jite) ... に応じます(応じる, 応じて); ... o nattoku shimásu (suru, shite) ... を納得します(する, して)

component n séibun 成分

compose v (*writes*) tsuzurimásu (tsuzuru, tsuzutte) 綴ります・つづります(綴る, 綴って), tsukurimásu (tsukúru, tsukutte) 作ります(作る, 作って)

composed adj (*unperturbed*) heiki (na) 平気(な); reisei (na) 冷静(な)

composite adj sōgō-teki (na) 総合的(な)

composition n (*writing*) sakubun 作文; (*constituency*) kōsei 構成

compound n (*word*) fukugō-go 複合語, jukugo 熟語

comprehend → understand → include → comprise → consist of

comprehension n rikai 理解

comprehension ability n rikái-ryoku 理解力

comprehensive adj (*composite*) sōgō-teki (na) 総合的(な)

compress v 1. (*constricts*) asshuku shimásu (suru, shíte) 圧縮します(する, して) 2. (*presses*) appaku shimásu (suru, shíte) 圧迫します(する, して) 3. (*shorten*) tanshuku shimásu (suru, shíte) 短縮します(する, して)

comprise v (*includes all items*) mōˊra shimásu (suru, shíte) 網羅します(する, して)

compromise 1. n dakyō 妥協; (*makes a compromise*) 2. v dakyō shimásu (suru, shíte) 妥協します(する, して)

compulsion n 1. (*psychology*) shōdō kyōhaku 衝動強迫 2. (*forcing*) kyōsei 強制

compulsive adj 1. (*psychology*) kyōhaku kan'nen no aru 強迫観念のある, osaerarenai 抑えられない 2. (*very interesting or compelling*) hito (no kokoro) o hikitsukeru 人(の心)を引きつける

compulsory adj 1. (*stipulated*) kitei (no) 規定(の) 2. (*obligatory*) gimu-teki (na) 義務的(な) 3. (*required*) hissu (no) 必須(の) 4. (*compelling*) kyōsei-teki (na) 強制的(な)
  compulsory education n gimu-kyōˊiku 義務教育

computation n keisan 計算

compute v keisan shimásu (suru, shíte) 計算します(する, して)

computer n konpyūˊta コンピュータ, konpyūˊtā コンピューター

computer game n konpyūˊta/konpyūˊtā gēmu コンピュータ/コンピューター・ゲーム

computerize v konpyūˊta-ka/konpyūˊtā-ka shimásu (suru, shíte) コンピュータ化/コンピューター化します(する, して)

computer programmer n konpyūˊta/konpyūˊtā puroguramā コンピュータ/コンピューター・プログラマー

computer science n konpyūˊta-ka/konpyūˊtā saiensu コンピュータ/コンピューター・サイエンス, jōhō kagaku 情報科学, jōhō kōgaku 情報工学

comrade n (...) dōˊshi (...)同志, (...) nakama (...)仲間

con n sagi 詐欺
  con man n sagi-shi 詐欺師・サギ師, peten-shi ペテン師

concave n ōmen 凹面

conceal → **hide** → **cover up**

conceit n [INFORMAL] unubore うぬぼれ, [FORMAL] kadai hyōka 過大評価

conceited person n tengu 天狗・てんぐ, unuboreta hito うぬぼれた人

concentrate v shūchū shimásu (suru, shíte) 集中します(する, して)

concentration n shūchū 集中

concept n gáinen 概念, shisō 思想

conception n 1. (*concept*) gáinen 概念, shisō 思想 2. (*fertilization*) jusei 受精 3. (*inception of pregnancy*) jutai 受胎, kainin 懐妊

concern 1. n (*relevance*) kankei 関係, (*interest*) kanshin 関心; (*worry*) shinpai 心配; (*business*) kaisha 会社 2. v (*relates to*) ... ni kanshimásu

(kansúru, kánshite) ... に関します(関する, 関して), (*centers on*) ... o megurimásu (meguru, megutte) ... を巡ります(巡る, 巡って)

concerning prep ... ni kán-shite ... に関して, ... o megutte ... を巡って

concert n ongáku(u) -kai 音楽会, ensōˊ-kai 演奏会, consāto コンサート
  concert hall n consāto hōru コンサート・ホール

concerto n koncheruto コンチェルト, kyōsō-kyoku 協奏曲

concession n 1. (*compromise*) jōho 譲歩 2. (*right*) tokken 特権

conciliate v nadamemásu (nadameru, nadamete) なだめます(なだめる, なだめて); wakai sasemásu (saseru, sasete) 和解させます(させる, させて); chōtei shimásu (suru, shíte) 調停します(する, して)

concise adj kanketsu (na) 簡潔(な)

conclude v (*brings to an end*) sumashimásu (sumásu, sumáshite) 済ます(済ます, 済まして); (*ends a discussion*) ketsuron shimásu (suru, shíte) 結論します(する, して); (*finalizes*) seiritsu shimásu (suru, shíte) 成立します(する, して)

conclusion n 1. (*of discussion*) ketsuron 結論; *in* ~ ketsuron to shite 結論として 2. (*finalization*) seiritsu 成立

concoct v koshiraemásu (koshiraeru, koshiraete) こしらえます(こしらえる, こしらえて), tsukuriagemásu (tsukuriageru, tsukuriagete) 作り上げます(作り上げる, 作り上げて)

concrete 1. n (*cement*) konkuríito コンクリート 2. adj (*not abstract*) gutai-teki(na) 具体的(な)
  concrete floor n takakí たたき

concubine n mekake 妾・めかけ, o-mekake(-san) お妾(さん), nígō(-san) 二号(さん)

concur v (*agrees*) dōi shimásu (suru, shíte) 同意します(する, して), (*coincides*) itchi shimásu (suru, shíte) 一致します(する, して)

concurrent adj (*occurring at the same time*) dōji ni okoru 同時に起こる

concurrently adv (*serves as*) ... o kanemásu (kanéru, kánete) を兼ねます(兼ねる, 兼ねて)

concussion n (*brain*) nō-shintō 脳しんとう

condemn v hinan shimásu (suru, shite) 非難します(する, して)

condense v 1. (*concentrates*) gyōshuku shimásu (suru, shíte) 凝縮します(する, して), nōshuku shimásu (suru, shite) 濃縮します(する, して) 2. (*liquefies*) ekika shimásu (suru, shite) 液化します(する, して) 3. (*summarizes*) yōyaku shimásu (suru, shíte) 要約します(する, して)

condensed milk n rennyū 練乳, kondensu miruku コンデンスミルク

condition n (*state*) ari-sama 有様・ありさま, jōtai 状態, jijō 事情, jissai 実際, guai 具合, chōshi 調子, (*weather*) hiyori 日和・ひより, (*stipulation*) jōken 条件; *best condition* zekkō-chō 絶好調; *be in good (bad) condition* chōshi ga ii (warui) 調子がいい(悪い)

condolence *n* okuyami お悔やみ

condom *n* kondōmu コンドーム

condominium *n* kondominiamu コンドミニアム, bunjō manshon 分譲マンション, bunjō apāto 分譲アパート

condone *v* mokunin shimás<u>u</u> (suru, shite) 黙認します(する, して)

conduct 1. *n* (*behavior*) okonai 行い・おこない **2.** *v* michibimás<u>u</u> (michibiku, michibiite) 導きます (導く, 導いて), sh<u>i</u>ki shimás<u>u</u> (suru, sh<u>i</u>te) 指揮します(する, して)

conductor *n* (*train*) shashō(-san) 車掌(さん); (*orchestra*) shik<u>i</u>sha 指揮者

cone *n* ensui(-kei) 円錐(形), kōn コーン; *ice cream cone* aisukuriimu kōn アイスクリームコーン

confection *n* (o-)káshi (お)菓子

confectionery *n* (*confectioner*) (o-)kashí-ya (お)菓子屋; (*candy*) (o-)kashí (お)菓子

confederacy *n* rengō 連合, dōmei(koku) 同盟(国)

confederate *n* (*person*) kyōhan-sha 共犯者, kyōbō-sha 共謀者

confer *v* **1.** hanashi-aimás<u>u</u> (hanashi-au, hanashi-atte) 話し合います(話し合う, 話し合って) **2.** → **grant**

conference *n* (*personal*) sōdan 相談; [FORMAL] káigi 会議, taikai 大会; (*discussion*) kyō´gí 協議, (*negotiation*) hanashi-ai 話し合い

confess *v* **1.** hák<u>u</u>jō shimás<u>u</u> (suru, sh<u>i</u>te) 白状します(する, して), jihaku shimás<u>u</u> (suru, shite) 自白します(する, して), kokuhaku shimás<u>u</u> (suru, shite) 告白します(する, して); (*confess the sin*) zángéshimás<u>u</u> (suru, sh<u>i</u>te) ざんげ・懺悔します (する, して) **2.** (*frankly reveals*) uchi-akemás<u>u</u> (uchi-akeru, uchi-akete) 打ち明けます(打ち明ける, 打ち明けて)

confession *n* hák<u>u</u>jō 白状; (*of sins*) zángé ざんげ・懺悔

confidence *n* shin'yō 信用, shinrai 信頼, tánomi 頼み; (*self-confidence*) jishin 自信; (*secure feeling*) anshin 安心

confidential *adj* naisho (no) 内緒(の)

confirm *v* (*a reservation*) (yoyaku o) kakunin shimás<u>u</u> (suru, sh<u>i</u>te) (予約を)確認します(する, して)

confirmation *n* kakunin 確認

conflict *n* tatakai 戦い

confluence *n* gōryū 合流

conform (*with/to*) *v* ... ni sh<u>i</u>tagaimás<u>u</u> (sh<u>i</u>tagau, sh<u>i</u>tagatte) ... に従います(従う, 従って), ... ni motozukimás<u>u</u> (motozúku, motozúite) ... に基づきます(基づく, 基づいて)

confront *v* ... ni tai-shimás<u>u</u> (tai-súru, tái-sh<u>i</u>te) ... に対します(対する, 対して); ... to tairitsu shimás<u>u</u> (suru, sh<u>i</u>te) ... と対立します(する, して); (*opposes*) ... ni taikō shimás<u>u</u> (suru, sh<u>i</u>te) ... に対抗します(する, して)

confrontation *n* taikō 対抗

confound *v* kondō shimás<u>u</u> (suru, sh<u>i</u>te) 混同します(する, して) **2.** (*perplexes*) konwaku sasemás<u>u</u> (saseru, sasete) 困惑させます(させる, させて)

Confucianism *n* Júkyō 儒教

Confucius *n* Kōshi 孔子

confused; gets ~ komaru 困る, komátte 困って, (*flustered*) awatemás<u>u</u> (awateru, awatete) 慌てます・あわてます(慌てる, 慌てて); (*in a panic, mistakenly*) mechamecha めちゃめちゃ

confusion *n* (*disorder*) konran 混乱, kónzatsu 混雑

congeal *v* **1.** *it congeals* katamarimás<u>u</u> (katamaru, katamatte) 固まります(固まる, 固まって) **2.** *congeals it* katamemás<u>u</u> (katameru, katamete) 固めます(固める, 固めて)

congenial *adj* aishō´ ga(/no) íi 相性が(/の)いい

congeniality *n* aishō´ 相性

conger eel *n* anago アナゴ・穴子

congested *n* (*traffic*) jūtai-jō´kyō 渋滞状況; *is ~* jūtai sh<u>i</u>te imás<u>u</u> (shiteiru, shiteite) 渋滞しています(している, していて)

congestion *n* jūtai 渋滞

conglomerate *n* konguromaritto コングロマリット, fukugō-kigyō 複合企業

congratulate *v* (o-)iwai shimás<u>u</u> (suru, sh<u>i</u>te) お祝いします(する, して)

congratulation *n* sh<u>u</u>kuga 祝賀, o-iwai お祝い; *Congratulations!* O-medetō gozaimás<u>u</u>. おめでとうございます

congregate *v* shūgō shimás<u>u</u> (suru, sh<u>i</u>te) 集合します(する, して)

congregation *n* atsumari 集まり, shūkai 集会

congress → **Diet; conference**

congruence *n* gōdō 合同

conjecture 1. *n* suisoku 推測, sas-shi 察し (o-sasshi お察し) **2.** *v* (*guesses, supposes*) sas-shimás<u>u</u> (sas-suru, sas-sh<u>i</u>te) 察します(察する, 察して)

conjugal *adj* fūfu (no) 夫婦(の), kon'in (no) 婚姻(の)

conjugate *v* (*grammar*) (dōshi o) katsuyō sasemás<u>u</u> (saseru, sasete) (動詞を)活用させます(させる, させて)

conjunction *n* setsuzokú-shi 接続詞

connect (*with*) *v* (... to) tsunagimás<u>u</u> (tsunagu, tsunaide) (... と)つなぎます(つなぐ, つないで); ... to renraku shimás<u>u</u> (suru, sh<u>i</u>te) ... と連絡します(する, して); tsū-jimás<u>u</u> (tsū-jiru, tsū-jite) 通じます(通じる, 通じて)

connected; is ~ (*with* ...) (...to) tsunagarimás<u>u</u> (tsunagaru, tsunagatte) (... と)つながります(つながる, つながって), (... ni) kan-shimás<u>u</u> (kan-súru, kán-sh<u>i</u>te) (... に)関します(関する, 関して)

connection *n* renraku 連絡; (*relevance*) kankei 関係; (*relation*) tsunagari つながり; (*link*) tsunagi つなぎ; (*"pull", avenue of influence*) kone コネ

conscience *n* ryō´shin 良心

conscientious *adj* majime (na) まじめ・真面目 (な); ryōshin-teki (na) 良心的(な)

consciousness *n* íshiki 意識, obóé 覚え; *loses ~* íshiki o ushinaimásu (ushinau, ushinatte) 意識を失います(失う, 失って)

conscription *n* (*for military service*) shōshū 召集・招集

consent *v* shōchi/shōdaku/dōi shimásu (suru, shite) 承知/承諾/同意します(する, して), nattoku shimásu (suru, shite) 納得します(する, して); [HUMBLE] uketamawarimásu (uketamawaru, uketamawatte) 承ります(承る, 承って)

consequence → **result**

conservative *adj* hoshu-teki (na) 保守的(な); shōkyoku-teki (na) 消極的(な); (*moderate*) uchiwa (na) 内輪(な)

conserve **1.** *v* (*saves*) setsuyaku shimásu (suru, shite) 節約します(する, して) **2.** *n* (*fruit jam*) jamu ジャム; *conserves boiled down from fish or seaweed* tsukuda-ni つくだ煮・佃煮・ツクダニ

consider *v* kangaemásu (kangáéru, kangáete) 考えます(考える, 考えて); (*takes into account*) kō´ryo ni iremásu (ireru, irete) 考慮に入れます (入れる, 入れて)

considerable *adj* sōtō (na) 相当(な), yohodo (no) 余程(の), yoppodo (no)よっぽど(の)

considerably *adv* kanari かなり, zuibun ずいぶん

consideration *n* (*being kind*) omoiyari 思いやり; (*thought*) kō´ryo 考慮, shíryo 思慮; *takes into ~* kō´ryo ni iremásu (ireru, irete) 考慮に入れます (入れる, 入れて)

consist; *~ of* ...kara nátte imásu (iru, ite) ... から成っています(いる, いて)

consolation *n* nagusame 慰め・なぐさめ, ian 慰安

console *v* nagusamemásu (nagusameru, nagusamete) 慰めます・なぐさめます(慰める, 慰めて)

consomme *n* konsome コンソメ

consonant *n* shion/shiin 子音

conspicuous *adj* ichijirushíi 著しい・いちじるしい; medátta ... 目立った..., medátte imásu 目立っています

conspicuously *adv* ichijirúshiku 著しく・いちじるしく; medátte 目立って

constant *adj* chakujitsu (na) 着実(な); fuhen (no) 不変の

constantly → **always**

constipation *n* benpi 便秘

constitute *v* kōsei shimásu (suru, shite) 構成します(する, して)

constitution *n* **1.** (*basic laws*) kénpō 憲法; *Constitution (Memorial) Day* (*3 May*) Kenpō-kinénbi 憲法記念日 **2.** (*physical*) taishitsu 体質 **3.** (*composition*) kōsei 構成

constrained *adj* kyū´kutsu (na) 窮屈・きゅうくつ(な)

constricted place, waist *n* kubire くびれ

construct → **build**

construction *n* (*work*) kō´ji 工事; *under construction* kōji-chū 工事中; (*building*) kensetsu 建設; (*constitution*) kōsei 構成

construe *v* káishaku shimásu (suru, shite) 解釈します(する, して)

consul *n* ryō´ji 領事

consul general *n* sō-ryō´ji 総領事

consulate *n* ryōjí-kan 領事館

consult *v* (*a person*) ... to sōdan shimásu (suru, shite) ... と相談します(する, して)

consultant *n* kómon 顧問, konsárutanto コンサルタント

consultation *n* ukagai 伺い (o-ukagai お伺い), sōdan 相談(go-sōdan ご相談); (*by appointment*) uchi-awase 打ち合わせ

consumer *n* shōhí-sha 消費者

consuming *adj* hageshii 激しい

consumption *n* shōhi 消費

consumption tax *n* (*duty*) shōhi-zei 消費税

contact **1.** *n* sesshoku 接触; *comes in ~ (with ...)* (... ni) furemásu (fureru, furete) (... に)触れます (触れる, 触れて), ses-shimásu (ses-suru, ses-shite) 接します(接する, 接して), sesshoku shimásu (suru, shite) 接触します(する, して) **2.** *contacts n* → **contact lenses** コンタクトレンズ **3.** *v* (*contacts a person*) ... to renraku shimásu (suru, shite)と連絡します(する, して), ... ni aimásu (áu, átte) ... に会います(会う, 会って)

contact lenses *n* kontakuto-rénzu コンタクトレンズ, kontákuto コンタクト; *wears ~* kontákuto o shite imásu コンタクトをしています

contagion *n* densen 伝染

contagious disease *n* densenbyō 伝染病

contain *v* ... ga háitte imásu (iru, ite) ... が入っています(いる, いて); ... o fukumimásu (fukúmu, fukúnde) ... を含みます(含む, 含んで)

container *n* ire-mono 入れ物, yō´ki 容器; (*box*) hako 箱; (*for transporting goods*) kóntena コンテナ

contamination *n* osen 汚染

contempt *n* keibetsu 軽蔑

contented *adj* ... de mánzoku shimásu (suru, shite) ... で満足します(する, して); osamarimásu (osamáru, osamátte) 治まります(治まる, 治まって)

contention *n* arasoi 争い

contents *n* nakámi 中身, naiyō 内容; (*table of contents*) mokuji 目次, midashi 見出し

contest *n* konkū´ru コンクール, kón-tesuto コンテスト; (*competition*) kyōsō 競争; (*sports*) kyō´gi 競技, (*match*) shō´bu 勝負, (*meet*) shiai 試合

contiguous *adj* *is ~ to* ... ni ses-shimásu (ses-suru, ses-shite) ... に接します(接する, 接して)

continent *n* tairiku 大陸

continuation *n* tsuzuki 続き

continue *v* (*it continues*) tsuzukimásu (tsuzuku, tsuzuite) 続きます(続く, 続いて); (*continues it*) tsuzukemásu (tsuzukeru, tsuzukete) 続けます(続ける, 続けて)

continuity *n* renzoku-sei 連続性

continuously *adv* taema-náku 絶え間なく・たえ まなく, táezu 絶えず・たえず; (*without resting*) yasumánaide 休まないで; tsuzukete 続けて

contraceptive *n* **1.** hinín-yaku 避妊薬, (*pills*) keikō-hinín-yaku 経口避妊薬 **2.** (*device*) hinín-gu 避妊具; (*condom*) kondō´mu コンドーム

contract **1.** *n* (*an agreement*) keiyaku 契約 **2.** *v* (*agrees to undertake work*) ukeoimásu (ukeóu, ukeótte) 請け負います(請け負う, 請け負って)

contractor *n* ukeoí-nin 請け負い人

contradict *v* ... ni sakaraimásu (sakaráu, sakarátte) ... に逆らいます(逆らう, 逆らって) → **deny**

contradiction *n* (*inconsistency*) mujun 矛盾

contradictory *adj* (*inconsistent*) mujun shite imásu (iru, ite) 矛盾しています(いる, いて)

contrary *adj* hantai (no) 反対(の), gyaku (no) 逆(の); **~ to** ... ni hán-shite... に反して; *acts ~ to* (*goes against*) ... ni han-shimásu (han-suru, han-shite) ... に反します(反する, 反して), ... ni sakaraimásu (sakaráu, sakarátte) ... に逆らいます (逆らう, 逆らって); **~ expectations** káette かえって

contrast **1.** *n* taishō/taihi (shimásu; suru, shite) 対照/対比(します; する, して) **2.** *v* (*compares*) kurabemásu (kuraberu, kurabete) 比べます(比べる, 比べて); *in ~ to/with* ... ni tái-shite ... に対して, ... ni hán-shite ... に反して

control **1.** *n* shíhai 支配, kánri 管理; (*of prices, etc.*) tōsei 統制 **2.** *v* (*supervises it*) tori-shimarimásu (tori-shimaru, tori-shimatte) 取り締まります (取り締まる, 取り締まって); (*restrains*) osaemásu (osáeru, osáete) 抑えます(抑える, 抑えて); (*operates equipment*) sōjū shimásu (suru, shite) 操縦します(する, して)

controversy *n* ronsō 論争

convenience *n* tsugō 都合 (go-tsugō ご都合), tsuide ついでに; *at your convenience* tsuide no sai ついでの際, tsuide no toki ni ついでの時に

convenience store *n* konbini コンビニ

convenient *adj* bénri (na) 便利(な), bén ga íi 便がいい; chō´hō (na) 重宝(な); (*easy to arrange*) tsugō ga íi 都合がいい

convent *n* shūdō´-in 修道院

convention → **conference, meeting**

conventional *adj* heibon (na) 平凡(な)

conversation *n* (*ordinary*) hanashí 話, danwa 談話; (*in language class, etc.*) kaiwa 会話

conversion *n* henkan 変換; *conversion key* henkan-kíi 変換キー

convert *v* hiki-kaemásu (hiki-káeru, hiki-káete) 引き変えます(引き換える, 引き換えて)

converter *n* henkan-ki 変換器; (*AC-DC*) henryū´-ki 変流器; (*transformer*) hen'atsú-ki 変圧器

convey *v* hakobimásu (hakobu, hakonde) 運びます (運ぶ, 運んで)

cook **1.** *n* ryōri-nin 料理人, kókku(-san) コック (さん), (*Japanese chef*) itamae 板前 **2.** *v* (*cooks it*) ryō´ri shimásu (suru, shite) 料理します(する, して), (*boils it*) nimásu (niru, nite) 煮ます(煮る,

煮て); (*rice, soup*) takimásu (taku, taite) 炊きま す(炊く, 炊いて) **3.** *v* (*it boils*) niemásu (nieru, niete) 煮えます(煮える, 煮えて)

cooked rice *n* meshí 飯, góhan ご飯

cooking *n* ryōri 料理

cooking stove *n* rénji レンジ

cool **1.** *adj* suzushíi 涼しい; (*calm*) reisei (na) 冷静(な); (*unperturbed*) heiki (na) 平気(な) **2.** *v it cools off/down* samemásu (saméru, sámete) 冷めます(冷める, 冷めて), hiemásu (hiéru, híete) 冷えます(冷える, 冷えて); (*cools it*) hiyashimásu (hiyású, hiyáshite) 冷やします(冷や す, 冷やして)

cooperation *n* kyōryoku 協力; (*joint activity*) kyōdō 共同

cop → **policeman**

copper *n* aka-gane アカガネ・銅, dō´ 銅

copula *n* shitei-shi 指定詞, keiji 繋辞 (= désu, dá, ná, nó, ní, dé, ... です, だ, な, の, に, で, ...)

copy **1.** *n* (*of a book*) ...-bu ... 部, ichí-bu 一部 **2.** *n* (*photocopy*) kópii コピー (*how many*) nán-mai 何枚) **3.** *n* (*reproduction*) fukusha 複写, fukusei 複製; *two-sided copy* ryōmen-kopii 両面コピー **4.** *v* (*copies it*) utsushimásu (utsúsu, utsúshite) 写します(写す, 写して), fukusha/fukusei shimásu (suru, shite) 複写/複製します(する, して); (*imitates*) nisemásu (niseru, nisete) 似せます (似せる, 似せて); (*makes a copy*) kópii o torimásu (tóru, tótte) コピーをとります(とる, とって)

coral *n* sángo サンゴ・珊瑚

cord *n* himo ひも・ヒモ・紐, nawá なわ・縄, kō´do コード

cordial *adj* shínsetsu (na) 親切(な), kokoro no komotta 心のこもった

core *n* shín しん・心・芯

cork *n* kóruku コルク, sén 栓, koruku-sen コル ク栓

corkscrew *n* korukú-nuki コルク抜き, sen-nuki 栓抜き

cormorant *n* u ウ・鵜

cormorant fishing *n* ukai 鵜飼い

corn *n* **1.** (*maize*) tō-mórokoshi トウモロコシ, kōn コーン **2.** (*on skin*) uonome 魚の目; (*callus*) táko たこ, (*bunion*) mamé まめ; soko-mame 底まめ

corner *n* (*outside*) kádo 角, (*inside*) súmi 隅

cornstarch *n* kōn-sutá´chi コーンスターチ, tōmorokoshí-ko トウモロコシ粉

corporation *n* **1.** (*joint-stock corporation*) kabushiki-gáisha 株式会社 **2.** (*incorporated association*) shadan 社団 **3.** (*public corporation*) kōdan 公団

corps *n* gundan 軍団; *Marine Corps* kaiheitai 海兵隊; *Peace Corps* heiwa-bútai 平和部隊; *medical corps* eisei-tai 衛生隊

corpsman *n* (*medical*) eiséi-hei 衛生兵

corpse *n* shitai 死体, nakigara なきがら・亡骸, shigai 死骸

correct   **1.** *adj* tadashíi 正しい   **2.** *v* atarimásu (ataru, atatte) 当たります(当たる、当たって); (*corrects it*) naoshimásu (naósu, naóshite) 直します(直す、直して), aratamemásu (arataméru, aratámete) 改めます(改める、改めて)

correction *n* naoshí 直し, teisei 訂正 (= *correcting*)

correctly *adv* tadáshiku 正しく

correspond (*to ...*) *v* (... ni) taiō shimásu (suru, shíte) (... に)対応します(する、して)

correspondence *n* (*messages*) tsūshin 通信; (*equivalence*) taiō 対応

corridor *n* rōka 廊下

corrugated cardboard *n* danbṓru 段ボール

cosmetics *n* keshṓ 化粧 (o-keshō お化粧), keshō-hin 化粧品

cost   **1.** *n* (*expense*) híyō 費用   **2.** *v it costs* (*how much*) (íkura) shimásu (suru, shíte) (いくら)します(する、して); (*requires*) yō-shimásu (yō-súru, yṓ-shite) 要します(要する、要して)

at any cost nán to shité mo 何としても、náni ga nánde mo 何が何でも

costly → **expensive**

costume *n* fukusō 服装

cotton *n* wata 綿, momen 木綿, kotton コットン; *absorbent cotton* dasshí-men 脱脂綿; *cotton-padded* (*garment*) wataíré 綿入れ

cotton belt *n* kotton beruto コットン・ベルト

couch *n* ne-isu 寝椅子, naga-isu 長椅子

cough *v* sekí o shimásu (suru, shíte) 咳をします(する、して)

could → **can; maybe**

counsel   **1.** *n* (*guide, coach*) shidōsha 指導者   **2.** *v* (*counsels them*) shidō shimásu (suru, shíte) 指導します(する、して)

count *v* kazoemásu (kazoéru, kazóete) 数えます(数える、数えて); *~ on one's fingers* yubí o ótte kazoemásu 指を折って数えます; *is counting on ...* o ate ni shite imásu (iru, ite) ... を当てにしています(いる、いて)

counter *n* (*shop counter*) uri-ba 売り場

counterclockwise *adj* hidari-máwari (ni) 左回り(に)

counterfeit   **1.** *adj* nise (no) 偽(の)   **2.** *v* nisemásu (niseru, nisete) 似せます(似せる、似せて) counterfeit bill *n* (*currency*) nisesatsu 偽札・にせ札・贋札

countless *adj* kazoe-kirenai 数え切れない, musū (no) 無数(の)

country *n* **1.** kuni 国;... -koku ... 国 (*how many countries* nan-kákoku 何カ国)   **2.** (*countryside*) inaka いなか・田舎; (*outdoors*) yagai 野外

county *n* gún 郡 (*U.S.*); shū́ 州 (*Britain*)

couple → **two; a couple** *n* (*husband and wife*) fū́fu 夫婦, (*on a date*) abékku アベック

coupon ticket *n* kaisū́-ken 回数券

courage *n* yū́ki 勇気

course *n* kṓsu コース; (*in school*) kamoku 科目; (*of action*) hōshin 方針; (*of time*) keika 経過;

(*development*) nariyuki 成り行き・なりゆき; *in the ~ ... of* (*during*) ...-chu (ni) 中(に)

course → **of course**

court *n* **1.** (*of law*) saiban-sho 裁判所, hōtei 法廷   **2.** (*sports*) kōto コート   **3.** (*imperial/royal*) kyūtei 宮廷

court dances and music *n* búgaku 舞楽

courtesy *n* reigí 礼儀

cousin *n* itóko いとこ・従兄弟・従姉妹

cover *n* (*lid*) futa ふた・蓋; kabā カバー; (*book, magazine, etc.*) hyōshi 表紙

cover *v* **1.** (*covers it*) ōimásu (ōu, ōtte) 覆[おお]います(覆う・おおう、覆って); (*includes all items*) mṓra shimásu (suru, shíte) 網羅します(する、して)   **2.** *~ with a roof ...* no yáne o fukimásu (fuku, fuite) ... の屋根をふきます(ふく、ふいて)   **3.** *~ up* (*conceals*) fusemásu (fuséru, fuséte) 伏せます(伏せる、伏せて)

cover charge *n* (*restaurant*) seki-ryō 席料, sābisu-ryō サービス料; (*admission*) nyūjṓ-ryō 入場料

cow *n* ushi 牛・ウシ (*how many* nán-tō 何頭)

coward *n* okubyō-mono 臆病[憶病・おくびょう]者; *cowardice* n okubyṓ 臆病・憶病・おくびょう; *cowardly* adj okubyṓ (na) 臆病(な)

crab *n* kani カニ・蟹 (**1:** ip-pikí 一匹, **2:** ní-hiki 二匹, **3:** sánbiki 三匹, *how many* nán-biki 何匹)

crack   **1.** *n* suki (-ma) 透き(間); (*wide*) ware-me 割れ目; (*fine*) hibí ひび・ヒビ; (*flaw*) kizu 傷   **2.** *it cracks* v waremásu (wareru, warete) 割れます(割れる、割れて)

crackers *n* kurákkā クラッカー, bisuketto ビスケット

cradle *n* yuri-kago ゆりかご・揺り籠

crag *n* iwá 岩

cram; *crams it in* v tsumemásu (tsuméru, tsúmete) 詰めます(詰める、詰めて); *it is crammed in* tsu-marimásu (tsumáru, tsumátte) 詰まります(詰まる、詰まって)

cram school *n* júku 塾

cramp *n* **1.** (*leg*) tsuru つる   **2.** (*stomach*) ikeiren 胃痙攣・胃けいれん

crane *n* **1.** (*bird*) tsúru ツル・鶴   **2.** (*machine*) kurḗn クレーン

crash *n* (*plane*) tsuiraku 墜落; (*collision*) shōtotsu 衝突

crass *adj* egetsunái えげつない

crate *n* wakú 枠, hako 箱

crater *n* funka -kō 噴火口

crawl *v* haimásu (háu, hátte) はいます・這います(はう、はって)

crawly *adj* múzumuzu (shimásu; suru, shíte) むずむず・ムズムズ(します; する、して)

crazy *adj* **1.** ki-chigái (no) 気違い・きちがい(の); **2.** *is crazy about ...* ni muchū́ désu ... に夢中です

cream *n* kurímu クリーム cream puff *n* shū-kurímu シュークリーム

crease *n* **1.** shiwa しわ・皺   **2.** (*pleat*) orimé 折り目

create *v* ts<u>u</u>kurimás<u>u</u> (ts<u>u</u>kúru, ts<u>u</u>kutte) 造[創]り ます(造[創]る, 造[創]って)

creator *n* (*god*) *sōzō-shu* 創造主, (*artists*) kurieitā クリエイター

creature *n* séibutsu 生物, kuriichā クリーチャー

credit *n* **1.** shin'yō 信用 **2.** (*one's credit*) noren の れん・暖簾 **3.** (*on credit*) kaké 掛け; *buys it on ~* (*on one's account*) ts<u>u</u>ké de kaimás<u>u</u> (kau, katte) つけで買います(買う, 買って)

credit sales *n* kakeuri 掛け売り, uri-kake 売り 掛け

credit card *n* kurejitto-kā´do クレジットカード

credit limit *n* kurejitto (kā´do) no gendo-gaku ク レジット(カード)の限度額

creed *n* shinjō 信条

creek *n* ogawa 小川

creep 1. *v* haimás<u>u</u> (hau, hatte) はい[這い]ます (這う, 這って); (*baby*) hai hai shimás<u>u</u> (suru, sh<u>i</u>te) はいはいします(する, して) **2.** *that creep n* aitsu あいつ

creeper *n* tsuru shokubutsu つる植物

creepy *adj* múzumuzu (shimás<u>u</u>; suru, sh<u>i</u>te) むずむず・ムズムズ(します; する, して)

cremation *n* kasō 火葬, shōkyaku 焼却

crematorium *n* kasō-ba 火葬場

crescent *n* mikazuki 三日月, shingetsu 新月

crest; *family crest* *n* monshō 紋章, món 紋, kamon 家紋

crested ibis *n* tóki トキ・朱鷺

crevice *n* ware-me 割れ目

crew *n* (*member*) norikumí-in 乗組員, (*of ship*) sen'in 船員

crew cut *n* kurū-katto クルーカット, kakugari 角刈り

crew neck *n* kurū-nekku クルーネック

crime *n* tsúmi 罪, hanzai 犯罪

criminal *n* (*culprit*) hánnin 犯人

crimson *adj* makká (na) 真っ赤・まっか(な)

cripple *n* shintai shōgaisha 身体障害者; *is crippled* ashí ga fú-jiyū des<u>u</u> 脚が不自由です

crisis *n* (*critical moment*) k<u>í</u>kí 危機

crisp *adj* paripari (no) パリパリ・ぱりぱり (の)

criterion *n* (*standard of judgment*) monosáshí も のさし・物差し・物指し, kijun 基準

critic *n* h<u>i</u>hyō-ka 批評家, (*judge*) h<u>i</u>hán-sha 批判 者; (*commentator*) hyōron-ka 評論家

critical *adj* (*judgmental*) h<u>i</u>han-teki (na) 批判的 (な); (*urgent*) kinkyū (na) 緊急(な)

critical moment *n* k<u>í</u>kí 危機

criticism *n* **1.** h<u>i</u>hyō 批評; (*favorable*) kōhyō 好評; (*unfavorable*) ak<u>u</u>hyō 悪評 **2.** (*commentary*) hyōron 評論

criticize *v* h<u>i</u>hyō shimás<u>u</u> (suru, sh<u>i</u>te) 批評します (する, して); (*judges*) h<u>i</u>han shimás<u>u</u> (suru, sh<u>i</u>te) 批判します(する, して); (*comments on*) hyōron shimás<u>u</u> (suru, sh<u>i</u>te) 評論します(する, して); (*censures*) sememás<u>u</u> (seméru, sémete) 責めます (責める, 責めて)

crock *n* tsubo つぼ・壷

crocodile *n* wáni ワニ・鰐

crony *n* nakama 仲間

crop *n* (*harvest*) minori 実り, shūkaku 収穫

cross 1. *n* (*symbol*) júji 十字; (*wooden*) jūji-ka 十字架 **2.** *n* ("×") bátsu ばつ (*vs.* maru 丸 "○")

cross *v* **1.** (*goes across*) watarimás<u>u</u> (wataru, watatte) 渡ります(渡る, 渡って), yoko-girimás<u>u</u> (yoko-gíru, yoko-gítte) 横切ります(横切る, 横切って); (*goes over a height*) koemás<u>u</u> (koeru, koete) 越えます(越える, 越えて) **2.** (*crosses one's legs*) kumimás<u>u</u> (kúmu, kúnde) 脚を組みます(組む, 組んで)

crossbeam *n* keta けた・ケタ・桁

crossing *n* (*street intersection*) kōsa-ten 交差点; (*crossing over*) ōdan 横断

crossroads *n* jūjí-ro 十字路, tsuji 辻 → **intersection**

cross-talk comedy *n* manzái 漫才

crossword puzzle *n* kurosuwādo (pazuru) クロスワード(パズル)

crotch *n* matá また・股

crouch *v* shagamimás<u>u</u> (shagamu, shagande) しゃ がみます(しゃがむ, しゃがんで); (*so as not to be seen*) mi o f<u>u</u>semás<u>u</u> (f<u>u</u>séru, f<u>u</u>séte) 身を伏せます (伏せる, 伏せて)

crow *n* kárasu カラス・烏・鴉

crowd *n* gunshū 群衆, renjū/renchū 連中; *in crowds* zórozoro ぞろぞろ

crowded; *gets ~* komimás<u>u</u> (kómu, kónde) こみ ます・混みます(こむ, こんで); *is ~* kónde imás<u>u</u> (iru, ite) こんで[混んで]います(いる, いて)

crown *n* ōkan 王冠

Crown Prince *n* Kōtáishi 皇太子, Kōtáishi-sama 皇太子様; *Crown Princess* Kōtáishi-hi 皇太子妃

crucian carp *n* fúna フナ・鮒

crude *adj* sómatsu (na) 粗末(な), zatsu (na) 雑(な)

cruel *adj* mugói むごい, tsurai つらい・辛い, hakujō (na) 薄情(な), zankoku (na) 残酷(な), zangyaku (na) 残虐(な)

cruelly *adv* h<u>í</u>doku ひどく

cruise *n* kurūzu クルーズ, funa-tabi 船旅

cruiser *n* kurūzā クルーザー

crumble *v* (*it crumbles*) kudakemás<u>u</u> (kudakéru, kudákete) 砕けます(砕ける, 砕けて); (*crumbles it*) kudakimás<u>u</u> (kudáku, kudáite) 砕きます(砕く, 砕いて)

crumb(s) *n* pan-kúzu パンくず・パン屑, pan-kó パン粉

crush *v* (*crushes it*) tsubushimás<u>u</u> (tsubusu, tsubu-sh<u>i</u>te) つぶします・潰します(つぶす, つぶして); (*it gets crushed*) tsuburemás<u>u</u> (tsubureru, tsuburete) つぶれます・潰れます(つぶれる, つぶれて)

crust *n* kawá 皮

crutch *n* matsuba-zúe 松葉杖

cry *v* nakimás<u>u</u> (naku, naite) 泣きます(泣く, 泣い て); (*cries out*) sakebimás<u>u</u> (sakébu, sakénde) 叫びます(叫ぶ, 叫んで)

cryptomeria n (*Japanese cedar*) sugi 杉・スギ

crystal n suishō 水晶, kesshō 結晶, kurisutaru クリスタル

cub n ko 子

cubbyhole n 1. (*snug room/place*) igokochi no yoi heya/basho 居心地の良い部屋/場所 2. (*small room/place*) chiisai heya/basho 小さい部屋/場所

cube n rippō (-tai) 立方(体)

cubic adj rippō-tai (*no*) 立方体(の), rippō (no) 立方(の)

cuckoo n kákkō カッコウ; (*little*) hototógisu ホトトギス

cucumber n kyū´ri キュウリ; (*sushi-bar term*) kappa カッパ

cuff n káfusu カフス

cuff link n kafusu botan カフスボタン

culprit n hánnin 犯人

cult n karuto カルト

cultivate v tagayashimásu (tagayasu, tagayashite) 耕します(耕す, 耕して)

cultural festival n bunká-sai 文化祭

cultural shock n karuchā-shokku カルチャーショック

culture n (*refinement*) kyōyō 教養; (*farming*) yōshoku 養殖; (*civilization*) búnka 文化; **Culture Day** (*3 November*) Búnka no hí 文化の日

culture center n karuchā sentā カルチャーセンター

cultured pearls n yōshoku-shínju 養殖真珠

cunning adj zurúi ずるい

cup n chawan 茶碗 (o-cháwan お茶碗), koppu コップ, (*with handle*) káppu カップ; (*cupful*) ... -hai ... 杯 (1: íp-pai 一杯, 2: ní-hai 二杯, 3: sánbai 三杯, *how many* nán-hai 何杯)

cupboard n (*enclosed shelves*) todana 戸棚; (*for dishes*) shokki-tódana 食器戸棚; (*closet*) oshi-ire 押し入れ

curb 1. n (*of road*) hodō´ no fuchí 歩道の縁・ふち → **sidewalk** 2. v yokusei 抑制します 3. v (*restrains*) yokusei shimásu (suru, shíte) 抑制します(する, して)

cure v naoshimásu (naósu, naóshite) 治します(治す, 治して)

curios n kottō-hin 骨董品 → **antiques**

curiosity n kōkíshin 好奇心

curious adj (*inquisitive*) monózukí (na) 物好き(な); (*novel*) mezurashíi 珍しい・めずらしい; *I'm curious about something.* Shiri-tái/Kiki-tai kotó ga arimásu. 知りたい/聞きたいことがあります.

curly v *become* ~ chijiremásu (chijireru, cnijirite) 縮れます(縮れる, 縮れて)

currant n rēzun レーズン; hoshibudō 干しブドウ

currency n (*bill/note*) satsu 札(o-satsu お礼); shíhei 紙幣

current 1. adj (*present*) génzai no ... 現在の..., gén (-) ... 現...; **current address** n gen-jū´sho 現住所 **current deposit** n tōza-yókin 当座預金

2. n (*tide*) chōryū 潮流

current affairs n jiji(mondai) 時事(問題)

currently adv génzai 現在

curriculum n karikyuramu カリキュラム

curriculum vitae n rirekisho 履歴書

curry n karē カレー; (*with rice*) karē-ráisu カレーライス

curry powder n karē ko カレー粉

curse 1. n noroi のろい・呪い 2. v (*utters a curse*) noroimásu (noróu, norótte) のろい[呪い]ます(のろう, のろって), (*reviles*) nonoshirimásu (nonoshíru, nonoshítte) ののしります・罵る(ののしる, ののしって)

cursor n (*computer*) kāsoru カーソル

cursory adj 1. (*hasty*) isogi (no) 急ぎ(の) 2. (*superficial*) hyōmen-teki (na) 表面的(な) 3. (*perfunctory*) ozanari (na) おざなり(な)

curt adj bu-áisō (na) 無愛想(な), bukkírábō (na) ぶっきらぼう(な)

curtail v herashimásu (herasu, herashíte) 減らします(減らす, 減らして)

curtain n kā´ten カーテン; (*bamboo*) sudare すだれ; (*stage*) makú 幕

curtain rod n kāten-róddo カーテンロッド

curtain time n kaien-jíkan 開演時間

curve 1. n magari 曲がり; (*road*) kābu カーブ; (*bend*) sorí そり・反り, (*arch*) yumi-gata 弓形 2. *it curves* v magarimásu (magaru, magatte) 曲がります(曲がる, 曲がって) 3. *curves it* v magemásu (mageru, magete) 曲げます(曲げる, 曲げて)

cushion n (*seat*) zabúton 座布団; (*spread*) shiki-mono 敷物; kusshon クッション

custard n kasutādo (kuriimu) カスタード (クリーム)

custard pudding n kasutādo purin カスタードプリン

custodian n 1. (*janitor*) kózukai 小使い, yōmu-in 用務員 2. (*administrator*) kanri-nin 管理人

custody n (*child custody*) yōiku-ken 養育権

custom n 1. shūkan 習慣 2. (*tradition*) dentō 伝統

customary adj jū´rai (no) 従来(の)

customer n (o-)kyaku (お)客, o-kyaku-samá お客様; (*patron*) otokui お得意, tokui-saki 得意先

customer center n kasutamā sentā カスタマーセンター

customer service n kasutamā sābisu カスタマーサービス

custom-made adj ōdā meido (no) オーダーメイド(の)

customs n (*place*) zeikan 税関; (*tariff*) kanzei 関税, zéi 税

customs duty n kanzei 関税

customs officer n zeikan shokuin 税関職員

customs official n zeimukan 税務官

cut 1. v kirimásu (kíru, kítte) 切ります(切る, 切って); (*mows*) karimásu (karu, katte) 刈ります

(刈る, 刈って); (*it cuts well*) kiremás<u>u</u> (kiréru, kírete) 切れます(切れる, 切れて) **2.** *n* (*of cloth*) kata 型; (*share*) wake-mae 分け前; (*percentage*) rítsu 率

cuts the price *v* makemás<u>u</u> (makeru, makete) 負けます(負ける, 負けて)

cut across *v* yoko-girimás<u>u</u> (yoko-gíru, yoko-gítte) 横切ります(横切る, 横切って)

cut back *v* sakugenshimás<u>u</u> (suru, shite) 削減します(する, して)

cut class *v* saborimás<u>u</u> (sabóru, sabótte) さぼります(さぼる, さぼって)

cut down *v* (*lessens*) herashimás<u>u</u> (herasu, herashite) 減らします(減らす, 減らして); (*reduces*) chijimemás<u>u</u> (chijiméru, chijímete) ちぢめます・縮めます(ちぢめる, ちぢめて); (*dilutes*) warimás<u>u</u> (waru, watte) 割ります(割る, 割って)

cut in (into) *v* wari-kómimás<u>u</u> (wari-kómu, wari-kónde) 割り込みます(割り込む, 割り込んで)

cut off *v* kirimás<u>u</u> (kíru, kítté) 切ります(切る, 切って); tachimás<u>u</u> (tátsu, tátte) 裁ちます・断ちます・絶ちます(裁[断・絶]つ, 裁[断・絶]って)

cut out *v* (*eliminates*) habukimás<u>u</u> (habúku, habúite) 省きます(省く, 省いて)

cutback *n* sakugen 削減

cute *adj* **1.** kawaíi かわいい・可愛い, kawairashíi かわいらしい・可愛らしい **2.** (*handsome*) kakkoii かっこいい

cuticle *n* **1.** (*nail*) amakawa 甘皮 **2.** (*hair*) kyutikuru キューティクル **3.** kuchikura クチクラ

cutlery *n* **1.** (*cutting instruments*) há-mono 刃物 **2.** (*tableware*) shokki-rui 食器類

cutlet *n* kátsu(retsu) カツ(レツ)

pork cutlet *n* tonkatsu 豚カツ・とんかつ・トンカツ

cutout *n* anzen sōchi 安全装置

cut-rate *adj* waribiki (no) 割引(の), yasu-uri (no) 安売り(の)

cutthroat *n* hitogoroshi 人殺し

cuttlefish *n* (*squid*) ika イカ

dried cuttlefish *n* surume スルメ

cyanide *n* shian kabutsu シアン化物, seisan kabutsu (na) 青酸化物

cyberspace *n* saibā-supēsu サイバースペース

cycle *n* (*circulation*) junkan 循環, saikuru サイクル

cycling *n* saikuringu サイクリング

cyclist *n* saikurisuto サイクリスト

cyclone *n* saikuron サイクロン, teikiatsu 低気圧

cygnet *n* wakai hakuchō 若いハクチョウ[白鳥]

cylinder *n* ts<u>u</u>tsu 筒, shirindā シリンダー

cymbal *n* shinbaru シンバル

cynic *n* hiniku-ya 皮肉屋

cynical *adj* hiniku (na) 皮肉(な), shinikaru (na) シニカル(な)

cynicism *n* shinikaru na taido シニカルな態度

cypress *n* **1.** hinoki ヒノキ・檜 **2.** itosugi イトスギ

Cypriot *adj* kipurosu (no) キプロス(の)

Cyprus *n* kipurosu キプロス

cyst *n* nōhō 嚢胞・のうほう; nōshu 脳腫・のうしゅ

cystitis *n* bōkō-en 膀胱炎

Czechoslovakia *n* chekosurobakia チェコスロバキア

Czechoslovakian *n* **1.** (*language*) chekosurobakia-go チェコスロバキア語 **2.** (*people*) chekosurobakia-jin チェコスロバキア人

D

dab *n* hitonuri ひと塗り・ひとぬり

daddy, dad *n* papa パパ

daffodil *n* rappa-zuisen ラッパズイセン

dagger *n* tanken 短剣

daily *n* **1.** (*newspaper*) nikkan(-shi) 日刊(紙) **2.** *adj* (*everyday*) mainichi(no) 毎日(の)

dainty *adj* **1.** (*delicate beauty*) yūbi (na) 優美(な), **2.** *n* (*something delicious*) oishii-mono おいしいもの・美味しいもの

dairy *n* (*milk shop*) *n* gyūnyū-ya 牛乳屋

dais *n* endai 演台

daisy *n* hinagiku ヒナギク・ひな菊, deijii デイジー

dam *n* dámu ダム

damage 1. *n* songai 損害; són 損・そん, gái 害, higai 被害・ひがい, daméji ダメージ **2.** *damages it* *v* itamemás<u>u</u> (itaméru, itámete) 傷めます(傷め

る, 傷めて), arashimás<u>u</u> (arásu, aréte) 荒らします・あらします(荒らす, 荒れて); sokonaimás<u>u</u> (sokonau, sokonátte) そこないます・損ないます(損なう, 損なって)

damascene *n* zō´gan 象眼・象嵌

damask *n* dónsu どんす・緞子

dame *n* (*woman, sometimes offensive*) onna 女・おんな

Damn! *interj* Shimátta! しまった!

damn (*fool*) *n* ...-me ...め; *damn idiot* baka-me ばかめ

damp 1. *adj* shimeppoi 湿っぽい・しめっぽい; **2.** *gets ~ v* shimerimás<u>u</u> (shimeru, shimette) 湿ります・しめります(湿る, 湿って), nuremás<u>u</u> (nureru, nurete) ぬれます・濡れます(ぬれる, ぬれて)

dampen *v* nurashimásu (nurasu, nurashite) ぬらします・濡らします(ぬらす, ぬらして), shimeshimásu (shimesu, shimeshite) 湿します (湿す, 湿して)

damp (hand-)towel *n* o-shíbori おしぼり

dampness *n* shikki 湿気, shikke 湿気・しっけ

dance 1. *n* odori 踊り・おどり, dansu ダンス **2.** *dances v* odorimásu (odoru, odotte) 踊ります・おどります(踊る, 踊って)

dancer *n* (*Japanese-style*) odori-te 踊り手; (*Western-style*) dansā ダンサー

dandelion *n* tánpopo タンポポ

dandruff *n* fuke ふけ

dandy 1. *n* (*fancy dresser*) osháre おしゃれ・お洒落 **2.** *v* oshåre (na) おしゃれ・お洒落(な)

Dane *n* (*people*) dēn-zoku デーン族, denmāku no minzoku デンマークの民族

danger *n* kiken 危険・キケン; (*crisis*) kyū 急; (*fear/worry lest …*) …osoré/shinpai …恐れ・おそれ/心配

dangerous *adj* abunai 危ない・あぶない, kiken (na) 危険(な); yabái やばい; (*delicate, ticklish*) kiwadói きわどい

dangle *v* (*dangles it*) sagemásu (sagéru, ságete) 下げます(下げる, 下げて), tarashimásu (tarásu, taráshite) 垂らします(垂らす, 垂らして); (*it dangles*) taremásu (taréru, tárete) 垂れます (垂れる, 垂れて)

dangling *adj* (*idly*) búrabura ぶらぶら・ブラブラ

Danish 1. *n* (*language*) denmāku-go デンマーク語; (*person*) denmāku-jin デンマーク人 **2.** *n* (*pastry*) denishu デニッシュ **3.** *adj* (*concerning Denmark*) denmāku-go(-jin) no デンマーク語 (人)の

dare (*to do*) *v* áete (shimásu) あえて(します)

dark 1. *adj* kurai 暗い; (*color*) kói [COLOR NAME] (no) 濃い・こい [COLOR NAME] (の) **2.** *the dark n* higure 日暮れ, yamí 闇; *it gets ~* hi ga kuremásu (kureru, kurete) 日が暮れます(暮れる, 暮れて)

dark blue *n* kón 紺・コン, kon-iro (no) 紺色(の)

dark glasses *n* sangurasu サングラス

darkness *n* (kura-)yami (暗)闇・(暗)やみ

darling *adj* kawaii かわいい・可愛い, kawairashíi かわいらしい・可愛らしい

darts *n* dātsu ダーツ

dash *n* dasshu ダッシュ

dashboard *n* dasshu-bōdo ダッシュボード

data *n* dḗta データ, shiryō 資料

database *n* dētabēsu データベース

date *n* **1.** (*of month*) hizuke 日付(け)・日づけ; (*complete*) nengáppi 年月日; *date of birth* seinen-gáppi 生年月日 **2.** (*engagement*) yakusoku 約束・やくそく(o-yakusoku お約束) **3.** (*a couple*) dēto (shimásu; suru, shite) デート(します; する, して)

date *n* (*fruit*) natsume なつめ

dated *adj* [DATE]-zuke [...日]付け

daughter *n* musume(-san) 娘・むすめ(さん); (*your*) ojō´ san お嬢さん; *eldest daughter* chōjo 長女

daughter-in-law *n* **1.** (*wife of your son*) musuko no tsuma 息子の妻 **2.** (*wife of someone's son*) o-yome-san お嫁さん・およめさん

dawn *n* yoaké 夜明け・夜あけ, akegata 明け方・あけがた

day *n* hi 日, …hí …日; (*daytime*) hirú 昼・ひる (o-híru お昼), hirumá 昼間・ひるま; *the day in question, that very day* tō´jitsu 当日; (*fixed*) hinichi 日にち・ひにち

day after tomorrow *n* asátte あさって・明後日, myō´go-nichi 明後日

day before last/yesterday *n* ototói おととい・一昨日, issakú-jitsu 一昨日

day in and day out aketémo kuretémo 明けても暮れても・あけてもくれても

day off *n* yasumí (no hí) 休み・やすみ(の日), kyūka 休暇

daybreak *n* akegata 明け方・あけがた, yoake 夜明け

daydream 1. *n* kūsō´ 空想, hakuchūmu 白昼夢 **2.** *v* bon'yári shimásu (suru, shite) ぼんやりします(する, して)

daylight *n* nitchū 日中, hiru no hikari 昼の光

days *n 1 day* ichi-nichí 一日, *2 days* futsuka 二日, *3 days* mikka 三日, *4 days* yokka 四日, *5 days* itsuka 五日, *6 days* muika 六日, *7 days* nanoka 七日, *8 days* yō´ka 八日, *9 days* kokonoka 九日, *10 days* tō´ka 十日, *14 days* jú-yokka 十四日, *24 days* ní-jū yokka 二十四日; (*others* …-nichi …日); *how many days* nán-nichi 何日

daytime *n* hirú 昼・ひる (o-híru お昼・おひる), hiru-má 昼間・ひるま

dazed; gets ~ bō´tto shimásu (suru, shite) ぼうっとします(する, して), madoimásu (madóu, madótte) 惑います・まどいます(惑う, 惑って)

dazzling *adj* mabushíi まぶしい・眩しい, mabayui まばゆい・眩い

DC, direct current *n* chokuryū 直流

dead 1. *adj* shinda …死んだ…; *is ~* shinde imásu (iru, ite) 死んでいます(いる, いて) **2.** *dead person n* nakunatta hitó 亡くなった人, shinda hitó 死んだ人, shinin 死人

deaden *v* **1.** (*becomes dead*) shinimásu (sinu, shinde) 死にます(死ぬ, 死んで) **2.** (*makes less sensitive*) mu-kankaku ni shimásu (suru, shite) 無感覚にします(する, して) **3.** (*weakens*) yowamarimásu (yowamaru, yowamatte) 弱まります(弱まる, 弱まって) **4.** (*makes impervious to sound*) bōon ni shimásu (suru, shite) 防音にします(する, して)

dead end *n* ikidomari 行き止まり

dead heat *n* dōchaku 同着

deadline *n* shimekiri 締め切り・〆切(り)・しめきり, (saishū-)kígen (最終)期限, kíjitsu 期日

deaf 1. *n* (*person*) mimi no kikoenai hito 耳の聞こえない人; *is deaf* mimi ga fú-jiyū desu 耳が不自由です **2.** *adj* mimi no kikoenai 耳の聞こえない, mimí ga fujiyū na 耳が不自由な

deafness *n* nanchō 難聴

deal 1. *n* (*transaction*) torí-hiki 取引 **2.** *v* (*cards*) kubarimásu (kubáru, kubátte) 配ります(配る, 配って); *a good/great deal* → **lots, much**

deal in (*sells*) urimásu (uru, utte) 売ります (売る, 売って), hanbai shimásu (suru, shite) 販売します(する, して)

deal with tori-atsukaimásu (tori-atsukau, tori-atsukatte) 取り扱います (取り扱う, 取り扱って); (*treats a person*) ashiraimásu (ashiráu, ashirátte) あしらいます(あしらう, あしらって); (*copes*) shóri/shóbun/shóchi shimásu (suru, shite) 処理/処分/処置します(する, して); (*disposes of a matter*) chímatsu chimásu (suru, chite) 始末します (する, して)

dealer *n* kouriten 小売店, (*retail outlet*) hanbái-ten 販売店, diirā ディーラー; (*seller of …*) …-shő´ …商, …-ya …屋

dealing *n* torihiki 取(り)引(き)

dean *n* gakubu-chō 学部長

dear *adj* **1.** (*beloved*) itoshíi いとしい・愛しい, natsukashíi 懐かしい・なつかしい **2.** (*precious*) taisetsu (na) 大切(な); *Dear Sir/Madam* Haikei 拝啓; *Dear dear!* *interj* Oyaoya! おやおや!; *Dear me! interj* (*feminine*) Mā! まあ! **3.** → **expensive**

dearly *adv* hijō (ni) 非常(に), kokoro-kara 心から

death *n* shí 死

death penalty *n* shí-kei 死刑

death toll *n* shibō-sha sū 死亡者数

debacle *n* hōkai 崩壊, dōraku 道楽

debatable *adj* giron no yochi ga aru 議論の余地がある

debate 1. *n* tō´ron 討論, ronsō´ 論争 **2.** *debates it* *v* ron-jimásu (ron-jiru, ron-jite) 論じます (論じる, 論じて)

debauchery *n* hōtō 放蕩

debit *n* fusai 負債, (*bookkeeping*) karikata 借方

debris *n* zangai 残骸・残がい

debt *n* shakkín 借金

debug *n* debaggu デバッグ

debut *n* debyū デビュー

decade *n* jū nen-kan 十年間・10年間

decadence *n* taihai 退廃

decaffeinated *adj* kafein nuki (no) カフェイン抜き(の)

decanter *n* mizusashi 水差し

decay 1. *v* kuchimásu (kuchiru, kuchite) 朽ちます (朽ちる, 朽ちて); kusarimásu (kusaru, kusátte) 腐ります・くさります(腐る, 腐って) **2.** *n* [BOOKISH] fuhai 腐敗

decayed tooth *n* mushi-ba 虫歯・ムシバ

deceased *n the deceased* kojin 故人

deceive → **cheat**

deceit *n* **1.** (*lie*) itsuwari 偽り・いつわり **2.** (*fraud*) sagi 詐欺・サギ

deceitful *adj* fu-shōjiki (na) 不正直(な)

deception *n* (*cheat*) gomakashi ごまかし, (*fraud*) sagi 詐欺・サギ

December *n* Jūni-gatsú 十二月・12月

decency *n* reigi 礼儀

decent *adj* (*respectable*) jō´hin (na) 上品(な), rippa (na) 立派・りっぱ(な)

decibel *n* deshiberu デシベル

decide *v* kimemásu (kimeru, kimete) 決めます・きめます(決める, 決めて); kettei shimásu (suru, shite) 決定します(する, して)

decider *n* **1.** (*person*) kettei-sha 決定者 **2.** (*game*) kettei-sen 決定戦

decimal *n* shōsū 小数; *decimal point* shōsū-ten 小数点

decision *n* kettei 決定

deck 1. *n* (*of ship*) kanpan 甲板, dékki デッキ **2.** → **pack** (*of cards*)

deckchair *n* dekki chea デッキチェア

decline 1. *v* **1.** (*refuses*) kotowarimásu (kotowáru, kotowátte) 断わります・ことわります(断わる, 断わって), jitai shimásu (suru, shite) 辞退します (する, して) **2.** (*it fades*) otoroemásu (otoróeru, otoróete) 衰えます(衰える, 衰えて)

declutch *v* kuratchi o kirimásu (kiru, kitte) クラッチを切ります(切る, 切って)

decode *v* kaidoku shimásu (suru, shite) 解読します(する, して)

decompose *v* (*rots*) fuhai shimásu (suru, shite) 腐敗します(する, して)

decor *n* sōshoku (hin) 装飾(品)

decorate *v* kazarimásu (kazaru, kazatte) 飾ります・かざります(飾る, 飾って)

decoration *n* kazari(-mono) 飾り・かざり(物), sō´shoku 装飾, dekōreshon デコレーション

decorative *adj* sōshoku teki (na) 装飾的(な)

decorator *n* sōshoku-sha 装飾者

decorum *n* reigi (sahō) 礼儀(作法)

decoy *n* otori おとり

decrease 1. *v* (*it decreases*) herimásu (heru, hette) 減ります(減る, 減って), genshō shimásu (suru, shite) 減少します(する, して); (*decreases it*) herashimásu (herasu, herashite) 減らします・へらします(減らす, 減らして) **2.** *n* genshō 減少

decrepit *adj* **1.** (*infirm*) rōsui shita 老衰した **2.** (*dilapidated*) rōkyūka shita 老朽化した

decry *v* kenashimásu (kenasu, kenashite) けなします(けなす, けなして)

dedicate *v* sasagemásu (sasageru, sasagete) 捧げます(捧げる, 捧げて)

dedication *n* kenshin 献身

deduct *v* hikimásu (hiku, hiite) 引きます・ひきます(引く, 引いて)

deed *n* (*act*) shiwaza 仕業・しわざ, kō´i 行為, okonai 行い

deep *adj* **1.** fukái 深い・ふかい **2.** (*saturated color*) kói 濃い・こい; *deep red* makká (na) 真っ赤・まっか(な)

deeply *adv* fukáku 深く・ふかく, (*feeling deeply*) shimijími (to) しみじみ(と)

deer *n* shika 鹿・シカ

deface *v* gaikan o sokonaimásu (sokonau, sokonatte) 外観を損ないます(損なう, 損なって)

301

defamation n chūshō 中傷; (*defamation of character*) meiyo-kison 名誉棄損

default n deforuto デフォルト, shoki-settei 初期設定

defeat 1. n make 負け・まけ, shippai 失敗・しっぱい 2. v (*defeats*) makashimásu (makasu, makashite) 負かします・まかします(負かす, 負かして), yaburimásu (yabúru, yabutte) 破ります・やぶります(破る, 破って); (*is defeated*) makemásu (makeru, makete) 負けます・まけます(負ける, 負けて), mairimásu (máiru, máitte) 参ります・まいります(参る, 参って), (*falls behind*) okure o torimásu (tóru, tótte) 遅れ[おくれ]を取[と]ります(取る, 取って)

defecate v daibén o shimásu (suru, shite) 大便をします(する, して); *defecation* n daibén 大便

defect n ketten 欠点, kizu 傷・きず

defective n furyō-hin 不良品, kekkan-hin 欠陥品

defend v mamorimásu (mamóru, mamótte) 守ります・まもります(守る, 守って); kabaimásu (kabau, kabatte) 庇います・かばいます(庇う, 庇って)

defendant n hikoku(-nin) 被告(人)

defense n (*military*) bōei 防衛, (*sport*) bōgyo 防御, difensu ディフェンス; *The Ministry of Defense* bōei-shō 防衛省

defensive adj bōei (no) 防衛(の), shubi (no) 守備(の)

defer v nobashimásu (nobásu, nobáshite) 延ばします・のばします(延ばす, 延ばして)

deference n 1. (*obedience*) fukujū 服従 2. (*respect*) keii 敬意

defiance n hankō 反抗

defiant adj hankō-teki (na) 反抗的(な)

deficiency n fusoku 不足・ふそく, ketsubō 欠乏, kekkan 欠陥

deficit (*figures*) n aka-ji 赤字

defile v yogoshimásu (yogosu, yogoshite) 汚します(汚す, 汚して)

define v teigi shimásu (suru, shite) 定義します(する, して)

definite adj (*certain amount of*) ittei (no) 一定(の)

definitely adv (*firmly*) kippári (to) きっぱり(と)

definitive adj kakujitsu (na) 確実(な)

deformity n kikei 奇形

defy v …ni sakaraimásu (sakaráu, sakarátte) …に逆らいます(逆らう, 逆らって)

degenerate adj daraku shiteiru 堕落している, daraku shita 堕落した

degrade v (*to lower in dignity*) otoshimemásu (otoshimeru, otoshimete) 貶めます・おとしめます(貶める, 貶めて)

degree n 1. (*extent*) téido 程度・ていど, dó 度, kagen 加減; … 2. *degrees* (*temperature*) …-do …度; (*higher learning*) gákúi 学位

dehydrate v dassui-jōtai ni narimásu (naru, natte) 脱水状態になります(なる, なって)

deify v shinkaku-ka shimásu (suru, shite) 神格化します(する, して), shinsei-shi shimásu (suru, shite)

神聖視します(する, して)

deity n shinsei 神性, kami 神

dejection n rakutan 落胆, iki shōchin 意気消沈

delay v (*delays it*) okurasemásu (okuraseru, okurasete) 遅らせます・おくらせます(遅らせる, 遅らせて); (*gets delayed*) okuremásu (okureru, okurete) 遅れます・おくれます(遅れる, 遅れて)

delegate 1. n (*representative*) daihyō 代表 2. n (*alternate*) dairi (-nin) 代理(人) 3. v (*commits to another*) inin shimásu (suru, shite) 委任します(する, して)

delete v tori-keshimásu (tori-kesu, tori-keshite) 取り消します・とりけします(取り消す, 取り消して)

deletion n tori-keshi 取り消し・取りけし, sakujo 削除

deliberate adj (*intentional*) kói (no) 故意(の); (*careful*) shinchō´ (na) 慎重・しんちょう(な)

deliberately adv wáza to わざと, wázawaza わざわざ, kói (ni) 故意(に)

delicate adj (*fine*) bimyō´ (na) 微妙(な); (*risky*) kiwadói きわどい・際どい

delicatessen n derikatessen デリカテッセン, chōri-zumi shokuhin (-ten) 調理済み食品(店)

delicious adj oishii おいしい・美味しい, [INFORMAL] umái/nmái うまい・んまい

delight 1. adj *is delighted* yorokobi-másu (yorokóbu, yorokónde) 喜びます・よろこびます(喜ぶ, 喜んで); *with great ~* ō´-yórokobi (de) 大喜び(で) 2. n yorokobi 喜び, tanoshimi 楽しみ

delightful adj ureshíi うれしい・嬉しい

delimit v kagirimásu (kagíru, kagítte) 限ります・かぎります(限る, 限って)

delinquency n hikō 非行

delinquent n (*juvenile delinquent*) hikō shōnen shōjo 非行少年少女, furyō 不良

deliria n (*pathology*) senmō せん妄

delirium n (*pathology*) seishin sakuran 精神錯乱, (*excitement*) kōfun 興奮; *delirium tremens* shinsen senmō 振戦せん妄

deliver v todokemásu (todokéru, todókete) 届けます・とどけます(届ける, 届けて)

delivered food n demae 出前

delivery n 1. haitatsu 配達, deribarii デリバリー; *restaurant delivery* (*service/person*) demae 出前; *delivery person* demáé-mochi 出前持ち 2. (*giving birth*) shussan 出産

delta n 1. (*Greek alphabet*) deruta デルタ 2. (*mathematics; incremental change*) sabun 差分 3. (*plain*) sankaku-su 三角州

deluge n (*great flood*) dai-kōzui 大洪水, (*downpour*) gōu 豪雨

delusion n sakkaku 錯覚

deluxe adj jō´ 上, jō´tō´ (no) 上等(の), gō´ka (na) 豪華(な)

deluxe article n tokutō-hin 特等品

deluxe coach n romansu-kā ロマンス・カー

deluxe edition n gōka-ban 豪華版

demand 1. n yō´kyū/seikyū (shimásu; suru, shite)

要求/請求(します; する, して) **2.** v motomemásu (motoméru, motómete) 求めます (求める, 求めて); *is in ~ (sells)* uremásu (ureru, urete) 売れます(売れる, 売れて)

demanding *adj (overly strict)* yakamashíi やかましい

democracy n minshu-shúgi 民主主義, demokurashii デモクラシー

democrat n minshu-shúgi-sha 民主主義者, minshu-tō-in 民主党員

democratic *adj* minshu-shúgi (no) 民主主義(の), minshu-teki (na) 民主的(な)

demolish v kuzushimásu (kuzúsu, kuzúshite) 崩します・くずします(崩す, 崩して); hakai shimásu (suru, shite) 破壊します・はかいします (する, して)

demon n akuma 悪魔, dēmon デーモン

demonize n warumono atsukai 悪者扱い・悪者 あつかい

denial n uchi-keshi 打ち消し・打ちけし, hitei 否定

denim n denimu デニム, denims jiinzu ジーンズ

denomination → **sect**

denominator n bunbo 分母

dense *adj* kói 濃い, mítsu (na) 密(な), missetsu (na) 密接(な)

density n mitsudo 密度

dent n kubomi 窪み・くぼみ

dentifrice n ha-mígaki 歯磨き・はみがき

dentist n há-isha 歯医者

dentistry n shika 歯科

denture n ireba 入れ歯

deny v uchi-keshimásu (uchi-kesu, uchi-keshite) 打ち消します・うちけします(打ち消す, 打ち消 して), hitei shimásu (suru, shite) 否定します (する, して)

deodorant n *(personal)* shō´shū-zai 消臭剤; *(household, etc.)* hōkō-zai 芳香剤

departing at/from v [TIME/PLACE] ... hátsu (no) ...発(の)

department n *(university, hospital)* ká 科; *(company, office)* bumon 部門, bu 部, ka 課; *Department of Health Education and Welfare* hoken kyōiku fukushi-shō 保健教育福祉省; *Department of Humanitarian Affairs* jindō mondai-kyoku 人道問題局

department store n depá´to デパート, hyakká-ten 百貨店

departure n shuppatsu 出発; [TIME/PLACE] ... hátsu (no ...) ...発(の...)
point of departure n shuppátsú-ten 出発点
departure platform n hassha-hōmu 発車ホーム
departure lobby n shuppátsú-robii 出発ロビー
departure time n shuppátsú-jikoku 出発時刻

depend; v ~ on (... ni) tayorimásu (tayóru, tayótte) (...に)頼ります(頼る, 頼って), izon shimásu (suru, shite) 依存します(する, して); *it depends (on ...)* (... ni) yorimásu (yoru, yotte) (...に)よります(よる, よって), ([NOUN], [VERB] -i

い) -shídai desu 次第です・しだいです

dependence n izon 依存

dependent n fuyō-kazoku 扶養家族

depiction n byōsha 描写

depilatory n datsumō´-zai 脱毛剤

deposit 1. v azukemásu (azukéru, azukete) 預け ます・あずけます(預ける, 預けて); *(money)* yokin/chokin shimásu (suru, shite) 預金/貯金し ます(する, して); tsumimásu (tsumu, tsunde) 積み ます・つみます(積む, 積んで) **2.** → **down-payment**

depositor n yokin-sha 預金者

depot n **1.** *(railroad station)* eki 駅 **2.** *(bus station)* basu hatchaku-jō バス発着場 **3.** *(warehouse)* sōko 倉庫

depressed *adj* **1.** *(feeling)* ki ga omoi 気が重 [おも]い **2.** *gets ~ (concave)* hekomimásu (heko-mu, hekonde) へこみます(へこむ, へこんで)

depressing *adj* yūtsu (na) 憂うつ・ゆうつ(な)

depression n *(hard times)* fukéiki 不景気; *(hollow)* kubomi くぼみ・窪み

depth n fukása 深さ; *(of color)* kósa 濃さ

derail v dassen shimásu (suru, shite) 脱線します (する, して); *derailment* n dassen 脱線

derision n azakeri あざけり, reishō 冷笑

derivative n *(word)* hasei-go 派生語

descend v kudarimásu (kudaru, kudatte) 下り ます(下る, 下って)

descendant n shíson 子孫

descent n **1.** *(going down)* kudari 下り・くだり **2.** *(family line)* kakei 家系

describe v *(pictures it)* byōsha shimásu (suru, shite) 描写します(する, して), *(elaborates)* (no kotó) o kuwáshiku iimásu (iu, itte/yutte) ...(のこ と[事])を詳しく言います(言う, 言って/ゆって); *(explains it)* setsumei shimásu (suru, shite) 説明し ます(する, して) → **relate**

description n setsumei 説明

desert n sabaku 砂漠・さばく

deserving *adj (proper)* tō´zen (no) 当然(の)

design 1. n *(sketch)* zuan 図案; dezain デザイン **2.** v *(plans it)* hakarimásu (hakáru, hakátte) 図り ます・はかります(図る, 図って); dezain shimásu (suru, shite) デザインします(する, して)

designate v atemásu (ateru, atete) 当てます・ あてます(当てる, 当てて), shitei shimásu (suru, shite) 指定します(する, して) → **name**

designation n shitei 指定, shimei 指名→ **name**

desirable *adj* nozomashii 望ましい・のぞましい, hoshíi 欲しい・ほしい; *most ~ (ideal)* motte-kói (no) もってこい(の)

desire 1. n nozomi 望み, omói 思い, nén 念; *(hope)* kibō 希望 **2.** *desires it* v (... ga) hoshíi (...が)欲しい; *(wants to do)* (shi-) tái desu (し) たいです; *(hopes for)* nozomimásu (nozomu, nozonde) 望みます(望む, 望んで)

desk n tsukue 机・つくえ, taku 卓; *(desk-top)* takujō´ 卓上; *desk lamp* sutando スタンド, denki sutándo 電気スタンド

despair *n* zetsubō´ 絶望, yáke やけ

desperate *adj* hisshi (no) 必死(の)

desperately *adv* (*hard*) isshō´-kénmei (ni) 一生懸命(に); (*out of despair*) yáke ni nátte やけになって

desperation *n* zetsubō´ 絶望, yáke やけ

despise *v* keibetsu shimásu (suru, shite) 軽蔑します(する, して)

despite (*that*) *prep* ...ni mo kakawarazu ...にもかかわらず・にも関わらず

despot *n* dokusai-sha 独裁者, bōkun 暴君

dessert *n* dezā´to デザート

destination *n* iki sakí 行き先, mokutekí chi 目的地; (*last stop*) shūten 終点

destiny *n* únmei 運命

destroy *v* kowashimásu (kowásu, kowáshite) 壊します(壊す, 壊して); hakai shimásu (suru, shite) 破壊します(する, して); horoboshimásu (horobosu, horoboshite) 滅ぼします(滅ぼす, 滅ぼして)

detach *v* hanashimásu (hanásu, hanáshite) 離します・はなします(離す, 離して)

detailed *adj* kuwashíi 詳しい・くわしい; bisai (na) 微細(な); (*machine, etc.*) seimitsu (na) 精密・せいみつ(な)

details *n* kuwashíi koto 詳しいこと, shō´sai 詳細; (*complexities*) ikisatsu いきさつ・経緯

detect → **see** → **smell** → **hear** → **discover** → **discern**

detective *n* 1. (*consulting detective*) tantei 探偵 2. (*police*) kéiji 刑事 3. (*investigator*) sōsa-kan 捜査官

detective agency *n* kōshin-jo 興信所

detective story (writer) *n* suiri-shōsetsu (sakka) 推理小説(作家)

deteriorate *v* (*weather*) kuzuremásu (kuzuréru, kuzúrete) 崩れます(崩れる, 崩れて)

determination *n* (*decision*) kettei 決定; (*resolve*) késshín 決心

determine (*to do*) *v* kettei shimásu (suru, shite) 決定します(する, して)

determined *adj* ketsuzen to shita 決然とした

detest *v* nikumimásu (nikúmu, nikúnde) 憎みます・にくみます(憎む, 憎んで)

detour *n* mawari-michi 回り道・まわり道, ukai 迂回・うかい, tō´máwari 遠回り・遠まわり

devastate *v* arashimásu (arásu, ará-shite) 荒らします(荒らす, 荒らして)

develop *v* 1. (*it unfolds*) hattatsu/hatten shimásu (suru, shite) 発達/発展します(する, して) 2. (*processes film*) genzō´ shimásu (suru, shite) 現像します(する, して)

developing nation *n* hatten tojō´koku 発展途上国, kōshinkoku 後進国

development *n* hattatsu 発達, hatten 発展, kaihatsu 開発, (*process*) nariyuki 成り行き・なりゆき, (*course*) keika 経過, *housing development* danchi 団地

deviate *v* soremásu (soréru, sórete) それます・逸れます(それる, それて)

device *n* (*gadget*) shikake 仕掛け・しかけ; (*scheme*) kufū 工夫

devil *n* (*ogre*) oní 鬼・オニ, (*Satan*) ákuma 悪魔・アクマ

devil's-tongue *n* (*root made into gelatin*) konnyákú コンニャク・蒟蒻

dew *n* tsúyu 露・つゆ

diabetes *n* tō´nyō´-byō´ 糖尿病

diagonal *adj* nanáme (no) 斜め・ななめ(の)

diagram *n* zu 図, zuhyō´ 図表, zukai 図解

dial *n* (*telephone*) daiyaru ダイヤル

dialect *n* hō´gén 方言; (*regional accent*) namarí なまり

dialogue *n* 1. (*lines*) serifu せりふ・台詞 2. (*conversation*) taiwa 対話, kaiwa 会話

dial tone *n* hasshin-on 発信音

diameter *n* chokkei 直径

diamond *n* daiya ダイヤ, daiyamóndo ダイヤモンド, kongō´-seki 金剛石・こんごうせき

diapers *n* oshíme おしめ, omútsu おむつ

diarrhea *n* geri 下痢・げり

diary *n* nikki 日記, daiarii ダイアリー

dice *n* saikóro さいころ・サイコロ

dichotomy *n* nibun 二分

dictation *n* kakítori 書き取り・かきとり, dikutēshon ディクテーション

dictator *n* dokusái-sha 独裁者, wánman ワンマン

dictatorship *n* dokusai-seiji 独裁政治, dokusai-seiken 独裁政権

dictionary *n* jibikí 字引(き), jishó 辞書・じしょ, jiten 辞典・じてん

dictionary entry *n* midashi 見出し・見だし, midashi-go 見出し語

did *v* shimáshita (shita, shite) しました(した, して)

didn't *v* shimasén deshita (shinákatta, shináide) しませんでした(しなかった, しないで)

die 1. *v* shinimásu (shinu, shinde) 死にます(死ぬ, 死んで), naku-narimásu (naku-naru, naku-natte) 亡くなります(亡くなる, 亡くなって); íki o híki-torimásu (híki-tóru, híki-tótte) 息を引き取ります(引き取る, 引き取って) 2. → **dice**

diesel *n* diizeru ディーゼル

diet *n* kitéi-shoku 規定食, daietto-shoku ダイエット食; daietto (shimásu; suru, shite) ダイエット(します; する, して)

Diet *n* (*parliament*) kokkai 国会, gikai 議会; (*building*) (kokkai) giji-dō´ (国会)議事堂

differ *v* kotonarimásu (kotonáru, kotonátta) 異なります(異なる, 異なって); *~ in opinion* íken ga chigaimásu (chigau, chigatte) 意見が違います(違う, 違って)

difference *n* chigai 違い, sō´i 相違, sa 差・さ, sái 差異; (*a big difference*) táisa 大差・たいさ; *difference in time* jísa 時差; *it makes no ~* kamaimasén (kamawánai, kamawánaide) 構いません・かまいません(構わない, 構わないで)

different *adj* *is ~* chigaimásu (chigau, chigatte)

違います・ちがいます(違う, 違って); kotonari-másu (kotonáru, kotonátte) 異なります・ことなります(異なる, 異なって); *a different direction* tahō´ 他方; *different opinion/view* iron 異論 (= *objection*)

differentiation *n* kúbetsu 区別

difficult *adj* muzukashii 難しい・むずかしい; kónnan (na) 困難(な); (*hard to do*) shi-nikúi しにくい, shi-gatai しがたい・し難い; (*requires much effort*) honé ga oremásu (oréru, órete) 骨が折れます(折れる, 折れて)

difficulty *n* kónnan 困難, (*hardship*) kurō´ 苦労; (*problem*) mondai 問題; (*nuisance*) mondō´ 面倒・めんどう; *with difficulty* yatto やっと

diffusion *n* fukyū´ 普及; *gets diffused* fukyū shimásu (suru, shite) 普及します(する, して)

dig *v* horimásu (hóru, hótte) 掘ります(掘る, 掘って)

digest *v* konashimásu (konasu, konashite) こなします(こなす, こなして), shō´ka shimásu (suru, shite) 消化します(する, して)

digestion *n* shō´ka 消化

digit *n* 1. (*Arabic figures*) (arabia) sūji (アラビア)数字 2. (*digit number*) ketasū 桁数 3. (*finger or toe*) yubi 指

digital *n* dejitaru デジタル

dignified *adj* igen no aru 威厳のある

dignitary *n* kōkan 高官

dignity *n* 1. (*nobility*) hin(-sei) 品(性), kihin 気品 2. (*respect and honor*) songen 尊厳; *death with dignity* songen-shi 尊厳死

digress *v* soremásu (soréru, sórete) それます・逸れます(それる, それて)

digression *n* dassen 脱線, yodan 余談

dike *n* (*levee*) tsutsumí 堤・つつみ, dote 土手, teibō´ 堤防・ていぼう

dilapidated; *gets ~* aremásu (areru, arete) 荒れます・あれます(荒れる, 荒れて)

dilemma *n* tō´waku 当惑, jirenma ジレンマ

diligent *adj* kinben (na) 勤勉(な), mame (na) まめ(な)

diligently *adv* kinben ni 勤勉に; sésse-to せっせと

dilute 1. *v* (*dilutes it*) (mizu de) warimásu (waru, watte) (水で)割ります(割る, 割って), usumemásu (usumeru, usumete) 薄めます(薄める, 薄めて) 2. *adj* (*dilute acid*) nōdo ga usui 濃度が薄い

dim 1. *adj* (*faint*) kásuka (na) かすか・微か(な), (*dark*) kurai 暗い・くらい 2. *v* (*gets dim, hazy*) kasumimásu (kasumu, kasunde) かすみます・霞みます(かすむ, かすんで)

dime *n* jussento kōka 10セント硬貨

dimple *n* ékubo えくぼ

din *n* sōon 騒音

dine *v* shokuji (o) shimásu (suru, shite) 食事(を)します(する, して)

diner *n* (*dining car*) shokudō´-sha 食堂車

dingey, dinghy *n* (*boat*) (kogata) bōto (小型)ボート

dining room *n* shokudō´ 食堂, daini'ngu rūmu ダイニングルーム

dinner *n* (*meal*) shokuji 食事, góhan ご飯・ごはん, (*supper*) ban góhan 晩ご飯・晩ごはん, yūshoku 夕食, yū gohan 夕ご飯・夕ごはん, yū-han/yū-meshi 夕飯

dinner jacket *n* takishiido タキシード

dinosaur *n* kyōryū 恐竜

diploma *n* 1. menjō´ 免状 2. (*graduation diploma*) sotsugyō-shōsho 卒業証書

diplomacy *n* gaikō´ 外交

diplomat *n* (*diplomatic official*) gaikō´-kan 外交官; (*diplomatic person*) gaikō´-ka 外交家

diplomatic *adj* gaikō´-teki (na) 外交的(な); gaikō´ (no) 外交(の); *~ in manner* sotsu no nai... そつのない

diplomatic relations *n* gaikō´ 外交

direct 1. *adj* chokusetsu (no) 直接(の); *goes ~* (*through to destination*) chokusetsu ikimásu 直接行きます 2. *v* (*tells the way*) (michi o) oshiemásu (oshieru, oshiete) (道を)教えます(教える, 教えて) 3. *v* (*guides, coaches*) shidō shimásu (suru, shite) 指導します(する, して); (*a film*) kantoku (suru, shite) 監督します(する, して)

direct current *n* chokuryu 直流

direction *n* 1. hō´kō´ 方向; kentō 見当; hō´mén 方面; ... (no) hō´ ...(の)方; hō´gaku 方角 2. *directions* (*instructions*) shíji 指示, oshie 教え; *gives ~ (to a destination)* michi o oshiemásu (oshieru, oshiete) 道を教えます(教える, 教えて)

directive *n* shirei 指令

directly *adv* chokusetsu (ni) 直接(に), zutto ずっと, jika-ni じかに・直に, (*immediately*) sugu すぐ, (*shortly*) ma-mó-naku 間もなく・まもなく

director *n* 1. (*coach*) shidō´-sha 指導者 2. (*of a film*) kantoku 監督, dirèkutā ディレクター

directory *n* (*telephone*) denwa-chō´ 電話帳; (*list of names*) meibo 名簿

dirt *n* yogore 汚れ・よごれ; (*filth*) doró 泥・ドロ; (*grime*) aká あか・垢; (*soil*) tsuchí 土

dirt-cheap *adj* kakuyasu (no) 格安(の), tada dōzen (no) ただ同然(の)

dirty 1. *adj* kitanái 汚い・きたない, fuketsu (na) 不潔(な) 2. *adj* (*dirty-minded*) gehin (na) 下品(な); étchi (na) エッチ(な); *dirty story* hiwai na hanashi 卑猥[ひわい]な話 3. *v gets ~* yogoremásu (yogoreru, yogorete) 汚れます・よごれます(汚れる, 汚れて) 4. *v dirties it* yogoshimásu (yogosu, yogoshite) 汚します・よごします(汚す, 汚して)

disability *n* shintai-shōgai 身体障害

disadvantage *n* són 損・そん, fúri 不利; (*shortcoming*) ketten 欠点, mainasu マイナス, tánsho 短所

disagreeable *adj* iyá (na) 嫌・いや(な), fuyukai (na) 不愉快(な)

disagreement *n* fu-itchí 不一致

disappointed *adj* zan'nen (na) 残念・ざんねん

(な); *gets ~* gakkári shimásu (suru, shite) がっか
りします(する, して)

disappointing *adj* shitsubō saseru 失望させる

disappointment *n* shitsubō´ 失望, kitai hazure
期待はずれ, rakutan 落胆; (*in love*) shitsuren 失恋

disapprobation *n* fu-sansei 不賛成

disapproval *n* **1.** (*disapprobation*) fu-sansei
不賛成, (*nonrecognition*) fu-shōnin 不承認
2. (*accusation*) hinan 非難

disarmament *n* busō-kaijo 武装解除, gunbi-
shukushō 軍備縮小

disarray *n* konran 混乱, mu-chitsujo 無秩序

disassemble *v* barashimásu (barásu, baráshite)
ばらします(ばらす, ばらして)

disaster *n* sō´nan 遭難・そうなん, sainán 災難・
さいなん, wazawai 災い・わざわい; *has a ~*
sō´nan shimásu (suru, shite) 遭難します・そうな
んします(する, して)

disaster area *n* hisai-chi 被災地

disastrous *adj* taihen (na) 大変・たいへん(な)

discard *v* sutemásu (suteru, sutete) 捨てます
(捨てる, 捨てて)

discern *v* **1.** (*discriminates*) shikibetsu shimásu
(suru, shite) 識別します(する, して) **2.** → **see**

discharge *v* (*from employment*) káiko shimásu
(suru, shite) 解雇します(する, して)

disciple *n* deshí 弟子・でし

discipline 1. *n* kiritsu 規律, chitsujo 秩序;
shitsuke しつけ **2.** *v* (*drills, trains*) kitaemásu
(kitaéru, kitáete) 鍛えます・きたえます(鍛える,
鍛えて), (*brings up children, …*) shitsukemásu
(shitsukéru, shitsúkete) しつけます(しつける, し
つけて)

disclose *v* (*public*) kōkai shímásu (suru, shite)
公開します(する, して); abakimásu (abaku,
abaite) 暴きます・あばきます(暴く, 暴いて); *is
disclosed* barémásu (baréru, baréte) ばれます(ば
れる, ばれて)

disco *n* disuko ディスコ

discomfort *n* fukai(-kan) 不快(感)

disconnect *v* hazushimásu (hazusu, hazushite)
外します・はずします(外す, 外して), hanashi-
másu (hanásu, hanáshite) 離します・はなします
(離す, 離して), kirimásu (kiru, kitte) 切ります・
きります(切る, 切って)

disconnected; *gets ~* (*comes off*) hazuremásu
(hazureru, hazurete) 外れます・はずれます
(外れる, 外れて)

discontent *n* (*grumbling*) fuhei 不平, fuman 不満

discontented *adj* fuman (na) 不満・ふまん(な)

discount *n* wari-biki 割引・わりびき, ne-biki 値
引き・ねびき

discourage *v* ki o kujikimásu (kujíku, kujíite)
気をくじきます(くじく, くじいて); *gets discour-
aged* ki ga kujikemásu (kujikéru, kujíkete) 気がく
じけます(くじける, くじけて)

discourtesy *n* búrei 無礼, shitsúrei 失礼

discover *v* **1.** (*finds*) mitsukemásu (mitsukeru,
mitsukete) 見つけます・みつけます(見つける,

見つけて), hakken shimásu (suru, shite) 発見し
ます(する, して) **2.** *is discovered*
barémásu (baréru, baréte) ばれます(ばれる, ばれ
て), abakaremásu (abakareru, abakarete) 暴かれま
す・あばかれます(暴かれる, 暴かれて)

discovery *n* hakken 発見; *Discovery Channel*
disukabarii channeru ディスカバリー・チャン
ネル

discrepancy *n* chigai 違い・ちがい, sa 差・さ,
sō´i 相違, kuichigai 食い違い・くいちがい; (*gap*)
zuré ずれ

discretion *n* tsutsushimi 慎み・つつしみ,
funbetsu 分別

discriminate *v* (*distinguishes them*) mi-wakemásu
(mi-wakeru, mi-wakete) 見分けます(見分ける,
見分けて), shikibetsu shimásu (suru, shite) 識別し
ます(する, して)

discrimination *n* sábetsu 差別・さべつ; kúbetsu
区別・くべつ; (*distinguishing*) shikibetsu 識別

discuss *v* (*talks it over*) hanashi-aimásu (hanashi-
au, hanashi-atte) 話し合います・はなしあいます
(話し合う, 話し合って), sō´dan shimásu (suru,
shite) 相談します(する, して); (*debates, argues*)
ron-jimásu (ron-jiru, ron-jite) 論じます(論じる,
論じて)

discussion *n* hanashi-ai 話し合い・はなしあい;
hanashí 話・はなし; kyō´gí 協議, (*argument*) rón
論, (*debate*) tō´ron 討論, ronsō´ 論争; (*roundtable
discussion*) zadán-kai 座談会

disease *n* byō´ki 病気

disembark *v* jō´riku shimásu (suru, shite) 上陸し
ます(する, して)

disgrace *n* hají 恥・はじ, chijoku 恥辱, ojoku
汚辱; *~ oneself* hají o kakimásu (káku, káite)
恥をかきます(かく, かいて)

disgraceful *adj* hazukashíi 恥ずかしい・はず
かしい

disgusted; *gets ~* akiremásu (akireru, akirete)
呆れます・あきれます(呆れる, 呆れて); iyá ni
narimásu (náru, nátte) 嫌になります・いやになり
ます(なる, なって)

disgusting *adj* iyá (na) 嫌・いや(な)

dish *n* sara 皿・さら(o-sara お皿); shokki 食器;
(*how many*) nán-mai 何枚)

dishcloth, dishtowel *n* fukín ふきん・布巾

dishearten → **discourage**

dishonest *adj* fu-seijitsu (na/no) 不誠実(な/の),
fu-shōjiki (na/no) 不正直(な/の), fusei (na/no)
不正(な/の)

dishpan *n* arai-óke 洗い桶・あらい桶

dish rack *n* shokkí-dana 食器棚

dishwasher *n* shokkí arai-ki 食器洗い機

disinfectant *n* shō´dokú-yaku/zai 消毒薬/剤

dislikable *adj* nikúi 憎い・にくい, iyá (na)
嫌・いや(な)

dislike *v* … ga kirai désu (iyá desu) …が嫌いで
す・…がきらいです(嫌です), …o iya-gari-másu
(iya-gáru, iya-gátte) …を嫌がります・…をいや
がります(嫌がる, 嫌がって)

dismal *adj* (*gloomy*) uttō´shíi うっとうしい

dismiss *v* (*from employment*) káiko shimásu (suru, shíte) 解雇します(する, して)

dismissal *n* (*from employment*) káiko 解雇; (*of servant*) hima 暇・ひま

disobedient *adj* hankō-teki (na) 反抗的(な)

disobey *v* … ni somukimásu (somúku, somúite) …に背きます・…にそむきます(背く, 背いて)

disorder *n* konran 混乱, kónzatsu 混雑, midaré 乱れ・みだれ, yamí 闇; *in disorder* mechamecha めちゃめちゃ

disorderly *adj* ranbō´ (na) 乱暴・らんぼう(な)

dispatched from/at [TIME/PLACE] hátsu (no) …発(の)

dispensary *n* yakkyoku 薬局

disperse *v* (*they scatter*) chirimásu (chiru, chitte) 散ります・ちります(散る, 散って)

display → **show**

displease *v* fu-yúkai ni shimásu (suru, shíte) 不愉快にします(する, して)

displeased *adj* fu-kigen (na) 不機嫌・ふきげん(な)

displeasing *adj* fu-yúkai (na) 不愉快・ふゆかい(な)

dispose *v* shímatsu shimásu (suru, shíte) 始末します(する, して); shóri shimásu (suru, shíte) 処理します(する, して)

disposition *n* 1. seishitsu 性質; (*nature*) táchi たち・質, shō´ 性; (*temperament*) ténsei 天性; (*attitude*) táido 態度 2. (*dealing with*) shóri 処理, shóbun 処分, shóchi 処置

dispute *n* arasoi 争い・あらそい, tō´ron 討論, sō´ron 争論

dissatisfied *adj* fuman (na) 不満・ふまん(な)

dissertation *n* ronbun 論文, (*for a degree*) gakui-rónbun 学位論文, (*doctoral*) hakase-rónbun 博士論文

dissipation *n* dō´raku 道楽

dissolve *v* (*dissolves it*) tokashimásu, tokáshite) 溶かします・とかします(溶かす, 溶かして); (*it dissolves*) tokemásu (tokéru, tókete) 溶けます・とけます(溶ける, 溶けて)

distance *n* kyóri 距離・きょり

distant *adj* (*far*) tō´i 遠い・とおい, háruka (na) はるか・遥か(な); *gets* ~ hedatarimásu (hedatáru, hedátte) 隔たります・へだたります(隔たる, 隔たって)

distilled liquor *n* (*from yam or rice*) shō´chū´ 焼酎

distilled water *n* jō´ryū´-sui 蒸留水

distinct *adj* hakkíri to shimásu (suru, shíte) はっきりとします(する, して)

distinctly *adv* hakkíri はっきり

distinguish *v* (*discriminates*) mi-wakemásu (mi-wakeru, mi-wakete) 見分けます(見分ける, 見分けて), shikibetsu shimásu (suru, shíte) 識別します(する, して)

distort *v* yugamemásu (yugameru, yugamete) ゆがめます・歪めます(ゆがめる, ゆがめて); *gets*

distorted yugamimásu (yugamu, yugande) ゆがみます・歪みます(ゆがむ, ゆがんで)

distortion *n* yugami ゆがみ・歪み

distract *v* ki o chirashimásu (chirasu, chirashite) 気を散らします(散らす, 散らして)

distress 1. *n* nayamí 悩み・なやみ, kurushimi 苦しみ・くるしみ 2. *v* (*afflicts*) kurushimemásu (kurushiméru, kurushímete) 苦しめます・くるしめます(苦しめる, 苦しめて); *gets distressed* kurushimimásu (kurushímu, kurushínde) 苦しみます・くるしみます(苦しむ, 苦しんで)

distribute *v* kubarimásu (kubáru, kubátte) 配ります・くばります(配る, 配って); wakemásu (wakéru, wákete) 分けます・わけます(分ける, 分けて)

distribution *n* ryūtsū 流通

district *n* chíhō´ 地方; hō´men 方面, …-hō´men …方面

disturb *v* (… no) jama o shimásu (suru, shíte) (…の)じゃま[邪魔]をします(する, して)

disturbance *n* (*intrusion*) (o-)jama (お)じゃま・邪魔; (*unrest*) sō´dō´ 騒動; (*strife*) arasoi 争い, rán 乱

disused *adj* fuyō (nó) 不要(の)

ditch 1. *n* mizo 溝, horí 堀 2. *v* mizo o horimásu (horu, hotte) 溝を掘ります(掘る, 掘って)

dive (*under*) *v* mogurimásu (mogúru, mogútte) 潜ります・もぐります(潜る, 潜って), tobikomi-másu (tobikomu, tobikonde) 飛び込みます・とびこみます(飛び込む, 飛び込んで), daibingu shimásu (suru, shíte) ダイビングします(する, して)

diver *n* daibā´ ダイバー; (*woman pearl diver*) áma 海女・あま

diverse *adj* sama zama (na) さまざま・様々(な)

divide *v* (*divides it*) warimásu (waru, watte) 割ります・わります(割る, 割って), wakemásu (wakéru, wákete) 分けます・わけます(分ける, 分けて); (*it divides*) waremásu (wareru, warete) 割れます・われます(割れる, 割れて); wakaremásu (wakaréru, wakárete) 分かれます・わかれます(分かれる, 分かれて); ~ *roughly* (*into main categories*) taibetsu shimásu (suru, shíte) 大別します(する, して)

diving (*sports*) *n* sensui 潜水, daibingu ダイビング

diving board *n* tobikomi-dai 飛び込み台, tobikomi-ban 飛び込み板

dividing line *n* wake-mé 分け目・わけめ

divine message *n* otsuge お告げ・おつげ

division *n* bú 部; (*army*) shídan 師団; (*branching*) wakaré 分かれ; (*math calculation*) warízan 割り算

divorce 1. *n* rikon 離婚; *gets divorced from* …to rikon shimásu (suru, shíte) …と離婚します(する, して) 2. *v* rikon shimásu (suru, shíte) 離婚します(する, して)

DIY *adj* (*do-it-yourself; building or repairing things for oneself*) nichiyō-daiku (no) 日曜大工(の)

dizzy *adj* 1. me ga mararu 目が回る; *feel dizzy*

memai ga shimásu (suru, shite) めまいがします（する，して）**2.** bakageta ばかげた

do v shimásu (suru, shite) します（する，して）; yarimásu (yaru, yatte) やります（やる，やって）; nashimásu (násu, náshite) なします（なす，なして）; (*performs*) okonaimásu (okonau, okonatte) 行います（行う，行って）; [HONORIFIC] nasaimásu (nasáru, nasátte, nasaimáshite) なさいます（なさる，なさって，なさいまして）; [HUMBLE, DEFERENTIAL] itashimásu (itasu, itashite, itashimáshite) 致します・いたします（致す，致して，致しまして）; *do it* (*deprecating object*) yarakashimásu (yarakasu, yarakashite) やらかします（やらかす，やらかして）; *do it over* (*again*) yari-naoshimásu (yari-naósu, yari-naóshite) やり直します・やりなおします（やり直す，やり直して）

docile *adj* súnao (na) すなお・素直（な）

dock *n* dókku ドック, ganpeki 岸壁・がんぺき

doctor *n* **1.** (*physician*) (o-)isha(-san) （お）医者（さん）, sensei 先生. **2.** (*Ph.D.*) hákase 博士・はかせ

doctor's office *n* (*clinic*) byō'in 病院, fín 医院

doctoral degree *n* hakase gō 博士号

doctoral dissertation *n* hakase rónbun 博士論文

doctrine *n* shúgi 主義

document *n* shorui 書類, bunsho 文書, bunken 文献

documentary *n* dokyumentarii ドキュメンタリー

dodge v (*turns it aside*) sorashimásu (sorásu, soráshite) そらします・逸らします（そらす，そらして）

does → do; **doesn't** → don't

dog *n* inú 犬・イヌ (**1:** ip-pikí 一匹, **2:** ní-hiki 二匹, **3:** sánbiki 三匹; *how many* nán-biki 何匹）

dog tag *n* (*dog license*) inú no kansatsu 犬の鑑札; (*name tag*) na fuda 名札

doll *n* ningyō' 人形・にんぎょう (o-ningyō' お人形); *festival doll* hina-níngyō' ひな人形・雛人形; Doll's Festival *n* (*3 March*) Hina-mátsuri ひな祭(り)・雛祭(り)

dollar *n* dóru ドル

dolphin *n* iruka イルカ

domestic *adj* (*not foreign*) kokúnai (no) 国内（の）; (*domestically made*) kokusan (no) 国産（の）; domestic help *n* otetsudai(-san) お手伝い（さん）, kaji-tetsudai 家事手伝い

domesticate v narashimásu (narásu, naráshite) 慣らします・ならします（慣らす，慣らして）

domino *n* domino ドミノ

done v (*ready*) dekimáshita 出来ました・できました, dékite imásu (iru, ite) 出来ています・できています（いる，いて）; (*finished*) (shi-) te shimaimáshita (shimatta, shimatte) （し）てしまいました（しまった，しまって）

half-done *adj* (*cooked medium*) han-yake (no) 半焼け（の）

underdone *adj* (*cooked rare*) nama-yake (no) 生焼け（の）, (*beef*) réa レア

well-done *adj* yóku yaketa 良［よ］く焼けた, (*beef*) wérudan ウェルダン

donkey *n* róba ロバ

don't v shimasén (shinai, shináide) しません（しない，しないで）

don't (do it)! *interj* (shité wa) damé desu/da （しては）だめです/だ, ikemasén (ikenai) いけません（いけない）; (shi-) náide kudasai （し）ないで下［くだ］さい; *Don't be shy/ reticent.* Go-enryo náku. ご遠慮なく・ごえんりょなく., *Don't feel you have to hurry.* Go-yukkúri. ごゆっくり., *Don't go to any trouble.* Okamai náku. お構いなく・おかまいなく. *Don't worry about it.* Go-shinpai náku. ご心配なく・ごしんぱいなく.

doodling *n* rakugaki 落書き・らくがき

door *n* to 戸, dóa ドア; (*hinged*) hiraki-do 開き戸・ひらき戸; (*opaque sliding*) fusuma ふすま・襖; door wing, door of a gate tobira 扉・とびら

doorbell *n* suzu 鈴・スズ, béru ベル, yobirin 呼び鈴

doorknob *n* doa nobu ドアノブ

dope *n* (*narcotic*) mayaku 麻薬

dormitory *n* kishúkusha 寄宿舎, ryō' 寮

dose *n* ikkai-ryō 一回量, ikkai-bun 一回分

dot *n* ten 点・てん, chóbo ちょぼ, póchi ぽち, pótsu ぽつ; (*with*) *dots* bótsu botsu ぼつぼつ

double 1. *adj* bai (no) 倍（の）, (*two-layer*) ni-jū (no) 二重（の）

double bed *n* daburu-béddo ダブルベッド

double boiler *n* nijū-nábe 二重鍋・二重なべ

double (room) *n* dáburu ダブル, daburu-rū'mu ダブルルーム, daburu-beddo-tsuki no heya ダブルベッド付きの部屋

doubles *n* (*tennis*) dáburusu ダブルス

double(-size) drink *n* dáburu ダブル **2.** *doubles it* v (...o) bai ni shimásu (suru, shite) （...を）倍にします（する，して）

double bass *n* kontorabasu コントラバス

double-breasted suit *n* dáburu ダブル

double-check v nén o oshimásu (osu, oshite) 念を押します（押す，押して）; saíkakunin shimásu (suru, shite) 再確認します（する，して）

double-cross 1. *n* (*treachery*) uragiri 裏切り・うらぎり **2.** v ura-girimásu (ura-giru, ura-gítte) 裏切ります（裏切る，裏切って）

double-decker *n* nikaidate basu 二階建てバス

double plug *n* (*two-way socket*) futamata-sókétto 二又ソケット

double suicide *n* shinjū 心中

doubt 1. *n* gimon 疑問, utagai 疑い・うたがい, fushin 不審 **2.** v utagaimásu (utagau, utagatte) 疑います（疑う，疑って）, fushin ni omoimásu (omóu, omótte) 不審に思います（思う，思って）

douche *n* chūsúi-ki 注水器

dough *n* pan-kiji パン生地

doughnut *n* dōnatsu ドーナツ

dove *n* háto 鳩・ハト

down *prep, adv* shita e 下へ; *down* (*lower in price*

by) ¥*100* hyaku én-yasu 百円安

get down orimás<u>u</u> (oríru, órite) 下ります・降ります（下りる、下りて）・おります（下りる、下りて）

go down kudarimás<u>u</u> (kudaru, kudatte) 下ります・くだります（下りる、下りて）, sagarimás<u>u</u> (sagáru, sagátte) 下ります・さがります（下る、下がって）

hang down taremás<u>u</u> (taréru, tárete) 垂れます・たれます（垂れる、垂れて）, sagemás<u>u</u> (sagéru, ságete) 下げます（下げる、下げて）

lie down nemás<u>u</u> (neru, nete) 寝ます・ねます（寝る、寝て）

take down oroshimás<u>u</u> (orósu, or<u>ó</u>sh<u>i</u>te) 下ろします・おろします（下ろす、下ろして）

download *v* (*computer*) *~ the file* (fairu o) daunrōdo shimás<u>u</u> (suru, sh<u>i</u>te)（ファイルを）ダウンロードします（する、して）

downpayment *n* atama-kin 頭金

downpour *n* gō´u 豪雨, doshaburi 土砂降り; *local downpour* shūchū-gō´u 集中豪雨

downstairs *n* kaika 階下

downtown *n* hanka-gai 繁華街

doze *v* úto uto shimás<u>u</u> (suru, sh<u>i</u>te) うとうと・ウトウトします（する、して）; *~ off* inemúri shimás<u>u</u> (suru, sh<u>i</u>te) 居眠りします・いねむりします（する、して）

dozen *n* (ichi-) dá su (一) ダース, jū-ní 十二・12

Dr.... *n* (*physician*) ... senséi ...先生

draft 1. *n* (*rough*) sh<u>i</u>tagaki 下書き, dorafuto ドラフト; (*military conscription*) shō´shū (shimás<u>u</u>; suru, sh<u>i</u>te) 召集（します；する、して）**2.** *n* (*beer*) náma 生, nama bíiru 生ビール **3.** *n* (*call-up*) shō´shū/chōhē (shimás<u>u</u>; suru, sh<u>i</u>te) 召集/徴兵（します；する、して）

drag *v* hipparimás<u>u</u> (hippáru, hippátte) 引っ張ります・ひっぱります（引っ張る、引っ張って）, h<u>i</u>kimás<u>u</u> (h<u>i</u>ku, hiite) 引きます・ひきます（引く、引いて）, h<u>i</u>ki-zurimás<u>u</u> (h<u>i</u>ki-zuru, h<u>i</u>ki-zutte) 引きずります（引きずる、引きずって）

dragnet *n* téhái 手配; *sets up a ~* téhái shimás<u>u</u> (suru, sh<u>i</u>te) 手配します（する、して）

dragon *n* ryū 竜・龍・りゅう, tatsu 竜・たつ, doragon ドラゴン

dragonfly *n* tonbo トンボ

drain 1. *n* (*kitchen*) gesui 下水; (*ditch*) mizo 溝 **2.** *it drains off* *v* hakemás<u>u</u> (hakéru, hákete) はけます（はける、はけて）; *it drains well* (mizu) haké ga íi dés<u>u</u> (水)はけがいいです

drain pipe *n* tói とい・樋

drama *n* engeki 演劇, géki 劇, dorama ドラマ

dramatic *adj* géki-teki (na) 劇的（な）

draperies *n* tanmono 反物

drapes *n* k<u>á</u>ten カーテン

draw 1. *v* (*a picture*) egakimás<u>u</u> (egáku, egáite) 描きます（描く、描いて）**2.** *v* (*pulls*) h<u>i</u>kimás<u>u</u> (h<u>i</u>ku, hiite) 引きます・ひきます（引く、引いて）; *~ out* h<u>i</u>ki-dashimás<u>u</u> (h<u>i</u>ki-dasu, h<u>i</u>ki-dash<u>i</u>te) 引き出します・ひきだします（引き出す、引き出して）; *~ an underline* kasen o h<u>i</u>kimás<u>u</u> (h<u>i</u>ku,

hiite) 下線を引きます（引く、引いて）**3.** *v* (*water etc.*) kumimás<u>u</u> (kumu, kunde) 汲みます・くみます（汲む、汲んで）**4.** *v ~ apart* h<u>i</u>ki-wakemás<u>u</u> (h<u>i</u>ki-wakeru, h<u>i</u>ki-wakete) 引き分けます・ひきわけます（引き分ける、引き分けて）**5.** *n* (*game*) h<u>i</u>kiwake 引き分け・ひきわけ

drawer *n* (*of desk, etc.*) h<u>i</u>ki-dashi 引き出し・ひきだし

drawers *n* (*underwear*) zubon-sh<u>i</u>ta ズボン下, momoh<u>i</u>ki 股引き, (*for woman*) zurō´su ズロース

drawing *n* (*diagram*) zu 図; (*picture*) é 絵

drawing room *n* (*parlor*) kyakuma 客間

draw near → approach

dread *v* **1.** osoremás<u>u</u> (osoreru, osorete) 恐れます・おそれます（恐れる、恐れて）

dreadful *adj* osoroshíi 恐ろしい・おそろしい, sugói すごい・凄い, hidoi ひどい・酷い

dream *n* yumé (o mimás<u>u</u>; míru, míte) 夢・ユメ（をみます；みる、みて）; *American dream* american doriimu アメリカンドリーム

dreary *adj* uttō´shíi うっとうしい

dregs *n* k<u>á</u>su かす; ori おり

dress 1. *n* ki-mono 着物; yō´-fuku 洋服, fukú 服, fuku<u>sō</u> 服装, (*woman's*) wanp<u>í</u>su ワンピース, dóresu ドレス **2.** *v* (*wears*) fukú o kimás<u>u</u> (kiru, k<u>i</u>te) 服を着ます（着る、着て）**3.** *v* (*dresses vegetables, fish*) aemás<u>u</u> (aéru, áete) あえます・和えます（あえる、あえて）

dressing gown *n* gaun ガウン

dressmaker *n* yō´sai-shi 洋裁師, doresu-mē´k<u>a</u> ドレスメーカー

dressmaking *n* yō´sai 洋裁

dried 1. *adj* hoshí-... 干し...; *dried persimmons* hoshi-gaki 干し柿・ホシガキ **2.** **→ dry**

dried bonito fish *n* katsuo-bushi カツオブシ・鰹節

dried gourd strips *n* kanpyō´ カンピョウ

drill 1. *n* (*tool*) kíri きり・錐 **2.** *n* (*practice*) doriru ドリル, (o-)kéi ko（お）けいこ・稽古; (*study*) renshū 練習; (*training*) kúnren 訓練 **3.** *v* (*trains*) nerimás<u>u</u> (néru, nétte) 練ります・ねります（練る、練って）, kúnren shimás<u>u</u> (suru, sh<u>i</u>te) 訓練します（する、して）, (*disciplines*) k<u>i</u>taemás<u>u</u> (k<u>i</u>taeru, k<u>i</u>táete) 鍛えます・きたえます（鍛える、鍛えて）

drink 1. *n* (*beverage*) nomí-mono 飲み物・のみもの; *one drink* h<u>i</u>tó-k<u>u</u>chi 一口; *has a drink* íp-pai nomimás<u>u</u>/yarimás<u>u</u> 一杯飲[の]みます／やります **2.** *v* nomimás<u>u</u> (nómu, nónde) 飲みます・のみます（飲む、飲んで）; [HONORIFIC] meshiagarimás<u>u</u> (meshiagaru, meshiagatte) 召し上がります・めしあがります（召し上がる、召し上がって）; [HUMBLE] itadakimás<u>u</u> (itadaku, itadaite) いただきます・頂きます（いただく、いただいて）

drinkable; is ~ nomemás<u>u</u> (noméru, nómete) 飲めます（飲める、飲めて）

drinking water *n* nomí-mizu 飲み水・のみ水

drip *v* taremás<u>u</u> (taréru, tárete) 垂れます・たれます（垂れる、垂れて）

drive 1. *v* (*a car*) unten shimásu (suru, shite) 運転します(する、して)、doraibu shimásu (suru, shite) ドライブします(する、して) **2.** *n* (*what one is driving at*) iitai-koto 言いたい事、nerai ねらい・狙い

drive-in *n* nori-komi 乗り込み

driver *n* untén-shu 運転手、doraibā ドライバー

driver license *n* untén-menkyo-shō 運転免許証

driveway *n* shadō´ 車道

drizzle *n* kosame 小雨; (*on-and-off*) shigure 時雨・しぐれ

droll *adj* yúkai (na) 愉快・ゆかい(な) → **funny**

drool *v is drooling* yodare ga deteimásu (déteiru, déteite) よだれが出ています(出ている、出ていて)

droop *v* naemásu (naéru, náete) 萎えます・なえます(萎える、萎えて)

drop 1. *v* (*drops it*) otoshimásu (otósu, otóshite) 落とします・おとします(落とす、落として)、(*lets it fall, spills*) tarashimásu (tarásu, taráshite) 垂らします・たらします(垂らす、垂らして) **2.** *v* (*it drops*) ochimásu (ochíru, óchite) 落ちます・おちます(落ちる、落ちて) **3.** *n* (*a drop*) tsúbu 粒、tamá 玉; (*counting*) …-teki …滴

drop in *v* yorimásu (yoru, yotte) 寄ります・よります(寄る、寄って)

drop off *v* (*a person from a vehicle*) oroshimásu (orósu, oróshite) 降ろします・おろします(降ろす、降ろして)

drown *v* obore-jini shimásu (suru, shite) おぼれ死にします(する、して)

drowse *v* útouto shimásu (suru, shite) うとうと・ウトウトします(する、して)

drowsy *adj* nemui 眠い; darui ダルい

drudge *v* ákuseku hatarakimásu (hataraku, hataraite) あくせく働きます・はたらきます(働く、働いて)

drug *n* (*for patient*) kusuri 薬(o-kusúri お薬)、(*chemical substances*) yakuhin 薬品

drug addict *n* mayaku-chūdoku-sha 麻薬中毒者

druggist *n* kusuri-ya (san) 薬屋(さん)

drugstore *n* kusuri-ya 薬屋、yakkyoku 薬局

drum *n* (*Japanese-style*) taiko 太鼓・たいこ、(*large*) ō´-daiko 大太鼓; (*hourglass-shaped*) tsuzumí 鼓・つづみ、(*small*) ko-tsúzumi 小鼓、(*Western-style*) doramu ドラム

drunk; gets ~ yopparaimásu (yopparau, yopparatte) 酔[よ]っぱらいます・酔っ払います(酔っぱらう、酔っぱらって); yoimásu (yóu, yótte) 酔います・よいます(酔う、酔って)

dry *v* (*it dries*) kawakimásu (kawáku, kawáite) 乾きます・かわきます(乾く、乾いて)、kansō shimásu (suru, shite) 乾燥します(する、して); (*dries it*) kawakashimásu (kawakásu, kawakáshite) 乾かします・かわかします(乾かす、乾かして)、(*foodstuff*) hoshimásu (hósu, hóshite) 干します・ほします(干す、干して)

dry cleaning *n* dorai-kuríníngu ドライクリーニング

dry goods *n* tanmono 反物、gofuku 呉服

dry land *n* oka おか・陸

dub *v* (*names*) nazukemásu (nazukéru, nazúkete) 名付けます・なづけます(名付ける、名付けて)

duck *n* (*wild*) kámo カモ・鴨、(*tame*) ahiru アヒル; (*canvas*) zúkku ズック

dude *n* mekashiya めかし屋; yatsu やつ・奴

due 1. *dues n* kaihi 会費、ryōkin 料金 **2.** *adj* (*payment*) kijitsu no 期日の(の)

due date → **deadline**

due to → **because**

dull *adj* nibúi 鈍い・にぶい、norói のろい; (*uninteresting*) taikutsu (na) 退屈・たいくつ(な)、(*long-winded*) kudói くどい; (*dull-witted*) wakarí ga warúi 分かりが悪い

dumb *adj* **1.** (*stupid*) baka (na) ばか・馬鹿(な) **2.** (*unable to speak*) kuchi no kikenai 口の利けない

dump 1. *v* (*discards*) sutemásu (suteru, sutete) 捨てます・すてます(捨てる、捨てて) **2.** *n* (*dump site*) sute-ba 捨て場

dumpling *n* dango だんご・団子(o-dango お団子); (*large stuffed bun*) manjū まんじゅう・饅頭; (*small meat-stuffed crescent*) gyō´za ギョウザ・餃子

dune *n* sakyū 砂丘・さきゅう

dung *n* kusó クソ・糞、fún フン・糞 → **excrement**

dupe *n* kámo カモ

duplicate *n*, *adj* **1.** (*double*) ni-jū (no) 二重(の) **2.** → **copy**

during *prep* (…) no aida (ni) (…)の間(に); …-chū (ni) …中(に); *during the war* senji-chū 戦時中

dust 1. *n* (*in air*) hokori ホコリ・埃; (*on ground, floor, etc.*) chiri チリ・塵; (*in house*) gomí ごみ **2.** *v* (*dusts it*) hatakimásu (hatáku, hatáite) はたきます・はたきます(はたく、はたいて)

dustbin *n* gomi-bako ゴミ箱・ごみばこ

dustcloth *n* zō´kin ぞうきん・雑巾

duster *n* zō´kin ぞうきん・雑巾; hataki はたき

dustpan *n* chiri-tóri ちり取り・塵取り・チリトリ

Dutch 1. *adj* Oranda no オランダの **2.** *n* (*language*) Oranda-go オランダ語 **3.** *n* (*person*) Orandá-jin オランダ人

Dutch treat *n* wari-kan 割り勘・ワリカン

duty *n* **1.** (*obligation*) gímu 義務 **2.** (*function*) yakumé 役目(o-yakume お役目)、yakú 役(o-yaku お役)、honbun 本分; (*job, post*) tsutomé 務め(o-tsutome お務め)、yakú 役(o-yaku お役); (*work, service*) kínmu 勤務; *those on duty* kinmú-sha 勤務者; *the person on duty* tō´ban 当番(o-tō´ban お当番) **3.** (*import tax*) kanzei 関税、yunyū-zei 輸入税 **4.** → **off duty**

dwarf trees *n* bonsai 盆栽

dwindle *v* herimásu (heru, hette) 減ります・へります(減る、減って)、sukúnaku narimásu (náru, nátte) 少なくなります・すくなくなります(なる、なって)

dye (*it*) *v* somemásu (someru, somete) 染めます・そめます(染める、染めて)

dysentery *n* sékiri 赤痢・セキリ

E

each *pron* [NUMBER, QUANTITY +] ...zútsu ...ずつ; (*every*) mai-...毎..., káku(-) ... 各..., ... goto (ni) ...毎・ごと(に)

each other *pron* o-tagai (ni) お互い・おたがい (に); [VERB-i] -aimásu (-au/-áu, -atte/-átte) [VERB-い]合います・あいます(合う, 合って)

eager *adj* nésshín (na) 熱心・ねっしん(な), setsubō shiteiru 切望している; *~ to* (*do*) zé-hi ... (shi-) tai ぜひ...(し)たい, (*concerning another person's behavior*) (shi-) tagarimásu (tagáru, tagátte) (し)たがります(たがる, たがって)

eager beaver *n* ganbari-ya 頑張り屋・がんばり 屋, (*workaholic*) shigoto no mushi 仕事の虫

eagerly *adv* nésshín (ni) 熱心・ねっしん(に)

eagerness *n* netsui 熱意, netsuretsu 熱烈, nesshin 熱心

eagle *n* washi ワシ・鷲

ear *n* mimí 耳・みみ

earache *n* mimi no itamí 耳の痛み・みみのい たみ

ear buzzing *n* mimi-nari 耳鳴り

ear doctor *n* jika-i 耳科医

ear pad *n* mimiate 耳あて・耳当て

eardrum *n* komaku 鼓膜・こまく

earl *n* hakushaku 伯爵・はくしゃく

earlier *adj* máe no ... 前の...・まえの...; [BOOKISH] zén(-) ... 前...・まえ...

early 1. *adj* hayái 早い・はやい **2.** *adv* háyaku 早 く・はやく; (*ahead of time*) hayame (ni) 早め・は やめ(に); *one's ~ years* kodomo no koro 子供の 頃・こどものころ

early bird *n* hayaoki (no hito) 早起き(の人)

earn *v* kasegimásu (kaségu, kaséide) 稼ぎます・ かせぎます(稼ぐ, 稼いで)

earnest *adj* majime (na) まじめ・真面目(な), (*serious*) honki (no) 本気(の)

earnings *n* (*income*) shūnyū 収入, shotoku 所得

earphone *n* iyahon イヤホン, iyahōn イヤホーン

earpick *n* mimi-kákí 耳かき・みみかき

earpiece *n* (*of glass frame*) (megane no) tsurú (めがねの)つる; (*telephone*) juwá-ki 受話器

earplug *n* iya-puragu イヤプラグ, mimi-sen 耳栓

earring *n* íyaringu イヤリング, mimi-kázari 耳飾 り・みみかざり

earshot *n* mimi no todoku kyori 耳の届[とど]く 距離, kikoeru kyori 聞こえる距離

earth *n* **1.** tsuchí 土, tochi 土地 **2.** *the Earth* chikyū 地球

earth and sand *n* dosha 土砂

earth axis *n* chi-jiku 地軸

what on earth *adv* ittai-zentai 一体全体

earthenware *n* doki 土器

earthenware pan *n* hōrókú ほうろく・焙烙; tōki 陶器

earthquake *n* jishin 地震

earthworm *n* mimizu ミミズ

ease 1. *n* (*comfort*) rakú 楽・らく

at ease jiyú (ni) 自由・じゆう(に), yukkúri ゆっ くり

2. ~ *it* *v* yasumemásu (yasuméru, yasúmete) 休め ます・やすめます(休める, 休めて)

easel *n* iizeru イーゼル, gaka 画架

easily *adv* **1.** tayásuku たやすく, wáke-naku わけ なく, kantan (ni) 簡単・かんたん(に), muzō´sa (ni) 無造作(に); assári (to) あっさり(と) **2.** → **undoubtedly**

easily broken koware-yasúi 壊れやすい・こわ れやすい

easily intoxicated sake ni yowái 酒に弱い [よわい]

east *n* higashi 東・ひがし, tō-... 東...; (*the east*) tōhō 東方, (*the eastern part*) tō´bu 東部

East Asia *n* Higashi-Ájia 東アジア, Tō´a 東亜

east coast *n* higashi-káigan 東海岸

Easter *n* iisutā イースター, fukkatsu-sai 復活祭

Easter egg *n* iisutā eggu イースターエッグ

Easter holidays *n* fukkatsu-sai no kyūka 復活祭 の休暇

easterly (*wind*) *n* higashi-yori (no kaze) 東寄り (の風)

East Europe *n* Higashi-yōroppa 東ヨーロッパ, Tō´ō 東欧

easy *adj* **1.** yasashii やさしい・易しい, tayasúi たやすい, wákenai わけない, kantan 簡単・かん たん, muzō´sa (na) 無造作(な); *~ (to do)* (shi-) yasúi (し)やすい; *~ to get to* ikiyasúi 行きやすい, *~ to understand* wakari-yasúi 分かりやすい

2. → **comfortable**

easy chair *n* anraku isu 安楽いす

easy death *n* anraku-shi 安楽死

easy delivery *n* anzan 安産

easygoing *adj* nónki (na) のん気・呑気(な), kiraku (na) 気楽・きらく(な)

easy money *n* abuku-zéni あぶく銭

eat *v* tabemásu (tabéru, tábete) 食べます・たべ ます(食べる, 食べて), (*vulgar form*) kuimásu (kuu, kutté) 食います・くいます(食う, 食って); (*has a meal*) shokuji shimásu (suru, shite) 食事し ます(する, して); [HONORIFIC] meshiagarimásu (meshiagaru, meshiagatte) 召し上がります・ めしあがります(召し上がる, 召し上がって); [HUMBLE] itadakimásu (itadaku, itadaite) いただき ます・頂きます(いただく, いただいて)

eat out *v* gaishoku shimásu (suru, shite) 外食し ます(する, して)

eat-in kitchen *n* dii-kē´ (DK) ディーケー, dainingu-kítchin ダイニングキッチン

eaves *n* noki 軒・のき, hisashi ひさし

ebauche *n* shitae 下絵

ebb 1. *n* hiki-shio 引き潮, kanchō 干潮

2. *v* otoroemásu (otoroeru, otoroéte) 衰えます (衰える, 衰えて)

ebb and flow *n* **1.** (*tide*) shio no michi-hiki 潮の満ち引き **2.** (*life*) (eiko) seisui (栄枯)盛衰

eccentric *n* **1.** fūgawari na hito 風変わりな人, ekisentorikku エキセントリック **2.** (*freak*) henjin 変人, ki-jin 奇人

echo 1. *n* hibikí 響き, kodama こだま, hankyō 反響, ekō エコー **2.** *v* (*it echoes*) hibikimásu (hibíku, hibíite) 響きます・ひびきます(響く, 響いて)

éclair *n* ekurea エクレア

eclipse *n* **1.** (*sun*) nisshoku 日食 **2.** (*moon*) gesshoku 月食

ecologist *n* seitai-gakusha 生態学者

ecology *n* seitai-gaku 生態学, ekorojii エコロジー, seitai-kankyō 生態環境

e-commerce *n* denshi shō-torihiki 電子商取引, ii komāsu e-コマース

economic *adj* keizai-gaku (no) 経済学(の), keizai (no) 経済(の)

economical *adj* keizai-teki (na) 経済的(な); toku (na) (お)徳・とく(な)

economics *n* kéizai 経済; (*science/study*) keizái-gaku 経済学

economize *v* ... o ken'yaku/setuyaku shimásu (suru, shite) ...を倹約/節約します(する, して), shimemásu (shiméru, shímete) 締めます・しめます(締める, 締めて)

economizing *n* (*saving*) setsuyaku 節約・せつやく

economy *n* **1.** (*saving*) setsuyaku 節約・せつやく **2.** (*economics*) keizai 経済

economy class *n* ekonomii-kurasu エコノミークラス

economy-class syndrome *n* ekonomii-kurasu shōkō-gun エコノミークラス症候群

economy hotel *n* bijinesu hoteru ビジネスホテル

economy size *n* o-kaidoku saizu お買い得サイズ, o-toku saizu お得サイズ

ecstasy *n* **1.** (*sexual ecstasy, name of drug*) ekusutashii エクスタシー **2.** kōkotsu 恍惚; *in an ~ of* muga-muchū (de) 無我夢中(で)

ecumenical *n* **1.** (*general*) fuhen-teki (na) 普遍的(な) **2.** (*ecumenical movement*) kyōkai itchi undō (no) 教会一致運動(の) **3.** (*of Christian unity throughout the world*) sekai no kirisuto-kyōkai (no) 世界のキリスト教会(の)

eczema *n* shisshin 湿疹・しっしん

edge *n* fuchí ふち・縁, hashi 端・はし, hashikko/hajikko 端っこ・はしっこ/はじっこ, háta 端・はた, ejji エッジ, (*rim*) herí へり・縁, (*brink*) kiwá 際, (*end*) tamotó たもと・袂, (*nearby*) sóba そば, (*of knife*) ha 刃, ha-saki 刃先

edacious *adj* kuishinbō (no) 食いしん坊・くいしんぼう(の)

edacity *n* taishoku 大食

edgy *adj* irairashita イライラした・苛々した

edible 1. *n* shokuryō-hin 食料品 **2.** *adj* shokuyō (no) 食用(の)

edict *n* **1.** (*government decree*) seirei 政令 **2.** (*act*) hōrei 法令 **3.** (*command*) meirei 命令

edifice 1. *n* (*large building*) dai-kenzōbutsu 大建造物, kyodai-kenchiku 巨大建築 **2.** (*complex system*) te no konda taikei 手の込んだ体系 **3.** (*complex organization*) te no konda soshiki 手の込んだ組織

edition *n* ban 版

editor *n* henshū-chō 編集長, editā エディター

editorial *n* shasetsu 社説

educate *v* (*rears*) sodatemásu (sodatéru, sodátete) 育てます・そだてます(育てる, 育てて) → **teach**

education *n* kyōiku 教育; (*learning*) gakúmon 学問, (*culture*) kyōyō 教養; (*bringing up*) yōiku 養育

Ministry of Education, Culture, Sports, Science and Technology *n* Monbú Kagaku-shō 文部科学省

educational *adj* kyōiku-teki (na) 教育的(な), kyōiku-jō (no) 教育上(の)

educational background *n* gakureki 学歴

education-related *adj* kyōiku-kanren (no) 教育関連(の)

eel *n* unagi ウナギ・鰻; (*conger eel*) anago アナゴ・穴子

broiled eel *n* kabayaki 蒲焼き, (*on rice in a lacquered box*) uná-jū うな重; (*on a bowl of rice*) una-don うな丼

effect *n* (*result*) kekka 結果; (*cause*) ... (no) séi ...(の)せい; (*effectiveness*) kiki-me 効き目, shirushi しるし, kōka 効果; (*gist*) muné 旨・むね

in effect yō-súru ni 要するに・ようするに

has/takes effect kikimásu (kiku, kiite) 効きます・ききます(効く, 効いて)

side/after-effect *n* fukú-sayō 副作用

effective *adj* yūkō (na) 有効・ゆうこう(な), kōka-teki (na) 効果的(な)

effeminate *adj* (*feminine*) memeshii 女々しい, onna no yō(na) 女のよう(な)

efficiency *n* nōritsu 能率; kōritsu 効率

efficient *adj* nōritsu-teki (na) 能率的・のうりつてき(な), kōritsu teki (na) 効率的・こうりつてき(な)

effort *n* hone-órí 骨折り・ほねおり (o-hone ori お骨折り), dóryoku 努力・どりょく; kúrō 苦労・くろう (go-kúrō ご苦労)

with much effort (but) sekkakú せっかく

requires much effort honé ga oremásu (oréru, órete) 骨が折れます・おれます(折れる, 折れて)

makes an effort doryoku shimásu (suru, shite) 努力します・どりょくします(する, して)

effortless *adj* muzó´sa (na) 無造作・むぞうさ(な); *effortlessly adv* muzó´sa (ni) 無造作・むぞうさ(に)

e.g. *adv* tatoeba 例えば・たとえば

egg *n* tamago 卵・玉子・タマゴ (*how many* nán-ko 何個)

egg on v sosonokashimásu (sosonokasu, sosonokashite) そそのかします(そそのかす、そそのかして)

hard-boiled adj (egg) katayude (no) 固ゆで(の)

soft-boiled adj (egg) hanjuku (no) 半熟(の)

egg cup n yude-tamago ire ゆで卵入れ、eggu-kappu エッグカップ

eggplant n násu ナス・茄子、násubi ナスビ

egg rolls n haru-maki 春巻・ハルマキ

eggshell n tamago no kara 卵の殻・たまごのから

ego n jíga 自我、ego エゴ

egoism n (selfishness) riko-shugi 利己主義、wagamama わがまま・我(が)侭 (= egotism)

egoist n riko-shugi-sha 利己主義者、egoisuto エゴイスト (= egotist)

Egypt n Ejiputo エジプト

Egyptian n 1. (language) Ejiputo-go エジプト語 2. (person) Ejiputo-jin エジプト人

eight n hachí 八・8、yattsú 八つ・やっつ; (8-oared racing boat) éito/ē'to エイト/エート; eight days yōka 八日

eight; 8 pieces (small things) hachi-ko, hák-ko 八個、**8 trees** (or long things) háp-pon 八本、**8 sheets** (flat things) hachí-mai 八枚; **8 cars** (or machines/vehicles) hachí-dai 八台; **8 copies** (books/magazines) has-satsú 八冊; **8 cats** (or small animals) hap-píki 八匹; **8 cows** (or large animals) hát-tō' 八頭; **8 birds/rabbits** háp-pa 八羽; **8 cupfuls** háp pai 八杯; **8 o'clock** hachi-ji 八時・8時; **8 hours** hachi-jíkan 八時間; **8 minutes** hachi-fun, háp-pun 八分・8分; **8 months** hachi-/hak-kágetsu 八ヶ月; hakkagetsú-kan 八ヶ月間; **8 years** hachi-nen 八年、hachí nén-kan 八年間; **8 years old** yattsú 八つ、hás-sai 八歳; **8 people** hachi-nín 八人; **8 yen** (money) hachi-en 八円; **8 degrees** hachi-dó 八度; **8 times** hachi-do 八度、hachi/hak-kai 八回; hap-pén 八遍; **8 floors/stories** hachi/hak-kai 八階

eighteen n jū-hachí 十八・18

eighth adj hachi-banmé (no) 八番目(の)、yattsu-mé (no) 八つ目(の)
the eighth day n yōka-mé 八日目、(the day of the month) yōka 八日

eight hundred n hap-pyakú 八百・800

eight thousand n has-sén 八千・8,000

eighty n hachi-jū 八十・80; **eighty thousand** n hachi-mán 八万・80,000

Eire n airurando アイルランド

either one adv dochira demo どちらでも

eke v yarikuri shimásu (suru, shite) やりくりします(する、して)、maniawasemásu (maniawaseru, maniawasete) 間に合わせます・まにあわせます(まにあわせる、まにあわせて)

elaborate 1. adj (complex) fukuzatsu (na) 複雑(な) 2. (diligent) kinben (na) 勤勉(な) 3. kuwashiku setsumei shimásu (suru, shite) 詳しく説明します(する、して)、kuwashiku nobe-másu (noberu, nobete) 詳しく述べます(述べる、述べて)

elapse v tachimásu (tátsu, tátte) 経ちます・たちます(経つ、経って)、hemásu (héru, héte) 経ます・へます(経る、経て)、keika shimásu (suru, shite) 経過します(する、して)

elastic n (material) → **rubber**
elastic band n wagomu 輪ゴム・わゴム

elation n jōkigen 上機嫌、ōyorokobi 大喜び

elbow n hijí 肘・肱・ひじ

eldest son n chō'nán 長男

elect v erabimásu (erábu, eránde) 選びます・えらびます(選ぶ、選んで)

election n sénkyo 選挙

electric adj dénki (no) 電気・でんき (の)

electric;
electric appliances n kaden 家電、denki-kígu 電気器具、denki-yō'hin 電気用品、denka-seihin 電化製品

electric car n densha 電車; (also electrified train, electric train)

electric fan n senpū'-ki 扇風機・せんぷうき

electric heater n denki-sutō'bu 電気ストーブ

electric hot plate n denki-kónro 電気コンロ

electric shaver n denki-kámisori 電気かみそり

electric vacuum cleaner n (denki) sōjíki (電気)掃除機

electric wire n densen 電線

electrician n denki-ya (san) 電気屋(さん)

electricity n dénki 電気・でんき

electron n dénshi 電子

electronic adj dénshi (no) 電子(の)
electronic account settlement n denshi-kessai 電子決済

electronic accounting n denshi-kaikei 電子会計

elegance n hin ása・ひん、(o-)jōhín (お)上品、fū'ryū 風流・ふうりゅう

elegant adj fū'ryū (na) 風流・ふうりゅう(な)、yū'bi (na) 優美・ゆうび(な)、yū'ga (na) 優雅・ゆうが(な); (o-)jōhín (na) (お)上品(な)

element n yō'so 要素、eremento エレメント

elementary school n (primary school) shōgákkō 小学校

elementary school student n shōgáku-sei 小学生

elephant n zō 象・ゾウ

elevator n erebē'tā' エレベーター

eleven n jū ichí 十一・11

eliminate v habukimásu (habuku, habúite) 省きます・はぶきます(省く、省いて)、nozokimásu (nozoku, nozoite) 除きます(除く、除いて); háijo shimásu (suru, shite) 排除します(する、して)

elimination n háijo 排除

elite 1. n eriito エリート 2. adj ichiryū (no) 一流(の)

else adv hoka (no/ni) 他・ほか(の/に)
or else mátá-wa または・又は、sore-tómo それとも、aruiwa 或いは・あるいは
somewhere else n (dokoka) yosó (no/ni) (どこか)よそ(の/に)、(dokoka) betsu no basho (no/ni) (どこか)別の場所・べつのばしょ(の/に)

email n mēru メール
embankment n teibō 堤防・ていぼう, tsutsumí 堤・つつみ
embarrass v komarasemásu (komaraséru, komarásete) 困らせます・こまらせます(困らせる, 困らせて), kurushimemásu (kurushiméru, kurushímete) 苦しめます・くるしめます(苦しめる, 苦しめて); ~ *oneself* hají o kakimásu (káku, káite) 恥をかきます(かく, かいて)
embarrassed; 1. *gets* ~ komarimásu (komáru, komátte) 困ります・こまります(困る, 困って); kurushimimásu (kurushímu, kurushínde) 苦しみます・くるしみます(苦しむ, 苦しんで) **2.** *feels* ~ teremásu (teréru, térete) 照れます・てれます(照れる, 照れて), kimari ga warúi (desu) きまりが悪い・きまりがわるい(です) **3.** *is* ~ (*ashamed, shy*) hazukashíi 恥ずかしい・はずかしい
embarrassment n tōwaku 当惑・とうわく; komáru kotó 困る事・こまること; hají 恥・はじ
embassy n taishí-kan 大使館
emblem n kishō 記章; (*symbol*) shōchō 象徴, hyōshō 表象; (*heraldic emblem*) monshō 紋章
embroidery n shishū 刺しゅう・刺繍
emerge v demásu (déru, déte) 出ます・でます(出る, 出て), arawaremásu (arawaréru, arawaréte) 現れます・あらわれます(現れる, 現れて)
emergence (*appearance*) n shutsugen 出現
emergency n hijō (jitai) 非常(事態), kinkyū (jitai) 緊急(事態), (*temporary*) rinji 臨時・りんじ; (*crisis*) kíki 危機
emergency brake n hijō-burḗki 非常ブレーキ
emergency exit n hijō-guchi 非常口
emergency phone n hijō-dénwa 非常電話
in an emergency tossa no toki (ni) とっさの時・とっさのとき(に)
for emergencies kyūkyū (no) 救急(の)
emery board n tsume-yásuri 爪やすり
emigrant n imin 移民, ijū-sha 移住者
Emoticon n (*computer*) kaomoji 顔文字, emōtikon エモーティコン
emotion n kanjō 感情・かんじょう; (*feeling*) kandō 感動・かんどう, kangeki 感激・かんげき
emotional adj kanjō-teki (na) 感情的・かんじょうてき(な)
Emperor n **1.** (*Japanese*) Tennō 天皇; *His Majesty the Emperor* Tennō-héika 天皇陛下 **2.** kōtei 皇帝
emphasis n kyōchō 強調
emphasize v kyōchō shimásu (suru, shíte) 強調します(する, して)
empire n téikoku 帝国
employ v **1.** tsukaimásu (tsukau, tsukatte) 使います・つかいます(使う, 使って), yatoimásu (yatóu, yattótte) 雇います・やといます(雇う, 雇って) **2.** *is employed* tsutómete imásu (iru, ite) 勤めています・つとめています(いる, いて); yatówarete imásu (iru, ite) 雇われています・やとわれています(いる, いて)

employee n jūgyō-in 従業員; (*of a company*) sha-in 社員, kaishá-in 会社員
employer n koyō-sha 雇用者, koyō-nushi 雇用主
employment n (*use*) shiyō 使用; (*hiring*) koyō 雇用, yatói 雇い・やとい; (*job*) tsutomé (o-tsutome) 勤め・つとめ(お勤め)
finding employment n shūshoku 就職
place of employment n tsutome-saki 勤め先
seeking employment n kyūshoku 求職
Empress n Kōgō (-sama) 皇后(様・さま); *Her Majesty the Empress* Kōgō-héika 皇后陛下
empty 1. adj kara (no) 空・から(の), karappo (no) 空っぽ・からっぽ(の); (*with nothing in it*) nani mo háitte inai … 何も入っていない…・なにもはいっていない…; (*hollow*) utsuro (na) 虚ろ・うつろ(な); (*futile*) munashii 空しい・虚しい・むなしい; (*is vacant*) aite imásu (iru, ite) 空いています・あいています(いる, いて) **2.** adj aki-…空[あ]き…
empty bottle n aki-bin 空[あ]き瓶
empty box n aki-bako 空[あ]き箱
empty can n aki-kan 空[あ]き缶
empty house n aki-ya 空[あ]き家
empty room/office n aki-ma 空[あ]き間, aki-shitsu 空[あ]き室
3. *gets* ~ akimásu (aku, aite) 空きます・あきます(空く, 空いて), sukimásu (suku, suite)すきます・空きます(すく, すいて) **4.** *empties it* v akemásu (akeru, akete) 空けます・あけます(空ける, 空けて); (*drinks to the bottom*) kanpai shimásu (suru, shíte) 乾杯します・かんぱいします(する, して)
enclose v (*in envelope*) dōfu shimásu (suru, shíte) 同封します(する, して)
encompass v fukumimásu (fukumu, fukunde) 含みます・ふくみます(含む, 含んで), kakomimásu (kakomu, kakonde) 囲みます(囲む, 囲んで)
encounter v … ni de-aimásu (de-áu, de-átte) …に出会います・…にであいます(出会う, 出会って), sōgū shimásu (suru, shíte) 遭遇します(する, して)
encourage v susumemásu (susumeru, susumete) 勧めます・すすめます(勧める, 勧めて) hagemashimásu (hagemásu, hagemashíte) 励まします・はげまします(励ます, 励まして)
encouragement n shōrei 奨励
encouraging adj kokoro-zuyoi 心強い・こころづよい
encroach upon v okashimásu (okasu, okashíte) 侵します・おかします(侵す, 侵して)
encyclopedia n hyakka-jíten 百科事典
end 1. n (*the ending*) owari 終わり・おわり, o-shimai おしまい, kirí 切り・きり; (*close*) sue 末・すえ; (*of street*) tsuki-atari 突き当たり・つきあたり; (*edge*) hashi/haji 端 = hashikko/hajikko 端っこ・はしっこ, tamotó 袂・たもと; (*purpose*) mokuteki 目的
end of the year n (toshi no) kure (年の)暮れ・

くれ, nenmatsu 年末
to the (very) end akú-made (mo) あくまで（も）
2. *v (it ends, ends it)* owarimásu (owaru, owatte)
終わります・おわります（終わる, 終わって）;
(comes to an end) sumimásu (súmu, súnde) 済みま
す・すみます（済む, 済んで）, *(runs out)* tskimásu
(tsukiru, tsukíte) 尽きます・つきます（尽きる,
尽きて）**3.** *v goes to the ~ (of a road, etc.)* tsuki-
atarimásu (tsuki-ataru, tsuki-atatte) 突き当たりま
す・つきあたります（突き当たる, 突き当たって）
end up (doing) *v* shite shimaimásu (shimau, shimatte) してしまいます（しまう, しまって）
endeavor *v* tsutomemásu (tsutoméru, tsutómete)
努めます・つとめます（努める, 努めて）, dóryoku
shimásu (suru, shite) 努力します・どりょくしま
す（する, して）
ending *n* owari 終わり, ketsumatsu 結末
ending address *n* shūryō adoresu 終了アドレス
ending balance *n* kimatsu-zandaka 期末残高
ending of a word *n* gobi 語尾
ending point *n* shūten 終点
happy ending *n* happii endo ハッピーエンド
endless *adj (no limit)* owari no nai 終わりのな
い・おわりのない, kirí ga nai 切りがない・きり
がない; *(forever)* eien (no) 永遠（の）
endorse → sign → support
endurance *n (patience)* shínbō 辛抱・しんぼう
endure *v (puts up with)* shínbō shimásu (suru,
shite) 辛抱します（する, して）
enema *n* kanchō 浣腸
enemy *n* teki 敵
energetic *adj* génki (na) 元気・げんき（な）,
enerugísshu (na) エネルギッシュ（な）; *(vigorous)*
sekkyoku-teki (na) 積極的（な）
energetically *adv* génki (ni) 元気・げんき（に）,
ikiói yóku 勢いよく・いきおいよく
energy *n* **1.** ikiói 勢い・いきおい **2.** enérúgii
エネルギー **3.** *(pep)* génki 元気(o-génki お元気)
engage *v* **1.** *(hires a professional)* tanomimásu
(tanómu, tanónde) 頼みます・たのみます
（頼む, 頼んで）**2. ~ in** *(an activity)* …ni jū'ji
shimásu (suru, shite) …に従事します（する,
して）**3. gets engaged** *(booked up, occupied)*
fusagarimásu (fusagáru, fusagátte) ふさがります
（ふさがる, ふさがって）
engaged *adj (to be married)* kon'yaku shite
imásu (iru, ite) 婚約しています（いる, いて）
engagement *n (date)* yakusoku 約束・
やくそく
engine 1. *n* kikan 機関, *(automobile)* énjin エン
ジン; *the ~ starts* énjin ga kakarimásu (kakáru,
kakátte) エンジンがかかります（かかる, かかっ
て）**2.** *n →* **fire engine 3.** *starts the ~* *v* énjin o
kakemásu (kakéru, kákete) エンジンをかけます
（かける, かけて）
engineer *n* gíshi 技師
engineering *n* kōgaku 工学
England *n* Igirisu イギリス, Eikoku 英国
English *n (language)* Eigo 英語; *(person)*

Igirisú-jin イギリス人
English conversation *n* eikaiwa 英会話・えいか
いわ
English-Japanese *n* ei-wa 英和; *English-
Japanese dictionary* eiwa-jíten 英和辞典
English-Japanese translation *n* eibun wayaku
英文和訳, nichiei-honyaku 日英翻訳
English text *n* eibun 英文
English translation *n* eiyaku 英訳
engrave *v* chōkoku shimásu (suru, shite) 彫刻し
ます（する, して）, kizamimásu (kizámu, kizánde)
刻みます・きざみます（刻む, 刻んで）
engraving → woodblock print
engrossed; *gets ~ in* … ni muchū ni narimásu
(náru, nátte) …に夢中になります（なる, なって）;
…ni korimásu (kóru, kótte) …に凝ります・…に
こります（凝る, 凝って）
enjoy *v* tanoshimimásu (tanoshímu, tanoshínde)
楽しみます・たのしみます（楽しむ, 楽しんで）;
enjói shimásu (suru, shite) エンジョイします（す
る, して）; *~ the company of …* to tsuki-aimásu
(tsuki-áu, tsuki-átte) …と付き合います・…とつ
きあいます（付き合う, 付き合って）
enjoyable *adj* tanoshíi 楽しい・たのしい
enjoyment *n* tanoshimi 楽しみ・たのしみ, enjói
エンジョイ
enlargement *n* zōdai 増大
enlightenment *n* satori 悟り・さとり
enliven; *~with* kakki-zukemásu (kakki-zukeru,
kakki-zukete) 活気づけます・かっきづけます
（活気づける, 活気づけて）; nigiyaka ni shimásu
(suru, shite) にぎやかにします（する, して）
enormous *adj* bakudai (na) 莫大・ばくだい
（な）; bōdai (na) 膨大・ぼうだい（な）; taihen (na)
大変・たいへん（な）
enough *adj* **1.** jūbun (na) 十分・じゅうぶん
（な）; tappúri たっぷり; kékkō 結構・けっこう
2. *is ~* tarimásu (tariru, tarite) 足ります・たり
ます（足りる, 足りて）**3.** *gets (more than) ~ of*
akimásu (akíru, ákite) 飽きます（飽きる, 飽きて）
enquiry *n* shitsumon 質問, toiawase
問い合わせ
enroll *(in school)* *v* nyūgaku shimásu (suru, shite)
入学します（する, して）
ensign *n (naval officer)* shōi 少尉
entangled; *gets ~* kojiremásu (kojiréru, kojírete)
こじれます（こじれる, こじれて）, motsuremásu
(motsureru, motsurete) もつれます（もつれる,
もつれて）
entanglement *n* motsure もつれ
enter *v* … (no naka) ni hairimásu (háiru, háitte)
… (の中[なか])に入ります（入る, 入って）;
(appears on stage) tōjō shimásu (suru, shite)
登場します（する, して）
entering *v*
entering a company nyūsha 入社
entering a country nyūkoku 入国
entering a hospital nyūin 入院
entering a school nyūgaku 入学

315

enterprise *n* jígyō 事業

entertain *v* (*with food*) gochisō shimásu (suru, shite) ごちそう[御馳走]します(する、して)

entertainer *n* geinō´-jin 芸能人

entertainment *n* entātei(n)mento エンターテイ(ン)メント, goraku 娯楽

enthusiastic *adj* nésshín (na) 熱心・ねっしん(な)

enthusiastically *adv* nésshín (ni) 熱心・ねっしん(に)

entire *adj* zentai (no) 全体・ぜんたい(の)
entire surface zenmen 全面
throughout the entire … …-jū …中

entirety *n* zenzen 全然・ぜんぜん; sokkúri そっくり → **all** → **completely**

entrance *n* iriguchi 入(り)口・いりぐち, toguchi 戸口; (*front entry*) génkan 玄関
entrance exam *n* (*school*) nyūgaku shikén 入学試験; (*company*) nyūsha-shikén 入社試験
entrance gate **1.** (*wicket*) madoguchi 窓口 **2.** (*station*) kaisatsuguchi 改札口

entranced; gets ~ with … ni muchū ni narimásu (náru, nátte) …に夢中になります(なる、なって)

entrust (*one with it*) *v* (sore o …ni) azukemásu (azukéru, azúkete) (それを…に)預けます・あずけます(預ける、預けて); yudanemásu (yudanéru, yudánete) 委ねます・ゆだねます(委ねる、委ねて); makasemásu (makaséru, makásete) 任せます・まかせます(任せる、任せて); tanomimásu (tanómu, tanónde) 頼みます・たのみます(頼む、頼んで); irai shimásu (suru, shite) 依頼します(する、して)

entry *n* **1.** (*head word of dictionary*) midashi 見出し・みだし, midashi-go 見出し語・見だし語 **2.** (*entry upon the stage*) tōjō 登場 **3.** sanka 参加 **4.** (*registration*) tōroku 登録 **5.** (*computer*) nyūryoku 入力 **6.** → **enter 7.** → **entrance**

envelope *n* fūtō 封筒・ふうとう (*how many* nánmai 何枚)

enviable/envious *adj* netamashíi ねたましい・妬ましい, urayamashíi うらやましい・羨ましい

environment *n* kankyō 環境・かんきょう
environmental pollution *n* kankyō-osen 環境汚染
environmental protection *n* kankyō-hogo 環境保護

environs *n* shūhen 周辺

envy *v* urayamimásu (urayamu, urayánde) うらやみ・ます(うらやむ、うらやんで); netamimásu (netámu, netánde) ねたみ[妬み]ます(ねたむ、ねたんで)

epidemic *n* ryūkō-byō 流行病; densenbyō 伝染病

episode *n* **1.** (*story*) episōdo エピソード, sōwa 挿話 **2.** (*TV series*) *a episode* ichi-wa 一話; *two episodes* ni-wa 二話; *final episode* saishū-kai 最終回

equal *adj* **1.** byōdō (na) 平等(な); (*on an ~ level*) taitō (no) 対等(の); (*equivalent to*) … to hitoshíi …と等しい **2.** (*extends to*) … ni oyobimásu (oyobu, oyonde) …に及び[および]ます(及ぶ、及ん

で) **3.** (*constitutes*) … désu (dá/ná/nó, dé, ní) …です(だ/な/の、で、に)

equality *n* byōdō 平等

equation *n* (*equation form*) hōtei-shiki 方程式

equator *n* sekidō 赤道

equilibrium *n* tsuriai 釣り合い・つりあい

equipment *n* (*apparatus*) sō´chi 装置, kiki 機器, (*facilities*) sétsubi 設備

equivalence *n* taiō 対応

equivalent *adj* taitō (no) 対等(の); **~ *to* …** to hitoshíi …と等しい・…とひとしい; … ni sōtō shimásu (suru, shite) …に相当します(する、して)

era *n* jidai 時代; …-jídai …時代
Edo-era *n* Edo-jídai 江戸時代

erase *v* keshimásu (kesu, keshite) 消します・けします(消す、消して), tori-keshimásu (tori-kesu, tori-keshite) 取り消します・とりけします(取り消す、取り消して)

eraser *n* (*pencil*) keshi-gomu 消しゴム; (*blackboard*) kokubán-fuki 黒板拭き・黒板ふき, kokubán-keshi 黒板消し・黒板けし

erasure *n* tori-keshi 取り消し・とりけし

erect *v* tatemásu (tatéru, tátete) 立てます・たてます(立てる、立てて), (*builds*) tatemásu (tatéru, tátete) 建てます(建てる、建てて)

erotic *adj* iroppói 色っぽい・いろっぽい, kōshoku (na) 好色(な)

err *v* ayamarimásu (ayamáru, ayamátte) 誤ります・あやまります(誤る、誤って)

errand *n* yōji 用事・ようじ, tsukai 使い, yō-táshí 用足し
errand runner *n* tsukai bashiri (tsukai-ppashiri) 使い走り

error *n* machigai 間違い・まちがい, ayamári 誤り・あやまり, erā エラー; *is in ~* machigaemásu (machigáeru, machigáete) 間違えます・まちがえます(間違える、間違えて)

erupt *v* funka shimásu (suru, shite) 噴火します(する、して)

eruption *n* funka 噴火; (*skin ~*) hasshin 発疹・はっしん; hosshin 発疹・ほっしん; fukidemono 吹き出物

escalator *n* esukarē˜tā エスカレーター

escape *v* nigemásu (nigéru, nígete) 逃げます・にげます(逃げる、逃げて); nukemásu (nukeru, nukete) 抜けます・ぬけます(抜ける、抜けて)
a convenient escape watari ni fúne 渡りに舟・わたりに舟

esoteric *adj* (*mysterious*) shinpi-teki (na) 神秘的(な)

especially *adv* tokubetsu (ni) 特別(に)・とくべつ(に), kóto(-ni) ことに・殊(に); toriwake とりわけ; sekkakú せっかく; *~ when* … sekkakú … na no ni せっかく…なのに

essay *n* zuihitsu 随筆, essē エッセー, zuisō-roku 随想録, sakubun 作文; shōron 小論

essential *adj* (*necessary*) hitsuyō (na) 必要・ひつよう(な)

essentials *n* (*supplies*) hitsuju-hin 必需品; daily

essentials 生活必需品

establish v tatemásu (tattéru, tátete) 建てます (建てる, 建てて); okoshimásu (okósu, okóshite) 起こします・おこします (起こす, 起こして)

establishment n 1. (founding) sōritsu 創立 2. (facility) shisetsu 施設・しせつ 3. → company

esteem n sonkei 尊敬・そんけい

estimate 1. n (an estimate) mitsumori 見積も り・みつもり, kentō´ 見当, suitei 推定, (forecast) yosoku 予測 2. v (estimates it) mi-tsumorimásu (mi-tsumoru, mi-tsumotte) 見積もります・みつも ります (見積もる, 見積もって), (makes a guess) kentō´ o tsukemásu (tsukéru, tsukéte) 見当をつ けます (つける, つけて), (infers) suitei shimásu (suru, shite) 推定します (する, して), (forecasts) yosoku shimásu (suru, shite) 予測します (する, して)

estimation n (inference, presumption) suitei 推定 → judgment

estrange v 1. gets estranged hedatarimásu (heda-táru, hedatátte) 隔たります・へだたります (隔た る, 隔たって) 2. becomes estranged from reality hedatemásu (hedatéru, hedatéte) 隔てます・へだてます (隔てる, 隔てて)

estranged adj utói うとい・疎い

eternal adj eien (no) 永遠・えいえん (の)

eternally adv eien (ni) 永遠・えいえん (に), eikyū (ni) 永久 (に)

eternity n eien 永遠・えいえん, eikyū 永久

ethics n rínri 倫理, dōtoku 道徳

ethnic n minzoku 民族

etiquette n reigí 礼儀, echikétto エチケット

etymology n gogen 語源

euro n yūro ユーロ

Europe n Yōróppa ヨーロッパ, Ō´shū 欧州 Europe and America n Ō-Bei 欧米, Séiyō 西洋

European n (person) Yōróppa-jin ヨーロッパ人, Ō´shū-jin 欧州人

European Union n Ō´shū-rengō 欧州連合

evacuate v (to escape) hinan shimásu (suru, shite) 避難します (する, して), (gets repatriated) hiki-agemá su (hiki-agéru, hiki-ágete) 引き揚げます・ ひきあげます (引き揚げる, 引き揚げて)

evacuation n (escape) hinan 避難, (repatriation) hikiage 引き揚げ・ひきあげ

evacuee n (refugee) hinan-min 避難民, (repatriated) hikiagésha 引き揚げ者

evaluation score n hyōten 評点

evaporated milk n eba-míruku エバミルク

even 1. adj (smooth, flat) taira (na) 平ら・たい ら (な) 2. adj dōtō (no) 同等 (の); ... to hitoshíi ...と等しい; kinitsu na 均一な 3. adj gokaku no 互角の 4. adv ... mo ...も; ... (de) sae (で) さえ; ~ doing adv (if it does) (shi-) té mo/(shi-) tátte (し) ても/(し) たって; ~ being adv (if it is) [ADJECTIVE] -kute mo/kutatte くても/くたって, [NOUN] démo/dátte でも/だって

even so (sore) démo (それ) でも

evening n ban 晩・ばん, yūgata 夕方・ゆうがた, yoi 宵・よい

evening at school n hōkago 放課後

evening paper n yūkan 夕刊

evening performance n yóru no bú 夜の部

evening dress n ibuningu doresu イブニングド レス, yakai-fuku 夜会服

evening meal n yūshoku 夕食

event n kotó 事・こと; (incident) jíken 事件; (case) dán 段; (ceremony) gyō´jí 行事, ibento イベント; (game) kyō´gí (shumoku) 競技 (種目)

eventually adv (come what may) nán to itté mo 何 [なん] と言っても; (in due time) sono uchi ni そのうちに; saishū-teki ni(wa) 最終的に (は) → finally, at last

ever 1. adv (always) ítsu-mo いつも; as ever aikawarazu 相変わらず・あいかわらず 2. adv (once) ítsu-ka いつか, ... kotó ga arimásu (áru, átte) 事 [こと] があります (ある, あっ て); 3. wh...ever ittai ...?! いったい・一体...?! Wherever have you been? Ittai dóko e itte imá shita ka. いったい [一体] どこへ行っていましたか. ever since adv ... irai ...以来・いらい

ever so many adv íkutsu mo いくつも, nán- [COUNTER] mo 何 [COUNTER] も

ever so much adv íkura mo いくらも; dōmo ど うも

every ... adj dóno ... démo どの...でも; ... goto (ni) ...ごと・毎 (に), mai-... 毎...; arayuru あらゆる

every chance one gets adv koto áru góto (ni) 事あるごと (に)

every day adv, n máinichi 毎日・まいにち, higoto (ni) 日毎 (に), híbi 日々; almost ~ máinichi no yō´ni 毎日のように

every month adv, n mai-tsuki 毎月, maigetsu 毎月

every morning adv, n mái-asa 毎朝

every night adv, n mai-ban 毎晩, mai-yo 毎夜

every other ... adv ... oki ni ...おきに

every station n kaku-eki 各駅

every time adv, n maido 毎度; ~ that ...tabí(ni) ...度 (に)

every week adv, n maishū 毎週

every which way adv hō´bō 方々・ほうぼう

every year adv, n mai-toshi 毎年, mainen 毎年

everybody pron mi(n)ná み (ん) な・皆, miná-san 皆さん・みなさん; dare demo 誰でも・だれでも (= everyone)

everyday ... adj (daily) máinichi no ... 毎日の...; (usual) fúdan no ... 普段の...・ふだんの... everyday clothes n fudán-gí 普段着・ふだん着

everyone pron zen'in 全員

everyplace → everywhere

everything pron minná みんな・皆, zénbu 全部・ぜんぶ, nan demo 何でも・なんでも, íssái 一切; monógoto 物事

everywhere adv doko demo どこでも, dóko ni

mo どこにも, hōʹbō 方々・ほうぼう

evidence *n* shōko 証拠; (*basis*) kónkyo 根拠・こんきょ

evil *n* 1. → **bad** 2. (*a devil*) ákú 悪
 evil spirit *n* ákuma 悪魔・アクマ

exact *adj* (*detailed*) kuwashíi 詳しい・くわしい, komakái 細かい・こまかい; (*correct*) seikaku (na) 正確・せいかく(な)

exactly *adv* chōdo ちょうど, mattakú 全く・まったく, pittári ぴったり, hakkíri はっきり; másani まさに・正に; ... daké...だけ

exaggerate *v* kochō shimásu (suru, shite) 誇張します(する, して)

exaggerated *adj* ōgesa (na) 大げさ・おおげさ(な), (go-)táisō (na) (ご)大層・たいそう(な)

exaggeration *n* kochō 誇張; (*bragging*) hóra ほら

examination *n* 1. (*test*) shikén 試験 2. (*inquiry*) chōʹsa 調査 3. (*inspection*) kénsa 検査, (*medical*) shinsatsu 診察
 examination place *n* shiken-jō 試験場
 examination room *n* shinsatsushitsu 診察室

examine *v* 1. (*investigates*) shirabemásu (shirabéru, shirábete) 調べます・しらべます(調べる, 調べて), kentō shimásu (suru, shite) 検討します・けんとうします(する, して) 3. (*medically*) mimásu (míru, míte) 診ます・みます(診る, 診て), shinsatsu shimásu (suru, shite) 診察します・しんさつします(する, して) 4. *examine tickets* (*at wicket*) kaisatsu shimásu (suru, shite) 改札します(する, して); (*aboard*) kensatsu shimásu (suru, shite) 検札します(する, して)

example *n* réi 例, ichi-rei 一例, tatoe 例え・たとえ, tatoi 例い・たとい; *follows* (*learns from*) *the ~ of ...* o mi-naraimásu (mi-narau, mi-naratte) ... を見習います(見習う, 見習って)
 for example tatóeba 例えば・たとえば

excavate *v* horimásu (hóru, hótte) 掘ります(掘る, 掘って)

exceed *v* sugimásu (sugíru, súgite) 過ぎます(過ぎる, 過ぎて), chōka shimásu (suru, shite) 超過します(する, して), koshimásu (kosu, koshite) 超します・こします(超す, 超して), uwa-mawari-másu (uwa-mawaru, uwa-mawátte) 上回ります(上回る, 上回って)

exceedingly *adv* móttómo 最も・もっとも, góku ごく・極, taihen 大変・たいへん, hijō ni 非常に・ひじょうに

excel *v* sugúrete imásu (iru, ite) 優れています・すぐれています(いる, いて)

excellent *adj* sugúreta 優れた・すぐれた, yūshū (na) 優秀(な); kékkō (na) 結構・けっこう(な); *is ~* sugúrete imásu (iru, ite) 優れています・すぐれています(いる, いて)

except (*for*) *prep* ...no hoka...の他, ...igai ...以外・...いがい

exception *n* reigai 例外; *without ~* (*all*) íssái 一切・いっさい

excess *n* chōka 超過, kajō 過剰; (*leeway, margin*) yoyū 余裕・よゆう; *is in ~* amarimásu (amáru, amátte) 余リます・あまります(余る, 余って)

excessive *adj* yokei (na) 余計・よけい(な), hōgai (na) 法外(な); (*extreme*) kageki (na) 過激(な), kyokután na 極端(な)

excessively *adv* yáke ni やけに, (*extremely*) kyokután (ni) 極端(に)・きょくたん(に)

exchange *v* (tori-)kaemásu (kaeru, kaete) (取り)替えます・(とり)かえます(替える, 替えて), hiki-kaemásu (hiki-káeru, hiki-káete) 引き換えます・ひきかえます(引き換える, 引き換えて), kōkan shimásu (suru, shite) 交換します(する, して)

exchange rate *n* kawase rēto 為替レート

excited 1. *gets ~* ki ga tachimásu (tátsu, tátte) 気が立ちます(立つ, 立って); nes-shimásu (nes-suru, nes-shite) 熱します(熱する, 熱して) 2. *is ~* kōfun shite imásu (iru, ite) 興奮しています(いる, いて)

excitement *n* kōfun 興奮

exciting *adj* wakuwaku saseru ワクワクさせる, kōfun saseru 興奮させる, kōfun suru 興奮する

exclude *v* háijo shimásu (suru, shite) 排除します(する, して)

excluded *adj* (*not included*) fukumarete inai 含まれていない・ふくまれていない

exclusion *n* háijo 排除

excrement *n* daibén 大便, kusó 糞・クソ

excursion *n* ensoku 遠足・えんそく, yūran 遊覧

excuse *n* ii-wake 言い訳・いいわけ, mōshiwake 申し訳・申しわけ; (*pretext*) kōjitsu 口実; *makes excuses* (*apologizes*) ii-wake o shimásu (suru, shite) 言い訳をします(する, して); (*declines*) kotowarimásu (kotowáru, kotowátte) 断ります・ことわります(断る, 断って)
 a convenient excuse watari ni fúne 渡りに舟

Excuse me. Sumimasén すみません; Osóre-irimásu. 恐れ入ります・おそれいります; Dōʹmo. どうも; Gomen nasái. ごめんなさい; Shitsúrei shimásu. 失礼します.
 Excuse me but I'll be on my way. Sore déwa shitsúrei (ita)shimásu. それでは失礼(いた)します.
 Excuse me for having interrupted/bothered you. O-jama shimáshita. おじゃま[お邪魔]しました.
 Excuse me for interrupting/bothering you. (*but*) O-jama deshō ga ... おじゃま[お邪魔]でしょうが....
 Excuse me for being the first to leave. O-saki ni shitsúrei shimásu. お先に失礼します.
 Excuse me for going first. O-saki ni. お先に・おさきに.

exempt *v* *is ~ from* ... o manukaremásu (manukaréru, manukárete) ... を免れます・まぬかれます(免れる, 免れて)
 tax-exempt *adj* menzei (no) 免税(の);

exercise 1. *n* (*physical*) undō 運動, (*calisthenics*)

taisō 体操; (*study*) renshū 練習・れんしゅう, (*practice*) dóríru ドリル, kéiko 稽古・けいこ (o-keiko お稽古) **2.** *v* undō shimásu (suru, shite) 運動します(する, して)

exercise book *n* nōto ノート, renshū-chō 練習帳

exert *v* (*exerts oneself*) tsutomemásu (tsutoméru, tsutó-mete) 努めます・つとめます(努める, 努めて); tsukushimásu (tsukúsu, tsukúshite) 尽くします・つくします(尽くす, 尽くして)

exhaust 1. *n* haiki 排気; (*fumes*) haiki-gásu 排気ガス **2.** ~ *it* *v* tsukai-hatashimásu (tsukai-hatásu, tsukai-hatáshite) 使い果たします・使いはたします(使い果たす, 使い果たして); (*runs out of*) kirashimásu (kirásu, kiráshite) 切らします・きらします(切らす, 切らして)

exhaust fan *n* haikí-sen 排気扇, kanki-sen 換気扇

exhaustive *adj* téttē´tékí (ná) 徹底的(な), mō´ra shita 網羅した

exhibit 1. *n* tenji(-kai) 展示(会), tenrán-kai 展覧会 **2.** *v* ~ *it* misemásu (miséru, mísete) 見せます・みせます(見せる, 見せて); shuppin shimásu (suru, shite) 出品します(する, して)

exhibition *n* tenji-kai 展示会, tenrán-kai 展覧会, hakuránkai 博覧会; (*display*) misemóno 見世物

exhibitor *n* shuppín-sha 出品者

exist *v* sonzai shimásu (suru, shite) 存在します(する, して)

existence *n* (*survives or does not survive*) sonzai 存在, seizon 生存; (*or exists or does not exist*) úmu 有無

exit 1. *n* dé-guchi 出口; *north/south/ east/west ~* kita/minami/higashi/nishi-guchi 北/南/東/西口 **2.** *v* taijō shimásu (suru, shite) 退場します(する, して)

exorbitant *adj* hogai (na) 法外(な)

expand *v* hirogarimásu (hirogaru, hirogatte) 広がります・ひろがります(広がる, 広がって); bōchō shimásu (suru, shite) 膨脹します(する, して) → **develop** → **grow** → **spread**

expansion → **development** → **growth**

expect (*awaits*) mátte imásu (iru, ite) 待っています・まっています(いる, いて), kitai shimásu (suru, shite) 期待します(する, して); (*anticipates*) yosō shimásu (suru, shite) 予想します(する, して); *as we might ~* sasuga (ni) さすが(に)

expect to (*do*) … (suru) tsumori dé su …(する)つもりです

expectation *n* mikomi 見込み・みこみ, tsumori つもり, ate 当て・あて, yosō 予想・よそう, yotei 予定・よてい; kitai 期待・きたい; …hazu …はず

expediency *n* (*convenience*) kōtsugō 好都合

expedient *adj* tsugō no yoi 都合のよい

expense *n* hiyó 費用, kei-hi 経費; …-hi …費

expensive *adj* (ne ga) takái (値が)高い

experience 1. *n* keiken 経験・けいけん, (*personal*) taiken 体験・たいけん; (*a sometime happening*) …kotó …事・こと; (*professional*) shokureki 職歴 **2.** *v* (*experiences, undergoes*) keiken shimásu (suru, shite) 経験します(する, して), …mé ni aimásu (áu, átte) …目にあいます(あう, あって)

experiment 1. *n* jikken (o shimásu; suru, shite) 実験・じっけん(をします; する, して); (*test*) shikén 試験, tameshí 試し **2.** *v ~ with* … o tameshimásu, (tamésu, taméshite) …を試します・…をためします(試す, 試して)

expert 1. *adj* jōzu (na) じょうず・上手(な), tassha (na) 達者(な) **2.** *n* meijín 名人, tsū 通, tsūjin 通人, (*veteran*) kūrō´to くろうと・玄人, okioupūto エキスパート, beteran ベテラン, (*specialist*) senmon-ka 専門家

expire *v* (*contract, rights, etc.*) shikkō shimásu (suru, shite) 失効します(する, して)

explain *v* setsumei shimásu (suru, shite) 説明します・せつめいします(する, して); tokimásu (tóku, tóite) 説きます(説く, 説いて); káishaku shimásu (suru, shite) 解釈します・かいしゃくします(する, して)

explanation *n* setsumei 説明・せつめい; (*interpretation*) kái-shaku 解釈; (*excuse*) ii-wake 言い訳・いいわけ

explanatory notes *n* hanrei 凡例・はんれい

explicit *adj* meihaku (na) 明白(な)

explicitly *adv* meihaku (ni) 明白(に)

explode *v* bakuhatsu shimásu (suru, shite) 爆発します(する, して)

exploit 1. *n* tegara 手柄 **2.** *v* riyō shimásu (suru, shite) 利用します(する, して)

explosion *n* bakuhatsu 爆発

export 1. *n* (*exporting*) yushutsu 輸出 **export goods** *n* yushutsu-hin 輸出品 **2.** *v exports it* yushutsu shimásu (suru, shite) 輸出します(する, して)

expose (*a secret*) *v* barashimásu (barásu, bará-shite) ばらします(ばらす, ばらして)

exposition *n* **1.** (*a fair*) hakurán-kai 博覧会 **2.** (*explanation*) káishaku 解釈

expound *v* káishaku shimásu (suru, shite) 解釈します(する, して)

express 1. *n* (*train, bus*) kyūkō 急行 **2.** *v* (*puts into words*) ii-arawashimásu (ii-arawásu, ii-arawashite) 言い表します・言いあらわします(言い表す, 言い表して), (*tells*) iimásu (iu, itte/yutte) 言います(言う, 言って/ゆって)

express mail *n* sokutatsu (yū-)bin 速達(郵)便
express train *n* kyūkō-ressha 急行列車

expression *n* (*way of saying*) iikata 言い方・言いかた, (*phrase*) hyōgen 表現・ひょうげん; (*on face*) hyōjō 表情・ひょうじょう, kao 顔・かお; *has/wears an ~ of* … (no) kao o shite imásu (iru, ite) …(の)顔をしています(いる, いて)

expressly *adv* (*clearly*) hakkiri (to) はっきり(と), (*specially*) tokubetsu (ni) 特別・とくべつ(に)

extend *v* **1.** (*extends it*) nobashimásu (nobásu, nobáshite) 延ばします・のばします(延ばす, 延ばして), enchō shimásu (suru, shite) 延長します(す

る、して) **2.** (*it extends*) nobimás̲u (nobíru, nóbite) 伸びます・のびます(伸びる、伸びて)、(*reaches*) oyobimás̲u (oyobu, oyonde) 及びます・およびます(及び、及んで)

extension *n* (*cord*) enchō-kō´do 延長コード; (*phone line, inside*) naisen 内線, (*outside*) gaisen 外線

extent *n* kágirí 限り・かぎり; hodo 程・ほど; teido 程度; kagen 加減 → **scope** → **degree**; *to what ~* dónna ni どんなに; *to this ~* konna ni こんなに; *to that ~* sonna ni そんなに, anna ni あんなに

exterior *n* gáibu 外部, gaimen 外面

external *adj* soto-gawa (no) 外側(の); gáibu/gaimen (no) 外部/外面(の); gai-… 外…

extinguish *v* keshimás̲u (kesu, kesh̲ite) 消します・けします(消す、消して); *gets extinguished* kiemás̲u (kieru, kiete) 消えます・きえます(消える、消えて)

extinguisher → fire extinguisher

extol *v* homemás̲u (homéru, hométe) 褒めます・ほめます(褒める、褒めて)

extortion *n* yusuri ゆすり

extra 1. *n* (*actor/actress*) ekisutora エキストラ **2.** *n* (*bonus*) omake おまけ **3.** *adj* yobun (no/ni) 余分・よぶん(に/の), betsu (no/ni) 別・べつ(の/に); (*special*) tokubetsu (no) 特別・とくべつ(の)

extra charge *n* betsu-ryō´kin 別料金

extract *n* ekisu エキス

extraordinary *adj* rinji (no) 臨時(の); namiha-zureta 並外れた・並はずれた

extravagance *n* muda-zúkai 無駄使い・むだづかい, rōhi 浪費

extravagant *adj* zeitákú (na) ぜいたく・贅沢(な); ogorimás̲u (ogoru, ogótte) おごります・驕ります(おごる、おごって)

extreme *adj* kyokután (na) 極端(な); (*radical*) kageki (na) 過激(な)

extremely *adv* hijō (ni) 非常・ひじょう(に), kiwámete 極めて・きわめて, hanahada 甚だ・はなはだ, góku ごく・極, shigoku しごく, itatte 至って・いたって, kyokután (ni) 極端・きょくたん(に), to(t)temo と(っ)ても, monosúgoku 物凄く・ものすごく, zúibun 随分・ずいぶん; (*more than one might expect*) nakanaka なかなか

extremist *n* kageki-ha 過激派

exultant *adj* (*proud*) tokui (na) 得意(な)

eye *n* **1.** mé 目[眼] **2.** (*detective*) tantei 探偵; (*of a needle*) médo めど; *(with) wide eyes* me o maruku shimás̲u (suru, sh̲ite) 目を丸くします(する、して)

public eye *n* seken no me 世間の目

typhoon's eye *n* taifū no me 台風の目

eye area *n* mejiri 目尻・めじり

eye ball *n* gankyū 眼球, medama 目玉・めだま

eyebrow *n* máyu(ge) 眉(毛)・まゆ(げ)

eye camera *n* ai kamera アイ・カメラ

eye doctor *n* mé-isha 目医者・眼医者

eye drops *n* me-gúsuri 目薬・めぐすり

eye fatigue *n* gansei-hirō 眼精疲労

eyeglasses *n* mégane 眼鏡・めがね・メガネ; *puts on* (*wears*) *~* mégane o kakemás̲u (kákete imás̲u) 眼鏡・メガネをかけます(かけています)

eyelashes *n* mátsuge まつげ

eyelid *n* mábuta まぶた

eye lotion *n* me-gúsuri 目薬

eye shadow *n* ai-shadō アイシャドウ

eyesight *n* shíryoku 視力

F

fable *n* gūwa 寓話

fabric *n* ori-mono 織物・おりもの, kíji 生地・きじ

fabrication *n* **1.** (*fiction*) tsukuri-banashi 作り話, detchiage でっちあげ **2.** (*making*) seizō 製造

fabulous *adj* subarashii すばらしい・素晴らしい, wakuwaku suru ワクワクする

face 1. *n* kao 顔・かお, tsurá つら・面; (*one's honor*) taimen 体面 **2.** *n* (*front*) shō´men 正面 **3.** *v* (*faces it*) mukimás̲u (muku, muite) 向きます・むきます(向く、向いて) **4.** *v* atarimás̲u (ataru, atatte) 当たります・あたります(当たる、当たって)

face cream *n* bigan kuriimu 美顔クリーム

face powder *n* oshiroi おしろい・白粉

face towel *n* fēsu taoru フェースタオル

Facebook *n* (*internet*) feisu bukku フェイスブック

facelift *n* biyō-seikei 美容整形, seikei-shujutsu 整形手術

facial *adj* kao (no) 顔(の)

facile *adj* tegaru (na) 手軽(な), tayasui たやすい

facility, facilities *n* sh̲isetsu 施設・しせつ, sétsubi 設備; bén 便・びん

facing *adv* mukai no 向かい・むかいの (o-múkai お向かいの)

facsimile *n* fakush̲imiri ファクシミリ, fákkusu ファックス → **fax**

fact *n* kotó 事・こと, jíjitsu 事実・じじつ; *in ~* jitsú wa 実は・じつは, jissai (wa) 実際・じっさい(は), iyó-iyo いよいよ, jitai 事態・じたい

faction *n* habatsu 派閥・はばつ

factory *n* kō´ba/kō´jō´ 工場

factory worker *n* kō´in 工員, shokkō´ 職工

fad *n* ichiji-teki ryūkō 一時的の流行

fade *v* **1.** samemás̲u (saméru, sámete) さめます(さめる、さめて), asemás̲u (aseru, asete) あせます・褪せます(あせる、あせて) **2.** (*grows weak*)

otoroemásu (otoróéru, otoróete) 衰えます・おと
ろえます(衰える、衰えて) **3.** (*vanishes*) kiemásu
(kieru, kiete) 消えます・きえます(消える、
消えて)

fade-in n fēdo in フェードイン

fade-out n fēdo auto フェードアウト

fail v **1.** shippai shimásu (suru, shite) 失敗します
(する、して) **2.** (*exam*) ochimásu (ochíru, óchite)
落ちます・おちます(落ちる、落ちて)、rakudai
shimásu (suru, shite) 落第します(する、して)
3. (*is wide off the mark*) hazuremásu (hazureru,
hazurete) 外れます・はずれます(外れる、外れて)
4. (*engine etc. breaks down*) koshō´ shimásu (suru,
shite) 故障します(する、して)
without fail zé-hi ぜひ・是非、kanarazu 必ず・
かならず

failed adj fugō´kaku (no) 不合格(の)

failure n **1.** shippai 失敗・しっぱい **2.** (*exam*)
rakudai 落第、fugō´kaku 不合格
power failure n teiden 停電

faint **1.** adj (*dim*) kásuka (na) かすか[微か](な)
2. v (*loses consciousness*) ki o ushinaimásu
(ushinau, ushinatte) 気を失い[うしない]ます
(失う、失って)

fair n (*market*) íchi 市、íchi-bá 市場・いちば、
(*temple festival*) én-nichi 縁日・えんにち

fair adj (*just, impartial*) kō´hei (na) 公平(な);
(*sunny*) hárete imásu (háreta …) 晴れています・
はれています(晴れた…); *fair weather* haré 晴
れ・はれ、(o-)ténki(お)天気・てんき

fairly adv (*rather*) kánari かなり、sō´tō´ 相当・
そうとう、zúibun 随分・ずいぶん

fairly well (*sufficiently*) kékkō´ 結構・けっこう

fairy n yōsei 妖精・ようせい

fairy tale n dōwa 童話、otogibánashi おとぎ話

faithful adj seijitsu (na) 誠実(な)、chūjitsu (na)
忠実(な)、makoto (no) 誠・まこと(の)

fake **1.** adj nise (no) 偽・にせ(の)、inchiki (na) い
んちき・インチキ(な) **2.** n (*thing*) nise-mono
偽物・にせもの、inchiki いんちき・インチキ、
feiku フェイク **3.** v detchiagemásu (detchiageru,
detchiagete) でっちあげます(でっちあげる、でっ
ちあげて)

falcon n taka タカ・鷹、hayabusa ハヤブサ・隼

falconry n taka-gari タカ狩り・鷹狩り

fall **1.** n (*autumn*) áki 秋 **2.** v (*it falls*) ochimásu
(ochíru, óchite) 落ちます・おちます(落ちる、落
ちて)、okkochimásu (okkochíru, okkóchite) 落
っこちます・おっこちます(落っこちる、落っこ
ちて) **3.** v (*falls and scatters*) chirimásu (chiru,
chitte) 散ります・ちります(散る、散って)

fall behind okuremásu (okureru, okurete)
遅れます・おくれます(遅れる、遅れて); okure o
torimásu (tóru, tótte) 後れを取ります・おくれを
とります(取る、取って)

fall down taoremásu (taoréru, taórete) 倒れます・
たおれます(倒れる、倒れて)、korobimásu
(korobu, koronde) 転びます・ころびます(転ぶ、
転んで)

fall in love with … ni horemásu (horeru, horete)
…にほれ[惚れ]ます(ほれる、ほれて)、kói ni
ochimásu (ochiru, ochite) 恋に落ちます[おちち
ます](落ちる、落ちて)

fallacy n goshin 誤信

fallout n **1.** (*radioactive particles*) hōsha-sei kōka-
butsu 放射性降下物、shi no hai 死の灰

falls n taki 滝・たき (= *waterfalls*)

false adj (*falsehood*) úso (no) うそ・嘘・ウソ
(の)、itsuwari (no) 偽り・いつわり(の); (*fake*)
nise (no) 偽・にせ(の)、(*artificial*) jinzō´ (no)
人造(の)

false alarm n go-keihō 誤警報

falsehood n úso うそ・嘘・ウソ、itsuwari 偽り・
いつわり

false teeth n ire-ba 入れ歯

falter v yoro-mekimásu (yoro-méku, yoro-méite)
よろめきます(よろめく、よろめいて)、yóro-yoro
shimásu (suru, shite) よろよろします(する、
して)

fame n **1.** (*reputation*) hyō´ban 評判 **2.** → honor

familiar adj shitashíi 親しい・したしい →
accustomed → **know**

family n úchi 家・うち、 uchí 宅(o uchi
お家); kázoku 家族・かぞく、(*household*) 家庭
(*clan*) úji 氏・うじ、…-ke …家; ~ *crest* (ka)món
(家)紋・(か)もん、monshō´ 紋章・もんしょう;
(*biological taxonomy*) ká 科

family circle n uchiwa 内輪・うちわ

family inn n minshuku 民宿・みんしゅく

family name n (*surname*) sei 姓、、(*as written*)
myō´ji, miyoji 名字・苗字、úji 氏、kámei 家名

family room n (*Japanese ~*) (o-)cha-no-ma (お)
茶の間

famine n ue 飢え、kikin 飢饉・ききん

famous adj yūmei (na) 有名・ゆうめい(な)、
na-dakái 名高い、hyoban (no) 評判・ひょうばん
(の); *gets ~* shiraremásu (shirareru, shirarete)
知られます・しられます(知られる、知られて)、
yūmei ni narimásu (náru, nátte) 有名になります
(なる、なって)

fan n **1.** ō´gí 扇・おうぎ、(*folding*) sensu 扇子・
せんす; (*flat*) uchíwa うちわ・団扇; (*electric*) senpū´-ki
扇風機・せんぷうき **2.** (*enthusiast*) fán ファン;
…-zuki …好き・…ずき

fan club n fan-kurabu ファンクラブ

fan letter n fan-retā ファンレター

baseball fan n yakyū-fan 野球ファン・やきゅう
ファン

fancy adj (*high-grade*) kō´kyū (no) 高級(の)

fancy dresser n osháre na hito おしゃれな人

fancy dress party n kasō pātii 仮装パーティー

fancy goods n kō´kyū-hin 高級品

fanfare n fanfāre ファンファーレ

fang n kiba 牙・キバ

fan shell n (*a kind of scallop*) taira-gí たいらぎ

fantastic n subarashii 素晴らしい

fantasy n (*imaginary*) kūsō 空想、fantajii ファン
タジー

far *adj* tō´i 遠い・とおい, háruka (na) はるかな・遥か(な); háruka (ni) はるかに・遥かに(に)
how far donogurai/donokurai どの位, dóko made どこまで
as far as it goes ichiō´ 一応
by far zutto ずっと, háruka (ni) はるか・遥か(に)

farce; traditional Noh ~ kyō´gén 狂言, chaban 茶番

fare *n* (*fee*) ryō´kin 料金, (*transportation*) únchin 運賃

Far East *n* kyokutō´ 極東

farewell *n* wakaré 別れ・わかれ (o-wakare お別れ)

farewell party *n* sō´bétsukai 送別会, o-wakare-kai お別れ会

farm *n* nō´jō´ 農場

farm house/family *n* nō´ka 農家

farm land *n* nō´chi 農地

farmer *n* nō´ka 農家, nō´min 農民

farmhand *n* nō´jō-rōdō-sha 農場労働者

farmhouse *n* nō´ka 農家

farming *n* 1. nō´gyō´ 農業 2. yōshoku 養殖

far-off *adj* tō´i 遠い・とおい, háruka (na) はるか・遥か(な)

farsighted *adj* enshi (no) 遠視(の); (*forward-looking*) mae-muki (no) 前向き・前むき(の); senken no mei (no/ga aru) 先見の明(の/がある)

fart *n* onara (o shimásu; suru, shíte) おなら(をします; する, して); hé (o hirimásu; híru, hítté) へ・屁(をひります; ひる, ひって)

fascinated *adj* uttóri (to) うっとり(と); *is ~* uttóri shimásu (suru, shíte) うっとりします(する, して)

fascination *n* miryoku 魅力

fascism *n* fashizumu ファシズム

fascist *n* fashisuto ファシスト

fashion 1. *n* (*way*) ryūkō´ 流行, hayari はやり[流行り], fásshon ファッション; (...) fū (...)風・ふう 2. *is in ~* hayari-másu (hayáru, hayátte) はやり[流行り]ます(はやる, はやって)

fashion show *n* fasshon shō ファッションショー

fashionable *adj* hayari (no) はやり[流行り](の), ryūkō´ (no) 流行(の); haikara (na) ハイカラ(な), sumā´to (na) スマート(な)

fast *adj* háyaku 速く・はやく; hayái 速い・はやい; (*clock runs fast*) susunde imásu (iru, ite) 進んでいます・すすんでいます(いる, いて)

fasten *v* 1. (*firmly attaches*) tomemásu (tomeru, tomete) 留めます・とめます(留める, 留めて) 2. (*tightens, secures*) shimemásu (shiméru, shímete) 締めます・しめます(締める, 締めて); *Fasten your seat belts.* Shiito béruto o shímete kudasai. シートベルトを締めて下さい[しめてください].

fastener *n* fasunā ファスナー, chakku チャック

fast food *n* fāsuto fūdo ファーストフード,

insutanto (shokuhin) インスタント(食品)

fastidious → choosy

fat 1. *n* (*grease*) abura あぶら・脂, (*lard, blubber*) shibō´ 脂肪・しぼう 2. *gets fat* *v* futorimásu (futóru, futótte) 太ります・ふとります(太る, 太って), koemásu (koéru, kóete) 肥えます・こえます(肥える, 肥えて); (*is fat*) futótte imásu (iru, ite) 太っています・ふとっています(いる, いて) 3. *adj* (*plump*) futói 太い・ふとい, debu (no) デブ(の), futotta 太った・ふとった

fate *n* ún 運, únmei 運命・うんめい, shukumei 宿命

father *n* otō´san お父さん・おとうさん, chíchí 父, chichi oya 父親・ちちおや

Father *n* (*Reverend*) ...shínpu san ...神父さん

father-in-law *n* gífu 義父

fatigue *n* hirō 疲労

fatso *n* debu でぶ・デブ

fatty *adj* abrakkói 脂っこい・あぶらっこい; *fatty tuna* tóro とろ・トロ

faucet *n* jaguchi 蛇口・じゃぐち

fault 1. *n* (*defect*) kizu きず; (*shortcoming*) tánsho 短所; (*guilt*) tsúmi 罪・つみ; (*cause*) ...séi ...せい 2. *at ~* warúi 悪い・わるい; *it is my ~* watashi ga warúi/wárukatta わたし[私]が悪[わる]い/悪[わる]かった 3. *finds fault with* toga-memásu (togaméru, togámete) とがめ[咎め]ます(とがめる, とがめて)

faust *adj* minikui 醜い・みにくい

faux pas *n* bu-sahō´ 無[不]作法・ぶさほう

favor 1. *n* (*kindness*) shínsetsu 親切・しんせつ (go-shínsetsu ご親切), (*goodwill*) kō´i 好意・こうい; (*request*) o-nagai お願い・おねがい 2. *does a ~* kō´i o misemásu (miséru, mísete) 好意を見せます[みせます](見せる, 見せて); *does me/us the ~ of ...ing* ...te kudasaimásu (kudasáru kudasátte)/kuremásu (kureru, kurete) ...て下さいます・...てくださいます(下さる, 下さって)/くれます(くれる, くれて) 3. *favors* *v* (*a choice*) ...(no) hō´ga íi to omoimásu (omóu, omótte) ...(の)方がいいと思います・...(の)ほうがいいとおもいます(思う, 思って)

favorite *adj* dái-suki (na) 大好き・だいすき(な), (ichiban) sukí (na) (一番)好き(な), o-kiniiri (no) お気に入り・おきにいり(の); konomí (o-kono-mi) no ...好み・このみ(お好み)の...; tokui (na/no) 得意・とくい(な/の)

favoritism *n* ekohiiki えこひいき

fax *n* fákkusu ファックス

fear 1. *n* (*a fear*) osoré 恐れ・おそれ, kyō´fu 恐怖・きょうふ; shinpai 心配・しんぱい 2. *fears it* *v* osoremásu (osoréru, osórete) 恐れます・おそれます(恐れる, 恐れて); kowagari-másu (kowagáru, kowagátte) 怖がります・こわがります(怖がる, 怖がって); (*worries about*) shinpai shimásu (suru, shíte) 心配します・しんぱいします(する, して)

fearful *adj* osoroshíi 恐ろしい・おそろしい

feat *n* waza 業・わざ; (*deed*) shiwaza 仕業・しわざ

feather *n* hane 羽, umō´ 羽毛・うもう; ke 毛

feature *n* tokuchō 特徴

feature article *n* tokushū-kiji 特集記事

feature film *n* chōhen-eiga 長編映画

February *n* Ni-gatsú 二月・2月

feces *n* kusó くそ・糞, fún ふん・糞; bén 便, daibén 大便

federation *n* renmei 連盟

fee *n* ryō´kin 料金; …-ryō´ …料; *(remuneration)* sharei 謝礼, rei 礼; *membership fee* kaihi 会費; *student fee* gakusei-ryō´kin 学生料金; *transportation fee* unsō´ryō 運送料

feeble → weak

feed *v* tabesasemásu (tabesaséru, tabesásete) 食べさせます・たべさせます(食べさせる, 食べさせて); [INELEGANT] kuwasemásu (kuwaséru, kuwasete) 食わせます・くわせます (食わせる, 食わせて)

feel 1. *v (by touch)* sawarimásu (sawaru, sawatte) さわり[触り]ます **2.** *(by emotion)* kan-jimásu (kan-jiru, kan-jite) 感じます・かんじます(感じる, 感じて) **3.** *(thinks)* omoimásu (omóu, omótte) 思います・おもいます(思う, 思って)・ぞんじます (zon-jiru, zon-jite) 存じます・ぞんじます(存じる, 存じて); zon-jiagemásu (zon-jíageru, zon-jiagéte) 存じあげます・ぞんじあげます(存じあげる, 存じあげて) **5.** *(body reaction)* moyō´shimásu (moyō´su, moyō´shite) 催します・もよおします(催す, 催して) **6.** *it feels good/bad* kimochi ga íi/warúi 気持ちがいい/悪い[わるい]

feeling *n* kimochi 気持ち・きもち, kanji 感じ・かんじ, ki 気, nén 念, nén´nen 念々・ねん; *(sense)* kimí 気味・きみ; kokóro 心・こころ, omói 思い・おもい; *(mood)* kokoro-mochi 心持ち・こころもち, kíbun 気分・きぶん; *(true inner)* honne 本音・ほんね, honshin 本心・ほんしん; *(one's inner)* íkō´ 意向; *(health)* (karada no) guai (体[からだ]の)具合・ぐあい; *(compassion)* nasake 情け・なさけ (o-násake お情け), nínjō´ 人情・にんじょう

fellow *n (person)* hito 人・ひと, … hitó 人…人; monó 者, yátsu やつ・奴; *(comrade)* fellow … … dō´shi …同志; *(man)* otoko 男

female *n* onná (no hito) 女・おんな(の人[ひと]), josei 女性; *female … (animal)* mesu no … メスの…

female flower *n* mebana 雌花

female impersonator *n (in Kabuki)* onna-gata 女形, óyáma おやま・女形

female student *n* jo (-shi) gákusei 女(子)学生

fence *n* kakíne 垣根・かきね, (wall) hei 塀・へい

fencing *n* fenshingu フェンシング; *the art of Japanese fencing (with bamboo swords)* kéndō´ 剣道・ケンドウ

fermented *adj* hakkō shita 発酵した
  fermented bean paste míso みそ・ミソ・味噌 (o-míso おみそ・お味噌)
  fermented soy beans nattō´ 納豆・ナットウ

fern *n* shída しだ・シダ

royal fern *n (osmund)* zenmai ぜんまい・ゼンマイ

ferry *(them over)* *v* watashimásu (watasu, wata-shíte) 渡します・わたします(渡す, 渡して)

ferryboat *n* watashi-búne 渡し舟[船]・わたしぶね

fester *v* umimásu (umu, unde) うみます・膿みます(うむ・膿む, うんで・膿んで)

festival *n* matsuri 祭り・まつり (o-matsuri お祭り)

feudal *(period, system)* *adj* hō´ken (-jídai/-séido) no 封建(時代/制度)の
  feudal lord *n* daimyō´ 大名 (o daimyō´ お大名)

fever *n* netsú 熱・ねつ (o-nétsu お熱); fiibā フィーバー; *became feverish* fiibā shimásu (suru, shíte) フィーバーします(する, して)

few *adj* sukóshi (no) 少し・すこし(の); sukunái 少ない・すくない
  a few wazuka わずか; sukoshi 少し → **several**
  a few days ago sendatté せんだって・先だって, senjitsu 先日・せんじつ

fewer *adj* (yori) sukunái (より)少ない・すくない

fib *n (lie)* úso うそ・嘘

fiber *n* sén´i 繊維, sén´i, (line) súji 筋・すじ
  synthetic fiber *n* kasen 化繊

fickle *adj* uwaki (na) 浮気・うわき(な)

fiction *n* shō´setsu 小説, tsukuri-banashi 作り話・つくりばなし, fikushon フィクション
  science fiction *n* saiensu fikushon サイエンスフィクション, esu-efu (shōsetsu) SF(小説)

fief *n* ryōchi 領地

field *n (dry)* hatake 畑・はたけ; nóhara 野原・のはら, háppara 原っぱ・はらっぱ; *(rice paddy)* tá 田・た, tanbo 田んぼ・たんぼ; *(specialty)* senmon 専門・せんもん; *(out in the field)* yagai 野外
  field day *n* **1.** *(military)* yagai enshū-bi 野外演習日 **2.** *(athletic festival)* undō-kai 運動会 **3.** *(picnic)* pikunikku ピクニック
  field study/trip/work *n* kengaku 見学

fielder *n* yashu 野手

fierce *adj* hageshíi 激しい・はげしい, sugói すごい・凄い

fifteen *n* jū´-go 十五・15

fifth *adj* go-banmé (no) 五番目(の), itsutsu-mé (no) 五つ目・いつつめ(の)
  the fifth day itsuka-me 五日目, *(of the month)* itsuka 五日

fifth floor *n* go-kai 五階

fifty *n* go-jū´ 五十・50
  fifty thousand go-mán 五万・50,000

fig *n* ichíjiku いちじく・イチジク

fight *v* tatakaimásu (tatakau, tatakatte) 戦います・たたかいます(戦う, 戦って) → **argue**

figure → count; number; think; shape; body; being, person; diagram

file *n* **1.** *(nail file, etc.)* yasuri やすり **2.** *(computer)* fairu ファイル **3.** → **folder** **4.** *v (grinds)* surimásu (súru, sutté) すります(する, すって)

5. *v* (*submit*) teishutsu shimás<u>u</u> (suru, sh<u>i</u>te) 提出します(提出する, 提出して); *file income tax* kakutei o shinkoku shimás<u>u</u> 確定申告をします
6. *v* (*store document*) shorui o tojimás<u>u</u> (tojíru, tojíte) 書類を綴じます(綴じる, 綴じて)

filet *n* (*of pork etc.*) hire ヒレ
Filipino *n* (*language*) Firipin-go フィリピン語; (*person*) Firipin-jin フィリピン人
fill *v* **1.** ippai ni shimás<u>u</u> (suru, sh<u>i</u>te) 一杯にします・いっぱいにします(する, して); mitashimás<u>u</u> (mitásu, mitásh<u>i</u>te) 満たします・みたします(満たす, 満たして); *fills the tank, fills it up* man-tan ni shimás<u>u</u> 満タンにします **2.** (*fulfills*) konashimás<u>u</u> (konasu, konash<u>i</u>te) こなします(こなす, こなして), *~ an order* chūmon o konashimás<u>u</u> 注文をこなします **3.** *~ in* (*information*) kaki-iremás<u>u</u> (kaki-ireru, kaki-irete) 書き入れます・かきいれます(書き入れる, 書き入れて), ki-nyū shimás<u>u</u> (suru, sh<u>i</u>te) 記入します(する, して)

filling station → gas station
film *n* f(u)irumu フィルム(フイルム); (*movie*) eiga 映画
filter **1.** *n* f(u)írutā フィルター(フイルター) **2.** *v* (*filters it*) koshimás<u>u</u> (kosu, kosh<u>i</u>te) こします(こす, こして)
filth *n* obutsu 汚物
filthy → dirty
fin *n* hire ひれ・ヒレ
final *adj* saigo (no) 最後・さいご(の), saishū (no) 最終(の)
finalization **1.** *n* seiritsu 成立; *gets finalized* seiritsu shimás<u>u</u> (suru, sh<u>i</u>te) 成立します(する, して)
finance **1.** *n* kin'yū 金融; kéizai 経済; zaisei 財政 Ministry of finance *n* Zaimú-shō 財務省; (*financing*) yūzū 融通 **2.** *finances it* *v* yūzū shimás<u>u</u> (suru, sh<u>i</u>te) 融通します(する, して)
financial circles *n* zaikai 財界
financial institution *n* kinyū-k<u>i</u>kan 金融機関
find **1.** *v* mits<u>u</u>kemás<u>u</u> (mits<u>u</u>keru, mits<u>u</u>kete) 見つけます・みつけます(見つける, 見つけて) **2.** *n* (*bargain*) horidashi-mono 掘り出し物・ほりだしもの
find fault with togamemás<u>u</u> (togaméru, togámete) とがめ[咎め]ます(とがめる, とがめて)
find out (*hears*) (… ga) mimí ni hairimás<u>u</u> (háiru, háitte) (…)が耳に入ります・(…)がみみにはいります(入る, 入って); (… ga) wakarimás<u>u</u> (wakáru, wakátte) (…)が分かります・(…)がわかります(分かる, 分かって)
fine **1.** *adj* (*small/detailed*) komakái 細かい・こまかい, (*minute*) bisai (na) 微細・びさい(な), (*delicate*) bimyō (na) 微妙・びみょう(な) **2. → OK, good, splendid, fair 3.** *n* (*penalty*) bakkin 罰金・ばっきん
finger *n* yubí 指・ゆび
finger food *n* o-tsúmami おつまみ, tsumami

つまみ・ツマミ
fingernail *n* (yubi no) tsume (指の)つめ・爪・ツメ
fingerprint *n* shimon 指紋・しもん
finish **1.** *n* **→ end 2.** *v* (*finishes …ing*) …te shimaimás<u>u</u> (shimau, shimatte) …てしまいます(しまう, しまって)
Finland *n* Finrando フィンランド
Finn *n* (*person*) Finrando-jin フィンランド人
Finnish *adj* (*language*) Finrando-go no フィンランド語の; (*person*) Finrando-jin no フィンランド人の
fir *n* mómi もみ・モミ
fire **1.** *n* hí 火, (*accidental*) káji 火事・かじ, kasai 火災; (*bonfire*) takibi たき火・たきび **2.** *v* (*lays off disemploys*) kubi ni shimás<u>u</u> (suru, sh<u>i</u>te) 首にします・くびにします(する, して), kotowarimás<u>u</u> (kotowáru, kotowátte) 断ります・ことわります(断る, 断って), káiko shimás<u>u</u> (suru, sh<u>i</u>te) 解雇します・かいこします(する, して); *got fired* kubi ni narimásh<u>i</u>ta 首になりました・くびになりました
fire alarm *n* kasai-kéihō 火災警報; (*device*) kasai-hō´ch<u>i</u>ki 火災報知器
fire department *n* shō´bō-sho 消防署
fire engine *n* shō´bō´-sha 消防車
fire extinguisher *n* shō´ká-ki 消火器
fire fighter *n* shō´bō´-shi 消防士
fire fighting *n* shō´bō´ 消防
fire house/station *n* shō´bō-sho 消防署
fireman → fire fighter
fireplug *n* shō´ka-sen 消火栓
firewood *n* taki-gi たき木・たきぎ, maki まき・薪
fireworks *n* hána-bi 花火・はなび
fireworks exhibition *n* hanabi-taikai 花火大会
firm **1.** *adj* jō´bu (na) 丈夫・じょうぶ(な); (*hard*) katai 固い・硬い・堅い・かたい **2.** *n* (*business*) **→ company**
firmly *adv* kataku 固く・硬く・堅く・かたく, (*securely*) chanto ちゃんと; (*resolutely*) sh<u>i</u>kkári しっかり; (*definitely*) kippári (to) きっぱり(と)
first *adj* hajime (no) 初め・はじめ(の), saisho (no) 最初・さいしょ(の), hatsu (no) 初・はつ(の); (*number one*) ichí-ban (no) 一番・いちばん(の); *the first* daiichi (no) 第一・だいいち(の) *adv* (*first of all*) dái-ichi (ni) 第一・だいいち(に), mázu ず・先ず・先ず; (*ahead of others*) saki (ni) 先・さき(に)
first aid *n* ō´kyū-téate 応急手当; *first-aid kit* kyūkyū´-bako 救急箱・きゅうきゅうばこ
first class *adj* ik-kyū 一級; (*ticket, seat*) it-tō´ 一等; (*hotel, school*) ichiryū (no) 一流・いちりゅう(の)
first day of the month *n* tsuitachí 一日・ついたち
first day of the year *n* ganjitsu 元日, gantan 元旦・がんたん
first floor *n* ik-kai 一階
first generation *n* is-sei 一世

first time adj hajímete (no) 初めて・はじめて(の)

first volume (of a set of 2 or 3) n jṓ-kan 上巻, jṓ-上

first-rate adj ichiryū (no) 一流・いちりゅう(の); jṓ-tṓ (no) 上等・じょうとう(の)

first-run movie n rṓdo-shṓ ロードショー

first-year student n ichinén-sei 一年生

fish 1. n sakana 魚・さかな (o-sakana お魚), uo 魚 (1: ip-piki 一匹, 2: ní-hiki 二匹, 3: sánbiki 三匹, how many nán-biki 何匹); sliced raw ~ sashimi 刺身・さしみ **2.** v (angles) tsurimásu (tsuru, tsutte) 釣ります・つります(釣る, 釣って)

fishballs n (for soup) tsumire つみれ・ツミレ

fish cake (steamed) kamaboko かまぼこ・カマボコ; (boiled) hanpen はんぺん・ハンペン; (broiled) chikuwa ちくわ・チクワ・竹輪; (deep-fried) Satsumá-age さつま[薩摩]揚げ・サツマアゲ

fish dealer/market n sakana-ya 魚屋・さかな屋

fish meal n soboro そぼろ・ソボロ

fisherman n ryṓshi 漁師, gyo´fu 魚夫

fishhook n tsuribari 釣り針・つりばり

fishing n (as sport) (sakaná-) tsuri (魚)釣り・つり, ryṓ 漁・りょう; (business) gyogyṓ 漁業

fishy adj (questionable) kusái 臭い・くさい; fishy-smelling namugusái 生臭い・なまぐさい

fist n kobushi こぶし・拳, genkotsu げんこつ・拳骨, genko げんこ

fit 1. adj (suitable) tekigi (no) 適宜・てきぎ(の); fits ... nicely ...ni yóku aimásu (aū, átte) ...に良く合います・...によくあいます(合う, 合って) **2.** v fits it to ... ni ate-hamemásu (ate-haméru, ate-hámete) ...に当てはめます・...にあてはめます(当てはめる, 当てはめて) **3.** n (a good fit) saizu ga atteiru サイズが合っている

five n gó 五・5; itsútsu 五つ・いつつ; fáibu ファイブ

five; five days itsu-ká 五日・いつか; 5 pieces (small things) gó-ko 五個, 5 trees (or long things) go-hon 五本; 5 sheets (flat things) go-mai 五枚; 5 cars (or machines/vehicles) go-dai 五台; 5 copies (books/magazines) gó-satsu 五冊; 5 cats (or small animals) gó-hiki 五匹; 5 cows (or large animals) go-tṓ 五頭; 5 birds/rabbits go-wa 五羽; 5 cupfuls go-hai 五杯; 5 days itsuka 五日, itsuka-kan 五日間; 5 o'clock go-jí 五時・5時; 5 hours go-jikan 五時間; 5 minutes go-fun 五分; 5 months go-kágetsu 五ヶ月, gokágetsu-kan 五ヶ月間; 5 years go-nen 五年, go nén-kan 五年間; 5 years old itsútsu 五つ, gó-sai 五歳; 5 people go-nín 五人; 5 yen (money) go-en 五円; 5 degrees gó-do 五度; 5 times go-dó 五度, go-kái 五回, go-hén 五遍; 5 floors/stories go-kai 五階

five hundred n go-hyakú 五百・500

five o'clock shadow n bushṓ-hige 無精/不精/ぶしょうひげ

five thousand n go-sén 五千・5,000

fix 1. v (repairs) naoshimásu (naósu, naóshite) 直します・なおします(直す, 直して); (makes) tsukurimásu (tsukúru, tsukutte) 作ります・つくります(作る, 作って); (prepares) sonaemásu (sonáéru, sonáete) 備えます・そなえます(備える, 備えて); (settles) sadamemásu (sadaméru, sadámete) 定めます・さだめます(定める, 定めて) **2.** n (plight) hamé 羽目・はめ, kukyō 苦境

fixed 1. adj (settled) ittei (no) 一定・いってい(の); (periodic) téiki (no) 定期・ていき(の); tei-...定... **2.** gets ~ (repaired) naorimásu (naóru, naótte) 直ります・なおります(直る, 直って); (settled) sadamarimásu (sadamáru, sadámátte) 定まります・さだまります(定まる, 定まって)

fixedly (staring) adv jitto じっと

fixture n kígu 器具

flag n hatá 旗・はた; (national) kokki 国旗

flame n honō´ 炎・ほのお

flannel n néru フランネル

flap 1. n (of envelope, etc.) futa ふた・蓋, furappu フラップ **2.** v flap the wings habatakimásu (habatáku, habatáite) 羽ばたきます(羽ばたく, 羽ばたいて)

flare n hatsuen-tō 発煙筒, furea フレア

flashing n pikápika ぴかぴか・ピカピカ

flashlight n kaichū-déntō 懐中電灯, dentō´ 電灯

flashy adj hadé (na) 派手・はで(な)

flask n furasuko フラスコ

flat 1. n heimén 平面 **2.** n (apartment) furátto フラット, apāto アパート **3.** v taira ni shimásu (suru, shite) 平らにします(する, して) **4.** adj taira (na) 平ら・たいら(な), hiratai 平たい・ひらたい; (flavorless) ajikenái 味気ない

flat land n heichi 平地

flat rate n kin'itsu-ryōkin 均一料金

flat tire n panku パンク; gets a ~ panku shimásu (suru, shite) パンクします(する, して)

flatfish n karei かれい・カレイ・鰈

flathead n (fish) kochi こち・コチ・鯒

flatter v o-seji o iimásu (iu/yū, itte/yutte) お世辞を言います・おせじをいいます(言う, 言って/ゆって); goma o surimásu (súru, sutté) ごま[胡麻]・ゴマをすります(する, すって)

flattery n o-seji お世辞・おせじ; gomasuri ごま[胡麻・ゴマ]すり

flatulate v onara o shimásu (suru, shite) おならをします(する, して), [IMPOLITE] hé o hirimásu (híru, hítte) 屁をひります(ひる, ひって)

flatulence n onara おなら・オナラ, hé へ・屁

flavor 1. n aji 味・あじ, fū´mi 風味; (seasoning) chō´mi 調味, kagen 加減 **2.** v (seasons it) ... ni aji o tsukemásu (tsukéru, tsukéte) ...に味を付け[つけ]ます(付ける, 付けて)

flavor sprinkles (to top rice) n furikake ふりかけ・フリカケ

flavorless adj ajike-nái 味気ない

flaw n kizu 傷・きず, (defect) ketten 欠点

flax n asá 麻・あさ

flea n nomí のみ・蚤・ノミ

flee *v* nigemásu (nigéru, nígete) 逃げます・にげます(逃げる, 逃げて)

fleet *n* (*fleet of ships*) kantai 艦隊

fleeting *adj* (*transitory*) hakánai はかない・儚い
  fleeting moments *n* hakánai isshun はかない[儚い]一瞬, tsukanoma つかの間

flesh *n* nikutai 肉体

flicker *n* chiratsuki ちらつき; chika-chikashita hikari チカチカした光

flies → fly

flight (*number …*) *n* …-bin …便

flight attendant *n* kyakushitsu jō´muin 客室乗務員, furaito-atendanto フライト・アテンダント

flint (*for lighter*) *n* (ráitā no) ishi (ライターの)石

float **1.** *v* (*it floats*) ukabimásu (ukabu, ukande) 浮かびます・うかびます(浮かぶ, 浮かんで), ukimásu, (uku, uite) 浮きます・うきます(浮く, 浮いて); (*floats it*) ukabemásu (ukaberu, ukabete) 浮かべます・うかべます(浮かべる, 浮かべて) **2.** *n* (*swimming float*) ukiwa 浮き輪

floating assets *n* ryūdō shisan 流動資産

floating exchange rate *n* hendō (kawase) rēto 変動(為替)レート, hendō kawase sōba 変動為替相場

flock **1.** *n* muré 群れ・むれ **2.** *v* they ~ together muragarimásu (muragáru, muragátte) 群がります(群がる, 群がって)

flood **1.** *n* kō´zui 洪水, ō´mízú 大水 **2.** *v* hanran shimásu (suru, shite) 氾濫します・はんらんします(する, して)

floor *n* yuka 床, furoa フロア; (*story*) (-)kai 階, **What floor?** nan-gai/kai 何階 (**1st floor** ik-kai 一階, **2nd floor** ni kai 二階, **3rd floor** san-gai 三階, san kai 三階; **mezzanine** (*floor*) chū-ní-kai 中二階

  floor lamp *n* (*denki*) sutándo (電気)スタンド

  floor mat(ting) *n* tatami 畳・タタミ

  floor space *n* taté-tsubo 建て坪・たてつぼ (*in units of tsubo; 3.954 sq. yards*)

floppy *n* furoppii (disuku) フロッピー・ディスク, FD

florist *n* haná-ya 花屋

flounder *n* hirame ひらめ・ヒラメ

flour *n* koná 粉・こな, kó 粉; (*wheat*) komugi-ko 小麦粉, meriken-ko メリケン粉

flourish *v* sakaemásu (sakáeru, sakáete) 栄えます・さかえます(栄える, 栄えて)

flourishing *adj* nigíyaka (na) にぎやか[賑やか](な)

flow **1.** *it flows v* nagaremásu (nagaréru, nagárete) 流れます・ながれます(流れる, 流れて) **2.** *it ~ v* nagashimásu (nagásu, nagáshite) 流します・ながします(流す, 流して) **3.** *n* (*outflow*) de 出, nagaré 流れ・ながれ

flower **1.** *n* haná 花・はな (o-hana お花) **2.** *v* (*blooms*) (hana ga) sakimásu (saku, saite) (花が)咲きます(咲く, 咲いて)

  flower arrangement *n* (*arranging*) o-hana お花, ikébana 生け花・いけばな, kadō 華道, furawā arenjimento フラワーアレンジメント; (*in a tall vase*) nage-ire 投げ入れ, (*in a low basin*) moribana 盛り花

  flower bed *n* kadan 花壇・花だん

  flower bud *n* tsubomi つぼみ・蕾

  flower cards *n* (*game*) haná-fuda 花札・はなふだ, hana-káruta 花かるた・花カルタ

  flowerpot *n* uekí-bachi 植木鉢・うえき鉢

  flower scissors *n* hana-basami 花ばさみ

  flower shop → florist

  flower vase *n* kabin 花瓶・かびん, káki 花器

  flower viewing *n* hana-mí 花見・はなみ (o-hana-miお花見)

flu *n* infuruénza インフルエンザ

fluent *adj* ryū´chō´ (na) 流ちょう[流暢](な); (*can speak it fluently*) jiyū (/ryū´chō´) ni hanasemásu (hanaséru, hanásete) 自由(/流暢)に話せます(話せる, 話せて)

fluent(ly) *adj* (*adv*) (*speaking*) perapera (to) ぺらぺら・ペラペラ(と); (*writing*) surasura (to) すらすら(と)

fluorescent light *n* keikō´-tō´ 蛍光灯

flush **1.** *n* (*the flush on one's face*) sekimen (shimásu; suru, shite) 赤面(します; する, して) **2.** *v* (*flush the toilet*) (toire o) nagashimásu (nagasu, nagashite) (トイレを)流します・ながします(流す, 流して)

  flush toilet *n* suisen-tóire 水洗トイレ

flustered; gets ~ awatemásu (awateru, awatete) あわてます・慌てます(あわてる, あわてて); **feels ~** teremásu (teréru, térete) 照れます・てれます(照れる, 照れて); **a person easily ~** awate-mono あわて者・慌て者

flute *n* fue 笛・ふえ; furúto フルート; **vertical bamboo ~** shakuhachi 尺八・しゃくはち

flutter; one's heart flutters dókidoki shimásu (suru, shite) どきどき[ドキドキ]します(する, して)

fly **1.** *n* (*insect*) hae 蝿・ハエ (**1:** ip-píkí 一匹, **2:** ní-hiki 二匹, **3:** sánbiki 三匹, *how many* nánbiki 何匹) **2.** *your ~ is open* (*unzipped/unbuttoned*) máe (chákku) ga aite imásu 前(チャック)が開いています **3.** *v* (*moves in air*) tobimásu (tobu, tonde) 飛びます・とびます(飛ぶ, 飛んで); (*flies it*) tobashimásu (tobasu, tobashite) 飛ばします・とばします(飛ばす, 飛ばして); *flies a kite* táko o agemásu (ageru, agete) 凧を揚げます・たこをあげます(揚げる, 揚げて); (*pilots*) sō´jū shimásu (suru, shite) 操縦します(する, して); (*goes by plane*) hikō´-ki de ikimásu (iku, itte) 飛行機で行きます・ひこうきでいきます(行く, 行って)

foam → bubble

focus **1.** *n* (*camera*) pinto ピント; (*focal point*) shō´ten 焦点; *out-of-focus* pinboke ピンぼけ **2.** *v* shōten o awasemásu (awaseru, awasete) 焦点を合わせます(合わせる, 合わせて); shūchū-sasemasu (shūchū-saseru, shūchū-sasete) 集中させます(集中させる, 集中させて)

fodder n shiryō 飼料

fog n kiri 霧・きり

foggy adj kiri ga fukái 霧が深い・きりがふかい

fold 1. n ori-mé 折り目 **2.** v (folds it) orimásu (óru, ótte) 折ります・おります(折る, 折って), (folds it up) tatamimás<u>u</u> (tatamu, tatande) 畳みます・たたみます(畳む, 畳んで); (it folds) oremás<u>u</u> (oréru, órete) 折れます(折れる, 折れて); folds one's arms udé o kumimás<u>u</u> (kúmu, kúnde) 腕を組みます(組む, 組んで)

folder n **1.** file folder kami-básami 紙挟み, fairu ファイル **2.** (computer) foruda フォルダ, forudā フォルダー

folding money n [INFORMAL] satsu 札・さつ, o-satsu お札

fold up v (ori-) tatamimás<u>u</u> (tatamu, tatande) (折り)畳みます・たたみます(畳む, 畳んで)

foliage n ha 葉

folk adj minkan no 民間の

folkcraft n mingei 民芸, mingei-hin 民芸品

folk dance n fōku dansu フォークダンス, minyō-buyō 民謡舞踊

folk dancer n minyō-buyō-ka 民謡舞踊家

folk medicine n (medicine) minkan-yaku 民間薬, (treatment) minkan-ryōhō 民間療法

folks → **people; parents; family**

folk song n min'yō´ 民謡, fōku songu フォークソング

follow v (follows it) … no áto o ts<u>u</u>kemás<u>u</u> (ts<u>u</u>kéru, ts<u>u</u>kete) …のあとをつけます(つける, つけて); (adheres to) … ni ts<u>u</u>kimás<u>u</u> (ts<u>u</u>kú, ts<u>ú</u>ite) … に付きます・… につきます(付く, 付いて), (conforms to) … ni sh<u>i</u>tagaimás<u>u</u> (sh<u>i</u>tagau, sh<u>i</u>tagatte) … に従います・… にしたがいます(従う, 従って); (runs along) … ni soimás<u>u</u> (sou, sotte) …に沿います・…にそいます(沿う, 沿って); ~ the example of … o mi-naraimás<u>u</u> (mi-narau, mi-naratte) …を見習います(見習う, 見習って)

follower n (adherent) shijisha 支持者; (follower of a stronger person or boss) kobun 子分

following 1. adj ts<u>u</u>gí (no) 次・つぎ(の), ika (no) 以下(の), kaki (no) 下記(の) **2.** n (a following) fan ファン **3.** prep … no ato ni ―の後に

folly n gukō 愚行, orokasa 愚かさ・おろかさ

fond of → **like**

fondness n konomi 好み

fondue n fondu フォンデュ

font n **1.** fonto フォント **2.** (church) senrei-ban 洗礼盤 (= baptismal bowl)

food n **1.** tabe-monó 食べ物・たべもの, góhan 御飯・ごはん, shokúmotsu 食物; (meal) shoku 食, (Western) yō´-shoku 洋食; (Japanese) wa-shoku 和食 **2.** n (stuff) → **groceries**

food cooked and served in a pan nabé-mono 鍋物

food delivered to order demae 出前

food poisoning shoku-chūdoku 食中毒, shoku-atari 食あたり

food with rice (food poured over rice) donburí-mono どんぶり物, don-mono 丼物

fool 1. n báka ばか・馬鹿, tónma とんま・頓馬

fool around v fuzakemás<u>u</u> (fuzakeru, fuzakete) ふざけます(ふざける, ふざけて) **2. ~ (someone)** v karakaimás<u>u</u> (karakau, karakatte) からかいます(からかう, からかって)

foolish adj baka-rashíi ばか[馬鹿]らしい, báka (na) ばか[馬鹿](な)

foolproof adj machigae yō no nai 間違えようのない, dare ni de mo dekiru 誰にでもできる

foot n ashí 足; (of a mountain) fumotó ふもと・麓; at the foot of … no fumotó(de) … のふもと[麓](で)

football n (American) (amerikan) futto-bōru (アメリカン) フットボール, amefuto アメフト

footing n ashi-ba 足場, kiso 基礎

footlight n futto-raito フットライト, kyakkō 脚光

footnote n kyakuchū 脚注

footprint n ashi-áto 足跡

foot sore (from shoe rubbing) n kutsu-zure 靴ずれ・靴擦れ

footstool n ashi nosé dai 足乗せ台

footwear n hakimono 履物・はきもの

for prep … (no) tamé (ni)… (の)ため(に); … ni (wa) … に(は); … ni tótte … にとって; …no… … の… ; (for the use of) …-yō´ (no) …用(の); (suitable for) …-muki (no) …向き・…むき (の); (bound/intended for) …-muke (no) …向け・…むけ(の)

do it for me/us, they do it for you … -te kuremás<u>u</u> (kureru, kurete) …てくれます(くれる, くれて)/[HONORIFIC] kudasaimás<u>u</u> (kudasáru, kudasátte) くださいます(くださる, くださって)

do it for you/them, you do it for them … -te agemás<u>u</u> (ageru, agete) …てあげます (あげる, あげて)/[HONORIFIC] sashi-agemás<u>u</u> (sashi-ageru, sashi-agete) さし[差し]あげます (さし[差し]あげる, さし[差し]あげて)

for a long time adv (now) zutto máe kara ずっと前から

for a while adv shibáraku しばらく; h<u>i</u>tómazu ひとまず

for example, for instance adv tatóeba 例えば・たとえば

for sure adv kanarazu 必ず・かならず, zéhi 是非・ぜひ, táshikani 確かに・たしかに; (not forgetting) wasurenáide 忘れないで・わすれないで

for the first time adv hajímete 初めて・はじめて

for the most part adv taigai 大概・たいがい, ō´kata おおかた・大方

for the reason that … adv to iu riyū de … という理由で, …yué ni …故に・ゆえに

for the time being adv tō´bun 当分, h<u>i</u>tómazu ひとまず

forbearance n shínbō´ しんぼう・辛抱

forbid *v* kin-jimásu (kin-jiru, kin-jite) 禁じます・きんじます(禁じる、禁じて)

force 1. *n* (*power*) jitsuryoku 実力 **2.** *v forces one* (*to do*) múri ni (or shíite) sasemásu (saseru, sasete) 無理に[強いて]させます(させる、させて)
forced landing *n* fujichaku 不時着

forceps *n* pinsetto ピンセット

forcible *adj* gō´in (na) 強引(な); *forcibly* gō´in ni 強引に、shíite 強いて・しいて

ford *n* asase 浅瀬

foreboding *n* yokan 予感・よかん

forecast 1. *n* yohō´ 予報, yosoku 予測; *weather forecast* tenki-yóhō´ 天気予報 **2.** *forecasts it* *v* (*predicts, estimates*) *it* yosoku shimásu (suru, shíte) 予測します(する、して)

forehead *n* hitai 額・ひたい, odéko おでこ

foreign *adj* gaikoku (no) 外国(の), gai-… 外…, (*Western*) yō´… 洋…
foreign currency operations *n* gaikoku-kawase (gaitame) 外国為替(外為)
foreign language *n* gaikoku-go 外国語
foreign minister *n* gaimu-daijin 外務大臣
Foreign Ministry *n* gaimu-shō 外務省
Foreign Office *n* gaikō-kikan 外交機関
foreign policy *n* gaikō-seisaku 外交政策
foreign student(s) *n* ryūgaku-sei 留学生

foreigner *n* gaijin 外人, gaikokú-jin 外国人
foreigner card *n* gáikokujin tōrokushō (kādo) 外国人登録証(カード)

forest *n* mori 森・もり, (*grove*) hayashi 林・はやし

forever *adv* ítsu mo いつも, eien ni 永遠に・えいえんに, eikyū ni 永久に・えいきゅうに

forwarding *adj* tensō (no) 転送(の), unsō (no) 運送(の)
forwarding address *n* tensō-saki (no) jūsho 転送先(の)住所
forwarding agency *n* unsō-gyōsha 運送業者
forwarding business *n* unsō-gyō 運送業
forwarding of e-mail *n* mēru (no) tensō メール(の)転送

foreword *n* jobun 序文, mae-gaki 前書き
forward planning *n* keikaku 計画

forge *v* **1.** (*a signature, document, etc.*) nisemásu (niseru, nisete) 似せます・にせます(似せる、似せて) **2.** (*tempers metal*) kitaemásu (kitáeru, kitáete) 鍛えます・きたえます(鍛える、鍛えて)

forger *n* gizō-sha 偽造者

forgery *n* (*making a fake copy*) gizō´ 偽造; (*a fake*) nise-mono 偽物・にせもの

forget *v* wasuremásu (wasureru, wasurete) 忘れます・わすれます(忘れる、忘れて); *don't forget to do it* wasurenáide shíte kudasai 忘れないでして下さい・わすれないでください

forgetful *adj* wasureppói 忘れっぽい・わすれっぽい

forget-me-not *n* wasurena-gusa 忘れな草・ワスレナグサ

forgive *v* yurushimásu (yurúsu, yurúshite) 許します・ゆるします(許す、許して)

forgiveness *n* yurushi 許し

fork *n* **1.** fō´ku フォーク **2.** (*forking, branching*) wakare 分かれ・わかれ, matá 又・又, futa-matá 二又[股]
fork out money (for ...) (... ni) okane o dashi-masu (dasu, dashite) (...に)お金を出して(出す、出して)

forked *adj* (*bifurcate*) futamata (no) 二又[股](の)

forklift *n* fōku rifuto フォークリフト

form 1. *n* katachi 形, katá 型, (*figure*) súgata 姿・すがた(o-súgata お姿), kakkō´ 格好・恰好・かっこう; narí なり(o-nári おなり), (*style*) tái 体; (*appearance*) teisai 体裁; (*blank paper*) yō´shi 用紙; (*document*) shorui 書類 **2.** *v* (*creates it*) nashimásu (násu, náshite) 成します・なします(成す、成して), tsukurimásu (tsukúru, tsukutte) 作ります・つくります(作る、作って)

formal *adj* seishiki (na/no) 正式・せいしき(な/の); fōmaru (na) フォーマル(な); keishikiteki (na) 形式的(な); (*procedure, red tape*) te-tsúzuki 手続き・てつづき

formality *n* fōmaru フォーマル; keishikiteki 形式的

format 1. *n* (*book, magazine*) teisai 体裁, hankei 版型; (*data*) fō´matto フォーマット **2.** *v* (*format a disk*) (disuku o) fōmatto(-ka) shimásu (suru, shíte) (ディスクを)フォーマット(化)します(する、して)

formation *n* (*getting formed*) seiritsu 成立

formed; gets ~ (*organized*) seiritsu shimásu (suru, shíte) 成立します(する、して)

former *adj* máe (no) 前・まえ(の); móto (no) もと[元](の); [BOOKISH] zén… 前…; *the former* zénsha 前者

formerly *adv* móto wa もと[元]は; kátsute かつて

fortnight *n* ni-shūkan 2週間・二週間

fortuitous (*accidental*) *adj* gūzen (no) 偶然・ぐうぜん(の)

fortunate *adj* saiwai (na) 幸い・さいわい(な)

fortunately *adv* saiwai ni (mo) 幸いに・さいわいに(も)

fortune *n* (*property*) zaisan 財産; (*luck*) ún 運, únmei 運命・うんめい; (*good luck*) saiwai 幸い・さいわい, shiawase 幸せ・しあわせ; (*written*) (o-)mikuji (お)みくじ
fortune-teller *n* uranai 占い・うらない = uranái-shi 占い師・うらない師
fortune-telling *n* uranai 占い・うらない

forty *n* yón jū 四十・40, shi-jū 四十

forty thousand *n* yon mán 四万・40,000

forward 1. *adv* (*ahead*) máe e/ni 前[まえ]へ/に; *goes ~* susumimásu (susumu, susunde) 進みます・すすみます(進む、進んで) **2.** *adj* (*pushy*) bu-énryo (na) 無遠慮・ぶえんりょ(な)

forwarding agent *n* unsō´-ya 運送屋

foster *v* yashinaimásu (yashinau, yashinatte) 養います・やしないます(養う、養って)

foster child *n* sodate-go 育て子, sato-go 里子
foster parent *n* sodate no oyá 育ての親・そだて
の親, sato-oya 里親
foul 1. *n* hansoku 反則 **2.** *v* hansoku shimásu
(suru, shíte) 反則します(する, して) → **dirty**
found 1. → **find**; *gets ~* mitsukarimásu, (mitsu-
karu, mitsukatte) みつかります・みつかります
(見つかる, 見つかって) **2.** → **establish**
foundation *n* (*base*) kisó 基礎・きそ, (*basis*)
konpon 根本, kíhon 基本・きほん; (*non-profit
organization*) zaidan 財団
fountain *n* funsui 噴水
fountain pen *n* mannén-hitsu 万年筆
four *n* yón 四・4, shí 四・4, yottsú 四つ・よっつ;
(*4-oared racing boat*) foa (fóʹ) フォア(フォー);
number four yo-ban (*also* yónban) 四番
four; 4 pieces (*small things*) yón ko 四個, (*long
things*) yón hon 四本; *4 sheets* (*flat things*) yónmai
(yo-mai) 四枚; (*machines/vehicles*) yón-dai 四台;
4 copies (*books/magazines*) yón-satsu 四冊; (*small
animals*) yón-hiki 四匹; (*large animals*) yón-tóʹ
四頭; *4 birds/rabbits* shí-wa/yón-wa 四羽;
4 cupfuls yón-hai 四杯; *4 days* yokka 四日, yokká-
kan 四日間; *4 o'clock* yó ji 四時・4時; *4 hours*
yo-jíkan 四時間; *4 minutes* yón -pun 四分・4分
(*also* yón-fun 四分・4分); *4 months* yon-kágetsu
四ヶ月; yonkagetsú-kan 四ヶ月間; *4 years* yo-nen
四年, yo-nén-kan 四年間; *4 years old* yottsú 四つ,
yón-sai 四歳; *4 yen* (*money*) yó(n)-en 四円;
4 people yo-nín 四人; *4 degrees* yón-do 四度;
4 times yón-do 四度, yón kái 四回 yónhén 四遍;
4 floors/stories yon-kai 四階; *four-and-a half mat
area* yo-jóʹ-han 四畳半
fourfold, two times doubled *n* yonbai 四倍
four hundred *n* yón-hyaku 四百・400
four or five *n* shi-go-… 四, 五…
fourteen *n* jūʹ-yón, jū-shí 十四・14; *fourteen
days* jū-yokka 十四日; *14th* (*day of month*)
jū-yokka 十四日; *fourteen people* jūʹ-yo-nin
十四人; *fourteen years, the year 14* jūʹyo-nen
十四年
fourteenth *adj* jūyo(m) -banmé (no) 十四番目
(の); *the fourteenth day* jūyokka-mé 十四日目,
(*of the month*) jūʹ-yokka 十四日
fourth *adj* yo-banmé (no) (*also* yonbanmé) 四番
目(の), yottsu-mé (no) 四つ目(の); *the fourth
day* yokka-mé 四日目, (*of the month*) yokka 四日;
fourth floor yon-kai 四階; *fourth time* yon do-mé
四度目, yon kai-mé 四回目; *fourth-year student*
yo-nén-sei 四年生
four thousand *n* yon-sén 四千・4,000
fowl *n* kakin 家禽・かきん
fox *n* kitsune きつね・キツネ・狐
fraction *n* **1.** ichibu 一部 **2.** (*mathematics*) bunsū
分数
fragile *adj* koware-yasúi 壊れやすい・こわれや
すい; (*thing*) koware-mono 壊れ物・こわれもの,
waremono 割れ物・われもの
fragrance *n* kaori 香り・かおり

fragrant *adj* kaorimásu (kaoru, kaotte) 香ります・
かおります(香る, 香って)
frail *adj* morói もろい・脆い; yowái 弱い・
よわい
frame *n* wakú 枠, fuchí ふち・縁, kamachí
かまち・框; (*of picture*) gaku-buchi 額縁;
(*of glasses*) mégane no fuchí 眼鏡の縁・メガネ
のふち
framework *n* kumi-tate 組み立て・くみたて,
honegumi 骨組み, furēmu wāku フレームワーク
France *n* Furansu フランス
frank *adj* sotchoku (na) 率直(な), assárishita …
あっさりした…; (*unreserved*) enryo ga/no nái
遠慮が/のない, enryo shinai 遠慮しない・えん
りょしない, bu-énryo (na) 無遠慮・ぶえんりょ
(な); (*uninhibited*) sappári shita … さっぱりし
た…
frankly *adv* sotchoku ni 率直に, assári (to) あっさ
り(と), (*unreservedly*) enryo shináide 遠慮しな
いで; zubari ずばり
frantically *adv* chi-mánako ni nátte 血眼にな
って・ちまなこになって
fraud *n* sági 詐欺・サギ, inchiki いんちき
freak *n* henjin 変人
freckle *n* sobakasu そばかす
free *adj* (*gratis*) táda (no) ただ(の), (*as part of the
service*) sābisu サービス, (*no fee/ charge*) muryóʹ
(no) 無料(の); (*unrestrained*) jiyū (na) 自由・
じゆう(な); (*unoccupied*) hima (na) 暇・ひま
(な); *sets ~* (*releases*) hanashimásu (hanásu,
hanáshite) 放します・はなします(放す, 放して)
→ **liberate**
free-of-charge, FOC *adj* muryō no 無料の
free parking muryō-chūshajō 無料駐車場
free seat (*unreserved*) jiyūʹ-seki 自由席
freedom *n* jiyūʹ 自由・じゆう
freelance, freelancing *n* (*work*) jiyūʹ-gyóʹ
自由業
freely *adv* jiyūʹ ni 自由に・じゆうに
freeway *n* kōʹsoku-dóʹro 高速道路
freeze *v* (*it freezes*) kōʹrimásu (kōʹru, kōʹtte)
凍ります・こおります(凍る, 凍って); (*freezes it*)
kōʹrasemásu (kōʹraseru, kōʹrasete) 凍らせます・
こおらせます(凍らせる, 凍らせて), reitō shimásu
(suru, shíte) 冷凍します(する, して)
Freeze! Ugokuna! 動くな!
freezer *n* reitōko 冷凍庫
freezer bags *n* reitō-yō baggu 冷凍用バッグ
French *n* (*language*) Furansu-go フランス語;
(*person*) Furansú-jin フランス人
French beans *n* (*kidney beans*) íngen インゲン・
隠元, ingénmame 隠元豆・インゲンマメ
French fries → **fried potatoes**
French kiss *n* furenchi-kisu フレンチキス
frequently → **often**
fresh *adj* atarashíi 新しい・あたらしい, shinsen
(na) 新鮮・しんせん(な), furesshu (na) フレッ
シュ(な); *~ from …* …-tate (no) …たて(の),
…-ágari (no) …上がり・…あがり(の)

freshman n 1. (*first year grade*) ichinén-sei 一年生 2. (*new student*) shinnyu-sei 新入生 3. (*new employee*) shinnyu-shain 新入社員

friction n masatsu 摩擦・まさつ

Friday n Kin'yōbi 金曜日
Friday prayers n kinyō-reihai 金曜礼拝
Friday the 13th n jūsan-nichi no Kin'yōbi 13日の金曜日

fried chicken n (tori no) kara-age (とりの・鶏の) 唐揚げ, furaido chikin フライドチキン

fried eggs n medama-yaki 目玉焼(き)

fried potatoes n furaido poteto フライドポテト

fried rice n chāʹhan チャーハン, yaki-meshi 焼き飯・ヤキメシ

fried shrimp n (*in batter*) ebi-ten えび[海老・エビ]天, (*in bread crumbs*) ebi-fúrai えび[海老・エビ]フライ

friend n tomodachi 友達・ともだち(o-tomodachi お友達); furendo フレンド; tómó 友・とも; yūjin 友人, (*pal*) nakama 仲間 (o-nakama お仲間); aibō 相棒・あいぼう; (*accomplice*) mikata 味方・みかた
best friend n ichiban no shinyū 一番の親友; muni no tomodachi 無二の友達
close friend n sinyū 親友

friendly adj yūkō-teki (na) 友好的(な); furendorii (na) フレンドリー(な)

friendship n (*keeping company*) tsuki-ai 付き合い・つきあい(o-tsukíai お付き合い)

frightened → afraid

frightful adj kowái 怖い・こわい

frizzy adj chijireta 縮れた・ちぢれた; *frizzy hair* chijireta kami(no ke) 縮れた[ちぢれた]髪(の毛)

frock n doresu ドレス

frog n 1. kaeru かえる・蛙・カエル 2. (*pinholder for flowers*) kénzan 剣山

frogman n daibā ダイバー

from prep ... kara ...から; *from now on* kore kara これから, kongo 今後・こんご; *from ... to ... ...* kara ...máde ...から...まで, [BOOKISH] ... náishi ... ...ないし...

front n 1. máe 前・まえ, (*ahead*) saki 先・さき; zenpóʹ 前方; (*side*) omoté 表・おもて 2. adj (*surface*) shōʹmén (no) 正面(の), zenmen (no) 前面(の)
front gate/entrance n seimon 正門, omote-mon 表門
front cover n hyōshi 表紙
front desk n furonto フロント
front door n omote-genkan 表玄関, shōmen-genkan 正面玄関, furonto-doa フロントドア
front entrance → front door

frontier n (*international border*) kokkyō 国境

frost n shimó 霜・しも

frostbite n tōshō 凍傷, shimo-yake 霜焼け・しもやけ

frosted glass n suri-garasu すりガラス

frosting n furosutingu フロスティング, aishingu アイシング

frown v 1. nigái/shibui kao o shimásu (suru, shite) 苦い/渋い顔[にがい/しぶいかお]をします(する, して), kao o shikamemásu (shikameru, shikamete) 顔をしかめます(しかめる, しかめて) 2. n jūmen 渋面, shibui kao 渋い面

frozen; is ~ kōʹtte imásu 凍っています・こおっています
frozen food n reitō-shokuhin 冷凍食品
frozen heart n reitan na kokoro 冷淡な心
frozen meal → frozen food

frugal adj tsumashíi つましい, ken'yaku (na) 倹約(な), shísso (na) 質素・しっそ(な)

fruit n 1. kudámono くだもの・果物; kí-no mi 木の実・きのみ, mi 実・ミ
fruit juice n kajū 果汁, furūtsu jūsu フルーツジュース
fruit market/shop n kudamonó-ya くだもの屋・果物屋
fruit salad n furūtsu sarada フルーツサラダ 2. (*product, outcome*) sanbutsu 産物 → result → crop

fruitful adj minori no ōi 実りの多い, yūeki (na) 有益(な)

frustrate v yaburimásu (yabúru, yabútte) 破ります・やぶります(破る, 破って), zasetsu sasemásu (saseru, sasete) 挫折させます・させつさせます(させる, させて); (*a plan*) kujikimásu (kujíku, kujíite) くじきます・挫きます(くじく, くじいて)

frustrated; gets ~ yaburemásu (yabureru, yaburete) 破れます・やぶれます(破れる, 破れて), zasetsu shimásu (suru, shite) 挫折します・させつします(する, して); (*a plan*) kujikemásu (kujikéru, kujíkete) くじけます・挫けます(くじける, くじけて)

frustration n zasetsu 挫折・ざせつ; (*feeling of ~*) zasetsú-kan 挫折感・ざせつかん; (*cause to lose hope*) shitsubo sasemásu (saseru, sasete) 失望させます(させる, させて), (*cause to despair*) rakutan sasemásu (saseru, sasete) 落胆させます(させる, させて)

fry v agemásu (ageru, agete) 揚げます・あげます(揚げる, 揚げて); (*pan fries, sautés*) itamemásu (itaméru, itámete) 炒めます・いためます(炒める, 炒めて)
frying pan n furai-pan フライパン

ftp n (= *file transfer protocol*) efu-tii-pii, ftp エフ・ティー・ピー

fuel n nenryōʹ 燃料, (*firewood*) taki-gi たきぎ・薪; (*gasoline*) gasorin ガソリン
fuel tank n nenryōʹ-tanku 燃料タンク

fugitive n tōbō-sha 逃亡者

Fujiyama n Fúji (-san) 富士(山)

fulfill v konashimásu (konasu, konashite) こなします(こなす, こなして) → accomplish; *a desire is fulfilled* nozomiga kanaimásu (kanáu, kanátte) 望みが叶います(叶う, 叶って)

full adj ippai (no) いっぱい[一杯](の); (*of people*) man'in (no) 満員(の); *gets ~* michimásu (michíru, míchite) 満ちます・みちます(満ちる, 満ちて)

full coverage insurance *n* zengaku-hoken 全額保険

full dinners *n* furu-kōsu フルコース

full moon *n* mangetsu 満月

full name *n* furu nēmu フルネーム, shimei 氏名

full stop *n* (*period*) shūshí-fu 終止符, piriodo ピリオド

full tank *n* man-tan 満タン

full-time Japanese housewife *n* sengyō-shufu 専業主婦

full-time worker *n* jōkin rōdō-sha 常勤労働者

fully *adv* tappúri たっぷり; mán(-) …満…, maru(-) …まる…; (*appreciating*) shimijími (to) しみじみ(と); *fully maturing* enjuku 円熟

fun *n* omoshirói (kotó) おもしろい[面白い]こと; asobi 遊び・あそび

function *n* **1.** yakumé 役目 (o-yakume お役目); hataraki 働き・はたらき; kinō 機能 **2.** (*mathematics*) kansū 関数; (*function as…*) …to shite kinō shimásu (suru, shite) …として機能します(する, して)

fund *n* shikín 資金, (*capital*) shihon 資本

fundamental *adj* konpon-teki (na) 根本的(な), kihon-teki (na) 基本的(な)

fundamentally *adv* konpon-teki (ni) 根本的(に), kihon-teki (ni) 基本的(に)

funeral *n* (o-)sō´shiki (お)葬式・そうしき

funeral home *n* (o-)sō´shiki-jō (お)葬式場, sō´gi-jō (お)葬儀場

funfair *n* yūen-chi 遊園地

funicular *n* kēburu-kā ケーブルカー

fun-loving *adj* omoshiroi-koto zuki (no) 面白いこと好き(の), omoshiroi-koto ga suki (na) 面白いことが好き(な), tanoshii-koto ga suki (na) 楽しいことが好き(な)

funnel *n* jō´go じょうご, [BOOKISH] rō´to ろうと・漏斗

funny *adj* okashíi おかしい, okashi na おかし

な; (*comical*) kokkei (na) こっけい・滑稽(な), hyōkín (na) ひょうきん(な), (*droll*) yúkai (na) 愉快・ゆかい(な), (*strange*) hén (na) 変・へん(な), fushigi (na) 不思議・ふしぎ(な)

fur *n* ke-gawa 毛皮

fur coat *n* ke-gawa no kōto 毛皮のコート, kega-wa no gaitō 毛皮の外套

furious *adj* gekido-shita 激怒した

furlough *n* hima 暇・ひま

furnace *n* ro 炉; kamado かまど; danbō´ (sō´chi) 暖房(装置)

furnish *v* (*provides*) sonaemásu (sonáeru, sonáete) 備えます・そなえます(備える, 備えて)

furnished *adj* (*with household goods*) kagu-tsuki (no) 家具付き・家具つき(の)

furniture *n* kágu 家具

furniture store *n* kagú-ya 家具屋

furry *adj* kegawa no yō (na) 毛皮のよう(な)

further **1.** *adv* (*more*) mótto saki (ni) もっと先(に), (*elsewhere*) hoka no basho (de) 他の場所(で) **2.** (*advances it*) *v* mótto susumemásu (susumeru, susumete) 進めます・すすめます(進める, 進めて)

fuse *n* hyū´zu ヒューズ

fusion *n* gō´dō´ 合同

fuss *n* sáwagi 騒ぎ・さわぎ, ō´-sáwagi 大騒ぎ・おおさわぎ

fussy *adj* ki-muzukashíi 気難しい・きむずかしい → **choosy**

futile *adj* muda (na) 無駄・むだ(な), munashii 空しい・虚しい・むなしい

futon *n* futon ふとん・布団

future *n* shō´rai 将来, mírai 未来・みらい, saki 先・さき (o-saki お先); zénto 前途, sue 末 **in the future** kongo 今後・こんご **in the near future** chikái uchí (ni) 近いうち・ちかいうち(に)

futures *n* sakimono-torihiki 先物取引

G

gabble *v* hayakuchi ni hanashimásu (hanasu, hanashite) 早口に話します(話す, 話して), pechakucha shaberimásu (shaberu, shabette) ぺちゃくちゃ[ペチャクチャ]喋ります[しゃべります](喋る, 喋って)

gable *n* kirizuma 切妻・きりづま

gaffe *n* bu-sahō´ 無作法・不作法・ぶさほう

gaiety *n* o-matsuri sawagi お祭り騒ぎ

gain **1.** *n* toku 得・とく (o-toku お得), (*income*) shotoku 所得 **2.** *v* → **get**

gait *n* aruki-kata 歩き方

gale *n* bōfú 暴風

gall bladder *n* (*medical*) tannō 胆囊・胆のう

gallery *n* gyararii ギャラリー, garō 画廊

gallon *n* garon ガロン

gallop **1.** *n* gyaroppu ギャロップ **2.** *v* kakemásu (kakéru, kákete) 駆けます・かけます(駆ける, 駆けて)

galoshes *n* amá-gutsu 雨靴・あまぐつ

gambling *n* kaké-(goto) 賭け事, tobaku とばく・賭博, bakuchi ばくち・博奕

game *n* **1.** asobi 遊び・あそび, gē´mu ゲーム; *card game* toranpu トランプ **2.** (*athletic*) kyōgi 競技

gang *n* renchū/renjū 連中, nakama 仲間

gangway *n* taráppu タラップ

gap *n* suki-ma すき間・隙間, suki すき・隙; ware-me 割れ目・われめ, kire-mé 切れ目・きれめ; zuré ずれ, gyáppu ギャップ

garage n gárē´ji ガレージ, sháko 車庫
garbage n gomí ごみ・ゴミ, (*kitchen waste*) nama-gomi 生ごみ
　garbage bag n gomi-búkuro ごみ袋
　garbage bin/can n gomi-bako ごみ箱
　garbage collector n gomí-ya (san) ごみ屋(さん)
　garbage dump n gomi-sute ba ごみ捨て場
garden n niwa 庭・にわ (o-niwa お庭・おにわ)
gardener n ueki-ya 植木屋, niwa-shi 庭師・にわし
gardening n engei 園芸, gēdeningu ガーデニング
gargle v ugai shimásu (suru, shite) うがいします (する, して)
garlic n ninniku にんにく・ニンニク・大蒜, gērikku ガーリック
garnishings n (*to go with sashimi*) tsumá つま・ツマ, tsukeawase つけ合わせ
garter n gā´tā ガーター
gas n 1. (*natural*) gásu ガス 2. (*a gas, vapor*) kitai 気体 3. (*gasoline*) gasorin ガソリン
　gas bill n gasú-dai ガス代
　gas company n gasu-gaisha ガス会社
　gas mask n gasu-masuku ガスマスク
　gas meter n gasu-mētē ガスメーター
　gas range n gasu-rénji ガスレンジ
　gas pedal ákuseru アクセル; **steps on the ~** ákuseru o fumimásu (fumu, funde) アクセルを踏みます[ふみます](踏む, 踏んで)
gas(oline) station n gasorin sutándo ガソリンスタンド
gasp v aegimásu (aégu, aéide) あえぎ[喘ぎ]ます (あえぐ, あえいで)
gate n món 門・もん, (*gateway*) deiriguchi 出入り口; (*of shrine*) torii 鳥居; (*front*) omote-mon 表門, (*back*) uramon 裏門, (*main [front]*) seimon 正門; (*at airport terminal*) gē´to ゲート
gatekeeper n mónban 門番
gather 1. v (*they gather*) atsumarimásu (atsumáru, atsumátte) 集まります・あつまります(集まる, 集まって), (*to make a set*) soroimásu (soróu, sorótte) 揃います・そろいます(揃う, 揃って), (*congregate*) shūgō shimásu (suru, shite) 集合します(する, して); (*gathers them*) atsumemásu (atsuméru, atsúmete) 集めます・あつめます(集める, 集めて), yosemásu (yoseru, yosete) 寄せます・よせます(寄せる, 寄せて) 2. v (*plucks, clips*) tsumimásu (tsumu, tsunde) 摘みます・つみます(摘む, 摘んで) 3. n (*pleat*) hida ひだ, gyazā ギャザー
gathering n shūgō 集合
　gathering place n tamari-ba たまり場
gaudy adj hadé はで・派手(な)
gauze n gā´ze ガーゼ
gave → **give**
gaze v mi-tsumemásu (mi-tsumeru, mi-tsúmete) 見つめます・みつめます(見つめる, 見つめて), nagamemásu (nagaméru, nagámete) 眺めます・ながめます(眺める, 眺めて)
gay adj 1. akarui 明るい・あかるい, yúkai (na) 愉快・ゆかい(な) 2. (*homosexual*) hómo (no) ホモ(の), gei n ゲイ(の)
gear n gí(y)a ギア[ギヤ], hagúruma 歯車・はぐるま
　gear box n gí(y)a bokkusu ギア[ギヤ]ボックス, hensoku-sōchi 変速装置
　high gear n kōsoku-gí(y)a 高速ギア[ギヤ]
　low gear n teisoku-gí(y)a 低速ギア[ギヤ]
gearshift n hensoku-rébā 変速レバー, shifuto-rébā シフトレバー
gecko n yámori やもり・ヤモリ・守宮
Gee! interj wā! わあ！, ā! ああ！, sugoi! すごい！
geisha n geisha 芸者
gel n geru ゲル, jeru ジェル
gelatine n zerachin ゼラチン; (*from tengusa* 天草・テングサ *seaweed*) kanten 寒天・カンテン
gem n hōseki 宝石
　gem dealer n hōsekí-shō 宝石商
Gemini n (*star sign*) Futago-za ふたご座・双子座
gender n séi 性
gene n idenshi 遺伝子
general 1. adj (*over all*) ippan (no) 一般(の); (*common*) kyōtsū (no) 共通(の) 2. n (*army*) táishō 大将
　in general daitai 大体・だいたい, taigai 大概・たいがい, ippan ni 一般に, futsū 普通 (= *generally*)
　the general public taishū 大衆
　general remarks (*outline*) sōron 総論
　major general shō´shō 少将
generally adv ippanteki ni 一般的に, zentai ni 全体に; daitai 大体・だいたい, taigai 大概・たいがい
generation n sedai 世代, dōjidai 同時代
　generations after generations, for generations dáidai 代々
generator n hatsudén-ki 発電機
generous adj kimae ga íi 気前がいい, kandai (na) 寛大・かんだい(な)
genius n tensai 天才
gentle adj yasashii 優しい・やさしい, (*well-behaved*) otonashíi おとなしい, (*docile*) súnao (na) すなお[素直](な); (*calm*) odáyaka (na) 穏やか・おだやか(な)
gentleman n dánsei 男性, shínshi 紳士・しんし; (*middle-aged man*) ojisan おじさん, (*old man*) ojíisan おじいさん
gently adv yasashíku 優しく・やさしく, otonáshiku おとなしく
gentry n shinshi-kaikyū 紳士階級, kizoku 貴族
gents' n shinshi-yō toire 紳士用トイレ, dansei-yō toire 男性用トイレ
gents' underwear n shinshi-yō shitagi 紳士用下着
genuine adj hontō (no) 本当・ほんとう(の), honmono (no) 本物・ほんもの(の), makoto (no) 真・まこと(の)
geoduck n (*surf clam*) mirú-gai みる貝・ミルガイ
geographical adj chiri-teki (na) 地理的(な), chiri-jō (no) 地理上(の)

geography n chíri 地理; (study/science) chirí-gaku 地理学

geology n (of a place) chishitsu 地質; (study/science) chishitsú-gaku 地質学

geranium n zeraniumu ゼラニウム

germ n saikin 細菌, baikin ばい菌・バイキン

German n (language) Doitsu-go ドイツ語; (person) Doitsú-jin ドイツ人

Germany n Dóitsu ドイツ

gesture n miburi 身振り・みぶり; jesuchā ジェスチャー, (hand gesture) temane 手まね, (motion) dōsa 動作

get v (receives) moraimásu (morau, moratto) もらいます・貰います(もらう、もらって), [HUMBLE] itadakimásu (itadaku, itadaite) いただき[頂き]ます(いただく、いただいて)

get (someone) **to do it** v **1.** (hito ni) shite moraimásu (morau, moratte) (人に)してもらいます(もらう、もらって) **2.** [BOOKISH] cmásu (éru, éte) 得ます・えます(得る、得て)

get caught (in) between v hasamarimásu (hasamáru, hasamátte) 挟まります・はさまります(挟まる、挟まって)

get down v (descends) orimásu (oríru, órite) 降ります・おります(降りる、降りて); (crouches) mi o fusemásu (fuséru, fuséte) 身を伏せます(伏せる、伏せて)

get in v (enters) hairimásu (háiru, háitte) 入ります・はいります(入る、入って); (puts it in) iremásu (ireru, irete) 入れます・いれます(入れる、入れて)

get into v (a vehicle) (… ni) norimásu (noru, notte) (…に)乗ります・のります(乗る、乗って)

get off v (gets down) orimásu (oríru, órite) 降ります・おります(降りる、降りて)

get old v toshi o torimásu (tóru, tótte) 年を取ります・としをとります(取る、取って), fukemásu (fukéru, fukéte) 老けます・ふけます(老ける、老けて)

get out v (leaves) demásu (déru, déte) 出ます・でます(出る、出て); (gets it out) dashimásu (dásu, dáshite) 出します(出す、出して)

get out of the way v dokimásu (doku, doite) どきます(どく、どいて), nokimásu (noku, noite) の[退]きます(の[退]く、の[退]いて)

get to be → **become**

get up v (arises) okimásu (okíru, ókite) 起きます・おきます(起きる、起きて)

getting aboard n (into a car, etc.) jōsha 乗車

getting a job n shūshoku 就職

Getting off! interj Orimásu! 降ります！

get-together party n konshín-kai 懇親会

get-up n (appearance) teisai 体裁

geyser n kankessen 間欠泉, kanketsu-onsen 間欠温泉

Ghana n Gēna ガーナ

ghastly adj sugói すごい・凄い; adv sugóku warúi すごく[凄く]悪い[わるい]

ghetto n gettō ゲットー

ghetto blaster n ōgata rajikase 大型ラジカセ

ghost n yū́rei 幽霊・ゆうれい, gōsuto ゴースト; (goblin) obáke お化け・オバケ, bake-mónó 化け物・ばけもの

giant n kyojin 巨人, ōotoko 大男; (baseball team) **the Giants** Kyójin-gun 巨人軍

gibberish n chinpunkanpun no/na hanashi ちんぷんかんぷんの/な話; detarame でたらめ

gift n purezento プレゼント gifuto ギフト → **present**

gift shop n miyagemono-ya みやげ[土産]物屋

gifted adj sugureta sainō no aru 優れた才能のある, sainō ni megumareta 才能に恵まれた

giga byte, GB n (computer) giga-baito ギガ・バイト

gigantic adj **1.** (vast amounts of) bōdai (na) 膨大・ぼうだい(な) **2.** kyodai (na) 巨大(な)

gill n era エラ・えら

gilt n kinpaku 金ぱく・金箔, kinmekki 金メッキ

gimmick n gimikku ギミック, shikake 仕掛け

gin n jin ジン

ginger n shōga しょうが・ショウガ・生姜

ginger ale n jinja-ēru ジンジャエール, jinjā-ēru ジンジャーエール

ginger beer n jinja-biiru ジンジャビール, jinjā-biiru ジンジャービール

Japanese ginger n (buds) myōga みょうが・ミョウガ・茗荷

pickled ginger n sushō´ga 酢しょうが, gári がり・ガリ

gingerbread n (bread) shōga-iri kashipan ショウガ入り菓子パン, shōga-iri kēki ショウガ入りケーキ

gingerbread man n (nigyō no katachi no) shōga-kukkii (人形のかたちの)ショウガクッキー

gingko n (tree) ichō いちょう・イチョウ・銀杏

gingko nuts n ginnán ぎんなん・ギンナン・銀杏

giraffe n kirin キリン

girder n keta けた・ケタ・桁; **under the girder** keta-shita けた下・桁下

girdle n **1.** (belt) óbi 帯 **2.** gādoru ガードル

girl n musume(-san) 娘(さん); onná-no-ko 女の子; jóshi 女子

girl friend n gāru-furéndo ガールフレンド; káno-jo 彼女

girlish adj shōjo rashii 少女らしい; onná-no-ko rashii 女の子らしい

giro system n furikae-seido 振替制度

girth n shūi 周囲

gist n muné 旨; yō 要, yō´shi 要旨, shushi 主旨, yōten 要点, yōryō´ 要領, kosshi 骨子

give v **1.** (they to you/me, you to me) kuremásu (kureru, kurete) くれます(くれる、くれて), kudasaimásu (kudasáru, kudasátte) 下さいます・くださいます(下さる、下さって) **2.** (I to you/them, you to them, they to them) agemásu (ageru, agete) あげます(あげる、あげて), yarimásu (yaru, yatte) やります(やる, やって); [HUMBLE, DEFERENTIAL] sashi-agemásu (sashi-ageru, sashi-agete) 差し上げます・さしあげます(差し上げる, 差し上げて) **3.** (*provides*) ataemásu (ataeru, ataete) 与えます・あたえます(与える, 与えて), motasemásu (motaséru, motásete) 持たせます・もたせます(持たせる, 持たせて); *give mercifully* (*in charity*) megu-mimásu (megumu, megunde) 恵みます(恵む, 恵んで) **4.** (*entrusts temporarily*) azukemásu (azukéru, azúkete) 預けます・あずけます(預ける, 預け て) **5.** (*a party, etc.*) (pātii o) hirakimásu (hiraku, hiraite) (パーティーを)開きます・ひらきます(開く, 開いて); moyōshimásu (moyōsu, moyōshite) 催します・もよおします(催す, 催して)

give birth to … o umimásu (umu, unde) …を生み[産み]ます(生む, 生んで)

give in/up *v* (*cedes, concedes*) yuzurimásu (yuzuru, yuzutte) 譲ります・ゆずります(譲る, 譲って)

give up (*on*) … o akiramemásu (akiraméru, akirámete) …を諦めます(諦める, 諦めて)

glacial *adj* hyōga-ki (no) 氷河[ヒョウガ]期(の)

glacial age *n* hyōga-ki 氷河[ヒョウガ]期

glacier *n* hyōga 氷河・ヒョウガ

glad *adj* ureshíi うれしい・嬉しい; *is glad* yorokobimásu (yorokóbu, yorokónde) 喜びます・よろこびます(喜ぶ, 喜んで)

glad to … *v* yorokonde … o shimásu (suru, shite) 喜んで…をします(する, して)

gladly *adv* yorokónde 喜んで・よろこんで

glamor *n* guramē グラマー

glamorous *adj* miryoku-teki (na) 魅力的(な), miwaku-teki (na) 魅惑的(な)

gland *n* sen 腺・せん

glare *v* … o niramimásu (nirámu, niránde) …をにらみ[睨み]ます(にらむ, に らんで)

glaring *adj* (*dazzling*) mabushíi まぶしい・眩しい

glass *n* (*the substance*) garasu ガラス; (*the container*) koppu コップ, gúrasu グラス

glass, glassful …-hai …杯 (**1:** íp-pai 一杯, **2:** ní-hai 二杯, **3:** sánbai 三杯; *how many* nán-bai 何杯)

glasses *n* mégane めがね・メガネ・眼鏡

glassy *adj* utsuro (na) うつろ・虚ろ(な), seiki no nai 生気のない, donyori (to) shita どんより(と)した, mu-hyōjō (na) 無表情(な)

glazier *n* garasu-ya ガラス屋

gleam, glitter *v* kagayakimásu (kagayáku, kagayáite) 輝きます・かがやきます(輝く, 輝いて)

glittering *adj* pikápika/kirakira kagayaku ぴかぴか・ピカピカ/きらきら・キラキラ輝く

glen *n* tani-ma 谷間

glider *n* guraidē グライダー

gliding *n* kakkū 滑空

glimmer *n* (*light*) kasuka na hikari かすかな光・微かな光

globe *n* (*shape*) tamá 球; (*map*) chikyū´-gi 地球儀

gloom *n* (*depression*) yūutsu 憂うつ[鬱]・ゆううつ

gloomy *adj* uttōshíi うっとうしい, kurai 暗い・くらい, yūutsu (na) 憂うつ[鬱]・ゆううつ(な), inki (na) 陰気(な)

glorious *adj* hanáyaka (na) 華やか・はなやか(な)

glory *n* méiyo 名誉

gloss *n* **1.** (*shine*) tsuya つや・ツヤ・艶 **2.** (*lipstick*) gurosu グロス

glove *n* tebúkuro 手袋・てぶくろ; (*baseball, boxing*) gúrabu グラブ, gúrōbu グローブ

glow 1. *v* hikarimásu (hikáru, hikátte) 光ります・ひかります(光る, 光って) **2.** *n* (*shine*) kagayaki 輝き, (*glow of sunset*) yūyake 夕焼け

glucose *n* budō-tō ブドウ糖, gurukōsu グルコース

glue 1. *n* setchakuzai 接着剤, nori のり・ノリ, nikawa にかわ・ニカワ・膠 **2.** *v* (*glues it*) setchakuzai de tsukemásu (tsukéru, tsukéte) 接着剤で付けます[つけます](付ける, 付けて), tsugimásu (tsugu, tsuide) 接ぎます(接ぐ, 接いで)

glum *adj* shibúi 渋い・しぶい, inki (na) 陰気(な)

glut *n* kajō 過剰

glutinous rice *n* mochi-gome もち米・モチゴメ

glutton *n* kúi-shínbō 食いしん坊・くいしんぼう, taishoku-ka 大食家

gluttonous *adj* kúi-shínbō (na) 食いしん坊・くいしんぼう(な)

gluttony *n* ōgui 大食い

glycerin *n* guriserin グリセリン

gnarl *n* fushí 節

gnat *n* buyo ブヨ

gnaw *v* kajirimásu (kajíru, kajítte) かじります・齧ります(かじる, かじって)

go *v* ikimásu (iku, itte) 行きます(行く, 行って)

go against … *v* ni somukimásu (somúku, somúite) …に背きます(背く, 背いて); …ni han-shimásu (han-súru, hán-shite) …に反します(反する, 反して)

go ahead *interj* (*to driver*) ōrai オーライ; sā dōzo さあどうぞ

go around *v* (*a curve*) magarimásu (magaru, magatte) 曲がります・まがります(曲がる, 曲がって); (*revolves*) mawarimásu (mawaru, mawatte) 回ります・まわります(回る, 回って)

go away *v* ikimásu (iku, itte) 行きます(行く, 行って); sarimásu (saru, satte) 去ります(去る, 去って)

go back *v* modorimásu (modóru, modótte) 戻ります・もどります(戻る, 戻って), kaerimásu (káeru, káette) 帰ります・かえります(帰る, 帰って)

go back *v* (*in time*) to … ni sakanoborimásu (sakanobóru, sakanobótte) … にさかのぼります・遡ります(さかのぼる, さかのぼって)

go back and forth *v* ittari kitari shimásu (suru, shite) 行ったり来たりします(する, して)

kayoimásu (kayou, kayotte) 通います・かよいます(通う、通って)

go down *v* orimásu (oríru, órite) 下ります・おります(下りる、下りて); kudarimásu (kudaru, kudatte) 下ります・くだります(下る、下って); sagarimásu (sagáru, sagátte) 下がります・さがります(下がる、下がって); (*on the price*) makemásu (makeru, makete) 負けます・まけます(負ける、負けて); (*dwindles*) herimásu (heru, hette) 減ります・へります(減る、減って)

go forward *v* susumimásu (susumu, susunde) 進みます・すすみます(進む、進んで)

go home *v* kaerimásu (káeru, káotte) 帰ります・かえります(帰る、帰って)

go in *v* hairimásu (hairu, háitte) 入ります・はいります(入る、入って), háitte ikimásu (iku, itte) 入って行きます・はいっていきます(行く、行って)

go out *v* demásu (déru, déte) 出ます・でます(出る、出て); déte ikimásu (iku, itte) 出て行きます・でていきます(行く、行って); (*of the house*) dekakemásu (dekakeru, dekakete) 出かけ[掛け]ます・でかけます(出かける、出かけて), gaishutsu shimásu (suru, shite) 外出します(する、して); (*appears*) arawaremásu (arawaréru, arawárete) 現れます・あらわれます(現れる、現れて); (*lights, fire, etc.*) kiemásu (kieru, kiete) 消えます・きえます(消える、消えて)

go over *v* (*exceeds*) sugimásu (sugíru, súgite) 過ぎます・すぎます(過ぎる、過ぎて), chōka shimásu (suru, shite) 超過します(する、して), koshimásu (kosu, koshite) 超[越]します(超[越]す、超[越]して); (*revises*) fukushū shimásu (suru, shite) 復習します(する、して)

go to *v* (*reaches*) itarimásu (itaru, itatte) 至ります・いたります(至る、至って)

go to bed *v* yasumimásu (yasúmu, yasúnde) 休みます・やすみます(休む、休んで), nemásu (neru, nete) 寝ます・ねます(寝る、寝て)

go too far *v* (*to excess*) do o koshimásu (kósu, kóshite) 度を超します・度をこします(超す、超して)

go too fast *v* (*clock*) susumimásu (susumu, susunde) 進みます・すすみます(進む、進んで)

go to the end of *v* (*a street*) tsuki-atarimásu (tsuki-atáru, tsuki-atátte) 突き当たります・つきあたります(突き当たる、突き当たって)

go to work *v* (*start work*) shigoto ni ikimásu (iku, itte) 仕事に行きます(行く、行って), shūrō shimásu (suru, shite) 就労します(する、して)

go up *v* agarimásu (agaru, agatte) 上がります・あがります(上がる、上がって), noborimásu (noboru, nobotte) 上ります・のぼります(上る、上って)

go upstream *v* (*goes against the stream*) sakanoborimásu (sakanobóru, sakanobótte) さかのぼります・さかのぼります(さかのぼる、さかのぼって)

Go *n* (*board game*) gó 碁・ご, ígo 囲碁・いご
  Go board *n* go-ban 碁盤

goal *n* mokuteki 目的, ate 当て; (*destination*) mokuteki-chi 目的地; (*sports*) gō´ru ゴール

goalkeeper *n* gōru kiipā ゴールキーパー

goat *n* yági やぎ・ヤギ・山羊

gobang *n* (*simplified version of Go*) gomoku-nárabe 五目並べ

go-between *n* (*intermediary*) chūkaisha 仲介者, nakadachí 仲立ち; (*match-maker*) nakō´do 仲人

goblin *n* (*long-nosed*) tengu 天狗・てんぐ・テング

goby *n* (*fish*) háze はぜ・ハゼ

God, gods *n* kámi(-sama) 神(様)・かみ(さま)

godchild *n* nazuke-go 名付け子

goddaughter *n* nazuke-musume 名付け娘・なづけむすめ

goddess *n* megami 女神

godfather *n* nazuke-oya 名付け親・なづけ親

godmother *n* nazuke-oya 名付け親・なづけ親

godown *n* (*storeroom*) kurá 蔵・倉・くら

godsend *n* ten no megumi 天の恵み

godson *n* nazuke-go 名付け子・なづけ子, nazuke-musuko 名付け息子・なづけむすこ

goggle *n* gōguru ゴーグル

Goh → Go

gold *n* kín 金, gorudo ゴールド

golden *adj* (*color*) kin-iro (no) 金色(の)

Golden Week (*29 April–5 May*) *n* gōruden-wíiku ゴールデンウィーク

goldfish *n* kíngyo 金魚・キンギョ

gold lacquer *n* (kin-)mákie (金)蒔絵

goldsmith *n* kin-zaiku shokunin 金細工職人

golf *n* górufu ゴルフ
  golf ball *n* gorufu-bōru ゴルフボール
  golf club *n* gorufu-kurabu ゴルフクラブ
  golf course *n* gorufu-jō ゴルフ場, gorufu-kōsu ゴルフコース

golfer *n* gorufā ゴルファー

gondola *n* gondora ゴンドラ

gong *n* gongu ゴング, dora どら

gone → go; *v is* ~ itte imásu (iru, ite) 行っています(いる、いて)

gonorrhea *n* rinbyō りん病・淋病

good *adj* íi いい・良い・好い・善い, yói 良い・好い・善い・よい
  good at (… ga) umái (…が)うまい, jōzú (na) じょうず[上手](な), o-jōzu お上手, tassha (na) 達者(な)
  a good deal *adv* yohodo よほど・余程, yoppodo よっぽど; *unto* うんと, takusán (no) たくさん・沢山(の)
  for the good of … *adv* no tamé ni …のため[為]に

Good afternoon. *interj* konnichi wa. こんにちは・今日は.

good-bye *interj* sayonara さよなら, sayōnára さようなら; sore déwa それでは; go- kigen yō´. ごきげんよう.

Good evening. *interj* konban wa. こんばんは・今晩は.

good-looking *adj* hansamu (na) ハンサム(な),

kakkoii かっこいい・格好いい, kakkōii かっこう いい・格好いい; rukkusu no ii ルックスのいい

Good morning. *interj* O-hayō (gozai-mású). おはよう[お早う]ございます.

Good night. *interj* O-yasumi nasái. おやすみ [お休み]なさい.

no good furyō (no) 不良(の)

good and evil *n* zén-aku 善悪

good fortune *n* kōun 幸運, saiwai 幸い・さい わい

good-hearted *adj* shinsetsu (na) 親切・しんせつ (な), omoiyari no aru 思いやりのある, yasashii 優しい・やさしい

good heavens/grief *interj* shimatta しまった, oya-mā おやまあ, *(feminine)* mā まあ

good-looking *adj* kírei (na) きれい[綺麗](な)

good-luck piece *n* o-mamori お守り・おまもり

good-natured *adj* kidate no yoi 気立ての良い・ きだてのよい

goodness *n* zén 善

good offices; *through the ~ of* ... no assen de ... のあっせん[斡旋]で

goods *n* shina(mono) 品(物); *(merchandise)* shōhin 商品

goodwill *n* kō'i 好意, kokorozashi 志・こころざ し, shínsetsu 親切・しんせつ(go-shínsetsu ご親切), zén'i 善意

goof 1. *n (blunder)* hema へま・ヘマ, doji どじ・ ドジ, chónbo ちょんぼ・チョンボ **2.** *v goof (up)* hema o shimású (suru, shite) へま(を)します(す る, して) **3.** *v goof off → loaf*

Google 1. *n (internet search engine)* gūguru グー グル **2.** *v* ... o gūguru de shirabemásu (shiraberu, shirabete) 〜をGoogleで調べます (調べる, 調べて)

goose *n* gachō がちょう・ガチョウ・鵞鳥

gorgeous *adj* gōka (na) 豪華(な); rippa (na) 立派・りっぱ(な); hanáyaka (na) 華やか・はな やか(な)

Gosh! *interj* wā わあ

gossip 1. uwasa うわさ・噂; muda-/baka-bánashi 無駄/ばか話 **2.** *(a gossip)* osháberi おし ゃべり

gourd *n* hyōtán ひょうたん・ヒョウタン・瓢箪

gourd strips *n (dried)* kanpyō かんぴょう・ カンピョウ・干瓢

sponge gourd *n* hechima へちま・ヘチマ・ 糸瓜

gourmand *n* taishokukan 大食漢

gourmet *n, adj* gurume (no) グルメ(の), shokutsū (no) 食通(の), bishokuka (no) 美食家(の)

govern *v* osaméru (osaméru, osámete) 治めま す・おさめます(治める, 治めて)

government *n* séifu 政府; *(cabinet)* náikaku 内閣; *(nation)* kuni (no) 国(の), *(national)* kokuritsu (no) 国立(の)・国上(の); *(the authorities)* tō'kyoku 当局, okámi お上

government office *n* (o-)yaku-sho (お)役所

government official *n* yakunin 役人

government worker/employee *n* kōmú-in 公務員

governor *n* chíji 知事

gown *n* gaun ガウン

grab → seize

graceful *adj* yū'bi (na) 優美(な)

gradation *n* guradēshon グラデーション

grade 1. *n (value, quality)* tōkyū 等級, *(class)* kyū 級, gakkyu 学級; *(step)* dán 段; *(evaluation score)* hyōten 評点, hyō'ka 評価; *(academic record)* seiseki 成績 **2.** *v (to grade a test paper)* saitenshimásu (suru, shite) 採点します(する, し て), seiseki o tsukemásu (tsukéru, tsukete) 成績を つけます(つける, つけて)

grade school *n* shōgakkō 小学校

grade school children *n* shōgaku-sei 小学生

gradually *adv* dandan だんだん, jojo ni じょじょ に, sukoshízútsu 少しずつ・すこしずつ, sórosoro (to) そろそろ(と); *(finally)* yōyaku ようやく

graduate 1. *v* sotsugyō shimásu (suru, shite) 卒業します(する, して); *~ from* (daigaku o) demásu (deru, dete) (大学を)出ます(出る, 出て) **2.** *n* sotsugyō´-sei 卒業生; *(graduate of ...)* ...no de ...の出

graduate school *n* daigakú-in 大学院

graduate student *n* daigakuín-sei 大学院生

graft 1. *n (bribery)* wáiro 賄賂・わいろ・ワイロ, oshoku 汚職 **2.** *n* tsugiki 接ぎ木 **3.** *v (attaches)* tsugimásu (tsugu, tsuide) 接ぎます・つぎます (接ぐ, 接いで)

grain 1. *n* tsúbu 粒 **2.** *(cereal)* kokúmotsu 穀物, kokúrui 穀類 **3.** *(texture)* kimé きめ・木目・肌理

gram *n* gúramu グラム

grammar *n* bunpō 文法, guramā グラマー

grand *adj* subarashíi すばらしい・素晴らしい, erái 偉い・えらい, sōdai (na) 壮大(な)

grandchild *n* magó 孫(o-mago-san お孫さん)

grandfather *n* ojíi-san おじいさん・お祖父さん, sófu 祖父

grandmother *n* obā´-san おばあさん・お祖母さ ん, sóbo 祖母

grandson *n* mago (musuko) 孫(息子)

grandstand *n (seats)* kanrán-seki 観覧席

grandstand play sutando-pure スタンドプレー

grand total *n* sōkei 総計

granite *n* kakō´-gan かこう岩・花崗岩・カコウ ガン, mikagé-ishi みかげ石・御影石・ミカゲイシ

grant 1. *n* hojokin 補助金, joseikin 助成金 **2.** *v (grants it)* ataemásu (ataeru, ataete) 与えま す・あたえます(与える, 与えて)

grapefruit *n* gurēpufurūtsu グレープフルーツ

grapes *n* budō ぶどう・ブドウ・葡萄

graph *n* grafu グラフ

graphic *n* zukei 図形, gurafikku グラフィック

grasp *v* tsukamimásu (tsukámu, tsukánde) つかみ ます・掴みます(つかむ, つかんで); nigirimásu (nigiru, nigitte) 握ります(握る, 握って)

grass *n* kusá 草・くさ; *(lawn)* shibafu 芝生・ しばふ

grasshopper n (locust) batta バッタ, inago イナゴ, (long-horned grasshopper) kirigirisu キリギリス

grassland n sōgen 草原・そうげん

grated v suri-oroshita すりおろした
grated radish n daikon-óroshi 大根おろし[下ろし]・ダイコンオロシ
grated yam n tororo とろろ・トロロ

grateful adj arigatái ありがたい・有り難い
I am grateful arigatáku zon-jimásu (zon-jiru, zon-jite) ありがたく存じます(存じる, 存じて)
feels grateful/obliged kyōshuku shimásu (suru, shite) 恐縮します(する, して)

grater n oroshí-gane 下ろし金

gratification n manzoku 満足

grating n kōshi 格子

gratis → **free**

gratitude n kansha 感謝・かんしゃ

gratuity n kokoro-zuke 心付け・こころづけ

grave n (tomb) haká 墓・はか (o-haka お墓)
graveyard n haka-bá 墓場, bóchi 墓地

grave adj (serious) omoi 重い・おもい, shinkoku (na) 深刻・しんこく(な)

gravel n jari 砂利・じゃり

gravy n taré たれ; (o-)sō´su (お)ソース; niku-jū/jíru 肉汁

gray adj hai-iro (no) 灰色(の), nezumi-iro (no) ねずみ色(の); gurē´ no グレーの

gray hair n shiragá 白髪・しらが

gray mullet n bora ぼら・ボラ

graze v kasurimásu (kasúru, kassute) かすります・掠ります(かする, かすって); kasumemásu (kasumeru, kasumete) かすめます・掠めます(かすめる, かすめて)

grease n abura 脂・油・アブラ

greasy adj aburakkói 脂っこい・あぶらっこい; kudói くどい

great adj (superior) idai (na) 偉大(な), erái 偉い・えらい; ōki (na) 大き(な)・おおきな, dai-大… → **big** → **good** → **grand**
a great difference taisa 大差
a great many táisō (na) たいそう・大層(な)
a great war taisen 大戦

Great Britain n Eikoku 英国, igirisu イギリス

great-grandfather n sō-sofu 曽祖父, hii ojiisan ひいおじいさん

great-grandmother n sō-sobo 曽祖母, hii obēsan ひいおばあさん

great-great-grandfather n hii hii ojiisan ひいひいおじいさん

great-great-grandmother n hii hii obēsan ひいひいおばあさん

greatly adv ōi ni 大いに・おおいに, unto うんと, totemo とても; hijō ni 非常に・ひじょうに → **extremely**

Greece n Gírisha ギリシャ

greed n yokubárí 欲張り・よくばり, yokú 欲

greedy adj yokubárí (na) 欲張り・よくばり(な), kúi-shínbō (na) 食いしん坊・くいしんぼう

(な); yokubarimásu (yokubáru, yokubátte) 欲張ります・よくばります(欲張る, 欲張って); a greedy person yokubárí 欲張り・よくばり

Greek 1. n (langage) Girisha-go ギリシャ語, (people) Girisha-jin ギリシャ人 **2.** adj Girisha-/-jin/-go (no) ギリシャ/人/語(の)

green adj **1.** mídori (no) 緑(の), aói 青い・あおい; guríin (no) グリーン(の) **2.** (inexperienced) osanái 幼い・おさない

Green Car n (deluxe coach) guríin-sha グリーン車

greengrocer n yao-ya 八百屋・ヤオヤ

greenhouse n onshitsu 温室

green light n (signal) ao-shíngō 青信号

green onion n nira にら・ニラ・韮; naga-nagi 長ねぎ[葱]・ナガネギ, négi ねぎ・ネギ・葱; (chives, scallion) asátsuki あさつき・アサツキ・浅葱

green pepper n píiman ピーマン

greens n náppa 菜っ葉・ナッパ, ná 菜・ナ; (boiled greens served cold with seasoning) o-hítashi おひたし・オヒタシ

green tea n (o-)cha (お)茶; a cup of green tea (in a sushi bar) agari 上がり

Green Window n (for special train tickets) mídori no madóguchi みどりの窓口

greet v (welcomes, receives) áisatsu (o) shimásu (suru, shite) あいさつ・挨拶(を)します(する, して); de-mukaemásu (de-mukaeru, de-mukaete) 出迎えます(出迎える, 出迎えて)

greeting n áisatsu あいさつ・挨拶; réi 礼

grenade n shuryūdan 手榴弾

grief n nagekí 嘆き・なげき, kanashimi 悲しみ

grievance n fuhei 不平, fuman 不満

grieve v nagekimásu (nagéku, nagéite) 嘆きます・なげきます(嘆く, 嘆いて); kokóro o itamemásu (itaméru, itámete) 心を痛めます(痛める, 痛めて)

grill v yakimásu (yaku, yaite) 焼きます・やきます(焼く, 焼いて), aburimásu (abúru, abútte) あぶります・炙ります(あぶる, あぶって)

grime n yogore 汚れ

grin 1. n (hanikanda) egao はにかんだ笑顔 **2.** v (nit-to, niyat-to) waraimásu (warau, waratte) (にっと/にやっと)笑います(笑う, 笑って)

grind v surimásu (súru, sútte) すります(する, すって); (into powder) hikimásu (hiku, hiite) ひきます(ひく, ひいて) → **sharpen** → **polish**

grip v nigirimásu (nigiru, nigitte) 握ります・にぎります(握る, 握って)

gripe 1. n (complaint) guchi ぐち・愚痴 **2.** v (complains) guchi o koboshimásu (kobósu, kobóshite) ぐち・愚痴をこぼします(こぼす, こぼして), gúzuguzu iimásu (yū, itte/yutte) ぐずぐず言います(言う, 言って/ゆって), boyakimásu (boyáku, boyáite) ぼやきます(ぼやく, ぼやいて)

groan 1. n (a groan) umekí うめき・呻き **2.** v (groans) umekimásu (uméku, uméite) うめきます・呻きます(うめく, うめいて); fuman o iimásu (iu, itte) 不満を言います(言う, 言って)

grocer *n* shokuryō-hin-ten 食料品店, shokuryō-zakka-shō 食料雑貨商

groceries *n* shokuryō-hin 食料品, shokuhin 食品

grocery (store) *n* shokuryō-hin-ten 食料品店

groin *n* matá 股・また

groom *n* hanamuko 花婿・はなむこ, shinrō 新郎

groove *n* mizo 溝

grope *v* sagurimásu (saguru, sagutte) 探ります・さぐります(探る, 探って)

groper *n* (*molester*) chikan 痴漢・チカン

gross *adj* (*crass*) egetsunai えげつない; (*rude*) gehin (na) 下品(な)

grotesque *n* gurotesuku グロテスク

grotto *n* dōkutsu 洞窟・洞くつ

ground 1. *n* (*land*) tochi 土地・とち, jí chi 地, (*earth*) tsuchí 土・つち, (*surface*) jímen 地面・じめん, (*playground*) guraundo グラウンド 2. *n* (*basecoat*) shitanuri 下塗り 3. *adj* hiita 挽いた 4. *v* (*to be grounded*) ...o gaishutsu kinshi ni shimásu (suru, shite) ...を外出禁止にします(する, して)

ground meat *n* hiki-niku 挽き肉・ヒキニク

ground floor *n* ik-kai 一階

groundless *adj* konkyo no nai 根拠のない

grounds *n* (*reason*) riyū 理由・りゆう, yué 故・ゆえ

group *n* gurū´pu グループ, dantai 団体; shūdan 集団; (*class*) kúrasu クラス; (*throng*, *flock*) muré 群れ

groupie *n* gurū´pii グルーピー, okkake 追っかけ

grove *n* hayashi 林・はやし

grow *v* 1. (*it grows*) seichō shimásu (suru, shite) 成長します(する, して); (*gets big*) ō´kiku/ō´ku narimásu (náru, nátte) 大きく[おおきく]/多く[おおく]なります(なる, なって); (*increases*) fuemásu (fuéru, fúete) 増えます・ふえます(増える, 増えて); (*teeth*, *hair*, *mold*, ...) haemásu (haéru, háete) 生えます・はえます(生える, 生えて); (*appears*) hassei shimásu (suru, shite) 発生します(する, して); (*develops*) hatten shimásu (suru, shite) 発展します(する, して) 2. (*grows it*) (*a plant*) uemásu (ueru, uete) 植えます・うえます(植える, 植えて), (*a crop*) tsukurimásu (tsukúru, tsukútte) 作ります・つくります(作る, 作って), (*hair*, *teeth*, ...) hayashi-másu (hayásu, hayáshite) 生やします・はやします(生やす, 生やして) 3. (*becomes*) (... ni, ...-ku) narimásu (náru, nátte) (...に, ...く)なります(なる, なって)

grow late *v* (yó ga) fukemásu (fukéru, fukéte) (夜が)更けます・ふけます(更ける, 更けて)

grow up *v* sodachimásu (sodátsu, sodátte) 育ち・そだちます(育つ, 育って); seichō shimásu (suru, shite) 成長します(する, して)

grower *n* saibai-sha 栽培者, shiiku-sha 飼育者

growing up *n* seichō 成長; sodachí 育ち・そだち

growl 1. *n* (*a growl*) unarí (goe) うなり・唸り(声) 2. *v* (*growls*) unarimásu (unáru, unátte) うなり[唸り]ます(うなる, うなって)

growth *n* seichō 成長; (*increase*) zōka 増加; (*development*) hatten 発展

grow thick(ly) *v* shigerimásu (shigéru, shigétte) 茂り[繁り]ます・しげります(茂[繁]る, 茂[繁]って)

grow weak *v* otoroemásu (otoróeru, otoróete) 衰えます・おとろえます(衰える, 衰えて)

grudge *n* uramí 恨み・うらみ

gruel *n* (*rice*) (o-)kayu (お)かゆ[粥]

grumble *v* boyakimásu (boyáku, boyáite) ぼやきます(ぼやく, ぼやいて), gúzuguzu shimásu (suru, shite) ぐずぐずします(する, して), (guchi o) kob-oshimásu (kobósu, kobóshite) (愚痴を)こぼします(こぼす, こぼして)

grumbling *n* fuhei 不平・ふへい

guarantee *n*, *v* hoshō (shimásu; suru, shite) 保証(します; する, して)

letter of guarantee *n* hoshō-sho 保証書

guard 1. *n* bán 番, gādo-man ガードマン, (*gate keeper*) mónban 門番, shuei 守衛; (*vigilance*) keikai 警戒 2. *v* *guards it* mamorimásu (mamóru, mamótte) 守ります(守る, 守って), keibi shimásu (suru, shite) 警備します(する, して); *guards against* ... o keikai shimásu (suru, shite) ...を警戒します(する, して)

guard dog *n* banken 番犬

guardian *n* hogo-sha 保護者, kōken-nin 後見人

guardian angel *n* shugo-tenshi 守護天使

guardian spirit *n* (*tutelary deity*) uji-gami 氏神

guarding *n* keibi 警備

guess 1. *n* (*conjecture*) sas-shi 察し・さっし (o-sasshi お察し), (*estimate*) suisoku 推測, kentō 見当 2. *v* (*guesses*) sas-shimásu (sas-suru, sas-shite) 察します・さっします(察する, 察して), suisoku shimásu (suru, shite) 推測します(する, して), kentō o tsukemásu (tsukéru, tsukéte) 見当をつけます(つける, つけて); (*correctly*) sas-shi ga tsukimásu (tsukú, tsúite) 察しがつきます・さっしがつきます(つく, ついて), atemásu (ateru, atete) 当てます・あてます(当てる, 当てて)

guest *n* (o-)kyaku (お)客・(お)きゃく, okyaku-san/-sámá お客[きゃく]さん/様・さま; (*caller*) raikyaku 来客

guest of honor *n* shuhin 主賓[ひん], kihin 貴賓[ひん]

guest room *n* kyakuma 客間

guesthouse *n* gesuto hausu ゲストハウス

guesstimate 1. *n* ate-suiryō 当て推量 2. *v* suisoku de mitsumorimásu (mitsumoru, mitsumotte) 推測で見積もります(見積もる, 見積もって)

guidance *n* annai 案内(go-annai ご案内); (*direction*, *counseling*) shidō 指導

guide 1. *n* (*person*) annai-gákari 案内係, annai-nin 案内人, annái-sha 案内者, gáido ガイド; (*coach*, *counsel*) shidō´-sha 指導者; (*book*) annai-sho 案内書, gaido bukku ガイドブック, (*travel*) ryokō-ánnai(-sho) 旅行案内(書); (*visual*) méate 目当て, meyasu 目安 2. *v* (*guides them*) annái shimásu (suru, shite) 案内します(する, して), michibikimásu (michibíku, michibíite) 導きます・みちびきます(導く, 導いて); (*directs, counsels*) shidō shimásu (suru, shite) 指導します(する, して)

guided tour *n* gaido-tsuki no tsue ガイド付きのツアー

guild *n* (*union*) kumiai 組合, girudo ギルド

guillotine *n* girochin ギロチン

guilt *n* tsúmi 罪・つみ; *feeling/sense of ~* záiaku-kan 罪悪感

guilty *adj* yūzai (no) 有罪(の)

guilty-feeling *n* yamashíi やましい

guinea pig *n* morumotto モルモット, jikken dōbutsu 実験動物

guitar *n* gitā ギター

guitarist *n* gitarisuto ギタリスト

gulf *n* wán 湾・ワン

gull *n* kamome かもめ・カモメ・鴎

gullet *n* shokudō 食道

gullible *adj* baka-shō´jiki (na) ばか正直(な)

gully *n* kyōkoku 峡谷

gulp 1. *n* ikki ni nomu 一気に飲む, hitoiki de nomu 一息で飲む **2.** *gulps down* *v* gutto/gabuga-bu nomimásu (nomu, nonde) ぐっと/がぶがぶ飲みます(飲む, 飲んで)

gum *n* (*chewing*) (chūin) gámu (チューイン)ガ

ム; (*mucus from eye*) me-yaní 目やに; (*teethridge*) háguki 歯茎

gum-boot *n* gomu(-naga) gutsu ゴム(長)靴

gun *n* jū´ 銃, teppō 鉄砲・てっぽう

gunfire *n* happō 発砲

gunpowder *n* kayaku 火薬

gunshot → gunfire

gush *v* hotobashirimásu (hotobashiru, hotoba-shitte) ほとばしります(ほとばしる, ほとばしって), wakimásu (waku, waite) わき[湧き・涌き]ます(わく, わいて)

guts *n* harawata はらわた・腸・腑, watá わた・腸; → **oourage**

gutter *n* mizo 溝; (*ditch*) dobu どぶ; (*drain pipe*) tói 樋・とい

guy *n* yátsu やつ・奴; *that guy* aitsu あいつ, (*polite*) sono/ano hitó その/あの人

gym *n* tai(í)kú-kan 体育館

gymnast *n* taisō-senshu 体操選手

gym shoe *n* undō-gutsu 運動靴, suniikē スニーカー

gymnasium *n* tai(í)kú-kan 体育館, jímu ジム

gymnastics *n* taisō 体操・たいそう

gyncoologist *n* fujin-ka 婦人科

gypsy *n* jipushii ジプシー

H

haberdashery *n* (*notions*) koma-mono 小間物, yōhin 洋品; (*shop*) yōhín-ten 洋品店, zakka-ya/-ten 雑貨屋/店

habit *n* shūkan 習慣; (*bad habit*) kusé 癖・くせ

habitable *adj* sumukoto ga dekiru 住むことができる; sumeru 住める

habitat *n* seisoku-chi 生息地; sumika 住処・すみか

habitation *n* kyojū-chi 居住地; sumai 住まい・すまい

habitual *adj* shūkan (no) 習慣(の); itsumono いつもの

hack *n* hakkingu ハッキング, (*computer*) hakkā ハッカー

hacker *n* (*computer*) hakkā ハッカー

had → have; *gets ~ (by …)* *v* (…ni) yararemásu (yarareru, yararete) (…に)やられます(やられる, やられて)

hag *n* (oni) baba (鬼)ばば

haggard *adj* yatsureta やつれた, yatsureteiru やつれている

haggle *n* ii-arasoi 言い争い, ronsō 論争

hail 1. *n* arare/hyō´ **2.** *v* arare/hyō´ ga furimásu (fúru, fútte) あられ・アラレ/ひょう・ヒョウが降ります(降る, 降って)

hailstone → hail

hair *n* (*on head*) kamí 髪・かみ, kamí no ke 髪の毛・かみのけ; (*general*) ke 毛

hair oil *n* kami ábura 髪油, pomā´do ポマード

hair spray *n* hea supurē ヘアスプレー

hair style *n* hea sutairu ヘアスタイル, kamigata 髪型

hairbrush *n* (hea) burashi (ヘア)ブラシ

haircut *n* rihatsu 理髪, sanpatsu 散髪, hea katto ヘアカット; *gets/gives a ~* rihatsu/sanpatsu shimásu (suru, shite) 理髪/散髪します(する, して)

hairdresser → beauty parlor → barber (*shop*)

hair-dryer *n* (hea) doraiyā (ヘア)ドライヤー

hairpin *n* heapin ヘアピン

hairspring *n* zenmai ぜんまい

hairy *adj* kebukai 毛深い

hale *adj* genki ga yoi 元気が良い・げんきがよい, genki (na) 元気・げんき(な)

half *n* hanbún 半分・はんぶん; *half a …* han-… 半-…, …no hanbún …の半分; *and a half* …- hán …半; *the first half* zenhan 前半

half a day *n* han-nichí 半日

half a month *n* han-tsukí 半月

half a week *n* sán-yokka 三, 四日 = *3 or 4 days*

half a year *n* han-toshí 半年

halfbeak *n* (*fish*) sayori さより・サヨリ

half brother *n* **1.** (*different mother*) ibo kyōdai

異母兄弟 **2.** (*different father*) ifu kyōdai 異父兄弟
half-cooked *adj* (*meat*) nama-nie (no) 生煮え(の)
half-done *adj* (*meat*) han'yake (no) 半焼け(の), namayake (no) 生焼け(の)
halfhearted *adj* ii-kagen (na) いい加減・いいかげん(な)
half-hour *n* san juppun 30分・三十分
half price *n* hangaku 半額; *half-price* hangaku (no) 半額(の)
half sister *n* **1.** (*different mother*) ibo shimai 異母姉妹 **2.** (*different father*) ifu shimai 異父姉妹
half term *n* chūkan kyūka 中間休暇
halfway *adj* tochū (no) 途中(の)
hall *n* (*building*) kaikan 会館; (*lecture hall*) kōdō 講堂, hōru ホール; (*entrance*) génkan 玄関
hallmark *n* ken'in 検印
hallucination *n* genkaku 幻覚
hallway *n* tsūro 通路, rōka 廊下
halt → **stop**
ham *n* hámu ハム
  ham and eggs *n* hamu éggu ハムエッグ
  ham sandwich *n* hamu sándo ハムサンド
hamburger *n* (*sandwich*) hanbá´gā ハンバーガー; (*ground beef*) hanbá´gu ハンバーグ
hamlet *n* chiisai mura 小さい村
hammer 1. *n* kanazuchi かなづち・金槌, hánmā/hánma ハンマー/ハンマ, tsuchí 槌・つち, (*small*) kózuchi 小槌
  claw hammer *n* kuginuki 釘抜き・くぎぬき
  2. *v* (*hits*) uchimásu (útsu, útte) 打ちます・うちます(打つ, 打って)
hamper *n* (*basket*) kago かご・カゴ
hamster *n* hamusutā ハムスター
hand *n* té 手; (*of clock*) hári 針・はり; *has on ~* (*in stock*) mochi-awasemásu (mochi-awaseru, mochi-awasete) 持ち合わせます・もちあわせます(持ち合わせる, 持ち合わせて)
  hand down *v* tsutaemásu (tsutaeru, tsutaete) 伝えます・つたえます(伝える, 伝えて); *gets handed down* tsutawarimásu (tsutawaru, tsutawatte) 伝わります・つたわります(伝わる, 伝わって)
  hand over *v* watashimásu (watasu, watashite) 渡します・わたします(渡す, 渡して); (*to me*) yokoshimásu (yokosu, yokoshite) よこします(よこす, よこして)
  hand up *v* kōsan shimásu (suru, shite) 降参します(する, して); *Hands up!* te o agero! 手を挙げろ!
handbag *n* hando bággu (hando bákku) ハンドバッグ(ハンドバック), tesage 手提げ・手さげ
handball *n* hando bōru ハンドボール
handbill *n* bira びら・ビラ
handbook *n* hando bukku ハンドブック, tebiki-sho 手引(き)書
handbrake *n* saido burē´ki サイドブレーキ
handcraft *v* kōsaku shimásu (suru, shite) 工作します(する, して)
handcrafted *adj* tesei (no) 手製(の)
handcuff *n* te jō 手錠

handful *n* shōryō 少量, hito-nigiri 一握り・ひとにぎり
handicap *n* handikyappu ハンディキャップ, handiikyappu ハンディーキャップ, handi ハンディ, handii ハンディー
handicapped *adj* (*physically*) karada ga fú-jiyū (na) 体が不自由(な)
  handicapped person *n* (shintai) shōgái-sha (身体)障害者
handicraft *n* shukōgei-hin 手工芸品
handiwork *n* te-záiku 手細工, saiku 細工, te-shigoto 手仕事
handkerchief *n* hankachi ハンカチ
handle 1. *n* totté 取っ手・とって, handoru ハンドル, tsurú つる・ツル・鉉, é 柄 **2.** *v* tori-atsukaimásu (tori-atsukau, tori-atsukatte) 取り扱います・とりあつかいます(取り扱う, 取り扱って); (*copes with it*) shóri shimásu (suru, shite) 処理します(する, して); (*uses a tool*) tsukaimásu (tsukau, tsukatte) 使います・つかいます(使う, 使って); (*controls, operates*) sōjū shimásu (suru, shite) 操縦します(する, して); (*receives*) …ni ses-shimásu (ses-suru, ses-shite) …に接します(接する, 接して) → **sell** → **touch**
handlebar *n* handoru ハンドル, sōsa rebā 操作レバー
Handle With Care Kowaremono chū´i こわれ物注意・コワレモノ注意
handling *n* tori-atsukai 取り扱い; (*operation*) sōjū 操縦; *handling charge* tesū´-ryō 手数料
hand luggage *n* te-nímotsu 手荷物
handshake *n* ákushu 握手・あくしゅ
handsome *n* hansamu ハンサム, nimai-me 二枚目
hand towel *n* te-nugui 手ぬぐい・手拭い, tefukí 手ふき・手拭き, o-téfuki お手ふき; (*damp*) o-shíbori お絞り・おしぼり
handwriting *n* te-gaki 手書き, niku-hitsu 肉筆
handy *adj* bénri (na) 便利・べんり(な)
handyman *n* (*or his shop*) benri-ya 便利屋・べんり屋
hang *v* **1.** *it hangs* kakarimásu (kakáru, kakátte) 掛かります・かかります(掛かる, 掛かって) **2.** *hangs it* kakemásu (kakéru, kakéte) 掛けます・かけます(掛ける, 掛けて), (*suspends it*) tsurimásu (tsuru, tsutte) 吊ります・つります(吊る, 吊って) **3.** *hangs one's head* utsumukimásu (utsumuku, utsumuite) うつむきます・俯きます(うつむく, うつむいて) **4.** *hangs around* urotsukimásu (urotsuku, urotsuite) うろつきます(つく, ついて)
  hang down *v* **1.** *it hangs down* taremásu (taréru, tárete) 垂れます・たれます(垂れる, 垂れて); sagarimásu (sagáru, ságatte) 下がります・さがります(下がる, 下がって); bura-sagarimásu (bura-sagaru, bura-sagatte) ぶら下がります(ぶら下がる, ぶら下がって) **2.** *hangs it down* sagemásu (sagéru, ságete) 下げます・さげます(下げる, 下げて); bura-sagemásu (bura-sageru, bura-sagete) ぶら下げます(ぶら下げる, ぶら下げて)

hang in there *v* ganbarimásu (ganbáru, ganbátte) がんばり[頑張り]ます(がんばる, がんばって)

hang up *v* (*phone*) (denwa o) kirimásu (kíru, kítté) (電話を)切ります・きります(切る, 切って)

hanger *n* (*clothes hanger*) hángā ハンガー

hang gliding *n* hangu-guraidā-nori ハンググライダー乗り

hanging scroll → scroll

hangout *n* tamari-ba 溜まり場・たまり場

hangover *n* futsuka-yoi 二日酔い

hankering *n* netsubō 熱望, setsubō 切望

haphazard *adj* ii-kagen (na) いい加減・いいかげん(な)

happen *v* okorimásu (okóru, okótte) 起こります・おこります(起こる, 起こって); *~ to see/ observe* mi-ukemásu (mi-ukeru, mi-ukete) 見受けます・みうけます(見受ける, 見受けて); *~ to see/ meet* de-aimásu (de-áu, de-átte) 出会います・であいます(出会う, 出会って)

happening *n* (*incident*) dekígoto 出来事・できごと, jíken 事件, hapuningu ハプニング; (*event*) koto 事

happi coat *n* happi はっぴ・ハッピ・法被, hantén 半天・ハンテン

happiness *n* kōfuku 幸福, shiawase 幸せ・しあわせ

happy *adj* ureshíi うれしい・嬉しい, yúkai (na) 愉快・ゆかい(な), kōfuku (na) 幸福(な), shiawase (na) 幸せ・しあわせ(な); (*cheerful*) yōki (na) 陽気(な); (*auspicious*) medetái めでたい・目出度い; (*is delighted*) yorokobimásu (yorokóbu, yorokónde) 喜びます・よろこびます(喜ぶ, 喜んで) → lucky

happy-go-lucky *adj* nónki (na) のん気(な), rakuten-teki (na) 楽天的(な), nōtenki (na) 能天気(な)

Happy New Year *interj* Shínnen/Akemáshite o-medetō gozaimásu. 新年/あけ[明け]ましておめでとうございます。

harakiri *n* seppuku 切腹・せっぷく, harakiri 腹切(り)・はらきり

harangue *n* netsuben 熱弁, sekkyō 説教

harbinger *n* mae-bure 前触れ・前ぶれ, zenchō 前兆

harbor → port

hard *adj* 1. katai 固い・硬い・堅い・かたい; (*difficult*) muzukashii 難しい・むずかしい, (*hard to do*) shi-nikúi しにくい; (*onerous*) kurushíi 苦しい・くるしい, (*trying*) tsurai つらい・辛い; (*requires much effort*) honé ga oremásu (oréru, órete) 骨が折れます・おれます(折れる, 折れて); (*cruelly, terribly*) hídoku ひどく 2. (*working ~*) yóku 良く・よく; (*laboriously*) ákuseku あくせく, sésse-to せっせと; (*intently*) shíkiri ni しきりに 3. *adv* (*zealously*) nesshín ni 熱心に; (*seriously*) majime ni まじめ[真面目]に; *works ~* hagemimásu (hagému, hagénde) 励みます・はげみます(励む, 励んで)

hard cash *n* genkín 現金, shōkin 正金

harden *v* 1. *it hardens* katamarimásu (katamaru, katamatte) 固まります・かたまります(固まる, 固まって) 2. *hardens it* katamemásu (katameru, katamete) 固めます・かためます(固める, 固めて)

hard disk *n* hādo disuku ハードディスク

hardly *adv* hotóndo ほとんど・殆ど + [NEGATIVE]

hardness *n* katasa 硬さ・かたさ

hard of hearing *adj* mimí ga tōi 耳が遠い・耳がとおい

hardship *n* kónnan 困難, kúrō 苦労

hard times *n* fukeıkı 不景気

hard to hear *adj* kiki-nikui 聞きにくい, kiki-zurai 聞きづらい

hardware *n* 1. kanamono 金物; (*items*) tekki 鉄器, tekkí-rui 鉄器類; (*store*) kanamono-ya 金物屋 → houseware; (*machine*) kikai setsubi 機械設備 2. (*computer*) hādowéa ハードウェア

hard work *n* kúrō 苦労 (go-kúrō ご苦労)

hard worker, hardworking staff *n* hataraki-mono 働き者・はたらき者

hardworking *adj* kinben (na) 勤勉(な)

hare *n* usagı うさぎ・ウサギ・兎

harm 1. *n* gái 害, songai 損害 2. *harms it* *v* sokonaimásu (sokonáu, sokonátte) 損ないます・そこないます(損なう, 損なって); *without ~* (*incident*) buji (ni) 無事・ぶじ(に); *no ~* ...shite mo mondai nai ...しても問題ない

harmful *adj* yūgai 有害(な)

harmless *adj* mugai (na) 無害(な)

harmonica *n* hāmonika ハーモニカ

harmony *n* chōwa 調和; *is in ~ with* ... to chōwa shimásu (suru, shite) ...と調和します(する, して)

harp *n* (*Japanese*) (o-)kóto (お)琴; (*Western*) hā'pu ハープ

harpoon *n* mori 銛・モリ

harpsichord *n* hāpushikōdo ハープシコード

harsh *adj* (*cruel*) zankoku (na) 残酷(な)

harvest 1. *n* minori 実り・みのり, shūkaku 収穫 2. *v* (*harvests it*) osamemásu (osaméru, osámete) 収めます・おさめます(収める, 収めて), shūkaku shimásu (suru, shite) 収穫します(する, して)

has → have

hash; *beef hash over rice* hayashi ráisu ハヤシライス

haste *n* isogí 急ぎ・いそぎ

hasten → hurry

hasty *adj* (*hurried*) isogí no 急ぎの; (*rash*) keisotsu (na) 軽率(な)

hat *n* bōshi 帽子; *bamboo hat* kása 笠・カサ

hatch *n* fuka 孵化

hatchet *n* nata なた, óno 斧・オノ, te-ono 手斧

hate *v* (... ga) iyádesu (...が) 嫌です; (... o) nikumimásu (nikúmu, nikúnde) (...を)憎みます・にくみます(憎む, 憎んで)

haughty *adj* gōman (na) 傲慢(な); *is/acts ~* ibari-másu (ibáru, ibátte) 威張ります・いばります(威張る, 威張って)

haul *n* (*goods in transit*) yusō-hin 輸送品

haunch *n* den-bu 臀部・でんぶ, koshi 腰・こし

haute couture *n* (*high fashion*) ōtokuchū´ru オートクチュール

have *v* (…ga) arimásu (áru, átte) (…が)あります (ある, あって), (…o) mótte imásu (iru, ite) (…を) 持っています・もっています(いる, いて); (*keeps, retains*) kakaemásu (kakaeru, kakaete) 抱えます・かかえます(抱える, 抱えて)

have someone do it *v* (hito ni sore o) sasemásu (saseru, sasete) (人にそれを)させます (させる, させて), (*as a favor*) shite moraimásu (morau, moratte) してもらいます(もらう, もらって)

have it done *v* (*by someone to another*) (hito ni sore o) saremásu (sareru, sarete) (人にそれを)されます(される, されて)

have no ... *v* (…ga) arimásén (nái, nákute) (…が)ありません(ない, なくて)

have to → must

Hawaii *n* Háwai ハワイ

hawk *n* taka たか・タカ・鷹

hay *n* magusa まぐさ・秣, hoshi-gusa 干し草・ホシグサ; ***hay fever*** kafun-shō 花粉症, arérúgii アレルギー

hazard *n* hazādo ハザード, (*danger*) kiken 危険・キケン

haze *n* móya もや・靄, (*mist*) kasumi かすみ・霞

hazelnut *n* hēzeru nattsu ヘーゼルナッツ

hazy; *gets* ~ kasumimásu (kasumu, kasunde) かすみます・霞みます(かすむ, かすんで)

he *n* káre 彼・かれ, anó-hito あの人 (*but use name, title, or role*; *often omitted*); (*that guy*) yátsu やつ・奴, yakko san やっこさん

he-... *n* no osú …のオス・…のオス

head *n* atamá 頭・あたま, kashirá 頭・かしら (o-kashira お頭); (*brains*) zunō 頭脳; (*leader*) kashirá 頭, chō´ 長, (*of a school*) kōchō 校長

head for ... *v* ni mukaimásu (mukau, mukatte) …に向かいます・…にむかいます(向かう, 向かって); … o mezashimásu (mezásu, mezáshite) …を目指します・をめざします(目指す, 目指して)

head over heels *adv* massáka-sama ni まっさかさまに・真っ逆さまに

headache *n* zutsū 頭痛; ***have a ~*** zutsū ga shimásu (suru, shite) 頭痛がします(する, して), atamá ga itái 頭が痛い

heading *n* (*caption*) midashi 見出し・みだし, (*title*) taitoru タイトル

headland *n* misaki 岬・みさき

headlight(s) *n* heddo ráito ヘッドライト, zenshōtō 前照灯; ***turns the ~ on/off*** heddo ráito o tsukemásu/ keshimásu ヘッドライトをつけます/ 消します

headline *n* midashi 見出し・みだし, heddo rain ヘッドライン

head office *n* honten 本店, (*corporate headquarter*) honsha 本社

headquarters *n* hónbu 本部; (*building; military*)

shiréi-bu 指令(司令)部; (*corporate headquarter*) honsha 本社

headstone *n* boseki 墓石, bohyō 墓標

headteacher *n* kōchō 校長

headway *n* zenshin 前進, shinpo 進歩

heady *adj* sēkyū (na) 性急(な)

heal *v* iyashimásu (iyasu, iyashite) 癒します・いやします(癒す, 癒して)

health *n* kenkō 健康, (*one's ~*) karada 体・身体・からだ; (*state of one's ~*) (go-)kigen (ご)機嫌, o-kagen お加減・おかげん; (*hygiene, sanitation*) eisei 衛生

health service *n* (*hospital*) byōin 病院

health insurance *n* kenkō hoken 健康保険

healthy *adj* kenkō (na) 健康・けんこう(な), génki (na) 元気・げんき(な), tassha (na) 達者 (な), mame (na) まめ(な); (*sturdy*) jōbu (na) 丈夫・じょうぶ(な); (*good for one's health*) karada ni íi 体にいい

heap 1. *n* yamá 山・やま, (*one*) hitó-yama 一山・ひとやま **2.** ~ *it up* *v* morimásu (moru, motte) 盛ります(盛る, 盛って)

hear *v* kikimásu (kiku, kiite) 聞きます・ひらきます(聞く, 聞いて); [HUMBLE] ukagaimásu (ukagau, ukagatte) 伺います・うかがいます(伺う, 伺って), uke-tamawaru (uke-tamawatte) 承ります・うけたまわります(承る, 承って)

hearer *n* kiki-te 聞き手

hearing test *n* **1.** (*checkup*) chōryoku kensa 聴力検査 **2.** (*exam*) hiyaringu tesuto ヒヤリング・テスト, hiyaringu shiken ヒヤリング試験, kikitori shiken 聞き取り試験

hearsay *n* (*rumor*) uwasa うわさ・噂

hearse *n* reikyū-sha 霊柩車

heart *n* shinzō 心臓; (*as seat of emotions*) kokóro 心・こころ(o-kokoro お心); (*the very center*) chūshin 中心; (*core, spirit*) shín 芯・シン; (*mind*) muné 胸, omói 思い; (*spirit*) ki 気

by heart *adv* (*from memory*) sóra de 空で・そらで

heartache *n* shintsū 心痛

heart attack *n* shinzō mahi 心臓麻痺, shinzō hossa 心臓発作

heartbreak *n* **1.** hitsū 悲痛 **2.** (*lost love*) shitsuren 失恋

heartburn *n* mune-yake 胸焼け

heartening *adj* kokoro-zuyoi 心強い・こころづよい

heartfelt *adj* kokóro kara (no) 心から・こころから(の)

heartless *adj* mujō (na) 無情(な), hakujō (na) 薄情(な)

heat 1. *n* atsu-sa 熱さ・暑さ・あつさ, netsú 熱 **2.** *heats it* *v* átsuku shimásu (suru, shite) 熱くします(する, して), nes-shimásu (nes-suru, nes-shite) 熱します(熱する, 熱して) **→ warm it up 3.** *it heats up* *v* átsuku narimásu (naru, natte) 熱く[暑く・あつく]なります(なる, なって), nes-shimásu (nes-suru, nes-shite) 熱します(熱する, 熱して)

heat island (effect) *n* hiito airando ヒートアイランド(現象)

heater *n* sutōˊbu ストーブ, híitā ヒーター, kanetsú-ki 加熱器

heath *n* are-chi 荒(れ)地

heating *n* (of room, etc.) danbō 暖房; *Japanese traditional quilt-covered heating device* kotatsu こたつ(o-kóta おこた)

heating saké *n* (o-)kan (お)燗, kán-zake 燗酒・かん酒

heatstroke *n* nissha-byō 日射病, nessha-byō 熱射病

heat wave *n* neppa 熱波

heaven *n* tén 天・てん; (sky) sóra 空・そら; (paradise) téngoku 天国・てんごく

heavy *n* omoi 重い・おもい; (onerous) kurushíi 苦しい・くるしい

heavy rain *n* ō-áme 大雨; (torrential downpour) gōˊu 豪雨

heavy snow *n* ō-yuki 大雪

heavy task *n* tsurai shigoto つらい仕事, kitsui shigoto きつい仕事, jūrōdo 重労働

heavy tax *n* jū-zei 重税

heavy work (load) → **heavy task**

heckling *n* yáji やじ・野次・ヤジ

hedge *n* ikegaki 生け垣・いけがき

hedonism *n* kairaku shugi 快楽主義, kyōraku shugi 享楽主義

heed *n* chūi 注意

heel *n* kakato かかと・踵

height *n* takasa 高さ; (stature) séi 背・せい = sé 背

heir *n* sōzoku-nin 相続人

helicopter *n* herikoputā ヘリコプター

helium *n* heriumu ヘリウム

hell *n* jigokú 地獄・じごく

hellish *adj* jigoku no yō (na) 地獄[じごく]のよう(な), hisan (na) 悲惨(な)

hello 1. (on phone) móshi moshi もしもし **2.** (saying at door) [FORMAL FORM] Gomen kudasái ごめん下さい. [CASUAL FORM] konnichi wa. こんにちは **3.** (on encounter) ā ああ + [NAME] and/or [TITLE]; yā やあ; gokigen yō ごきげんよう.

help 1. *n* (assistance) tetsudái (otétsudai) 手伝い・てつだい(お手伝い); (good offices) assen あっせん・斡旋, sewá 世話; (aid) énjo 援助, hójo 補助; (support) ōen 応援; *with the ~ of ...* no assen/ sewá de ...の あっせん/世話で **2.** *v* (assists) tetsudaimásu (tetsudáu, tetsudátte) 手伝います・てつだいます(手伝う, 手伝って); (rescues) tasukemásu (tasukéru, tasukéte) 助けます・たすけます(助ける, 助けて), sukuimásu (sukū, sukutte) 救います(救う, 救って); (supports) ōen shimásu (suru, shite) 応援します(する, して)

helper *n* joshu 助手; *household helper* o-tétsudai(-san) お手伝い・おてつだい(さん)

helping; *a second ~* (of rice, etc.) o-káwari お代わり・おかわり

hem *n* suso 裾・すそ

hemorrhoids *n* ji 痔・ぢ

hen *n* mendori 雌鳥・メンドリ

henchman *n* kó-bun 子分

hepatitis *n* kan'en 肝炎

her → **she**; **herself** → **oneself**

herb *n* kusá 草・クサ; yakusō 薬草・ヤクソウ, hāˊbu ハーブ

herd *n* mure 群れ

here *n* koko ここ; kochira こちら, kotchí こっち; *is ~* kitéimásu (iru, ite) 来ています(いる, いて); *Here!* (answering roll call) *exclam* Hái! はい! *Here (you are)!* Hái (kore désu)! はい(これです)! [HONORIFIC] Dōzo (kochira désu)! どうぞ(こちらです)!

here and there achí-kóchi あちこち; (various places) tokoro dókoro ところどころ・所々

hero *n* eiyū 英雄, hiirō ヒーロー

heroine *n* eiyū 英雄, hiroin ヒロイン

herpes *n* hōshin 疱疹, hérupesu ヘルペス

herring *n* níshin にしん・ニシン・鰊

hers (= of her) → **she**

hesitate *v* tameraimásu (tameráu, tamerátte) ためらいます・躊躇います(ためらう, ためらって); chūcho shimásu (suru, shite) ちゅうちょ[躊躇]します(する, して); enryo shimásu (suru, shite) 遠慮します・えんりょします(する, して)

hey! *interj* (masculine) óí! おい!, tchotto! ちょっと!, (feminine) nē! ねえ!, ano né! あのね!

hi! *interj* (masculine) yáˊ やあ! → **hello** → **hey**

Hibiya *n* Hibiya 日比谷
 Hibiya Park *n* Hibiya kōˊen 日比谷公園

hiccup *n* shákkuri しゃっくり

hide 1. *v* (hides it) kakushimásu (kakusú, kakushite) 隠します・かくします(隠す, 隠して); (it hides) kakuremásu (kakuréru, kakúrete) 隠れます・かくれます(隠れる, 隠れて) **2.** *n* (skin of an animal) kawa 皮, híkaku 皮革, (skin of a human) hifu 皮膚

hi-fi *n* haifai ハイファイ, sutereo ステレオ

high *adj* takái 高い・たかい; kō-... 高...; *highest* (maximum, top) saikō (no) 最高(の), saijō (no) 最上(の); *higher by ¥100* hyakuén-daka 百円高; *the highest (degree)* saikō-gendo 最高限度

high (barometric) pressure *n* kō-kíatsu 高気圧

high blood pressure *n* kō-kétsúatsu 高血圧

highball *n* haibōˊru ハイボール; (of shōchū´ 焼酎) chū-hai 酎ハイ・チューハイ; (whisky-and-water) mizuwari 水割り

highbrow 1. *n* interi インテリ **2.** *adj* (intellectual) chiteki (na) 知的(な)

high-class *adj* (high-grade/-ranking) kōkyū (na) 高級(な), haikurasu (no) ハイクラス(の)

high degree *n* kōˊdo 高度

highest *adj/adv* ichiban takái 一番高い, saikō (no) 最高(の); ichiban ue 一番上, saijō (no) 最上(の)

high fashion *n* ōtokuchūru オートクチュール

high-fiber *adj* sen'i no ōi 繊維の多い

high-fidelity *adj* kōseinō (no) 高性能(の)

high gear *n* kōsoku gí(y)a 高速ギア[ヤ]

highhanded *adj* gōin (na) 強引（な）
highhandedly *adv* gōin ni 強引に
highland *n* kōchi 高地
highlight *n* midokoro 見所, medama 目玉, hairaito ハイライト
highly *adv* ōi ni おおいに, hijō ni 非常に・ひじょうに, kiwamete 極めて
highpoint *n* chō´ten 頂点
highrise *adj* kōsō (no) 高層（の）
high-rise (office) building *n* kōsō ofisubiru 高層（オフィス）ビル
high school *n* kōtō-gákkō 高等学校, kō-kō 高校
high school student *n* kōkō´-sei 高校生
high sea *n* taikai/daikai 大海; soto-umi/gaiyō 外洋
high speed *adj* kōsoku 高速
highway *n* kaidō 街道, kokudō 国道, kōdō 公道; (*expressway*) kōsoku-dōro 高速道路
hijack 1. *v* (*airplane*) nottorimásu (nottóru, nottótte) 乗っ取ります（乗っ取る、乗っ取って）2. *n* haijakku ハイジャック
hijacker *n* nottorí-han 乗っ取り犯
hijacking *n* nottori-jíken 乗っ取り事件
hike, hiking *n* háikíngu (o shimásu; suru, shite) ハイキング（をします; する、して）
hilarious *adj* yukai (na) 愉快（な）
hilarity *n* tanoshii/yukai na kibun 楽しい/愉快な気分
hill *n* (*slope*) saká 坂; (*small mountain*) oka 丘・おか, koyama 小山
hilt *n* tsuká 塚・つか
him → **he; himself** → **oneself**
hind *adj* ushiro (no) 後ろの・うしろの
hind leg *n* ato-ashi 後肢, ushiro ashi 後ろ肢・うしろあし
hinder *v* samatagemásu (samatageru, samatagete) 妨げます・さまたげます（妨げる、妨げて）
hindrance *n* sashitsukae 差し支え・さしつかえ; (o-)jama (お)じゃま[邪魔]; koshō 故障; shōgai 障害
hinge 1. *n* chō-tsúgai ちょうつがい・蝶番 2. *v* hinge on ... ni sayū-saremásu (sayū-sareru, sayū-sarete) ...に左右されます（左右される、左右されて）
hinged door *n* hiraki-do 開き戸
hint 1. *n* hínto ヒント, honomekashí ほのめかし, anji 暗示, tegakari 手掛かり 2. *v* (*hints it*) honomekashimásu (hono-mekásu, hono-mekáshite) ほのめかします（ほのめかす、ほのめかして）, anji shimásu (suru, shite) 暗示します（する、して）
hinterland *n* oku-chi 奥地, nairiku-chi 内陸地
hip 1. *n* (*buttock*) shirí 尻・しり (o-shiri お尻), (*thigh*) mómo もも・股; (*loins*) koshi 腰・こし, hippu ヒップ 2. *adj* [SLANG] (*cool*) ikashita いかした, iketeru イケてる
hippopotamus *n* kaba かば・カバ・河馬
hiragana *n* hirágána ひらがな・平仮名
hire *v* yatoimásu (yatóu, yatótte) 雇います・やといます（雇う、雇って）; (*a professional*)

tanomimásu (tanómu , tanónde) 頼みます・たのみます（頼む、頼んで）
his (*of him*) → **he**
historian *n* rekishi-ka 歴史家
history *n* rekishi 歴史; *one's personal ~* rireki 履歴, keireki 経歴, (*resume*) rirekisho 履歴書
hit 1. *n* híttó ヒット; atari 当たり 2. *v* butsukemásu (butsukeru, butsukete) ぶつけます（ぶつける、ぶつけて）, uchimásu (útsu, útte) 打ちます・うちます（打つ、打って）; (*strike*) tatakimásu (tatáku, tatáite) 叩きます・たたきます（叩く、叩いて）; atemásu (ateru, atete) 当てます・あてます（当てる、当てて）3. *v* atarimásu (ataru, atatte) 当たります・あたります（当たる、当たって）; *gets ~* (*robbed, beset, wounded, killed*) yararemásu (yarareru, yararete) やられます（やられる、やられて）
hit and run *adj* 1. hikinige ひき逃げ 2. (*baseball*) hitto endo ran ヒット・エンド・ラン
hitch 1. *n* (*knot*) musubi-me 結び目・むすび目 2. *n* (*barrier*) shōgai 障害 3. *n,v* (*hitchhike*) hit-tchi-haiku (shimásu; suru, shite) ヒッチハイク（します; する、して）
hitherto *n* jū´rai 従来
hit home (*with/to one*) pin to kimásu (kúru, kité) ぴんときます（くる、きて）
hives *n* jinmashin じん麻疹・じんましん
hoard *v* takuwaemásu (takuwaeru, takuwaete) 蓄えます・たくわえます（蓄える、蓄えて）, (*buys up*) kaidame shimásu (suru, shite) 買いだめします（する、して）
hoarse *adj* hasukii (na) ハスキー（な）; shiwagareta しわがれた
hobby *n* shúmi 趣味・しゅみ, hobii ホビー; ohako おはこ・十八番 (= *hobbyhorse*)
hoe *n* kuwa くわ・クワ・鍬
Hokkaido *n* Hokkáidō 北海道
hold 1. *v* (*té ni*) mochimásu (mótsu, mótte) (手に)持ちます・もちます（持つ、持って）, mótte imásu (iru, ite) 持っています・もっています（いる、いて）; (*in arms*) dakimásu (daku, daite) 抱きます・だきます（抱く、抱いて）, (*or under the arm*) kakaemásu (kakaeru, kakaete) 抱えます・かかえます（抱える、抱えて）; (*an open umbrella*) sashimásu (sásu, sáshite) 差します・さします（差す、差して）; (*keeps in reserve*) tótte okimásu (oku, oite) 取って置きます（置く、置いて）; (*gives an event*) moyōshimásu (moyōsu, moyōshite) 催します・もよおします（催す、催して）; *~ in the mouth* (kuchi ni) fukumimásu (fukúmu, fukúnde) (口に)含みます（含む、含んで）2. *n* (*place to hold on*) tegákari 手掛かり
hold back *v* (*hesitates*) (go-)enryo shimásu (suru, shite) (ご)遠慮・えんりょします（する、して）
hold it *v* (sonomama de) machimásu (matsu, matte) (そのままで)待ちます（待つ、まって）, taiki shimásu (suru, shite) 待機します（する、して）
hold it up *v* (*lift*) sashi-agemásu (sashi-ageru,

sashi-agete) 差し上げます・さしあげます(差し
上げる, 差し上げて)

hole n aná 穴・あな; (*opening*) kuchi 口・クチ

hole-punch n kíri きり・キリ・錐

holiday n yasumí 休み・やすみ, kyūjitsu 休日;
(*official*) saijitsu 祭日, shukujitsu 祝日

Holland n Oranda オランダ

hollow 1. adj (*empty*) utsuro (na) うつろ(な)
2. n (*a dent*) kubomi くぼみ・窪み; *gets ~*
hekomimásu (hekomu, hekonde) へこみます・凹
みます(へこむ, へこんで)

holly n hiiragi ヒイラギ

holocaust n dai-gyakusatsu 大虐殺; *the*
Holocaust yudaya-jin (no) dai-gyakusatsu ユダヤ
人(の)大虐殺

home n uchi 家 (o-uchi お家), ... uchí ...家;
(*one's residence*) jitaku 自宅; (*household*) katei
家庭; (*of a product/crop*) sánchi 産地; *goes ~*
kaerimásu (káeru, káette) 帰ります・かえります
(帰る, 帰って)

home and abroad náigai 内外

(one's) **home area** kuni 国(o-kuni お国), inaka
いなか・田舎 (= *hometown*)

one's **parent's home** jikka 実家

home appliance n katei yō´gu/yō´hin 家庭用
具/用品

homebody n de-bushō 出不精

home help n hōmu herupā ホームヘルパー

homeland n sókoku 祖国, (*motherland*) bókoku
母国

homeless n hōmuresu ホームレス, furō´-sha
浮浪者

homely adj (*ugly*) bu-kíryō (na) 不器用[ぶきよ
う](な)

homemade adj tesei (no) 手製(の), tezúkuri (no)
手作り・てづくり(の)

homemade cake n jikasei kēki 自家製ケーキ,
hōmu-meido kēki ホームメイドケーキ

homemaker n shufu 主婦

homesick adj hōmu shikku (no) ホームシック
(の)

home stay n hōmu sutei ホームステイ

hometown n kōkyō 故郷; hōmu taun ホームタ
ウン; (*countryside*) inaka いなか・田舎; sato 里
(o-sato お里)

homework n (*student*) shukudai 宿題

homicide n **1.** (*murder*) satsujin 殺人 **2.** (*killer*)
satsujin-han 殺人犯

homosexual 1. n hómo ホモ **2.** adj dōséi ai (no)
同性愛(の)

homosexuality n dōséi ai 同性愛

honest adj shōjíkí (na) 正直・しょうじき(な),
katagi (na) 堅気(な); (*proper*) tadashíi 正しい・
ただしい; (*earnest*) majime (na) まじめ[真面目]
(な)

honestly adv shōjíki ni 正直に

honewort n mitsuba 三ツ葉・ミツバ

honey 1. n mítsu 蜜・ミツ, hachi-mitsu 蜂蜜・
ハチミツ **2.** interj hanii ハニー

Hong Kong n Hónkón ホンコン・香港

Honolulu n Honoruru ホノルル

honor n méiyo 名誉; (= "*face*") taimen 体面;
(*sense of obligation*) girí 義理

honorable adj (*respectable*) sonkeidekiru 尊敬で
きる, rippa na 立派な; (*famous*) chomei na 著名な

honorific (word) n keigo 敬語; *honorific prefix*
o- お・御; go- ご・御; (*for a few words*) on- 御,
mi- み・御, o-mi- おみ・御, gyo- 御

Honshu n Hónshū 本州

hood n **1.** (*of car*) bonnétto ボンネット **2.** (*for*
head) fūdo フード

hoodlum n yotamono よたもの・与太者; chinpíra
ちんぴら・チンピラ

hoof n hizume ヒヅメ・蹄

hook n **1.** n kagí カギ・鉤; (*snap*) hókku ホック;
fishing hook tsuribari 釣り針 **2.** v (*to hook a fish*)
(sakana o) trurimásu (tsuru, tsutte) 釣ります(釣る,
釣って); *~ up* setsuzoku shimásu (suru, shite) 接
続します(する, して) **3.** v (*to hang*) tsurushimásu
(tsurusu, tsurushite) 吊るします(吊るす, 吊るし
て), hikkakémásu (hikkakéru, hikkakéte) 引っ掛
けます(引っ掛ける, 引っ掛けて)

hookey, *plays ~* saborimásu (sabóru, sabótte)
さぼります(さぼる, さぼって), zuru-yásumi
shimásu (suru, shite) ずる休みします(する, して)

hoop n wa(-ka) 輪(っか); *a barrel hoop* n tagá
たが

hope 1. n nozomi 望み・のぞみ, kibō 希
望, (*anticipation*) mikomi 見込み, (*ambition*)
kokorozashi 志 **2.** *hopes for* v nozomimásu
(nozomu, nozonde) 望みます・のぞみます(望む,
望んで), kibō shimásu (suru, shite) 希望します
(する, して); *I ~ that ...* (da) to íi desu ...(だ)と
いいです

horizon n (*sea*) suihei sen 水平線, (*land*) chihei
sen 地平線

horizontal adj suihei (no) 水平(の)

hormone n horumon ホルモン

horn n (*of animal*) tsunó 角・ツノ; (*of car*) keiteki
警笛, kurakushon クラクション; (*music*) hórun
ホルン

hornet n suzumé-bachi スズメバチ・雀蜂

horrible adj osoroshíi 恐ろしい・おそろしい

horse n umá 馬 (**1:** i-tō, **2:** ni-tō, **3:** sán-tō; *how*
many nán-tō 何頭)

horse mackerel n áji アジ・鯵

horseman n kishu 騎手

horsepower n bariki 馬力

horse racing n keiba 競馬

horseradish n (*seiyō*) wásabi (セイヨウ)ワサ
ビ・山葵

hose n hōsu ホース → **stockings**

hospital n byōin 病院; *~ admission* nyūin 入院;
is in the ~ nyūin shite imásu (iru, ite) 入院してい
ます(いる, いて)

hospital head/director n ínchō 院長

hospitality n o-motenashi おもてなし, kantai
歓待

host *n* shújin 主人, téishu 亭主

hostage *n* (*captive*) hitojichi 人質

hostelry *n* minshuku 民宿

hostess *n* onna shújin 女主人; hósutesu ホステス

hostile *adj* tekii/tekitaishin/hankan o motta 敵意/敵対心/反感を持った

hostility *n* tekii 敵意

hot *adj* 1. atsúi 熱い・暑い・あつい; (*pungent, spicy*) karai からい・辛い 2. *gets* ~ nes-shimásu (nes-suru, nes-shite) 熱します・ねっします(熱する, 熱して)

hot air *n* (*idle talk*) baka-/muda-bánashi ばか/無駄話

hot blast *n* neppū 熱風

hot blood *n* tanki 短気

hot cake *n* hotto-kēki ホットケーキ, pan-kēki パンケーキ; *sells like hot cakes* (*popular*) ninki no aru 人気のある

hot dog *n* hotto-doggu ホットドッグ

hotel *n* hóteru ホテル

hotel bill *n* hoterú-dai ホテル代

hothouse *n* onshitsu 温室

hotline *n* hottorain ホットライン

hot plate *n* (*electric*) denki kónro 電気こんろ・電気コンロ, hotto purēto ホットプレート, (*gas*) gasu kónro ガスこんろ・ガスコンロ

hot spring *n* onsen 温泉

hot-spring cure tōji 湯治

hot water *n* oyu お湯, yú yu 湯・ゆ, (*burning hot water*) nettō 熱湯

hot-water bottle *n* yu-tánpo 湯たんぽ・ゆたんぽ

hour *n* jikan 時間・じかん (o-jíkan お時間)

hourglass *n* suna-dokei 砂時計

house *n* uchi 家 (o-uchi お家), ... uchi ...家, ié 家 (1: íkken 一軒, 2: ní-ken 二軒, 3: sán-gen 三軒; *how many* nán-gen 何軒); taku 宅, ...-ya ...家

house addition/extension *n* tatemashi 建て増し

house dust *n* (ie no) hokori (家の)ほこり

house refuse *n* gomí ごみ・ゴミ

house rent *n* yá-chin 家賃

rental house *n* (*house for rent or rented house*) kashi-ya 貸家

your house o-taku お宅

housefly *n* hae はえ・ハエ・蝿

household *n* katei 家庭; shotái 所帯

household altar *n* (*Buddhist*) butsudan 仏壇, (*Shinto*) kami-dana 神棚

household helper *n* otétsudai(-san) お手伝い・おてつだい(さん)

household budget *n* 家計

housekeeper *n* kaséi-fu 家政婦

housekeeping *n* kasei 家政, shotái 所帯

housekeeping book *n* kakei-bo 家計簿

house sit; *is house sitting* (*for*) (...no) kawari ni súnde imásu (...の)代わりに住んでいます

houseware *n* (*store*) nichiyōhin-ten 日用品店

housewife *n* shúfu 主婦

housework *n* kaji 家事

housing development *n* danchi 団地

housing project *n* (kōei) danchi (公営)団地

how *adv* dō どう, [DEFERENTIAL] ikága いかが・如何

How are you (feeling)? *interj* Go-kigen (wa) ikága desu ka. ご機嫌(は)いかが[如何]ですか. O-génki desu ka. お元気ですか.

how come *adv* dō´-shite どうして

How do you do? *interj* (*on first being introduced*) Hajimemáshite. 初めまして・はじめまして.

how far/long *adv* (*distance*) dono-gurai/kurai どの位・どのくらい

how long *adv* (*time length*) ítsu made いつまで; ítsu kara いつから

how many *adj* íkutsu いくつ (o-ikutsu おいくつ); (*small things*) ~ *pieces* nán-ko 何個; (*long things*) nán-bon 何本; (*flat things*) ~ *sheets* nán-mai 何枚; (*small animals, fish/bugs*) nán-biki 何匹; (*large animals*) nan-tō 何頭; (*birds, rabbits*) nán-ba 何羽; (*machines, vehicles*) nán-dai 何台; (*books, magazines*) ~ *copies* nán-satsu 何冊; ~ *days* nán-nichi 何日; ~ *people* nán-nin 何人, nánmei 何名; ~ *times* nán-do 何度, nán-kai 何回, nánbén 何遍 (*how many fold*) nán-bai 何杯; ~ *cupfuls* nán-bai 何杯; ~ *years* nán-nen 何年; ~ *years old* íkutsu いくつ (o-ikutsu おいくつ), nán-sai 何歳

how much *adj* íkura いくら (o-ikura おいくら), dono-gurai どの位, ika-hodo いか程; dónna ni どんなに

how old *adj* íkutsu いくつ (o-ikutsu おいくつ); nán-sai 何歳

how true *interj* naru-hodo (sō desu né) なるほど[成る程](そうですね)

however *adv* kéredo (mo) けれど(も), shikáshi しかし, démo でも, dátte だって, tokoróga ところが, tádashi ただし・但し; (*to be sure*) móttómo もっとも

hug *v* daki-shimemásu (daki-shiméru, daki-shíme-te) 抱き締めます・だきしめます(抱き締める, 抱き締めて)

huge *adj* kyodai (na) 巨大(な), bakudai (na) 莫大・ばくだい(な)

huh?! *exclam* hóra! ほら!; hē へー; *Interesting, huh?!* Omoshiroi-desho!? 面白いでしょ!?, (*male*) Omoshiroi-daro!? 面白いだろ!?

hull *n* 1. (*of grain, etc.*) kawa 皮, kara 殻, (*of strawberry*) heta へた 2. (*of boat*) sentai 船体

human being *n* ningen 人間; jínrui 人類

humankind → **human being**

human feelings/nature *n* nínjō 人情

humanities *n* jinbun kagaku 人文科学

humanity *n* ningen-sei 人間性, hyūmanitii ヒューマニティ

human rights *n* jinken 人権

humble *adj* (*modest*) kenkyo (na) 謙虚(な)

humid *adj* (*in summer*) mushi-atsúi 蒸し暑い, (*gets sultry*) mushimásu (músu, múshite) 蒸します

(蒸す, 蒸して) ; (*in winter*) shimeppoi 湿っぽい・しめっぽい

humidity *n* shikki/shikke 湿気, shitsúdo 湿度

humiliating *adj* kuyashíi 悔しい・くやしい

humor *n* yū´moa ユーモア

humorous *adj* yū´morasu na ユーモラスな, yū´moa no aru ユーモアのある, kek-kei na 滑稽[こっけい]な

hunch up se o maruku shimásu (suru, shite) 背を丸くする(する, して)

hundred *n* hyakú 百・100; *how many hundred* nán-byaku 何百

hundred million *n* óku 億

hundred thousand *n* jū-mán 十万・100,000

hungry 1. *n* gets ~ o-naka ga sukimásu (suku, suite) おなかがすきます(すく, すいて), hara ga heri-másu (heru, hette) 腹が減ります・腹がへります(減る, 減って) **2.** *adj* kūfuku (no) 空腹(の)

hunt *v* kári/ryō´ o shimásu (suru, shite) 狩り/猟をします(する, して) → **look for**

hunter *n* káriudo 狩人, ryō´-shi 猟師, hantā ハンター

hunting *n* kári 狩り, ryō´ 猟

hurdle *n* (*obstacle*) ohōgai(butsu) 障害物, (*sport*) hādoru ハードル

hurray! *exclam* banzái! 万歳・バンザイ!

hurricane *n* bōfū 暴風, harikēn ハリケーン

hurry *v* isogimásu (isógu, isóide) 急ぎます・いそぎます(急ぐ, 急いで) ; tobashimásu (tobasu, tobashite) 飛ばします・とばします(飛ばす, 飛ばして)

in a big hurry ō-ísogi (de/no) 大急ぎ(で/の)

hurt 1. *v it hurts* (*is painful*) *v* itái 痛い・いたい **2.** *v gets hurt* kegá o shimásu (suru, shite) けが[怪我]をします(する, して) **3.** *adj* (*injures*) itamemásu (itaméru, itámete) 傷めます(傷める, 傷めて) ; (*damages*) sokonaimásu (sokonáu, sokonátte) 損ないます・そこないます(損なう, 損なって) **4.** *n* kizu 傷, kega けが, kutsū 苦痛

husband *n* otto 夫, shújin 主人, danna-san/-sama 旦那さん/様, téishu 亭主

husband and wife n fū´fu 夫婦; *both ~* fūfu-tomo 夫婦共・夫婦とも

my husband otto 夫, shújin 主人, taku 宅

your husband go-shújin ご主人

hut *n* koya 小屋・こや

hydrant → **fireplug**

hydrogen *n* súiso 水素

hygiene *n* eisei 衛生

hypothesis *n* katei 仮定・かてい, zentei 前提

I

I *n* [FORMAL *for male*] watashi わたし・私, [FORMAL] watakushi わたくし・私; [HUMBLE] temae 手前; (*male*) boku ぼく・僕; (*male, unrefined*) ore おれ・オレ・俺; (*female*) atashi あたし

I see! *interj* naru-hodo なるほど・成る程, wakatta わかった・分かった

...-ic, ...-ical ...-teki (na) ...的(な)

ibis *n* toki トキ・鴇

ice *n* kōri 氷・こおり

iceberg *n* hyō´zan 氷山

icebox *n* reizō´ko 冷蔵庫, reitō´ko 冷凍庫 → **refrigerator**

ice cream *n* aisu-kuríimu アイスクリーム

ice cube *n* kaku-hyō 角氷・かくひょう

ice hockey *n* aisu-hokkē アイス・ホッケー

ice rink *n* sukēto-rinku スケート・リンク

ice skate *n* aisu-sukēto アイス・スケート

icicle *n* tsurara つらら・ツララ・氷柱

icing *n* aishingu アイシング

icon *n* **1.** (*computer*) aikon アイコン; *icon box* aikon-bokkusu アイコン・ボックス **2.** (*image*) zō 像

icon memory *n* zanzō 残像

iconify *v* aikon-ka shimásu (suru, shite) アイコン化します(する, して)

iconoclast *n* seizō-hakai-sha 聖像破壊者

idea *n* (*thought*) kangáe 考え・かんがえ, omóitsuki 思いつき; kokoro atari 心当たり; (*opinion*) íken 意見, (*your opinion*) go-íken ご意見; aidéa アイデア; (*intention, aim*) nerai 狙い → **rough idea**

ideal *adj* risō-teki (na) 理想的(な); (*most desirable*) motte-kói (no) もってこい(の)

idealism *n* risō-shugi 理想主義

idealist *n* risō-shugi-sha 理想主義者

identical *adj* hitoshíi 等しい・ひとしい → **same**

identical twins *n* ichiransei-sōsēji 一卵性双生児

identified; *gets ~*shiremásu (shireru, shirete) 知れます(知れる, 知れて)

identity card *n* mibun-shōmei-sho 身分証明書, ai dii-kādo IDカード

ideologist *n* kannen ron-sha 観念論者

ideology *n* ideorogii イデオロギー, kannen 観念, shisō 思想, kangae 考え

idiot *n* (*fool*) báka ばか・バカ, manuke 間抜け・まぬけ

idle 1. *v* (*is lazy*) namakemásu (namakéru, namákete) 怠けます・なまけます(怠ける, 怠けて); (*useless, unavailing*) **2.** *adj* muda (na) 無駄・むだ(な)

idle talk baka/muda-bánashi ばか/無駄話

idleness *n* taida 怠惰, bushō 無精

idly *adv* búrabura ぶらぶら・ブラブラ

i.e. *adv* sunawachi すなわち, iikaereba 言い換え
れば

if *conj* móshi … (shi-) tára もし…(し)たら; …
(no) ba(w)ai … (の)場合;
  if by any chance *conj* mán'ichi 万一
  if you prefer/like *conj* nan-nára なんなら
  if I remember rightly *conj* táshika 確か・たしか
  if you don't mind *conj* yoroshíkáttara よろしか
  ったら・宜しかったら; nan-nára なんなら
  if you don't want to/if you like *conj* nan-nára
  なんなら
  if there be *conj* áreba あれば, árya ありゃ

ignition *n* tenka 点火; ~ *switch* (kuruma no)
tenka suítchi (車の)点火スイッチ; *turns on the* ~
tenka suítchi o iremásu (ireru, irete) 点火スイッチ
を入れます(入れる, 入れて)

ignorance *n* muchi 無知

ignore *v* múshi shimásu (suru, shite) 無視します
(する, して)

ikebana *n* ikebana 生け花・いけばな

ileac *adj* kaichō (no) 回腸(の)

ileus *n* (*medical*) ireusu イレウス, chō-heisoku
腸閉塞

ill → sick; bad

illegal *adj* fuhō (no) 不法(の), ihō (no) 違法(の)
  illegal work(er) *n* fuhō shūrō(-sha) 不法就労
  (者)

illicit *adj* yamí no 闇の・やみの, fuhō (na) 不法
(な), mumenkyo (no) 無免許(の),

illness *n* byōki 病気

ill-tempered *adj* ijí ga warúi 意地が悪い・意地
がわるい

illuminate *v* terashimásu (terásu, teráshite) 照らし
ます・てらします(照らす, 照らして)

illumination *n* iruminēshon イルミネーション,
shōmei 照明

illustration *n* zukai 図解, irasuto (rēshon) イラス
ト(レーション)

illustrator *n* irasutorētā イラストレーター

ill-will *n* (*resentment*) uramí 恨み・うらみ,
(*hostile feeling*) teki-i 敵意

image *n* (ga)zō (画)像, imēji イメージ, (*video
picture*) eizō 映像; (*psychological, social*) imē´ji
イメージ

imagery *n* 1. (*image*) imēji イメージ, shinshō 心
象 2. (*figure of speech*) hiyu 比喩・比ゆ

imaginary *adj* kakū (no) 架空(の), sōzōjō (no)
想像上(の)

imagination *n* sōzō 想像, (*imaginative power*)
sōzō-ryoku 想像力

imagine *v* sōzō shimásu (suru, shite) 想像します
(する, して) → **suppose, think**

imbalance *n* fu-antei 不安定, anbaransu アンバ
ランス

imbecile 1. *adj* teinō (na) 低脳(な) 2. *n* teinō na
hito 低脳な人

imitate *v* … no mane o shimásu (suru, shite) …の
まね[真似]をします(する, して), …o manemásu
(maneru, manete) …をまね[真似]します(する,

して); nisemásu (niseru, nisete) 似せます(似せる,
似せて)

imitation *n* 1. (*man-made*) jinzō 人造; (*fake*) nise
偽, mozō-hin 模造品, nise-mono 偽物 2. (*mimicry*)
mane まね・真似

imitator *n* mohō-sha 模倣者

immediate *adj* tōmen (no) 当面(の), mokuzen
(no) 目前(の)

immediately *adv* súgu (ni) すぐ(に), sassokú
早速・さっそく, jiki (ni) じき(に), tádachi-ni
直ちに・ただちに, tachimachi (ni) たちまち
(に); (*without waiting*) matánaide 待たないで

immense *adj* tái-shita 大した・たいした; bakudai
(na) 莫大・ばくだい(な)

immigrant *n* imin 移民
  immigrant laborer *n* imin-rōdō-sha 移民労
  働者

immigrate *v* ijū shimásu (suru, shite) 移住します
(する, して)

immigration *n* (*entry*) nyūkoku 入国
  immigration office *n* nyūkoku kanri-kyoku 入国
  管理局
  immigration control office *n* nyūkoku-kanri-
  jimú-sho 入国管理事務所

imminent *adj* sashisematta 差し迫った・さしせ
まった, majika (no) 間近(の)

immoderately *adv* múyami ni むやみに

immoral *adj* fu-dō´toku (na) 不道徳(な)

immorality *n* fu-dō´toku 不道徳

immortal *adj* fu-shi (no) 不死(の); fu-metsu (no)
不滅(の); fu-kyū (no) 不朽(の)
  immortal poetry *n* fu-metsu no si 不滅の詩
  immortal soul *n* fu-shi no tamashii 不死の魂
  immortal words *n* fu-kyū no kotoba 不朽の言葉
  immortal work *n* fu-kyū no meisaku 不朽の名作

immunization *n* yobō-chūsha 予防注射

impartial *adj* kōhei (na) 公平(な); kōsei (na)
公正(な)

impartiality *n* kōsei 公正

impatient *adj* ki ga mijikái 気が短い・気がみじ
かい

impediment *n* shōgai 障害; (*hindrance*)
sashitsukae 差し支え・さしつかえ

imperial *adj* téikoku (no) 帝国(の)

imperialism *n* teikoku-shúgi 帝国主義, teisei
帝政

impertinent *adj* namaiki (na) 生意気・なまい
き(な)

impetus *n* hazumi 弾み・はずみ

impish *adj* itazura na いたずらな, wanpaku na
わんぱくな

implant 1. *n* (*tooth*) sáshi-ba 差し歯, (*medical*)
ishoku 移植 2. *v* umekomimásu (umekomu,
umekónde) 埋め込みます(埋め込む, 埋め込ん
で), ishoku shimásu (suru, shite) 移植します
(する, して)

implement 1. *n* (*tool*) yō´gu 用具; (*apparatus*)
kígu 器具 2. *v* jik-kō shimásu (suru,
shite) 実行します(する, して)

imply *v* **1.** fukumimás<u>u</u> (fukúmu, fukúnde) 含みます・ふくみます(含む, 含んで) **2.** → **hint**

impolite *adj* búrei (na) 無礼(な), shitsúrei (na) 失礼・しつれい(な)

import *v* yunyū shimás<u>u</u> (suru, sh<u>i</u>te) 輸入します(する, して); (*goods*) yunyū-hin 輸入品

importance; *a matter of* ~ dáijí 大事, jū-dái-ji 重大事

important *adj* jūyō (na) 重要(な), taisetsu (na) 大切・たいせつ(な), jūdai (na) 重大(な), (*precious*) daijí (na) 大事(な); tái-sh<u>i</u>ta (kotó) 大した・たいした(事[こと]); omoi 重い・おもい

importune *v* kongan shimás<u>u</u> (suru, sh<u>i</u>te) 懇願します(する, して), segamimás<u>u</u> (segamu, segande) せがみます(せがむ, せがんで)

impose; ~ *it* *v* kuwaemás<u>u</u> (kuwaeru, kuwaete) 加えます・くわえます(加える, 加えて)

imposition *n* **1.** (*forcible*) kyōsei 強制 **2.** (*obligation*) gimu 義務

impossible *adj* dekínai 出来ない・できない, fukánō (na) 不可能(な)
impossible! *interj* másaka まさか

imposter *n* sagi-shi 詐欺師

impotence *n* inpotensu インポテンス

impotent *adj* muryoku (na) 無力(な)

impression *n* inshō 印象

impressionism *n* inshō-shugi 印象主義

impressive *adj* inshō-teki (na) 印象的(な)

imprisonment *n* tōgoku 投獄

improve *v* **1.** (*it improves*) naorimás<u>u</u> (naóru, naótte) 直ります・なおります(直る, 直って), yóku narimás<u>u</u> (náru, nátte) 良くなります・よくなります(なる, なって) **2.** (*improves it*) naoshimás<u>u</u> (naósu, naósh<u>i</u>te) 直します・なおします(直す, 直して), yóku shimás<u>u</u> (suru, sh<u>i</u>te) 良くします・よくします(する, して)

improvement *n* kaizen 改善

impudent *adj* atsukamashii 厚かましい・あつかましい, zūzūshii ずうずうしい・図々しい

impulse *n* hazumi 弾み・はずみ, shigeki 刺激, shōdō 衝動

impulsive *adj* shōdō-teki (na) 衝動的(な)

impunity *n* buji 無事

in *prep* ... de ... で, (*located in*) ...ni ...に; (*inside*) ...no náka (de/ni) ...の中・...のなか (で/に); (*resident in*) zai- ... 在...
come in *v* (... ni) háitte kimás<u>u</u> (kúru, k<u>i</u>té) (...に)入って来ます・はいってきます(来る, 来て)
go in *v* (... ni) hairimás<u>u</u> (háiru, háitte) ...に入ります(入る, 入って), háitte ikimás<u>u</u> (iku, itte) 入って行きます(行く, 行って)
let/put in *v* (... ni) iremás<u>u</u> (ireru, irete) (...に)入れます(入れる, 入れて)

inadvertently *adv* tsúi つい, ukkari うっかり

inadvisable *adj* mazúi まずい

inbound (*to Tokyo*) *adj* nobori (no) 上り(の)

incense *n* kō 香・コウ; (o-)sénkō お線香, sénkō 線香・センコウ

inception *n* kaishi 開始, hajimari はじまり・始まり

incessantly *adv* sh<u>i</u>kiri-ni しきりに

incest *n* kinshin sōkan 近親相姦

incentive *n* dōki 動機

inch **1.** *n* (...)ínchi (...)インチ; (*Japanese*) (...-)sún (...)寸 **2.** *v* (*to make very slowly*) yukkuri/ sukoshi zutsu/ noronoro ugokimás<u>u</u> (ugoku, ugoite) ゆっくり/少しずつ/ノロノロ動きます (動く, 動いて)

incident *n* jíken 事件, jíhen 事変

incidentally *adv* (*by the way*) sore wa sō´ to それはそうと, tokoró de ところで, chinami ni ちなみ[因み]に, tsuide ni ついでに, tokí ni 時に・ときに

incision *n* sekkai 切開

incite *v* aorimás<u>u</u> (aóru, aótte) あおります(あおる, あおって), shigeki shimás<u>u</u> (suru, sh<u>i</u>te) 刺激します(する, して)

inclination *n* katamuki 傾き・かたむき; (*intention*) íkō 意向

include *v* iremás<u>u</u> (ireru, irete) 入れます・いれます(入れる, 入れて), komemás<u>u</u> (koméru, kómete) 込めます(込める, 込めて), fukumemás<u>u</u> (fukuméru, fukúmete) 含めます・ふくめます(含める, 含めて); (*covers all items*) mō´ra shimás<u>u</u> (suru, sh<u>i</u>te) 網羅します(する, して)

including ... *prep* o irete/fukúmete ... を入れて/含めて; ...-tsuki ...付き・つき

income *n* shotoku 所得, shūnyū 収入
income tax *n* shotokú-zei 所得税

inconsistency *n* mujun 矛盾

inconsistent *adj* **is ~** mujun sh<u>i</u>te imás<u>u</u> (iru, ite) 矛盾しています(いる, いて)

inconvenience **1.** *n* (*trouble taken*) tesū´ 手数 (o-tesū お手数), tékazu 手数, futsugō 不都合 **2.** ... ni meiwaku/tesū o kakemás<u>u</u> (kakeru, kakéte) ...に迷惑/手数を掛けます(掛ける, 掛けて)

inconvenient *adj* fúben (na) 不便(な); fú-jiyū (na) 不自由(な)

increase **1.** *v* (*it increases/increases it*) mashimás<u>u</u> (masu, mash<u>i</u>te) 増します・まします(増す, 増して); (*it /they increase(s)*) fuemás<u>u</u> (fuéru, fúete) 増えます・ふえます(増える, 増えて), (*increases it/them*) fuyashimás<u>u</u> (fuyásu, fuyásh<u>i</u>te) 増やします・ふやします(増やす, 増やして) **2.** *n* (*an increase*) mashi 増し; zōka 増加, zōdai 増大, zōshin 増進

increasingly *adv* masú-masu ますます・益々

incur *v* (*unfair treatment, tribulation*) kōmurimás<u>u</u> (kōmúru, kōmútte) 被ります・こうむります(被る, 被って)

indecent *adj* gehín (na) 下品(な); (*obscene*) waisetsu (na) わいせつ・猥褻(な)

indeed *adv* honto ni ほんとに・本当に, hontō ni ほんとうに・本当に, jitsú ni 実に・じつに, tashika ni 確かに・たしかに; (*of course*) móttomo もっとも・最も; (*as we might expect*) sasuga (ni) さすが(に)

indefinite adj fu̱tei (no) 不定(の), fumeiryō (na) 不明瞭(な)

indemnify v hoshō shima̱su̱ (suru, shi̱te) 保証します(する, して)

indemnity n baishō(-kin) 賠償(金), (indemnity allowance) hoshō-kin 補償金

indemnity insurance n songai hoken 損害保険

indemnity issue n baishō-kin mondai 賠償金問題

indemnity period n hoshō kikan 補償期間

independence n dokuritsu 独立

independent adj dokuritsu shi̱ta … 独立した…; is ~ dokuritsu shi̱te ima̱su̱ (iru, ite) 独立しています(いる, いて)

index n sakuin 索引・さくいん, midashi 見出し・みだし, indekkusu インデックス

index card n sakuin kādo 索引カード

index finger n hitosashi yubi 人差し指・ひとさしゆび

index function n shisū kansū 指数関数

India n Índo インド

Indian n 1. Indó-jin インド人 2. American indian Índian インディアン

India ink n sumí 墨; India ink painting sumi-e 墨絵

indicate v shimeshima̱su̱ (shimesu, shimeshi̱te) 示します・しめします(示す, 示して); sashima̱su̱ (sásu, sáshi̱te) 指します・さします(指す, 指して); shi̱teki shima̱su̱ (suru, shi̱te) 指摘します(する, して), shíji shima̱su̱ (suru, shi̱te) 指示します(する, して)

indication n shíji 指示, (token, sign) shirushi しるし・印

indicator n (car) uinkā ウインカー

indict v kiso shima̱su̱ (suru, shi̱te) 起訴します(する, して)

indictment n kiso 起訴

indifferent to … adj ni mu-kánshin (no) …に無関心(の)

indigent n (people) hinkon-sha 貧困者

indigestion n shōka-fúryō 消化不良

indignant; adj gets ~ fungai shima̱su̱ (suru, shi̱te) 憤慨します(する, して), ikidorima̱su̱ (ikidó'ru, ikidó'tte) 憤ります・いきどおります(憤る, 憤って)

indignation n fungai 憤慨, ikidóri 憤り・いきどおり

indignity n bujoku 侮辱, kutsujoku 屈辱

indigo n (Japanese indigo plant) ái 藍・アイ; (Japanese indigo dye) ái zome 藍染め

indirect adj kansetsu (no) 間接(の)
indirect kiss n kansetsu kisu 間接キス
indirect lighting n kansetsu shōmei 間接照明
indirect medical cost n kansetsu iryōhi 間接医療費

indirectly adv kansetsu ni 間接に

indiscreet adj keisotsu (na) 軽率(な)

indiscriminate adj musabetsu (no) 無差別(の), yatara na やたらな, mechaku̱cha (na) めちゃくちゃ・メチャクチャ(な)

indiscriminately adv yatara ni やたらに, múyami ni むやみに

indispensable adj hissu (no) 必須(の), fukaketsu (no) 不可欠(の)

indispensability n fukaketsu 不可欠

individual 1. adj kojin-teki (na) 個人的(な) 2. n (a person) kójin 個人

individuality n kosei 個性

individually adv betsu betsu ni 別々に

indolence n taida 怠惰, namake 怠け・なまけ

Indonesia n Indonéshia インドネシア

Indonesian n (language) Indonesia-go インドネシア語, (person) Indonéshiá-jin インドネシア人

indoors adv uchi (no náka) de/ni 家(の中)で/に

indoor shoes n 1. (in school) uwabaki 上履き 2. (in room) shi̱tsunaibaki 室内履き

indulgent adj kandai (na) 寛大(な), amai 甘い

industrialization n kō´gyō-ka 工業化, sangyō-ka 産業化

industrious adj kinben (na) 勤勉(な)

industry n kō´gyō 工業, sangyō 産業, gyōkai 業界
industry analyst n gyōkai anarisuto 業界アナリスト
industry bookkeeping n kōgyō boki 工業簿記

in effect yō-súru ni 要するに・ようするに

inept adj hetá (na) へた[下手](な)

inequality n hu-kōhei 不公平, fu-byōdō 不平等

inequilateral triangle n hu-tōhen sankakkei 不等辺三角形

inequity n hu-kōhei 不公平, fu-kōsei 不公正

inertia n (physics) kansei 慣性, dasei 惰性

inevitable adj yondokoro-nái よんどころない・拠ん所無い, shi̱kata-nái 仕方ない・しかたない

inevitably adv kanarazu 必ず・かならず; nán to shi̱témo 何としても・なんとしても; iyaō-naku いやおう[否応]なく

inexpensive adj yasui 安い

inexperience n mu-keiken 無経験

inexperienced adj keiken busoku (no) 経験不足(の)

inexpert adj hetá (na) へた[下手](な)

infancy n (childhood) yōnen-ki 幼年期

infant n yō´ji 幼児, shō´ni 小児, akanbō 赤ん坊・あかんぼう, aka-chan 赤ちゃん

infantile paralysis n shōni-máhi 小児麻痺

infantry n hohei 歩兵

infect v utsushima̱su̱ (utsúsú, utsúshi̱te) 移します・うつします(移す, 移して)

infection n 1. kansen 感染 2. (infectious disease) densenbyō 伝染病
virus infection uirusu kansen ウイルス感染

infer v suitei shima̱su̱ (suru, shi̱te) 推定します(する, して)

inference n suitei 推定

inferior adj furyō (no) 不良(の); is ~ ochima̱su̱ (ochíru, óchi̱te) 落ちます・おちます(落ちる, 落ちて), otorima̱su̱ (otoru, ototte) 劣ります・おとります(劣る, 劣って); yuzurima̱su̱ (yuzuru, yuzutte) 譲ります・ゆずります(譲る, 譲って) makema̱su̱ (makeru, makete) 負けます・まけます(負ける、負けて)

inferiority complex n konpurekkusu コンプレックス, rettō-kan 劣等感

inflation n infure インフレ

influence n (*effect*) eikyō 影響, ...séi ...せい; (*power*) séiryoku 勢力

influential adj yūryoku (na) 有力(な)

influenza → flu

inform v kikasemásu (kikaseru, kikasete) 聞かせます(聞かせる、聞かせて), shirasemásu (shiraseru, shirasete) 知らせます・しらせます (知らせる、知らせて), tsugemásu (tsugeru, tsugete) 告げます・つげます(告げる、告げて); (*instructs*) oshiemásu (oshieru, oshiete) 教えます・おしえます(教える、教えて); (*tells*) mimí ni iremásu (ireru, irete) 耳に入れます(入れる、入れて)

informal adj hi-kō´shiki (no) 非公式(の)

information n jōhō 情報, shirase 知らせ・しらせ; (*guidance*) annái 案内; (*reception desk*) uke-tsuke 受付

information desk n annai-jo 案内所, furonto フロント

information technology n jōhō gijutsu 情報技術, jōhō kogaku 情報工学, infomēshon tekunorojii インフォメーション・テクノロジー

informed adj chishiki no aru 知識のある, jōhō ni motozuita 情報にもとづいた

informer n mikkoku-sha 密告者, jōhō-ya 情報屋, jōhō-teikyō-sha 情報提供者

infotainment n (*documentary film*) dokyumentarii dorama ドキュメンタリードラマ

infraction n (*violation*) ihan 違反

infrared rays n sekigai-sen 赤外線

infrequent adj tama no たまの, mare na まれ [稀]な

infrequently adv tama ni たまに, mare ni まれ [稀]に

infringement n ihan 違反

infusion n chūnyū 注入, yueki 輸液

ingredient n (*component*) séibun 成分; (*raw material*) zairyō´ 材料; (*cooking ingredient*) shokuzai 食材

inherit v (*succeeds to*) tsugimásu (tsugu, tsuide) 継ぎます(継ぐ、継いで)

injection n chūsha 注射
preventive injection yobō-chūsha 予防注射

injure v 1. kega (o) saseru 怪我(を)させる, itamemásu (itaméru, itámete) 傷めます(傷める、傷めて); (*damages it*) sokonaimásu (sokonáu, sokonátte) 損ないます(損なう、損なって) 2. ~ *it* kizu tsukemásu (tsukeru, tsukete) 傷つけます(傷つける、傷つけて); kega o sasemásu (saseru, sasete) 怪我をさせます(させる、させて)

injured adj kizutsuita 傷ついた, fōshōshita 負傷した
injured person n kega-nin けが人

injury n kegá けが・怪我; (*damage*) gái 害, higai 被害

ink n inki インキ, inku インク
ink stick, India ink n sumí 墨

inkjet printer n inkujetto purintā インクジェット・プリンター

inkstone n suzurí 硯・スズリ
inkstone case n suzurí-bako 硯箱

inlaid work n zōgan 象眼・象嵌

inland adj (*domestic*) kokúnai (no) 国内(の)

Inland Sea n Seto-náikai 瀬戸内海

...-in-law n girí no ... 義理の...

inlet n (*opening*) kuchi 口

inn n (*Japanese-style*) ryokan 旅館; yado-ya 宿屋, yádo 宿 (o-yado お宿)

inner adj 1. (*inside*) naibu no 内部の, uchigawa no 内側の 2. (*secret*) kakureta 隠れた 3. (*one's mind*) naimen-teki na 内面的な
inner cloth n shitagi 下着
inner moat n uchi-bori 内堀(り)

innocent adj (*naive*) mújaki (na) 無邪気(な); múku (na) 無垢(な); (*not guilty*) múzai (no) 無罪(の)
innocent baby n muku na akanbō 無垢な赤ん坊
innocent lie n warugi no nai uso 悪気のない嘘 [うそ]
innocent mischief n warugi no nai itazura 悪気のない悪戯[いたずら]

innumerable adj musū (no) 無数(の), kazoe-kire nai 数え切れない

inoculation n yobō-chū´sha 予防注射

inordinate adj hogai (na) 法外(な)

in other words → word

in particular → particular

inpatient n nyūin-kanja 入院患者

in pieces → piece

inquire v toimásu (tou, tōte) 問います(問う、問うて) **→ ask**

inquiry n (o-)toiawase (お)問い合わせ; (o-)ukagai (お)伺い; (*survey*) chō´sa 調査

inquisitive adj monózuki (na) 物好き(な)

inquisitiveness n kōkíshin 好奇心

in rapid succession → succession

insane adj ki-chigái (no) 気違い(の); *goes* ~ ki ga kuruimásu (kurū´, kurútte) 気が狂います(狂う、狂って)

insect n konchū 昆虫・コンチュウ, (*bug*) mushi 虫・ムシ (**1:** ip-píki 一匹, **2:** ní-hiki 二匹, **3:** sánbiki 三匹, *how many* nán-biki 何匹)

insecticide n bōchū-zai 防虫剤

insect repellent n mushi-yoke 虫よけ

insert v sashi-komimásu (sashi-komu, sashi-konde) 差し込みます・さしこみます(込む、込んで); (*puts it between*) hasamimásu (hasámu, hasánde) 挟みます・はさみます(挟む、挟んで)

in short → short

inside adj, adv, prep (... no) náka (de/ni) (...の)中(で/に), ...-nai ...内; (*among*) (... no) uchí(de/ni) (...の)中(で/に); *the* ~ uchi-gawa 内側, uchiwa 内輪, okunai 屋内, (*back/deep inside*) óku 奥; *is* ~ háitte imásu (iru, ite) 入っています(いる、いて)

inside and out *adv* **1.** náigai no 内外の
2. nani mo ka mo 何もかも
inside corner *n* súmi 隅・すみ
inside information *n* naibu-jōhō 内部情報
inside-out *adj* uragaeshi (no) 裏返し(の)
insipid *adj* ajike-nái 味気ない
inspect *v* kénsa/kansatsu shimásu (suru, shite)
検査/監察します(する, して)
inspection *n* kénsa 検査, kansatsu 監察
install *v* sonaemásu (sonáeru, sonáete) 備えます・
そなえます(備える, 備えて)
installation *n* shisetsu 施設
installment(s) *n* kappu/wappu 割賦; (*monthly payments*) geppu 月賦, bunkatsu barai 分割払い
installment savings *n* tsumitatekin 積立金
instance *n* (*example*) tatoe 例え・たとえ, tatoi
例い・たとい, réi 例, ichi-rei 一例
for instance tatóeba 例えば・たとえば
instant *n* (*moment*) shunkan 瞬間, sétsuna せつな・刹那
(at) the instant that … totan ni 途端に
in an instant tachimachi (ni) たちまち(に), súgu
すぐ, tossa ni とっさに
instantly *adv* tachimachi (ni) たちまち(に)
instead *adv* (sono) kawari ni (その)代わりに
institute *n* (*research*) kenkyū-jo 研究所
institute director *n* shochō 所長
institution *n* shisetsu 施設
instruct → teach
instruction *n* (*teaching*) oshie 教え; (*leading*)
shidō 指導
instructions *n* (*directions*) sáshizu 指図, shíji
指示; (*written explanation*) setsumei-sho 説明書
instructor *n* **1.** kyō´shi 教師, senséi 先生
2. (*sports*) insutorakutā インストラクター
instrument *n* (*implement*) yō´gu 用具;
(*instrumentality*) kíkai 機械, kíkan 機関; (*musical*)
gakki 楽器
insufficiency *n* fusoku 不足, …-búsoku …不足
insufficient *adj* tarimasén (tarinai) 足りません・
たりません(足りない)
insulate *v* zetsuen shimásu (suru, shite) 絶縁します
(する, して)
insult **1.** *n* bujoku 侮辱 **2.** *v* (*insults one*) bujoku
shimásu (suru, shite) 侮辱します(する, して)
insurance *n* hoken 保険
insure (*it*) *v* (… ni) hoken o kakemásu (kakéru,
kákete) (…に)保険をかけます(かける,
かけて)
intact *adj* sono mamá (de/no) そのまま(で/の),
mu-kizu (no) 無傷の
integrate *v* … o matomemásu (matomeru, matomete) …をまとめます(まとめる, まとめて),
tōitsushimásu (tōitsuru, tōitsushite) 統一します
(統一する, 統一して)
integrity *n* seijitsu 誠実, shōjiki 正直
intellectual *adj* chiteki (na) 知的(な)
intelligence *n* **1.** (*information*) jōhō 情報
2. chisei 知性, chinō 知能; → knowledge

intelligent *adj* chiteki (na) 知的(な), rikō (na)
利口(な)
intelligentsia *n* (*intellectual(s)*) chishiki-jin
知識人, interi インテリ
intelligibility *n* rikaido 理解度
intend *v ~ (to do)* (suru) tsumori désu (tsumori da,
tsumori de) (する)つもりです(つもりだ,
つもりで)
intent *n* muné 旨 → **intention**
intention *n* tsumori つもり, íto 意図, íshi 意思,
kokoro-zashi 志・こころざし; (*aim*) nerai
狙い・ねらい
That was not my intention. *interj* sonna
tsumori dewa arimasendeshita. そんなつもりでは
ありませんでした
intentionally *adv* wazato わざと, takuránde 企ん
で → **[on] purpose**
intently *adv* shikiri-ni しきりに; jitto じっと
intercourse *n* (*social*) shakō 社交; (*sexual*) seikō
性交
interest **1.** *n* (*on money*) risoku 利息, ríshi 利子,
rí 利; (*pleasure*) kyō´mí 興味, shúmi 趣味;
(*relevance*) kankei 関係, (*concern*) kanshin 関心
2. *v* … no kyōmi o hikimásu (hiku, hiite) …の興味
を引きます(引く, 引いて)
interesting *adj* omoshirói おもしろい・面白い,
kyōmi-bukái 興味深い
(Oh?) How interesting! Sō´ desu ka. そうですか.
interfere *v* jama ni narimásu (náru, natte) じゃま[
邪魔]になります(なる, なって), jama o shimásu
(suru, shite) じゃま[邪魔]をします
(する, して), kanshō shimásu (suru, shite) 干渉し
ます(する, して)
interference *n* jama じゃま・邪魔; (*meddling*)
kanshō 干渉
interior *n* okunai 屋内, shitsunai 室内; uchigawa
内側
interior decoration interia dezain インテリアデ
ザイン
interjection *n* (*word*) kantō´shi 間投詞
intermediary *n* chūkai-sha 仲介者, shōkai-sha
紹介者
intermission *n* (*between acts*) makuai 幕あい・
幕間
internal *adj* **1.** uchi (no) 内(の), náibu (no) 内部
(の), nai-teki (na) 内的(な) **2.** (*to the nation*)
kokúnai (no) 国内(の), náichi (no) 内地(の)
3. (*within the office/company*) shánai (no) 社内(の)
internal evidence nai-teki shō´ko 内的証拠
international *adj* kokusai-teki (na) 国際的(な);
intānashonaru (na/no) インターナショナル
(な/の);(*worldwide*) sekai-teki (na) 世界的(な)
Internet *n* (*world wide web*) (intā)netto (インタ
ー)ネット
interpret *v* tsū´yaku shimásu (suru, shite) 通訳し
ます(する, して); (*explains, construes*) káishaku
shimásu (suru, shite) 解釈します(する, して)
interpretation *n* tsū´yaku 通訳; (*explanation,
understanding*) káishaku 解釈

interpreter *n* (*translator*) tsū´yaku(-sha) 通訳(者)
interrupt *v* (*with a remark*) …no hanashí no kuchi o hasamimásu (hasamu, hasande) (…の話に)口をはみます(はさむ, はさんで)
  Am I interrupting you? *interj* (o-)jama-datta? (お)邪魔だった?, jama-shita? 邪魔した? [FORMAL] O-jama-deshitaka? お邪魔でしたか?
interruption *n* shadan 遮断; (*suspension*) teishi 停止; (*remark*) sashideguchi 差し出口
intersect *v* yoko-girimásu (yoko-gíru, yoko-gítte) 横切ります(横切る, 横切って)
intersecting *n* ōdan 横断
intersection (*of streets*) *n* kōsaten 交差点, yotsu-kado 四つ角
interval *n* aida 間・あいだ, ma 間; kankaku 間隔
interview *n* **1.** kaiken 会見 **2.** taimen 体面 **3.** (*meeting with*) menkai 面会 **4.** (*job interview*) mensetsu 面接, intabyū インタビュー
  interviewing *n* (*questioning*) shimon 諮問
  press interview *n* kisha kaiken 記者会見
intestines *n* harawata はらわた・腸, watá わた・腸, chō 腸
intimate *adj* shitashíi 親しい・したしい; missetsu (na) 密接(な)
in time → **time**
intimidate *v* kowagarasemásu (kowagaraseru, kowagarasete) 怖がらせます(怖がらせる, 怖がらせて)
intolerable *adj* tamarimasén (tamaranai) たまりません(たまらない), taeraremasén (taerarenai) 耐えられません(耐えられない)
intolerably *adv* yáke ni やけに; hidoku ひどく
intoxicated → **drunk**; *is easily intoxicated* sake ni yowái 酒に弱い
intoxication *n* yoi 酔い
intramural *adj* kō´nai (no) 校内(の), chō´nai/shinai (no) 町/市内(の)
intransitive verb *n* jidō´shi 自動詞
intravenous *n* jōmyaku (chūsha) 静脈(注射), tenteki 点滴
intravenous anesthesia *n* jōmyaku masui 静脈麻酔
intricate *adj* (*situation, subject*) komi-itta 込み入った
introduce *n* shōkai shimásu (suru, shite) 紹介します(する, して)
  Let me introduce you. Go-shōkai shimásu. ご紹介します。
introduction *n* shōkai 紹介 (go-shōkai ご紹介)
intrude *v* (*to force*) oshi-tsukémásu (oshi-tsukéru, oshi-tsukéte) 押し付けます・おしつけます(付ける, 付けて)
intrusive *adj* (o-)jama (na) (お)じゃま[邪魔] (な)
intuition *n* chokkan 直観・直感
in vain → **vain**
invalid 1. *adj* (*not valid*) mukō (na) 無効(な) **2.** *n* (*ill person*) byōnin 病人
invasion *n* shinryaku 侵略

invention *n* hatsumei 発明
inventory *n* mokuroku 目録, zaiko 在庫; (*inventory list*) zaiko-hyō 在庫表
invest *v* oroshimásu (orósu, oróshite) 下ろします・おろします(下ろす, 下ろして); tōshi shimásu (suru, shite) 投資します(する, して)
investigate *v* shirabemásu (shirabéru, shirábete) 調べます・しらべます(調べる, 調べて); kiwamemásu (kiwaméru, kiwámete) 究めます(究める, 究めて); kentō shimásu (suru, shite) 検討します(する, して)
investigation *n* **1.** (*research*) chōsa 調査 **2.** (*study*) kenkyū 研究
investment *n* tōshi 投資
invisible *n* (mé ni) miemasén (miénai) (目に)見えません(見えない)
invitation *n* sasoi 誘い, shō´tai 招待; (*card*) shōtái-jō 招待状
invite *v* yobimásu (yobu, yonde) 呼びます・よびます(呼ぶ, 呼んで), sasoimásu (sasou, sasotte) 誘います・さそいます(誘う, 誘って), manekimásu (manéku, manéite) 招きます・まねきます(招く, 招いて), shōtai shimásu (suru, shite) 招待します(する, して), mukaemásu (mukaeru, mukaete) 迎えます・むかえます(迎える, 迎えて)
involuntary *adj* muíshiki (no/na) 無意識(の/な)
iodine *n* yō´do ヨード
i.q. 1. *adj* dōyō (no) 同様(の) **2.** *adv* dōyō ni 同様に
Iran *n* Iran イラン
Iraq *n* Iraku イラク
Ireland *n* Airurándo アイルランド
Irelander *n* Airurando-jin アイルランド人
iris *n* **1.** (*plant*) shō´bu しょうぶ・ショウブ・菖蒲, ayame アヤメ・菖蒲 **2.** (*eye*) kōsai 虹彩
Irish *n* (*language*) Airurando-go アイルランド語; (*person*) Airurando-jin アイルランド人
Irish potato *n* jagaimo じゃがいも・ジャガイモ・じゃが芋
iron *n* (*metal*) tetsu 鉄・てつ; (*clothes iron*) airon アイロン; *irons a shirt* wai-shatsu ni airon o kakemásu (kakéru, kákete) ワイシャツにアイロンをかけます(かける, かけて)
iron bar *n* tetsu-bo 鉄棒・てつぼう
iron bridge *n* tekkyō 鉄橋
ironic *adj* hiniku (na) 皮肉(な)
irregular *adj* fukísoku (na) 不規則(な)
irrelevant to … *adj* to mu-kánkei (no) …と無関係(の)
irresponsible *adj* mu-sékinin (na) 無責任(な)
irrigation *n* kangai 灌漑・かんがい
irritate *v* jirashimásu (jirashimásu, jirashite), iraira sasemásu (saseru, sasete); *gets irritated/is irritating* shaku ni sawarimásu (sawaru, sawatte) しゃく[癪]にさわります(さわる, さわって)
is (*am, are, be*) *v* **1.** (*it is*) …désu (dá/nó/ná, dé, ní) です(だ/の/な, で, に); [DEFERENTIAL] …de gozaimásu (de gozaimáshite) …でございます(で

ございまして), [HONORIFIC] … de irasshaimásu (de irassháru, de irasshátte/iráshite) …でいらっしゃいます(でいらっしゃる, でいらっしゃって/いらして) **2.** (*there is; it is there*) arimásu (áru, átte) あります(ある, あって); [DEFERENTIAL] gozaimásu (gozaimá-shite) ございます(ございまして) **3.** (*person is there*) imásu (iru, ite) います(いる, いて), [DEFERENTIAL, HUMBLE] orimásu (óru, ótte/orimáshite) おります(おる, おって/おりまして), [HONORIFIC] irasshaimásu (irassháru, irasshátte/irasshaimáshite) いらっしゃいます(いらっしゃる, いらっしゃって/いらして/いらっしゃいまして) **4.** (*is doing*) …te imásu (iru, ite)…ています(いる, いて), …te orimásu (óru, ótte/orimáshite) …ております(おる, おって/おりまして), …te irasshaimásu (irassháru, irasshátte/iráshite/irasshaimáshite) … ていらっしゃいます(いらっしゃる, いらっしゃって/いらして/いらっしゃいまして) = …te oide ni narimásu (náru, nátte/narimáshite) …ておいでになります(なる, なって/なりまして)

Islam *n* Isuramu-kyō イスラム教, kaikyō 回教

island *n* shimá 島; (*group of*) *islands* …-shótō …諸島, (*archipelago*) rettō 列島, …-réttō …列島

(-)ism *n, suffix* shúgi 主義

isn't (*aren't*) **1.** *v* (*it isn't*) …ja arimasén (ja nái, ja nákute)…じゃありません(じゃない, じゃなくて) **2.** (*there isn't*) arimasén (nái, nákute) ありません(ない, なくて)

isolation *n* koritsu 孤立

Israel *n* Isuraeru イスラエル

Israeli *n* Isuraeru-jin イスラエル人

issuance *n* hakkō 発行

issue 1. *n* hakkō(butsu) 発行(物); (*magazine issues*) -gatsu-gō 月号 **2.** *v* (*publishes*) hakkō shimásu (suru, shite) 発行します(する, して) → **put out**

it *pron* sore それ (*but usually omitted*)

Italian 1. *n* (*language*) Itaria-go イタリア語; (*person*) Itariá-jin イタリア人 **2.** *adj* Itaria (no) イタリア(の)

italic *n* itarikku(-tai) イタリック(体); shatai 斜体

Italy *n* Itaria イタリア

itch *n* kayúmi かゆみ・痒み

itchy *adj* kayúi かゆい・痒い; múzumuzu suru むずむずする

item *n* **1.** kōmoku 項目 **2.** (*sports*) shumoku 種目 **3.** (*game*) aitemu アイテム

itinerary *n* nittei 日程

its *pron* sore no それの, are no あれの

itself *pron* sore jíshin/jítai それ自身/ 自体; … ~ (*as we might expect*) sasuga no …さすがの…; …(*in*) ~ … sono-mónó …そのもの, (sore) jítai (それ) 自体; *of/by* ~ hitori-de ni ひとりでに・独りでに

ivory *n* zōge 象牙・ゾウゲ

ivy *n* tsuta つた・ツタ・蔦

J

jab *n* **1.** tsuki 突き **2.** (*boxing*) jabu ジャブ

jacket *n* uwagi 上着, jákétto ジャケット; *traditional workman's jacket* hantén 半天・ハンテン, happi はっぴ・法被・ハッピ

jackknife *n* jakku naifu ジャックナイフ

jade *n* hísui ひすい・ヒスイ・翡翠

jail *n* keimú-sho 刑務所, rōgoku 牢獄, rōya 牢屋, [*uncommon*] orí おり・檻

jailer *n* kanshu 看守

jam *n* (*to eat*) jámu ジャム

Jamaica *n* jamaika ジャマイカ

janitor *n* kózukai 小使い, yōmúin 用務員; kanri-nin 管理人

January *n* Ichi-gatsú 一月・1月

Japan *n* Nihón 日本・にほん, Nippón 日本・にっぽん; *made in Japan* Nihon-sei (no) 日本製(の), meido in japan (no) メイド・イン・ジャパン(の), kokusan (no) 国産(の)

Japan Airlines, JAL *n* Nihon Kōkū 日本航空, Járu ジャル

Japan-bashing *n* Nihon-tátaki 日本叩き[たたき]

Japanese 1. *n* (*language*) Nihon-go 日本語; (*person*) Nihon-jín 日本人 **2.** *adj* (*of Japan*) Nihón no 日本の; wa-… 和;, nichi-; 日…

Japanese cakes/sweets *n* wa-gáshi 和菓子

Japanese celery *n* údo うど・ウド・独活

Japanese clothes *n* wa-fuku 和服

Japanese cuisine *n* Nihon-ryō´ri 日本料理, kappō´ 割烹; kaiseki-ryō´ri 懐石料理

Japanese-English dictionary *n* waei-jíten 和英辞典

Japanese food *n* wa-shoku 和食

Japanese ginger (*buds*) *n* myōga みょうが・ミョウガ・茗荷

Japanese grapefruit *n* (*pomelo*) natsu-míkan 夏みかん・ナツミカン・夏蜜柑

Japanese harp *n* (o-)kóto (お)琴

Japanese music *n* hōgaku 邦楽; (*traditional to the imperial court*) gágaku 雅楽, (*and dances*) búgaku 舞楽

Japanese noodles *n* (*wheat-flour*) udon うどん・ウドン; (*buckwheat-flour*) soba そば(o-soba おそば)

Japanese paper *n* wáshi 和紙

Japanese parsley *n* serí せり・芹

Japanese pepper n (*mild*) sanshō さんしょう・サンショウ・山椒

Japanese restaurant n kappō´ 割烹, (nihon) ryōrí-ya (日本) 料理屋

Japanese style adj wafū 和風, nihon-fū 日本風

Japanese-style room n wa-shitsu 和室, Nihonma 日本間

Japanese-style wrestling n sumō 相撲・スモウ (= *Sumo wrestling*)

Japan Travel Bureau, JTB n Jei tii bii, JTB (JTB Corp.)

jar n (*with a large mouth*) kamé かめ・瓶; (*with a small mouth*) tsubo つぼ・壺; (*glass*) garasu-hin ガラス瓶, bín びん・瓶

jargon n senmon-go 専門語; tawagoto 戯言・たわごと

jaundice n ōdan 黄疸・おうだん

jaunt n ensoku 遠足

javelin n nage-yari 投げ槍・投げやり

jaw n agó あご・顎

jazz n jazu ジャズ

jealous adj urayamashii 羨ましい・うらやましい; **gets ~** (yaki-móchi o) yakimásu (yaku, yaite) (焼きもちを) 焼きます (焼く, 焼いて), urayamimásu (urayamu, urayande) 羨みます・うらやみます (羨む, 羨んで)

jealousy n yaki-móchí 焼きもち・やきもち, shitto 嫉妬

jeans n jiinzu ジーンズ, jiipan ジーパン

jeep n jiipu ジープ

jeer 1. n hiyakashi 冷やかし 2. v hiyakashimásu (hiyakasu, hiyakashite) 冷やかします (冷やかす, 冷やかして)

jelly n zérii ゼリー, jérii ジェリー

jellyfish n kurage くらげ・水母・クラゲ

jeopardy n kiki 危機, kiken 危険

jerk; with a ~ gutto ぐっと

jerky 1. adj gikushakushita ぎくしゃくした 2. n (*smoked/dried meat*) jākii ジャーキー

jersey n jāji ジャージ

Jesus Christ n iesu kirisuto イエス・キリスト

jet (*plane*) n jettō-ki ジェット機

jet lag n jisa-boke 時差ぼけ

jet black adj makkúro (na) 真っ黒・まっくろ (な)

jetty n bōha-tei 防波堤

Jew n Yudayá-jin ユダヤ人

jewel n hōseki 宝石, tamá 玉

jeweler n hōseki-shō 宝石商

jigsaw puzzle n jigusō-pazuru ジグソーパズル

job n shigoto 仕事 (o-shígoto お仕事), tsutomé 勤め・つとめ (o-tsutome お勤め), (*place*) tsutome-saki 勤め先

getting a job shūshoku 就職

job hopping n tenshoku 転職

job hunting n kyūshoku 求職

job transfer n tenkin 転勤, tennin 転任

jockey n kishu 騎手

jockstrap n (*athletic supporting underwear*) sapō´tā サポーター

jog(ging) n jogingu (o shimásu; suru, shite)

ジョギング (をします; する, して), marason マラソン

join v (*joins them together*) awasemásu (awaséru, awásete) 合わせます・あわせます (合わせる, 合わせて), (*grafts, glues*) tsugimásu (tsugu, tsuide) 接ぎます (接ぐ, 接いで); (*enters*) …ni hairimásu (háiru, háitte) … に入ります (入る, 入って); (*in cooperation*) tsukimásu (tsukú, tsúite) 付きます・つきます (付く, 付いて); **~ (forces)** gōdō shimásu (suru, shite) 合同します (する, して)

joint 1. n fushí 節; (*of two bones*) kansetsu 関節; (*of pipe; seam*) tsugi-me 接ぎ目・つぎめ 2. adj (*combined*) gōdō no … 合同の…

joint venture, JV n kyōdō/gōben jigyō 共同/合弁事業

joke n jōdán 冗談, share しゃれ・洒落

joss stick n (o-)sénkō (お)線香, sénkō 線香・せんこう

journal n 1. jānaru ジャーナル 2. (*diary*) nikki 日記 3. (*newspaper*) shinbun 新聞 4. (*magazine*) zasshi 雑誌

journalist n 1. jānarisuto ジャーナリスト 2. (*newspaper journalist*) shinbun-kishá 新聞記者 3. (*reporter*) kichú 記者

journey n tabi 旅, ryokō 旅行 → **trip**

jovial adj yōki (na) 陽気 (な)

joy n yorokobi 喜び・よろこび

joyful adj ureshii 嬉しい・うれしい, tanoshii 楽しい・たのしい, yorokondeiru 喜んでいる・よろこんでいる

Judaism n Yudaya-kyō ユダヤ教

judge 1. n hánji 判事, saibánkan 裁判官 2. v (*gives judgment*) hándan shimásu (suru, shite) 判断します (する, して), (*criticizes*) hihan shimásu (suru, shite) 批判します (する, して)

judgment n hándán 判断; (*criticism*) hihan 批判

judicious adj kenmei (na) 賢明 (な)

judo n jū´dō 柔道; **~ outfit/suit** jūdō´-gí 柔道着

jug n mizusashi 水差し

juggler n 1. (*magician*) tejiná-shi 手品師 2. (*magic*) **jugglery** n téjina 手品 3. jagurā ジャグラー

juice n jū´su ジュース; shíru 汁; *juice of bitter orange* pónsu ポンス, ponzu ポン酢

juicy adj jū´shii (na) ジューシー (な), shiruke no/ga ōi 汁気の/が多い

jujitsu n jūjutsu 柔術 (= **judo**)

July n Shichi-gatsú 七月・7月

jumble n gotchamaze ごちゃ混ぜ, yoseatsume 寄せ集め・よせあつめ

jumbo shrimp n kurumá-ebi 車えび [海老・エビ]

jump v tobimásu (tobu, tonde) 跳びます・とびます (跳ぶ, 跳んで), janpu shimásu (suru, shite) ジャンプします (する, して); *jumps out* tobi-dashimásu (tobi-dásu, tobi-dáshite) 飛び出します・とびだします (飛び出す, 飛び出して)

jumper n janpā ジャンパー

June n Roku-gatsú 六月・6月

jungle *n* mitsurin 密林, jánguru ジャングル
jungle gym *n* janguru-jímu ジャングルジム
junior *adj* (*younger*) toshi-shíta (no) 年下(の);
(*colleague, fellow student*) kōhai 後輩; (*3rd-year
student*) sannén-sei 三年生
junior college *n* tanki-dáigaku 短期大学
junior high school *n* chūgákkō 中学校; **junior
high school student** chūgáku-sei 中学生
junk *n* kúzu くず・クズ, kuzu-mono くず物,
garakuta がらくた・ガラクタ
junk food *n* janku-fūdo ジャンクフード
junkyard *n* sute-ba 捨て場
jurisconsult *n* hō gaku-sha 法学者
jurisdiction *n* shihō-ken 司法権
jurisprudence *n* hō(ritsu-)gaku 法(律)学
jurist *n* hōritsu-ka 法律家
juror *n* baishin-in 陪審員
jury *n* baishin (-in dan) 陪審員団

just **1.** *adv* (*exactly*) chōdo ちょうど・丁度, mása
ni まさに・正に; (*only*) …daké …だけ, (*merely*)
táda ただ **2.** *adj* (*equal, fair*) tadashii 正しい,
kōsei na 公正な
just a moment chótto ちょっと
just did it (shi-)ta bákari desu (し)たばかり
です
just now tatta-íma たった今, tadáima ただ今・只
今, tsúi imashígata つい今しがた
just right pittári ぴったり; uttetsuke (no) うって
つけ(の); is just right for me watashi ni pittári
desu わたし[私]にぴったりです
just the (*one/thing/ticket, …*) uttetsuke (no) うっ
てつけ(の)
justice *n* **1.** (*rightness*) seigi 正義, seitō-sei 正当性
2. (*judiciary*) shihō 司法
juvenile delinquent *n* hikō-shōnen 非行少年,
chinpira ちんぴら・チンピラ

K

kana *n* kana かな・仮名・カナ
kangaroo *n* kangarū カンガルー
karate *n* (*weaponless self defense*) karate 空手・
カラテ; **karate outfit/suit** karaté-gí 空手着
katakana *n* katákána カタカナ・かたかな・
片仮名
kayak *n* kayakku カヤック
keen *adj* nesshin (na) 熱心(な)
keenly *adv* shimijími (to) しみじみ(と)
keep *v* tamochimásu (tamótsu, tamótte) 保ち
ます・たもちます(保つ, 保って); (*retains*)
kakaemásu (kakaeru, kakaete) 抱えます・か
かえます(抱える, 抱えて); (*takes in trust*)
azukarimásu (azukaru, azukátte) 預かります・あ
ずかります(預かる, 預かって); (*raises animals*)
kaimásu (káu, kátte) 飼います・かいます(飼う,
飼って)
keep away from *v* yokemásu (yokéru, yókete)
よけます・避けます(よける, よけて)
keep company with *v* (…o) chíka-zukemásu
(chíka-zukéru, chíka-zúkete) (…を)近付けます
(近付ける, 近付けて)
keep cool *v* (*calms down*) ochi-tsukimásu
(ochi-tsuku, ochi-tsuite) 落ち着きます(落ち着く,
落ち着いて)
keep doing *v* (shi-)te imásu (iru, ite) (し)てい
ます(いる, いて); (shi)-tsuzukemásu (-tsuzukéru,
-tsuzúkete) (し)続けます・つづけます(続ける,
続けて)
Keep it up! ganbare! 頑張れ!
keepsake *n* **1.** (*legacy*) katami 形見
2. (*remembrance*) kinen no shina 記念の品,
kinen-hin 記念品
keg *n* taru たる・樽

kelp *n* kónbu 昆布・コンブ; **kelp flakes**
tororo-kónbu とろろ昆布
kennel *n* inu-goya 犬小屋
kerchief *n* nekkachiifu ネッカチーフ
kernel *n* koku-tsubu 穀粒
kerosene *n* tōyu 灯油, sekiyu 石油
kerosene heater *n* sekiyu sutō'bu 石油ストーブ
ketchup *n* kecháppu ケチャップ
kettle *n* (*teakettle*) yakan やかん・ヤカン・薬缶,
yu-wákashi 湯沸かし; (*cauldron*) kama かま・釜
key *n* kagí 鍵, kíi キー
keyhole *n* kagí-ana 鍵穴
"key money" (*to obtain rental lease*) kenri-kin
権利金
kick *v* kerimásu (kéru, kétte) 蹴ります・けります
(蹴る, 蹴って)
kick out *v* (*company*) kubi ni shimásu (suru,
shíte) クビにしますし(する, して), (*school*)
yame/taigaku-sasemásu (-saseru, -sasete) 辞め/退
学させます(させる, させて)
kick the habit *v* (tabako, sake o) yamemásu
(yameru, yamete) (たばこ, 酒)やめます(やめる,
やめて)
kid *n* kodomo 子供・子ども, kozō 小僧・こぞう
→ **child**
kid around fuzakemásu (fuzakeru, fuzakete)
ふざけます(ふざける, ふざけて)
kids oneself about … (*underestimates*) … o
amaku mimásu (míru, míte) …を甘く見ます・…
をあまくみます(見る, 見て)
no kidding! másaka まさか, uso (da/darō)
うそ(だ/だろう)!
kidnap **1.** *n* yūkai 誘拐 **2.** *v* yūkai shimásu (suru,
shíte) 誘拐します(する, して)

kidnapper *n* yūkai-han 誘拐犯

kidnapping *n* yūkai 誘拐, rachi 拉致

kidney *n* jinzō 腎臓

kidney beans *n* íngen いんげん・インゲン, ingén mame いんげん豆・インゲンマメ

kill *v* koroshimásu (korosu, koroshíte) 殺します (殺す, 殺して); [SLANG] barashimásu (barásu, baráshíte) ばらします (ばらす, ばらして)

killjoy *n* tanoshimi ni mizu o sasu hito 楽しみに水を差す人, ba o shirakesaseru hito 場をしらけ [白け] させる人

killed; gets ~ korosaremásu (korosareru, korosarete) 殺されます (殺される, 殺されて), yararemásu (yarareru, yararete) やられます (やられる, やられて)

killer *n* satsujin-han 殺人犯

kiln *n* kama かま・釜

kilogram *n* kíro キロ, kiroguramu キログラム

kilometer *n* kíro キロ, kirométoru キロメートル

kiloliter *n* kíro キロ, kirorittoru キロリットル

kilowatt *n* kíro キロ, kirowatto キロワット

kimono *n* 1. (*Japanese attire*) wa-fuku 和服, ki-mono 着物・キモノ; (*long-sleeved*) furisode 振り袖・ふりそで 2. (*light, for summer*) yukata ゆかた・浴衣, (*gown*) tánzen 丹前

kin *n* (*relatives*) shinseki 親戚, ketsuen 血縁

kind 1. *n* (*variety*) shúrui 種類, tó 手
a kind of … no ís-shu …の一種 (ís-shu no … 一種の…)
all kinds of samazama (na) 様々・さまざま (な), iroiro (na/no) 色々・いろいろ (な/の)
kinds of …-rui …類
2. *adj* (*nice*) (go-)shínsetsu (na) (ご) 親切・しんせつ (な)

kindness *n* shinsetsu 親切・しんせつ, omoiyari 思い遣り・おもいやり

kindergarten *n* yōchíen 幼稚園・ようちえん

kindling *n* taki-tsuke たきつけ

kindly *adv* atatakáku あたたかく・温かく; (*kindly does*) (shi-) te kuremásu (kureru, kurete) (し) てくれます (くれる, くれて), kudasaimásu (kudasáru, kudasátte) /下さいます・くださいます (下さる, 下さって)

kindness *n* ón 恩・おん (go-ón ご恩), kokorozashi 志・こころざし (o-kokorozashi お志), shínsetsu 親切・しんせつ (go-shínsetsu ご親切)

king *n* ō 王, ō-sama 王様

kingdom *n* ō-koku 王国

king-size *adj* kingu-saizu (no) キングサイズ (の), tokudai (no) 特大 (の)

kink *n* nejire ねじれ・捩れ

kinky *adj* 1. (*twisted*) nejireta ねじれた・捩れた 2. (*sexually perverse*) hentai (no) 変態 (の), seiteki ni tōsakushita 性的に倒錯した

kinsfolk → kin

kinship *n* shinzoku 親族

kiosk *n* (*selling things*) baiten 売店, kiosuku キオスク

kiss *n* ki(s)su (shimásu; suru, shíte) キ (ッ) ス (します; する, して); seppun (shimásu; suru, shíte) 接吻 (します; する, して)

kit (*of tools*) *n* yō´gu 用具, kitto キット; *kit bag* yōgu-búkuro 用具袋

kitchen *n* daidokoro 台所, katte 勝手 (o-katte お勝手), (*Western-style*) kitchin キッチン

kitchen door *n* katte-guchi 勝手口

kitchen range/stove *n* (*old Japanese style*) kamado かまど; (*gas, electricity*) konro コンロ, renji レンジ

kitchen sink *n* nagashí 流し

kitchen utensils *n* daidokoro-dō´gu 台所道具

kitchenware *n* daidokoro yō´hin 台所用品

kite *n* táko 凧・たこ・タコ; *flies a ~* táko o agemásu (ageru, agete) 凧を揚げます (揚げる, 揚げて); *kite-flying* takó-ágé 凧揚げ・凧あげ

kitten *n* konéko 子猫・コネコ

Kleenex *n* (*tissue*) tísshu-pē´pā ティッシュペーパー; hanagami 鼻紙, chiri-gami ちり紙・チリガミ

knack *n* kotsú こつ; yōryō´ 要領

knapsack *n* 1. ryúkku リュック, ryukkusákku リュックサック 2. (*elementary school bag*) randóseru ランドセル

knead *v* nerimásu (néru, nétte) 練ります・ねります (練る, 練って)

knee *n* hiza ひざ・膝

kneecap *n* hizagashira ひざがしら・膝頭

kneel *v* hizamazukimásu (hizamazuku, hizamazuite) 跪きます・ひざまずきます (ひざまずく, ひざまずいて)

knew → know

knife *n* 1. náifu ナイフ 2. (*kitchen knife*) hōchō 包丁・ホウチョウ, (*butcher knife*) nikukiri-bō´chō 肉切り包丁

knight *n* naito ナイト, kishi 騎士

knit *n* amimásu (ámu, ánde) 編みます・あみます (編む, 編んで)

knitted goods *n* meriyasu メリヤス, amí-mono 編み物・あみもの

knob *n* (*bump*) kobú こぶ, (*gnarl*) fushí 節; *door knob* hiki-te 引き手, totte 取っ手・とって, doa nobu ドアノブ

knock 1. *v* (*hits*) nagurimásu (nagúru, nagútte) 殴ります・なぐります (殴る, 殴って) 2. *v* (*on door*) (to o) tatakimásu (tatáku, tatáite) (戸を) 叩きます・たたきます (叩く, 叩いて), nókku shimásu (suru, shíte) ノックします (する, して) 3. *n* nókku ノック

knock down *v* taoshinásu (taósu, taóshite) 倒します・たおします (倒す, 倒して)

knockout *n* (*boxing*) nokkuauto ノックアウト

knot *n* musubi (-me) 結び (目)・むすび (め); (*gnarl*) fushí 節

know *v*… o shíte imásu (iru, ite) …を知っています・…をしっています (いる, いて), [DEFERENTIAL] zon-ji(age)másu (zon-ji(age)ru, zon-ji(agé)te) 存じ (あげ) ます (存じ (あげ) る,

存じ(あげ)て), [HONORIFIC] gozónji (désu)
ご存じ・ごぞんじ (です), (*understands*)…ga
wakarimásu (wakáru, wakátte) …が分かりま
す・…がわかります(分かる, 分かって); ***doesn't
know*** shirimasen (shiranai, shiranáide) 知り
ません・しりません(知らない, 知らないで),
wakarimasén (wakaránai, wakaránaide) 分かりま
せん・わかりません
(分からない, 分からないで)

know-it-all *n* shittakaburi 知ったかぶり

know-how *n* nōhau ノウハウ; yarikata やり方

knowledge *n* chíshiki 知識; (*learning, academics*)
gakúmon 学問

knowledgeable (*about …*) ni kuwashíi …に詳し
い・…にくわしい

known; *gets ~* shiremásu (shireru, shirete) 知れ
ます・しれます(知れる, 知れて), (*widely*) shiraremásu (shirareru, shirarete) 知られます・しら
れます(知られる, 知られて)

known as … (*so-called*) iwáyuru … いわゆる

knuckle *n* yubi-kansetsu 指関節

knuckle down *v* isshōkenmei yarimásu (yaru,
yatte) 一生懸命やります(やる, やって)

knuckle under *v* kōsan shimásu (suru, shite)
降参します(する, して)

Kobe *n* Kōbe 神戸; *the port of kobe* Kōbé-kō
神戸港; *Kobe Station* *n* Kōbé-Eki 神戸駅

Korea *n* 1. (*South Korea*) Kánkoku 韓国 2. (*North
Korea*) Kita-chōsen 北朝鮮

Korean *n* (*person*) Kankokú-jin 韓国人;
(*language*) Kankoku-go 韓国語

kumquat *n* kinkan きんかん・キンカン

Kurile (*Islands*) *n* Chishíma 千島, Chishíma-réttō
千島列島

Kyoto *n* Kyōto 京都; *Kyoto Station* Kyōtó-Eki
京都駅; *Kyotoite* *n* Kyōtó-jin 京都人; *Kyoto-style
cooking/dishes* *n* Kyō ryō´ri 京料理

Kyūshu *n* Kyū´shū 九州

L

lab *n* rábo ラボ; (*research*) kenkyūjo 研究所;
(*testing*) shiken jo 試験所

label 1. *n* retteru レッテル, (*tag*) fuda 札・ふだ,
rabel ラベル 2. *n* (*record*) rēberu レーベル
3. *v* raberu o tsukemásu/harimásu (tsukeru,
tsukete/haru, hatte) ラベルを付けます/貼りま
す(付ける, 付けて/貼る, 貼って)
label requirement *n* hinshitsu hyōji 品質表示
grade labeling *n* tōkyū hyōji 等級表示

labor *n* rōdō 労働; *Labor Thanksgiving Day*
Kinrō kánsha no hí 勤労感謝の日
labor union *n* rōdō kumiai 労働組合

laboratory *n* 1. (*research room*) kenkyū-shitsu
研究室 2. (*experimental laboratory*) jikken-shitsu
実験室, rabo ラボ

laborer *n* rōdō-sha 労働者

laboring *adj* 1. (*hard*) hone ga oreru 骨が折れる
2. (*painful*) kurushii 苦しい

laboriously *adv* ákuseku あくせく

lace *n* 1. rē´su レース, mō´ru モール 2. → **shoelace**

lack 1. *n* (*shortage*) fusoku 不足 2. *v* (*is not available*) …ga arimasén (nái) …がありません(ない)
lacks the finishing touch (*idiom*) garyū tensei o
kaku 画竜点睛を欠く

lackey *n* tsuishō-sha 追従者, gomasuri ごますり

lackluster *adj* 1. saenai さえない, patto shinai ぱ
っとしない 2. (*object*) tsuya no nai つやのない

lacquer 1. *n* urushi 漆・ウルシ, nuri 塗り・ぬり;
raised lacquer maki-e 蒔絵
lacquer ware nuri mono 塗り物, shikki 漆器 2. *v*
(*lacquers it*) nurimásu (nuru, nette) 塗ります・ぬ
ります(塗る, 塗って)

lad *n* 1. (*boy*) shōnen 少年 2. (*young man*)
wakamono 若者, seinen 青年

ladder *n* hashigo はしご・ハシゴ・梯子

laden *adj* tsunda 積んだ

laden weight *n* sekisai jūryō 積載重量

ladle *n* 1. hishaku ひしゃく・柄杓; (*large wooden*)
shákushi しゃくし・杓子 2. *~ it* *v* kumimásu
(kumu, kunde) 汲みます・くみます(汲む, 汲んで)

lady *n* fujin 婦人, óku-san/-sama 奥[おく]さ
ん/様; (*young*) ojō-san お嬢さん, redii レディ,
(*middle-aged*) oba-san おばさん, (*old*) obāsan お
ばあさん → **woman**

lady-killer, ladies' man *n* onna(t)tárashi 女(っ)
たらし

lag 1. *n* (*a lag*) okure 遅れ・おくれ, [FORMAL]
chien 遅延 2. *v* (*lags behind*) okuremásu (okureru,
okurete) 遅れます・おくれます(遅れる, 遅れて)
time lag *n* jisa 時差

lake *n* mizū´mi 湖・みずうみ, …-ko …湖
lake-side *n* kohan 湖畔
lakeshore *n* kogan 湖岸
lake trout *n* masú ます・マス・鱒

lamb *n* ko-hítsuji 子羊・コヒツジ; (*meat, includes
mutton*) yōniku 羊肉; ramu ラム
lamb chop *n* yōniku 羊肉; ramu niku ラム肉

lame 1. *adj* ashí ga fú-jiyū (na) 足が不自由(な) →
cripple(d) 2. *n* (*fabric*) rame ラメ

lament *v* nagekimásu (nagéku, nagéite) 嘆きま
す・なげきます(嘆く, 嘆いて)

lamentation *n* nagekí 嘆き・なげき

lamp *n* ránpu ランプ; akari 明かり・あかり; dentō
電灯・電燈; *desk/floor lamp* (denki-) sutándo
(電気)スタンド

lampoon n fūshi 風刺, hiniku 皮肉

lampshade n ránpu no kasa ランプのかさ

lance n yari 槍・やり

land 1. n riku 陸・りく, oka 丘・おか, jí 地; (a piece of ~) tochi 土地 → **country** → **earth** → **place** 2. v (comes ashore) jōriku shimásu (suru, shite) 上陸します(する, して); (from the air) chakuriku shimásu (suru, shite) 着陸します (する, して)

landing n chakuriku 着陸, jōriku 上陸

landing gear n chakuriku sōchi 着陸装置

landlady n 1. (traditional Japanese inn, etc.) okámi おかみ・女将, okami-san おかみさん・女将さん 2. (apartment, etc.) ō'ya(-san) 大家・おおや(さん), yanushi 家主 3. (rental manager) kanri-nin 管理人

landlord n ō'ya(-san) 大家・おおや(さん), yanushi 家主; (owner) ōnā オーナー; (rental manager) kanri-nin 管理人

landmark n mejirushi 目印

landowner n ji-nushi 地主

landscape n fū'kei 風景・ふうけい, keshiki 景色

landslide n (earth slide) ji-súberi 地滑り・地すべり 2. adj (overwhelming) taisa (no) 大差(の), attō-teki (na) 圧倒的(な)

lane n (traffic, swim) kō'su コース; (path) komichi 小道; Lanes Merge "Gōryū Chū´i" "合流注意"

language n 1. kotobá 言葉・ことば, [FORMAL] géngo 言語; ...-go ...語; what language nani-go 何語; how many languages nan-kákokugo 何ヵ国語; language learning gogaku gakushū語学学習 2. (foreign language) gaikoku-go 外国語; How many languages do you know? Gaikoku-go wa íkutsu dekimásu ka. 外国語はいくつできますか.

languid adj (ke-)darui (気)だるい

lanky adj yaseta やせた・痩せた, hosoi 細い・ほそい

lantern n (of paper) chōchín ちょうちん・堤灯; (traditional night-light) andon あんどん・行灯

lap n hiza ひざ・膝

lapel n eri 襟・えり

lapse n 1. (time lapse) toki no keika 時の経過 2. (small error) kashitsu 過失, chiisana machigai 小さな間違い・小さなまちがい

laptop n rapputoppu (-gata) pasokon ラップトップ(型)パソコン, nōto (-gata) pasokon ノート(型)パソコン

larceny n settō (-zai) 窃盗(罪)

large adj ōkíi 大きい・おおきい, ō'ki-na 大きな・おおきな; (wide, spacious) hirói 広い・ひろい

large crowd n ōzéi 大勢

large number n tasū 多数

large quantity n taryō 多量, tairyō 大量

large-size (model) n ō'gata 大型

lasso n nage-nawa 投げ縄・なげなわ, wána わな・ワナ・罠

last adj 1. (final) owari no 終わりの・おわりの, sáigo no 最後の; (the tail end) bíri (no) びり(の)

2. (the preceding ...) kono máe no この前の, sen-...先...・...さき..., saru 去る (+ DATE); it lasts mochimásu (mótsu, mótte) 持ちます・もちます (持つ, 持って)

at last tō'tō とうとう, yatto (no kotóde) やっと(のことで), iyó-iyo いよいよ, tsúini ついに, yōyaku ようやく

last breath n (deathbed) rinjū 臨終

last call n rasuto ōdā ラスト・オーダー

last century n zenseiki 前世紀

last chance n saigo no chansu 最後のチャンス, rasuto chansu ラストチャンス

last day (of month) n, adv getsumatsu 月末, misoka みそか・晦日; (of year) ō-mísoka 大みそか・大晦日; the Last Day saigo no shinpan (no hi) 最後の審判(の日)

last month n, adv séngetsu 先月

last night n, adv kinō no ban きのう[昨日]の晩, kinō no yoru きのう[昨日]の夜, sakúban 昨晩, yūbé ゆうべ・昨夜

last stop n shūten 終点

last time adv kono máe この前

last volume n (of a set of 2 or 3) gekan 下巻, gé 下

last week n, adv senshū 先週

last year n, adv kyónen 去年, sakunen 昨年

late 1. adj osoi 遅い・おそい; (lags, fails to be on time) okuremásu (okureru, okurete) 遅れます・おくれます (遅れる, 遅れて); is too ~ (for it) ma ni aimasén (awánai, awánaide) 間に合いません・まにあいません (合わない, 合わないで); till ~ osokú made 遅くまで・おそくまで; till ~ at night yóru osokú made 夜遅くまで, shín'ya made 深夜まで; the night grows ~ yó ga fukemásu (fukéru, fukéte) 夜が更けます (更ける, 更けて) 2. adv osoku 遅く・おそく; ~ for chikoku shimásu (suru, shite) 遅刻します(する, して)

lately adv 1. (other day) kono aidá この間, konaidá こないだ 2. (recently) chikágoro 近頃, saikin 最近

later (on) adv áto (de) 後・あと(で), áto no ...後の..., [FORMAL] nochihodo 後程・のちほど, [BOOKISH] kō´(-)... go ...; does for ~ (shi-)teokimásu (-teoku, -teóite) (し)ておきます(ておく, ておいて), (shi-)tokimásu (-toku, -tóite) (し)ときます(とく, といて)

See you later. interj Jā mata. じゃあまた, Jāne. じゃあね

Talk to you later. interj Jā mata. じゃあまた, Jāne. じゃあね

latest 1. n saishin (no mono) 最新(の物・もの) 2. adj (newest) saishin (no) 最新(の)

at the latest ... máde ni wa ...まで[迄]には, osóku tomo 遅くとも・おそくとも

Latin n Raten-go ラテン語; Latin letters rōmá-ji ローマ字

latter adj áto no ...後の・あとの..., [BOOKISH] kō´(-) ... go ...; the latter kō'sha 後者

laugh v ~ at (... o) waraimásu (warau, waratte) (...を)笑います(笑う, 笑って)

loud laugh (*laugh out loud*) ōwarai 大笑, bakushō 爆笑

laugh maker *n* o-warai sakka お笑い作家

laughingstock *n* (o-)warai-gusa（お）笑い草, warai mono 笑いもの

laughter *n* warai 笑い

launch *n* hassha 発射, uchiage 打ち上げ

launder *v* sentaku shimásu (suru, shíte) 洗濯します（する, して）

laundry *n* sentaku(-mono) 洗濯（物）, o-séntaku お洗濯; (*a laundry*) sentaku-ya 洗濯屋; (*cleaner*) kuriiningu-ya クリーニング屋

laurel *n* gekkei 月桂・ゲッケイ, gekkéi-ju 月桂樹・ゲッケイジュ

lava *n* yōgan 溶岩

lavatory *n* (*to wash up in*) senmen-jo 洗面所, keshō-shitsu 化粧室 → **bathroom**, **toilet**

law *n* hōritsu 法律, hō 法; (*rule*) hōsoku 法則; (*science/study*) hōgaku 法学 → **...-in-law**

lawn *n* shiba 芝・しば, shibafu 芝生・しばふ

lawn mower *n* shibakarí-ki 芝刈り機

lawsuit *n* soshō 訴訟; uttae 訴え・うったえ

lawyer *n* bengó-shi 弁護士

lax *adj* yurúi 緩い・ゆるい

laxative *n* gezai 下剤

lay *v* (*puts*) okimásu (oku, oite) 置きます・おきます（置く, 置いて）; (*did lie down*) nemáshita (neta) 寝ました（寝た）

lay aside *v* sutemásu (suteru, sutete) 捨てます（捨てる, 捨てて）, mizu ni nagashimásu (nagasu, nagashite) 水に流します（流す, 流して）

lay down *v* yoko ni shimásu (suru, shite) 横にします（する, して）, yokotaemásu (yokotaeru, yokotaete) 横たえます（横たえる, 横たえて）

lay it face down *v* fusemásu (fuséru, fuséte) 伏せます・ふせます（伏せる, 伏せて）;

lay off *v* kaiko shimásu (suru, shite) 解雇します（する, して）

lay on its side *v* nekashimásu (nekasu, neka-shite) 寝かします（寝かす, 寝かして）

layman *n* mongái-kan 門外漢

layout *n* (*format*) teisai 体裁, reiauto レイアウト

lazy *adj* namaketa 怠けた; **gets ~** namakemásu (namakéru, namákete) 怠けます・なまけます（怠ける, 怠けて）; (*shirks*) okotarimásu (okotaru, okotatte) 怠ります・おこたります（怠る, 怠って）; *lazy person* namake-mono 怠け者・なまけもの

lead 1. *n* (*metal*) namari 鉛・なまり **2.** *v* (*guides them*) annái shimásu (suru, shite) 案内します（する, して）, michibikimásu (michibíku, michibíite) 導きます・みちびきます（導く, 導いて）, riído shimásu (suru, shite) リードします（する, して）; (*coaches them*) shidō shimásu (suru, shite) 指導します（する, して）; (*commands them*) hiki-imásu (hiki-íru, híki-iite) 率います・ひきいます（率いる, 率いて）

leader *n* chō 長; (*director, coach*) shidō´-sha 指導者; ríídā リーダー

group leader *n* han chō 班長

leader of a sect *n* kyōso 教祖

team leader *n* han chō 班長, chiimu ríídā チームリーダー

leadership *n* (*guidance*) shidō 指導; ríídāshippu リーダーシップ

leading *adj* (*chief*) shuyō (na) 主要（な）, omo (na) 主（な）

leaf *n* happa 葉っぱ・はっぱ, ha 葉・は (*how many leaves*) nán-mai 何枚）

leaflet *n* chirashi ちらし・チラシ, bira びら・ビラ

leak *v* **1.** *it leaks* morimásu (móru, mótte) 漏ります・もります（漏る, 漏って）, moremásu (moréru, mórete) 漏れます・もれます（漏れる, 漏れて） **2.** *leaks it* morashimásu (morásu, moráshite) 漏らします・もらします（漏らす, 漏らして）

lean 1. *v* katamuku 傾く; ... o katamukeru ～を傾ける; **~ against** ... ni motaremásu (motaréru, motárete) ...にもたれます（もたれる, もたれて）; **~ toward** ... no hō´ni katamukimásu (katamúku, katamúite) ...の方に傾きます（傾く, 傾いて）; (*to one side*) kata-yorimásu (kata-yóru, kata-yótte) 片寄ります・かたよります（片寄る, 片寄って）; **~ out of...** ... kara nori-dashimásu (nori-dásu, nori-dáshite) ...から乗り出します（乗り出す, 乗り出して） **2.** (*meat/fish*) *adj* akami (no) 赤味（の）

leap → **jump**

leap year *n* urū´doshi うるう[閏]年・うるうどし

learn *v* naraimásu (naráu, nárátte) 習います・ならいます（習う, 習って）, manabimásu (manabu, manande) 学びます（学ぶ, 学んで）; (*finds out*) shirimásu (shiru, shitte) 知ります・しります（知る, 知って）, (*hears*) ... ga mimí ni hairimásu (háiru, háitte) ...が耳に入ります（入る, 入って）

learning *n* gakúmon 学問, gaku 学; (*study of a basic subject*) gakushū 学習

least *adj* (*smallest*) saishō (no) 最小（の）

at least sukúnáku-tomo 少なくとも・すくなくとも, sémete せめて; (*anyway*) tó-ni-kaku とにかく

leather *n* kawá 皮・革・カワ

leave *v* demásu (déru, déte) 出ます・でます（出る, 出て）; sarimásu (saru, satte) 去ります・さります（去る, 去って）; (*for a far place*) tachimásu (tátsu, tátte) 発ちます・たちます（発つ, 発って）; (*to go home*) kaerimásu (káeru, kátte) 帰ります（帰る, 帰って）; (*withdraws*) hiki-agemásu (hiki-agéru, hiki-ágete) 引き揚げます（引き揚げる, 引き揚げて）, hiki-torimásu (hiki-tóru, hiki-tótte) 引き取ります・ひきとります（引き取る, 引き取って）; (*~ one's seat*) seki o hazushimásu (hazusu, hazushite) 席を外します（外す, 外して）

leave it behind *v* nokoshimásu (nokósu, nokóshite) 残します（残す, 残して）; (*forgetfully*) wasure-mono o shimásu (suru, shite) 忘れ物をします（する, して）, oki-wasurémásu (oki-wasuréru, oki-wasuréte) 置き忘れます・おきわすれます（忘れる, 忘れて）

leave it empty *v* akemás̱u (akeru, akete) 空けます・あけます(空ける、空けて)

leave it intact *v* (*untouched*) sono mamá ni shimás̱u (suru, s̱hite) そのままにします(する、して)

leave it undone *v* shináide okimás̱u (oku, oite) しないでおきます(おく、おいて)

Leave me alone! *interj* hōtteoite/hottoite (kudasai) 放っておいて/ほっといて(ください)、(watashi ni) kamawanaide (kudasai) (私に)構わないで・かまわないで(ください)、hitori ni shite (oite) (kudasai) 一人[独り・ひとり]にして(おいて)(ください)

leave out (*skips*) nukashimás̱u (nukasu, nukasẖite) 抜かします・ぬかします(抜かす、抜かして)

leave-taking *n* itoma 暇・ひま

lecherous *adj* s̱ukébē (na) すけべ(え)な・助平(な)・スケベ(な), kōshoku (na) 好色(な)

lecture *n* kogi 講義、(*talk*) kōen 講演; *lecture platform* endan 演壇, kōdan 講壇

lecturer *n* **1.** (*instructor*) kō´shi 講師 **2.** (*public speaker*) kō´en-sha 講演者

ledger *n* daichō 台帳

leech *n* híru ひる・ヒル・蛭

leek *n* nira にら・ニラ・韮; négi ねぎ・ネギ・葱 (= naga-negi 長ねぎ[葱・ネギ])

leeway *n* yoyū 余裕, yochi 余地

left 1. *adj* (*not right*) hidari (no) 左の **2.** → **leave 3.** → **rest**

left; *gets ~ behind* nokorimás̱u (nokóru, nokótte) 残ります・のこります(残る、残って); *gets ~ over* (*in excess*) amarimás̱u (amáru, amátte) 余ります・あまります(余る、余って) → **left behind**

left-handed (*person*) hidari-kiki/-giki (no) 左利き(の); gícho (no) ぎっちょ(の)

leftover *n* nokorí 残り・のこり; (*surplus*) amarí 余り・あまり; *leftovers* n nokori-mono 残り物

leg *n* ashí 脚・足・あし、(*shin*) suné すね・脛・臑

legacy *n* isan 遺産

legal *adj* **1.** hōritsu-jō (no) 法律上(の), hōteki (na) 法的(な) **2.** (*lawful*) gōhō (na) 合法(な)

legend *n* mukashi-bánashi 昔話, densetsu 伝説, monogátari 物語

leisure *n* **1.** (*spare time*) hima 暇, ma 間, yoka 余暇 **2.** réja レジャー

leisure center *n* reja sentā レジャーセンター

leisure land *n* reja rando レジャーランド

leisure time *n* hima na jikan 暇な時間, yoka 余暇

lemon *n* remon レモン; *lemonade* remón-sui レモン水, remonē´do レモネード; *lemon soda* ramune ラムネ

lend *v* kashimás̱u (kasu, kasẖite) 貸します・かします(貸す、貸して); *lends money* (*finances it*) yūzū shimás̱u (suru, s̱hite) 融通します(する、して)

length *n* nágasa 長さ

lengthen *v* (mótto) nágaku shimás̱u (suru, s̱hite) (もっと)長くします(する、して); (*prolongs it*)

nobashimás̱u (nobás̱u, nobás̱hite) 伸ばします・のばします(伸ばす、伸ばして); enchō shimás̱u (suru, s̱hite) 延長します(する、して)

lengthwise *adj* táte (no/ni) 縦(の/に)

lenient *adj* yurúi ゆるい・緩い; amai 甘い・あまい

lens *n* **1.** rénzu レンズ (*how many* nán-ko 何個) **2.** (*eye*) suishōtai 水晶体

contact lens *n* kontakuto renzu コンタクトレンズ

eye lens *n* gan renzu 眼レンズ

lens eye *n* suishōtai 水晶体

Leo *n* (*star sign*) shishi-za 獅子座

leopard *n* hyō ひょう・ヒョウ・豹

lesbian *n* rezu(-bian) レズ(ビアン)

less *adj* (yori) s̱ukunái (より)少ない・すくない; (*minus*) mainasu マイナス

less than (…) íka (…)以下, …míman …未満

no less than (…) íjō (…)以上, ... mo no ... もの (= *as many as*)

lessee *n* chinshaku-nin 賃借人

lessen *v* s̱ukúnaku/chísaku shimás̱u (suru, s̱hite) 少なく/小さくします(する、して); herashimás̱u (herasu, herasẖite) 減らします・へらします(減らす、減らして)

lesson *n* …-ka …課, réssun レッスン; *takes lessons (in)* (…o) naraimás̱u (naráu, narátte) (…を)習います・ならいます(習う、習って)

lessor *n* chintai-nin 賃貸人

let *v* *lets (one) do it* (… ni sore o) sasemás̱u (saseru, sasete) (…にそれを)させます(させる、させて), yurushimás̱u (yurús̱u, yurúsẖite) 許します・ゆるします(許す、許して); (*as a favor*) (…ni sore o) sasete (…にそれを)させて + [GIVE]

let approach *v* yosemás̱u (yoseru, yosete) 寄せます(寄せる、寄せて)

let fly *v* tobashimás̱u (tobasu, tobasẖite) 飛ばします・とばします(飛ばす、飛ばして)

let get away *v* nigashimás̱u (nigásu, nigásẖite) 逃がします・にがします(逃がす、逃がして)

let go *v* (*releases*) hanashimás̱u (hanásu, hanásẖite) 放します・はなします(放す、放して)

let in *v* (*air, the sun, light*) iremás̱u (ireru, irete) 入れます・いれます(入れる、入れて); *~ through/in* tōshimás̱u (tōsu, tōsẖite) 通します・とおします(通す、通して)

let off/out *v* (*of a vehicle*) oroshimás̱u (orósu, orósẖite) 降ろします・おろします(降ろす、降ろして)

let me know *interj* [FORMAL] O-shirase kudasai お知らせください; Go-renraku kudasai ご連絡ください

let me see *interj* (*well now*) sā´ さあ; Sō´ desu ne. そうですね。

let's (*do it*) (-shi-)mashō´ (し)ましょう

lethal *adj* chimei-teki (na) 致命的(な)

lethargy *n* mukiryoku 無気力

letter *n* tegami 手紙・てがみ (o-tégami お手紙)、(*news*) táyori 便り・たより; (*of alphabet*) móji 文字, (*character*) jí 字; *letter of guarantee* hoshō-sho 保証書; *letter of recommendation*, *reference letter* suisen-jō 推薦状

letter box *n* yūbin posuto 郵便ポスト

love letter *n* rabu retā ラブレター, [FORMAL] koibumi 恋文

letter paper and envelope *n* retā setto レターセット

lettuce *n* rétasu レタス

level *adj* (*flat*) taira (na) 平ら・たいら(な); (*extent*) téido 程度・ていど; (*standard*; *water level*) suijun 水準, reberu レベル; *advanced level* jōkyū 上級, *academic level* kyōiku suijun 教育水準

lever *n* teko てこ・挺子, rébā レバー

levity *n* keisotsu 軽率

levy *v* chōshū shimásu (suru, shite) 徴収します (する, して)

levying *n* chōshū 徴収

lewd *adj* sukébe (na) すけべ(え)・助平(な)・スケベ(な), midara (na) 淫ら・みだら(な), hiwai (na) 卑猥・ひわい(な)

liable to (*do*) → **apt to**

liaison *n* renraku 連絡

liar *n* usó-tsuki うそ[嘘]つき

liberate *v* kaihō shimásu (suru, shite) 解放します (する, して)

liberation *n* kaihō 解放

libertine *n* hōtō-mono/sha 放蕩者

libido *n* ribidō リビドー, seiteki shōdō 性的衝動

Libra *n* (*star sign*) tenbin-za 天秤座・てんびん座

librarian *n* tosho-gákari 図書係, toshokán-in 図書館員, shisho 司書

library *n* (*building*) toshó-kan 図書館; (*room*) toshó-shitsu 図書室, (*home study*) shosai 書斎; (*collection*) zōsho 蔵書

main library *n* chūō-toshokan 中央図書館

National Diet Library *n* kokuritsu kokkai toshokan 国立国会図書館

lice *n* shirami しらみ・シラミ・虱

license *n* ménkyo 免許, ráisensu ライセンス, menkyo-shō/-jō 免許証/状; menjō 免状; *license (tag)* kansatsu 鑑札; (*car*) *license plate* nánbā ナンバー, nanbā-purē'to ナンバープレート

driver's license *n* unten menkyo(-shō) 運転免許(証), menkyo(-shō) 免許(証)

license agreement *n* raisensu keiyaku ライセンス契約

lick *v* namemásu (naméru, námete) なめます・舐めます(なめる, なめて)

lid *n* futa ふた・蓋 (*how many* nánmai 何枚)

lie 1. *n* (*falsehood*) úso うそ・嘘, itsuwari 偽り・いつわり; *a lie comes to light* uso ga baremásu (baréru, baréte) うそがばれます(ばれる, ばれて) 2. *v* ~ (*down*) nemásu (neru, nete) 寝ます(寝る, 寝て); yoko ni narimásu (náru, nátte) 横になります(なる, なって); yoko-tawárimásu (yoko-tawáru, yoko-tawátte) 横たわります(横たわる, 横たわって)

lieutenant *n* (*1st Lt, Lt JG*) chū´i 中尉; (*2nd Lt*) shō´i 少尉; (*navy full*) dáii/táii 大尉

lieutenant colonel *n* chūsa 中佐

lieutenant commander *n* shōsa 少佐

lieutenant general *n* chūjō 中将

life *n* ínochi 命, seimei 生命; (*daily living*) seikatsu 生活; (*lifetime*) shō´gai 生涯, isshō 一生, yo 世; (*a one's life*) jínsei 人生; *brings ~ to* … o ikashimásu (ikásu, ikáshite) …を生かします (生かす, 生かして)

life boat *n* kyūmei bōto 救命ボート

life care *n* raifu kea ライフケア

lifeguard *n* raifu gādo ライフガード, kyūjo-in 救助員

life insurance *n* seimei hoken 生命保険

life partner *n* (*spouse*) shōgai no hanryo 生涯の伴侶

life preserver *n* kyūmei (yō-)gu 救命(用)具

lifestyle *n* raifu sutairu ライフスタイル, ikikata 生き方

lift 1. *v* mochi-agemásu (mochi-ageru, mochi-agete) 持ち上げます・もちあげます(持ち上げる, 持ち上げて), agemásu (ageru, agete) 上げます・あげます(上げる, 上げて) 2. → **elevator**

light 1. *n* hikarí 光・ひかり, akari 明かり・あかり, (*ray*) kōsen 光線; (*electric*) dénki 電気, dentō 電灯; *in the ~ of* … ni teráshite …に照らして 2. *lights it up* v terashimásu (terásu, teráshite) 照らします(照らす, 照らして) 3. *adj* (*not heavy*) karui 軽い・かるい; (*bright*) akarui 明るい・あかるい; (*pale*) usui 薄い・うすい; (*simple*) assári shita あっさりした…; *light rain* kosame 小雨・こさめ

lightbulb *n* denkyū 電球

lighter *n* (*cigarette*) ráitā ライター

lighthearted *adj* kigaru (na) 気軽・きがる(な)

lighthouse *n* tōdai 灯台

lighting *n* (*illumination*) shōmei 照明, raitingu ライティング; *lighting fixtures* shōmei kígu 照明器具

lighting-up time *n* tentō jikoku 点灯時刻

lightning *n* inabíkari 稲光り・イナビカリ, inazuma 稲妻・イナズマ

like 1. *v* (*is fond of*) …ga sukídesu … が好きです, … o konomimásu (konómu, konónde) …を好みます(好む, 好んで); *would like* → **want, wish** 2. *prep* (*similar*) … no yō´(na) …の様(な); (*is similar to*) … ni nite imásu (iru, ite) …に似ています(いる, いて)

like that *adj* sō (sō´ + [PARTICLE]/désu) そう (そう+ [PARTICLE]/です); sonna … そんな…; ā (ā´ + [PARTICLE]/désu) ああ(ああ + [PARTICLE]/です), anna …あんな…

like this *adj* kō (kō´ + [PARTICLE]/désu) こう (こう + [PARTICLE]/です); konna … こんな…

likely 1. *adj* ari-sō´(na) ありそう(な), (shi-) sō´(na) (し)そう(な) 2. *adv* (*probably*) tábun たぶん・多分

like(ly) as not *adv* taigai 大概・たいがい

likely to *adv* (*do*) (shi-) yasúi (し)やすい

liking *n* (*a fancy*) shikō 志向, konomí 好み (o-konomi お好み)

lily *n* yuri ゆり・ユリ・百合

lime 1. *n* (*fruit*) ráimu ライム **2.** (*mineral*) sékkai 石灰

limit 1. *n* kágiri 限り, seigén 制限; géndo 限度; hodo 程・ほど; hán'i 範囲; rimitto リミット; *time limit* taimu rimitto タイムリミット, seigen (jikan) 制限（時間） **2.** *limits* (*delimits*) *it v* kagirimásu (kagíru, kagítte) 限ります・かぎります（限る, 限って）; (*restricts*) gentei shimásu (suru, shite) 限定します（する, して）, seigén shimásu (suru, shite) 制限します（する, して）

limitation *n* gentei 限定, seigén 制限

limited edition *n* gentei-han 限定版

limited time offer *n* kikan gentei 期間限定

limited-time product *n* kisetsu gentei shōhin 季節限定商品

limousine for hire *n* háiyā ハイヤー

line *n* sén 線, rétsu 列, (*of letters*) gyō´ 行; (*plot*) súji 筋; (*in a play*) serifu せりふ・台詞; *the ~ is busy* (o-)hanashi chu (お)話し中です・はなしちゅうです; (*of work*) shokúgyō 職業, gyō´業

lined garment *n* (*kimono*) awasé あわせ・袷

linen *n* **1.** áma 亜麻・アマ, asa 麻・アサ, rinneru リンネル **2.** (*sheet*) shiitsu シーツ

line up *v* (*they line up*) narabimásu (narabu, narande) 並びます・ならびます（並ぶ, 並んで）; (*lines them up*) narabemásu (naraberu, narabete) 並べます・ならべます（並べる, 並べて）

linguist *n* **1.** gogaku ni tannōna hito 語学に堪能な[たんのうな]人 **2.** (*language scholar*) gengo gakusha 言語学者

linguistics *n* (*language learning*) gogaku 語学; (*science of language*) gengó-gaku 言語学

lining *n* urá 裏; (*material*) ura-ji 裏地 **lining of a sleeve** *n* sode ura 袖裏

link 1. *n* wá 輪 **2.** *links them v* tsunagimásu (tsunagu, tsunaide) つなぎます・繋ぎます（つなぐ, つないで）

link address *n* (*computer*) rinku adoresu リンクアドレス, rinku saki リンク先

linked; is ~ (*with …*) (*… to*) tsunagarimásu (tsunagaru, tsunagatte) つながります・繋がります（つながる, つながって）

lion *n* raion ライオン, shíshi 獅子・シシ

lip *n* kuchibiru くちびる・唇

lipstick *n* kuchi-beni 口紅・くちべに

liquid *n* eki(-tai) 液(体), mizu 水

liquor *n* (o-)sake (お)酒, (*Western*) yōshu 洋酒; (*distilled from yam or rice*) shōchū´ 焼酎

lisp *v* shi tága motsuremásu (motsuréru, motsúrete) 舌がもつれます（もつれる, もつれて）

list 1. *n* (*of items*) hyō 表, mokuroku 目録, rísuto リスト; (*of names*) meibo 名簿 **2.** *v* (*lists them*) hyō ni shimásu (suru, shite) 表にします（する, して）, (*puts it in a list*) (rísuto ni) iremásu (ireru, irete) (リストに)入れます（入れる, 入れて）

listen *v* kikimásu (kiku, kiite) 聞きます（聞く, 聞いて）; [HUMBLE] uketamawarimásu (uketamawaru, uketamawatte) 承ります・うけたまわります（承る, 承って）

listener *n* kiki-te 聞き手, risunā リスナー

lit; is ~ tsúite imásu (iru, ite) ついています・点いています（いる, いて）

liter *n* rittoru リットル

literary 1. *adj* (*literature*) búngaku (no) 文学（の）; (*bookish*) bungo-tcki (na) 文語的(な) **2.** *n literary style* bungo-tai 文語体

literature *n* búngaku 文学

litter 1. *n* (*rubbish*) kúzu くず・屑, kuzu-mono くず物・屑物, garakuta がらくた **2.** *n* (*stretcher*) tánka 担架 **3.** *v* (*to throw litter*) (gomi o) chirakashimásu (chirakasu, chirakashite) (ゴミを)散らかします（散らかす, 散らかして）

little *adj* (*in size*) chiisái 小さい, chíisa-na 小さな; chítchái ちっちゃい, chítcha-na ちっちゃな; (*in quantity*) sukunái 少ない, sukóshi (no) 少し（の） *a little* sukóshi 少し, wazuka わずか; (*somewhat*) yáya やや

a little at a time sukoshí-zútsu 少しずつ

a little while ago saki-hodo 先程, sákki さっき

little by little sukoshí zútsu 少しずつ; sórosoro そろそろ

live 1. *v* (*resides*) súnde imásu (iru, ite) 住んでいます（いる, いて）; (*is alive*) íkite imásu (iru, ite) 生きています（いる, いて）; (*gets along*) kurashimásu (kurasu, kurashite) 暮らします（暮らす, 暮らして）; *lets/makes it ~* ikashimásu (ikásu, ikáshite) 生かします（生かす, 生かして） **2.** *adj* (*animal*) ikita 生きた, (*broadcast*) raibu (no) ライブ（の）, nama/jikkō hōso (no) 生/実況放送（の） **3.** *adv* (*broadcast*) raibu de ライブで, nama/jikkō hōso de 生/実況放送で, (*live performance*) 生で

livelihood *n* seikei 生計

lively *adj* (*cheerful*) yōki (na) 陽気（な）, (*peppy*) kappatsu (na) 活発（な）, ikiiki (to) shita 生き生き（と）した, génki (na) 元気（な）, (*flourishing*) nigíyaka (na) 賑やか・にぎやか（な）

live-out *adj* kayoi (no) 通い（の）

liver *n* kimó 肝, kanzō 肝臓, (*as food*) rébā レバー **liver transplant** *n* kan(-zō) ishoku 肝（臓）移植

livestock *n* kachiku 家畜

living allowance *n* seikatsu-hi teate 生活費手当(て)

living costs *n* seikatsú-hi 生活費

living room *n* ímá 居間, (*Japanese-style*) zashíkí 座敷(o-zashiki お座敷), (*Western-style*) ribingu (rūmu) リビング（ルーム）

living thing *n* ikímono 生き物・いきもの

lizard *n* tokage とかげ・トカゲ・蜥蜴

loach *n* dojō どじょう・ドジョウ

load 1. *n* nímotsu 荷物 (o-nímotsu お荷物), ní 荷 **2. ~ it** *v* (*piles it on*) tsumimásu (tsumu, tsunde) 積みます・つみます（積む, 積んで）, (*puts it aboard*) nosemásu (noseru, nosete) 載せます・のせます（載せる, 載せて）

loaf *v* (*around*) búrabura shimásu (suru, shite) ぶらぶらします（する, して）; (*on the job*) saborimásu (sabóru, sabótte) さぼります・サボります（さぼる、さぼって）

loaf n (of bread) katamari 固まり・塊・かたまり, hitó-kátamari 一固まり[塊]・ひとかたまり

loaf cake n rōfu kēki ローフケーキ

sandwich loaf n shoku-pan 食パン

loan → lend

lobby n róbii ロビー

lobster n ise ebi 伊勢えび[海老・エビ]・イセエビ, robusutā ロブスター

local 1. adj chihō´ (no) 地方（の）, rō´karu (na) ローカル（な）; (of the city) machí (no) 町（の）, (within the city) shínai (no) 市内（の） **2.** n jimoto 地元

local downpour n shūchū-gō´u 集中豪雨

local paper n chihō´-shi 地方紙, chihō´-shinbun 地方新聞

local specialty n méibutsu 名物

local telephone call n shinai dénwa 市内電話

local train n kakueki téisha (no ressha) 各駅停車（の列車）; (non-express) futsū dénsha 普通電車

location n **1.** íchi 位置, basho 場所 **2.** (computer) rokēshon ロケーション **3.** (shooting place) rokechi ロケ地

location of offices n kaisha (no) shozai-chi 会社（の）所在地, jimusho (no) shozai-chi 事務所（の）所在地

lock 1. n jō(-mae) 錠（前）, kagí 鍵, rokku ロック **2. locks** v (a door) (ni) kagí o kakemásu (kakéru, kákete) (戸に)鍵を掛けます・かぎをかけます（掛ける、掛けて）; (shuts it) shimemásu (shiméru, shímete) 閉めます・しめます（閉める、閉めて） **3. it locks** v kagí ga kakarimásu (kakáru, kakátte) 鍵が掛かります・かぎがかかります（掛かる、掛かって）, (it shuts) shimari másu (shimáru, shimátte) 閉まります・しまります（閉まる、閉まって）

locker n rókkā ロッカー; (coin-operated) **baggage lockers** koin rókkā コインロッカー

lodging n (lodging house) geshuku (-ya) 下宿（屋）

log n maruta 丸太 (**1:** íp-pon 一本, **2:** ní-hon 二本, **3:** sánbon 三本, **how many** nán-bon 何本)

logic n rónri 論理, rikutsu 理屈

logical adj ronri-teki (na) 論理的（な）, rojikaru (na) ロジカル（な）

login n (computer) roguin ログイン, setsuzoku 接続

loincloth n fundoshi ふんどし・褌, sarumata 猿股, koshi-maki 腰巻き

loin(s) n koshi 腰

London n Róndon ロンドン

loneliness n kodoku 孤独・こどく

lonely adj hitori (no) ひとり・独り（の）, sabishíi 寂しい・淋しい・さびしい, wabishíi わびしい・侘びしい, kokoro-bósói 心細い

feel lonely sabishíi 寂しい・淋しい・さびしい

long 1. adj nagái 長い **2.** adv nágaku 長く **3. long for** v machi-kogaremásu (machi-kogareru, machi-kogarete) 待ち焦がれます・まちこがれま

す（待ちこがれる、待ちこがれて）

for a long time adv nágaku 長く・ながく, nagái aida 長い間, (in the past) máe kara 前から

after a long time adv (of absence) hisashi-buri ni 久しぶりに・ひさしぶり

how long (a time) adv dono-gurai どの位・どのくらい

long ago adv mukashi 昔・むかし; súde-ni 既に・すでに

long and slender/narrow adj hosói 細い・ほそい

long awaited adj machidōshíi 待ち遠しい

long before adv daibu máe ni だいぶ[大分]前に; súde-ni 既に・すでに; ma-mó-naku 間もなく・まもなく, sórosoro そろそろ, yagate やがて

long-distance adj chō-kyóri (no) 長距離（の）

long distance telephone n chō-kyori denwa 長距離電話

long distance runner n chō-kyori rannā 長距離ランナー

longer adj mótto (nágaku) もっと（長く）; **no ~, not any ~** mō´ もう + [NEGATIVE]

long-nosed goblin n tengu 天狗・テング

long-period adj (time) chō´ki 長期

long-range adj chō´ki 長期

longsighted → farsighted

longsleeved kimono n furisode 振り袖・ふりそで

long-term contract n chō´ki keiyaku 長期契約

long-time bills n chō´ki-tegata 長期手形

long-winded adj kudó´i くどい

loofah → luffa

look 1. n (appearance) yōsu 様子・ようす; (personal appearance) kíryō 器量, kao 顔; (a look in one's eyes) mé-tsuki 目付き・目つき **2. it looks like** v (as though) ... yō´/mítai desu (da/na, de, ni) ...よう/みたいです（だ/な、で、に）; [NOUN] dátta yō´/mítai desu (da/na, de, ni) ...だったよう/みたいです（だ/な、で、に）; [VERB] -(r)u/-ta yō´/mítai desu (da/na, de, ni) う[る]/たよう/みたいです（だ/な、で、に）; [ADJECTIVE] -i/-kátta yō´/mítai desu (da/na, de, ni) い/かったよう/みたいです（だ/な、で、に） **3. look (at)** v (... o) mimásu (míru, míte) (...を)見ます（見る、見て）, [HUMBLE] haiken shimásu (suru, shite) 拝見します（する、して）, [HONORIFIC] goran ni narimásu (náru, nátte) ご覧になります（なる、なって）

look after v ... no sewá o shimásu (suru, shite) ...の世話をします（する、して）, ... no mendō´ o mimásu (míru, míte) ...の面倒を見ます・...のめんどうをみます（見る、見て）, (a matter) shóri o shimásu (suru, shite) 処理をします（する、して）; (takes over) hiki-torimásu (hiki-tóru, hiki-tótte) 引き取ります（引き取る、引き取って）

look around for v (shop around for) busshoku shimásu (suru, shite) 物色します（する、して）

look back v furi-kaerimásu (furi-kaeru, furi-kaétte) 振り返ります・ふりかえります（振り返る、振り返って）

look down v utsumukimásu (utsumuku,

utsumuite) うつむきます・俯きます（うつむく、うつむいて）

look for **1.** (searches) sagashimásu (sagasu, sagashite) 捜します［探す］ます(捜す・探す, 捜し［探し］て); motomemásu (motoméru, motóme-te) 求めます・もとめます(求める, 求めて), tazunemásu (tazunéru, tazúnete) 尋ねます・たずねます(尋ねる, 尋ねて)・うかがいます (伺う, 伺って) **2.** (expects) machimásu (mátsu, mátte) 待ちます・まちます(待つ, 待って)

look out on, look out to v … o nozomimásu (nozomu, nozónde) …を望みます・…をのぞみます(望む, 望んで)

look up v (a word) hikimásu (hiku, hiite) 引きます・ひきます(引く, 引いて)

loom n hatá 機

loop n **1.** (ring) wá 輪 **2.** (shape) kanjō 環状; loop line kanjō-sen 環状線 **3.** (computer) rūpu ループ

loophole n (hole) aná 穴・アナ

loose 1. adj yurúi ゆるい・緩い, bára (de) ばら(で) **2.** lets it ~ v (releases) hanashimásu (hanásu, hanashite) 放します・はなします(放す, 放して) **3.** gets/comes ~ v zuremásu (zuréru, zúrete) ずれます(ずれる, ずれて), (slack) tarumimásu (tarumu, tarunde) たるみ[弛み]ます(たるむ, たるんで)

loot n ryakudatsu-hin 略奪品

looting n ryakudatsu 略奪

loquacious adj taben (na) 多弁(な), oshaberi (na) おしゃべり・お喋り(な)

loquat n bíwa びわ・ビワ・枇杷

lord n (feudal) daimyō 大名; ryōshu 領主; go-shujin-sama ご主人様; Lord ~ ~ kyō ~ 卿

lorry n torakku トラック

Los Angeles n Rosanzérusu ロサンゼルス, Rosu ロス

lose v nakushimásu (nakusu, nakushite) なくします・なくします(なくす, なくして), ushinaimásu (ushinau, ushinatte) 失います・うしないます(失う, 失って); (gets defeated) makemásu (makeru, makete) 負けます・まけます(負ける, 負けて), mairimásu (máiru, máitte) 参ります・まいります(参る, 参って)

lose color v (iró ga) samemásu (saméru, sáme-te) 色がさめます(さめる, さめて)

lose consciousness v ki/íshiki o ushinaimásu (ushinau, ushinatte) 気/意識を失います(失う, 失って)

lose patience v shibire o kirashimásu (kirásu, kiráshite) しびれを切らします(切らす, 切らして)

loss n **1.** songai 損害, sonshitsu 損失 **2.** (defeat) make 負け shippai 失敗

lost 1. it gets ~ v naku-narimásu (naku-naru, naku-natte) なくなります(なくなる, なくなって) **2.** (a person) gets ~ v (michi ni) mayoimásu (mayóu, mayótte) (道に)迷います・まよいます(迷う, 迷って) **3.** n (item) otoshimono 落とし物

lost child n máigo 迷子

lot 1. n (in a lottery) kúji くじ・クジ; (vacant land) aki-chi 空き地; parking lot chūsha-jō 駐車場 **2.** a lot, lots adj (much/many) takusán (no) たくさん[沢山](の), ṓi 多い・おおい, ṓ ku no 多くの・おおくの; ṓku 多く・おおく, tábun ni 多分に; yóku よく

lottery n takará-kuji 宝くじ・宝クジ, fukubiki 福引(き)

lotus n hasu はす・ハス・蓮; lotus root renkon れんこん・レンコン・蓮根

loud adj (noise) ōkíi 大きい・おおきい, ṓ ki-na 大きな・おおきな, in a ~ voice ṓ gúe de 大声で, kowadaka (ni) 声高(に); (color) hadé(na) はで[派手](な)

loudspeaker n kakuséi-ki 拡声器, supíikā スピーカー

lounge n **1.** (break room) kyūkći-shitsu 休憩室 **2.** (in a hotel, etc.) raunji ラウンジ **3.** (chair) ne-isu 寝椅子

louse → lice

lovable adj kawaíi かわいい・可愛い, kawairashíi かわいらしい・可愛らしい

love 1. n kói 恋, ren'ai 恋愛, ai 愛, rabu ラブ; ~ marriage ren'ai-kékkon 恋愛結婚 **2.** n (tennis) rabu ラブ; fifteen ~ fifutiin rabu フィフティーン・ラブ **3.** v aishimásu (aisúru, áishite) 愛します(愛する, 愛して); kawai-garimásu (kawai-gáru, kawai-gátte) かわい[可愛]がります(かわいがる, かわいがって), kói ni ochimásu (ochiru, ochite) 恋に落ちます(落ちる, 落ちて) → like; falls in ~ (with) … ni horemásu (horeru, horete) …に惚れ[ほれ]ます(惚れる, 惚れて), kói ni ochimásu (ochiru, ochite) 恋に落ちます(落ちる, 落ちて)

love affair n ren'ai-kánkei 恋愛関係, rómansu ロマンス

lovely adj **1.** airashii 愛らしい **2.** (beautiful) utsukushii 美しい・うつくしい **3.** (pretty) kawaii 可愛い・かわいい

lover n koibito 恋人, íi-hito いい人; (devotee of …) (…no) aikō-ka (…の)愛好家, …-zuki …好き; lovers' suicide shinju 心中

low adj (short) hikúi 低い; (cheap) yasúi 安い; low gear teisoku gí(y)a 低速ギア[ヤ]

low (barometric) pressure n tei-kíatsu 低気圧

low blood pressure n tei-kétsúatsu 低血圧

low voice n kogoe 小声

low-wage adj tei-chingin (no) 低賃金(の)

lower 1. adj shita no 下(の); (cheaper) by ¥100 hyakuén-yasu 百円安 **2.** ~ it v sagemásu (sagéru, ságete) 下げます・さげます(下げる, 下げて), oroshimásu (orósu, oróshite) 下ろします・おろします(下ろす, 下ろして); ~ one's eyes mé o fusemásu (fuséru, fusete) 目を伏せます(伏せる, 伏せて), utsumukimásu (utsumuku, utsumuite) うつむきます・俯きます（うつむく、うつむいて）

lowest adj (minimum, minimal) sáika (no) 最下(の), (bottom) saitei (no) 最低(の); the lowest (degree) saitei géndo 最低限度

lowly *adj* (*shabby*) iyashii 卑しい・いやしい
loyal *adj* chūjitsu (na) 忠実(な), seijitsu (na) 誠実(な)
luck *n* **1.** ún 運 **2.** (*fate*) únmei 運命 **3.** (*happiness*) shiawase 幸せ・しあわせ
  good luck **1.** *interj* ganbatte (kudasai). 頑張って下さい・がんばってください **2.** *n* kōun 幸運
  bad luck **1.** *adj* un ga warui 運が悪い **2.** *n* akuun 悪運, fu-un 不運
luckily *adv* ún-yoku 運良く・運よく
lucky *adj* ún ga íi 運がいい; shiawase (na) 幸せ・しあわせ(な); (*strikes it lucky*) tsúite imás̲u (iru, ite) ついています(いる, いて)
  lucky bag *n* fuku-bukuro 福袋
  lucky charm *n* o-mamori お守り
  lucky seventh *n* rakkii sebun ラッキー・セブン
  lucky star *n* kōun no hoshi 幸運の星
  lucky shot *n* magure atari まぐれ当たり
luffa *n* (*sponge gourd*) hechima へちま・ヘチマ・糸瓜
luggage *n* (te-)nímotsu (手)荷物, temáwari 手回り, temawari-hin 手回り品
lukewarm *adj* nurúi ぬるい
lumber *n* zaimoku 材木, zái 材
lump *n* katamari 固まり・塊・かたまり
lunch *n* hiru góhan 昼御飯・昼ごはん (hirú 昼,

o-híru お昼), chūshoku 昼食, ránchi ランチ; (*box*) bentō´ 弁当 (o-bentō お弁当)
lunch break *n* hiru yasumi 昼休み・昼やすみ, hiru kyūkei 昼休憩
luncheon special *n* ranchi sā´bisu ランチサービス
lung cancer *n* hai-gan 肺がん・肺癌
lungs *n* hai 肺
lure 1. *n* (*decoy*) otori おとり **2.** *n* (*fishing*) ruā ルアー **3.** *v* obikidashimás̲u (obikidásu, obikidáshite) おびき出します(おびき出す, おびき出して)
lurid *adj* **1.** (*horrible*) zottosuru ぞっとする **2.** (*shocking*) shokkingu (na) ショッキング(な) **3.** (*bright red*) makka (na) 真っ赤(な)
luscious *adj* **1.** (*delicious*) oishii 美味しい・おいしい **2.** (*good smell*) kaori ga/no yoi 香りが/の良い・かおりが/のよい **3.** (*sensual*) kannōteki (na) 官能的(な)
lush *adj* (midori no) shigetta (緑の)茂った, aoao to shita 青々とした, mizumizushii みずみずしい
lute *n* (*Japanese lute*) bíwa 琵琶・ビワ
luxury, luxurious *adj* zeitákú (na) ぜいたく[贅沢](な); (*deluxe*) gō´ka (na) 豪華(な)
luxury goods, luxuries *n* zeitaku-hin ぜいたく[贅沢]品
lyrics *n* kashi 歌詞

M

macabre *adj* zotto suru ぞっとする
macaroni *n* makaroni マカロニ
machination *n* inbō 陰謀, keiryaku 計略, takurami たくらみ
machine *n* k̲ikái 機械, mashin マシン (*how many* nán-dai 何台)
machine gun *n* k̲ikan-jū 機関銃, mashin gan マシンガン
machiner *n* k̲ikái kō 機械工
machinery *n* k̲ikái 機械
mackerel *n* saba サバ・鯖
  mackerel pike *n* sanma サンマ・秋刀魚
mad *adj* (*insane*) ki-chigái (no) 気違い(の); (*goes mad*) ki ga kuruimás̲u (kurū´, kurútte) 気が狂います(狂う, 狂って); muchū ni narimás̲u (náru, nátte) 夢中になります(なる, なって); *gets ~* (*angry*) okorimás̲u (okóru, okótte) 怒ります(怒る, 怒って)
Madam *n* óku-san/-sama 奥さん/様, madamu マダム
made → make
made in ...-sei; ...製; *made in Japan* Nihon-sei (no) 日本製(の), meido in japan メイド・イン・ジャパン
madman *n* kichigai 気違い
madness *n* kyōki 狂気

maestro *n* (*great musician/artist*) ... senséi ...先生, maesutoro マエストロ
magazine *n* zasshi 雑誌 (*how many* nán-satsu 何冊), magajin マガジン
magic (*tricks*) *n* téjina 手品; majikku マジック
magical *adj* mahō (no) 魔法(の); *magical world* mahō no sekai 魔法の世界
magician *n* tejiná-shi 手品師
magistrate *n* hanji 判事
magnate *n* yūryokusha 有力者
magnesium *n* maguneshium マグネシウム
magnet *n* jíshaku 磁石, magunetto マグネット
  magnetic *adj* jíki (no) 磁気(の), jíshaku (no) 磁石(の)
magnificent *adj* subarashíi すばらしい・素晴らしい; sōdai (na) 壮大(な)
magnifying *adj* kakudai (shita) 拡大(した)
magnifying glass *n* rūpe ルーペ, mushi megane 虫メガネ; *magnifying glass icon* mushi megane no aikon 虫メガネのアイコン
magnitude *n* magunichūdo マグニチュード
magnolia *n* mokuren モクレン・木蓮
magpie *n* kasasagi カササギ・鵲
mahjong *n* majan マージャン・麻雀
  mahjong parlor *n* mājan-ya マージャン[麻雀]屋
  mahjong tile *n* pái パイ

mahogany *n* mahoganii マホガニー

maid *n* (*servant*) otétsudai(-san) お手伝い（さん）, mḗ´do/meido メード／メイド

maiden *n* otome 乙女・おとめ, (*girl*) shōjo 少女

maiden name *n* kyūsei 旧姓

mail **1.** *n* yūbin 郵便 **2.** *v* (*mails it*) (tegami o) dashimásu (dásu, dáshite) （手紙を）出します・だします (出す, 出して), yūsō shimásu (suru, shite) 郵送します (する, して)

  mail box *n* yūbínbako 郵便箱, pósuto ポスト

  mail drop *n* pósuto ポスト

  mail officer *n* yūbin kyoku-in 郵便局員

  mail ordor *n* tsūshin hanbai 通信販売

mailing *n* yūsō 郵送

mailman, mail deliverer *n* yūbin-ya (san) 郵便屋（さん）

main *adj* ómo (na) 主（な）, shuyō (na) 主要（な）; hon-... 本...

  main course *n* mein kōsu メインコース

  main road/route *n* honsen 本線; *main road to a shrine* omote sándō 表参道

  main store *n* honten 本店

  main street *n* ōdō´ri 大通り; mein sutoriito メインストリート

mainland *n* hondo 本土

mainly *adv* ómo ni 主に

mainstay *n* (*person*) daikokubashira 大黒柱

mainstream *n* honryū 本流

maintain *v* (*preserves*) hóshu shimásu (suru, shite) 保守します (する, して); (*supports*) shíji shimásu (suru, shite) 支持/維持します (する, して); (*insists*) shuchō shimásu (suru, shite) 主張します (する, して)

maintenance *n* (*preservation*) hóshu 保守; (*support*) shíji 支持, (*upkeep*) íji 維持

majesty *n* ō zoku 王族

  Your Majesty *interj* Heika 陛下

major *n* (*army*) shōsa 少佐; (*line/field/study*) senmon 専門; (*mainstream*) mejā メジャー; (*study*) senkō (shimásu; suru, shite) 専攻 (します; する, して) → **main** → **big**

  major city *n* shuyō tóshi 主要都市

  major general *n* shō´shō 少将

  Major League Baseball *n* mejā riigu メジャーリーグ

majority *n* dai-búbun 大部分, dai-tasū´ 大多数, (*more than half*) kahansū 過半数

make **1.** *v* (*does*) shimásu (suru, shite) します (する, して), (*creates*) tsukurimásu (tsukúru, tsukutte) 作ります (作る, 作って), (*concocts*) koshiraemásu (koshiraeru, koshiraete) こしらえます (こしらえる, こしらえて) **2.** *n* seizō 製造, (*type*) kata(-shiki) 型 (式)

  make a fire *v* (hí o) takimásu (taku, taite) （火を）焚きます・たきます (焚く, 焚いて)

  make a living *v* kurashimásu (kurasu, kurashite) 暮らします (暮らす, 暮らして)

  make do *v* (*with* ...) (...de) ma-ni-awasemásu (ma-ni-awaséru, ma-ni-awásete) (...で) 間に合わ

  せます（間に合わせる, 間に合わせて）

  make good, make up for *v* ...o oginaimásu (ogináu, oginátte) ...を補います (補う, 補って)

  make money *v* (*profit*) (kane o) mōkemásu (mōkéru, mō´kete) （金を）もうけ [儲け] ます (もうける, もうけて)

  make one do *v* (... ni ... o) sasemásu (saseru, sasete) (...に...を) させます (させる, させて)

  make sure *v* tashikamemásu (tashikaméru, tashikámete) 確かめます (確かめる, 確かめて)

  make the most of ... *v* o ikashimásu (ikásu, ikáshite) ...を生かします (生かす, 生かして)

make-believe *adj* mise-kake (no) 見せかけ・みせかけ (の)

maker *n* (*manufacturer*) mḗ´ka メーカー, seizō-moto 製造元

makeshift *adj* ma-ni-awase 間に合わせ・まにあわせ

makeup *n* keshō´ 化粧 (o-keshō お化粧), mēkyáppu メーキャップ; (*cosmetics*) keshō hin 化粧品; (*structure*) kumi-tate 組み立て, kōzō 構造

  makeup exam *n* tsui-shikén 追試験, sai-shikén 再試験

malady *n* byōki 病気

malaria *n* mararia マラリア

male **1.** *n* otokó 男, dansei 男性; (*animal*) (...no) osú (...の) 雄; *male and female* dánjo 男女 **2.** *adj* (*gender*) otokó (no) 男 (の), dansei (no) 男性 (の); (*animal*) osú (no) 雄 (の)

malefactor *n* **1.** (*bad man*) akunin 悪人 **2.** (*criminal*) hannin 犯人

malevolence *n* akui 悪意

malevolent *adj* akui no aru 悪意のある

malfunction *n* koshō 故障

malice *n* ákui 悪意

malicious *adj* akui no aru 悪意のある, iji no warui 意地の悪い

malignant *adj* akushitsu (na) 悪質 (な)

mall *n* (*shopping*) mōru (ショッピング)モール

mallet *n* kizuchi 木槌

  mallet of luck *n* uchide no kozuchi 打ち出の小槌

malt *n* bakuga 麦芽

  malt beer *n* moruto biiru モルトビール

  malt beverage *n* bakugashu 麦芽酒

malum *n* byōki 病気, shikkan 疾患

mama *n* mama ママ, o-kāsan おかあさん・お母さん, o-kāchan おかあちゃん・お母ちゃん

mammal *n* honyū-rui 哺乳類, honyū dōbutsu 哺乳動物

mammoth *n* manmosu マンモス

man *n* **1.** (*male*) otokó 男, otoko no hitó/katá 男の人/方, dánshi 男子, (*middle-aged*) oji-san おじさん, (*old*) ojíisan おじいさん, (*young*) o-níi-san お兄さん **2.** (*person*) hito 人, ... hitó ...人

manage *v* (*treats*) tori-atsukaimásu (tori-atsukau, tori-atsukatte) 取り扱います (取り扱う, 取り扱って); (*copes with*) shóri shimásu (suru, shite) 処理します (する, して); (*runs a business*) keiei shimásu (suru, shite) 経営します (する, して); (*a* *team*) kantoku shimásu (suru, shite) 監督します（する，して）

manage to (*do*) dō´ni ka shimásu (suru, shite) どうにかします（する，して）; konashimásu (konasu, konashite) こなします（こなす，こなして）

management n keiei 経営; manējimento マネージメント; (*control*) shíhai 支配; (*handling*) tori-atsukai 取り扱い

manager n shíhai-nin/-sha 支配人/者, kanri-nin 管理人, máné´jā マネージャー; (*sports*) kantoku 監督

Manchuria n Mánshū 満州

Mandarin Chinese n Mandarin マンダリン, Chūgoku hyōjun-go 中国標準語, pekin-go 北京語

mandarin orange → tangerine

mandate n shirei 指令

mandatory adj kyōsei-teki (na) 強制的(な)

mane n tategami たてがみ

man-eater n (*seductress*) otoko tárashi 男たらし

maneuver n sakusen 作戦, enshū 演習

manga n (*comic*) manga 漫画・まんが・マンガ

manganese n mangan マンガン

mangle v zutazuta ni shimásu (suru, shite) ずたずたにします（する，して）, mechamecha ni shimásu (suru, shite) めちゃめちゃにします（する，して）

mango n mangō マンゴー

mangy adj kitanarashii 汚らしい, misuborashii みすぼらしい, fuketsu (na) 不潔(な)

manhandle v teara ni atsukaimásu (atsukau, atsukatte) 手荒に扱います（扱う，扱って）

manhood n 1. (*manly*) otoko rashisa 男らしさ 2. (*adult male*) seijin danshi 成人男子, seinen dansei 成年男性

mania n mania マニア

maniac n maniakku マニアック

manicure n manikyua マニキュア

manifest 1. adj akiraka (na) 明らか・あきらか(な) 2. v arawaremásu (arawaréru, arawárete) 現れます（現れる，現れて）, (*make it clear*) akiraka ni shimásu (suru, shite) 明らかにします（する，して）

manifestation n meiji 明示, hyōmei 表明

manifesto n sengen 宣言, seimei 声明

Manila n Mánira マニラ

manipulate v sōjū shimásu (suru, shite) 操縦します（する，して）, (*a person*) (hito o) ayatsuru (人を)操る・あやつる

mankind n jinrui 人類

manliness n otokorashisa 男らしさ

manly adj otokorashii 男らしい

mannequin n manekin (ningyō) マネキン(人形)

manner (*of doing*) n yari-kata やり方, shi-kata 仕方; furí ふり; (*fashion*) (…) fū (…)風・ふう

manners n gyōgi 行儀, sáhō 作法, manā マナー; **→ etiquette**

manor n shōen 荘園

manpower n rōdō-ryoku 労働力

mansion n daigōtei 大邸宅

mantelpiece n rodana 炉棚, danro no mae no tana 暖炉の前の棚

mantis shrimp n sháko しゃこ・シャコ・蝦蛄

manual n manyuaru マニュアル, tebikisho 手引き書

manufacture v seisan/seizō shimásu (suru, shite) 生産/製造します（する，して）, tsukurimásu (tsukúru, tsukutte) 作[造]ります・つくります（作[造]る，作[造]って）

manuscript n genkō 原稿

many adj takusán (no) たくさん［沢山］(の), ō´ku (no) 多く(の); *are/have many …* ga ō´i …が多い; *how many* íkutsu いくつ, nán-… 何…

map n chízu 地図, mappu マップ; (*diagram*) zu 図; (*how many*) nán-mai 何枚)

maple n kaede かえで・カエデ・楓, mómiji もみじ・モミジ・紅葉

maple syrup n mēpuru shiroppu メープルシロップ

marathon n marason マラソン; *marathon runner* marason senshu マラソン選手, marason rannā マラソンランナー; *marathon relay race* ekiden 駅伝

marble n (*marble stone*) dairi-seki 大理石

marbles n o-hájiki おはじき, biidama ビー玉

march 1. n kōshin 行進, māchi マーチ 2. (*music*) kōshin kyoku 行進曲 3. v kōshin shimásu (suru, shite) 行進します（する，して）

March n Sán-gatsu 三月・3月

mare n (*horse*) meuma 雌馬

margarine n māgarin マーガリン

margin n (*white space*) yohaku 余白; (*leeway*) yoyū 余裕, yochi 余地; (*price difference*) rizáya 利鞘・利ざや, májin マージン

marijuana n marifana マリファナ

marina n mariina マリーナ

marine(s), Marine Corps n kaihei tai 海兵隊

mariner n suifu 水夫

marionette n ayatsuri ningyō 操り人形・あやつり人形, marionetto (ningyō) マリオネット(人形)

marital adj kon'in (no) 婚姻(の)

mark 1. n (*sign*) shirushi 印, kigō 記号, māku マーク, ato 跡 2. n (*vestige*) konseki 痕跡; *leaves a ~* konseki o nokoshimásu (nokósu, nokóshite) 痕跡を残します（残す，残して） 3. n (*score point*) ten ten 点, (*score*) tensū´ 点数; (*school grades*) seiseki 成績 4. v (*makes a mark on*) (… ni) shirushi/kigō/ten o tsukemásu (tsukéru, tsukéte) (…に)印/記号/点を付けます（付ける，付けて）

market n íchi(-bá) 市(場), shijō 市場, mā´ketto マーケット; *vegetable ~* seika íchiba 青果市場

marketing n māketingu マーケティング

marketplace n íchi-bá 市場

marksman n shashu 射手

marmalade n māmarēdo マーマレード

maroon n, adj kuri iro (no) 栗色・くり色(の)

marriage n kekkon 結婚; *marriage proposal* endan 縁談

marron glacé n marongurasse マロングラッセ

marrow *n* kotsuzui 骨髄; spinal ~ sekizui 脊髄

marry *v* (… to) kekkon shimásu (suru, shite) (…と) 結婚します(する, して)

Mars *n* kasei 火星
　Martian *n* kaséijin 火星人

marsh *n* numa (chi) 沼 (地)

marshy *adj* nukarunda ぬかるんだ

martial arts *n* bújutsu 武術, búdō 武道; *martial arts hall* dō jō 道場

marvelous *adj* suteki (na) すてき[素敵](な), sugói すごい・凄い

mask *n* men 面 (o-men お面), kamen 仮面, másuku マスク; (*Noh drama*) nō-men 能面

mash *v* suritsubushi másu (suritsubusu, suritsubushite) すり潰します・すりつぶします (すりつぶす, すりつぶして)

mashed potatoes *n* masshu poteto マッシュポテト

marshmallow *n* mashumaro マシュマロ

masochism *n* mazo(-hizumu) マゾ(ヒズム), jigyaku 自虐

mason *n* sekkō 石工

masque *n* kamen geki 仮面劇

masquerade *n* kasō pātii 仮装パーティ, kamen budō kai 仮面舞踏会

mass *n* 1. (*Buddhist*) hōji 法事, (*Catholic*) mísa ミサ 2. (*lump*) katamari 固まり・塊; (*people*) taishū 大衆, kōshū 公衆, minshū 民衆
　mass communications *n* masu-komi マスコミ
　mass media *n* マスメディア
　mass meeting *n* taikai 大会

massacre 1. *n* daigyakusatsu 大虐殺, mina-goroshi 皆殺し 2. *v* gyakusatsu shimásu (suru, shite) 虐殺します(する, して)

massage 1. *n* massá´ji マッサージ, anma あんま・按摩 2. *v* (*rubs with both hands*) momimásu (momu, monde) 揉みます・もみます(揉む, 揉んで)

masseur *n* massájí-shi マッサージ師, anma あんま・按摩

massive *adj* bōdai (na) 膨大(な)

mast *n* hashira 柱, masuto マスト

master *n* 1. (*of house*) shújin 主人, danna-san/-sama 旦那さん/様 2. (*of shop*) masutā マスター, danna 旦那 3. (*owner*) (mochí-)nushi (持ち)主 4. (*college degree*) shū´shi 修士 5. (*maestro*) senséi 先生, (*artisan*) oyakata 親方, shishō 師匠; *grand master* (*martial arts*) shihan 師範

masterpiece *n* kessaku 傑作, meisaku 名作

master's thesis *n* shūshi-rónbun 修士論文

mastery *n* 1. (*conversance*) seitsū 精通 2. (*control*) shihai 支配

masturbate *v* jíí/shuin o shimásu (suru, shite) 自慰/手淫をします(する, して), onanii o shimásu (suru, shite) オナニーをします(する, して)

mat *n* shiki-mono 敷物・しきもの, mátto マット; (*Japanese floor*) tatami 畳・タタミ, (*thin*) gozá ござ・ゴザ; (*how many* nán-mai 何枚)

match 1. *n* (*sports*) shiai 試合, kyō´gi 競技; (*contest*) shō´bu 勝負 2. *v* (*matches, equals, is a match for*) … ni kanaimásu (kanáu, kanátte) …にかないます(かなう, かなって) …to yóku aimásu (áu, átte) …とよく合います(合う, 合って)

matchbook *n* kami-mátchi 紙マッチ (*how many* íkutsu いくつ)

matchbox *n* matchí-bako マッチ箱

match(es) *n* (*for fire*) mátchi マッチ; (1: íppon 一本, 2: níhon 二本, 3: sánbon 三本; *how many* nán-bon 何本)

matchmaker *n* 1. matchí seizō gyō-sha マッチ製造業者 2. nakōdo 仲人・なこうど

mate *n* 1 (*friend*) nakama 仲間, tomodachi 友達・友だち 2. (*spouse*) haigū-sha 配偶者
　classmate *n* dōkyū-sei 同級生, kurasu meito クラスメイト
　workmate *n* shigoto nakama 仕事仲間, (*colleague*) dōryō 同僚

material *n* 1. (*cloth*) kíji 生地 2. *raw material* zairyō 材料, zái 材 3. (*topic*) táne 種; → **substance**

material *adj* (*physical*) busshitsuteki (na) 物質的(な)

materialism *n* busshitsu chúgi 物質主義

materialize *v* genjitsu-ka shimásu (suru, shite) 現実化します(する, して)

materials *n* zairyō´ 材料, genryō´ 原料, shíryō 資料

mathematical *adj* sūgaku (no) 数学(の)

mathematics *n* 1. sūgaku 数学; *mathematician* sūgáku-sha 数学者 2. (*subject of elementary school, calculation*) sansū 算数・さんすう

matinee *n* máchíne マチネー; hiru no bú 昼の部

matter *n* 1. kotó 事・こと, (*problem*) mondai 問題・もんだい 2. (*something that is*) *the matter* (*amiss, wrong*) ijō 異常, (*hitch*) kómatta kotó 困った事・こまったこと, (*bad aspect/point/thing*) warúi tokoró/ten/kotó 悪いところ/点/事
　What's the matter? *interj* Dō´shita *n* desu ka. どうしたんですか.
　It doesn't matter. *interj* Kamaimasén 構いません・かまいません.

mattress *n* mattoresu マットレス

mature *v* (*growth, developed*) seijuku shimásu (suru, shite) 成熟します(する, して); *fully matures* enjuku shimásu (suru, shite) 円熟します(する, して)

maturity *n* seijuku 成熟

maudlin *adj* kanshō-teki (na) 感傷的(な), namida moroi 涙もろい

mausoleum *n* (*an Imperial tomb*) ryō´ 陵, (dai) reibyō 霊廟

maxim *n* kakugen 格言

maximal *adj* (*greatest*) saidaigen (no) 最大限 (の); (*highest*) saikō (no) 最高(の)

maximum 1. *n* saidai-gén 最大限 2. *adj* → **maximal**

May *n* Gó-gatsu 五月・5月

may *v* (*perhaps*) …kámo shiremasén …かもしれ

ません; (*it is OK to do*) (shi)-témo íi desu (し)て もいいです

maybe *adv* tábun (… deshō´) 多分 (…でしょう), … kámo shiremasén …かもしれません; hyótto shita ra/shite/suru to ひょっとしたら/して/する と; arúi-wa あるいは・或いは

mayonnaise *n* mayonēzu マヨネーズ

mayor *n* shíchō´ 市長

maze *n* meiro 迷路, meikyū 迷宮

me *pron* watashi わたし・私, wata-kushi わたく し・私; (*male*) boku ぼく・僕, *[unrefined]* ore おれ・オレ・俺; watashi/watakushi (o/ni) 私 (を/に); (*male*) boku/ore (o/ni) 僕/俺 (を/に)

meadow *n* sōgen 草原・そうげん, kusahara 草原, kusachi 草地

meager *adj* sukunái 少ない, toboshii 乏しい

meal *n* (o-)shokuji (お)食事; (o-)shokuji o shimásu; suru, shite (お)食事をします; する, し て), góhan ご飯 (góhan o tabemásu; tabéru, tábete ご飯を食べます; 食べる, 食べて); (**1:** is-shoku 一食, **2:** ní-shoku 二食, **3:** sán-shoku 三食, *how many*; nán-shoku 何食)

a set/complete meal *n* teishoku 定食; *a set meal (of house choices)* sétto セット, kō´su コース with meals (*included*) *adj* shoku(-ji) tsuki (no) 食事付き・食事つき (の)

meal ticket *n* shokken 食券 (*how many*; nán-mai 何枚)

mean *v it means …* … to iu ími desu …という意 味です; … o ími shimásu (suru, shite) …を意味 します (する, して); *what I mean is …* ii-tai kotó wa … 言いたい事は…・いいたいことは…

meaning *n* ími 意味, wáke 訳・わけ; (*significance*) ígi 意義; (*what one wants to say*) ii-tai kotó 言いたい事・いいたいこと

meaningful *adj* ími ga aru 意味がある, yūigi (na) 有意義 (な)

meaningless *adj* mu-ími (na) 無意味 (な)

means *n* **1.** shúdan 手段, hōhō 方法, shi-kata 仕方, shi-yō 仕様 **2.** → **mean** by all means zé-hi 是非・ぜひ by some means (*or other*) nán to ka shite 何とか して・なんとかして means of transportation *n* kōtsū shudan 交通手 段; kōtsū kikan 交通機関 use any means hudan o erabimasen (erabanai, erabanaide) 手段を選びません (選ばない, 選ばな いで)

mean-spirited *adj* (*mean spirited*) ijí no warúi 意地の悪い → **stingy**

meantime *n* aida 間・あいだ in the meantime *adv* sono aida (ni) そのあいだ・ その間 (に), sono-uchi (ni) そのうち (に)

meanwhile *adv* sono-uchi (ni) そのうち (に); (*on the other hand*) ippō´ 一方

measles *n* hashika はしか

measure 1. *n* → **a means 2.** *n* (*ruler*) mono-sáshi 物差し, mejā メジャー **3.** *measures it* *v* hakari-másu (hakáru, hakátte) 計ります (計る, 計って)

measuring tape *n* maki-jaku 巻き尺

measurement(s) *n* sunpō 寸法

meat *n* nikú 肉・ニク (o-níku お肉); *grilled meat* yaki-niku 焼肉・ヤキニク

meatballs *n* (*Chinese*) niku-dángo 肉団子, miito bōru ミートボール

meat cleaver *n* nikukiri-bō´chō 肉切り包丁

mechanic *n* (*car repairman*) shūrí kō 修理工, seibi-shi 整備士; *automobile mechanic* jidōsha seibishi 自動車整備士

mechanical *adj* kikai-teki (na) 機械的 (な), kikai (no) 機械 (の)

mechanics *n* rikigaku 力学

medal *n* medaru メダル, kunshō 勲章; *gold medal* kin medaru 金メダル; *silver medal* gin medaru 銀 メダル; *bronze medal* dō medaru 銅メダル

medallion *n* ōgata medaru 大型メダル

meddle *v* o-sékkai o yakimásu (yáku, yaíte) おせ っかい[お節介]を焼きます (焼く, 焼いて)

meddling *n* o-sékkai おせっかい・お節介; kan-shō 干渉; sewá 世話・せわ (o-séwa お世話)

media *n* (masu-)media (マス)メディア → **mass**

mediation *n* (*good offices*) assen あっせん・斡 旋; chōtei 調停

mediator *n* assen-sha あっせん・斡旋者; chōtei-sha 調停者; chūsai-nin 仲裁人

medical *adj* igaku no 医学の, naika no 内科の medical department *n* ígaku bu 医学部, íkyoku 医局 medical examination *n* shinsatsu 診察, kenkō´ shindan 健康診断

medicine *n* **1.** kusuri 薬・くすり (o-kusúri お薬), [FORMAL] yakuzai 薬剤 **2.** (*doctoring*) ígaku 医学

meditation *n* mokusō 黙想; meisō 瞑想; meditēshon メディテイション; (*ascetic training*) shugyō 修行, gyō´ 行; (*Zen*) zazen 座禅

Mediterranean *n* chichū-kai 地中海

medium 1. *adj* chūkan (no) 中間 (の) **2.** *n* chūkan 中間; baitai 媒体 medium-fat tuna *n* chū-toro 中とろ・中トロ medium-rare *adj* (*meat*) han-yake (no) 半焼け (の), midiamu rea ミディアム・レア medium-size *n* (*model*) chūgata 中型

medley *n* (*music*) medorē メドレー

meek *adj* súnao (na) すなお[素直] (な)

meet *v* **1.** (*sees a person*) …ni aimásu (áu, átte) …に会います (会う, 会って); (*welcomes*) …o mukaemásu (mukaeru, mukaete) …を迎えます (迎える, 迎えて), … o de-mukaemásu (de-mukaeru, de-mukaete) …を出迎えます (出 迎える, 出迎えて) (*happens to meet*) de-aimásu (de-au, de-atte) 出会います (出会う, 出会って), (*encounters*) ses-shimásu (ses-suru, ses-shite) 接します (接する, 接して) **2.** (*they assemble*) atsumarimásu (atsumáru, atsumátte) 集まります (集まる, 集まって), shūgō shimásu (suru, shite) 集合します (する, して)

meeting *n* **1.** kái 会; (*mass meeting*) taikai 大会; (*conference*) káigi 会議, miitingu ミーティング

370

2. (*interview*) menkai 面会; (*of prospective bride and groom*) miai 見合い **3.** (*by prior arrangement*) uchi-awase 打ち合わせ

megahertz (MHz) *n* megaherutsu メガヘルツ

megaphone *n* megahon メガホン

melancholy *n, adj* yūutsu (na) 憂うつ・ゆううつ (な), merankorii (na) メランコリー(な)

mellow *v* (*gets mellow*) enjuku shimásu (suru, shite) 円熟します(する, して)

melodrama *n* merodorama メロドラマ

melody *n* merodii メロディー, senritsu 旋律

melon *n* méron メロン; úri 瓜・ウリ

melt *v* (*it melts*) tokemásu (tokéru, tókete) 溶け ます(溶ける, 溶けて); (*melts it*) tokashimásu (tokásu, tokáshite) 溶かします(溶かす, 溶かして)

member *n* ménbā メンバー, kai-in 会員; (*ichi-*) in (一)員

membership *n* ménbā shippu メンバーシップ, kai-in 会員

memo(randum) *n* mémo メモ

memorial *n* kinen hi 記念碑

memorial service *n* (*remembrance ceremony*) tuitō-shiki 追悼式; (*funeral*) kokubetsu-shiki 告別式; (*100 days after the death*) hyákkanichi 百か日

memorize *v* anki shimásu (suru, shite) 暗記しま す(する, して)

memory *n* obóe 覚え・おぼえ, monoóboe 物覚 え・ものおぼえ, kioku 記憶, (*computer*) memori メモリ, memorii メモリー, (*capacity*) kiokú-ryoku 記憶力; (*a recollection*) omoide 思い出; *by/from memory* sóra de そらで, anki shite 暗記して

memory stick *n* memori stikku メモリスティ ック

men → **man**

mend *v* ~ *it* naoshimásu (naósu, naóshite) 直し ます・なおします(直す, 直して), tsukuroimásu (tsukuróu, tsukurótte) 繕います・つくろいます(繕う, 繕って)

mending *n* shū́ri 修理, naoshí 直し → **repair**

menstruation *n* gekkei 月経, seiri 生理

menswear *n* otoko mono 男物

mental *adj* séishin (no) 精神(の)

mental care *n* seishin-teki na kea 精神的なケア, mentaru kea メンタルケア

mental disease *n* seishin-byō 精神病, seishin shōgai 精神障害, seishin shikkan 精神疾患

mentality *n* shínri 心理, kangaekata 考え方

mention 1. *v* ... ni furemásu (fureru, furete) ...に 触れます(触れる, 触れて); [BOOKISH] ...ni gen-kyū shimásu (suru, shite) ...に言及します (する, して) **2.** → **say**
Don't mention it. *interj* Dṓ itashimashite. どういたしまして.

mentor *n* (*yoki*) jogen-sha (良き)助言者, shidō-sha 指導者, senpai 先輩

menu *n* kondate 献立・こんだて, ményū メニ ュー

merchandise *n* shōhin 商品

merchant *n* shṓnin 商人

mercy *n* megumi 恵み・めぐみ; nasake 情け・ なさけ

mere *adj* hon no ... ほんの...; táda ただ; [BOOK-ISH] tán naru ... 単なる...

merely *adv* táda ただ, tatta たった; [BOOKISH] tán ni 単に

merge *v* (*they unite*) gappei shimásu (suru, shite) 合併します(する, して); (*they flow together*) gōryū shimásu (suru, shite) 合流します(する, して) Lanes Merge (*Ahead*), Merge (*Lanes*) "Gōryū chū́i" "合流注意"

merger *n* gappei 合併; (*confluence*) gōryū 合流

merit *n* (*strong point*) chṓsho 長所

merry *adj* yúkai (na) 愉快・ゆかい (な), (*bustling*) nigíyaka (na) にぎやか[賑やか] (な) Merry Christmas. *interj* Kurísúmásu omedetō クリスマスおめでとう

mess *n* (*disorder*) konran 混乱; (*predicament*) komátta koto 困った事・こまったこと, (*plight*) (kurushíi) hamé (苦しい) 羽目; (*bungle*) héma へま・ヘマ; *makes a damn ~ of it* héma o yarakashimásu へま[ヘマ]をやらかします; *It's a ~.* Taihen désu né. 大変ですね. *I'm in a ~.* Komátte imásu. 困っています.

message *n* kotozuke ことづけ・言付け, kotozute ことづて・言伝て, mésséji メッセージ, o-tsuge お告げ

message board *n* dengonban 伝言板, (*bulletin board*) keijiban 掲示板

messenger *n* tsukai 使い, (*internet*) messenjā メッセンジャー

messenger boy *n* tsukaihashiri (no shōnen) 使い走り (の少年)

messenger of God *n* kami no tsukai 神の使い

messenger RNA *n* messenjā āru enu ē メッセン ジャーRNA

messiah *n* kyūsei-shu 救世主, meshia メシア

messy *adj* kitanái 汚い・きたない, chirakatte(i)ru 散らかって(い)る

messy situation *n* konran 混乱

metal *n* kínzoku 金属, metaru メタル heavy metal *n* (*music*) hebimeta ヘビメタ

meter *n* **1.** (*of length*) mētoru メートル **2.** (*device*) kéiki 計器, mētā メーター

method *n* shi-kata 仕方; shi-yō 仕様, hōhō 方法, ... hō ...法

metro(politan) *adj* tokai (no) 都会(の); (*run by Tokyo*) toei 都営

Mexico *n* mekishiko メキシコ

mezzanine (*floor*) *n* chū-ní-kai 中二階

microcomputer *n* maikuro konpyūta/konpyūtā マイクロコンピュータ/コンピューター

microphone *n* maiku マイク, maikurohon マイ クロホン

microscope *n* kenbi-kyō 顕微鏡

microwave *n* **1.** (*wave*) maikuro-ha マイクロ波 **2.** (*kitchen microwave*) denshi renji 電子レンジ

midday *n* mahiru 真昼, shōgo 正午

middle 1. *n* náka 中, mannaka 真ん中・まんなか, chūshin 中心; naka ba 半ば; chūkan 中間; (*medium size*) chū´ 中 **2.** *adj* mannaka (no) 真ん中・まんなか(の), chūkan (no) 中間(の)
the middle of (*month*) *n* chūjun 中旬, nakaba 半ば・なかば
middle of the night *n* (ma)yonaka 真夜中
middle volume *n* (*of a set of three*) *n* chū-kan 中巻, chū´ 中
middle age *n* chū-nen 中年
middle-aged *adj* chū-nen (no) 中年(の)
middle school *n* (*junior high*) chūgakkō 中学校
midget *n* chíbi ちび・チビ
midnight *n* ma-yónaka 真夜中
midst *n* (… no) sáichū (…の)最中
midsummer/midyear gift *n* (o-)chūgen (お)中元
might 1. *n* → **perhaps 2.** *v* → **power**
mild *adj* yawarakái 柔らかい・やわらかい; (*taste*) maroyaka まろやか; (*moderate*) odayaka (na) 穏やか(な)
mildew *n* kabi かび・カビ
mile *n* mairu マイル
military *n, adj* gunrai (no) 軍隊(の), gunjin (no) 軍人(の)
military base *n* (gunji) kíchí (軍事)基地
military occupation *n* senryō 占領
military officer *n* shō´kō 将校
military person *n* gunjin 軍人
military uniform *n* gunpuku 軍服
milk *n* míruku ミルク, gyūnyū 牛乳; *mother's milk* chíchí 乳, bonyū 母乳, [BABY TALK, SLANG] óppai おっぱい
milkman *n* gyūnyū-ya 牛乳屋, gyūnyū haitatsu (-nin) 牛乳配達(人)
milkshake *n* miruku sē´ki ミルクセーキ
millet *n* áwa あわ・アワ・粟
milligram *n* miriguramu ミリグラム
million *n* hyaku mán 百万・1,000,000
millionaire *n* mirionērā ミリオネラー, hyaku man chōja 百万長者
million city *n* hyaku man toshi 百万都市
million dollar *n* mirion darā ミリオン・ダラー, ichi oku-en purēyā 1億円プレーヤー
million-seller *n* mirion serā ミリオンセラー
mimic *n* … no mane (o shimásu; suru, shite) …のまね[真似](をします; する, して)
mimicry *n* mane まね・真似
minced meat *n* hiki-niku 挽き肉・ヒキニク
mincing (*fish/meat*) *n* tatakí 叩き, …-tátaki …叩き
mind *n* kokóro 心, omói 思い・想い, séishin 精神; muné 旨・むね; ki 気; kokorozashi 志, (*what one has in mind*) tsumori つもり, ikō 意向
bear/keep in mind fukumimásu (fukúmu, fukúnde) 含みます(含む, 含んで); oboemásu (oboéru, obóete) 覚えます(覚える, 覚えて)
Do you mind? *interj* Íi desu ka? いいですか?
if you don't mind *adv* nan-nára なんなら, yoroshikáttara よろし[宜し]かったら

Never mind. *interj* Kamaimasén 構いません・かまいません.
one's right mind *n* shōki 正気
set one's mind *v* kokoro-zashimásu (kokoro-zasu, kokoro-zashite) 志します・こころざします (志す, 志して)
mine *pron* (*my*) wata(ku)shi no わた(く)しの・私の
mine *n* (*coal, etc.*) kō´zan 鉱山
miner *n* tankō sagyōin 炭坑作業員
mineral water *n* mineraru wōtā ミネラルウォーター
minimal *adj* (*smallest, least*) saishō no 最小の; (*lowest*) saitei (no) 最低(の), sáika (no) 最下(の)
minimum 1. *n* (*degree*) saishō-gén 最小限 **2.** *adj* → **minimal**
minimum rate *n* saitei chingin 最低賃金
minimum standard of living *n* saitei seikatsu suijun 最低生活水準
minister *n* (*pastor*) bokushi 牧師; (*cabinet*) dáijin 大臣
Ministry *n* …-sho …省
Ministry of Agriculture, Forestry and Fisheries of Japan (MAFF) *n* Nōrin-Suisan-shō 農林水産省
Ministry of Defense *n* Bōei-shō 防衛省
Ministry of Economy, Trade and Industry *n* Keizai Sangyō-shō 経済産業省
Ministry of Education, Culture, Sports, Science and Technology (MEXT) *n* Monbú Kagaku-shō 文部科学省
Ministry of Finance *n* Zaimú-shō 財務省
Ministry of Health, Labour and Welfare *n* Kōsei-Rōdō-shō 厚生労働省
Ministry of Internal Affairs and Communications (MIC) *n* Sōmu-shō 総務省
Ministry of Justice *n* Hōmu-shō 法務省
Ministry of Land, Infrastructure, Transport and Tourism (MLIT) *n* Kokudo-Kōtsū-shō 国土交通省
Ministry of the Environment (MOE) *n* Kankyō-shō 環境省
minus *n* mainasu マイナス
minute *n* …-fun …分 (1: íp-pun 一分, 2: ni-fun 二分, 3: sánpun 三分, 4: yónpun 四分, 5: gó-fun 五分, 6: róp-pun 六分, 7: naná-fun 七分, 8: háp-pun 八分, 9: kyū´-fun 九分, 10: júp-pun 十分; *how many* nán-pun 何分)
in a minute *adv* súgu (ni) すぐ(に); tadáima ただ今・只今・ただいま
minutes after *adv* chokugo (ni) 直後(に)
minute *adj* (*fine, detailed*) bisai (na) 微細(な), seimitsu (na) 精密(な)
minutes *n* gijiroku 議事録
mirror 1. *n* kagamí 鏡・カガミ **2.** *v* (*reflects it*) utsushimásu (utsúsú, utsúshite) 映します(映す, 映して)
side mirror *n* (*car*) saido mirā サイドミラー
rearview mirror *n* (*car*) bakku mirā バックミラー

miscarriage n ryū´zan 流産

miscast v haiyaku o ayamarimásu (ayamaru, ayamatte) 配役を誤ります・あやまります(誤る, 誤って)

miscellaneous adj samazama (na) 様々・さまざま(な), zatta (na) 雑多(な); *miscellaneous goods* zakka 雑貨

mischief n itazura いたずら・悪戯

mischievous adj wanpaku (na) 腕白・ワンパク (な); *mischievous child* itazurakko いたずらっ子

miserable adj wabishíi わびしい・侘しい; nasake-nái 情けない・なさけない, míjíme (na) みじめ・惨め(な)

"Les Miserables" n (title) "ā mujō" 『ああ無情』

misfortune n fukō´ 不幸, wazawai 災い・わざわい

mishap n kegá けが・怪我(o-kéga おけが・お怪我), wazawai 災い・わざわい → **accident**

misrepresent v gomakashimásu (gomakásu, gomakáshite) ごまかします・誤魔化しします(ごまかす, ごまかして)

miss 1. n (mistake) mísu ミス **2.** v (goes wide off the mark) hazuremásu (hazureru, hazurete) 外れます・はずれます(外れる, 外れて), (fails) shippai shimásu (suru, shite) 失敗します(する, して) **3.** v (is not in time for) (…ni) ma ni aimasén (awánai, awánaide) (…に)間に合いません・まにあいません(合わない, 合わないで) **4.** v (yearns for) …ga natsukashíi …が懐かしい; (feels lonely without) …ga inakute/nákute sabishíi …がいなくて/なくて寂しい

Miss n … san …さん, … san no ojō´-san …さんのお嬢さん

missing 1. n (person) yukue fumei no hito 行方不明の人, yukue fumei-sha 行方不明者; (it) is ~ arimasén (nái, nákute) ありません(ない, なくて); (he) is ~ imasén (inai, ináide) いません(いない, いないで) **2.** adj yukue fumei (no) 行方不明(の), miataranai 見当たらない, mitsukaranai 見つからない, fusoku shita 不足した

mission n (task) ninmu 任務, (operation) sakusen 作戦, (Christianity) fukyō (katsudō) 布教(活動)

missionary n senkyō´shi 宣教師

mist n kasumi かすみ・霞, kiri きり・霧, móya もや・靄

mistake 1. n machigái 間違い・まちがい, ayamárí 誤り・あやまり, ayamáchí 過ち・あやまち, mísu ミス, misuteíku ミステイク **2.** v (makes a mistake) machigaimásu (machigáu, machigátte) 間違います・まちがいます(間違う, 間違って), ayamarimásu (ayamáru, ayamátte) 誤ります・あやまります(誤る, 誤って) **3.** mistakes it v machigaemásu (machigáeru, machigáete) 間違えます・まちがえます(間違える, 間違えて)

mistletoe n yadorigi ヤドリギ

mistreat v gyakutai shimásu (suru, shite) 虐待します(する, して)

mistress n **1.** (Madam) óku-san/-sama 奥さん/様 **2.** (lover) káno-jo 彼女; (concubine) mekaké 妾・めかけ, o-mekake-san お妾さん, nígó(-san) 二号(さん)

misty; gets ~ kasumimásu (kasumu, kasunde) かすみます・霞みます(かすむ, かすんで)

misunderstand v gokai shimásu (suru, shite) 誤解します(する, して)

mix v (mixes it in with) (… ni sore o) mazemásu (mazéru, mázete) (…にそれを)混ぜます・まぜます(混ぜる, 混ぜて); (it mixes) mazarimásu (mazáru, mazátte) 混ざります・まざります(混ざる, 混ざって), majirimásu (majíru, majítte) 混じります・まじります(混じる, 混じって); *mixing one's foods/drinks* chánpon ちゃんぽん mixed bathing kon'yoku 混浴

mixture n (assortment) kumiawase 組み合わせ・くみあわせ, kongō 混合

moan v nagekimásu (nagéku, nagéite) 嘆きます・なげきます(嘆く, 嘆いて)

moat n horí 堀; *inner moat* uchi-bori 内堀, *outer moat* soto-bori 外堀

mobile 1. n keitai (denwa) 携帯(電話) **2.** adj mochi-hakoberu 持ち運べる

mobile phone n keitai (denwa) 携帯(電話)

model n mohan 模範, tehón 手本(o-tehon お手本); (mold) mokei 模型; (type) katá 型, …-gata …型, …-kei …型; móderu モデル

fashion model n fasshon moderu ファッション・モデル

supermodel n sūpā moderu スーパーモデル

moderate 1. adj (reasonable) tekido (no) 適度 (の); (properly limited/restrained) odayaka (na) 穏やか・おだやか(な); (conservative) hikaeme (na) 控えめ・ひかえめ(な) **2.** moderates it v kagen shimásu (suru, shite) 加減します(する, して)

moderation n tékido 適度, setsudo 節度; kagen 加減

modern adj géndai (no) 現代(の), kindai (no) 近代(の), modan モダン

modern dance n modan dansu モダンダンス

modern music n kindai ongaku 近代音楽

modern people n gendai-jin 現代人

modern state n kindai kokka 近代国家

modernization n gendai-ka 現代化, kindai-ka 近代化

modest adj kenkyo (na) 謙虚(な), hikaeme (na) 控え目・ひかえめ(な), uchiki (na) 内気(な); (small) ō´kiku nái 大きくない

Mohammed n mohameddo モハメッド, muhanmado ムハンマド

moisten v shimeshimásu (shimesu, shimeshite) 湿します・しめします(湿す, 湿して)

mold 1. n (pattern) katá 型; (model) mokei 模型 **2.** (growth) kabi かび・カビ, 黴; is moldy kabi ga háete imásu かびが生えています **3.** v katachizukurimásu (katachi-zukuru, katachi-zukútte) 形作ります(形作る, 形作って)

mole *n* (*on skin*) hokuro ほくろ・ホクロ; (*rodent*) mogura もぐら・モグラ・土竜

molester *n* (*sexual*) chikan 痴漢・ちかん・チカン

moment *n* (*instant*) shunkan 瞬間, sétsuna せつな・刹那

at the moment isshun 一瞬

just a moment chótto matte kudasai ちょっと待って下さい

on the spur of the moment tokí no hazumi de 時の弾みで

(at) the moment that ... totan ni ... とたん[途端]に

momentum *n* hazumi 弾み・はずみ

Monday *n* Getsuyō′(-bi) 月曜(日); *Monday-Wednesday-Friday* ges-sui-kin 月水金

money *n* (o-)kane (お)金; (*money given as a New Year's gift*) otoshi-dama お年玉 → **cash** → **finance**

money-changer *n* (*money-changing machine*) ryōgaé-ki 両替機

money changing/exchange *n* ryōgae 両替

money market *n* kin'yū shíjō 金融市場

money offering (*to a shrine*) *n* (o-)saisen (お)さい銭・(お)賽銭

money order *n* kawase 為替; (*postal*) yūbin káwase 郵便為替

Mongolia *n* Mongoru モンゴル

monk *n* (*Buddhist*) bō′zu 坊主, obō-san お坊さん; *young monk* kozō′ 小僧, kozō-san 小僧さん

monkey *n* sáru 猿・サル(o-saru お猿)

monorail *n* monorē′ru モノレール

monster *n* kaibutsu 怪物, kaijū 怪獣, monsutā モンスター

month *n* tsukí 月, ...-getsu ...月 (*how many months*) nan-kágetsu 何ヵ月)

month after next *n* sarai-getsu 再来月

month before last *n* sensén-getsu 先々月

monthly *adj* maitsuki (no) 毎月(の); *monthly installments/payments* geppu 月賦; *monthly salary* gekkyū 月給

monument *n* monyumento モニュメント, kinen hi 記念碑

mood *n* kíbun 気分, kokoro-mochi 心持ち, mūdo ムード

good mood *n* jō-kigen 上機嫌, (go-)kigen (ご)機嫌

moody *adj* kigen ga warúi 機嫌が悪い

moon *n* tsukí 月, ó-tsuki-sama お月様

moon-faced *adj* marugata (no) 丸型(の); marugao (no) 丸顔(の); (*moon-faced woman*) okáme おかめ

moonlight night *n* tsukí-yo 月夜

moonrise *n* tsuki no de 月の出

moon viewing *n* tsuki-mí 月見 (o-tsukimi お月見)

mop *n* móppu モップ

moral 1. *n* moraru モラル 2. *adj* dōtoku-teki (na) 道徳的(な)

morality, morals *n* dōtoku 道徳; (*ethics*) shū′shin 修身

more *adj* mótto もっと, mō sukóshi もう少し, mō mō う + [NUMBER]; (*some ~*) sára-ni さらに・更に

a little more *adj* mō sukóshi もう少し

a lot more *adj* mótto takusán もっとたくさん[沢山]

all the more ..., still/much ~ ... *adv* issō ... 一層・いっそう, nao-sara なおさら・尚更

the more ... the more *adv* ...-suréba suruhodo/dake ...すればする程/だけ... (issō ... 一層・いっそう...)

more and more *adv* masú-masu ますます・益々, iyó-iyo いよいよ

more or less *adv* tsúmari つまり; tashō 多少

more than anything *adv* náni yori mo 何よりも・なによりも

more than enough *adv* tappúri たっぷり

moreover *adv* sono ue (ni) その上・そのうえ(に), matá 又・また, náo 尚・なお, shiká-mo しかも, kótoni ことに・殊に

morning *n* ása 朝・あさ, go zen 午前; *this ~* kesa 今朝

Good morning. O-hayō (gozaimásu). おはよう[お早う]ございます.

morning glory *n* (*flower*) ásagao 朝顔・アサガオ

morning meal *n* chōshoku 朝食, asa-góhan 朝ご飯

morning paper *n* chōkan 朝刊

morning sun *n* ásahi 朝日

morphine *n* moruhine モルヒネ

mortar *n* (*utensil*) úsu うす・臼; suríbachi すり鉢; (*material*) morutaru モルタル, shikkui しっくい・漆喰

mortifying *adj* kuyashíi 悔しい

Moscow *n* Mosukuwa モスクワ

mosquito *n* ka 蚊・カ

mosquito net *n* kaya かや・カヤ・蚊帳

moss *n* koke こけ・コケ・苔

most *adj* ichiban 一番, móttómo 最も

most of the ... *adj* ... no daibúbun ...の大部分

at most *adv* ō′kute 多くて, sémete せめて, séizei せいぜい

for the most part *adv* ōkata おおかた, taigai 大概・たいがい, ō′ku 多く

the most *adj* (*largest*) saidai (no) 最大(の)

most recent *adj* (+ [DATE]) saru ... 去る...; kono mae/aida (no) この前/間(の); tsui saikin (no) つい最近(の)

moth *n* ga が・ガ・蛾; (*clothes moth*) íga いが・イガ・衣蛾, shimi しみ・衣魚, mushi 虫・ムシ

mothballs *n* bōchū′-zai 防虫剤; mushi-yoke 虫よけ

mother *n* okā′-san お母さん, háha 母, haha-oya 母親; ofukuro おふくろ・お袋

mother country *n* bókoku 母国, sókoku 祖国

mother-in-law *n* gíbo 義母; (*husband or wife's mother*) shūtome しゅうとめ・姑, o-shūtome-san お姑さん

mother's milk n chichí 乳, bonyū 母乳; [baby talk] óppai おっぱい

motion n ugokí 動き・うごき; mō´shon モーション; *motion sickness* norimono-yoi 乗物酔い

motivation, motive n dōki 動機; yaruki やる気

motor n hatsudō´-ki 発動機, mō´tā モーター → **automobile**

motorcycle n ōtóbai オートバイ (*how many* nán-dai 何台)

motor race, motor racing n jidōsha rēsu 自動車レース, kā rēsu カーレース

motto n hyōgo 標語, mottō モットー

mould → mold

mound n tsuká 塚; (*burial*) ryō´ 陵

mount v (*ride*) ... ni norimásu (noru, notte) ...に乗ります(乗る, 乗って); (*sits astride*) ... ni matagarimásu (matagáru, matagátte) ...にまたがります・跨ります(またがる, またがって); (*climb*) ... ni noborimásu (noboru, nobotte) ...に登ります(登る, 登って)

mountain n yamá 山; ...-san ...山

mountain bicycle/ bike n maunten baiku マウンテンバイク

mountain-climber n tozán-sha 登山者

mountain-climbing n yama nóbori 山登り・山のぼり, tozan 登山; *mountain-climbing rope* záiru ザイル

mountain lodge n yama-goya 山小屋

mountain pass n tōgé 峠

mountain range n sanmyaku 山脈

Mount Fuji n Fúji-san 富士山

mouse n 1. nezumi ねずみ・ネズミ・鼠, hatsuka nézumi 二十日ねずみ[鼠・ネズミ] 2. (*computer*) mausu マウス

mousetrap n nezumí-tori ねずみ[鼠]取り[捕り]

mouth n 1. (*human*) kuchi 口 2. (*river mouth*) kakō 河口

mouthful n (*one ~*) hitó-kuchi 一口

mouth organ n hāmonika ハーモニカ

movable type n katsuji 活字

move 1. v (*it moves*) ugokimásu (ugóku, ugóite) 動きます(動く, 動いて); (*moves it*) ugokashimásu (ugokásu, ugokáshite) 動かします(動かす, 動かして) 2. (*moves residence*) utsurimásu (utsúru, utsútte) 移ります(移る, 移って), (*changes residence*) hikkoshimásu (hikkósu, hikkóshite) 引っ越します(引っ越す, 引っ越して); (*moves into an apartment*) nyūkyo shimásu (suru, shite) 入居します(する, して)

movement n ugokí 動き; katsudō 活動; undō 運動; (*gesture*) miburi みぶり・身振り, dōsa 動作

mover n (*household ~*) hikkoshi-ya 引っ越し屋, (*hikkoshi no*) unsō-ya 引っ越しの)運送屋

movie(s) n eiga 映画
  movie theater n eigá-kan 映画館
  movie projector n eishá-ki 映写機
  movie actor/actress n eigá haiyū/joyū 映画俳優/女優

moving n (*one's household*) hikkoshi 引っ越し;

moving man → **mover**

mover's van n hikkoshi torákku 引っ越しトラック

mow v karimásu (karu, katte) 刈ります(刈る, 刈って)

moxibustion n (o-)kyū (お)きゅう・(お)灸・キュウ

Mr. n ... san ...さん; *Mrs.* ... san (no óku-san) ...さん(の奥さん), ...-fujin ...夫人; *Mr. and Mrs.* ... fusái ... 夫妻; *Ms.* ... san ...さん, ...jóshi ...女史

much adj, adv takusán (no) たくさん[沢山](の), ō´ku (no) 多く・おおく(の), un to うんと

is/has much adj ... ga ō´i ...が多い

not (very) much adv anmari あんまり + [NEGATIVE]

how much adv íkura いくら・幾ら(o-ikura おいくら), dono-gurai どの位・どのくらい

as much as adv ... gúrai ...位, ...no yō´ni ...のように[様]に; *~ one likes* (omóu) zonbun ni (思う)存分に

much more adj mótto takusán もっとたくさん[沢山], zutto ō´ku ずっと多く; (*still more*) issō いっそう・一層, nao-sara なおさら・尚更

much → how much

muck → mud

mucus n (*nasal*) hana (mizu) 鼻(水)

mud n doró 泥・ドロ

muddy adj doro-dárake (no) 泥だらけ(の); *gets ~* nigorimásu (nigóru, nigótte) 濁ります(濁る, 濁って)

mudfish n dojō どじょう・ドジョウ

muffin n mafin マフィン

muffler n mafurā マフラー

mug n 1. (*cup*) magu kappu マグカップ 2. (*beer mug*) jokki ジョッキ

mugged; *gets ~* (*robbed*) gōtō ni osowaremásu (osowareru, osowarete) 強盗に襲われます(襲われる, 襲われて)

muggy adj mushi-atsúi 蒸し暑い

mulberry n kúwa くわ・クワ・桑

mule n (*animal*) raba ラバ・騾馬

multiply v 1. (*grows*) fuemásu (fuéru, fúete) 増えます・ふえます(増える, 増えて) 2. (3 by 5 sán ni góo) kakemásu (kakéru, kákete) (3に5を)かけます・掛けます(掛ける, 掛けて) 3. (*increases*) fuyashimásu (fuyásu, fuyáshite) 増やします(増やす, 増やして)

mummy n miira ミイラ

mumps n otafuku kaze おたふく風邪

municipal adj shí (no) 市(の), shiritsu (no) 市立(の), kōritsu (no) 公立(の), (*urban*) shínai (no) 市内(の)

municipality n chihō jichitai 地方自治体

mural painter n hekiga-ka 壁画家

mural painting n hekiga 壁画

murder n satsujin 殺人, hitogóroshi 人殺し → **kill**

murmur → whisper

muscle n kínniku 筋肉, súji 筋; (*power*) kínryoku 筋力, chikará 力

muscle pains *n* kinniku-tsū 筋肉痛
museum *n* hakubútsú-kan 博物館; (*art gallery*)
bijútsú-kan 美術館
mushroom *n* kínoko きのこ・キノコ・茸;
(*thumb-like*) matsutake 松茸・マツタケ; (*large
brown*) shíitake 椎茸; (*straw*) enokí-dake/-take え
のき[榎・エノキ]茸
music *n* óngaku 音楽, myūjikku ミュージック,
(*traditional to the imperial court*) gágaku 雅楽
musical *n* myūjikaru ミュージカル
musical instrument *n* gakki 楽器; *musical
instrument score* gakufu 楽譜
musician *n* ongaku-ka 音楽家, myūjishan ミュー
ジシャン
musk *n* jakō ジャコウ
muskmelon *n* masuku meron マスクメロン
Muslim *n* **1.** isuramu kyōto イスラム教徒, kai
kyōto 回教徒 **2.** isuramu kyō(no) イスラム教
(の), kai kyō(no) 回教(の)
mussel *n* igai イガイ; *blue mussel* mūru-gai ム
ール貝
must *verbal auxiliary* ~ *do* (shi-) nákereba
narimasén (し)なければなりません; ~ *not* (*do*)
(shi-)té wa ikemasén (し)てはいけません
mustache *n* kuchi hige 口ひげ[髭]

mustard *n* karashi からし・カラシ・芥子,
masutādo マスタード
mutt *n* (*dog*) zasshu (ken) 雑種(犬)
mutton *n* maton マトン, hitsuji no niku 羊の肉
→ **lamb**
mutual *adj* o-tagai (no) お互い・おたがい(の);
[BOOKISH] sō´go (no) 相互(の)
mutually *adv* o-tagai ni お互いに・おたがいに;
[BOOKISH] sō´go ni 相互に
my *pron* wata(ku)shi no わた(く)し[私](の); *my
wife* kánai 家内
My my! My goodness! [EXCLAM] Sore wa sore
wa それはそれは
myopic *adj* kingan (no) 近眼(の), kinshi (no) 近
視(の)
myringa *n* (*medical*) komaku 鼓膜
myself *pron* jibun 自分, (watakushi) jíshin (私)
自身
by myself jibun jíshin de 自分自身で
mysterious *adj* (*strange*) fushigi (na) 不思議
(な); (*esoteric*) shinpi-teki (na) 神秘的(な)
mystery *n* nazo 謎・ナゾ, misuterii ミステリー,
(*secret*) himitsu 秘密・ヒミツ
myth *adj* shinwa 神話
mythologist *n* shinwa gakusha 神話学者

N

Nagasaki *n* Nagásaki 長崎; *Nagasaki City*
Nagasakí-shi 長崎市; *Nagasaki Prefecture*
Nagasakí-ken 長崎県
nail *n* kugi 釘・くぎ; (*finger, toe*) tsume 爪・ツメ
nail clippers *n* tsumekírí 爪切り
nail polish *n* manikyua (eki) マニキュア(液)
nail polish remover *n* jokō eki 除光液, manikyua
otoshi マニキュア落とし
naive *adj* mújaki (na) むじゃき・無邪気(な),
soboku (na) 素朴(な), naiibu (na) ナイーブ(な)
naked *adj* hadaka (no) 裸(の) → **nude**
naked eye *n* ragan 裸眼
name 1. *n* namae 名前 (o-namae お名前), na 名
2. *v* (*calls*) (…to) yobimásu (yobu, yonde)
呼びます(呼ぶ, 呼んで), (*dubs*) nazukemásu
(nazukéru, nazúkete) 名付けます(名付ける, 名付
けて); (*says the name of*) …no namae o iimásu
(iú, itte/yutte) …の名前を言います(言う, 言っ
て/ゆって)
list of names *n* meibo 名簿
name card *n* meishi 名刺
name plate/tag *n* na fuda 名札
name seal/stamp *n* ("*chop*") hankó はんこ・判
こ・判子
nameless *adj* mumei (no) 無名(の)
namely *adv* sunáwachi すなわち・即ち; tsumari
つまり

namesake *n* dōmei no hito 同名の人
nap *n* hiru-ne (o shimásu; suru, shite) 昼寝(をしま
す; する, して) 一眠り
napkin *n* nápukín ナプキン, fukín ふきん・布巾
narcotic(s) *n* mayaku 麻薬
narration *n* narēshon ナレーション
narrative *n* monogatari 物語; naratibu ナラティブ
narrator *n* narētā ナレーター; katari-te 語り手
narrow *adj* semái 狭い・せまい; hosói 細い・
ほそい
narrow mind *n* henkyō na kokoro 偏狭な心;
kyōryō na kokoro 狭量な心
narrow road *n* hosomichi 細道
NASA *n* nasa NASA; beikoku kōkū uchū kyoku
米国航空宇宙局
nasal mucus *n* hana-jiru 鼻汁 → **snivel**
nasty *adj* iyá (na) 嫌(な), akuratsu (na) 悪らつ・
悪辣(な)
nation *n* (*country*) kuni 国, kókka 国家; (*people*)
kokumin 国民; *how many nations* nan-kákoku
何か国
national *adj* kuni (no) 国(の); koku-…国…;
kokuritsu (no) 国立(の); kokumin (no) 国民の;
nashonaru ナショナル
national defense *n* kokubō 国防
National Foundation Day *n* (*11 February*)
Kenkoku-kínen no hi 建国記念の日

national park *n* kokuritsu kōen 国立公園
nationalist *n* kokka shugi-sha 国家主義者; (*patriot*) aikoku shugi-sha 愛国主義者
nationality *n* kokuseki 国籍
national(s) *n* kokumin 国民
nation-wide zénkokuteki (na/ni) 全国的 (な/に)
native *adj* bokoku (no) 母国 (の); umaretsuki (no) 生まれつき (の); neitibu ネイティブ
native American *n* Amerika senjūmin アメリカ先住民, Indian インディアン
native land *n* bokoku 母国
native language *n* bokoku-go 母国語
native place *n* shusshin chi 出身地; kuni 国 (o-kuni お国)
natural *adj* **1.** shizen (no, na) 自然 (の, な); tennen (no) 天然 (の); nachuraru ナチュラル **2.** *adj* (*proper, deserved*) tōzen (no) 当然 (の) **3.** (*to be expected*) … (suru) monó desu … (する) ものです
natural food *n* shizen shoku (-hin) 自然食 (品)
natural gas *n* tennen-gásu 天然ガス
naturally *adv* shizen ni 自然に; (*by nature*) motomoto もともと・元々 → **spontaneously** → **of course**
nature *n* **1.** shizen 自然 **2.** seishitsu 性質, shō 性, séi 性; (*quality*) shitsú 質; (*disposition*) táchi 質; *human nature* nínjó 人情 **3.** *by nature* mótó-yori もとより, motomoto もともと・元々
naughty *adj* wanpaku (na) 腕白・わんぱく (な), itazura (na) いたずら・悪戯 (な)
naughty child *n* itazurákko いたずらっ子・悪戯っ子; (*boy*) wanpaku-bōzu 腕白坊主, (*girl*) otenba お転婆
nausea *n* hakike 吐き気, (*medical term*) oshin 悪心, ōki 嘔気
nauseate *v feels nauseated* hakiké (o moyō-shimásu; moyōsu, moyōshuite) 吐き気 (を催します; 催す, 催して) → **queasy**
navel *n* (o-)heso (お) へそ
navigate *v* kōkai shimásu (suru, shite) 航海します (する, して); annái shimásu (suru, shite) 案内します (する, して)
navigation *n* kōkai 航海; (*car navigation system*) kānabi カーナビ
navy *n* káigun 海軍
navy blue *n* neibii burū ネイビーブルー, (nō) kon (濃) 紺
near *adj* chikái 近い; *adv* chikaku (ni) 近く (に)
near-miss *n* niamisu ニアミス
near (by) *adj* sóba (no) そば・側 (の); chikáku (no) 近く (の)
nearly *adv* hotóndo ほとんど・殆ど; mázu まず; hóbo ほぼ
nearsighted *adj* (*myopic*) kingan (no) 近眼 (の), kinshi (no) 近視 (の)
neat *adj* (*tidy*) kichín-to shite imásu (iru, ite) きちんとしています (いる, いて); (*attractive*) kírei (na) きれい[綺麗] (な)
necessarily *adv* kanarazu 必ず; *not ~* kagiri-masen (kagiranai) 限りません (限らない)

necessary *adj* hitsuyō (na) 必要 (な), (*needed*) nyūyō (na) 入用 (な); …ga irimásu (iru, itte) …が要ります (要る, 要って)
necessity *n* hitsuyō 必要
neck *n* kubi 首; (*of a bottle*) kubire くびれ
necklace *n* kubi-kázari 首飾り, nékkuresu ネックレス
necktie *n* nékutai ネクタイ; *puts on* (*wears*) *a ~* nékutai o musubimásu (musubu, musunde) ネクタイを結びます (結ぶ, 結んで), nékutai o shimásu (suru, shite) ネクタイをします (する, して)
need 1. *v needs to do* (… ga) irimásu (iru, itte) (…が) 要ります (要る, 要って), (… o) yō-shimásu (yō-súru, yṓ-shite) (…を) 要します (要する, 要して); (suru) hitsuyō ga arimásu (áru, átte) (する) 必要があります (ある, あって), (shi)-nákereba narimasén (し) なければなりません; *needs not do* (shi) nákute mo íidesu (し) なくてもいいです **2.** *n* (*necessity*) hitsuyō 必要; (*poverty*) hinkon 貧困, fújiyū 不自由; *is in ~* (*of help*) komarimásu (komáru, komátte) 困ります (困る, 困って)
needle *n* hári 針
sewing needle *n* núibari 縫い針
needlework *n* hari-shígoto 針仕事
needy *adj* mazushíi 貧しい, fú-jiyū (na) 不自由 (な), hinkon (na) 貧困 (な)
negation *n* uchi-keshi 打ち消し, hitei 否定
negative 1. *adj* shōkyoku-teki (na) 消極的 (な), hitei-teki (na) 否定的 (な), negatibu (na) ネガティブ (な) **2.** *n* (*film*) nega ネガ
neglect 1. *v* (*disregards*) múshi shimásu (suru, shite) 無視します (する, して); (*leaves undone*) hōtte okimásu (oku, oite) 放っておきます (おく, おいて); (*shirks*) okotarimásu (okotaru, okotatte) 怠ります (怠る, 怠って); *~ to write/visit* (go-) busata shimásu (suru, shite) (ご) 無沙汰します (する, して) **2.** *n* ikuji-hōki 育児放棄
neglectful *adj* taiman (na) 怠慢 (な); *I have been ~* (*in not keeping in touch with you*). Go-busata itashimáshita. ご無沙汰しました.
negligee *n* negurije ネグリジェ
negligence *n* taiman 怠慢; (*carelessness*) yudan 油断, fuchūi 不注意
negligent *adj* taiman (na) 怠慢 (な), zubora (na) ずぼら (な)
negligible *adj* wazuka (na) わずか (な)
negotiable *adj* kōshō no yochi ga aru 交渉の余地がある
negotiate *v* hanashi-aimásu (hanashi-au, hanashi-atte) 話し合います (話し合う, 話し合って); kōshō 交渉
negotiation *n* hanashi-ai 話し合い, kōshō (shimásu; suru, shite) 交渉 (します; する, して)
negotiator *n* kōshō-nin 交渉人
neighborhood *n* (go-)kínjo (ご) 近所
neighbor(ing) *adj* tonari (no) 隣り (の)
neither … nor … *adv* … mo… mo… も…も + [NEGATIVE]

neither one dóchira (no …) mo どちら（の…）も + [NEGATIVE]

nephew n oi おい・甥; *your nephew* oigo-san 甥子さん

nerve n shínkei 神経; *gets on one's nerves* shínkei ni sawarimásu (saware, sawatte) 神経に障ります（障る, 障って）

nervous adj **1.** shinkéi-shitsu (na) 神経質（な） **2.** (*feels self-conscious*) agarimásu (agaru, agatte) 上がります（上がる, 上がって） **3.** (*gets agitated*) dōyō shimásu (suru, shite) 動揺します（する, して） → **flustered 4.** (*feeling apprehensive*) kimí ga warúi 気味が悪い → **worried**

nervous breakdown n shinkei suijaku 神経衰弱

nest n su 巣

nest egg n hesokuri へそくり

nested boxes n jūbako 重箱 (o-jū お重)

net n **1.** ami 網, nétto ネット **2.** = *internet* nettó ネット

Netbook n (*computer*) netto-bukku ネットブック

Netherlander n Oranda-jin オランダ人

Netherlandic n, adj (*language*) Oranda-go (no) オランダ語（の）; (*person*) Oranda-jin (no) オランダ人（の）

Netherlands n Oranda オランダ

Netizen n (*internet*) netto-shimin ネット市民 (*from internet + citizen*)

net price n séika 正価

network n **1.** nettowāku ネットワーク, jōhō-mō 情報網 **2.** (*human network*) jinmyaku 人脈
network administrator n nettowāku kanri-sha ネットワーク管理者
computer network n konpyūta/konpyūtā nettowāku コンピュータ/コンピューターネットワーク

neurotic adj noirōze (no) ノイローゼ（の）

neutral(ity) adj chūritsu (no) 中立（の）, nyūtoraru ニュートラル

never adv kesshite 決して + [NEGATIVE]; *has ~ (done)* (shi)-ta kotó ga arimasén (nái) （し）た事がありません; *~ (does)* (su)-ru kotó wa arimasén (nái) （す）る事はありません; *~ mind* kamaimasén (kamawánai) 構いません（構わない）

never-ending adj owari no nai 終わりのない

nevertheless adv sore náno ni それなのに, tó-ni-kaku とにかく

new adj ataráshii 新しい; shín(-) … 新…; shínki (no) 新規（の）, nyū ニュー
new address n **1.** (*home*) shin-jūsho 新住所 **2.** (*email*) atarashii adoresu 新しいアドレス
new age n nyū eiji ニューエイジ
newborn baby n shinseiji 新生児
new moon n shin-getsu 新月, mikazuki 三日月
new movie n shin-saku (eiga) 新作（映画）
new version n atarashii bājon 新しいバージョン, shin bājon 新バージョン
new world n shin-sekai 新世界
new year n shínnen 新年; *Happy new year.* (Shínnen/Akemáshite) o-medetō（新年/明けまして）おめでとう.

New Year's (day) n ganjitsu 元日, gantan 元旦; O-shōgatsu お正月

New Year's eve ō-mísoka 大みそか・大晦日

newcomer n shinjin 新人

newest adj saishin (no) 最新（の）

newly adv ataráshiuku 新しく, aratámete 改めて・あらためて

newlyweds n shinkon fūfu 新婚夫婦

news n nyū´su ニュース, tsūshin 通信; (*newspaper item*) kíji 記事; (*word from*) táyori 便り, shōsoku 消息

news agency n tsūshin-sha 通信社

newscaster n nyūsu kyasutā ニュースキャスター

newsflash n nyūsu sokuhō ニュース速報

newsletter n nyūsu retā ニュースレター, kaihō 会報

newspaper n shinbun 新聞; (*morning*) chōkan 朝刊, (*evening*) yūkan 夕刊; (*company*) shinbún-sha 新聞社; *newspaper bill* shinbun-dai 新聞代

newsperson n shinbun-kísha 新聞記者

newsstand n (*at the station*) baiten 売店, (*kiosk*) kiosuku キオスク

news vendor n shinbun-úri 新聞売り

newt n imori イモリ

New York n Nyūyōku ニューヨーク

New Zealand n Nyūjiirándo ニュージーランド; *New Zealander* Nyūjiirandó-jin ニュージーランド人

next adj (*in time/order*) tsugí (no) 次（の）, (*date etc.*) yóku(-) … 翌…; (*the next one*) tsugí 次, tsugí no 次の; (*going on to the ~*) tsuzukete 続けて; ~ *to* (*in space*), ~ *door to …* no tonari (no) …の隣り（の）; ~ *on the left/right* hidari-/migi-dónari (no) 左/右隣り（の）; ~ *after/to …* (*in importance*) … ni tsúide (no) …に次いで（の）
next day n, adv yokujitsu 翌日, tsugi no hi 次の日
next evening n, adv yokuban 翌晩, tsugi no hi no yo(ru) 次の日の夜
next month n, adv ráigetsu 来月
next morning n, adv yokuasa 翌朝, tsugi no hi no asa 次の日の朝
next time n, adv kóndo 今度, jikai 次回, kono-tsugí この次
next week n, adv raishū 来週
next year n, adv rainen 来年

nibble v kajirimásu (kajiru, kajitte) かじります・齧ります（かじる, かじって）

nice adj **1.** ii/yoi いい/良い → **good 2.** oishii おいしい → **delicious 3.** kirei (na) きれい（な）, utsukushii 美しい, hare (no) 晴れ（の） → **fair 4.** shinsetsu (na) 親切（な）, yasashii やさしい → **kind 5.** → **delicate**

nice weather n íi ténki（いい）天気 (o-tenki お天気)

nicely adv shinsetsu (ni) 親切に, kirei (ni) 綺麗に・きれいに

nick *v* kizamimásu (kizamu, kizande) 刻みます (刻む, 刻んで)

nickname *n* adana あだ名, aishō 愛称, nikkunēmu ニックネーム

niece *n* méi めい・姪; *your niece* meigo-san めいごさん・姪子さん

night *n* yóru 夜, yó 夜; ban 晩; *(at)* ~ yakan 夜間, *late at* ~ yóru osoku 夜遅く, shín'ya 深夜; ~ *before last* issakú-ban/-ya 一昨晩/夜; *the* ~ *before* (… no) zen'ya (…の)前夜; *one night* hitóban 一晩, *two nights* futá-ban 二晩

night(s) of lodging …-haku …泊 (**1:** ip-paku 一泊, **2:** ni-haku 二泊, **3:** sanpaku 三泊; *how many nights (will you stay?)* Nánpaku shimásu ka. 何泊 (しますか.)

night bus *n* yakō basu 夜行バス

nightcap *n* naito kyappu ナイトキャップ; nezake 寝酒

nightclothes *n* pajama パジャマ

nightclub *n* (*cabaret*) kyábarē キャバレー; naito kurabu ナイトクラブ

nightdress → nightclothes

night duty *n* shukuchoku 宿直

night game *n* (*of baseball*) náitū ナイター

night-light (*Japanese traditional paper-covered*) *n* andon あんどん・行灯

nightmare *n* akumu 悪夢

night school *n* yakan gakkō 夜間学校

night shift *n* yakin 夜勤

night-watch(man) *n* yakei 夜警; yakei-in 夜警員

Nikko *n* Níkkō 日光

nil *n* zero ゼロ

nimble *adj* kíyō (na) 器用(な)

nine *n* kyū 九・9, kú 九・9, kokónotsu 九つ; náin ナイン

nine; 9 pieces (*small things*) kyū´-ko 九個, **9 trees** (*or long things*) kyū-hon 九本, **9 sheets** (*flat things*) kyū´-mai 九枚; **9 cats** (*or small animals*) kyū-híki 九匹; **9 cows** (*or large aminals*) kyū-tō 九頭, **9 birds/rabbits** kyū-wa 九羽; **9 cars** (*or machines/vehicles*) kyū-dai 九台; **9 copies** (*books/magazines*) kyū´-satsu 九冊; **9 floors/stories** kyū-kai 九階; **9 people** kyū´-nin, ku-nín 九人, kyū´-mei 九名; **9 fold** kyū-bai 九倍; **9 degrees** kyū´-do 九度; **9 times** kyū-dó 九度 kyū´-kái 九回, kyū´-hén 九遍; **9 o'clock** kú-ji 九時; **9 hours** kú-jíkan 九時間; **9 days** kokonoka 九日; **9 weeks** kyū´-shūkan 九週間; **9 months** kyū´-ká-getsu 九ヶ月; **9 years** kyū´-nen 九年, kyū-nénkan 九年間; **9 years old** kokónotsu 九つ, kyū´-sai 九歳

nine hundred *n* kyū´-hyaku 九百・900

nineteen *n* jū-ku 十九・19, jū-kyū´ 十九・19

nine thousand *n* kyū-sén 九千・9,000

ninety *n* kyū´-jū 九十・90, ku-jū´ 九十; *ninety thousand* kyū-mán 九万・90,000

ninja *n* nínja 忍者

ninjitsu, ninjutsu *n* nínjutsu 忍術

ninth *adj* kyū-banme (no) 九番目(の)・9番目(の) ku-banmé (no) 九番目(の), kokonotsumé (no)

九つ目(の); *the ninth day* kokonoka-mé 九日目・9日目, (*of the month*) kokonoka 九日・9日

no *adv* iie いいえ (*or just say the negative verb*); **no charge/fee** *n, adj* múryō (no) 無料(の), tada (no) ただ(の)

no doubt *adv* (*surely*) kitto きっと; *There's no doubt about it.* sore wa machigai arimasen. それは間違いありません.

No kidding! *interj exclam* Másaka! まさか!, (*male*) Jōdan daro! 冗談だろ!, (*female*) Jōdan desho! 冗談でしょ!

no good *adj* tsumaránai つまらない; damé (na) だめ[駄目](な); furyō (na) 不良(な), (*futile*) muda (na) 無駄(な); (*worthless*) yákuza (na) やくざ(な)

no later than *adj* … máde ni wa …までには

no need to worry *interj, adj* daijō´bu (na) 大丈夫(な); shinpai nai/(go-)muyō 心配ない/(ご)無用

No parking chūsha kinshi 駐車禁止

No passing oi-koshi kinshi 追越し禁止

No smoking kin'en 禁煙

No, thank you. *interj* Kékkō desu. 結構です.

No trespassing tachiiri kinshi 立ち入り禁止

no use *adj* damé (na) だめ[駄目](の)

No war! *interj* Sensō hantai! 戦争反対!

No way! *interj* Tonde-mo arimasén (nái) とんでもありません(ない); (*Absolutely not.*) Zettai ni dame desu. 絶対にだめです.

noble *adj* kidakai 気高い, kōketsu (na) 高潔(な), sūkō (na) 崇高(な)

nobody *pron* dare mo 誰も + [NEGATIVE]

nod *v* unazukimásu (unazuku, unazuite) うなずきます・頷きます(うなずく, うなずいて)

Noh *n* (*Japanese classical theater*) nō 能, o-nō お能; *traditional Noh farce* kyōgén 狂言

noise *n* otó 音; (*unwanted*) sōon 騒音, (*static*) zatsuon 雑音; (*boisterous*) sáwagi 騒ぎ

noisy *adj* yakamashíi やかましい, sōzōshíi 騒々しい, urusai うるさい

nomad *n* yūboku-min 遊牧民

nomadic *adj* yūboku-min (no) 遊牧民(の)

nominal *adj* meimoku-jō (no) 名目上(の)

nominate *v* shimei shimásu (suru, shite) 指名します(する, して); mei-jimásu (mei-jiru, mei-jite) 命じます(命じる, 命じて); suisen shimásu (suru, shite) 推薦します(する, して); nominēto shimásu (suru, shite) ノミネートします(する, して)

non- *prefix* fu- 不

non-alcohol *n, adj* sofuto dorinku (no) ソフトドリンク(の); non arukōru (no) ノンアルコール(の)

noncommittal *adj* (*beats around the bush*) hanashi o bokashimásu (bokásu, bokáshite) 話をぼかします(ぼかす, ぼかして)

nondrinker *n* geko 下戸; (o-)sake o nomanai hito (お)酒を飲まない人

none *pron* (*nothing*) nani mo 何も + [NEGATIVE]; (*not even one*) hitotsu mo 一つも + [NEGATIVE], (*person*) hitori mo 一人も + [NEGATIVE]

non-fatty tuna (maguro no) aka-mi（まぐろ[鮪・マグロ]の）赤身

nonetheless *adv* sore náno ni それなのに

nonsense *n* baka na kotó ばかなこと; baka-bánashi ばか話; detarame でたらめ; tawagoto たわごと・戯言; nansensu ナンセンス

nonsmoker *n* non-sumōkā ノンスモーカー; tabako o suwanai hito たばこ[タバコ・煙草]を吸わない人; hi-kitsuen-sha 非喫煙者

no(n)-smoking *n* kin'én seki 禁煙席

no(n)-smoking car *n* kin'én-sha 禁煙車

nonspecialist *n* mongái-kan 門外漢

nonstop *adj* (*flight*) mu-chákuriku (no) 無着陸(の)

noodles *n* mén(-rui) めん[麺](類); (o-)sóba（お）そば・蕎麦; (*Japanese wheat-flour*) udon うどん(o-údon おうどん), (*thin*) sōmen そうめん; (*chilled*) hiya-múgi 冷や麦・ヒヤムギ; (*Chinese*) rā'men ラーメン

  cup noodle *n* kappu nūdoru カップヌードル

  noodle shop *n* (o-)sobá-ya （お）そば[蕎麦]屋; udon-ya うどん屋

noon *n* hirú 昼 (o-híru お昼); (*exactly noon*) shō'go 正午

nope *adv* (*no*) iya いや

no place → **nowhere**

norm *n* (*standard*) kikaku 規格, hyōjun 標準

normal *adj* hyōjun (no) 標準（の）, futsū (no) 普通 (の), nōmaru (no) ノーマル(の) → **usual**

normally *adv* hyōjun-teki (ni) 標準的（に）, futsū (ni) 普通(に)

north *n* kita 北, hoku-… 北…; (*the north*) hoppō 北方, (*the northern part*) hókubu 北部; *north and south* nánboku 南北

North America *n* Kita-Ámerika 北アメリカ, Hoku-Bei 北米

northeast *n* hokutō 北東

northerly *adj* (*wind*) kita-yori (no kaze) 北寄り（の風）

North Pole *n* Hokkyoku 北極

North Sea *n* Hokkai 北海

northwest *n* hokusei 北西

Norway *n* Noruwei ノルウェイ

Norwegian *n* (*language*) Noruwei-go ノルウェイ語; (*person*) Noruwei-jin ノルウェイ人

nose *n* hana 鼻 (o-hana お鼻)

nosebleed *n* hanaji 鼻血

nose hair *n* hanage 鼻毛

not *adv does not* [VERB]-masén (-nai, -náide) ません(ない, ないで); *is not* [ADJECTIVE]-ku arimasén (-ku nái, -ku nákute) くありません(くない, くなくて); [NOUN] ja arimasén (ja nái, ja nákute じゃありません(じゃない, じゃなくて)

  not as/so much as … *adj*…hodo… ほど・程 + [NEGATIVE]

  not at all *adv* **1.** sappári さっぱり; kesshíte 決して + [NEGATIVE] **2.** (*you're welcome*) dō' itashimashíte どういたしまして

  not working properly *adj* guai ga warúi 具合が悪い

not yet *adv* máda まだ + [NEGATIVE] non-past (… -masén …ません, …-nai …ない)

notch 1. *v* (*makes a notch*) kizamimásu (kizamu, kizande) 刻みます(刻む, 刻んで), kizami-me/ kirikomi o iremásu (ireru, irete) 刻み目/切り込みを入れます(入れる, 入れて) **2.** *n* kizami-me 刻み目

note *n* (*memorandum*) mémo メモ; chū'i 注; (*reminder*) chū'i 注意; (*promissory note*) tegata 手形 → **letter** → **notice, explanatory notes** → **sound**

notebook *n* nō'to ノート, nōtobúkku ノートブック

noted *adj* chomei (na) 著明(な)

note pad *n* memo-chō メモ帳

nothing *pron* nani mo 何も + [NEGATIVE]; **~ (at all)** nan to mo 何とも + [NEGATIVE]

  there is nothing like (*better than*) … ni kagirimásu (kagíru, kagítte) …に限ります(限る, 限って)

notice 1. *v* … ni ki ga tsukimásu (tsukú, tsúite) …に気が付きます(付く, 付いて), kizukimásu (kizúku, kizúite) 気付きます(気付く, 気付いて) **2.** *n* (*notification*) shirase 知らせ (o-shirase お知らせ), todoké届け (o-todoke お届け), tsūchi 通知; (*reminder*) chū'i 注意

  with short notice *adv* kyū na (o-)shirase (de) 急な(お)知らせ(で); totsuzen no shirase (de) 突然の知らせ(で)

  without notice *adv* mudan de 無断で; kotowári mo náku 断りもなく

notification → **notice**

notify *v* shirasemásu (shiraseru, shirasete) 知らせます(知らせる, 知らせて), (*notifies formally or officially*) tsūchi shimásu (suru, shite) 通知します(する, して); todokemásu (todokéru, todókete) 届けます(届ける, 届けて)

notion *n* kangae 考え, iken 意見 → **idea** → **concept**

notions *n* (*haberdashery*) koma-mono 小間物

noun *n* meishi 名詞

nourish *v* yashinaimásu (yashinau, yashinatte) 養います(養う, 養って)

nourishment *n* eiyō 栄養

novel 1. *n* (*fiction*) shōsetsu 小説 **2.** (*curious*) *adj* mezurashíi 珍しい

novelist *n* shōsetsu-ka 小説家, sak-ka 作家

November *n* Jūichi-gatsú 十一月・11月

now *adv* íma 今, (*already*) mō' もう

  from now on kore kara これから, kongo 今後

  just now tadáima ただ今, tsúi imashígata つい今しがた

  until now ima-máde 今まで

  well now (sore) ja （それ）じゃ, jā' じゃあ, déwa では, sá-te さて

  now then, and now sá-te さて

  now and then tama ni たまに

nowhere *adv* doko (de/ni/e) mo どこ(で/に/へ)も + [NEGATIVE]

nuclear *adj* káku (no) 核(の)
nuclear weapon *n* kaku hēki 核兵器
nude **1.** *adj* hadaka (no) 裸(の), nūdo (no) ヌード(の); ratai (no) 裸体(の) **2.** *n* nū′do ヌード; (*picture*) ratai-ga 裸体画 → **naked**
nuisance *n* mendō 面倒・めんどう
numb *adj* mu-kánkaku (na) 無感覚(な); *goes/gets* ~ shiremásu (shiberéru, shiberete) しびれます (しびれる, しびれて)
number *n* kázu 数, sū′ 数, nanbā ナンバー; bán 番, …-ban …番; (*written numeral*) sūji 数字; (*assigned*) bangō′番号, (*on an athlete*) zékken ゼッケン; (*large and/or small*) tashō 多少
a number of … ikutsu ka no … いくつかの…, nan-[COUNTER] ka no … 何 [COUNTER] かの…, sū-[COUNTER] no … 数 [COUNTER] の…
in large numbers ōzéi 大勢, dóndon どんどん, zorozoro ぞろぞろ
the number of days nissū′ 日数, hinichi 日にち
the number of people nínzū 人数
the number of times kaisū 回数

numbering *n* nanbaringu ナンバリング
number one *adj* ichí-ban (no) 一番(の)
numbness *n* shibiré しびれ
numeral *n* sūji 数字, sū′ 数
numerous → **many**
nun *n* áma 尼
nurse **1.** *n* kangó-fu 看護婦, nāsu ナース **2.** *v* (*nurses a patient*) kángo shimásu (suru, shite) 看護します(する, して)
nursery *n* takuji-jo 託児所
nursery school *n* (*pre-kindergarten*) hoikú-en 保育園
nursing (*a patient*) *n* kángo 看護, kanhyō 看病
nutrition *n* eiyō 栄養
nuts **1.** *n* náttsu ナッツ, kurumi くるみ・クルミ・胡桃; kí-no-mi 木の実・キノミ (*includes fruits and berries*), mi 実・ミ **2.** *adj* (*mad*) (atama no) ikareta (頭の)イカれた; *Are you nuts?* atama okashiinjanai? 頭おかしいんじゃない?
nylon *n* náiron ナイロン
nymph *n* ninfu ニンフ

O

Oahu *n* Oafu-tō オアフ島
oak *n* ōku オーク
oar *n* kai 櫂・かい, ōru オール
oasis *n* oashisu オアシス
oat *n* ōto mugi オートムギ, karasu mugi カラスムギ
oath *n* chikai (no kotoba) 誓い(の言葉)
obedient *adj* súnao (na) すなお[素直](な)
obeisance *n* (*salute*) keirei 敬礼
obelisk *n* oberisuku オベリスク
obesity *n* himan 肥満
obey (*a person*) *v* (… ga) yū/iu kotó o kikimásu (kiku, kiite) (…が)言う事を聞きます・いうことをききます(聞く, 聞いて)
obituary *n* shibō kiji 死亡記事
object **1.** *n* taishō 対象; (*thing*) monó 物; buttai 物体; obujekuto オブジェクト; (*objective, goal*) mokuteki 目的, ate 当て; (*aim*) nerai 狙い **2.** *v* ~ *to* (*opposes*) … ni hantai shimásu (suru, shite) …に反対します(する, して)
objective *n* mokuhyō 目標
obligation *n* (*duty*) gímu 義務, (*responsibility*) sekinin 責任; (*sense of* ~) girí 義理 (o-giri お義理); (*for a kindness*) ón 恩 (go-ón ご恩)
obliged *adj* **1.** *becomes* ~ (*to … for help*) (…no) sewá ni narimásu (naru, natte) (…の)お世話になります(なる, なって); *I'm much obliged for all your help.* Iroiro o-séwa ni narimáshita. いろいろ[色々]お世話になりました。 **2.** *feels* ~ (*grateful*) kyōshuku shimásu (suru, shite) 恐縮します(する, して)

oblique *adj* (*diagonal*) nanáme (no) 斜め(の), (*slanting*) hasu (no) はす(の); (*oblique statement*) tōmawashi (no) 遠回し(の)
obliquely *adv* nanáme ni 斜めに, hasu ni はすに
oblong *n* **1.** (*box*) chōhō-kei 長方形 **2.** (*oval*) chōdaen-kei 長だ円形・長楕円形
obscene *adj* waisetsu (na) わいせつ(な)
obscure *adj* (*unknown*) fumei (no) 不明(の); (*unrenowned*) mumei (no) 無名(の) → **dark**
observation *n* kansatsu 観察, kansoku 観測
observatory *n* (*astronomical*) tenmon-dai 天文台; (*weather station*) sokkó-jo 測候所, kishō-dai 気象台; (*sightseeing*) tenbō-dai 展望台
observe *v* **1.** (*happens to see*) kizukimásu (kizuku, kizuite) 気付きます・気づきます(気付く, 気付いて) **2.** (*watches*) kansatsu/kansoku shimásu (suru, shite) 観察/観測します(する, して) **3.** → **say**
observe a rule *v* okite o mamorimásu (mamoru, mamotte) 掟を守ります(守る, 守って)
observer *n* kansatsú-sha 観察者; tachiai-nin 立会人
obstacle *n* sashitsukae 差し支え・さしつかえ; (o-)jama (お)じゃま[邪魔]; shōgai 障害 → **hindrance**
obstruct *v* (*hinders*) samatagemásu (samatageru, samatagete) 妨げます・さまたげます(妨げる, 妨げて); *gets obstructed* (*clogged*) tsukaemásu (tsukáéru, tsukáete) つかえます(つかえる, つかえて)
obstruction *n* shōgai 障害, samatage 妨げ・さまたげ

obtain *v* té ni iremás<u>u</u> (ireru, irete) 手に入れます（入れる、入れて）→ **get**

obvious *adj* meihaku (na) 明白（な）, akiraka (na) 明らか・あきらか（な）

obviously *adv* (*clearly*) meihaku (ni) 明白（に）, akiraka (ni) 明らか・あきらか（に）→ **certainly, of course**

occasion *n* (*time*) tokí 時・とき, (*at that time*) koro 頃・ころ; (*event*) sétsu 節, sái 際, orí 折・おり, jísetsu 時節; (*opportunity*) k<u>i</u>kái 機会; tsuide ついで; (*circumstance*) ba(w)ai 場合; *on the ~ of …* ni sái-sh<u>i</u>te … に際して

occasional *adj* (*infrequent*) tama no たまの; tokidoki no 時々・ときどきの

occasionally *adv* tamatama たまたま; tama ni たまに; tokidoki 時々・ときどき

Occident *n* (*the West/Western*) Séiyō 西洋; *Occidental adj* yō-… 洋…

occult *n* okaruto オカルト

occultism *n* shinpi-gaku 神秘学

occultist *n* okaruto shinkō-sha オカルト信仰者

occupant *n* kyojū-sha 居住者

occupation *n* (*job*) shokúgyō 職業, shoku 職; (*military*) senryō 占領

occupied *adj* **1.** *is ~* (*toilet, etc.*) shiyōchū 使用中; (*I'm in here*) Háitte imás<u>u</u> 入っています **2.** (*a seat*) (*They're coming!*) Kimás<u>u</u> 来ます **3.** → **busy 4.** *gets ~* (*booked up*) fusagarimás<u>u</u> (fusagaru, fusagatte) ふさがります（ふさがる、ふさがって）

occur *v* okorimás<u>u</u> (okóru, okótte) 起ります（起こる、起こって）, hassei shimás<u>u</u> (suru, sh<u>i</u>te) 発生します（する、して）, shōjimás<u>u</u> (shō-jiru, shō-jite) 生じます（生じる、生じて）; genjitsu-ka shimás<u>u</u> (suru, sh<u>i</u>te) 現実化します（する、して）

occurrence *n* hassei 発生

ocean *n* taiyō 大洋, taikai/daikai 大海

o'clock *adv* …-ji …時 (4 ~ yó-ji 四時)

October *n* Ju-gatsú 十月・10月

octopus *n* táko たこ・タコ・蛸; *baby octopus* íidako イイダコ・飯蛸

oculist *n* mé-isha 目[眼]医者

odd *adj* (*peculiar, strange*) hén (na) 変（な）, kawatta 変わった; kawatteiru 変わっている; okashina おかしな

odor → **smell**

of *… prep* … no …の

of course mochíron もちろん・勿論, muron むろん・無論, móttómo もっとも

off; time ~ yasumí 休み; *time ~ in lieu of* daikyū 代休; *day ~* ofu (no hi) オフ（の日）, hiban (no hi) 非番（の日）; *~ (down in price by) ¥100* hyakeún-yasu 百円安

off *adv* (*turns*) *~* (*light, radio, etc.*) …o keshimás<u>u</u> (kesu, kesh<u>i</u>te) …を消します（消す、消して）; (*button, etc.*) *comes ~* toremás<u>u</u> (toreru, tórete) 取れます（取れる、取れて）, (*slips off*) nukemás<u>u</u> (nukeru, nukete) 抜けます（抜ける、抜けて）; *gets ~* (*a vehicle*) orimás<u>u</u> (oríru, órite) 降ります（降りる、

降りて）; *takes ~* (*clothes, shoes*) nugimás<u>u</u> (núgu, núide) 脱ぎます（脱ぐ、脱いで）; *does/is ~ and on* … -tári/-káttari/dáttari shimás<u>u</u> (suru, sh<u>i</u>te) …たり/かったり/だったりします（する、して）; *gets ~ the track* dassen shimás<u>u</u> (suru, sh<u>i</u>te) 脱線します（する、して）

off duty (*taxi*) kaisō(-chū) 回送（中）; *~ taxi* kaisō´-sha 回送車

Off Limits "tachiiri kinshi" "立入り禁止"

off-line *n* ofu rain オフライン

off screen 1. *adj* gamen-gai (no) 画面外（の） **2.** *adv* gamen-gai de 画面外で

off season *n* ofu shiizun オフシーズン, kansanki 閑散期

off the record *n* ofureko オフレコ

offend *v* **1.** (*violates*) … ni ihan shimás<u>u</u> (suru, sh<u>i</u>te) …に違反します（する、して） **2.** → **displease 3.** → **anger**

offense *n* burei 無礼; ihan 違反

offensive *adj* shaku ni sawaru しゃく[癪]に障る

offer 1. *n* mōshi-komi 申し込み, ofā オファー; (*makes an offer*) mōshidemás<u>u</u> (mōshideru, mōshidete) 申し出ます（申し出る、申し出て） **2.** *v* (*propose*) teian shimás<u>u</u> (suru, sh<u>i</u>te) 提案します（する、して）, (*recommend*) susumemás<u>u</u> (susumeru, susumete) 勧めます（勧める、勧めて）

job offer *n* saiyō 採用

offering *n* mōshi-de 申し出, mōshi-komi 申し込み; (*public*) mōshi-ire 申し入れ; o-sonae お供え

office *n* (*business*) jimú-sho 事務所; (*government*) yak<u>u</u>sho 役所（o-yak<u>u</u>sho お役所）; (*within the company*) shánai 社内, ofisu オフィス; (*job*) shoku 職, tsutomé 勤め（o-tsutome お勤め）, (*post*) yakú 役; (*place of employment*) tsutome-saki 勤め先

office attendance *n* sh<u>u</u>kkin 出勤

office clerk/worker *n* jimú-in 事務員

office lady *n* ōeru OL・オーエル

officer *n* (*military*) shō´kō 将校; *police officer* omáwari-san おまわりさん, [FORMAL] keikan 警官

office work *n* jímu 事務

official 1. *adj* (*public*) ōyake (no) 公（の） **2.** *n* (*a government official*) kōmu-in 公務員; yak<u>u</u>nin 役人

offing, offshore *n* oki 沖; *offshore from* no oki …の沖

often *adv* yóku よく, tabitabi たびたび, hinpan (ni) 頻繁（に）, sh<u>i</u>bashiba しばしば, sésse-to せっせと

ogre *n* oní 鬼・オニ

oh *interj* wā わあ; ā´ ああ; *oh?* sō´des<u>u</u> ka そうですか, árá あら; *oh well* mā´ まあ (*tends to be a female expression*)

oil *n* abura 油, (*petroleum, machine oil*) sekiyu 石油, (*for lubricating cars*) óiru オイル; *hair oil* pomā´do ポマード

ointment *n* nuri-gúsuri 塗り薬, nankō 軟膏

O.K. 1. *adv* íi des<u>u</u> いいです; (*I approve*) sansei (dés<u>u</u>) 賛成（です）; (*safe; functioning*) daijōbu

(désu) 大丈夫(です); ōkē (désu) オーケー(です)
2. *adj O.K.!* Yóshi! よし!

Okhotsk *n* Ohōtsuku オホーツク; *Sea of Okhotsk*
Ohōtsuku-kai オホーツク海

Okinawa *n* Okinawa 沖縄; Ryūkyū′ 琉球

old 1. *adj* (*not new*) furúi 古い, (*from way back*)
mukashi karáno 昔からの; kyū′(-) … 旧…
2. *adj* (*not young*) toshi-tótta 年取った, rō-…
老…; *gets ~* toshi o torimásu (tóru, tótte) 年を取
ります(取る, 取って), fukemásu (fukéru, fukéte)
老けます(老ける, 老けて) **3.** *n* (*old person*) rōjin
老人

how old íkutsu いくつ(o-ikutsu おいくつ), nán-
sai 何歳, (*age*) toshí 年

old friend *n* mukashi kará no tomodachi/yūjin 昔
からの友達/友人, furuku kará no yūjin 古くから
の友人; [BOOKISH] kyū′yū 旧友

old maid *n* (*card game*) baba-núki ばば抜き

older *adj* toshi-ue (no) 年上(の)

older brother *n* áni 兄; (o-)nii-san (お)兄さん

older sister *n* ane 姉; (o-)né-san (お)姉さん

oldest *adj* ichiban (toshi-)ue (no) 一番(年)上(の)

old person *n* toshiyóri 年寄り (o-toshiyori お年
寄り), rōjin 老人, kōrei-sha 高齢者, kōrei no hito/
kata 高齢の人/方, (*man*) ojii-san おじいさん,
(*woman*) obā′-san おばあさん

olive *n* oríibu (no ki) オリーブ(の木)

olive oil *n* oríibu-yu オリーブ油, oríibu-oiru
オリーブオイル

olive branch *n* *offer an olive branch* wakai o
mōshideru 和解を申し出る

...ology *n* ...-gaku …学; *biology* seibutsu-gaku
生物学

omelet *n* omuretsu オムレツ; *omelet wrapped
around rice* omu-ráisu オムライス

omen *n* engi 縁起, zenchō 前兆

omission *n* shōryaku 省略, ryaku 略

omit *v* **1.** otoshimásu (otósu, otóshite) 落とします
(落とす, 落として), habukimásu (habúku,
habúite) 省きます(省く, 省いて), nokemásu
(nokeru, nokete) のけ[除け]ます(のける, のけ
て), nukimásu (nuku, nuite) 抜きます(抜く, 抜
いて), nozokimásu (nozoku, nozoite) 除きま
す(除く, 除いて); (*skips*) tobashimásu (tobasu,
tobashite) とばします・飛ばします(とばす,
とばして); (*curtails*) ryakushimásu (ryakúsú,
ryakúshite) 略します(略す, 略して) **2.** *gets
omitted* ochimásu (ochíru, óchite) 落ちます(落ち
る, 落ちて); nukemásu (nukeru, nukete) 抜けます
(抜ける, 抜けて); moremásu (moréru, mórete)
漏れます・もれます(漏れる, 漏れて)

on *prep* **1.** … de …で, (*located*) … ni …に; (*atop*)
… no ue (de/ni) …の上(で/に) **2.** *has/puts on*
(*clothes, etc.*) → **wear 3.** *turns on* (*light, radio,
etc.*) … o tsukemásu (tsukéru, tsukéte) …を付けま
す(付ける, 付けて)

on the way tochū 途中

on the whole daitai だいたい・大体

once *adv* ichi-dó 一度・いちど, ik-kái 一回; ichiō

ichiō・いちおう; (*sometime*) ítsu ka いつか; *~ did*
shitakotó ga arimásu (áru, átte) した事がありま
す・したことがあります(ある, あって); *~ in a
while* tama ni たまに

one *n* ichí 一; hitótsu 一つ・ひとつ; hito-… 一…,
ichi-… 一…; wán ワン; (*person*) hitóri 一人・ひ
とり (o-hitori お一人・おひとり), ichí-mei 一名;
~ of a pair, the other ~ katahō 片方, katáppō 片一
方, katáppo 片っぽ・かたっぽ

one after another tsugí-tsugi ni 次々に, zokuzoku 続々, áitsuide 相次いで

one and the same hitótsu 一つ・ひとつ

one by one ichi-ichi 一々; (*objects*) hitotsu-zutsu
一つずつ・ひとつずつ, (*people*) hitori-zutsu
一人ずつ・ひとりずつ

one; 1 piece (*small thing*) ík-ko 一個, *1 tree* (*or
long things*) íp-pon 一本, *1 sheet* (*flat thing*) ichí-
mai 一枚; *1 cat* (*or small animals*) ip-piki 一匹;
1 cow (*or large aminals*) ít-tō 一頭, *1 bird/rabbit*
ichí-wa 一羽; *1 car* (*or machines/vehicles*) ichi-dai
一台; *1 copy* (*book/magazine*) is-satsú 一冊;
1 person hitó-ri ひとり・一人, ichí-mei 一名;
1 time ichi-dó 一度, ik-kái 一回, ip-pén 一遍;
1 degree ichí-do 一度; *1 o'clock* ichi-ji 一時;
1 hour ichí-jikan 一時間; *1 day* ichi-nichí 一日;
1 week ís-shūkan 一週間; *1 month* íkkágetsu
一ヶ月, íkkagetsu-kan 一ヶ月間; *1 year* ichí-nen
一年, ichí-nénkan 一年間; *1 year old* hitótsu 一つ,
ís-sai 一歳; *1 yen* ichi-en 一円

one day *n* ichi-nichí 一日; (*a certain day*) áru hi
ある日; (*someday*) ichijitsú 一日

one leg/foot *n* kata-ashi 片足

one-room (studio) apartment *n* wan-rū′mu
ワンルーム

oneself *pron* jibun 自分, wáre 我; *~ (as we might
expect*) sasuga no … さすがの…; *talking to ~*
hítori-goto 独り言

one side *n* ippō′ 一方

one-time *adj* ichí-ji (no) 一時(の); kátsute (no)
かつて(の), ízen (no) 以前(の)

one word *n* ichí-go 一語

one-way *adj* (*ticket*) katamichi(-kíppu) 片道(切符);
(*traffic*) ippō-tsū′kō 一方通行

onion *n* (*green*) négi ねぎ・ネギ・葱, naga-negi
長ねぎ[葱・ネギ]; (*green chive*) nira にら・
ニラ・韮; (*round bulb*) tama- négi 玉ねぎ[葱]・
タマネギ

only *adj* táda … ただ…, tatta … たった…, …
daké…だけ, …bákari …ばかり; … ni sugínai
(sugimasén) …に過ぎない(過ぎません)

Ontario *n* Ontario オンタリオ

oops *interj* otto おっと, o′ おっ, a′ あっ

opaque *adj* futōmei (na) 不透明(な)

opal *n* opāru オパール

OPEC *n* (*Organization of Petroleum Exporting
Countries*) Sekiyu yushutsu-koku kikō 石油輸出
国機構

open *v* **1.** *opens it* akemásu (akeru, akete) 開け
ます(開ける, 開けて), (*opens it up*) hirakimásu

(hiráku, hiráite) 開きます(開く、開いて); (*begins it*) hajimemásu (hajimeru, hajimete) 始めます(始める、始めて) **2.** *it opens* akimásu (aku, aite) 開きます(開く、開いて); (*it begins*) hajimarimásu (hajimaru, hajimatte) 始まります(始まる、始まって), (*a place, an event*) ō´pun shimásu (suru, shite) オープンします(する、して), kaijō shimásu (suru, shite) 開場します(する、して), (*a shop/business*) kaiten shimásu (suru, shite) 開店します(する、して) **3.** *~ to the public* kōkai (no) 公開(の); *opens it to the public* kōkai shimásu (suru, shite) 公開します(する、して)

open door *n* (*admission free*) nyūjō muryō 入場無料

open-minded *adj* **1.** (*broad-minded*) kokoro no hiroi 心の広い **2.** (*unprejudiced*) henken no nai 偏見のない

open-mouthed *adj* (*dumbfounded*) azen to shita 唖然とした

opener *n* (*can*) kan-kírí 缶切り・缶きり; (*bottle*) sen-nuki 栓抜き・栓ぬき

opening *n* **1.** (*inlet*) kuchi 口 **2.** (*gap*) suki(-ma) 透き/隙(間) **3.** (*of a place*) kaijō 開場, ō´pun オープン; *opening ceremony* kaijō/kaikai-shiki 開場/開会式; *opening time* kaijō-jíkan 開場時間 **4.** (*book*) bōtō 冒頭

job opening *n* shūshoku-guchi 就職口

open(ly) *adv* (*publicly*) kōzen (no/to) 公然(の/と), ōyake (no/ni) 公(の/に); (*candid*) ō´pun (na/ni) オープン(な/に), sotchoku (na/ni) 率直(な/に)

open (public) space *n* (*plaza*) híro-bá 広場
open space parking *n* okugai chūsha-jō 屋外駐車場

opera *n* kágeki 歌劇, ópera オペラ

operate *v* (*machinery*) sōjū shimásu (suru, shite) 操縦します(する、して); (*vehicle*) unten shimásu (suru, shite) 運転します(する、して); (*machinery*) ugokashimásu (ugokásu, ugokáshite) 動かします(動かす、動かして); (*business*) keiei shimásu (suru, shite) 経営します(する、して)

operation *n* (*surgical*) shújutsu 手術; (*driving*) unten 運転; (*handling*) sōjū 操縦; (*management*) keiei 経営; (*working*) sagyō 作業, shigoto 仕事

operator *n* **1.** (*telephone*) (denwa) kōkánshu (電話)交換手; operḗtā オペレーター **2.** (*vehicle*) unténshu 運転手 **3.** (*business*) keiéisha 経営者

opinion *n* íken 意見(go-íken ご意見), kangáe 考え; hyō´ka 評価; (*outlook*) mikomi 見込み, (*observation*) kansoku 観測; *public ~* yóron 世論

opium *n* ahen アヘン・阿片

opponent *n* (*sports*) aité 相手(o-aite お相手); taikō-sha 対抗者; (*rival*) teki 敵

opportunity *n* kikái 機会; chansu チャンス; (*opening*) suki(-ma) 透き/隙(間); (*opportune time*) jíki 時機, jísetsu 時節; (*convenience*) tsugō 都合, tsuide ついで

oppose *v* ... ni hantai shimásu (suru, shite) ...に反対します(する、して), ... o kobamimásu

(kobámu, kobánde) ...を拒みます(拒む、拒んで); (*resists*) ... ni hankō shimásu (suru, shite) ...に反抗します(する、して); ... to tairitsu shimásu (suru, shite) ...と対立します(する、して), ...ni taikō shimásu (suru, shite) ...に対抗します(する、して); (*faces*) ... ni mukaimásu (mukau, mukatte) ...に向かいます(向かう、向かって)

opposite *adj* (*facing*) mukō (no) 向こう(の), (o-)múkai (no) (お)向かい(の); (*contrary*) gyaku (no) 逆(の), (*opposing*) hantai (no) 反対(の)

opposite side *n* hantai-gawa 反対側, mukō-gawa 向こう側

opposition *n* (*resistance*) hankō 反抗; (*confrontation*) taikō 対抗; *in ~ to* ... ni taikō shite ...に対抗して; *opposition party* yatō 野党

oppress *v* appaku shimásu (suru, shite) 圧迫します(する、して)

oppression *n* appaku 圧迫

optimism *n* rakkan/rakuten (shugi) 楽観/楽天(主義)

optimistic *adj* rakkan-teki (na) 楽観的(な)

optional *adj* zuii (no) 随意(の), nin'i (no) 任意(の)

or *conj* ... ka ...か; máta-wa または・又は
or else sore-tómo それとも, máta-wa または・又は, arúiwa あるいは・或いは
or something (*like it*) ... tó ka ... とか

oral *adj* **1.** kuchi no 口の, kuchi kará no 口からの; keikō(-) 経口; *oral contraceptive* keikōhinín'yaku 経口避妊薬 **2.** (*verbal*) kōtō (no) 口頭(の); *oral examination* kōtō-shímon 口頭試問

orange *n* orénji オレンジ; (*Mandarin orange, tangerine*) míkan みかん・ミカン・蜜柑; (*bitter*) daidái だいだい・ダイダイ・橙

orange drink/soda pop (*orange juice*) orenji-jū´su オレンジジュース

orbit *n* kidō 軌道

orchestra *n* ōkesutora オーケストラ

orchid *n* rán 蘭・ラン

order **1.** *n* júnjo 順序, jun 順; *alphabetical order* ē-bii-shii (ABC)-jun エービーシー[ABC]順; (*turn*) junban 順番 **2.** *n* (*grade, step*) dán 段, dankai 段階 **3.** *n* (*procedure*) tejun 手順 **4.** *n* (*rule*) kimari 決まり; chitsujo 秩序 **5.** *n* (*command*) meirei 命令 **6.** *v* (*clothes, meal, etc.*) chūmon shimásu (suru, shite) 注文します(する、して) **7.** *v* (*a person to do something*) ... ni ii-tsukemásu (ii-tsukéru, ii-tsukéte) ...に言い付けます・言いつけます(言い付ける、言い付けて), meijimásu (meijiru, meijite) 命じます(命じる、命じて)

puts in order (*tidies up*) katazukemásu (katazukéru, katazúkete) 片付けます(片付ける、片付けて); (*arranges as a set*) soroemásu (soroéru, soroete) 揃えます・そろえます(そろえる、そろえて)

ordinarily *adv* heijō (ni) 平常(に), futsū (ni) 普通・ふつう(に), fúdan (wa) 普段・ふだん(は)

ordinary *adj* futsū (no) 普通・ふつう(の), tsūjō

(no) 通常(の), tsúne (no) 常(の), fúdan (no) 普段・ふだん(の); táda (no) ただ(の); (*average*) nami (no) 並(の)

organic *adj* ōganikku (no) オーガニック(の), yūki (no) 有機(の)

organization *n* (*setup*) soshiki 組織; (*structure*) kumi-tate 組み立て・くみたて, kōzō 構造; (*group*) dantai 団体

organize *v* (*sets up*) kumi-tatemásu (kumi-tateru, kumi-tatete) 組み立てます・くみたてます(組み立てる, 組み立てって); hensei shimásu (suru, shite) 編成します(する, して)

Orient *n* Tō´yō 東洋; Oriento オリエント

Orient Express *n* Óriento kyūkō オリエント急行

Oriental *adj* Tō´yō (no) 東洋(の)

origin *n* kígen 起源, (*cause*) gen'in 原因, moto 元, okorí 起こり, hassei 発生; (*historical ~*) engi 縁起; (*a person's origins*) de 出

originally *adv* móto wa 元は・もとは, motomoto 元々・もともと, hónrai wa 本来は, gánrai wa 元来は; (*in itself*) jitai 自体

Orion *n* 1. orion オリオン 2. (*star sign*) Orion-za オリオン座

ornament *n* kazari(-mono) 飾り(物), sōshoku-hin 装飾品, (*decoration*) sōshoku 装飾, (*bric-a-brac*) oki-mono 置き物

ornamentation *n* sōshoku-hin 装飾品

ornate *adj* karei (na) 華麗(な)

orphan *n* kóji 孤児; *orphanage* *n* kóji-in 孤児院

Osaka *n* Ōsaka 大阪; *~ Station* Osaká-Eki 大阪駅

Oscar *n* Osukā オスカー

Oslo *n* Osuro オスロ

other *adj* hoka (no) 他(の), betsu (no) 別(の); [BOOKISH] tá (no) 他(の); *other companies* tásha 他社 → **every other**

in other words *conj* sunáwachi すなわち, 即ち

the other day *adv* kon[o]aidá こないだ[この間]

the other fellow *n* aité 相手(o-aite お相手)

the other side *n* senpō 先方

on the other hand tahō de wa 他方では

other than ... yóri ...より

otherwise *adv* sá-mo nákereba さもなければ, sō´shinai to そうしないと, [INFORMAL] sō´ja nái to そうじゃないと

otherwise known as *adj* betsumei 別名

Ottawa *n* Otawa オタワ

otter *n* kawauso カワウソ

ouch! *interj* itái! 痛い・いたい!, itái! 痛(っ)・い た(っ)!

ought to *auxiliary verb ~ (do)* (shi)-ta hō´ga íi deshō(し)た方がいいでしょう, [BOOKISH] (su)-ru béki desu (す)るべきです

ounce *n* onsu オンス

our(s) *pron* watakushí-tachi no (watashí-táchi no) わたくし[私]達の(わたし[私]達の)

out 1. *adv* sóto e/ni 外へ/に; (*away from home*) (o-)rúsu (desu) (お)留守(です), gaishutsu-chū (désu) 外出中(です); *come/go out* (... kara) demásu (déru, déte) (...から)出ます(出る, 出て);

let out (*of a vehicle*) oroshimásu (orosu, oroshite) 降ろします(降ろす, 降ろして) 2. *adj* (*baseball*) áuto (no) アウト(の)

out loud *adv* kóe o dáshite 声を出して

out of order; gets ~ kuruimásu (kurū´, kurútte) 狂います(狂う, 狂って); (*broken machine*) koshō shiteimásu (shiteiru, shiteite) 故障しています(している, していて)

out of place *adj* ba-chígai (no) 場違い・場ちが い(の); *slips ~* zuremásu (zuréru, zúrete) ずれま す(ずれる, ずれて)

out of service *n, adj* kaisō(-chū) 回送(中); *a car ~* kaisō-sha 回送車

out of the way; gets ~ dokimásu (doku, doite) どきます(どく, どいて), nokimásu (noku, noite) のきます・退きます(のく, のいて)

out of touch with ... *adj* ni utói ...に疎い・うと い

outage *n* (*power outage*) teiden 停電

out-and-out *adv* kanzen (na) 完全(な); tettei-teki (na) 徹底的(な); tettei-shita 徹底した

outback *n* okuchi 奥地

out-box *n* (*e-mail*) sōshin bokkusu 送信ボックス

outbound *adj* (*from Tokyo*) kudari 下り

outbreak *n* toppatsu 突発; hassei 発生

outbuilding *n* hanare 離れ

outburst *n* bakuhatsu 爆発

outcome *n* (*of situation*) ketsumatsu 結末; (*result*) séika 成果; (*product*) sanbutsu 産物; (*medical diagnosis*) tenki 転帰

outdoor(s) *adj* (*adv*) sóto no (/de/ni/e) 外の (/で/に/へ); yagai no (/de) 野外の(/で); autodoa (no) アウトドア(の); okugai no (/de/ni/e) 屋外の(/で/に/へ); *outdoor bath* noten-búro 野 天風呂

outer *adj outer appearance* uwabe うわべ・上辺; *outer lane/track* auto-kō´su アウトコース; *outer moat* soto-bori 外堀; *outer side/surface* omoté 表; *outer space* úchū 宇宙

outfit *n judo outfit* jūdō´-gi 柔道着; *karate outfit* karaté-gí 空手着

outflow *n* de 出; ryūshutsu 流出

outing *n* (*picnic etc.*) ensoku 遠足・えんそく

outlet *n* 1. déguchi 出口; (*for water/emotion/ goods*) haké-kuchi/-guchi はけ口; (*sales~*) ure-kuchi 売れ口; (*store*) chokubái-ten 直売店 2. (*electric ~*) kónsénto コンセント; (*plug*) sashi-komi 差し込み・さしこみ, puragu プラグ

outline *n* 1. (*synopsis*) gaiyō 概要, auto rain アウ トライン 2. (*line*) rinkaku 輪郭

outlook *n* mikomi 見込み・見こみ, mitōshi 見通し

output *n* auto putto アウトプット, seisan 生産, sanshutsu 産出

outrage *n* ranbō 乱暴 → **indignation**

outrageous *adj* tonde-mo nái とんでもない, tonda とんだ

outset *n* (*beginning*) hána はな・端, saisho 最初, shoppana 初っ端・しょっぱな

outside 1. *adv* sóto (de/ni) 外(で/に); **~ of** (*other than*) … no hoka …の他、…ígai …以外 **2.** *adj* soto-gawa 外側(の)、sóto (no) 外(の) **3.** *n* **the outside** soto-gawa 外側、hata はた・端、gáibu 外部、gaimen 外面

outside corner *n* kádo 角

outsider *n* (*stranger*) yosó no hitó よその人、yoso-mono よそ者、tanin 他人、mongái-kan 門外漢、bugaisha 部外者

outsize *adj* tokudai (no) 特大(の)

outskirts *n* (*suburb*) shígai 市外、kōgai 郊外、(tóshi no) shūhen (都市の)周辺

outsourcing *n* autosōshingu アウトソーシング、gyōmu itaku 業務委託、gaichū 外注、gaibu hatchū 外部発注

outspread *adj* hirogatta 広がった

outstanding *adj* medátta 目立った・めだった、kencho (na) 顕著(な)、medátte imásu 目立っています・めだっています

outstandingly *adv* medátte 目立って・めだって、ichijirushiku 著しく・いちじるしく

outward 1. *adj* soto (no) 外の、(*ostensible*) mikake jō (no) 見かけ・みかけ上(の)、hyōmen jō (no) 表面上(の) **2.** *adv* soto e 外へ

outward appearance *n* mikake 見かけ・みかけ

outwardly *adv* mikake wa 見かけは・みかけは

outwitted; gets ~ (*tricked*) gomakasaremásu (gomakasáreru, gomakasárete) ごまかされます・誤魔化されます(ごまかされる、ごまかされて)

oval 1. *n* daen(-kei) 楕円(形)・だ円(形) **2.** *adj* daen-kei (no) 楕円[だ円]形(の)

ovation *n* daikassai 大喝采; **standing ~** sutandingu obēshon スタンディング・オベーション

ovary *n* ransō 卵巣、(*plant*) shibō 子房

oven *n* ōbun オーブン、témpi 天火、kama かま・窯、kamado かまど・竈

oven-proof *adj* ōbun tainetsu-sei (no) オーブン耐熱性(の)

over 1. *prep* (*above*) … no ue (de/ni) …の上(で/に)、… o ōimásu (ōu, ōtte) …を覆います(覆う、覆って); (*more than*) … ijō 以上、... yori ōku …より多く; … o sugimásu (sugiru, sugite) …を過ぎます(過ぎる、過ぎて)、... o koemásu (koeru, koete) …を超えます(超える、超えて) **2.** *adj* (*above*)… no ue (no) …の上(の) **3.** *adv* (*above*) ue (ni) 上(に); (*covered*) ichimen (ni) 一面(に); (*finished*) owarimashita (owatta, owatte) 終わりました(終わった、終わって); (*run over*) kurikaeshimásu (kurikaesu, kurikaeshite) 繰り返します(繰り返す、繰り返して) **4.** *v* (*recover*) (byōki ga) naorimásu (naoru, naotte) (病気が)治ります(治る、治って)
over there mukō 向こう、mukai 向かい、sochira/sotchi そちら/そっち、achira/atchi あちら/あっち; (*other side*) mukō gawa ni 向こう側に
over again → again

overage *adj* tekirei(-ki) o sugita 適齢(期)を過ぎた、nenrei seigen o koeta 年齢制限を越えた

overall 1. *adj* (*composite*) sōgō-teki (na) 総合的

(な)、zentai-teki (na) 全体的(な) **2.** *adv* sōgō-teki (ni) 総合的(に)、zentai-teki (ni) 全体的(に)

overalls *n* (*coveralls*) tsunagi つなぎ

overcharge *v* **~ (for)** fukkakemásu (fukkakéru, fukkákete) ふっかけます(ふっかける、ふっかけて); **gets overcharged for** fukkakeraremásu (fukkakeraréru, fukkakerárete) ふっかけられます(ふっかけられる、ふっかけられて)

overcoat *n* ōˋbā オーバー、kōto コート、gaitō 外套、

overcome *v* uchikachimásu (uchikatsu, uchikatte) 打ち勝ちます(打ち勝つ、打ち勝って)、koku-fukushimásu (suru, shite) 克服します(する、して)

overdo *v* **~ (it)** múri o shimásu (suru, shite) 無理をします(する、して)、(sore o) múri ni yarimásu (yaru, yatte) (それを)無理にやります(やる、やって)

overeducate *v* kajō (ni) kyōiku shimásu (suru, shite) 過剰(に)教育します(する、して)

overestimate 1. *n* kadai hyōka 過大評価 **2.** *v* kadai hyōka shimásu (suru, shite) 過大評価します(する、して)

overemphasize *v* kyōchōshisugimásu (shisugiru, shisugite) 強調し過ぎます・強調しすぎます(しすぎる、しすぎて)

overexcited *adj* kajō ni kōfun shita 過剰に興奮した

overexpose *v* roshutsu shisugimásu (shisugiru, shisugite) 露出し過ぎます・露出しすぎます(しすぎる、しすぎて)

overexposure *n* roshutsu kado 露出過度

over-familiar *adj* narenareshii なれなれしい・馴れ馴れしい

overflow *v* afuremásu (afuréru, afúrete) あふれ[溢れ]ます(あふれる、あふれて); hanran shimásu (suru, shite) 氾濫します(する、して)

overflowing *n* hanran 氾濫

overheat 1. *n* kanetsu 過熱、(*engine, etc.*) ōbā hiito オーバーヒート **2.** *v* kanetsu shimásu (suru, shite) 過熱します(する、して)、(*engine, etc.*) ōbā hiito shimásu (suru, shite) オーバーヒートします(する、して)

overhype *v* hade ni senden shimásu (suru, shite) 派手に宣伝します(する、して)

overlap *v* kasanarimásu (kasanaru, kasanatte) 重なります(重なる、重なって)、[INFORMAL] daburimásu (dabúru, dabútte) だぶります(だぶる、だぶって)

overly *adv* amari ni mo あまりにも; … -sugimásu (-sugíru, -súgite) …過ぎます(過ぎる、過ぎて); **~ strict** yakamashíi やかましい

over-optimism *n* chō rakkan shugi 超楽観主義、chō rakuten-teki/ka 超楽天的/家

overprice *v* takane o tsukesugimásu (tsukesugiru, tsukesugite) 高値を付け過ぎます・つけすぎます(付け過ぎる、付け過ぎて)

overprint *v* **1.** surikasanemásu (surikasaneru, surikasanete) 刷り重ねます(刷り重ねる、刷り重

ねて) **2.** surisugimásu (surisugiru, surisugite) 刷り過ぎます(刷り過ぎる, 刷り過ぎて)

overseas *adj* káigai 海外; *overseas travel* kaigai-ryokō 海外旅行

oversee *v* kantoku shimásu (suru, shite) 監督します(する, して)

overseer *n* kantoku 監督

overshoes *n* ōbāshū´zu オーバーシューズ

overshoot *v* ikisugimásu (ikisugiru, ikisugite) 行き過ぎます(行き過ぎる, 行き過ぎて)

overtake *v* … ni oi-tsukimásu (oi-tsukú, oi-tsúite) …に追い付きます(追い付く, 追い付いて)

overthrow *v* taoshimásu (taósu, taóshite) 倒します(倒す, 倒して), hikkuri kaeshimásu (kaésu, kaéshite) ひっくり返します(返す, 返して)

overtime; runs ~ jikan ga ō´bā shimásu (suru, shite) 時間がオーバーします(する, して); *overtime work* zangyō 残業

overwork *v* múri o shimásu (suru, shite) 無理をします(する, して)

owe *v* (*borrow money*) (hito ni kane o) karite imásu (iru, ite) (人に金を)借りています(いる, いて)

owing *adj* ~ *to* … (no) séi de…(の)せいで → **because**

owl *n* fukúrō´ ふくろう・フクロウ・梟

own 1. *v* (*possesses*) mótte imásu (iru, ite) 持っています(いる, いて) **2.** *adj* (*one's own*) jibun no 自分の, shoyū no 所有の

owner *n* (mochí-)nushi (持ち)主, shoyūsha 所有者; (*master*) shújin 主人, ōnā オーナー; (*landowner*) ji-nushi 地主

ox *n* (*cattle*) ushi 牛・ウシ, (*male*) o-ushi 雄牛 (*plural; oxen*) (*how many* nán-tō 何頭)

oxidant *n* sanka-zai 酸化剤, okishidanto オキシダント

oxter *n* waki no shita 脇の下・わきのした

oxydol *n* okishidōru オキシドール

oxygen *n* sánso 酸素

oxygenate *v* sanka shimásu (suru, shite) 酸化します(する, して)

oxygen mask *n* sanso masuku 酸素マスク

oyster *n* káki かき・カキ・牡蠣, oisutā オイスター

ozone *n* ozon オゾン

ozone layer *n* ozon sō オゾン層

P

pace *n* pēsu ペース, hochō 歩調

walking pace *n* aruku hayasa 歩く速さ, aruku sokudo 歩く速度

pacemaker *n* pēsu mēkā ペースメーカー

Pacific Ocean *n* Taihéiyō 太平洋

pacifier *n* (*for baby*) o-sháburi おしゃぶり

pacifism *n* heiwa shugi 平和主義

pacifist *n* heiwa shugi-sha 平和主義者, hansen shugi-sha 反戦主義者

pacify *v* shizumemásu (shizuméru, shizúmete) 静[鎮]めます(静[鎮]める, 静[鎮]めて); (*soothes*) nadamemásu (nadaméru, nadámete) なだめます・宥めます(なだめる, なだめて); (*suppresses an uprising*) osamemásu (osaméru, osámete) 収めます(収める, 収めて)

pack 1. *n* (*of cards*) (toránpu) hitó-kumi (トランプ)一組; (*package of cigarettes*) (tabako) hitó-hako (たばこ)一箱 **2.** *v* (*one's bags*) ni-zúkuri o shimásu (suru, shite) 荷造りをします(する, して) **3.** *v* (*wraps it up*) tsutsumimásu (tsutsúmu, tsutsúnde) 包みます(包む, 包んで), hōsō shimásu (suru, shite) 包装します(する, して)

package *n* kozútsumi 小包, nimotsu 荷物, pakkēji パッケージ → **packet**

package deal *n* setto hanbai セット販売

package tour *n* pakkēji tsuā パッケージツアー, pakku ryokō パック旅行

packed *adj* **1.** (*full*) tsumatte(i)ru 詰まって(いる), tsumatta 詰まった **2.** (*crowded*) konde(i)ru 混ん

で(い)る, konda 混んだ

packed train *n* man'in densha 満員電車

packer *n* (*person*) konpō gyōsha 梱包業者

packet *n* (kogata) hōsō´-butsu (小型)包装物, kozútsumi 小包

pact *n* kyōtei 協定, jōyaku 条約

pad *n* (*note pad*) memo-chō メモ帳

sketch pad *n* suketchi bukku スケッチブック

shin pad *n* sune-ate 脛当て・すね当て

shoulder pad *n* kata-ate 肩当て, kata paddo 肩パッド

padded; *padded garment* wata-iré 綿入れ; *padded bathrobe* tánzen 丹前, dotera どてら; *padded quilt* futon 布団 (o-futón お布団)

paddle *n* kai 櫂

paddy *n* suiden 水田

padlock *n* nankinjō 南京錠

page *n* pēji ページ・頁

pagoda *n* tō´ 塔

pagurian *n* yadokari ヤドカリ

pail *n* te-oke 手桶

pain 1. *n* itamí 痛み; (*suffering*) kurushimi 苦しみ, (*trouble, bother*) mendō 面倒; *takes (great) pains* honé o orimásu (óru, ótte) 骨を折ります(折る, 折って) **2.** *v* (*distresses*) kurushimemásu (kurushiméru, kurushímete) 苦しめます(苦しめる, 苦しめて)

painful *adj* itái 痛い; kurushíi 苦しい, tsurai 辛い

paint 1. *n* penki ペンキ, enogu 絵の具, tosō 塗装

paintbox   **ENGLISH–JAPANESE**

2. *v* (penki o) nurimásu; nuru, nutte) (ペンキを)
塗ります(塗る,塗って); (*picture*) (e o kakimásu
(káku, káite) 絵を描きます(描く,描いて)
paintbox *n* enogubako 絵の具箱
paintbrush *n* efude 絵筆
painter *n* (*artist*) gaka 画家; (*house-painter*)
penki-ya ペンキ屋
painting *n* (*picture*) é 絵, (*oil color*) abura e 油絵,
…-ga …画; (*watercolor*) suisai-ga 水彩画
pair *n* (it-) tsui 〈一〉対; pea ペア; (*of foot-wear*)
is-sokú 一足 → **two**
a pair of *n* (it-)tsui (no) 〈一〉対(の); hitokumi
(no) 一組(の); (*animal*) tsugai (no) つがい(の)
paisley *n, adj* pēzurii (moyō) (no) ペーズリー
(模様) (の)
pajamas *n* pajama パジャマ; nemaki 寝巻き
Pakistan *n* Pakisutan パキスタン
Pakistani *adj* Pakisutan (no) パキスタン(の),
(*person*) Pakisutan-jin (no) パキスタン人(の)
pal *n* nakamá 仲間(o-nakama お仲間)
pen pal *n* pen paru ペンパル, pen furendo ペ
ンフレンド, buntsū nakama 文通仲間, buntsū
tomodachi 文通友達
palace *n* (*in Tokyo*) kō´kyo 皇居; (*in Kyoto*) gósho
御所; (*in general*) kyūden 宮殿, paresu パレス
Palau *n* (*republic nation of south Pacific ocean*)
Parao パラオ
pale *adj* **1.** (*color*) (iro ga) usui (色が)薄い; usui
[…iro] (no) 薄い[…色](の) **2.** (*face*) (kao ga) aói
(顔が)青い, (kao ga) aojiroi (顔が)青白い; *turns
pale* kao ga áoku narimásu (náru, nátte); 顔が青く
なります(なる,なって)
Palestine *n* Paresuchina パレスチナ
palette *n* paretto パレット
palindrome *n* kaibun 回文
palladium *n* parajiumu パラジウム
palm *n* (*tree*) yáshi ヤシ・椰子; (*~ of hand*) té-nó-
hira 手のひら・掌
palmistry *n* tesō 手相
pamper *v* amayakashimásu (amayakasu, amay-
akashíte) 甘やかします(甘やかす,甘やかして)
pamphlet *n* pánfurétto パンフレット; (*leaflet,
handbill*) bira びら・ビラ, chirashi ちらし・
チラシ
pan *n* nábe 鍋(o-nabe お鍋); *food cooked and
served in a pan* nabé-mono 鍋物; nabe-ryōri
鍋料理
panacea *n* bannō-yaku 万能薬
Panama *n* Panama パナマ
Panama Canal *n* Panama unga パナマ運河
pancake *n* pankēki パンケーキ, hottokēki ホッ
トケーキ; *seasoned pancake* okonomiyaki お好
み焼き; *pancake mix* hottokēki no moto ホット
ケーキの素
pancreas *n* suizō 膵臓・すい臓
panda *n* panda パンダ
Pandora's box *n* pandora no hako パンドラの箱
pandowdy *n* (*baked fruit pie*) appuru pai アップ
ルパイ

panel *n* paneru パネル
panel discsssion *n* paneru disukasshon パネルデ
ィスカッション
panel house *n* baishun yado 売春宿
panelist *n* kaitō-sha 解答者・回答者, shutsujō-sha
出場者
pan-fry *v* itamemásu (itaméru, itámete) 炒めます
(炒める,炒めて)
panic *n* pánikku パニック, [BOOKISH] kyōkō 恐慌
pant *v* (*for breath*) aegimásu (aégu, aéide) あえぎ
[喘ぎ]ます(あえぐ,あえいで)
panther *n* hyō 豹・ヒョウ, pyūma ピューマ
panties *n* pántii パンティー, pántsu パンツ
pantomime *n* pantomaimu パントマイム
pantry *n* (*dish cupboard*) shokki(tó)dana
食器(戸)棚; (*room*) shokuryō´-ko 食料庫
pants *n* zubón ズボン, (*slacks*) surákkusu ス
ラックス; (*underpants*) zubon-shita ズボン下;
(*women's*) pántaron パンタロン
panty hose *n* pantii stokukkingu (pansuto) パン
ティーストッキング(パンスト)
papa *n* papa パパ, o-tōsan おとうさん・お父さん,
o-tōchan おとうちゃん・お父ちゃん
papaya *n* papaiya パパイヤ
paper *n* **1.** kamí 紙; yōshi 用紙, (*squared*)
genkyō´shi 原稿用紙; (*tissues*) chiri-gami ちり
紙, tisshu ティッシュ; (*Japanese*) wáshi 和紙;
colored ~ irógami 色紙 **2.** (*newspaper*) shinbun
新聞, (*morning*) chōkan 朝刊, (*evening*) yūkan
夕刊 **3.** (*research report*) happyō 発表 **4.** →
document
paper bag *n* kami-búkuro 紙袋
paperclip *n* kami-básami 紙挟み, kuríppu クリ
ップ
paperfolding (art) *n* orígami 折り紙・おりがみ
paper-hanger/-repairer *n* hyōgu-ya 表具屋
(*picture-framer*)
paper money *n* shihei/shíhei 紙幣, (o-)satsu (お)
札; (*currency bills*) …-satsu …札 (*two $100 bills*
hyakudóru-satsu ní-mai 百ドル札二枚)
paperweight *n* bunchin 文鎮・ブンチン
Papist *n* katorikku kyōto カトリック教徒
paprika *n* papurika パプリカ
Papua New Guinea *n* Papua nyūginia パプアニ
ューギニア
papyrus *n* papirusu パピルス
parable *n* [BOOKISH] gūwa 寓話
parabola *n* hōbutsu sen 放物線
parabola antenna *n* parabora antena パラボラア
ンテナ
parachute *n* parashūto パラシュート
parade *n* parēdo パレード, gyōretsu 行列,
(*march*) kōshin 行進; demo kōshin デモ行進
fancy-dress parade *n* kasō gyōretsu 仮装行列
parade ground *n* [BOOKISH] eppei-jō 閲兵場
paradise *n* téngoku 天国, gokuraku 極楽,
paradaisu パラダイス
paradox *n* paradokkusu パラドックス,
gyakusetsu 逆説, mujun 矛盾

388

paraffin n parafin パラフィン
paraglider n paraguraidā パラグライダー
paragraph n danraku 段落, setsu 節, paragurafu パラグラフ
Paraguay n Paraguai パラグアイ
parakeet n inko インコ
parallel n heikō 並行
　parallel bars n heikō bō 並行棒
　parallel lines n heikō sen 並行線
paralysis n (medical) máhi 麻痺; *infantile paralysis* (polio) shōni-máhi 小児麻痺
paralytic n mahi kanja 麻痺患者
Paramatman n (Hindu belief) taiga 大我
paramecium n zōri mushi ゾウリムシ
parameter n paramēta パラメータ, paramētā パラメーター; hensū 変数
paramount adj saikō (no) 最高(の); shijō (no) 至上(の)
paraphrase n parafurēzu パラフレーズ
parasite n parasaito パラサイト, isōrō 居候, (worm) kiseichū 寄生虫
parasol n hi-gása 日傘; (beach umbrella) parasoru パラソル
parcel n kozútsumi 小包, nimotsu 荷物
parcel post n kozutsumi-yū´bin 小包郵便
parchment n yōhishi 羊皮紙
pardon v yurushimás̱u (yurúsu, yurúsh̲ite) 許します(許す, 許して)
　Pardon? (say once more) [POLITE] Mō ichido osshatte kudasai. もう一度おっしゃって下さい。; (male) Nandatte! 何だって!; (female) Nandesutte! 何ですって!; Sh̲itsúrei desu ga. 失礼ですが. → **Sorry?, Excuse me.**
　Pardon, me! Sh̲itsúrei shimás̱u. 失礼します; Sumimasén すみません; Gomennasai. ごめんなさい.
pare v (peels it) mukimás̱u (muku, muite) むきます・剥きます(むく、むいて)
paregoric n (medicine) geri-dome 下痢止め
parent n oyá 親, kata oya 片親, *your parent* oyagosan 親御さん; *one's parents* oyátachi 親達, (father and mother) ryō´shin 両親, *your parents* go-ryō´shin ご両親
　parent and child n óyako 親子
　parent directory n (computer) oya direkutori 親ディレクトリ
　parent-teacher association n pii tii ei PTA
parentage n kakei 家系; umare 生まれ
parenthesis n (maru) kakko （丸)括弧・カッコ
parenting n ikuji 育児; kosodate 子育て
paresthesia n (medical) kankaku ijō 感覚異常; chikaku ijō 知覚異常
parfait n pafe パフェ
Paris n Pári パリ
parish n kyō´(-kai) ku 教(会)区
park 1. n kōen 公園; (parking lot) chūsha-jō 駐車場 2. v (a car) chūsha shimás̱u (suru, sh̲ite) 駐車します(する、して)
parking n chūsha 駐車

free parking n muryō chū´shajō 無料駐車場
No parking n chūsha kinshi 駐車禁止
paid parking n yūryō chūshajō 有料駐車場
parking fee n chūsha ryōkin 駐車料金
parking lot n chūsha-jō 駐車場
parking meter n pākingu mētā パーキングメーター, chūsha ryōkin-kei 駐車料金計
parking ticket n chūsha ihan no kippu 駐車違反の切符
parliament → **Diet**
parliamentary adj gikai (no) 議会(の)
parlor n (drawing room) kyakuma 客間
　beauty parlor n biyōin 美容院, byūtii saron ビューティサロン
　ice-cream parlor n aisu kuriimu-ten アイスクリーム店, aisu kuriimu pārā アイスクリームパーラー
　mahjong parlor mājan-ya マージャン[麻雀]屋; jansō 雀荘
parody n parodii パロディ; mojiri もじり
parrot n ōmu おうむ・オウム・鸚鵡
parsley n paseri パセリ; *Japanese parsley* serí せり・セリ・芹
part n 1. bubun 部分, ishi bu 一部, (portion) búnbun 分, (section) bú 部; *I for my* de watashi [私]はわたし[私]で 2. (passage of a text) …tokoró …所; *this ~* koko ここ 3. (parting of hair) wake-me 分け目 4. (role) yakuwari 役割, yakú 役 5. v (to divide) wakemás̱u (wakéru, wákete) 分けます(分ける, 分けて); (they separate) wakaremás̱u (wakaréru, wakárete) 別れます(別れる, 別れて); *~ with …* o hanashimás̱u (hanásu, hanásh̲ite) …を離します(離す, 離して)
Parthenon n (ancient Greek temple) Parutenon shinden パルテノン神殿
partial adj ichibu (no) 一部(の), ichibubun 一部分
participant n sanká-sha 参加者
participate v sanka shimás̱u (suru, sh̲ite) 参加します(する, して)
particle n 1. (auxiliary word) joshi 助詞 2. (physics) ryūshi 粒子
particular adj 1. (especial) tokubetsu no 特別の; (separate) betsu no 別の; (peculiar, unique) tókushu na 特殊な, tokuyū no 特有の 2. (specific) áru … ある…, kore to iú/yū … これと言う/ゆう… → **choosy**
　in particular adv tóku-ni 特に, toriwake とりわけ
particularly adv toku ni 特に, tokubetsu ni 特別に, toriwake とりわけ, koto ni 殊に; *not ~* betsu ni 別に + [NEGATIVE]
particulars → **details**
parting n (separation) wakaré 別れ(o-wakare お別れ)
partition n sh̲ikiri 仕切り, (computer) pātishon パーティション
partner n aité 相手(o-aite お相手), pātonā パートナー
parts n buhin 部品; bubun 部分, pātsu パーツ

part-time *adj* arubáito (no) アルバイト(の), baito (no) バイト(の); pāto taimu (no) パートタイム(の); hi-jōkin (no) 非常勤(の)

part-time high school *n* teiji-sei kōkō 定時制高校

part-time job *n* arubáito (no shigoto) アルバイト(の仕事), baito バイト; pāto taimu (no shigoto) パートタイム(の仕事), pāto (no shigoto) パート(の仕事)

part-time teacher *n* hi-jōkin kōshi 非常勤講師, rinji kyōin 臨時教員

part-time worker *n* arubáito (no hito) アルバイト(の人), baito (no hito) バイト(の人); pāto (no hito) パート(の人), [BOOKISH] hi-jōkin (kinmu-sha) 非常勤(勤務者)

party *n* 1. enkai 宴会, pā´ti パーティ, pā´tii パーティー, …-kai …会 → **reception** 2. *political party* seitō 政党

birthday party *n* tanjōbi kai 誕生日会, bāsudē pāti/pāti(i) バースデー・パーティ/パーティー

drinking party *n* nomi kai 飲み会, enkai 宴会

farewell party *n* sōbetsu kai 送別会

opposition party *n* yatō 野党

ruling party *n* yotō 与党

year-end party *n* bōnen kai 忘年会

welcome party *n* kangei kai 歓迎会

parvenu *n* (*newly-rich*) narikin 成金

pass 1. *n* (*commuter ticket*) teikíken 定期券 2. *n* (*mountain pass*) tōge 峠, …-tō´ge …峠 3. *n* (*sexual overture*) kudoku 口説く, iiyoru 言い寄る; *makes a pass at …* o kudokimásu (kudóku, kudóite) …口説きます(口説く, 口説いて); nanpa shimásu (suru, shíte) ナンパします(する, して) 4. *v* (*goes past*) …o tōrimásu (tō´ru, tō´tte) …を通ります(通る, 通って); (*exceeds*) sugimásu (sugíru, súgite) 過ぎます(過ぎる, 過ぎて); (*hands over*) watashimásu (watasu, wata-shite) 渡します(渡す, 渡して); (*hands around*) mawashimásu (mawasu, mawa-shite) 回します(回す, 回して); (*salt, sugar, etc.*) torimásu (tóru, tótte) 取ります(取る, 取って) 5. *v* (*exam*) (shiken ni) gōkaku shimásu (suru, shite) (試験に)合格します(する, して), ukarimásu (ukáru, ukátte) 受かります(受かる, 受かって), (shikén o) pásu-shimásu (pásu-suru, pásu-shite) (試験を)パスします(パスする, パスして) 6. *v* (*time passes*) tachimásu (tátsu, tátte) 経ちます(経つ, 経って), hemásu (héru, héte) 経ます(経る, 経て), keika shimásu (suru, shite) 経過します(する, して); (*passes time*) sugoshimásu (sugósu, sugóshite) 過ごします(過ごす, 過ごして) 7. *v* (*overtakes and passes a vehicle*) …o oi-koshimásu (oi-kósu, oi-kóshite) …を追い越します(追い越す, 追い越して); *No passing* oi-koshi kinshi 追い越し禁止 8. *v* ~ *it on* tsutaemásu (tsutaeru, tsutaete) 伝えます(伝える, 伝えて); *is passed on* tsutawarimásu (tsutawaru, tsutawatte) 伝わります(伝わる, 伝わって)

pass out 1. (*loses consciousness*) íshiki o ushinaimásu (ushinau, ushinatte) 意識を失います(失う, 失って) 2. → **distribute**

passage *n* tsūkō 通行; (*thorough-fare*) tōri通り, tsū´ro 通路, (*corridor*) rōka 廊下; (*of text*) …tokoró…ところ, issetsu 一節

passbook *n* tsūchō 通帳

passenger *n* jōkyaku 乗客, ryokyaku 旅客; ~ *car* (*automobile*) jōyō-sha 乗用車, (*train*) kyakusha 客車; ~ *ticket* jōshá-ken 乗車券

passer-by *n* tsūkō-nin 通行人

passion *n* jōnetsu 情熱, gekijō 激情, netchū 熱中

passionate *adj* jōnetsu-teki (na) 情熱的(な)

passive *adj* judō-teki (na) 受動的(な), shōkyoku-teki (na) 消極的(な)

passive voice *n* judō-tai 受動態, ukemi 受身

passport *n* ryoken 旅券, pasupō´to パスポート

password *n* pasuwādo パスワード

past *adv* (*the ~*) káko 過去; (*… ~ the hour*) …-(fún-) sugi …(分)過ぎ

pasta *n* pasuta パスタ

paste 1. *n* nori のり・ノリ・糊 2. (*pate*) pēsuto ペースト, neri-mono 練り物 3. *v* (*pastes it*) norízukeshimásu (norizukéru, norizukéte) のり付けします(のり付けする, のり付けて)

pastel *n* pasuteru パステル

pastel color *n* pasuteru karā パステルカラー

pasties *n* (*covering for nipples*) supankōru スパンコール

pastime *n* dōráku 道楽; goraku 娯楽, shúmi 趣味

pasting *n* [BOOKISH] kanpai 完敗

pastor *n* bokushi 牧師

pastry *n* (o-)káshi (お)菓子, kashi-pan 菓子パン, pesutorii ペストリー, pai kiji パイ生地

pat *v* (*karuku*) tatakimásu (tataku, tataite) (軽く)叩きます・たたきます(たたく, たたいて)

patch 1. *v* (*patches it*) (… ni) tsugi o atemásu (ateru, atete) (…に)継ぎを当てます(当てる, 当てて), tsuzurimásu (tsuzuru, tsuzutte) つづり[綴り]ます(つづる, つづって) 2. *n* (*a patch*) tsugi 継ぎ, patchi パッチ 3. → **field**

patent *n* tokkyo 特許, tokkyo-ken 特許権

path *n* 1. komichi 小道, michi 道 2. (*computer*) pasu パス

patience *n* gáman 我慢, konki 根気, [BOOKISH] nintai 忍耐, shinbō 辛抱; *loses ~* shibiré o kirashimásu (kirásu, kiráshite) しびれを切らします(切らす, 切らして)

patient 1. *adj* (*puts up with it*) gáman shimásu (suru, shite) 我慢します(する, して); (*has patience*) gaman-zuyói 我慢強い, nintai-zuyói 忍耐強い 2. *n* (*medical*) kanja 患者, (*ill person*) byōnin 病人, byōki no hito 病気の人

patiently *adv* jitto じっと; gáman shite 我慢して

patina *n* [BOOKISH] rokushō 緑青

patio *n* nakaniwa 中庭; terasu テラス

patriot *n* aikoku-sha 愛国者

patriotism *n* aikoku-shin 愛国心

patrol *n* patorōru パトロール; junkai 巡回

patrol car *n* patokā パトカー

patrolman *n* junsa 巡査

patron *n* (*customer, client*) tokui-saki 得意, suponsā スポンサー; patoron パトロン

pattern *n* patā´n/patán パターン/パタン, moyō 模様, tehón 手本(o-tehon お手本), katá 型, gara 柄

paulownia *n* (*tree/wood*) kiri 桐

pauper *n seikatsu-hogo-sha* 生活保護者, hinmin 貧民; "The Prince and The Pauper" "Ōji to Kojiki" 『王子と乞食』(→ **beggar**)

pause 1. *n* (*rest*) yasumí 休み (o-yasumi お休み); pōzu ポーズ; (*break in talk etc.*) kire-mé 切れ目 **2.** *v* hitoiki-tsukimásu (hitoiki-tsúku, hitoiki-tsuite) 一息つきます(一息つく, 一息ついて); tameraimásu (tameráu, tameratte) ためらいます(ためらう, ためらって)

pavement *n* (*roadway*) shadō 車道; (*walkway*) hodō 歩道

paw *n* ashi 足; te 手

pawn *n* **1.** (*something pawned*) shichí 質 **2.** (*chess*) pōn ポーン

pawnbroker/pawnshop *n* shichí-yá 質屋

pay 1. *n* (*one's wage*) kyū´ryō 給料 (o-kyūryō お給料), chingin 賃金 **2.** *adj* (*not free*) yūryō (no) 有料(の) **3.** *v* ~ (*out*) haraimásu (haráu, harátte) 払います(払う, 払って), dashimásu (dásu, dáshite) 出します(出す, 出して); (*taxes*) osamemásu (osaméru, osámete) 納めます(納める, 納めて); ~ *attention to* ... ni chū´i o haraimásu (haráu, harátte) ...に注意を払います(払う, 払って), ... ni nén o iremásu (ireru, irete) ...に念を入れます(入れる, 入れて); ~ *compliments* o-seiji o iimásu (iu, itte/yutte) お世辞を言います(言う, 言って/ゆって); ~ *one's share* buntan shimásu (suru, shite) 分担します(する, して); (*profitable*) wari ni aimásu (au, atte) 割に合います(合う, 合って)

pay parking *n* yūryō-chū´shajō 有料駐車場

pay phone *n* kōshū-dénwa 公衆電話 (*public telephone*)

pay raise *n* bēsu-appu (béa) ベースアップ(ベア)

payday *n* kyūryō´-bi 給料日

payment *n* shiharai 支払い, (*of taxes*) [BOOKISH] nōzei 納税

peace *n* heiwa 平和, heion 平穏, heian 平安; ~ *of mind* anshin 安心

Peace Corps *n* heiwa-bútai 平和部隊; (*member*) heiwa-butái-in 平和部隊員

peaceful *adj* (*calm*) odáyaka (na) 穏やか(な), nódoka (na) のどか(な)

peach *n* momo もも・モモ・桃

peacock *n* kujaku くじゃく・クジャク・孔雀

peak *n* itadaki 頂, chōjō´ 頂上; miné 峰; (*highpoint*) chō´tén 頂点

peanuts *n* píinátsu ピーナツ, píináttsu ピーナッツ, rakkasei 落花生,

pear *n* nashí なし・ナシ・梨

pearl *n* shinju 真珠, pāru パール

pearl diver *n* (*woman*) áma 海女

Pearl Harbor *n* Shinjú-wan 真珠湾

peas *n* éndō えんどう・エンドウ・豌豆, endō´-

mame えんどう豆・エンドウマメ・豌豆豆

pebble *n* koishi 小石; jari 砂利

peck (*at*) *v* **1.** (... o) tsu(t)tsukimásu (tsu(t)tsúku, tsu(t)tsúite) (...を)つ(っ)つきます(つ(っ)つく, つ(っ)ついて)

peculiar *adj* okashíi おかしい・可笑しい, okashina おかしな・可笑しな, kímyō (na) 奇妙(な), hén (na) 変(な) → **particular**

pedal *n* **1.** pédaru ペダル **2.** → **gas pedal**

pedestrian *n* hokō-sha 歩行者

pedestrian crossing *n* ōdan hodō 横断歩道

pediatrician *n* shōniká-i 小児科医

pediatrics *n* shōni ka 小児科

pedometer *n* manpo-kei 万歩計

peek *v* (... o) nozokimásu (nozoku, nozoite) (...を)のぞき[覗き]ます(のぞく, のぞいて)

peel 1. *n* (*rind*) kawá 皮 **2.** *v peels it* ...no kawá o mukimásu (muku, muite) ...の皮をむきます(むく, むいて); *peels it off* hagimásu (hágu, háide) はぎ[剥ぎ]ます(はぐ, はいて); *it peels off* hagemásu (hagéru, hágete) はげ[剥げ]ます(はげる, はげて)

peep (*at/into*) → **peek**

peephole *n* nozoki aná のぞき[覗き]穴

peeping Tom *n* nozoki-ya のぞき[覗き]屋

peewee *n* (*small kids*) (o)chíbi-(san) (お)ちび(さん)

peg *n* kugi くぎ・釘

Peking *n* Pékin ペキン・北京

pen *n* pén ペン; (*ballpoint*) bōrupen ボールペン; (*fountain*) mannén-hitsu 万年筆

penalty *n* **1.** (*fine*) bakkin 罰金 **2.** batsu 罰; penarutii ペナルティ

pence *n* pensu ペンス

pencil *n* enpitsu 鉛筆 (**1:** íp-pon 一本, **2:** ní-hon 二本, **3:** sánbon 三本, **10:** jíp-pon 十本; *how many* nánbon 何本)

penetrate *v* **1.** tōrimásu (tō´ru, tōtte) 通り[透り]ます(通[透]る, 通[透]って), tōshimásu (tō´su, tō´shite) 通し[透し]ます(通[透]す, 通[透]して) **2.** (*soaks in, permeates*) shimimásu (shimiru, shimite) 染みます(染みる, 染みて) **3.** minukimásu (minuku, minuite) 見抜きます(見抜く, 見抜いて)

penguin *n* pengin ペンギン

peninsula *n* hantō 半島

penis *n* pénisu ペニス, dankon 男根; [BABY TALK] (o-)chínchin (お)ちんちん, chínko ちんこ; (*medical*) inkei 陰茎

pension *n* **1.** nenkin 年金, taishoku-nénkin 退職年金 **2.** (*bed & breakfast*) penshon ペンション

people *n* hito 人, ... hitó... 人, hitó-tachi 人達・人たち; hitóbitto 人々, (*at large*) séken 世間; (*of a nation*) kokumin 国民; (*populace, civilians*) minshū 民衆; [COUNTED] ...-nin ...人, [BOOKISH] ...-mei ...名 (**1:** *person* hitóri 一人, ichi-mei 一名, **2:** futarí 二人, ni-mei 二名, **3:** san-nín 三人, sanmei 三名; *how many* nán-nin 何人, nanmei 何名)

pep *n* génki 元気

pepper *v* (*black*) koshō´ こしょう・コショウ・胡椒, (*Japanese mild*) sanshō さんしょう・サンショウ・山椒; (*green/bell*) píiman ピーマン; (*red*) tōgarashi とうがらし・トウガラシ・唐辛子

peppermint *n* hakka はっか・ハッカ・薄荷. pepāminto ペパーミント

pepper sprout *n* kí-no-me/kónome 木の芽

peppery *adj* karái 辛い

perceive *v* **1.** kizukimasu (kizuku, kizuite) 気付きます・気づきます(気づく, 気づいて) **2.** ...o rikai shimásu (suru, shite) 〜を理解します(する, して)

perceivable *adj* chikaku dekiru 知覚できる

percent *n* (...-) pāsénto (...)パーセント; *ten percent* ichí-wari 一割, *one percent* ichí-bu 一分

percentage *n* wari 割, wariai 割合; rítsu 率

perfect 1. *adj* kanzen (na) 完全(な), kanpeki (na) 完璧(な), pāfekuto (no/na) パーフェクト(の/な) **2.** *v* *perfects it* kansei sasemásu (saseru, sasete) 完成させます(させる, させて)

perfect circle, perfectly round manmaru (no) 真ん丸・まんまる(の)

perfectly *adv* kanzen ni 完全に, kanpeki (ni) 完璧(に), píttari ぴったり, píttáshi ぴったし → **absolutely, totally**

perform *v* okonaimásu (okonau, okonatte) 行います(行う, 行って); (*act*) enjimásu (enjiru, enjite) 演じます(演じる, 演じて); (*music, etc.*) ensō shimásu (suru, shite) 演奏します(する, して); *~ an operation* shújutsu shimásu (suru, shite) 手術します(する, して)

performance *n* **1.** (*of a task, duty*) jikkō 実行 **2.** (*daytime/evening ~*) (hirú/yóru no) bú (昼/夜の)部 **3.** (*artistic*) éngi 演技, pafōmansu パフォーマンス; (*musical instrument*) ensō 演奏; *beginning a ~* kaien 開演; *during the ~* kaien-chū 開演中 → **show**

performer *n* engí-sha 演技者, (*musical performer*) ensō-sha 演奏者

perfume *n* kōsui 香水

perfunctory *adj* ii-kagen (na) いい加減(な)

perhaps *adv* ... ká mo shiremasén/shirenai ...かも知れません/知れない, ... ká mo wakarimasén/wakaránai... かも分かりません/分からない, moshi-ka-shitara もしかしたら, moshi-ka-suru to もしかすると, tábun ... (deshō) 多分...(でしょう), [BOOKISH] osoraku ... (deshō) 恐らく・おそらく ...(でしょう)

peril *n* kiken 危険, [BOOKISH] kiki, 危機

perilla *n* (*plant*) shiso しそ・シソ・紫蘇

period *n* (*of time*) kikan 期間, (*limit*) kígen 期限; (*era*) jidai 時代, ...-jídai ...時代; (*punctuation*) shūshí-fū 終止符; (*end*) owari 終わり, oshimai おしまい; ijō 以上

periodic *adj* téiki (no) 定期(の)

perish *v* horobimásu (horobiru, horobite) 滅びます(滅びる, 滅びて)

permanent *adj* eien (no) 永遠(の); funen (no) 不変(の); kawaranai 変わらない

permanent residence *n* eijū 永住, honseki 本籍; *permanent place* *n* honséki-chi 本籍地

permanent visa *n* eijū biza 永住ビザ

permanent wave *n* pā´ma パーマ

permanently *adv* eien (ni) 永遠(に), eikyū (ni) 永久(に)

permission *n* kyóka 許可, ninka 認可; menkyo 免許, ráisensu ライセンス; *without ~* mudan de 無断で, kotowári mo náku 断りもなく

permissive *adj* amai 甘い

permit *n* kyoka (-shō) 許可(証), ráisensu ライセンス → **allow** → **permission** → **license**

pernicious *adj* akushitsu (na) 悪質(な)

perpendicular *adj* suichoku (no) 垂直(の)

perpetrate *v* (tsumi o) okashimásu (okasu, okashite) (罪を)犯します(犯す, 犯して)

perplexed; gets ~ komarimásu (komáru, kómátte) 困ります(困る, 困って); mayoimásu (mayóu, mayótte) 迷います(迷う, 迷って)

persecute *v* hakugai shimásu (suru, shite) 迫害します(する, して)

persecution *n* hakugai 迫害

perseverance *n* gáman 我慢

persevere *v* gáman shimásu (suru, shite) 我慢します(する, して)

persist *v* koshitsu shimásu (suru, shite) 固執します(する, して), jizoku shimásu (suru, shite) 持続します(する, して)

persimmon *n* (*fruit*) kaki 柿・カキ

person *n* hito 人, ... hitó ...人; (*honored*) ...katá ...方; ... monó ...者, ...yátsu ...やつ・奴; ko 個, te 手; ...-jin ...人, ...-nin ...人; ...-sha ...者; hitóri 一人, (*being*) sonzai 存在 → **people**

personage *n* jínbutsu 人物, (*being*) sonzai 存在

personal *adj* kojin-teki (na) 個人的(な); kojin-yō (no) 個人用(の), (*for one's own use*) jibun-yō (no) 自分用(の); shiteki (na) 私的(な)

Act for Protection of Computer Processed Personal Data held by Administrative Organs *n* kojin jōhō hogo hō 個人情報保護法

personal appearance *n* (mi-) narí (身)なり, kíryō 器量

personal business *n* shiyō 私用, shiji 私事

personal computer *n* paso-kon パソコン, pii shii PC

personal effects *n* temáwari 手回り, temawari-hin 手回り品

personal experience *n* taiken 体験, kojin-teki na keiken 個人的な経験

personal history *n* rireki 履歴; (*resume*) rireki-sho 履歴書

personal opinion *n* kojin-teki na iken 個人的な意見, [BOOKISH] kojin-teki (na) kenkai 個人的(な)見解

personality *n* kosei 個性, pāsonaritii パーソナリティ

personally *adv* jíka-ni じか[直]に, kojin-teki ni 個人的に

personnel *n* *personnel department* jinji-ka

人事課; *personnel cost* jinken-hi 人件費

person-to-person *adj* man tsū man マンツーマン, ittaiichi 一対一

person-to-person call *n* shimei-tsū´wa 指名通話

perspire → sweat

persuade *v* settoku shimásu (suru, shite) 説得します(する、して), (… ni sore o) nattoku sasemásu (…にそれを)納得させます

persuasion *n* settoku 説得 → **belief**

pertain *v ~ to* … ni kan-shimásu (kan-súru, kán-shite) …に関します(関する、関して)

pessimism *n* hikan 悲観; *pessimistic adj* hikan-teki (na) 悲観的(な)

pessimist *n* hikan ron-sha 悲観論者

pessimistic *adj* hikan-teki (na) 悲観的(な)

pet 1. *n* pétto ペット **2.** *v (strokes, pats)* nademásu (nadéru, nádete) なで[撫で]ます(なでる、なでて)

petrol → gasoline

petroleum *n* sekiyu 石油

petticoat *n* pechikōto ペチコート

petty *adj* sásai (na) ささい[些細]な, sasáyaka (na) ささやか(な); *petty cash* koguchi-genkin 小口現金

pharmaceuticals *n* yakuzai 薬剤

pharmacist *n* yakúzai-shi 薬剤師

pharmacy *n* yakkyoku 薬局

pheasant *n* kiji きじ・キジ・雉

phenomenon *n* genshō 現象

phial *n* kusuri bin 薬瓶

Philippines *n* Fírípin フィリピン

philosopher *n* tetsugákú-sha 哲学者

philosophy *n* tetsugaku 哲学

phone *n* denwa 電話; *(cell-phone, mobile-phone)* keitai dénwa 携帯電話 **→ telephone**

phone book *n* denwa-chō 電話帳

phone booth *n* kōshū denwa 公衆電話

phone number *n* denwa bangō 電話番号

phonograph *n* chikuón-ki 蓄音機

phony *adj* nise (no) にせ・偽(の)

photo, photograph 1. *n* shashin 写真 (*how many* nánmai 何枚); *~ of a wanted criminal* tehaisháshin 手配写真 **2.** *v (takes a photograph of)* … no shashin o torimásu (tóru, tótte) …の写真を撮ります(撮る、撮って)

photographer *n* shashin-ka 写真家, kamera-man カメラマン

phrase *n* mónku 文句, kú 句, furēzu フレーズ

physical *adj* karada (no) 体(の), shíntai (no) 身体(の)

physical assault *n* bōkō-jiken 暴行事件

physical exam *n* shintai-kénsa 身体検査

physical exercises *n* taisō 体操

physician *n* isha 医者, o-isha(-san) お医者(さん)

physicist *n* butsuri gákú-sha 物理学者

physics *n* butsuri-gaku 物理学

physiology *n* seiri-gaku 生理学; seiri (kinō) 生理(機能)

physiological *adj* seiri-teki (na) 生理学的(な)

physique *n* taikaku 体格

pianist *n (professional)* pianisuto ピアニスト

piano *n* piano ピアノ; *plays ~* piano o hikimásu (hiku, hiite) ピアノを弾きます(弾く、弾いて)

pick *v* **1. → choose 2.** *(plucks)* tsumimásu (tsumu, tsunde) 摘みます(摘む、摘んで); *picks it up* … o hiroimásu (hirou, hirotte) …を拾います(拾う、拾って); *picks one up (by car, etc.)* mukae ni ikimásu (iku, itte) 迎えに行きます(行く、行って); tsumamimásu (tsumamu, tsumande) つまみます(つまむ、つまんで); *picks one's pocket* surimásu (súru, sútté) すります(する、すって)

pickle 1. *n* tsukemono 漬物・つけもの; o-shinko おしんこ・お新香; *(Chinese)* zāsai ザーサイ **2.** *pickles it v* tsukemásu (tsukeru, tsukete) 漬けます(漬ける、漬けて)

pickled daikon *(radish)* *n* takú(w)an たくあん(わ)ん・タクアン(ワン)・沢庵

pickled ginger *n* gári ガリ, amazu shō´ga 甘酢しょうが[生姜・ショウガ]

pickled plum/apricot *n* umeboshi 梅干し・うめぼし・ウメボシ

pickpocket *n* súri すり

picnic *n* ensoku 遠足, píkuníkku ピクニック; *picnic boxes* jūbako 重箱(o-jú お重)

picture *n* é 絵; *(photo)* shashin 写真; *(diagram, drawing)* zu 図; *(films)* eizō 映像; *picture book* e-hón 絵本; *picture postcard* e-hágaki 絵葉書; *the picture quality* utsurí 映り; *takes a ~* shashin o torimásu (tóru, tótte) 写真を撮ります(撮る、撮って); utsushimásu (utsúsú, utsúshite) 映します(映す、映して)

picture-framer *n* hyōgu-ya 表具屋

pie *n* pái パイ

piece *n (one)* ~ (ík)-ko (一)個, (hitó)-tsu (一)つ; *(a cut)* kiré 切れ, hitó-kire 一切れ

in pieces *adv* barabara (ni) ばらばら(に), mechamecha めちゃめちゃ・メチャメチャ

into pieces *adv* barabara ni narimásu (naru, natte) ばらばらになります(なる、なって)

pier *n* sanbashi 桟橋, hato-ba 波止場

pierce *v* tōshimásu (tō´su, tō´shite) 通します(通す、通して)

pig *n* buta 豚・ブタ

pigeon *n* háto 鳩・ハト

pile *n* **1.** *(stake)* kúi くい・杭 **2.** *(heap)* (hitó)-yama (一)山

pile *v* **1.** *piles them up* kasanemásu (kasaneru, kasanete) 重ねます(重ねる、重ねて); *they pile up* kasanarimásu (kasanaru, kasanatte) 重なります(重なる、重なって) **2.** *piles it up* tsumimásu (tsumu, tsunde) 積みます(積む、積んで), morimásu (moru, motte) 盛ります(盛る、盛って)

piles → hemorrhoids

pill *n (medicine)* kusuri 薬, o-kusúri お薬, *(specifically)* gan'yaku 丸薬, jōzai 錠剤; *(contraceptive)* keikō-hinin-yaku 経口避妊薬, piru ピル

pillar *n* hashira 柱 (**1:** íp-pon 一本, **2:** ní-hon 二本, **3:** sánbon 三本; *how many* nánbon 何本)

pillow *n* mákura まくら・枕 (*how many* nán-ko 何個)

pilot *n* pairótto パイロット; (*plane captain*) kichō´ 機長

pimp *n* ponbiki/ponpiki ぽん引き

pimple *n* níkibi にきび, dekímónó できもの・出来物, o-déki うお的

pin *n* (*for hair*) (hea-)pín (ヘア)ピン, pin-dome ピン留め; (*for sewing*) hári 針; mushi-pin 虫ピン
　pin money *n* kózukai 小遣い
　pin number *n* pasuwādo パスワード, anshō bangō 暗証番号
　pin shell *n* (*a kind of scallop*) taira-gi たいらぎ

pinball (machine) *n* (*Japanese style*) pachinko パチンコ

pincers *n* yattoko やっとこ

pinch 1. *n* pínchi ピンチ, [BOOKISH] kíki 危機
2. *v* tsunerimásu (tsunéru, tsunétte) つねります (つねる, つねって), tsumamimásu (tsumamu, tsumandé) つまみます(つまむ, つまんで)

pine *n* (*tree*) mátsu (no kí) 松(の木)

pineapple *n* paináppuru パイナップル

pinholder *n* (*frog for flowers*) kénzan 剣山

pink *n* (*adj*) momo-iro (no) 桃色(の), pínku (no) ピンク(の)

pinpoint *v* seikaku ni shimeshimásu (shimesu, shimeshite) 正確に示します(示す, 示して)

pinup *n* pinnappu shashin ピンナップ写真

pioneer *n* paionia パイオニア, kaitaku-sha 開拓者, senku-sha 先駆者

pipe *n* páipu パイプ; (*tube*) tsutsu 筒, kúda 管

pipeline *n* páipu rain パイプライン; rūto ルート, yusōkanro 輸送管路

pipsqueak *n* chíbi ちび

pirate *n* kaizoku 海賊
　pirate ship *n* kaizoku-sen 海賊船

pirated *adj* kaizoku-ban (no) 海賊版(の)

Pisces *n* (*star sign*) Uo-za 魚座・うお座

piss *n* shōbén 小便; [BABY TALK] shikko しっこ (o-shikko おしっこ) → urine; urinate

pissoir → urinal

pistol *n* pisutoru ピストル, kenjū 拳銃

pitch *n* (*baseball*) tōkyū 投球, (*cricket*) pitchi ピッチ

pitcher *n* tōshu 投手; pitchā ピッチャー; *water pitcher* mizu-sáshi 水差し; *saké pitcher* (*decanter*) tokkuri とっくり・トックリ・徳利

pith *n* shín 芯

pitiful, pitiable *adj* kawai-sō´ (na) かわいそう・可哀想(な), (o-)ki no dókú (na) (お)気の毒(な)

pittance *n* shōryō 少量
　small pittance *n* wazuka na teate/shūnyū わずかな手当/収入

pituitary *n* kasuitai 下垂体

pity 1. *v* (*pities*) dōjō shimásu (suru, shite) 同情します(する, して) **2.** *n* (*it is a pity*) zannen (na) ...残念(な)..., kinodoku 気の毒, dōjō 同情

pizza *n* píza ピザ

pizza crust, pizza dough *n* píza no kiji ピザの生地

pizza delivery *n* píza no haitatsu ピザの配達, píza no takuhai ピザの宅配

place 1. *n* tokoró 所, basho 場所; (*assigned seat*) seki 席(o-séki お席); (*for something*) ba 場, ...-ba ...場; (*to put something*) oki-ba 置き場 (*how many places*) nan-kásho 何か所・何箇所)
2. *v* → put
　out of place, not from the right/best place *adj* ba-chígai (na/no) 場違い(な/の)
　takes place *v* happen
　takes the place of *v* ... ni kawari-másu (kawaru, kawatte) ...に代わります(代わる, 代わって)

place of employment *n* tsutomesaki 勤め先; [BOOKISH] kinmu saki 勤務先, shoku-ba 職場

place of residence *n* kyojū-chi 居住地

plain 1. *adj* (*not gaudy*) jimí (na) 地味(な), (*simple, frugal*) shísso (na) 質素(な) **2.** *n* (*flat land*) heiya 平野, heichi 平地

plain taste *n* tanpaku na aji 淡白な味

plain yogurt *n* purēn yōguruto プレーンヨーグルト

plainly *adv* (*clearly*) hakkíri (to) はっきり(と); (*simply*) assári (to) あっさり(と)

plan 1. *n* keikaku 計画; kikaku 企画; puran プラン; (*schedule*) yotei 予定; (*scheme*) takurami たくらみ・企み, kuwadate 企て; (*intention*) tsumori つもり, íto 意図 **2.** *v* keikaku shimásu (suru, shite) 計画します(する, して); kikaku shimásu (suru, shite) 企画します(する, して); kuwadatemásu (kuwadáteru, kuwadátete) 企てます(企てる, 企てて); (*schedule*) yotei shimásu (suru, shite) 予定します(する, して); (*devises*) takuramimásu (takurámu, takuránde) たくらみ[企み]ます(たくらむ, たくらんで)

plane *n* (*airplane*) hikō-ki 飛行機
　plane crash *n* tsuiraku (jiko) 墜落(事故)

planet *n* wakusei 惑星

planetarium *n* puranetariúmu プラネタリウム

plank *n* íta 板

plant 1. *n* (*a plant*) shokúbutsu 植物; (*herb*) kusá 草, (*shrub*) kí 木; (*garden/potted*) ueki 植木 **2.** *n* (*factory*) kōjō 工場 **3.** *v* (*plants it*) uemásu (ueru, uete) 植えます(植える, 植えて)

plaster *n* **1.** sekkō 石こう[膏]; *adhesive plaster* bansōkō ばんそうこう・絆創膏 **2.** (*stucco*) shikkui しっくい・漆喰

plastic *n* purásuchikku プラスチック; (*vinyl*) bíniru/biníiru ビニル/ビニール; (*polyethylene*) pori(-) ポリ; *plastic bag* poribúkuro ポリ袋, biniirubúkuro ビニール袋; *plastic model* puramóderu プラモデル

plate *n* sara 皿 (o-sara お皿); shokki 食器, purēto プレート

platform *n* **1.** (*at station*) hō´mu ホーム, nori-ba 乗り場; (*non-passenger entry*) ticket nyūjō´-ken 入場券 **2.** (*lecture ~*) endan 演壇, kōdan 講壇

platonic *adj* puratonikku (na) プラトニック(な); kannen-teki (na) 観念的(な)

platonic love *n* puratonikku rabu プラトニックラブ

plausible *adj* mottomorashii もっともらしい

play *v* asobimás<u>u</u> (asobu, asonde) 遊びます(遊ぶ、遊んで); (*a game*) shimás<u>u</u> (suru, sh<u>i</u>te) します(する、して); (*a stringed instrument or piano*) hikimás<u>u</u> (h<u>i</u>ku, hiite) 弾きます(弾く、弾いて); (*musical instrument*) ensō shimás<u>u</u> (suru, sh<u>i</u>te) 演奏します(する、して); (*baseball, football, hookey, etc.*) (yakyū, sakkā, hokkē,...) o shimás<u>u</u> (suru, sh<u>i</u>te) (野球、サッカー、ホッケー)をします(する、して); **~ it safe** daijō torimás<u>u</u> (tóru, tótte) 大事をとります(とる、とって)

play *n* (*drama*) shibai 芝居, engeki 演劇
Shakespeare's plays *n* sheikusupia no gikyoku シェイクスピアの戯曲

playboy *n* purei bōi プレイボーイ

player *n* (*sports*) sénshu 選手, (*instrument*) purēyā プレーヤー
CD player *n* shiidii purēyā CDプレーヤー
music player *n* myūjikku purēyā ミュージックプレーヤー
video player *n* bideo purēyā ビデオプレーヤー

playground *n* undō jō 運動場

playing cards *n* toránpu トランプ

playmate *n* asobi nakama 遊び仲間

plaza *n* híró-bá 広場; puraza プラザ

pleasant *adj* tanoshíi 楽しい; omoshirói おもしろい・面白い; ureshíi うれしい・嬉しい; kaiteki (na) 快適(な)

Please ... *interj* Dṓzo ... どうぞ...; *Do me a favor.* O-negai shimás<u>u</u>. お願いします。; ...(shi) te kudasái ...(し)て下さい, [INFORMAL] ...(shi)te chōdái. ...(し)てちょうだい。

pleasure *n* tanoshimi 楽しみ(o-tanoshimi お楽しみ)

pleat *n* ori-mé 折り目; puriitsu プリーツ

pledge 1. *n* chíkai 誓い **2.** *v* (*swears it*) chikaimás<u>u</u> (chikau, chikatte) 誓います(誓う、誓って) **→ promise**

Pleiades *n* (*cluster of stars*) Pureadesu プレアデス, Pureiadesu プレイアデス

plentiful *adj* yútaka (na) 豊か(な)

plenty *n* takusán たくさん・沢山

pliers *n* (*pincers*) pénchi ペンチ, yattoko やっとこ・鋏

plight *n* (*one gets into*) hamé はめ・羽目

plot *n* (*story line*) súji 筋; (*scheme, trick*) keiryaku 計略, hakarigoto はかりごと・謀, inbō 陰謀

plop *v* **1.** (*it drops*) dosun (dosa', dobun, pochan, poton, *etc.*) to ochimás<u>u</u> (ochiru, ochite) ドスン(ドサッ、ドブン、ポチャン、ポトン)と落ちます(落ちる、落ちて) **2.** (*drops it*) dosun (dosa', dobun, pochan, poton, *etc.*) to otoshimás<u>u</u> (otosu, otoshite) ドスン(ドサッ、ドブン、ポチャン、ポトン)と落とします(落とす、落として)

plow 1. *n* (*a plow*) suki すき・鋤 **2.** *v* (*plows it*) tagayashimás<u>u</u> (tagayásu, tagayásh<u>i</u>te) 耕します(耕す、耕して), s<u>u</u>kimás<u>u</u> (s<u>u</u>ku, suite) すき[鋤き]ます(すく、すいて)

pluck *v* tsumimás<u>u</u> (tsumu, tsunde) 摘みます(摘む、摘んで)

plug *n* sén 栓; (*electricity*) puragu プラグ, sash<u>i</u>komi 差し込み, kónsénto コンセント

plum *n* **1.** sumomo すもも・スモモ・李 **2.** (*Japanese apricot*) ume 梅・ウメ; *pickled plum* ume-boshi 梅干し・ウメボシ; *plum tree* ume 梅・ウメ; *plum wine* ume-shu 梅酒・ウメ酒

plumber *n* suidō-ya (san) 水道屋(さん); (*city water department*) suidō-kyoku 水道局

plumbing *n* (*water line*) suidō (sétsubi) 水道(設備)

plump *adj* f<u>u</u>tói 太い

plunder *v* ubaimás<u>u</u> (ubáu, ubátte) 奪います(奪う、奪って), ryakudatsu shimás<u>u</u> (suru, shite) 略奪します(する、して)

plural *n* fukusū 複数

plus *n* purasu プラス

p.m. *adv* (*afternoon*) gógo 午後, pii emu PM

pneumonia *n* haien 肺炎

poached eggs *n* pōchido-eggu ポーチドエッグ

poacher *n* (*person*) [BOOKISH] mitsuryō-sha 密猟者

pocket *n* pokétto ポケット; kaichū (no) 懐中(の)

pocketbook *n* **1.** handobággu ハンドバッグ **→ purse 2.** (*paperback*) bunko-bon 文庫本

pocket money *n* kózukai 小遣い・こづかい, (o-)kózukai (お)小遣い

pockmark *n* abata あばた

pockmarked face *n* abata-zura あばた面

pod *n* sáya さや・サヤ

podium *n* endan 演壇, shiki dai 指揮台

poem *n* shi 詩, utá 歌 **→ verse**

poet *n* shijin 詩人, kajin 歌人

point *n* ten 点, (*points obtained*) tokuten 得点; (*in a statement*) fushí 節; (*gist*) yōten 要点; (*tip, end*) saki 先; *to the point* tekisetsu (na/ni) 適切(な/に)

point *v* (*puts a point on*) togarasemás<u>u</u> (togaráseru, togarásete) とがらせ[尖らせ]ます(とがらせる、とがらせて); *~ at/to ...* o sashimás<u>u</u> (sásu, sásh<u>i</u>te) ...を指します(指す、指して); *~ out* sh<u>i</u>teki shimás<u>u</u> (suru, sh<u>i</u>te) 指摘します(する、して); shíji shimás<u>u</u> (suru, sh<u>i</u>te) 指示します(する、して)

pointed; *gets ~* togarimás<u>u</u> (togáru, togátte) とがり[尖り]ます(とがる、とがって)

point of departure *n* shuppátsúten 出発点

poison *n* dokú 毒, [BOOKISH] doku-so 毒素

poke *v* ts<u>u</u>kimás<u>u</u> (ts<u>u</u>ku, tsuite) 突きます(突く、突いて); *~ fun at* karakaimás<u>u</u> (karakáu, karakátte) からかいます(からかう、からかって)

pole *n* (*rod*) bō 棒, saó さお・竿, pōru ポール; *telephone/light ~* denchū 電柱

police *n* keisatsu 警察; *police box* kōban 交番; *police station* keisatsu-sho 警察署
police car *n* patokā パトカー
policeman, police officer *n* omáwari-san お巡り

[おまわり]さん, keikan 警官, [BOOKISH] junsa 巡査

policy n hōshin 方針, tatémae 建て前, porishii ポリシー, (*political*) seisaku 政策; *makes ... one's ~* ... o tatémae to shimásu (suru, shíte) ...を建て前とします(する, して)

polio n shōni-máhi 小児麻痺

polish v (*shines*) migakimásu (migaku, migaite) 磨きます(磨く, 磨いて); (*grinds*) togimásu (tógu, tóide) 研ぎます(研ぐ, 研いで)

polished rice n hakúmai 白米

polite adj (go-)téinei téinei (na) (ご)丁寧(な), (*well-behaved*) otonashíi おとなしい・大人しい, reigi-tadashíi 礼儀正しい

politely adv téinei ni 丁寧に, otoná-shiku おとなしく・大人しく, yasashiku 優しく・やさしく

politician n seiji-ka 政治家

politics n seiji 政治

pollution n osen 汚染, kō´gai 公害

  air pollution n taiki-osen 大気汚染

  environmental pollution n kankyō-osen 環境汚染

  water pollution n suishitsu-osen 水質汚染

polyethylene n pori(-) ポリ, poriechiren ポリエチレン

polyvinyl n bíniru ビニル, biníiru ビニール

pomade n pomā´do ポマード

pomelo n (*Japanese*) natsu-míkan 夏みかん・夏蜜柑・ナツミカン

pond n iké 池

pony n ponii ポニー

ponytail n (*hairstyle*) ponii tēru ポニーテール

pool; *motor pool* (*parking* (*lot*)) mōtā pū´ru モータープール, chūsha-jō 駐車場; *swimming pool* pū´ru プール

poor adj (*needy*) bínbō (na) 貧乏(な), mazushíi 貧しい; (*clumsy*) hetá (na) へた[下手](な); (*bad*) warúi 悪い; (*pitiful*) kawaisō (na) かわいそう[可哀相](な)

pop **1.** n (*soda water*) sōda ソーダ, jūsu ジュース **2.** v (*it pops*) hajikemásu (hajikéru, hajíkete) はじけます(はじける, はじけて) **3.** v (*pops it*) hajikesasemásu (hajikesaséru, hajikesásete) はじけさせます(はじけさせる, はじけさせて)

popcorn n poppukō´n ポップコーン

popular adj **1.** ninki (no aru) 人気(のある); taishū (no) 大衆(の); zoku (na) 俗(な); hayari (no) はやり・流行り(の); hyoban (no) 評判(の) **2.** *is ~* ninki ga arimásu (áru, átte) 人気があります(ある, あって); hayatteimásu (íru, ítte) はや[流行]っています(いる, いて); ureteimásu (iru, ite) 売れています(いる, いて); (*a person is well liked*) motemásu (motéru, mótete) もてます(もてる, もてて)

popularity n ninki 人気; ryūkō 流行

popularization n fukyū 普及; *gets popularized* fukyū shimásu (suru, shíte) 普及します(する, して)

popular music n poppusu ポップス

population n **1.** jinkō 人口; nínzu 人数, nínzū 人数 **2.** (*populace*) → **people**

porcelain n setomono 瀬戸物, jíki 磁器 → **china(ware)**

porch n **1.** (*entrance hall*) génkan 玄関, pōchi ポーチ, beranda ベランダ **2.** (*veranda*) engawa 縁側

pork n buta-niku 豚肉, pōku ポーク

  pork cutlet n ton-katsu 豚カツ・とんかつ

  pork dumpling n (*meatballs steamed in thin pastry*) shūmai シューマイ・焼売

porno film n poruno-éiga ポルノ映画

pornography n póruno ポルノ, ero-hon エロ本; (*traditional*) shunga 春画

porpoise n iruka イルカ

porridge n (o-)kayu (お)かゆ[粥]

port n minato 港; *Port of (Yokohama)* (Yokohama)-kō (横浜)港

portable shrine n (*for festival parades*) (o-)mikoshi (お)みこし[御輿]

porter n pō´tā ポーター; (*redcap*) akabō 赤帽

portion n búbun 部分, bún 分, ichí-bu 一部, wari-mae 割り前; (*serving*) ...-ninmae ...人前

portrait n shōzō(-ga) 肖像(画), zō 像

position n **1.** íchi 位置, pojishon ポジション **2.** (*status, rank*) chíi 地位 **3.** → **place** → **job**

positive adj **1.** sekkyoku-teki (na) 積極的(な), pojitibu ポジティブ **2.** → **sure**

  positive thinking n maemuki (na) shikō 前向き(な)思考, pojitibu shinkingu ポジティブ・シンキング

possess v **1.** *is possessed of* shoyūshiteimásu (shoyūsuru, shoyūshíte) 所有しています(所有する, 所有して) → **have** → **own** **2.** sonaemásu (sonáeru, sonáete) 備えます(備える, 備えて)

possessed adj toritsukareta 取り憑かれた

possession n (*thing owned*) shoyū-butsu 所有物, shoyū-hin 所有品

possibility n kanō-sei 可能性, jitsugen-sei 実現性

possible adj kanō (na) 可能(な); *is ~* dekimásu (dekíru, dékite) でき[出来]ます(できる, できて), kanaimásu (kanáu, kanátte) かない[叶い]ます(かなう, かなって)

possibly adv hyótto shitára/shite/suru to ひょっとしたら/して/すると; arúi-wa あるいは・或いは

possum n fukuro nezumi フクロネズミ

post n **1.** yūbin 郵便; *a post* yūbin-bustu 郵便物; (*mailbox*) yūbin-posuto 郵便ポスト → **mail** **2.** hashira 柱 → **pole, stake** **3.** (*duty*) yakú 役, (*job*) shoku 職

postage n yūbin-ryō´kin 郵便料金, yūsō´-ryo 郵送料; *postage stamp* kitte 切手, yūbin-kítte/-gítte 郵便切手/切手

postal; *postal savings* yūbin-chókin 郵便貯金; *postal transfer* yūbin-fúrikae 郵便振替

postcard n hagaki 葉書(o-hágaki お葉書); (*picture*) e-hágaki 絵葉書

poster n posutā ポスター

posterity n shíson 子孫

postman *n* yūbin-ya (san) 郵便屋(さん)
post office *n* yūbín-kyoku 郵便局
postpone *v* enki shimásu (suru, shite) 延期します(する, して), nobashimásu (nobasu, nobashite) 延ばします(延ばす, 延ばして)
postponement *n* enki 延期
posture *n* shisei 姿勢
postwar *adj* sengo (no) 戦後(の)
pot *n* **1.** (*piece of pottery*) yakimono 焼き物 **2.** (*for cooking*) kama かま・釜; (*pan*) nábe 鍋 (o-nabe お鍋); (*kettle*) pótto ポット **3.** (*for plants*) hachí 鉢; *potted plant* hachiue 鉢植え, hachí-mono 鉢物, ueki 植木
potage *n* (*thick soup*) potā´ju ポタージュ
potassium *n* kariumu カリウム
potato *n* póteto ポテト; (*Irish*) jagaimo じゃがいも(o-jága おじゃが)・ジャガイモ; (*sweet*) imó 芋・イモ(o-imo お芋), Satsuma-imo さつま[薩摩]芋・サツマイモ; (*baked sweet potato*) yaki-imo 焼き芋・ヤキイモ
potato starch *n* katakúriko 片栗粉
pot-au-feu *n* (*food*) potofu ポトフ
potency *n* senzai-ryoku 潜在力
potential *n* (*possibility*) kanōsei 可能性, (*potentiality*) senzaisei 潜在性
potential ability *n* senzai nōryoku 潜在能力
potter's wheel *n* rokuro ろくろ
pottery *n* yaki-mono 焼き物, tō´ki 陶器
pouch *n* póchi ポーチ, fukuro 袋
pouch of a kangaroo *n* kangarū no fukuro カンガルーの袋
pouched animal *n* [BOOKISH] yūtai-rui (dōbutsu) 有袋類(動物)
poultice *n* shippu 湿布
poultry *n* [BOOKISH] kakin 家禽
pound 1. *n* (*weight or money*) póndo ポンド **2.** *pounds it v* tatakimásu (tatáku, tatáite) 叩きます(叩く, 叩いて)
pour *v* **1.** tsugimásu (tsugu, tsuide) つぎ[注ぎ]ます(つぐ, ついで), sosogimásu (sosogu, sosoide) そそぎ[注ぎ]ます(そそぐ, そそいで); *pouring the saké/beer* (o-)shaku (お)酌 **2.** *~ on* abisemásu (abiseseru, abisesete) 浴びせます(浴びせる, 浴びせて)
pout *v* fukuremásu (fukureru, fukurete) ふくれます(ふくれる, ふくれて)
poverty *n* hinkon 貧困, binbō 貧乏
powder *n* koná 粉(o-kóna お粉); funmatsu 粉末; paudā パウダー; (*face*) oshiroi おしろい・白粉
powder magazine *n* kayaku-ko 火薬庫, danyaku-ko 弾薬庫
powder snow *n* kona yuki 粉雪
powder soap *n* kona sekken 粉石鹸・粉せっけん
powdered arrowroot *n* kuzuko くず粉
powdered medicine *n* kona-gúsuri 粉薬
powdered milk *n* kona-míruku 粉ミルク
powdered sugar *n* kona zatō 粉砂糖
power *n* chikará 力, jituryoku 実力; kenryoku 権力; (*person of power*) kenryoku-sha 権力者;

(*energy, influence*) séiryoku 勢力; (*electricity*) dénki 電気
power company *n* denryoku-gaisha 電力会社
power failure/outage *n* teiden 停電
power line *n* densen 電線
powerful *adj* yūryoku (na) 有力(な); kyōryoku (na) 強力(な); pawafuru (na) パワフル(な)
practical *adj* jitchi (no) 実地(の), jissenteki (na) 実践的(な); jitsuyōteki (na) 実用的(な)
practical use *n* jitsuyō 実用
practically *adv* taigai 大概・たいがい; jitsuyōteki (ni) 実用的(に)
practice *n* **1.** (*drill*) renshū 練習, (*artistic*) (o-)kéiko (お)けいこ[稽古] **2.** (*realization*) jikkō 実行, (*reality*) jissai 実際, (*habit*) shūkan 習慣; *(putting to)* ~ jitchi 実地; *puts to* ~ jisshi shimásu (suru, shite) 実施します(する, して)
Practice makes perfect. *idiom* Narau yori nareyo. 習うより慣れよ。
praise 1. *n* (*homage*) home-kótoba ほめ[褒め]言葉, homé ほめ・褒め, [BOOKISH] shōsan 称賛 **2.** *v* (*lauds*) homemásu (homéru, hómete) ほめ[褒め]ます(ほめる, ほめて)
prank *n* itazura いたずら・悪戯
prawn *n* kurumá-ebi 車えび[海老]・クルマエビ
pray *v* inorimásu (inóru, inótte) 祈ります(祈る, 祈って)
prayer *n* inorí 祈り(o-inori お祈り)
preach *v* sekkyō shimásu (suru, shite) 説教します(する, して), (oshie o) tokimásu (tóku, tóite) (教えを)説きます(説く, 説いて)
preacher *n* (*priest*) bokushi(-san) 牧師(さん)
preamble *n* maeoki 前置き
prearrange *v* uchi-awasemásu (uchi-awaséru, uchi-awásete) 打ち合わせます(打ち合わせる, 打ち合わせて)
precaution *n* (*care*) yō´jin 用心, keikai 警戒, nén念; (*prevention*) yobō 予防; *as a* ~ nen no tamé (ni) 念の為(に)
precedent *n* senrei 先例, zenrei 前例, réi 例
precious *adj* taisetsu (na) 大切(な), daijí (na) 大事(な), kichō (na) 貴重(な); oshíi 惜しい
precipice *n* (*cliff*) zeppeki 絶壁; kiki 危機
precipitate *v* (*rains, snows*) furimásu (fúru, fútté) 降ります(降る, 降って)
precipitous *adj* kyu (na) 急(な), kewashíi 険しい
precise *adj* seimitsu (na) 精密(な)
precisely *adv* kíchin-to きちんと; seikaku ni 正確に; kikkari (ni) きっかり(に)
precision *n* seikaku 正確; [BOOKISH] seimitsu 精密
predicament *n* kyūchi 窮地, kukyō 苦境
predicate *n* jutsugo 述語; jutsubu 述部
predict *v* yogen shimásu (suru, shite) 予言します(する, して)
prediction *n* (*weather, etc.*) yohō 予報, yogen 予言
prefabricated house *n* purehabu-jūtaku プレハブ住宅

preface n jobun 序文, maegaki 前書き

prefectural adj kenritsu (no) 県立(の), kōritsu (no) 公立(の)

prefecture n kén 県, ...-ken ...県; **prefecture office** kenchō 県庁

prefer v ... no hō´ ga sukídesu ...の方が好きです; ... no hō´ o konomimásu (konómu, konónde) ...の方を好みます(好む, 好んで)

preferably adv isso いっそ, múshiro むしろ

prefix n settō-go 接頭語, settō-ji 接頭辞

pregnancy n ninshin 妊娠; (gets pregnant) ninshin shiteimásu (shiteiru, shiteite) 妊娠しています(している, していて)

prehistoric adj senshi jidai (no) 先史時代(の), yūshi izen (no) 有史以前(の)

prehistory n senshi jidai 先史時代, [BOOKISH] yūshi izen 有史以前

prejudice n henken 偏見, sennyūkan 先入観, sabetsu 差別

pre-kindergarten n hoikú-en 保育園

preliminary n yosen 予選

prelude n (music) pureryūdo プレリュード, zensō kyoku 前奏曲, jokyoku 序曲

premature adj hayasugiru 早過ぎる, [BOOKISH] jiki shōsō (no) 時期尚早(の)
premature baby n sōzan-ji 早産児, mijuku-ji 未熟児

premeditated adj (not accidental, pre-planned) keikakuteki (ni) 計画的(に); (intentionally) koi (ni) 故意(に)

premiere n puremia プレミア, (film) hatsu kōkai 初公開

premise n zentei 前提, katei 仮定

premium n puremiamu プレミアム, (bonus) [BOOKISH] hōshōkin 報奨金; shōhin 賞品; omake おまけ, keihin 景品

premonition n yokan 予感

preparation(s) n yō´i 用意, júnbi 準備; shitaku したく・支度; (anticipatory steps) yóbi 予備; (advance study) yoshū 予習; (provisions) sonáe 備え

prep(aratory) school n yobi-kō 予備校

prepare v 1. ... no yō´i/júnbi o shimásu (suru, shite) ...の用意/準備をします(する, して) 2. (arranges) ...no shitaku o shimásu (suru, shite) ...のしたく[支度]をします(する, して) 3. (studies ahead) yoshū shimásu (suru, shite) 予習します(する, して) 4. (readies it) totonoemásu (totonóeru, totonóete) 整えます(整える, 整えて) 5. (makes it) tsukurimásu (tsukúru, tsukútte) 作ります(作る, 作って) 6. (sets up, provides) mōkemásu (mōkéru, mōkete) 設けます(設ける, 設けて)

prepared; is ~ for (resigned to) kákúgo shimásu (suru, shite) 覚悟します(する, して)

prescribe v 1. (prescribes medicine) shohō shimásu (suru, shite) 処方します(する, して) 2. (stipulates) kitei shimásu (suru, shite) 規定します(する, して)

prescription n shohō 処方; (~ slip) shohō-sen 処方せん[箋]

present 1. adj (the present time) génzai (no) 現在(の); íma (no) 今(の); kóndo (no) 今度(の) **2.** adj (in attendance) shusseki (no) 出席(の) **3.** n génzai 現在; íma 今; hon- ...本..., kon-... 今...; at ~ íma wa 今は, génzai wa 現在は(; up to the ~ imamáde 今まで, koremáde これまで; the ~ conditions/state genjō 現状

present n (gift) okuri-mono 贈り物, purézento プレゼント; o-rei お礼; kokoro-zashi 志 (o-kokorozashi お志); (as a souvenir) (o-)miyage (お)みやげ[土産], [BABY TALK] o-míya おみや; (midyear) (o-)chūgen (お)中元, (year-end) (o-)seibo (お)歳暮

present v (gives) agemásu (ageru, agete) あげます(あげる, あげて), sashi-agemásu (sashi-ageru, sashi-agete) 差し上げます(差し上げる, 差し上げて); okurimásu (okuru, okutte) 贈ります(贈る, 贈って)

presently adv 1. (by and by) íma ni 今に, yagate やがて → **soon** 2. (at present) íma wa 今は

preservation n [BOOKISH] hozon 保存; hogo 保護 **Peace Preservation Law** n Chian iji hō 治安維持法

preservation of environment n kankyō hogo 環境保護, kankyō hozen 環境保全

preservation of order n chitsujo no iji 秩序の維持

preservation of the species n shu no hozen 種の保全

wildlife preservation n yasei seibutsu no hogo 野生生物の保護

preservative n bōfu-zai 防腐剤; hozon-ryō 保存料

preserve v tamochimásu (tamótsu, tamótte) 保ちます(保つ, 保って), hozon shimásu (suru, shite) 保存します(する, して); mamorimásu (mamóru, mamótte) 守ります(守る, 守って)

president n (of a nation) daitō´ryō 大統領; (of a company) shachō 社長; (of a university, college, etc.) gakuchō 学長; (of a school) kōchō 校長

press 1. v ~ (on) oshimásu (osu, oshite) 押します(押す, 押して); (press ... (up)on ...) oshitsukémásu (oshitsukéru, oshistukétte) 押し付けます(押し付ける, 押し付けて) **2.** v (iron) airon o atemásu (ateru, atete) アイロンをあてます(あてる, あてて); (hug) daki-shimemásu (daki-shiméru, daki-shimete) 抱きしめます(抱きしめる, 抱きしめて) **3.** n (printing press) insatsu-ki 印刷機; (publishing) shuppan-kai 出版界; (press corps) kishadan 記者団

pressed; feels ~ aserimásu (aséru, asétte) 焦ります(焦る, あせって)

pressure n atsuryoku 圧力; appaku 圧迫; puresshā プレッシャー; puts ~ on appaku shimásu (suru, shite) 圧迫します(する, して)

prestige n méiyo 名誉; meiyo 名誉

presumably adv dōmo... rashii どうも...らしい;

tabun … da to omou たぶん … だと思う

presume v **1.** suitei/yosō shimásu (suru, shite) 推定/予想します(する, して) → **think 2.** ~ *on someone's goodwill* amaemásu (amaéru, amaéte) 甘えます(甘える, 甘えて)

presumption n suitei 推定, yosō 予想; katei 仮定

pret à porter n (*ready to wear*) puretapórute プレタポルテ

pretend v … (no) furí o shimásu (suru, shite) …(の)ふりをします(する, して)

pretend(ed) adj (*sham*) mise-kake (no) 見せかけ(の); (*fake*) nise (no) ニセ(の), omocha (no) おもちゃ(の)

pretense n furí ふり; misekake 見せかけ

pretension n misekake 見せかけ

pretext n kōjitsu 口実; iiwake 言い訳

pretty 1. adj kírei (na) きれい[綺麗](な), kawaii かわいい → **fairly, rather 2.** adv (*very*) kanari かなり, [BOOKISH] hijō ni 非常に

prevalence n fukyū 普及

prevalence of diseases n byōki no ryūkō 病気の流行

prevalence of the internet n intānetto no fukyū インターネットの普及

prevalence rate n fukyū ritsu 普及率, (*disease*) [BOOKISH] rikan ritsu 罹患率, yūbyō ritsu 有病率

prevent v **1.** (*hinders*) (… no) jama o shimásu (suru, shite) (…の)じゃま[邪魔]をします(する, して); (*thwarts*) habamimásu (habámu, habánde) 阻みます(阻む, 阻んで) **2.** (*blocks*) fusegimásu (fuségu, fuséide) 防ぎます(防ぐ, 防いで), (*wards off*) yobō shimásu (suru, shite) 予防します(する, して)

prevention n yobō 予防, bōshi 防止

preview n **1.** shitami 下見 **2.** shisha 試写

preview party n shisha-kai 試写会

preview room n shisha-shitsu 試写室

previous adj máe no 前の

previous appointment/engagement sen'yaku 先約

previous story n (*TV, etc.*) zenkai no (o-)hanashi 前回の(お)話・はなし

previously adv izen ni 以前に, maemotte 前もって

prewar adj senzen (no) 戦前(の)

prey n (*sacrifice*) gisei 犠牲

price n nedan 値段 (o-nédan お値段), kakaku 価格, ne 値; (*the set/regular/net price*) teika 定価; *commodity prices* bukka 物価

price control n kakaku/bukka-tōsei 価格/物価統制

price difference/differential n rizáya 利ざや

price index n bukka-shisū 物価指数

price rise n ne-age 値上げ

price tag n shō-fuda 正札, ne fuda 値札

price war n kakaku-kyōsō 価格競争

pride n hokori 誇り; puraido プライド, (*boast*) jiman 自慢; (*strong point*) tokui 得意

priest n (*Christian*) shínpu(-san) 神父(さん),

bokushi 牧師; (*Buddhist*) sō´(ryo) 僧侶; (*Shinto*) kánnushi 神主

priggish adj katakurushii 堅苦しい, kuchi urusai 口うるさい

prim adj kichintoshita きちんとした, totonotta 整った

primrose adj sakurasō サクラソウ

primarily adv gánrai 元来, zéntai 全体

primary adj daiichi (no) 第一(の); shokyū (no) 初級(の)

primary cancer n (*medical*) genpatsu-gan 原発がん・原発癌

primary election n yobi-sénkyo 予備選挙

primary school → elementary school

prime minister n sōri-dáijin 総理大臣, shushō 首相

prince n miya(-sama) 宮(様), ōji(-sama) 王子(様), purinsu プリンス; *Crown Prince* kōtaishi (-sama) 皇太子(様)

"The Little Prince" n "Hoshi no ōji-sama" 『星の王子さま』

princess n híme 姫, ohíme-sama お姫様; ōjo (-sama) 王女(様), purinsesu プリンセス; *Crown Princess* kōtaishi-hi 皇太子妃

principal 1. n (*head of a school*) kōchō 校長; shuyaku 主役 **2.** adj (*main*) ómo (na) 主(な)

principally adv ómo ni 主に, moppara もっぱら・専ら

principle n (*policy*) hōshin 方針; (*doctrine*) gensoku 原則, shúgi 主義

print n (*woodblock*) mokuhan (-ga) 木版(画), hanga 版画; insatsu 印刷

print v (*prints it*) insatsu shimásu (suru, shite) 印刷します(する, して), purinto shimásu (suru, shite) プリントします(する, して), surimásu (súru, sútte) 刷ります(刷る, 刷って); (*in print*) katsuji ni shimásu (suru, shite) 活字にします(する, して)

printed matter n insatsú-butsu 印刷物

printer n (*for personal computer*) purínta プリンター

prior adj jizen (no) 事前(の), saki (no) 先(の)

prior arrangement n uchi-awase 打ち合わせ

priority n yūsen(-ken) 優先(権); *first priority* sai-yūsen 最優先; *order of priority* yūsen-jun('i) 優先順(位)

prism n purizumu プリズム

prison n keimusho 刑務所, (*slang*) musho ムショ, buta-bako ブタ箱, [BOOKISH] kangoku 監獄 → **jail**

privacy n puraibashii プライバシー; shiseikatsu 私生活

private adj (*use*) jibun-yō (no) 自分用(の), shiyō (no) 私用(の); (*undisturbed*) jama sarenai じゃま[邪魔]されない; (*confidential*) naishō (no) 内緒(の), (*secret*) himitsu (no) 秘密(の), puraibēto プライベート; (*within the family*) uchiwa (no) 内輪(の); (*privately established*) watakushí-ritsu/shiritsu (no) 私立(の), shisetsu (no) 私設(の)

private company *n* minkan kigyō 民間企業

private railroad *n* shitetsu 私鉄

private room *n* koshitsu 個室

private school *n* shiritsu (gakkō) 私立学校, watakushiritsu 私立・わたくしりつ

private talk *n* uchiwa no hanashí 内輪の話, naisho-bánashi 内緒話

private time *n* jibun no jikan 自分の時間

privatization *n* min'eika 民営化

privilege *n* tokken 特権, tokuten 特典, kenri 権利

prize 1. *n* shō´賞, …-shō …賞, (*object*) shōhin 賞品, (*money*) shōkin 賞金; *prize contest* konkū´ru コンクール; *grand prize* taishō 大賞, guranpuri グランプリ 2. *n* (*reward*) go-hō´bi ごほうび・ご褒美 3. *v* (*highly esteems it*) daijí ni shimásu (suru, shite) 大事にします(する, して)

pro *n* 1. = *professional* puro プロ 2. (*supporter*) shiji-sha 支持者

probably *adv* tábun 多分・たぶん, osóraku 恐らく・おそらく, ōkata おおかた・大方, taigai 大概・たいがい; … (surú/shíta) deshō´ …(する/した)でしょう

problem *n* mondai 問題, kadai 課題

difficult problem *n* nanmon 難問

If you have any problems, please let me know. *interj* Nani ka mondai ga arimashitara (dōzo) oshirasekudasai. 何か問題がありましたら(どうぞ)お知らせください.

No problem at all. *interj* Mattaku mondai arimasen. 全く問題ありません.

problematic *adj* mondai no aru 問題のある

procedure *n* (*formalities*) tetsúzuki 手続き; (*program*) tejun 手順

proceed *v* 1. susumimasu (susumu, susunde) 進みます(進む, 進んで) 2. tsuzukemásu (tsuzukeru, tsuzukete) 続けます(続ける, 続いて)

proceeding *n* gijiroku 議事録; sinkō 進行

process 1. *n* (*method*) yari-kata やり方, hōhō 方法, (*course, stage*) katei 過程, purosesu プロセス, (*development*) nariyuki 成り行き 2. *v* (*handles*) shóri shimásu (suru, shite) 処理します(する, して); (*industrially treats*) kakō shimásu (suru, shite) 加工します(する, して)

produce 1. *v* (*produces it*) … ga dekimásu (dekíru, dékite) …ができ[出来]ます(できる, で きて), … o tsukurimásu (tsukúru, tsukútte) …を作 ります(作る, 作って), … o seizō/seisaku shimásu (suru, shite) …を製造/制作します(する, して) 2. *v* (*brings it about*) … o shō-jimásu (shō-jiru, shō-jite);…を生じます(生じる, 生じて) 3. → **product**

producer *n* seisan-sha 生産者; (*movie, drama, etc.*) seisaku-sha 制作者, purodyūsā プロデューサー, enshutsuka 演出家

product *n* (*sei*)sanbutsu (生)産物; seihin 製品

production *n* (*manufacture*) seisan 生産, seizō 製造; (*movie, drama, etc.*) seisaku 制作, purodakushon プロダクション

production company *n* seisaku-gaisha 制作会社

profession *n* (*vocation*) shokúgyō 職業

professional *n* (*an expert*) kúrō´to くろうと・玄人, púro プロ

professional baseball *n* puro yakyū プロ野球

professional experience *n* (*career*) shokureki 職歴

professional wrestling *n* puro-resu プロレス

professor *n* kyōju 教授

proficiency *n* jitsuryoku 実力

profile *n* purofiiru プロフィール; (*face in profile*) yokogao 横顔; (*side view*) sokumen (zu) 側面(図)

profit 1. *n* ríeki 利益; toku 得 (o-toku お得); (*interest*) rí ri 利 2. *v* (*makes a profit*) mōkemásu (mōkeru, mō´kete) もうけ[儲け]ます(もうける, もうけて)

profit and loss *n* son eki 損益, son toku 損得

profit-and-loss arithmetic *n* son toku kanjō 損得勘定

profit-and-loss statement *n* son eki keisansho 損益計算書; pii eru P/L

profit-earning *adj* shūeki-sei no aru 収益性のある

profitable *adj* yū´ri (na) 有利(な), toku (na) 得 (な); umái うまい; (*pay*) rieki ni naru 利益になる; mōkaru 儲かる; wari ga íi 割がいい

profound *adj* fukai 深い, [BOOKISH] shin'en (na) 深遠(な)

program *n* (*TV, etc.*) bangumi 番組, puroguramu プログラム; (*plan*) keikaku 計画, (*itinerary, routine*) nittei 日程; (*procedure*) tejun 手順; (*computer program*) puroguramu プログラム, sofuto(wea) ソフト(ウェア)

programmer *n* (*computer program*) purogurámā プログラマー

progress 1. *n* shinkō 進行, shínpo 進歩, shínchoku 進捗; keika 経過 2. *v* (*it progresses*) susumimásu (susumu, susunde) 進みます(進む, 進んで), shínpo shimásu (suru, shite) 進歩します(する, して)

progression *n* zenshin 前進, shinkō 進行

prohibit *v* kinshi shimásu (suru, shite) 禁止します(する, して)

prohibition *n* kinshi 禁止

project 1. *v* (*a picture/movie*) utsushimásu (utsúsu, utsúshite) 映します(映す, 映して); keikaku shimásu (suru, shite) 計画します(する, して) 2. *n* keikaku 計画, kikaku 企画, purojekuto プロジェクト

projection *n* (*movie*) eishá 映写, tōei 投影

projector *n* (*movie*) eishá-ki 映写機, purojekutā プロジェクター

prologue *n* purorōgu プロローグ, jomaku 序幕, joron 序論

prolong → **lengthen**

promethium *n* puromechiumu プロメチウム

prominent *adj* ichijirushíi 著しい, medatta 目立った・めだった, (*famous*) chomei (na) 著名(な)

prominently *adv* ichijirúshiku 著しく

promise 1. *n* (o-)yakusoku (お)約束, yakusoku-goto 約束事; (*outlook*) mikomi 見込み 2. *v*

400

promises it yakusoku shimásu (suru, shite) 約
束します（する、して）; *fulfills a ~* yakusoku o
hatashimásu (hatasu, hatashite) 約束を果たします
（果たす、果たして）

promising *adj* mikomi no aru 見込みのある、
shōraisei no aru 将来性のある、kitai dekiru 期待
できる、[BOOKISH] yūbō (na) 有望（な）、zento yūbō
(na) 前途有望（な）
  promising candidate *n* yūbō na kōho-sha 有望な
候補者
  promising enterprise *n* yūbō (na) kigyō 有望
（な）企業
  promising future *n* akarui mirai 明るい未来
  promising job *n* shōraisei no aru shigoto 将来性
のある仕事
  promising youth *n* zento yūbō na wakamono 前
途有望な若者、mikomi no aru wakamono 見込み
のある若者

promontory *n* misaki 岬

promotion *n* (*salary rise*) shōkyū 昇給;
(*incentive*) shōrei 奨励; (*betterment, increase*)
zōshin 増進、hanbai sokushin 販売促進

prompt *adj* sassokú (no) 早速（の）、[BOOKISH]
jinsoku (na) 迅速（な）、(*instant*) tossa (no) とっ
さ（の）
  prompt reply *n* jinsoku na hentō 迅速な返答

promptly *adv* binsokú ni 敏速に、jinsoku ni
迅速に、(*instantly*) tossa ni とっさに

pronoun *n* daiméishi 代名詞

pronounce *v* hatsuon shimásu (suru, shite) 発音
します（する、して）

pronunciation *n* hatsuon 発音
  pronunciation practice *n* hatsuon (no) renshū
発音（の）練習
  pronunciation symbol *n* hatsuon kigō 発音記号

proof *n* shōko 証拠、shōmei 証明

proofread *v* kōsei shimásu (suru, shite) 校正しま
す（する、して）

proofreader *n* kōsei-sha 校正者

prop **1.** *n* (*a support*) sasae 支え **2.** *n* kodōgu
小道具 **3.** *v* **props it** (*up*) *v* sasaemásu (sasaeru,
sasaete) 支えます（支える、支えて）

propaganda *n* senden 宣伝、senden katsudō 宣
伝活動

propane *n* purópan プロパン; *propane gas*
puropan-gásu プロパンガス

propel *v* susumasemásu (seru, sete) 進ませます
（せる、せて）; suishin shimásu (suru, shite) 推進し
ます（する、して）

propeller *n* puropera プロペラ

proper *adj* (*appropriate*) tekitō (na) 適当（な）、
tekisetsu (na) 適切（な）、kichintoshita きちん
とした、chanto shita ちゃんとした; (*expected,
deserved*) tōzen (no) 当然（の）; (*correct*) tadashíi
正しい・ただしい
  proper noun *n* koyū meishi 固有名詞

properly *adv* tadáshiku 正しく・ただしく; tekitō
ni 適当に、tekisetsu ni 適切に、kichinto きちんと、
chanto ちゃんと

property *n* (*fortune*) zaisan 財産; shoyū(ken)
所有（権） → **belongings** → **land**

prophet *n* yogen-sha 預言者
  the prophet Muhammad *n* yogen-sha
Mahometto 預言者マホメット

proportion *n* rítsu 率; wariai 割合; puropōshon
プロポーション

proposal *n* **1.** mōshi-komi 申し込み、mōshi-de
申し出 **2.** (*public*) mōshi-ire 申し入れ
3. (*suggestion*) kikaku (an) 企画（案）、kikaku-sho
企画書、teian-sho 提案書; (*of marriage*) endan
縁談; kyūkon 求婚; puropōzu プロポーズ

propose *v* **1.** teian shimásu (suru, shite) 提案しま
す（する、して）; mōshi-komimásu (mōshi-komu,
mōshi-konde) 申し込みます（申し込む、申し込ん
で）、mōshi-demásu (mōshi-deru, mōshi-dete) 申
し出します（申し出る、申し出て）; (*publicly*) mōshi-
iremásu (mōshi-ireru, mōshi-irete) 申し入れま
す（申し入れる、申し入れて） **2. ~ to** (*marriage*)
kyūkon shimásu (suru, shite) 求婚します（する、
して）

proprietor *n* keiéi-sha 経営者

prosecutor *n* kénji 検事

prospect(s) *n* (*outlook*) mikomi 見込み、mitōshi
見通し、[BOOKISH] zentó 前途

prospective *adj* mikomi no aru 見込みのある、
kitai sareru 期待される
  prospective customer *n* mikomi kyaku
見込み客

prosper *v* sakaemásu (sakáeru, sakáete) 栄えます
（栄える、栄えて）

prosperity *n* (*relative business conditions*) keiki
景気; (*good business conditions*) kō-kéiki 好景気

prosperous *adj* sakan (na) 盛ん（な）

prostitute *n* baishún-fu 売春婦

prostitution *n* baishun 売春

protect *v* mamorimásu (mamóru, mamótte)
守ります（守る、守って）; (*safeguards*) hógo
shimásu (suru, shite) 保護します（する、して）;
kabaimásu (kabau, kabatte) 庇います・かばいま
す（庇う、庇って）

protection *n* bōei 防衛、bōgyo 防御、
purotekushon プロテクション

protein *n* tanpakú-shitsu たんぱく[蛋白]質・タ
ンパク質

protest *n* kō'gí (shimásu; suru, shite) 抗議（しま
す; する、して）

protester *n* kō'gí-sha 抗議者

Proteus *n* (*Greek god in mythology*) Puroteusu
プロテウス

protocol *n* purotokoru プロトコル、gaikō girei
外交儀礼

proton *n* yōshi 陽子

protrude *v* tsuki-demásu (tsuki-déru, tsuki-déte)
突き出ます（突き出る、突き出て）、tobi-dashi-
amásu (tobi-dásu, tobi-dáshite) 跳び[飛び]出しま
す（跳び[飛び]出す、跳び[飛び]出して）

protruding tooth *n* (*bucktooth*) déppa 出っ歯、
sóppa 反っ歯

proud adj **1.** tokui (na) 得意(な) **2.** *is proud of* …
o jiman shimásu (suru, shite) …を自慢します
(する, して)

prove v shōmei shimásu (suru, shite) 証明します
(する, して)

proverb n kotowaza ことわざ・諺

provide v (*provides one with*) motasemásu
(motaséru, motásete) 持たせます(持たせる, 持た
せて); ataemásu (ataeru, ataete) 与えます(与える,
与えて) → **give** → **prepare**; ~ *a treat* gochisō
shimásu (suru, shite) ごちそう[ご馳走]します
(する, して)

provided conj moshi もし, tádashi ただし・但し
→ **if**

province n (*of old Japan*) (… no) kuni (…の)
国; (*modern prefecture*) kén 県, …-ken …県; (*of
Canada*) shū 州, …-shū …州; (*region*) chihō 地方

provision n (*supply*) kyōkyū 供給; (*allowance*)
téate 手当(o-téate お手当); (*stipulation*) jōken 条
件; (*preparations*) sonáe 備え

provoke; *gets provoked*, *is provoking* shaku ni
sawarimásu (sawaru, sawatte) しゃく[癪]に障り
ます(障る, 障って)

prowess n (*ability*) udemae 腕前; yūki 勇気

prudence n tsutsushimi 慎しみ・つつしみ

pseudo-... ese-... えせ..., gi-... 偽...

psyche n séishin 精神

psychiatric adj séishin-ka (no) 精神科(の)

psychiatrist n seishin-ka-i 精神科医

psychic powers n nenriki 念力, shinrei nōryoku
心霊能力, saikikku pawā サイキックパワー

psychologist n shinrigákú-sha 心理学者

psychology n shínri 心理; (*science/study*) shinrí-
gaku 心理学

pub n (*Western-style*) pabu パブ; (*Asian-style*)
izakaya 居酒屋

public 1. adj kōshū (no) 公衆(の); kōkai (no)
公開(の); ōyake (no) 公(の); kōkyō (no) 公共
(の); (*open*) kōzen (no) 公然(の); (*officially
established*) kōritsu (no) 公立(の) **2.** n (*society*)
yo-nó-naka 世の中, yo 世, séken 世間

public bath n séntō 銭湯, (o-)furo-ya (-san) (お)
風呂屋(さん), (kōshū-)yokujō (公衆)浴場

public hall n kaikan 会館

public holiday n shukujitsu 祝日, saijitsu 祭日

public opinion n yóron 世論, séron 世論

public park n kōen 公園

public transportation n kōkyō no kótsū kikan
公共の交通機関

publication n shuppan 出版; (*things*) shuppán-
butsu 出版物; (*publishing*) hakkō 発行; (*books*)
shoseki 書籍

publicity n senden 宣伝

publish v **1.** arawashimásu (arawásu, arawáshite)
著します(著す, 著して), shuppan shimásu (suru,
shite) 出版します(する, して); hakkō shimásu
(suru, shite) 発行します(する, して) **2.** (*puts it in
a newspaper*) nosemásu (noseru, nosete) 載せます
(載せる, 載せて) → **announce**

publisher n (*person*) shuppán-sha 出版者,
hakkō´-sha 発行者; (*company, etc.*) shuppan-moto
出版元

publishing 1. n shuppán-gyō 出版業 **2.** adj
shuppan (no) 出版(の)

publishing company n shuppán-sha 出版社

publishing industry n shuppan gyōkai 出版業界

pucker v *puckers it up* subomemásu (subomeru,
subomete) すぼめます(すぼめる, すぼめて);
it puckers up subomarimásu (subomaru, subomat-
te) すぼまります(すぼまる, すぼまって)

pudding n pudingu プディング, purin プリン

puddle n mizutamari 水たまり

puff n (*cream puff*) shū-kuríimu シュークリーム

puffer fish n (*globefish*) fúgu ふぐ・フグ・河豚

puke → **vomit**

pull v hipparimásu (hippáru, hippátte) 引っ張りま
す(引っ張る, 引っ張って); hikimásu (hiku, hiite)
引きます(引く, 引いて); ~ *out* hikidashimásu
(hikidasu, hikidashite) 引き出します(引き出す,
引き出して); ~ *up* (*refloats it*) hiki-agemásu (hiki-
agéru, hiki-ágete) 引き上げます(引き上げる, 引き
上げて); (*stop*) tomemásu (tomeru, tomete) 止め
ます(止める, 止めて)

pull n (*connnections*) kone コネ; *has ~* (*with …*)
kao ga kikimásu (kíku, kiíte) 顔がききます(きく,
きいて), kóne ga arimásu (áru, átte) コネがありま
す(ある, あって)

pullover n sētā セーター, puruōbā プルオーバー

pulp n (*a material of paper*) parupu パルプ

pulse n myakú 脈, myakuhaku 脈拍

pulverize v funmatsu ni shimásu (suru, shite)
粉末にします(する, して), kona-gona in shimásu
(suru, shite) こなごなにします(する, して)

pumice n karuishi 軽石

pump n pónpu ポンプ

pumpkin n kabocha かぼちゃ・カボチャ・南瓜

pun n hiyase しゃれ・洒落, dajare だじゃれ・駄洒
落, goro-áwase ごろ[語呂]合わせ

punch n panchi パンチ

punctual adj jikan o mamoru 時間を守る,
jikandōri (no) 時間通り(の)

punctually adv kichín-to きちんと, jikandōri ni
時間通りに

punctuation n kugiri 区切り, kutō ten 句読点

puncture n (*of tire*) panku パンク

pungent adj karái からい・辛い

punish v bas-shimásu (bas-suru, bas-shite)
罰します(罰する, 罰して), (*punishes one's child*)
oshioki (o) shimásu (suru, shite) お仕置き(を)し
ます(する, して)

punishment n batsu 罰; (*abuse*) gyakutai 虐待,
(*physical punishment*) táibatsu 体罰, oshioki お
仕置き

punk n chinpira ちんぴら・チンピラ

pupil n **1.** (*student*) séito 生徒; (*apprentice,
disciple*) deshi 弟子 **2.** (~ *of the eye*) hitomi
ひとみ・瞳

puppet n ayatsuri ningyō 操り人形

puppet show *n* ningyō-geki 人形劇; (*Japanese traditional*) búnraku 文楽

puppy *n* koinu 小犬・コイヌ

purchase → buy

pure *adj* junsui (na) 純粋(な), jún (na) 純(な); (*clean*) seiketsu (na) 清潔(な)

purgative *n* gezai 下剤

purge *n* tsuihō 追放

purple *adj* murásaki (no) 紫(の)

purport *n* muné 旨

purpose *n* (*intention*) tsumori つもり (o-tsumori おつもり), íto 意図, kokorozashi 志; (*goal*) mokuteki 目的; *for the ~ of* (no) tamé (ni) …(の)ため[為](に); *on* ~ wáza-to わざと, wázawaza わざわざ, ito-teki ni 意図的に, takuránde たくらんで・企んで; *serves a ~* → useful

purse *n* saifu 財布, gamaguchi がまぐち

pursue *v* oimásu (ou, otte) 追います(追う, 追って)

pus *n* (*medical*) umí うみ・膿

push 1. *v* oshimásu (osu, oshite) 押します(押す, 押して); (*thrusts*) tsukimásu (tsuku, tsuite) 突きます(突く, 突いて); oshitsukémásu (oshitsukéru, oshitsukéte) 押し付けます(押し付ける, 押し付けて); *push a good thing too far* zu ni norimásu (noru, notte) 図に乗ります(乗る, 乗って) 2. *n* oshi 押し; (*recommend*) osusume おすすめ・お勧め; (*pressure*) atsuryoku 圧力

pusher *n* oshiuri 押し売り

pushy *adj* zūzūshíi ずうずうしい・図々しい, bu-énryo (na) 無遠慮(な)

put *v* okimásu (oku, oite) 置きます(置く, 置いて)

put aboard nosemásu (noseru, nosete) 載せます(載せる, 載せて)

put aside tótte okimásu (oku, oite) 取っておきます(おく, おいて)

put away shimaimásu (shimau, shimatte) しまいます(しまう, しまって)

put in iremásu (ireru, irete) 入れます(入れる, 入れて); ~ *a call* denwa o iremásu (ireru, irete) 電話を入れます(入れる, 入れて)

put in order soroemásu (soroéru, soróete) 揃えます(揃える, 揃えて); (*tidies it up*) katazukemásu (katazukéru, katazúkete) 片付けます(片付ける, 片付けて)

put into words ii-arawashimásu (ii-arawásu, ii-arawáshite) 言い表します(言い表す, 言い表して)

put it another way ii-kaemásu (ii-kaéru, ii-káete) 言い換えます(言い換える, 言い換えて)

put it on its side nekashimásu (nekasu, nekashite) 寝かします(寝かす, 寝かして)

put it together (*assembles it*) kumi-tatemásu (kumi-tateru, kumi-tatete) 組み立てます(組み立てる, 組み立てて)

put it to use yakú ni tatemásu (tatéru, tátete) 役に立てます(立てる, 立てて)

put on (*clothes*) kimasu (kiru, kite) 着ます(着る, 着て); (*footwear*) hakimásu (haku, haite) はきます・履きます(はく・履く, はいて・履いて); (*headwear*) kaburimasu (kaburu, kabutte) かぶり[被り]ます(かぶる・被る, かぶって・被って); (*glasses*) kakemasu (kakeru, kakete) かけます・掛けます(かける・掛ける, かけて・掛けて) → wear

put on airs kidorimásu (kidoru, kidotte) 気取ります(気取る, 気取って)

put one on top of another kasanemásu (kasaneru, kasanete) 重ねます(重ねる, 重ねて)

put out dashimásu (dasu, dáshite) 出します(出す, 出して); (*extinguishes*) keshimásu (kesu, keshite) 消します(消す, 消して)

put pressure on appaku shimásu (suru, shite) 圧迫します(する, して)

put to bed/sleep nekashimásu (nekasu, nekashite) 寝かします(寝かす, 寝かして)

put together awasemásu (awaséru, awásete) 合わせます(合わせる, 合わせて); (*sets up*) kumimásu (kúmu, kúnde) 組みます(組む, 組んで)

put someone up overnight tomemásu (tomeru, tomete) 泊めます(泊める, 泊めて)

put up with gáman shimásu (suru, shite) 我慢します(する, して); shinobimásu (shinobu, shinonde) 忍びます(忍ぶ, 忍んで), taemásu (taéru, táete) 耐えます(耐える, 耐えて), shínbō shimásu (suru, shite) 辛抱します(する, して); sumashimásu (sumásu, sumáshite) 済まします(済ます, 済まして)

puzzle *n* nazo なぞ・謎, pázuru パズル

puzzling *adj* yayakoshíi ややこしい

pyramid *n* piramíddo ピラミッド

Q

quack doctor *n* yabu isha やぶ医者

quadrangle *n* 1. shikakukei, shikakkei 四角形 2. (*yard*) naka-niwa 中庭

quagmire *n* shitchi 湿地

quail *n* uzura ウズラ・鶉

qualification(s) *n* (*competency*) shikaku 資格

qualified *adj* tekishita 適した, shikaku ga aru 資格がある

qualify *v* (*suitable*) teki-shimásu (teki-súru, tekí-shite) 適します(適する, 適して)

qualitative *adj* shitsu-teki (na) 質的

quality *n* shitsu 質, hin 品, hinshitsu 品質; *best quality* tokkyū (no) 特級(の)

quality control *n* hinshitsu kanri 品質管理

qualm *n* fuan 不安

quantitative *adj* ryō-teki (na) 量的(な)

quantity *n* ryō 量; taká 多寡; (*large*) taryō 多量; tairyō 大量; (*large and/or small*) tashō 多少

quantum *n* (*physics*) ryōshi 量子

quarrel *n, v* kenka (shimásu; suru, shite) けんか［喧嘩］(します; する, して), kuchi-genka (shimásu; suru, shite) 口げんか［口喧嘩］(します; する, して), kōron (shimásu; suru, shite) 口論 (します; する, して) → **argument** → **dispute**

quarrelsome *adj* 1. (*inclined to quarrel*) kenka-zuki (no/na) 喧嘩好き (の/な) 2. (*argumentative*) giron-zuki (no/na) 議論好き (の/な)

quart *n* kuwōto クォート

quarter *n* 1. yonbun-no-ichi 四分の一・4分の1; (*of a year*) shihanki 四半期・4半期; (*time*) jūgo-fun 15分 2. (*district*) hōmen 方面, …-hō´men …方面 → **area**

quartet *n* karutetto カルテット; (*music*) shijū-sō kyoku 四重奏曲; (*group*) shijū-sō-dan 四重奏団

quartz *n* (*crystal*) suishō 水晶

quay *n* hato-ba 波止場; futō 埠頭

queasy *adj* 1. (*feels nauseated*) múkamuka shimásu (suru, shite) むかむかします(する, して), haki-kéga shimásu 吐き気がします, haki-ké o moyōshimásu (moyōsu, moyoshite) 吐き気を催します(催す, 催して) 2. (*feels anxious*) shinpai (na) 心配(な), ochitsukanai 落ち着かない

queen *n* joō 女王, (card) kuiin クイーン

queen-size *adj* kuiin saizu (no) クイーンサイズ(の)

queer *adj* hén (na) 変(な), okashíi おかしい; (*wondrous*) myō´ (na) 妙(な)

quest *n* tankyū 探求, tansaku 探索, tsuikyū 追求

question *n* shitsumon 質問; (*problem*) mondai 問題; (*doubt, query*) gimon 疑問

questionable *adj* ayashii 怪しい・あやしい, ikagawashíi いかがわしい, utagawashíi 疑わしい; (*fishy*) kusái くさい・臭い

questioning *n* (*interviewing*) shimon 試問

question mark *n* gimón-fu 疑問符

questionnaire *n* ankēto アンケート

queue *n* rétsu 列; *forms a* ~ rétsu o tsukurimásu (tsukuru, tsukutte) 列を作ります(作る, 作って)

quick *adj* hayái 速い・早い・はやい

quickly *adv* háyaku 速く・早く・はやく

quick-witted *adj* kitten no kiku 機転のきく, atama no kaiten no yoi/hayai 頭の回転のよい/速い

quiet 1. *adj* shízuka (na) 静か・しずか(な), odáyaka (na) 穏やか・おだやか(な), nódoka (na) のどやか(な); *gets quiet* shizumarimásu (shizumaru, shizumatte) 静まります・しずまります (静まる, 静まって) 2. *v quiets it, makes it quiet* shizumemásu (shizumeru, shizumete) 静めます・しずめます(静める, 静めて)

quietly *adv* shízuka ni 静かに・しずかに; jitto じっと

quilt *n* (*padded*) futon ふとん・布団(o-fútón お布団); *bottom quilt* shiki-búton 敷布団; *top quilt* kake-búton 掛け布団, yágu 夜具

quinine *n* kiníine キニーネ

quirk *n* kusé 癖・くせ

quit *v* yamemásu (yameru, yamete) やめ［止め, 辞め］ます(やめる, やめて)

quite *adv* sōtō 相当, daibu だいぶ・大分, zúibun ずいぶん; (*completely*) mattakú 全く・まったく → **very** → **almost**; *quite a …* chótto shita … ちょっとした…; *~ so* naru-hodo なるほど・成る程

quitter *n* okubyō-mono 臆病者, ikuji nashi 意気地なし

quiver *v* furuemásu (furueru, furuete) 震えます(震える, 震えて)

quiz *n* kuizu クイズ

quota *n* wariate 割り当て, noruma ノルマ

quotation *n* ínyō 引用

quote *v* in'yō shimásu (suru, shite) 引用します(する, して)

R

rabbi *n* rabi ラビ

rabbit *n* usagi ウサギ・兎
  rabbit hole *n* usagi no suana ウサギ・兎の巣穴
  rabbit hutch *n* usagi-goya ウサギ・兎小屋

raccoon *n* araiguma アライグマ

raccoon dog *n* tanuki たぬき・タヌキ・狸

race 1. *n* kyōsō 競争, rēsu レース; (*bike*) keirin 競輪; (*horse*) keiba 競馬 2. *n* (*of people*) jinshu 人種, minzoku 民族; *the human race* jinrui 人類 3. *v* kyōsō shimásu (suru, shite) 競争します (する, して); *~ the engine* énjin o fukashimásu (fukásu, fukáshite) エンジンを吹かします(吹かす, 吹かして)
  boat race *n* kyōtei 競艇; bōto rēsu ボートレース

race of stars *n* hoshi no unkō 星の運行

race discrimination *n* jinshu-teki henken 人種的偏見

race issue *n* jinshu mondai 人種問題

racehorse *n* kyōsō-ba 競走馬

racetrack *n* keiba-jō 競馬場

racial *adj* jinshu (no) 人種(の)

racing car *n* rēshingu kā レーシングカー

racing driver *n* rē´sā レーサー

racism *n* jinshu sabetsu 人種差別

rack *n* tana 棚
  coat rack *n* kōto-kake コート掛け
  hat rack *n* bōshi-kake 帽子掛け
  magazine rack *n* magajin rakku マガジンラック

racket *n* (*tennis, etc.*) rakétto ラケット

radar *n* rēdā レーダー

radiation *n* hōsha 放射; hōsha-sen 放射線

radiator *n* (*in house, etc,*) danbō(-sōchi) 暖房
(装置); (*car*) rajiētā ラジエーター

radical *adj* (*extremist*) kageki (na) 過激(な)
the radicals *n* kagekí-ha 過激派

radio *n* rajio ラジオ
radio program *n* rajio-bangumi ラジオ番組
radio cab *n* musen takushii 無線タクシー
radio calisthenics *n* rajio taisō ラジオ体操
radio cassette player *n* rajikase ラジカセ
radio station *n* rajio hōsō kyoku ラジオ放送局
radio wave *n* denpa 電波

radioactive *adj* hōsha-sei (no) 放射性(の)
radioactive waste *n* hōsha-sei haikibutsu
放射性廃棄物

radioactivity *n* hōsha-sen 放射線, hōsha-nō
放射能

radiograph *n* hōsha-sen shashin 放射線写真,
rentogen shashin レントゲン写真

radiotelegram *n* musen denpō 無線電報

radish *n* (*the giant white*) daikon 大根; *radish
pickles* taku(w)an たくあ(わ)ん・タクア(ワ)
ン・沢庵, (*radish, etc.*) (o-)shinko (お)しんこ
[新香]

radium *n* rajiumu ラジウム

radius *n* hankei 半径

raffle *n* (*lottery*) fukubiki 福引き

raft *n* ikada いかだ・筏

rag *n* bóro ぼろ; kuzu くず・屑; (*dust cloth*) zōkin
ぞうきん・雑巾

rage 1. *v* abaremásu (abareru, abarete) 暴れます
(暴れる, 暴れて), aremásu (areru, arete) 荒れま
す(荒れる, 荒れて), (*be angry*) ikarimásu (ikaru,
ikatte) 怒ります(怒る, 怒って), (*be furious*)
ikarikuruimásu (ikarikurū, ikarikuruttc) 怒り狂
います(怒り狂う, 怒り狂って) 2. *n* (*outrage*)
gekido 激怒; (*passion*) jōnetsu 情熱

ragged *adj* boroboro (no) ボロボロ(の)

ragpicker *n* kuzu-hiroi くず拾い・屑拾い

raid 1. *n* (*attacking*) shūgeki 襲撃, kōgeki 攻撃;
(*bombing*) bakugeki 爆撃 2. *v raids it* shūgeki/
kōgeki/bakugekí shimásu (suru, shite) 襲撃/攻撃/
爆撃します(する, して); (*invades, makes a raid
on*) fumi-komimásu (fumi-kómu, fumi-kónde)
踏み込みます(踏み込む, 踏み込んで)

rail *n* rēru レール

railroad, railway *n* tetsudō 鉄道; *railway line/
track* sénro 線路; *railway station* éki 駅, sutēshon
ステーション

rain 1. *n* áme 雨; *light rain* kosame 小雨; *heavy
rain* ō-ame 大雨, gō'u 豪雨 2. *v* (*it rains*) áme
gafurimásu (fúru, fútté) 雨が降ります(降る,
降って)

rain boots *n* amá-gutsu 雨靴

rainbow *n* niji 虹
rainbow colors *n* niji iro 虹色

rain check; *takes a* ~ enryo shite okimásu (oku,
óite) 遠慮しておきます(おく, おいて)
I'll take a rain check. *interj* Mata (kondo) sasotte
kudasai. また(今度)誘ってください.

rain cloud *n* amagumo 雨雲

raincoat *n* reinkō'to レインコート

raindrop *n* amatsubu 雨粒

rainfall *n* kōu 降雨

rain shutters *n* amádo 雨戸

rain storm *n* bōfūu 暴風雨

rainy season *n* (*in Japan*) tsuyu つゆ・梅雨,
nyūbai 入梅, (*outside Japan*) uki 雨季

raise 1. *v* agemásu (ageru, agete) あげ[上げ,
挙げ, 揚げ]ます(あげる, あげて); (*arouses*)
okoshimásu (okósu, okóshite) 起こします(起こ
す, 起こして); (*increases*) mashimásu (másu,
mashite) 増します(増す, 増して), (*price, wage,
fee*) híki-agemásu (híki-agéru, híki-ágete) 引き
上げます(引き上げる, 引き上げて); (*erects*)
tatemásu (tatéru, tátete) 立てます(立てる, 立てて)
2. *v* (*fosters, nourishes*) yashinaimásu (yashinau,
yashinatte) 養います(養う, 養って); (*rears a
child*) sodatemásu (sodaféru, sodátete) 育てます
(育てる, 育てて); (*keeps animals, etc.*) kaimásu
(káu, katte) 飼います(飼う, 飼って); *is raised*
(*reared*) sodachimásu (sodátsu, sodátte) 育ちます
(育つ, 育って) 3. *v* (*collects money*) tsunorimásu
(tsunoru, tsunotte) 募ります(募る, 募って)
4. *n* (*salary increase*) shōkyū 昇給; (*price increase*)
neagari 値上り

raised lacquer *n* maki-e 蒔絵

raising *n* yōshoku 養殖; *raising silkworms* yōsan
養蚕

raisin(s) *n* hoshi-búdō 干しぶどう[葡萄], rēzun
レーズン

rake 1. *n* kumade くまで・熊手 2. *v* (*rakes
them up*) kaki-atsumemásu (kaki-atsuméru, kaki-
atsumete) かき集めます(かき集める, かき集めて)

rally *n* shūkai 集会, kaigō 会合

ram *n* rámu ラム, hitsuji 羊・ヒツジ, o-hitsuji
雄羊

ramp *n* surō'pu スロープ, ránpu ランプ

rampage 1. *n* bōryoku 暴力, bōsō 暴走
2. *v* abaremásu (abareru, abarete) 暴れます
(暴れる, 暴れて)

ranch *n* dai-bokujō 大牧場, dai-nōen 大農園

rancher *n* bokujō (no) keieisha 牧場(の)経営者,
nōen (no) keieisha 農園(の)経営者

random *adj* iikagen (na) いいかげん・いい加減
(な); detarame (na) でたらめ・出鱈目(な);
yatara (na) やたら(な); (*math, computer*) musakui
(no) 無作為(の); *at* ~ musakui (ni) 無作為(に),
tekitō (ni) 適当(に), teatarishidai (ni) 手当たり次
第(に), randamu (ni) ランダム(に)

randomly *adv* yatara ni やたらに

range *n* (*kitchen*) kamado かまど・竃, rénji レ
ンジ; (*gas*) gasurénji ガスレンジ; (*mountains*)
sanmyaku 山脈; (*scope*) han'i 範囲
age range *n* nenrei haba 年齢幅
a range of *adj* ichiren (*no*) 一連(の)

firing range *n* shatei 射程
long-range *adj* chōkyori (no) 長距離(の)
mountain range *n* sanmyaku 山脈
price range *n* kakaku haba 価格幅
short-range *adj* tankyori (no) 短距離(の)
rank 1. *n* kuraiā 位, …-i …位; chíi 地位, kaikyū 階級, kaisō 階層, ranku ランク **2.** *v* (*to grade*) chii o shimemásu (shiméru, shimete) 地位を占めます(占める, 占めて)
first rank *n* ikkyū 一級; ichiryū 一流
high rank *n* kōkyū 高級; kōi 高位
high-ranked officer *n* kōkyū kanryō 高級官僚, kōkan 高官
ransom *n* minoshirokin 身代金
rape 1. *n* (*plant*) náppa 菜っ葉・ナッパ, ná 菜 **2.** *n* (*forcible intercourse*) gōkan 強姦, reipu レイプ **3.** *v rapes* gōkan shimásu (suru, shite) 強姦します(する, して)
rapid *adj* subayai 素早い; jinsoku (na) 迅速(な); kyūsoku (na) 急速(な) → **fast**
in rapid succession *adv* zokuzoku ぞくぞく・続々
rapid response *n* jinsoku na hentō 迅速な返答
rapids *n* (*river*) kyūryū 急流
rare *adj* (*infrequent*) mare (na) まれ[稀](な), (*precious, curious*) mezurashíi 珍しい; (*uncooked*) náma no 生の, (*little cooked*) nama-yake (no) 生焼け(の), réa (no) レア(の)
rare case *n* mare na kēsu まれな[稀な]ケース
rare chance *n* zekkō no chansu 絶好のチャンス
rarely *adv* mare ni まれ[稀]に; (*occasionally*) tama ni たまに
rash 1. *n* (*medical*) hosshin 発疹・ほっしん, hasshin 発疹・はっしん **2.** *adj* (*hasty*) keisotsu (na) 軽率(な), métta (na) めった(な), mukō´-mizu (na) 向こう見ず・むこうみず(な)
skin rash *n* (*medical*) hishin 皮疹
rasp *n* yasuri やすり
raspberry *n* razuberii ラズベリー
rat *n* nezumi ねずみ・ネズミ・鼠; dobu nezumi ドブネズミ・溝鼠
rate 1. *n* (*ratio*) rítsu 率, (*percentage*) wariai 割合; (*charge*) ryōkin 料金 **2.** *v* (*estimates it*) mitsumorimásu (mitsumoru, mitsumotte) 見積もります(見積もる, 見積もって) **3.** → **at any rate**
admission rate *n* nyūin ritsu 入院率
discount rate *n* waribiki ritsu 割引率
employment rate *n* koyō ritsu 雇用率
infection rate *n* kansen ritsu 感染率
mortality rate *n* shibō ritsu 死亡率
tax rate *n* zei ritsu 税率
unemployment rate *n* shitsugyō ritsu 失業率
rather *adv* múshiro むしろ; (*preferably*) isso いっそ; (*fairly*) kánari かなり, ii-kagen いい加減 → **pretty, moderate**
ratio *n* ritsu 率, hiritsu 比率, (*percentage*) wariai 割合
birth ratio *n* shussei ritsu 出生率
ratio method *n* hiritsu hō 比率法

ration 1. *n* haikyū 配給 **2.** *v* (*rations it*) haikyū shimásu (suru, shite) 配給します(する, して)
rational *adj* gōri-teki (na) 合理的(な); risei-teki (na) 理性的(な)
rationalization *n* gōri-ka 合理化
rationalize *v* gōri-ka shimásu (suru, shite) 合理化します(する, して)
rattan *n* tō´ 藤・フジ
rattle *v* gáragara narimásu (naru, natte) がらがら鳴ります(鳴る, 鳴って); (*clatters*) gátagata shimásu (suru, shite) がたがたします(する, して)
rattlesnake *n* garagara hebi ガラガラヘビ
ravine *n* kyōkoku 峡谷
raving *n* uwagoto うわごと・うわ言
raw *adj* náma (no, de) 生(の/で); *sliced raw fish* (o-)sashimí (お)刺身刺身
raw material *n* zairyō 材料
raw silk *n* kí-ito 生糸
ray *n* kōsen 光線
a ray of sunlight *n* hizashi 日差し
X-ray *n* ekkusu sen X線, rentogen レントゲン
rayon *n* rēyon レーヨン
razor *n* kamisórí かみそり・剃刀; *razor blade* kamisórí no ha かみそりの刃
razor shell *n* (*a kind of scallop*) taira-gi たいらぎ
re-… *prefix* sai-… saimásu (suru, shite) 再…します(する, して); mō ichi-do… shimásu (suru, shite) もう一度…します(する, して); (*improves*) (shi-)naoshimásu ((shi-)naósu, (shi-)náoshite) (し)直します((し)直す, (し)直して)
reach 1. *v* (*it is delivered*) todokimásu (todoku, todóite) 届きます(届く, 届いて); (*it extends to*) … ni oyobimásu (oyobu, oyonde) …に及びます(及ぶ, 及んで), nobimásu (nobíru, nóbite) 伸びます(伸びる, 伸びて); (*arrives at*) …ni tsukimásu (tsukú, tsúite) …に着きます(着く, 着いて); (*achieves*) …ni tas-shimásu (tas-suru, tas-shite) …に達します(達する, 達して) **2.** *n* (*within reach*) (te no) todoku hani/kyori (手の)届く範囲/距離
react *v* hannō shimásu (suru, shite) 反応します(する, して)
reaction *n* (*response*) hannō 反応; (*repercussion*) handō 反動
adverse reaction *n* (*medical*) yūgai hannō 有害反応
allergic reaction *n* arerugii hannō アレルギー反応
anaphylactic reaction *n* (*medical*) anafirakishii hannō アナフィラキシー反応
reactionary *adj* handō-teki (na) 反動的(な); *the reactionaries* *n* handō-ha 反動派
read *v* yomimásu (yómu, yónde) 読みます(読む, 読んで)
read aloud *v* ondoku shimásu (suru, shite) 音読します(する, して)
read rapidly *v* sokudoku shimásu (suru, shite) 速読します(する, して)
read with pleasure, like to read *v* aidoku shimásu (suru, shite) 愛読します(する, して)

read silently *v* mokudoku shimás<u>u</u> (suru, shite) 黙読します(する、して)

read thoroughly *v* jukudoku shimás<u>u</u> (suru, shite) 熟読します(する、して)

read through *v* ichidoku shimás<u>u</u> (suru, shite) 一読します(する、して)

readable *adj* yomiyasui 読みやすい; yonde omoshiroi 読んで面白い

reader *n* (*person*) dokusha 読者; (*book*) tok<u>u</u>hon 読本

readily *adv* (*easily*) wáke-naku 訳なく・わけなく, muzó´sa ni 無造作に

reading *n* dokusho 読書

ready 1. *adj* (yō´i ga) dék<u>í</u>te imás<u>u</u> (iru, ite) (用意が)出来ています(いる、いて), dekimásh<u>í</u>ta 出来ました; (*is arranged*) totonoimás<u>u</u> (totonoú, totonótte) 整います(整う、整って) **2.** *adj* (*easy*) wáke-nai 訳ない **3.** *adv* (*ready made*) kisei (no) 既成(の), kizon/kison (no) 既存(の) **4.** *v ~ it* (*provides*) sonaemás<u>u</u> (sonáeru, sonáete) 備えます(備える、備えて), (*arranges it*) totonoemás<u>u</u> (totonóeru, totonóete) 整えます(整える、整えて)

ready cash/money *n* genkín 現金

ready-made 1. *n* kisei<u>h</u>in 既製品 **2.** *adj* kisei (hin) (no) 既製(品)(の), dekiai (no) 出来合い(の)

ready to wear (*off the rack*) k<u>i</u>seifuku (hin) 既製服(品), turushi つるし・吊し

real *adj* **1.** hontō (no) 本当(の); riaru リアル → **genuine**; *the real thing* honmono 本物 **2.** (*actual*) genjitsu (no) 現実(の)

real estate *n* fudōsan 不動産

real income *n* jisshitsu shotoku 実質所得

real intention *n* honne 本音; honshin 本心; shin'i 真意

real service *n* shin no sābisu 真のサービス

real world *n* jisshakai 実社会; genjitsu shakai 現実社会; genjitsu (no) sekai 現実(の)世界

realistic *adj* genjitsu-teki (na) 現実的(な)

realistic person *n* genjitsu-teki na hito 現実的な人

realistic plan *n* genjitsu-teki na keikaku/puran 現実的な計画/プラン

reality *n* jissai 実際; genjitsu 現実; riaritii リアリティ

realization *n* **1.** jikkō 実行; genjitsu-ka 現実化 **2.** → **understanding, enlightenment**

realize *v* **1.** (*comprehends*) ... ga wakarimás<u>u</u> (wakáru, wakátte) ...が分かります(分かる、分かって), satorimás<u>u</u> (satoru, satotte) 悟ります(悟る、悟って) **2.** (*carries out*) genjitsu-ka shimás<u>u</u> (suru, sh<u>i</u>te) 現実化します(する、して) **3.** (*notices*) k<u>i</u>zukimás<u>u</u> (kizuku, kizuite) 気づきます(気づく、気づいて) → **accomplish**; *a desire is realized* nozomi ga kanaimás<u>u</u> (kanáu, kanátte) 望みが叶い[かない]ます(叶う、叶って)

really *adv* hontō/honto (ni) 本当/ほんと(に), jitsú (ni) 実(に); *Really??* (*No kidding!*) [EXCLAM] másaka まさか

realm *n* ryōdo 領土, kok<u>u</u>do 国土

reap *v* osamemás<u>u</u> (osaméru, osámete) 収めます(収める、収めて), shūkaku shimás<u>u</u> (suru, sh<u>i</u>te) 収穫します(する、して)

reaped; *gets* ~ osamarimás<u>u</u> (osamáru, osamátte) 収まります(収まる、収まって), shūkaku saremás<u>u</u> (sareru, sarete) 収穫されます(される、されて)

rear 1. → **back, behind** → **tail end 2.** → **raise**

rear admiral *n* shō´shō 少将

rearview mirror *n* bakku-mírā バックミラー

reason *n* wáke わけ・訳, riyū 理由; (*what is sensible*) dōrí 道理; (*logic*) rik<u>u</u>tsu 理屈, ronri 論理; (*meaning*) yóshi 由; (*grounds*) yué 故, konkyo 根拠; *for the ~ that* ...to iu riyū de ...という理由で, ...yuéni ...故[ゆえ]に

good reason *n* seitō na riyū 正当な理由

without reason *adv* riyū naku 理由なく

reasonable *adj* (*natural, proper*) atarimae (no) 当り前(の); tekisetsu (na) 適切(な); datō (na) 妥当(な); (*rational*) gōri-teki (na) 合理的(な); tegoro (na) 手頃(な) → **moderate** → **suitable** → **sensible**

reasonable price *n* tegoro na kakaku 手頃な価格, datō na nedan 妥当な値段

rebate *n* haraimodoshi 払い戻し, ribēto リベート

tax rebate *n* zeikin (no) kanpu 税金(の)還付

rebel 1. *n* hangyaku-sha 反逆者 **2.** *v* (*against*) ...ni somukimás<u>u</u> (somúku, somúite) ...に背き[そむき]ます(背く、背いて), hangyaku shimás<u>u</u> (suru, sh<u>i</u>te) 反逆します(する、して), hanran o okoshimás<u>u</u> (okosu, okosh<u>i</u>te) 反乱を起こします(起こす、起こして)

rebellion *n* hangyaku 反逆

rebuke 1. *n* (o-)togamé (お)とがめ・(お)咎め, hinan 非難, [BOOKISH] shisseki 叱責 **2.** *v* (*blames*) togamemás<u>u</u> (togaméru, togámete) とがめ[咎め]ます(とがめる、とがめて)

recall 1. *n* (*of defective products*) rikōru リコール **2.** *v* (*remembers*) omoi-dashimás<u>u</u> (omoi-dasu, omoi-dash<u>i</u>te) 思い出します(思い出す、思い出して)

receipt *n* uke-tori 受け取り, ryōshū-sho 領収書, juryō´-shō 受領書, resh<u>í</u>to レシート

receive *v* moraimás<u>u</u> (morau, moratte) もらいます(もらう、もらって), ukemás<u>u</u> (ukéru, úkete) 受けます(受ける、受けて), uke-torimás<u>u</u> (uke-toru, uke-totte) 受け取ります(受け取る、受け取って), uke-ts<u>u</u>kemás<u>u</u> (uke-ts<u>u</u>keru, uke-ts<u>u</u>kete) 受け付けます(受け付ける、受け付けて); h<u>í</u>ki-torimás<u>u</u> (h<u>í</u>ki-tóru, h<u>í</u>ki-tótte) 引き取ります(引き取る、引き取って), ses-shimás<u>u</u> (ses-suru, ses-sh<u>i</u>te) 接します(接する、接して)

receiver *n* (*telephone*) juwá-ki 受話器

recent *adj* saikin no 最近の, kono-goro no この頃の, ch<u>í</u>kágoro no 近頃の

the most recent *adj* saishin no 最新の

recently *adv* saikin 最近, kono-goro この頃, ch<u>í</u>kágoro 近頃; (*a few days ago*) sendatté 先立って, senjitsu 先日

receptacle *n* yō´ki 容器, utsuwa 器

reception n resépushon レセプション; uketsuke 受付, (*get-together party*) konshín-kai 懇親会; (*welcome party*) kangéi-kai 歓迎会; (*farewell party*) sōbétsú-kai 送別会; (*engagement, wedding, etc.*) hirō´-kai 披露会, hirō´-en 披露宴
reception room n ōsetsuma 応接間; ōsetsushitsu 応接室
receptionist n uketsuke no hito 受付の人; uketsuke-gakari 受付係
recess n yasumí 休み; [BOOKISH] kyūkei 休憩
recession n fukéiki 不景気; keiki (no) kōtai 景気(の)後退
recipe n reshipi レシピ
reciprocal adj o-tagai (no) お互い(の); [BOOKISH] sō´go (no) 相互(の)
reciprocally adv o-tagai ni お互いに; [BOOKISH] sō´go ni 相互に
recital n risaitaru リサイタル
recite v utaimásu (utau, utatte) 歌います(歌う, 歌って); tonaemásu (tonáéru, tonáete) 唱えます (唱える, 唱えて); anshō shimásu (suru, shite) 暗唱します(する, して)
reckless adj mubō (na) 無謀(な), múcha (na) むちゃ[無茶](な), métta (na) めった[滅多] (な), yatara (na) やたら(な), mukō´-mizu (na) 向こう見ず・むこうみず(な)
recklessly adv yatara ni やたらに, múyami ni む やみ[無闇]に, mukō´-mizu ni 向こう見ずに・む こうみずに
reckon v kazoemásu (kazoeru, kazoete) 数えます (数える, 数えて)
reclamation n kaikon 開墾
recognition n ninshiki 認識
recognize v mitomemásu (mitomeru, mitomete) 認めます(認める, 認めて)
recoil v atozusarimásu (atozusaru, atozusatte) 後ず さります(後ずさる, 後ずさって), [BOOKISH] kōtai shimásu (suru, shite) 後退します(する, して)
recollect v omoidashimásu (omoidasu, omoidashite) 思い出します(思い出す, 思い出して)
recommend v susumemásu (susumeru, susumete) 勧め[薦め]ます(勧め[薦め]る, 勧め[薦め]て)
recommendation n suisen 推薦, (*letter*) suisen-jō 推薦状
recompense v benshō shimásu (suru, shite) 弁償 します(する, して)
reconcile v nakanaori shimásu (suru, shite) 仲直 りします(する, して), [BOOKISH] wakai shimásu (suru, shite) 和解します(する, して)
reconfirm 1. n sai-kákunin 再確認, (*flight*) rikonfāmu リコンファーム **2.** v (*reservations*) (yoyaku o) sai-kákunin shimásu (suru, shite) (予約を)再確認します(する, して)
reconfirmation n sai-kákunin 再確認
record 1. n (*phonograph*) rekō´do レコード; (*results, marks*) seiseki 成績; (*historic*) kiroku 記録; *a new ~* (*an event*) shin-kiroku 新記録 **2.** v *records it* (*sound*) rokuon shimásu (suru, shite) 録音します(する, して); (*event*) kiroku shimásu

(suru, shite) 記録します(する, して)
birth record n shussei kiroku 出生記録
death record n shibō kiroku 死亡記録
recorder n rokuón-ki 録音機; *tape recorder* tēpu rekōdā テープレコーダー
recording n (*video*) rokuga 録画; (*music*) rokuon 録音
record player n (rekōdo) purēyā (レコード)プ レーヤー
recover v kaifuku shimásu (suru, shite) 回復しま す(する, して)
recovery n kaifuku 回復
recreation n goraku 娯楽; ian 慰安; réjā レジャ ー, rekuriē´shon レクリエーション
recruit 1. n shinnyū-shain 新入社員 **2.** v boshū shimásu (suru, shite) 募集します(する, して); sai- yō shimásu (suru, shite) 採用します(する, して)
recruitment n boshū 募集; saiyō 採用; rikurūto リクルート
recruitment agency n jinzai-gaisha 人材会社
recuperate → recover
recuperation → recovery
recycle n, v risaikuru (shimásu; suru, shite) リサイクル(します; する, して); sairiyō (shimásu; suru, shite) 再利用(します; する, して)
red adj akai 赤い; áka (no) 赤(の); *deep red* makká (na) 真っ赤(な); *the red* (*deficit figures*) aka-ji 赤字
red bean n azukí あずき・アズキ・小豆; *soup with ~ paste* shiruko 汁粉(o-shiruko お汁粉)
redcap n (*porter*) akabō 赤帽
Red Cross n Sekijū´ji 赤十字
Junior Red Cross n Seishōnen Sekijū´ji 青少年 赤十字
red light n (*signal*) aka-shíngō 赤信号
red snapper n tái たい・タイ・鯛
redo v (*does it over* (*again*)) yari-naoshimásu (yari-naósu, yari-naóshite) やり直します(やり 直す, やり直して)
reduce v **1.** herashimásu (herasu, herashite) 減らします(減らす, 減らして), (*curtails*) habukimásu (habúku, habúite) 省きます(省く, 省いて); (*summarizes*) tsuzumemásu (tsuzuméru, tsuzúmete) つづめます(つづめる, つづめて) → **lessen → lower → shorten 2.** (*loses weight*) yasemásu (yaseru, yasete) やせ[痩せ]ます(やせる, やせて)
Reduce Speed. "Sókudo otóse" "速度落とせ"
reduction → discount
reed n áshi/yóshi アシ/ヨシ・葦
reed organ n riido orugan リードオルガン
reef n anshō 暗礁
coral reef n sango-shō サンゴ礁・珊瑚礁
reel 1. n (*spool*) ito maki 糸巻き, riiru リール; (*frame*) waku 枠 **2.** v (*reels it*) kurimásu (kúru, kútté) 繰ります(繰る, 繰って) **3. → stagger**
reentry n (*into the country*) sainyūkoku 再入国
reentry permit n sainyūkoku kyoka 再入国許可
reentry visa n sainyūkoku biza 再入国ビザ

refer v ~ *to* ... ni furemás̱u (fureru, furete) ...に触れます(触れる, 触れて); [BOOKISH] ... ni genkyū shimás̱u (suru, shi̱te) ...に言及します(する, して); (*reference*) sanshō shimás̱u (suru, shi̱te) 参照します(する, して)

referee n refurii レフリー, shinpan (-in) 審判(員)

reference n sanshō 参照
reference book n sankō-sho 参考書
reference literature n sankō bunken 参考文献

refined adj (*genteel*) (o-)jōhín (na) (お)上品(な), yū´ga (na) 優雅(な)

refinement n hin 品, jōhín 上品; (*culture*) kyōyō 教養

refinery n (*oil*) seiyu-sho 製油所

reflect v (*mirrors it*) utsushimás̱u (uts̱ús̱ú, uts̱úshi̱te) 映します(映す, 映して); *gets reflected* utsurimás̱u (uts̱úru, uts̱úi̱te) 映ります(映る, 映って); (*ponders*) hansha shimás̱u (suru, shi̱te) 反射します(する, して); *reflects on* hansei shimás̱u (suru, shi̱te) 反省します(する, して)

reflection n uts̱urí 写り; hansha 反射; kage 影; (*consideration*) kō´ryo 考慮; hansei 反省

refloat v hi̱ki-agemás̱u (hi̱ki-agéru, hi̱ki-ágete) 引き上げます(引き上げる, 引き上げて)

reform v (*starts a new life*) kōsei shimás̱u (suru, shi̱te) 更生します(する, して)

reformation n 1. (*improvement*) kairyō 改良, kaizen 改善 2. (*innovation*) kaikaku 改革 3. (*remedy*) kōsei 更生

reformatory n shōnen-in 少年院

refrain; ~ *from* ... o enryo shimás̱u (suru, shi̱te) ...を遠慮します(する, して)

refresh v sawáyaka na kibun ni shimás̱u (suru, shite) さわやか[爽やか]な気分にします(する, して)

refreshing adj sawáyaka (na) さわやか・爽やか(な)

refreshments n (*food*) tabe-monó 食べ物; (*drink*) nomí-mono 飲み物; (*tea*) o-cha お茶

refrigerate v hiyashimás̱u (hiyás̱u, hiyáshi̱te) 冷やします(冷やす, 冷やして)

refrigerator n reizō´ko 冷蔵庫 (*how many* nán-dai 何台)

refugee n hinán-sha 避難者, nanmin 難民
asylum for refugees n nanmin higo 難民庇護
place of refuge n hinan-jo 避難所
refugee camp n nanmin kyanpu 難民キャンプ
refugee support n nanmin shien 難民支援

refund 1. n harai-modoshi 払い戻し, henkin 返金 2. v (*refunds it*) harai-modoshimás̱u (harai-modosu, harai-modoshi̱te) 払い戻します(払い戻す, 払い戻して), henkin shimás̱u (suru, shi̱te) 返金します(する, して)
tax refund n zeikin (no) kanpu 税金(の)還付

refusal n kotowárí 断り; kyóhi 拒否; kyozetsu 拒絶

refuse 1. n (*rubbish*) kuzu くず・屑, gomi ごみ・ゴミ 2. v kotowarimás̱u (kotowáru, kotowátte) 断ります(断る, 断って); kyóhi shimás̱u (suru,

shi̱te) 拒否します(する, して); jitai shimás̱u (suru, shi̱te) 辞退します(する, して); (*rejects it*) kobamimás̱u (kobámu, kobánde) 拒みます(拒む, 拒んで)

regain v (*waste*) kúzu くず・屑

regard 1. v mimás̱u (miru, mite) 見ます(見る, 見て); kangaemasu (kangaeru, kangaete) 考えます(考える, 考えて); sonkei 尊敬, keii 敬意; *regards to* ... ni yoroshi̱ku (itteku-dasái, o-tsutae kudasái) ...によろしく[宜しく](言って下さい, お伝え下さい)

regarding prep *in/with regard to* ... ni tái-shi̱te (tai-súru ...) ...に対して(対する...), ... ni tsuite (no) ...について(の)

regardless → **nevertheless; (doesn't) matter**

regatta n regatta レガッタ

regeneration n kōsei 更生

reggae n regē レゲエ

region n chihō 地方, chíiki 地域

regional adj chíhō (no) 地方(の), chíiki (no) 地域(の)

register 1. n (*of names*) meibo 名簿, (*enrollment*) kiroku 記録 2. v (*checks into hotel*) chekkúín shimás̱u (suru, shi̱te) チェックインします(する, して); (*enrolls, signs up*) tōroku shimás̱u (suru, shi̱te) 登録します(する, して); ~ *a letter* tegami o kakí-tome ni shimás̱u (suru, shi̱te) 手紙を書留にします(する, して)

registered adj tōroku/tōki sareta 登録/登記された
registered mail n kakí-tome 書留
registered mail for cash n genkin kakí-tome 現金書留

registration n tōroku 登録, tō´ki 登記

regret 1. n kō´kai 後悔 2. v (*regrets it*) kōkai shimás̱u (suru, shi̱te) 後悔します(する, して), kuyamimás̱u (kuyámu, kuyánde) 悔やみます(悔やむ, 悔やんで); *I regret that* ... zannen/ikan nagara ...残念/遺憾ながら...

regrettable adj oshíi 惜しい, zannén (na) 残念(な), ainiku (na) あいにく(な), [BOOKISH] ikan (na) 遺憾(な)

regrettably adv zannen nagara 残念ながら, [BOOKISH] ikan nagara 遺憾ながら

regular 1. adj (*usual*) fu̱tsū no 普通の, (*ordinary*) nami no 並の, régyurā レギュラー; (*periodic/scheduled*) téiki no 定期の 2. n (*customer*) jōren (-kyaku) 常連(客), otokui-sama お得意(様), sei-kaiin 正会員; *regulars* (*army*) jōbi-gun 常備軍

regular customer n jōren kyaku 常連客, kotei kyaku 固定客, tokuisaki 得意先
regular employee n seishain 正社員
regular exam, regular examination n teiki shiken 定期試験
regular life n kisoku tadashii seikatsu 規則正しい生活
regular size n fu̱tsū saizu 普通サイズ

regulate v (*adjusts*) totonoemás̱u (totonóeru, totonóete) 整えます(整える, 整えて)

regulation *n* kísoku 規則, kítei 規定; kimari 決まり

rehabilitation *n* rihabiri リハビリ

rehearsal *n* rihāsaru リハーサル

reincarnation *n* umarekawari 生まれ変わり

reindeer *n* tonakai トナカイ

reign *n* chisei 治世

rein(s) *n* tázuna 手綱・たづな

reject *v* kobamimásu (kobámu, kobánde) 拒みます(拒む, 拒んで); kyóhí shimásu (suru, shite) 拒否します(する, して)

rejection *n* kyozetsu 拒絶
  acute rejection *n* (*medical*) kyūsei kyozetsu hannō 急性拒絶反応

rejoice *v* yorokobimásu (yorokóbu, yorokónde) 喜びます(喜ぶ, 喜んで)

relate *v* 1. (*tells*) katarimásu (kataru, katatte) 語ります(語る, 語って), nobemásu (nobéru, nóbete) 述べます(述べる, 述べて) 2. (*is connected/relevant to*) … ni kanshimásu (kansúru, kánshite) …に関します(関する, 関して)

relation(ship) *n* kankei 関係; tsunagari つながり; (*between people*) náka 仲, aidagara 間柄

relative 1. *n* (*person*) shinrui 親類, shinseki 親戚 2. *adj* kankei/kanren no aru 関係/関連のある

relatively *adv* wari (ai) ni 割(合)に, híkaku-teki ni 比較的に

relative merits *n* yūretsu 優劣

relax *v* (*looses tension*) tarumimásu (tarumu, tarunde) たるみ[弛み]ます(たるむ, たるんで); (*gets comfortable*) kutsurogimásu (kutsurógu, kutsuróide) くつろぎ[寛ぎ]ます(くつろぐ, くつろいで); (*rests oneself*) yasumimásu (yasúmu, yasúnde) 休みます(休む, 休んで), rirakkusu shimásu (suru, shite) リラックスします(する, して), (*enjoys oneself*) asobimásu (asobu, asonde) 遊びます(遊ぶ, 遊んで)

relay race *n* rirē リレー
  relay broadcast *n* chūkei hōsō 中継放送
  relay race *n* rirē kyōsō リレー競争

release 1. *n* (*publication*) hatsubai 発売, (*movie*) kōkai 公開; *press release* puresu ririisu プレスリリース 2. *v* (*announce*) happyō shimásu (suru, shite) 発表します(する, して); (*let go*) kahō shimásu (suru, shite) 解放します(する, して)
  release date *n* hatsubai bi 発売日, kōkai-bi 公開日

relevance *n* renraku 連絡, kanren 関連

relevant *adj* (*related*) kanren/kankei no aru 関連/関係のある; *is relevant to* … ni kanren shimásu (suru, shite) …に関連します(する, して)

reliability *n* shinrai-sei 信頼性

reliable *adj* (*steady*) te-gatai 手堅い; (*trustworthy*) shinrai dekíru 信頼できる, *is highly ~* shinrai-sei ga takái 信頼性が高い

reliance *n* ate 当て, tánomi 頼み, shinrai 信頼

relief *n* (*rescue*) kyū´jo 救助; (*from worry*) anshin 安心; *breathes a sigh of ~* hóttó shimásu (suru, shite) ほっとします(する, して)

relieve *v* 1. *is relieved* anshin shimásu (suru,

shite) 安心します(する, して); (*gets saved*) tasukarimásu (tasukáru, tasukátte) 助かります(助かる, 助かって) 2. *relieves oneself* (*goes to the bathroom*) yō´ o tashimásu (tasu, tashite) 用を足します(足す, 足して)

religion *n* shū´kyō 宗教, …-kyō …教

relish *n small dish of ~* tsukeawase 付け合せ

rely; *~ on …* ni tayorimásu (tayóru, tayótte) …に頼ります(頼る, 頼って), (*requests*) tanomimásu (tanómu, tanónde) 頼みます(頼む, 頼んで), irai shimásu (suru, shite) 依頼します(する, して)

remain *v* (*gets left behind*) nokorimásu (nokóru, nokótte) 残ります(残る, 残って), (*is in excess*) amarimásu (amáru, amátte) 余ります(余る, 余って); (*stops*) todomarimásu (todomáru, todomátte) とどまります(とどまる, とどまって); (*stays*) imásu (iru, ite) います(いる, いて), (*rather than go*) ikimasén (ikanai, ikanáide) 行きません(行かない, 行かないで)

remainder *n* (*leftover*) nokorí 残り, (*surplus*) amarí (o-ámari) 余り(お余り); áto no (mono, hító, …) 後の(物人, …)

remains *n* (*what remains*) nokori-mono 残り物; *the remaining* … áto/nokori no …後/残りの…

remark 1. *a remark n* kotobá 言葉, … (*yū/iu/itta*) kotó… (言う/言った) 言葉; *uncalled-for ~* sashideguchi 差し出口 2. *v →* **say**

remarkable *adj* ijō (na) 異常(な); ichijirushíi 著しい

remember *v* (*recalls*) omoi-dashimásu (omoidasu, omoi-dashite) 思い出します(思い出す, 思い出して); (*retains in memory*) obóete imásu (iru, ite) 覚えています(いる, いて)
  Remember me to … … ni yoroshíku (itte kudasái, o-tsutae kudasái) …によろしく[宜しく](言って下さい, お伝え下さい)

remind; *~ one of … …* o omowa-semásu (omowaséru, omowásete) …を思わせます(思わせる, 思わせて); kizukasemásu (kizukaséru, kizukásete) 気付かせます(気付かせる, 気付かせて)

reminder *n* hínto ヒント, chū´i 注意, saisoku-jō 催促状, rimaindā リマインダー

remissness *n* yudan 油断

remit *v* sōkin shimásu (suru, shite) 送金します(する, して)

remittance *n* sōkin 送金

remodel *v* kaichiku shimásu (suru, shite) 改築します(する, して), rifōmu shimásu (suru, shite) リフォームします(する, して)

remote *adj* enkaku-chi 遠隔地
  remote access *n* rimōto akusesu リモートアクセス, enkaku akusesu 遠隔アクセス
  remote area *n* hekichi へき地・僻地
  remote control *n* 1. enkaku seigyo 遠隔制御 2. (*TV, etc.*) rimo-kon リモコン,

remove *v* torimásu (tóru, tótte) 取ります(取る, 取って), nozokimásu (nozoku, nozoite) 除きます(除く, 除いて); sarimásu (saru, satte) 去ります(去る, 去って), háijo shimásu (suru, shite) 排除し

ます(する, して) → **take off** → **omit** → **move (house)**

snow removal *n* josetsu 除雪

remover *n* hakuri-zai 剥離剤

hair remover *n* datsumō-zai 脱毛剤

remuneration *n* sharei 謝礼; (*salary*) kyūryō 給料

renew *v* kōshin shimásu (suru, shite) 更新します (する, して)

renewal *n* kōshin 更新, rinyūaru リニューアル

contract renewal *n* keiyaku (no) kōshin 契約 (の)更新

license renewal *n* menkyo (no) kōshin 免許 (の)更新

renewal fee *n* kōshin-ryō 更新料

rent 1. *n* (*cost*) karí-chin 借り賃, (*house*) yá-chin 家賃; *rented/rental house* kashi-ya 貸家; *rented/ rental room* kashi-ma 貸間 2. *v* (*rents it out to*) kashimásu (kasu, kashite) 貸します (貸す, 貸して); (*rents it from*) karimásu (kariru, karite) 借ります(借りる, 借りて)

rental *n, adj* chintai (no) 賃貸(の), rentaru (no) レンタル(の)

rental car *n* rentákā レンタカー

rental fee *n* shiyōryo 使用料, rentaru ryōkin レンタル料金

rental house *n* kashiya 貸家

rental safe *n* kashi-kinko 貸金庫

rental shop *n* rentaru shoppu レンタルショップ

rental video *n* rentaru bideo レンタルビデオ

renovate *v* 1. (*repair*) shūri shimásu (suru, shite) 修理します(する, して) 2. (*rebuild*) rifōmu shimásu (suru, shite) リフォームします(する, して)

reorder 1. *v* (*adjusts*) séiri shimásu (suru, shite) 整理します(する, して) 2. *n* sai-chūmon 再注文; tsuika-chūmon 追加注文

reorganization *n* sai-hensei 再編成

reorganize → **reorder**

repaint *v* nuri-kaemásu (nuri-káeru, nuri-káete) 塗り替えます(塗り替える, 塗り替えて)

repair 1. *n* (*repairing*) naoshí z(e)i na, shū´ri 修理, shūzen 修繕, tsukurói 繕い; (*upkeep, care*) te-iré 手入れ 2. *v repairs it* naoshimásu (naósu, naó-shite) 直します(直す, 直して); (*mends, patches, sews*) tsukuroimásu (tsukuróu, tsukurótte) 繕い ます(繕う, 繕って); shū´ri/shūzen shimásu (suru, shite) 修理/修繕します(する, して); (*it gets repaired*) …ga naorimásu (naóru, naótte) … が 直ります(直る, 直って), (*gets it repaired*) … o naóshite moraimásu (morau, moratte) … を直して もらいます(もらう, もらって)

repairman *n* shūrí-kō 修理工, shūzén-kō 修繕工

reparation *n* (*provision*) téate 手当て (o-téate お 手当て); (*money*) baishō-kin 賠償金

repay *v* (*compensates*) mukuimásu (mukuíru, mukúite) 報います(報いる, 報いて)

repeat 1. *v* mō ichi-do iimásu (iu/yū, itte/yutte) もう一度言います(言う, 言って/ゆって); kuri-

kaeshimásu (kuri-kaesu, kuri-káeshite) 繰り返し ます(繰り返す, 繰り返して) 2. *n* ripiito リピー ト; kurikaeshi 繰り返し; [BOOKISH] hanpuku 反復

repeat function *n* ripiito kinō リピート機能

repeatedly *adv* (*often*) shíbashiba しばしば; (*ever so many times*) nán-do/-kai mo 何度/回も

repeater *n* ripiitā リピーター

repel *v* (*water, etc.*) hajikimásu (hajíku, hajíite) 弾きます(弾く, 弾いて)

repercussion *n* handō 反動

repertory *n* repātorii レパートリー

repetition *n* kurikaeshi 繰り返し, hanpuku 反復

rephrase *v* ii kaemásu (ii kaéru, ii káete) 言い換 えます(言い換える, 言い換えて)

replace *v* tori-kaemásu (tori-kaeru, tori-kaete) 取り換えます(取り換える, 取り換えて)

replacement *n* torikae 取り換え, sashikae 差し替 え, [BOOKISH] chikan 置換

replica *n* fukusei (-hin) 複製品, mozō(-hin) 模造 品, repurika レプリカ

reply 1. *n* kaitō 回答 2. *v ~ to* kaitō shimásu (suru, shite) 回答します(する, して) → **answer**

report 1. *n* (*notice*) shirase (o-shirase) 知らせ (お知らせ), tsūchi 通知, todoké (o todoke) 届け (お届け); (*announcement*) hōkoku 報告, repō´to レポート; (*message*) dengon 伝言; (*research paper*) happyō 発表; (*claim*) mōshi-de 申し出 2. *v* (*announces*) hōkoku shimásu (suru, shite) 報 告します(する, して), (*relays, tells*) tsutaemásu (tsutaeru, tsutaete) 伝えます(伝える, 伝えて), (*is reported*) tsutawarimásu (tsutawaru, tsutawatte) 伝わります(伝わる, 伝わって), (*notifies*) todokemásu (todokéru, todókete) 届けます(届ける, 届けて); (*presents research*) happyō shimásu (suru, shite) 発表します(する, して); (*claims*) mōshi-demásu (mōshi-deru, mōshi-dete) 申し出ます(申し 出る, 申し出て) → **inform** → **tell**; ~ *for work* shukkin shimásu (suru, shite) 出勤します(する, して)

report card *n* seisekí-hyō 成績表

reportedly *adv* … (da) sō desu …(だ)そうです

reporter *n* ripōtā リポーター, (*news reporter*) shinbun-kíshá 新聞記者, (shuzai) kíshá (取材) 記者

representative 1. *n* daihyō 代表, daihyō´-sha 代表者 → **agent** 2. *adj* (*typical, model*) daihyō-teki (na) 代表的(な)

repress *v* osaemásu (osáeru, osáete) 抑えます (抑える, 抑えて)

reprint *n, v* zōsatsu (shimásu; suru, shite) 増刷 (します; する, して)

reproach *n, v* hínan (shimásu; suru, shite) 非難 (します; する, して), sememásu (seméru, sémete) 責めます(責める, 責めて)

reproduce *v* (*replay*) saisei shimásu (suru, shite) 再生します(する, して); (*replicates/copies it*) fukusei/fukusha shimásu (suru, shite) 複製/複写し ます(する, して)

reproduction *n* (*replication*) fukusei 複製, (*copy*) fukusha 複写; (*replay*) saisei 再生

reprove v togamemásu (togaméru, togámete) とがめ[咎め]ます(とがめる, とがめて)

reputation n hyōban 評判

request 1. n negái 願い, tanomí 頼み, irai 依頼, rikuesuto リクエスト; (a demand) yōkyū 要求, seikyū 請求; (requesting) kói 請い 2. v (asks a favor) negaimásu (negáu, negátte) 願います(願う, 願って), tanomimásu (tanómu, tanónde) 頼みます(頼む, 頼んで), irai shimásu (suru, shite) 依頼します(する, して); (demands) seikyū shimásu (suru, shite) 請求します(する, して)

require v 1. (demands) yōkyū shimásu (suru, shite) 要求します(する, して) 2. → need → take (time/money) → stipulate

requirement n yōkyū 要求; (qualification) shíkaku 資格
   admission requirements n nyūgaku shikaku 入学資格
   entry requirements n tōroku hitsuyō jōken 登録必要条件
   job requirements n shokumu yōken 職務要件

rescue 1. n kyū´jo 救助 2. v tasukemásu (tasukéru, tasukéte) 助けます(助ける, 助けて), sukuimásu (sukū, sukutte) 救います(救う, 救って); kyū´jo shimásu (suru, shite) 救助します(する, して)

research 1. v kenkyū shimásu (suru, shite) 研究します(する, して), chōsa shimásu (suru, shite) 調査します(する, して), risāchi shimásu (suru, shite) リサーチします(する, して) 2. (investigation) n chō´sa 調査
   researcher n kenkyū-in 研究員, kenkyū-sha 研究者, chōsa-in 調査員

resemblance n ruiji 類似

resemble v … ni nite imásu (iru, ite) …に似ています(いる, いて), nimásu (niru, nite) 似ます(似る, 似て); … ni/to ruiji shimásu (suru, shite) …に/と類似します(する, して); closely ~ … ni/to ni-kayoimásu (ni-kayóu, ni-kayótte) …に/と似通います(似通う, 似通って)

resent v fungai shimásu (suru, shite) 憤慨します(する, して); ikidōrimásu (ikidō´ru, ikidō´tte) 憤ります(憤る, 憤って); uramimásu (urámu, uránde) 恨みます(恨む, 恨んで)

resentment n fungai 憤慨, ikidōri 憤り, uramí 恨み

reservation n (booking) yoyaku 予約, mōshí-komi 申し込み

reserve n 1. (reticence) enryo 遠慮; shows ~ enryo shimásu (suru, shite) 遠慮します(する, して) 2. (spare) yobi 予備

reserve adj (spare) yóbi (no) 予備(の)
   reserve fund n tsumitate-kin 積立金

reserve v (makes a reservation) yoyaku shimásu (suru, shite) 予約します(する, して), mōshí-komimásu (mōshí-komu, mōshí-konde) 申し込みます(申し込む, 申し込んで); (puts aside, holds) tótte okimásu (oku, oite) 取って置きます(置く, 置いて)

reserved seat(s) n shitei-seki 指定席

reservoir n chosúi-chi 貯水池, jōsúi-chi 浄水池

reside → live

residence n 1. (place) súmai 住まい(o-súmai お住まい), jū´sho 住所, jūtaku 住宅; one's ~ (home) jitaku 自宅 2. (residing) zairyū 在留; status of ~ zairyū-shíkaku 在留資格; permanent residence honseki 本籍, (place) honséki-chi 本籍地

resident n (person) kyojū´-sha 居住者, jūmin 住民; (apartment tenant) nyūkyó-sha 入居者; ~ in … zai-… 在…

resign v (job) (shigoto o) yamemásu (yameru, yamete) (仕事を)辞めます(辞める, 辞めて), jishoku shimásu (suru, shite) 辞職します(する, して)

resignation n 1. (quitting a job) jishoku 辞職 2. (acceptance) akirame 諦め, kákugo 覚悟

resigned; is ~ to … o kákúgo shimásu (suru, shite) …を覚悟します(する, して), akiramemásu (akiraméru, akirámete) 諦めます(諦める, 諦めて)

resin n yaní やに・ヤニ, (pine) matsuyani 松やに・マツヤニ; (synthetic resin) gōsei jushi 合成樹脂

resist v … ni hankō/teikō shimásu (suru, shite) …に反抗/抵抗します(する, して), kobamimásu (kobámu, kobánde) 拒みます(拒む, 拒んで)

resistance n hankō 反抗, teikō 抵抗

resolutely adv shíkkári しっかり

resolution n (preparation) kákúgo 覚悟

resolve 1. n (determination) késshín 決心 2. v resolves to do (shiyō to) késshín shimásu (suru, shite) (しようと)決心します(する, して) 3. v (medical) shōsan shimásu (suru, shite) 消散します(する, して)

resolved; is ~ (to do) kákúgo shimásu (suru, shite) 覚悟します(する, して)

resonance n hankyō 反響, kyōmei 共鳴, zankyō 残響

resonate v kyōmei shimásu (suru, shite) 共鳴します(する, して)

resound v (echo) hibikimásu (hibíku, hibíite) 響きます(響く, 響いて)

respect 1. n sonkei 尊敬, uyamai 敬い 2. v sonkei shimásu (suru, shite) 尊敬します(する, して), uyamaimásu (uyamáu, uyamátte) 敬います(敬う, 敬って); ogamimásu (ogámu, ogánde) 拝みます(拝む, 拝んで); Respect-for-the-Aged Day (the 3rd Monday of September) Keirō no hí 敬老の日 3. → with respect to

respectable adj katagi (na) 堅気(な); (proper) chanto shita …ちゃんとした…; (considerable) chótto shíta … ちょっとした…

respective adj sorézore no … それぞれの…, onóono no … 各々[おのおの]の…, kaku … 各…

respectively adv sorézore それぞれ, onóono 各々・おのおの

respiration n kokyū 呼吸

respond v kotaemásu (kotáeru, kotáete) 答えます(答える, 答えて), ō-jimásu (ō-jiru, ō-jite) 応じます(応じる, 応じて)

response n kotáe 答え, resuponsu レスポンス,
resu レス
  audience response n 1. (*at stadium, theater,
etc.*) kankyaku no hannō 観客の反応 2. (TV, etc.)
shichō-sha no hannō 視聴者の反応

responsibility n sekinin 責任; (*charge*) tantō
担当; (*cause*) gen'in 原因
  sense of responsibility n sekinin-kan 責任感

responsible; ~ **for** (*is in charge of*) ... o tantō
shite imásu (iru, ite) ... を担当しています(いる,
いて); (*is the cause of*) ... no gen'in desu ...の原
因です
  responsible person n sekinín-sha 責任者; (*the
one in charge*) tantō´-sha 担当者

rest 1. n (*a break/pause*) yasumí 休み(o-yasumi
お休み), [BOOKISH] kyukei 休憩 2. n the rest
(*remainder*) nokorí 残り; (*thereafter*) sore kara
áto (wa) それから後(は) 3. v (*takes a rest*)
yasumimásu (yasúmu, yasúnde) 休みます(休む,
休んで)
  rest room n toire トイレ, keshō´-shitsu 化粧室,
(o-)teárai (お)手洗い → **toilet**

restaurant n résutoran レストラン, shokudō 食堂,
ryōrí-ten/-ya 料理店/屋

restless adj ochi-tsukimasén 落ち着きません
(ochi-tsukanai 落ち着かない)

restoration n kaifuku 回復, fukugen 復元

restrain v osaemásu (osáeru, osáete) 抑えます
(抑える, 抑えて); **properly restrained** iikagen
(na) いい加減(な)

restrict v seigén/gentei shimásu (suru, shite) 制限/
限定します(する, して)

restricted adj fú-jiyū (na) 不自由(な)

restriction n seigén 制限, gentei 限定

result n kekka 結果; (*outcome*) séika 成果;
(*marks, grades*) seiseki 成績
  experimental result n jikken kekka 実験成果
  laboratory results n kensa kekka 検査結果
  study results n kenkyū seika 研究成果

resume 1. n rireki-sho 履歴書 2. v (*continue*)
saikai shimásu (suru, shite) 再開します(する, して)

retail 1. n ko-uri 小売 2. v (*retails it*) ko-uri
shimásu (suru, shite) 小売りします(する, して)
  retail price n 小売価格
  retail shop n 小売店

retailer n ko-uri gyōsha 小売業者

retain v (*keeps it*) kakaemásu (kakaeru, kakaete)
抱えます(抱える, 抱えて)

retentiveness n (*of memory*) kiokú-ryoku 記憶力

reticence n enryo 遠慮 (go-enryo ご遠慮)

retire v 1. (*from job*) intai/taishoku shimásu (suru,
shite) 引退/退職します(する, して) 2.(*withdraws*)
shirizokimásu (shirizoku, shirizóite) 退きます
(退く, 退いて)híki-torimásu (híki-tóru, híki-tótte)
引き取ります(引き取る, 引き取って)

retirement n intai 引退, taishoku 退職
  retirement allowance n taishokukin 退職金
  retirement pension n taishoku-nénkin 退職年金

retort 1. v (*refute*) hanron shimásu (suru, shite)
反論する, iikaeshimásu (iikaesu, iikaeshite) 言い
返します(言い返す, 言い返して) 2. v (*revenge*)
shikaeshi o shimásu (suru, shite) 3. n (*answer
back*) iikaeshi 言い返し 4. *retort food* n retoruto
shokuhin レトルト食品

retreat 1. n (*escape*) hinan 避難, (*retirement*) intai
引退, (*stay-at-home*) hikikomori 引きこもり
2. v shirizokimásu (shirizoku, shirizóite) 退きます
(退く, 退いて)

retribution n bachi 罰・ばち

return v 1. (*reverses direction*) modorimásu
(modósu, modótte) 戻ります(戻る, 戻って); (*goes
back/home*) kaerimásu (káeru, káette) 帰ります
(帰る, 帰って); (*comes back to where one is now*)
itte kimásu (kúru, kité) 行って来ます(来る, 来て);
~ **from abroad** kíkoku shimásu (suru, shite) 帰国
します(する, して) 2. ~ **it** kaeshimásu (káesu,
káeshite) 返します(返す, 返して); modoshimásu
(modósu, modóshite) 戻します(戻す, 戻して);
(*turns back*) hiki-kaeshimásu (hiki-káesu, hiki-
káeshite) 引き返します(引き返す, 引き返して)
3. n (*response*) hentō 返答; (*replacement*)
henkyaku 返却; (*restoration*) kaifuku 回復
  return ticket n ōfuku kíppu 往復切符
  return trip n ōfuku ryokō 往復旅行

returnee n kikokushijo 帰国子女

reveal v morashimásu (morásu, moráshite) 漏らし
ます(漏らす, 漏らして); (*shows*) arawashimásu
(arawásu, arawáshite) 現(わ)します(現(わ)す, 現
(わ)して); (*makes it public*) akíraka ni shimásu
(suru, shite) 明らかにします(する, して)

revelation n otsuge お告げ

revenge v (... no) fukushū o shimásu (suru, shite)
(...の)復讐をします(する, して)

revenue n 1. (*governmental revenue*) sainyū 歳入
2. (*income*) shūnyū 収入, shūeki 収益
  revenue stamp n shūnyū-ínshi 収入印紙

revere v uyamaimásu (uyamáu, uyamátte) uyamai
敬います(敬う, 敬って)

reverence n sonkei 尊敬

Reverend n ... bokushi ...牧師, ...shínpu ...神父

reverse 1. n, adj hantai (no) 反対(の), gyaku (no)
逆(の); (*back; lining*) urá (no) 裏(の), uragawa
(no) 裏側(の) 2. v (*to turn around*) gyaku
[sakasama, hanten, hantai] shimásu (suru, shite)
逆[逆さま・反転・反対]にします(する, して);
uragaeshimásu (uragaesu, uragáe-shite) 裏返しま
す(裏返す, 裏返して)

reversible adj ribāshiburu (no) リバーシブル(の)

revert v modorimásu (modóru, modótte) 戻ります
(戻る, 戻って)

review 1. n rebyū レビュー, (*study*) fukushū 復習;
(*criticism*) híhyō 批評, (*commentary*) hyōron 評論
2. v (*studies it*) fukushū shimásu (suru, shite) 復習
します(する, して); (*criticizes it/comments on it*)
híhyō/hyōron shimásu (suru, shite) 批評/評論し
ます(する, して); (*considers it*) kentō shimásu
(suru, shite) 検討します(する, して)
  book review n shohyō 書評

movie review *n* eiga hyōron 映画評論

reviewer *n* hyōron-ka 評論家

revise *v* kaitei shimásu (suru, shite) 改訂します (する, して)

revival *n* (*regeneration*) fukkatsu 復活, saisei 再生, ribaibaru リバイバル → **recover**

revive *v* (*brings back to life*) ikashimásu (ikásu, ikáshite) 生かします (生かす, 生かして)

revoke *v* tori-keshimásu (tori-kesu, tori-keshite) 取り消します (取り消す, 取り消して)

revolt 1. *n* hanran 反乱, hankō 反抗
2. *v* somukimásu (somúku, somúite) 背きます (背く, 背いて); hanran o okoshimásu (okosu, oko-shite) 反乱を起こします (起こす, 起こして)

revolution *n* (*political*) kakumei 革命, reboryūshon レボリューション; (*revolving*) kaiten 回転

French Revolution *n* Furansu kakumei フランス 革命

revolve *v* mawarimásu (mawaru, mawatte) 回りま す (回る, 回って), kaiten shimásu (suru, shite) 回転します (する, して)

revolver *n* pisutoru ピストル, riborubā リボル バー

reward 1. *n* shōkin 賞金, shō'yo 賞与; sharei 謝礼; (go-)hō'bi (ご)ほうび・褒美 **2.** *v ~ for* (...shita) kai ga arimásu (aru, atte) (...した) かいがあります (ある・あって)

rewards and punishments shōbatsu 賞罰

rewrite; *~ it* kakí-naoshimásu (kaki-naosu, kaki-naoshite) 書き直します (書き直す, 書き直して), kakí-kaemásu (kakí-káeru, kakí-kaete) 書き換えま す (書き換える, 書き換えて)

rhino *n* sai サイ・犀

rhubarb *n bog ~* fuki ふき・フキ・蕗

rhythm *n* rízumu リズム

rhythmical *adj* rizumikaru (na) リズミカル (な)

rib *n* rokkotsu ろっ骨・肋骨, abarabone あばら 骨・肋骨

ribbon *n* himo ひも・紐, ríbon リボン

ink ribbon *n* inku ríbon インクリボン

rice *n* komé (o-kome) 米 (お米); (*cooked*) góhan ご飯, meshí 飯, (*on plate*) ráisu ライス; (*at store*) o-kome お米; (*hulled*) komé 米, (*unhulled*) momí もみ・籾; (*unpolished*) génmai 玄米, (*polished*) hakúmai 白米, (*plant*) íne 稲; *Chinese fried rice* chā'han チャーハン・炒飯; *rice boiled in a soup* zōsui 雑炊; *rice boiled with red beans* sekíhan (o-sekíhan) 赤飯 (お赤飯); *rice topped with something* donburi どんぶり・丼, dom(buri)-mono どん(ぶり)もの・丼もの; (*with chicken and onion cooked in egg*) oyako-dónburi/don 親子どん ぶり [丼]; (*with pork cutlet cooked in egg*) katsu-don カツ丼; (*with tenpura shrimp on top*) ten-don 天丼; *rice with hot tea* (o-)chazuke (お) 茶漬け

rice bowl *n* chawan 茶碗, o-cháwan お茶碗

rice bucket/tub *n* meshi-bitsu 飯びつ [櫃], o-hítsu おひつ [櫃], o-hachi お鉢

rice cake *n* (o-)mochi (お) もち・モチ・餅;

toasted rice cake yaki-móchí 焼き餅; *rice cakes in vegetable soup* zōni 雑煮・ぞう煮 (o-zōni お雑煮)

rice cooker *n* suihanki 炊飯器

rice crackers *n* sénbe(i) せんべ(い)・煎餅・セ ンベイ, o-sénbe(i) おせんべ(い); (*cubes, tidbits*) arare あられ・アラレ

rice curry *n* (*rice with curry*) karē-ráisu カレーラ イス

rice dealer *n* komé-ya (o-komeya) 米屋 (お米屋)

rice field *n* tá 田, tanbo 田んぼ, suiden 水田

rice gruel/porridge *n* (o-)kayu (お) かゆ [粥]

rice paper *n* (*stationery*) hánshi 半紙

rice planting *n* taué 田植え

rice scoop *n* shamoji しゃもじ

rice straw *n* wára わら・藁

rice wine → saké

riceball *n* musubi むすび・結び (o-músubi お むすび・お結び); nigiri-meshi にぎり [握り] 飯, o-nígiri おにぎり・お握り; *riceball lunch(box)* makunóuchi(bentō) 幕の内 (弁当)

rich *adj* (*wealthy*) kanemóchí (no) 金持ち (の), yūfuku (na) 裕福 (な), ritchi (na) リッチ (な); (*abundant*) yútaka (na) 豊か (な), hōfu (na) 豊富 (na); *is rich/abundant in …* ni tomimásu (tómu, tónde) …に富みます (富む, 富んで)

richi person *n* okanemochi お金持ち

rickshaw *n* jinríkísha 人力車

riddle *n* nazo 謎, nazonazo なぞなぞ

ride 1. *n* (*~ a vehicle*) jōsha 乗車, (*driving*) doraibu ドライブ, (*horse riding*) jōba 乗馬 **2.** *v … ni* norimásu (noru, notte) …に乗ります (乗る, 乗っ て), … ni notte ikimásu (iku, itte) …に乗って行 きます (行く, 行って); (*sits astride*) matagarimásu (matagáru, matagátte) またがり [跨り] ます (また がる, またがって) **3.** *gives a ride to … v* o nosemásu (noseru, nosete) … を乗せます (乗せる, 乗せて)

ridge *n* (*of roof*) mune 棟

ridiculous *adj* bakageta ばかげた, bakabakashii ばかばかしい

rifle *n* shōjū 小銃, raifurú (-jū) ライフル (銃), teppō 鉄砲

right 1. *adj* (*adv*) (*not left*) migi (no) 右 (の) **2.** *adj* (*correct*) tadashíi (tadáshíku) 正しい (正しく), fii いい, yóku 良く **3.** *n* (*privilege*) kénri 権利

just right *adj* píttari ぴったり

That's right. *interj* Sō' desu. そうです。, Sonotō'ri desu. その通りで。

right after *adv* chokugo (ni) 直後 (に)

right there *adv* chōdo (a)soko (ni) ちょうど (あ) そこ (に)

voting right *n* tōhyō-ken 投票権, senkyo-ken 選挙権

You are so right. *interj* Naruhodo. なるほど。

right and wrong *n* zén-aku 善悪

right away *adv* (*at once*) sassokú 早速

right click *n* migi kurikku 右クリック

right-handed *adj* migi-kíki (no) 右利き (の)

right mind; *in one's ~* shōki (no) 正気 (の)

right or wrong *n* zé-hi 是非
rightful *adj* seitō (na) 正当 (な)
rightly *adv* tadashiku 正しく
rightness *n* (*justice*) seigi 正義
rigid *adj* katai 堅い・硬い
rim *n* herí へり・縁, fuchí ふち・縁
rind *n* kawa 皮
ring 1. *n* (*on finger*) yubi-wa 指輪, ringu リング; (*circle*) wá 輪, maru 丸・円・まる, en 円・えん
  engagement ring *n* konyaku yubi-wa 婚約指輪, engēji ringu エンゲージリング
  ring finger *n* kusuri yubi 薬指
  wedding ring *n* kekkon yubi-wa 結婚指輪
  2. *v* (*a bell sounds*) narimásu (naru, natte) 鳴ります (鳴る, 鳴って); (*sounds a bell*) narashimásu (narasu, narashite) 鳴らします (鳴らす, 鳴らして)
ringleader *n* óyá-bun 親分
ring-shaped *adj* kanjō (no) 環状 (の)
ringtone *n* chaku mero 着メロ, chakushin-on 着信音
ringworm *n* tamushi たむし・タムシ・田虫, mizu-mushi 水虫・ミズムシ
rink *n* aisu sukēto-jō アイススケート場, (rōrā) sukēto-jō (ローラー) スケート場
rinse *v* yusugimásu (yusugu, yusuide) ゆすぎます (ゆすぐ, ゆすいで); susugimásu (susugu, susuide) すすぎます (すすぐ, すすいで)
riot *n* bōdō 暴動, sōdō 騒動
ripen *v* (*it gets ripe*) jukushimásu (jukúsú, jukúshite) 熟します (熟す, 熟して), seijuku shimásu (suru, shite) 成熟します (する, して); minorimásu (minoru, minotte) 実ります (実る, 実って)
ripped; gets ~ off (*overcharged*) borare másu (boraréru, borárete) ぼられます (ぼられる, ぼられて), (*robbed*) yararemásu (yarareru, yararete) やられます (やられる, やられて)
rise 1. *n* (*in price, wage, fee*) hǐki-age 引き上げ; **gives ~ to** … o okoshimásu (okósu, okóshite) …を起こします (起こす, 起こして), shō-jimásu (shō-jiru, shō-jite) 生じます (生じる, 生じて) **2.** *v* (*gets up*) okimásu (okíru, ókite) 起きます (起きる, 起きて); (*goes up*) agarimásu (agaru, agatte) 上がります (上がる, 上がって), (*climbs, sun rises*) noborimásu (noboru, nobotte) 登り [昇り] ます (登 [昇] る, 登 [昇] って); (*stands up*) tachi-agarimásu (tachi-agaru, tachi-agátte) 立ち上がります (上がる, 上がって); (*looms*) sobiemásu (sobiéru, sobíete) そびえます・聳えます (そびえる, そびえて)
rising 1. *n* (*riot*) hanran 反乱, bōdō 暴動 **2.** *n, adj* (*uprise*) jōshō (shita) 上昇 (した)
  rising smoke *n* tachinoboru kemuri 立ち昇る煙
  rising yen *n* endaka 円高
rising sun *n* ásahi 朝日; noboru taiyō 昇る太陽
  flag of the Rising Sun *n* hi no maru 日の丸, [BOOKISH] nisshōki 日章旗
risk *n* risuku リスク; kiken 危険
risky *adj* risukii (na) リスキー (な); kiken (na) 危険 (な)

rival *n* teki 敵; kyōgōsha 競合者, raibaru ライバル
rivalry *n* kyōsō 競争; **in ~ with …** ni taikō shite …に対抗して
river *n* kawá 川・河
riverbank *n* kawagishi 川岸
river trout *n* áyu あゆ・アユ・鮎, ái あい・アイ
rivet *n* ribetto リベット; byō 鋲・びょう
revision *n* kaitei (-ban) 改訂 (版), kōsei 校正
road *n* michi 道, dō´ro 道路, (*main road*) kaidō 街道; (*roadway*) shadō 車道; (*roadside*) tsuji 辻, michibata 道端
road rage *n* kōtsūjūtai de no iraira 交通渋滞でのイライラ
road-show attraction *n* rōdo-shō ロードショー
roadside *n* michibata 道端, robō 路傍, tsuji 辻
road sign *n* dōro-hyō´shǐki 道路標識, rojō hyōshiki 路上標識
roam *v* idō 移動
roar 1. *n* (*a roar*) unarí うなり・唸り **2.** *v* (*roars*) unarimásu (unáru, unátte) うなり [唸り] ます (うなる, うなって) **3.** *v* (*rumbles*) todorokimásu (todoróku, todoróite) とどろき [轟き] ます (とどろく, とどろいて)
roast 1 *n* yaki- 焼き -yaki 焼き; rō´suto ロースト; **~ beef/chicken** rōsuto-bíifu/-chíkin ローストビーフ/チキン **2.** *v* (*roasts it*) yakimásu (yaku, yaite) 焼きます (焼く, 焼いて); irimásu (íru, ítte) いり [炒り] ます (いる, いって)
roasted chestnuts *n* yaki-guri 焼き栗
rob *v* (*steals*) nusumimásu (nusúmu, nusúnde) 盗みます (盗む, 盗んで); (*plunders*) ubaimásu (ubáu, ubátte) 奪います (奪う, 奪って); (*robs it of …*) kasume-torimásu (kasume-tóru, kasume-tótte) かすめ取ります (かすめ取る, かすめ取って); **gets robbed** (*hit with a robbery*) (gōtō ni) yararemásu (yarareru, yararete) (強盗に) やられます (やられる, やられて)
robber *n* gōtō 強盗, dorobō どろぼう・泥棒; zoku 賊
robbery *n* gōtō 強盗
robin *n* komadori コマドリ
robot *n* robotto ロボット
rock *n* (*stone*) ishí 石, (*crag*) iwá 岩; (*music*) rókku ロック (also *rock'n'roll* rokkun-rōru ロックンロール)
rock *v* (*it rocks*) yuremásu (yureru, yurete) 揺れます (揺れる, 揺れて)
rock-climbing *n* rokku kuraimingu ロッククライミング, iwanobori 岩登り
rocket *n* rokétto ロケット
rocking chair *n* yuriisu 揺り椅子
rocking horse *n* yurimokuba 揺り木馬
rocky *adj* iwa no ōi 岩の多い
Rocky Mountains *n* Rokkii maunten ロッキーマウンテン, Rokkii sanmyaku ロッキー山脈
rod *n* saó さお・竿; (*curtain, etc.*) róddo ロッド
roe *n* (*caviar*); **salmon ~** ikura イクラ, (*salmon/trout*) sujiko すじこ・スジコ・筋子, suzuko すずこ・スズコ, **cod ~** tarákó たらこ・タラコ・鱈子

role *n* yakuwari 役割, yakú 役, o-yakume お役目; tsutomé 務め (o-tsutome お務め)

roll **1.** *v (it rolls)* korogarimásu (korogaru, korogatte) 転がります (転がる, 転がって), *(sways)* yuremásu (yureru, yurete) 揺れます (揺れる, 揺れて); *(rolls it)* korogashimásu (korogasu, korogashite) 転がします (転がす, 転がして); *(rolls it up)* makimásu (maku, maite) 巻きます (巻く, 巻いて) **2.** *n (bread)* rōru-pan ロールパン, (batā-)rō´ru (バター)ロール **3.** *n (a roll of toilet paper)* (toiretto-pē´pā) hitó-maki (トイレットペーパー)一巻; *~ of (currency)* bills satsu-taba 札束 **4.** *n (list of names)* meibo 名簿

roller *n* rō´rā ローラー
  roller coaster *n* jetto kōsutā ジェットコースター
  roller blade *n* rōrā burēdo ローラーブレード
  roller skates *n* rōrā sukēto gutsu ローラースケート靴
  roller-skating *n* rōrā sukēto ローラースケート

ROM (read only memory) *n (computer)* romu ロム

romance *n* rómansu ロマンス, ren'ai 恋愛, roman ロマン, rōman 浪漫
  romance gray *n* romansu gurei ロマンスグレイ
  romance novel *n* romansu shōsetsu ロマンス小説, ren'ai shōsetsu 恋愛小説

Romania *n* Rūmania ルーマニア

romanization *n* rōmá-ji ローマ字

romantic *adj* romanchikku (na) ロマンチック (な)

Rome *n* Ró´ma ローマ

roof **1.** *n* yáne 屋根; *(rooftop floor)* okujō 屋上 **2.** *v roofs a house* uchi no yáne o fukimásu (fuku, fuite) 家の屋根をふき [葺き] ます (ふく, ふいて)

roofed *adj* yanetsuki (no) 屋根付き (の)
  roofed passageway *n* ā´kēdo アーケード

rookie *n* **1.** shinjin 新人 **2.** *(player)* shinjin senshu 新人選手, rūkii ルーキー

room *n* **1.** heyá 部屋 (o-heya お部屋), (...-) ma (...) 間; ...-shítsu ...室; *(tatami room)* zashíkí 座敷 (o-zashíki お座敷) **2.** *(extra space)* yochi 余地, *(leeway)* yoyū 余裕

Japanese-style room *n* washitsu 和室

room and board *n* geshuku 下宿

rooming/boarding house *n* geshuku-ya 下宿屋

roommate *n* dōshítsú-sha 同室者, rūmu-meito ルームメイト

room number *n* heya (no) bangó´ 部屋 (の) 番号; ...-gō shitsu ...号室; *Room No. 3* san-gō´shítsu 三号室

room service *n* rūmu-sā´bisu ルームサービス

rooms for rent *n* kashi-ma 貸間

tatami room *n* zashíkí (o-zashiki) 座敷 (お座敷)

Western-style room *n* yōshitsu 洋室, yōma 洋間

root *n* né 根, *near the ~* ne-motó 根元; *(cause)* gen'in 原因
  root of all evil *n* shoaku no kongen 諸悪の根源
  roots of a tree *n* ki no ne 木の根

root of a word *n* gogen 語源

rope *n* nawá 縄, nō, tsuná 綱・つな; rō´pu ロープ; *mountain-climbing rope* záiru ザイル

rose *n* bara (no haná) ばら [薔薇・バラ] (の花)

rosy *adj* barairo (no) ばら色 (の)

rot *v* kuchimásu (kuchiru, kuchite) 朽ちます (朽ちる, 朽ちて), kusarimásu (kusáru, kusátte) 腐ります (腐る, 腐って)

rotary → traffic circle

rotate *v* kaiten shimásu (suru, shite) 回転します (する, して)

rotation *n* kaiten 回転

rouge *n* béni べに・紅

rough **1.** *adj (coarse; wild)* arai 荒い [粗い], zatsu-... 雑...; *(in texture)* zárazara (shíta ...) ざらざら (した...); *(bumpy)* dekoboko (no) でこぼこ・凸凹 (の); *(rambunctious)* ranbō (na) 乱暴 (な); *(approximate)* ōyoso (no) おおよそ (の); ōmaka na おおまかな; daitai (no) 大体 (の); *(sloppy)* zonzai (na) ぞんざい (な), ōzáppa (na) おおざっぱ (な) **2.** *gets ~* aremásu (areru, arete) 荒れます (荒れる, 荒れて); *gets a ~ idea of it* kentō´ga tsukimásu (tsukú, tsúite) 見当がつきます (つく, ついて)
  rough manners *n* busahō 不作法
  rough road *n* dekoboko (shita) michi でこぼこ (した) 道
  rough schedule *n* ōmaka na yotei おおまかな予定, daitai no yotei 大体の予定
  rough work *n* arashigoto 荒仕事

roughly *adv* ōyoso おおよそ; daitai 大体; zatto ざっと; hóbo ほぼ; ...-kéntō ...見当

roughneck *n* abare-mono 暴れ者, abarenbō 暴れん坊

round **1.** *n, adj* enkei (no) 円形 (の), wa 輪, marui 丸い; *round thing* tamá 玉・珠; *make ~* maruku shimásu (suru, shite) 丸くします (する, して) **2.** *n (game, match)* raundo ラウンド, shiai 試合 **3.** *~ off* v shishagonyū shimásu (suru, shite) 四捨五入します (する, して) **4.** *adv (during)* ... no aida-jū ...の間中; marumeru 丸める
  final round *n* kesshō-sen 決勝戦
  first-round match *n* (dai) ikkai-sen 第1回戦, yosen 予選
  round-up amount *n* gaisan 概算
  round-eyed *adj* me o marukushita 目を丸くした
  round face *n* marugao 丸顔
  round figure *n* gaisū 概数
  round screw *n* maru neji 丸ネジ
  round shape *n* enkei 円形; marui katachi 丸い形
  round-table *n* maru tēburu 丸テーブル, [BOOKISH] en taku 円卓
  round-the-world *adj* sekai isshū (no) 世界一周の
  round trip (ticket) *n* ōfuku(-kíppu) 往復 (切符)

roundabout → traffic circle

roundly *adv* maruku 丸く

roundtable discussion *n* zadán-kai 座談会

rouse *v* okoshimásu (okósu, okóshite) 起こします (起こす, 起こして)

route *n* sén 線; rūto ルート; keiro 経路; (*bus*, *train*) rosen 路線
  administration route *n* (*medicine*, *etc.*) tōyo keiro 投与経路
routine *n* 1. nikka 日課 2. (*computer*) rūchin ルーチン
  routine work *n* o-kimari no shigoto お決まりの仕事, kima(riki)tta shigoto 決ま(りき)った仕事; [BOOKISH] nichijō gyōmu 日常業務
roux *n* rū ルー
row 1. *n* (*line*) rétsu 列, narabi 並び, (*of trees*) namiki 並木; ... *are in a row* ... narande imás̱u (iru, ite) 並んでいます(いる、いて); (*linked*) *in a row* tsunagatte つながって 2. *v* (*a boat*) kogimás̱u (kógu, kóide) こぎ[漕ぎ]ます(こぐ、こいで) 3. *v* (*to quarrel*) kenka shimás̱u (suru, s̱h̲ite) けんかします(する、して), kōron shimás̱u (suru, s̱h̲ite) 口論します(する、して)
  first row of seats *n* saizenretsu (no seki) 最前列(の席)
royal *adj* ō (no) 王(の)
  royal family *n* 1. ōzoku 王族, ōshitsu 王室 2. (*Japanese*) kōshitsu 皇室
royalty *n* chosakuken ryō 著作権料, (*on a book*) inzei 印税
  royalty basis *n* inzei hōshiki 印税方式
  royal blend *n* roiyaru burendo ロイヤルブレンド
  royal flush *n* roiyaru furasshu ロイヤルフラッシュ
  royal jelly *n* roiyaru zerii ロイヤルゼリー
  royal road *n* ōdō 王道, (*shortcut*) chikamichi 近道, (*easy way*) raku na hōhō 楽な方法; *There is no royal road to learning.* [IDIOM] Gakumon ni ōdō nashi. 学問に王道なし。
  royal rule *n* ōsei 王政・王制
rub 1. masatsu 摩擦; (*difficulty*) konnan 困難 2. *v* (*rubs it*) kosurimás̱u (kosúru, kosútte) こすります(こする、こすって), surimás̱u (súru, sútte) 擦ります(擦る、擦って), masatsu shimás̱u (suru, s̱h̲ite) 摩擦します(する、して); (*with both hands*) momimás̱u (momu, monde) もみ[揉み]ます(もむ、もんで) 3. *v* (*it rubs*) suremás̱u (suréru, súrete) 擦れます(擦れる、擦れて)
rubber *n* gómu ゴム; (*condom*) sákku サック; *rubber band* wa-gomu 輪ゴム
rubbish *n* 1. gomí ごみ・ゴミ; kúzu くず・屑, kuzu-mono くず物・屑物, garak̲uta がらくた 2. (*failure*) dasaku 駄作 3. *v* (*to rubbish a rumor*) ... o kenashimás̱u (kenaru, kenashite) ...をけなします(けなす、けなして)
  rubbish bin *n* gomí-bako ごみ・ゴミ箱
  rubbish vehicle *n* gomí kaishū-sha ごみ・ゴミ回収車
rubella *n* hashika はしか; fūshin 風疹
ruble *n* rūburu ルーブル
ruby *n* rubii ルビー, kōgyoku 紅玉
rucksack *n* ryukkusakku リュックサック
rudder *n* káji かじ・舵
rude *adj* búrei (na) 無礼(な); buénryo (na) 無遠慮(な)

rudiment *n* (*basic*) kiso 基礎
ruffian *n* abare-mono 暴れ者
rug *n* shík̲i-mono 敷物, jū´tan じゅうたん・絨毯
rugby *n* ragubii ラグビー
ruin 1. *ruins it v* damé ni shimás̱u (suru, s̱h̲ite) だめ[駄目]にします(する、して); arashimás̱u (arásu, aréte) 荒らします(荒らす、荒れて); ~ *one's health* karada o kowashi-más̱u (kowás̱u, kowás̱h̲ite) 体を壊します・からだをこわします(こわす、こわして) 2. *goes to ~ v* aremás̱u (areru, arete) 荒れます(荒れる、荒れて) 3. **ruins** *n* iseki 遺跡
ruined; gets ~ damé ni narimás̱u (náru, nátte) だめ[駄目]になります(なる、なって)
rule 1. *n* (*regulation*) kísoku 規則, kítei 規定, rū´ru ルール; (*law*) hōsoku 法則, hō´ 法 2. *v* shihai shimás̱u (suru, s̱h̲ite) 支配します(する、して)
ruler *n* (*to measure with*) jō´gi 定規, (*foot rule*) monosás̱hí 物差し
ruling party *n* yōtō 与党
rum *n* ramu-shu ラム酒
rum-soaked raisins *n* ramu-zuke (no) rēzun ラム浸け(の)レーズン
rumble *v* todorokimás̱u (todoróku, todoróite) とどろき[轟き]ます(とどろく、とどろいて)
rumor *n* uwasa うわさ・噂
run 1. *n* (*dash*) kyōsō 競走; (*exercise*) ranning ランニング; *a run for one's money* doryoku ni miatta mikaeri 努力に見合った見返り 2. *v* hashirimás̱u (hashíru, hash̲ítte) 走ります(走る、走って), (*gallops*) kakemás̱u (kakéru, kákete) 駆けます(駆ける、駆けて); *runs a marathon* marason o shimás̱u (suru, s̱h̲ite) マラソンをします(する、して) 3. *v* (*connects*) tsū-jimás̱u (tsū-jiru, tsū-jite) 通じます(通じる、通じて) 4. *v* (*operates a machine*) unten shimás̱u (suru, s̱h̲ite) 運転します(する、して) 5. *v* (*manages*, *operates a business*) keihei shimás̱u (suru, s̱h̲ite) 経営します(する、して)
  run along *v* (*side*) soimás̱u (sou, sotte) 沿います(沿う、沿って)
  run away *v* (*flees*) nigemás̱u (nigéru, nígete) 逃げます(逃げる、逃げて), ochimás̱u (ochíru, óchíte) 落ちます(落ちる、落ちて); (*from home*) (uchi o) tobi-dashimás̱u (tobi-dásu, tobi-dash̲ite) (家を)飛び出します(飛び出す、飛び出して), iede shimás̱u (suru, s̱h̲ite) 家出します(する、して)
  run fast *v* (*timepiece*) susumimás̱u (susumu, susunde) 進みます(進む、進んで)
  run into *v* 1. → **collide** 2. → **meet** 3. (*comes to the end of a street*) tsuki-atarimás̱u (tsuki-ataru, tsuki-atatte) 突き当たります(突き当たる、突き当たって)
  run out *v* 1. (*dashes out*) tobi-dashimás̱u (tobi-dásu, tobi-dásh̲ite) 跳び[飛び]出します(跳び[飛び]出す、跳び[飛び]出して) 2. *it runs out* (*stock is exhausted*) kiremás̱u (kiréru, kírete) 切れます(切れる、切れて), (*gets used up*) tsukimás̱u (tsukiru, tsukite) 尽きます(尽きる、尽きて)

3. *runs out of* ... o kirashimásu (kirásu, kiráshite) ...を切らします(切らす, 切らして), ... o tsukaitsukushimásu (tsukaitsukúsu, tsukaitsukúshite) ...を使い尽くします(使い尽くす, 使い尽くして), tsukaihatashimásu (tsukaihatasu, tsukaihatashite) 使い果たします(使い果たす, 使い果たして); (*it sells out*) uri-kiremásu (uri-kiréru, uri-kírete) 売り切れます(売り切れる, 売り切れて)

run over *v* **1.** (*a person*) híkimásu (híku, hiite) ひきます・轢きます(ひく, ひいて); ***gets run over by*** ... ni híkaremásu (híkareru, híkarete) ...にひかれ[轢かれ]ます(ひかれる, ひかれて) **2.** → **exceed**

run overtime *v* jikan ga ṓbā shimásu (suru, shite) 時間がオーバーします(する, して), jikan o sugimásu (sugiru, sugite) 時間を過ぎます(過ぎる, 過ぎて)

run slow *v* (*it lags*) okuremásu (okureru, okurete) 遅れます(遅れる, 遅れて)

runaway *n* **1.** (*from home*) iede-nin 家出人 **2.** (*escapee*) tōbō-sha 逃亡者

rune *n* rūn moji ルーン文字

runlet *n* ogawa 小川

runner *n* rannā ランナー; sōsha 走者
     long-distance runner *n* chōkyori rannā 長距離ランナー; chōkyori sōsha 長距離走者

running *n* ranningu ランニング
     running togs *n* ranningu wea ランニングウェア
     running water *n* suidō 水道

runt *n* (*deprecating a short person*) chíbi ちび

rupee *n* rupii ルピー

rural *adj* inaka (no) いなか・田舎(の)

rush *v* isogimásu (isógu, isóide) 急ぎます(急ぐ, 急いで); ō-ísogi de shimásu (suru, shite) 大急ぎで

しますする, して); ***with a ~*** (*suddenly*) dotto どっと; ***feels rushed*** aserimásu (aséru, asétte) 焦ります(焦る, 焦って)

rush hour *n* rasshu-áwā ラッシュアワー

Russia *n* Róshia ロシア; (*Soviet Union*) Sóren ソ連

Russian *n* (*person*) Roshiá-jin ロシア人; (*language*) Roshia-go ロシア語

rust **1.** *n* sabí さび・錆 **2.** *v* (*it rusts*) sabimásu (sabíru, sábite) さびます・錆びます(さびる, さびて)

rustic *adj* inaka (no) 田舎・いなか(の), shísso (na) 質素(な); yábo (na) やぼ[野暮](な), yábottai やぼったい[野暮ったい]

rusticity *n* inaka rashisa 田舎らしさ・いなからしさ

rustle *n* sarasara/kasakasa to iu oto サラサラ/カサカサという音

rustless **1.** (*rustproof*) sabínai さびない・錆びない **2.** sabiteinai さびていない・錆びていない

rustproof *adj* sabínai さびない・錆びない

rusty *n* sabita さびた・錆びた

rut *n* wa-dachi わだち・轍

rutabaga *n* rutabaga ルタバガ

ruthless *adj* mujihi (na) 無慈悲(な); reikoku (na) 冷酷(な)

ruthlessly *adv* mujihi ni 無慈悲に; reikoku ni 冷酷に

Rwanda *n* Ruwanda ルワンダ

rye *n* raimugi ライ麦・ライムギ
     rye bread *n* raimugi pan ライ麦・ライムギパン; kuro pan 黒パン
     rye whisky, rye whiskey *n* rai wisukii ライウィスキー

Ryukyu (islands) *n* Ryūkyū́ 琉球 (= Okinawa)

S

Sabbath *n* ansoku-bi 安息日

sabbatical **1.** *n* ichinen kyūka 一年休暇 **2.** *adj* Sabbatical ansokubi (no) 安息日の

sabotage *n* bōgai kōsaku 妨害工作, hakai kōsaku 破壊工作, sabotāju サボタージュ

saccharin *n* sakkarin サッカリン

sack **1.** *n* (*bag*) fukuró 袋, (*large bag*) ōkina fukuro 大きな袋 **2.** *n* (*pillage*) ryakudatsu 略奪 **3.** *n* (*dismissal from employment*) kaiko 解雇 **4.** *n* (*bed*) beddo ベッド, shindai 寝台 **5.** *v* kaiko shimásu (suru, shite) 解雇します(する, して) **6.** *v* [INFORMAL] kubi ni shimásu (suru, shite) 首にします(する, して)

sacking *n* **1.** (*laying off*) kaiko 解雇 **2.** (*cloth*) asa nuno 麻布

sacrament *n* seireiten 聖礼典

sacred *adj* **1.** (*holy*) shinsei (na) 神聖(な)

2. (*religious*) shūkyō-teki (na) 宗教的な, shūkyō (no) 宗教の

sacred building *n* sei-dō 聖堂

sacrifice **1.** *n* gisei 犠牲, ikenie 生(け)贄・いけにえ; ***makes a ~*** (*scapegoat*) of ... o gisei ni shimásu (suru, shite) ...を犠牲にします(する, して); ***offers a ~*** ikenie ni shimásu (suru, shite) 生(け)贄にします(する, して) **2.** ***is sacrificed*** *v* gisei ni narimásu (náru, nátte) を犠牲になります(なる, なって)

sacrificial *adj* gisei (no) 犠牲(の), ikenie (no) 生(け)贄・いけにえ(の)

sacrilege *n* [BOOKISH] bōtoku 冒涜・ぼうとく

sacrosanct *adj* shinsei fukashin (no) 神聖不可侵(の)

sad *adj* **1.** kanashii 悲しい・かなしい; ***to be ~*** kanashimimásu (kanashimu, kanashinde) 悲しみ

ます・かなしみます(悲しむ,悲しんで)
2. (*regrettable*) zannen (na) 残念(な)
3. (*miserable*) mijime (na) 惨め・みじめ(な)
4. (*deplorable*) nagekawashii 嘆かわしい・なげかわしい

look sad *v* kanashisō ni miemásu (mieru, miete) 悲しそうに見えます(見える, 見えて)

sadden *v* kanashimasemásu (kanashimaseru, kanashimasete) 悲しませます・かなしませます(悲しませる, 悲しませて); kanashikunarimásu (kanashikunaru, kanashikunatte) 悲しくなります・かなしくなります(悲しくなる, 悲しくなって)

saddle 1. *n* (*for horse*) kurá くら・鞍 **2.** *n* (*of bicycle*) sadoru サドル **3.** *v* owasemásu (owaseru, owasete) 負わせます(負わせる, 負わせて)

saddlebag *n* sadorubaggu サドルバッグ

sadism *n* sadizumu サディズム, sado サド

sadist *n* sadisuto サディスト, sado サド

sadistic *adj* sadisuto-teki (na) サディスト的(な), kagyaku-teki (na) 加虐的(な)

sadness *n* kanashimi 悲しみ・かなしみ

sae *n* = *self-addressed envelope* henshiyō fūtō 返信用封筒

safari *n* safari サファリ, shuryō (ryokō) 狩猟(旅行), tanken (ryokō) 探検(旅行)

safari park *n* safari pāku サファリパーク

safe 1. *adj* (*harmproof*) anzen (na) 安全(な); (*reliable*) dai-jō´bu (na) 大丈夫・だいじょうぶ(な), jōbu (na) 丈夫(な); (*steady*) te-gatai 手堅い; (*certain*) táshika (na) 確か(な); kakujitsu (na) 確実(な) **2.** *n* (*strongbox*) kínko 金庫 **3.** **to be on the ~ side** nen no tamé (ni) 念のため[為](に); **plays it ~** daijí o torimásu (tóru, tótte) 大事をとります(とる, とって)

safe-conduct *n* (anzen) tsūkō kyoka-shō (安全)通行許可証

safe and sound *adj* buji (ni) 無事(に)

safeguard 1. *n* (*protection*) hogo 保護 **2.** *n* (*safety device*) anzen sōchi 安全装置 **3.** *v* hógo shimásu (suru, shite) 保護します(する, して)

safely *adv* (*harmfree, without incident*) búji (ni) 無事(に); (*for sure*) chanto ちゃんと, táshika (ni) 確かに

safety *n* anzen 安全
safety assessment *n* anzen-sei hyōka 安全性評価
safety belt *n* anzén beruto 安全ベルト
safety driving *n* anzén na unten 安全な運転
safety first *n* anzen daiichi 安全第一
safety pin *n* anzénpin 安全ピン
safety zone *n* anzen-chítai 安全地帯

safflower *n* benibana 紅花

saffron *n* safuran サフラン

sag *v* tarumimásu (tarumu, tarunde) たるみます(たるむ, たるんで), tawamimásu (tawamu, tawande) たわみます(たわむ, たわんで)

saga *n* **1.** sāga サーガ **2.** (*tales of adventure*) bōken monogatari 冒険物語 **3.** *n* (*tale of heroism*) eiyūden 英雄伝, eiyū monogatari 英雄物語

sagacity *n* kibin (sa) 機敏(さ), meibin (sa) 明敏(さ), sōmei (sa) 聡明さ, kashikosa 賢さ, chisei 知性

sage *n* **1.** (*wise person*) kenja 賢者, kenjin 賢人 **2.** (*saint*) seija 聖者, seijin 聖人 → **saint**

Sagittarius *n* (*star sign*) Ite-za 射手座・いて座

Sahara *n* Sahara サハラ; *Sahara desert* Sahara sabaku サハラ砂漠

said *v* iimáshita (itta/yutta) 言いました(言った/ゆった) → **say**

sail 1. *n* ho 帆 **2.** *v* (*makes a voyage*) kōkai shimásu (suru, shite) 航海します(する, して)

sailboard *n* sērū bōdo セールボード

sailboat *n* (kogata) hansen (小型)帆船, yotto ヨット

sailing *n* kōkai 航海

sailing boat *n* yotto ヨット

sailor *n* funánori 船乗り, súifu 水夫, sērā セーラー; (*member of the crew*) sen'in 船員; (*navy enlisted person*) súihei 水兵

saint *n* seija 聖者, seijin 聖人

saintly *adj* seija no yō (na) 聖者のよう(な), seijin no yō (na) 聖人のよう(な)

saké *n* (*rice wine*) (o-)sake (お)酒, Nihon shu 日本酒; *sweet saké* (*for cooking*) mirin みりん・ミリン・味醂; *saké bottle/pitcher* (*decanter*) tokkuri とっくり・徳利; *saké cup* (o-)chóko (お)ちょこ, sakazuki 杯(o-sakazuki お杯); *saké offered to the gods* miki 神酒 = o-miki お神酒・おみき

sake; for the ~ of … no tamé ni …のため[為]に, **for the ~ of doing …** suru tamé ni …するため[為]に

Sakhalin *n* (*an island in the Sea of Okhotsk*) saharin サハリン, karafuto 樺太

salad *n* sárada サラダ
fruit salad *n* furūtsu sarada フルーツサラダ
salad bowl *n* sarada bōru サラダボウル
salad cream → salad dressing
salad dressing *n* sarada (yō) doresshingu サラダ(用)ドレッシング
salad oil *n* sarada oiru サラダオイル, sarada abura サラダ油
vegetable salad *n* yasai sarada 野菜サラダ

salamander *n* sanshō-uo 山椒魚・サンショウウオ

salami sausage *n* sarami サラミ, sarami sōseji サラミソーセージ

salaried man *n* sararii man サラリーマン, kaisha-in 会社員, kyūryō-tori 給料取り・給料とり

salary *n* hōkyū 俸給, (o-)kyū´ryō (お)給料, sárarii サラリー; (*monthly*) gekkyū 月給

sale *n* hanbai 販売; hatsubai 発売; (*special*) uridashi 売り出し, (bāgen)seru (バーゲン)セール; *sale goods/item*, (*something*) *for sale* uri-mono 売り物

sales agency *n* hanbai-moto 販売元, hanbai dairi-ten 販売代理店

sales assistant, salesclerk, salesperson *n*
ten'in 店員, uriko 売り子, hanbai-in 販売員

sales outlet *n* hanbái-ten 販売店

sales tax *n* uriage-zei 売上税

sales volume *n* hanbái-daka 販売高

saliva *n* tsúba つば・ツバ・唾, tsubakí つばき・ツバキ・唾, [BOOKISH] daeki 唾液・だえき

salmon *n* sáke さけ・サケ・鮭, sāmon サーモン, sháke シャケ・鮭; *salmon roe* ikura イクラ; sujiko すじこ・スジコ・筋子, suzuko すず子・スズコ

salon *n* saron サロン

saloon *n* 1. (*great hall*) (ō-) hiroma (大)広間 2. (*bar*) sakaba 酒場

salt *n* shió sháke ・しお, o-shío お塩・おしお; *table salt* shokúen 食塩

salt shaker *n* shió-ire 塩入れ・しおいれ

salty *adj* shio-karái 塩辛い・塩からい, shoppái しょっぱい・塩っぱい

salute 1. *n* keirei 敬礼 2. *v* keirei shimásu (suru, shíte) 敬礼します(する, して)

salvage *n* hiki-age 引き揚げ

salvation *n* kyūsai 救済

Salvation Army *n* kyūsei gun 救世軍

salve *n* 1. (*ointment*) nankō 軟膏 2. (*comfort*) nagusame 慰め・なぐさめ

salvo *n* issei shageki 一斉射撃

samba *n* sanba サンバ

same 1. *pron* onaji … 同じ…・おなじ…, [BOOKISH] dō´(-) … 同… 2. *adj/adv* onaji yō´ (na/ni) 同じ様・おなじよう(な/に); *one and the same* hítotsu 一つ・ひとつ; *same period* dō´ki 同期; *same time* dōji 同時

sample 1. *n* mihon 見本, sanpuru サンプル 2. *n* (*free sample*) shikyō-hin 試供品 3 *v* (*samples; tries doing*) (shi)-te mimásu (míru, míte) (し)てみます(みる, みて)

samurai *n* (*Japanese warrior*) samurai 侍・サムライ, búshi 武士・ぶし; *the way of the samurai* bushi-dō 武士道

sanatorium *n* sanatoriumu サナトリウム; hoyōchi 保養地; ryōyō-jo 療養所

sanctify *v* shinseika shimásu (suru, shíte) 神聖化します(する, して)

sanction *n* [BOOKISH] seisai (sochi) 制裁(措置)

sanctity *n* shinseisa 神聖さ

sanctuary *n* 1. sei-iki 聖域 2. (*asylum*) hinanjo 避難所 3. (*church*) kyōkai 教会

sand *n* suna 砂・すな; *sand dune* sakyū 砂丘・さきゅう

sandbag *n* suna-búkuro 砂袋

sandbox *n* suna-ba 砂場

sandcastle *n* suna no shiro 砂の城

sandstone *n* sagan 砂岩

sandal *n* sandaru サンダル; (*Japanese traditional style*) *straw sandals* zōri 草履

sandalwood *n* byakudan びゃくだん・ビャクダン・白壇

sandpaper *n* sandopē´pā サンドペーパー, kami-yásuri 紙やすり, yasurí-gami やすり紙

sandwich 1. *n* sandoítchi サンドイッチ; …-sándo …サンド; *tuna-fish sandwich* tsuna-sándo ツナサンド, *egg sandwich* tamago-sando たまご・タマゴ[卵]サンド, *vegetable sandwich* yasai-sando 野菜サンド, cutlet sandwich katsu-sando カツサンド 2. *becomes sandwiched (in)* *v between* hasa-marimásu (hasamáru, hasamátte) はさ[挟]まります(はさ[挟]まる, はさ[挟]まって)

sandy *adj* suna no 砂の, suna no yō (na) 砂のよう(な)

sane *adj* shōki (no) 正気(の)

San Francisco *n* Sanfuranshísuko サンフランシスコ

sanguine 1. *adj* kaikatsu (na) 快活(な), (*happy-go-lucky*) rakuten-teki (na) 楽天的(な) 2. (*optimistic*) rakkan-teki (na) 楽観的(な)

sanitary *adj* eisei-teki (na) 衛生的(な), eisei (no) 衛生(の); *sanitary napkin* (seiri-yō) nápukín (生理用)ナプキン

sanitation *n* eisei 衛生, kōshū eisei 公衆衛生

sanity *n* shōki 正気, funbetsu 分別

Santa Claus *n* Santa (kurōsu) サンタ(クロース), Santa-san サンタさん

"Santa Claus Is Comin' To Town" *n* "Santa ga machi ni yattekuru" 『サンタが街にやって来る』

sap *v* yowarasemásu (yowaraseru, yowarasete) 弱らせます(弱らせる, 弱らせて)

sapling *n* 1. (*tree*) naegi 苗木 2. (*person*) wakamono 若者

sapphire *n* safaia サファイア

sapphism *n* (*lesbianism*) rezubian レズビアン, rezu レズ

sarcasm *n* hiniku 皮肉, iyami 嫌味・いやみ

sarcastic *adj* hiniku (na) 皮肉(な), iyami (na) 嫌味・いやみ(な), iyamippoi 嫌味っぽい・いやみっぽい

sardine *n* iwashi いわし・イワシ・鰯; (*baby*) shirasu しらす・シラス・白子; (*large, usually dried*) urume(-íwashi) うるめ(いわし)・潤目(鰯)・ウルメ(イワシ)

sase *n* = *self-addressed stamped envelope* kitte o hatta henshiyō futō 切手を貼った返信用封筒

sash *n* (*girdle*) óbi 帯・おび; (*military*) sukā´fu スカーフ; (*window-sash*) mado-waku 窓枠, sásshi サッシ, sásshu サッシュ

Satan *n* satan サタン, ákuma 悪魔・アクマ

satanic *adj* satan (no) サタン(の), ákuma (no) 悪魔・アクマ(の)

satchel *n* kaban かばん・鞄

sate 1. *v* (*satiate*) tannō sasemásu (saseru, sasete) 堪能させます(させる, させて) 2. *n* (*skewered food*) saté サテー

satellite *n* eisei 衛星; sateraito サテライト artificial satellite *n* jinkō eisei 人工衛星 satellite transmission *n* eisei chūkei 衛星中継 satellite TV *n* eisei terebi 衛星テレビ

satellize *v* eisei-ka shimásu (suru, shíte) 衛星化します(する, して)

satiate *v* (sate) tannō sasemás̠u (saseru, sasete) 堪能させます(させる, させて)

satin *n* shús̠u しゅす・シュス・繻子, sáten サテン

satire *n* fūshi 風刺

satirical *adj* fūshi (no) 風刺(の), fūshi-teki (na) 風刺的(な)

satisfaction *n* manzoku 満足

satisfactory *adj* yoroshii よろしい・宜しい, mánzoku (na) 満足(な), mánzoku dekiru 満足できる, nattoku (no) iku 納得の)いく

satisfied; *v gets ~* mánzoku shimás̠u (suru, sh̠ite) 満足します(する, して)

satisfy *v* mánzoku sasemás̠u (saseru, sasete) 満足させます(させる, させて); (fulfills) mitashi-más̠u (mitásu, mitásh̠ite) 満たします(満たす, 満たして)

saturate *v* (soaks) zubunure ni sasemás̠u (saseru, sasete) ずぶ濡れにさせます(させる, させて)

saturated *adj* kói 濃い

saturation *n* [BOOKISH] hōwa 飽和
saturation point *n* hōwa ten 飽和点
saturation state *n* hōwa jōtai 飽和状態

Saturday *n* Doyō´bi 土曜日; *Saturday-Sunday* dō-nichi 土日

Saturn *n* Dosei 土星

sauce *n* sō´su ソース; (cooking) taré たれ・タレ; *soy sauce* (o-)shōyu (お)しょうゆ [醤油]

saucepan *n* nabe 鍋・ナベ

saucer *n* ko-zara 小皿 (o-kózara お小皿), sara 皿 (o-sara お皿); (for cup) uké-zara 受け皿
flying saucer *n* sora tobu enban 空飛ぶ円盤

Saudi Arabia *n* Saujiarabia サウジアラビア

Saudi Arabian **1.** *adj* Saujiarabia (no) サウジアラビア(の) **2.** *n* (person) Saujiarabia-jin サウジアラビア人

sauna *n* sauna サウナ → **steam bath**

saurel *n* áji あじ・アジ・鯵

saury *n* sanma 秋刀魚・サンマ

saury-pike *n* kamás̠u かます・カマス

sausage *n* sō´sē´ji ソーセージ

sauté **1.** *n* sotē ソテー **2.** *v* itamemás̠u (itaméru, itámete) 炒めます(炒める, 炒めて)

savage **1.** *adj* yaban (na) 野蛮(な) **2.** *a savage* yaban-jín 野蛮人

savanna *n* sabanna サバンナ

save *v* **1.** (saves up, hoards) takuwaemás̠u (takuwaeru, takuwaete) 蓄えます(蓄える, 蓄えて), (deposits money) chokin shimás̠u (suru, sh̠ite) 貯金します(する, して); (accumulates) tamemás̠u (tameru, tamete) ため[溜め]ます(ためる, ためて) **2.** (curtails, omits) habukimás̠u (habúku, habúite) 省きます(省く, 省いて); (economizes on) setsuyaku shimás̠u (suru, sh̠ite) 節約します(する, して), ken'yaku shimás̠u (suru, sh̠ite) 倹約します(する, して) **3.** → **rescue**

savings *n* takuwae 蓄え・たくわえ; *savings account* chokin 貯金; *installment savings* tsumi-tate-kin 積立金

savings account *n* yokin-kō´za 預金口座, tsumi-

tate-chókin 積立貯金; *savings book* yokin-tsū´chō 預金通帳

savings box *n* chokin-bako 貯金箱

savior *n* **1.** (saver) kyūsai-sha 救済者 **2.** (messiah) kyūsei-shu 救世主

savor *v* (tastes) ajiwaimás̠u (ajiwau, ajiwatte) 味わいます(味わう, 味わって); ajiwai-tanoshi-mimás̠u (ajiwai-tanoshimu, ajiwai-tanoshinde) 味わい楽しみます(味わい楽しむ, 味わい楽しんで)

saw **1.** *n* (tool) nokogíri のこぎり・鋸 **2.** *v* (saws it) nokogíri de h̠ikimás̠u (h̠iku, h̠iite) のこぎり「鋸」で引きます(引く, 引いて)

sawdust *n* ogakuzu おがくず・おが屑

sawmill *n* seizai kōjō 製材工場, seizaisho 製材所

sawman *n* nokogiri shokunin のこぎり職人

sawmill machine, sawmill machinery *n* seizai kikai 製材機械

saw *v* (did see) mimásh̠ita (míta) 見ました(見た); (met a person) ... ni aimásh̠ita (átta) …に会いました(会った)

saxophone *n* sakkusu サックス; sakusuhōn サクスホーン

saxophone player *n* sakkusu sōsha サックス奏者; sakusuhōn sōsha サクスホーン奏者

saxophonist → **saxophone player**

say *v* (that ...) (... to) iimás̠u (iu/yu, itte/yutte) (...と) 言います(言う/ゆう, 言って/ゆって); [HUMBLE] mōshimás̠u (mō´su, mōsh̠ite/mōshimásh̠ite) 申します(申す, 申して/申しまして), mōshi-agemás̠u (mōshi-ageru, mōshi-agete) 申し上げます(申し上げる, 申し上げて); [HONORIFIC] osshaimás̠u (ossháru, osshátte/osshaimásh̠ite) おっしゃいます(おっしゃる, おっしゃって/おっしゃいまして)

say it another way *v* ii-kaemás̠u (ii-kaéru, ii-káete) 言い換えます・言いかえます(言い換える, 言い換えて)

Say there! *interj* Móshi-moshi! もしもし!

saying *n* kotowaza ことわざ・諺; kakugen 格言

scab *n* kasabuta かさぶた

scaffold *n* **1.** (for the execution) shokei dai 処刑台; shikei dai 死刑台; kōshu dai 絞首台 **2.** (framework) ashi ba 足場

scaffold *n* kasabuta かさぶた

scald **1.** *n* (mark on the skin) yakedo やけど・火傷 **2.** *v* (scalds) yakimás̠u (yaku, yaite) 焼きます(焼く, 焼いて), (gets scalded) yakemás̠u (yakeru, yakete) 焼けます(焼ける, 焼けて)

scale **1.** *n* sukēru スケール **2.** (fish) uroko うろこ・ウロコ・鱗

scale down *v* shukushō shimás̠u (suru, sh̠ite) 縮小します(する, して)

scale insect *n* kaigaramushi カイガラムシ

scale up *v* kakudai shimás̠u (suru, shite) 拡大します(する, して)

scales *n* (weighing) hakarí 秤・はかり

scallion *n* asátsuki あさつき・アサツキ・浅葱

scallop(s) *n* hotaté-gai ほたて［帆立・ホタテ］貝; (*pin/razor/fan shell*) taira-gi たいらぎ

scalp *n* atama no kawa 頭の皮, [BOOKISH] tōhi 頭皮

scalpel *n* (geka-yō) mesu (外科用) メス

scamper *v* awatete hashirimásu (hashiru, hashitte) 慌てて走ります（走る, 走って）, isoide hashirimásu (hashiru, hashitte) 急いで走ります（走る, 走って）

scan *v* sukyan shimásu (suru, shite) スキャンします（する, して）

scandal *n* sukyándaru スキャンダル, [BOOKISH] fushōji 不祥事; (*disgrace*) ojoku 汚辱

Scandinavia *n* Sukanjinabia スカンジナビア; *Scandinavia peninsula* Sukanjinabia hantō スカンジナビア半島

scanner *n* sukyanā スキャナー

scant, scanty *adj* toboshii 乏しい・とぼしい

scapegoat *n* sukēpugōto スケープゴート; migawari 身代わり → **sacrifice**

scar *n* kizu-ato 傷跡

scarce *adj* sukunái 少ない・すくない, toboshii 乏しい・とぼしい

scarcely *adv* hotóndo 殆ど・ほとんど + [NEGATIVE]

scarcity *n* (*shortage*) fusoku 不足; (… ga) sukunái kotó (…が)少ない事・すくないこと

scare *v* odorokashimásu (odorokásu, odoroká-shite) 驚かします・おどろかします（驚かす, 驚かして）; bikkuri sasemásu (saseru, sasete) びっくりさせます・吃驚させます（させる, させて）; harahara sasemásu (saseru, sasete) はらはらさせます（させる, させて）

scarecrow *n* kakashi カカシ・案山子

scared *adj* obieta おびえた・怯えた

scarf *n* sukā´fu スカーフ

scarlet *n, adj* sukāretto (no) スカーレット(の), hiiro 緋色(の)

scarlet eggplant *n* kazarinasu カザリナス

scarlet fever *n* shōkō netsu 猩紅熱・しょうこうねつ

scarlet letter *n* hi moji 緋文字

scatter *v* chira(ka)shimásu (chira(ka)su, chira(ka)shite) 散ら（か）します（散ら（か）す, 散ら（か）して）; barabara ni narimásu (naru, natte) ばらばらになります（なる, なって）

scatterbrain *n* awate-mono 慌て者・あわてもの

scenario *n* shinario シナリオ; kyakuhon 脚本 **scenario writer** *n* shinario raitā シナリオライター; kyakuhon-ka 脚本家

scene *n* (*story, play*) shíin シーン; dán 段; bamen 場面; (*sight*) arisama 有り様・ありさま

scenery *n* késhiki 景色, fū´kei 風景, (*view*) nagamé 眺め・ながめ

scent *n* kaori 香り・かおり, hōkō 芳香

schedule 1. *n* (*plan*) yotei 予定, sukejūru スケジュール **2.** *n* (*time-table*) yotei-hyō 予定表, sukejūru-hyō スケジュール表, jikan-hyō 時間表 **3.** *n* (*daily routine*) nittei 日程 **4.** *n* (*train*) daiya ダイヤ; (*train time-table*) jikoku-hyō 時刻表; (*list*) hyō 表 **5.** *v* yotei shimásu (suru, shite) 予定します（する, して）, sukejūru o tatemásu (tateru, tatete) スケジュールを立てます（立てる, 立てて）, keikaku shimásu (suru, shite) 計画します（する, して）

scheduled *adj* (*periodic*) téiki (no) 定期(の)

scheme 1. *n* (*plan*) keikaku 計画; (*device*) kufū 工夫; (*plot, trick*) keiryaku 計略, hakarigoto はかりごと・謀 **2.** *v* (*plot, plan*) ... no keikaku o tatemásu (tateru, tatete) ...の計画を立てます（立てる, 立てて）

schizophrenia *n* (*medical*) tōgōshitchōshō 統合失調症

scholar *n* gakusha 学者; *scholarly society* gakkai 学会

scholarship *n* shōgaku-kin 奨学金; sukarashippu スカラシップ

school *n* (*educational establishment*) gakkō 学校; sukūru スクール; *primary school* shōgákkō 小学校, *middle* (*junior high*) *school* chūgákkō 中学校; *high school* kōtō-gákkō 高等学校, kōkō 高校; *tutoring/cram school* júku 塾; *in school* zaigaku (-chū) 在学(中)

boys' school *n* danshikō 男子校

coed school *n* kyōgaku 共学

cooking school *n* ryōri gakkō 料理学校; kukkingu sukūru クッキングスクール

driving school *n* (jidōsha) kyōshūjo (自動車) 教習所; (jidōsha) kyōshū gakkō (自動車) 教習学校

girls' school *n* joshikō 女子校

school activity *n* kōnai katsudō 校内活動

school age *n* gakurei (ki) 学齢(期); shūgaku nenrei 就学年齢

school bag *n* randoseru ランドセル; tsūgaku kaban 通学かばん

schoolboy *n* danshi seito 男子生徒

school committee *n* kyōiku iinkai 教育委員会

school committee for discipline *n* fūki iinkai 風紀委員会

school festival *n* gakuen-sai 学園祭

school flag *n* kōki 校旗

schoolgirl *n* jo(shi) seito 女(子)生徒

school grounds, school field *n* kōtei 校庭

school hours *n* jugyō-jíkan 授業時間

school-house *n* kōsha 校舎

school teacher *n* gakkō no senséi 学校の先生

school textbook *n* (gakkō no) kyōkasho (学校の)教科書

school uniform *n* gakuséi-fuku 学生服, seifuku 制服

school year *n* gakunen 学年

schoolchild *n* gakudō 学童

schooling *n* (gakkō) kyōiku (学校)教育

schoolroom *n* kyōshitsu 教室

schoolmaster *n* sensei 先生, kyōshi 教師

schoolmate *n* gakuyū 学友

science *n* kágaku 科学, sáiensu サイエンス, (*study*) gaku 学, ríka 理科

science fiction n esu-efu SF (エス・エフ), saiensu fikushon サイエンス・フィクション
scientific adj kagaku-teki (na) 科学的(な)
scientist n kagákusha 科学者, saientisuto サイエンティスト
scissors n hasamí はさみ・鋏 (*how many pairs* nán-chō 何丁)
scold v shikarimásu (shikaru, shikatte) しかり[叱り]ます(しかる, しかって)
scolding n kogoto 小言・こごと (o-kógoto お小言), o-shikari おしかり[叱り]; (*abuse*) warú-kuchi/-guchi 悪口
scone n sukōn スコーン
scoop 1. n sukoppu スコップ; [BOOKISH] hishaku ひしゃく・柄杓, (*one scoopful*) hitó-mori 一盛り・ひともり **2.** v (*scoops it up*) kumimásu (kumu, kunde) くみ[汲み]ます(くむ, くんで), sukuimásu (sukū, sukutte) すくいます・掬います(すくう, すくって)
scooter n sukūtā スクーター
scope n hán'i 範囲
scorch v **1.** (*scorches it*) kogashimásu (kogásu, kogáshite) 焦がします(焦がす, 焦がして) **2.** (*it gets scorched*) kogemásu (kogéru, kógete) 焦げます(焦げる, 焦げて)
score 1. n sukoa スコア, (*game*) tokuten 得点; (*score points*) tensū 点数; (*musical score*) gakufu 楽譜 **2.** v (*makes a score*) ten o torimásu (tóru, tótte) 点を取ります・点をとります(取る, 取って)
scoreboard n sukoa bōdo スコア・ボード, tokuten keiji-ban 得点掲示板
Scorpio n (*star sign*) Sasori-za さそり座
scorpion n sasori サソリ
scotch n (*whisky*) sukotchi スコッチ
scotch tape n serohan tēpu セロハンテープ, serotēpu セロテープ
Scotland n sukottorando スコットランド
scoundrel n akutō 悪党
scramble v **1.** (*mixes*) kakimazemásu (kaki-mazeru, kakimazete) かき混ぜます・掻き混ぜます(かき混ぜる, かき混ぜて) **2.** (*climbs*) hainoborimásu (hainoboru, hainobotte) 這い登ります・はいのぼります(はいのぼる, はいのぼって) **3.** (*fights*) ubaiaimásu (ubaiau, ubaiatte) 奪い合います・奪いあいます(奪いあう, 奪いあって)
scrambled eggs n iri-támago いり卵・炒り卵, sukuranburu-éggu スクランブルエッグ
scrap 1. n kúzu くず・屑, danpen 断片, kuzu-mono くず物・屑物; (*refuse*) sukurappu スクラップ **2.** v sukurappu ni shimásu (suru, shite) スクラップにします(する, して)
scrap book n sukurappu bukku スクラップブック
scrape v kosurimásu (kosúru, kosútté) こすります・擦ります(こする, こすって)
scratch 1. v (*scratches it*) hikkakimásu (káku, káite) (ひっ)かきます(かく, かいて) **2.** n (*a scratch*) hikkaki-kizu 引っかき傷・ひっかき傷

scrawl 1. n hashiri-gaki 走り書き, *naguri-gaki* 殴り書き・なぐり書き **2.** v hashirigaki shimásu (suru, shite) 走り書きします(する, して), nagurigaki shimásu (suru, shite) 殴り書きします・なぐり書きします(する, して)
scrawny adj yase(koke)teiru 痩せ(こけ)ている・やせ(こけ)ている, yaseta 痩せた・やせた
scream 1. v himei o agemásu (ageru, agete) 悲鳴を上げます・悲鳴をあげます(上げる, 上げて), sakebimásu (sakébu, sakénde) 叫びます・さけびます(叫ぶ, 叫んで), (*feminine*) kyā(t)to sakebimásu (sakébu, sakénde) きゃー(っ)[キャー(ッ)]と叫びます[さけびます](叫ぶ, 叫んで) **2.** n himei 悲鳴・ひめい
screen 1. n (*folding*) byōbu びょうぶ・屏風 **2.** n (*TV, computer*) gamen 画面 **3.** n (*movie*) sukuríin スクリーン **4.** v (*examine*) kensa shimásu (suru, shite) 検査します(する, して) **5.** v (*movie*) ... o jōē shimásu (suru, shite) ...を上映します(する, して)
screen door n amí-do 網戸・あみど → **window screen**
screenplay n (*scenario*) kyakuhon 脚本, shinario シナリオ
screw 1. n néji ねじ・ネジ **2.** v (*tighten*) (kataku) shimemásu (shimeru, shimete) (堅く)締めます(締める, 締めて)
screw up v dainashi ni shimásu (suru, shite) 台無しにします(する, して), [INFORMAL] mechamecha ni shimásu (suru, shite) めちゃめちゃにします(する, して)
screwdriver n neji-máwashi ねじ回し・ネジまわし
scribble n hashirigaki 走り書き, nagurigaki 殴り書き
scribbling n rakugaki 落書き・らくがき
script n kyakuhon 脚本, daihon 台本
scroll n maki-mono 巻(き)物・まきもの; (*hanging*) kaké-mono 掛け物, kakéjiku 掛軸, kakéji 掛け字
scrubbing brush n tawashi たわし・タワシ
scrum n sukuramu スクラム
scuba n sukyūba スキューバ
scuba diving n sukyūba daibingu スキューバダイビング
sculptor n chōkoku-ka 彫刻家
sculpture n chōkoku 彫刻
scuffle n tsukamiai 掴み合い・つかみあい, tokkumiai 取っ組み合い・とっくみあい
scurry v (*goes in haste*) awatete ikimásu (iku, itte) 慌てて行きます・あわてていきます(いく, いって), (*goes quickly*) isoide ikimásu (iku, itte) 急いで行きます・いそいでいきます(いく, いって)
sea n úmi 海・うみ, ...-kai ...海; *high sea* taikai (daikai) 大海; *Inland Sea* Seto-náikai 瀬戸内海, *Sea of Japan* Nihon-kai 日本海
sea bass n suzuki すずき・スズキ・鱸
sea bathing n kaisuiyoku 海水浴
sea bream n tái たい・タイ・鯛

sea calf *n* azarashi アザラシ

sea captain *n* senchō 船長

sea chart *n* kaizu 海図

seadiver *n* (*woman seadiver*) áma 海女・アマ

seafood *n* shiifūdo シーフード, gyokairui 魚介類・魚貝類

seagull *n* kamome かもめ・カモメ・鴎

sea horse *n* tatsu no otoshigo タツノオトシゴ・竜の落(と)し子

sea lion *n* ashika アシカ

sea level *n* kaibatsu 海抜

seamail *n* funabin 船便

seaman *n* súifu 水夫; (*navy*) súihei 水兵

seashell *n* kaigara カイガラ・貝殻

seashore *n* kaigan 海岸

seasick; *gets* ~ (fúne ni) yoimásu (yóu, yótte) (船に)酔います(酔う, 酔って)

seasickness *n* funayoi 船酔い

seaside *n* umibe 海辺

sea urchin *n* úni うに・ウニ・海胆

seawater *n* kaisui 海水

seaweed *n* kaisō 海藻・カイソウ; (*green*) norí のり・ノリ・海苔; wakáme わかめ・ワカメ・若布; (*kelp*) kónbu 昆布・コンブ

seaweed-gelatin strips *n* tokoroten ところてん・トコロテン

seaweed-rolled sushi *n* norí-maki のり巻き; (*with cucumber*) kappa-maki かっぱ巻き; (*with tuna*) tekka-maki 鉄火巻き

seal **1.** *n* (*for stamping one's name*) hán(kó) はん(こ)・判(子), ín ín 印 **2.** *n* (*animal*) azárashi あざらし・アザラシ・海豹. ottosei オットセイ **3.** *v* (*seals a letter*) (tegami no) fū´ o shimásu (suru, shite) (手紙の)封をします(する, して), mippū shimásu (suru, shite) 密封します(する, して), fusagimásu (fusagu, fusaide) ふさぎます(ふさぐ, ふさいで)

seam *n* nui-mé 縫い目・ぬいめ, tsugi-me 接ぎ目・つぎめ

seamless *adj* nui-me no nai 縫い目のない, tsugi-me no nai 接ぎ目のない, tsunagi-me no nai つなぎ目のない, shiimuresu (no) シームレス(の)

seamy *adj* **1.** uramen (no) 裏面(の) **2.** (*unpleasant*) fukai (na) 不快(な)

sear *n* yakekoge 焼け焦げ

search **1.** *n* sōsaku 捜索 **2.** *n* (*internet*) kensaku 検索 **3.** *v* - *for* (*seeks*) ... o sagashinású (sagasu, sagashite) ...を探し[捜し]ます・...をさがします(探[捜]す, 探[捜]して); *a* ~ *for a criminal* téhái 手配

searching for a criminal *n* hannin-sagashi 犯人捜し

searching for a missing person/thing *n* sōsaku 捜索

searching for one's lost child *n* maigo-sagashi 迷子捜し

search party *n* sōsaku-tai 捜索隊

search warrant *n* sōsaku (rei-) jō 捜索(令)状, sashiosae 差(し)押さえ

search window *n* kensaku uindou 検索ウインドウ

searchlight *n* sāchi raito サーチライト, [BOOKISH] tanshōtō 探照灯

season **1.** *n* kisétsu 季節; shízun シーズン; jíki 時季; jísetsu 時節 **2.** *v* (*flavors it*) ... ni aji o tsukemásu ... (tsukéru, tsukéte) ...に味を付けます(付ける, 付けて)

four seasons *n* shiki 四季

off-season *n* shiizun ofu シーズンオフ

season for traveling *n* ryokō shiizun 旅行シーズン

season ticket *n* teikí-ken 定期券

seasoning *n* (*food*) chō´mi 調味, aji 味・あじ; kagen 加減・かげん

seat *n* seki 席, (o-séki お席), zaseki 座席, shiito シート, koshi-káké 腰掛け; (*bottom, butt*) shiri 尻 (o-shiri お尻); (*taking a seat*) chakuseki 着席; *takes a* ~ chakuseki shimásu (suru, shite) 着席します(する, して); *Are there seats (available)?* Suwaremásu ka? 座れますか・すわれますか?

seat belt *n* zaseki-béruto 座席ベルト; siíto-béruto シートベルト

seat number *n* zaseki-bángō 座席番号

secluded *adj* hotozato-hanareta 人里離れた, kakurisareta 隔離された

seclusion *n* kakuri 隔離

second **1.** *adj* ni-banmé (no) 二番目(の), futatsu-mé (no) 二つ目の; *the second day* futsuka-mé (no) 二日目, (*of the month*) futsuka 二日 **2.** *n* (*of a minute*) -byō 秒; *one second* ichí-byō 一秒

second class *adj* ni-tō 二等; *second class seat* nitō´-seki 二等席; *second class ticket* nitō´ (seki)-ken 二等(席)券

second floor *n* ni-kai 二階 (o-níkai お二階)

second generation *n* ní-sei 二世

second helping *n* o-káwari お代わり・おかわり

second opinion *n* sekando opinion セカンド・オピニオン, hoka no ishi no iken 他の医師の意見, betsu no ishi no shindan 別の医師の診断

second time *n* nido-mé 二度目, nikai-mé 二回目

secondary school *n* chūtō kōtō gakkō 中等高等学校

secondhand **1.** *adj* chūko/chūburu (no) 中古(の), furúi 古い **2.** *n* (*goods*) chūko-hin 中古品

secondhand book *n* huruhon 古本

secondhand car *n* chūko-sha 中古車

secondhand shop, secondhand store *n* risaikuru shoppu リサイクル・ショップ

secondment *n* haichigae 配置換え, haken 派遣

secrecy *n* himitsu 秘密, [BOOKISH] kimitsu 機密

secrecy agreement *n* shuhi gimu keiyaku 守秘義務契約

secret **1.** *n* himitsu 秘密, shiikuretto シークレット **2.** *n the secret* (*trick to it*) táne 種 **3.** *adj* (*confidential*) naisho (no) 内緒(の)

secret agent *n* himitsu kōsaku-in 秘密工作員

secretariat *n* jimu-kyoku 事務局

secretary *n* shóki 書記; (*private*) hishó 秘書

secretary of foreign affairs *n* gaimu chōkan 外務長官

secretion *n* bunpi 分泌

secretly *adv* kossori (to) こっそり（と）; himitsu (ni/de) 秘密（に/で）

sect *n* shūha 宗派, ha 派, habatsu 派閥

section *n* bú bó 部; ká shon sekushon セクション, …-ka …課; (*area*) chíkú 地区

section manager *n* ka-chō 課長

sector *n* (*area*) chíkú 地区; sekutā セクター

secure *adj* 1. *is ~* chanto shite imásu (iru, ite) ちゃんとしています（いる、いて） 2. *feels ~* anshin shimásu (suru, shite) 安心します（する、して） 3. → get

securely *adv* chanto ちゃんと; (*firmly*) shikkári しっかり

security *n* (*stock*, *bond*) shōken 証券; (*secure feeling*) anshin 安心

security deposit *n* (*for rental*) shikí-kin 敷金

sedan *n* sedan セダン

sedate *adj* ochitsuita 落ち着いた

sedation *n* chinsei 鎮静; chinsei sayō 鎮痛作用

sedative *n* chinsei-zai 鎮静剤; chintsū-zai 鎮痛剤

sedentary *adj* suwarigachi (no/na) 座りがち（の/な）

sediment *n* kásu かす・滓; ori おり・澱; chinden-butsu 沈殿物

sedition *n* sendō 扇動・せんどう

seduce *v* tarashi-komimásu (tarashi-komu, tarashi-konde) たらし込みます（たらし込む、たらし込んで）, yūwaku shimásu (suru, shite) 誘惑します（する、して）

seducer *n* yūwakusha 誘惑者, (*men*) onna-tárashi 女たらし

seduction *n* yūwaku 誘惑

seductress *n* yūwakusha 誘惑者, (*women*) otoko-tárashi 男たらし

see *v* mimásu (míru, míte) 見ます（見る、見て）, [HONORIFIC] goran ni narimásu (náru, nátte) ご覧になります（なる、なって）; [HUMBLE] haiken shimásu (suru, shite) 拝見します（する、して） 2. (*meets a person*) … ni aimásu (áu, átte) …に会います（会う、会って）; [HUMBLE] o-me ni kakarimásu (kakáru, kakátte) お目にかかります（かかる、かかって） 3. (*understands*) wakarimásu (wakáru, wakátte) 分かります（分かる、分かって）; *I see!* Naru-hodo! なるほど 4. *see one off* (mi-) okurimásu (okuru, okutte) (見)送ります（送る、送って）

seed *n* táne 種・タネ

seedling *n* náe 苗・ナエ

seedy *adj* 1. tane ga ōi 種が多い 2. misuborashiii みすぼらしい

seeing-eye dog *n* mōdō-ken 盲導犬・盲どう犬

seek *v* 1. busshoku shimásu (suru, shite) 物色します（する、して） → search (for) 2. → aim at

seem *v* (*like*) … to miemásu (miéru, míete) …と見えます（見える、見えて）, … (no) yō´desu …（の）よう［様］です, … rashíi desu …らしいです

seemingly *adv* (*outwardly*) mikake wa 見かけは・見掛けは, mikake-jō 見かけ上・見掛け上

seemly *adj* fusawashii ふさわしい, jōhin (na) 上品（な）

seep *v* shintō shimásu (suru, shite) 浸透します・しんとうします（する、して）, shimidemásu (shimideru, shimidete) 染み出ます・しみでます（しみでる、しみでて）, moremásu (moreru, morete) 漏れます・もれます（もれる、もれて）

seer *n* yogen-sha 預言者・予言者

seesaw *n* shiisō シーソー

see-through *adj* (*garment*) shiisurū no (fuku) シースルーの(服)

segment *n* bubun 部分; segumento セグメント

segregate *v* bunri shimásu (suru, shite) 分離します・ぶんりします（する、して）, hanashimasu (hanasu, hanashite) 離します（離す、離して）

seize *v* tsukamimásu (tsukámu, tsukánde) つかみます・掴みます（つかむ、つかんで）, toraemásu (toráeru, toráete) 捕らえます（捕らえる、捕らえて）, tsukamaemásu (tsukamaeru, tsukamaete) 捕まえ［つかまえ］ます（捕まえる、捕まえて）; (*plunders*) ubaimásu (ubáu, ubátte) 奪います・うばいます（奪う、奪って）; (*illegally takes over*) nottorimásu (nottóru, nottótte) 乗っ取ります・乗っとります（乗っ取る、乗っ取って）

seizure *n* 1. (*illegal takeover*) nottorijíken 乗っ取り事件・乗っとり事件 2. (*medical*) hossa 発作

seldom *adv* métta ni めった [滅多]に + [NEGATIVE], hotóndo 殆ど・ほとんど + [NEGATIVE]; (*infrequently*) tama ni たまに

select → **choose**; **selection** → **choice**

selection *n* sentaku 選択; serekushon セレクション

selective buying (*of stocks*, …) busshoku-gai 物色買い

self *n* jibun 自分; ji-… 自…; onore 己; jíko 自己; hon-nin 本人

self-abandonment *n* sute-bachi 捨て鉢; jibō-jiki 自暴自棄

self-analysis *n* jiko bunseki 自己分析, deshabari 出しゃばり・でしゃばり

self-assertion *n* jiko shuchō 自己主張

self-centered *adj* jiko chūshin-teki (na) 自己中心的（な）

self-confidence *n* jishin 自信

self-conscious; *feels ~* agarimásu (agaru, agatte) 上がり［あがり］ます（上がる、上がって）

self-defense *n* jiei 自衛, jiko bōei 自己防衛; (*weaponless*) ~ *art* goshin-hō 護身法 (*also* jū´dō 柔道, karate 空手, aikídō 合気道)

Self-Defense Forces *n* Jiei-tai 自衛隊

self-disgust, self-hatred *n* jiko ken'o 自己嫌悪

self-discipline *n* [BOOKISH] jiko tanren 自己鍛錬

self-employed *adj* jiei (no) 自営（の）, jieigyō (no) 自営業（の）

self-esteem *n* jisonshin 自尊心

self-evident fact *n* jimei no jijitsu 自明の事実

self-pity *n* [BOOKISH] jiko renbin 自己憐憫

self-portrait *n* jiga zō 自画像

self-interested *n* jiko hon'i (no) 自己本位(の)

self-respect *n* [BOOKISH] jison-shin 自尊心

self-satisfaction *n* jiko manzoku 自己満足

self-service *adj* serufu sābisu (no) セルフサービス(の)

self-sufficiency *n* jikyū jisoku 自給自足

self-taught *adj* dokugaku (no) 独学(の)

selfish *adj* katte (na) 勝手(な), jibun-kátte/-gátte (na) 自分勝手(な), waga-mámá (na) わがまま・我が侭(な)

sell *v* **1.** *sells it* urimásu (uru, utte) 売ります(売る, 売って) **2.** *it sells* (*well*) (yóku) uremásu (ureru, urete) (良く)売れます(売れる, 売れて); hakemásu (hakéru, hákete) はけます(はける, はけて)

sell out *v* uri-kiremásu (uri-kiréru, uri-kírete) 売り切れます(売り切れる, 売り切れて)

sellout *n* uri-kire 売り切れ

sell retail *v* ko-uri shimásu (suru, shite) 小売りします(する, して)

sell wholesale *v* oroshi-uri shimásu (suru, shite) 卸売りします(する, して)

seller *n* uri-te 売り手; uri-nushi 売り主; (*dealer*) hanbai-nin 販売人

semen *n* sei eki 精液; *semen test* sei eki kensa 精液検査

semester *n* gakki 学期

end of semester *n* gakki-matsu 学期末

semester final examination *n* kimatsu shiken 期末試験

semicircle *n* hanshū 半周

semicolon *n* semikoron セミコロン

semifinal *n* jun-kesshō 準決勝

seminar *n* zémi ゼミ, zemináˊru ゼミナール, seminā セミナー, kōshūkai 講習会

seminary *n* shingakkō 神学校

senate *n* jōin 上院

senator *n* jōin giin 上院議員

send *v* okurimásu (okuru, okutte) 送ります(送る, 送って), yarimásu (yaru, yatte) やります(やる, やって), yosemasu (yoseru, yosete) 寄せます(寄せる, 寄せて); (*a telegram*) uchimásu (útsu, útte) 打ちます(打つ, 打って); (*a person*) ikasemásu (ikaseru, ikasete) 行かせます(行かせる, 行かせて)

send here yokoshimásu (yokósu, yokóshite) よこします(よこす, よこして)

sender *n* **1.** (*mail, etc.*) hassōnin 発送人, okurinushi 送り主 **2.** (*mail, e-mail, etc.*) sashidashinin 差出人, sōshin-sha 送信者

send-off *n* (*farewell*) sōbetsu 送別, *send-off party* sōbétsú-kai 送別会

senior *adj* (*older*) toshi-ue (no) 年上(の); (*colleague, fellow student*) senpai 先輩; (*4th-year student*) yonén-sei 四年生; *senior essay* gakushi-rónbun 学士論文

senior citizen *n* toshiyóri 年寄り (o-toshiyori お年寄り), rōjin 老人, kōrei-sha 高齢者, kōrei no hito 高齢の人

senior high school *n* kōtō-gákkō 高等学校, kō-kō 高校; *senior high school student* kōkōˊ-sei 高校生

sensation *n* (*feeling*) kimochi 気持ち・気持, kimí 気味; (*sense*) kankaku 感覚; (*excitement*) senséˊshon センセーション

sensational *adj* senséˊshonaru (na) センセーショナル(な), [BOOKISH] senjōteki (*na*) 扇情的(な)

sense *n* sénsu センス; *common sense* jōshiki 常識; *sense of honor* taimen 体面, [BOOKISH] renchí-shin 廉恥心; *sense of obligation* girí 義理(o-giri お義理) → **feel(ing)** → **meaning** → **significance** → **reason** → **consciousness**

sense of humor *n* yūmoa no sensu ユーモアのセンス

senses; *come to one's* ~ (*recovers consciousness*) ki ga tsukimásu (tsúku, tsúite) 気が付きます(付く, 付いて), me ga samemásu (saméru, sámete) 目が覚めます(覚める, 覚めて)

sensibility *n* kankaku 感覚

sensible *adj* gōri-teki (na) 合理的(な), atarimae (no) 当り前(の); *what is* ~ dōri 道理

sensitive *adj* **1.** binkan (na) 敏感(な) **2.** (*easily pained*) kizutsukiyasui 傷つきやすい, sensai (na) 繊細(な), derikēto (na) デリケート(な) **3.** (*easily annoyed*) shinkei kabin (no) 神経過敏(の) **4.** (*requiring caution*) chūi ga hitsuyō na 注意が必要な, chūi o haraubeki 注意を払うべき, shinchō o kisu 慎重を期す

sensual *adj* kannō-teki (na) 官能的(な)

sentence *n* **1.** (*written*) bún(shō) 文(章); (*spoken*) kotó 事・こと, kotoba 言葉・ことば **2.** (*linguistic*) séntensu センテンス **3.** (*judicial verdict*) hanketsu 判決

sentiment *n* kanshō 感傷

sentimental *adj* senchiméntaru (na) センチメンタル(な); o-senchi (na) おせんち(な); kanshōteki na 感傷的(な)

sentry *n* mihari 見張り, hoshō 歩哨

Seoul *n* Sóuru ソウル

separate 1. *adj* (*different*) betsu (no) 別(の); barabara (ni) ばらばら(に) **2.** *v* (*separates them*) wakemásu (wakéru, wákete) 分けます(分ける, 分けて); (*gets them apart*) hedatemásu (hedatéru, hedátete) 隔てます・へだてます(隔てる, 隔てて) **3.** *v* (*they separate*) wakaremásu (wakaréru, wakárete) 分かれ[別れ]ます(分かれ[別れ]る, 分かれ[別れ]て); (*gets distant*) hanaremásu (hanaréru, hanárete) 離れます(離れる, 離れて) **4.** *v* ~ *it* (*from*) … o hanashimásu (hanásu, hanáshite) …を離します(離す, 離して)

separate bill *n* betsu-ryōˊkin 別料金

separated; *is* (*lives*) ~ *from* … to bekkyo shimásu (suru, shite) …と別居します(する, して)

separately *adv* wakárete 分かれて; hanárete 離れて; *quite* ~ *from* … tówa betsu ni (shite) …とは別に(して)

separation *n* bun-ri 分離; bekkyo 別居

sepsis *n* (*medical*) haikesshō 敗血症

September *n* Ku-gatsú 九月・9月
septic *adj* (*medical*) haiketsu-sei (no) 敗血性(の)
sequel *n* tsuzuki 続き・つづき, renzoku 連続
sequence *n* shiikuensu シークエンス, renzoku
連続, (*order*) júnjo 順序, zéngo 前後
in sequence *adv* jun (ni) 順(に), junban (ni) 順
番(に)
serenade *n* serenādo セレナード, sayo-kyoku
小夜曲
serene *adj* odayaka (na) 穏やか(な)・おだやか
(な), shizuka (na) 静か・しずか(な)
sergeant *n* 1. (*army*) gunsō 軍曹 2. (*police*) junsa
buchō 巡査部長
serial *n, adj* rensai (no) 連載(の), renzoku (no)
連続
serial killer *n* renzoku satsujin(-han) 連続殺人
(犯)
serial number *n* shiriaru nanbā シリアルナンバ
ー; tōshi bangō 通し番号
serial port *n* shiriaru pōto シリアルポート
serialize *v* rensai shimásu (suru, shite) 連載しま
す(する, して)
sericulture *n* yōsan 養蚕・ヨウサン
series *n* (hito-)tsuzuki (ひと)続き; renzoku 連続;
shiriizu シリーズ
drama series *n* renzoku dorama 連続ドラマ
TV series *n* renzoku terebi bangumi 連続テレビ
番組
serious *adj* (*character*) majime (na) まじめ[真
面目](な); *He's serious.* 彼は本気です。*I'm
serious.* honki desu. 本気です。, (*not joking*) jōdan
ja arimasén (nái) 冗談じゃありません(ない);
(*heavy, grave*) omoi 重い, jūdai (na) 重大(な),
shinkoku (na) 深刻(な); taihen (na) 大変(な), tái-
shita ... 大した...・たいした...; (*medical*) jūtoku
(na) 重篤(な)
seriously *adv* majime (ni) まじめ[真面目](に);
honki (de) 本気(で); hontō (ni) 本当(に); jōdan
de wa naku 冗談ではなく; (*INFORMAL*) maji (de)
まじ(で); *takes it ~* ... o honki ni shimásu (suru,
shite) ...を本気にします(する, して)
sermon *n* sekkyō 説教
serpent *n* 1. (*snake*) hebi 蛇・ヘビ 2. (*devil*)
akuma 悪魔・アクマ
serum *n* kessei 血清
servant *n* meshi-tsúkai 召し使い; shiyō-nin
使用人; yōmú-in 用務員, kózukai 小使い
serve *n* 1. (*games*) sābu サーブ 2. *v* (*a meal*)
dashimásu (dásu, dáshite) 出します(出す, 出し
て); *meals are served* shokuji ga demásu (déru,
déte) 食事が出ます(出る, 出て); *~ the rice wine,
pour the saké* (o-)shaku o shimásu (suru, shite)
(お)酌をします(する, して)
serve a purpose *v* yakúni tachimásu (tátsu, tátte)
役に立ちます(立つ, 立って), yaku-dachimásu
(yaku-dátsu, yaku-dátte) 役立ちます(役立つ, 役立
って)
serve the purpose *v* mokuteki ni kanaimásu

(kanáu, kanátte) 目的に適います・目的にかない
ます(かなう, かなって)
server *n* sābā サーバー
service *n* 1. (*in restaurant, etc.*) sā´bisu サービ
ス 2. (*maintenance and repair*) afutāsābisu アフター
サービス 3. (*utility*) yakú 役 4. (*armed forces*)
gúntai 軍隊 5. (*duty, work*) kínmu 勤務
6. (*games*) sābu サーブ
service area *n* sā´bisu eria サービスエリア
service charge *n* tesū´-ryō 手数料, sābisu-ryō サ
ービス料
service industry *n* sābisu sangyō サービス産業
serviceman, service personnel *n* 1. (*military*)
gunjin 軍人 2. → repairman
spirit of good service *n* sābisu seishin サービス
精神
service station → **gas station**
servicing *n* afutā-sā´bisu アフターサービス
... serving(s) ... -nínmae ...人前
serviette *n* (*shokutaku yō*) napukin (食卓用)ナ
プキン
servile *adj* iyashii いやしい・卑しい, hikutsu (na)
卑屈(な), dorei no yō (na) 奴隷のよう(な)
sesame *n* goma ごま・ゴマ・胡麻
session *n* 1. sesshon セッション 2. (*sitting of a
court*) kaitei 開廷 3. (*assembly*) kai 会, kaigō
会合 4. (*meeting, conference*) kaigi 会議
set 1. *n* (*collection*) kumí 組, hitó-kumi 一組;
(*array*) soroi 揃い・そろい; *makes (up) a set*
soroimásu (soróu, sorótte) 揃い[そろい]ます
(揃う, 揃って), *makes into a set* soroemásu
(soroéru, soróete) 揃え[そろえ]ます(揃える,
揃えて) 2. *n* (*hair*) sétto セット 3. *v sets it* (*puts
it there*) okimásu (oku, oite) 置きます(置く,
置いて) 4. → **sit** → **settle** → **decide**
set aside *v* atemásu (ateru, atete) 当てます・あ
てます(当てる, 当てて)
set free *v* hanashimásu (hanásu, hanáshite) 放し
ます(放す, 放して)
set off/out *v* (*departs*) dekakemásu (dekakeru,
dekakete) 出かけます(出かける, 出かけて)
set up *v* tatemásu (tatéru, tátete) 立てます
(立てる, 立てて); (*provides*) mōkemásu (mōkéru,
mō´kete) 設けます(設ける, 設けて); (*assembles*)
kumi-tatemásu (kumi-tateru, kumi-tatete) 組み立
てます(組み立てる, 組み立てて)
set back *n* zasetsu 挫折・ざせつ
set meal *n* teishoku 定食; *set series of chef's
choices* kō´su (ryōri) コース(料理)
set price *n* teika 定価
setting *n* settingu セッティング, settei 設定
settle *v* (*decides it*) kimemásu (kimeru, kimete)
決めます(決める, 決めて), (*fixes*) sadamemásu
(sadaméru, sadámete) 定めます(定める, 定めて);
(*completes*) matomemásu (matomeru, matomete)
まとめます(まとめる, まとめて); (*disposes of*)
shímatsu shimásu (suru, shite) 始末します(する,
して); (*solves, resolves*) kaiketsu shimásu (suru,
shite) 解決します(する, して); (*gets relaxed/

calm) ochitsukimásu (ochi-tsuku, ochitsuite) 落ち着きます(落ち着く、落ち着いて); ~ *down/in* osamarimásu (osamáru, osamátte) 収[治・納]ま ります・おさまります(収[治・納]まる、収[治・納]まって)

settled *adj* 1. ittei (no) 一定(の) 2. *gets* ~ kimarimásu (kimaru, kimatte) 決まります(決まる、決まって), sadamarimásu (sadamáru, sadamátte) 定まります(定まる、定まって); matomarimásu (matomaru, matomatte) まとまります(まとまる、まとまって)

settlement *n* kimari 決まり; (*solution*) kaiketsu 解決

settling accounts *n* késsan 決算

setup *n* 1. (*organization*) soshiki 組織 2. (*arrangement*) settoappu セットアップ, junbi 準備, settei 設定

seven *n* nána 七・7, shichí 七・7, nanátsu 七つ・ 7 つ; sébun セブン

seven; *seven days* nanoka 七日・7日; *7 pieces* (*small things*) naná-ko 七個, *7 trees* (*or long things*) nanáhon 七本; *7 sheets* (*flat things*) nanámai 七枚, *7 cats* (*or small animals*) naná-hiki 七 匹, *7 cows* (*or large aminals*) naná-tō 七頭; *7 birds/rabbits* naná-wa 七羽, *7 cars* (*or machines/vehicles*) naná-dai 七台, *7 copies* (*books/magazines*) naná-satsu 七冊; *7 floors/stories* nanákai 七階; *7 people* naná-nin 七人, naná-mei 七名; *7 fold* nana-bai 七倍, *7 degrees* naná-do 七度; *7 times* naná-dó 七度, naná-kái 七回, naná-hén 七遍; *7 o'clock* shichí-ji/naná-ji 七時; *7 hours* shichí-jíkan/naná-jíkan 七時間; *7 weeks* naná-shūkan 七週間; *7 months* naná-ká-getsu 七ヶ月; *7 years* shichí-nen/naná-nen 七年, naná-nénkan 七年間; *7 years old* nanátsu 七つ, naná-sai 七歳

seven hundred *n* naná-hyaku 七百・700

seventeen *n* jū-nána 十七・17, jūshichi 十七・17

seventeen-syllable poem *n* (*Japanese traditional poem*) senryū 川柳

seventh *adj* nana-banmé (no) 七番目(の), nana-tsu-mé (no) 七つ目(の); *the 7th day* nanoka-mé 七日目・7日目, (*of the month*) nanoka 七日・7日; *7th floor* nana-kai 七階

seven thousand *n* nana-sén 七千・7,000

seventy *n* naná-jū 七十・70, shichi-jū´七十・70; *seventy thousand* nana-mán 七万・70,000

several *adj* futatsú-mi(t)tsu (no) 二つ三つ(の), ní-san (no) 二三(の), jakkan (no) 若干(の); íkutsu ka (no) いくつか(の); sū-… 数…(*several days* sū-jitsu 数日, *several people* sū-nin 数人, *several years* sū-nen 数年)

severally *adv* sorézóre それぞれ, onóono 各々・おのおの

severe *adj* kibishíi 厳しい・きびしい, kitsui きつい; (*terrible*) hidói ひどい・酷い; sibia シビア, (*medical*) jūdo (no) 重度(の)

sew *v* nuimásu (nū´, nútte) 縫います(縫う、縫って); ~ *together/up* tsuzurimásu (tsuzuru, tsuzutte) 綴ります・つづります(綴る、綴って)

sewage *n* gesui 下水, osui 汚水; *sewage treatment plant* gesui shori-jō 下水処理場

sewer *n* gesui-kan 下水管

sewing *n* saihō 裁縫

sewing machine *n* míshin ミシン (*how many* nán-dai 何台)

sewing needle *n* núibari 縫い針

sewing set *n* saihō-dōgu 裁縫道具

sex *n* sei 性, sékkusu セックス; (*the erotic*) iró 色, éro エロ; *has sex* sékkusu o shimásu (suru, shite) セックスをします(する、して), [VULGAR] yarimásu (yaru, yatte) やります(やる、やって)

sexual *adj* sei-teki (na) 性的(な); *make (a)* ~ *advance(s)* kudokimasu (kudoku, kudoite) 口説きます(口説く、口説いて)

sexual harassment *n* sekuhara セクハラ, sekusharu harasumento セクシャル・ハラスメント

shabby *adj* 1. (*worn*) tsukaifurushita 使い古した 2. (*wearing worn clothes*) boro (boro no fuku) o kita ぼろ(ぼろの服)を着た, boro (boro no fuku) o kiteiru ぼろ(ぼろの服)を着ている, (minari no) misuborashii 身なりのみすぼらしい 3. (*unworthy*) somatsu (na), o-somatsu (na) 粗末(な)・お粗末(な)

shack *n* hottate goya 掘っ立て小屋・ほったて小屋

shackle 1. *n* (*fetter*) sokubaku 束縛, ashi kase 足枷・足かせ, kōsoku dōgu 拘束道具 2. *v* soku-baku shimásu (suru, shite) 束縛します(する、して), kōsoku shimásu (suru, shite) 拘束します(する、して), ashikase o kakemásu (kakeru, kakete) 足枷・足かせをかけます(かける、かけて)

shad *n* kohada こはだ

shade *n* káge 陰・かげ; (*of trees*) kíno káge 木の陰, kokage 木陰・こかげ; *window shade* (mádo no) hiyoke (窓の)日よけ

shadow *n* káge 影・かげ, shadō シャドー, shadou シャドウ, (*from sunlight*) hi-kage 日影; (*of a person*) káge-bō´shi 影法師

shady *adj* (*questionable*) ayashii 怪しい, ikagawashii いかがわしい

shaft *n* shafuto シャフト, e 柄

shaggy 1. *adj* mojamoja (no) もじゃもじゃ(の), kemukujara (no) 毛むくじゃら(の) 2. *n* (*hairstyle*) shagii シャギー

shake 1. *v* (*shakes it*) furimásu (furu, futte) 振ります・ふります(振る、振って); yusaburimasu (yusaburu, yusabutte) 揺さぶります(揺さぶる、揺さぶって); ~ *hands* ákushu shimásu (suru, shite) 握手します(する、して); ~ *out* haraimásu (haráu, harátte) 払います(払う、払って) 2. *v* (*it shakes*) furuemásu (furueru, furuete) 震えます(震える、震えて), (*sways*) yuremásu (yureru, yurete) 揺れます・ゆれます(揺れる、揺れて) 3. *n* (*milkshake*) (miruku-)sē´ki (ミルク)セーキ; sheiku シェイク

shall 1. *Shall I/we do it?* Shimashō´ka. しましょうか. 2. → **will**

shallow *adj* asai 浅い・あさい; *shallows* n asase 浅瀬

sham *adj* mise-kake (no) 見せかけ・みせかけ(の)

shamble *n* yoromeita aruki よろめいた歩き

shame *n* hazukashíi (kotó) 恥ずかしい・はずかしい(事・こと), hají 恥・はじ; (*scandal*) ojoku 汚辱 *That's a shame.* Sore wa ikemasén ne. それはいけませんね.

shameful *adj* nasake-nái 情けない; hazukashíi 恥ずかしい・はずかしい; mittomo-nai みっともない

shameless *adj* zūzūshíi ずうずうしい・図々しい

shampoo 1. *n* shámpū シャンプー 2. *v* kami o araimásu (araru, aratte) 髪を洗います(洗う, 洗って)

Shanghai *n* Shánhái シャンハイ・上海

shape *n* katachi 形, katá 型; (*figure*) súgata 姿, kakkō かっこう・格好・恰好; (*condition*) guai 具合

shapely *adj* kakkoíi かっこいい・カッコいい格好いい・恰好いい

shape-up *n* sheipu appu シェイプアップ

share 1. *n* (*portion*) toribún 取り分, wake-mae 分け前・わけまえ; (*allotment*) buntan 分担; *one's ~ wari-ate* 割り当て 2. *v* **divide → Dutch** 3. *v* shares in, pays/does one's share buntan shimásu (suru, shite) 分担します(する, して)

shark *n* same さめ・サメ・鮫, fuka ふか・フカ・鱶, shāku シャーク

sharp *adj* surudói 鋭い・するどい, shāpu シャープ(な); (*clever*) rikō (na) 利口(な); *gets ~* (*pointed*) togarimásu (togáru, togátte) 尖り[とがり]ます(尖る, 尖って)

sharpen *v* (*pencil*) kezurimásu (kezuru, kezutte) 削ります(削る, 削って), togarashimásu (togarásu, togaráshite) 尖らし[とがらし]ます(尖らす, 尖らして); (*blade*) togimásu (tógu, tóide) 研ぎます(研ぐ, 研いで)

shave *v* hige o sorimásu (sóru, sótte) ひげを剃ります(剃る, 剃って)

shaver *n* (*electric*) denki-kámisori 電気かみそり

shaving cream *n* higesori-yō kuríimu ひげ剃り用クリーム

shawl *n* shōru ショール

she *pron* káno-jo 彼女, anó-hito あの人, anó-ko あの子 (*but use name, title, or role; often omitted*)

she-... (*animal*) ... no mesú ...の雌

sheaf *n* taba 束・たば

shear *n* ōbasami 大鋏・大ばさみ・オオバサミ

sheath *n* sáya さや・鞘

shed *n* naya 納屋; (*storehouse*) mono-óki 物置; (*hut*) koya 小屋

sheep *n* hitsuji 羊・ヒツジ

sheet *n* (*of paper, glass, etc.*) (ichí)-mai (一)枚; (*bed ~*) (beddo) shíitsu (ベッド)シーツ, shikifu 敷布

sheet of paper *n* ichimai no kami 一枚の紙

shelf *n* tana 棚; *enclosed shelves* to-dana 戸棚

book shelf *n* hon-dana 本棚, sho-dana 書棚

shell *n* kara 殻・カラ; (*of shellfish*) kái 貝・カイ, kai-gara 貝殻・カイガラ; (*of tortoise etc.*) kōra 甲羅・コウラ; *eggshell* tamago no kara 卵[玉子]の殻; *bombshell* hōdan 砲弾

shellfish *n* kái 貝, ...-gai ...貝, kōkaku-rui 甲殻類

shelter *n* sherutā シェルター, hinanjo 避難所

shepherd *n* hitsujikai 羊飼い

sherbet *n* shābetto シャーベット

sheriff *n* hoankan 保安官

sherry *n* sherii-shu シェリー酒

Shiba *n* Shíba 芝; *Shiba Park* Shiba-Kō'en 芝公園

Shibuya *n* Shibuya 渋谷; *Shibuya Station* Shibuyá-Eki 渋谷駅

shield 1. *n* táte 盾・たて, shiirudo シールド 2. *v* (*protects*) hógo shimásu (suru, shite) 保護します(する, して); (*covers*) ōimásu 覆い[おおい]ます(ōu, oou 覆う・おおう, ōtte 覆って・おおって)

shift 1. *v* (*it shifts*) utsurimásu (utsúru, utsútte) 移ります(移る, 移って) 2. *v* (*shifts/changes it*) ten-jimásu (ten-jiru, ten-jite) 転じます(転じる, 転じて) 3. *v* (*alternates*) kōtai shimásu (suru, shite) 交替・交代します(する, して) 4. *n* idō 移動 5. *n* henka 変化, shifuto シフト

day shift *n* nikkin 日勤

night shift *n* yakin 夜勤

shift key *n* (*keyboard*) shifuto kii シフトキー

shift system *n* shifuto-sei シフト制, kōtai-sei 交代制

Shikoku *n* Shikoku 四国

shilling *n* shiringu シリング

Shimbashi *n* Shínbashi 新橋; *Shimbashi Station* Shinbashí-Eki 新橋駅

shimmer 1. *n* yurameki 揺らめき・ゆらめき 2. *v* yuramekimásu (yurameku, yurameite) 揺らめきます・ゆらめきます(揺らめく, 揺らめいて)

shin *n* sune すね・脛

shine 1. *n* (*gloss*) tsuya つや・ツヤ・艶 2. *v* (*it shines*) hikarimásu (hikáru, hikátte) 光ります(光る, 光って); (*gleams*) kagayakimásu (kagayáku, kagayáite) 輝きます・かがやきます(輝く, 輝いて); (*the sun*) terimásu (téru, tétte) 照ります(照る, 照って); (*polishes it*) migakimásu (migaku, migaite) 磨きます(磨く, 磨いて) 3. *n ~ on* (*illuminates*) ...o terashimásu (terásu, teráshite) ...を照らします(照らす, 照らして)

shingle *n* íta 板; *shingles a roof* íta de yáne o fukimásu (fuku, fuite) 板で屋根をふき[葺き]ます(ふく, ふいて)

shingles *n* (*herpes zoster*) (taijō-) hō'shin (帯状)疱疹, herupesu ヘルペス

Shinjuku *n* Shinjuku 新宿; *Shinjuku Station* Shinjukú-Eki 新宿駅

Shinto(ism) *n* Shíntō/Shíndō 神道; *Shinto music and dances* kágura 神楽

Shinto shrine *n* jínja 神社; (o-)miya (お)宮

shiny *adj* hikaru 光る, hikatte(i)ru 光って(い)る, kagayaku 輝く・かがやく, kagayaite(i)ru 輝いて(い)る・かがやいて(い)る

ship 1. *n* fúne 船・舟, (*steamship*) kisen 汽船, …-sen …船; (*how many* nán-seki 何隻, nán-sō 何艘) 2. *v* (*loads/carries*) (fune ni) nosemásu (noseru, nosete) (船に)載せます(載せる, 載せて)

ship building *n* zōsen 造船

ship's crew *n* sen'in 船員

shipwreck *n* nanpa 難破・ナンパ, sōnan 遭難

shipwrecked vessel *n* nanpa sen 難破船

shipyard *n* zōsen-jo 造船所

shirk *v* 1. okotarimásu (okotaru, okotatte) 怠ります (怠る, 怠って), namakemásu (namakeru, namakete) 怠けます (怠ける, 怠けて) 2. noga-remásu (nogareru, nogarete) 逃れます・のがれます (逃れる, 逃れて), sakemásu (sakeru, sakete) 避けます (避ける, 避けて), [BOOKISH] kaihi shimásu (suru, shite) 回避します(する, して)

shirk one's job *v* shigoto o okotarimásu (okotaru, okotatte) 仕事を怠ります・おこたります (怠る, 怠って)

shirk payment *v* (shiharai o) fumitaoshimásu (fumitaosu, fumitaoshite) 支払いを踏み倒します (踏み倒す, 踏み倒して)

shirk responsibility *v* sekinin o nogaremásu (nogareru, nogarete) 責任を逃れます (逃れる, 逃れて), sekinin o kaihi shimásu (suru, shite) 責任を回避します (回避する, 回避して)

shirt *n* wai-shatsu Yシャツ, (*undershirt*) shátsu シャツ; (*how many* nánmai 何枚)

shit → dung, feces → defecation → defecate

shiver 1. *v* zotto shimásu (suru, shite) ぞっとします, furuemásu (furueru, furuete) 震えます (震える, 震えて), miburui (o) shimásu (suru, shite) 身震い(を)します(する, して), ononokimásu (ononoku, ononoite) 慄きます・おののきます (おののく, おののいて) 2. *n with a ~* zotto ぞっと, samuke 寒け

shock *n* shókku ショック, [BOOKISH] shōgeki 衝撃; *the oil shock* oiru-shókku オイルショック

shocking *adj* tonde-mo nai … とんでもない…; shokkingu (na) …ショッキング(な)…; tonda … とんだ…

shoe *n* kutsú 靴・くつ, (*outdoor shoes*) shita-baki 下履き; (1: pair is-sokú 一足, 2: ní-soku 二足, 3: sán-zoku/ -soku) 三足; *how many* nán-zoku/-soku 何足)

shoe box *n* (*at entryway*) getabako 下駄箱・ゲタ箱

shoehorn *n* kutsu-bera 靴べら・靴ベラ

shoelace *n* kutsú-himo 靴ひも・靴紐

shoe-repair(er) *n* kutsu-náoshi 靴直し・靴なおし

shoeshine *n* kutsu-mígaki 靴磨き・靴みがき

shoe shop/store *n* kutsú-ya 靴屋

shoesole *n* kutsu no urá 靴の裏, kutsu-zoko 靴底

shogunate *n* bákufu 幕府; bakufu-jídai 幕府時代

shoot *v* 1. uchimásu (útsu, útte) 撃ちます (撃つ, 撃って) 2. (*arrow*) irimásu (íru, itte) 射ります (射る, 射って) 3. (*~ to death*) uchi-koroshimásu (uchi-korosu, uchi-koroshite) 撃ち殺します (撃ち殺す, 撃ち殺して) 4. barashimásu (barásu, baráshite)

barashimásu (barásu, barashite) 5. (*film*) satsuei shimásu (suru, shite) 撮影します(する, して)

shoot a dice *v* saikoro o furimásu (furu, futte) サイコロを振ります (振る, 振って)

shoot a film *v* eiga o satsuei shimásu (suru, shite) 映画を撮影します(する, して)

shoot for the stars *v* takanozomi o shimásu (suru, shite) 高望みをします(する, して),

shooting *n* shageki 射撃

shooting game *n* shūtingu gēmu シューティング・ゲーム

shooting star *n* nagaré-boshi 流れ星

shop *n* (*store*) misé 店, uri-ba 売り場, shō'ten 商店, shoppu ショップ; …-ya …屋, …-ten …店; (1: ík-ken 一軒, 2: ní-ken 二軒, 3: sán-gen 三軒; *how many* nán-ken 何軒)

shop *v* (*does the shopping*; *buys*) kai-mono shimásu (suru, shite) 買い物します(する, して)

shop around for … *v* o busshoku shimásu (suru, shite) …を物色します(する, して)

shop clerk *n* ten'in 店員

shop curtain *n* noren のれん・暖簾

shopgirl *n* (joshi-)ten'in (女子)店員

shopkeeper *n* tenshu 店主; …-ya (san) …屋(さん)

shoplift *v* kapparaimásu (kapparau, kapparatte) かっぱらいます(かっぱらう, かっぱらって), man-biki o shimásu (suru, shite) 万引き[まんびき]をします(する, して)

shoplifting, shoplifter *n* manbiki 万引き

shopping *n* kaimono 買い物, shoppingu ショッピング

shopping bag *n* shoppingu-bággu ショッピングバッグ

shopping center *n* shoppingu-séntā ショッピングセンター

shopping area, shop street(s) *n* shōtén-gai 商店街

shop window *n* shō uindō ショー・ウインドウ

shore *n* kishí 岸・きし, [BOOKISH] kishíbe 岸辺・きしべ; (*seashore*) kaigan 海岸, [BOOKISH] (*seaside*) umibe 海辺・うみべ; [BOOKISH] (*lakeshore*) kogan 湖岸

short *adj* (*not long*) mijikái 短い; (*not tall*) (séga) hikúi (背が)低い; (*deficient*) … ga tarimasén (tarinai) …が足りません(足りない)

in short *adv* tsúmari つまり, yōsúru ni 要するに・ようするに

shortage *n* fusoku 不足, …-búsoku …不足

water shortage *n* mizu-búsoku 水不足

shortcake *n* shōto kēki ショートケーキ

shortchange *v* tsuri-sen o gomakashimásu (gomakásu, gomakáshite) 釣(り)銭を誤魔化します(ごまかす, ごまかして), kozeni o gomakashimásu (gomakasu, gomaká-shite) 小銭を誤魔化します・ごまかします(ごまかす, ごまかして)

short circuit *n* (*electric*) (denki ga) shō'to (shimásu; suru, shite) ショート(します; する, して)

shortcoming n tánsho 短所, ketten 欠点

shortcut n 1. chiká-michi 近道 2. (computer) shōto katto ショートカット

shorten v 1. *shortens it* mijíkaku shimásu (suru, shite) 短くします・みじかくします(する、して); chijimemásu (chijimeru, chijimete) 縮めます(縮める、縮めて); herashimásu (herasu, herashite) 減らします・へらします(減らす、減らして); (abbreviates) ryakushimásu (ryakúsu, ryakúshite) 略します(略す、略して) 2. mijíkaku narimásu (naru, natte) 短くなります・みじかくなります(なる、なって); chiji-márimasu (chijimaru, chijimatte) 縮まります (縮まる、縮まって)

shorthand n sokki 速記

short-handed adj hitode ga tarinai 人手が足りない、hitode ga fusoku shiteiru 人手が不足している、hitode-busoku (no) 人手不足(の)

short hair n 1. mijikai kami 短い髪 2. (hair style) shōto katto ショートカット

shortly adv ma-mó-naku 間もなく・まもなく、chikáku 近く・ちかく

short-necked clam n asari あさり・アサリ・浅蜊

shortness n fusoku 不足

shortness of breath n (medical) ikigire 息切れ

shorts n 1. (outerwear) shōtopántsu ショートパンツ; tanpan 短パン 2. (undershorts) zubon-shita ズボン下

shortsighted adj (myopic) kinshi (no) 近視(の)、kingan (no) 近眼(の); (not thinking ahead) shō'rai o kangaemasén (kangáenai) 将来を考えません(考えない)

shortstop n (baseball) shō'to ショート

short story n tanpen shōsetsu 短編小説; shō'to sutōrī ショートストーリー

short-tempered adj tanki (no/na) 短気(の/な)

shortwave adj tanpa (no) 短波(の)

shot n 1. (fire) hassha 発射; happō 発砲 2. (for a goal) shūto シュート 3. (TV scene, film) katto カット

　big shot n ōmono 大物; ōgosho 大御所

　give it one's best shot v zenryoku o tsukushite (yatte) mimásu (miru, mite) 全力を尽くして[つくして](やって)みます(みる、みて)

　Good shot! interj Naisu shotto! ナイスショット!

　have a shot at v (tries) tameshite mimásu (tamesu, tameshite) 試してみます(試す、試して)

　long shot n kanōsei no hikui 可能性の低い

shotgun n shotto-gan ショットガン; [BOOKISH] sandan-jū 散弾銃

should → ought

shoulder 1. n káta 肩・かた 2. v (carries on shoulders) shoimásu (shou, shotte) しょいます (しょう、しょって)、seoimásu (seou, seotte) 背負います(背負う、背負って)、hikukemásu (hikiukeru, hikiukete) 引き受けます(引き受ける、引き受けて) over-the-shoulder adj katagoshi (no) 肩ごし・肩越し(の)

shoulder bag n shorudābaggu ショルダーバッグ

shoulder blade n kenkōkotsu 肩甲骨

shout 1. v (calls out) sakebimásu (sakébu, sakénde) 叫びます・さけびます(叫ぶ、叫んで); (chants) tonaemásu (tonáeru, tonáete) 唱えます・となえます(唱える、唱えて); (yells) donarimásu (donáru, donátte) どなります・怒鳴ります(どなる、どなって) 2. n sakebi-goe 叫び声, ōgoe 大声

shove n, v tsuyoku oshimásu (osu, oshite) 強く押します(押す、押して)

shovel n sháberu シャベル

show 1. (display) mié 見栄・ミエ 2. (an exhibit) mise-mónó 見せ物, shō ショー 3. ~ *movie* ~ *play*

show v 1. (displays it) misemásu (miséru, mísete) 見せます(見せる、見せて); [HUMBLE] o-me ni kakemásu (kakéru, kákete) お目にかけます(かける、かけて) 2. (reveals) arawashimásu (arawásu, arawáshite) 表します(表す、表して); (indicates) shimeshimásu (shimesu, shimeshite) 示します(示す、示して) 3. (tells) oshiemásu (oshieru, oshiete) 教えます(教える、教えて)

show in v (ushers) tōshimásu (tō'su, tōshite) 通します(通す、通して)、annai shimásu (suru, shite) 案内します(する、して)

show off v jiman shimásu (suru, shite) 自慢します(する、して)、misebirakashimásu (misebirakasu, mísebirakashite) 見せびらかします(見せびらかす、見せびらかして); [BOOKISH] koji shimásu (suru, shite) 誇示します(する、して)

show up v arawaremásu (arawaréru, awárete) 現れます(現れる、現れて); (comes) miemásu (miéru, míete) 見えます(見える、見えて)

Showa era n Shōwa jidai 昭和時代

showcase n shō kēsu ショー・ケース, tenji-yō kēsu 展示用ケース, [BOOKISH] chinretsu-dana 陳列棚

showdown n taiketsu 対決, dotanba 土壇場

shower 1. n (bath) sháwā シャワー; *rain shower* yūdachi 夕立(ち); *sudden shower* niwaka-áme にわか雨 2. v (takes a shower) sháwā o abimásu (abiru, abite) シャワーを浴びます(浴びる、浴びて); ~ *on* abisemásu (abiseru, abisete) 浴びせます(浴びせる、浴びせて)

showing n (movie) jōei 上映

showroom n shō rūmu ショー・ルーム, tenji-shitsu 展示室, chinretsu-shitsu 陳列室

showy adj hanáyaka (na) 華やか・はなやか(な)、hadé (na) 派手・はで(な)

shred n kirehashi 切れ端

shredder n shureddā シュレッダー

shrew n gamigami on'na がみがみ女

shrewd adj josai nai 如才ない

shrill adj kandakai 甲高い shrill voice n kiiroi koe 黄色い声, kandakai koe 甲高い声, kanakiri-goe金切り声

shrimp n ebi えび・エビ・海老; (batterfried) ebi-ten えび天・エビテン; (fried in bread crumbs) ebi-fúrai えびフライ・エビフライ; *giant shrimp*

(*prawn*) kurumá-ebi 車えび・車海老・クルマエ
ビ; *tiny shrimp* shiba ebi 芝えび・芝海老・シ
バエビ; *mantis shrimp* sháko しゃこ・シャコ・
蝦蛄

shrine *n* (*Shinto*) (o-)miya (お)宮; jínja 神社,
(*large*) jingū´ 神宮

shrink *v* chijimimásu (chijimu, chijinde) 縮みます
(縮む, 縮んで), chijimárimásu (chijimaru, chijimatte) 縮まります(縮まる, 縮まって), (*shortens,
abridges*) tsuzumarimásu (tsuzumáru, tsuzumátte)
つづまり[約まり]ます(つづまる, つづまって)

shrivel *v* chijimimásu (chijimu, chijinde) 縮みま
す(縮む, 縮んで), shioremásu (shioreru, shiorete)
しおれます(しおれる, しおれて)

shrub *n* kanboku 潅木・かんぼく, yabu やぶ・藪

shudder *v* zotto shinmásu (suru, shite) ぞっとし
ます・ゾッとします(する, して); *with a ~* zotto
ぞっと・ゾッと

shuffle *v* mazemásu (mazéru, mazete) 混ぜます
(混ぜる, 混ぜて); *~ the cards* toránpu o kiri-másu
(kíru, kítté) トランプを切ります(切る, 切って)

shut *v* **1.** (*shuts it*) shimemásu (shiméru, shímete)
閉めます(閉める, 閉めて); (*a book, etc.*) tojimásu
(tojíru, tójite) 閉じます(閉じる, 閉じて) **2.** (*it
gets shut*) shimarimásu (shimáru, shimátte) 閉
まります(閉まる, 閉まって); (*it puckers up*)
tsubomarimásu (tsubomaru, tsubomatte) つぼま
ります(つぼまる, つぼまって); *~ one's eyes* mé
o tsuburimásu (tsuburu, tsubutte) 目を瞑ります・
目をつぶります(つぶる, つぶって); *~ up* (*not
speak*) damarimásu (damáru, damátte) 黙ります
(黙る, 黙って)

shutter *n* (*camera, etc.*) sháttā シャッター;
(*horizontal house or vertical storefront metal
shutters*) yoroi-do よろい[鎧]戸, (*rain shutters*)
amádo 雨戸・あまど

shuttle bus *n* shatoru basu シャトルバス

shuttlecock *n* hane 羽根 → **battledore**

shy *adj* uchíki (na) 内気(な), shai (na) シャイ
(な), hazukashíi 恥ずかしい・はずかしい; *acts ~*
hanikamimásu (hanikámu, hanikánde) はにかみま
す(はにかむ, はにかんで), enryo shimásu (suru,
shite) 遠慮します(する, して)

shyness *n* enryo 遠慮 (go-enryo ご遠慮)

Siberia *n* Shiberia シベリア

sibling *n* (*brother*) kyōdai 兄弟, (*sister*) shimai
姉妹

sick *adj* byōki (no) 病気(の); *gets sick and tired*
unzári shimásu (suru, shite) うんざりします(す
る, して) → **queasy**

sickly *adj* byōki-gachi (na) 病気がち(な)

sickness *n* byōki 病気

side *n* **1.** yoko 横, -gawa 側 **2.** (*beside, nearby*)
sóba そば・側・傍, (*off to the side*) hata 端
3. (*of body*) wakí わき・脇
both sides ryō-gawa 両側
that side achira-gawa あちら側
(the) left side hidari-gawa 左側
(the) right side migi-gawa 右側

the other side mukō-gawa 向こう側・むこうが
わ

this side (*my/our side*) kochira-gawa こちら側

one side … the other side ippō´… (mō) ippō 一
方…(もう)一方; (*party*) senpō 先方

which side dochira-gawa どちら側

your side sochira-gawa そちら側

sideboard *n* shokki-tódana 食器戸棚

sideburns *n* momiage もみあげ・揉み上げ

side dish *n* (*to go with the rice*) okazu おかず

side effect *n* fukusayō 副作用

side hill *n* san-puku 山腹

side job, sideline *n* arubáito アルバイト

side light *n* saido raito サイドライト

sidestep *v* sakemásu (sakeru, sakete) 避けます
(避ける, 避けて), [BOOKISH] kaihi shimásu (suru,
shite) 回避します(する, して)

side street *n* yokochō 横丁

sidetracked; *gets ~* dassen shimásu (suru, shite)
脱線します(する, して)

sidewalk *n* hodō 歩道

sideways, sidewise *adj, adv* yoko (no/ni)
横(の/に)

siege *n* hōi 包囲, hōi kōgeki 包囲攻撃

sieve, sifter *n* furui ふるい・篩, zarú ざる

sight *n* (*scene*) ari-sama ありさま・有り様;
(*scenery*) késhiki 景色; (*eyesight*) shíryoku
視力; *sees the sights* kenbutsu shimásu (suru,
shite) 見物します(する, して)

sightseeing *n* kenbutsu 見物, kankō 観光; *sightseeing bus* kankō-básu 観光バス; *sightseeing tour*
kankō-tsuā 観光ツアー

sightseer *n* kankō´-kyaku 観光客

sign 1. *n* (*symptom*) shirushi しるし[徴], chōkō
徴候; (*omen*) zenchō 前兆 **2.** *n* (*signboard*)
kanban 看板 **3.** *n* (*marker*) hyōshiki 標識
4. *n* (*symbol*) kigō 記号 **5.** *v* (*writes one's name*)
shomei shimásu (suru, shite) 署名します(する,
して)

sign language *n* (*hand language*) shuwa 手話

signs and symptoms *n* (*medical*) chōkō to shōjō
徴候と症状

signal *n* shingō 信号, aizu 合図, shigunaru シグ
ナル

signature *n* shomei 署名, sain サイン

signboard *n* kanban 看板・かんばん, taté-fuda
立て札

signer *n* shomei-sha 署名者

significance *n* ígi 意義

signpost *n* dōhyō 道標, dōro (annai) hyōshiki
道路(案内)標識

silencer *n* (*gun*) sairen-sā サイレンサー

silent; *is ~* (*not speak*) damarimásu (damáru,
damátte) 黙ります(黙る, 黙って)

silhouette *n* shiruetto シルエット

silicon *n* shirikon シリコン

silk *n* kínu 絹・きぬ, shiruku シルク; *raw silk*
kí-ito 生糸・きいと

silkworm *n* (o-)káiko (お)蚕・カイコ; *raising*

silkworms, *silk farming* yōsan 養蚕

silky *adj* kínu no yō (na) 絹[きぬ]のような,
yawarakai やわらかい・柔らかい

sill *n* (*window/door*) *sill* (mádo/to no) shikii
(窓/戸の)敷居

sillago *n* (*fish*) kisu きす・キス・鱚

silly *adj* bakabakashii ばかばかしい, bakageteiru
ばかげている・馬鹿げている

silver 1. *n* gín 銀・ぎん, shirubā シルバー **2.** *adj*
(*color*) gin-iro (no) 銀色(の)

similar *adj* onaji yō (na) 同じよう[様]な・おな
じような, hitoshíi 等しい・ひとしい, nita 似た,
ruiji no 類似の

similarity *n* ruiji 類似

simile *n* tatóe 例え・たとえ, tatói 例い・たとい

simple *adj* kantan (na) 簡単・かんたん(な),
tanjun (na) 単純(な), shínpuru (na) シンプル
(な); (*easy*) wáke-nai 訳ない・わけない; (*plain*)
assári shita あっさりした; (*frugal*) shísso (na)
質素・しっそ(な); (*naive*) soboku (na) 素朴
(な); (*tastefully restrained*) shibúi 渋い・しぶい;
simple (modest) tastes wabi わび・侘び

simplehearted *adj* tanjun (na) 単純(な)

simple-minded *adj* tanjun (na) 単純(な),
(o-)medetái (お)めでたい[目出度い]

simply *adv* **1.** kantan ni 簡単に・かんたんに;
(*easily*) wáke-naku 訳なく・わけなく; assári
(to) あっさり(と) **2.** (*merely*) táda ただ, ... ni
sugimasén (sugínai) …に過ぎません(過ぎない)

simultaneous *adj* dōji (no) 同時(の)
simultaneous translation n dōjitsu´yaku 同時
通訳

sin *n* tsúmi 罪; záiaku 罪悪

since 1. *prep* ... kara …から; (*sono*) áto/go
(その)後; (*sono*) sono-go その後; (...) írai (…)
以来 **2.** *conj* ... shite kara …してから
3. → **because**

sincere *adj* makoto (no) 誠(の), seijitsu (na) 誠実
(な); (*heartfelt*) kokóro kara 心から(の)

sincerity *n* seii 誠意, magokoro 真心

sing *v* utaimásu (utau, utatte) 歌います(歌う,
歌って)

singer *n* kashu 歌手, shingā シンガー

single 1. *adj* (*for one person*) hítori no 一人
[独り]の **2.** *n* (*unmarried*) hitori-mónó 独り者,
dokushin 独身
single (room) n shínguru シングル, shinguru-
rū´mu シングルルーム

sink 1. *n* (*in kitchen*) nagashí 流し **2.** *v* (*it sinks*)
shizumimásu (shizumu, shizunde) 沈みます(沈
む, 沈んで); (*sinks it*) shizumemásu (shizumeru,
shizumete) 沈めます(沈める, 沈めて)

sip *v* suimásu (sū, sutte) 吸います(吸う, 吸って)

sir... ... sama ...様・さま, ... san ...さん

siren *n* (*sound*) sairen サイレン

sirloin *n* sāroin サーロイン
sirloin steak n sāroin-sutēki サーロインステ
ーキ

sister *n* **1.** onna no kyō´dai 女の兄弟; (*older*) ane
姉・あね, (o-)nē´-san (お)姉さん・おねえさん;
(*younger*) imōtó 妹・いもうと, (o-)imōto-san
妹さん **2.** (*nun*) sisutā シスター

sister-in-law *n* giríno ane/imōtó 義理の姉/妹
(*older/younger*)

sit *v* (*especially Japanese-style*) suwarimásu
(suwaru, suwatte) 座ります・すわります(座る,
座って), (*on a cushion*) shikimásu (shiku, shiite)
敷きます(敷く, 敷いて); (*in chair*) (koshi-)
kakemásu (kakéru, kákete) (腰)掛けます(掛ける,
掛けて); ~ *astride* ... ni matagarimásu (matagáru,
matagátte) …に跨がり[またがり]ます(跨がる,
跨がって)

site *n* (*building lot*) shiki-chi 敷地; genba 現場;
basho 場所

sit-in (strike) *n* suwarikomi 座り込み

situation *n* jōtai 状態, jōkyō 状況, jítai 事態;
(*circumstance*) ba(w)ai 場合; (*stand-point*) tachi-
ba 立場; (*stage*) kurai 位; (*location*) íchi 位置

six *n* rokú 六・6, muttsú 六つ; shíkkusu シッ
クス

six; 6 pieces (*small things*) rók-ko 六個; *6 trees*
(*or long things*) róp-pon 六本; *6 sheets* (*flat
things*) roku-mai 六枚; *6 cats* (*or small animals*)
rop-piki 六匹; *6 cows* (*or large animals*) rokú-tō
六頭; *6 birds/rabbits* róp-pa 六羽; *6 cars* (*or
machines/vehicles*) rokú-dai 六台; *6 copies* (*books/
magazines*) rokú-satsú 六冊; *6 people* rokú-nin
六人, rokú-mei 六名; *6 floors/stories* rok-kai
六階; *6 fold* rokú-bai 六倍; *6 days* muika 六日・
6日; *6 degrees* rokú-do 六度; *6 times* rokú-dó
六度, rok-kái 六回, rop-pén 六遍; *6 o'clock* rokú-ji
六時; rokú-jíkan 六時間; *6 days* muika 六日;
6 weeks rokú-shūkan 六週間; *6 months* rokú-ká-
getsu 六ヶ月; *6 times* rokudo-mé 六度目,
rokkai-mé 六回目; *6 years* rokú-nen 六年,
rokunén-kan 六年間; *6 years old* muttsú 六つ,
rokú-sái 六歳

six hundred *n* rop-pyakú 六百・600

sixteen *n* jū-rokú 十六・16

sixth *adj* roku-banmé (no) 六番目(の), muttsu-mé
(no) 六つ目(の); *the sixth day* muika-mé 六日目,
(*of the month*) muika 六日

six thousand *n* roku-sén 六千・6,000

sixty *n* rokú-jū´ 六十・60; *sixty thousand* roku-
mán 六万

size *n* ōkisa 大きさ, sáizu サイズ; (*model*) katá 型,
...-gata ...型

skate, skating 1. *n* sukē´to スケート, rōrā sukē´to
ローラースケート **2.** *v* sukē´to o shimásu (suru,
shite) スケートをします(する, して); suberimásu
(subéru, subétte) 滑ります(滑る, 滑って)
ice skating n aisu sukēto アイススケート
skateboard n sukēto bōdo スケートボード

sketch *n* shasei 写生; suketchi スケッチ; shitae
下絵

skewer *n* yaki-gushi 焼き串

ski, skiing *n* sukíi (o shimásu; suru, shite) スキー
(をします; する, して)

figure skating *n* figyua sukēto フィギュアスケート

ski resort *n* sukii-jō スキー場; sukii rizōto スキー・リゾート

ski wear *n* sukii uea スキーウエア, sukii wea スキーウェア

skill *n* udemae 腕前; ginō 技能; sukiru スキル

skillful *adj* jōzú (na) じょうず[上手] (な) (o-jōzu おじょうず), umái うまい, takumi (na) 巧み (な); (*proficient*) tassha (na) 達者 (な); (*nimble*) kíyō (na) 器用 (な)

skim *v* (*grazes*) kasumemásu (kasumeru, kasumete) かすめ[掠め]ます (かすめる, かすめて); **~ off** kasume-torimásu (kasume-tóru, kasume-tótte) かすめ[掠め]取ります (かすめ[掠め]取る, かすめ[掠め]取って)

skim milk *n* dasshí-nyū 脱脂乳

skin **1.** *n* hifu 皮膚; (*of animal, potato, …*) kawá 皮 **2.** *v* (*pares/peels it*) mukimásu (muku, muite) むきます・剥きます (むく, むいて), hagimásu (hagu, haide) はぎます・剥ぎます (はぐ, はいで)

human skin *n* hada (hito) 肌 (人) 肌・はだ

skin cancer *n* (*medical*) hihu gan 皮膚がん・皮膚癌

skin care *n* sukin kea スキン・ケア

skinflint *n* kéchinbo(u) けちんぼ(う)・けちん坊, kéchi けち

skip *v* (*leaves out*) nukashimásu (nukasu, nukashite) 抜かします (抜かす, 抜かして), tobashimásu (tobasu, tobashite) 飛ばします (飛ばす, 飛ばして); **skip school** gakkō o saborimásu 学校をさぼります (さぼる, さぼって), zuruyásumi shimásu (suru, shite) ずる休みします (する, して)

skirt *n* sukā́to スカート

sky *n* sóra 空; (*heaven*) tén 天; (*blue, empty*) aozóra 青空

skydiving *n* sukai daibingu スカイ・ダイビング

skyscraper *n* kōsō-bíru 高層ビル

slack *adj* yurúi 緩い・弛い・ゆるい; **gets ~** taruminásu (tarumu, tarunde) たるみ[弛み]ます (たるむ, たるんで)

slacks *n* surákkusu スラックス, zubon ズボン

slander **1.** *n* warú-kuchi/-guchi 悪口, [BOOKISH] hibō ひぼう・誹謗 **2.** *v* … o chūshō shimásu (suru, shite) …を中傷します (する, して)

slang *n* zokugo 俗語, surangu スラング

slant **1.** *n* katamuki 傾き・かたむき **2.** *v* (*leans*) katamukimásu (katamúku, katamúite) 傾きます・かたむきます (傾く, 傾いて)

slanting *adj* nanáme (no) 斜め・ななめ (の), [BOOKISH] hasu (no) はす[斜] (の)

slap *v* hatakimásu (hatáku, hatáite) はたき[叩き]ます (はたく, はたいて); hippatakimasu (hippataku, hippataite) 引っぱたきます (引っぱたく, 引っぱたいて); (*one's face*) … no kao o uchimásu (útsu, útte) …の顔を打ちます (打つ, 打って), … ni binta shimasu (suru, shite) ビンタします (する, して)

slash *n* surasshu スラッシュ; shasen 斜線, "/"

slave *n* dorei 奴隷; yakko やっこ・奴

sled *n* sóri そり・ソリ・橇

sleep **1.** *n* (*sleeping*) nemuri 眠り, ne 寝, suimin 睡眠; *not enough sleep* ne-búsoku 寝不足 **2.** *v* (*sleeps*) nemurimásu (nemuru, nemutte) 眠ります (眠る, 眠って); yasumimásu (yasúmu, yasúnde) 休みます (休む, 休んで); (*goes to bed*) nemásu (neru, nete) 寝ます (寝る, 寝て); (*a leg, etc.*) *goes to ~* (*gets numb*) shibiremásu (shibiréru, shibírete) しびれます・痺れる (しびれる, しびれて)

sleep soundly → **sound asleep**

sleeping bag *n* nebukuro 寝袋

sleeping car *n* shindái-sha 寝台車

sleeping pill *n* suimin-zai 睡眠剤, suimín-yaku 睡眠薬

sleepy *adj* nemui 眠い・ねむい

sleet *n* mizore みぞれ

sleeve *n* (o-)sode (お) 袖・そで; (*end of kimono sleeve*) tamotó 袂・たもと; *sleeve cord* tasuki たすき

slender *adj* hosói 細い・ほそい

slice **1.** *n* suraisu スライス **2.** *v* → **cut; piece**

sliced raw fish *n* sashimí 刺身・さしみ (o-sashimi お刺身)

slick *adj* subekkói すべっこい・滑っこい

slide **1.** *n* suberí-dai すべり台・滑り台, o-súberi お滑り **2.** *v* suberimásu (subéru, subétte) 滑ります (滑る, 滑って)

slider *n* suraidā スライダー

sliding panel/door *n* **1.** (*translucent*) shōji 障子・しょうじ **2.** (*opaque*) fusuma ふすま・襖

slight *adj* chótto shita … ちょっとした…

slip **1.** *n* → **slide** **2.** *slip out of …* *v* nuke-dashimásu (nuke-dásu, nuke-dashite) 抜け出します (抜け出す, 抜け出して)

slippers *n* suríppa スリッパ, uwabaki うわばき・上履き

slippery *adj* suberi yasui すべりやすい・滑りやすい; subekkói すべっこい・滑っこい; *Slippery (Area)* "Surippu-jíko ṓshi" "スリップ事故多し"

slipshod *adj* zusan (na) ずさん[杜撰] (な)

slogan *n* surṓgan スローガン, hyōgo 標語

slope *n* saká 坂

sloping road *n* saka-michi 坂道

sloppy *adj* zonzái (na) ぞんざい (な), zusan (na) ずさん[杜撰] (な)

slot *n* kuchi 口, aná 穴

slot machine *n* (*vending machine*) (jidō-)hambái-ki (自動)販売機; (*gambling*) surotto mashiin スロットマシーン

slovenly *adj* zonzái (na) ぞんざい (な); darashinai だらしない; zusan (na) ずさん[杜撰] (な)

slow *adj* osoi 遅い, surṓ (na) スロー(な); (*sluggish*) norói のろい, yurúi 緩い; (*clock runs slow*) okurete imásu (iru, ite) 遅れています (いる, いて)

slow motion *n* (*film, etc.*) surō mōshon スローモーション

slowly adv yukkúri ゆっくり; (tardily, late) osoku 遅く・おそく

slug n (coin) tamá 玉

sluggish adj norói のろい

slum n suramu(-gai) スラム(街). [BOOKISH] hinmín-kutsu/-gai 貧民窟/街

sly adj zurúi ずるい; **sly dog/person** zurúi-yatsu ずるいやつ, tanuki たぬき・タヌキ・狸

small adj (little) chiisái/chítchái 小さい/ちっちゃい, chíisa-na/chítcha-na …小さな/ちっちゃな …; ko-… 小; (fine) komakái 細かい; (small-scale) sasáyaka (na) ささやか(な)

small boat n kobune 小舟

small change n komakái (o-)kane 細かい(お)金, ko-zeni 小銭; o-tsuri お釣り・おつり, tsuri-sen 釣り銭

smallpox n (medical) tennentō 天然痘・てんねん痘

small restaurant n (Japanese traditional) koryō-rí-ya 小料理屋

small-size adj (model) kogata (no) 小型(の)

smart 1. adj (intelligent) atamá ga íi 頭がいい, rikō (na) 利口(な); (stylish) sumā´to (na) スマート(な), iki (na) いき[粋](な) 2. v (it smarts) shimimásu (shimiru, shimite) 染みます(染みる, 染みて)

smartphone n (multifunctional mobile phone) sumátofon スマートフォン

smash v 1. (breaks it) kowashimásu (kowásu, kowáshite) 壊します(壊す, 壊して), kudakimásu (kudáku, kudáite) 砕きます(砕く, 砕いて); (crushes it) tsubushimásu (tsubusu, tsubushite) 潰し[つぶし]ます(潰す, 潰して) 2. (it breaks) kowaremásu (kowaréru, kowárete) 壊れます(壊れる, 壊れて), kudakemásu (kudakéru, kudákete) 砕けます(砕ける, 砕けて); (it crushes) tsuburemásu (tsubureru, tsuburete) 潰れ[つぶれ]ます(潰れる, 潰れて)

smell 1. n (odor) niói におい・臭い・匂い 2. v (it smells) nioimásu (nióu, nióte) におい[臭い・匂い]ます(におう, におって), niói ga shimásu (suru shite) におい[臭い・匂い]がします(する, して) 3. v (smells it) kagimásu (kagu, kaide) 嗅ぎます(嗅ぐ, 嗅いで)

smelly adj kusái 臭い・くさい

smile 1. v níkoniko shimásu (suru, shite) にこにこします・ニコニコします(する, して); hohoe-mimásu (hohoému, hohoénde) 微笑みます・ほほえみます(微笑む, 微笑んで) 2. n (smiling face) e-gao 笑顔; hohoemí 微笑み・ほほえみ; [BOOKISH] bishō 微笑・びしょう

smoke 1. v (tobacco) tabako o nomimásu (nómu, nónde) たばこを飲み[呑み]ます(飲[呑]む, 飲[呑]んで), tabako o suimásu (sū, sutte) たばこを吸います(吸う, 吸って); kitsuen shimásu (suru, shite) 喫煙します(する, して) 2. v ibu-shimásu (ibusu, ibushite) いぶし[燻し]ます(いぶす, いぶして) 3. n kemurí 煙・けむり

smoker n (person who smokes) kitsuén-sha 喫煙者

smokestack n entotsu 煙突

smoking n kitsuen 喫煙

  smoking corner n kin'en kōnā 喫煙コーナー

  smoking prohibited n kin'en 禁煙

  nonsmoking seat n kin'en seki 禁煙席

smoky adj kemui 煙い・けむい, kemutai 煙たい・けむたい

SMON n (subacute myelo-optico neuropathy) súmon スモン, súmon-byō スモン病

smooth 1. adj naméraka (na) 滑らか・なめらか(な), sube sube shita , (flat) taira (na) 平ら(な), (slippery) subekkói 滑っこい・すべっこい; **not smooth** arai 粗い・あらい 2. v narashimásu (narasu, narashite) ならし[均し]ます(ならす, ならして); (pats) nademásu (naderu, nádete) なで[撫で]ます(なでる, なでて)

smorgasbord n ("Viking") báikingu バイキング

smudge n yogore 汚れ・よごれ

smuggle v mitsuyu shimásu (suru, shite) 密輸します(する, して)

snack n keishoku 軽食, karui monó/tabemónó/shokuji 軽い物/食べ物/食事; (mid-afternoon) o-sánji お三時, o-yátsu おやつ

snack bar, snackshop n sunákku スナック

snake n hébi 蛇・ヘビ

snap v 1. (it snaps) hajikemásu (hajikéru, hajíkete) はじけ[弾け]ます(はじける, はじけて) 2. (snaps it) hajikimásu (hajíku, hajíite) はじき[弾き]ます(はじく, はじいて)

snapping turtle n suppon すっぽん・スッポン

sneakers n suniikā スニーカー, zukkú-gutsu ズック靴

sneeze n, v kushámi (o shimásu; suru, shite) くしゃみ(をします; する, して)

snivel n hana はな・洟・鼻, hana-mizu 鼻水

snore n, v ibikí (o kakimás; káku, káite) いびき・鼾(をかきます; かく, かいて)

snoring n ibiki いびき・鼾; **snoring away** gu´gu ぐうぐう

snow n yukí (ga furimás; fúru, fútté) 雪(が降ります; 降る, 降って)

snowslide n yuki-nádare 雪なだれ, nadare なだれ・雪崩

snowstorm n fúbuki 吹雪・ふぶき

snow white adj masshíro (na) 真っ白・まっしろ(な)

so adv 1. (like that) sō´ そう (sō そう + [VERB]), (like this) kō´ こう (kō こう + [VERB]) 2. (that much) sonna ni そんなに, (this much) konna ni こんなに, 3. (and so) …kara …から, …-te …って (…-kute …くて, … de…で); dá kara (sa) だから(さ)

  so as to be [NOUN] ni に, [ADJECTIVE]-ku く; …yō ni …よう[様]に

  so to speak adv iwaba いわば・言わば

soak v 1. soaks it tsukemásu (tsukeru, tsukete) 漬けます(漬ける, 漬けて) 2. it soaks tsukari-másu (tsukaru, tsukatte) 漬かります(漬かる, 漬かって) 3. it soaks in shimimásu (shimiru, shimite) 染みます(染みる, 染みて)

so-and-so *n* **1.** dáredare だれだれ・誰々, dáresore だれそれ・誰それ; yátsu やつ・奴; (*scoundrel*) yarō 野郎 **2.** náninani なになに・何々

soap *n* sekken 石けん・石鹸, shabon シャボン, sōpu ソープ

soap bubble *n* shabon-dama シャボン玉

soap opera *n* hōmu-dorama ホームドラマ, mero dorama メロドラマ

sober *adj* (*in one's right mind*) shōki (no) 正気 (の); (*plain*) jimí (na) 地味(な); (*undrunk*) shirafu (no) しらふ(の)

so-called *adj* iwayuru いわゆる

soccer *n* sákkā サッカー

soccer ball *n* sakkā bōru サッカーボール

soccer player *n* (*professional*) sakkā senshu サッカー選手

sociable *adj* aisó (/aisóˊ) ga (/no) íi あいそ(う) [愛想]が(/の)いい, shakō-teki (na) 社交的(な)

social *adj* shákai (no) 社会(の); *social company* tsuki-ai 付き合い(o-tsukíai お付き合い), (*~ friendly intercourse/relations*) kōsai 交際; *social standing* míbun 身分, shakai-teki chíi 社会的地位

social intercourse *n* shakō 社交

socialism *n* shakai-shúgi 社会主義

socialist *n* shakaishugí-sha 社会主義者

social science(s) *n* shakai-kágaku 社会科学

society *n* shákai 社会; (*association*) kyōkai 協会, (*scholarly*) gakkai 学会; ...-kai ...会

socket *n* sokétto ソケット; *two-way socket* futamata-sokétto 二又ソケット

socks *n* kutsu-shita 靴下, (*anklets*) sókkusu ソックス, (*split-toe*) tábi たび・足袋; (**1:** pair is-sokú 一足, **2:** ní-soku 二足, **3:** sán-zoku/-soku 三足; *how many* nán-zoku/-soku 何足)

soda water *n* tansán-sui 炭酸水; sōda ソーダ, sōdá-sui ソーダ水

soft *adj* yawarakái 柔らかい・やわらかい, sofuto (na) ソフト(な); *soft ice cream* sofuto-kuríimu ソフトクリーム

software *n* sofutowéa ソフトウェア

soil 1. *n* (*earth*) tsuchí 土, tochi 土地; (*stain*) 汚れ **2.** *v* (*makes it dirty*) yogoshimásu (yogosu, yogoshite) 汚します(汚す, 汚して); (*gets dirty*) yogoremásu (yogoreru, yogorete) 汚れます(汚れる, 汚れて)

sojourn *v* taizai (shimásu; suru, shite) 滞在します (する, して)

sold → **sell**; *~ out* uri-kire (no) 売り切れ(の)

soldier *n* heishi 兵士, hei 兵, gunjin 軍人

sole 1. *n* (*fish*) shita-bírame 舌平目・シタビラメ **2.** *n* (*of foot*) ashi no urá 足の裏; (*of shoe*) kutsu no urá 靴の裏, kutsu-zoko 靴底 **3.** *adj* → **only** (*one*)

solicitude *n* omoi-yari 思いやり; *thanks to your ~* okage-sama de おかげ[お蔭]さまで; *a visit of ~* (o-)mimai (お)見舞い

solid 1. *adj* (*firm*) katai 固い・硬い・堅い・かたい **2.** *n* (*a solid*) kotai 固体, rittai 立体

solid-color *adj* múji (no) 無地(の)

solstice *n* *summer solstice* geshi 夏至, *winter solstice* tōji 冬至

solution *n* kaiketsu (saku) 解決(策)

solve *v* **1.** tokimásu (tóku, tóite) 解きます(解く, 解いて); *gets solved* tokemásu (tokéru, tókete) 解けます(解ける, 解けて) **2.** kaiketsu shimásu (suru, shite) 解決します(する, して)

Somalia *n* Somaria ソマリア

somber *adj* **1.** inki (na) 陰気(な) **2.** (*color*) kusunda くすんだ

some 1. *adj* (*pron*) (*a little*) sukóshi 少し (*but often omitted*); (*certain*) nánráka no ... なんらか の...; (*a certain amount*) íkura ka (no) いくらか・幾らか(の), (*a certain number*) íkutsu ka (no) いくつか・幾つか(の); tashō (no) 多少(の) **2.** *pron* (*particular*) áru ...ある...; *some people* áru hito ある人, ... hitómo arimásu (áru, átte) ...人もあります(ある, あって)

somebody → **someone**

someday *adv* izure いずれ, ítsu-ka いつか; [BOOKISH] ichijitsú 一日

somehow *adv* dō´ni ka どうにか; (*vaguely*) dō´mo どうも; *~ or other* nán to ka shite 何とかして, (*necessarily*) dō-shitemo どうしても

someone *pron* dáre ka 誰か; (...) hito (...)人; *~ or other* dáredare だれだれ・誰々, dáresore だれそれ・誰それ

some other time izure いずれ

something *pron* náni ka 何か; (...) monó (...)物; something or other náninani なにない・何々; something the matter, something wrong n ijō 異常

something to drink *n* nomí-mono 飲み物

something to talk about *n* hanashí 話

sometime *adj* ítsu ka いつか; izure いずれ

sometimes *adv* tokidoki 時々, tokí ni 時に; (*occasionally*) tama ni たまに...; ... (suru) kotó ga arimásu (áru, átte) ...(する)事があります(ある, あって); *~* (*intermittently*) *does/is* ... -tári/...-káttari/... dáttari shimásu (suru, shite) ...たり /...かったり/...だったりします(する, して)

somewhat *adv* sukóshi 少し, chótto ちょっと → **somehow**

somewhere *adv* doko ka どこか

somewhere else yosó よそ

somewhere or other dókodoko どこどこ, dókosoko どこそこ

son *n* musuko 息子; (*your son*) bótchan 坊ちゃん; *eldest son* chō´nán 長男

song *n* utá 歌, songu ソング

songwriter *n* sakushi-ka 作詞家

son-in-law *n* múko 婿 (o-múko-san お婿さん)

soon *adv* ma-mó-naku 間もなく・まもなく, mō (súgu) もう(すぐ), jiki ni じき[直]に; *as soon as* ... (suru) to (súgu) (する)と(すぐ), (shite) kara súgu (して)からすぐ, ([VERB]-i)-shídai (ni) ([VERB]い) 次第(に)

soot *n* súsu すす・スス・煤

soothe *v* shizumemásu (shizumeru, shizumete) 静めます・鎮めます(静[鎮]める、静[鎮]めて)、nadamemásu (nadaméru, nadámete) なだめ[宥め]ます(なだめる、なだめて)

sophisticated *adj* tokaiteki (na) 都会的(な)、senrensareta 洗練された

sophomore *n* ninén-sei 二年生

sore 1. *adj* itái 痛い 2. *n* (*a sore spot*) itái tokoró 痛い所、(*from shoe rubbing*) kutsu-zure 靴ずれ → **boil → wound**

sorry *adj* (*for you/him*) (o-)ki-no-dókúdesu (お)気の毒です
Sorry! *interj* Sumimasén. すみません。、Gomennasai. ごめんなさい。

sort *n* (*kind*) shúruí 種類、ís-shu 一種

so-so *adj* mā-mā まあまあ

soul *n* séishin 精神, támashii 魂・たましい; (*person*) hito 人, ningen 人間
soul mate *n* sōru meito ソールメイト

sound 1. *n* (*noise*) otó 音; ne 音 2. *n* (*audio*) onkyō 音響; saundo サウンド 3. *v it sounds* narimásu (naru, natte) 鳴ります(鳴る、鳴って)、(*makes an animal sound*) nakimásu (naku, naite) 鳴きます(鳴く、鳴いて) 4. *v sounds it* narashimásu (narasu, narashíte) 鳴らします(鳴らす、鳴らして)
sound asleep *adj* gussúri ぐっすり, gūgū (nemutte imásu) ぐうぐう(眠っています)
sound effect *n* saundo efekuto サウンド・エフェクト; onkyō kōka 音響効果
sound out *v* (*a person*) dashin shimásu (suru, shite) 打診します(する、して)
soundscape *n* saundo sukēpu サウンドスケープ; oto (no) fūkei 音(の)風景, onkei 音景
sound track *n* santora サントラ; saundo torakku サウンド・トラック
sound wave *n* onpa 音波

soup *n* (*Western-style*) sū´pu スープ、(*Japanese opaque broth and rice meat broths, etc.*) shíru 汁, (o-)tsúyu (お)つゆ[汁]; (*Japanese clear*) sui-mono 吸い物; (*Japanese bean-paste*) miso-shíru みそ[味噌]汁; (*sweet redbean-paste*) (o-)shiruko お汁粉・おしるこ; (*thick Western*) potā´ju ポタージュ; (*thin Western*) konsome コンソメ
soup pan *n* sūpu nabe スープ鍋
soup plate *n* sūpu-zara スープ皿
soup stock *n* dashi だし・ダシ

sour 1. *adj* suppái 酸っぱい・すっぱい 2. *v it sours* kusarimásu (kusáru, kusátte) 腐ります(腐る、腐って)

source *n* moto もと・元, táne 種; okorí 起こり

south *n* minami 南, nan-... 南...; (*the south*) nanpō 南方, (*the southern part*) nánbu 南部

southeast *n* nantō 南東

southerly *adj* minami-yori (no kaze) 南寄り(の風)

southwest *n* nansei 南西

souvenir *n* (o-)miyage (お)みやげ[土産], miyage-mono みやげ[土産]物; kinen-hin 記念品

sow 1. *v* (*seeds*) makimásu (máku, máite) まき

[蒔き]ます(まく、まいて) 2. *n* (*female pig*) mesubuta 雌豚・メスブタ

soy *n* daizu 大豆・ダイズ

soybean *n* daizu 大豆・ダイズ; *fermented soybean* nattō´納豆・ナットウ

soybean flour *n* kínako きなこ・キナコ・黄な粉

soy sauce *n* (o-)shōyu (お)しょうゆ[醤油・ショウユ]; (*in sushi restaurant*) murasaki 紫・ムラサキ

spa *n* supa スパ; onsen 温泉, tōji-ba 湯治場

space *n* 1. (*available*) ma 間; (*between*) aida 間, (*innerspace*) kūkan 空間, sukima すき間, supēsu スペース; (*outer space*) úchū 宇宙; (*room, leeway*) yochi 余地 2. → **blank**

Spain *n* Supéin スペイン

span 1. *n* (*term*) kikan 期間, supan スパン 2. *v* (*stretches over it*) ... ni matagarimásu (matagáru, matagátte) ...に跨り[またがり]ます(跨がる、跨がって)

Spaniard, Spanish *n* (*person*) Supéin-jín スペイン人

Spanish *n* (*language*) Supein-go スペイン語

Spanish paprika *n* tōgarashi 唐辛子

spare 1. *adj* (*reserve*) yóbi (no) 予備(の) 2. *n* (*leeway, surplus*) yoyū 余裕; *spare time* hima 暇, yoka 余暇 3. → **save**

spark *n* híbana 火花

sparkle *n* kirameki きらめき・煌き, kagayaki 輝き

sparrow *n* suzume 雀・すずめ・スズメ

speak *v* hanashimásu (hanásu, hanáshite) 話します(話す、話して), iimásu (iu, itte) 言います(言う、言って)

speaker → **loudspeaker**

speaking ability *n* kaiwaryoku 会話力

speaking of ... ... wa ...は; ...no kotó/hanashí desu ga ...の事[こと]/話ですが

spear *n* yari 槍・ヤリ

special *adj* tokubetsu (no) 特別(の); supesharu (na) スペシャル(な), toku-... 特...; (*peculiar*) tokushu (no) 特殊(の); (*favorite*) tokui (na/no) 得意(な/の); (*emergency*) rinji (no) 臨時(の)
special class *n* tokubetsu kurasu 特別クラス; tokkyū 特級
special delivery *n* sokutatsu 速達
special express (*train*) *n* tokkyū 特急; *special express ticket* tokkyū´-ken 特急券
special feature/quality *n* tokushoku 特色, tokuchō 特徴・特長
special lunch *n* ranchi sā´bisu ランチ・サービス
special menu *n* supesharu menyū スペシャル・メニュー, tokubetsu menyū 特別メニュー
special offer *n* tokubetsu hōshi-hin 特別奉仕品
special price *n* tokubetsu kakaku 特別価格

specialist *n* senmon-ka 専門家; supesharisuto スペシャリスト; (*medical*) senmón-i 専門医

specialty *n* senmon 専門, (*forte*) tokui 得意, (*trick*) ohako おはこ・十八番

species …-rui …類; *a species of* … no ís-shu …の一種

specific *adj* (*particular*) kore to iu …これという; hakkiri to shita はっきりとした; gutaiteki (na) 具体的(な)

spectator *n* kankyaku 観客

spectrum *n* supekutoru スペクトル

speculation *n* (*venture*) yamá やま、tōki 投機

speech *n* hanashí 話し、kotobá 言葉, kuchi 口; (*public*) enzetsu 演説, kōen 講演, supiichi スピーチ

speed *n* háyasa 速さ, sókudo 速度, supído スピード; jisoku 時速

spell *v* (jí o) tsuzurimásu (tsuzuru, tsuzutte) (字を)綴り[つづり]ます(綴る, 綴って)

spellbound; is ~ uttóri shimásu (suru, shite) うっとりします(する, して)

spelling *n* tsuzuri 綴り・つづり, supéru スペル; (*way written*) kaki-kátá 書き方, (*letters*) jí 字

spend *v* tsukaimásu (tsukau, tsukatte) 使います(使う, 使って), (*pays*) dashimásu (dásu, dáshite) 出します(出す, 出して); (*uses time*) sugoshimásu (sugósu, sugóshite) 過ごします(過ごす, 過ごして); okurimásu (okuru, okutte) 送ります(送る, 送って)

spermatozoon *n* seishi 精子

sphere *n* kyū 球, kyūtai 球体

sphinx *n* sufinkusu スフィンクス

sphygmomanometer *n* ketsuatsukei 血圧計

spice *n* kō´(shin)ryō´ 香(辛)料, chōmi(-ryō) 調味(料), supaisu スパイス

spice box *n* yakumi-ire 薬味入れ

spiced saké *n* (o-)tóso (お)とそ・トソ・屠蘇

spicy *adj* karai からい・辛い, supaishii スパイシー

spider *n* kúmo くも・クモ・蜘蛛; *spider web* → **cobweb**

spill *v* (*it spills*) koboremásu (koboréru, kobórete) こぼれます・零れます(こぼれる, こぼれて); (*spills it*) koboshimásu (kobósu, kobóshite) こぼします・零します(こぼす, こぼして); tarashimásu (tarásu, taráshite) 垂らします(垂らす, 垂らして)

spinach *n* hōrénsó ほうれん草・ホウレンソウ; (*boiled and seasoned*) o-hitashi おひたし・お浸し

spine *n* sebone 背骨

spinning *n* bōseki 紡績; *spinning mill* bōseki-kō´jō 紡績工場

spiral *n* rasen 螺旋・らせん

spirit *n* séishin 精神, kokóro 心, támashii 魂, supiritto スピリット, kokoro-mochi 心持ち; ki 気

spit *n* (*skewer*) kushí 串, yakigushi 焼き串

spit 1. *n* (*spittle*) tsúba つば・ツバ・唾, tsubakí つばき・ツバキ・唾 **2.** *v* (*spits out*) (tsúba o) hakimásu (háku, háite) (つばを)吐きます(吐く, 吐いて)

spite; in ~ of … (ná) no ni …(な)のに

splendid *adj* rippa (na) 立派・りっぱ(な), subarashíi すばらしい・素晴らしい, suteki (na) すてき・素敵(な), mígoto (na) 見事(な), sakan (na) 盛ん・さかん(な), kékkō (na) 結構(な)

splendidly *adv* rippa ni 立派に・りっぱに, subaráshiku すばらしく・素晴らしく

split *v* **1.** (*splits it*) sakimásu (sáku, sáite) 裂きます(裂く, 裂いて), warimásu (waru, watte) 割ります(割る, 割って); (*divides it*) wakemásu (wakéru, wákete) 分けます(分ける, 分けて) **2.** (*it splits*) sakemásu (sakéru, sákete) 裂けます(裂ける, 裂けて), waremásu (wareru, warete) 割れます(割れる, 割れて); (*it separates*) wakaremásu (wakaréru, wakárete) 別れます(別れる, 別れて)

splitting the bill *n* wari-kan 割り勘・ワリカン

split-toe socks *n* tábi たび・タビ・足袋

spoil *v* **1.** *spoils it* wáruku (damé ni) shimásu (suru, shite) 悪く(駄目に)します(する, して); itememásu (itaméru, itámete) 傷めます(傷める, 傷めて); *~ a person's mood* kíbun o kowashimásu (kowásu, kowáshite) 気分を壊します(壊す, 壊して), kíbun o gaishimásu (gaísu, gaíshite) 気分を害します(害す, 害して) **2.** *it gets spoiled* wáruku narimásu (náru, nátte) 悪くなります(なる, なって), itamimásu (itámu, itánde) 傷みます(傷む, 傷んで) **3.** *it spoils* (*sours*) kusarimásu (kusáru, kusátte) 腐ります(腐る, 腐って); (*rots*) itamimásu (itámu, itánde) 傷みます(傷む, 傷んで)

spoke → speak; spoken language kōgo 口語

sponge *n* kaimen 海綿, suponji スポンジ

sponge gourd *n* hechima へちま・ヘチマ・糸瓜

spongecake *n* kasutera カステラ; suponji kēki スポンジケーキ

spontaneously *adv* hitori-de ni 独りでに・ひとりでに, onozukara 自ずから・おのずから

spool *n* itomaki 糸巻き

spoon *n* supū´n スプーン, sájí さじ・サジ・匙 (**1:** íp-pon 一本, **2:** ní-hon 二本, **3:** sánbon 三本; *how many* nánbon 何本)

spoonful *n* (hitó)-saji (一)匙・(ひと)さじ; *how many spoonfuls* nán-saji 何匙, nan-hai 何杯

sport(s) *n* supō´tsu スポーツ, undō 運動; *Sports Day* (*2nd Monday of October*) Taiiku no hí 体育の日

spot *n* **1.** ten 点; (*spotted*) madara (no) まだら[班](の), (*blot*) shimi 染み・しみ, (*with*) *spots* bótsubotsu ぼつぼつ・ボツボツ **2.** (*place*) basho 場所

sprain *v* (*an ankle*) (ashí o) kujikimásu (kujíku, kujíite) (足を)挫き[くじき]ます(挫く, 挫いて); *gets a sprained ankle* ashí ga kujikemásu (kujikéru, kujíkete) 足が挫け[くじけ]ます(挫ける, 挫けて)

spread *v* **1.** (*spreads it*) hirogemásu (hirogeru, hirogete) 広げます(広げる, 広げて), (*diffuses it*) hiromemásu (hiroméru, hirómete) 広めます(広める, 広めて); (*spreads it out*) nobashimásu (nobásu, nobáshite) 伸ばします(伸ばす, 伸ばして), nobemásu (nobéru, nóbete) 伸べます(伸べる, 伸べて); (*spreads it on*) harimásu (haru, hatte) 張ります(張る, 張って) **2.** (*it spreads*) hirogarimás<u>u</u> (hirogaru, hirogatte) 広がります(広がる, 広がって); (*it gets diffused*) hiromarimás<u>u</u> (hiromáru, hiromátte) 広まります(広まる, 広まって), f<u>u</u>kyū shimás<u>u</u> (suru, sh<u>i</u>te) 普及します(する, して); (*it spreads out*) nobimás<u>u</u> (nobíru, nóbite) 伸びます(伸びる, 伸びて); (*it spreads on*) (batā o) nurimás<u>u</u> (núru, nútte) (バターを)塗ります(塗る, 塗って)

spread *n* shiki-mono 敷物

spring 1. *n* (*season*) háru 春; (*device*) bane(-jíkake) ばね・バネ(仕掛け), (*of clock*) zenmai ぜんまい; *hot spring* onsen 温泉 **2.** *v ~ forth* (*gushes*) wakimás<u>u</u> (waku, wa<u>i</u>te) わき[湧き]ます(わく, わいて) **3.** *v ~ from* … kara okorimás<u>u</u> (okóru, okótte) …から起こります(起こる, 起こって)

spring → jump

springtime *n* háru 春

sprinkle; *~ it v* furi-kakemás<u>u</u> (furi-kakéru, furi-kákete) 振りかけます(振りかける, 振りかけて)

sprout(s) → pepper sprout

spy *n* supai スパイ, [BOOKISH] kanbō 間諜

square *n* sh<u>i</u>kaku 四角; *adj* sh<u>i</u>kakú (no) 四角(の), sh<u>i</u>kakúi 四角い; kakú 角; (*plaza*) híró-bá 広場

squared paper *n* genkō-yō´shi 原稿用紙

squash *v* tsuburemás<u>u</u> (tsubureru, tsuburete) つぶれます・潰れます(つぶれる, つぶれて)

squat 1. *n* sukuwatto スクワット **2.** *v* shagami-más<u>u</u> (shagamu, shagande) しゃがみます(しゃがむ, しゃがんで)

squeeze *adj* tsubushimás<u>u</u> (tsubusu, tsubush<u>i</u>te) 潰し[つぶし]ます(潰す, 潰して); (*squeezes out*) shiborimás<u>u</u> (shibóru, shibótte) 絞ります・しぼります(絞る, 絞って)

squid *n* ika いか・イカ・烏賊

squilla *n* (*mantis shrimp*) sháko しゃこ・シャコ・蝦蛄

squirrel *n* rísu りす・リス・栗鼠

Sri Lanka *n* Suriránka スリランカ

stab *v* (tsuki-)sashimás<u>u</u> (sásu, sásh<u>i</u>te) (突き)刺します(刺す, 刺して)

stable 1. *adj* anteish<u>i</u>ta 安定した **2.** *n* uma-goya 馬小屋, kyūsha 厩舎

stadium *n* kyōgi-jō 競技場; *baseball stadium* yakyū-jō 野球場, kyūjō 球場

stage *n* bútai 舞台; sutēji ステージ, (*of a process*) dankai 段階; *gets ~ fright* agarimás<u>u</u> (agaru, agatte) 上がります(上がる, 上がって)

stagger *v* yoro-mekimás<u>u</u> (yoro-méku, yoro-méite) よろめきます(よろめく, よろめいて)

staggered work hours *n* jisash<u>ú</u>kkin 時差出勤

staggering *adj* yóroyoro (no) よろよろ(の), chidori-ashi (no) 千鳥足(の)

staging *n* (*play, movie*) ensh<u>u</u>tsu 演出

stain 1. *n* shimi 染み・しみ **2.** *v* (*paints it*) nurimás<u>u</u> (nuru, nutte) 塗ります(塗る, 塗って); (*soils it*) yogoshimás<u>u</u> (yogosu, yogosh<u>i</u>te) 汚します(汚す, 汚して), (*gets soiled*) yogoremás<u>u</u> (yogoreru, yogorete) 汚れます(汚れる, 汚れて)

stairs, stairway *n* kaidan 階段; (*wooden*) hashigo-dan はしご[梯子]段

stake *n* (*post*) kúi 杭

stale *adj* (*not fresh*) furúi 古い

stalk *n* k<u>u</u>ki 茎・クキ

stamp *n* **1.** (*postal*) kitte 切手 (*how many* nánmai 何枚); *stamp album* kitte-chō 切手帳 **2.** (*seal*) ín 印; (*cancellation mark*) keshi-in 消印 **3.** sutanpu スタンプ

stand 1. *n* (*sales booth*) uri-ba 売り場, baiten 売店, s<u>u</u>tando スタンド; (*food stall*) yatai 屋台 **2.** *v* (*stands up*) tachimás<u>u</u> (tátsu, tátte) 立ちます(立つ, 立って); *stands it up* tatemás<u>u</u> (tateru, tátete) 立てます(立てる, 立てて) **3.** *stands it v* (*tolerates*) gáman shimás<u>u</u> (suru, sh<u>i</u>te) 我慢します(する, して), koraemás<u>u</u> (koráeru, koráete) こらえます(こらえる, こらえて), taemás<u>u</u> (taéru, táete) 耐えます(耐える, 耐えて), shínbō shimás<u>u</u> (suru, sh<u>i</u>te) 辛抱します(する, して)

stand against (*opposes*) … ni taikō shimás<u>u</u> (suru, sh<u>i</u>te) …に対抗します(する, して)

stand firm ganbarimás<u>u</u> (ganbáru, ganbátte) がんばり[頑張り]ます(がんばる, がんばって)

stand out (*prominently*) medachimás<u>u</u> (medátsu, medátte) 目立ちます(目立つ, 目立って)

stand still tachi-domarimás<u>u</u> (tachi-domaru, tachi-domatte) 立ち止まります(立ち止まる, 立ち止まって)

standard 1. *adj* hyōjun (no) 標準(の); *standard Japanese* hyōjun-go 標準語 **2.** *n* meyasu 目安; k<u>i</u>kaku 規格; kijun 基準

standardization *n* k<u>i</u>kaku-ka 規格化; tōitsu 統一

standardize *v* tōitsu shimás<u>u</u> (suru, sh<u>i</u>te) 統一します(する, して); k<u>i</u>kaku-ka shimás<u>u</u> (suru, sh<u>i</u>te) 規格化します(する, して)

standee *n* tachimi no kyaku 立ち見の客; *sees it as a ~* tachimi shimás<u>u</u> (suru, sh<u>i</u>te) 立ち見します(する, して)

standing room tachimí-seki 立ち見席

standpoint *n* tachi-ba 立場, kanten 観点

staple *n* (hochikisu no) hári (ホチキスの)針

stapler *n* hóchikis<u>u</u> ホチキス

star *n* hoshi 星; (*symbol*) hoshi-jírushi 星印; (*actor*) s<u>u</u>tā´ スター, hanágata 花形; **Hollywood star** *n* hariuddo sutā ハリウッド・スター

star chart *n* seizu 星図

star sign *n* seiza 星座

starch 1. *n* (*laundry*) norí 糊・のり **2.** (*food*) denpun でんぷん・澱粉; *potato starch* katakúriko 片栗粉 **→ cornstarch**

No starch please. Norízukékinshi. 糊付け禁止.

stare *v ~ (at)* (…*at*) jíro-jiro mimás<u>u</u> (míru, míte) (…を)じろじろ見ます(見る, 見て); mi-tsume-más<u>u</u> (mi-tsumeru, mi-tsúmete) 見詰め[見つめ]ます(見詰める, 見詰めて), nagamemás<u>u</u> (nagaméru, nagámete) 眺めます(眺める, 眺めて)

start 1. *n* hajimari 始まり; sh<u>u</u>ppatsu 出発; *at (from) the ~* shoppana kara しょっぱなから; *from* *the* ~ hajime kara 始めから, hónrai 本来 **2.** *v* (*it starts*) hajimarimásu (hajimaru, hajimatte) 始まります(始まる, 始まって); (*sets out*) demásu (déru, déte) 出ます(出る, 出て) **3.** *v* (*starts it*) hajimemásu (hajimeru, hajimete) 始めます(始める, 始めて), (*starts doing it*) shi-hajimemásu (shi-hajiméru, shi-hajímete) し始めます(し始める, し始めて); *it starts to rain* áme ga furi-hajimemásu (furi-hajimeru, furi-hajimete) 雨が降り始めます(降り始める, 降り始めて), áme ni narimásu (náru, nátte) 雨になります(なる, なって); **starts the engine → engine 4. → startle**

starting *n* (*a performance*) kaien 開演

startle *v* bikkúri sasemásu (saseru, sasete) びっくりさせます・吃驚させます(させる, させて); *gets startled* bikkúri shimásu (suru, shite) びっくりします・吃驚します(する, して)

start off/out *v* (*departs*) dekakemásu (dekakeru, dekakete) 出かけます(出かける, 出かけて)

starve *v* uemásu (uéru, úete) 飢えます(飢える, 飢えて)

state 1. *n* (*of the U.S.*) shū´ 州, ... -shū ...州; (*status*) bún 分; ~ *of affairs* jōkyō 状況, jítai 事態 **→ condition → nation 2.** *v expressly states* utaimásu (utau, utatte) うたい[謳い]ます(うたう, うたって) **→ say**

static (*noise*) *n* zatsuon 雑音

station *n* **1.** (*rail*) éki 駅・えき; (*box lunches sold at railroad stations*) eki-ben 駅弁 **2. → gas station**

stationary *adj* (*not moving*) ugokanai 動かない, (*not moving*) henkanai 変化しない

stationery *n* (*letter paper*) binsen 便箋; (*writing supplies*) bunbō´-gu 文房具; (*shop*) bunbōgu-ya 文房具屋

stationmaster *n* ekichō 駅長; *stationmaster's office* ekichō-shitsu 駅長室

statistics *n* tōkei 統計

statue *n* zō 像, chōzō 彫像, (*bronze*) dōzō 銅像

stature *n* (*height*) séi/sé 背・せ(い)

status *n* bún 分, (*social, personal*) míbun 身分, (*position*) chíi 地位; *the status quo* genjō 現状

stay 1. *n* (*away from home*) taizai 滞在 **2.** *v* taizai shimásu (suru, shite) 滞在します(する, して) **3.** *v* imásu (iru, ite) います(いる, いて), [DEFERENTIAL/HUMBLE] orimásu (óru, ótte/orimáshite) おります(おる, おって/おりまして), [HONORIFIC] irasshaimásu (irassháru, irasshátte/iráshite/irasshaimáshite) いらっしゃいます(いらっしゃる, いらっしゃって/いらして/いらっしゃいまして) = oide ni narimásu (náru, nátte/narimáshite) おいでになります(なる, なって/なりまして) **4.** *v* todomarimásu (todomáru, todomátte) とどまります[止まり・留まり]ます(とどまる, とどまって); (*overnight*) tomarimásu (tomaru, tomatte) 泊まります(泊まる, 泊まって)

stay away *v* (*from school, etc.*) yasumimásu (yasúmu, yasúnde) 休みます(休む, 休んで); (*skips work*) saborimásu (sabóru, sabótte) サボります(サボる, サボって)

stay up all night *v* tetsuya shimásu (suru, shite) 徹夜します(する, して); *stay up late* yofúkáshi (o) shimásu (suru, shite) 夜更し(を)します(する, して)

steadily *adv* jitto じっと; zutto ずっと

steady *adj* katagi (na) 堅気(な), tegatai 手堅い; chakujitsu (na) 着実(な)

steak *n* sutēki ステーキ, (*beef-steak*) biifutēki ビーフ・ステーキ

steak sandwich *n* sutēki-sándo ステーキ・サンド

steal *v* nusumimásu (nusúmu, nusúnde) 盗みます(盗む, 盗んで), kapparaimásu (kapparau, kapparatte) かっぱらいます(かっぱらう, かっぱらって)

stealth *n* (*espionage*) *the art of stealth* nínjutsu 忍術; *a master of stealth* nínja 忍者

steam 1. *n* jō´ki 蒸気, yúge 湯気 **2.** *v* (*steams food*) fukashimásu (fukásu, fukáshite) ふかします(ふかす, ふかして), mushimásu (músu, mú-shite) 蒸します(蒸す, 蒸して)

steam bath *n* mushiburo 蒸し風呂, suchiimu basu スチーム・バス, sauna サウナ

steamed bun *n* manjū´ まんじゅう・饅頭; (*stuffed with bean jam*) anman あんまん, (*ground pork*) niku-man 肉まん

steamed custard *n* (*from broth and eggs*) chawan-mushi 茶碗蒸し

steamed fish cake *n* kamaboko かまぼこ・カマボコ

steamed foods *n* mushí-mono 蒸し物

steamship *n* kisen 汽船

steel *n* hagane 鋼・はがね・ハガネ, kōtetsu 鋼鉄, tetsu 鉄

steep *adj* (*precipitous*) kyū (na) 急(な), kewashíi 険しい

steering wheel *n* handoru ハンドル

stem *n* (*of plant*) kuki 茎・クキ

step 1. *n* (*stairs*) kaidan 階段, dan 段 **2.** *n* suteppu ステップ **3.** *v* (*walk*) arukimásu (arúku, arúite) 歩きます(歩く, 歩いて) **→ measure → stage 4.** *v* steps into/on fumi-komimásu (fumi-kómu, fumi-kónde) 踏み込みます(踏み込む, 踏み込んで); *steps on the gas* ákuseru o fumimásu アクセルを踏みます

stepchild *n* mama-ko まま[継]子

stepfather *n* mama-chíchi まま[継]父

stepmother *n* mama-haha まま[継]母

steps → stairs

stereo *adj* (*phonic/scopic*) rittai-onkyō (no) 立体音響(の); sutereo (onkyō) (no) ステレオ(音響)(の)

stereo *n* (*sound/player*) sutereo ステレオ

sterilization *n* sakkin 殺菌

stew *n* shichū シチュー

steward *n* bōi ボーイ, kyū´ji 給仕, suchuwādo スチュワード

440

stewardess *n* suchuwā́desu スチュワーデス

stick **1.** *n* (*club*) bō(-kkire) 棒(っ切れ); (*staff*) tsúe 杖 *or* (*cane*) sutékki ステッキ **2.** *n* (*of gum, candy, etc.*) … ichí-mai …一枚, (*of yakitori, etc.*) íp-pon 一本 **3.** *n* (*lipstick*) kuchibeni 口紅 **4.** *v* (*it sticks to*) … ni kuttsukimásu (kuttsúku, kuttsúite) …にくっつきます(くっつく, くっついて) **5.** *v* (*sticks it on*) tsukemásu (tsukéru, tsukéte) 付けます(付ける, 付けて); (*pastes it on*) harimásu (haru, hatte) 貼ります(貼る, 貼って)

stickiness *n* nebarí 粘り

stick out (*sticks it out*) tsuki-dashimásu (tsuki-dásu, tsuki-dáshite) 突き出します(突き出す, 突き出して) → **protrude**

sticky; *is* ~ nébaneba shimásu (suru, shite) ねばねばします(する, して)

stiff *adj* **1.** → **hard** **2.** (*shoulder*) *gets* ~ (katá ga) korimásu (kóru, kótte) 肩が凝ります(凝る, 凝って); *~ shoulder, stiffness of shoulder* kata no kori 肩の凝り

still *adv* (*yet*) máda まだ; (*but*) (sore) démo (それ)でも; *still better* issō/náo íi 一層[いっそう]/尚[なお]いい; *still more* mótto もっと; náo 尚・なお, Isso 一層・いっそり

still image *n* seishi ga (-zō) 静止画(像)

still-life painting *n* seibutsu ga 静物画

still object *n* seibutsu 静物

still → **quiet**; *interj Stand still!* (Tatta mama) ugo-kánaide kudasai. (立ったまま)動かないで下さい., Jitto tatteite kudasai. じっと立っていて下さい.

stillness *n* seishi 静止

stimulate *v* unagashimásu (unagásu, unagáshite) 促します(促す, 促して)

stimulation *n* shigeki 刺激

sting **1.** *v* sashimásu (sásu, sáshite) 刺します(刺す, 刺して) **2.** *n* (*bee's sting*) hari 針

stingy *adj* kéchi (na) けち(な); *stingy person* kéchinbo けちんぼ, kéchinbō けちんぼう

stinking *n* kusái 臭い・くさい

stipulate *v* kitei shimásu (suru, shite) 規定します(する, して)

stipulation *n* kitei 規定 → **provision** → **condition**

stir *v* **1.** ~ *it* kaki-mawashimásu (kaki-mawasu, kaki-mawashite) かき回します(かき回す, かき回して) **2.** ~ *up* (*fans, incites*) aorimásu (aóru, aótte) あおり[煽り]ます(あおる, あおって)

stock *n* **1.** (*financial*) kabu 株, (*soup*) dashí だし・ダシ; (*on hand*) zaiko(-hin) 在庫(品), sutokku ストック; mochiawase (no) 持ち合わせ(の) **2.** *has in* ~ (*on hand*) zaiko ga arimásu (aru, atte) 在庫があります(ある, あって); mochi-awasemásu (mochi-awaseru, mochi-awasete) 持ち合わせます(持ち合わせる, 持ち合わせて); motte imásu (iru, ite) 持っています(いる, いて); oite imásu (iru, ite) 置いています(いる, いて)

stockings *n* kutsu-shita 靴下・くつした; (*1 pair*) is-sokú 一足, **2:** ní-soku 二足, **3:** sán-zoku/-soku 三足; *how many pairs* nán-zoku/-soku 何足)

stomach *n* i-búkuro 胃袋, i 胃; (*strictly, belly*) o-naka おなか, hará 腹; ~ *band* hará-maki 腹巻き; *stomach and intestines* ichō 胃腸; *develops stomach trouble* o-naka o kowashimásu (kowásu, kowáshite) おなかを壊します(壊す, 壊して)

stomach cancer *n* (*medical*) i-gan 胃がん・胃癌

stone *n* ishí 石

stone lantern *n* tōrō 灯篭; ishi-dōrō 石灯籠

stop **1.** *v* (*it comes to rest*) tomarimásu (tomaru, tomatte) 止まります(止まる, 止まって), todomarimásu (todomáru, todomátte) とどまり[止まり・留まり]ます(とどまる, とどまって) → **stand still**; (*it ceases*) yamimásu (yamu, yande) 止みます(止む, 止んで) **2.** *v* (*stops it*) tomemásu (tomeru, tomete) 止めます(止める, 止めて), todomemásu (todoméru, todométe) とどめ[止め]ます(とどめる, とどめて), yoshimásu (yósu, yóshite) よします(よす, よして); (*stops doing*) … o yamemásu (yameru, yamete) …を止めます(止める, 止めて) **3.** *n* (*halting place*) teiryū-jo 停留所; (*end*) owari 終わり

stop up fusagimásu (fusagu, fusaide) ふさぎます(ふさぐ, ふさいで); *gets stopped up* fusa-garimásu (fusagáru, fusagátte) ふさがります(ふさがる, ふさがって)

stoppage of electricity (*power failure*) teiden 停電

stopper *n* (*cork*) kuchi 口; (*plug, cork*) sén 栓

store *n* (*shop*) misé 店; sutoa ストア

storeroom *n* (*storehouse*) kurá 倉・蔵

storm **1.** *n* árashi 嵐・あらし, [BOOKISH] bōfū́ 暴風 **2.** *v* (*rages*) abaremásu (abareru, abarete) 暴れます(暴れる, 暴れて)

story *n* **1.** hanashí 話, sutōrii ストーリー **2.** → **floor**

storyteller *n* hanashi-ka 噺家, sutōrii terā ストーリー・テラー

stove *n* sutṓbu ストーブ, (*kitchen*) kamado かまど・竈, kama かま・釜, rénji レンジ; (*portable cooking*) kónro コンロ

straddle *v* … ni matagarimásu (matagáru, matagátte) …に跨がり[またがり]ます(跨がる, 跨がって)

straight *adj* massúgu (na) まっすぐ・真っ直ぐ (な)

straight line *n* chokusen 直線

straighten *v* (*tidies it*) ~ *it up* katazukemásu (katazukéru, katazúkete) 片付けます(片付ける, 片付けて)

strain **1.** *n* (*tension*) kinchō 緊張 **2.** *v* (*forces*) múri ni shimásu (suru, shite) 無理にします(する, して); (*filters*) koshimásu (kosu, koshite) こし[漉し](through cloth) shiborimásu (shibóru, shibótte) 絞ります・しぼります(絞る, 絞って)

strait(s) *n* kaikyō 海峡

strange *adj* hén (na) 変(な), fushigi (na) 不思議 (な); (*peculiar*) kímyō (na) 奇妙(な), okashíi

おかしい; (*wondrous*) myō´ (na) 妙(な); (*alien*) yosó (no) よそ(の); (*unknown*) shiranai 知らない

stranger *n* (*unknown person*) shiranai hitó 知らない人; (*outsider*) yosó no hitó よその人, tanin 他人

strap *n* himo ひも・紐; (*to hang on to*) tsuri-kawa 吊り革; (*watch-band, etc.*) bando バンド

straw *n* wára わら・ワラ・藁, mugiwara 麦わら[藁]; (*to drink with*) sutórō ストロー

straw bag *n* tawará 俵・たわら

strawberry *n* ichigo いちご・イチゴ・苺

straw mat *n* (*thin floor mat*) gozá ござ・ゴザ

straw mushrooms *n* enokí-take/-dake えのき茸・榎茸[エノキタケ/エノキダケ]

straw raincoat *n* míno みの・蓑・ミノ

straw sandals *n* zōri 草履・ゾウリ

stray 1. *n* (*child*) maigo ; (*animals*) mayoi-inu (-neko) 迷い犬(猫) **2.** *adj* michi ni mayotta 道に迷った, hagureta はぐれた **3.** *v* (*digresses*) soremásu (soréru, sórete) 逸れ[それ]ます(逸れる, 逸れて)

stream *n* nagaré 流れ; **in streams** zorozoro ぞろぞろ

streamline *v* (*procedures, ...*) gōri-ka shimásu (suru, shite) 合理化します(する, して)

street *n* michi 道, tōrí 通り, shadō 車道, tsuji 辻; (*on*) *the* **~** gaitō (de) 街頭(で)

streetcar *n* romen densha 路面電車

street stall *n* yatai 屋台

strength *n* tsuyosa 強さ, (*power*) chikará 力・ちから (o-chikara お力); (*real* **~**) jitsuryoku 実力; (*of saturation*) kósa 濃さ

strengthen *v* ~ (*it*) tsúyoku shimásu (suru, shite) 強くします(する, して), katamemásu (katameru, katamete) 固めます(固める, 固めて)

stretch 1. *v* (*stretches it*) nobashimásu (nobásu, nobáshite) 伸ばします(伸ばす, 伸ばして); (*it stretches*) nobimásu (nobíru, nóbite) 伸びます(伸びる, 伸びて), (*taut*) harimásu (haru, hatte) 張ります(張る, 張って) **2.** *n* nobi 伸び, senobi 背伸び

stretch over (*extends over*) ... ni matagarimásu (matagáru, matagátte) ...に跨がり[またがり]ます(跨がる, 跨がって)

stretcher *n* tánka 担架

strew *v* chirashimásu (chirasu, chirashite) 散らします(散らす, 散らして)

stricken area *n* higái-chi 被害地

strict *adj* (*severe*) kibishíi 厳しい, katai 固い・堅い, yakamashíi やかましい; (*precise*) genmitsu (na) 厳密(な); genjū (na) 厳重(な)

stride; ~ over matagimásu (matágu, matáide) 跨ぎ[またぎ]ます(跨ぐ, 跨いで)

strife *n* arasoi 争い, [BOOKISH] sō´dō 騒動

strike 1. *n* (*job action*) sutó スト, sutoraiki ストライキ; (*baseball*) sutoraiku ストライク **2. → hit**

striking *adj* (*outstanding*) ichijirushíi 著しい

strikingly *adv* ichijirúshiku 著しく

string 1. *n* (*thread*) íto 糸; (*cord*) himo ひも・紐; (*of violin or bow*) tsurú つる・弦 **2.** (*linked*) *in*

a string tsunagatte つながって **3. *string up*** *v* (*suspends*) tsurimásu (tsuru, tsutte) 吊ります(吊る, 吊って)

stripe *n* shimá しま・縞, sutoraipu ストライプ **stripe pattern** *n* shima-moyō 縞模様

striptease, strip show *n* sutoríppu ストリップ

strive *v* tsutomemásu (tsutoméru, tsutómete) 努めます(努める, 努めて), dóryoku shimásu (suru, shite) 努力します(する, して), tsukushimásu (tsukúsu, tsukúshite) 尽くします(尽くす, 尽くして)

stroke 1. *n* (*sounds of bell*) (kane no) hibiki (鐘の)響き **2.** *n* (*sports*) ichida 一打 **3.** *v* nademásu (náderu, nádete) なで[撫で]ます(なでる, なでて) **4.** *v* (*strike*) uchimásu (utsu, utte) 打ちます(打つ, 打って) **5.** *v* (*draw*) kakimásu (kaku, kaite) 描きます(描く, 描いて)

stroke order *n* kakijun 書き順

stroll *v* sanpo (shimásu; suru, shite) 散歩します(する, して)

strong *adj* tsuyói 強い; (*coffee, etc.*) kói 濃い; (*influential*) yūryoku (na) 有力(な)

strong point *n* (*merit*) chō´sho 長所

strong wind *n* ō-kaze 大風

structure *n* kōzō 構造; (*setup*) kumi-tate 組み立て; (*system*) soshiki 組織

struggle 1. *n* (*contention*) arasoi 争い **2.** *v* **~** *for* (*contends*) ... o arasoimásu (arasóu, arasótte) ...を争います(争う, 争って)

stucco *n* shikkui しっくい・漆喰

stuck; gets ~ (*clogged*) tsumarimásu (tsumáru, tsumátte) 詰まります(詰まる, 詰まって)

stuck-up *adj* (*affected*) kidotte imásu 気取っています, kidotta ...気取った...

student *n* gakusei 学生, ...-sei ...生, (*pupil*) séito 生徒; *student between schools* rōnin 浪人; *a student of the teacher's*, *one of the teacher's student* senséi no oshiego 先生の教え子; *the student of English* (*in general*) Eigo (no) gakushū´-sha 英語(の)学習者

studio *n* (*private*) atorie アトリエ; (*public*) sutajio スタジオ

studio apartment *n* wan-rū´mu ワンルーム

studious person *n* benkyō-ka 勉強家

study 1. *n* benkyō 勉強; gakushū 学習; **~** *by observation*, *field* **~** kengaku 見学 **2.** *n* (*room*) shosai 書斎 **3.** *v* (*studies it*) benkyō shimásu (suru, shite) 勉強します(する, して), manabimásu (manabu, manande) 学びます(学ぶ, 学んで), (*is tutored/taught*) osowarimásu (osowaru, osowatte) 教わります(教わる, 教わって); (*a basic subject*) gakushū shimásu (suru, shite) 学習します(する, して) **4.** *v* → **research** → **science**

stuff 1. *n* (*thing*) monó 物 **2.** *v* (*crams*) tsumemásu (tsuméru, tsúmete) 詰めます(詰める, 詰めて)

stumble *v* tsuma-zukimásu (tsuma-zuku, tsuma-zuite) つまずきます・躓きます(つまずく, つまずいて)

stump *n* (*tree*) kiri-kabu 切り株

stumped; is ~ mairimás<u>u</u> (máiru, máitte) 参ります(参る, 参って) → **perplexed**

stunt n kyokugéi 曲芸; **horseback stunts** kyokuba 曲馬

stupid adj báka (na) ばか・バカ・馬鹿(な)

sturdy adj jōbu (na) 丈夫(な)

style n **1.** ... fū´/...-fū ...風; ... sh<u>i</u>ki/ ...-sh<u>i</u>ki ...式; **Japanese ~** Nihon-fū (no) 日本風(の) **2.** (form) tái 態

stylish adj sumā´to (na) スマート(な), iki (na) いき[粋](な), otsu (na) おつ(な)

styptic pencil n chi-dome 血止め; sh<u>i</u>ketsu-zai 止血剤

subject n (topic) mondai 問題, (of conversation) wadai 話題; táne 種; (school) kamoku 科目; (grammar) shúgo 主語

subjective adj sh<u>u</u>kan-teki (na) 主観的な; **subjectivity** n sh<u>u</u>kan 主観

submarine n sensui-kan 潜水艦

submissive adj súnao (na) すなお[素直](な)

subordinate n búka 部下, (follower) kó-bun 子分

subscribe v yoyaku shimás<u>u</u> (suru, sh<u>i</u>te) 予約します(する, して), mōshi-komimás<u>u</u> (mōshi-komu, mōshi-konde) 申し込みます(申し込む, 申し込んで)

subscription n yoyaku 予約

subsequently adv ts<u>u</u>ide 次いで → **later** → **next**

substance n (material) bussh<u>i</u>tsu 物質

substantial adj **1.** (concrete) gutaiteki (na) 具体的(な) **2.** → **considerable**

substitute n kawari 代わり; daiyōhin 代用品

subtle adj wazuka (na) わずか(な), kasuka (na) 微か・かすか(な), (delicate) bimyō (na) 微妙(な)

subtract v h<u>i</u>kimás<u>u</u> (h<u>i</u>ku, hiite) 引きます(引く, 引いて)

suburb n kō´gai 郊外, sh<u>i</u>gai 市外, (outskirts) basue 場末; (bedroom community) beddotáun ベッドタウン

subway n ch<u>i</u>ka-tetsu 地下鉄

succeed v (is successful) seikō shimás<u>u</u> (suru, sh<u>i</u>te) 成功します(する, して); **~ to** (takes over for) uketsugimás<u>u</u> (uketsugu, uketsuide) 受け継ぎます(受け継ぐ, 受け継いで), tsugimás<u>u</u> (tsugu, tsuide) 継ぎます(継ぐ, 継いで); (in a projection) h<u>i</u>ki-tsugimás<u>u</u> (h<u>i</u>ki-tsúgu, h<u>i</u>ki-tsúide) 引き継ぎます(引き継ぐ, 引き継いで); (in a test) ukárimás<u>u</u> (ukáru, ukátte) 受かります(受かる, 受かって)

success n seikō 成功; gōkaku 合格; **making a ~ out of life** sh<u>u</u>sse 出世

success story n seikō-dan 成功談; sakusesu sutórii サクセス・ストーリー

successful adj umái うまい; umakuiku うまくいく; **is ~** → **succeed**

successfully adv úmaku うまく

succession; in ~ ts<u>u</u>ide 次いで・ついで, tsuzuite 続いて; tsunagatte つながって; tsuzukete 続けて

in rapid succession adv zokuzoku ぞくぞく・続々

such adj sonna そんな, sono yō´na そのよう[様]な, sō yū そうゆう; (like this) konna こんな, kono yō´na このよう[様]な, kō yū こうゆう

such-and-such a place dókodoko どこどこ, dókosoko どこそこ

suck v suimás<u>u</u> (sū, s<u>u</u>tte) 吸います(吸う, 吸って); shaburimás<u>u</u> (shaburu, shabutte) しゃぶります(しゃぶる, しゃぶって)

It sucks! saitē da 最低だ, hidoi ひどい

sucker n (dupe) kámo かも・カモ・鴨

sudden adj (unexpected) totsuzen (no) 突然(の), níwaka にわか; (urgent) kyū (na) 急(な); **sudden shower** yūdachi 夕立・ゆうだち, niwaka ame にわか雨

sudden illness n kyūbyō 急病

suddenly adv fui ni 不意に, totsuzen 突然; (unexpectedly) níwaka ni にわかに, (immediately) tachimachi (ni) たちまち(に); (urgently) kyū ni 急に; (with a rush) dotto どっと; (with a jerk/gulp) gutto ぐっと; (with a sudden start of surprise) hatto (sh<u>i</u>te) はっと(して)

sue v uttaemás<u>u</u> (uttaeru, uttaete) 訴えます(訴える, 訴えて)

suffer v kurushimimás<u>u</u> (kurushímu, kurushínde) 苦しみます(苦しむ, 苦しんで), nayamimás<u>u</u> (nayámu, nayánde) 悩みます(悩む, 悩んで), wazuraimás<u>u</u> (wazurau, wazuratte) 煩います(煩う, 煩って); (incurs) kōmurimás<u>u</u> (kōmúru, kōmútte) 被り[こうむり]ます(被る, 被って), ukemás<u>u</u> (ukéru, úkete) 受けます(受ける, 受けて)

suffer from ... o wazuraimás<u>u</u> (wazurau, wazuratte) ...を煩い[わずらい]ます(煩う, 煩って) → **incur**

suffering n kurushimi 苦しみ, (anguish) nayamí 悩み

suffice, sufficient v, adj tarimás<u>u</u> (tariru, tarite) 足ります(足りる, 足りて)

suffix n setsubi-go/-ji 接尾語/辞

sugar n satō´ 砂糖・サトウ (o-satō お砂糖)

suggest(ion) → **propose** (proposal) → **hint**

suicide n jisatsu 自殺

double suicide n shinjū 心中

suicidal wishes n jisatsu ganbō 自殺願望, [BOOKISH] kishi nenryo 希死念慮

suit 1. n yō-fuku 洋服 (o-yō´fuku お洋服), fuku 服, (business) sebiro 背広, sū´tsu スーツ, (esp. woman's two-piece) tsūpíisu ツーピース; (diving suit) sensui fuku 潜水服, daibingu sūtsu ダイビング・スーツ **2.** n (of playing cards) kumí 組 **3.** v (matches with) ...ni aimás<u>u</u> (áu, átte) ...に合います(合う, 合って); **suits one's taste** k<u>u</u>chi ni aimás<u>u</u> 口に合います **4.** v (is becoming to) ...ni ni-aimás<u>u</u> (ni-áu, ni-átte) ...に似合います(似合う, 似合って)

suitable adj f<u>u</u>sawashíi ふさわしい, tekitō (na) 適当(な), tekigi (na) 適宜(な); (moderate) kakkō

443

(na) 格好(な); *is ~* teki-shimásu (teki-súru, tekí-shite) 適する, 適します, 適して); *the most ~* uttetsuke (no) うってつけ(の)

suitably *adv* fusawáshiku ふさわしく, tekitō ni 適当に

suitcase *n* kaban かばん・鞄, sūtsukḗsu スーツケース; (*luggage*) (te-)nímotsu (手)荷物

sulk *v* fukuremásu (fukureru, fukurete) 膨れます (膨れる, 膨れて)

sullen face *n* butchō-zura 仏頂面

sultry *adj* (*weather*) mushi-atsúi 蒸し暑い; (*behavior*) jōnetsúteki (na) 情熱的(な); *gets sultry* mushimásu (músu, múshite) 蒸します(蒸す, 蒸して)

sum 1. *n* gáku 額 **2.** *to ~ it up* yōsúru ni 要するに

sumac *n* (*plant*) háze はぜ・ハゼ

summarize *v* yōyaku shimásu (suru, shite) 要約します(する, して), tsumamimásu (tsumamu, tsumande) つまみます(つまむ, つまんで), tsuzumemásu (tsuzuméru, tsuzúmete) つづめ[約め]ます(つづめる, つづめて)

summary *n* taiyō 大要, yōyaku 要約, (*gist*) yō´shi 要旨; gaiyō 概要; *in ~* yōsúru ni 要するに・ようするに

summer *n* natsú 夏; *summer gift* (o-)chūgen (お)中元; *summer period/term* káki 夏期; *summer school* kaki-kōshū 夏期講習; *summer solstice* geshi 夏至; *summer vacation/holidays* natsuyásumi 夏休み

summit *n* itadaki 頂・いただき, chōjō´ 頂上, mine 峰・みね

summon *v* yobimásu (yobu, yonde) 呼びます (呼ぶ, 呼んで)

sumo → wrestling, wrestler

sun *n* táiyō 太陽・たいよう, hi 日, o-ténto-sama おてんとさま・お天道様, [BABY TALK] o-hi-sama お日様

sunbathing *n* (*enjoying the warmth of the sun*) hinata-bókko ひなた[日向]ぼっこ, (*sunbathing, tanning*) nikkōyoku 日光浴

sunburn *n* hiyake 日焼け

Sunday *n* Nichiyō´bi 日曜日

sundry *adj* zatta (na) 雑多(な); *sundries* zakka 雑貨

sunglass *n* sangurasu サングラス

sunny *adj* (*room, etc.*) hiatari ga íi 日当りがいい

sunrise *n* hinode 日の出

sunset *n* hinoiri 日の入り, nichibotsu 日没; (*time*) higure 日暮れ

sunshade *n* hiyoke 日よけ, hi-gasa 日傘・ひがさ

sunshine *n* hinata ひなた・日向, níkkō 日光, sanshain サンシャイン

super *adj* chō 超, sūpā スーパー
superman *n* sū´pāman スーパーマン, chōjin 超人
supernatural *n* chō shizen (no) 超自然(の)
supernatural power *n* chō nōryoku 超能力

superfluous *adj* yokei (na) 余計・よけい(な); (*surplus*) kajō (no) 過剰(の)

superintendent *n* kantoku 監督

superior 1. *adj* yūshū (na) 優秀(な); jōtō (no) 上等(の); ue (no) 上(の), meue (no) 目上(の) **2.** *adj* erái 偉い; masatte iru 勝っている **3.** *n a superior* menue no hító 目上の人

supermarket *n* sū´pā スーパー, sū´pā-mā´ketto スーパーマーケット

supervise *v* kantoku shimásu (suru, shite) 監督します(する, して)

supervisor *n* kantoku 監督, sū´pā-baizā スーパーバイザー, esu bui, esu vii SV

supper *n* ban-góhan 晩ご飯, yūshoku 夕食, yū-han 夕飯

supplement *n* hosoku 補足, zōho 増補; (*pills*) sapuriment サプリメント, sapuri サプリ; *food supplements* eiyōhojo-shokuhin 栄養補助食品

supplies *n* ...-yō´hin ...用品, (*necessities*) hitsuju-hin 必需品, (*expendables*) shōmō-hin 消耗品

supply 1. *v supplies it* kyōkyū shimásu (suru, shite) 供給します(する, して); hokyū shimásu (suru, shite) 補給します(する, して) **→ provide → give → sell 2.** *supply(ing)* *n* kyōkyū 供給; hokyū 補給
supply and demand *n* juyo to kyōkyū 需要と供給

support 1. *n* (*approval*) sansei 賛成, sandō 賛同; (*backing, help*) kōen 後援, bákku-appu バックアップ, ōen 応援; (*aid*) énjo 援助, sapōto サポート **2.** *v* (*supports it*) ōen shimásu (suru, shite) 応援します(する, して), bákku-appu shimásu (suru, shite) バックアップします(する, して); (*props it*) sasaemásu (sasaeru, sasaete) 支えます(支える, 支えて); (*endorses*) shíji shimásu (suru, shite) 支持します(する, して)

supporter *n* (*football*) fan ファン; *athletic supporter* (*jockstrap*) sapō´tā サポーター

suppose *v* ... to shimásu (suru, shite) ...とします (する, して); sō omoimásu (omou, omotte) そう思います(思う, 思って) **→ think → imagine**

supposed *adj* katei (no) 仮定(の)

supposition *n* katei 仮定; (*conjecture*) suisoku 推測

suppress *v* appaku shimásu (suru, shite) 圧迫します(する, して)

suppression *n* appaku 圧迫

surcharge *n* tsuika-ryōkin 追加料金

sure *adj* táshika (na) 確か・たしか(な)
for sure *adv* kanarazu 必ず・かならず, táshika ni 確かに・たしかに, zé-hi ぜひ・是非
makes sure *v* tashikamemásu (tashikaméru, tashikámete) 確かめます(確かめる, 確かめて); *to make sure* nen no tamé (ni) 念のため[為](に)
to be sure *adv* móttómo もっとも **→ of course**

surely *adv* kitto きっと

surf 1. *n* yoseru-nami 寄せる波 **2.** *v* sā´fin o shimásu (suru, shite) サーフィンをします(する, して); (*to surf the internet*) netto sā´fin o shimásu (suru, shite) ネットサーフィンをします(する、して)

surface 1. *n* mén 面, hyōmén 表面; (*top*) uwabe うわべ・上辺; *entire surface* zenmen 全面 **2.** *v* (*becomes known*) barémásu (baréru, baréte) ばれます(ばれる、ばれて)

surfboard *n* sāfubōdo サーフボード, sāfínbōdo サーフィンボード

surf clam *n* (*geoduck*) mirú-gai みる貝・ミルガイ

surfer, surfrider *n* sāfā サーファー

surfing, surfriding *n* nami-nori 波乗り, sāfín サーフィン

surgeon *n* geká-i 外科医

surgery *n* (*surgical operation*) shújutsu 手術; (*as a medical specialty*) geka 外科

surmise 1. *n* suisoku 推測 **2.** *v* suisoku shimásu (suru, shite) 推測します(する、して)

surpass *v* suguremásu (suguréru, sugúrete) 優れ [すぐれ]ます(優れる、優れて), nukimásu (nuku, nuite) 抜きます(抜く、抜いて), masarimásu (masaru, masatte) 勝ります(勝る、勝って)

surplus *n* yoyū 余裕; kajō (no) 過剰(の)

surprised; gets ~ bikkúri shimásu (suru, shite) びっくりします(する、して), odorokimásu (odoróku, odoróite) 驚きます(驚く、驚いて)

surprising *adj* omoigakénai 思いがけない

surrender *n, v* kōfuku/kōsan (shimásu; suru, shite) 降伏/降参します(する、して)

surround *v* kakomimásu (kakomu, kakonde) 囲みます(囲む、囲んで); (*centers on*) megurimásu (meguru, megutte) 巡ります(巡る、巡って)

surrounding 1. *adj the ~* ... shūhen no ... 周辺の... **2.** *adj* (*centering on*) ... o megutte ...を巡って **3.** *surroundings* *n* shū´i 周囲

sushi *n* (o-)súshi (お)すし[寿司・鮨], sushí すし・寿司・鮨; *covered with fish tidbits* chirashí-zushi ちらし[鮨]; *in a bag of aburage* (*fried bean curd*) inarí-zushi いなりずし・稲荷鮨; *rolled in seaweed* norí-maki のり巻き; (*with cucumber*) kappa(-maki) かっぱ(巻き); (*around tuna tidbit*) tekka(-maki) 鉄火(巻き); *hand-packed into small balls* nigirí-zushi にぎりずし[鮨]; *pressed with marinated fish in squarish molds* oshi-zushi 押しずし[鮨]

sushi bar *n* sushí-ya すし[寿司・鮨]屋(o-sushi-ya おすし[寿司・鮨]屋)

suspect 1. *v* utagaimásu (utagau, utagatte) 疑います(疑う、疑って) **2.** *n* yōgí-sha 容疑者

suspend *v* **1.** (*hangs it*) tsurimásu (tsuru, tsutte) 吊ります(吊る、吊って), burasagemásu (bura-sageru, burasagete) ぶら下げます(ぶら下げる、ぶら下げて) **2.** (*stops in the midst*) chūshi shimásu (suru, shite) 中止します(する、して)

suspenders *n* zubón-tsuri ズボンつり, sasupendā サスペンダー

suspense *n* sasupensu サスペンス

suspense film *n* sasupensu eiga サスペンス映画

suspension *n* (*stoppage*) teishi 停止, (*abeyance*) chūshi 中止

suspicious *adj* fushigi (na) 不思議(な), ayashii 怪しい, ikagawashíi いかがわしい

sustain *v* (*incurs*) kōmurimásu (kōmúru, kōmútte) 被り[こうむり]ます(被る、被って)

sutra *n* (*Buddhist scripture*) o-kyō お経, kyōten 経典

swab *n* (*scrub*) tawashi たわし・タワシ, (*mop*) móppu モップ; (*cotton*) watá 綿, (*sponge*) suponji スポンジ; (*earpick*) mimikáki 耳かき

swagger *v* ibarimásu (ibáru, ibátte) 威張ります(威張る、威張って)

swallow 1. *n* (*the bird*) tsubame つばめ・ツバメ・燕 **2.** *v* (*ingests*) nomi-komimásu (nomi-komu, nomi-konde) 飲み込みます(飲み込む、飲み込んで)

swamp *n* numá 沼

swan *n* hakuchō 白鳥・ハクチョウ

sway *v* **1.** (*it sways*) yuremásu (yureru, yurete) 揺れます(揺れる、揺れて) **2.** (*sways it*) yusu-burimásu (yusuburu, yusubutte) 揺すぶります(揺すぶる、揺すぶって), yurimásu (yuru, yutte) 揺ります(揺る、揺って)

swear *v* **1.** (*vows*) chikaimásu (chikau, chikatte) 誓います(誓う、誓って) **2.** (*reviles*) nonoshirimásu (nonoshíru, nonoshítte) ののしります・罵ります (ののしる、ののしって)

sweat *n, v* áse (ga demásu; déru, déte) 汗(が出ます; 出る、出て)

sweater *n* sē´tā セーター (*how many* nánmai 何枚)

sweep *v* sōji shimásu (suru, shite) 掃除します (する、して); hakimásu (háku, háite) 掃きます (掃く、掃いて)

sweeper *n* sōjí-ki 掃除機

sweeping *n* sōji 掃除(o-sō´ji お掃除)

sweet *adj* amai 甘い

sweet and sour *adj* amazuppai 甘酸っぱい

sweet and sour pork *n* su-buta 酢豚・スブタ

sweet rice wine *n* mirin みりん・ミリン・味醂

sweet roll with beanjam inside *n* anpan あんパン

sweetfish *n* (*river trout*) áyu あゆ・アユ・鮎, ái あい

sweetheart *n* ii-hito いい人, koibito 恋人

sweet potato *n* satsuma-imo さつま[薩摩]芋・サツマイモ → **potato**

sweets *n* (*pastry, candy*) (o-)káshi (お)菓子

swell *adj* (*splendid*) suteki (na) すてき[素敵](な), (*terrific*) sugói すごい・凄い

swell *v ~ (up)* haremásu (hareru, harete) 腫れ[はれ]ます(腫れる、腫れて); fukuramimásu (fukura-mu, fukurande) 膨らみ[ふくらみ]ます(膨らむ、膨らんで), fukuremásu (fukureru, fukurete) 膨れ [ふくれ]ます(膨れる、膨れて); [BOOKISH] bōchō shimásu (suru, shite) 膨脹します(する、して); ō´kiku narimásu (náru, nátte) 大きくなります (なる、なって) → **increase**

swelling *n* hare-mono 腫れ物; dekí-mónó できも の・出来物, o-déki おでき; (*bump*) kobú こぶ・瘤

445

swim 1. *n* (hitó-)oyogi (ひと)泳ぎ **2.** *v* oyogimásu (oyógu, oyóide) 泳ぎます (泳ぐ, 泳いで)
swim suit *n* mizu-gi 水着
swimming *n* oyogí 泳ぎ, suiei 水泳, suimingu スイミング; *swimming pool* pū´ru プール
swimming meet *n* suiei taikai 水泳大会, suiei kyōgi kai 水泳競技会
swing 1. *v* (*it swings*) yuremásu (yureru, yurete) 揺れます (揺れる, 揺れて) **2.** *v* (*swings it*) yusuburimásu (yusuburu, yusubutte) 揺すぶります (揺すぶる, 揺すぶって), yurimásu (yuru, yutte) 揺ります (揺る, 揺って) **3.** *n* (*a swing*) búranko ぶらんこ **4.** *gets into the ~ of things* chōshi ni norimásu (noru, notte) 調子に乗ります (乗る, 乗って), chōshi ga demásu (déru, déte) 調子が出ます (出る, 出て)
swipe *v* kapparaimásu (kapparau, kapparatte) かっぱらいます (かっぱらう, かっぱらって); nusumimásu (nusúmu, nusúnde) 盗みます (盗む, 盗んで)
Swiss 1. *adj* Súisu no スイスの **2.** *n* (*person*) Suisú-jin スイス人
switch *n* suítchi スイッチ → **change** → **turn on/off**
Switzerland *n* Súisu スイス
sword *n* kataná 刀; (*double-edged*) kén/tsurugí 剣; yaiba やいば・刃
sword battle *n* chanbara ちゃんばら
swordfish *n* kájiki かじき・カジキ
sword-guard *n* tsúba つば・ツバ・鍔
syllable *n* onsetsu 音節
symbol *n* shinboru シンボル, [BOOKISH] shōchō 象徴; (*mark*) kigō 記号

symbol of peace *n* heiwa no shōchō 平和の象徴, heiwa no shinboru 平和のシンボル
symbol of the nation *n* kuni no shōchō 国の象徴
symmetry *n* tsuriai 釣り合い・つりあい; taiō 対応
sympathize *v* ~ *with* … ni dōjō shimásu (suru, shite) …に同情します (する, して); (*takes into consideration*) … o kumimásu (kumu, kunde) …を汲みます (汲む, 汲んで); sas-shimásu (sas-suru, sas-shite) 察します (察する, 察して)
sympathy *n* dōjō 同情, kyōkan 共感
symptom *n* (*sign*) shirushi しるし [徴]; shōjō 症状; (*unusual state*) ijō 異常
syndicate *n* shinjikēto シンジケート
syndrome *n* (*medical*) shōkōgun 症候群, shindorōmu シンドローム
synonym *n* dōi-go 同義語, dōgi-go 同義語
synthesis *n* sōgō 総合
synthesized *adj* (*composite*) sōgōteki (na) 総合的 (な)
synthetic fiber *n* kagaku sen'i 化学繊維, kasen 化繊
syphilis *n* (*medical*) baidoku 梅毒
Syria *n* shiria シリア
syringe *n* (*for injections*) chūsháki 注射器; (*for water*) chūsúiki 注水器
syrup *n* shíroppu シロップ
system *n* soshiki 組織, séido 制度, taikei 体系, chítsujo 秩序, shisutemu システム
systematic *adj* kichōmen na きちょうめんな, kisoku-tadashii 規則正しい, tejundōri no 手順通りの (= *orderly*)

T

tab *n* tsumami つまみ; tábu タブ → **bill**
tabby *n* tora neko トラ猫
table *n* **1.** tēburu テーブル, táku 卓; (*dinner table*) shokutaku 食卓, (*low meal table*) (shoku)zen (食)膳 (o-zen お膳, gó-zen ご膳) **2.** (*list*) hyō 表; (*inventory*) mokuroku 目録
multiplication table *n* kakezan hyō 掛け算表
tablecloth *n* tēburú-kake テーブル掛け; teburukurosu テーブルクロス
table d'hôte *n* (*meal of the house/day*) teishoku 定食
table knife *n* tēburu naifu テーブルナイフ, shokutaku-yō naifu 食卓用ナイフ
table lamp *n* denki sutando 電気スタンド
table of contents, TOC *n* mokuji 目次
table salt *n* shokúen 食塩, shokutakú-en 食卓塩
tablespoon *n* ō-saji 大さじ・大匙
table tennis *n* takkyū 卓球
tableware *n* shokki 食器

tablet *n* (*pill*) jōzai 錠剤, taburetto タブレット; (*note pad*) memo-chō メモ帳
taboo *n* tabū タブー; kinki 禁忌
taciturn *adj* mukuchi (na) 無口 (な); [BOOKISH] kamoku (na) 寡黙 (な)
tack 1. *n* byō´ びょう・鋲; (*sewing*) shi-tsuke 仕付け **2.** *v tacks it on the wall* … o kabe ni byō´ de tomemásu (tomeru, tomete) …を壁にびょう [鋲] で留めます (留める, 留めて); (*with thread*) shi-tsukemásu (shi-tsukéru, shi-tsúkete) 仕付けます (仕付ける, 仕付けて)
tacking (*with thread*) *n* shi-tsuke 仕付け; *tacking thread* shitsuke-íto 仕付け糸
tackle *n* takkuru タックル
tact *n* **1.** kiten 機転, saiki 才気 **2.** kanshoku 感触
tactful *adj* kiten no kiku 機転のきく
tactician *n* senjutsu-ka 戦術家
tactics *n* (*strategy*) senjutsu 戦術, sakusen 作戦
teddy bear *n* tedii bea テディベア

tadpole *n* otamajakushi オタマジャクシ

tag *n* fuda 札; (*baggage/package ~*) ní-fuda 荷札, tagu タグ

name tag *n* na fuda 名札

price tag *n* ne fuda 値札

tail *n* shippó しっぽ・尻尾, ó 尾; *the tail end* びり, ketsu けつ・尻

tailor *n* shitate-ya 仕立屋, yōfuku-ya 洋服屋

Taisho era *n* Taishō jidai 大正時代

Taiwan *n* Taiwan 台湾; *a Taiwanese* Taiwán-jin 台湾人

Tajikistan *n* Tajikisutan タジキスタン

take *v* **1.** torimásu (tóru, tótte) 取ります(取る, 取って), totte/motte ikimásu (iku, itte) 取って/持って行きます(行く, 行って) **2.** hipparimásu (hippáru, hippátte) 引っ張ります(引っ張る, 引っ張って) **3.** (*requires*) yō-shimásu (yō-súru, yō´-shite) 要します(要する, 要して); (*requires time/money*) (jikan/kane ga) kakarimásu (kakáru, kakátte) (時間/金が)かかります(かかる, かかって) **4.** (*incurs*) ukemásu (ukéru, úkete) 受けます(受ける, 受けて); (*accepts; understands*) uke-torimásu (uke-toru, uke-totte) 受け取ります(受け取る, 受け取って); *~ it seriously* honki ni shimásu (suru, shite) 本気にします(する, して); *~ one's blood pressure* ketsuatsu o hakarimásu (hakáru, hakátte) 血圧を計ります(計る, 計って); *~ a bath* fúró ni hairimásu (hairu, háitte) 風呂に入ります(入る, 入って); *~ a shower* shāwá o abimásu (abiru, abite) シャワーを浴びます(浴びる, 浴びて); *~ medicine* kusuri o nomimásu (nómu, nónde) 薬を飲みます(飲む, 飲んで); *~ a picture* shashin o torimásu (tóru, tótte) 写真を撮ります(撮る, 撮って), utsushimásu (utsúsu, utsúshite) 写します(写す, 写して)

take advantage of *v* ... o riyō shimásu (suru, shite) ...を利用します(する, して); zu ni norimásu (noru, notte) 図に乗ります(乗る, 乗って)

take away *v* totte ikimásu (iku, itte) 取って行きます(行く, 行って); (*confiscates, deprives of*) tori-agemásu (tori-ageru, tori-agete) 取り上げます(取り上げる, 取り上げて); (*clears from table*) sagemásu (sagéru, ságete) 下げます(下げる, 下げて)

take aim *v* nerai o tsukemásu (tsukéru, tsukéte) 狙いをつけます(つける, つけて)

take apart *v* barashimásu (barásu, baráshite) ばらします(ばらす, ばらして)

take care of *v* **1.** (*handles*) ... o shóri shimásu (suru, shite) ...を処理します(する, して) **2.** (*~ a person*) ... no sewá o shimásu (suru, shite) ...の世話をします(する, して), ... no mendó o mimásu (míru, míte) ...の面倒をみます(みる, みて)

Take care (of yourself). *interj* O-daiji ni! お大事に!

take charge of ... *v* ... o hiki-ukemásu (hiki-ukéru, hiki-úkete) ...を引き受けます(引き受ける, 引き受けて), tannin/tantō shimásu (suru, shite) 担任/担当します(する, して)

take down *v* oroshimásu (orósu, oróshite) 下ろし[降ろし]ます(下ろす, 下ろして)

take effect *v* (*is effective*) kikimásu (kíku, kiite) 効きます(効く, 効いて)

take fright *v* kowagarimásu (kowagáru, kowagátte) 怖がり[こわがり]ます(怖がる, 怖がって)

take in(to) *v* iremásu (ireru, irete) 入れます(入れる, 入れて); *takes into consideration/account* kōryo ni iremásu (ireru, irete) 考慮に入れます(入れる, 入れて)

take in trust *v* azukarimásu (azukáru, azukátte) 預かります(預かる, 預って)

Take it easy. *interj* **1.** Go-yukkúri. ごゆっくり. **2.** → good-bye

take off *v* **1.** (*removes*) hazushimásu (hazusu, hazushíte) 外します(外す, 外して); (*clothes, shoes, etc.*) nugimásu (núgu, núide), 脱ぎます(脱ぐ, 脱いで) **2.** (*plane*) ririku shimásu (suru, shite) 離陸します(する, して)

take-off *n* (*of a plane*) ririku 離陸

take offense *v* shaku ni sawarimásu (sawaru, sawatte) しゃく[癪]にさわり[障り]ます(さわる, さわって)

take over *v* hiki-tori/tsugimásu (hiki-tóru/tsúgu, hiki-tótte/tsuide) 引き取り/継ぎます(引き取る/継ぐ, 引き取って/継いで); (*illegally seizes*) nottorimásu (nottóru, nottótte) 乗っ取ります(乗っ取る, 乗っ取って)

takeover *n* (*illegal seizure*) nottorijíken 乗っ取り事件

take pains *v* honé o orimásu (óru, ótte) 骨を折ります(折る, 折って)

take refuge *v* hínan shimásu (suru, shite) 避難します(する, して)

take responsibility for *v* (*responsibility for situation*) ... o hiki-ukemásu (hiki-ukéru, hiki-úkete) ...を引き受けます(引き受ける, 引き受けて), ... no sekinin o tori/oimásu (toru/ou, totte/otte) ...の責任を取り/負います(取る/負う, 取って/負って)

take revenge *v* fukushū shimásu (suru, shite) 復讐します(する, して)

take time off *v* yasumimásu (yasúmu, yasúnde) 休みます(休む, 休んで)

take up *v* tori-agemásu (tori-ageru, tori-agete) 取り上げます(取り上げる, 取り上げて)

takeaway, takeout *n* (*food*) (o-)mochikaeri (お)持ち帰り

tale *n* (o-)hanashí (お)話, monogátari 物語

fairy tale *n* yōsei monogatari 妖精物語, otogi-banashi 御伽噺・おとぎ話

old tale *n* mukashi-banashi 昔話

The Tale of the Bamboo-Cutter *n* Taketori monogatari 竹取物語

The Tale of Genji *n* Genji monogatari 源氏物語

talent *n* sainō 才能, sái 才; (*personality*) tarento タレント; *talent agency* *n* geinō purodakushon 芸能プロダクション

talented *adj* sainō (no) aru 才能(の)ある

taleteller *n* (*liar*) usotsuki 嘘つき

talisman (*of a shrine*) *n* o-fuda お札, go-fu 護符, o-mamori お守り

talk 1. *n* hanashí 話; (*conference, discussion*) hanashi-ai 話し合い, (*consultation*) sōdan 相談 → **speech** 2. *v* (*speaks*) hanashimásu (hanásu, hanáshite) 話します(話す, 話して); **~ together** hanashi-aimásu (hanashi-au, hanashi-atte) 話し合います(話し合う, 話し合って)

talk back *v* kuchi-gotae o shimásu (suru, shite) 口答えをします(する, して)

talk big *v* (*boost*) hora o fukimásu (fuku, fuite) ほらを吹く

talk show *n* tōku shō トークショー, taidan bangumi 対談番組

talkative *adj* hanashizuki (na) 話し好き(な), oshaberi (na) おしゃべり・お喋り(な)

tall *adj* takái 高い; (*of body height*) sé ga takái 背が高い

tall story *n* (*unbelivable story*) hora ほら[法螺]

tambourine *n* tanbarin タンバリン

tame *v ~ it* narashimásu (narásu, naráshite) 馴らします(馴らす, 馴らして), kainarashimásu (kainarásu, kainaráshite) 飼い慣らします(飼い慣らす, 飼い慣らして)

tan *n* hiyake 日焼け

tanned *adj* hiyakeshita 日焼けした

tandem *n* tandemu タンデム, futarinori-yō (no) jitensha/jidensha 二人乗り用(の)自転車

tangerine *n* (*Mandarin orange*) míkan みかん・ミカン・蜜柑

tangible *adj* gutai-teki (na) 具体的(な)

tangle *n* (*entanglement*) motsure もつれ・縺れ

tangled *adj* (*complicated*) yayakoshíi/yaya(k)koshíi ややこしい/ややっこしい → **entangled**

tango *n* tango タンゴ

tank *n* tanku タンク

tank top *n* tanku toppu タンクトップ

tanka *n* tanka 短歌

tanker *n* tankā タンカー

tantalum *n* (*metal*) tantaru タンタル

Tanzania *n* Tanzania タンザニア

tap 1. *v* (*karuku*) tatakimásu (tataku, tataite) (軽く)叩きます・たたきます(たたく, たたいて) 2. *v* tōchō shimásu (suru, shite) 盗聴します(する, して) 3. *n* jaguchi 蛇口 4. *n* (*tap-daicing*) tappu dansu タップダンス

tap water *n* suidōsui 水道水

tape *n* tē´pu テープ; himo ひも・紐

adhesive tape *n* bansōkō 絆創膏・ばんそうこう

adhesive cellophane tape *n* serohan tēpu セロハンテープ

gum tape *n* gamu tēpu ガムテープ

tape measure *n* makijaku 巻き尺, mejā メジャー

tape recorder *n* tēpu-rekō´dā テープレコーダー

tapestry *n* tapesutorii タペストリー

tapping *n* (*medical exam*) dashin 打診

tar *n* tāru タール

target *n* mato 的, taishō 対象; (*goal*) mokuhyō 目標, tāgetto ターゲット

tariff *n* kanzei 関税

tart *n* (*pie*) taruto タルト

tart pastry *n* taruto kiji タルト生地

tartan *n* tātan タータン

tartan check *n* tātan chekku タータンチェック

task *n* shigoto 仕事; tasuku タスク

task allocation *n* shigoto (no) haibun 仕事(の)配分; tasuku (no) haibun タスク(の)配分

Tasman Peninsula *n* (*Australia*) Tasuman hantō タスマン半島

tassel *n* fusa 房

taste 1. *n* (*flavor*) aji 味, fūmi 風味; (*has flavor*) aji ga shimásu (suru, shite) 味がします(する, して) 2. (*liking*) shúmi 趣味; tēsuto テースト, sensu センス. konomí 好み (o-konomi お好み); *simple* (*modest*) *tastes* wabi わび・侘び

There is no accounting for taste. [IDIOM] Tade kuu mushi mo sukizuki. たで食う虫も好き好き.

bad taste *n* akushumi 悪趣味

bitter taste *n* nigai aji 苦い味, [BOOKISH] nigami 苦味

bitter taste of life *n* (*jinsei no*) nigai keiken (人生の)苦い経験

good taste *n* yoi shumi 良い趣味, ii sensu いいセンス

sweet taste *n* amai aji 甘い味, [BOOKISH] kanmi 甘味

sour taste *n* suppai aji 酸っぱい味, [BOOKISH] sanmi 酸味

taste *v* (*tastes it*) ajiwaimásu (ajiwau, ajiwatte) 味わいます(味わう, 味わって), namemásu (naméru, námete) なめ[舐め]ます(なめる, なめて); (*tries eating it*) tábete mimásu (míru, míte) 食べてみます(みる, みて)

tasty *adj* oishii おいしい・美味しい, umái うまい・旨い・美味い, bimi 美味

tatami *n* tatami たたみ・畳

tatami room *n* zashíki 座敷(o-zashiki お座敷)

tattoo *n* ire-zumi 入れ墨・刺青

Taurus *n* (*star sign*) Oushi-za 牡牛座・おうし座

taught → **teach; is taught** osowarimásu (oso-waru, osowatte) 教わります(教わる, 教わって)

taut; stretched ~ pin-to hatta ピンと張った

tavern *n* nomí-ya 飲み屋; izaka-ya 居酒屋

tax *n* zéi 税, zeikin 税金; *tax* (*revenue*) *stamp* shūnyū-ínshi 収入印紙

consumption tax *n* shōhi zei 消費税

corporation tax *n* hōjin zei 法人税

income tax *n* shotoku zei 所得税

national tax *n* koku zei 国税

residential tax *n* jūmin zei 住民税

regional taxation bureau *n* kokuzei-kyoku 国税局

sales tax *n* uriage zei 売上税

tax-free *adj* menzei (no) 免税(の); **~ goods** menzei-hin 免税品; **~ shop** menzei-ten 免税店

448

tax office *n* zeimusho 税務署

tax refund *n* zeikin (no) kanpu 税金(の)還付

withheld tax *n* gensen chōshū-zei 源泉徴収税

taxi *n* tákushii タクシー; *taxi stand/station* takushii nori-ba タクシー乗り場

TB *n* (hai-)kekkaku (肺)結核, haibyō 肺病

tea *n* cha 茶; (*green*) ryoku-cha 緑茶, o-cha お茶, (*coarse*) bancha 番茶, (*bitter*) shibucha 渋茶; (*black*) kōcha 紅茶, tii ティー; (*powdered green, for tea ceremony*) matcha 抹茶; (*weak powdered*) usu-cha 薄茶, o-úsu お薄; *a cup of green tea* [*sushi bar term*] agari 上がり; *makes ~* o-cha o iremásu (ireru, irete) お茶を入れます(入れる, 入れて)

Japanese tea *n* nihon cha 日本茶

tea bag *n* tii baggu ティーバッグ

teacake *n* (o-)cha-gáshi (お)茶菓子

tea canister/caddy *n* cha-ire 茶入れ; (*for tea ceremony*) natsume 棗・なつめ

tea ceremony *n* o-cha お茶, chano-yu 茶の湯, sadō 茶道; *tea ceremony procedures* temae 点前 (o-témae お点前)

teacup *n* yunomí 湯飲み, yunomi-jáwan 湯飲み茶碗; (*also ricebowl*) chawan 茶碗 (o-cháwan お茶碗)

teakettle *n* yakan やかん, yuwákashi 湯沸し

teapot *n* do-bin どびん・土瓶, kyūsu きゅうす・急須, cha-bin ちゃびん・茶瓶

tearoom *n* kissa-ten 喫茶店; (*for tea ceremony*) (o-)chashitsu (お)茶室

tea scoop *n* (*for tea ceremony*) chashaku 茶杓

tea party *n* o-chakai お茶会

teaspoon *n* sájí さじ・匙, ko-saji 小さじ・小匙 cha-saji 茶さじ・茶匙, tii supūn ティースプーン

teatime *n* tii taimu ティータイム, o-cha no jikan お茶の時間

tea whisk *n* (*for tea ceremony*) chasen 茶筅

teach *v* oshiemásu (oshieru, oshiete) 教えます (教える, 教えて)

teacher *n* senséi 先生; (*school-teacher*) gakkō no senséi 学校の先生, (*instructor*) kyō´shi 教師

head teacher *n* kōchō (sensei) 校長(先生)

teaching *n* kyōju 教授, oshie 教え; *classroom teaching* júgyō 授業; *teaching hours* jugyō-jíkan 授業時間

teaching materials *n* kyōzai 教材

team *n* chíimu チーム

team up (*with*) (... to) kumimásu (kúmu, kúnde) (...と)組みます(組む, 組んで)

teamwork *n* chiimu-wā´ku チームワーク, kyōdō sagyō 共同作業

tear 1. *n* (*in eye*) námida 涙

burst into tears *v* watto nakidashimásu (nakidasu, nakidashite) わっと泣き出します(泣き出す, 泣き出して)

tear gland *n* ruisen 涙腺

tears of joy *n* ureshinamida 嬉し涙

tears of mortification *n* kuyashinamida 悔し涙

2. *v* (*tears it*) sakimásu (sáku, sáite) 裂きます(裂

く, 裂いて), yaburimásu (yabúru, yabútte) 破ります(破る, 破って); *tears into pieces* chigirimásu (chigiru, chigitte) 千切ります(千切る, 千切って)

3. *v* (*it tears*) sakemásu (sakéru, sákete) 裂けます (裂ける, 裂けて), yaburemásu (yaburéru, yabúrete) 破れます(破れる, 破れて)

teardrop *n* namida no tsubu 涙の粒

teardrop-shaped (diamond) *adj* namida-gata no (daiyamondo) 涙型の(ダイヤモンド)

tearful *adj* namidagunda 涙ぐんだ

tearful eyes *n* namidagunda me 涙ぐんだ目

tearful farewell *n* namida no wakare 涙の別れ

tearful look *n* nakisō na kao 泣きそうな顔

teartul story *n* shimeppoi hanashi 湿っぽい話

tease *v* (*pokes fun at*) karakaimásu (karakáu, karakátte) からかいます(からかう, からかって); (*torments*) ijimemásu (ijimeru, ijimete) いじめます・苛めます(いじめる, いじめて)

technical *adj* senmon-teki (na) 専門的(な); tekunikaru (na) テクニカル(な)

technical term *n* senmon-yōgo 専門用語; tekunikaru na yōgo テクニカルな用語

technician *n* gijutsu-ka 技術家

technique *n* gíjutsu 技術; waza 技; tekunikku テクニック

teenager *n* tiin eijā ティーンエイジャー; jūdai (no hito) 10代(の人); jūsan sai kara jūkyū sai 13歳から19歳

teens *n* (*teenager*) jūdai (no hito) 10代(の人); jūsan sai kara jūkyū sai 13歳から19歳

teeth → **tooth**

teething ring *n* osháburi おしゃぶり

Teheran *n* Teheran テヘラン

telecast *n* terebi hōsō テレビ放送

telecommunication *n* (denki) tsūshin (電気)通信

teleconference *n* denwa kaigi 電話会議; terebi kaigi テレビ会議

telegram *n* denpō (o uchimásu; útsu, útte) 電報 (を打ちます; 打つ, 打って)

telephone 1. *n* = *telephone call* denwa 電話 (o-dénwa お電話); *mobile telephone/cell-phone* keitai denwa 携帯電話; *touch-tone telephone* *n* pusshúhon プッシュホン

telephone book/directory *n* denwa-chō 電話帳

telephone booth *n* denwa-bókkusu 電話ボックス

telephone card *n* terehon kādo テレホンカード

telephone company *n* denwa-gaisha 電話会社

telephone line *n* denwa-sen 電話線

telephone number *n* denwa-bángō 電話番号

telephone operator *n* (denwa-)kōkán-shu (電話)交換手, (denwa) operētā (電話)オペレーター

telephone wire(s) *n* denwa-sen 電話線

2. *telephones* *v* (... ni) denwa o kakemásu (suru, shite) (...に)電話をかけます(かける, かけて)/します(する, して)

teleport *v* tensō shimásu (suru, shite) 転送します(する, して)

teleportation *n* (*psychic powers, etc.*) terepōto テレポート

telescope *n* bōenkyō 望遠鏡

television *n* térebi テレビ, terebíjon テレビジョン

telex *n* terekkusu テレックス

tell *v* **1.** iimásu (iu/yū, itte/yutte) 言います(言う, 言って/ゆって); (*relates*) nobemásu (nobéru, nóbete) 述べます(述べる, 述べて); katarimásu (kataru, katatte) 語ります(語る, 語って) **2.** (*informs one of*) ... no mimí ni iremásu (ireru, irete) ...耳に入れます(入れる, 入れて), ... ni kikasemásu (kikaseru, kikasete); ...に聞かせます (聞かせる, 聞かせて), ... ni tsugemásu (tsugeru, tsugete) ...に告げます(告げる, 告げて) **3.** (*instructs*) oshiemásu (oshieru, oshiete) 教えます(教える, 教えて); ~ *on* (*tattles*) ii-tsukemásu (ii-tsukéru, ii-tsukete) 言い付けます(言い付ける, 言い付けて)

teller *n* **1.** (*narrator*) hanashite 話し手; katarite 語り手 **2.** (*bank*) (ginkō no) suitō-gakari (銀行の)出納係

story teller *n* sutōrii terā ストーリー・テラー

telop *n* teroppu テロップ

temper 1. *n* (*disposition*) ijí 意地; táchi たち・質, ténsei 天性, táido 態度 **2.** *v* (*forges metal*) kitaemásu (kitaéru, kitáete) 鍛えます(鍛える, 鍛えて)

be in a bad temper *v* kigen ga warui desu (kigen ga warui, kigen ga warukute) 機嫌が悪いです (機嫌が悪い, 機嫌が悪くて)

be in a good temper *v* kigen ga ii desu (kigen ga ii, kigen ga yokute) 機嫌がいいです(機嫌がいい, 機嫌が良くて)

hot temper, short temper *n* tanki 短気

lose one's temper *v* tanki o okoshimásu (okosu, okoshite) 短気を起こします(起こす, 起こして)

temperament *n* ténsei 天性; kishitsu 気質

temperature *n* óndo 温度; (*of body*) taion 体温; (*fever*) netsú 熱; (*air*) kion 気温; (*room air*) shitsuon 室温

temple *n* **1.** (*Asian*) terá 寺, o-tera お寺; ...-ji ...寺 **2.** shinden 神殿; *temple of Jupiter Caesar* Yupiteru shinden ユピテル神殿 **3.** (*flat part on each side of the head*) komekami こめかみ

temple bell *n* tsurigane 釣り鐘

temple fair *n* énnichi 縁日

temple gate *n* sanmon 山門

tempo *n* tenpo テンポ, hayasa 速さ

temporal *adj* **1.** ichiji-teki (na) 一時的(な) **2.** sokutō-bu (no) 側頭部(の)

temporary *adj* rinji (no) 臨時(の), tōza (no) 当座(の); (*passing*) ichíji (no) 一時(の), ichiji-teki (na) 一時的(な); (*tentative*) kari (no) 仮(の), ka-... 仮...

temporary availability *n* ichiji-teki ni riyō kanō 一時的に利用可能, ichiji-teki ni nyūshu kanō 一時的に入手可能

temporary ceasefire *n* ichiji teisen 一時停戦

temporary expedient *n* ichiji shinogi 一時しのぎ, maniawase まにあわせ

temporary office *n* kari (no) jimusho 仮(の)事務所

temporary work *n* rinji (no) shigoto 臨時(の)仕事

tempt *v* sasoimásu (sasou, sasotte) 誘います(誘う, 誘って)

temptation *n* sasoi 誘い, yūwaku 誘惑

tempura *n* (*food fried in batter, especially shrimp*) tenpura てんぷら・テンプラ・天麩(婦)羅

tempura bowl *n* tendon 天丼

ten *n* jū´ 十・10, tō´ 十・10; *ten days* tōka 十日・10日

ten; 10 pieces (*small things*) júk-ko 十個; **10 trees** (*or long things*) júp-pon 十本; **10 sheets** (*flat things*) jū´-mai 十枚; **10 cats** (*or small animals*) júp-piki 十匹; **10 cows** (*or large animals*) jút-tō 十頭; **10 birds/rabbits** júp-pa 十羽; **10 cars** (*or machines/vehicles*) jū´-dai 十台; **10 copies** (*books/magazines*) jus-satsú 十冊; **10 people** jū´-nin 十人, jū´-mei 十名; **10 floors/stories** juk-kai 十階; **10 fold** jū´-bai 十倍; **10 degrees** jū´-do 十度; **10 times** jū´-dó 十度, juk-kái 十回, jup-pén 十遍; **10 o'clock** jū´-ji 十時; **10 hours** jū-jíkan 十時間; **10 weeks** jús-shūkan 十週間; **10 months** júk-ká-getsu 十ヶ月; **10 years** jū´-nen 十年, jū´-nenkan 十年間; **10 years old** tō´ 十, jús-sai 十歳

tenacity *n* shūchaku 執着

tenant *n* (*of apartment, room*) magari-nin 間借人, nyūkyó-sha 入居者, tenanto テナント

tenant owner *n* tenanto no ōnā テナントのオーナー

tend (*to do/happen*) *v* yóku ... (shimásu) よく...(します); (shi)-yasúi desu (し)やすいです

tendency *n* keikō 傾向

tender → gentle, soft → hurt

tenderness *n* nasake 情け (o-násake お情け)

tendon *n* sújí 筋

Achilles' tendon *n* akiresu ken アキレス腱

tenement house *n* naga-ya 長屋

tennis *n* ténisu テニス

tennis court *n* tenisu kōto テニスコート

tennis player *n* tenisu senshu テニス選手, tenisu purēyā テニスプレーヤー

tennis racket *n* tenisu raketto テニスラケット

tennis shoes *n* tenisu shūzu テニスシューズ

tenor *n* ténā テナー, tenōru テノール

tense *v* (*taut*) hatte imásu (iru, ite) 張っています (いる, いて); (*strained*) kinchō shite imásu (iru, ite) 緊張しています(いる, いて); (*situation*) kinpaku shimásu (suru, shite) 緊迫します(する, して)

tension *n* kinchō 緊張; tenshon テンション

tent *n* ténto テント

tentative *adj* kari (no) 仮(の)

tenth *adj* jū-banmé (no) 十番目(の), tō-mé (no) 十目(の); *the tenth day* tōka-mé 十日目, (*of the month*) tōka 十日・10日; *tenth floor* juk-kai 十階

ten thousand *n* mán 万・10,000, ichi-mán 一万・10,000

ten-thousandfold *adj* (ichi)manbai (一)万倍

term *n* (*period*) kíkan 期間, (*time limit*) kígen 期限; (*of school*) gakki 学期; (*technical word*) senmon-yōgo 専門用語, yōgo 用語; (*stipulation*) jōken 条件

terminal (*place*), **terminus** *n* shūten 終点; hatchaku-chi 発着地; tāminaru ターミナル

terminology *n* senmon yōgo 専門用語

terms *n* (*between people*) náka 仲; *they are on good/bad ~* náka ga íi/warúi desu 仲がいい/悪いです

terrace *n* terasu テラス

terrible *adj* (mono-)sugói (もの)すごい・(物)凄い, taihen (na) 大変(な); (*severe*) hidoi ひどい・酷い; (*frightening*) osoroshíi 恐ろしい; (*shocking*) tonde-mo nái とんでもない, tonda とんだ

terribly *adv* súgoku すごく・凄く, mono-súgoku ものすごく・物凄く, taihen 大変; hídoku ひどく・酷く; osoróshiku 恐ろしく; (*extremely, completely*) to(t)temo と(っ)ても; (*unbearably*) yáke ni やけに

terrific *adj* sugói すごい/凄い, kowái こわい・怖い

territorialism *n* nawabari araeoi 縄張り争い

territory *n* ryō´do 領土, ryō´chi 領地, teritorii テリトリー, nawabari 縄張り

terror *n* kyō´fu 恐怖
  balance of terror *n* kyō´fu no kinkō 恐怖の均衡
  holy terror *n* (*child*) itazurakko いたずらっ子, te ni amaru ko(domo) 手にあまる子(供), te ni oenai ko(domo) 手に負えない子(供)
  reign of terror *n* kyō´fu jidai 恐怖時代

terrorism *n* téro テロ

terrorist *n* terorisuto テロリスト

test *n* **1.** shikén 試験, tésuto テスト; (*check of blood, etc.*) kénsa 検査 → **trial** → **experiment 2.** → **try**
  achievement test *n* gakuryoku shiken 学力試験
  blood test *n* ketsueki kensa 血液検査
  DNA test *n* dii enu ei kantei DNA 鑑定
  eye test *n* shiryoku kensa 視力検査
  hearing test *n* **1.** (*checkup*) chōryoku kensa 聴力検査 **2.** (*exam*) hiyaringu tesuto ヒヤリングテスト, hiyaringu shiken ヒヤリング試験, kikitori shiken 聞き取り試験
  routine test *n* (*examination*) teiki shiken 定期試験
  test pilot *n* shaken sōjū-shi 試験操縦士, shaken hikō-shi 試験飛行士, shaken pairotto 試験パイロット
  test tube *n* shiken-kan 試験管

testament *n* (*will*) yuigon 遺言; *the Old/New Testament* Kyū-/Shin-yaku 旧/新約

testicle(s) *n* kintamá 金玉, (*medical*) kōgan 睾丸

testifier *n* shōgen-sha 証言者

testify *v* shōgen shimásu (suru, shite) 証言します (する, して)

testimony *n* shōgen 証言

Texas *n* Tekisasu テキサス

text 1. *n* bun 文, (*computer*) tekisuto テキスト **2.** *v* (mēru o) uchimásu (utsu, utte) (メールを)打ちます (打つ, 打って)
  text book *n* tekisuto テキスト, kyōkā-sho 教科書
  text file *n* tekisuto fairu テキストファイル

textile *n* ori-mono 織物
  textile industry *n* sen'i sangyō 繊維産業, bōseki kōgyō 紡績工業

texture *n* jí ji 地, ori-ji 織地; kimé きめ・肌理; (*touch*) tezawari 手触り・手ざわり, shitsukan 質感

…th *adj* …-mé (no) …目(の); *fifth* itsutsu-mé 五つ日

Thai *n* (*language*) Tai-go タイ語; (*person*) Tai-jin タイ人

Thailand *n* Tai タイ

than … … yóri …より

thank *v* o-rei o iimásu (iu/yū, itte/yutte) お礼を言います(言う/ゆう, 言って/ゆって)
  I thank you. *interj* Arígatō gozaimásu. ありがとう[有り難う]ございます; Dō´mo. どうも; Sumimasén すみません; osóreirimásu. 恐れ入ります.
  Thank you for everything you have done for me. *interj* Iroiro (to) (o-)sewa ni narimashita. いろいろ(と)(お)世話になりました.
  Thank you for the hard work. *interj* Go-kúrō-sama (deshita). ご苦労さま(でした).
  Thank you for the treat. *interj* Gochisō-sama (déshita). ご馳走[ごちそう]さま(でした).
  "thank-you money" (*to obtain rental*) rei-kin 礼金
  Thank you in advance. *interj* Yoroshiku onegaishimasu. 宜しくお願いします・よろしくお願いします.

thank-you letter *n* o-rei no tegami お礼の手紙, sankyū retā サンキューレター; [BOOKISH] kansha-jō 感謝状, reijō 礼状

thanks *n* (*gratitude*) kansha (no kotobá) 感謝(の言葉), (o-)rei (お)礼; *~ to your solicitude* okagesama de お蔭さまで

thanksgiving *n* **1.** (*gratitude*) kansha 感謝 **2.** (*day*) kansha-sai 感謝祭

that *pron* **1.** (*one*) sore それ, soitsu そいつ, (*of two*) sochira/sotchí そちら/そっち; (*over there; obvious*) are あれ, (*of two*) achira/atchí あちら/あっち; *that damn one* soitsu そいつ, aitsu あいつ, kyátsu きゃつ; anna ni あんなに; *to ~ extent* sonna ni そんなに; anna ni あんなに **2.** *that …* sono … その…; ano … あの…; (*said/thought that*) … to … と; (*which/who*) — *not translated*
  that is to say *adv* sunáwachi すなわち・即ち
  that kind of *adj* sono/ano yō na その/あのよう[様]な, sō/ā yū そう/ああゆう, sonna/anna そんな/あんな
  that place *pron* **1.** soko そこ; sochira/sotchí そちら/そっち **2.** (*over there; obvious*) asoko あそこ, asuko あすこ; achira/atchí あちら/あっち
  that side *n* achira-gawa あちら側
  that sort of → that kind of

That's right *interj* sō´ (desu) そう (です)

that time *adv, n* sono tókí その時, tō´ji 当時

that very day *adv, n* tōjitsu 当日

that way *n* (*like that*) sō そう (sō´ そう + [PARTICLE] or désu です); (*over there; obvious*) ā ああ (ā ああ + [PARTICLE] or désu です); (*that direction*) sochira/atchí あちら/あっち, (*over there; obvious*) achira/atchí あちら/あっち

that... 1. sono ...その...; (*over there; obvious*) ano ... あの...; [*said/thought that*] ... (sono yō ni) itta/kangaeta, omotta (そのように)言った/考えた・思った 2. [RELATIVE PRONOUN] = **which...**, **who...**

thatch 1. *n* káya かや・茅, (*straw*) wára わら・藁, (*grass*) kusá 草 2. *v* **thatches a roof** káya/wára/kusá de yáne o fukimásu (fuku, fuite) かや/わら/草で屋根をふきます(ふく, ふいて)

thaw *v* (*it thaws*) tokemásu (tokéru, tókete) 解(溶)けます(解(溶)ける/解(溶)けて); (*thaws it*) tokashimásu (tokásu, tokáshite) 解(溶)かします(解(溶)かす, 解(溶)かして)

the *article* (*usually not translated*); ano ... あの..., hon- 本...

theater *n* (*building*) gekijyō 劇場, za 座; (*drama*) engeki 演劇, (*play*) shibai 芝居, (*traditional*) kabuki 歌舞伎; **theater people** engekí-jin 演劇人; **the Kabuki theater** (*building*) Kabuki-za 歌舞伎座

theft *n* nusumí 盗み, tōnan 盗難

them, they *pron* (*people*) anóhito-tachi あの人達, káre-ra 彼等 (*or name/title/role* + -tachi 達・たち); (*things*) soré-ra それら

theme *n* (*topic*) tē´ma テーマ, shudai 主題; (*composition*) sakubun 作文

theme park *n* tēma pāku テーマパーク; yūenchi 遊園地

theme song *n* tēma songu テーマソング; shudai-ka 主題歌

then *adv* (*at that time*) sono tókí その時, tō´ji 当時; (*after that*) sore kara それから; (*in that case*) sore nára それなら; *and/well then* sá-te さて

theology *n* shingaku 神学

theoretic *adj* riron (no) 理論(の)

theoretical *adj* rironteki (na) 理論的(な), riron-jō (no) 理論上(の)

theory *n* riron 理論, rikutsu 理屈, seorii セオリー, ...-ron ...論

there *adv* soko (ni) そこ(に); (*over there*) asoko/asuko (ni) あそこ/あすこ(に)

therefore *adv* dákara (sa) だから(さ); (*accordingly*) shitagatte したがって・従って

there is/are ... *adv* ...ga arimásu (áru, átte) ...があります(ある/あって); [DEFERENTIAL] gozaimásu (gozaimáshite) ございます(ございまして); *~ no* ... ga arimasén (nái, nákute) ...が(/は)ありません(ない, なくて)

thermal *adj* netsu (no) 熱(の)

thermal conduction *n* netsu dendō 熱伝導

thermal conductivity *n* netsu dendō ritsu 熱伝導率

thermal energy *n* netsu enerugii 熱エネルギー

thermometer *n* ondo-kei 温度計; (*room*) kandán-kei 寒暖計; (*body*) taion-kei 体温計

thermos bottle *n* mahō´-bin 魔法びん・魔法瓶

these *pron* ... kono ... この...; ~ (*ones*) koré-ra これら; *~ damn ones* koitsú-ra こいつら

thesis *n* ronbun 論文, gakuirónbun 学位論文; *master's* ~ shūshi-rónbun 修士論文

they → **them**

thick *adj* atsui 厚い, buatsui 分厚い・部厚い, atsubottai 厚ぼったい; (*and round*) futói 太い; (*dense, close*) kói 濃い, mítsu (na) 密(な), missetsu (na) 密接(な); (*greasy*) kudói くどい

thicket *n* yabu やぶ・ヤブ・薮

thief *n* dorobō どろぼう・泥棒; [BOOKISH] zoku 賊, tōzoku 盗賊

sneak thief *n* koso-doro こそどろ・こそ泥; akisu 空き巣

thigh *n* mómo もも・股, futomomo 太股・ふともも

thimble *n* yubi-núkí 指ぬき

thin 1. *adj* usui 薄い; (*and round*) hosói 細い 2. *gets* ~ (*loses weight*) yasemásu (yaseru, yasete) やせ[痩せ]ます(やせる/やせて)

thing *n* monó 物, yátsu やつ・奴; (*fact, matter*) kotó 事; *things* monógoto 物事

just the thing *n, adj* (*ideal*) motte-kói (no) もってこい(の)

think *v* (*that ...*) (*... to*) omoimásu (omóu, omótte) (...と)思います(思う, 思って), kangaemásu (kangáeru, kangáete) 考えます(考える, 考えて); [DEFERENTIAL] zon-jimásu (zon-jiru, zon-jite) 存じます(存じる, 存じて); [HUMBLE] zon-jiagemásu (zon-jíageru, zon-jiagéte) 存じあげます(あげる, あげて)

thinking *n* shikō 思考

Man is a thinking animal. [IDIOM] Ningen wa kangaeru ashi de aru. 人間は考える葦である.

thinking-over *n* hansei 反省

third *adj* sanbanmé (no) 三番目, mittsu-mé (no) 三つ目(の); *the third day* mikka-mé 三日目, (*of the month*) mikka 三日・3日; *third or fourth* san-yo-banmé (no) 三, 四番目(の)

third class *adj* san-tō (no) 三等(の)

third floor *n* san-gai 三階

third generation *n* sán-sei 三世

third time *n* sando-mé 三度目, sankai-mé 三回目

third-year student *n* sannén-sei 三年生

thirsty *adj* nódo ga kawaita のど[喉]が渇いた, nódo ga kawaite(i)ru のど[喉]が渇いて(い)る

thirteen *n* jū-san 十三・13

thirty *n* san-jū 三十・30

thirty or forty *n* san-shi-jū 三, 四十; *~ thousand* san-yo(m)-man 三, 四万

thirty percent *n* sán-wari 三割, sanjup-pāsénto 三十パーセント・30%

this *pron* 1. (*one*) kore これ, hon-... 本...; (*of two*) kochira/kotchí こちら/こっち; *~ damn one* koitsu こいつ; *to ~ extent* konna ni こんなに 2. *this ...* kono ... この...

this afternoon *adv, n* kyō´no gógo 今日の午後
this evening *adv, n* kónban 今晩
this kind of *adj* kono yō´na このよう[様]な, kō yū こうゆう, konna こんな
this month *adv, n* kongetsu 今月
this morning *adv, n* késa 今朝; kyō´no ása 今日の朝
this much *adv* konna ni こんなに
this place *pron* koko ここ; kochira/kochí こちら/こっち
this side *n* kochira-gawa こちら側; *~ of …* no temae …の手前
this sort of → this kind of
this time *adv, n* kóndo 今度, íma 今, kono tabí このたび[度]
this way *n* (*like this*) kō こう (kō´kou + [PARTICLE] *or* désu です); (*this direction*) kochira/kochí こちら/こっち
this week *adv, n* konshū 今週
this year *adv, n* kotoshi 今年
thong *n* **1.** (kawa) himo (皮)紐・ひも **2.** (*on geta* [下駄]) hanao 鼻緒
thorium *n* toriumu トリウム
thorn *n* togé とげ・トゲ・棘
thorny *adj* **1.** togé no ōi とげ[トゲ・棘]の多い **2.** ibara (no) イバラ・茨(の) **3.** yakkai (na) 厄介(な), muzukashii 難しい
thorny path *n* ibara (no) michi いばら[イバラ](の)道, kon'nan na michi 困難な道
thorny problem *n* nandai 難題
thorough *adj* tettei-teki (na) 徹底的(な); (*detailed*) seimitsu (na) 精密(な)
thoroughbred *n* sarabureddo サラブレッド
thoroughfare *n* tsū´ro 通路, ōrai 往来
thoroughly *adv* tettei-teki ni 徹底的(に)
those → them
those … *pron* sono … その…, ano … あの…; *~ (ones)* soré-ra それら, aré-ra あれら; *~ damn ones* soitsú-ra そいつら, aitsú-ra あいつら; *~ present* shussékí-sha 出席者
those days *n* tō´ji 当時
though *conj* démo でも, kéredo (mo) けれど(も)
thought 1. *n* kangáe 考え, omói 思い, shikō 思考; shisō 思想; (*fulness*) shíryo 思慮 **2.** → think
thousand *n* sén 千・1,000, is-sén 一千・1,000; *a thousand yen* sen-en 千円・1,000円
thousandfold *adj* senbai (no) 千倍(の)
thread *n* íto 糸
threat *n* odoshi 脅し, [BOOKISH] kyōhaku 脅迫
threaten *v* odo(ka)shimásu (odo(ka)-su, odo(ka)shite) 脅(か)します・脅(か)す, 脅(か)して)
threatening *adj* kyōhaku-teki (na) 脅迫的(な)
threatening call *n* kyōhaku denwa 脅迫電話
threatening e-mail *n* kyōhaku mēru 脅迫メール
threatening letter *n* kyōhaku-jō 脅迫状
three *n* san 三・3, mittsú 三つ; san-… 三…, mi-… 三…; surī スリー; (*people*) san-nín 三人, [BOOKISH] sánmei 三名
three; *3 pieces* (*small things*) sán-ko 三個; *3 trees*

(*or long things*) sánbon 三本; *3 sheets* (*flat things*) sánmai 三枚; *3 cats* (*or small animals*) sánbiki 三匹; *3 cows* (*or large aminals*) san-tō 三頭; *3 birds/rabbits* sánba 三羽; *3 cars* (*or machines/vehicles*) sán-dai 三台; *3 copies* (*books/magazines*) sán-satsu 三冊; *3 floors/stories* san-gai 三階; *3 people* san-nín 二人, san-mei 三名; *3 fold* sánbai 三倍; *3 degrees* san-do 三度; *3 times* sán-dó 三度, sán-kái 三回, sánbén 三遍; *3 o'clock* sán-ji 三時; *3 hours* sán-jíkan 三時間; *3 days* mikka 三日: *~ from now* shiasátte しあさって・明々後日; *the first ~ of the new year* sanganichi 三が日; *~ ago* mikka máe 三日前; *3 weeks* sán-shūkan 三週間; *3 months* sán-ká-getsu 三ヶ月; *3 years* san-nen 三年, san-nen-kan 三年間: *~ ago* san-nen máe 三年前, saki-otótoshi さきおととし・一昨々年; *~ old* mittsú 三つ, sán-sai 三歳
three-dimensional *adj* rittai (no) 立体(の)
three hundred *n* sánbyaku 三百・300
three nights ago *adv* mikka máe no ban/yoru 三日前の晩/夜; saki-ototói no ban/yoru さきおとい・一昨々日の晩/夜
three or four *n* san-shi- 三、四, *except for…* *3-4 hours* san yo-jíkan 二、四時間, *3-4 o'clock* san-ji ka yó-ji 三時か四時; *3-4 people* san-yo-nín 三、四人, *3-4 servings* san-yo-ninmae 三、四人前; *3-4 times* san-yon-kai 三、四回, *3-4 times as much* san-yo-bai 三、四倍 = sanbai ka yo(m)-bai 三倍か四倍, *3-4 yen* san-yo-en 三、四円, *3-4 days* san-yokka 三、四日, *3-4 hundred* san-shíhyaku 三、四百 = sánbyaku ka yónhyaku 三百か四百
three thousand *n* san-zén 三千・3,000
threshold *n* **1.** shikii 敷居 **2.** (*threshold value*) ikichi 閾値
thrifty *adj* tsumashíi つましい・倹しい, ken'yaku (na) 倹約(な), komakái 細かい
thrill 1. *n* súríru スリル **2.** *adj* (*is thrilled*) waku-waku/zokuzoku shimásu (suru, shite) わくわく/ぞくぞくします(する/して)
thrilling *adj* suriru o kanjisaseru スリルを感じさせる, waku-waku/zokuzoku suru わくわく/ぞくぞくする
thrive *v* sakaemásu (sakáeru, sakáete) 栄えます(栄える/栄えて); uremásu (ureru, urete) 売れます(売れる/売れて)
throat *n* nódo のど・喉 [BOOKISH] inkō 咽喉
throb *v* dokidoki shimásu (suru, shite) どきどき・ドキドキします(する/して)
throne *n* ōi 王位, ōza 王座
throng 1. *n* ōzéi 大勢; (*flock*) muré 群れ **2.** *they throng together* *v* muragarimásu (muragáru, muragátte) 群がります(群がる/群がって)
through 1. *prep* *putting ~* … o tō´shite …を通して; *gets ~* tsū-jimásu (tsu-jiru, tsū-jite) 通じます(通じる, 通じて); *coming ~* … o tō´tte …を通って(*via*) … o héte …を経て; … kéiyu (de/no) … 経由(で/の) **2.** *prep* (*throughout*) …-jū …じゅう・中; …no aida-jū …の間じゅう [間中]; *all the way ~* zutto ずっと **3.** (*by means of*) … de …で,

… o tsukatte …を使って **4.** (*extending ~*) … ni kákete …にかけて **5.** adv (*is finished*) dekimáshita 出来ました, (shi)-te shimaimáshita（し）てしまいました

throughout *prep* (*the entire* [PLACE/TIME]) …-jū …じゅう・中; *~ the world* sekai-jū 世界じゅう 〔中〕

throw *v* nagemásu (nagéru, nágete) 投げます(投げる/投げて); *~ away* sutemásu (suteru, sutete) 捨てます(捨てる/捨てて); *~ in extra* soemásu (soeru, soete) 添えます(添える/添えて); *~ into disorder* midashimásu (midásu, midáshite) 乱します(乱す/乱して)

throwaway *adj* tsukaisute (no) 使い捨て(の)
throwaway chopsticks *n* wari-bashi 割りばし 〔箸〕

throw up → vomit

thrush *n* tsugumi ツグミ

thrust *v* tsukimásu (tsuku, tsuite) 突きます(突く/突いて)
thrust stage *n* haridashi butai 張り出し舞台

thumb *n* oya-yubi 親指

thumb drive *n* (*small computer storage*) samu-doraibu サムドライブ

thumbprint *n* (*when used to stamp a document*) boin 母印・拇印

thumbtack *n* gabyō 画びょう・画鋲

thunder *n* kaminári (ga narimásu; naru, natte) 雷(が鳴ります; 鳴る, 鳴って)

thunderstorm *n* ráiu 雷雨

Thursday *n* Mokuyō´bi 木曜日

thwart *v* habamimásu (habámu, habánde) 阻みます(阻む, 阻んで)

Tibet *n* Chibetto チベット

tick *n* chekku チェック

tick mark *n* chekku māku チェックマーク, re ten レ点

tick-tack *n* kachi kachi カチカチ

ticket *n* kippu 切符, chikétto チケット; …-ken …券; *just the ~* (*ideal*) motte-kói (no) もってこい(の), (*most suitable*) uttetsuke (no) うってつけ(の); *admission ticket* nyōjō-ken 入場券
ticket agency *n theater ~* pureigáido プレイガイド ("*Play Guide*")
ticket book *n* (*for commuting*) kaisū´-ken 回数券
ticket collecting *n* shūsatsu 集札
ticket examining *n* (*at wicket*) kaisatsu 改札, (*aboard*) kensatsu 検札
ticket seller *n* kippú-uri 切符売り
ticket vending machine *n* kenbáiki 券売機
ticket wicket *n* kaisatsu-guchi 改札口

tickle *v* kusugurimásu (kusuguru, kusugutte) くすぐります(くすぐる, くすぐって)

ticklish *adj* kusuguttái くすぐったい; (*dedicate*) kiwadói 際どい

tide *n* shió 潮; chōryū 潮流

tidy 1. *adj* kírei (na) きれい(な) **2.** *tidies it up* *v* katazukemásu (katazukéru, katazúkete) 片付けま

す(片付ける, 片付けて); *it gets tidy* katazukimásu (katazúku, katazúite) 片付きます(片付く, 片付いて)

tie 1. *v* musubimásu (musubu, musunde) 結びます(結ぶ, 結んで); (*fastens*) tsunagimásu (tsunagu, tsunaide) つなぎます(つなぐ, つないで) **2.** *n* (*necktie*) nékutai ネクタイ; (*game*) hikiwake 引き分け

tie up (*binds*) shibarimásu (shibáru, shibátte) 縛ります(縛る, 縛って)

tiff *n* mome-goto もめ事・揉め事

tiger *n* tora 虎・トラ; taigā タイガー

tight *adj* (*tight-fitting*) kitsui きつい; (*hard*) katai 堅い; (*skimpy*) semái 狭い → **drunk**

tighten, tighten up on *v* shimemásu (shiméru, shímete) 締めます(締める, 締めて)

tights *n* taitsu タイツ

tile 1. *n* (*roof*) kawara 瓦; *tile-roofed* kawara-buki (no) 瓦ぶき・瓦葺き(の) **2.** *n* (*floor, wall*) táiru タイル **3.** *v* tiles a roof kawara de yáne o fukimásu (fuku, fuite) 瓦で屋根をふき〔葺き〕ます(ふく, ふいて)

timber *n* zaimoku 材木

time 1. *n* tokí 時, … tókí …時, jikan 時間 (o-jíkan お時間), jibun 時分; (*specified*) jíkoku 時刻; (*season*) jíki 時期; (*opportunity*) jíki 時機, (*appropriate occasion*) jísetsu 時節; (*free*) hima 暇, ma 間; (*taken up*) temá 手間 (o-téma お手間); (*interval, time while* …) aida 間; *Do you have/ know the time?* Nán-ji ka wakari-másu ka. 何時か分かりますか. **2.** *n* (*occasion*) tabí たび・度, orí 折, sái 際, tokoró ところ; (*period*) koro 頃; *at one ~* kátsute かって, kátte かって; *at the ~ of* … ni sái-shite …に際して; *for the ~ being* tōbun 当分, íma no tokoró wa 今のところは; *is in ~* yagate やがて; *is in ~ (for* …) (… ni) ma ni aimásu (áu, átte) (… に)間に合います(合う, 合って); (*the trend of*) *the times* jisei 時勢 (go-jísei ご時世)
how many times *adv, n* nán-do 何度, nán-kai 何回, nánbén 何遍 (**1**: ip-pén 一遍, **2**: ni-hen 二遍, **3**: sánbén 三遍); *~ doubled* nanbai 何倍
in a short time *adv* mamonaku まもなく, sugu (ni) すぐ(に)
in time *adv* (*eventually*) yagate やがて
on time *adv* jikandōri ni 時間通りに, teikoku ni 定刻に
this/next time *adv, n* kóndo 今度
what time *adv, n* nán-ji 何時
time and again *adv* nando mo (nando mo) 何度も(何度も), [BOOKISH] saisan saishi 再三再四
time deposit *n* teiki-yókin 定期預金
time difference, time-lag *n* jísa 時差
Time is money. [IDIOM] Toki wa kane nari. 時は金なり.
time killer *n* hima tsubushi (ni naru mono) 暇つぶし(になるもの), hima tsubushi (ni suru mono) 暇つぶし(にするもの)
time limit *n* taimu rimitto タイムリミット, seigen jikan 制限時間

time loan *n* teiki kashitsuke-kin 定期貸付金
time machine *n* taimu mashin タイムマシン
time management *n* jikan (no) kanri 時間（の）管理
time off *n* yasumi 休み
timepiece *n* tokei 時計
time schedule *n* jikoku-hyō 時刻表
timetable *n* jikoku-hyō 時刻表; (*school*) jikan-wari 時間割（り）
time travel *n* taimu toraberu タイムトラベル
timekeeper *n* (*person*) jikan kiroku-gakari 時間記録係
timely 1. *adj* taimurii (na) タイムリー（な）2. *adj, adv* taimurii ni タイムリーに
timer *n* taimā タイマー
timid *adj* (*shy*) uchiki (na) 内気（な）, (*cowardly*) okubyō (na) 臆病（な）
timid animal *n* okubyō na dōbutsu 臆病な動物
timid attitude *n* ozuozushita taido おずおずした態度
tin *n* buriki ブリキ, suzu すず・スズ・錫
tin opener *n* kankiri 缶きり・缶切り
tinhorn *n* hattari (ya) はったり（屋）
tinkle *n* chirin chirin (to iu oto) チリンチリン（という音）
tint *n* iroai 色合い
tiny *adj* totemo chiisana とても小さな, chippoke (na) ちっぽけ（な）
tiny tot *n* chibikko ちびっ子
tip 1. *n* (*money*) chíppu チップ, kokoro-zuke 心付け, chadai 茶代; (*point*) saki 先 2. *v it tips over* hikkuri-kaerimásu (hikkuri-káeru, hikkuri-káette) ひっくり返ります（ひっくり返る, ひっくり返って）, *tips it over* hikkuri-kaeshimásu (hikkuri-káesu, hikkuri-káeshite) ひっくり返します（ひっくり返す, ひっくり返して）
tips *n* kotsu こつ・コツ, hiketsu 秘訣
tire *n* (*of wheel*) taiya タイヤ
tire chain *n* taiya chēn タイヤ・チェーン
tired; *gets ~* tsukaremásu (tsukaréru, tsukárete) 疲れます（疲れる, 疲れて）, kutabiremásu (kutabiréru, kutabírete) くたびれます（くたびれる, くたびれて）; *gets ~ of* ... ni akimásu (akíru, ákite) ...に飽きます（飽きる, 飽きて）; *dead ~* ku (t) takuta く（っ）たくた; hetoheto へとへと
tireless *adj* tsukarenai 疲れない
tiresome *adj* akiakisaseru 飽き飽きさせる, taikutsu (na) 退屈な
tissue *n* tisshu-pē̄pā ティッシュペーパー; hanagami 鼻紙, chirigami ちり紙
Titan *n* Taitan タイタン
titanate *n* (*chemical*) chitan san'en チタン酸塩
title *n* (*of book*, *article*, ...) hyōdai 表題・標題, daimei 題名, midashi 見出し; (*job title*) katagaki 肩書; (*of anything*, *esp. movie*, *person*, *athlete*) táitoru タイトル; *~ page* tobira 扉
end-title credit *n* kurejitto クレジット
end-title roll *n* endo rōru エンドロール
title catalogue *n* tosho mokuroku 図書目録

title match *n* taitoru matchi タイトルマッチ
to *prep* ... ni ...に, ... e ...へ
toad *n* hikigaeru ヒキガエル
toast 1. *n* tṓsuto トースト; ("*bottoms up*") kanpai 乾杯 2. *v* (*toasts it*) yakimásu (yaku, yaite) 焼きます（焼く, 焼いて）
toaster *n* tṓsutā トースター
tobacco *n* tabako たばこ・煙草; *tobacco shop* tabako-ya たばこ屋・煙草屋
today *n* kyṓ 今日; [BOOKISH] honjitsu 本日
toe *n* ashi no yubí 足の指; (*toe-tip*) tsumasaki つま先・爪先
Toei Line *n* (*bus*) Toei basu 都営バス, (*subway*) Toei-chikatetsu 都営地下鉄; (*streetcar*) toden 都電
tofu *n* tōfu 豆腐
together *adv* issho ni いっしょ［一緒］に, tomo ni 共に
Togo *n* Tōgo トーゴ
toilet *n* tóire トイレ, tóirétto トイレット; keshō-shitsu 化粧室, teárai 手洗(o-teárai お手洗), benjó 便所
toilet paper *n* toiretto-pē̄pā トイレットペーパー, kami 紙
token *n* (*sign, indication*) shirushi しるし・印・徴(o-shirushi おしるし)
Tokyo *n* Tōkyō 東京; *Tokyo Station* Tōkyṓ-Eki 東京駅; *the metropolis of Tokyo* Tōkyṓ-to 東京都
Tokyoite *n* Tōkyṓ-jin 東京人; tomin 都民
Tokyo Metro (Line) *n* (*subway lines of Tokyo*) Tōkyō metoro 東京メトロ; Marunouchi-sen 丸ノ内線; Ginza-sen 銀座線; Hibiya-sen 日比谷線; Tōzai-sen 東西線; Chiyoda-sen 千代田線; Yūrakuchō-sen 有楽町線; Hanzōmon-sen 半蔵門線; Nanboku-sen 南北線; Fukutoshin-sen 副都心線
Tokyo University *n* Tōkyō-Dáigaku 東京大学, Tō-dai 東大
told → tell
tolerate *v* gáman shimásu (suru, shite) 我慢します（する, して）, taemásu (taeru, taete) 耐えます（耐える, 耐えて）
toll *n* tsūkō-ryō 通行料; (*telephone charge*) tsūwa-ryō 通話料
toll-free *adj* tsūwa-ryō muryō (no) 通話料無料（の）; furii daiyaru (no) フリーダイヤル（の）
tollgate *n* ryōkin-jo 料金所
tomato *n* tomato トマト
tomb *n* (o-)haka （お）墓, boketsu 墓穴
tomboy *n* otenba おてんば・お転婆
tombstone *n* boseki 墓石, [BOOKISH] bohi 墓碑
tomcat *n* osu neko 雄猫・オスねこ
tomorrow *n* ashitá あした・明日, asú 明日; [BOOKISH] myṓnichi 明日
  Tomorrow is another day. [IDIOM] Ashita wa ashita no kaze ga fuku. 明日は明日の風が吹く.
tomorrow morning ashita no ása あした［明日］の朝; [BOOKISH] myōchō 明朝

tomorrow night *ashita no ban* あした[明日]の晩; [BOOKISH] *myō´ban* 明晩

tone *n* (*sound*) neiro 音色, tōn トーン; (*coloring*) iro-ai 色合い; (*physical condition*) tai-chō 体調; (*voice*) kuchō 口調

tongs *n* (*for fire*) hí-bashi 火ばし[箸]; tongu トング

tongue *n* shíta 舌; *barbed/spiteful tongue* doku-zetsu 毒舌
ox tongue *n* gyūtan 牛タン

tonight *n* kónban 今晩; kón'ya 今夜
tonight's guest *n* kónya no gesuto 今夜のゲスト

tonsil *n* hentō-sen 扁桃腺

too *adv* (*also*) … mo …も; (*overly*) anmari あんまり, amari (ni) あまり(に); ...-sugimásu (-sugíru, -súgite) ...すぎます(すぎる,すぎて)
too bad zannen (na) 残念(な); (*in commiseration*) ikemasén (ikenai) いけません(いけない)
too many ō-sugimásu (ō-sugíru, ō-súgite) 多すぎます(多すぎる,多すぎて)
is too much te ni amarimásu (amáru, amátte) 手に余ります(余る,余って)

took → **take**

tool *n* dōgú 道具(o-dōgu お道具), yō´gu 用具, utsuwa 器; tsūru ツール
tool box *n* dōgu-bako 道具箱, yōgu-bako 用具箱

tooth *n* há 歯; *protruding (buck) tooth* déppa 出っ歯
toothache *n* ha-ita 歯痛; *has a ~* há ga itái 歯が痛い
toothbrush *n* ha-búrashi 歯ブラシ
toothpaste *n* neri-hamígaki 練り歯磨き; (*toothpowder*) hamígaki(-ko) 歯磨き(粉)
toothpick *n* tsuma-yōji つまようじ・爪楊枝, yōji ようじ・楊枝

top 1. *n* ue 上; (*top side*) jōmen 上面, hyōmen 表面; (*highest part*) teppén てっぺん, (*summit*) chōjō´ 頂上 2. *n* (*toy*) kóma こま・独楽; *top-spinning* koma-máwashi こま[独楽]回し 3. *adj* (*topmost, best*) saijō (no) 最上(の), saikō (no) 最高(の), toppu (no) トップ(の)

topaz *n* topāzu トパーズ
topcoat *n* ō´bā(kōto) オーバー(コート)
topflight *adj* (*elite*) ichiryū (no) 一流(の)
topic *n* (*of talk*) wadai 話題, topikku トピック; daimoku 題目, (*hanashi no*) táne (話の)種; (*problem*) mondai 問題
topmost *adj* saijō (no) 最上(の)
topping *n* toppingu トッピング
tops *adj* (*best*) saikō (no) 最高(の), saijō (no) 最上(の)
torch *n* táimatsu たいまつ・松明 → **flashlight**
tore, torn → **tear**
torment 1. *n* (*suffering*) nayamí 悩み; (*teasing*) ijime いじめ・苛め 2. → **tease**
tornado *n* torunēdo トルネード, tatsumaki 竜巻
Toronto *n* Toronto トロント

torrential downpour *n* doshaburi 土砂降り; gō´u 豪雨
tortoise *n* káme 亀・カメ; *tortoise shell* bekkō べっこう・ベッコウ・鼈甲
toss → **throw**
tot *n* (*tiny tot*) chibikko ちびっ子
total 1. *adj* zénbu (de/no) 全部(で/の); (*absolute*) zettai (no) 絶対(の) 2. *n* zén(-) …全; tōtaru トータル, (*sum*) gōkei 合計, (*grand total*) sōkei 総計
totter *v* yoro-mekimásu (yoro-méku, yoro-méite) よろめきます(よろめく, よろめいて); *tottering* *adj* yóroyoro (to) よろよろと
touch *v* sawarimásu (sawaru, sawatte) 触ります (触る, 触って); … ni (téo) f018 furemásu (fureru, furete) ...に(手を)触れます(触れる, 触れて), … ni tsukimásu (tsukú, tsúite) ...に付きます(付く, 付いて); atemásu (ateru, atete) 当てます(当てる, 当てて); (*comes in contact with*) ses-shimásu (se-suru, ses-shite) 接します(接する, 接して), sesshoku shimásu (suru, shite) 接触します(する, して); kandō sasemásu (saseru, sasete) 感動させる(させる, させて); *gets in ~ with* … to renraku shimásu (suru, shite) …と連絡します(する, して), … to renraku o torimásu (toru, totte) …と連絡を取ります(取る, 取って); *touches upon* … ni furemásu (fureru, furete) …に触れます(触れる, 触れて), [BOOKISH] … ni genkyū shimásu (suru, shite) …に言及します(する, して); *out of ~ with* … ni utói …に疎い・うとい
tough *adj* katai 固い・堅い → **hard** → **strong**
tough guy *n* tafu gai タフガイ
tour *n* ryokō (shimásu; suru, shite) 旅行(します; する, して); (*sight-seeing*) kankō 観光, tsúā ツアー; (*official, duty*) shutchō 出張
tourist *n* kankō´-kyaku 観光客; tsūrisuto ツーリスト
tourist lodge *n* minshuku 民宿
tournament *n* taikai 大会; shiai 試合; senshuken 選手権; tōnamento トーナメント
tow *v* hikimásu (hiku, hiite) 引[曳]きます(引[曳]く, 引[曳]いて)
toward *prep* … no hō´ e …の方へ; (*towards, confronting*) … ni tái-shite …に対して, tai-…対…
towel *n* te-nugui 手拭い・てぬぐい, táoru タオル, fukín 布きん・ふきん; *hand towel* (o-)tefukí (お)手拭き, (*damp*) o-shíbori おしぼり
tower *n* tō´ 塔; tawā タワー
Tokyo Tower *n* Tōkyō tawā 東京タワー
town *n* machí 町, tokai 都会
town mayor *n* chō´chō 町長
tow truck *n* rékkā レッカー, rekkā´-sha レッカー車
toy *n* omócha おもちゃ・オモチャ・玩具
trace *n* (*clue*) tegakari 手掛かり, ate 当て; (*vestige*) konseki 痕跡, ato 跡; *trace it back to sore o … ni sakanoborimásu*

(sakanobóru, sakanobótte) それを…にさかのぼり
[遡り]ます(さかのぼる, さかのぼって)

tracing paper *n* torepe トレペ, torēshingu-pē´pā
トレーシングペーパー

track 1. *n* (*railtrack*) sénro 線路; (*for running*)
torákku トラック; (*remains*) ato 跡; *track number
(six)* (roku)-bansen (六)番線; *what (number of)
track* nanbansen 何番線 **2.** *v* (*to go back and
investigate*) ato o tsumemásu (tsukeru, tsurete) 跡
を付けます(付ける, 付けて), (*to track an online
the transaction of something*) suiseki shimásu
(suru, shite) 追跡します(する, して)

tracking number *n* torakkingu nanbā トラッキン
グナンバー, tsuseki bangō 追跡番号

tracks *n* ashi ato 足跡

tractable *adj* atsukaiyasui 扱いやすい

tractate *n* (*treatise*) ronbun 論文

tractile *adj* hikinobasukoto ga dekiru 引き伸ばす
ことができる

tractor *n* torakutā トラクター

trade 1. *n* (*international*) bōeki 貿易; (*business*)
shō´bai 商売, (*commerce*) shō´gyo 商業;
(*transaction*) tórí-hiki 取り引き **2.** *v* tórí-hiki
shimásu (suru, shite) 取り引きします(する, し
て); (*exchanges A for B*) A o B ni kōkan shimásu
(suru, shite) A を B と交換します(する, して)

trademark *n* shōhyō 商標; torēdo māku トレー
ドマーク

trader *n* (*merchant*) shō´nin 商人; (*international*)
bōékí-shō 貿易商; (*stock*) tōki-ka 投機家

tradition *n* dentō 伝統; (*legend*) densetsu 伝説

traditional *adj* dentō-teki (na) 伝統的(な);
(*accustomed*) imamade no 今までの, koremade no
これまでの, [BOOKISH] jū´rai (no) 従来(の)

traditional agriculture *n* dentō nōgyō 伝統農業

traditional approach *n* jūrai no yarikata 従来の
やり方

traditional arts *n* dentō geijutsu 伝統芸術

traditional event *n* dentō gyōji 伝統行事

traditional garment *n* dentō-teki na (i)fuku
伝統的な(衣)服

traditional lifestyle *n* dentō-teki na seikatsu
yōshiki 伝統的な生活様式

traffic *n* kōtsū 交通; ōrai 往来

traffic accident *n* kōtsū jiko 交通事故

traffic circle *n* rō´tarii ロータリー

traffic jam *n* kōtsū-jū´tai 交通渋滞

traffic sign *n* (dōro) kōtsū hyō´shiki (道路)
交通標識

traffic signal, traffic light *n* shingō-ki 信号機

tragedy *n* hígeki 悲劇

tragic *adj* hígeki-teki (na) 悲劇的(な); hísan (na)
悲惨(な); aénái あえない・敢えない; *tragically
enough* aénaku mo あえなくも・敢えなくも

trailer *n* (*movie*) yokoku-hen 予告編, (eiga no)
torērā (映画の)トレーラー

train 1. *n* densha 電車; ressha 列車; (*nonelectric/
steam*) kishá 汽車; (*train numbers*) ...-gō´sha ...号
車 **2.** *v* (*drills*) kúnren shimásu (suru, shite) 訓練

shimasu (suru, shite), (*practices*) renshū shimásu
(suru, shite) 練習します(する, して); (*brings up
children, disciplines*) shitsukemásu (shitsukéru,
shitsúkete) しつけ[躾け]ます(しつける, しつ
けて)

bullet train *n* shinkansen 新幹線

local train *n* kakueki (densha) 各駅(電車)

night train *n* yakō ressha 夜行列車

rapid train *n* kaisoku (densha) 快速(電車)

train going downtown *n* kudari (densha) 下り
(電車)

train going uptown *n* nobori (densha) 上り
(電車)

train wreck *n* ressha-jíko 列車事故

trainee *n* kenshū-in 研修員, minarai 見習い

trainee doctor *n* kenshū-i 研修医

trainee teacher *n* kyōiku jisshū-sei 教育実習生

trainer *n* torēnā トレーナー

training *n* kúnren 訓練; (*practice*) renshū 練習;
(*imparting discipline*) shitsuke しつけ・躾;
(*in ascetic practices*) shugyō 修行

training course *n* kenshū kōsu 研修コース

training manual *n* kunren-yō manyuaru 訓練用
マニュアル

training period *n* kenshū kikan 研修期間

tram *n* romen densha 路面電車

trampoline *n* toranporin トランポリン

trance *n* toransu jōtai トランス状態; *in a ~*
muchū (no/de) 夢中(の/で)

tranquil *adj* nódoka (na) のどか・長閑(な)

transacting *n* (*dealing with*) shóri 処理

transaction *n* tori-atsukai 取扱い; (*business*) tórí-
hiki 取り引き

transfer 1. *v* (*trains, etc.*) nori-kaemásu (nori-
káeru, nori-káete) 乗り換えます(乗り換える, 乗
り換えて); (*job*) tennin (shimásu; suru, shite) 転
任(します; する, して), ten-jimásu (ten-jiru,
ten-jite) 転じます(転じる, 転じて); (*transfers it*)
utsushimásu (utsusú, utsúshite) 移します(移す, 移
して); furi-kaemásu (furi-kaeru, furi-kaete) 振替
えます(振替える, 振替えて) **2.** *n* idō 移動, nori-
kae 乗り換え

transformer *n* (*electric*) hen´átsu-ki 変圧器

transformer station *n* hendensho 変電所

transforming factor *n* (*biology*) keishitsu tenkan
inshi 形質転換因子

transmigrant *n* imin 移民, ijūsha 移住者

transmigration *n* **1.** ijū 移住 **2.** (*metempsychosis*)
rin'ne 輪廻. tensei 転生

transmigration of souls *n* rin'ne 輪廻

transmission *n* sōshin 送信, dentatsu 伝達, denpa
伝播

transit *n* tsukō 通行

transitive verb *n* tadō´shi 他動詞

transitory *adj* hakanái はかない

translate *v* yakushimásu (yakúsú, yakúshite)
訳します(訳す, 訳して), hon´yaku shimásu (suru,
shite) 翻訳します(する, して); (*Japanese into
English*) wayaku shimasu (suru, shite) 和訳します

(する, して)

translate freely *v* iyaku shimás<u>u</u> (suru, sh<u>i</u>te) 意訳します(する, して),

translate literally *v* chokuyaku shimás<u>u</u> (suru, sh<u>i</u>te) 直訳します(する, して),

translation *n* hon'yaku 翻訳, yakú 訳

automatic translation *n* jidō hon'yaku 自動翻訳

English-Japanese translation *n* einichi hon'yaku 英日翻訳, eibun wayaku 英文和訳

Japanese-English translation *n* nichiei hon'yaku 日英翻訳, wabun eiyaku 和文英訳

machine translation *n* kikai hon'yaku 機械翻訳

translator hon'yákú-sha 翻訳者, yaku-sha 訳者

transmit *v* tsutaemás<u>u</u> (ts<u>u</u>taeru, ts<u>u</u>taete) 伝えます(伝える, 伝えて), tsūji-más<u>u</u> (tsū-jiru, tsū-jite) 通じます(通じる, 通じて)

transmitted; gets ~ tsutawarimás<u>u</u> (ts<u>u</u>tawaru, ts<u>u</u>tawatte) 伝わります(伝わる, 伝わって)

transom window (*opening*) ranma 欄間・らんかん

transparent *adj* tōmei (na) 透明(な)

transport(ation) *n* unsō 運送, unpan 運搬, yusō 輸送; (*traffic*) kōtsū 交通

trap 1. *n* wána わな・罠 **2.** *v* (*traps it*) wána ni kakemás<u>u</u> (kakéru, kákete) わな[罠]にかけます(かける, かけて); (*gets trapped*) wána ni kakarimás<u>u</u> (kakáru, kakátte) わな[罠]にかかります(かかる, かかって)

trash *n* (*scrap, junk*) kuzu くず・屑, gomi ごみ

trash box *n* gomi-bako ごみ箱

travel *n* ryokō (shimás<u>u</u>; suru, sh<u>i</u>te) 旅行(します; する, して)

travel agency *n* ryokō dairiten 旅行代理店

travel vendor *n* ryokō-gaisha 旅行会社

traveler *n* ryokō'sha 旅行者, ryok(y)aku 旅客, tsūrisuto ツーリスト

traveler's check *n* ryokōsha-yō kogítte 旅行者用小切手; toraberāzu chekku トラベラーズチェック

tray *n* (o-)bon (お)盆, torei トレイ; (*dining tray, low meal table*) (o-)zen (お)膳(gó-zen ご膳) → **ash tray**

treachery *n* (*acts of treachery*) ura-giri 裏切り, haishin-kōi 背信行為

treasure *n* takará 宝, (o-takara お宝), takara-mono 宝物, [BOOKISH] zaihō 財宝

national treasure *n* kokuhō 国宝

treasure box *n* takará-bako 宝箱, tamate-bako 玉手箱

treasure hunt *n* takara sagashi 宝さがし

treasure island *n* takara-jima 宝島

treat 1. *n* gochisō (shimás<u>u</u>; suru, sh<u>i</u>te) ごちそう[ご馳走](します; する, して) **2.** *v* (*pays the bill*) ogorimás<u>u</u> (ogoru, ogotte) おごります(おごる, おごって); (*medically*) chiryō shimás<u>u</u> (suru, sh<u>i</u>te) 治療します(する, して) → **handle**

treatise *n* ronbun 論文, rón 論

treatment *n* téate (o-téate お手当); (*handling*) toriats<u>u</u>kai 取り扱い; (*reception*) taigū 待遇; (*medical*) chiryō 治療, ryōhō 療法

drug treatment *n* yakubutsu ryōhō 薬物療法

treaty *n* jōyaku 条約

tree *n* kí 木 (**1:** íp-pon 一本, **2:** ní-hon 二本, **3:** sánbon 三本; *how many* nánbon 何本); **trees** kígi 木々

tree-ears *n* (*an edible fungus*) k<u>i</u>kúrage きくらげ・キクラゲ・木耳

trefoil leaves *n* mitsuba 三つ葉・ミツバ

tremble *v* furuemás<u>u</u> (furueru, furuete) 震えます(震える, 震えて), yuremás<u>u</u> (yureru, yurete) 揺れます(揺れる, 揺れて)

tremor *n* yure 揺れ

trench coat *n* torenchi kōto トレンチコート

trend *n* (*tendency*) keikō 傾向, (*inclination*) katamuki 傾き, chōshi 調子; (*current*) chōryū 潮流; (*movement*) ugokí 動き; (*fashion*) ryūkō 流行; torendo トレンド

trendy *adj* torendii (na) トレンディ(な), ryūkō (no) 流行(の)

trespass; No Trespassing. "Tachiiri kinshi." 「立ち入り禁止.」

trespass (*on*) *v* fumi-komimás<u>u</u> (fumi-kómu, fumi-kónde) 踏み込みます(踏み込む, 踏み込んで)

trial *n* (*legal*) sáiban 裁判; (*test*) sh<u>i</u>kén 試験, (*trying*) tameshi 試し, kokoromi 試み, toraiaru トライアル

trial version *n* taiken-ban 体験版; toraiaru-ban トライアル版

triangle *n* **1.** sánkaku 三角, sankaku-kei, sankakkei 三角形 **2.** (*instrument*) toraianguru トライアングル

love triangle *n* sankaku kankei 三角関係

tribe; the ~ (*group, gang*) **of ...** ...-zoku ...族

trick *n* **1.** (*feat*) waza 業, géi 芸, torikku トリック, **one's favorite trick** ohako おはこ・十八番; (*move*) té 手; (*knack*) kotsú こつ・コツ, téguchi 手口; (*plot, scheme*) keiryaku 計略, hakarigoto 謀・はかりごと; **~ to it** (*the secret of it*) táne 種 **2. → cheat**

Trick or Treat. *interj* Okashi o kurenakya itazura suruzo. お菓子をくれなきゃ悪戯するぞ., Okashi o kurenaito itazura suruyo. お菓子をくれないと悪戯するよ.

tricky *adj* zurúi ずるい, torikkii トリッキー, bimyō (na) 微妙(な), (*difficult*) muzukashii 難しい

tricky politician *n* kōkatsu na seijika 狡猾な政治家

tricky question *n* kōmyō na shitsumon 巧妙な質問

tricycle *n* sanrín-sha 三輪車

trifling *adj* sásai (na) ささい[些細](な)

trigger *n* h<u>i</u>kigane 引き金, kikkake きっかけ

trigger finger *n* hitosashiyubi 人差し指・ひとさし指

trigger-happy *adj* kōsen-teki (na) 好戦的(な); (*critic*) arasagashi no sukina あら捜しの好きな

triggerman *n* koroshiya 殺し屋

trill *n* toriru トリル

trip *n* ryokō 旅行; *business trip* shutchō 出張

triple *n* sanbai 三倍; *adj* sanbai (no) 三倍(の); toripuru トリプル
　triple time *n* sanbyōshi 三拍子

trite *adj* heibon (na) 平凡(な)

trivial *adj* tsumaránai つまらない, chótto shita ちょっとした; sásai (na) ささい[些細](な) → **unimportant**

trolley *n* torokko トロッコ

trombone *n* toronbōn トロンボーン

troops *n* (*army*) gúntai 軍隊, gún 軍; (*detachment*) bútai 部隊

trophy *n* torofii トロフィー

tropic(s) *n* nettai(-chíhō´) 熱帯(地方)

tropical *adj* nettai (no) 熱帯(の); toropikaru (na) トロピカル(な)
　tropical fish *n* nettai-gyo 熱帯魚
　tropical flora *n* nettai shokubutsu 熱帯植物
　tropical fruits *n* toropikaru furútsu トロピカルフルーツ
　tropical island *n* nettai no shima 熱帯の島
　tropical rainforest *n* nettai urin 熱帯雨林; **~ climate** nettai urin kiko 熱帯雨林気候
　tropical region *n* nettai chihō 熱帯地方

trouble *n* (*inconvenience*) tékázu 手数, tesū´手数(o-tesū お手数); (*time taken up*) temá 手間(o-téma お手間); (*nuisance*) (go-)méiwaku (ご)迷惑, (go-)mendō´ (ご)面倒, toraburu トラブル; (*care*) sewá 世話 (o-séwa お世話, o-sewa-sama お世話様); (*bother*) (go-)yákkai (ご)やっかい・厄介; (*difficulty*) kónnan 困難, komáru kotó 困ること; (*ailment*) wazurai 煩い・わずらい, byōki 病気 → **worry**
　goes to much trouble honé o orimásu (óru, ótte) 骨を折ります(折る, 折って)
　is troubled by (*an ailment*), **has trouble with ...** o wazuraimásu (wazurau, wazuratte) …を煩います(煩う, 煩って)

troublemaker *n* toraburu mēkā トラブルメーカー; momegoto o okosu hito 揉め事[もめごと]を起こす人; gotagota o okosu hito ごたごたを起こす人

troublesome *adj* yaya(k)koshii やや(っ)こしい; méiwaku (na) 迷惑(な); yákkai (na) やっかい・厄介(な); mendō (na) 面倒(な); wazurawashii 煩わしい; hanzatsu (na) 煩雑(な)

trough shell *n* aoyagi あおやぎ・アオヤギ・青柳

trousers *n* zubón ズボン

trout *n* másu ます・マス・鱒

truck *n* torákku トラック; (*3-wheeled*) ōto-sánrin オート三輪

truck driver *n* torákku (no) untenshu トラック(の)運転手

true *adj* honto/hontō (no) ほんと(う)/本当(の); *how true* naru-hodo なるほど・成る程

truly *adv* honto (hontō) ni ほんと(ほんとう)に・本当に, makoto ni 誠に, jitsúni 実に

trumpet *n* toranpétto トランペット, rappa ラッパ

trumpet-shell *n* hóra ほら・ホラ・法螺, horá-gai ほら貝・ホラガイ・法螺貝

trunk *n* (*of tree*) miki 幹; (*of elephant*) hana 鼻; (*baggage*; *car ~*) toránku トランク

trunks *n* (*sports*) tanpan 短パン; (*swin*) suiei-pantsu 水泳パンツ; (*underwear*) torankusu トランクス, pantsu パンツ

trust 1. *n* tánomi 頼み, irai 依頼; shin'yō 信用, shinrai 信頼, ate 当て; anshin 安心 **2.** *v* (*trusts them*) shin'yō shimásu (suru, shite) 信用します(する, して), shin-jimásu (shin-jiru, shin-jite) 信じます(信じる, 信じて); *gives in ~* azukemásu (azukéru, azukete) 頂けます(頂ける, 頂けて), *takes in ~* azukarimásu (azukáru, azukátte) 預かります(預かる, 預かって)

truth *n* shinjitsu 真実, honto/hontō no kotó ほんと/ほんとう[本当]の事

try *v* **1.** (*attempt*) tameshimásu (tamésu, taméshite) 試します(試す, 試して); [BOOKISH] kokoromimásu (kokoromíru, kokorómite) 試みます(試みる, 試みて) **2.** (*doing*) (shi)-te mimásu (míru, míte) (し)てみます(みる, みて) **3.** (*to do*) (shi)-yō/(ya)-rō toshimásu (suru, shite) (し)よう/(や)ろうとします(する, して)
　try hard(er) ganbarimásu (ganbáru, ganbátte) がんばり[頑張り]ます(がんばる, がんばって); dóryoku shimásu (suru, shite) 努力します(する, して)

trying *adj* (*hard to bear*) tsurai つらい・辛い

T-shaped *adj* tii-ji gata (no) T字型(の)

T-shirt *n* tii shatsu Tシャツ

Tsukuba *n* Tsukúba つくば・筑波; *Tsukuba University* Tsukuba Dáigaku 筑波大学

tsunami *n* tsunami 津波

tub *n* óke 桶・おけ; (*basin*) tarai たらい; (*bathtub*) yúbune 湯船; (*rice tub*) o-hachi お鉢, o-hitsu おひつ・お櫃, meshi-bitsu 飯びつ・飯櫃

tuba *n* chūba チューバ

tube *n* kúda 管, kán 管; (*flexible, squeezable, inflatable*) chū´bu チューブ; *test tube* shikenkan 試験管; *TV tube* buraunkan ブラウン管

tuberculosis *n* kekkaku (haikékkaku) 結核(肺結核), haibyō 肺病; = *TB*

Tuesday *n* Kayō´bi 火曜日; *Tuesday-Thursday* Kā-Moku 火木

tug; *~ at* hipparimásu (hippáru, hippátte) 引っ張ります(引っ張る, 引っ張って)

tugboat *n* hiki-fune 引き船・曳き船; tagu-bōto タグボート

tulip *n* chūrippu チューリップ

tumble *v* korogarimásu (korogaru, korogatte) 転がります(転がる, 転がって); taoremásu (taoréru, taórete) 倒れます(倒れる, 倒れて), korobimásu (korobu, koronde) 転びます(転ぶ, 転んで)

tummy *n* onaka おなか; (*baby talk*) ponpon ポンポン

tumult *n* sō´dō 騒動

tuna *n* maguro まぐろ・マグロ・鮪; (*fatty*) tóro とろ・トロ, (*pink, medium-fat*) chū-toro 中と

ろ・中トロ, (*red, unfatty*) aka-mi 赤身; (*canned tunafish*) tsúna ツナ
fresh slices of raw tuna *n* maguro no sashimi まぐろ[マグロ・鮪]の刺身
tunafish sandwich *n* tsuna-sándo ツナサンド
tundra *n* tsundora ツンドラ
tune *n* kyoku 曲; chōshi 調子; tōn トーン, fushí 節
tuner *n* **1.** (*person*) chōritsu-shi 調律師 **2.** (*tool*) chūnā チューナー
tunnel *n* tonneru トンネル
turban shell, turbo *n* sázae さざえ・サザエ・栄螺; ~ *cooked in its shell* tsubo-yaki つぼ焼き・壷焼き
turbot *n* karei かれい・カレイ・鰈
turf *n* shiba 芝・シバ, shibafu 芝生・シバフ
turkey *n* shichimen-chō 七面鳥・シチメンチョウ
Turkey *n* Tóruko トルコ
turn 1. *n* (*order*) junban 順番; (*spin*) kaiten 回転; (*corner*) magarikado 曲がり角 **2.** *v* (*changes directions*) magarimásu (magaru, magatte) 曲がります(曲がる, 曲がって); (*goes round*) mawarimásu (mawaru, mawatte) 回ります(回る, 回って) **3.** *v* (*makes it go round*) mawashimásu (mawasu, mawashite) 回します(回す, 回して); (*directs one's face/eyes/attention to*) … ni mukemásu (mukeru, mukete) …に向けます(向ける, 向けて)
turn aside (*diverts*) sorashimásu (sorásu, soráshite) 逸らし[そらし]ます(逸らす, 逸らして)
turn back hiki-kaeshimásu (hiki-káesu, hiki-káeshite) 引き返します(引き返す, 引き返して)
turn inside out ura-gáeshimásu (ura-gáesu, ura-gáeshite) 裏返します(裏返す, 裏返して)
turn into **1.** (*becomes*) ([NOUN] ni に, [ADJECTIVE]-ku く) narimásu (náru, nátte) なります(なる, なって) **2.** (*makes it into*) ([NOUN] ni に, [ADJECTIVE]-ku く) shimásu (suru, shite) します(する, して)
turn left/right sasetsu/usetsu shimásu (suru, shite) 左折/右折します(する, して)
turn loose nigashimásu (nigásu, nigáshite) 逃がします(逃がす, 逃がして)
turn off (*light, radio, etc.*) … o keshimásu (kesu, keshite);を消します(消す, 消して); ~ *the ignition* suítchi o kirimásu (kíru, kítté) スイッチを切ります(切る, 切って)
turn on (*light, etc.*) … o tsukemásu (tsukéru, tsukéte) …を付けます(付ける, 付けて); ~ *the ignition* suítchi o iremásu (ireru, irete) スイッチを入れます(入れる, 入れて)
turn over ura-gaeshimasu (ura-gaesu, ura-gaeshite) 裏返します(裏返す, 裏返して)
turn up (*it gets found*) mitsukari-másu (mitsu-karu, mitsukatte) 見付かります(見付かる, 見付かって); ~ *one's nose at* … o hana de ashiraimásu (ashiráu, ashirátte) …を鼻であしらいます(あしらう, あしらって)
turning point *n* kawarime 変わり目, tenki 転機
turnip *n* kabu かぶ・カブ・蕪, kabura かぶら・カブラ・蕪

turtle *n* káme 亀・カメ; (*snapping*) suppon すっぽん・スッポン
turtleneck *n* tātoru nekku タートルネック
tusk *n* kiba 牙・キバ
tutelary deity *n* (*guardian spirit*) uji-gami 氏神
tutor *n* kateikyō´shi 家庭教師, chūtā チューター
tutoring school *n* júku 塾
tuxedo *n* takishiido タキシード
TV *n* térebi テレビ
tweed *n* tsuiido ツイード
tweet 1. *v* (*internet*) (tsuittā de) tsubuyaku (ツイッターで)つぶやく **2.** (*bird*) saezurimásu (saezuru, saezutte) さえずります(さえずる, さえずって) **3.** (*bird*) (kotori no) saezuri (小鳥の)さえずり
tweezers *n* pinsétto ピンセット
twelve *n* jū-ní 十二・12
twentieth *adj* nijū-banmé (no) 二十番目(の); *the twentieth day* hatsukamé 二十日目, (*of the month*) hatsuka 二十日・20日
twenty *n* ní-jū 二十・20, futá-jū 二十; (*20 years old*) hátachi 二十歳・20歳, níjús-sai 二十歳・20歳
twenty thousand *n* ni-mán 二万・20,000, futa-mán 二万・20,000
twice *adv* (*two times*) ni-dó 二度, ni-kái 二回; (*double*) ni-bai 二倍
twilight *n* yūgata 夕方; tasogare たそがれ・黄昏
twin(-bed) room *n* tsúin ツイン, tsuin-rū´mu ツインルーム
twin beds *n* tsuin-béddo ツインベッド
twine 1. *n* → string **2.** *v* (*twists*) yorimásu (yóru, yótte) よります・縒ります(よる, 縒って・縒って)
twinkle 1. *n* kirameki きらめき・煌き **2.** *v* kirameki másu (kirameku, kirameite) きらめきます・煌きます(きらめく, きらめいて), kagayakimásu (kagayaku, kagayaite) 輝きます(輝く, 輝いて)
twins *n* futago 双子・ふたご
twist *v* nejirimásu (nejíru, nejítte) ねじります・捻ります(ねじる, ねじって), hinerimásu (hinéru, hinétte) ひねります・捻ります(ひねる, ひねって), yorimásu (yóru, yótte) よります(よる, よって); *gets twisted* (*entangled*) kojiremásu (kojiréru, kojírete) こじれます・拗れます(こじれる, こじれて)
Twitter *n* (*internet*) tsuittā ツイッター
two *n* ní 二・2, futatsú 二つ・2つ; futa-... 二..., ni-... 二...; (*people*) futarí 二人, [BOOKISH] ní-mei 二名
two; 2 pieces (*small things*) ní-ko 二個, **2 trees** (*or long things*) ní-hon 二本; **2 sheets** (*flat things*) ní-mai 二枚; **2 fish/bugs/cats** (*or small animals*) ní-hiki 二匹; **2 cows** (*or large aminals*) ní-tō 二頭; **2 birds/rabbits** ní-wa 二羽; **2 cars** (*or machines/vehicles*) ní-dai 二台; **2 copies** (*books/magazines*) ní-satsu 二冊; **2 people** futa-rí ふたり・二人, ní-mei 二名; **2 floors/stories** ni-kai 二階; **2 fold**

ni-bai 二倍; *2 degrees* ní-do 二度; *2 times* ni-dó 二度, ni-kái 二回, ni-hén 二遍; *2 o'clock* ní-ji 二時; *2 hours* ní-jíkan 二時間; *2 days* fútsuka 二日; *2 weeks* ní-shūkan 二週間; *2 months* ni-ká-getsu 二ヶ月; *2 years* ní-nen 二年, ninén-kan 二年間; *2 years old* futatsú 二つ, ní-sai 二歳

two hundred *n* ní-hyaku 二百・200, futá-hyaku 二百・200

two-piece woman's suit *n* tsū-píisu ツーピース; *ugly woman* búsu ぶす・ブス

two thousand *n* ni-sén 二千・2,000, futa-sén 二千・2,000

two-way socket *n* futamata-sokétto 二又ソケット

two-way traffic *n* ryōmen-kōtsū 両面交通

two-year college (*education*) *n* tanki-dáigaku 短期大学, tan-dai 短大

U

Ueno *n* Ueno 上野; *Ueno Park* Ueno-Kō´en 上野公園; *Ueno Station* Ueno-Eki 上野駅

ugly *adj* (*look*) minikúi 醜い・みにくい; mazúi まずい; *ugly woman* búsu ぶす・ブス

uh *interj* ē-to えと; *uh* … anō あのう…; *uh-huh* *n* ん; *uh-uh, huh-uh* nn んん

UK *n* igirisu イギリス, eikoku 英国

ulcer *n* (*gastric*) i-káiyō 胃潰瘍・胃かいよう

ultimate 1. *n* kyūkyoku 究極 **2.** *adj* kyūkyoku no 究極の

ultimately *adv* saishū-teki ni 最終的に, kekkyoku 結局

ultimatum *n* saigo tsūchō 最後通牒, saishū tsūkoku 最終通告

ultrasound *n* **1.** chōonpa 超音波 **2.** (*ultrasound diagnosis*) chōonpa shindan 超音波診断

ultraviolet *n* shigaisen 紫外線, *adj* shigaisen (no) 紫外線(の)

umbrella *n* kása かさ・傘, amagása 雨傘; (*parasol*) hi-gása 日傘; (*oilpaper*) ban-gasa 番傘, kara-kása 唐傘; (*western-style*) kō´mori (-gása) こうもり・コウモリ(傘), yō-gása 洋傘

umpire *n* shinpan(-in) 審判(員)

UN → United Nations

un- *prefix* fu- 不

unacceptable *adj* mitomerarenai 認められない

unaccountable *adj* setsumei dekinai 説明できない

unanimous *adj* manjō itchi (no/de) 満場一致(の/で), zen'in itchi (no/de) 全員一致(の/で)

unanticipated *adj* omowánu … 思わぬ・おもわぬ…

unapproachable *adj* chikayorigatai 近寄りがたい・近寄り難い, chikazukinikui 近づきにくい

unarmed *adj* hibusō (no) 非武装(の)

unassuming *adj* kidoranai 気取らない

unavoidable *adj* yamu-o-énai やむを得ない

unbalanced *adj* fuantei (na) 不安定(な), katayotta 偏った, katayotteiru 偏っている, baransu no warui バランスの悪い

unbeatable *adj* muteki (no) 無敵(の)

unbelievable *adj* shinjirarenai 信じられない

unbiased *adj* katayori no nai 偏りのない, sennyū-kan no nai 先入観のない

unbusy *adj* isogashikunai 忙しくない, hima (na) 暇(な)

unbutton *v* … no botan o hazushimásu (hazusu, hazushite) …のボタンを外します(外す, 外して); *comes unbuttoned* akimásu (aku, aite) 空きます(空く, 空いて), … no botan ga hazuremásu (hazureru, hazurete) …のボタンが外れます(外れる, 外れて)

uncalled-for *adj* yokei (na) 余計・よけい(な)

uncanny *adj* sugói すごい・凄い; fushigi 不思議・ふしぎ

uncertain *adj* futei (no) 不定(の); ayashii 怪しい・あやしい

unchaste *adj* futei (na) 不貞(な)

uncle *n* oji(-san) おじ[叔父, 伯父](さん)

unclean *adj* fuketsu (na) 不潔(な)

Uncle Tom *n* hakujin ni hikutsu na taido o toru kokujin 白人に卑屈な態度を取る黒人

uncomfortable *adj* kimochi ga warúi 気持ちが悪い; (*not feel at home*) igokochi ga warui 居心地が悪い; (*to wear*) kigokochi ga warui 着心地が悪い; (*constrained*) kyūkutsu (na) 窮屈(な)

uncommon *adj* mezurashíi 珍しい・めずらしい

unconcerned *adj* **1. → calm 2. ~ with** … ni mu-kánshin (na) …に無関心(な)

unconditional *adj* mu-jō´ken (no) 無条件(の)

unconditionally *adv* mu-jō´ken de 無条件で

unconnected *adj* … to mukánkei ni …と無関係(の)

unconscious *adj* íshiki fumei (no) 意識不明(の); (*involuntary*) mu-íshiki (no/na) 無意識(の/な)

type *n* táipu タイプ, (*sort*) shúrui 種類; (*model*) katá 型, …-gata …型; (*print*) katsuji 活字; *different type n betsu no taipu* 別のタイプ; chigau taipu 違うタイプ, [BOOKISH] kotonaru shurui 異なる種類

type (*write*) *n* táipu (shimásu; suru, shite) タイプ(します; する, して)

typewriter *n* taipuráitā タイプライター, táipu タイプ; (*how many*) nán-dai 何台)

typhoon *n* taifū´ 台風

typhus *n* chifusu チフス

typical *adj* tenkei-teki (na) 典型的(な), daihyō-teki (na) 代表的(な), (*usual*) futsū (no) 普通(の)

typist *n* taipisuto タイピスト

tyrant *n* bōkun 暴君

uncooked *adj* náma (no) 生(の)

uncork *v* (… no sén o) nukimásu (nuku, nuite) (…の栓を)抜きます(抜く, 抜いて); (… no kuchi o) akemásu (akeru, akete) (…の口を)空けます (空けて, 空けて)

uncover *v* bakuro shimásu (suru, shite) 曝露します(する, します)

uncultivated *adj* kyōyō no nai 教養のない; mukyōyō (no) 無教養(の); (wild) soya (na) 粗野 (な)

undecided *adj* (indefinite) futei (no) 不定(の)

under *prep, adv* … no shitá (de/ni/no) …の下(で/ に/の); (the tutelage of) … no motó (de) …の下 (で); ~ (doing) ...-chū (no) ...中(の)

undercut *v* 1. (cuts under) shita o kirimásu (kiru, kitte) 下を切ります(切る, 切って) 2. (offers at a lower price) yasune de urimásu (uru, utte) 安値 で売ります(売る, 売って) 3. (golf) andā katto shimásu (suru, shite) アンダーカットします (する, して)

underdog *n* makeinu 負け犬

underdone *adj* nama-yake (no) 生焼け(の)

underestimate *v* (kids oneself about) amaku mimásu (míru, míte) 甘く見ます・あまくみます (見る, 見て), (person) mikubirimásu (mikubiru, mikubitte) みくびります(みくびる, みくびって), kashōhyōka shimásu (suru, shite) 過小評価します (する, して)

undergo *v* (experiences) keiken shimásu (suru, shite) 経験します(する, して); … mé ni aimásu (áu, átte) …目に会います(会う, 会って)

undergraduate (student) *n* daigáku-sei 大学生

underground 1. *adj* chiká (no) 地下(の) 2. → **subway**

underline *n, v* kasen (o hikimásu; hiku, hiite) 下線 (を引きます; 引く, 引いて)

underneath 1. *n* shita 下 2. *prep, adv* shita ni 下に

underpants *n* zubon-shita ズボン下, pantsu パンツ

undershirt *n* shátsu シャツ

understand *v* (… ga) wakarimásu (wakáru, wakátte) (…が)分かります(分かる, 分かって); (… o) rikai shimásu (suru, shite) (…を)理解しま す(する, して)

understanding *n* rikai 理解, (ability) rikái-ryoku 理解力 → **agreement**

understood; *is* ~ tsū-jimásu (tsū-jiru, tsū-jite) 通じます(通じる, 通じて)

undertake *v* (plan, attempt, scheme) kuwa-datemásu (kuwadatéru, kuwadátete) 企てます (企てる, 企てて)

undertaker *n* (funeral director) sōgi-ya 葬儀屋

undertaking *n* shigoto 仕事; (enterprise) jígyō 事業, kuwada te 企て

undertone *n* kogoe 小声

undervalue *v* kashōhyōka shimásu (suru, shite) 過小評価します(する, して)

underwater 1. *adj* suichū (no) 水中(の) 2. *adv* suichū de 水中で

underwear *n* shita-gi 下着, hadagí 肌着; (underpants) shitabaki 下穿き, pántsu パンツ, (women's drawers) zurō´su ズロース, (panties) pántii パンティー

underworld *n* 1. (another world) anoyo あの世 2. (gang land) ankoku-gai 暗黒街

undeserving *adj* (Also; What a waste!) mottai-nái もったいない

undisturbed *adj* sono mamá (de/no) そのまま (で/の)

undo *v* hazushimásu (hazusu, hazushite) 外します (外す, 外して); moto ni modoshimásu (modosu, modoshite) 元に戻します(戻す, 戻して); (unties) hodokimásu (hodóku, hodóite) ほどきます(ほど く, ほどいて), tokimásu (tóku, tóite) 解きます(解 く, 解いて)

undone; *comes* ~ tokemásu (tokéru, tókete) 解け ます(解ける, 解けて); *leaves it* ~ shinai de okimásu (oku, oite) しないでおきます(おく, おいて)

undoubtedly *adv* utagai náku 疑いなく, táshika ni 確かに・たしかに, kitto きっと

undress *v* 1. (takes off one's clothes) fuku o nugimásu (nugu, nuide) 服を脱ぎます(脱ぐ, 脱いで) 2. (takes off someone's clothes) fuku o nugasemásu (nugaseru, nugasete) 服を脱がせます (脱がせる, 脱がせて)

unduly *adv* yatara ni やたらに

uneasiness *n* shinpai 心配

uneasy *adj* shinpai (na) 心配(な), fuan (na) 不安(な)

unemployed; ~ *person* shitsugyō-sha 失業者; ~ *samurai* rōnin 浪人

unemployment *n* shitsugyō 失業

uneven *adj* dekoboko (no) でこぼこ・凸凹(の)

unexpected *adj* igai (na) 意外(な), omoigakénai 思いがけない; (sudden) níwaka (no) にわか (の); (but welcome) mezurashíi 珍しい

unexpectedly *adv* igai ni 意外に, futo ふと, (suddenly) níwaka ni にわかに

unfair *adj* fu-kōhei (na) 不公平(な); (unjustified) futō (na) 不当(な); fea dewanai フェアではない

unfaithful *adj* (to her husband) futei (na) 不貞(な)

unfasten *v* hazushimásu (hazusu, hazushite) 外し ます・はずします(外す, 外して)

unfavorable *adj* fúri (na) 不利(な); (unlikable) konomashikúnai 好ましくない

unfazed (by …) 1. *v* (…-témo) dō-jimasén (dō-jinai, dō-jináide) (…ても)動じません(動じな い, 動じないで) 2. *adj* heiki (na) 平気(な)

unfeeling *adj* hakujō (na) 薄情(な)

unfixed *adj* futei (no) 不定(の)

unfortunate *adj* (unlucky) fukō´ (na) 不幸(な), fu-un (na) 不運(な); (regrettable, inopportune) ainiku (na) あいにく(な) → **pitiful**

unfortunately *adv* ainiku あいにく, zannen nagara/desuga 残念ながら/ですが, [BOOKISH] ikan nagara 遺憾ながら

unfriendly adj fushinsetsu (na) 不親切(な), buaisō (na) 無愛想(な), sokkenai そっけない

ungrateful adj on shirazu (na/no) 恩知らず (な/の), kansha shinai 感謝しない

unhandy adj fúben (na) 不便(な)

unhappy adj (unlucky) fukó´ (na) 不幸(な), (gloomy) inki (na) 陰気(な), (moody) kigen ga warúi 機嫌が悪い, (dissatisfied) fuman (na) 不満(な)

unhealthy adj 1. fu-kenkō (na) 不健康(な) 2. (bad for one's health) karada ni warúi 体に悪い 3. (sickly) byōki-gachi (na) 病気がち(な)

unhulled rice n mómi もみ・籾

unification n tōitsu 統一

uniform 1. n seifuku 制服, yunifōmu ユニフォーム; (military) gunpuku 軍服, (school) gakuséi-fuku 学生服 2. adj (the same) byōdō 平等 (な), taitō (no) 対等(の) 3. v (equal) soroemásu (soroéru, soroete) そろえます(そろえる・そろえて)

unify v tōitsu shimásu (suru, shite) 統一します (する, して)

unimportant adj (matter) mondai ni naránai 問題にならない

unintentionally adv tsúi つい, ukkari うっかり, mu-ishiki ni 無意識に, itosezu ni 意図せずに

union n (labor) kumiai 組合, rōdōkúmiai 労働組合; (alliance) rengō 連合, renmei 連盟, (joint) kyōdō 共同, (merger) gappei 合併, gōdō 合同

unique adj yúitsu (no) 唯一(の); yuniiku (na) ユニーク(な)

unit n tán'i 単位; (military) bútai 部隊

unite v (they merge) gappei/gōdō shimásu (suru, shite) 合併/合同します(する, して); (combines dual functions as) ... o kanemásu (kanéru, kánete) ...を兼ねます(兼ねる, 兼ねて); (partner) kumimásu (kúmu, kúnde) 組みます(組む, 組んで)

United Nations n Kokusai-Réngō 国際連合

United States n Amerika(-Gasshū´koku) アメリカ(合衆国)

universe n úchū 宇宙; yunibāsu ユニバース

university n daigaku 大学; at ~ zaigaku(-chū) 在学(中)

unjustified adj futō (na) 不当(な)

unkind adj fu-shínsetsu (na) 不親切(な) → **mean**

unknown adj fumei (no) 不明(の); shiranai 知らない

unless conj (shi)-nákereba (し)なければ, (shi)-nai to (し)ないと

unlikely adj ari-sō´mo nái ありそうもない; (shi)-sō mo nái (し)そうもない

unload v oroshimásu (orósu, oróshite) 降ろします (降ろす, 降ろして)

unlock v ... no kagí o akemásu (akeru, akete) ...の鍵を開けます(開ける, 開けて)

unlocked; comes ~ ... (no kagí ga) akimásu (aku, aite) ...(の鍵が)開きます(開く, 開いて)

unluckily adv ún-waruku 運悪く

unlucky adj ún ga warúi 運が悪い; (fails to strike it lucky) tsúite imasén (inai, inákute) ついていません(いない, いなくて)

unmarried adj hitori-mónó 独り者, dokushin 独身

unnatural adj fu-shízen (na) 不自然(な)

unnecessary, unneeded adj iranai いらない, muyō (na) 無用(な), fuyō (na) 不要(な); (superfluous) yokei (na) 余計(な)

unoccupied adj (free of business) hima (na) 暇(な)

unofficial adj hi-kō´shiki (no) 非公式(の)

unpack v nimotsu o hodokimásu (hodoku, hodóite) 荷物を解きます・ほどきます(ほどく, ほどいて)

unperturbed adj heiki (na) 平気(な)

unpleasant adj iyá (na) 嫌(な); fuyúkai (na) 不愉快(な)

unpolished rice n génmai 玄米

unprofitable adj wari ga warúi 割が悪い

unqualified adj mushíkaku (no) 無資格(の); (unlimited) mujōken (no) 無条件(の)

unreasonable adj múri (na) 無理(な); múcha (na) むちゃ[無茶](な); hidói ひどい

unrelated (to ...) adj (... to wá) mukánkei (nó) (...とは)無関係(の)

unreliable adj ayashii 怪しい, detarame (na) でたらめ(な)

unreserved adj (frank; rude) buénryo (na) 無遠慮(な)

unreserved seat(s) n jiyū´-seki 自由席

unrest n sō´dō 騒動; fuan 不安; shinpai 心配

unsafe adj (troubled) bussō´ (na) 物騒(な)

unsavory rumors n tokaku no uwasa とかくのうわさ[噂]

unscrupulous adj akuratsu (na) 悪らつ(な)・悪辣(な)

unseemly, unsightly adj migurushíi 見苦しい

unsentimental adj dorai (na) ドライ(な)

unskillful adj hetá (na) へた[下手](な), mazúi まずい

unsociable adj bu-áisō (na) 無愛想(な)

unsophisticated adj sekenshirazu (na) 世間知らず(な); mújaki (na) 無邪気・むじゃき(な), soboku (na) 素朴(な)

unsuitable adj kakkō ga warúi かっこう・格好[恰好]が悪い

untangle v motsure o tokimásu (tóku, tóite) もつれを解きます(解く, 解いて), kaiketsu shimásu (suru, shite) 解決します(する, して)

untasty adj mazúi まずい

untidy adj kitanái 汚い; chirakatte(i)ru 散らかって(い)る

untie v tokimásu (tóku, tóite) 解きます(解く, 解いて), hodokimásu (hodóku, hodóite) ほどきます(ほどく, ほどいて)

until prep ... máde ...まで・迄; ~ now ima-made 今まで[迄]

untouched adj sono mamá (de/no) そのまま(で/の)

unusual *adj* (*abnormal*) ijō (na) 異常（な）; (*extreme*) hijō (na) 非常（な）, (*novel*) kawatta 変わった, mezurashí 珍しい

unusually *adv* mezuráshiku 珍しく・めずらしく; (*extremely*) hijō ni 非常に

unwell; feeling ~ kimochi ga warúi 気持が悪い

unwilling (*to do*) *adj* (shi)-taku arimasén (nái, nákute) （し）たくありません（ない, なくて）

unzipped *adj comes ~* (chákku ga) akimásu (aku, aite) （チャック が）空きます（空く, 空いて）; *to unzip a file* (*computer*) fairu o kaitō shimásu (suru, shite) ファイルを解凍します（する, して）

up *prep* (… no) ué e (…の）上へ; *up* (*higher by*) ¥100 hyakuén-daka 百円高

bring up *v* (*trains*) shitsukemásu (shitsukéru, shitsúkete) しつけ［躾け］ます（しつける, しつけて）, (*rears*) sodatemásu (sodatéru, sodátete) 育てます（育てる, 育てて）

get up *v* okimásu (okíru, ókite) 起きます（起きる, 起きて）; (*gets one up*) okoshimásu (okósu, okóshite) 起こします（起こす, 起こして）

go up *v* agarimásu (agaru, agatte) 上がります（上がる, 上がって）, noborimásu (noboru, nobotte) 上り［昇り］ます（上［昇］る, 上［昇］って）

make up for *v* oginaimásu (ogináu, oginátte) 補います（補う, 補って）

up to now jū´rai 従来, ima-máde 今まで[迄]

up-to-date *adj* (*modern*) géndai (no) 現代（の）; (*latest*) saishin (no) 最新（の）

upbringing *n* shitsuke しつけ・躾; sodachí 育ち

update 1. *n* kōshin 更新; saishin (-ban) 最新(版) 2. *v* kōshin shimásu (suru, shite) 更新します（する, して）, saishin (-ban) ni shimásu (suru, shite) 最新(版)にします（する, して）, appudēto shimásu (suru, shite) アップデートします（する, して）

upfront money *n* atama-kin 頭金

upkeep *n* íji 維持; (*expense*) ijí-hi 維持費; (*care, repair*) te-iré 手入れ

upload *v* (*computer*) appurōdo shimásu (suru, shite) アップロードします（する, して）

upon → **on**

upper *adj* ue (no) 上（の）

upping the (*base*) **pay** bēsu-áppu ベースアップ, béa ベア

upright *adj* katai 堅い → **honest**

upright piano *n* appuraito piano アップライトピアノ

uprising *n* bōdō 暴動, hanran 反乱

upset 1. *v* (*it overturns*) hikkuri-kaerimásu (hikkuri-káeru, hikkuri-káette) ひっくり返ります（ひっくり返る, ひっくり返って）, (*overturns it*) hikkuri-kaeshimásu (hikkuri-káesu, hikkuri-káeshite) ひっくり返します（ひっくり返す, ひっくり返して） → **spill** 2. *v* (*disturbs*) midashimásu (midásu, midáshite) 乱します（乱す, 乱して）; (*is disturbed*) midaremásu (midaréru, midárete) 乱れます（乱れる, 乱れて）, (*gets nervous*) dōyō shimásu (suru, shite) 動揺します（する, して）; *has an ~ stomach* (o-naka no) guai ga warúi

(おなかの）具合が悪い 3. *n* (*stomach upset*) imotare 胃もたれ, muneyake 胸焼け

upsetting *adj* dōyō saseru 動揺させる

upshot *n* shímatsu しまつ・始末

upside *n* 1. jōbu 上部, ue-no-hō 上のほう 2. riten 利点

upside down *adv* sakasa(ma) (ni) 逆さ(ま)（に）, abekobe (ni) あべこべ(に)

upstairs *adv* ni-kai 二階, o-níkai (de/ni, e, no) お二階（で/に, へ, の）

uptown (*Tokyo*) *n* yama-te 山手, yama-no-te 山の手

up until *adv* (…) ízen (…)以前

upwards of (…) íjō (…)以上

urban *adj* toshi (no) 都市（の）; shínai (no) 市内（の）

urbanite *n* tokai-jin 都会人

urge *v* (*bustles up*) sekitatemásu (sekitateru, sekitatete) せき立てます・急き立てます（せき立てる, せき立てて）; susumemásu (susumeru, susumete) 勧めます（勧める, 勧めて）; (*persuades*) unagashimásu (unagasu, unagáshite) 促します（促す, 促して）

urgency *n* shikyū 至急, kinkyū 緊急

urgent *adj* kyū (na) 急（な）, kinkyū (na) 緊急（な）, shikyu (na) 至急（の）

urgent business *n* kyūyō 急用

urgently *adv* kyū´ ni 急に, shikyū (ni) 至急（に）

urinal *n* (*place*) shōben-jo 小便所; (*thing*) shōben-ki 小便器, (*bedpan*) shibin しびん・し瓶

urinate *v* shōben shimásu, shonben shimásu (suru, shite) 小便します（する, して）, (*medical*) hainyō shimásu (suru, shite) 排尿します（する, して）

urine *n* shōben, shonben 小便, (*medical*) nyō 尿; [BABY TALK] (o-)shikko (お) しっこ

urn *n* tsubo つぼ・壷

us *pron* watáshí-táchi わたしたち[私達], watakúshí-tachi [私達]; ware-ware われわれ・我々

U.S. *n* Amerika アメリカ, Beikoku 米国; Bei-…, …-Bei …米

usable *adj* shiyō dekiru 使用できる, shiyō kanō (na) 使用可能（な）, riyō dekiru 利用できる, riyō kanō (na) 利用可能（な）

usage *n* shiyō 使用, kanyō 慣用

use 1. *n* (*the use*) shiyō 使用; (*utilization*) riyō 利用; (*putting to use*) ōyō 応用 2. *n* (*for the use of*) …-yō …用 3. *n* (*service*) (go-)yō （ご)用, yakú 役 (o-yaku お役) 4. *v* tsukaimásu (tsukau, tsukatte) 使います（使う, 使って）, mochiimásu (mochiiru, mochiite) 用います（用いる, 用いて）; (*makes use of*) riyō shimásu (suru, shite) 利用します（する, して）

used *adj* (*secondhand*) chūko (no) 中古（の）, furúi 古い

used to (do) (shi)-ta monó/món desu （し)たもの/もんです; *gets used to* … ni naremásu (naréru, nárete) …に慣れます（慣れる, 慣れて）

useful *adj* yaku ni tatsu 役に立つ; yakudatsu 役立つ, yūyō (na) 有用（な）, chō´hō (na)

重宝(な); *is* ~ yakú ni tachimásu (tátsu, tátte) 役に立ちます(役立つ, 役立って), yaku-dachimásu (yaku-dátsu, yaku-dátte) 役立ちます(役立つ, 役立って); chō´hō shimásu (suru, shite) 重宝します(する, して)

useless *adj* 1. (*wasteful*) muda (na) 無駄(な) 2. (*of no use, unworthy*) muyō (no) 無用(の) 3. (*unworthy of no value*) fuyō (no) 不用(の)

user *n* shiyō´-sha 使用者; riyō´-sha 利用者; (*computer*) yūza ユーザ, yūzā ユーザー

usher 1. *n* toritsugi 取り次ぎ・とりつぎ; (*greeter*) annai-gákari 案内係, annai-nin 案内人 2. *v* (*ushers one*) annái shimásu (suru, shite) 案内します(する, して)

usual *adj* futsū (no) 普通(の), ítsumo (no) いつも(の), heijō (no) 平常(の), fúdan (no) 普段(の); tsūjō (no) 通常(の), tsúne (no) 常(の); *as* ~ ítsumo no yō´ni いつものよう[様]に, aikawarazu 相変らず・あいかわらず

usually *adv* (*normally*) futsū (wa) 普通・ふつう (は), tsūjō (wa) 通常(は), (*mostly*) taitei (wa)

たいてい・大抵(は), (*daily*) fúdan (wa) 普段・ふだん(は), higoro (wa) 日頃(は), (*always*) ítsumo (wa) いつも(は)

utensil *n* utsuwa 器; ...-yōhin ...用品

utilities (*bills*) *n* kōkyō-ryō´kin 公共料金

utility *n* jitsuyō 実用

utilization *n* riyō 利用

utilize *v* riyō shimásu (suru, shite) 利用します (する, して)

utmost; *to the* ~ ákú-made (mo) あくまで(も); *does one's* ~ saizen o tsukushimásu (tsukúsu, tsukúshite) 最善を尽くします(尽くす, 尽くして)

utter → speak, say; ~ a curse noroimásu (noróu, norótte) 呪います(呪う, 呪って)

utterly *adv* mattaku 全く・まったく, sukkári すっかり, zenzen 全然・ぜんぜん; ~ *exhausted* ku(t)takuta く(っ)たくた

U-turn *n* yūtā´n ユーターン・Uターン; *makes a* ~ yūtā´n shimásu (suru, shite) ユーターン・[Uターン]します(する, して)

V

vacant *adj* 1. (*open*) aite imásu (iru, ite) 空いています(いる, いて) 2. (*hollow*) utsuro (na) う つろ・虚ろ(な) 3. *vacant* ... aki-... 空き...; *vacant car* (*available taxi*) kūsha 空車; *vacant house* aki-ya 空き家; *vacant lot* aki-chi 空き地; *vacant room(s)* aki-ma 空き間, *vacant room/office* aki-shitsu 空き室

vacate *v* akemásu (akeru, akete) 空けます(空け る, 空けて)

vacation *n* yasumí 休み, kyūka 休暇, bakēshon バケーション

vacationer *n* gyōraku kyaku 行楽客

vaccination *n* wakuchin sesshu ワクチン接種

vaccine *n* wakuchin ワクチン

vacuum *v* sōjiki o kakemásu (kakeru, kakete) 掃 除機をかけます(かける, かけて)

vacuum bottle *n* mahō´bin 魔法瓶

vacuum cleaner *n* (denki) sōjiki (電気)掃除機

vagabond, vagrant *n* furō´-sha 浮浪者

vagina *n* chitsu 膣

vague *adj* aimai (na) あいまい(な)・曖昧(な), ii-kagen (na) いい加減(な)

vaguely *adv* aimai ni あいまいに・曖昧に; (*somehow*) dō´mo どうも

vain (*conceited*) *adj* unbore ga tsuyói うぬぼれ が強い; *in vain* *adj, adv* munashii 空しい・虚しい・む なしい, muda (na/ni) 無駄(な/に)

Valentine's Day *n* barentain dē バレンタインデー

valiant *adj* yūkan (na) 勇敢(な)

valid *adj* yūkō (na) 有効(な)

valley *n* tani(-ma) 谷(間)

valuable *adj* taisetsu (na) 大切(な), kichō (na) 貴重(な) → **expensive**

valuables *n* kichō-hin 貴重品

value 1. *n* káchi 価値, neuchi 値打ち 2. *v values* (*cherishes*) *it* chōhō shimásu (suru, shite) 重宝し ます(する, して), chōhō-garimásu (chōhō-gáru, chōhō-gátte) 重宝がります(重宝がる, 重宝が って)

valued *adj* chō´hō (na) 重宝(な) → **valuable**

valve *n* bén 弁

van *n* (*car*) raito ban ライトバン

vanilla *n* bánira バニラ

vanish *v* (*from sight*) miénaku narimásu (náru, nátte) 見えなくなります(なる, なって); (*from existence*) náku narimásu (náru, nátte) なくなり ます(なる, なって); (*gets extinguished*) kiemásu (kieru, kiete) 消えます(消える, 消えて)

vanity *n* kyoei-shin 虚栄心, unbore うぬぼれ

vapor *n* kitai 気体 → **steam**

various *adj* iroiro (na/no) いろいろ[色々] (な/の), ironna いろんな, samazama (na) さまざ ま・様々(な); *various places* tokorodókoro とこ ろどころ・所々

varnish *n* nísu ニス = wánisu (o nurimásu; nuru, nutte) ワニス(を塗ります; 塗る, 塗って); nuri 塗り

vase *n* bin 瓶; (*for flowers*) kabin 花瓶, káki 花器

vast *adj* bakudai (na) 莫大(な)

vaudeville *adj* (*theater*) yose 寄席; engei(-jō) 演芸(場)

vegetable *n* yasai 野菜 (o-yásai お野菜); (*greens*) aó-mono 青物, náppa 菜っ葉, ná 菜

vegetarian *n* bejitarian ベジタリアン; saishoku shugi-sha 菜食主義者; *vegetarian cuisine* shōjin-ryō´ri 精進料理

vehicle *n* nori-mono 乗り物, kuruma 車 (o-kúruma お車), …-sha … 車; (*how many* nán-dai 何台)

vein *n* (*vena*) jōmyaku 静脈

veil *n* bēru ベール

velocity *n* sokudo 速度, hayasa 速さ, supiido スピード

velvet *n* birōdo ビロード, berubetto ベルベット

vending machine *n* hanbái-ki 販売機; *ticket vending machine* kenbái-ki 券売機

vendor *n* uriko 売り子 → **seller, dealer**

venereal disease *n* seibyō 性病

Venezuela *n* benezuera ベネズエラ

vengeance *n* fukushū 復讐

ventilation *n* kanki 換気; *ventilation system* kanki-sō´chi 換気装置

venture *n* bōken 冒険; tōkiteki jigyō 投機的事業; tōki 投機; (*speculation, wild guess*) yamá やま・山

Venus *n* (*planet*) kinsei 金星

veranda *n* beranda ベランダ; engawa 縁側

verb *n* dōshi 動詞

verbal *adj* (*spoken*) kōtō (no) 口頭 (の)

verbally *adv* kōtō (de) 口頭 (で)

verification *n* shōmei 証明; kenshō 検証

verify *v* shōmei shimásu (suru, shite) 証明します (する, して)

vermifuge *n* mushi-kúdashi 虫下し

vermilion *n* shu(iro) 朱 (色)

vernal equinox *n* shunbun 春分; *Vernal Equinox Day* Shunbun no hí 春分の日

versatility *n* yūzū 融通; *is versatile* yūzū ga kikimásu (kiku, kiite) 融通がききます (きく, きいて)

verse *n* shi 詩; (*17-syllable*) haiku 俳句, hokku 発句; (*31-syllable*) wáka 和歌, tánka 短歌; (*longer*) chō´ka 長歌

versus *prep* tai-… 対…

vertex *n* chōjō 頂上. chōten 頂点

vertical *adj* táte (no) 縦 (の), suichoku (no) 垂直 (の)

vertically *adv* táte ni 縦に, suichoku ni 垂直に

vertigo *n* memai めまい・眩暈・目眩

very *adv* zúibun ずいぶん・随分, taihen たいへん・大変, totemo とても, hijō ni 非常に, táisō たいそう・大層, góku ごく; amari (ni) あまり (に); ōi-ni 大いに・おおいに; *the very* + [NOUN] = the [NOUN] *itself* … sono-mónó… そのもの

at very beginning/first saisho (no/ni) 最初 (の/に)

very well (*satisfactory*) yoroshii よろしい・宜しい; (*OK*) yóshi 良し

vest *n* chokki チョッキ; besuto ベスト

vestige *n* konseki 痕跡

vet *n* jū-i 獣医

veteran 1. *n* taieki gunjin 退役軍人; **2.** *adj* (*experienced*) beteran (no) ベテラン (の)

veto 1. *n* kyóhi 拒否 **2.** *v* (*rejects it*) kyóhi shimásu (suru, shite) 拒否します (する, して)

vexatious *adj* haradatashíi 腹立たしい

via … *prep* kéiyu (de) …経由 (で); …o tō´tte …を通って, … o héte …を経て

vibrate *v* shindō shimásu (suru, shite) 振動します (する, して)

vibration *n* shindō 振動; (*cell-phone, etc.*) baiburēshon バイブレーション, baibu バイブ

vibrato *n* (*music*) biburāto ビブラート

vice *n* warúi shūkan 悪い習慣, akufū 悪風

vice admiral *n* chū´jō 中将

vice-president *n* (*of company*) fuku-sháchō 副社長; (*of nation*) fuku-daitō´ryō 副大統領

vice versa *adv* hantai ni 反対に, gyaku ni 逆に, gyaku mo onaji 逆も同じ, gyaku mo dōyō 逆も同様

vicinity *n* fukín 付近, kínjo 近所, chikáku 近く, … hen …辺

vicious *adj* warúi 悪い, hidói ひどい

victim *n* (*of sacrifice*) giséi-sha 犠牲者, (*of injury*) higái-sha 被害者; *falls ~ to* … no gisei ni narimásu (náru, nátte) …犠牲になります (なる, なって)

victor *n* shōrí-sha 勝利者, yūshō-sha 優勝者

victory *n* shōri 勝利, yūshō 優勝; *wins the ~* yūshō shimásu (suru, shite) 優勝します (する, して)

video *n* videótēpu ビデオテープ; *video recorder* bideo ビデオ; *video camera* bideó kamera ビデオカメラ

vie → **compete**

view 1. *n* (*scenery*) nagamé 眺め; *in ~ of* … ni teráshite …に照らして, … o kangáete …を考えて **2.** *v* (*gazes at*) nagamemásu (nagaméru, nagámete) 眺めます (眺める, 眺めて) **3.** → **opinion** → **outlook** → **look** → **standpoint**

viewpoint *n* kénchi 見地, mi-kátá 見方, tachi-ba 立場

vigilance *n* keikai 警戒

vigor *n* génki 元気, katsuryoku 活力

vigorous *adj* sakan (na) 盛ん・さかん (な); sekkyoku-teki (na) 積極的 (な) → **energetic** → **healthy** → **strong**

villa *n* bessō´ 別荘

village *n* murá 村; …-son …村; sato 里

villain *n* warumono 悪者; akutō´ 悪党

vine *n* **1.** tsurú つる・ツル・蔓 **2.** (*grape tree*) budō no ki ブドウ [葡萄] の木

vinegar *n* sú 酢, o-su お酢

vineyard *n* budō-en ブドウ園・葡萄園

vintage 1. *n* bintēji ビンテージ **2.** *adj* gokujō (no) 極上 (の)

vinyl *n* biníiru ビニール, bíniru ビニル

violate *v* (*breaks the law*) okashimásu (okasu, okashite) 犯します (犯す, 犯して); yaburimásu (yabúru, yabútte) 破ります (破る, 破って); … ni ihan shimásu (suru, shite) …に違反します(する, して), … ni somukimásu (sumúku, somúite) …に背きます(背く, 背いて)

violation n ihan 違反

violence n (*brute force*) bōryoku 暴力
domestic violence n katei-nai bōryoku 家庭内暴力, domesutikku baiorensu ドメスティック・バイオレンス

violent adj (*severe*) hageshíi 激しい・はげしい; (*unruly*) ranbō (na) 乱暴(な); múri (na) 無理(な)

violet n sumire スミレ・菫

violin n baiorin バイオリン

virgin n (*female*) shójo 処女, bajin バージン, ki-músume 生娘; (*male*) dōtei 童貞

Virgo n (*star sign*) Otome-za 乙女座・おとめ座

virtue n bitoku 美徳, toku 徳

virus n bírusu ビールス, uirusu ウイルス

visa n bíza ビザ, [BOOKISH] sashō 査証

visible adj (mé ni) mieru (目に)見える

vision n 1. (*eyesight*) shíryoku 視力 2. (*dream*) kūsō 空想 3. (*foresight*) bijon ビジョン

visit 1. v hōmon shimásu (suru, shite) 訪問します(する, して); tazunemásu (tazunéru, tazúnete) 訪ねます(訪ねる, 訪ねて), [HUMBLE] ukagaimásu (ukagau, ukagatte) 伺います・うかがいます(伺う, 伺って), mairimásu (máiru, máitte) 参ります・まいります(参る, 参って) 2. n hōmon 訪問, (o-)asobi (お)遊び, (o-)ukagai (お)伺い・うかがい; (*of solicitude*) (o-)mimai (お)見舞い; (*interview*) menkai 面会

visiting card n meishi 名刺

visitor n o-kyaku (お)客, o-kyaku-san/sámá お客さん/様; raikyaku 来客; (*solicitous*) mimái-kyaku 見舞い客; (*for interview*) menkai-nin 面会人

vitamin(s) n bitamin ビタミン; (*pills*) bitamin-zai ビタミン剤

vivid adj senmei (na) 鮮明(な); azayaka (na) 鮮やか(な); ikiiki to shita 生き生きとした

vividly adv senmei (ni) 鮮明(に); azayaka (ni) 鮮やか(に); ikiiki to 生き生きと

vixen n kuchi urusai onna 口うるさい女

vocabulary n kotobá 言葉, gói 語彙, tango 単語

vocal adj koe no 声の, ónsei 音声(の)

vocalist n vōkaru ヴォーカル, bōkaru ボーカル, (*classical music*) seigaku-ka 声楽家

vocation n shokúgyō 職業

vocational adj shokugyō (no) 職業(の), shoku-gyō-jō (no) 職業上(の)

vocational sickness n shokugyō-byō 職業病

vogue n ryūkō 流行

voice n kóe 声

voice mail n boisu mēru ボイスメール

voice-over n boisu ōbā ボイスオーバー, narētā no koe ナレーターの声

voiceprint n seimon 声紋

voice training n hassei renshū 発声練習, boisu torēningu ボイストレーニング

void → **invalid**

volcanic ash n kazánbai 火山灰

volcano n kazan 火山, borukěno ボルケーノ

volley n issei shageki 一斉射撃

volleyball n barēbō´ru バレーボール

volt n boruto ボルト

voltage n den'átsú 電圧
high-voltage cable n kōatsu-sen 高圧線
high-voltage current n kōatsu denryū 高圧電流

voltage converter n hen'átsú-ki 変圧機

volume n (*book*) hón 本, …-bon …本; (*of a set*) (dái …-) kan (第…)巻; (*quantity*) ryō´ 量

voluntarism n borantia seishin ボランティア精神

voluntary adj mizukara 自ら・みずから; (*optional*) zuii (no) 随意(の)

volunteer n borantia ボランティア

vomit 1. n hédo へど・反吐, (*medical*) ōto 嘔吐 2. v modoshimásu (modósu, modóshite) 戻します(戻す, 戻して) 3. v (hédo o) hakimásu (háku, háite) (へどを)吐きます(吐く, 吐いて)

vote 1. n tōhyō 投票 2. v tōhyō shimásu (suru, shite) 投票します

voter n tōhyō-sha 投票者, yūken-sha 有権者

vow → **pledge**

vowel n boin 母音, boon 母音

voyage n kōkai 航海; *makes a ~* kōkai shimásu (suru, shite) 航海します(する, して)

Voyager n boijā ボイジャー

V-shaped adj bui-ji gata (no) V字形(の), kusabi gata (no) くさび形(の)

V sign n bui sain Vサイン

vulgar adj gehín (na) 下品(な); iyashii 卑しい・いやしい; (*mundane*) zoku (na) 俗(な)

vulgarities n gehín 下品; zoku 俗; soya 粗野

vulture n kondoru コンドル; hagewashi ハゲワシ; hagetaka ハゲタカ

W

wad *n* (chiisana) katamari (小さな・ちいさな)か
たまり

wadding *n* tsumemono 詰め物・つめもの

waddle *v* yotayota arukimás<u>u</u> (aruku, aruite) よた
よた歩きます(歩く, 歩いて), yochiyochi
arukimás<u>u</u> (aruku, aruite) よちよち歩きます(歩く,
歩いて)

wade *v* arúite ikimás<u>u</u> (iku, itte) 歩いて行きます
(行く, 行って), (*across*) arúite watarimás<u>u</u>
(wataru, watatte) 歩いて渡ります(渡る, 渡って)

wadge *n* (*lump, mass*) katamari 固まり・かたまり

wafer *n* (*sweet*) uehāsu ウエハース

waffle *n* (*sweet*) waffuru ワッフル

wag *v* yuremás<u>u</u> (yureru, yurete) 揺れます・
ゆれます(揺れる, 揺れて), yureugokimás<u>u</u>
(yureugoku, yureugoite) 揺れ動きます・ゆれう
ごきます(揺れ動く, 揺れ動いて), (*tail*) furimás<u>u</u>
(furu, f<u>u</u>tte) 振ります(振る, 振って)

wage *n* chíngin 賃金, (*salary*) kyūryō 給料 →
salary

waggish *adj* odoketa おどけた, hyōkin (na) ひょう
きん(な), itazura (na/no) いたずら・悪戯(な/の)

Wagner *n* Wagunā ワグナー

wagon *n* **1.** ni basha 荷馬車 **2.** (*station wagon*)
sutēshon wagon ステーションワゴン; wagon-sha
ワゴン車

wagtail *n* sekirei セキレイ

Wahabi, Wahhabi *n* Wahhābu-ha no shinto ワッ
ハーブ派の信徒

Waikiki *n* Waikiki ワイキキ

Wain *n* Hokuto shichisei 北斗七星

waist *n* koshi 腰 (= **loins**), uésuto ウエスト;
(*specifically*) koshi no kubire 腰のくびれ; kubire
くびれ

waist band *n* uesuto bando ウエストバンド,
beruto ベルト

waistcoat *n* besuto ベスト, chokki チョッキ

waist line *n* koshi no rain 腰のライン, uesuto rain
ウエストライン

waist pocket *n* waki poketto 脇ポケット

waiter *n* uéˊtā ウエーター; ueitā ウエイター;
bōi(-san) ボーイ(さん) → **wait person**

wait; *v* ~ **for**... o machimás<u>u</u> (mátsu, mátte) ...を
待ちます(待つ, 待って)

Please wait a moment. *interj* [FORMAL] Shōshō
omachikudasai. 少々お待ちください。, [INFOR-
MAL] Chotto mattekudasai. ちょっと待ってくだ
さい。

Please wait for a little while longer. *interj* [FOR-
MAL] Mō shōshō omachikudasai. もう少々お待ち
ください。, [INFORMAL] Mō chotto mattekudasai.
もうちょっと待ってください。

Please wait to be seated. *interj* (*restaurant*)
Kakarinomono ga (o-seki ni) go-an'nai suru made
omachikudasai. 係りの者が(お席に)ご案内する
までお待ちください。

waiting *n* taiki 待機

waiting for a long time *adj* machidōshíi 待ち遠
しい

waiting line *n* machi gyōretsu 待ち行列

waiting list *n* kyanseru machi meibo キャンセ
ル待ち名簿, weitingu risuto ウェイティング・
リスト

waiting room *n* machiái-shitsu 待合室

waiting time *n* machi jikan 待ち時間

wait person *n* kyūˊji 給仕; sekkyaku-gakari
接客係; kakari (no mono) 係(の者)

waitress *n* uéˊtoresu ウエートレス; ueitoresu
ウエイトレス → **wait person**

wake up *v* méga samemás<u>u</u> (saméru, sámete)
目が覚めます・さめます(覚める, 覚めて), (*rises*)
okimás<u>u</u> (okíru, ókite) 起きます(起きる, 起き
て); (*wakes a person up*) ... o okoshimás<u>u</u> (okósu,
okóshite) ...を起こします(起こす, 起こして)
Please wake me up. *interj* Okoshite kudasai.
起こしてください。

wake-up call *n* mōningu kōru モーニングコール

Wales *n* wēruzu ウェールズ, uēruzu ウエールズ

walk 1. *v* arukimás<u>u</u> (arúku, arúite) 歩きます(歩
く, 歩いて), arúite ikimás<u>u</u> (iku, itte) 歩いて行き
ます(行く, 行って) **2.** *v* (*strolls*) sanpo (shimás<u>u</u>;
suru, sh<u>i</u>te) 散歩(します; する, して); goes for a
~ sanpo ni ikimás<u>u</u> (iku, itte) 散歩に行きます
(行く, 行って) **3.** *n* (*way*) hodō 歩道 **4.** *n* (*walking*)
hokō 歩行

walkaway *n* rakushō 楽勝

walking *n* hokō 歩行, wōkingu ウォーキング
fire walking *n* hiwatari 火渡り・火わたり
race walking *n* kyōho 競歩
walking shoes *n* wōkingu shūzu ウォーキング
シューズ
walking stick *n* (*cane*) s<u>u</u>tékki ステッキ, tsúe 杖

Walkman *n* Wōkuman ウォークマン

walkway *n* hodō 歩道

wall *n* (*of house*) kabe 壁; (*around courtyard, etc.*)
hei 塀・へい

wallet *n* saifu 財布・さいふ, gamaguchi がまロ,
(*billfold*) satsu-ire 札入れ

wallpaper *n* kabegami 壁紙

Wall Street *n* Wōru sutoriito ウォールストリー
ト; Wōru-gai ウォール街

walnut *n* kurumi クルミ・胡桃

waltz *n* warutsu ワルツ

wander *v* (*walks around*) arukimawarimás<u>u</u>
(arukimawaru, arukimawatte) 歩き回ります
(歩き回る, 歩き回って), (*hangs round*) bura-
tsukimás<u>u</u> (buratsuku, buratsuite) ぶらつきます
(ぶらつく, ぶらついて), buraburashimás<u>u</u>
(buraburasuru, buraburashite) ぶらぶらします
(ぶらぶらする, ぶらぶらして), samayoimás<u>u</u>
(samayóu, samayótte) さまよいます・彷徨います
(さまよう, さまよって)

want *v* **1.** … ga irimásu (iru, itte) …が要ります(要る、要って)、(*desires something*) hoshigarimásu (hoshigáru, hoshigátte) 欲しがります(欲しがる、欲しがって); … ga hoshíi desu …が欲しいです; (*looks for, seeks to buy*) motomemásu (motoméru, motómete) 求めます(求める、求めて) **2.** *wants to do* (*it*) (…ga) shi-tái desu (shi-tai, shi-tákute) (…が)したいです(したい、したくて)、(… o) shi-tagarimásu (shi-tagaru, shi-tagátte) (…を)したがります(したがる、したがって); *wants to have* (*it*) *done* (*by…*) (…ni) … o shi-te morai-tái desu (morai-tai, morai-tákute) (…に)…をしてもらいたいです (もらいたい、もらいたくい) **3. → need, poverty**
does as one wants *v* katte ni shimásu (suru, shite) 勝手にします(する、して)

wanted criminal *n* shimei-tehai(nin) 指名手配 (人); *photograph of wanted criminal* shimei-tehai sháshin 指名手配写真

war *n* sensō 戦争、rán, ran 乱; *after/since the war* sengo (no) 戦後(の); (*after*) *the end of the war* shūsen(-go) 終戦(後); *before the war* senzen (no) 戦前(の); *during the war* senji-chū 戦時中
a great war taisen 大戦; *world war* sekai-táisen 世界大戦; *World War II* Dai ni-ji Sekai-Táisen 第二次世界大戦

warbler; *bush warbler* *n* ugúisu うぐいす・ウグイス・鶯・鴬

ward *n* (*city district*) kú 区、…-ku …区

ward office *n* ku-yákusho 区役所

wardrobe *n* yōfuku dansu 洋服箪笥・洋服だんす、ishō dansu 衣装箪笥・衣装だんす

ware *n* saiku 細工; (*ceramic ware*) tō´ki 陶器、setomono 瀬戸物、…-yaki …焼き

warehouse *n* sō´ko 倉庫、kurá 倉

warless *adj* sensō no nai 戦争のない

warlike *adj* kōsen-teki (na) 好戦的(な)

warm **1.** *v ~ it up* *v* ata-tamémásu (ata-taméru, ata-tamete) あたため[温め・暖め]る、(あたため[温め・暖め]る、あたため[温め・暖め]て)、nes-shimásu (nes-suru, nes-shite) 熱します(熱する、熱して); *warms the rice wine* (o-)kán o tsukemásu/shimásu (お)燗をつけます/します **2.** *v warms up* ata-tamárimásu (ata-tamáru, ata-tamátte) あたたまり[温まり・暖まり]ます(あたたまる・温まる・暖まる、あたたまって・温まって・暖まって) **3.** *adj* atatakai/attakai あたたかい/あったかい・(*not cool*) 暖かい・(*not cold*) 温かい; (*lukewarm liquids*) nurúi ぬるい; (*dedicated*) nessin (na) 熱心(な)

warmhearted *adj* kokoró ga atatakái 心が温かい、atsui 厚い・篤い

warmheartedness *n* atsu-sa 厚さ・篤さ; nínjō 人情

warmly *adv* atatakáku あたたかく・暖かく・温かく

warmth *n* (*heat*) átsu-sa 熱さ・暑さ

warn *v* keikoku shimásu (suru, shite) 警告します (する、して)、chūi shimásu (suru, shite) 注意します(する、して)

warning *n* keikoku 警告; (*alert*) keihō 警報; (*notice*) kotowári 断り

warning label *n* keikoku hyōji 警告表示、keikoku raberu 警告ラベル

warning message *n* keikoku messēji 警告メッセージ、keikoku tsūchi 警告通知

warp **1.** *n* sorí そり・反り **2.** *v* (*it warps*) sorimásu (sóru, sótte) そり[反り]ます(そる、そって); (*warps it*) sorashimásu (sorásu, soráshite) そらし[反らし]ます(そらす、そらして)、yugamemásu (yugameru, yugamete) 歪め[ゆがめ]ます(歪める、歪めて) **3.** *gets warped* *v* (*distorted*) yugamimásu (yugamu, yugande) 歪み[ゆがみ]ます(歪む、歪んで); (*crooked*) kuruimásu (kurū´, kurútte) 狂います(狂う、狂って) **4.** *n* (*vertical threads*) tate-ito たて糸・縦糸

warranty *n* hoshō(-sho) 保証(書)

warrior *n* **1.** senshi 戦士 **2.** (*Japanese*) samurai 侍・サムライ、búshi 武士・ぶし

warship *n* gunkan 軍艦

wartime *n* sénji(chū) 戦時(中)、sensō no toki 戦争の時・とき

was *v* … déshita (.., dátta) ,,,でした(…だった)・arimáshita (átta) ありました(あった); imáshita (ita) いました(いた) **→ is**

wash **1.** *v* araimásu (arau, aratte) 洗います(洗う、洗って); (*launders*) sentaku shimásu (suru, shite) 洗濯します(する、して) **2.** *n the wash*(*ing*) *n* sentaku 洗濯、sentaku-mono 洗濯物

wash basin *n* senmén-ki 洗面器

wash towel *n* wosshu taoru ウォッシュタオル

wash tub *n* sentaku tarai 洗濯たらい

washable *adj* sentaku (no) dekiru 洗濯(の)できる、araeru 洗える

wash-and-wear *adj* wosshu ando wea ウォッシュ・アンド・ウェア、airon no iranai アイロンの要らない、airon fuyō (no) アイロン不要(の)

washcloth *n* (*hand towel*) te-nugui 手拭い、(*dishcloth*) fukín ふきん・布巾

washer *n* (*washing machine*) sentakú-ki 洗濯機

washing machine → washer

Washington *n* Washínton ワシントン

washout *n* **1.** (*big mistake*) daishippai 大失敗 **2.** (*a failure*) shippai-sha 失敗者

washroom *n* (o-)teárai (お)手洗い、senmen-jo 洗面所

washstand *n* senmen dai 洗面台

wasn't *v*… ja/dewa arimásén deshita (…ja nákatta) …じゃ/ではありませんでした(…じゃなかった); arimásén deshita (nákatta) ありませんでした(なかった); imasén deshita (inákatta) いませんでした(いなかった) **→ isn't**

wasp *n* hachi 蜂・ハチ、suzume-bachi 雀蜂・スズメバチ

waspish *n* suzume-bachi no yō (na) 雀蜂のよう(な)、(スズメバチのよう(な)、(*having a hot temper*) okorippoi 怒りっぽい

waste **1.** *n* (*trash*) kúzu 屑・くず、kuzu-mono 屑物・くず物; (*extravagance*) mudazukai 無駄

遣い, rōhi 浪費 **2.** v (wastes it) muda ni shimás<u>u</u> (suru, sh<u>i</u>te) 無駄にします(する, して); (is extravagant with) muda-zúkai shimás<u>u</u> (suru, sh<u>i</u>te) 無駄使いします(する, して), rōhi shimás<u>u</u> (suru, sh<u>i</u>te) 浪費します(する, して) **3. falls to ~** aremás<u>u</u> (areru, arete) 荒れます(荒れる, 荒れて)

waste away v shōmō shimás<u>u</u> (suru, sh<u>i</u>te) 消耗します(する, して)

waste of effort n mudabone 無駄骨, torō´ 徒労

waste of money n (o-)kane no muda-zukai (お)金の無駄遣い, (o-)kane no rōhi (お)金の浪費

waste of talent n takara no mochigusare 宝の持ち腐れ

waste of time n jikan no muda 時間の無駄・むだ

What a waste! interj Mottainai! もったいない!

wastebasket n kuzú-kago くずかご

wasteful adj mottai-nái もったいない, muda (na) 無駄・むだ(な)

wastepaper n kamikúzu 紙くず・紙屑; **wastepaper basket** kuzú-kago くずかご

wastewater n gesui 下水, osui 汚水, haisui 排水

watch 1. n (timepiece) tokei 時計 **2.** v (looks at/after) mimás<u>u</u> (miru, mite) 見ます・観ます・みます(みる, みて); (guards it) … no bán o shimás<u>u</u> (suru, sh<u>i</u>te) …の番をします(する, して) **3.** v (observes) kansatsu shimás<u>u</u> (suru, sh<u>i</u>te) 観察します(する, して)

night watch, night watchman yakei (-in) 夜警(員), yakan keibiin 夜間警備員, yo-máwari 夜回り・夜まわり

watch for neraimás<u>u</u> (nerau, neratte) 狙います・ねらいます(狙う, 狙って); **~ a chance** k<u>i</u>kái o ukagaimás<u>u</u> (ukagau, ukagatte) 機会を窺い[うかがい]ます(うかがう, うかがって)

watch out for (guards against) keikai shimás<u>u</u> (suru, sh<u>i</u>te) 警戒します(する, して)

Watch out! Abunai! 危ない・あぶない!

Watch your step! Ashi-mótó ni ki o ts<u>u</u>kéte! 足元に気を付けて!

watcher n (nurse) kango-nin 看護人; (observer) kansatsu-sha 観察者; (researcher) kenkyū-sha 研究者

fire-watcher n kasai keibiin 火災警備員

watchful; keeps a ~ eye (on the situation) (jōkyō o) ukagaimás<u>u</u> (ukagau, ukagatte) (状況・情況を)窺い[うかがい]ます(うかがう, うかがって)

watchman n bannín 番人, keibiin 警備員; (gatekeeper) mónban 門番 → **night watch, night watchman**

watch tower n monomi no tō 物見の塔・ものみの塔

watchword n (motto) mottō モットー; hyōgo 標語; (password) aikotoba 合言葉

water n mizu 水; hot water o-yu お湯, yú yu 湯; drinking water nomí-mizu 飲み水, o-híya お冷や・おひや

water gate n suimon 水門

waterfall n taki 滝・たき

water fowl n mizutori 水鳥・ミズトリ

waterfront n kashi 河岸

waterhole, watering hole n mizu tamari 水溜り・水たまり

water imp n kappa かっぱ・カッパ・河童

water level n suii 水位; suijun 水準

waterline n suii sen 水位線

water mill n suisha 水車

water pistol n mizu-déppō 水鉄砲

water pitcher n mizu-sáshí 水差し・みずさし

waterpower n suiryoku 水力; **~ plant** suiryoku hatsudensho 水力発電所

waterproof adj bōsui (no) 防水(の)

waterproofing n bōsui kakō 防水加工

waterscape n suikei-ga 水景画

water service → **waterworks**

watershed n bunkiten 分岐点

water-skiing n suijō sukii 水上スキー

waterworks n suidō 水道; **Waterworks Bureau** suidō´-kyoku 水道局; **turn on the ~** namida o nagasu 涙を流す (= to cry, in order to get sympathy)

waterweed n mizukusa 水草

waterwheel n suisha 水車

watchmaker n tokei-ya 時計屋

watermelon n suika すいか・スイカ・西瓜

watt n watto ワット

wattage n watto-ryō ワット量

watt-hour n watto-ji ワット時

watt meter n denryoku-kei 電力計

wave 1. n namí 波 **2.** n (permanent) páma パーマ **3.** v (waves a hand) té o furimás<u>u</u> (furu, f<u>u</u>tte) 手を振ります(振る, 振って)

waveform n hakei 波形

wavelength n hachō 波長

wavelet n sazanami さざなみ

waver n yure 揺れ

wax n (bee wax) mitsurō みつろう・ミツロウ・蜜蝋, rō´ ろう・ロウ・蝋

waxwork n rō-zaiku 蝋細工・ろう細工, rō´ ningyō 蝋人形・ろう人形

way n michi 道; (method) shi-kata 仕方, shi-yō 仕様, yari-kata やり方; (means) shúdan 手段; (manner) tō´ri 通り, (fashion) fū´ 風, (trick) téguchi 手口

any way adv nanraka no hōhō (de) 何らか[なんらか]の方法で

all the way adv (from far) harubaru はるばる, tōi tokoro 遠いところ

by way of … → **via**

by the way adv, conj **1.** (incidentally) sore wa sō´ to それはそうと, tokoróde ところで, chinami ni ちなみに, tsuide ni ついでに, tokí ni 時に **2.** adv (way of) … o tō´tte … を通って; (via) … keiyu (de/no) … 経由(で/の)

gets in the way v (o-)jama ni narimás<u>u</u> (náru, nátte) (お)じゃま[邪魔]になります(なる, なって), (o-)jama o shimás<u>u</u> (suru, sh<u>i</u>te) (お)じゃま[邪魔]をします(する, して)

get out of the way dokimás<u>u</u> (doku, doite) どき

ます・退きます(どく、どいて)、nokimás<u>u</u> (noku, noite) のきます・退きます(のく、のいて)

give way *v* yuzurimás<u>u</u> (yuzuru, yuzutte) 譲ります・ゆずります(譲る、譲って)

make way *v* (*goes forward*) zenshin shimás<u>u</u> (suru, shite) 前進します(する、して)

in a way *adv* aru imi ある意味

No way! → no

on the way tochū (de) 途中(で)

one's way *adv* (*one's*) jikoryū de 自己流で, jibun no omou yarikata de 自分の思うやり方で

the way I am arugamama no jibun あるがままの自分, arinomama no jibun ありのままの自分

way above… *adj* …o haruka ni koeta …をはるかに超えた

way ahead *adv* zutto saki (ni) ずっと先(に)

way back *adv* (*before*) zutto máe (ni) ずっと前(に), zutto izen (ni) ずっと以前(に), zutto mukashi (ni) ずっと昔(に)

way of …ing [VERB INFINITIVE] + -kata …方; ~ *of saying/telling/putting it* ii-kata 言い方

wayside *n* michibata 道端; robō 路傍; gaitō 街頭

we *pron* watáshí-tachi わたしたち・私達, jibun-tachi 自分たち・自分達, [INFORMAL] uchira うちら, [BOOKISH] watak<u>u</u>shí-tachi わたくしたち・私達; ware-ware われわれ・我々

weak *adj* 1. yowái 弱い・よわい; fú-jiyū (na) 不自由(な); (*coffee, etc.*) usui 薄い・うすい 2. *grows* ~ otoroemás<u>u</u> (otoróéru, otoróete) 衰えます・おとろえます(おとろえる、おとろえて)

weak point (*shortcoming*) tánsho 短所; (*weakness*) yowami 弱み・よわみ; jakuten 弱点; yowai tokoro 弱いところ

wealth *n* tómi 富, zaisan 財産, zái 財

wealthy → rich

weapon *n* heiki 兵器; buki 武器; kyōki 凶器

wear 1. *n* fuku 服; irui 衣類 2. *v* (*on body*) kiteimás<u>u</u> (kiteiru, kite(i)te) 着ています(着ている、着て(い)て), [HONORIFIC] o-meshi ni narimás<u>u</u> (náru, nátte) お召しになります(なる、なって); (*pants, footwear*) haiteimás<u>u</u> (haiteiru, haiteité) はいています・履いています(はいている・履いている、はいていて・履いていて), (*hat, headwear*) kabutteimás<u>u</u> (kabútteiru, kabute(i)té) かぶっています・被っています(かぶっている・被っている、かぶって(い)て・被って(い)て), (*a pin, ornament, etc.*) ts<u>u</u>keteimás<u>u</u> (ts<u>u</u>kéteiru, ts<u>u</u>kéteite) 付けています(付けている、付けていて), (*necktie, belt*) shimeteimás<u>u</u> (shiméteiru, shímeteite) 締めています(締めている、締めていて), (*on hands, fingers*) hameteimás<u>u</u> (hameteiru, hameteite) はめています(はめている、はめていて)

weary 1. *adj* → tired 2. *v wearies* (*of …*) (*be sick of*) (… ni) akimás<u>u</u> (akíru, ákite) (…に)飽きます(飽きる、飽きて)

weather *n* ténki 天気 (o-ténki お天気); kishō 気象; hiyori 日和

Nice weather, isn't it? *interj* Ii (o-)ténki desu ne. いい(お)天気ですね.

weather forecast *n* tenki-yóhō 天気予報

weather observatory/station *n* sokkō-jo 測候所; kishō-dai 気象台

weave *v* orimás<u>u</u> (óru, ótte) 織ります・おります(織る、織って)

weaver *n* (*person*) orite 織り手, (*machine*) hataori 機織り

the Festival of the Weaver Star Tanabata 七夕・たなばた (*7 July*)

web 1. → cobweb, spiderweb 2. → internet

wedding *n* kekkon 結婚, wedingu ウェディング, (*ceremony*) kekkón-shiki 結婚式

wedding invitation *n* kekkonshiki (no) shōkai-jō 結婚式(の)紹介状

wedding party *n* kekkon shukuga-kai 結婚祝賀会, wedingu pātii ウェディングパーティ

wedding photo *n* kekkonshiki no shashin 結婚式の写真

wedding reception *n* kekkon hirōen 結婚披露宴

Wednesday *n* Suiyō'bi 水曜日, Suiyō' 水曜

weed *n* k<u>u</u>sá 草・くさ, zassō 雑草

week *n* shūkan 週間; shū' 週, …-shū …週; *how many weeks* nan-shū'kan 何週間

week after next *n, adv* saraishū 再来週

week before last *n, adv* sensén-shū 先々週

weekend *n, adv* shūmatsu 週末

Have a nice weekend! *interj* Yoi shūmatsu o! 良い[よい]週末を!

weep *v* nakimás<u>u</u> (naku, naite) 泣きます(泣く、泣いて); (*laments*) nagekimás<u>u</u> (nagéku, nagéite) 嘆きます・なげきます(嘆く、嘆いて)

weigh 1. *v it weighs …* …no omosa ga … arimás<u>u</u> (áru, átte) (…の)重さが…あります(ある、あって); *How much does it* (*do you*) *weigh?* (…) no omosa ga dono-gurai arimás<u>u</u> ka (…の)重さがどの位ありますか 2. *v weighs it* (…)no omosa o hakarimás<u>u</u> (hakáru, hakátte) (…の)重さを量ります・おもさをはかります(量る、量って) 3. *n* omosa 重さ, mekata 目方, jūryō 重量; (*of body*) taijū 体重; (*object*) omoshi 重し・おもし

weight-lifting *n* jūryō-age 重量挙げ・重量あげ, weito rifutingu ウェイトリフティング; *weight-lifter* jūryōage-sénshu 重量挙げ[重量あげ]選手

weight/weighing scales *n* hakarí はかり・秤・ハカリ

weird *adj* ayashii 怪しい・あやしい, f<u>u</u>shigi (na) 不思議・ふしぎ(な), sugói すごい・凄い; (*feeling*) kimí ga warúi 気味が悪い

welcome 1. *n* (*a welcome*) mukae 迎え・むかえ, kangei 歓迎 2. *adj* (*it is welcome*) nozomashii 望ましい, arigatái ありがたい・有り難い 3. *v* (*welcomes one*) … o mukaemás<u>u</u> (mukaeru, mukaete) …を迎えます・をむかえます(迎える、迎えて), … o de-mukaemás<u>u</u> (de-mukaeru, de-mukaete) …を出迎えます・をでむかえます(出迎える、出迎えて)

Welcome! *interj* Yóku irasshaimásh<u>i</u>ta! よくいらっしゃいました!; Yō'koso! ようこそ!; Irasshaimáse! いらっしゃいませ!

You're welcome! *interj* Dō´ itashimáshite. どういたしまして.

Welcome back/home! *interj* O-kaeri nasái. お帰りなさい.

welfare *n* fukúshi 福祉; *welfare policy* fukushi-séisaku 福祉政策

well 1. *n* (*for water*) ído 井戸 **2.** *adj* (*good, nice*) yóku よく・良く; (*healthy*) génki (na) 元気 (な); (*splendid*) rippa (na/ni) 立派(な/に); *gets ~* naorimásu (naóru, naótte) 治り[直り]ます(治[直]る, 治[直]って) **3.** *adv* (*come on*) sá´さあ; *~ now/then* (sore) déwa (それ)では, (sore) jā (それ)じゃあ, jā じゃあ, sáte さて; ē-to ええと; tokoró-de ところで; (*let me think*) sō´desu né そうですね; (*maybe*) mā まあ

very well (*satisfactory*) yoroshii よろしい・宜しい

well versed in tsū-ji(tei)másu (tsū-ji(tei)ru, tsū-ji(tei)te) 通じ(てい)ます(通じ(てい)る, 通じ(てい)て)

well-behaved *adj* otonashíi おとなしい・大人しい

well-known *adj* yūmei (na) 有名(な), chomei (na) 著明(な)

well-liked; *is ~* motemásu (motéru, mótete) もてます(もてる, もてて)

west *n* nishi 西, sei-... 西...; (*the west*) seihō 西方, (*the western part*) séibu 西部, (*the Occident*) Séiyō 西洋, (*Europe and America*) O-Bei 欧米; *Western Japan* Kánsai 関西

West Indies *n* Nishi indo shotō 西インド諸島

westerly (*wind*) *adj* nishi-yori (no kaze) 西寄り(の風)

western 1. *adj* nishi (no) 西(の) **2.** *n* seibu-geki 西部劇

western paper *n* yōshi 洋紙

western style *n* (*Occidental*) Seiyō-fū 西洋風, yō-fū 洋風; yō- 洋...; *western-style building* yōkan 洋館; *western-style room* yō-ma 洋間; *western-style clothes* yō-fúku 洋服

wet 1. *adj* nureta ... ぬれた・濡れた (*moist*) shimetta 湿った, shimeppoi 湿っぽい **2.** *it gets wet* v nuremásu (nureru, nurete) 濡れます(濡れる, 濡れて) **3.** *makes it wet* v nurashimásu (nurasu, nurashite) 濡らします(濡らす, 濡らして), (*dampens it*) shimeshimásu (shimesu, shimeshite) 湿します(湿す, 湿して)

whale *n* kujira くじら・クジラ・鯨

wharf *n* hato-ba 波止場

what *pron* náni 何・なに [nán if *before* t, d, n]; nán no ... 何の..., náni-... 何... [*before any sound*]; (*which*) dóno ... どの...; (*in what way*) dō´dō どう

what ... (*one/fact that*) ... (no) monó/kotó... (の)物/事, ...no ...の

what color nani-iro 何色, dónna iró どんな色

what day (*of the week*) nan-yō´bi 何曜日; (*of the month*) nán-nichi 何日

whatever nan demo 何でも・なんでも; *~ you like* nan demo sukina mono (o) 何でも[なんでも]好きな物(を), dore demo sukina mono (o) どれで

も好きな物(を), nan demo hoshii mono (o) 何でも[なんでも]欲しい物[ほしいもの](を), [BOOKISH] dore demo nozomu mono (o) どれでも望む物[のぞむもの](を), náni (ga/o) ...-témo 何(が/を)...ても

what kind of dono yō´na どのよう[様]な, dō´yū どうゆう, dónna どんな

what language nani-go 何語

what month nán-gatsu 何月

what nationality naní-jin 何人, doko no kuni no hito どこの国の人, [HONORIFIC] dochira no (o-) kuni no kata どちらの(お)国の方

what part **1.** (*where*) dóko どこ **2.** (*thing*) dono búbun どの部分

what place dóko どこ; dóchira どちら, dótchi どっち

what's-his/her-name dáredare だれだれ・誰々, dáresore だれそれ・誰それ

what's-it(s-name) náninani 何々・なになに

what sort of → what kind of

what time nán-ji 何時

what university nani-dáigaku 何大学

what year nán-nen 何年

wheat *n* komúgi 小麦・コムギ; múgi 麦・ムギ

wheedle *v* tarashi-komimásu (tarashi-komu, tarashi-konde) たらし込みます(たらし込む, たらし込んで)

wheel *n* wá 輪, sharin 車輪, hoiiru ホイール; (*steering wheel*) handoru ハンドル

wheelchair *n* kuruma isu 車椅子・車いす

when *pron* ítsu いつ

about when itsugoro いつ頃・いつごろ

since when ítsu kara いつから

until when ítsu made いつまで

by when ítsu made ni いつまでに

when ... *adv* (*the time that ...*) ... (no) tóki... (の)時; (*where upon*) ... (suru) to ... (する)と, (shi)-tára ... (し)たら, ... (shi)-ta tókí... (し)た時; (*and then*) (shi)-te (し)て, (shi)-tékara (し)てから, (shi)-te sore kara (し)てそれから; (*on the occasion of*) ... ni sái-shite ...に際して

where *pron* dóko どこ; [DEFERENTIAL] dóchira どちら

where ... *adv* (*the place that ...*) ... (no) tokoró... (の)所; (*and there*) ...-te soko (de/ni) ...てそこ(で/に)

whereabouts *n* shozai 所在

whereupon 1. *adv* → when ... **2.** ... tokoró ga ...ところが

whether *conj* ... ka dō´ka ...かどうか

which *pron* (*of two*) dóchira/dótchi no ... どちら/どっちの... (*or* ... no dóchira/dótchi ... のどちら/どっち); (*of more than two*) dóno ... どの... (*or* ... no dóre ...のどれ)

which damn (*one*) dóitsu どいつ

which ... 1. → that ... **2.** (*and that*) (soshite) sore (ga/wa) (そして)それ(が/は)

while ... *conj* (no) aida ...(の)間; ... (shi)-nagara ...(し)ながら; ...-chu (ni) ...中(に)

(for) a while *n* shibáraku しばらく

a little while ago sakíhodo 先程, sákki さっき

whip *v* múchi (de uchimásu; útsu, útte) むち[鞭] (で打ちます; 打つ, 打って)

whipping cream *n* hoippu-kuríimu ホイップクリーム

whirlpool *n* uzú-maki 渦巻き・うずまき, úzu 渦・うず

whirlwind *n* sempū 旋風, tsumují-kaze つむじ風

whisky *n* uísúkíi ウイスキー, wísukii ウィスキー; *whisky and water* mizuwari 水割り

whisper 1. *n* (*a whisper*) kogoe 小声, sasayaki ささやき・囁き **2.** *v* (*whispers it*) sasayakimásu (sasayaku, sasayaite) ささやき[囁き]ます (ささやく, ささやいて), mimiuchi shimásu (suru, shíte) 耳打ちします(する, して)

whistle *n* fue 笛; (*v*) (*with lips*) kuchibue (o fukimásu; fukú, fúite) 口笛を吹きます(吹く, 吹いて); (*steam*) kiteki 汽笛

white *adj* shiróí 白い; shíro (no) 白(の); howáito (no) ホワイト(の); *snow ~* masshíro (na) 真っ白(な); *the ~ of an egg* shírómi 白身

whitebait *n* shirasu しらす・シラス・白子

who *pron* dáre 誰; |DEFERENTIAL| dónata どなた, dóchira (sama) どちら(様)

who … 1. → that … 2. (*and he/she/they*) … (soshite) sonó-hito ga/wa …(そして)その人が/は

whole *adj* zentai (no) 全体(の); zén(-) … 全…; *the whole thing* (*all of it*) zénbu 全部

one's whole life isshō 一生

wholesale *adj* óroshi (de) 卸し(で); *selling wholesale* oroshi-uri 卸し売り

wholly *adv* zentai (teki) ni 全体(的)に

whore *n* baishun-fu 売春婦, jorō´ 女郎 → **prostitute**

whorehouse *n* baishún-yado 売春宿

whose *pron* dáre no 誰の

whose … 1. → that … 2. (*and his/her/ their*) … (soshite) sonó-hito no …(そして)その人の

why *adv* dō´shite どうして, náze なぜ, dō´zó ; *that's why* dákara (sá) だから(さ)

wicker trunk *n* kō´ri 行李

wicket *n* kído 木戸; (*ticket*) kaisatsu-guchi 改札口; (*window*) mádó-guchi 窓口, …-guchi …口

wide 1. *adj* (haba ga) hiróí (幅が)広い **2.** *adj* hiroku 広く; *widely* *adv* hiroku 広く

widow *n* mibō´-jin 未亡人, yamome やもめ, goke(-san) 後家(さん)

widower *n* otoko-yámome 男やもめ

width *n* hírosa 広さ, haba 幅; yoko 横; yoko haba 横幅

wife *n* (*your/his wife*) óku-san/-sama 奥さん/様, fujin 夫人; (*my wife*) kánai 家内, sái/tsúma 妻, nyō´bo/nyō´bō 女房; wáifu ワイフ

wig *n* katsura かつら・鬘

wild *adj* **1.** wairudo ワイルド; (*disorderly*) ranbō (na) 乱暴(な); (*rough*) arai 荒い; (*roughneck*) abare-mono 暴れ者; (*not cultivated*) yasei no 野性の **2.** *gets ~* aremásu (areru, arete) 荒れます (荒れる, 荒れて)

wild duck *n* kámo かも・カモ・鴨

wild goose *n* gán がん・ガン・雁

wildlife *n* yasei dōbutsu 野生動物, yasei seibutsu 野生生物

wild person *n* abare-mono 暴れ者・あばれ者

will *n* (*intention*) íshi 意志, omói 思い; (*testament*) yuigon 遺言

will be … … désu (dá/nó/ná, dé, ní) …です(だ/の/な, で, に)

will do shimásu (suru, shíte) します(する, して)

willow *n* yanagi 柳・ヤナギ; *budding willow* aoyagi/ ao-yánagi 青柳・アオヤナギ

win *v* (*game/war*) … ni kachimásu (kátsu, kátte) …に勝ちます(勝つ, 勝って); (*prize*) jushō shimásu (suru, shíte) 受賞します(する, して), o (kachi) torimásu (tóru, tótte) …を(勝ち)取ります(取る, 取って) → **victory**

wind 1. *v* magarimásu (magáru, magátte) 曲がります(曲がる, 曲がって) **2.** *v wind it* (*around/up*) makimásu (maku, maite) 巻きます(巻く, 巻いて); (*reel*) kurimásu (kúru, kútté) 繰ります(繰る, 繰って) **3.** *n* (*breeze*) kaze 風; *seasonal wind* 季節風; *strong (heavy) wind* 強風

wind up (*concludes it*) shimemásu (shimeru, shimete) 締めます(締める, 締めて), keri o tsukemásu (tsukéru, tukéte) けりをつけます(つける, つけて); (*ends up doing*) (shi)-te shimaimásu (shimau, shimatte) (し)てしまいます(しまう, しまって)

against the wind sakaraimásu (sakaráu, sakarátte) 逆らいます(逆らう, 逆らって)

windbreaker *n* (*jacket*) uindo-burēkā ウインドブレーカー, jánpā ジャンパー

wind-chimes *n* fūrin 風鈴・風りん

window *n* mádo 窓; (*opening*, *wicket*) madó-guchi 窓口; *transom window* ranma 欄間

windowpane *n* mado-gárasu 窓ガラス

window screen *n* amido 網戸; bōchū-ami 防虫網, mushiyoké-ami 虫よけ網

windshield wiper *n* waípā ワイパー

windy *adj* kaze ga tsuyóí 風が強い

wine *n* **1.** wáin ワイン, budō´shu ぶどう[葡萄・ブドウ]酒 **2. → rice wine, saké**

wine cup *n* (*saké cup*) sakazuki 杯(o-sakazuki お杯), chóko ちょこ(o-chóko おちょこ)

wing *n* (*of bird or plane*) tsubasa 翼・つばさ; (*of insect*) hane 羽・羽根・翅; (*of door/gate*) tobira 扉・とびら

wink *n* ma-bátaki まばたき・瞬き, uínku/wínku (shimásu; suru, shíte) ウインク/ウィンク(します; する, して)

winner *n* (*victor*) shōrí-sha 勝利者, yūshō-sha 優勝者; (*awardee*) jushō´sha 受賞者

winter *n* fuyú 冬; *~ solstice* tōji 冬至

winter vacation *n* fuyu yasumi 冬休み, |BOOKISH| tōki kyūka 冬期休暇

win-win relationship *n* win win no kankei ウィン・ウィンの関係; sōhō ga rieki o eru kankei

双方が利益を得る関係; sōhōga kachigumi ni naru kankei 双方が勝ち組になる関係

wipe v fukimásu (fuku, fuite) 拭きます・ふきます (拭く, 拭いて); ~ *away* nuguimásu (nugū´, nugútte) 拭います・ぬぐいます (拭う, 拭いて)

wire n harigane 針金・はりがね; (*electric*) densen 電線, (*telephone line*) denwa-sen 電話線 → **telegram**

wisdom n chié 知恵・ちえ

wise adj kashikói 賢い・かしこい, kenmei (na) 賢明 (な)

wish n (o-)negai (お)願い, kibō 希望
  my best wishes to … (*please send*) …ni (dō´zo) yoroshiku …に (どうぞ) よろしく [宜しく]
  wish for … ga hoshíi desu (hoshíi, hóshikute) …が欲しいです (欲しい, 欲しくて)
  wish that … (it does) (shi)-tára íi desu (ga) (し) たらいいです (が); … (*it had done*) (shi)-tára yókatta desu (ga) (し) たら良かったです (が) or yókatta no ni 良かったのに・よかったのに
  wish to do (shi)-tái desu (shi-tai, shi-tákute) (し) たいです (したい, したくて)
  wish to have it done (shi)-te morai-tái desu (し) てもらいたいです

wisteria n fuji ふじ・フジ・藤

wit n yū´moa ユーモア, kichi 機知, witto ウィット
  to wit sunáwachi すなわち・即ち

with prep … to …と, to issho ni … と一緒に; (*by using*) … de …で; (*with … attached/included*) … ga tsúita …が付いた, …-tsuki (no) …付き (の); ~ *its being* … de …で; ~ (*it had done*) ~ *bath* furo/basu-tsuki (no) 風呂/バス付き (の); ~ *difficulty* yatto やっと; ~ *forethought* mitōshíte 見通して; ~ *great delight* ō-yórokobi de 大喜びで; ~ *meals* (*included*) shoku (ji)-tsuki (no) 食(事)付き (の); ~ *much devotion/ effort* (*but*) sekkaků せっかく; ~ *a shudder/shiver* zotto ぞっと
  with respect to … ni kákete wa … にかけては; … ni kán-shite … に関して

withdraw v 1. (*leaves*) hiki-agemásu (hiki-agéru, hiki-ágete) 引き上げます(上げる, 上げて), hiki-torimásu (hiki-tóru, hiki-tótte) 引き取ります(引き取る, 引き取って) 2. (*takes out money*) (yokin/okane o) oroshimásu (orósu, oróshite) (預金/お金を) 下ろします(下ろす, 下ろして); (yokin/okane o) hiki-dashimásu (hiki-dasu, hiki-dashite) (預金/お金を) 引き出します(引き出す, 引き出して)

wither v karemásu (kareru, karete) 枯れます(枯れる, 枯れて), naemásu (naéru, náete) 萎え[なえ] ます(萎える, 萎えて)

within prep (…) ínai (…) 以内; …-nai …内; … no náka (de/ni/no) …の中 (で/に/の); *within (time)* …-chu (ni) …中(に)
  within the city shínai 市内
  within the metropolis (*of Tokyo*) tónai 都内
  within the office/company shánai (no) 社内(の)

without prep (*excluding*) … no hoka ni …のほか [他・外]に; (*not having*) … ga nái to …がないと, … ga náku (te) …がなく(て), … náshi ni …なし

に; (*omitting*) …-nuki (de/no) …抜き(で/の)

without exception (*all*) reigai náku 例外なく, íssái いっさい・一切

without fail zé-hi 是非・ぜひ

without interruption (*continuously*) taemanáku 絶え間なく, táezu 絶えず

without notice/permission mudan de 無断で

witness n (*in court*) shōnin 証人; shōko 証拠

wolf 1. n ō´kami おおかみ・オオカミ・狼 2. v (*impose*) tsukekomimásu (tsukekomu, tsukekonde) つけ込みます (つけ込む, つけ込んで)

woman n onná 女, onna no hitó/katá 女の人/方; josei 女性, jóshi 女子; (*lady*) fujin 婦人; okámi おかみ・お内儀

womanizer n onna-tárashi 女たらし

women's bath n onna-yu 女湯

women's college n joshi-dai(gaku) 女子大(学); *women's college student* joshi-dáisei 女子大生

women's language (*terms*) joseigo 女性語; onna kotoba 女言葉・女ことば

womenswear n onna-mono 女物

wonder 1. v odorokimásu (odoróku, odoróite) 驚きます(驚く, 驚いて); *I wonder* … ka shira … かしら, … ka ne …かね 2. n odoroki 驚き; fushigi 不思議; *it is no wonder that* … … no mo múri wa arimasén (nái) …のも無理はありません (ない)

wonderful adj subarashíi すばらしい・素晴らしい, suteki (na) すてき・素敵(な), sugói すごい・凄い; (*delightful*) ureshíi うれしい・嬉しい; (*wondrous*) fushigi (na) 不思議(な), myō (na) 妙(な)

won't do v shimasén (shinai, shináide) しません (しない, しないで); *it* ~ ikemasén (ikenai, ikenáide) いけません(いけない, いけないで); damédesu (da/na, de, ni) だめです(だ/な, で, に)

wood n kí 木, mokuzai 木材, (*lumber*) zaimoku 材木 → **firewood**

woodblock print n mokuhan-ga 木版画, hanga 版画

wooden adj 1. mokusei no 木製の 2. muhyōjō no 無表情の
  wooden bucket n óke 桶
  wooden shoes n getá げた・下駄
  wooden stairs n hashigo-dan はしご[梯子]段

woods n (*forest*) mori 森・もり

woof n (*horizontal threads*) yokoito 横糸

wool n ū´ru ウール, ke 毛, keito 毛糸, yōmō 羊毛

woolen goods, woolens n keorimono 毛織物

word n 1. kotobá 言葉・ことば, tango 単語; …-go …語; (*one's words/speech*) kuchi 口; (*written characters*) jí 字; (*compound word*) jukugo 熟語 2. (*news*) táyori 便り・たより, shōsoku 消息
  in other words adv sunáwachi すなわち・即ち, iikaeruto 言い換えると

word processor n wā-puro ワープロ

work 1. n hataraki 働き・はたらき; (*job*) shigoto 仕事 (o-shígoto お仕事); (*operations*) ságyō 作業; *place of work* kinmú-saki 勤務先; shoku-ba 職場

construction work kōˊji 工事; *work in progress*
kōji-chū 工事中 **2.** *n a work* (*of literature or art*)
sakuhin 作品 **3.** *n* (*workmanship*) saiku 細工
4. *v* (*does work*) shigoto o shimásu (suru, shite)
仕事をします(する、して); (*labors*) hatarakimásu
(hataraku, hataraite) 働きます(働く、働いて);
kínmu shimásu (suru, shite) 勤務します(する、
して); (*is employed at/by*) … ni tsutómete imásu
(iru, ite) … に勤めています(いる、いて); (*hires
oneself out for pay*) kasegimásu (kaségu, kaséide)
稼ぎます(稼ぐ、稼いで); ~ *as* (*a …*) (… o)
tsutomemásu (tsutoméru, tsutométe) (…を)務め
ます(務める、務めて) **5.** *v* (*it works*) (*is effective*)
kikimásu (kiku, kiite) 効きます(効く、効いて)
6. *v* → **study**
workaholic *n* wākahorikku ワーカホリック;
hataraki-sugi (no hito) はたらきすぎ・働き過ぎ
(の人); shigoto chūdoku (-sha) 仕事中毒(者)
worker *n* (*laborer*) hiyatoi 日雇い; rodo-sha 労働
者; (*workman*) koin 工員, shokko 職工; (*employee,
staff*) shain 社員, shokuin 職員
workflow *n* sagyō no nagare 作業の流れ; wāku
furō ワークフロー
working *n* hataraki 働き; (*duty, job*) tsutomé
勤め(o-tsutome お勤め); (*operating*) unten 運転,
ságyō 作業; *working hours* sagyō-jíkan 作業時
間, kinmu-jíkan 勤務時間; *working mom* wāking
mazā ワーキング・マザー
world *n* sékái 世界; (*at large*) yo (no naka)
世(の中)・よのなか; (*people*) séken 世間; ~ *war*
sekai-táisen 世界大戦
World Cup *n* Wārudo kappu ワールドカップ
worldwide *adj* sekai-teki (na) 世界的(な), sekai-
jū 世界中
worm *n* mushi 虫・ムシ; *worm remedy* mushi-
kúdashi 虫下し・ムシくだし
worry 1. *n* shinpai 心配・しんぱい, ki-zúkái
気遣い・気づかい, wazurai 煩い・わずらい
2. *worries* (*about …*) *v* (… o) shinpai shimásu
(suru, shite) (…を)心配します(する、して),
wazuraimásu (wazurau, wazuratte) 煩い[わずら
い]ます(煩う、煩って); ki-zukaimásu (ki-zúkáu,
ki-zukátte) 気遣います・気づかいます(気遣う、
気遣って); kokoró o itamemásu (itaméru, itámete)
心を痛めます(痛める、痛めて) *Don't worry
about it.* Goshinpai náku. ご心配なく・ごしんぱ
いなく, Shinpai shinaide (kudasai). 心配・しんぱ
いしないで(ください).
worse *adj, adv* móttо warúi もっと悪い;
otorimásu (otoru, ototte) 劣ります・おとります
(劣る、劣って); *is no ~ off even if … …*-témo
motomoto désu …てももとより[元々]です; *grow
~* akka shimásu (suru, shite) 悪化します(する、
して)
worsen *v* (*illness gets worse*) kojiremásu
(kojiréru, kojírete) こじれます(こじれる、こじ
れて); akka shimásu (suru, shite) 悪化します
(する、して)
worship 1. *n* sūhai 崇拝, (*service*) raihai 礼拝

2. *v* ogamimásu (ogámu, ogánde) 拝みます(拝む、
拝んで)
worst *adj* ichiban warúi 一番悪い; saiaku (no)
最悪(の); (*lowest*) saitei (no) 最低(の)
worth → **value**
worthless *adj* tsumaránai つまらない, yákuza
(na) やくざ(な)
would → **perhaps**
would like → **want, wish**
wound 1. *n* (*injury*) kizu 傷, kegá けが・怪我
2. *v* (*gets wounded*) kizu-tsukimásu (kizu-tsúkú,
kizu-tsúite) 傷付きます(傷付く、傷付いて);
yararemáxu (yararoru, yararote) やられます(やら
れる、やられて); (*injures*) kizu-tsukemásu (kizu-
tsukéru, kizu-tsúkéte) 傷付けます(傷付ける、
傷付けて)
wound it → **wind it**
Wow! *interj* wā! わあ!
wrap *v* tsutsumimásu (tsutsúmu, tsutsúnde) 包みま
す(包む、包んで), hōsō shimásu (suru, shite)
包装します(する、して); (*something around it*)
makimásu (maku, maite) 巻きます(巻く、巻いて)
wrapper *n* (*traditional cloth*) furoshiki ふろし
き・風呂敷; (*package paper*) hōsōshi 包装紙
wrapping *n* rappingu ラッピング; hōsōshi 包装紙
wreath *n* (*lei*) hanawa 花輪; *wreath shell* sázae
さざえ・サザエ・栄螺
wreck 1. *n* (*accident*) jíko 事故, (*collision*)
shōtotsu 衝突, (*ship wreck*) nanpa 難破, sōnan
遭難, (*train wreck*) ressha-jíko 列車事故, sōnan
遭難; (*the wreckage*) zangai 残骸 **2.** *v* (*ruins it*)
kowashimásu (kowásu, kowáshite) 壊します
(壊す、壊して); *wrecks a car* kuruma o kowashimásu 車を壊します
wrecker *n* (*tow truck*) rékkā レッカー, rekkāˊ-sha
レッカー車
wrench *n* rénchi レンチ, supána スパナ
wrestler *n* *sumo wrestler* sumōˊ-tóri 相撲取り,
o-sumō-san お相撲さん; (*ranking*) seki-tórí 関
取; (*champion*) ōˊ-zeki 大関; (*grand champion*)
yokozuna 横綱
wrestler's belt *n* (*loincloth*) mawashi まわし・
回し
wrestling *n* résuringu レスリング; (*professional*)
puro-resu プロレス; (*Japanese*) sumō 相撲・スモ
ウ・すもう
wrestling ring *n* (*sumo*) dohyō 土俵
wrestling tournament *n* basho 場所; *grand ~*
ō-zúmō 大相撲
wretch *n* yátsu やつ・奴
wretched *adj* nasake-nái 情けない・なさけない
wring (*out*) *v* shiborimásu (shibóru, shibótte) 絞り
ます(絞る、絞って)
wrinkle 1. *n* shiwa しわ・シワ・皺 **2.** *v* (*it
wrinkles*) shiwa ga dekimásu (dekíru, dékite) しわ
[皺]ができます(できる、できて)
wrist *n* té-kubi 手首
wristwatch *n* ude-dókei 腕時計
write *v* kakimásu (káku, káite) 書きます(書く、

書いて); (*composes*) ts<u>u</u>kurimás<u>u</u> (ts<u>u</u>kúru, ts<u>u</u>kútte) 作ります (作る, 作って), tsuzurimás<u>u</u> (tsuzuru, tsuzutte) 綴ります・つづります(綴る, 綴って); (*publishes*) arawashimás<u>u</u> (arawásu, arawáshite) 著します(著す, 著して)

writer *n* sakka 作家, chósha 著者; (*the author*) h<u>í</u>ssha 筆者

writing *n* (*written characters*) mój<u>i</u> 文字, j<u>í</u> 字; shorui 書類; ~ *a composition/theme* sakubun 作文

writing brush *n* fude 筆・ふで

writing paper *n* binsen 便せん・便箋

written explanation *n* setsumeisho 説明書

wrong **1.** *adj* (*mistaken*) machigátta 間違った・まちがった, (*is in error*) machigaemás<u>u</u> (machigátte) 間違えます・まちがえます(間違う, 間違って); (*different*) chigatta 違った・ちがった; (*wrongful*) warúi 悪い; (*amiss*) (… no) guai ga warúi (…の)具合が悪い; *something wrong* ijō 異常 **2.** *n* (*malfunction*) koshō 故障

wry *adj* shibúi 渋い・しぶい, nigái 苦い・にがい; *wry face* shibúi/nigái kao 渋い・しぶい/苦い・にがい顔

X

X *n* (*symbol "wrong"*) bátsu ばつ・バツ, battén ばってん・罰点

Xanadu *n* tōgenkyō 桃源郷

xanthic flowers *n* kiiroi hana 黄色い花

Xavier *n* Zabieru ザビエル

x-axis *n* ekkusu jiku X軸

X box *n* ekkusu bokkusu エックスボックス

xenophobia *n* (*hatred of foreign people*) gaikoku-jin girai 外国人嫌い

xenophobic *adj* gaikoku girai (no) 外国嫌い(の), (*hatred of foreign goods*) hakuraihin girai (no) 舶来品嫌い(の), (*hatred of foreign people*) gaikoku-jin girai (no) 外国人嫌い(の)

xerography *n* zerogurafii ゼログラフィー

Xerox *v* kopiishimás<u>u</u> (suru, sh<u>i</u>te) コピーします(する, して)

Xian *v* shiian 西安・シーアン

Xmas *n* (*Christmas*) kurisumás<u>u</u> クリスマスプレゼント

Xmas cake *n* (*Christmas*) kurisumasu kēki クリスマスケーキ

Xmas gift *n* (*Christmas*) kurisumasu purezento クリスマスプレゼント

X-rating *n* seijin muke eiga shitei 成人向き映画指定

xylitol *n* kishiritōru キシリトール

X-ray **1.** *n* ekkūsu-sen X線, rentogen (shashin) レントゲン(写真) **2.** *v* ekkūsu-sen (de) kensa shimás<u>u</u> (suru, sh<u>i</u>te) X線(で)検査します(する, して), rentogen (shashin) o torimás<u>u</u> (toru, totte) レントゲン(写真)を撮ります(撮る, 撮って)

Y

yacht *n* **1.** (*sailboat*) yotto ヨット **2.** (*motor cruiser*) kurūzā クルーザー
luxury yacht *n* gōka kaisoku-sen 豪華快速船

yahoo *interj* yahhō ヤッホー

Yahoo! *n* Yahū (kensaku enjin) ヤフー(検索エンジン)

yak *n* (*animal*) yaku ヤク

yam *n* imó イモ・芋 (o-imo お芋), yamu imo ヤムイモ

Yankee *n* Yankii ヤンキー

yap *v* hoemás<u>u</u> (hoeru, hoete) 吠えます・ほえます(吠える, 吠えて)

yard *n* niwa 庭

yard goods *n* tanmono 反物・たんもの

yard sale *n* garējisēru ガレージセール (= *garage sale*)

yarn *n* ito 糸; (*for knitting*) ke-ito 毛糸・けいと

yawn **1.** *n* akubi あくび[欠伸] **2.** *v* akubi o shimás<u>u</u>

(suru, sh<u>i</u>te) あくび[欠伸]をします(する, して)

yeah *interj* ā ああ; un うん

year *n* tosh<u>í</u> 年; nén 年, …-nen … 年; *years old* … -sai …歳; *1 year old* h<u>i</u>tótsu 一つ・ひとつ, *10 years old* tō´ 十・とお, *20 years old* hátachi/nijús-sai 二十歳・はたち; *how many years old* <u>í</u>kutsu いくつ・幾つ((o-ik<u>u</u>tsu おいくつ・お幾つ), nán-sai 何歳

year after next *n* sarainen 再来年・さ来年

year before last *n* otótoshi おととし・一昨年 issakú-nen 一昨年

Zodiac Years *n* jūnishi 十二支

Year of the Boar *n* idoshi 亥年

Year of the Cock *n* toridoshi 酉年

Year of the Dog *n* inudoshi 戌年

Year of the Dragon *n* tatsudoshi 辰年

Year of the Horse *n* umadoshi 午年

Year of the Monkey *n* sarudoshi 申年

Year of the Ox *n* ushidoshi 丑年
Year of the Rabbit *n* udoshi 卯年
Year of the Rat *n* nedoshi 子年
Year of the Sheep *n* hitsujidoshi 未年
Year of the Snake *n* midoshi 巳年
Year of the Tiger *n* toradoshi 寅年
year-end *adj* kure (no) 暮れ(の), nenmatsu (no) 年末(の); **~ party** bōnen-kai 忘年会; **~ gift** (o-) seibo (お)歳暮
yearly 1. *adj* nén ichido (no) 年1度(の), nen ikkai (no) 年1回(の) **2.** *adv* nen (ni) ichido 年(に)1度, maitoshi 毎年, mainen (no) 毎年(の)
yearn; **~ for** akogaremásu (akogareru, akogarete) あこがれ[憧れ]ます(あこがれる, あこがれて)
year period *n* néndo 年度
yeast *n* iisuto イースト
yell *v* wamekimásu (waméku, waméite) わめき[喚き]ます(わめく, わめいて), sakebimásu (sakébu, sakénde) 叫びます・さけびます(叫ぶ, 叫んで) → **shout**
yellow 1. *n* kiiro 黄色 **2.** *adj* kiiroi 黄色い; kiiro (no) 黄色(の) **3.** *adj* (*coward*) okubyō (na) 臆病(な)
yellowtail *n* (*fish*) búri ぶり・ブリ・鰤, (*baby*) inada いなだ・イナダ, (*young*) hamachi はまち・ハマチ
Yemen Arab Republic *n* Iemen arabu kyōwa-koku イエメン・アラブ共和国
yen *n* én 円, …-en …円
　high value of the yen *n* en-daka 円高
　low value of the yen *n* en-yasu 円安
　yen basis *n* endate 円建て
　yen credit *n* enshakkan 円借款
yes *adv* hái はい, ē´ ええ; sō´desu そうです; (*or just say the verb*) *Yes, I see./Yes, I will (comply).* Wakarimáshita. わかりました.
　Yes and no. *interj* Dochiratomo iemasen. どちらとも言えません., Sā dōdeshō. さあどうでしょう.
　Yes, sir/ma[d]am. *interj* Shōchi shimáshita. 承知しました
yes-man *n* iesu man イエスマン, gomasuri ゴマすり
yesterday *n, adj, adv* kinō´ (no) きのう・昨日(の)

yet *adv* máda まだ, *and yet* sore démo それでも, shiká-mo しかも → **but**
yew *n* ichii いちい・イチイ・櫟
yield 1. *n* (*product; income*) dekiagari 出来上がり・できあがり **2.** *v* (*gives in/up*) yuzurimásu (yuzuru, yuzutte) 譲ります(譲る, 譲って) **3.** *v* (*produces*) sanshutsu shimásu (suru, shite) 産出します(する, して)
yin and yang *n* in yō 陰陽
YMCA *n* Wai emu shii ei YMCA, Kirisuto-kyō seinen-kai キリスト教青年会
yoga *n* yoga ヨガ
yogurt *n* yōguruto ヨーグルト
Yokohama *n* Yokohama 横浜; *the port of ~* Yokohamá-kō 横浜港
yolk *n* (*of egg*) kimi 黄身・キミ
yonder *adv* achira あちら, atchí あっち
you *pron* anáta あなた, ánta あんた (*but use name, title, or role whenever possible*); sochira (sama) そちら(様); o-taku お宅, o-taku sama お宅様; (*intimate*) kimi 君; (*condescending*) omae お前・おまえ
　you all miná-san 皆さん・みなさん, anáta-tachi あなた達[たち], anáta-gata あなた方
young 1. *adj* wakái 若い・わかい; *very young* osanái 幼い・おさない; *young boy* shōnen 少年, *young girl* shō´jo 少女; *young novelist* wakate-sákka 若手作家 **2.** *the young* → **youth**
younger *adj* toshi-shita (no) 年下(の); *younger brother* otōtó 弟, (*your*) otōto-san 弟さん; *younger sister* imōtó 妹, (*your*) (o-)imōto-san (お)妹さん
youngest *adj* ichiban wakái 一番若い, (toshi-)shita (no) (年)下(の)
young lady *n* ojō´-san お嬢さん; musume(-san) 娘(さん)
young man *n* seinen 青年
young person → **youth**
youngster *n* (*young person*) waka-mono 若者
your(s) *pron* anáta-tachi/anata-gata no mono あなた達[たち]/あなた方の物
yourself, yourselves *pron* anáta-jishin あなた自身
youth hostel *n* yūsu-hósuteru ユースホステル

Z

Zaire *n* Zeiiru ザイール
Zambia *n* Zanbia ザンビア
zany *n* dōke-shi 道化師
zap *v* **1.** (*shoots someone dead*) uchikoroshimásu (uchikorosu, uchikoroshite) 撃ち殺します(撃ち殺す, 撃ち殺して) **2.** (*defeats*) (uchi) makashimásu (makasu, makashite) (打ち)負かします(負かす, 負かして) **3.** (*deletes*) sakujo

shimásu (suru, shite) 削除します(する, して)
zapped 1. *adj* (*dead tired*) tsukarehateta 疲れ果てた・つかれはてた **2.** *n* (*vigor*) genki 元気, katsuryoku 活力
zapper *n* (*remote control*) rimokon リモコン
zeal *n* (*enthusiasm*) netsui 熱意; netsujō 熱情; nesshin 熱心
zebra *n* shimauma シマウマ・縞馬

Zen *n* (*Buddhism*) Zén 禅
Zen Buddhist *n* Zen sō 禅僧
zero *n* réi 零, zéro ゼロ; (*written symbol*) maru 丸
zest *n* **1.** (*enthusiasm*) netsui 熱意 **2.** (*interest*) tsuyoi kyōmi 強い興味 **3.** (*enjoyment*) yorokobi 喜び
Zeus *n* Zeusu ゼウス
ZIP, zip code *n* yūbinbángō 郵便番号
zipper *n* chákku チャック, jíppā ジッパー; fásunā ファスナー
zinc *n* aen 亜鉛
zodiac *n* (*horoscope*) jūnikyū-zu 十二宮図
　Zodiac Years *n* jūnishi 十二支 → year

zombie *n* (*person in a trance-like state*) zonbi ゾンビ
zone *n* chítai 地帯, kúiki 区域; zōn ゾーン; tái 帯, ...-tai ...帯
zoo *n* dōbutsú-en 動物園
zoology *n* dōbutsú-gaku 動物学
zoom *n* kakudai 拡大, (*camera*) zūmu ズーム
　zoom lens *n* (*camera*) zūmu-renzu ズームレンズ
Zoroastrianism *n* Zoroasutā-kyō ゾロアスター教
zucchini *n* (*vegetable*) zukkīni ズッキーニ
zygote *n* (*human egg*) setsukōshi 接合子・せつごうし
zzz *n, interj* gūgū グーグー, ぐうぐう